AMT AUSLAND/ABWEHR
Admiral Wilhelm Canaris
Adjutant: Lieutenant Colonel Jenke

ABTEILUNG II (SECTION II)

Sabotage, subversion and special duties
Major Helmuth Groscurth (1938-39)
Colonel Erwin Lahousen (1939-43)
Colonel Wessel von Freytag-Loringhoven (1943-44)
Functions: Sabotage, active countersabotage, planning of commando operations

BRANDENBURG DIVISION

(Special formation employed in sabotage and commando operations)
Major General Alexander von Pfuhlstein

ABTEILUNG III (SECTION III)

Counterespionage, counterintelligence
Major Rudolf Bamler (1933-39)
Colonel Franz-Eccard von Bentivegni (1939-44)
Functions: Armed Forces security, combating of espionage and treason, infiltration of foreign intelligence services

IIA
Central Office

WEST

EAST

SOUTHEAST

OVERSEAS

TECHNICAL

IIIA
Staff and administration

IIIC
Military security; liaison with RSHA; OKW passport office

IIIU
Internal evaluation (of results of counterespionage)

IIIW
Counterespionage in Armed Forces

IIIN
Liaison with press, cinema, postal authorities, censorship

IIID
Disinformation

IIIKgF
Security in POW camps

IIIG
Assessment of treasonable acts

IIIF
Counterespionage (combating foreign intelligence services)
Colonel Joachim Rohleder

from 1943 onwards, controlled

IIIH
Army Security

IIIM
Naval Security

IIIL
Air Force Security

CANARIS

CANARIS

by

Heinz Höhne

Translated from the German by
J. Maxwell Brownjohn

Doubleday & Company, Inc., Garden City, New York
1979

Canaris: Patriot im Zwielicht by Heinz Höhne © 1976 by
C. Bertelsmann Verlag Gmbh, München

Library of Congress Cataloging in Publication Data

Höhne, Heinz, 1926–
  Canaris: a biography of Hitler's chief of espionage.

  Bibliography: p. 672
  Includes index.
  1. Canaris, Wilhelm, 1887–1945. 2. Admirals—Germany—Biography. 3. Anti-
Nazi movement—Biography. DD247.C35H6313   355.3′43′0924 [B]
ISBN: 0-385-08777-2
Library of Congress Catalog Card Number 76–56303

For my wife Christine,
without whose patience and understanding
this book would never have been written.

CONTENTS

LIST OF ILLUSTRATIONS

TRANSLATOR'S NOTE

German technical terms, titles and ranks have in most cases been re-tained. On the first occasion when such words appear, a translation is given in brackets. Appendix 2 provides a glossary of the German words and phrases regularly used in this book.

Where the Notes refer to English editions of German works, many passages in the text have been freshly translated from the original. Where they refer to English-language works containing recorded quotations from German, some of the latter have also been rendered afresh.

FOREWORD

What prompts one person to write about another? Gordon Shepherd, who wrote a life of Dollfuss, once said that there were two motives for producing a biography: admiration or detestation of the hero, or the discovery of material which revises existing ideas. My own motives are historiographic rather than emotional. I have unearthed fresh documentary evidence and new information which reveal my elusive subject in an unaccustomed light.

This may seem strange in view of the many writers who have portrayed Adolf Hitler's inscrutable spy-master through the medium of film, radio and the written word. Few members of the Third Reich's executive hierarchy have captured the imagination of our contemporaries or taxed the deductive powers of historians more thoroughly than Canaris, the admiral and military intelligence chief. It was only too tempting to try and fathom a personality which seemed to defy rational explanation and remained obscure to most observers. Ever cryptic and reluctant to commit himself, Canaris operated in a sort of no man's land, alternately paving the way for Hitler's wars of conquest and planning Hitler's overthrow with resistance groups opposed to the regime.

Many have tried to account for these inconsistencies, sometimes with apparent success, but only two of these numerous interpretations have proved durable: Karl Heinz Abshagen's life of Canaris, which first appeared in 1949 and was long regarded as a reliable standard work; and Gert Buchheit's history of German military intelligence, published seventeen years later. Working on a somewhat sounder documentary basis, Buchheit amplified what Abshagen had gleaned by word of mouth alone, but both authors took the same view of their subject. Canaris was construed as an early opponent of the National Socialist regime and one of the leaders of the German Resistance, while the Abwehr was upgraded into a dissident organization and its jurisdictional clashes with the SS and police into a politico-moral conflict.

Given that ordinary Germans had been shocked by the defeat and delinquencies of the Hitler regime, this view accorded perfectly with their need for a luminous figure capable of suppressing their personal sense of guilt and making them seem better, wiser and more humane than they really had been. The boosting of men like Canaris—indeed, their apotheosis—performed a largely defensive function. Its purpose was to prove that not all Germans had fallen under the spell of what was significantly called the "despotism" of National Socialism (as if the Nazi regime had clung to power by force alone and not been founded on the consent of an overwhelming majority drawn from all social classes and occupational categories). Even serious historians contributed to the growth of these myths by producing seemingly firm evidence, but they too laboured under a widespread tendency to overrate the German Resistance and the role played within it by Admiral Canaris.

I have never been satisfied with such an interpretation because it restricts the Admiral's many-sided and colourful career to a single theme, namely, that of opposition to Hitler. As soon as I investigated the theory and practice of the so-called SS state, I came to distrust the oversimple explanations with which so many authors had sought to encompass the complex reality of the Third Reich. However well it suited the apologetic requirements of Canaris's biographers to represent him as an honest, decent patriot locked in unremitting combat with Heydrich, the evil and satanic boss of the SD, this image was false. My own attitude resembled that of the *Welt am Sonntag* reviewer who, after seeing the much acclaimed German film production *Canaris*, wrote: "Watching Canaris (O. E. Hasse) and Heydrich (Martin Held), one experiences an occasional flash of recognition. Then they become curios in a specimen cabinet. The masks, circumstances and outward appearances are there, but the reality is missing. Where is that passionate desire to gamble with life and death—where is that struggle for power which ultimately inspired the enigma called Canaris?"

It became increasingly clear to me that no reliance on stereotypes would help to capture such a will-o'-the-wisp. My proper course was to expose the layers of political and social consciousness which alone could account for the innumerable ties between Hitler's regime and the man whom his most recent biographer has described as "the inspiration, patron and brains of the Resistance." But the task could not be accomplished with the traditional material of the Canaris biographer. The sources adduced by earlier writers were too incomplete and the documentary foundations on which they erected their theories too unstable. Hardly any key event in the Admiral's life had been buttressed with solid evidence. Whatever the biographer's object of scrutiny—his role as an extreme right-wing conspirator under the Weimar Republic or his first steps as a secret agent, his contacts with the Allies in World War II or the reasons for his downfall—conjecture often stood proxy for fact and legend for certainty.

I have striven to explore new sources of information about Canaris and breathe new life into his withered historical remains. I have spent six years researching in archives and private libraries, reading the transcripts of postwar trials, obtaining statements from important witnesses and enlisting the help of so many people that I can only thank them collectively. Little by little, a new picture of Canaris took shape, furnishing me with an insight into half a century of German history whose course could be traced in parallel with the fascinating career of a man who was more than the "untypical loner," as one eminent historian has called him: a man who was a child of his time, a product of his generation and a representative of thought- and behaviour-patterns common to an entire military caste.

What Canaris was, and what he became, I have set down in the following pages with the caution that should distinguish the historian from the public prosecutor. I have also eschewed the German academic's besetting sin and refrained from nailing every blunder and misinterpretation to which earlier biographers have succumbed. This would be not only captious but incompatible with the respect I owe to those who kept faith with their hero in a faithless age. Besides, where would any biographer be without the efforts and endeavours of his predecessors, little as he may sometimes agree with their theories?

So let the story of Wilhelm Canaris begin. It is a story of human dreams and illusions, fears and achievements, corruptibility and self-deception. It is such a many-faceted tale that its prospects of gaining access to our theory-laden history books may be slender, but it is true nonetheless—as true as Benjamin Disraeli's advice to the young in his novel *Contarini Fleming*, published in 1832: "Read no history: nothing but biography, for that is life without theory."

1

The Kaiser's Cadet

Lieutenant Arnold Böker was the first to sight smoke. Training his binoculars on the skyline, he saw what he had feared: a three-funnelled ship. Böker knew what to do. He seized the tiller and swung the steam-pinnace around in a tight circle, then chugged at full speed to where the light cruiser *Dresden* lay anchored at the far end of Cumberland Bay. It was a sunlit Sunday morning, March 14, 1915.[1]

Böker hurried to his commanding officer, Captain Fritz Lüdecke, and reported that a British cruiser of the *Newcastle* class was approaching the bay from the west.[2] The significance of this news was not lost on Lüdecke. Sole survivor of the Falkland Islands engagement, the *Dresden* had been hunted by the Royal Navy for months. Short of food and virtually immobilized by lack of coal after repeatedly dodging her pursuers, she had finally sought refuge in a bay off the Pacific island of Más a Tierra, where Daniel Defoe's literary imagination had once marooned Robinson Crusoe.

Lüdecke did not expect the British to attack because Más a Tierra, being part of the Juan Fernández group, was neutral Chilean territory. He had further expressed his readiness to have the *Dresden* and her crew interned by the Chilean authorities. By rights, a British attack was out of the question, but Lüdecke was wary enough to sound the alarm.[3]

The cruiser's hull vibrated to the howl of sirens and the blare of klaxons. The gun crews mustered on deck but did not go to action stations because Lüdecke's primary concern was to demonstrate his vessel's non-belligerent status. Steam was raised in a second boiler and the pinnace secured by hawser to the stern so that the *Dresden*, whose guns were pointing inland, could be towed round in the event of an attack. At the same time, boats were swung out in readiness to ferry superfluous stokers and engine-room personnel ashore.[4]

Then Böker reappeared with ominous tidings: a second British cruiser was heading for Cumberland Bay from the east.[5] Before long, Lüdecke ascertained that no less than three Royal Navy ships—the heavy cruiser *Kent*, the light cruiser *Glasgow* and the auxiliary cruiser *Orama*—were preparing to destroy the *Dresden*. The British drew steadily nearer. Already, the German captain could estimate their time of arrival at the mouth of the bay. For a little while longer he clung to the hope that the British would shrink from violating Más a Tierra's neutrality. All such illusions were dispelled at 0840, when puffs of dirty brown smoke sprouted from the enemy cruisers' guns. The British had opened fire.[6]

Lüdecke ordered his gun crews to action stations and all unwanted stokers into the boats. British shells were already screaming overhead and exploding far beyond the *Dresden*, mostly in the Chilean fishing village.[7] The second salvo was better-ranged. It struck the afterpart of the ship, mangled the German cruiser's only combat-ready guns and transformed the stern into a "shapeless ruin," as Lieutenant Otto Schenk later recalled.[8] From then on the *Dresden* shuddered under a succession of hammer blows. Shells rent the ship's hull and "exploded with a sound like subterranean thunder" (to quote another eyewitness), flames licked over the stern and fire broke out in Nos. 2 and 3 magazines.[9]

Lüdecke urged the crew of the pinnace to swing the cruiser's stern round, but in vain—the current was too strong.[10] By now, the captain could issue no more orders because the fire-control system and voice-pipe circuit had been put out of action. The ship was being ripped to pieces. Her shell-torn ensign was temporarily secured to the yard of the foremast but one gun after another fell silent.[11] None of the *Dresden*'s main armament could be brought to bear on the attackers—even the crew's small arms were inaccessible, buried beneath the ruins of the blazing stern.

Captain Lüdecke was faced with the possibility that the British would board and seize his defenceless ship. This had to be prevented at all costs. To an officer schooled in the strict precepts of naval tradition, there was no alternative: the *Dresden* must be scuttled. First, though, the fires below deck would have to be extinguished to enable a demolition squad to open enough sea cocks and lay the explosive charges required to send the ship to the bottom. In addition, the dead, wounded and surviving members of the crew had to be ferried ashore. Lüdecke needed time—plenty of it—but he could not afford to excite the enemy's suspicions. He decided on a *ruse de guerre*.

The man he chose to carry it out was an officer to whose boundless ingenuity and imagination the *Dresden* had largely owed her survival since August 1914, when the outbreak of war cut her off from Germany. Wilhelm Canaris was a taciturn, rather insignificant-looking young man, barely of medium height and almost squat in build. His round-shouldered and unathletic bearing tempted casual observers to underrate him, but they should have been alerted by his keen gaze and large, imposing head with its luxuriant fair hair. "Short and somewhat frail in appearance," was how Lüdecke's confidential report described him on December 1, 1913. "He would seem to have little physical stamina."[12]

A closer working relationship with Lieutenant Canaris, whom he ultimately appointed his adjutant, or personal staff officer, prompted Lüdecke to amend his initial verdict on this "frail" officer. Whenever the *Dresden* had to be extricated from the enemy's clutches, whenever provisions had to be obtained for the crew and fuel for the ship, Canaris had an ace up his sleeve. Thus, nothing could have been more natural than that Lüdecke should call on his closest aide to perform one last service for the doomed ship. His plan was that Canaris should head for the *Glasgow* and distract the British until preparations for scuttling were complete.

While Canaris got ready for his mission, Lüdecke ordered signal flags to be run up the German cruiser's mast. "Am sending negotiators," they said, but the enemy's sole response was to continue firing.[13] Undeterred by the shells screaming overhead and mindful only of Lüdecke's order to gain time, Canaris jumped into the pinnace and cast off. The little boat steamed across Cumberland Bay at an almost defiantly slow turn of speed. Passing the Chilean fort of San Juan Bautista and the Punto San Carlos, it headed straight for the *Glasgow*, which was still firing.[14]

The closer Canaris drew to the British cruiser, the more he dragged his feet. Once clear of the bay, he had time to reflect on himself and his surroundings. So this was how the end looked—the end of his doomed and beloved *Dresden*, the end of all the hopes and dreams that had once impelled him to join the ranks of the Imperial Navy. Few German naval officers had elected to serve in one of His Majesty's ocean-going cruisers with keener expectations of release from the constraints of home or a greater yearning to sample the southern latitudes.

Canaris had been fascinated by the sea and the exotic ever since he could remember. Reared in a family of businessmen, engineers and industrialists whose enthusiasm was reserved for production figures and output quotas, he felt drawn towards remote and unexplored regions still innocent of the din of machinery. In him there was a revival of the restless spirit of the Canarisi, as his ancestors were originally known, when they first appeared in the silk-spinners' village of Sala on the western shores of Lake Como at the beginning of the sixteenth century.[15] They were a talented and inventive family which produced many successful merchants as well as many craftsmen and sailors.

The Canarisi, who were notorious for their wanderlust, never stayed put for long. They spread across Northern Italy, and many of them emigrated. One branch of the family moved to Greece, another to Corsica and a third—the line from which Wilhelm Canaris himself was descended—to Germany.[16] Canaris blood flowed in the veins of Napoleon, and Constantine Kanaris, Minister of Marine and later Prime Minister, became one of the co-founders of modern Greece.[17] By contrast, the German branch of the family steered clear of political ventures and favoured an average middle-class existence. Resident in the neighbourhood of Trèves, they became "chamberlains" to the Elector of that territory, factory managers, lawyers and civil servants.[18]

The Industrial Revolution lured the family farther north and plunged it into the thick of modern industrial life. From the mid-nineteenth century onwards, Wilhelm Canaris's forebears belonged to the managerial elite of the West German coal-mining and iron-smelting industries. His grandfather, Johann Joseph Canaris (1817–94), a royal "mining counsellor" at Dortmund, rated as one of the pioneers of the Ruhr mining area. His father, Carl (1852–1904), was managing director and board member of the Lower Rhine Smelting Works at Duisburg-Hochfeld, and his brother Carl August (1881–1934) became one of Germany's most able steel men and managing director of the Henschel locomotive and machine factory. Even his sister Anna (1883–1964) remained true to family tradition by marrying Rudolf Buck, an engineer who subsequently headed the Buderus Ironworks.[19]

So the world into which Wilhelm Franz Canaris was born in the Ruhr village of Aplerbeck near Dortmund on January 1, 1887, was a mining world where winding engines, boiler houses and drilling rigs assailed the eye at every turn.[20] It was a world in which boundless faith in progress and fanatical creative drive were translated into action by an army of sweating labourers and a corps of production-minded engineers dedicated to a single goal: maximizing output and extracting higher production quotas.

Wilhelm's father, the engineer Carl Canaris, had married Auguste Amélie Popp, daughter of a Franconian forestry superintendent. It was soon borne in on Wilhelm—if only by their frequent changes of abode —that his parents and their three young children were "going places" in every sense. Originally technical director of the Aplerbeck Smelting

Works, his father transferred in January 1892 to the Lower Rhine Smelting Works at Duisburg-Hochfeld, a subsidiary of the Rheinisches Bergbau- und Hüttenwesen A.G., where his first appointment was that of chief engineer.[21] The family followed him, first to 13a Düsseldorfer Kreuzstrasse; then, in April 1892, to Duisburg's Hüttenstrasse; and finally, in January 1893, to 110 Wörthstrasse, a sumptuous villa complete with grounds, kitchen garden, stables and tennis court—Wilhelm Canaris's future and never-to-be-forgotten boyhood paradise.[22]

Wilhelm's father offered his youngest son a life of luxury and upperclass stability. Even in later years, Wilhelm was fond of recalling drives with his brother and sister through the grounds of the Villa Canaris. He often took over the reins of the goat cart and regaled the other two with samples of his dry humour. "None of us could help laughing at Willy," his sister said later.[23] His parents were equally entertained by his comical ideas. His father, always on the reserved and unapproachable side, was impressed by Wilhelm's knowledge of history and geography, while his mother was captivated by his charm. He sometimes warded off a maternal scolding with some such remark as "Mummy, you've got X rays darting out of your eyes."[24]

For all that, we have no record of any youthful pranks on his part. This is no mere accident. There was an aura of precocity about the boy which tended to form a barrier between him and his peers. Finding it hard to make friends with other children, he spent most of his time reading or playing in the grounds by himself. Best of all he enjoyed the company of the family's dogs, usually wire-haired dachshunds.[25] Like Frederick the Great, he soon came to feel that "dogs have all men's good qualities without possessing any of their failings."[26]

Wilhelm Canaris was too irritable and highly strung, too much the hyperaesthete, to bare his soul readily. The classical angularity of his profile with its long prominent nose and receding brow and chin, coupled with his oval face and gracefully slender physique, betrayed what the psychiatrist Ernst Kretschmer christened schizothymia, or spiritual dichotomy. This makes people react in an unpredictable and often ultrasensitive manner. Canaris combined an excess of opposites; the sober calculation of a line of merchants and entrepreneurs, the refinement of the educated Franconian bourgeoisie, the blithe catholicity of his Italian forebears and his mother's brooding, mystically inclined religious sense. Auguste Amélie Popp had introduced a metaphysical—indeed, almost ascetic—tendency into a family whose general attitude was briskly and cheerfully down-to-earth. She was also responsible for that "un-Prussian" flavour which subsequent observers detected in Canaris. Her mother had been Katharina Ronge, sister of the German Catholic rebel-priest Johannes Ronge (1813–87) and a descendant of Silesian farmers from Bischofswalde in Kreis Neisse, a district whose inhabitants "had never become genuine Prussians but always remained Austrians at heart."[27] This varied genetic background made Wilhelm Canaris an inscrutable person. Volatile and abrupt, he concealed the often dreamy nature of his inner thoughts behind a mask of wry humour and incapsulated himself against the personal advances of his fellow men.

He remained just as much of an outsider at Duisburg's Steinbart Gymnasium, the school he attended from 1898 onwards, and made little impression on his contemporaries. He was quiet and taciturn youth. Many people found him reserved and uncommunicative, though he was one of the best pupils in his class and did well enough in his university entrance examination to be excused an oral. The only fellow pupil who knew him at all well was Anton Marcotty, later a Ruhr ophthalmologist, who gained his confidence and was generally regarded as his best friend. To most of his classmates he remained an enigma tinged with opulence and exoticism. The carriage that brought the industrialist's son to school in the Louisen-Strasse every morning whisked him away again at noon.[28]

The only time Canaris unbent was when Headmaster Steinbart signalled the start of the annual school excursion to Kettwig, which always developed—as it could hardly fail to in Wilhelminian Germany—into a quasi-military exercise.[29] Led by so-called platoon and section commanders drawn from the two senior forms, the various classes worked their way along the wooded slopes bordering the Ruhr. Suspense and excitement reigned until the first of the columns reached its appointed objective: Kettwig Station. Canaris, who eagerly assisted "Commander in Chief" Steinbart, discovered a surprising fact about himself: he not only had a talent for leadership but took pleasure in man management and tactics.

Carl Canaris noted his son's interest in military matters with some surprise. Before long, he learnt that Wilhelm wanted to join the armed forces. This genuinely astonished him because no Canaris in the family annals had ever become a regular officer—not that he had anything against Wilhelm's choice of career. A staunch monarchist and National Liberal, apart from being a lieutenant of the reserve in Sapper Battalion No. 7 based at Köln-Deutz, Carl Canaris did not share the antipathy of his Ruhr and Rhine industrialist friends for the Prusso-German officer caste.[30] All would have been well, therefore, if the boy had not pledged himself to a service whose future his father did not rate particularly highly: the Imperial Navy.

But that was the object of Wilhelm's fervent enthusiasm and the key to his conception of a life of liberty. His passion stemmed from a visit made to Greece with his parents during the summer vacation of 1902.[31] In Athens he had come across a monument to someone who bore his own name: Kanaris. What he learnt about the man aroused his curiosity and made him wonder if they were related. The exploits of Admiral Constantine Kanaris (1790–1877) stimulated his imagination. With a boy's imitative instinct, Wilhelm re-enacted the privateering raids of the ship's captain who rose from commanding a small merchantman to become his country's head of government. He was familiar with every one of the admiral's heroic deeds in the Greek War of Independence: the night attack on the Turkish fleet in the Chios Channel on June 18–19, 1822, the destruction of the enemy flagship in the harbour of Tenedos the following November, the burning of a fleet of Turkish troopships off Samos in August 1824.[32]

Wilhelm became so engrossed in the Greek admiral's world of ideas that his father presented him with a model of the Athenian monument. (Even as head of the Abwehr, Wilhelm Canaris hung a coloured engraving of Constantine Kanaris in the living room of his Berlin home and would jocularly refer to the Greek as his grandfather.[33]) Not even the discovery that they were unrelated could prevent him from dreaming himself into the role of a latter-day Admiral Kanaris. He was hell-bent on going to sea.

Canaris Sr., who did not wish him to join the Navy, made repeated attempts to divert him from his aim. He painted a glowing picture of life in the cavalry and presented him with a horse (which he learnt to ride well).[34] In the end, he even prevailed on his son to apply for a commission in the Bavarian 1st Heavy Cavalry Regiment, based in Munich.[35] Although Wilhelm seemed to have abandoned his plans for a naval career, he secretly continued to hope that his father could be won over.

From all he read in newspapers and books, he could not help feeling strengthened in the belief that his original choice was the right one. The whole of Germany resounded to the slogans of a mass movement whose aim was to translate the Kaiser's dictum—"Our future lies on the water"—into action. Europe and Bismarck's Reich had become too cramped for the Germans, who now yearned for the soaring and supposedly less constricted heights of intercontinental politics. Weltpolitik was the great watchword of the time. It was "the vogue, the dream, a burning expectation—almost an ideology and a religion,"[36] and nothing could better satisfy this basic attitude, which was common to wide sections of the population, than the "floating weapon" or fleet of Emperor Wilhelm II.

Ever since the first German Navy, the North Sea squadron under Admiral Brommy, had been formed during the revolutionary turmoil of 1848 and speedily auctioned off thereafter, warships had symbolized the German dream of power and unity. Germany had never before possessed a national navy. After the Empire was founded in 1871, it became the darling of the middle classes. Seemingly unencumbered by the feudal traditions of the Prusso-German military, it was exempt from the bickering that went on between federalistic authorities, exclusively under national control (hence its "Imperial" designation) and an aid to Germany's future world-power status.

It was a long time before the small force of German warships, which were commanded by Prussian generals and largely manned by Britons and Swedes, transcended the role of floating coastal artillery. The Oberkahnführer [head bargee], as Army officers scornfully nicknamed the Navy's commander in chief, could hardly hope to intimidate an enemy with his assortment of corvettes, frigates and gunboats.[37] The naval establishment plan of 1872 itself declared that the Navy's function was "not to take offensive action against the major European states, but to sustain our authority only insofar as we ourselves have minor interests to uphold."[38]

Even in the 1880s, when Germany began to pick up the crumbs left by the great powers' empire-building activities and found colonies of her own, including overseas naval bases, the fleet's role remained defensive. This was now referred to as direct and indirect coastal defence: the fleet was to exert direct deterrence against a potential foe by means of warships, torpedo boats, mines and coastal fortifications, but it was also to conduct economic warfare and threaten enemy colonies. Leopold von Caprivi, the last Prussian general to head the Admiralty, was still insisting in 1888 that all that mattered to Germany, "both now and in the immediate future, is how small our fleet can be, not how large."[39]

But Germany's explosive economic development swept the Navy along in the wake of worldwide expansion. The German population explosion (an increase of nearly 30 million, or 90 per cent, between 1850 and 1910), together with the growth of industrial output and the never-ending rise in employment figures, cried out for fresh solutions.[40] These could only be found overseas, in wider export markets and new areas of colonization. But who was to lead the Germans there and guarantee them a share in this future paradise? There was only one sure guarantor: the Navy.

The expansionists felt entitled to hope for the fulfilment of their desires from 1888 onwards, for the accession of Emperor Wilhelm II ("the trident belongs in our hand") meant that a Navy fan had come to power. "The ocean," he announced, "is essential to German greatness. But the ocean also demonstrates that, far away thereon and beyond it, no major decision may any longer be taken without Germany and the German Emperor."[41] Many of Wilhelm's gestures proclaimed that there were glorious times in store for the Navy. He was the first German emperor to appear in naval officer's uniform, he created the

Reichsmarineamt [a species of Admiralty] and an Imperial Navy Cabinet because "I have resolved to wield supreme personal command over my Navy," and he also put naval officers in charge of the fleet.[42]

So the ground was already prepared for the great seducer who sent millions of Germans into a lather of pro-Navy enthusiasm from 1897 onwards. Alfred von Tirpitz, admiral and State Secretary at the Reichsmarineamt, was a battleship fetishist. Only "a fighting force that can stand between Heligoland and the Thames," he assured the Emperor, would be capable of instilling respect into the British and making them allies of Germany. No cruisers, however powerful, could achieve anything because Germany did not possess enough overseas bases.[43] The Emperor took his point. From now on, the German fleet could never be large enough. The Reichstag naval bills introduced by Tirpitz became more and more extravagant in scope.[44]

The British admirals took fright. They could calculate when the Germans would achieve parity with the Royal Navy, the world's most powerful maritime force. Even the German naval legislation of 1898 provided for an Imperial Navy of nineteen capital ships, eight coastal defence vessels, twelve heavy and thirty light cruisers. The naval legislation of 1900 went still further: it envisaged the construction of two flagships, four squadrons each of eight capital ships, eight heavy and twenty-four light cruisers, a distant waters fleet comprising three heavy and twenty-four light cruisers, and a reserve fleet of four capital ships, three heavy and four light cruisers.[45] This bill was tantamount to a declaration of war on the one country in the world whose good will was absolutely essential to Germany's overseas trade.

So manifold were the interests served by Admiral von Tirpitz's naval policy that scarcely a single German politician protested. Tirpitz had promises on tap for all: he aimed to secure international markets for the German export industry, large-scale orders for heavy industry and shipyards, full employment for the working class and relief from the pressure of political and social reforms for a Prusso-German system of government which was then in a state of crisis. At the turn of the century, there was no sector of the population which did not expect Tirpitz's plans to provide a solution to its problems.

Those who persisted in their lack of comprehension were steamrollered by a propaganda machine the like of which had never before been seen in German history. Supervised by the information bureau of the Reichsmarineamt, a deluge of pro-Navy pamphlets and articles descended on schools and universities, editorial offices and government departments. Backed by a combination of heavy industry and the Marineamt, the 900,000 members of the powerful Navy League busily ensured that every last German received a glowing picture of the Tirpitz-style Navy's future prospects.[46]

This debate was enriched by the appearance of a new figure: the "naval expert," ever on hand to produce some apt catch phrase from his store of scientific knowledge. Historians predominated among those who depicted the new utopia of the German fleet. Englert confidently asserted in 1900 that it was the Imperial Navy's "exalted and sacred national task" to provide the Germans with new colonial territories overseas and thus to create a "greater Germany." His colleague Erich Marcks went so far as to proclaim that naval construction was an aid to "character-building by means of international politics." It was conducive to "manliness on a mighty scale"—indeed, it was becoming "an inward boon to our nation."[47]

Who could blame a youth of seventeen for being carried away by the naval fervour of his time? Wilhelm Canaris felt sure that his future must lie with the Navy, but his father had barred the way and was still insisting that he should become a cavalry officer. At this point, disaster smote the family. Only fifty-two years old, Carl Canaris died of a stroke on September 26, 1904, while taking the waters at Bad Nauheim.[48] From Wilhelm's point of view, his father's death unlocked the door to a naval career. His widowed mother soon abandoned her opposition and submitted his name to the [Executive] Naval Cadets' Admission Board at Kiel even before he successfully matriculated at Easter 1905.

To the Board, which made a practice of examining every applicant with sedulous care, the industrialist's son was an almost ideal candidate. He came of "good" family (something the Navy regarded as almost more important than academic ability), he possessed a pleasant social manner, he had passed his university entrance and, last but not least, he was a scion of that indefatigable sponsor of Tirpitz's plans, the world of heavy industry. Equally welcome was the fact that Frau Canaris could readily sign the covenant committing her to support her son financially for the first four years of his career. This entailed an outlay of 4,800 marks—in those days a substantial sum which effectively debarred "undesirable" elements such as members of the lower middle class, let alone working class, from admission to the elite executive officer corps.[49] Canaris was accepted and happily set off for Kiel.

On April 1, 1905, he presented himself at the grim-looking premises of the old Warrant Officers' School in Kiel's Muhliusstrasse, where every officer in the Imperial Navy traditionally began his career.[50] Through its portals streamed another 158 matriculates, sixth-formers and officer cadets, all of them members of the same future *Crew*, as each Naval Academy vintage was known.[51] A new life stretched ahead of Wilhelm Canaris. His early months in the Navy were ruled by severity and discipline, absolute obedience and a relentless insistence on driving oneself to the verge of physical collapse—all these things only slightly mitigated by a sense of comradeship.

The cadets cut their teeth on dry land. They underwent basic infantry training, were subjected to the monotony of arms drill, route marches and fieldcraft, suffered the torments of constant inspections, night exercises and weapon-cleaning sessions.[52] After four weeks the new cadets were distributed among Germany's three sail-training ships in groups of fifty. Canaris was posted to the cruiser-corvette *Stein*, probably the toughest training ship in the Imperial Navy. Manned by 20 officers, 449 petty officers and seamen, 50 naval cadets and 210 boy apprentices, the 2,843-ton vessel was reputed to be hard to handle and would only sail well in a stiff quartering breeze.[53]

The cadets, who now wore short blue jackets with gold buttons and, at their side, that most important attribute the "cheese knife" or naval dirk, were only too prone to believe that they had already attained the status of naval officers and gentlemen. The *Stein's* instructors soon dispelled any such misconception. Even before breakfast, all cadets were obliged to climb the ship's three masts. Each had to be scaled on one side and descended on the other, and always at lightning speed: the foretop in 1 minute 20 seconds, the maintop in 1 minute 30 and the mizzentop in 1 minute 10. Many cadets missed their footing in the shrouds and plunged to the deck, while others trampled on the fingers of the overeager classmates following at their heels.[54]

Cadets were forever expected to perform fresh tests of personal courage and increasingly hazardous manoeuvres. They learnt how to stand poised on the topmost royal yard or perch astride a yardarm backwards. Always slightly out of breath, they welcomed spells of navigational instruction or gun drill with the old cannons of the corvette, which had been built between 1878 and 1880. Most idyllic of all, however, were the night watches, when the average cadet contrived to doze on his feet.

Once the basic drills had been mastered, the *Stein* put to sea. She headed for Skagen, Iceland and, ultimately, the Mediterranean.[55] But the cadets were never left idle for a moment. Fluctuating between seasickness, vertigo during masthead climbs and surges of resentment at their instructors' harsh tone, they were chivvied from one manoeuvre to another. Whether ordered to reef topsails or holystone the decks, they felt permanently harried and unable to relax. Some of them cracked under the strain and others fell sick after watch-keeping in wet gear for excessive periods, either at the helm or as lookouts.[56]

Canaris, too, found difficulty in surviving these drills and tests of courage aboard the *Stein*. He had never been an athletic type, and physical prowess meant little to him. However often nausea may have overcome him while aloft in the dizzy world of rope, spar and canvas, and however much the heavy oars of the *Stein's* longboat may have sapped his energy, he had a cast-iron determination to succeed. His standard of performance steadily improved and his slight frame gained strength week by week. This struggle for self-mastery earned him the respect of one of his instructors, Warrant Officer Richard Protze, who later became a personal friend and one of his closest associates in the Abwehr.[57]

Canaris attracted no special attention among his classmates. He was not unpopular, thanks to his sense of humour and obliging attitude, but he left the talking to others.[58] One of these was Karlgeorg Schuster, who scented a rival in the reserved and ironical Canaris. "They were poles apart from the outset," recalls another member of their class. It was true. Even after Canaris's death, Schuster continued to impugn his former classmate and fellow admiral for "treachery" under the Third Reich.[59] But Canaris ignored Schuster's gibes. He was, as his classmate and friend Otto Benninghof put it, "quick to hear but slow to speak and slower still to anger."[60]

He could not get his own back until the Stein returned to Kiel early in 1906 and his eighteen-month course at the Naval Academy began. Canaris was now able to demonstrate that few of his classmates could surpass him in intellectual ability. "Theoretically very well endowed and unremittingly hard-working" was how one instructor's confidential report described him.[61] Physics, mathematics, navigation, naval construction—Canaris did well in all these subjects. To quote another entry in his personal file, he was "of very good general education and constantly at pains to improve himself in every respect."[62] He also acquitted himself well in the social-cum-sporting field. Riding was one of his favourite activities, though he lacked the temperament for dancing.

Once at the Naval Academy, however, Canaris must soon have spotted the importance of subjects other than those connected with science and weaponry. Many branches of instruction were totally neglected. The teaching of foreign languages had been dropped in 1905, and there were no lectures on domestic or social policy.[63] Even the military sciences received quite cursory treatment. Typically enough, all efforts were focused on training cadets to become officers and gentlemen. Every lecture was designed to imbue them with the feeling that they were members of a military elite ordained for political and social leadership.

Every inmate of the Academy had to grasp that the executive officer corps enjoyed supreme status in the Empire, not unlike the guards officers of old Prussia whom the naval authorities deliberately emulated. The officers of the Imperial Navy saw themselves as the Reich's future order of chivalry, answerable to the Emperor alone and insulated from the currents and conflicts of the age: an exclusive club whose members were enjoined to abstinence in all spheres of life but accorded the right to settle alleged points of honour by force. Indebtedness was forbidden, marriage below the rank of senior lieutenant seldom permitted and the consumption of alcohol curbed by a series of official directives.[64]

The naval executive officer had to be ready to uphold the prestige of his corps at all times and against all comers, if necessary by force of arms. Even cadets were compelled to accept challenges to duel. As one naval court of honour declared: "Anyone who picks a quarrel with officers must feel that, so far from embarking on a game, he is placing his life in jeopardy."[65] The executive officer was also expected to stand up to other members of the Navy if any threat to the club's reputation arose. Above all, engineer, specialist and warrant officers must be taught to respect the omnipotence of the executive branch.

The fact was that the Imperial Navy contained officers and officers. Its leadership was strictly compartmentalized into a four-class system. Lowest of all were the warrant or "deck" officers, who, being quartermasters and the like, did not hold commissioned rank despite their designation. Then came the gunnery and torpedo officers (specialist officers), who handled the storage and administration of the tools of war. Above them, again, came a third category comprising the engineer officers who supervised all things mechanical.[66] Finally, at the apex of the pyramid, there was the executive officer caste or military-cum-navigational command corps. Given the existence of such a caste system, the executive officers tended to feel threatened by their "inferiors" and engaged in fierce skirmishes over privileges, uniforms and mess conventions.

Executive officers wore a black mohair band round their caps and specialist officers a dark blue one—reason enough for the former to press the Emperor for a change in caps on the grounds that it was unthinkable for a specialist officer to be mistaken for an executive officer at night.[67] They also did their utmost to prevent the granting of officer status to warrant officers and even to get them downgraded to the lower deck, although warrant officers had been assured by a royal command dated 1854 that they ranked "below officers and above chief petty officers."[68]

Naval engineers were a particular thorn in the side of the executive branch. Incensed by the fact that engineers had been granted commissioned status at all, the executive branch now banned any further fraternization. No engineer officer was suffered to give orders to a sublieutenant and none was admitted to the executive officers' mess at a naval base.[69] "We shall see to it," insisted Vice-Admiral von Coerper, Inspector of Naval Training, "that the engineers return of their own accord to the subordinate status that befits them."[70] The naval authorities duly ensured that no executive officer maintained social contact with officers of the engineering branch. Post Captain Wilbrandt fulminated that one ship's captain had "actually invited his chief engineer home to meet the family!"[71]

Executive officers had to draw an equally sharp distinction between themselves and the lower deck, who were always tainted with the suspicion of being in league with the accursed Social Democrats (in fact, many seamen and stokers in capital ships were organized along trade union lines). Although officers were forbidden to engage in party politics, they regarded it as their natural duty to combat Social Democratic aspirations.[72] Any officer suspected of sympathizing with the lower deck, let alone of being a "Red" himself, could kiss his career goodbye. In this respect as in others, the executive officer corps proved itself "a faithful reflection of Wilhelminian society."[73]

Hour by hour, the Kiel cadets were taught that their vocation was to cement the supremacy of the executive branch. Canaris, too, became imprinted with the doctrines and behaviour patterns of the Imperial Navy's officer corps. Having grown up in isolation from the "lower" classes and been reared in critical and uncomprehending aloofness from the working class in a parental home where the master-and-servant attitude reigned supreme, he found it only natural that a gentleman caste should wield absolute power in the ships of His Imperial Majesty.

By October 1907 he was ready to put his Kiel-inculcated precepts into practice. After passing his final examination, Midshipman Canaris joined his classmates on the Naval Academy's parade ground and, facing a German naval ensign that fluttered in the breeze, swore the oath of allegiance. From that moment on, Wilhelm Franz Canaris undertook "loyally and worthily to serve His Majesty the German Emperor, Wilhelm II, my Supreme Commander, in each and every instance, on land and water, in time of war and peace and in whatsoever places it may be; to promote His Majesty's advantage and welfare, to shield Him from injury and detriment, and faithfully to comply with the Articles of War that have been read to me and the instructions and orders given me."[74]

A kindly providence absolved Canaris from ever having to submit the Naval Academy's maxims to a serious test in that arena where the Navy's internal class struggle assumed particular intensity behind a façade of discipline: the battleship. He was never to experience the awful tedium pervading those armour-plated monsters which assembled each spring and autumn to carry out naval exercises of unvarying sameness in the North Sea and Baltic—to quote Vice-Admiral Eberhard von Mantey, "a Prussian army corps transplanted into iron barracks."[75] Canaris served in a Navy which had practically ceased to exist and counted for little from the Tirpitz standpoint: that of the cruiser and torpedo boat.

A whiff of seafaring romanticism and exoticism still clung to this arm of the service. The German Emperor's ocean-going cruisers sustained the last vestiges of that mission which was supposed to characterize the pre-Tirpitz Navy: that of being envoys of the Reich and a link between the Bismarckian state and millions of Germans overseas. This was what had lured Canaris into the Navy. A quirk of naval personnel policy brought him nearer the object of his desires. Still in October 1907, Midshipman Canaris received orders to report to the light cruiser *Bremen*.[76]

The 3,816-ton cruiser, one of the German Navy's most modern ships (built 1902–4), headed for the Southwest Atlantic. She was destined for service on the East American Station, which meant upholding German interests along the eastern shores of South and Central America by showing the flag and maintaining a permanent presence there.[77] Canaris's job in the *Bremen* was to train seamen, deliver lectures to the crew and, in the event of international complications, place his not inconsiderable linguistic skills at the captain's disposal (he spoke good English, passable French and a smattering of Russian).[78] His habitual enthusiasm, coupled with an unfailingly earnest but unobtrusive manner, quickly endeared him to his superior officers.

"He is small of stature and very modest and retiring," noted the *Bremen*'s commander, Captain Alberts, "so one takes a little time to get to know him. Extremely efficient and conscientious."[79] The other ship's officers also liked having the new midshipman around and extolled his abilities. The navigating officer called him "a most reliable assistant" and the gunnery officer was equally full of praise.[80] What surprised them, however, was Canaris's diffidence and reluctance to emerge from his shell. Alberts: "He promises to be a good officer once he acquires a little more confidence and self-assurance."[81]

Even after being commissioned sublieutenant on September 28, 1908, Canaris preferred to spend most of his spare time in his cabin, pursuing studies of a private nature.[82] The proximity of Latin America inspired him to learn Spanish, and it was not long before he could express himself so fluently that a superficial observer might have thought he had spoken the language for years.

This stood the *Bremen* in good stead when she joined the blockading fleet assembled by Britain, Italy and Germany to put pressure on the Venezuelan President, Cipriano Castro, whose nationalization policy had provoked the Great Powers. Canaris, who had meanwhile become the *Bremen*'s adjutant [v. Glossary], proved himself an adroit negotiator during talks with the Venezuelans. He had an almost unrivalled talent for dealing with foreigners. Even General Juan Vicente Gómez, who succeeded Castro on the latter's removal from office, presented the young officer with a token of his respect. On May

13, 1909, Canaris was invested by him with the Order of Bolívar, Fifth Class—his first-ever decoration.[83]

It began to dawn on the Bremen's officers that they had an artist in man management on board. The cruiser's new commander, Captain Albert Hopmann, became another Canaris admirer. He credited him with "good military and social conduct" and praised him for his "unassuming civility and courtesy."[84] Hopmann assigned Canaris new and wider responsibilities. He involved him in the mobilization duties which normally devolved on the senior officer in the East American Station. Once again Canaris proved his mettle and displayed "far more skill and understanding than were to be expected in someone so new to the service" (Hopmann). The captain drew closer to his ship's adjutant on a personal level too. With Canaris—"whom I grow to like more and more," as Hopmann noted in his diary—he visited friends and relations in Argentina and Brazil. Before long, Hopmann never attended a party ashore without his staff officer in tow.[85]

Canaris enjoyed his weeks and months on board the Bremen. The world of the South had cast its spell over him. He never forgot the unconstrained atmosphere and easy gaiety of those prewar days: lavish receptions at the homes and clubs of German immigrants, parades and shipboard rituals beneath the imperial ensign, visits to foreign warships. A twenty-two-year-old lieutenant could be forgiven for numbering himself among the lords of creation and seriously believing that he personified a Germany whose power and glory were virtually unbounded.

Although he was too realistic to share the condescension with which his brother officers regarded foreign nations and navies, Canaris did subscribe to many of the clichés current in ships of the Imperial Navy: a grudging admiration for Great Britain, whose power was respected—and overrated—but whose parliamentary and democratic institutions defied German understanding; scant regard for the French; and contempt for Russia's naval officers, most of whom were dismissed as corrupt. Canaris differed from the bulk of his fellows in only one distinct respect. He was magically attracted by the culture and temperament of the Latins. Their gaiety—their whole natural disposition—struck chords within him which he had never heard before.

But his idyll beneath the hot southern sun was rudely interrupted by the naval rotation system. In January 1910 Canaris was posted as second watch-keeping officer to torpedo boat V162, which soon left to join Division III for spring exercises in the North Sea.[86] This was an uncomfortable experience because he had always shunned cold weather since suffering two bouts of malaria in Venezuela and Mexico in 1909.[87] In June he changed horses again, this time becoming divisional and watch-keeping officer in torpedo boat S145, which belonged to Division II.[88]

The stormy autumn weather in the North Sea proved too much for his health and enforced a break in his career. The medical diagnosis: catarrhal apicitis of the lung. Canaris was granted six months' sick leave.[89] On his return in 1911, he again distinguished himself by his devotion to duty. Flattering assessments reappeared in his confidential reports, as witness the following by Lieutenant Nieden of Division II: "He has displayed skill and a sure eye for specialized service in torpedo boats, and would lend himself to future employment as a boat commander."[90] Even before his final exertions in the North Sea were behind him, Canaris received a new commission: he had been promoted to full lieutenant.[91]

Then the Southern Hemisphere reclaimed him. In December 1911 he was assigned to serve in a ship which became his second home, the light cruiser *Dresden*.[92] He first set eyes on the 361-man vessel in Kiel. Built by the Blohm & Voss yard during 1907–8, she was 387 feet long and 11 feet in the beam, had a displacement of 3,664 tons and could make at least twenty-four knots. The gunnery officer in Canaris was quick to note the cruiser's armament of ten 10.5-centimetre [4.1-inch] guns and four torpedo tubes.[93]

He was not given long to dwell on the sight of the cruiser lying peacefully in her berth. On April 6, 1913, the outbreak of the Second Balkan War took the *Dresden* to the Eastern Mediterranean, bound for Constantinople.[94] Commander Lüdecke, her captain, was under orders to safeguard German interests during the Balkan disturbances and maintain contact with Germany's Turkish allies. Lieutenant Canaris received a special assignment: he was to observe the progress of construction work on the Daghdad Railway in Anatolia, which was being financed by German capital.[95]

By the end of 1913 the *Dresden* was back in Kiel. A new captain, Commander Erich Köhler, arrived on board together with fresh orders from Naval Staff: sail at once and head for the east coast of Mexico.[96] The *Dresden* was to relieve the *Bremen* on the East American Station and extend protection to German nationals in Mexico, which had been rent by civil war since February 1913. Naval Staff were so insistent that, although the ship had been continuously in service since 1908, Köhler was obliged to curtail her overhaul, which had already begun.[97] The *Dresden's* mission was not, admittedly, expected to be a long one, and the naval authorities guaranteed that she would be relieved by the new cruiser *Karlsruhe* in a few months' time.

At 0600 on December, 27, 1913, Köhler gave the order to raise steam. The cruiser cast off, negotiated the Kaiser Wilhelm Canal and by 1700 had reached the Brunsbüttel Lock. The North Sea lay ahead. The *Dresden* rapidly picked up speed. After putting in at St. Thomas in the Virgin Islands, she made for the Gulf of Mexico via Haiti,

Jamaica and Cuba. On January 21 Köhler reached his destination, the Mexican port of Veracruz, where the Bremen was already waiting to be relieved.[98] Two days later, Canaris's first ship headed for home.[99]

But hardly was the Dresden on station when the Mexican civil war hastened to its sanguinary climax. More and more foreigners imperilled by the fighting requested the Dresden to pick them up and convey them to a place of safety. As ship's adjutant, Canaris took charge of negotiations, helping foreign nationals in distress and acting as interpreter during their exchanges with Köhler. The Dresden was soon transformed into a floating Babel. Germans, Austrians, Dutch and Americans sought refuge aboard the German cruiser, which then transported them to the safety of Tampico.[100]

Canaris's services as an interpreter were again in demand at the end of April, when two thousand U.S. citizens had to be accommodated in the German ship—a successful operation for which President Wilson expressed his gratitude.[101] The diplomatic skill of the Dresden's commander and his aide eventually earned their vessel a delicate mission which, as it were, set the seal on the Mexican civil war. On July 14, 1914, the Dresden received orders to bring out the man who had unleashed it in the first place: General Victoriano Huerta, the country's ex-President.[102]

Two days later the Dresden entered Puerto México, where Huerta, his War Minister Blanquet and their respective families were to embark. But Huerta was in no hurry to leave. He sent his presidential retinue on ahead, and a swarm of vociferous womenfolk and servants took possession of the Dresden. The ship's band was frequently called upon to keep the exiles in good spirits. At last the ex-dictator appeared—only to disappear again. Growing uneasy, Köhler angrily sent Canaris to coax Huerta aboard. By July 20 he had succeeded, and the Dresden sailed. Three days later she put the Mexicans ashore at Kingston, Jamaica.[103]

At Port-au-Prince in Haiti on July 25, the Dresden finally met up with the cruiser Karlsruhe, which was to relieve her. The Dresden's former captain, Lüdecke, who had been commanding the Karlsruhe and was now resuming command of his old ship, came aboard.[104] On July 26, after taking on guns and ammunition from the Dresden, the Karlsruhe steamed out of harbour again.[105] Fritz Lüdecke was in a hurry, because his orders were to get the Dresden home as fast as possible.

The cruiser was just embarking the last of her supplies when the wireless officer dashed out of his cabin clutching a signal. The word "war" ran round the ship like wildfire. Naval Staff reported that Austria-Hungary and Serbia had broken off diplomatic relations and that war was looming between all the European Great Powers. The Dresden must head for home with the utmost speed.[106] It was July 28, 1914, only four days before the outbreak of World War I.

Eager to reach Germany before the worst happened, Lüdecke immediately recalled his shore parties and raised steam.[107] A few hours later the *Dresden* left harbour and headed for St. Thomas, near Puerto Rico, where she topped up her stocks of food and coal.[108] On the afternoon of July 31 the ship sailed again, bound for home, but three hours later a new W/T message put paid to Lüdecke's plans. He read: "War imminent Great Britain, France, Russia. Allies: Austria-Hungary, probably Italy. Do not return home. Conduct cruiser warfare in accordance with mobilization provisions."[109]

This was tantamount to an order to commit suicide. Menaced by the guns of the world's most powerful navy, wholly dependent on her own resources, thousands of miles from home and in poor mechanical condition, the *Dresden* was expected to disrupt and, where possible, paralyse the enemy's overseas trade—as the phrase "cruiser warfare" implied. Germany would now have to pay dearly for the fact that her battleship-crazy admirals had neglected cruiser construction for so many years. Only second-rate ships (like the *Dresden*) had been assigned to foreign service and few supply ships provided for their replenishment.

The crew of the *Dresden* knew only too well what the new order portended. As Petty Officer Heinrich Schneider said later: "How long would we be able to hold out? Not long, was the general verdict, because it had to be assumed that enemy warships were already after us."[110] But Lüdecke had no thought of surrender—"Nobody hauls down our ensign!"[111]—and the rest of the crew shared his attitude as a matter of course. Their sense of duty and patriotism, still fully intact, left them no choice but to stick it out, hunt for prey and hope for a miracle.

Lüdecke promptly devised a new plan. The *Dresden* would head south and lie off the La Plata estuary, where freighters left Argentina bound for England.[112] The only flaw in his plan—a major one—was that the *Dresden*'s stocks of coal were insufficient to allow her to operate off the coast of Argentina.

Coal . . . To a warship, this had meant the difference between life and death ever since the age of steam began. The sailing ships of old had sometimes waged war for years on end, remaining operational for as long as their supplies of fresh water, food and tackle lasted. The modern cruiser was lost as soon as her fuel ran out, which it quickly did. To maintain a speed of twenty knots the *Dresden* required 170 tons of coal every twenty-four hours, yet her bunkers could not hold more than 850.[113]

To ensure the survival of their ocean-going cruisers, Naval Staff planners had begun to establish prewar *Etappen* ["staging posts" or bases] on the coasts of maritime countries. These were commanded by a naval officer who was kept informed of the operations and requirements of German warships. He also compiled intelligence reports on the enemy with the aid of V(*ertrauens*)-*Männer* ["trusted persons" or informants] and maintained contact with German shipping companies and their vessels. German merchantmen berthed in the harbours of a base area had to be ready at all times to convey coal, food or other supplies to a warship on the high seas and transfer them at a predetermined spot.[114] It was naturally essential that such arrangements be kept from the enemy because advance notice made it only too easy for them to ambush a German warship or at least disrupt a rendezvous.

Information about the enemy was a prime requirement, but this was just what the *Dresden* lacked. The British had cut Germany's five transatlantic cables as soon as war broke out.[115] The *Dresden* was dependent on reports from South and Central American radio stations which themselves relied largely on British news agencies and often played the Royal Navy's game. Given this situation, there was no alternative. The *Dresden* must obtain information of her own, and Lüdecke knew of only one person with sufficient contacts on the South American mainland to provide it.

Lieutenant Canaris was instructed to establish a network of informants who could submit reasonably accurate reports about the enemy's dispositions and intentions. He had already engaged in one such venture with Hopmann, the captain of the *Bremen*. That was in 1908, when Hopmann had been building up the *Bremen's* intelligence network in Argentina and Brazil. One of the captain's relations, simply referred to in his diary as "Uncle Rudolf," had set up the requisite contacts, though Hopmann's notes also disclose that he regarded secret service rituals with some scepticism. Entry dated November 21, 1908: "Spent morning with Canaris . . . went through V.M. [informant] matters . . . Afternoon, read G. [secret] papers, much of them rubbish." November 25, 1908: "Went ashore with Canaris and settled cipher matters with Uncle Rudolf. The system now being introduced is complicated in the extreme and bound not to work." December 24, 1908: "Went ashore with Canaris and negotiated with Herr Georgius about V. [informant] matters . . . and recruited him as an informant."[116]

Canaris, who was fascinated by these cat-and-mouse games with the enemy, did not share his former captain's scepticism. As one who had experimented with invisible inks and assumed false names in his boyhood,[117] he was fond of the mysterious—of veiled allusions and the concealment of ulterior motives and intentions. He proceeded to get in touch with a number of business men in Brazil and Argentina by radio, all of them contacts dating from his service in the *Bremen*.

At the same time, he was at pains to ensure that the *Dresden* covered her tracks while heading south. The U.S. wireless station at San Juan in Puerto Rico received a false report that the *Dresden* was continuing her homeward voyage via the Azores, while another—encoded —signal informed the Brazilian base that the cruiser would henceforth communicate under the cover name *Sierra Salvada*. It also stated that her first step would be to make for the island of Rocas, off the northeast coast of Brazil, and take on fresh supplies of coal there.[118] The *Dresden's* security was so effective that not even the aides and associates of the Brazilian base guessed what lay behind the name *Sierra Salvada*. On August 7, when fears that the cruiser might not make it to Rocas prompted a request for an earlier rendezvous, the German freighter *Corrientes*, which had been alerted in the North Brazilian port of São Luis do Maranhão, suspected a trap.[119]

Captain Mehring of the *Corrientes* was reluctant to leave harbour, even though the *Dresden* purported to be a German warship, because he thought a British cruiser might be trying to lure him under her guns.[120] Then his bosun Julius Fetzer had a bright idea. Fetzer, who had served in the *Dresden* during 1911, requested her to radio the names of the captain and executive officer at that time. When the correct answers came back, Mehring abandoned his opposition. On August 10 the two vessels met in a bay off Jericoacoara and the *Dresden* took on 570 tons of coal.[121]

Fetzer submitted a report to Canaris, who was so impressed by his knowledge that he invited him to join the *Dresden*. A Cape-Horner, Fetzer was well acquainted with the Patagonian archipelago, the *Dresden's* future operational area. The proposition appealed to him, so he transferred to the cruiser as a supernumerary lieutenant and became Canaris's closest aide.[122] Not that he realized it, the Third Reich's future spy-master had acquired his first subordinate (Fetzer later joined the Abwehr as a senior naval lieutenant).[123]

The *Dresden* resumed her southward progress. On August 13 she reached the island of Rocas, where the freighter *Baden* was already awaiting her with more coal. When the Rocas lighthouse-keeper became too inquisitive (the *Dresden* had passed herself off as a Swedish ship), the cruiser steamed on.[124] Her new destination: the Brazilian island of Trinidad. And so the *Dresden* worked her way from base to base, serviced by a succession of German freighters and screened from the enemy by misleading radio messages.

But when the cruiser finally swooped across the mouth of the Río de la Plata at the end of August, disappointment lay in store: there was not a sign of a British ship. The *Dresden's* score to date had been meagre. She had sunk one British freighter south of Rocas and another north of the La Plata estuary. Three more British vessels had been stopped but released because they were carrying neutral cargoes.[125]

Since then, not a single Britisher had been sighted. Unbeknown to Lüdecke and Canaris, even their few early successes had scared British captains into quitting the harbours of Argentina and Brazil.

Then, early in September, Canaris's intelligence network reported that Royal Navy ships were mustering with the intention of putting paid to the *Dresden*. The British heavy cruisers *Good Hope* and *Monmouth* and the auxiliary cruiser *Otranto* were steaming down from the north and would shortly be arriving in Montevideo.[126] Lüdecke promptly took his ship farther south. One of Canaris's aides, Sublieutenant Neiling, cargo-master aboard the steam collier *Santa Isabel*, hurried to Punta Arenas, Chile's southernmost port, to glean more information and obtain fresh supplies, while the *Dresden* herself withdrew to a bay in Hoste Island, at the extreme tip of South America, to carry out essential repairs.[127]

Neiling returned on September 12, bringing bad news. The British warships *Good Hope*, *Monmouth* and *Glasgow* were cruising off the eastern entrance of the Magellan Strait, some two hundred miles from the *Dresden*'s lair.[128] Lüdecke decided to dodge them by heading northwest into the Pacific. This accorded with Naval Staff advice. Neiling produced a signal from Berlin which had reached Punta Arenas on September 9. It recommended "joint operations with the *Leipzig*," a light cruiser based in the eastern Pacific.[129]

Lüdecke weighed anchor and steamed to meet the *Leipzig*. By so doing, he ultimately joined forces with a German squadron which was ploughing through the watery wastes of the Pacific, rather aimlessly and to little strategic purpose. Bound from the Far East and commanded by Vice-Admiral Count Maximilian von Spee, it was a sizeable armada comprising the heavy cruisers *Scharnhorst* and *Gneisenau*, the light cruisers *Nürnberg* and *Leipzig*, the auxiliary cruiser *Prinz Eitel Friedrich*, the fleet auxiliary *Titania* and eight steam colliers—too large for mercantile warfare but too small for a pitched battle at sea.[130]

Quite as taken aback by the outbreak of war as the *Dresden*, Spee had long debated the best way of deploying his squadron. Instead of disbanding it and allowing each cruiser to act as an independent commerce raider, thereby fragmenting the enemy forces, he waged mercantile warfare with his entire force. This made him the focus of every enemy naval unit within reach, and his link-up with the *Dresden* lured the British West Atlantic Squadron into the Pacific as well. A clash became inevitable.

By virtue of his permanent contacts with German bases in Argentina and Chile, Canaris was among the first to learn of the enemy's redeployment. It was largely thanks to him that Spee received news of the enemy's movements. *Dresden* to commander in chief, night of October 6–7: "*Newcastle* at La Paz September 16. Four British warships reported heading westwards off Cape Horn."[131] Soon afterwards came another report: "From freighter in Corral (Chile), unconfirmed: British cruiser squadron rumoured intending wait for German Far East Squadron off Easter Island . . . Two enemy cruisers passed Punta Arenas morning of October 5."[132]

The *Dresden's* reports became so numerous that Spee dispatched her to comb the bays along the Chilean coast for enemy warships. Canaris improved his intelligence network by contacting merchantmen owned by German shipping companies at Mollendo, Antofagasta, Valparaiso, Talcahuano, Coronel and Corral. All equipped with radio, these vessels reported sightings of any suspicious warships.[133]

Reports from Canaris and the *Leipzig* enabled Spee to surprise the British off Coronel, south of Valparaiso, and hit them hard. Attacking in heavy seas, the German squadron opened fire at 1834 on November 1, 1914. The *Good Hope* sank and the *Monmouth* followed her ninety minutes later.[134] Only the *Glasgow* and *Otranto* managed to escape under cover of darkness. Germany had won the first naval battle of the war and "destroyed the aura of British naval invincibility."[135]

Spee sailed proudly into Valparaiso with several of his ships and received a jubilant welcome from Chile's German colony.[136] Canaris, who was decorated with the Iron Cross Second Class, remained cautious. "A fine success, undoubtedly. It has gained us a temporary breathing space and may also influence the general situation," he wrote to his mother. "However, the chances of peace are still extremely slender. It will probably be a long time before England is finished."[137] Spee, on the other hand, was made reckless by his victory at Coronel. Believing that the enemy's (alleged) confusion had opened up his homeward route, he planned to penetrate the South Atlantic and fight his way back to Germany with the entire squadron.

To make matters worse, the Admiral's thirst for action was aggravated by a rumour that rebellion had broken out in South Africa, compelling the British fleet in the South Atlantic to go to the aid of Britain's hard-pressed settlers there.[138] If true, this meant that Britain's naval base off the southern extremity of Latin America—Port Stanley in the Falkland Islands—would be denuded of protection. Spee promptly decided to destroy Port Stanley en route for the South Atlantic.[139]

In vain did Lüdecke and his fellow captains advise against such an attack, pointing out that nobody knew the enemy's local strength. Their counterproposal was that the squadron should be disbanded and its cruisers released for independent commerce-raiding operations.[140] But nothing could dissuade Spee from attacking. Early on the morning of December 8, the *Gneisenau* and *Nürnberg* headed at full speed for Port Stanley—and perdition. Only the night before, a British squadron had dropped anchor off the Falkland Islands without any inkling of the Germans' proximity. It was a substantial force consisting of two battle cruisers, three heavy cruisers and three other cruisers.[141]

Spee spotted the danger and fled eastwards at full speed, but the damage was done. Though caught unawares, the British warships quickly raised steam. By 1000 they were already under way and had taken up the chase. The Royal Navy's faster vessels quickly overhauled the Germans and cut them down. British salvoes blew Spee's cruisers to pieces one by one. The German ships sank, leaving their crews to struggle vainly in the icy water. At 1617 Spee's flagship went down. A last semaphore message from the doomed squadron commander was addressed to the critics of his Falkland Islands venture: "Admiral to Captain: you were right after all."[142]

Only the *Dresden* remained unscathed. She sped from the British shells and torpedoes like a will-o'-the-wisp, seizing every opportunity to escape disaster. Lüdecke drove his crew to the limit. The cruiser's engines pounded fit to burst as her stokers and engineers expended their last reserves of energy. Little by little, the distance between the *Dresden* and her pursuers increased.[143]

Towards 1700, visibility deteriorated. Darkness fell swiftly. The *Dresden* sped on into the unknown, British gunfire still flickering astern and British shells still sending up great geysers of water all around. Lüdecke maintained a south-southwesterly course in the hope of gaining Tierra del Fuego and seeking refuge from his pursuers in its maze of rocky inlets.[144] But was it the right course? Before long, Lüdecke came to doubt it. He had to assume that the British would cut off his direct route to Tierra del Fuego, and that British cruisers were already patrolling the mouth of the Strait of Magellan and the Beagle Channel, the most obvious approaches to his chosen sanctuary. He altered course in favour of a detour which would take him to Tierra del Fuego from the Pacific side, or via the Cockburn Channel.[145]

Towards afternoon the next day, the *Dresden* rounded Cape Horn. Dense fog enveloped her shortly afterwards, completely eliminating the risk of detection, but Lüdecke kept his men at full stretch. On and on he went, now heading northwestwards along the rocky coast of Tierra del Fuego in an unremitting search for somewhere to veer off. What with the fog, darkness and heavy seas, his initial attempts to find a suitable inlet were frustrated. The ship groped her way cautiously along, ten to twenty miles offshore. Finally, at dawn on December 10, the lookouts spotted a narrow passage between some cliffs and reefs not far from the Lion Rocks and the West Furies.[146]

But the *Dresden*'s navigating officers had no charts of Tierra del Fuego's labyrinthine fjords. Lüdecke crept slowly along, guided by Lieutenant Schenk, who manned the forward crow's-nest and swiftly re-

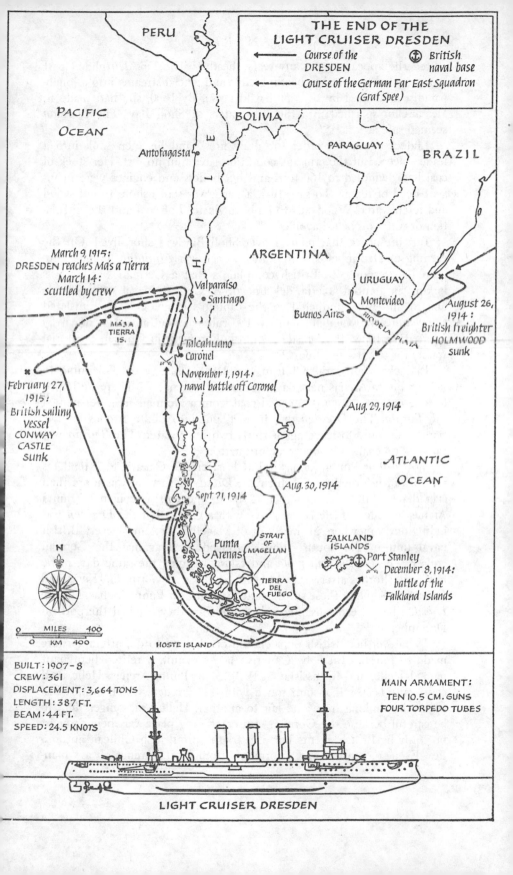

THE END OF THE
LIGHT CRUISER DRESDEN

⟵————— Course of the
DRESDEN

⊕ British
naval base

⟵- - - - - Course of the German Far East Squadron
(Graf Spee)

PERU

PACIFIC
OCEAN

BOLIVIA

PARAGUAY

BRAZIL

C H I L E

Antofagasta

ARGENTINA

URUGUAY

March 9, 1915:
DRESDEN reaches Más a Tierra
March 14:
scuttled by crew

Valparaíso
Santiago

Montevideo

Buenos Aires

RÍO DE LA PLATA

August 26,
1914:
British freighter
HOLMWOOD
sunk

MÁS A
TIERRA
IS.

Talcahuano
Coronel

November 1, 1914:
naval battle off Coronel

Aug. 29, 1914

February 27,
1915:
British sailing
vessel
CONWAY
CASTLE
sunk

ATLANTIC
OCEAN

Aug. 30, 1914

Sept. 21, 1914

N

STRAIT
OF
MAGELLAN

FALKLAND
ISLANDS

Punta
Arenas

Port Stanley
December 8, 1914:
battle of the
Falkland Islands

TIERRA
DEL
FUEGO

MILES   400

KM   400

HOSTE ISLAND

BUILT: 1907-8
CREW: 361
DISPLACEMENT: 3,664 TONS
LENGTH: 387 FT.
BEAM: 44 FT.
SPEED: 24.5 KNOTS

MAIN ARMAMENT:
TEN 10.5 CM. GUNS
FOUR TORPEDO TUBES

LIGHT CRUISER DRESDEN

ported the appearance of any reefs ahead.[147] The *Dresden* glided past
snow-covered mountains, beetling cliffs and glacial streams into a lonely
paradise inhabited by seals and wild geese. By 1600, she had made it.
Her anchor splashed into the still waters of Sholl Bay. The *Dresden*
seemed safe at last.[148]

Lüdecke gave the order to "draw fires" and his men sank into a
leaden sleep. But the cruiser's condition gave him no rest. Her stock of
coal had dwindled to 160 tons and her boilers and engines were in urgent need of repair. To save fuel, a party was sent ashore to cut wood
and fetch water. Wood was to be burnt instead of coal and the distillation of water on board avoided.[149]

But the peace that reigned over Sholl Bay was short-lived. On the
evening of December 11 the Chilean destroyer *Almirante Condell* appeared in response to British complaints that a German warship was
lurking in neutral Tierra del Fuego. A Chilean naval officer came
aboard and was conducted to the captain's cabin. Canaris translated
the visitor's message: pursuant to the rules of neutrality laid down by
international law, the *Dresden* could only remain in Chilean territorial
waters for twenty-four hours.[150]

Lüdecke assured the Chilean that he was in any case planning to
sail for Punta Arenas next day—he had no alternative. There he hoped
to take on some urgently needed coal from a German freighter named
the *Turpin*. The *Dresden* did, in fact, put into Punta Arenas on December 12, only to leave again thirty-two hours later. The *Turpin* was
carrying no coal, only low-grade briquettes.[151]

This call at Punta Arenas did at least enable Canaris to extend his
network of informants, on which the *Dresden's* survival was more than
ever dependent. On December 12 itself, the British consul in Punta
Arenas had alerted the Royal Navy with a report that the *Dresden* was
hiding out somewhere in the Strait of Magellan.[152] Almost every British
naval unit in the South Atlantic arrayed itself against the German
cruiser. The *Bristol*, *Inflexible* and *Glasgow* sailed the same day, to be
followed shortly afterwards by the *Carnarvon*, *Cornwall*, *Kent* and
Orama.[153] Some of these ships headed straight for Punta Arenas, but the
Dresden had already disappeared by the time they reached the port on
December 14.[154]

Whatever her British pursuers did or planned to do, attempts were
made to forestall them by Canaris's latest recruit, a retired lieutenant
named Helle, and his assistants.[155] Based in Punta Arenas, Helle used
couriers to keep in constant touch with the *Dresden*, which evaded discovery by slinking from one lair to another. Helle's messengers had to
be careful because the German cruiser's hiding place was being sought
not only by British agents but also by the pro-British Chilean authorities. Even so, couriers and informants from Punta Arenas always man-

aged to find their way to Canaris—"with extreme devotion and outstanding skill," to quote the official history written by Erich Raeder, who later headed Hitler's Navy.[156]

Helle also alerted the bases at Valparaiso and La Plata with a view to obtaining coal. In mid-December they received the following telegram: "*Dresden* needs steam collier in three weeks at latest. Freighter to seek wireless contact with *Dresden* immediately on entering Smyth Channel. Reply at once whether possible. Do your utmost."[157] The bases reacted promptly. On December 18 the La Plata base dispatched the freighter *Sierra Cordoba* with coal, and other coal ships were also promised.[158]

But hardly any of them eluded the British blockade. Only the *Sierra Cordoba* managed to break through. On the evening of January 18, 1915, she met up with the *Dresden*, which had withdrawn to a remote and still wholly uncharted anchorage (named "Christmas Bay" by her crew)[159] The *Sierra Cordoba's* coal put new heart into Lüdecke. Early in February he telegraphed Naval Staff: "Will attempt break-through to west coast of South America with *Sierra Cordoba* on February 3. Intend transfer commerce-raiding operations to East Indies given availability of sufficient coal."[160]

This plan, too, was frustrated because the bases were unable to dispatch any coal ships to the South Pacific, Lüdecke's proposed area of operations. However, the *Dresden's* commander had no wish to loiter idly in his place of concealment. An early departure was dictated by many factors including the ship's deteriorating condition, the risk of discovery, frequent snowstorms and a steady decline in the crew's morale. Rather than rot away completely, the *Dresden* would have to gain the open sea.

Canaris and his small band of informants did their best to divert the enemy's attention from the western part of Tierra del Fuego. A rumour was spread in Punta Arenas that the *Dresden* had been sighted heading north past Cabo de las Virgenes at the eastern end of the Strait of Magellan.[161] At 0530 on February 14, under cover of a severe blizzard, the cruiser weighed anchor and set off. Once again she weaved her way through a maze of uncharted islands and rocks. At last, just as dusk was falling, she reached the open sea.[162]

The *Dresden* was free once more. Lüdecke ordered full speed ahead, and the cruiser steamed westwards with renewed vigour. A few days later she reached the busy sailing-ship lanes which ran two hundred miles off the coast of southern Chile. On February 27 the *Dresden* scored her first kill, the British full-rigged ship *Conway Castle*, which was carrying 2,400 tons of barley. The vessel was sunk and her crew later transferred to a Peruvian sailing ship.[163]

By the beginning of March, the *Dresden's* coal stocks had again dwindled to the point where she had to radio for help. On March 7 she contacted the freighter *Gotha*, which had been dispatched by the Valparaiso base with 1,200 tons of coal and was urgently requesting a rendezvous. Lüdecke signalled the co-ordinates of the spot in the Pacific where the two vessels were to meet. Heartened by this prospect of a further lease of life, he kept a sharp lookout for more prizes.[164] Little could be seen next day because the sea was shrouded in a dense pall of fog. "At lunch," Schenk recalls, "everyone was cheerful and in high spirits. The *Flying Dutchman* had acquired a worthy rival."[165]

Suddenly the fog lifted. At the same instant, Lieutenant Böker's voice rang through the afterpart of the ship: "Suspicious vessel sighted to starboard, two points abaft the beam—looks like a British cruiser!"[166] The officers grabbed their binoculars and dashed on deck. There was no doubt about it: the silhouette of a British cruiser stood out clearly against the skyline. A swift succession of orders rent the air: "Alarm!", "Action stations!", "Raise steam in all boilers!"[167] It was 1500 hours on March 8, 1915.

Lüdecke soon ascertained that the ship which had surprised him was the heavy cruiser *Kent*. The *Dresden* was virtually defenceless against such an adversary, so his only recourse was flight. He drove his crew and taxed his engines to the limit, just as he had during the battle of the Falkland Islands. Summoning up every ounce of power she possessed, the German cruiser turned and sped from her foe. Lüdecke stared spellbound at the range finder. "Range decreasing . . . range constant . . . range increasing . . ."[168]

Although the *Kent*'s guns could have reached the *Dresden*, they remained unused. The British vessel pursued the German in silence, growing smaller and smaller as she fell behind. The *Kent* did not fire a single shell, clearly frustrated by the light, which was against her.

The *Dresden* had escaped yet again, but Lüdecke had long been aware that her days were numbered. No rendezvous with the *Gotha* was possible, and heavy wireless traffic betrayed that the *Kent* was not the only British warship operating in this area. The *Dresden*'s condition left Lüdecke no choice: she had given her all during that final dash to safety. Her coal stocks had shrunk to eighty tons and most of her ammunition was expended. Steam pipes were leaking, several furnaces were out of action and the ship had lost her combat capacity.[169]

"There was no question of remaining operational," Lüdecke wrote later. "The immediate and imperative need was to seek out a safe harbour."[170] He had, as quickly as possible, to find a neutral country which would intern the *Dresden* before she fell into British hands. But where to find such a place in the middle of the Pacific? The only possibility was to steer north for the Juan Fernández Islands, four hundred miles from the Chilean coast. The scene of Robinson Crusoe's literary adventures, this group was partly uninhabited, but the main island of Más a Tierra boasted a canning factory for crayfish.

Doggedly, Lüdecke headed for Más a Tierra. Although the *Dresden*'s speed was down to twenty knots, she reached there without incident. At about 0830 on March 9, her anchor chains rattled into the waters of Cumberland Bay on the north side of the island.[171] She had escaped yet again, if only temporarily.

Soon afterwards the Chilean harbour master, a cigar dealer, came aboard and informed the Germans that their warship must conform to international practice by quitting the bay within twenty-four hours. Lüdecke explained that lack of coal made this impossible and that he wished the *Dresden* and her crew to be interned.[172] Although amenable to this idea, the Chilean merely shrugged when asked what protection he could offer the ship against a British attack. The island possessed no military installations.

Lüdecke then proposed sending for some Chilean warships. The harbour master agreed, but added that it would be days before he could get a letter to the competent authorities in Chile. Lüdecke offered to put the *Dresden*'s radio equipment at his disposal, but the Chilean declined on the grounds that he possessed no code. Lüdecke had no choice but to wait. The Chilean drafted a letter to his superiors on the mainland and an auxiliary-powered sailing vessel set off with it the same evening.[173]

Days went by, but no word came. Meanwhile, Lüdecke demobilized his ship. All boilers except one were extinguished and some of the crew allowed ashore. Any officer who chose to make his own way back to Germany was permitted to do so. The executive officer, senior gunnery officer and two other members of the wardroom chartered a sailing boat and left for Valparaiso, where they managed to get a passage home.[174] The possibility of scuttling the *Dresden* was also explored after approval had been obtained from Naval Staff. A signal received from Berlin during the night of March 9–10 stated: "His Majesty the Emperor leaves you free to put your vessel out of commission."[175]

But the British wanted to preclude this possibility. The *Kent* had soon discovered where the *Dresden* was lurking and summoned reinforcements. Directed by the captain of the light cruiser *Glasgow*, the bombardment in Cumberland Bay on the morning of March 14 finally showed what scant regard the British paid to the neutrality of an undefended Chilean island. The *Dresden* was done for. Shell-torn, immobilized and on fire, she could only be preserved from capture by a *coup de grâce*.

Accordingly, Lieutenant Canaris was instructed to parley with the *Glasgow* until the *Dresden*'s scuttling charges were in place. Standing in the cruiser's steam-pinnace, he steered for the *Glasgow*'s belching guns. They did not cease firing until he was close to the enemy vessel's side.[176] A sudden and unearthly hush descended. Canaris climbed aboard.

A few minutes later he was face to face with Captain John Luce, the Glasgow's commanding officer. Canaris launched into a lengthy verbal protest. By attacking His Imperial Majesty's Ship Dresden, British naval forces had committed a blatant breach of international law because the German cruiser was in Chilean territorial waters and thus enjoyed the protection of Chilean neutrality. What was more, the ship and her crew had already been provisionally interned. "Captain Luce's answer," relates the official British naval history of World War I, "was —as the tradition of the service demanded—that he could treat on no basis but that of unconditional surrender."[177]

Canaris objected that the British attitude violated all the provisions of international law, Chile being a neutral country. To this, Luce retorted: "My orders are to destroy the Dresden wherever I find her. Other matters are not my concern—the diplomats will have to settle those later."[178]

Artfully, Luce asked Canaris whether the Dresden had not in any case struck her colours (the British had evidently noticed that the German cruiser's ensign had been shot down). Canaris took Luce to the rail and pointed out that her ensign had been resecured to the foremast.[179] There was no more to be said. Silently, the British officers saluted as the German Emperor's lieutenant left the ship.

Canaris hurried back to the Dresden. Lüdecke had by now completed his preparations for scuttling and sent the crew ashore. The sea cocks were opened and the fuses of the scuttling charges ignited. Lüdecke was the last to leave. At 1115, two mighty detonations shook the hull. Then came a dazzling eruption of flame followed by dirty yellow clouds of smoke. A few seconds later the Dresden's bow dipped, the stern and screws rose high into the air, and the entire hull slid beneath the surface to the traditional cheers of the crew mustered ashore.[180]

But Lüdecke was a broken man. Almost apathetically, he left his adjutant to handle everything from evacuating the wounded (whom the British took to Valparaiso), to burying the seven dead and providing the crew with makeshift accommodation in the huts of the local fishing village.[181] The Germans had to wait another five days before plumes of smoke on the horizon betrayed the approach of two Chilean cruisers, the Zenteno and the Esmeralda, which were to transport them to the mainland.[182]

The bulk of the Dresden's crew were embarked in the Esmeralda. Only Lüdecke and Canaris travelled in the Zenteno. They were astonished to be welcomed aboard in flawless German by two Chilean naval officers with German names. Captain Schröder, commanding the *Zenteno*, and his executive officer, Lieutenant Günther, raided their own lockers to provide the Germans with underwear and other comforts.[183] Their orders were to take the *Dresden*'s crew to Talcahuano, but fresh instructions received en route redirected them to Valparaiso.[184]

The British were at pains to ensure that the Germans did not slip off home and rejoin the fray. As soon as the British Ambassador in Chile heard that the *Dresden*'s crew were to be lodged aboard the German steamer *York* in Valparaiso harbour like any shipwrecked sailors, he brought pressure to bear on the weak-kneed Chilean authorities.[185] A new order reached the Germans: they were to be interned on Quiriquina, off the Central Chilean city of Concepción.

On March 24 the Germans caught their first glimpse of the Isla Quiriquina, a barren and sparsely inhabited island which had once been the site of a Chilean naval academy. Its rugged cliffs sloped gradually down to form a valley in the east. The *Esmeralda*, to which all the Germans had now been transferred, headed for this valley. A landing stage came into view, and beyond it a rough track leading to some huts where the internees were to be accommodated.[186]

Canaris, together with Lüdecke and the remaining officers, was billeted in a house ten minutes' walk from the huts. Although Chilean sentries were posted, the Germans were left to run the camp themselves. The officers assigned duties and held muster parades to keep the men on their toes. Lüdecke to his crew: "The Chilean government has assigned us this island as a place of residence. No one may leave it without special permission. The Chilean sentries are only here to prevent attempts to escape, which I would strongly caution you against. And now, join me in the cry: His Majesty the Emperor, hurrah!"[187] Lüdecke did not allow his men to idle. Some working parties improved the island's water mains while others laid roads, repaired roofs or built kitchens.

The officers supervised these tasks or devoted their time to riding, for the German landowners on the mainland—Concepción was the centre of a large German colony—had insisted on putting horses at the disposal of the *Dresden*'s wardroom.[188] Officers were even permitted to pay occasional visits to Concepción at the invitation of German residents, and many a party on German-owned estates helped to console them against the rigours of internment.

But Canaris gradually became bored with life on Quiriquina. He had not joined the Navy to rot in idleness on some godforsaken island in the Pacific. Thoughts of escape had preoccupied him (and many others) ever since his arrival, but Lüdecke was careful to ensure that no one left the island. It took Canaris some time to persuade the captain that it was pointless to detain him there any longer. Lüdecke finally abandoned his opposition when Erckert, the German diplomatic representative, also agreed that Canaris should escape and try to make his way back to Germany. He did, however, contrive to be absent from Quiriquina when the escape actually took place. Early in August Lüdecke travelled to Valparaiso with the Chilean authorities' permission, there to transact some official business at the embassy and spend a month's vacation as the guest of a local German doctor.[189] Lüdecke was hardly off the island when Canaris embarked on preparations for his own hazardous journey.

On the night of August 3–4, 1915, he crept silently out of the officers' quarters.[190] Like almost every member of the *Dresden*'s crew, he knew the escape route by heart. Evading the Chilean sentries, who only cordoned off the valley, he headed for the rougher and more precipitous ground in the northeast. From there a path led down to a place on the shore where a tall cliff jutted into the sea. At low tide, a small beach became exposed—just big enough to enable a fishing boat to land. The mainland was only a couple of hours away, and plenty of fishermen were ready to earn twenty pesos by ferrying someone across.[191]

Sure enough, a fisherman was waiting there. Canaris jumped in. The boat slid quietly into the water and crossed the bay. Then came a stretch which was visible to the sentries and within range of their rifles. Nothing stirred. Minute by minute Wilhelm Canaris drew farther away from his sterile island prison and nearer the adventures that lay ahead.

2

Mission in
the Mediterranean

The route had been selected and money was waiting. As soon as Canaris landed on a quiet beach near Concepción, he was passed from one helping hand to another. Once his plan to escape became known to them, many local Germans had advised him on the best way of evading Chilean surveillance and pursuit.

The first essential was to cross the usually snowbound Cordilleras (Andes), a natural frontier and barrier between Chile and her more pro-German neighbour Argentina. This was where most would-be escapers came to grief. "Some of them died on the way," recalls a member of the *Dresden's* crew, "while others perished in the passes and tunnels of the Andes and were buried who knows where."[1]

Canaris had made some preliminary contacts while visiting the German landowners who maintained large estates in the lowlands near Concepción. It was on the winegrowing estate of San Cristóbal and at the home of its owner, a German named Puffe, that Canaris had first glimpsed a vague chance of escaping internment. A couple of his host's friends had volunteered to provide everything necessary to put him as quickly as possible beyond reach of the Chilean police.[2] They kept their word. When Canaris turned up during the early hours of August 4, 1915, all was ready—money, a rail ticket and letters of recommendation to friends in Argentina.

The man who left for the South a few hours later bore little outward resemblance to the fugitive German naval officer named Wilhelm Canaris. Attired in a travelling outfit of local cut, he was seated with apparent nonchalance in the carriage of a train bound for the South Chilean provincial capital of Osorno, a centre frequented by the German immigrants who had turned its environs into a farmer's and cattle breeder's El Dorado.[3] But Canaris did not yield to a false sense of security. It would not be long before his absence from Quiriquina was spotted and the Chilean police reacted. After a brief rest at Osorno, Canaris bought a horse and galloped off. He had to gain the shelter of the Cordilleras before his pursuers picked up his trail.

Canaris rode east and then northeast, consistently avoiding the larger townships and spending the night at secluded inns. Villages sped past, figures loomed up and vanished like phantoms. Canaris seldom paused to rest. He trekked across highland plateaux, skirted salt lakes and plodded on through snowstorms. He could not afford to feel even temporarily secure until a fortnight later, when he reached Argentine soil. Then he headed for an estate owned by Herr von Bülow, a German-Argentinian settler to whom one of his letters of recommendation was addressed.[4] Bülow took the exhausted fugitive in and urged him to rest up, but Canaris did not linger.

Accepting the offer of a fresh horse, he rode to the Central Argentinian cathedral town of Neuquén, at the confluence of the rivers Neuquén and Limay, and boarded a train to Buenos Aires, where he arrived on August 21.[5] He immediately reported to the naval attaché at the German Embassy, who made the necessary travel arrangements. Canaris was issued with a passport representing him as a Chilean widower named Reed Rosas, son of a Chilean father and a British mother. The naval attaché also found a ship capable of getting him safely through the Allied blockade of the eastern Atlantic and home to Germany. The Dutch steamship *Frisia*, which was due to sail in the next few days, circuitously bound for Amsterdam by way of the Brazilian, Portuguese and British coasts, still had a cabin to spare for Señor Rosas.[6]

Canaris soon got a chance to try out his new passport. He told the captain of the *Frisia* that he had to visit Holland urgently to settle matters arising from an inheritance left him by a relative of his British mother.[7] The captain, who saw no reason to refuse such a well-connected Chilean a passage to Rotterdam, welcomed Reed Rosas aboard. At the end of August, the *Frisia* cast off and sailed out of Buenos Aires.

The events of the next few weeks form part of the Canaris legend. None of his biographers omits to embroider this transatlantic voyage with a wealth of dramatic detail designed to adumbrate him as a master spy in the making. He is reputed to have played the part of a Chilean so perfectly and made such friends with the British on board that the

Royal Navy intelligence officers who examined the *Frisia*'s crew and passengers at Plymouth passed him without hesitation—indeed, he is even said to have helped the British security men check on a Chilean whose accent had aroused their suspicions.[8]

Fact or fiction, there is no doubt that Canaris reached Amsterdam on September 30 after a lengthy passage via Montevideo, Santos, Rio de Janeiro, Bahia, Pernambuco, Lisbon and Falmouth. With some difficulty, he secured an entry visa to Germany and finally reached home on October 4, 1915. Tremulous with mental strain and physical exhaustion, he turned up on the doorstep of his aunt Dorothea Popp's house in Hamburg. But Canaris's temperament would not allow him to rest even then. After a little refreshment at his aunt's home, he reported to the Naval Staff and submitted a personal account of the *Dresden*'s last voyage.

The relevant Naval Staff department recorded this in the form of an official memorandum. A far from rosy report, it was tinged with the fierce resentment of a man who was still smarting from the loss of his ship and looking for scapegoats to explain why, despite her successful escape after the battle of the Falkland Islands, the *Dresden* had so quickly succumbed to her enemies and the problem of coal supplies. Canaris knew of one such scapegoat· Caesar Wehrhahn, managing director of the Cosmos steamship company, whom he accused of insufficiently supporting the *Dresden* with his vessels and their crews. In particular, he claimed, Wehrhahn had made inadequate use of the freighter *San Sacramento*, which was supposed to keep Spee's squadron supplied with fuel and information. Canaris boldly accused the managing director of "prejudicing national interests." A Naval Staff officer took the following denunciation down in writing: "The managing director of the Cosmos line, Herr Wehrhahn, conducted himself in an extremely unsatisfactory manner, in that, by compromising his subordinates Sielfeld and Derp and refusing to assign the steamship *Sacramento* as instructed by the Cosmos line, he ran the risk of exposing our entire network of informants. The *Sacramento* was hopelessly compromised by this behaviour on Herr W's part."[9]

Canaris's superiors rewarded the *Dresden*'s former adjutant for his perseverance by promoting him to Kapitänleutnant [senior lieutenant] on November 16.[10] They did not, however, seem to have any suitable outlet for his drive and enthusiasm. After posting him to No. 1 Naval Inspection Department in Kiel, they gave him a few brief assignments afloat and ashore.[11]

Further plagued by a recurrence of his old malaria, Canaris restrained his impatience with difficulty. This was not his idea of how to fight a war. He had not ridden hundreds of miles and endured extremes of hunger and fatigue in order to be wasted on sterile military routine.

He itched to serve his country on a ship's bridge and prove himself in action. An official memorandum recorded: "His personal wish is to command a torpedo boat."[12]

At the end of November, his impatience was dispelled by an order from the Naval Staff. Canaris had caught the attention of its Intelligence Section (Naval Staff N). German naval intelligence officers had evidently learned of the skill with which Canaris had employed informants and agents on behalf of the naval authorities. The growth of naval warfare in the Mediterranean called for a new intelligence and supply organization, and Canaris seemed the ideal person to set it up.

Ever since Italy entered the war in May 1915, German naval operations had been extended to cover enemy commerce in the Mediterranean as well. Submarine warfare promised to yield a particularly rich harvest in that area because weather conditions in the Mediterranean were more favourable than those of the stormy Atlantic. The one great impediment to successful economic warfare against the Entente was that Germany's allies on the Mediterranean seaboard, Austria-Hungary and Turkey, possessed virtually no operational submarines. What was more, four thousand miles of sea separated the German U-boat fleet from the nearest Austro-Hungarian base of Cattaro (now Kotor) in the South Adriatic.[13]

The approach route for German U-boats was so circuitous and laborious that the Naval Staff at first doubted whether they could be successfully deployed in the Mediterranean. April 1915 saw the first German submarine depart for this new theatre of operations. *U21*, commanded by Lieutenant Otto Hersing, was assigned to support the Turkish defenders of the Dardanelles in their fight against the Anglo-French expeditionary force. Hersing chose a complicated route round the north of the British Isles. He reached the Central Mediterranean unscathed, only to run out of fuel. *U21* had to put in at Cattaro and replenish before proceeding to the Dardanelles.[14] Total duration of passage: one month.

The success of *U21* (she sank two British capital ships and damaged a third, thereby contributing to the Dardanelles victory) encouraged the Naval Staff to transfer more U-boats to the Mediterranean.[15] To cut out the long passage by sea, ten small B- and C-class boats were transported by rail to the Austro-Hungarian naval base of Pola (southwest of Trieste) and reassembled at a shipyard there.[16] They then sallied forth into the Adriatic and Eastern Central Mediterranean. Being unsuitable for major operations, however, they were generally used as small-scale ammunition transports and served to maintain contact with Turkey by sea.

In summer 1915 the German naval authorities decided to intervene in the Mediterranean with larger U-boats dispatched by sea. Because growing American opposition to German submarine warfare in the Atlantic had prompted Berlin to limit operations against shipping in the North Sea, more U-boats became available for the Mediterranean. By October 1915, five large U-boats (*U33, 34, 35, 38,* and *39*) had reached Cattaro. A month later Lieutenant Commander Kophamel of *U35* relinquished his boat to Lieutenant Lothar von Arnauld de la Perière and assumed command of "U-Flotilla Mediterranean."[17]

Kophamel used his small force to wage economic warfare on a broad front. Not content to operate in the Adriatic and near the Dardanelles, he was soon thrusting farther and farther afield. *U21* operated off the Syrian coast while other U-boats penetrated the Western Mediterranean and opened up new hunting grounds in the sea area west of Gibraltar. *U38* destroyed some British and French warships in the port of Funchal, Madeira, and before long the Germans were threatening the coasts of Morocco.[18]

As soon as the first Class C II transport U-boats became available, U-Flotilla Mediterranean carried out a number of special missions in the field of psychological warfare. Their main objective was British- and French-controlled North Africa, whose restive inhabitants were to be incited against their colonial overlords. Lieutenant Franz Becker and his transport U-boat *UC20* maintained contact with native opponents of the French on the Moroccan coast, while tribes in Tripolitania, which had risen in revolt against Italian rule under Turkish leadership, were supplied with arms by Kophamel's boats.[19]

Operations on this ambitious scale required an efficient supply organization. U-boats patrolling the Western Mediterranean, many hundreds of miles from the Adriatic bases of Cattaro and Pola, were particularly dependent on receiving supplies and spares in good time. They could only operate if enough fuel, ammunition and food were available, but what if they had fired all their torpedoes, exhausted their fuel or were having engine trouble? In such cases, a clandestine supply organization went to work. This, in turn, could only operate from the one neutral country in the Western Mediterranean: Spain.

Immediately after the outbreak of war, German naval intelligence had established a Spanish base whose agents had the task of providing German warships with supplies and information about the enemy.[20] Its director was Lieutenant Commander Hans von Krohn, a forty-four-year-old officer who had been sent to Madrid in August-September 1914 after a brief spell of training.[21] Although Krohn had no secret service experience, Naval Staff set store by his knowledge of Spain and social contacts. Through his father-in-law, a Portuguese businessman and honorary consul, he had access to commercial circles in the Iberian Peninsula.[22]

But Krohn, who had to work in the shadow of the German naval attaché in Madrid and did not take over the latter's job until February 1918, lacked the imagination and gift for improvisation of the true secret serviceman, nor was he tough enough to hold his own against the German Embassy's military attaché and espionage chief proper, Major Kalle, who represented the interests of the secret intelligence service of the Army High Command.[23] Canaris was brought in to remedy this. His instructions were to help develop the Madrid "centre" and set up a supply system for U-boats operating in the Western Mediterranean, but he also had to create an improved reconnaissance service capable of providing firm information about enemy shipping movements.[24]

Canaris set off on November 30, 1915, and reached Madrid a few days later, having travelled overland via Italy and France.[25] The lieutenant, who was again using his Chilean passport, shunned the German Embassy in Calle Castellana for security reasons. He rented various apartments in the name of Reed Rosas and switched addresses frequently.[26] All in all, he led the life of a secret agent. His immediate boss, Krohn, never saw him except at home. Informants and couriers he met at secluded spots, generally employing the weird and wonderful pseudonym "Kika"—something which must surely have gratified a boyhood devotee of coded messages and invisible inks.[27]

Only a handful of embassy personnel knew who Kika was. Canaris maintained contact with Kalle and the latter's two closest associates, Lieutenant Colonel von Winterfeld and Secretary Eberhard von Stohrer, who was destined to work with (and against) Canaris as Germany's Ambassador in Madrid during World War II.[28] Few of them shared the newcomer's great expectations. Major Kalle considered Spain an unproductive intelligence field and had put in several requests for a transfer because "the transmission of intelligence from here is of only minor value."[29] Even thirteen years later, Major von Koss—another member of the same circle—was cautioning higher authority against Canaris's exaggerated enthusiasm: despite his past achievements, he would rather "not entrust Herr C. with a big and responsible assignment."[30]

Kika quickly made a name for himself in the small Madrid community of German agents and their Spanish patrons. Madrid society, young Spanish naval officers and the business world in particular, helped Canaris to fulfil his special mission with success. Many doors in Madrid were open to the fair-haired *extranjero* with his partiality for Hispano-American culture and the Latin way of life. "In Spain," the Duquesa de la Torre wrote to a French diplomat shortly before Canaris's arrival, "'society' is pro-German—but it is so without being anti-French in consequence. The Germans have the women and priests on their side . . . The women are pro-German mainly because the Queen Mother, being Austrian, naturally cherishes Austro-German sympathies.

To please the Queen Mother, who still wields great influence, people are pro-German—simply because she is. It's the done thing!"[31]

Alfonso XIII of Spain, too, regarded the Germans with some benevolence although he sometimes expressed sympathy for the Allies as well. Major Kalle knew how to foster pro-German sentiments in this highest of all quarters because he had become the pleasure-loving monarch's almost constant companion and could claim to be his personal friend.[32] They were on such close terms that it alarmed the British intelligence chief in Spain, Captain F. Touhy. "The King talks too much," Touhy reported, "and it is to be feared that he conveys information acquired from Allied naval and military attachés to enemy ears." In addition, he was "surrounded by a completely pro-German court clique and a like-minded General Staff."[33]

Given this favourable climate of opinion, Canaris could conduct an almost carefree tour of the Spanish ports in quest of recruits for an improved reconnaissance service. He was assisted by Kalle's military intelligence centres in Madrid, Barcelona and San Sebastián as well as a V-Mann in Bilbao.[34] Little by little, the recruitment of new informants enabled the naval intelligence service to establish a network of its own. Its focal point was in southern Spain. Carlos Fricke, later vice-consul, kept watch in Valencia, the businessman Ricardo Classen submitted reports from Cádiz and Captains Meyer and Stahl kept enemy naval movements under observation from their ships the *Roma* and *Caesar*.[35]

By early 1916, all the principal ports in Spain had agents ready to gather information about the enemy and transmit it to Kika. Sailors from Allied ships were pumped, Spanish labourers at the British naval base in Gibraltar were put on Kika's payroll and Spanish seamen worked for the Germans with alacrity.[36] At Krohn's home, Canaris drafted almost weekly reports on the subject of probable Allied naval operations. These reports were always addressed to Naval Staff N.[37] From Berlin they were usually forwarded to the staff of U-Flotilla Mediterranean at Cattaro.

Canaris's second problem—the establishment of a supply network—proved more intractable. Few Spanish dealers were prepared to furnish German warships with food and equipment, and it was hard to find enough boats and small vessels capable of transporting supplies to German submarines operating in the Mediterranean. Then, unexpectedly, the key to Canaris's problem was provided by one of the biggest ship-owners in Spain.

Prince Max von Ratibor, the German Ambassador in Madrid, had connections with a Hispano-German banking group, though it would be hard to say who was more dependent on whom. The ambassador owed the Kocherthaler-Ullmann-Lewin group repayments on a debt of 250,000 pesetas, whereas the bankers needed Ratibor's approval in order to export graphite products to France.[38] Ullmann not only heard about Canaris's transport problem and came up with an answer but was destined to figure frequently in his life.[39]

Ullmann introduced Canaris to the industrialist Horacio Echevarrieta, one of the most influential men in Spain. Echevarrieta was a press tycoon, a friend of the King's and a liberal (his private secretary, Indalecio Prieto, later became the leader of the Socialist Party).[40] From Canaris's angle, this man of many parts fulfilled an even more important function: he owned the shipbuilding firm of Echevarrieta y Lariniaga, which controlled shipyards at Cádiz, Barcelona and Ferrol.[41] Writing of him ten years later, Canaris said: "He is a Basque by birth, extremely proud and ambitious, and the wealthiest industrialist in Spain."[42] Echevarrieta was not averse to the proposal that his company should build some small auxiliary and supply ships for the Germans.

He finally agreed on condition that the deal could be kept secret from the Spanish authorities (Spain was, after all, a neutral country) and from Echevarrieta y Lariniaga's British customers. Canaris provided plenty of camouflage. During his frequent visits to the Echevarrieta yards, Señor Rosas purported to be a South American marine construction expert who welcomed the Spanish shipbuilding industry's readiness to take some of the pressure off its Latin American counterpart, which was overburdened with Allied war contracts.[43] The engineers and employees of Echevarrieta's firm genuinely believed they were working for a South American customer.

Meanwhile, presumably with Echevarrieta's help, Canaris recruited the Spanish crews who were to man his miniature fleet of supply ships. The first vessels were ready to sail in spring 1916. Their captains, all Spaniards, were under strict orders to fly the Spanish flag and never stray far from their ports of origin.[44] As floating U-boat bases, they now became indispensable aids to Germany's conduct of the war at sea. Operating primarily in the Cádiz area and off the Canary Islands, these Madrid-controlled auxiliaries were always on hand when U-boats needed provisions, ammunition and spares. The Canaris-Echevarrieta partnership had passed its first test. Ten years later, it was to make another important contribution to Germany's naval requirements.[45]

But Canaris had no wish to await the fruition of his work in Spain. He longed to quit the backwoods of the war and cease acting as a mere purveyor to his comrades fighting on the high seas. Eager to be one of their number and command a vessel in action against the enemy, he put in for a transfer to the torpedo boat arm and urged his superior, Krohn, to back this request. Although Krohn was reluctant to lose his best man, he finally agreed—especially as HQ Baltic Station in Kiel were showing a keen interest in the competent young officer.[46]

Without waiting for a U-boat to pick him up so that he could return to Germany via Cattaro, Canaris conceived the idea of making his own way home. Again relying on his South American alias, he hoped to sneak through France and Italy in the role of a consumptive Chilean seeking treatment at a Swiss sanatorium.[47] On February 21 he left Madrid.[48] He travelled through France and northern Italy by train until he was only a few miles from the Swiss border.

At this juncture, HQ Baltic Station received an alarming report that Canaris had been detained by the Italian police. An immediate query addressed to the Naval Staff's Intelligence Section proved unproductive. On February 28 Berlin telegraphed Kiel: "Lieutenant Canaris left Spain for Genoa February 21. Nothing has since been heard of him. Will advise you as soon as something is known. Naval Staff N."[49] It was not until two days later that the Naval Staff received a dispatch whose gist was that Canaris had been arrested in Genoa on February 24.[50] The root of the mystery: the French secret service had discovered the true identity of Reed Rosas and warned the Italian frontier authorities.[51]

French counterespionage in Spain had succeeded in "turning" an associate of the German Embassy in Madrid who noted anything he could glean at the Calle Castellana and passed it on to the French.[52] He had obviously heard references to the mysterious Reed Rosas without exactly knowing what he did. This information was sufficient for the French to alert the Italians, but the French evidence must have been so sketchy that the Italian police remained dubious. On March 3 Naval Staff N were told: "To all appearances, his release is probable."[53]

Krohn, who nonetheless considered his ex-assistant to be in the gravest danger, promptly urged his friends in the Spanish Government and Navy to intervene in Rome on Canaris's behalf. It is also probable that intermediaries approached the Vatican and protested that Reed Rosas was indeed a Chilean, not a German spy.[54] These moves could not have fully convinced the Italian authorities, because Canaris's return took such a dramatic form that it bred the most colourful legends during his own lifetime. According to one account he locked the prison chaplain in his cell, killed him and escaped in his cassock. Another version is that the Italians released him but put him aboard a Spanish ship bound for Marseilles, and that Canaris persuaded the captain to alter course and head straight for Spain.[55]

There is no proof of this. Only one extant document, a naval medical report dated 1924, relates to Canaris's sojourn in Genoa and implies that he did, at least, escape from his prison cell. Preserved in telegraphic form by his doctor, Canaris's comments on his imprisonment at Genoa are as follows: "Detained in Italy during return journey, very harsh conditions, rigorous questioning, badly treated; escaped again."[56] The fact is that Canaris reappeared in Madrid on March 15. Five days later Naval Staff N telegraphed Baltic HQ: "Return via Switzerland impossible. Having regard to circumstances governing a journey from Spain . . . he will be advised to attempt a return via Holland or America and Norway."[57]

Safe but frustrated, Canaris was obliged to continue his work for the Madrid centre. German naval intelligence was not displeased at having its agent Kika back in Spain. On March 20, 1916, Naval Staff N stated: "Lieutenant Canaris has no choice but to remain in Spain for the present."[58] In any case, Krohn had a number of new assignments for his aide. Naval Staff were planning to dispatch some more large U-boats into the Mediterranean, and the east coast of Spain was looming ever larger in the strategic considerations of those responsible for supplying them by sea. For Canaris, this meant building up his network of informants in ports along the Spanish Mediterranean seaboard.[59]

Again his intermediaries set about establishing caches of spare parts for submarines and recruiting helpers for the conveyance of supplies and equipment. Even the Spanish port authorities were enlisted, and many a harbour master looked the other way when a U-boat tied up in quest of assistance. Captain Touhy of British intelligence furiously protested that the U-boat problem was "extremely grave. German U-boat commanders do as they please in Spanish waters and ports."[60]

Krohn and Canaris, too, expanded their intelligence activities. Their agents compiled information about the British (whereas espionage against France was Kalle's preserve).[61] The Madrid centre's radius of action extended to South America. Canaris reactivated his Latin American connections dating from the *Dresden* period and kept watch on the loyalty of German expatriates across the Atlantic.[62]

As time went by, the Madrid centre became additionally responsible for sabotage assignments. Its leading lights toyed with the idea of staging bomb explosions in Britain. The Spanish newspaper *El Liberal* later hinted that a naval officer not attached to the German Embassy (clearly a reference to Canaris) had engaged in sabotage, but Canaris denied it.[63] This much he did concede: "I still vaguely recall Krohn telling me that he was thinking of smuggling explosives into ore carriers bound for England [from northern Spain] so as to blow up some blast furnaces there."[64]

Canaris continued to weave his tangled web, but his heart was not in it. HQ Baltic Station, too, became fractious and requested Canaris's speedy return "in view of the great need for U-boat commanders."[65] Naval Staff began by playing hard to get (as late as September it informed HQ Baltic that Canaris's return could not be guaranteed "in the immediate future") but eventually recalled Krohn's aide from Spain.[66] The officer commanding U-Flotilla Mediterranean was instructed to send one of his U-boats to southern Spain and pick Canaris up at a prearranged spot.

Flotilla Commander Kophamel transmitted this order to *U34*, which was then operating in the Western Mediterranean under Lieutenant Rücker. Rücker was instructed to pick up Canaris off the port of Cartagena, but bad weather frustrated the venture.[67] The order was then passed to Lieutenant von Arnauld de la Perière, whose *U35* was preying on merchantmen near the Balearics. Arnauld's instructions were to rendezvous with Canaris in the Bay of Salitrona west of Cartagena. The sailing boat carrying Canaris would identify itself by hoisting a red signal flag and repeatedly dipping its mainsail.[68] Date: September 30.

But the plan was betrayed even before Canaris and two companions, Sublieutenant Sievers and Acting Officer Badewitz, could prepare for the trip and charter a boat through an agent in Cartagena.[69] The French agent in the German Embassy had evidently kept his ears open. Soon afterwards the French submarine *Opale*, under Commandant Pradeau, headed for the Bay of Salitrona escorted by an auxiliary cruiser disguised as a trawler.[70] When September 30 dawned, both French vessels were lying in wait. Their orders were brief and to the point: the craft carrying Germany's most dangerous agent in Spain must be destroyed.

U35 had been delayed by a counterattack in the strait between the Balearic islands of Majorca and Ibiza, while Canaris had found it difficult to slip out of Cartagena harbour in the tender of the German steamship *Roma* and get aboard the sailing boat unobserved. Arnauld, who vainly kept watch, noted in his patrol report: "Lay stopped in Salitrona Bay, did not see Lieut. Canaris . . . Lay on surface at rendezvous line, cruised east and west inshore during night. Not having found Canaris yet, intend conduct renewed search of Salitrona Bay after midnight."[71]

The French auxiliary cruiser was the first vessel to sight Canaris's boat gliding down the coast on the morning of October 1. The spurious trawler headed for the craft at once. "The trawler quickly drew nearer," Canaris records. "We hid in the sand ballast inside the boat. The trawler hove to just astern of us and the captain peered inside. Seeing only the Spanish crew, he slowly proceeded southeast towards a vessel which was coming into view there"—Pradeau's submarine.[72] Canaris climbed cautiously out of his hiding place. Soon afterwards he sighted what he had been looking for: a periscope unobtrusively breaking surface.

Still submerged, Arnauld could make out Canaris and his companions screened from the French by the boat's sail. He could also see the red identification signal, but how was he to pick up the party of Ger-

mans without courting a French attack? There was only one way. He
would have to surface in the lee of the sailing boat, take them quickly
aboard and dive in the twinkling of an eye. Arnauld gave the requisite
orders and U35 surfaced. The French auxiliary cruiser promptly alerted
the Opale with a series of strident blasts from her siren.[73]

Canaris, Sievers and Badewitz stared spellbound at the German submarine. "We jumped aboard at 0640," Canaris recalled later. "The entire manoeuvre took about three or four minutes."[74] The U-boat's steel
hull was already subsiding into the depths by the time Pradeau grasped
what had happened. He had "not noticed the boat because, seen from
my position, it was right in line with the setting sun, which badly
dazzled me," as Pradeau wrote after the war—a flattering piece of self-
delusion because the incident occurred in the morning and not at
sunset.[75] After briefly debating whether to attack the French, Arnauld
decided to head for Cattaro. U35 returned to base on October 9. Canaris was safe at last.[76]

A few days later he reported on the Spanish mission to his Naval
Staff superiors. Vice-Admiral Reinhard Koch of naval intelligence glow-
ingly stated that Canaris had carried out his special assignment "with
exceptional skill, vigour and circumspection, so I have recommended
him for a decoration at the highest level."[77] On October 20 he was "respectfully placed under imperial orders," as a letter to HQ Baltic Station put it, and four days later a decoration arrived in the shape of the
Iron Cross First Class.[78] Canaris had made it. His route to the bridge of
a warship was open at last.

Although his dream of commanding a torpedo boat never materialized, he was appointed to command a submarine instead. After all its
sanguinary setbacks on the battlefields of Europe, the German High
Command had decided that U-boats were its last hope of laying the
British low before the Americans acted on their already discernible intention of joining forces with the Entente. Naval Staff had long been
planning to wage unrestricted submarine warfare, For this, competent
officers were needed. Anyone in the Imperial Navy worth his salt—
anyone who had shown courage and ingenuity—was seconded to the
U-boat arm. Canaris qualified admirably.

On October 24, 1916, Naval Staff assigned him to the Inspectorate
of Submarines, and Canaris took up his duties in a U-boat soon afterwards.[79] He learnt the rudiments of submarine warfare and took one
course after another: first the commander's course at the Submarine
School in Eckernförde, then the observer's course and finally a course of
practical instruction in a training boat.[80] The head of the Submarine
School, Lieutenant Commander Eschenburg, rated Canaris "a very
gifted officer, both theoretically and practically, and endowed with outstanding qualities which render him particularly suited to the U-boat

arm." General assessment: "Particularly well suited to command a large submarine or submarine cruiser."[81]

The Inspectorate of Submarines could hardly withhold such a talented officer from operational duties. Canaris had only just passed his practical examination at the Submarine School on September 11, 1917, when he was posted to a theatre of war whose intelligence and supply problems could not have been more familiar to him. On September 16 he was assigned to the chief of U-Flotilla Mediterranean for employment as a submarine commander.[82]

Canaris found it harder to leave Kiel than he would ever have suspected on his return from Spain. He had since met a girl—the first to restore his self-confidence since an abortive liaison with Edith Hill, an American businessman's daughter to whom he had become engaged after his digression into the Balkan War in December 1913. The new girl's name was Erika Waag, and she was a friend of the sister of one of Canaris's brother officers, who had introduced the couple.[83] Born on January 26, 1893, Erika was the daughter of a Pforzheim manufacturer. Cultivated, interested in art and fond of music, she had an austere beauty which strangely attracted the sensitive young lieutenant. Her firm and often masterful manner supplied what Canaris (and many of his superiors) found so sorely wanting in himself.[84]

But the progress of the war did not allow him to tie the knot at this stage. Late in September Canaris reported to Captain Theodor Püllen, who had since taken over the Mediterranean flotilla from Kophamel, at Pola. There Canaris learnt that he would be given command of a U-boat within the next few weeks. Until then, he was to perform staff duties at the U-boat base in Cattaro.[85] His new chief was Lieutenant Commander Rudolf Ackermann, who exercised military supervision over the operational U-boats at Cattaro and was currently engaged in building some large stone huts for the temporary accommodation of German submariners there.[86]

Ackermann soon took to his new assistant. "With great aptitude, swiftness of perception and keen judgement," wrote Ackermann, "he has very quickly familiarized himself with his duties and achieved excellent results."[87] Although no lover of paperwork, Canaris patiently stuck at his desk in the knowledge that he would soon be assigned to combat duties. He was not disappointed. On November 28 he was given command of the transport submarine *UC27* and left on his first patrol. His task: the mining of Allied sea routes.[88]

He acquitted himself so well that Ackermann appointed him deputy commander of *U34* in the absence of her captain, Lieutenant Johannes Klasing. Canaris spent two days working with his unfamiliar crew. Then, on January 19, 1918, *U34* put to sea and headed for the Western Mediterranean.[89] The submarine lay in wait east of Gibraltar, but no enemy vessel was sighted. On January 30 Canaris noted in his patrol report: "I propose to spend the remaining moonlight nights on the Oran-Cabo de Gata or Cabo Sabinal line because that is where I suspect the heaviest traffic to be."[90]

Canaris had guessed right. At 1430 he sighted a British convoy of five large freighters steadily zigzagging westwards. He dived, firmly resolved to attack the convoy despite its strong escort. A new entry appeared in his patrol report: "I shall dive into position between the two lines of freighters from ahead, maintaining the same course and tacking with them so as to keep my ahead position. If the gap between the two leading ships is big enough, I shall try a bow shot at one and a stern shot at the other."[91]

He selected as his first victim a ship of the British *Foxglove* class, the 7,293-ton freighter *Maizar*. At 1547 his word of command rang down the voice pipe and Torpedo No. 9371 sped hissing from its bow tube. Canaris saw it hit the *Maizar* amidships and promptly ordered *U34* to 120 feet. Enemy depth charges were not slow to follow.[92] Canaris waited for two hours and then surfaced. The *Maizar* was sinking, but the rest of the convoy had vanished over the horizon.

U34 turned away and altered course, this time towards Oran. Five days later Canaris had another stroke of luck. A British convoy of eighteen ships was steaming along north of Oran. Canaris fired another torpedo and the armed merchantman *General Church* was rocked by an explosion. The escorting British destroyers at once counterattacked with depth charges but the U-boat managed to elude them.[93] Canaris went in search of more targets.

He returned to Cattaro on February 16, fully entitled to pride himself on a notable success: *U34* had sunk three enemy ships totalling 16,174 tons and severely damaged another. "The patrol," Ackermann wrote approvingly, "was conducted in a competent and highly successful manner. The results merit special recognition in view of the fact that the captain was commanding a large boat for the first time."[94] From that time on, Canaris could number himself among the elite of the German submarine commanders whose commerce-raiding operations in the Mediterranean filled the enemy with almost superstitious dread. Although he lacked the brilliance of Arnauld de la Perière, Forstmann, Valentiner or Hersing, his superiors regarded him as a U-boat commander who could be relied on to produce "good results" at all times.[95] Even the Emperor pricked up his ears at Canaris's name and asked if he was related to the hero of the Greek War of Independence.[96]

Canaris was now operating with such assurance that U-Flotilla Mediterranean at last gave him a boat of his own (Klasing had resumed command of *U34*).[97] In May 1918 he travelled to Kiel and reported to the Submarine Acceptance Board (UAK) to collect his new boat and submit her crew to prior training. "Thanks to his unflagging enthusiasm," the UAK affirmed on August 1, "the technical preparedness of his boat and the training of his crew were fully up to standard at the time of the boat's release."[98] *UB128*, as Canaris's new command was designated, put to sea at the end of July and reached Cattaro just a month later.[99]

But Canaris arrived too late. The military defeat of his country and its allies was already casting shadows over German submariners long accustomed to the taste of victory. During August, the sinking of 165,000 tons of enemy cargo space took them to a new but ultimate pinnacle of success.[100] From mid-September onwards the figures steadily declined. French forces in Salonika opened a Balkan offensive which first compelled Bulgaria to surrender and then shook Austria-Hungary to its foundations. The Habsburg empire disintegrated. On October 8 the Poles, Czechs and Yugoslavs proclaimed their demand for independence. At the end of the month the Austro-Hungarian Emperor tendered his country's surrender.

The collapse of Austria-Hungary robbed the German U-boat flotilla of its bases in the Adriatic. Captain Püllen instructed his officers to strike camp and head for home. Ten unserviceable U boats were scuttled by their crews and the flotilla's installations at Cattaro and Pola blown up.[101] Sixteen German submarines assembled for the dismal voyage home, among them Canaris's *UB128*. Canaris received sad tidings en route: *U34*, his first command, had sunk for reasons which were never explained.[102]

Then came a flurry of alarming signals from home. The U-boat crews learned of Germany's surrender and the imperial regime's collapse. Revolution had triumphed in the land of Bismarck.

3

Counterrevolution

At 0720 on November 29, 1918, Captain Theodore Püllen signalled the start of his flotilla's last voyage. His order was flashed to the U-boats assembled in the Northwest Baltic. One after another, they got under way: fifteen German submarines, the survivors of U-Flotilla Mediterranean, were heading for home.[1]

Three hours later, Kiel's first harbour installations appeared on the skyline. Shortly before reaching the harbour entrance Canaris saw a steam-pinnace making for the flotilla leader at high speed. Standing foursquare aboard the boat was a tall, rugged, slightly stooping figure with a lank moustache—a man described by the French historian Gentizon as personifying "those ancient Germans of whom Tacitus reports that they dressed in animal skins and settled every quarrel with their powerful fists alone."[2] This giant symbolized the new political regime in revolutionary Germany. He was Gustav Noske, the Social Democratic Party's defence expert and governor of Kiel.

Püllen brought his boat to a stop and Noske came aboard. The voyage continued. At 1030 the submarines entered harbour and headed for their allotted berth.[3]

Canaris noted in *UB128*'s war diary: "Tied up at the Blücherbrücke. Crew went ashore. Address by Governor Noske."[4] Noske later recalled that the bearded submariners gathered on the jetty, "begrimed as they were from their arduous duties, so that I could deliver some words of welcome and apprise them of events at home, about which they were very ill-informed despite notification by wireless."[5]

Noske's voice seemed to emanate from a fog as he tried, with growing vehemence, to explain what had happened to Germany in recent days. The ex-patrollers of the Mediterranean listened blankly to his recurrent key words. He spoke of chaos and revolution, appealed to the Navy's proven discipline and conjured up a picture of the Fatherland's downfall and disintegration. Only the most perceptive members of his audience began to realize that they had entered a new and unfamiliar world which bore little resemblance to the one they used to call Germany.

Bewildered rather than enlightened by this half-hour harangue, the men doubled back to their boats to perform a last duty. Canaris's entry in the war diary reads: "1200. Decommissioning. Captain's address. Ensign and pennant were hauled down with three cheers."[6] But the questions raised by Noske continued to gnaw at the submariners—so much so that Püllen called on Noske the same afternoon and asked him to give his men "further information about the sudden upheaval in Germany." The governor duly agreed to address his officers and men next day.[7]

"On Saturday evening," Noske writes, "the men assembled in a small hall in the Schlosshof. They sat there side by side, every last one of them, spick and span, orderly and well-disciplined."[8] Noske was embarking on an account of what had led up to the collapse of the monarchy and the proclamation of a republic when a policeman burst into the hall and reported to him that some coastal gunners were mustering in Friedrichsort at the entrance to Kiel Bay with the intention of attacking him. They might march off at any moment unless they were stopped.[9]

Although Noske dismissed the report as "nonsense," it made a deep impression on his audience. "When I had finished my speech, the commanding officer added a few words about the incident and asked how many of his men were ready to stand by the governor. As though shot from the barrel of a gun, several hundred smart and stalwart fellows leapt to their feet."[10]

The homecomers had grasped the truth at last. This scene in the Schlosshof of Kiel conveyed what had happened in Germany more eloquently than any verbal explanation. The rule of law was shattered and the country had become the plaything of mutinous soldiers and fanatical agitators. Only a few courageous souls—men like Noske—were attempting to stem the drift towards disaster. Germany was tottering on the brink of chaos, coerced into surrender by the superiority of the Allied war coalition, robbed of her wonted political system and paralysed by the fury of a wide section of the population which had been embittered by four years of war, hunger and official grin-and-bear-it propaganda.

Nowhere could the rudiments of a new political system or genuine concentration of authority be discerned. The November revolutionaries had destroyed a centuries-old system but were incapable of creating an adequate substitute. From the very outset, the German upheaval lacked the prime essentials of any revolution: unified leadership, a universally accepted strategy and a common conception of the future. The revolution of November 1918 was not, in fact, a revolution at all, merely a chain reaction of uncontrolled mutinies staged by leaderless and aimless ex-servicemen whose only bond was rage and disappointment at the years they had squandered in trenches and stokeholds.

They vented their emotions by savaging officers and middle-class civilians, dominated the streets and cities and incited returning soldiers to disobedience on an ever wider scale. Their numbers were swelled, week after week, by urban rowdies and bully-boys, malcontents from military bases and ragged front-line soldiers who, tormented by cold and hunger, were roaming the countryside unfed, unhoused and ready to follow anyone who promised them a brighter future. Military discipline had ceased to exist. Barracks degenerated into brothels and black markets, arsenals became the preserve of revolutionaries and the old military establishment was largely a prisoner of Germany's new Red masters.

Kiel and Hamburg, Wilhelmshaven and Berlin—almost every North German city presented the same picture: military vehicles careering around with red flags and vociferous soldiers on board, barricades and machine-gun nests, shots and explosions. Gangs of youngsters chased officers and ripped off their medals and insignia, and many columns of demonstrators carried poles adorned with the bloodstained tunics of murdered officers—unmistakable indications of who and what ruled the streets of Germany in November 1918.

Lieutenant Wilhelm Canaris, who saw what he had lived and fought for trampled underfoot in the gutters of Kiel, was outraged by these acts of mutiny and terrorism. The scenes in Red-controlled Kiel made an indelible impression on him. To Canaris they symbolized, once and for all, the shame and humiliation of the Imperial Navy. Seamen and stokers had taken up arms against superiors who had yielded to their mutinous onslaught without a fight. Wherever in North Germany the decaying fabric of the monarchical system collapsed, and wherever terrorism was the order of the day, sailors were always to be found with cigarettes dangling from their lips and rifles slung muzzle-down—"the iron spearhead of the revolution," as their Kiel ringleaders called them.[11]

Once the Emperor's darling and an aid to German self-aggrandizement, the Navy had blazed a trail to violent revolution. Canaris took a long time to recover from this shock. He realized only too well that his service and its officer corps were temporarily down and out. Gone were the dreams and aspirations that had united the officers of the executive branch under the German naval ensign. At the same time, everything in Canaris rebelled against the idea of meekly accepting the Navy's downfall. He was ceaselessly haunted by the question of how it had all come to pass and who was responsible.

Other executive officers, no less shocked than Canaris, asked themselves the same question, many of them with merciless honesty and unblinkered by tradition. "Anything is tolerable today except the people who seek to prevent us from reshaping our ideas," wrote Captain von Egidy, head of the Cadet School at Mürwik. He warned against putting the blame on others. "It is not a courageous or, above all, a decent thing to do when one has made a hash of things (as 'we' have) and been forced to quit the stage."[12] Another captain and long time opponent of Tirpitz, Lothar Persius, already foresaw how the Navy's search for scapegoats would end: "Memories are short-lived among comrades. One is quick to forgive robbery, theft and betrayal, but one never forgets political activities that conflict with one's own interests."[13]

Canaris himself was reluctant to draw any conclusions. Like so many of his brother officers, he bitterly contested the view that the officer corps had substantially contributed to its own downfall. In this respect he was an authentic product of naval tradition. It never occurred to him that the Imperial Navy had foundered on its internal conflicts and antitheses. The more he brooded on the causes of the disaster, the more plausible he found the alibi theories devised by other officers. It was a cast-iron article of the traditionalist faith that the Navy had succumbed to an exogenous conspiracy. The Marxist-Communist foe had surreptitiously infiltrated the fleet and subverted it with the aid of undercover accomplices on board.

This theory bred a living lie which enabled a whole generation of German naval officers to persist in the same old attitude. Canaris not only yielded to it but did so more wholeheartedly than many others. He had never served in a large vessel, had no experience of the class struggle on board battleships and knew nothing of the bitter skirmishes over food, privileges and human dignity. He was only familiar with small ocean-going cruisers and submarines where naval life and the relations between wardroom and lower deck had still been in good working order.

Hence the eagerness with which he rejected all imputations of autocracy among the officers of the Imperial Navy. As late as 1926, he was vehemently assuring Reichstag members that the Navy had been "inwardly sound" and that the seeds of rebellion were imported "from outside."[14] He found it "monstrous" to talk of a failure on the part of the executive branch. Of one thing he was firmly convinced: "Until the end . . . with a few exceptions, an unclouded relationship of mutual trust prevailed between officers and men."[15]

In reality, Canaris's clichés were wide of the mark. Far from being inwardly sound, the Imperial Navy was disastrously riven by groups who fulfilled different functions and whose fierce conflicts of interest were in part a reflection of the Empire's social antitheses. Devoid of psychological understanding, many executive officers totally disregarded the everyday problems of their men on the principle that—as the captain of the battleship *Rheinland* put it—"men are of secondary importance because we can get as many as we want."[16] To officers, all that mattered was discipline, standards of training and implicit obedience.

These tensions were exacerbated by the inactivity of the High Seas Fleet and the collapse of German food supplies during the "turnip winter" of 1916–17, which showed up the inequality of shipboard rations with particular blatancy and brought the conflict to a head. Fired by the example of the March revolutionaries in Russia, who had turned their guns on their own officers, rebellious stokers and seamen banded together in a resolve to impress higher authority with the power of the rank and file and demonstrate their own indispensability. Being experienced trade unionists, their leaders were familiar with only one weapon, the strike, so they used it. On July 20 and August 1, 1917, the crews of several warships at Wilhelmshaven swarmed ashore.[17]

The trouble was over in a few hours. Few officers took a very serious view of the seamen's strike because similar incidents had occurred at every stage in the German Navy's history. But Admiral Reinhard Scheer, commander of the High Seas Fleet and one of the Navy's strictest disciplinarians, saw things differently. To him the strike was an ideal opportunity. When detained and questioned, its ringleaders admitted to having been in prior contact with the leaders of the USPD (Independent Social Democratic Party of Germany), a revolutionary and pacifist splinter group of the SPD.[18]

Scheer's lawyers duly cobbled together an indictment for treason in which the striking sailors were represented as tools of the allegedly traitorous USPD. They could not prove that the party and the sailors had actually planned an insurrection. They could not even demonstrate the existence of a revolutionary organization in the High Seas Fleet, still less the conspiratorial participation of prominent USPD functionaries like Haase and Dittmann, but that was immaterial to the squadron court-martial. It found that there had been "treasonable incitement to rebellion." The result: five "principal ringleaders" of the naval strike were sentenced to death and two of them executed.[19]

But the Navy's social problems remained unsolved and the naval authorities ignored the smouldering conflict. Their energies were engaged elsewhere. In autumn 1918 the new Directorate of Naval Warfare under Scheer still hoped to end the war in Germany's favour by throwing in all its reserves of naval strength. Then, when the Army's final offensive in France collapsed and even the autocratic General Erich Ludendorff, Germany's undeclared ruler, government and emperor, called for an armistice, the admirals staged what they had so strongly condemned a year before: a mutiny against the government.

The new Chancellor, Prince Max von Baden, was already negotiating an armistice with the Allies when the Directorate of Naval Warfare resolved to send the High Seas Fleet on a dramatic suicide mission which would rouse the country and force its leaders' hand. It acted without government approval. Only three staff officers were assigned to draw up a plan of operations and the crucial orders were transmitted by word of mouth—even the squadron commanders were at first kept in ignorance. On October 27 the High Seas Fleet—three squadrons of battleships crewed by sixty thousand men took station in the Schilling roads off Wilhelmshaven in readiness for the ultimate battle.[20]

Even before the final orders were issued, the ships' companies mutinied. Rumours of their officers' plans had spread like wildfire, and the "suicide mission" catch phrase proved too much for men who had no intention of being immolated on the very threshold of peace. The mutineers seized ship after ship, and revolution was proclaimed on many vessels by "servicemen's councils," or soviets. Although the authorities crushed this mutiny within a few hours, the damage was done. Crews infected with the bacillus of revolution steamed back to their home ports, there to join with workers of revolutionary persuasion in rising against an imperial regime which had been discredited by war and starvation.

It was a dispute over the arrested mutineers, who had been taken to Kiel, which triggered the German Revolution on November 4, 1918. Armed contingents from Kiel's dockyard and torpedo depots occupied the city's strategic key points, crews took over their ships and the governor of Kiel surrendered to the mutineers soon afterwards A workers' and servicemen's council seized power.[21] Revolution spread to other parts of Germany as fast as trains could travel and ships put to sea. On November 5 mutinous sailors occupied Lübeck. Twenty-four hours later they were in Hanover, Braunschweig and Cologne, and by November 8 they had extended their grasp to Breslau, Dresden and Darmstadt.[22]

Next day they joined forces with insurgent workers in Berlin and dealt the Hohenzollern monarchy its *coup de grâce*. Max von Baden resigned, leaving the remnants of power to Friedrich Ebert, leader of the SPD. To forestall an extreme left-wing coup under the Spartacist leader Karl Liebknecht, Ebert's friend Philipp Scheidemann proclaimed a republic. From now on, it depended largely on the steady nerves and tactical skill of the Social Democratic leaders whether or not the country extricated itself from chaos, revolution and political dissolution.[23] Ebert and his friends were determined to preserve Germany's national integrity and scope for development.

This determination to maintain public order was well exemplified by Gustav Noske, a former woodworker and leading Social Democrat from Brandenburg. Catapulted into Red Kiel by a party directive, he acted so swiftly that he became the turbulent city's central figure within a few days. Noske tamed the workers' and servicemen's council, got himself elected its chairman and supplanted the feeble governor of Kiel.[24]

Noske knew, however, that his authority reposed on shifting sands and that law and order had far from been restored. Indiscipline was rife in the naval units controlled by the servicemen's council, some of which would barely tolerate officers in their ranks. Noske asserted his authority gradually, unit by unit, with the help of a few officers and moderates on the servicemen's council. He was further assisted by a young naval lieutenant named Canaris, who had been seconded to the Inspectorate of Submarines since December 1 and was soon afterwards appointed liaison officer between HQ Baltic and the new governor.

Although the two men were poles apart in temperament and social background, Noske's straightforward approach to law and order held an almost magical appeal for Canaris, who was fascinated by men with the ability to assert themselves and win respect. Shortly after returning to Kiel he had joined a circle of naval officers dedicated to smashing the power of the workers' and servicemen's councils.[25]

Lieutenant Commander Wilfried von Loewenfeld, a member of Scheer's staff, had begun to recruit other like-minded officers immediately after the upheaval in Kiel. At secret meetings in various apartments there, Loewenfeld and his friends formed a loose-knit organization with the aim of protecting officers from the whims of the new masters and restoring the Navy's traditional hierarchy.[26] Loewenfeld himself had something even more ambitious in mind: "To become the nucleus of the new Navy after restoring order in the country—that was my aim."[27]

The lieutenant commander enjoyed a good reputation in the Navy. Formerly executive officer of the heavy cruiser *Prinz Heinrich* and wartime commander of the auxiliary mine layer *Deutschland*, Loewenfeld was respected by the lower deck as well.[28] Many sailors joined his circle, among them such prominent members of the U-boat commanders' elite as Lieutenant Lothar von Arnauld de la Perière, who had retrieved Canaris from Spain in 1916.[29]

Canaris, too, joined the Loewenfeld set. His diplomatic skill—his ability to resolve clashes of temperament and eliminate sources of personal friction—made him one of Loewenfeld's indispensable aides. He also knew what slogans to feed his brother officers, most of whom tended to be hazy on the subject of politics. Thanks not least to his efforts, Loewenfeld's organization gradually developed to the point where he pressed his superiors for permission to form a unit of his own.[30]

But Station HQ at Kiel refused. Loewenfeld's activities were hampering the naval authorities in their efforts to reaccustom the servicemen's councils to the idea of military discipline and gain their support for a return to routine duties. In fact, Loewenfeld's political associates made it quite clear that their ultimate aim was to dry up what Arnauld called the "Red swamp." Loewenfeld saw the crucial motivation of his work as a struggle, "both overt and surreptitious, against those in power"—indeed, against "the November government . . . which brought the revolution about."[31]

There could be no plainer way of saying that Loewenfeld—like Canaris—aspired to a political system dissimilar from the one established in November 1918. He later gave an indication of the grievances that dominated his thinking: "The Navy was the germ cell of the mutiny in summer 1918 [read 1917] and became that of the November Revolution because the then Reichstag declared the authors of the mutiny, Deputies Haase, Barth and Dittmann, immune instead of summarily hanging them à la Clemenceau. Patriotic members of the old Imperial Navy . . . endeavoured . . . to make amends for this disgrace."[32] It is hardly surprising that HQ Baltic Station, being intent on conciliation and compromise, should have found such sentiments unwelcome.

As for Canaris, he was too intelligent not to grasp at once that Loewenfeld was manoeuvring himself into a blind alley. While still maintaining contact with the Loewenfeld circle, he gambled on Noske the Social Democratic champion of law and order, who offered a more realistic means of neutralizing the ultra-Red servicemen's councils. As early as November, Noske had got Captain Roehr to form a disciplinary unit composed of reliable Navy personnel. These were recruited for the governor by the Warrant Officers' Association and the Association of Regular Navy Ratings.[33]

By late December Roehr had built up a force of 1,200 men, all of them naval volunteers. They comprised warrant officers, petty officers, long-service men and engineer officer candidates and applicants.[34] No. 1 Naval Brigade, or the "Iron Brigade" as they liked to be known, were issued with field-grey uniforms and arms from depots in Kiel. They were the only unit in the port on whom Station HQ could rely in an emergency.[35] Noske, who had returned to Berlin to assume cabinet responsibility for the Army and Navy, put his faith in them too.

At this stage the Brigade was alerted by reports that Karl Liebknecht and Rosa Luxemburg were about to lead a Spartacist insurrection in Berlin. Roehr, his second-in-command Captain von Schlick, and Petty Officer Hirschmann, the Brigade volunteers' official representative, travelled to Berlin on January 3, 1919, and offered Noske their unit's support.[36] Noske accepted because he was hourly expecting a revolt by the Communists, as the Spartacists now styled themselves in the wake of the party conference that had just founded the KPD [Communist Party of Germany].

Once again, revolutionary ammunition had been supplied by Navy personnel. After wavering between the Communists and the Socialist government, the so-called People's Naval Division had mutinied against the latter on December 23, 1918—ostensibly because its pay was in arrears. Armed sailors forced their way into Ebert's office, demanded money and sealed off the Chancellery. Ebert requested assistance from army units stationed in Berlin, who opened fire on the sailors' barricades. The mutineers were just hoisting the white flag when a Berlin mob bore down on the soldiers and disarmed them.[37]

Ebert's USPD cabinet members resigned in protest at his having called out the military, whereupon he demanded the resignations of all USPD members holding key posts in the police service. The struggle between the two related but warring parties reached its climax at Berlin's police headquarters, which was headed by USPD official Emil Eichhorn. The government demanded his resignation, but he refused.[38] At this juncture the Communist Party entered the lists. Its party newspaper, the Rote Fahne [Red Flag], advocated "revolutionary measures" and the "arming of the proletariat," while Communists and Independent Socialists issued concerted calls for mass demonstrations against the government.[39]

Noske realised that both the extreme left-wing parties contained elements who were flirting with the idea of a coup. Although Rosa Luxemburg was still advising her comrades against such a hazardous policy, many Communists felt only too tempted to impose by force what they had failed to secure by peaceful means: a Red soviet republic.[40] Noske thus had every reason to accept the Iron Brigade's offer of assistance. He wrote Roehr and Schlick the necessary operational orders and issued them with new passes signed by Ebert. On Noske's authority, No. 1 Naval Brigade was to be transferred to the capital.[41]

But even before the Brigade could receive its marching orders from Berlin, the Communists struck. During the night of January 5–6, armed KPD shock troops occupied the Berlin newspaper quarter, evidently on their own initiative. Their action left Rosa Luxemburg and her partner

Liebknecht no alternative. With some misgivings, they unleashed the so-called Spartacist Revolt. KPD contingents stormed the city's main-line stations, seized barracks and wheeled guns in front of police head-quarters, now the headquarters of a revolutionary council which pro-claimed that the government had been deposed.[42]

However, their most important blow went astray: two companies of loyal volunteers repulsed an attempt to storm the Chancellery. Confu-sion reigned in Ebert's office, where ministers were helplessly debating how to quell the insurrection. At last, Noske insisted that a decision be made. "All right," retorted one cabinet member, "do the job yourself." "Very well," said Noske. "Somebody has to be hard-nosed and I won't shirk the responsibility." Minutes later, armed with extraordinary powers, Noske took over the erstwhile premises of the Grand General Staff and—heedless of the extreme left-wing demonstrators milling around outside—took command.[43]

Noske was soon joined by Roehr and Schlick, whose promise of sup-port encouraged him to hope that the young republic would withstand its gravest crisis to date. But the Naval Brigade failed to appear. Civil-ian authorities and railwaymen in Kiel were refusing to sanction the unit's transfer to Berlin, and not even Canaris could clear the obstruc-tion. Petty Officer Hirschmann had to return from Berlin and produce Noske's movement order before the Brigade could be entrained at Kiel's central station. It moved into the villages round Teltow, south of Berlin, on January 9.[44]

The Brigade's absence had been partly instrumental in Noske's deci-sion to transfer his headquarters to a Berlin suburb at noon on January 6 itself.[45] Now based at the Luisenstift girls' school in Dahlem, he was effectively a general without an army because the government no longer possessed any regular troops. The field army had almost entirely dispersed after returning home. Held together with difficulty until the final parade in Berlin at the beginning of December, it had taken only a few days to disintegrate under the strain of conflicts that had been papered over for years. Much to the horror of the country's military traditionalists, many soldiers threw in their lot with the revolutionaries; others simply went home.

Some commanders quickly recovered from their shock and began to form units composed of volunteers from the remnants of the field army. Popular officers who had preserved close contacts with their men were quick to gather a following. A name or a slogan was often sufficient to recall soldiers to duty. A motley collection of individuals, many of an adventurous disposition, reassembled under the banners of famed com-manders. Usually grouped in regiments numbering no more than five or six hundred men, they styled themselves Freikorps [Volunteer Corps] and soon became the bane of left-wing street fighters.

These new units bore little resemblance to the old Army, whose traditions and standards had long been destroyed. The command-and-obey system was replaced by an unpredictable form of modern mercenarydom, and traditional military discipline yielded to a do-it-yourself administration of justice which gave short shrift. Human life—one's own or another's—counted for little; Freikorps personnel were inured to the infliction and acceptance of death. They seldom took prisoners. "Ruthless action against armed and unarmed masses and opponents and an infinite disregard for the so-called sanctity of human life"—to quote the Freikorps bard Ernst von Salomon—were deemed to be an expression of soldierly toughness.[46]

This injected a murderous element into the German civil war which had previously, in spite of all its excesses, been absent. Fraught with the resentment of defeat and the fears of classes threatened with social degradation, the Freikorps were potential vehicles of counterrevolution. Disgust at the prewar middle-class world and abhorrence of the "Red rabble" in their tattered uniforms were allied with anarcho-terrorist patterns of behaviour which rendered them ideally suitable for employment by resolute right-wing conspirators. Men "on whom the war has never released its grip, who will always carry it in their veins" (Salomon) were in no way bound to the Republic. They entered the government's service of their own free will and could leave it in the same way.[47] Their loyalty did not belong to the government, only to the leader whose authority they accepted.

Hatred of the Communists and Noske's "strong man" reputation were all that attracted the Freikorps to the government's side. For a minimum payment of thirty marks they pledged themselves to spend—initially—one month's tour of duty in Berlin and to obey all military laws enacted prior to the revolution.[48] One Freikorps after another formed up to march on the rebellious capital. Still at his girls' school headquarters, Commander in Chief Noske was happily informed by his aides that ten thousand men under General Walther von Lüttwitz were on the way.[49]

Quartered at Teltow, Canaris was fascinated to watch the advance of the Freikorps, which impressed him as a new and creative form of soldiery. The outwardly free-and-easy ways of the Freikorps personnel appealed to a man who had never been unduly fond of rigid military discipline. "He was always telling me about the joys of life in the Freikorps," recalls Canaris's friend Otto Wagner.[50] The informal atmosphere of the Naval Brigade, which was, after its own fashion, a precursor of the Freikorps, temporarily distracted Canaris from other outstanding problems. Then an order from Noske brought him into full association with the Freikorps movement.

On January 10 Noske inspected the Brigade and discussed the situation with its officers. This had become extremely awkward thanks to an unexpected move on the part of the rank and file, whose evident mistrust of their own superiors had prompted a request that they be replaced with Army officers.[51] An Army officer, Colonel von Roden, assumed command of the Brigade itself and most of its companies and platoons were reassigned to other experienced soldiers. Roehr and his naval officers bowed out and placed themselves at Noske's disposal.[52] The commander in chief at once found a job for Canaris. He was to maintain contact with the staff of the Guards Cavalry Rifle Division (GKSD), to which the Naval Brigade had meanwhile been subordinated.

Next day Canaris found himself face to face with a small wiry officer who was as responsible as anyone for introducing him to the world of political conspiracy and intrigue. Captain Waldemar Pabst, born 1880, son of a Berlin museum director and a product of Germany's leading cadet academy, was now the GKSD's General Staff Officer, Grade 1, and its commander in all but name. He was also a perfect example of the politically minded officer. His division had been recruited from the old guards regiments of the monarchy. Having tailored it into the most effective "model unit" (Lüttwitz) in the Freikorps movement, he now dreamt of launching a *coup d'état* against the Socialist Republic.[53] Pabst, who saw at once that Canaris could help to further his plans, described him in later years as "my best man."[54]

Canaris never left his mentor's side. He was there on January 11 when Noske moved into the western quarters of the capital with three squadrons of the GKSD and the Naval Brigade and launched the battle for Berlin. He was there when the bulk of the GKSD overran Communist positions in the south of Berlin on the same day and prepared to storm police headquarters. He was there on January 13, when Noske's final orders reached GKSD headquarters. They were to cut off the south of Berlin from the working-class districts in the north and use the Division to occupy the area bounded by the Spree, Reichstag, Ringbahn and Potsdamer Platz.[55]

The GKSD columns set off at dawn on January 15 but encountered little resistance. Strategic points were occupied, squares and intersections secured with machine guns and armoured cars. Unopposed, Pabst and Canaris reached the Eden Hotel, their objective and future divisional headquarters, near the Tiergarten [Zoological Gardens].[56]

The Berlin revolt had collapsed but the civil war continued. Traditionalist officers and men who had suppressed their hatred since November 1918 now vented it on their largely defenceless opponents. Freikorps raiding parties conducted house-to-house searches and ruthlessly gunned down anyone suspected of Communist sympathies.

Former insurgents were fair game. "Like wild animals," writes the historian Benoist-Méchin, "they were hunted from one quarter to the next, herded into back yards and there shot in batches of fifteen or twenty. A veritable manhunt began . . ."[57]

Search parties were also on the lookout for the KPD leaders Karl Liebknecht and Rosa Luxemburg, who had been in hiding since January 13.[58] As Freikorps General Maercker put it: "The threat is a dire one. Rosa Luxemburg is a she-devil and Liebknecht the type who will stop at nothing."[59] The Polish Jewess with the Prussian passport tallied perfectly with the caricature of a "rootless" female agitator which haunted the military mind. Her "shrill invective" against German customs and conditions, which even frayed the nerves of Moscow envoy Karl Radek and many other comrades, her venomous diatribes against the "miserably beaten men of Flanders and the Argonne," her persistent and fanatical demands that senior officers be tried by a revolutionary tribunal and all officers excluded from elections—these pronouncements could not fail to infuriate an officer corps brimming with resentment and the spirit of revenge.[60]

Pabst was determined to render the two fugitives "harmless." Attendance at several KPD demonstrations addressed by Liebknecht and Luxemburg had, he said later, "driven me to conclude that both were extremely dangerous and could not be matched on their own ground."[61] Troops and units of the Einwohnerwehr [Home Guard] received orders from Pabst to step up their hunt for the two Communist leaders. Late on the night of January 15, the news he had been awaiting reached the Eden Hotel: between 9 and 10 P.M., militiamen had found and detained Liebknecht and Luxemburg at the apartment of a family named Markussohn, No. 43 Mannheimer Strasse in the Wilmersdorf district of Berlin.[62]

A few minutes later the two prisoners were delivered to Pabst's quarters on the first floor of the Eden Hotel. After questioning them briefly, he reached a decision. Two escort parties, one to each prisoner, were instructed to take them out on the pretext of delivering them to the Moabit Prison and shoot them on the way "while attempting to escape." Two cars drew up outside the hotel. One of them—Liebknecht's—was manned by Lieutenant Horst von Pflugk-Hartung, his brother Heinz and three other lieutenants from the Naval Brigade. Frau Luxemburg's escort consisted of Lieutenant Kurt Vogel and five men.[63]

The murders were arranged with such secrecy that few of Pabst's staff officers had prior knowledge of them. Captain Petri, the divisional railway transport officer, even suspected that Pabst planned to release the Communists, so he gave a simple-minded soldier named Runge a hundred marks to club them to death.[64] When Liebknecht and Luxemburg were led downstairs, Runge rushed out of a side entrance and set about them with his rifle butt. Although Liebknecht was bleeding badly and the woman critically injured, they were dragged to the cars and dumped inside.[65]

At about 10:45 P.M. the vehicle containing Liebknecht and his naval escort drove off. The murder went according to plan. In the middle of the darkened Tiergarten the car stopped, ostensibly because of a flat tyre. Liebknecht was compelled to proceed on foot ahead of his escorts, who opened fire at once. Horst von Pflugk-Hartung fired first, followed by the rest of his party. Rosa Luxemburg's liquidation, which took place an hour later, went awry. Unnerved by Runge's intervention, her escorts dispatched the half-dead woman only a hundred yards from the Eden, where the shots could be heard by hotel guests. One man leapt on to the car's running board and fired. Escort-commander Vogel, who completely lost his head, drove to the Landwehr Canal and had the corpse thrown into the water.[66]

Pabst angrily reprimanded Vogel for disobeying orders when he came back to report. Vogel advised him to put out a story that Luxemburg's car had been mobbed by an angry crowd who had fired at the woman and then borne her off to an unknown destination. This line was duly followed by a divisional communiqué issued on January 16: Luxemburg had been killed and abducted by a mob, Liebknecht shot while attempting to escape.[67]

It was typical of the moral decline of the time that few of the dead Communists' opponents protested against this double murder. When Pabst reported to Noske, the Social Democrat commander in chief was not displeased. "He shook my hand," Pabst recalled later.[68] Noske snapped at his worried colleagues: "You've got nerves like hysterical old women. War's war. Ah well, you never were a game bunch."[69] As for the Social Democrats' central press organ, *Vorwärts*, it wrote of the two victims: "They were self-confessed instigators of civil war, murderers of the proletariat, fratricides, and their ears must ring forever with the fearful words: 'A fugitive and a vagabond shalt thou be in the earth.'"[70]

Did Canaris know of the crime or actually take part? He always denied it, and his biographers are at great pains to locate their hero as far from the scene of the gruesome deed as possible. They claim that he was in South Germany at the relevant time, not in Berlin at all, but they fail to agree on dates. Gert Buchheit times his departure as early as "late December 1918," André Brissaud makes him board a train "during the night of January 14–15," and Karl-Heinz Abshagen transposes his trip to the period after he moved into the Eden, or January 15 at the earliest.[71] None of this seems too convincing, especially in default of any documentary evidence.

It is nonetheless conceivable that Pabst may have released his "best man" for a trip to the south once the fighting in Berlin had ended—

which it did in the course of January 15. The circumstances of Canaris's trip may present us with a clue to the truth.

Canaris was preoccupied with the new concept of Einwohner- wehren [Home Guard units]. These had come into being during De- cember 1918 on the initiative of Berlin citizens who formed small armed bands to protect banks, warehouses and important buildings from thieves and looters. When fighting broke out in Berlin, these mili- tia units were taken over by the Army. The GKSD, in particular, pushed through plans to set up Einwohnerwehren on a larger scale and in sufficient strength to relieve the pressure on its own men. Noske, who was also in favour of the idea, issued a public appeal on January 13 calling upon all the capital's citizens to join these units.[72]

Before long the streets were alive with members of the new militia. Men wearing civilian clothes or old uniforms and white arm bands turned out with rifles, truncheons, steel helmets and hand grenades. They were placed under the supervision of Freikorps section command- ers.[73] But the GKSD's plans went still further. They envisaged the es- tablishment of Einwohnerwehren all over Germany as reliable aids to the suppression of Red chaos. A start had already been made on their formation in Bavaria—reason enough to send Canaris on a recon- naissance trip. But who wrote out his travel warrant and who had been appointed by Pabst to organise these militia units? None other than Pabst's senior orderly officer and the murderer of Liebknecht, Horst von Pflugk-Hartung, with whom Canaris was on good terms.[74] The events of the night of January 15 must have left an emotional mark on him. Would he really have refrained from confiding its nature to a friend like Canaris?

Whether or not Canaris knew of the double murder, he must have welcomed this chance of a brief respite from the bloodshed in Berlin. He also had personal reasons for going south. At Pforzheim he saw Erika Waag, who was as charming and regally self-assured as ever. The reunion proved a success, and they celebrated their engagement a few days later (they were to marry in the same year, on November 22, 1919).[75] But Canaris did not linger in Pforzheim because news from Bavaria hastened his departure. Plans by Erhard Auer, Bavaria's SPD Minister of the Interior, to set up a Bürgerwehr [militia] were in jeop- ardy. Auer was barely holding his own against radicals inside the gov- ernment and on the workers' councils, and Bavaria was steadily drifting towards the chaos of a soviet republic.[76] Despite this, Canaris received a universally attentive hearing when he outlined the GKSD's Einwohner- wehr plans and urged citizens to take action.

Canaris's mission to the South of Germany must have been success- ful, because Pabst entrusted him with the task of pushing the Einwoh- nerwehr idea in public. Back in Berlin at the beginning of February, he found a new brief awaiting him: he was to go to Weimar as divisional liaison officer and lobby the National Assembly on behalf of the new defence plan.[77] Meanwhile, on January 19, SPD-sponsored elections had yielded a majority for the parties of the democratic centre. The National Assembly was to give the Republic a constitution, and the crux of all controversy was the form to be taken by the new armed forces—the future Reichswehr [v. Glossary].

If Noske was finding it hard enough to render plans for a new army founded on old notions of discipline and obedience palatable to the left wing of his own party, there seemed no prospect at all of gaining the far-left parties' support for the Einwohnerwehren, with their strong flavour of civil strife. This was where Canaris came in. The National Assembly had only just begun its deliberations on February 6 when he turned up to cement support, dispel opposition and feed propaganda material into the right channels.

Canaris displayed immense skill in presenting his case, even to the most reluctant audience. His chameleon-like capacity for outward adaptation to all who conversed with him left many visitors to his office convinced that they had found a kindred spirit. "He could handle anyone," an admiring colleague said later. "He struck the right note with them all—with the German Nationalist who was just leaving by one door or the Independent who was simultaneously entering by the other."[78]

This type of gentle persuasion helped to secure a parliamentary majority in favour of establishing Home Guard units. Noske, soon to become Minister of Defence, could happily dictate a new proclamation to the country at large: "The Einwohnerwehren   are designed to embrace all inhabitants of a non-seditious character with the aim of supporting government troops and maintaining peace and good order."[79] The naval officer's adroitness had impressed the SPD man, who kept an eye on him from now on.

Canaris's success at Weimar strengthened his position on the staff of the GKSD. More than that, it made him a central contact man for all who sought access to the new military or planned to use them for their own political ends. His room in the Eden Hotel resembled a PR office. People came and went, confidential information was exchanged, alliances were forged and appointments made. Before long, many aspiring and ambitious individuals found it useful to know this unobtrusive naval lieutenant.

Canaris was particularly courted by naval officers because he held a key to the Reichsmarine [Republican Navy] established by the Weimar Constitution. On February 15 he was appointed to the Reichsmarineamt [Navy Office], which was renamed the Admiralität a few months later and became the Marineleitung [Navy Directorate] from 1920 onwards.[80] Although he remained on the staff of the GKSD as the

Reichsmarineamt's liaison officer, he played a part in building up the new Navy from its very inception.

March saw the appearance of Rear Admiral Adolf von Trotha, spiritual father of the abortive naval sortie of October 1918, whom the Republic had perversely appointed to head the Admiralität. A fanatical Tirpitz supporter and confirmed monarchist, Trotha advocated a nationalistic naval programme in which the Navy's sacred function was to be a "token of German national vigour."[81] He was only too happy to adopt the idea for which Canaris and Loewenfeld had paved the way at Kiel—that of securing the Navy a new cadre by forming naval brigades.

As early as February 18, Noske had at last authorized Loewenfeld to establish a naval land force in the style of a Freikorps. The first unit, which sprang into being at once, comprised the crew of the light cruiser *Breslau* plus an assortment of executive and engineer officers, petty officers, junior ratings and ex-soldiers. Rapidly swelling in strength from 400 to 1,200 men, it was incorporated in the Navy establishment as No. 3 Naval Brigade.[82] But it had a competitor. Lieutenant Commander Hermann Ehrhardt, formerly commanding No. 9 Torpedo Flotilla, had also been commissioned to recruit a brigade. Drawing on Navy personnel, he quickly formed two regiments and grouped them into No. 2 Naval Brigade.[83]

A renewed threat of Communist uprisings prompted the Admiralität to transfer both units to Berlin. Ehrhardt's brigade arrived at the Jüterbog training area in March and Loewenfeld's followed a month later.[84] Both brigades were subordinated to the GKSD, which effectively brought them into Canaris's orbit.[85] Loewenfeld valued him so highly that he appointed him his liaison officer at the Admiralität even though Canaris was not technically a member of his unit, and Ehrhardt worked closely with him too.[86]

These contacts assured Canaris of an unusual key position in the antechambers of the Republic's budding military leadership. As a member of the Reichsmarineamt he influenced the plans of the Admiralität, as Trotha's liaison officer he held a post on the politically ambitious staff of the Guards Cavalry Rifle Division, and as liaison officer of No. 3 Naval Brigade and Ehrhardt's confidant he had access to the innermost thoughts of two prominent Freikorps commanders.

And so Canaris gradually built up a network of contacts and connections which made him one of the best-informed men in turbulent postwar Berlin. Whenever military plans were discussed, officers plotted and politicized or military and political pundits conferred, Canaris was there, saying little but listening patiently in his sphinxlike and inscrutable way.

To his few friends, Canaris showed himself an invariably dependable partner. He soon gave proof of this unhesitating readiness to help.

In April Pabst's position was threatened by a judicial inquiry. As time went by a sizeable number of people became aware of the macabre role which GKSD officers had played in the murder of the two Communists Liebknecht and Luxemburg. This crime now rebounded on the killers and their principals. Canaris became so inextricably entangled in the affair—after the event, as it were—that he never managed to scotch the erroneous rumour that he himself had been one of the assassins.

The divisional commander, Lieutenant General von Hofmann, had not been privy to the murders. Next day, on January 16, he enraged Pabst by appointing Kriegsgerichtsrat [Court-Martial Counsel] Kurtzig to investigate the case. He also proposed that the executive of the Berlin workers' and servicemen's councils should participate in the inquiry. The councils duly appointed two observers named Wegmann and Rusch and sent them to the GKSD. Kurtzig, who at once suspected that something was wrong with the official version (Liebknecht shot "while escaping," Rosa Luxemburg shot and abducted by a mob), became convinced that the GKSD's story was at variance with the facts.[87]

On January 16 Kurtzig ordered the arrest of Lieutenant Vogel, who had driven the car carrying Rosa Luxemburg. His grounds: "Adequate reason to suspect that he omitted to do what was necessary to protect those in custody."[88] The officer in charge of Liebknecht's car, Lieutenant Horst von Pflugk-Hartung, was likewise arrested on orders from Kurtzig.[89] The Kriegsgerichtsrat was already engaged in looking for other suspects on the staff when Pabst blocked him. He introduced a second investigator, ostensibly "to speed up inquiries." Kriegsgerichtsrat Jorns, an ambitious legal officer who had formerly served with the Imperial Defence Force [colonial troops] in Africa, sympathized with the GKSD officers. What was more, he treated the prisoners' and suspects' defence pleas with a forbearance that verged on deliberate obstruction.

The two legal officers split the murders between them (Jorns took over the Liebknecht case), but Jorns was soon complaining that Kurtzig's interrogation methods were overrigorous.[90] On January 18 he asked General von Hofmann to put him in charge of both inquiries. Hofmann agreed and Kurtzig withdrew.[91] From now on, Jorns conducted the investigation on his own. Having promptly released Vogel and Pflugk-Hartung, he embarked on a leisurely review of the evidence and questioned a few witnesses.[92] Nothing, however, could induce him to doubt the murderers' statements.

Even when witnesses came forward to dispute Vogel's version of events, Jorns remained unmoved. Members of the hotel staff testified that no "angry mob" had been present at Rosa Luxemburg's departure: Jorns did not react.[93] One Rifleman Dreger testified that Vogel's companions told him they had thrown her body off the bridge: Jorns made no comment.[94] On February 4 Wegmann and Rusch insisted that the chief investigator should arrest Vogel because he was strongly suspected "of having disposed of the murdered woman's body so as to cover the traces of the crime": Jorns refused to budge.[95]

Instead of questioning Vogel, Jorns systematically squeezed the two observers out. He ignored all proposals for the summoning of new witnesses and held interrogations in the absence of representatives from the workers' and servicemen's councils. His boycott finally bore fruit. On February 15 Wegmann and Rusch withdrew after lodging a formal protest: "We decline to participate in legal proceedings which enable traces of the crime to be obliterated and the murderers to escape the reach of justice."[96]

But now the government jibbed. It called for vigorous action and urged Jorns to take sworn statements from soldiers who claimed to have seen Vogel's party throw Luxemburg into the water.[97] Jorns had at last run out of delaying tactics. On February 18 he questioned the said witnesses, and shortly afterwards Vogel made a half confession: yes, he had given orders for the body to be thrown into the water; yes, he and his companions had agreed to spread a false account of what had taken place.[98]

On February 20 Jorns ordered the lieutenant's arrest and detention in the Moabit Prison.[99] A week later Vogel got company because strong pressure exerted on Jorns by the justice ministers of the Reich and Prussia compelled the chief investigator to arrest one suspect after another. On February 28 Jorns ordered the arrest of Liebknecht's entire escort, and the remainder of Luxemburg's captors followed within a few days. The last to be detained was Captain Heinz von Pflugk-Hartung, who had not only been "editing" Jorns's findings until the time of his arrest, but had helped his joint principal, Runge, to disappear by furnishing him with money and false papers.[100]

The officers took full advantage of their detention. Since cell doors were left open and the guards allowed them to mingle freely, they were able to confer almost every day and bring their statements into line. They also received frequent visits and messages of encouragement from outsiders, prominent among whom was Canaris, who repeatedly called on his friend Horst von Pflugk-Hartung—"to discuss Home Guard matters," as he later put it.[101]

Jorns took no exception to this until the jealous wife of one prisoner complained to him on March 14 that her husband was receiving visits from other women.[102] What really infuriated him, however, was the sight of another prisoner, Liepmann, striding gaily towards him from the Kolibri bar in Wittenbergplatz on the night of March 25.[103] Jorns now showed a different side of his character. On March 27 he deprived the two chief suspects, Vogel and Pflugk-Hartung, of visiting rights, and five days later he complained to General von Hofmann about lax prison conditions.[104] Jorns became tougher week by week, and all Pabst's doubts were finally dispelled when Runge was run to earth at the beginning of April: a trial was imminent.

A public hearing posed threats to Pabst and the Division, especially as Jorns was not altogether dependable. His recent behaviour was a clear indication that he would play ball only for as long as, and to the extent that, his legal reputation remained untarnished. Only one man could ward off impending disaster, and that was Canaris. Pabst got the consultative council of the GKSD to elect Canaris an associate judge on the relevant court-martial and left the rest to him.[105]

Even before the court convened on May 8, 1919, in Berlin's Landgericht I [Higher District Court No. 1], Canaris staged a run-through of the trial in the Moabit Prison. Some prisoners took the part of judges and prosecuting counsel while others played the accused. Each man had to learn his lines because every statement needed memorizing in detail if the prisoners were to prevent the full facts of the Liebknecht-Luxemburg murders from coming out. Runge, who had been persuaded to attack the two Communist leaders, had to be taken through his part again and again.[106] Most of these rehearsals were directed towards obscuring the role played by the chief instigators of the double crime. Any trails leading to Pabst had to be obliterated and outside witnesses employed to confuse the court rather than enlighten it.

Canaris may not have had complete faith in his talent for stage management, because he provided the chief suspects with another line of escape. Contacts in government and military departments were tapped for ways and means of spiriting them out of the country. This meant procuring false passports, recruiting accomplices, exploring escape routes and finding emergency quarters abroad. An obscure intermediary named Bredereck supplied the necessary funds.

A former Berlin lawyer, wanted by the prewar public prosecutor's department for embezzlement and forgery, Bredereck had joined the Army under a false name in 1914, been dismissed by the Emperor and then pardoned. He now sat on the committee of the ultra-conservative National Association of German Officers, which had first broached the escape plan.[107] The committee members included friends of the Pflugk-Hartung family who thought it intolerable that scions of such a house should be subjected to court-martial proceedings. As Bredereck put it, these gentlemen doubted if it would be "expedient to allow proceedings against the officers to reach a conclusion."[108]

Somebody proposed that money be collected to finance the prisoners' escape. Bredereck succeeded in raising thirty thousand marks, not from the coffers of the National Association but from "a quarter" whose identity the ex-lawyer later refused to disclose.[109] Five thousand or fifteen thousand marks (Bredereck could not recall the exact sum) were to be made available at once and the balance remitted to the fugitives once they were safely abroad.[110] Elli von Pflugk-Hartung, a sister of the two accused officers, played the go-between and often went with Bredereck to visit them in prison.[111] This must have come to Canaris's attention, because he not only advised her to ask for the balance to be paid at once but accompanied her when she took receipt of Bredereck's money.[112]

By now, all undetained members of the GKSD's staff were hard at work on the grand escape plan. Pabst and an officer named Dr. Grabowski alerted contacts on the escape route, Captain Janssen of Section VIII stamped the false passports and driver Janschkow (a witness for the defence) sold the Division his private car.[113] The officers could feel safe in their cells. One of them said later that he and his companions "consoled themselves against the indictment preferred by Kriegsgerichtsrat Jorns with mutual assurances that nothing could happen to them as long as . . . Canaris was one of their judges."[114]

The eight accused finally appeared before the court-martial looking relaxed and confident. "Instead of being conducted to the dock by the usual route," noted one critical observer, "they cross the courtroom from the judges' chambers. They enter smiling broadly, chests adorned with medals, looking as if they are bound for a wedding rather than the dock."[115] Associate Judge Canaris made very sure that the court, which was presided over by Kriegsgerichtsrat Ehrhardt, did not uncover every last secret of the Liebknecht-Luxemburg murders.

Canaris's stage directions paid off. None of the prisoners or witnesses implicated Captain Pabst and no rifts appeared in their united front. All the accused denied having deliberately planned or occasioned the deaths of the two Communists. Canaris obfuscated the question of guilt in the Luxemburg murder with particular skill. Vogel was made to take the centre of the stage and become the focus of the court's attention—a safe enough gambit because it was doubtful if he had fired the fatal shot. This, at least in Canaris's opinion, had come from the man who leapt on to the running board at the last moment, and it was Vogel's job to unsettle the court with vague allusions to this shadowy figure.

Kriegsgerichtsrat Ehrhardt was quick to take the bait. Ehrhardt: "Lieutenant Vogel, who was the third person sitting in the car?"

Vogel: "I stand by the statement made during my last interrogation. That is to say, I refuse to testify on the subject."

Ehrhardt: "Accused, I submit that the evidence against you is extremely strong, and not only in consequence of witnesses' statements. If you committed the crime, I advise you to admit it."

Vogel: "I did not commit it and I decline to testify about the said person."

Ehrhardt: "You stated earlier that someone jumped on and jumped off again?"

Vogel: "I did."

Ehrhardt: "You admit to having described this person and said that he was not a soldier but a civilian? At all events, you saw nothing shiny? The said person wore no steel helmet or arm band which might have enabled you to infer a military function of some kind?"

Vogel: "That is correct."

Ehrhardt: "Yet you still insist that you are not guilty of the crime and, on the other hand, decline to state who the third person is?"

Vogel: "I do."[116]

Intervention from Prosecuting Counsel Jorns: "Gentlemen, I also find it impossible to accept that the unidentified person, who was, at all events, an officer, would have failed to give himself up after reading newspaper reports of the extremely damaging allegations made against Lieutenant Vogel. I, at least, refuse to accept that an officer could be so cowardly as to leave a comrade stranded in this way."[117] Jorns did not know that Associate Judge Canaris was deliberately holding back the third man, whom he, at least, assumed to be the murderer. Sublieutenant Souchon did not make an appearance in the trial until the subject of the Luxemburg murder had been dealt with and the other passengers in the Luxemburg car, who could have identified him, had left the courtroom.[118]

So the judges had a guilty party but could not be certain that he had fired the shot. This uncertainty was echoed by their findings on May 14, 1919: Lieutenant Kurt Vogel was summarily dismissed the service and sentenced to "a total of two years four months' imprisonment for gross dereliction of duty in the field coupled with acting as an accessory while in the performance of his duty, for abuse of authority . . . and the disposal of a body, as well as, in another instance, for wilfully submitting an inaccurate official report." Runge received a similar sentence for attempted murder and another of the accused was given six weeks' close confinement to quarters for "arrogation of authority." The remaining prisoners were acquitted without a single reference to murder or the callous destruction of human lives—without even the mildest condemnation of such a reprehensible crime. Canaris had guessed right.[119]

Vogel, the scapegoat, felt ill at ease in his new role and yearned to be free. Having procured a Foreign Office trilingual passport in the name of Kurt Velsen at the end of January, he lived in daily hopes of release. Vogel was in such a hurry that he drove to the Dutch Consulate General—unhindered by his guards—and got himself a visa. But word of this spread quickly. On May 14 the Independent Social Democrat deputy Dr. Cohn warned Minister Noske that the officer detainees possessed false papers and were planning to escape.[120]

In a directive issued the same day, Noske strictly impressed on the relevant authority, HQ Reichswehr Group I, that no negligence or carelessness must be allowed to facilitate the prisoners' escape.[121] Pabst got his hands on Noske's order within twenty-four hours, but he inferred from a conversation with Jorns that Vogel's time was running out fast. Jorns had decided to transfer him to another prison and reinforce the guard on his cell.[122] Again Pabst called on Canaris, and again Canaris helped after his fashion.

On the afternoon of Saturday, May 17, a car drew up outside the cell block in Moabit's Lehrter Strasse and an officer climbed out. Introducing himself as Lieutenant Lindemann, he reported to the central guardhouse and presented an order signed by Kriegsgerichtsrat Jorns authorizing him to convey Vogel to another prison. Lindemann left with the prisoner a few minutes later, as Jorns was shocked to discover when he visited the prison next day. He did not know any Lieutenant Lindemann and had not ordered Vogel's transfer. The man was as spurious as the documents he had presented, and the man was Canaris himself, who had devised this masquerade as a means of getting Vogel to safety in Holland.[123]

Judges who released the men they had helped to convict were something new in German legal history. Nothing could have dented the law more gravely or dealt the administration of justice a fouler blow. Noske took it as a personal challenge and reacted swiftly. He ordered Heeresanwalt [Army Legal Officer] Sohl to arrest Canaris and convey him to the Moabit Prison, but Canaris spent only four days there because friends intervened on his behalf and demanded his release.[124]

Brigade Commander Loewenfeld succeeded in getting Canaris's imprisonment converted into a sort of house arrest in the former royal palace, his own headquarters. After another week, a board of inquiry was appointed to discover whether Canaris had been guilty of abetting Vogel's escape.[125] But who conducted the investigation? Court-martial officers from the Guards Cavalry Rifle Division, on whose behalf Canaris had been acting. They cleared Canaris of all complicity, largely on grounds that have become an old favourite with his biographers: he had not been in Berlin at the time in question. Pabst knew better and maintained until his dying day that Canaris and Lindemann were one and the same person.[126]

Canaris's part in winding up the Liebknecht-Luxemburg case reinforced his reputation as a man of legendary skill. Now thirty-three, the lieutenant was more and more coming to be regarded as a dark horse by military men and right-wing conservatives with an itch to impose their will on a tottering political system. Canaris knew how to translate political influence into action, especially as he had long been on the closest terms with Noske, whose name so many people associated with their hazy dreams of dictatorship by a man capable of redeeming Germany from the evils of defeat and revolution. Noske had made Canaris a member of his personal staff, in which capacity he dealt with Naval Brigade matters under the Minister's chief aide, Major Erich von Gilsa.[127]

Now based at 38–42 Königin-Augusta-Strasse, Berlin, the complex of buildings occupied by the Reichswehr Ministry, Canaris received many visitors anxious to commend their schemes to Noske and hopeful of gaining access to the Minister via his naval aide. The broad mindedness shown by Noske, a Social Democrat who treated his largely conservative military associates as partners and defended the various Freikorps from critics in his own party, fostered an illusion that this right-wing "comrade" would be amenable to a *coup d'état* against the forces of the Left. Rossbach, a Freikorps commander who was impressed by the brusque way in which Noske repelled emotional attacks by left-wing Social Democrats on the military, pronounced him "a real man."[128]

Pabst was another who put his faith in Noske. He welcomed the presence of his former assistant in the Reichswehr Minister's outer office and repeatedly urged Canaris to solicit Noske's approval of plans for a dictatorship. This underlying aim was not lost on Noske. During a conversation with Pabst, for whom he cherished a fundamental respect, he jocularly accused the captain of wanting to put the entire government under lock and key. Pabst: "Not you, Minister—far from it." Noske: "You see, Captain, there's quite a difference between us. I can't guarantee I won't have *you* arrested one of these days."[129]

Then a national trauma carried hopes of a Noske dictatorship still further: the victorious Allies dictated their peace terms at Versailles—harsh, foolish, self-righteous demands involving large territorial concessions, the recognition of Germany's alleged war guilt, the extradition of high-ranking "war criminals" and disarmament to the level of a 100,000-strong Army. This came as a particular blow to the Freikorps. Resentment of national humiliation went hand in hand with fears for their own continued existence. There would be no more Freikorps if the victors had their way, but that was the whole point. Whether or not to sign the Versailles Treaty was a question that split the nation and rent families, political parties and cabinets asunder.

Military opinion was almost unanimous that only Noske could save the situation. On June 23, shortly before the cabinet made its decision, Freikorps General Maercker drove to see Noske and begged him to ensure that the government rejected the peace treaty. He must "take the destiny of the Fatherland into his own strong hand and appoint himself dictator"; the Reichswehr would "back him to a man." Noske's eyes filled with tears. He shook Maercker's hand, exclaiming, "General, I've had enough of this rotten business too."[130] He promised to block the signature of the Versailles Treaty, if necessary by threatening to resign.

The cabinet accepted the Allied terms, but the government and President prevailed on Noske to remain at his post. The military accused him of betrayal, and the alliance between the SPD Reichswehr Minister and the Freikorps broke up. On June 24 General von Lütt-witz, GOC Reichswehr Group I and effectively the commander in chief of all combat units, informed Noske that he had set himself at odds with the Army and deprived the officer corps of faith in the government.[131] Noske was the target of hostile comment at a commanders' conference the same afternoon. Pabst insisted that the government should adopt the Army's policy, and Lieutenant Commander Ehrhardt fulminated that the government was in gross violation of its pact with the Freikorps, which had only been concluded on the understanding that its members could continue to discharge their duties in an honourable manner.[132]

Noske was now paying dearly for his failure to make any serious attempt to curb the power of the Freikorps and combat them by building up a Republican army. Having quelled the Red insurrections in Berlin, West Germany and the South, the Freikorps felt strong enough to dictate terms to the government. But Noske refused to be intimidated. He left the conference determined to unload his former allies, now grown too powerful for comfort.

The first step was to relieve himself from the pressure of the GKSD, which had since expanded into the Guards Cavalry Rifle Corps [GKSK] and was three divisions strong. It seemed far too risky to leave an ambitious coup strategist like Pabst in control of a force whose forty thousand men made it the strongest in Germany.[133] On the other hand, its strength was also its weakness. The GKSK's political power resided solely in the personality of its leader. With Pabst out of the way, the Reichswehr Ministry would be able to bring it under full government control.

Noske acted accordingly. In mid-July Pabst was informed that he had been relieved of his post and dismissed the service. The little captain lost his head and, on July 21, moved some GKSK units into Berlin on the pretext that Bolshevik-inspired disturbances were imminent. These units had already occupied the suburbs when Maercker hurried to Pabst and persuaded him to call off his coup.[134] Shortly after Pabst had left the scene, Noske disbanded the GKSK, subdivided it into four brigades and distributed them throughout the area covered by Reichswehr Group I (Berlin and parts of North Germany).[135]

The breach between Noske and Pabst put Canaris in an awkward position. The fact that he had joined Noske's staff as a Freikorps confidant but was pledged to keep faith with his Minister placed him in the line of fire between the two adversaries. Firm decisions and pitched battles had never been his forte. Fond of manoeuvring, he always tried to defer his own decisions by tactical means and compromise formulas. It was characteristic of him to avoid choosing between Noske and Pabst, especially as he must have realized that Pabst had no practical policy to offer. The only alternative to signing the Versailles Treaty was a resumption of hostilities, at least in the east, and that would have been folly.

Canaris had to use every evasive tactic in the book to retain his own position because Pabst persisted in trying to involve him in his political schemes. Pabst had by now gone over to the group centred on Wolfgang Kapp of East Prussia, a wan and ailing man who dreamed of restoring the Empire's old hierarchical system and re-establishing the supremacy of the civil servant and officer class. Once a co-founder, with Tirpitz, of the Fatherland Party, he had preserved its remains from the November revolution in the guise of a "National Union," which maintained several offices in Berlin's Schellingstrasse.[136]

Pabst now transformed this into the "National Alliance." As its manager in chief, he proclaimed that the party's headquarters in Schellingstrasse were to become an administrative center for "right-minded, enterprising and patriotic officers."[137] Pabst's eloquence and talent for organization did indeed turn the Schellingstrasse offices into a sort of conspirators' headquarters. The National Alliance attracted all in Germany who kicked against the parliamentary system and felt dispossessed by the Revolution. It gradually built up a motley assortment of Freikorps commanders, adventurers, right-wing politicians and industrialists, former court chaplains and ex-police commissioners.

Members of the Alliance included Canaris's one-time helper Bredereck, Ludendorff's erstwhile chief of operations ex-Colonel Max Bauer, Ehrhardt and his young aide Franz Liedig, and the Freikorps littérateur Friedrich Wilhelm Heinz—all of them destined to play a part in Canaris's future career. Canaris sat in on the plotters' deliberations and listened to their chatter without taking it too seriously.

Pabst himself took the view that a coup would stand no chance before autumn 1920,[138] but he had reckoned without the wounded pride of General von Lüttwitz, who had been a member of the National Alliance since autumn 1919 and, as "Father of the Freikorps," felt increasingly provoked by Noske. In February 1920 the Allies had appeared in Berlin and insisted that the Naval Brigades be disbanded. Noske was not averse to this. Now that the GKSK had been neutralized, the Naval Brigades—and especially Ehrhardt's, which was stationed at Döberitz, near Berlin—were the sole potential backers of a coup by the

Freikorps leaders.[139] On February 29 Noske gave orders that the Brigades should be disbanded by March 10.[140]

Noske's directive robbed Lüttwitz of his last personal fief in the Freikorps, and one which he needed in his jurisdictional battle with Lieutenant General Hans von Seeckt, head of the Reichswehr's Truppenamt [Army General Staff]. "Technically a Bonaparte but psychologically a Captain from Köpenick,[141] Lüttwitz was prepared for the direst consequences. He ostentatiously drove to Döberitz on March 1 to attend an anniversary parade of the Ehrhardt Brigade and called for resistance to Noske's disbandment order: "I will not tolerate the destruction of such a crack unit in such threatening times!"[142]

Lüttwitz was now immune to misgivings. Nothing could hold him back, not even a warning from his Chief of Staff that he and other officers at Group HQ would not support a coup.[143] Kapp was also ready to strike (unlike the more realistic Pabst). One of the National Alliance's leading theoreticians, Dr. Schnitzler, worked out plans for a coup while Lüttwitz formulated demands for submission to the government: dissolution of the National Assembly and fresh elections, the appointment of specialist departmental ministers, his own appointment as commander in chief of the Reichswehr and the retraction of the disbandment order.[144]

Although the general's demands left no more room for compromise, President Ebert invited Lüttwitz to call on him and submit his ideas in person at 6 P.M. on March 10.[145] However, Noske and Lüttwitz's opponent Seeckt had laid their countermines well in advance. On the morning of March 10 Noske withdrew the Ehrhardt Brigade from General von Lüttwitz's command and placed it under Trotha—much to the annoyance of the admiral, who felt that Noske had taken unfair advantage of him.[146] Not only had the disbandment of the Naval Brigades been decreed behind his back (while he was visiting relatives in Brandenburg), but he had now been burdened with the task of implementing the unpopular disbandment order.[147]

Worse than this personal ill feeling was the fact that Noske's order conflicted with Trotha's own plans. The admiral had always hoped to use the bulk of the Naval Brigades as a cadre for the new Reichsmarine. Now Noske was insisting on their instantaneous and total disbandment. This infuriated not only Trotha but Canaris, whose status as co-founder of the Loewenfeld Naval Brigade and an intimate of Ehrhardt's put him in an awkward position vis-à-vis his friends. It was not surprising that Trotha and Canaris showed no particular eagerness to carry out Noske's orders.

But Noske and Gilsa increased their pressure on Canaris when it became more and more apparent that Ehrhardt was not averse to acting as the spearhead of a coup led by Lüttwitz. Ehrhardt had frankly admitted in conversation with Gilsa that he and his brigade would occupy Berlin if Lüttwitz gave the order,[148] and there was then no more resolute or better-equipped unit than the Ehrhardt Brigade. Five thousand strong, led by outstanding officers and imbued with the reactionary ideals of discipline and obedience, it reserved its loyalty for a paternally popular commander who could only conceive an ordered existence within the framework of a monarchic and authoritarian state.[149]

It was this man, Hermann Ehrhardt, whom Canaris and Trotha were now supposed to dissuade from reckless action and, if possible, from launching a coup. They could hardly be blamed for approaching the task in a halfhearted manner. Trotha summoned Ehrhardt and asked him if he was planning such a move. When Ehrhardt said nothing, Trotha did not press the point.[150] Canaris, too, cautioned the brigade commander, but so vaguely that Ehrhardt could not tell whether he was acting on instructions or expressing a personal opinion. "He [Ehrhardt] often talked to me about the problems of the period," Canaris wrote later, "but he never used the sort of language which might have occasioned fears that he had become entangled in some kind of political liaison."[151] Canaris did not, he said, believe that Ehrhardt cherished "insurrectionist aims."[152] Can any friend of Captain Pabst's have been so utterly naive?

Whatever the truth, Lüttwitz had little time for further manoeuvre. On the evening of March 10 he reported to Ebert and Noske and brusquely submitted his demands. Noske's vehement response was that Lüttwitz's programme amounted to an ultimatum and must be rejected out of hand. Ebert seconded this. The Naval Brigade had been withdrawn from Lüttwitz's command, Noske thundered, and the general must obey orders. Lüttwitz stalked out in a fury.[153]

By now, disaster was almost inevitable. Early on the morning of March 11 the Republican chief of the Army Command Staff, Major General Reinhardt, called on Noske and advised him to suspend Lüttwitz from duty because the general was contemplating a resort to force.[154] Seeckt, who had come to a similar conclusion, drew up warrants for the arrest of Lüttwitz's fellow conspirators (Pabst, Kapp, Bauer and Schnitzler) and got Noske to sign them.[155] Although Pabst's police contacts managed to warn the conspirators in time, Noske pressed on regardless. Lüttwitz was suspended from duty and a secret telegram to his successor, Lieutenant General von Oldershausen, cautioned all Group HQs and military district commanders against any attempt to overthrow the government by force of arms.[156]

But Canaris and Trotha were still reluctant to commit themselves. Trotha went on leave on March 11 while Canaris remained with Noske and Gilsa, outwardly a loyal associate of the Reichswehr Minister's but privately tormented by doubts and fears—an inscrutable and, to many observers, an enigmatic figure.[157] Trotha's personal staff officer, Captain Erich Raeder, saw Canaris often at this period, and it may have been his indecision and divided loyalties that prompted the future head of the German Navy to follow his career with persistent mistrust and uneasiness.

Meanwhile, Lüttwitz had met Ehrhardt on the way to Döberitz. He informed the brigade commander of his altercation with the President and asked if he was ready to march on Berlin. Ehrhardt agreed. He pronounced it impossible to move out the same day, March 11, because his men were exhausted after a long route march, but promised that they would be at the Brandenburg Gate by Saturday morning, March 13.[158] He then drove back and embarked on preparations for the Brigade's departure.

There was much activity at Döberitz Camp next day. Lorries were loaded, baggage wagons and ambulances assembled. These preparations did not pass unnoticed. They came to the attention of Captain Baron von Freiberg, commander of the air base at Döberitz, who reported his observations to HQ Reichswehr Group I, whence they were passed to Oldershausen in Berlin.[159]

Oldershausen alerted Reinhardt, who went with him to dig Noske and Trotha (recalled from leave) out of a cabinet meeting late on the afternoon of March 12.[160] Noske had an idea: Trotha must call on Ehrhardt and appeal to his conscience. The head of the Admiralität objected that he had no wish to go to Döberitz. "If Ehrhardt is determined to march tonight, I consider it impossible to talk him out of it by discussion or persuasion—on the contrary, it will only make a bad impression on him."[161]

"Will you go or won't you?" Noske snapped. Trotha: "Of course. If it's decided that an attempt should be made, I'll drive out there and do my best."[162] Reinhardt offered to go too, but Trotha declined the company of a Republican who was so unpopular with the military. Gilsa had a better suggestion: why not take Canaris instead?[163] The two men duly drove to the Naval Brigade camp and were admitted by the guard at 7:30 P.M. Trotha went to see Ehrhardt in his hut while Canaris inspected the camp.[164]

Trotha could have been in no doubt that Ehrhardt was poised for a descent on Berlin. If "[he] warned me against plans for a coup," as Ehrhardt later recalled,[165] he must have done so for a very good reason. Canaris must have been equally convinced, but the two emissaries— still manoeuvring between Noske and his opponents—decided to turn a blind eye on all they had seen at Döberitz. When Trotha and Canaris reported back to Noske and Gilsa at 8:30 P.M., they were so vague that the Reichswehr Minister could only conclude that Ehrhardt's Brigade presented no immediate threat.[166]

"On arriving at Döberitz," Trotha reported, "I encountered a perfectly peaceful camp. Off-duty personnel were coming and going through the gates, and the general impression was one of complete tranquillity."[167] He even alleged that "Lieutenant Commander Ehrhardt's original plans for a coup have been abandoned owing to a loss of confidence." Trotha felt strengthened by Canaris's reference to his own inability to detect "any signs of an intended coup in conversation with the Brigade's officers."[168] Canaris obligingly added that "The camp made . . . a peaceful impression" on him.[169] However, the two scouts allowed for all eventualities by leaving a back door open. Canaris: "In the case of a unit as good as the Brigade, this meant nothing at all. It could have been ready to march at very short notice."[170]

Whatever Canaris and Trotha may have produced in the way of palliative remarks, Noske was reassured. Noske: "As long as he [Ehrhardt] doesn't march tonight, we shall have boosted morale so much by tomorrow that the danger will have passed."[171] It was a fatal error. Two hours later the Ehrhardt Brigade took to the road and its marching columns headed for Berlin. Soon after midnight, Noske learned that the coup was under way. The Reichswehr Minister felt that he had been hoodwinked by his two envoys, and his faith in Trotha and Canaris was abruptly transmuted into the direst suspicion.

Canaris was not even invited to the emergency meeting at the Reichswehr Ministry which Noske called at 1:30 A.M., and Trotha's presence was barely tolerated.[172] Noske asked, "Which of you gentlemen is ready to go to the troops and call on them to resist the Naval Brigade?" Only Reinhardt and Gilsa raised their hands. Trotha and the other armed forces representatives remained silent. "Personally," said Trotha, "I never assumed that the question could possibly be addressed to me because I don't have a single unit in Berlin under my command."[173]

Shortly after 3 A.M., when the cabinet was again debating whether to parley with Ehrhardt, Trotha found himself completely excluded. Noske barred him from the conference room because—according to the head of the Chancellery—"confidence in him had been shaken by prior events, notably his negotiations with the Naval Brigade."[174] An hour later Gilsa and Noske had gone and the government was on its way to Stuttgart. March 13, 1920, dawned to reveal what historians refer to as the Kapp Putsch.

Within a few hours Ehrhardt's troops had occupied Berlin and friends of the National Alliance had usurped government authority. Power seemed to have fallen so completely into the hands of the new masters that Canaris felt bound to join them. Trotha, too, was ready, "with secret reluctance, to place myself at the service of the authorities currently in possession of military power," as he chose to interpret his conduct after the event.[175] Trotha's reluctance was certainly not perceptible in his fiery exhortations to the Navy to co-operate loyally with the Kapp regime. In fact, no such appeals were needed because the naval officer corps went over to the rebels almost *en bloc*. Loewenfeld telegraphed Ehrhardt "hearty congratulations on your success" and the officers of the North Sea Station assured Kapp of their allegiance. Rear Admiral von Levetzow, the station commander at Kiel, followed their example soon afterwards.[176]

What happened next was to live in the naval officers' memories forever afterwards—a spectacle unique in the annals of German military history: the officers' revolt was succeeded by a counterrevolt on the part of their men. At Wilhelmshaven, after warrant officers and ratings had removed the station commander and his staff, a petty officer engineer took command. At Kiel, ratings joined dockyard workers and a workers' militia unit in opposing Station Commander von Levetzow, who enlisted help from elements of the Loewenfeld Brigade and escaped in a torpedo boat after heavy fighting. In many ships, notably mine sweepers, the lower deck seized command and elected their own officers.[177]

At a stroke, the naval officers' breach of faith annihilated what it had taken months of effort to create: a new Republican Navy. The officers were virtually prisoners of their crews, the rudiments of a new style of discipline had been destroyed and—as Noske bitterly remarked —"the whole thing [was] in ruins."[178] The officers had gambled away their Navy to no purpose because the rebels held out for only a few days. A general strike, coupled with the loyalty of most of the Reichswehr generals, banished the Kapp-Lüttwitz spectre for good.[179]

Lieutenant Canaris found himself back behind bars, reunited in the cells of Berlin's police headquarters with many brother officers who had also been arrested on suspicion of high treason.[180] Canaris was released after a few days, but that was only the prelude to a series of embarrassing interviews and interrogations. On April 20 Labour Secretary Christian Stock was appointed a junior minister at the Reichswehr Ministry and instructed to form a "Board of Inquiry into the Events of March" which investigated the conduct of every officer suspect.[181] Stock's committee began by purging the Reichswehr Ministry itself. Each officer was scrutinized in turn, and one of the first to appear before the Board was Canaris. Although he had offered his services to Kapp, there was no proof that he had taken any part in preparations for the coup. Since he could also claim to have acted on Admiral von Trotha's orders, the Board let him go.[182]

Otto Gessler, who had taken over the Reichswehr Ministry now that Noske had been dropped by his own party, was quite happy to employ the rehabilitated Canaris when he proceeded to restore order in the Navy. The latter was in such bad shape that even Tirpitz had warned Gessler off. "Leave it alone—it's rotten from the bottom up. Nothing healthy will ever grow in that soil."[183] But Gessler indefatigably visited one naval station after another, reinstating officers in the teeth of stubborn opposition from their men.[184]

Gessler did not keep Canaris in his entourage for long because his South German liberal temperament was distasteful to most ex-members of Noske's staff. Gessler soon got rid of his overcondescending principal aide, Gilsa, and Canaris had to go too.[185] On July 23, 1920, the Marineleitung transferred him to Baltic Station Headquarters at Kiel as a Naval Staff Officer, Grade 1.[186]

His task, which was clearly defined, consisted in removing the final traces of the recent Kiel upheaval and helping to build up a German Baltic Fleet. When Canaris reported to his new chief, Lieutenant Commander Meusel, the Baltic Station's chief of staff, he was confronted by a caricature of a fleet. Ships and depots had been extensively looted, ratings—who still held sway over the Navy—had almost lost the habit of discipline, and important posts ashore and afloat remained unfilled because of a widespread lack of qualified personnel. The once powerful force had dwindled to a meagre "defensive formation" comprising light cruisers and torpedo boats, and the only vessels rated operational were one cruiser and one obsolete battleship.[187]

Virtually shore-based, the Fleet had swiftly reverted to a condition resembling that of the nineteenth-century Prusso-German Navy. Its strength reposed, not in ships, but in the naval units ashore, most of them recruited from the crews of large warships which Germany had either scuttled or surrendered to the Allies. Although it was only logical that the Navy's coastal defence forces should have taken over the duties once performed by Army units,[188] the German naval ensign had vanished from the Baltic.

Ambitious executive officers could not fail to resent this because the Baltic had been the German Navy's focal point. With the North Sea and the world's oceans barred to it since the defeat of 1918, the small Reichsmarine's immediate future lay in the Baltic alone. Now that German supremacy in this area had been destroyed, it was faced with a number of insoluble problems. These were to maintain contact with East Prussia, which had now been severed from the Reich, compensate for the loss of the Gulf of Danzig and offset the emergence of a Polish Navy. But the agents and spies of the Allied Naval Control Commission ensured that the Reichsmarine did not possess a single gun or rifle more than it had been granted by the Versailles Treaty.

Canaris, Meusel and their colleagues were not disheartened. Doggedly, they proceeded to put backbone into the Baltic Fleet. Depots were reorganized, thefts stopped and undesirables weeded out. Canaris was particularly adept in expounding the Navy's common ties, either in lectures or in conversation with individual ratings. "With purposeful and unflagging energy . . . and an unerring and farsighted talent for organization," Meusel wrote, "he has, under difficult circumstances, made an outstanding contribution to our successes in restoring discipline."[189]

Displaying exceptional drive, Canaris procured all that was needed to fit out the small fleet and collected enough ammunition and equipment from secret arms dumps to equip the first naval units at sea and ashore. The depots of the Baltic Station were soon so full that its gunnery officers had every reason to fear surprise visits from Allied inspectors.[190] Canaris also exploited his vast range of personal contacts for the benefit of the Baltic Fleet. After the disbandment of the Naval Brigades in autumn 1920, he endeavoured to secure Ehrhardt's and Loewenfeld's best staff officers for service with the Baltic Station.[191]

By December the Baltic Fleet was ready to incorporate such naval units as the Reichsmarine still possessed. Kiel Station was assigned the old battleships Schleswig-Holstein and Hessen, the cruisers Thetis and Berlin, six torpedo boats and a reserve force comprising one battleship, one cruiser and one torpedo boat.[192] These were followed in March 1921 by other vessels including eight torpedo boats.[193] They were grouped into a squadron and placed under the command of a "Commander of Naval Forces in the Baltic" based at Swinemünde (and later Kiel).[194] Although it was largely a paper organization because most of the vessels lacked crews owing to a severe shortage of seagoing personnel, there was a reluctance to fall back on the naval units ashore.

These newly acquired ships fired the ambitions of the Kiel Station. While politicians in the Reichstag were still debating whether the Reichsmarine's functions should be limited to those of a naval police force (as the leftists wanted) or whether it should assume the role of an active coastal defence force, Canaris and his friends were already laying plans for a fully operational Grand Fleet. Never having abandoned their utopian dreams of German world-power status, they found it quite natural that their country should require a powerful Navy. This only intensified their refusal to accept the realities of 1921: the Allies had sanctioned a Reichsmarine establishment of 15,000, including 1,500 officers—not one man more.[195]

But Canaris knew a way out. This was to build up a secret (or "black") personnel reserve and use well-directed propaganda to keep alive the idea of a powerful and combat-ready fleet. Restricted to the non-political and abstract performance of its duties after the bitter experiences of the Kapp Putsch, the Navy could not undertake this publicity campaign itself. It needed willing helpers who had no outward connection with Baltic Command, and these it found in the maze of extreme right-wing groups which were leading an obscure existence on the fringes of legality.

Canaris's ideas were enthusiastically endorsed by a colleague, Lieutenant Otto Schuster, who had belonged to the Ehrhardt Brigade and marched at Ehrhardt's side during the Kapp Putsch.[196] Schuster and Canaris won over the senior officers at Baltic Command, though the station commander, Rear Admiral Baron von Gagern, and his Chief of Staff, Meusel, preferred to stand aloof. It was later stated in a confidential naval publication that Gagern and Meusel had "eschewed any detailed knowledge because, given the prevailing political situation, they had at all times to be ready to issue an official denial of their involvement in illicit political activity."[197]

Baltic Command's main deficiency was financial, so Canaris began by remedying this. Because his scheme could not be officially funded by the Navy, he had to fall back on the abundance of arms and equipment stored in naval depots and sell them abroad. He knew, for instance, that Gunnery Captain (ret.) Jung maintained a large and illicit stock of weapons and equipment in the naval arsenal at Kiel. It comprised several thousand rifles, hundreds of machine guns and a quantity of optical instruments and mines.[198] Jung helped Canaris to market some of this equipment abroad.

An old acquaintance of Canaris's, Lieutenant (formerly Warrant Officer) Richard Protze, who headed a small intelligence section at station headquarters, supervised this transaction. Intelligence chief Protze, who was quite his ex-pupil's equal in guile and subterfuge, maintained a ring of agents and informants in Kiel and other Baltic ports. Their task was to keep untrustworthy Navy personnel under surveillance, guard caches of arms against betrayal and shadow the Kiel section of the Allied Naval Control Commission.[199]

Protze now put his agents to work for Canaris. Gunnery and optical equipment was loaded into boats which delivered it to Bendix, a Copenhagen-based firm of Danish forwarding agents. There the equipment was taken over and marketed by the firm of Daug & Company. Some items were sold in Finland, Estonia and Sweden, others as far afield as China.[200] The first sales transactions went off so well that customers were soon asking for more. Canaris and Protze continued to supply them for as long as Jung deemed it safe. The Danish middlemen were also interested in further deals because they did well out of them. Sixty per cent of the proceeds went to the Navy and the Danes pocketed the rest.[201]

At the same time, Canaris got his friend Protze to ensure that enough weapons were available to equip the secret personnel reserve. In the naval establishment at Kiel-Wik, rooms were vacated in the detention barracks and Stores A and B so that Canaris's helpers could concentrate their illegal stock of arms and equipment.[202] Only the most trusted assistants of Construction Officer Kelm of the Kiel Naval Arsenal were allowed access to this secret depot. An alarm system was devised to preserve the cache from confiscation by Allied inspectors. At a given code word, its entire contents—apart from 2,400 rifles—were to be promptly removed and taken out to sea in a barge.[203]

With finance secured and arms readily available, Canaris could now tap the human reservoir from which he hoped to recruit the Navy's clandestine reserve. As an erstwhile co-founder of the Loewenfeld Brigade and joint organizer of the Einwohnerwehr, he knew of no more suitable material than the disbanded Freikorps men who had vanished into the Republic's political underground. A largely aimless bunch, they were ripe for any antidemocratic venture and fundamentally ignorant of any *raison d'être* but a military one. The prototype of this forlorn and rootless horde was Ehrhardt's private army.

In September 1920, after Ehrhardt's flight from justice, an "Association of Former Ehrhardt Officers" had been founded. A cross between a paramilitary unit and a secret political sect, it was designed to accommodate the bulk of the former Brigade in provincial "syndicates" (mainly in Bavaria) and to preserve solidarity among those officers who had been admitted to the Reichsmarine.[204] The latter objective was pursued by Lieutenant Commander Wolf von Trotha, who recruited ex-members of the Ehrhardt Brigade into an organization based at Wilhelmshaven.[205] Its aim: to imbue the Navy with the "Ehrhardt spirit" and reshape it along nationalistic and reactionary lines.

However, the new Marineleitung succeeded in putting a stop to this infiltration, whereupon many of Ehrhardt's officers left the service in the summer of 1921.[206] The Association of Former Ehrhardt Officers then became dominated by even more extreme elements who fashioned the scattered remnants of the Brigade into a secret politico-military combat unit intended to provide the spearhead of a future right-wing coup.[207] Because these men were constantly in need of money and no coup was feasible without the help of the Reichswehr, they offered their services to the military authorities as a secret reserve army in the event of war. A new organization had come into being, muddleheaded and romantic but nonetheless dangerous because it did not balk at the murder of prominent opponents. Its name, Organisation Consul (OC), derived from the pseudonym used by its leader, Ehrhardt, who had gone to earth in Munich.[208]

OC combat units took shape in North Germany too—reason enough for Canaris to contact them at an early stage. He did not find it hard to penetrate the mysterious gloom in which this peculiar sect enshrouded itself. In Kiel Schuster introduced him to Lieutenant (ret.) Wende, who was a leading member of the OC and its so-called

Gauleiter [regional director] for Holstein, Mecklenburg and Pomerania.[209] Canaris was impressed by what the OC Gauleiter told him about his organization and its personnel. Here, quite obviously, was a ready-made unit from whose ranks the Baltic Station could recruit the personnel reserve it needed.

Canaris and Wende came to terms, and Organisation Consul gladly accepted a firm assignment from the Navy. It was soon on the payroll of Baltic Command. Indeed, Canaris proved such a generous paymaster that insiders came to regard him as the real financial boss of the Ehrhardt organization.[210] The cash was usually passed by one of his confidants, Lieutenant (ret.) von Werner, mostly in Danish kroner drawn from the arms-deal fund. Only the leaders of the organization were paid in Germany currency. The OC's leading man in Holstein, Captain of Cavalry (ret.) Kurt Lieder, received 250 marks a month.[211] His comrade-in-arms Werner Voss, the Mecklenburg OC commander, was also subsidized by Canaris.[212]

Lieder was regarded as the Kiel Command's most important agent. He held a key to the naval station's secret entrance and was also entitled to enter the camouflaged arms depot maintained by Construction Officer Kelm.[213] The coastal units of the OC were largely under naval command. OC combat units held military exercises and OC standing orders enjoined the clandestine organization to work closely with the Navy in the event of war. Protze was the chief beneficiary of this cooperation because numerous OC men entered the service of his espionage network.

But the closer his links with the OC became, the more Canaris became embroiled in its political machinations. His loyalty to the democratic system was definitely compromised. However understandable one may find it that an officer should have worried about the operational efficiency of his service and pursued a personal line which conflicted with the German government's avowed intention to disarm, it was a clear breach of faith to collaborate with an antigovernment organization and a man who was still wanted for high treason by the republic's legal authorities. Worse still, Canaris did not withdraw his support from the OC even when young and fanatical members of that organization took to murdering prominent politicians for alleged betrayals of the Fatherland and terrorizing the population by means of secret tribunals.

Could he have failed to experience a twinge of embarrassment when he saw the police hunting murderers and murderers' accomplices who had once enjoyed his confidence or crossed his official path? Lieutenant Erwin Kern, the assassin of Foreign Minister Walther Rathenau, had once been personal aide to the same OC Gauleiter Wende with whom Canaris had concluded an alliance between the Baltic Station and the OC.[214] Lieutenant (ret.) Manfred von Killinger, who procured the murder of Finance Minister Matthias Erzberger, had led the assault company that occupied the Reichswehr Ministry on the day of the Kapp Putsch.[215] Ex-Warrant Officer Voss had been privy to Rathenau's murder and was one of Canaris's confidants.[216] Last but not least, there was Lieutenant von Bergen, one of Canaris's many informants, who was currently engaged in preparations for a gas-bomb attack on Army Chief Seeckt.[217]

Being intent on his scheme for naval reconstruction, Canaris was as unconcerned by this as he was by the fact that Ehrhardt had meanwhile lent his officers to an aggressive but seemingly insignificant party leader named Adolf Hitler for the purpose of forming a paramilitary unit whose marching columns were later to sap the Republic's strength: SA or Sturm-Abteilungen [Assault Detachments]. It was Ehrhardt's officers who founded and trained Hitler's brown-uniformed, truncheon-wielding guard, watched with interest by the naval lieutenant in Kiel, who was quick to note any newcomer to the jungle of extreme right-wing organizations.[218]

Was Canaris already in touch with Hitler? This must remain an open question. Canaris biographer Heinz Kiel claims that the two men met in Munich during 1923 but fails to supply evidence of such an encounter.[219] What is certain, however, is that Canaris was adequately informed about Hitler's movement and, more especially, about the SA. After Ehrhardt broke with Hitler in May 1923 (the Nazi leader would not submit to further dictation from Ehrhardt's officers), a Sublieutenant Hans-Ulrich Klintzsch turned up in Kiel.[220] A co-founder of the SA after being compulsorily retired from the Navy, Klintzsch succeeded Lieder as commander of the Holstein OC and kept in close touch with Canaris.

Hitler's plans for a Munich Putsch also influenced the course of further negotiations between Canaris and the OC. Ehrhardt's representatives in North Germany steadily increased their pressure on the officers of Baltic Command to support a revolutionary coup against the Berlin government. The prospects for revolution seemed favourable. Passive resistance to the French and Belgian occupation of the Ruhr had brought the country to the brink of economic chaos, and Bavaria and West and Central Germany were in a ferment. Friends of the OC were eager to prepare for an antigovernment coup in Schleswig-Holstein too.

Canaris bowed to their insistence, and one of his representatives, Lieutenant Commander Schultze, made an arrangement with Lieder. In the event of a coup in Kiel, Baltic Command and the OC would take concerted action. The Navy assumed responsibility for financing and arming OC combat units and Lieder placed himself under naval command without altogether relinquishing control over his own men.[221] Baltic Command entrusted the OC with the task of deploying right-wing forces in the event of a Putsch. To this end, the organization was issued with twelve machine guns. The Navy also deposited more weapons at several places in Kiel.[222] Extreme right-wing conspirators and naval officers of the Republic, to whose defence the latter were pledged by oath,.could hardly have drawn much closer.

In the very midst of these preparations Canaris received a routine order from the Marineleitung in Berlin: he was relieved of his duties in June 1923 and appointed executive officer of the training cruiser *Berlin*, based in Kiel.[223] Schuster, who succeeded him as Naval Staff Officer, Grade 1, took over his secret deals and contacts as well. Canaris unenthusiastically reported to the *Berlin* to find himself awaited with interest by an old acquaintance and new commanding officer, Wilfried von Loewenfeld.[224]

Canaris was surprised at the severity and strictness with which Captain von Loewenfeld ran the *Berlin*. He brooked no argument and waged an embarrassing war of words with Lieutenant Warzecha, his senior instructor, whose methods he disliked.[225] Behind it all, however, lay Loewenfeld's eagerness to present himself as faithful officer of the Reichsmarine. He had never forgotten his unpleasant sessions with the Stock committee and knew full well that President Ebert was still contesting his reinstatement as an ex-supporter of the Kapp Putsch.[226]

From all this, Loewenfeld had concluded that his flirtation with the Freikorps must cease for good. Although he aimed to modify the Republic's naval (and general) policy in a gradual and conservative manner, he wanted no doubts cast on his loyalty to the democratic state. This ran counter to all Canaris had thought and felt while at Baltic Command. He found it hard to come to terms with Loewenfeld's new "rational Republicanism."

Divorced from political activity and exposed to the tedium of life afloat, Canaris drew no comfort even from a trip to his beloved Spain aboard the *Berlin*. Indeed, he felt more depressed and out of sorts than ever, partly because his old malaria was troubling him but more especially because the post-Ruhr crisis in Germany's internal affairs was coming to a head. Rebels would soon be on the march in Munich and Kiel, but he was pinned down on board the *Berlin*. If the ship had been berthed in Kiel he could have resumed contact with his old friends at Baltic Command. As it was, he had no strings left to pull.

All that occasionally cheered him were the civil, almost servile attentions of a lanky cadet whose personal appearance became indelibly imprinted on his mind and was to haunt him like a nightmare in years to come. The long face surmounting the overlong neck looked like a composite of two different halves. Common to both were a large nose, prominent cheekbones and bad front teeth.

Cadet Reinhard Heydrich, born 1904, was the offspring of an opera singer and an actress. He had a capacity for charm and self-ingratiation, and Canaris was in the mood to be courted.[227] Never a good judge of human nature and readily impressed by civility in others, he could be predisposed in their favour by the bestowal of a titbit or a kind word on one of his omnipresent wire-haired dachshunds.

Heydrich had good reason to enlist Canaris's good will. Nicknamed "Ziege" [Goat] on account of his high-pitched voice, he felt isolated because his arrogant but obsequious manner, coupled with his artistic leanings, had made him the most unpopular cadet on board.[228] Canaris, who had a soft spot for loners, took to the young man. They hit it off politically as well. Heydrich had served as a runner in General Maercker's Freikorps and later joined the Halle Freikorps. As a nationalist, Canaris was unworried by his brief membership of the anti-Semitic Deutsch-völkischer Schutz- und Trutzbund [German Nationalist Defence and Offence Association].[229]

Heydrich also possessed an attribute which endeared him to Erika Canaris: he was an excellent violinist. Canaris's marriage was not an outstanding success, and the couple's relationship became little more cordial after the birth of their first daughter, Eva.[230] They did not lead a congenial family life. Erika was more interested in Kiel society than in her husband's profession, while Wilhelm felt happier with his brother officers than in Erika's conventional middle-class world. There was nothing to keep him at home. He had taken no leave since 1913 and seldom went travelling with his wife in later years.[231]

But Heydrich's courtesy calls at the couple's home did occasionally brighten their family life. Erika's trained ear at once perceived the young man's musical talent. "A soft and gentle performer, Heydrich displayed excellent style and marked sensitivity as a violinist," his biographer records.[232] Although Canaris himself had no ear for music ("Music is just something for musicians, I suppose," he used to say), he enjoyed watching his wife and Heydrich play together and would sometimes retire to the kitchen in his white chef's hat to prepare a meal.[233]

These convivial evenings were rare, however. Canaris was more often overwhelmed by a mood of hopelessness and depression. He felt isolated and far removed from the events that were stirring the nation. Hitler's beer-hall Putsch on November 8, 1923, misfired and an OC-led insurrection by right-wing associations in Holstein collapsed with lamentable speed. Canaris was still further infuriated when the Marineleitung severed all links between Baltic Command and Organisation Consul. The picaresque era of the Freikorps and the *coup d'état* was over at last.

Canaris could see no future for himself in the Navy. He decided to quit the service, citing his recurrent attacks of malaria as a pretext. On January 15, 1924, by which time he had been promoted lieutenant commander, he wrote to Baltic Station HQ: "Because I no longer feel physically equal to the demands of service in the Reichsmarine, I request my discharge at the end of March with statutory maintenance as provided by the WVG [Armed Forces Welfare Law]."[234] The *Berlin's* doctor, Dr. Schulte-Ostrop, noted that Canaris displayed signs of "physical fatigue and mental exhaustion." His report went on: "Loss of mental resilience, volatile changes of mood, irritable, easily upset by trifles and unduly sensitive to the same. Furthermore, lack of energy and concentration."[235]

But Station Commander von Gagern had no wish to lose Canaris. "Quite simply," Gagern wrote to him on February 6, "I should like to keep you, your intelligence, drive and efficiency for the Navy's benefit." He realized that things could not go on as they were—"I am referring to our political, etc., circumstances in Kiel"—but he would "try, and I think successfully, to change that." He then alluded vaguely to assignments in the Far East "which are to be dealt with this summer and will probably take six months to complete. I think I can definitely assure you that I shall entrust them to you."[236]

Canaris took the point and withdrew his offer of resignation. The final sentence in Gagern's letter instructed him to burn it after reading. That smacked of espionage and intelligence work, and Canaris was pretty near the mark. Ahead of this outwardly listless man lay a new field of operations perfectly designed to rekindle his imagination and whet his thirst for action: the secret rearming of the German Navy.

4

The Exploits of
Herr Kika

Rear Admiral von Gagern kept his word. Only a few weeks after receiving Gagern's letter, Lieutenant Commander Canaris was instructed by the Marineleitung to leave the *Berlin* and embark on a confidential mission so secret that it had to be disguised as one of the professional *voyages d'études* on which naval officers were customarily sent. In May 1924 Canaris donned civilian clothes and boarded the Norddeutscher Lloyd vessel *Rheinland*, bound for the Far East. His destination: the Japanese port of Osaka.[1]

Normally used for cargo-carrying purposes only, the small freighter took its time over the long voyage. This gave Canaris, now in the guise of a tourist, ample opportunity to mull over what he had been told by his superiors in Kiel and Berlin. A few hours' briefing had sufficed to initiate him into the secrets of the banned German submarine service.

The victorious Allies of 1918 had looked upon submarines as the Germans' most aggressive weapon and the most sinister embodiment of German imperialism. German U-boats, with their advanced technology, had almost brought the British to their knees. They had also carried the imperial ensign into the safest backwaters of the British and U.S. spheres of influence. Consequently, the victors of Versailles dictated that the Reich should maintain no submarines and be forbidden to build any more. Existing U-boats were handed over to the Allies or broken up, dockyards were demolished and blueprints largely destroyed.[2]

But not even the close-meshed network of informants employed by the Allied Disarmament Commission could prevent German naval officers and civilian designers from sneaking off to foreign countries where, far beyond the inspectors' range of vision, they embarked on plans for a new U-boat arm—to begin with, only on paper. The drawing offices of Germany's two most important U-boat yards, Kiel's Germania and Hamburg's Vulcan, which had salvaged the plans of the last U-boats to be built and tested before the war's end, conceived the idea of offering them to foreign navies and, thus, of ensuring that they were built with the assistance of German personnel. This, it was argued, would be Germany's only chance of preserving the requisite know-how in submarine construction.[3]

The Marineleitung agreed, and the chief designer of the Germania yard, Diplomingenieur Techel, soon landed a big potential customer: the Kawasaki Sb. Co., a Japanese yard at Tanagawa/Osaka.[4] More than any country on earth with the exception of the United States, Japan had been bitten by the navy bug. Cheap successes gained at the expense of scattered German warships and colonial possessions in the Far East had strengthened Japanese politicians and military leaders in the belief that only a powerful fleet could assure their country of world power status and break the Pacific supremacy of Britain and the United States. In 1922 they decided on an ambitious naval construction programme under which Japan would acquire eight new battleships and eight new battle cruisers in as many years.[5]

Still dissatisfied, Japan's admirals aspired to supplement their projected fleet with a strong submarine arm. Examination of a few German submarines which fell into their hands at the end of the war convinced them that the Germans possessed the boats their country needed: large and heavy enough to cope with the watery wastes of the Pacific and additionally suitable for use in combined operations with the battle fleet.[6] The German Navy had, in fact, built outsize submarine cruisers and submarine mine layers—reason enough for the Germans to lure representatives from Japanese shipyards to Europe and allow them to forage for components in the remains of the German U-boat fleet.

The Japanese were also interested in German drawings, which suited Techel perfectly. In 1920 he offered to sell the Kawasaki representatives blueprints of the submarine cruiser *U142* and the submarine mine layer *U117*, and the Japanese snapped them up.[7] Assisted by German design engineers, the Osaka firm started work on Japan's first submarine cruisers in the Itto-Sensui-Kan series, which were initially used as mine layers.[8]

This early success encouraged Techel and his friends to set up a company abroad, where it would be safe from Allied surveillance. The

Germania, Weser and Vulcan yards established a design office for submarine construction entitled Ingenieurskantoor voor Scheepsbouw (IvS) and based at The Hague.[9] Techel joined the firm as technical director and two experienced U-boat officers, Lieutenant Commanders Blum and Bartenbach (both retired), took over its management. Before long, IvS had thirty marine and design engineers hard at work on new submarine drawings.[10]

But work at the Kawasaki yard progressed slowly because German engineers at Osaka were often hampered by the suspicious and bureaucratic attitude of the Japanese naval authorities. Canaris had orders to pinpoint and remedy these problems and, at the same time, gauge how far Japan might be interested in closer collaboration with the IvS. He reached Osaka with only twelve days in which to fulfil his assignment because the Rheinland was due to sail for Europe barely a fortnight later.[11]

Canaris contacted the German U-boat personnel in Osaka and called on the Japanese naval authorities, who treated him with extreme courtesy. He learned that Japan was counting on continued German assistance in developing a submarine fleet—more so than ever, in fact. During 1921–22, economic setbacks and pressure from their British and U.S. rivals in the Pacific had forced the Japanese to conclude a naval standstill agreement under which U.S., British and Japanese naval forces would be frozen in a ratio of 5:5:3.[12] Tonnage restrictions applied only to battleships, cruisers and aircraft carriers, however, so the Japanese were doubly eager to offset their concessions in regard to large warships by stepping up submarine construction.[13]

On board the Japanese liner Nagasaki Maru, which took him from Kobe to Shanghai and the waiting Rheinland, Canaris had time to reflect that his trip had been a success despite some initial difficulties.[14] The report he submitted on returning to Germany in autumn 1924 was so optimistic in tone that a year later the IvS dispatched one of its leading submarine experts, Lieutenant (ret.) Robert Bräutigam, to supervise work at the Kawasaki yard.[15]

Unwilling to dispense any longer with the services of its versatile emissary to Japan, the Marineleitung assigned him to headquarters in Berlin. On October 4, 1924, Canaris took over the desk responsible for mobilizational planning (AIIm), a small office in the Marineleitung's Flottenabteilung [Fleet Section].[16] His new job brought him into contact with a circle of naval officers who were doggedly engaged in strengthening and expanding the Reichsmarine after their own fashion: quietly and unobtrusively, with an eye to what was feasible and realistic.

But Canaris had difficulty in adapting to the Marineleitung atmosphere. He was used to the Freikorps, with their indisciplined freebooter's mentality, and had for too long rubbed shoulders with right-wing conspirators to relish the prosaic daily round of life at headquarters. His sympathies still lay with the clamorous naval officers' clubs and veterans' associations which cherished dreams of a German naval renaissance and recollections of the so-called glories of the imperial era. More than that, he preserved a heartfelt attachment to the monarchical system and the ex-Kaiser, who for him (as for most naval officers) remained a legitimate head of state who had merely been driven into exile by force of circumstance.

He, Wilhelm Canaris, was now required to serve in an admiralty which demanded his unqualified co-operation under a democratic system of government. Like Rear Admiral von Levetzow, he may well have asked himself whether this new system was fostering "the tradition of our old Navy . . . or a new spirit which cannot serve to uphold well-established principles."[17] In wanting to resign during 1923, he had been motivated largely by problems of political adjustment.

He also suffered from the fighting man's prejudice against armchair warriors who expended their energies on bureaucratic minutiae and interdepartmental bickering—who lacked any grand design or desire for a resurgence of German naval strength. Naval units ashore and afloat were still imbued with the aggressive spirit of the erstwhile Naval Brigades and dominated, as one historian puts it, by "extremist Brigade officers who aspired to immediate liberation, both internally and externally, who made no bones about their anti-Republican sentiments and rejected all compromise as weakness."[18] Canaris's last commanding officer in the *Berlin*, Lieutenant Commander Paul Wülfing von Ditten, complained that "Everyone concentrates jealously on his own department and its powers. Inability to take an over-all view is very common."[19] Canaris might have voiced the same criticism.

In reality, the Marineleitung was just as anxious to strengthen the Reichsmarine. "In view of our straitened circumstances," wrote one of its officers, "every Navy department has a natural duty to make the naval arm as strong as possible."[20]

Germany's postwar position precluded any other course. Threatened in the west by a heavily armed France and confronted in the east by the turbulent chauvinism of Poland, the almost defenceless country needed a strong navy. In the Marineleitung's view, this could only be created by slow degrees, "with a firm and resolute heart, not with strong but futile words," as Reichswehr Minister Gessler wrote encouragingly to Vice-Admiral Paul Behnke, head of the Marineleitung, in 1921.[21] Step by step, the naval authorities divested the Reichsmarine of its worst liabilities. It began by recommissioning old vessels and putting the Navy back on a fully operational footing, revived the tradition of foreign visits by German warships and, finally, planned the construction of new cruisers and torpedo boats insofar as the Versailles Treaty allowed.[22] At the same time, it discouraged excessive naval propaganda and suppressed monarchist utterances by Navy personnel—a policy dictated less by personal conviction than by a tactical regard for the pacifist Left and fear of Allied eavesdroppers. Extreme traditionalists regarded even this as weak-kneed middle-of-the-roadism and unworthy of the German naval officer corps.

Canaris could not fail to be still further disheartened by the fact that his own appointment to the Marineleitung almost coincided with that of a new chief who took a guarded view of clandestine efforts at rearmament on IvS lines. Vice-Admiral Adolf Zenker, Behnke's successor, doubted whether illegal rearmament was of any real value to the Navy. He celebrated his new appointment on October 3, 1924, by rejecting precisely what Canaris had arranged during his visit to the Far East, namely, closer relations between the German and Japanese navies.[23]

Zenker's reasoning: "Reliance on the Anglo-Saxons in the immediate future is an urgent necessity. Any wavering in our views on military policy will come to their notice and make them suspicious."[24] Unlike Behnke, who had striven for co-operation with the Soviet Navy, Zenker wanted to base the future of the German Navy on co-operation with that of Great Britain. His argument was that, since the British had drafted the humiliating naval provisions of the Versailles Treaty, they alone could release the Reichsmarine from its bonds.[25]

To rearm the German Navy in secret would inevitably vitiate any accommodation with Britain because the British secret service was bound, sooner or later, to detect the Marineleitung's furtive essays in rearmament. Zenker was also alarmed by the entrepreneurial nature of this rearmament, which confined itself to business deals by naval officers of whom most were retired and thus exempt from adequate supervision by the Marineleitung. He noted the activities of the IvS with particular uneasiness. Though initially prepared to tolerate them, he later warned senior officers at headquarters that official policy "must not be governed by the business interests of the IvS. The Marineleitung must not act as a shop sign for the IvS. Greater heed should be paid to this than before."[26] There could have been no clearer definition of the gulf between Canaris and his chief.

But the new head of mobilizational planning was not the type to court an open conflict with higher authority. He readily performed the tasks assigned him. His predecessor in the post had been a flop, and the head of the Flottenabteilung, Captain Arno Spindler, was haunted by distasteful memories of his bureaucratic blunders.[27]

Lieutenant Commander Canaris provided a doubly convincing demonstration of how statistics should be laid out, operational lists compiled, items of information collated and documents neatly filed. The head of the Flottenabteilung soon had a reliable summary of the strengths and weaknesses of German naval mobilization plans at his finger tips. Spindler commended his subordinate as follows: "He has tackled this job conscientiously, clear-sightedly and expertly, and initiated all requisite measures in a purposeful, swift and enterprising manner."[28]

Canaris did not, however, enjoy his duties. He felt bored behind a desk and hated paper work. His forte was human contact and private intercourse, the fathoming and exploration of personal and political ambitions. Spindler realized this too. "I formed the impression," he noted in 1925, "that this kind of straightforward desk work, which consists largely of sifting and collation, does not suit him. As previous reports imply, he is a restless soul who is stimulated by difficult and out-of-the-ordinary assignments."[29] Because Spindler had no such assignments to bestow, Canaris went looking for them on his own initiative.

He now had a sufficient grasp of conditions inside the Marineleitung to realize that not all its officers shared Zenker's aversion to secret rearmament ventures. Canaris sought out like-minded colleagues at headquarters, especially as he heard that the IvS was in urgent need of backing. After its early successes in Japan, Spain and Turkey, the firm's financial reserves were running dangerously low.[30] In a neighbouring section with which he worked closely—BS, the Marine Transport Section of the Allgemeines Marineamt [General Navy Office]—he found someone who was willing to help the IvS: Captain Walter Lohmann.

The two men collaborated on joint assignments because Lohmann's section also dealt with mobilization problems. His office was responsible for marine transport and supplies, for navigational matters, coastal intelligence and communication with merchant shipping. The task of BS was to prepare emergency mobilization plans under which civilian cargo space would be requisitioned for military purposes and merchant vessels detailed for use as auxiliary cruisers, transport ships, auxiliary mine sweepers, hospital ships, et cetera.[31]

This last range of functions overlapped those of Canaris's desk, which was how the two men came into contact. Canaris soon realized that he had found a kindred spirit. Imaginative, secretive, restless, insatiably ambitious and filled with extravagant plans for the future, Captain Lohmann had established a power base which was independent of all the Marineleitung's departments and sections and often made him seem more influential than the admiral himself.[32] Lohmann reported to the chief direct, but the latter exercised no supervision over his activities. Though ambitious, he planned to use his power solely in the fulfilment of what he, with messianic fervour, regarded as his historic mission: to deliver the Fatherland from the restraints of the Versailles Treaty and restore the Navy's strength.

Lohmann's depressing experiences aboard the British battleship *Hercules* on December 8, 1918, when he took delivery of the Allies' harsh demands as a member of the German Armistice Commission, had made him a fanatical opponent of the Entente.[33] That same day, he vowed to the commander of the cruiser *Emden* that he would oppose and strive to mitigate the Entente's terms by all and every means.[34] Chance, coupled with the turmoil of the postwar period, had given him an opportunity to do so.

As soon as the war ended, Lohmann revealed his ample talent for organization, management and the tapping of all those contacts which linked him, as the son of a former managing director of Norddeutscher Lloyd, with the world of shipping and industry. He quickly succeeded in demobilizing 2,700 auxiliary vessels which had been pressed into service with the Imperial Navy, thereby saving the Reich "many millions [of marks] without the institution of long and costly legal proceedings."[35]

Lohmann was tireless in his efforts to release German shipping from the constraints of war. He introduced the "Panac" system which first enabled German merchantmen to pass through the Allied naval blockades. He transported Allied prisoners of war to their countries of origin and brought German prisoners of war home from all over the world—in eighteen German ships which had been captured by the Entente and which, with the approval of King George V, he bought back. He also extracted German prizes and interned vessels from the custody of former enemy states, notably the Soviet Union, with which he concluded secret agreements on his own authority.[36]

Lohmann's covert dealings with the Russians gave him the idea of outflanking the strict disarmament provisions of the Versailles Treaty by way of countries that were either pro-German or neutral. He planned to establish plants and commercial fronts in various neighbouring countries, where they could augment Germany's arms potential screened by an omniscient secret service which he himself aspired to head.

Walter Lohmann had a romantic love of espionage and a passion for secrecy.[37] He was so immersed in the world of informants, clandestine rendezvous and conspiratorial activities that he regarded himself as a man of mystery. As head of the Marine Transport Section and director of the coastal intelligence network since October 1920, he had built up a personal intelligence service additional to the counterespionage desk of the Marineleitung and largely staffed by businessmen and retired officers.[38] Not the least important function of Lohmann's service was to disguise the captain's activities from his own colleagues and superiors. He refrained from divulging the full extent of his operations even to his closest associates, each of whom was restricted to a knowledge of his particular field and strictly forbidden to discuss official business with the rest.[39]

The brisk flow of information from Lohmann's network earned him a reputation for wide experience in conspiratorial dealings, so Navy Chief Behnke had no qualms about entrusting him with confidential assignments. Lohmann made two tours of the Soviet Union on Behnke's behalf, established contacts with foreign intelligence services and was always on tap when the Marineleitung had something "hush-hush" in the offing.[40]

His great moment came in March 1923, when the German authorities were organizing passive resistance to the Franco-Belgian invaders of the Ruhr. The Chancellery evolved the idea of providing the Reichswehr with secret funds for purposes of national defence from sources extraneous to the budget, which was subject to Entente scrutiny.[41] Lohmann noted: "Various discussions took place within the Marineleitung about the size of the sum required for this. The original estimate of 200–250 million marks was reduced in the course of discussion to 100 million . . . It [eventually] turned out that the Navy would have to make do with 10 million marks."[42]

Major General Wurzbacher, who administered the secret "Ruhr fund" at the Reichswehr Ministry, was instructed to pay out 10,039,767 marks 74 pfennigs to the head of the Marineleitung. Behnke could think of no more suitable recipient than his trusted associate Lohmann, who collected the money from Wurzbacher and incorporated it in his own secret fund.[43] Lohmann: "I was told that the funds came from a highly secret source whose existence must under no circumstances become known because this would be simply disastrous for the department which had provided them."[44]

Behnke's instructions on the purpose and employment of the Wurzbacher fund were equally vague. Although the Navy chief issued Lohmann with "guidelines for relevant measures," he left him free "to arrange, on his own initiative, the ways and means most suitable to the implementation of the tasks assigned him," as Zenker put it later.[45] From now on Lohmann was sole master of the secret fund. The budgetary department of the Marineleitung had been short-circuited and the audit office could run no checks on expenditure.[46]

Lohmann now had enough money to put his wild schemes for rearmament into practice. He created a jigsaw puzzle of firms and factories, organizations and cover addresses, each more opaque than the next but all harnessed to the single aim of encouraging and implementing the rearmament forbidden to the Reichsmarine by the Versailles Treaty.

In 1923 Lohmann founded Navis GmbH, a "front" company designed to act as the administrative headquarters of his various concerns.

This supervised the construction of high-speed launches, acquired premises and sites in Berlin and arranged the formation of other companies.[47] It was followed in 1924 by Trayag A.G. of Travemünde, whose purpose was "Practical maintenance of . . . high-speed launches and [the provision of a] base for these vessels in peacetime and in case of emergency."[48] Two other organizations were charged with secretly recruiting and training the necessary personnel: former Navy Chief von Trotha's high seas transport association Hansa and ex-Admiral Hopmann's Motor-Yachtklub.[49]

Lohmann continued to conjure up firms and businesses, planning and founding them at an ever more feverish rate. His Baltische Segelschiffs-Reederei sponsored the construction of powered sailing vessels and his Berliner Öltransport GmbH was designed to increase tanker tonnage.[50] Firms established elsewhere included a Bergungs-Studiengesellschaft" [Salvage Study Corporation] and a Neustädter-Slip GmbH.[51] Even the aircraft and film industries were invaded by Lohmann's tireless spirit of enterprise. He bought up the bankrupt Caspar-Werke and acquired shares in the Phoebus film company because a sense of patriotism convinced him that it was part of his mission to carry on pro-Navy propaganda and preserve the German economy from "American infiltration."[52]

It took little urging from Canaris to persuade an industrious entrepreneur like Lohmann that the Ingenieurskantoor voor Scheepsbouw would neatly fill a gap in his empire. Never having ventured into the field of submarine construction, Lohmann jumped at the idea. He diverted nearly 1 million marks into the coffers of the IvS and used another 20,000 as starting capital for the Mentor-Bilanz GmbH, which was to maintain permanent contact with the IvS, and to that end acquired a holding in the company.[53]

Canaris and Lohmann got on so well that they were soon debating where Germany could best engage in clandestine submarine construction. As a onetime frequenter of the Mediterranean, Canaris knew of only one country that claimed his sympathies and stirred his imagination. Spain was currently waging a disastrous colonial war in its Moroccan possessions, so the hard-pressed kingdom and its strong man, the dictator-general Primo de Rivera, would surely be interested in German money and military know-how. Since Canaris had renewed his friendly wartime relations with Spanish military circles, it seemed obvious that he should travel to Spain and carry out an immediate reconnaissance.

An opportunity soon arose. In January 1925 IvS chief Blum was requested by one of the company's joint owners, the Germania shipyard, to visit Spain and explore the possibility of building German submarines there.[54] Blum was reluctant to go alone and insisted that a

Spanish expert should accompany him—undoubtedly thinking of Canaris. He applied to Zenker, the head of the Marineleitung, who granted Canaris leave of absence because his misgivings about IvS activities were outweighed by his unwillingness to miss a chance of timely involvement in any schemes for submarine construction.[55]

The Marineleitung let Canaris go, but not before entrusting him with a second mission. His duties as head of AIIm included the precautionary task of re-establishing the secret foreign outstations which had rendered such good service to naval units operating far from home during World War I. No one could have been better qualified for the job than the man who had once created an efficient intelligence and supply network in Spain, so Canaris received orders which finally transferred him to the arena that was destined to become his professional stamping ground: the world of espionage.

On January 28, 1925, Canaris left for Spain accompanied by Lieutenant Commander (ret.) Blum.[56] It took him only a few days to reassemble his old wartime associates and informants and instruct them in their tasks. He defined the duties of his new organization as follows: "1. The dispatching of agents to France. 2. M[obilization]-geared preparation of an N [intelligence] centre in Spain. These preparations to apply mainly to agents' duties, interrogation duties in ports and S[abotage] duties. 3. Submission of regular reports (three or four times monthly) on political and economic matters of a general nature."[57] One of Canaris's friends from the Freikorps days, a retired Army officer and ex-member of the Loewenfeld Brigade named Conrad Meyer, had recently turned up in Madrid to take over the small espionage group there—the nucleus of the legendary ND [Nachrichtendienst Intelligence Service] network which Canaris later maintained in Spain as head of the Abwehr.[58]

Canaris made it his personal business to provide agent-supervisor Meyer with the necessary tools of the trade. He reported to Berlin: "I have given him the G [secret] inks . . . required for agent's work and instructed him in their use. In addition, as a further basis for his work, I have handed him the military questionnaire I was given."[59] In return for a monthly salary of two hundred marks, the agent-supervisor was to submit regular reports to "Schäfer," a Marineleitung intelligence centre in Berlin, under the not particularly imaginative code name "Conrad."[60]

Many people welcomed this renewed opportunity of working for "Kika," as Canaris once more styled himself in Spain. Information for the Reichsmarine was collected in Barcelona by Carlos Baum (code name "Martha"), who owned an export firm, in Valencia by Consul-to-be Carlos Fricke (code name "Fernando") and in Cartagena by ex-Sublieutenant Alfred Menzel (code name "Edoardo"), manager of a subsidiary of Minerales y Productos Metalúrgicos S.A., while Ricardo Classen (code name "Ricardo"), an agent of the firm Baquera, Kuschke y Martin, recorded anything he deemed useful to the Navy in Cádiz. Another of Canaris's confidants, Reserve Lieutenant Rüggeberg, was based in Barcelona, and the Navy's interests were represented in Madrid by Lieutenant (ret.) Mayrhofer, a personal friend.[61]

What proved harder was to commend German plans for submarine construction to Spain's political and military establishment. Although Canaris gained access to the royal court and to Primo de Rivera's official residence through the good offices of influential friends like Captain Mateo García y los Reyes, commander of the Spanish submarine base at Cartagena, and Max Bauer, the Kapp rebel who had fled from German justice and was now military adviser to King Alfonso XIII, Germany's U-boat plans excited little apparent interest among the Spanish naval authorities.[62]

Britain had long been the Spanish Navy's arms supplier and the Spanish naval scene was dominated by British submarines, British designs, British instructors and engineers. The firm Constructora Naval —backed by British capital—monopolized Spain's submarine construction with the benevolent encouragement of Cornejo, the pro-British Minister of the Navy.[63] The Germans could hardly hope to prevail against such competition. In April 1924 the IvS had—with support from Krupp—joined a Spanish consortium in forming the Unión Naval de Levante (UNL), but the hoped-for orders had not been forthcoming.[64]

Canaris's conversations with Spanish naval officers nonetheless made it plain to him that German submarine designers might well have a chance in Spain. The younger officers were particularly dissatisfied with British submarine types and displeased at their Navy's strong dependence on British capital and armaments. Apart from that, German U-boats' wartime successes in the Mediterranean were still fresh enough in the memories of many Spanish naval officers for them to want to boost their country's prestige there by the acquisition of similar vessels.

This mood had to be exploited for the benefit of German submarine projects, but Canaris considered the UNL far too lethargic and uninfluential to persuade Madrid to build any German-designed submarines. Even its financial resources struck him as suspect. "The UNL-owned bank, Banco de Cataluña, is a third-rate institution which no one takes seriously,"[65] he wrote, and flatly stated that UNL managing director Ziegelasch was incapable of pushing German interests in a sufficiently forceful manner. He went on to note, doubtless with polemical intent: "Z. himself quite exhausted—muddled—swamped with paper work. His energies are clearly being exploited to the full by Spain. Cannot see the wood for the trees."[66]

Canaris concluded that the IvS should withdraw from the Unión Naval de Levante and be harnessed to another Spanish partner with better prospects of implementing German plans.[67] He already knew of such a partner—someone who had been of service to him in the war: the shipowner and industrialist Horacio Echevarrieta. The Madrid banker Ullmann, another wartime acquaintance, had advised him to join forces with Echevarrieta on the grounds that he was "firmly resolved to establish an armaments industry in Spain, independent of foreigners" and wanted "to build submarines at all costs."[68]

Canaris promptly put his shirt on Echevarrieta and bombarded the Marineleitung with reports describing the Basque as the most influential and dependable partner the Reichsmarine could wish for. "At the present time," he wrote, "he is a political force of the first order because he has earned the gratitude of the Spanish people by purchasing the release of Spanish prisoners of war in Morocco . . . at considerable risk to his own person. He is . . . the wealthiest industrialist in Spain. Since Echevarrieta merits special attention from the general German standpoint, an attempt must be made to influence him in our favour."[69] An informant had already conveyed that "Echev.'s influence [is] likewise paramount in regard to submarines. Said to have an order for twelve submarines in his pocket."[70]

This was a gross exaggeration, the fact of the matter being that Echevarrieta was on the verge of bankruptcy and *persona non grata* at court because of his republican sympathies. Von Jess, Hapag's Madrid representative, also warned of "that great big fraud" Echevarrieta, who made all kinds of promises with no intention of keeping them.[71] However, the industrialist was under such pressure that he unscrupulously staked everything on the German card and sought financial aid for his ailing companies from Germany alone. It did not, therefore, displease him to be wooed by Canaris, who pulled out all the stops in an effort to win this ostensibly reluctant and vacillating ally for the German cause.

Bauer, who was another of Canaris's confidants, vigorously helped to interest Echevarrieta in German submarine designs and simultaneously drew the Spanish authorities' attention to the new Canaris-Echevarricta duo. Primo de Rivera was initially cautious, but his deputy, Admiral Antonio Conde de Magáz, warmed to the idea of introducing German submarine types into the Spanish Navy.[72] Canaris was able, with some satisfaction, to report to Berlin: "The Spanish Navy has finally decided on the German type. The officer with the greatest say in this matter, Captain Don Mateo García y los Reyes, wants to build a German-type submarine of approximately 1,000 ts., extremely fast and with a long range."[73]

Back in Berlin on February 17, 1925, Canaris advocated extensive co-operation between the Reichsmarine and the Spanish Navy. He skilfully neutralized Navy Chief Zenker's objections to the IvS by proposing that the Marineleitung should itself participate in the construction of Spanish submarines based on German designs and that Echevarrieta and the IvS should co-operate only if the Marineleitung came in.[74] Zenker concurred. In a subsequent memorandum, Canaris noted that the Spanish Navy was to be supported "because strengthening Spain is to Germany's advantage. Hence the interest in the IvS and its successes."[75]

But Echevarrieta's competitor, the UNL, was reluctant to abandon the struggle and declined to release the IvS for a joint project with the Basque industrialist. In March Ziegelasch turned up at the Marineleitung and insisted that the UNL was on the verge of landing a big order for the construction of several submarines. The Germania yard, which had an interest in the IvS, considered the UNL's prospects so bright that it had given Ziegelasch the drawings of a new submarine which he wanted to submit to the Spanish naval authorities.[76] He now requested the Marineleitung to supply official confirmation that the IvS projects enjoyed its backing. Zenker had the appropriate certificate drafted but kept it on file because Ziegelasch refused to make a firm commitment on the quid pro quo which the Marineleitung demanded in return, to wit, the release of the IvS.[77]

Canaris used this fuss over the Marineleitung's certificate to push Echevarrieta's candidature in Madrid as well. Meanwhile, Berlin had been visited by a Spanish naval board which soon grasped that Canaris alone could provide Spain with access to Germany's wartime experience in submarine, torpedo boat and torpedo construction.[78] This meant that Canaris had a decisive say in whom the Spanish naval authorities entrusted with orders for submarines because that person must also enjoy the confidence of the Germans—and "that person" was none other than Don Horacio Echevarrieta.

Canaris was recalled to Spain in April 1925 by a letter from Daniel Araoz, one of Echevarrieta's closest associates.[79] The industrialist was pressing Madrid to reach a decision and asking for binding German guarantees. Canaris offered him IvS co-operation (behind the UNL's back) but insisted that he should sever his business connections with the Blohm & Voss yard, which had turned down an interest in the IvS. Echevarrieta agreed.[80] At that precise moment, Canaris played his trump card: he called at the Ministry of the Navy and handed over the document which now linked the Marineleitung with the Spanish Navy.[81]

Game, set and match to Canaris, who seemed to have clinched the deal. He reported on the outcome of his mission as follows: "1. The Spanish Navy and the Directorate are firmly resolved to build the German submarine type developed by the IvS. 2. What clinched this decision was the memorandum drafted by the Marineleitung, which was construed as a military guarantee. 3. The UNL, which submitted the IvS project, has no prospect of being commissioned to build these submarines because their prices are too high. 4. The Spanish Directorate is determined to place the submarines' construction with Echevarrieta."[82]

The next task was to cement Echevarrieta's commitment to the German cause. Ex-Colonel Bauer proposed that the industrialist should travel to Germany and enter into direct negotiations with the Marineleitung, so Echevarrieta's yacht *Kosmo Jacinta* was soon heading for Kiel with its owner on board.[83] "A great deal depends," Bauer wrote to Canaris on July 20, "on his being well received and permitted to see everything without gaining the impression that something is being forced on him."[84] Canaris and Lohmann ensured that Echevarrieta was respectfully courted during his visit to Germany in August 1925, mindful of Bauer's admonition that they must "keep emphasizing that, as a Spanish patriot, he is especially welcome to us Germans."[85]

Echevarrieta and the German naval officers hit it off from the start, and the Spaniard complied with most of Canaris's and Lohmann's suggestions. Since Madrid had yet to make a final decision on building submarines, the new partners resolved to start collaborating in the field of torpedo manufacture. It now transpired that the "wealthiest industrialist in Spain" was short of capital, so Lohmann granted him a loan.[86] On February 22, 1926, Canaris noted: "The firm of Echevarrieta y Lariniaga has been commissioned by royal decree to build a torpedo factory for the Spanish Navy at Cádiz."[87]

Canaris could justly feel pleased with himself. For the first time since the war, a foreign navy had proved ready to ally itself with the accursed Germans—not least because of his personal influence. Even the fall of Magáz, Primo de Rivera's rival, and the postponement of the decision to build submarines failed to shake Canaris's position in Spain. He kept in touch with Magáz on the (false) assumption that he would stage a comeback and clung doggedly to the belief that Echevarrieta would land an order for at least a dozen submarines.[88] Such was his influence that the Marineleitung never made a move on the Spanish question without consulting him first.

In March 1926 Lohmann enlisted his aid. Echevarrieta had reappeared in Berlin with fresh financial demands.[89] He lacked the capital to build the torpedo factory. Worse still, the British had offered to fill the breach with capital and patents. Echevarrieta skilfully played on Lohmann's anti-British syndrome by declaring that he needed Germany's assistance because he had "made it his aim to break British influence on the Spanish munitions industry."[90] This time, however, his credit requirements exceeded Lohmann's resources. Canaris suggested a way out of the dilemma: they must procure Echevarrieta a credit from the Deutsche Bank (DB).

"To attain our objective in Spain," Canaris had written earlier in the year, "it is absolutely essential that . . . a bank (DB) should be interested in granting Echevarrieta credits by analogy with the Bank of England."[91] Lohmann thereupon proposed to the head of the Marineleitung that the government should, by guaranteeing repayment, persuade the Deutsche Bank to grant Echevarrieta a large credit on condition that he undertook to work exclusively with the IvS and use German designs alone.[92] The Marineleitung and the cabinet agreed, largely because they were impressed by Canaris's argument that Echevarrieta might defect at any moment: "Is at present pro-German but will, if difficulties arise in this quarter, unhesitatingly . . . procure the assistance of others and thereby gravely jeopardize the adoption of the German type."[93]

In May DB director Luck visited Spain under the careful guidance of Canaris.[94] It was hardly surprising that final negotiations on the Echevarrieta credit were also attended by Ullmann, the banker who had long formed a link between Canaris and the Spanish industrialist.[95] Echevarrieta signed the credit agreement on May 17, a day after he had signified his acceptance of all the German terms in writing.[96] With cool and characteristic self-assurance, Canaris suffered himself to be acclaimed by the leaders of Spanish society as their country's liberator from British financial pressure.

"General Primo de Rivera," he reported in mid-June, "expressed his gratitude for the great assistance bestowed by the German Navy on the Spanish Navy through the medium of Herr Echevarrieta. He told me that this accommodating attitude had been instrumental in prompting him to conclude a favourable trade agreement with Germany."[97] The King, too, expressed his good will and considered it "axiomatic that, in gratitude for our readiness to oblige, the Spanish Navy will allow us to participate in all experiments and trials." To sum up: "Constructora Naval [the pro-British firm] is in strong disfavour, primarily because of the pressure it exerted in respect of recent construction orders placed against the Navy's wishes. The Navy has clearly recognized that its expansion is being tailored to the interests of Constructora Naval rather than to national requirements."[98]

The Spaniards were now so keen to collaborate with the Reichsmarine that Canaris thought it safe for Lohmann, the clandestine rearmer, to be introduced to the Spanish scene. In August Canaris arranged a meeting between Lohmann, who had been hankering to meet the Spanish individuals and authorities bent on co-operation with the Reichsmarine, and King Alfonso and his naval chiefs. The occasion of

Lohmann's visit to Spain was a demonstration of the German rotor ship *Barbara* in Santander harbour.[99]

For this high spot of Lohmann's trip on August 18, 1926, Canaris had mustered some of the most prestigious figures in Spain. The King himself, members of the royal family, commanders of numerous Spanish warships and leaders of the Spanish shipbuilding industry—all turned out to welcome Lohmann.[100] Alfonso XIII actually permitted the *Barbara* to hoist the royal standard. Lohmann proudly noted that this was "a very special honour which had never before been granted to a foreign merchantman."[101]

The King proved just as gracious in conversation. Spain was anxious to develop a "national munitions industry with German help." As for Echevarrieta, he was to form a Committee for National Defence and exploit Germany's modern naval projects for the benefit of Germany as well as Spain.[102] Lohmann, who wanted to supply Spain with the new German fire-control system, proposed that Germany should start by building six torpedo boats and two fast ten-thousand-ton tankers for the Spanish Navy.[103] He was so gratified by Alfonso's disclosures that he entrusted him with a secret Marineleitung film on torpedo boats. As soon as it dawned on him how rash this was, he gave instructions that the film should be "unobtrusively retrieved through the good offices of [Echevarrieta's friend] Araoz . . . and safely returned by way of the embassy."[104]

Wherever Lohmann went in Spain, Canaris was always at his shoulder with a knowledge of the right strings to pull, the best doors to open and the most convincing arguments to employ. If Echevarrieta asked Lohmann for a list of new German naval weapons, Canaris produced one. If the Spaniards wanted papers on fire-control systems, tankers and the rotor principle, Canaris had already drafted them. If Lohmann wondered what Navy Minister Cornejo thought of the German fire-control system, Canaris had already traveled to Madrid to sound him out.[105]

Lohmann was considerably surprised to observe the ease with which Canaris moved in Spanish social and military circles. "Lieutenant Commander Canaris," he wrote on his return, "[has] underpinned the development of our co-operation with Spain by means of his personal relations . . . notably with Echevarrieta, with Lieutenant Commander Daniel Araoz Baron del Sacro Lirio, gentlemen in waiting to the King, and with the King himself."[106] Better than any German officer of his day, Canaris knew the rules of Spanish politics and could manipulate the Spanish mentality and love of tradition.

This was not lost on the man who had once been close to him in the turmoil of civil war and had again become his immediate superior: Captain Wilfried von Loewenfeld, the new head of the Flottenabteilung. Writing of Canaris on September 30, 1926, Loewenfeld said: "Highly sensitive to the psychology and mentality of foreigners and an exceptionally good linguist as well, he has an exemplary capacity for dealing with foreigners (from the man in the street to those in high places), whose confidence he quickly gains. Once entrusted with such an assignment, he balks at no obstacle and is undeterred by any bout of fever. No office is too remote for him to penetrate and gain access to the relevant person. In a surprisingly short space of time he is there in the saddle, looking childishly innocent."[107] Spain provided a rich field of operations for Canaris's manifold talents because no other country appealed so strongly to what lay within him: the art of man management, a craving for romance and adventure, and a childish delight in covering his tracks.

Secret messages, pseudonyms and ciphers had fascinated Canaris since boyhood. In Spain he made use of everything he deemed indispensable to the secret envoy's armoury. "Kika" was everywhere and nowhere. He stayed at small and inconspicuous hotels, met informants at remote and secluded rendezvous, instructed his agents in the ABC of dead-letter boxes and invisible inks. Although (or perhaps because) he had never undergone secret service training, he evinced an insatiable appetite for the rituals and rigmaroles of intelligence work.

With some imagination and naivety, he evolved an intricate code which would, he believed, disguise his Spanish activities from outside observers but was more apt to bewilder his readers in the Marine-leitung. He reported, for instance, that "a decree issued in Schulzen-dorf" had "requested Hausknecht [hotel porter] to offer the Richard system for sale," or that a certain aircraft had been "christened by the Bishop with Alex, Mogul and the Prince of Wales in attendance."[108] This gibberish could only be deciphered by consulting the code list. "Schulzendorf" was the Spanish Navy Ministry, "Hausknecht" Eche-varrieta and "Richard" the German fire-control system. "Mogul" shrouded the identity of Primo de Rivera and "Alex" was none other than King Alfonso.[109] However, the rest of the wording was so straightforwardly rendered "in clear" that any secret service pro could have fathomed the interplay of pseudonyms with ease.

Be that as it may, Canaris was so familiar a figure to the Spanish intelligence and police machines that they gladly enlisted his aid. General Severiano Martínez Anido, the dictatorship's Minister of the Interior, often took the German lieutenant commander's advice. Early in 1928—to anticipate slightly—the general sent for Canaris and suggested that he work out an agreement on co-operation between the German and Spanish political police authorities.[110] Although the official aim of this agreement was to combat the Communist menace, Martínez Anido was primarily interested in neutralizing seditious Spanish expatriates who might be planning to assassinate prominent figures at home.

After consulting the German Embassy, Canaris agreed to help draft the document. Martínez Anido then passed him on to General Bazan, the *Jefe de la Seguridad* or chief of the Spanish security police, who joined Canaris in drafting the first anti-Comintern pact in German history.[111]

The parties to this agreement on "Mutual Relations Between the Police Authorities of Germany and Spain" (to quote its official title) undertook to exchange information on "the planning of insurrections and seditious campaigns" in both countries and assist one another in the surveillance or pursuit of politically suspect persons. Communications from the German and Spanish police were to be signed "Tristan" and "Siegfried" and "Alonso" and "Sancho" respectively. The twin texts stipulated that "in either case, messages are to be inserted in two envelopes of which the first shall bear the agreed address and the second the word 'Especial' only."[112]

The secret Canaris-Bazan agreement of February 17, 1928, established a lifelong link between the future German Abwehr chief and the Spanish secret police which was to survive two systems of government, monarchic and republican. The Seguridad was not, however, Canaris's sole partner among the Spanish intelligence services. His confidant Mayrhofer also provided a direct entree to the intelligence and counterespionage section of the Navy Ministry, whose chief, Lieutenant Commander Manuel de Vierna, was a friend of long standing. As Mayrhofer reported to Berlin: "One can sometimes learn useful things from him."[113]

Canaris still lacked proper contact with the Spanish Army and its intelligence service, but this too developed as the Reichswehr authorities sent Canaris on more and more confidential missions. As early as 1925 the Truppenamt—the organization which had replaced the old General Staff after its prohibition by the Versailles Treaty—requested Canaris to get German Air Force officers enrolled in the aviation units of the Spanish Army, preferably those engaged in the Moroccan War.[114] This mission took him to the War Ministry in Madrid, where the Spanish air forces were commanded by Lieutenant Colonel Alfredo Kindelán.

Kindelán familiarized Canaris with the problems of the colonial war in Morocco and approved the admission of German officers to the aviation units operating there.[115] Morocco and the other Spanish possessions in Africa remained on Canaris's agenda from then on. He was later instructed to promote German commercial interests in Ifni and Spanish Guinea and secure permission for the establishment of Hispano-German commercial concerns in Northwest Africa, which brought him into contact with General Count Jordana, the stiff-necked Minister for the Colonies.[116]

Morocco was also a staple topic of conversation among the young Army officers whom Canaris met in Madrid at this period. In the view of ambitious captains like Juan Vigón and Martínez Campos, the early defeats and losses of the Moroccan War had shown up the hidebound and ineffectual nature of the entire Spanish military system.[117] The same topic enthralled a young colonel whom Canaris often encountered at the royal palace although they had yet to become personally acquainted. One of the King's favourite officers, this colonel commanded the 1st Regiment of the 1st Division and went by the name of Francisco Franco y Bahamonde.[118]

Without realizing it, Canaris had forged links with men who were to form the ruling elite of the Franco regime a decade later. General Kindelán became the Caudillo's "king-maker," General Jordana rose to become Foreign Minister and Canaris's friends Vigón and Martínez Campos reached the top of the General Staff and Spanish military intelligence respectively. Even older acquaintances of Canaris occupied key posts in Franco's Spain. Martínez Ánido became the Caudillo's first Minister of Security and Admiral Magáz his ambassador to Berlin.

Admiral Zenker could not leave an officer with Canaris's connections and influence buried in a minor department like AIIm. On October 1, 1926, he was appointed adviser to the Chief of Staff of the Marineleitung, Captain Peter Donner, and thus became something akin to the Navy's Foreign Minister.[119] Donner defined his adviser's functions more modestly: "Dealing with matters relating to foreign attachés, co-ordinating communication with foreigners and deputizing for the Chief of Staff."[120] This "staff officer with exceptional qualities of intellect and character" (Zenker) had now joined the supreme hierarchy of the Marineleitung.[121]

Canaris spent most of his time in Spain, as before. His assignments multiplied, as did his Spanish partners' requests, which became steadily more ambitious. Torpedoes, tankers, fire-control systems, special engines, torpedo boats—there was no end to Spanish requirements. Canaris also attracted the attention of German industrial concerns for which he had to set up contacts, secure concessions and scout new markets.

He was able to chalk up one success after another. "Funds for the two oilers (combined tankers) have been approved by Mogul and the Consejo de Defensa further to our meeting at Zarzuela," he reported in May 1927. Another message followed soon afterwards: "Apart from the factory for torpedoes, one for torpedo planes—ordinary aircraft and engines—is to be built at Cádiz. The [German] torpedo boats are also to undergo trials at this experimental station."[122] A third report signalled "the possibility of channelling major orders to German industry via him

[Echevarrieta], e.g. coal distillation and liquefaction plant, tanker-freighter contracts and possibly funding operations as well."[123]

The German aircraft industry, in particular, found Canaris an indefatigable champion of its interests. As he noted on August 8, 1927: "Despite vigorous efforts on the part of British, French and Italian airline companies, Herr E[chevarrieta] has now managed to obtain government consent to the formation of a Spanish airline company in association with Germany's Luft-Hansa . . . Moreover, preliminary discussions between E. and Luft-Hansa have established a basis for the continuing development of this company in respect of overseas traffic with South America."[124]

Experiments with German weapons and designs had shown such promise that Canaris was soon taken with the idea of extending them to South America. In Madrid in spring 1927 he had met Argentina's Navy chief, Admiral Galindez, who told him he had just placed an order for two modern destroyers with Constructora Naval.[125] Canaris inferred that he must have given preference to the Spanish shipbuilding industry for reasons of Hispanic tradition, because British and Dutch yards had offered him far better terms.

"So in order to work in S.A. [South America]," Canaris declared firmly, "we must definitely have a springboard in Sp[ain]. An opening now exists, and the most favourable one imaginable. With the Johnny constructions [tankers] we can build up a first-class yard in Cádiz which will not only meet the requirements of the Sp. Schulzendorf [Spanish Navy Ministry] but, in addition, turn our fraternization with S.A. circles to practical use."[126] Canaris duly kept in touch with Galindez and encouraged his Spanish friends to sing the praises of German expertise in armaments and shipbuilding.

He even roped in King Alfonso. "[Galindez] told me," he noted after a conversation with the admiral, "that the King had drawn his attention to the torpedo under construction with Echevarrieta, also to the tankers. The King had spoken most disparagingly of Constructora Naval and expressed his pleasure at Echevarrieta's collaboration with German firms."[127] Canaris introduced the Argentinian to Don Horacio and urged him to build some German-designed submarines. Galindez showed interest. Canaris later visited Argentina and paved the way for contacts between the IvS and the Argentine naval authorities to such good effect that the firm based a senior employee in Buenos Aires as its permanent representative there.[128]

But Canaris, forever hastening from one secret mission to the next, was already devoting himself to new tasks and topics. Nothing seemed to halt him in his tracks. Heedless of family ties and home comforts, he shuttled between Berlin, Spain, Argentina and the Mediterranean. He seldom went on leave and displayed such incurable restlessness that even his superiors became worried. "Care will have to be taken," wrote Captain Donner, "to ensure that this valuable officer does not prejudice his career in the executive branch by exclusive assignment to duties of a domestic and foreign policy nature, as well as by employment on special missions. There is also a risk of overtaxing him physically and mentally."[129]

Canaris was not fettered to his Berlin desk until summer 1927, when Donner took several months' leave. He now had to deputize for the absent Chief of Staff.[130] He also learnt to assess the policy and strategy of the Reichsmarine from a higher standpoint and gained an insight into the workings of the various sections and desks. Familiarity with the daily decision-making process sharpened his perception of what was feasible and necessary. Seen at this level, many a naval officer's personal initiative and many a bold infringement of the Versailles provisions dwindled to the true importance it assumed in the Marineleitung's general scheme of things.

Quite suddenly, no officer at headquarters impressed Canaris as a greater potential source of trouble than Lohmann, the comrade-in-arms with whom he had shared so many secrets. A rift had opened between them in recent months. Canaris now found Lohmann overintense and romantic. He may also have felt uneasy because, despite their close working relationship, Lohmann had never initiated him into his ultimate aims and objectives. Months before, Lohmann had sent ex-Lieutenant Messerschmidt (code name "Ebi") to Madrid with instructions to report regularly to Canaris and the Marine Transport Section on the progress of operations in Spain.[131] Canaris now saw his colleague in a new light.

We shall never really know what prompted Canaris to turn against Lohmann. Perhaps he caught wind of the concern felt by Lohmann's closest associates, who were appalled to see how their chief, poised on the brink of a nervous breakdown, was slowly coming apart as he steered his increasingly labyrinthine complex of business ventures from one commercial disaster to the next. Lieutenant Commander Flies complained that Lohmann was "drunk with work," a mental state which would not let him rest: he raced from car to train, train to plane and plane back to car, constantly in touch with his innumerable firms and operations by telephone.[132]

In fact, Lohmann now flitted through his world of schemes and fancies like a ghost. He was a sick man, and barely capable of performing his duties. As early as November 1925, doctors at the garrison hospital in Berlin had noted that he was suffering from "speech defects, headaches and arterial rigidity." Early in 1926 his symptoms of arteriosclerosis increased, and by the end of the year he was again suffering from speech defects.[133] Even electropathic treatment failed to bring a permanent improvement in his condition. To make matters worse, his memory deteriorated. He often found it hard to concentrate and forgot important points.[134]

A sick man who singlehandedly directed a whole chain of mysterious enterprises and operations was a potential threat to the Reichsmarine at large. Canaris could not shake off a sense of impending disaster. He did not know what ventures Lohmann was still involved in, but even his limited knowledge of the captain's activities was sufficient for him to raise the alarm.

As soon as Donner returned from leave in July, Canaris reported to him. He had, as he put it later, "formed the impression that BS was engaged in ventures unknown to us and, more particularly, to the head of the Marineleitung."[135] He also recalled that he "suggested . . . to Captain Donner that the head of the Marineleitung should order Captain Lohmann to submit information about all his enterprises."[136] Donner acted on Canaris's suggestion and went to see Zenker. At the end of July Lohmann was instructed to put all his cards on the table.[137]

Lohmann's preliminary and partial revelations were disturbing enough for Zenker and Donner to decide to take him out of circulation before his escapades became public knowledge. Zenker planned to take advantage of Lohmann's promotion to rear admiral, which was due that autumn, to neutralize him. In practice, this meant assigning him a Chief of Staff to help run the Marine Transport Section, detaching his commercial empire from the Navy and amalgamating it into a holding company. Lohmann's immediate subordinate, Oberinspektor [Senior Inspector] Schneider, was to be officially retired from the Navy and appointed managing director of the new conglomerate.[138]

Before this scheme could be set in motion, the Navy was overtaken by the disaster which Canaris had vaguely foreseen: one of Lohmann's more bizarre enterprises, the Phoebus film company, went bankrupt.[139] Lohmann was still debating whether to come clean with his superiors when the *Berliner Tageblatt* saved him the trouble. On August 8 the paper reported that the film company, "which has debts of 4 or 5 million marks," had been "financed to the tune of at least 6½ to 8 million marks from the secret Marineleitung fund at the Reichswehr Ministry."[140]

The Ministry promptly denied this story and the Marineleitung made soothing noises, but the Marineleitung's credulous complacency was short-lived. Canaris clarified the situation by going to Schneider over Lohmann's head and getting him to produce documentary evidence of Phoebus's business dealings.[141] The files and accounts in Schneider's safe told a story of commercial ineptitude and political charlatanism unique in German naval history.

In 1922 a number of small German film companies had merged to form the Phoebus-Film A.G. In 1924, after initially limiting its activities to film production and distribution. Phoebus had begun to build or acquire cinemas of its own. The company was running short of capital when one of its directors, Correll, met Captain Lohmann. Impressed by Correll's talk of close contacts with Russia and his disquisitions on the "national responsibility" of the German film industry, Lohmann scented that Phoebus might prove a source of secret intelligence about the Soviet Union and financed the firm without informing the head of the Marineleitung.[142]

Lohmann at first confined himself to granting Phoebus some substantial loans, which by January 1925 amounted to 870,000 marks. He then acquired a major holding in the firm. Lohmann and the Phoebus board agreed to increase the company's share capital by 2.8 million marks of which Lohmann took up 1.3 million. He also acquired a batch of old shares with a nominal value of 320,000 marks, but not even this disguised subsidy got Phoebus off the hook. Early in 1926 the company again ran into financial difficulties, and again Lohmann came to the rescue—this time with a credit of 3 million marks guaranteed by the Marineleitung. A year later Phoebus appealed to Lohmann for further assistance and was granted another two credits totalling 4.4 million marks.[143]

But all Lohmann's disbursements failed to save the company from collapse. As the official board of inquiry later declared: "The total loss incurred by the country as a result of this involvement with Phoebus-Film A.G. may thus be roughly put at 8 million marks exclusive of forfeited interest and indirect losses."[144]

However, readers of the Schneider documents could not fail to be particularly incensed by the crafty way in which Lohmann had wangled his government-backed credit of 3 million marks in 1926. Deutsche Girozentrale had refused to advance this sum unless the state stood guarantor in the event of the company's inability to repay it. Lohmann thereupon approached Finance Minister Reinhold and requested his approval of such a guarantee by the Reichswehr Ministry on the grounds that government consent was immaterial because the guarantee could be underwritten by Lignose, a film-manufacturing company with which he was closely associated. To dispel Reinhold's lingering doubts, Lohmann produced yet another argument: in the unlikely event of the state's having to shell out, "the Marineleitung would furnish any necessary funds out of its intelligence budget." Reinhold agreed.[145]

Lohmann drafted a declaration of surety signed on behalf of the Marineleitung by himself alone, but the Girozentrale board wanted this countersigned by the Finance Minister. However, Reinhold declined to endorse the document unless Reichswehr Minister Gessler did so too.[146]

This put Lohmann on the spot because Gessler was ignorant of the guarantee ostensibly under consideration by his own ministry and had never been apprised of Lohmann's dealings with Phoebus.

The only course open to Lohmann was to play the two unsuspecting ministers off against each other. He pretended to Reichswehr Minister Gessler that the declaration of surety had already been agreed with Reinhold and to the Finance Minister that Gessler had already approved the whole transaction.[147] Gessler later testified that Lohmann had allayed Reinhold's misgivings by hinting "that his signature was only a formality and that he would undertake no binding commitments thereby . . . Conversely, Captain Lohmann represented the matter to me in a light which suggested that my signature was merely the fulfilment of a formality."[148] The result: both ministers signed.

The contents of the Schneider documents were so explosive that Zenker and Donner genuinely feared that relations between Gessler and the Navy would be ruined if they became known. Hoping to bury the Phoebus affair as quickly as possible, they decided to withhold the truth about Lohmann's stroke of genius from the minister. This meant that he must be informed—or rather, disinformed—accordingly, and no one was better equipped for the job than Canaris, whose experience in dealing with the stolid Swabian dated from his days as an aide at the Reichswehr Ministry. Canaris was duly instructed to visit Gessler, who was vacationing on the North Sea island of Sylt, and present a wordy but noncommittal report.

Canaris must have pulled off a brilliant stroke of rhetoric and man management, because Gessler never for one moment suspected that a crisis was looming. The subsequent board of Inquiry found that he showed "scant concern" at Canaris's report.[149] Seeing no reason to return to Berlin, the minister continued to sun himself on Sylt until August 16, when he travelled to Kiel to attend a naval exercise.[150] Nothing and no one warned him that he was fast approaching the gravest crisis in his political career.

It had meanwhile become obvious that the Lohmann genie conjured up by the *Berliner Tageblatt* could not be returned to its bottle. Press disclosures about the Reichsmarine's secret commercial empire multiplied week by week. One firm after another was bathed in a glare of publicity. Reporters and leader writers unearthed a "fine old tangle of firms and businesses, each shadier than the other," as Gessler himself came gradually to accept.[151] There seemed to be few fields of entrepreneurial activity in which the Navy had not become involved. Banking, canned pork products, property speculation, mining, the construction of mills for pulverized coal, the production of "patriotic" films—Lohmann had dabbled in all of these.

He was promptly suspected of lining his own pockets. The *Berliner*

Tageblatt insinuated that he had been "allotted and, to our knowledge, paid 10 per cent of all net revenues received by Phoebus-Film A.G. and its Marmorhaus-Theater."[152] These press revelations, most of which were only too accurate, would have been incomplete without a *femme fatale* in the person of Else Ekimoff, the ex-wife of a tsarist general.[153] For her, Lohmann had obligingly spent 900,000 marks on a desirable piece of Berlin real estate known as No. 3 Lützowufer. He had also employed her as his secretary at the then princely salary of 1,000 marks a month.[154]

Worse still, Lohmann had directed his thirty companies with no commercial success. Nearly all of them were in the red. He had been compelled to dip repeatedly into his secret fund and resort to dubious business practices "in the belief that he could master the commercial side of things by dint of military daring and an unbridled disregard for legal and commercial considerations which to him smacked of red tape," as an official auditor phrased it.[155] Total loss to the German taxpayer: 26 million marks.[156]

A storm of public protest broke over Lohmann and his superiors as the Navy lurched into its worst crisis since the Kapp Putsch. Lohmann was dismissed and later brought before a naval court of honour (which acquitted him), Reichswehr Minister Gessler's head rolled and even Zenker's days at the Marineleitung were numbered.[157] But public anger was not so readily appeased. Under pressure, the Chancellor appointed ex-Minister Saemisch, the head of the Public Audit Office, to conduct an investigation. He was soon joined by a second inquisitor, ex-State Secretary Fritze.[158]

However, the government could have no interest in exposing the whole system of clandestine naval rearmament. Saemisch and Fritze were only permitted to scratch the surface. They were also obliged to help detach Lohmann's unmasked enterprises from the Navy and incorporate them under cover names in private industry, where they largely retained their previous function. The investigators' reports were appropriately mild. Fritze on Lohmann: "He is guilty of having put too many pans on the stove. He consequently failed to notice—and could not, in fact, have noticed—when one of his many pans caught or boiled over."[159]

The mood at Marineleitung headquarters was less clement. The new Reichswehr Minister, General (ret.) Wilhelm Groener, was not a man to tolerate the proximity of officers who hoodwinked their superiors. He called for a detailed list of all secret naval rearmament projects and grew hot under the collar when the Marineleitung's Munitions Section replied in writing that such enterprises could "not be listed on paper."[160] Groener insisted on the most punctilious compliance with his orders. He further required all officers in the Marineleitung to submit a detailed account of their relations with Lohmann and the extent to which they had been informed of his activities. Canaris was among those questioned.

His statement contained an admission that he had taken part in some of Lohmann's operations in Spain. However: "I had no personal connection with the rest of Captain Lohmann's activities. His links with Travag did not come to my notice until recently. I was further aware of the existence of Navis, Mentor and the involvement with the IvS. I heard nothing about the film ventures, the banking company and the many other concerns of which I learned in the course of the inquiry."[161]

At the same time, Canaris thought it wiser to dissociate himself from his erstwhile comrade-in-arms. Being an expert manipulator, he knew only too well how to jettison ballast and sever burdensome human ties. Whenever the recollection of his former partnership became an embarrassment, his listeners were told how badly he had got on with Lohmann. From now on, he cautioned them against "Leo" (Lohmann's code name) and his schemes. He was in "no doubt that a business venture tackled by Leo is doomed to failure from the outset."[162]

When Echevarricta complained to Canaris that Lohmann was making repeated offers of partnership and getting on his nerves, Canaris promptly undertook to relieve the Spaniard of Lohmann's presence. "The one thing we must do our utmost to prevent," he said soothingly, "is his interference in current transactions of interest to the Marineleitung." It had, after all, been "proved that Leo had far exceeded his authority, kept his superiors in ignorance of important measures and conducted irresponsible financial transactions resulting in substantial losses and detriment to the Navy."[163]

Donner, too, confirmed that, so far from having been involved in the Lohmann affair, his immediate subordinate had "actively helped to clear it up and earned great credit by so doing."[164] For all that, Canaris's disengaging manoeuvre was not an unqualified success. His sworn opponents in the left-wing press found it intolerable that he should "dodge behind his friend Lohmann's long-suffering back with the agility of his Hellenic ancestors," as the *Weltbühne* put it.[165]

This mouthpiece of radical pacifists and Socialists, which demanded the abolition of the Reichswehr and was not averse to deliberate treason,[166] had set out to illustrate the arrogance of German militarists by citing Canaris's alleged machinations as a case in point. On one occasion the *Weltbühne* accused him of having offered incriminating evidence against Zenker to the editors of "a leading democratic newspaper," on another it insinuated that he was manipulating the naval counterespionage network for the benefit of right-wing extremists, on another it suspected him of masterminding the Swedish operations of the Junkers aircraft company and on yet another it claimed that he had been the real wire-puller behind Lohmann's nationalistic and conservative film-making policy.[167]

Although most of these "disclosures" were wide of the mark, they brought Canaris some highly unwelcome publicity. Many a credulous Republican found it easy to believe in the dangerous potentialities of this "last key witness for the dark age" because he knew from reading the *Weltbühne* that Canaris, "that shrewdest member of the warrior caste," had actually prevailed upon Gustav Noske to rehabilitate the old military establishment in 1919.[168] Other left-wing papers adopted a similar stance, with the result that few German naval officers of the period attracted more vituperation or greater antipathy in the Socialist and pacifist press.

The anti-Canaris campaign was not unprovoked, of course. Canaris had never concealed his dislike of the Left and his fundamental belief that it was "nationally unreliable." As an officer, he had no time for anyone who wanted to deprive his country of essential military safeguards, let alone called for the abolition of the armed forces or pronounced a German fleet "not only an expensive luxury but a downright public menace."[169] His hatred of the "Reds" had outlasted the German civil war. In his eyes, the extreme Left was enduringly burdened with the original sin of responsibility for the naval disorders of 1917–18.

The extent to which he was still dominated by the prejudices of the revolutionary period, even early in 1926, is apparent from his violent altercation with Social Democrats on the parliamentary committee appointed to investigate the causes of the German collapse. During a discussion of the naval strike of 1917, the SPD deputy Wilhelm Dittman, once a prominent independent Socialist in contact with the strike leaders, launched a vitriolic attack on the Imperial Navy's judicial system and repeated what he had been saying for years, namely, that the strike leaders had been unjustly sentenced to death and that unrest in the Fleet had resulted from internal abuses, not from the activities of the USPD.[170]

To many naval officers, Dittmann's name was an emotive reminder of one of their most painful wartime reverses. Immediately after the naval strike of 1917, HQ High Seas Fleet had requested the Chancellor to institute proceedings against Dittmann and two other USPD officials for having incited sailors to commit high treason in the face of the enemy. The evidence against Dittmann was so scanty that no charges were ever brought.[171] The same man, who had since returned to the Social Democratic fold, was now renewing his assault on the Navy. The Marineleitung reacted fiercely.

Canaris was selected to deliver a stinging retort before the committee of inquiry. Officially described as a Marineleitung expert on matters relating to the naval disorders, he turned up at the Reichstag on January 23, 1926, looking brisker and more pugnacious than his colleagues could remember. His very first words were a challenge. "Deputy Dittmann," he began, "has endeavoured to prove that the collapse of the Fleet was attributable, not to revolutionary influences but to adverse factors of all kinds, notably shortcomings on the part of its officers . . . I must begin by emphatically rejecting these monstrous accusations."[172]

Laughter rang out among the Social Democrat committee members. "Disprove them, then!" shouted one deputy, but the Left's hilarity did not last. The longer Canaris spoke, the more vehemently and angrily he was heckled by Social Democrats and Communists.[173]

"First and foremost," Canaris continued, "I shall bring evidence to show that the ringleaders of the mutiny in the Fleet were in close touch with the USPD, that the influences emanating from that quarter were gravely prejudicial to the Fleet and that further impairment of discipline and gradual collapse were attributable to the same." He proceeded to quote from the record of the court-martial which had originally convicted the strike leaders. Almost all the accused had admitted that contact with USPD members was the factor that had first encouraged them to strike and given them the feeling that their campaign enjoyed party support. "There can be no doubt that the very fact of these links between serving naval personnel and a party which opposed the government and wanted to bring about peace at any price . . . was sooner or later bound to induce collapse because it bred an aversion to military activity."[174]

Contact between the three USPD deputies and the "mutineers" had "substantially strengthened the ringleaders' resolve, exerted a detrimental effect on discipline and prompted others to join in," Canaris declared. The High Seas Fleet authorities had thus been right to call for the arrest of the three USPD leaders. Canaris's voice rose: "The Navy was convinced that immediate action would have proved successful. No such immediate action was taken. The blame rests with those who neglected to act."[175]

Although Canaris could hardly make his arguments stick (most of the arrested strike leaders' statements had been made under duress), his words enraged the left-wing deputies present. Dittmann sprang threateningly to his feet and his party colleague Moses asked "if Lieutenant Commander Canaris is identical with the Lieutenant Canaris who acted as an associate judge at the trial of the murderers of Liebknecht and Rosa Luxemburg, and who is credited with having done most to ensure that Vogel got away."[176]

One deputy shouted: "Ugh! What's he doing here?" and others

joined in with shouts of "Outrageous!", "Murderers' accomplice!" and
similar epithets. The Communist deputy Rosenberg requested an ad-
journment "because in my estimation the majority of the committee
find it incompatible with their dignity to confer with a government representative such as Captain [sic] Canaris." One SPD colleague suspected "an affront to the committee by the Reichswehr Ministry" and
another deputy expressed surprise at the "unprecedented fact" that the
Reichswehr Minister had seen fit to send a representative against whom
"extremely grave accusations of a criminal nature" were being made.
When a Liberal deputy tried to come to grips with Canaris's arguments, Moses cut him short. "It's a question of his person, not his
remarks. We refuse to confer with his person any longer."[177]

From one moment to the next, the committee room had been invaded by the spectre of civil war and a resurgence of the old antipathies
that seemed to have been mollified, if nothing more, by years of recon-
ciliatory endeavour on the part of various centrist governments. Canaris: "The wholly unjustified attacks that have been made on me can be
readily disposed of by consulting my superiors at the Marineleitung. I
shall not defend myself. Any reply will be given by the Reichswehr
Ministry." So saying, he marched out of the room.[178]

Sure enough, the committee received a prompt denial from the
Reichswehr Minister, who wrote: "The personal accusation made
against Lieutenant Commander Canaris, to wit, that he was involved in
the escape of Lieutenant Vogel, is wholly unfounded, as established by
a judicial hearing instituted by my predecessor. This inquiry found that
Lieutenant Commander Canaris was completely innocent."[179] Although Canaris could feel safe with such a testimonial under his belt, it
was soon borne in on him that his performance in front of the Reichstag committee had cost him dear. From now on, he was constantly
under fire from the politicians and polemicists of the Left.

Left-wing speakers never tired of denouncing Canaris as a politically
untrustworthy officer who had for years been working to overthrow the
Republic. Moses accused him in the Reichstag of having planned a
coup in collaboration with the anticonstitutional Wiking-Bund, a successor of Ehrhardt's Organisation Consul, during his tour of duty at
Kiel.[180] SPD deputy Philipp Scheidemann disclosed numerous details
of this working relationship, and the journalist Carl von Ossietzky even
insinuated that the Canaris circle had in November 1923 asked the
British Government to occupy Schleswig-Holstein and support the rebels
against Berlin in the event of a Kiel coup backed by the naval station
there.[181]

"We have shown," the *Weltbühne* summed up in September 1927,
"that it was always one man who maintained these links and, above all,
caused public money to be disbursed to extreme right-wing organi-

zations: Lieutenant Commander Canaris."[182] Left-wing newspapers continually reverted to his part in the judicial closure of the Liebknecht-Luxemburg murder inquiry. To quote a diatribe in the Communist *Welt am Abend:* "Although Herr Canaris has been repeatedly accused in the past ten years of having committed a penal offence while acting in a judicial capacity . . . no German court in all these years has been prepared to punish that penal offence."[183]

Canaris's critics painted him in ever darker colours. He seemed an embodiment of all they abhorred so deeply. To them he typified the politically active anti-Republican officer who preserved a thousand links with the old monarchical overlord-and-underling state and did not shrink from acclaiming judicial murders like the conviction of the naval strike leaders of 1917 as shining examples of "the great and exceptional consideration bestowed on the feelings of the lower ranks."[184]

The anti-Canaris campaign was, in fact, directed less at its object's person than at the cause he represented. The German Social Democratic Party was dominated by a group of extreme Marxists and pacifists who found it utterly nonsensical to maintain a navy. With an abhorrence worthy of the Prophets, they resisted any attempt by the Reichsmarine to improve its arms and equipment and compelled the more moderate party leaders to oppose all Navy appropriations in the Reichstag.[185]

The Navy's treacherous attitude during the Kapp Putsch, coupled with extravagant monarchist and nationalist pronouncements by members of the officer corps which raised fresh doubts about their allegiance to the Republic, had prejudiced the SPD leaders against all Navy requests. The party's left wing, which paid homage to utopian pacifism, rejected any navy as a putative tool of imperialism and went so far as to oppose all national defence in a bourgeois democratic context.[186] Personal factors were also involved. The SPD's naval policy owed its direction to left-wing comrades who in 1918–19—when most of them were members of the USPD—had wielded the reins of revolution and seen them wrested from their grasp by the Naval Brigades.[187]

Their spokesman was the ex-leading stoker Bernhard Kuhnt, who had once elbowed his way to the top of the revolutionary government at Wilhelmshaven and later fled from the Ehrhardt Brigade.[188] Ever since then, as an SPD Reichstag deputy, he had preached downright hatred of the Navy and its officers. To Kuhnt, the naval officer corps consisted exclusively of murderers and criminals, Huns and Vandals. As he once declared in the Reichstag: "Wherever we go in Germany, and wherever we encounter a capital offence, we find naval officers."[189] It was his influence rather than that of the Communist Party which made the SPD such an implacable opponent of the Navy.

Whenever parliamentary debate centred on naval expenditure, the construction of new warships or matters affecting Navy personnel, the Social Democratic Party consistently voted nay.[190] Its spokesmen even withheld approval of expenditure on repairs to existing naval equipment and called for drastic cuts in the officer corps—true to the line laid down by Deputy Künstler, the SPD's naval expert: "The battle fleet is utterly superfluous. Germany can defend her shores without a navy."[191] The possibility of threats from France and Poland was flatly denied, just as misgivings about the Republic's external security were dismissed as the chimera of an incorrigible and warlike military caste.

Any policy as unconcerned with national interests stood in constant need of slogans and whipping boys designed to justify it in public. Lieutenant Commander Canaris's exploits and missions in the twilit obscurity of Reichswehr policy made him an ideal bogyman of the Left. His past career amid the shadows of revolution and counterrevolution perfectly fitted him for the role of a coup-hungry traitor to the Republic and hopeless reactionary. "Men like you," the *Weltbühne* declared accusingly, "have for twelve years had a finger in every deal that has harmed the Republic."[192]

The more left-wing polemicists hammered away at Canaris the edgier the Marineleitung's reactions became. Although colleagues may at first have admired his staunch defence of the Navy against Socialists and pacifists, their admiration soon yielded to displeasure. The Marineleitung could not remain indifferent to the fact that one of its officers was an object of ceaseless public invective and that his name had become a focus of anti-Navy sentiment. There was bitter irony in the situation that now arose: Canaris, the Navy's champion, was becoming the Navy's burden.

Then something happened which made his position quite untenable. On May 20, 1928, the SPD emerged victorious from the new Reichstag elections. The Marineleitung had to allow for the possibility that a Social Democrat would form the next government and that his party would bring pressure to bear on naval policy. SPD leader Hermann Müller did, in fact, assume the Chancellorship. It now became essential to take account of his party's attitude, the more so because Müller showed every intention of defying left-wing Socialist opposition and perpetuating the armed forces policy adopted by previous governments.[193] However, this necessitated the removal of all obstacles to agreement between the Navy and the new SPD Chancellor. In other words, Canaris had to quit Berlin.

On June 22, 1928, Zenker appointed him executive officer of the old battleship *Schlesien*, which was serving in the North Sea under the command of Captain Max Bastian. Canaris's transfer was a purely opportunist act of naval policy. "Consequent upon his performance of assignments of a discreet nature," Donner wrote in his personal file on

June 18, "frequent allusions to his name have lately appeared in pacifist newspapers, et cetera, usually in conjunction with wholly false conjectures. For this reason . . . it is necessary . . . to employ him solely in an active capacity."[194] A sop followed twelve months later in the shape of promotion to the rank of commander.[195]

Donner and his chief were reluctant to lose Canaris just when messages from friends in Spain suggested that his efforts in Madrid had been crowned with success. Echevarrieta was commissioned by the King and dictator to build a 750-ton German-designed submarine for the Spanish Navy, and other boats were to follow.[196] "Please give A.Z. [Admiral Zenker] the glad tidings," Canaris's friend Araoz wrote to Donner on May 13, 1928. "It is a great triumph to have succeeded in overcoming the opposition which has persisted throughout the twenty-five years I have been working here."[197]

Under the impact of such news, Zenker and Donner felt doubtful whether it would be right to dissociate Canaris from all special missions of a political nature. As soon as the Spaniards expressed a renewed desire to deal with their old favourite, they caved in. Zenker repeatedly allowed Canaris to visit Spain or negotiate with Spanish representatives on board the *Schlesien*.[198] This meant that Donner had, with some embarrassment, to solicit HQ Wilhelmshaven's approval of extramural activities by the *Schlesien*'s executive officer—as, for instance, in a letter dated August 27, 1928: "Although the Chief wishes to keep Canaris out of these transactions in principle, it matters so much to him in the present instance that he is sanctioning this exception."[199]

Suddenly, however, the Marineleitung imposed a ban on all further Spanish assignments for Canaris. Reliable reports had appeared on Zenker's desk which fanned the Navy chief's suspicions that, while in Spain, Canaris had fallen far short of the discretion which alone could preserve the Marineleitung from public annoyance. The master spy's prestige sank to an all-time low. His so-called secret activities had apparently become an everyday topic at social functions in Madrid.

Months before, on November 22, 1927, the *Weltbühne* had published an article whose anonymous author betrayed a disquieting familiarity with Canaris's exploits in Spain. Satirically camouflaged as a fairy tale, it told of a cunning and indefatigable warrior "who had powerful kinsmen in the lands of Spain and Greece and bore the name 'Nauarchos,' though the people called him simply 'the Canarian.'" Having brooded "day and night" on another war, he decided "first and foremost to procure himself some ships"—abroad. "So he embarked and headed for Spain with all sail set. There he had a friend whom the Spanish people called 'the Ash' [*Esche*] after the beautiful tree of that name. The Ash owned many slaves, mines and smelting ovens and built ships which could swim under water like fish." The Ash (an obvious al-

lusion to Echevarrieta) had undertaken to build some of these ships for
the Canarian too, "and the Canarian promised to send him a great deal
of money." So the Ash had busily constructed ships for the great war to
come. "At the request of this man he kept their building a secret and
hid the completed vessels from the gaze of other nations because he
was well aware that the Canarian had been compelled to swear the
other nations a sacred oath that he would do nothing of the kind."[200]

It dawned on the upper reaches of the Marineleitung that Canaris
was anything but the master of concealment he purported to be. This
suspicion was reinforced by Ministerialrat [Section Head] Frerich of
the Reichswehr Ministry, who had just returned from a *voyage d'études*
to Spain. Frerich reported on April 16, 1928, that numerous representatives of German industry in Madrid doubted whether Canaris was
working with the right Spanish partners. Echevarrieta "operates unscrupulously, using all available means" and was associated with many shipyards "under British management and British influence (Vickers)."[201]

The Frerich report, which was distributed to several departments in
the Marineleitung, read so ominously that Donner promptly recalled
every copy on the grounds that "in part, it contains data which, if they
fell into the wrong hands, might give rise to the gravest inferences regarding our foreign and economic policy."[202] But Donner could not
shake off his own misgivings about Canaris, and these received fresh
confirmation when a former Marineleitung agent set out to track down
the mysterious Señor Kika.

In spring 1928 Canaris's old desk (AIIm) and the Marineleitung's
naval intelligence desk (AIIk) had recruited the German-Spanish journalist Dr. Ritter von Goss as an "intelligence agent." Goss was to supply military information while the maintenance of secret contacts with
the Spanish Navy was reserved for Messerschmidt, Canaris's representative.[203] It was hardly surprising that the two agents clashed, especially as Goss was a fanatical Teutomaniac who could not abide Canaris and considered that his partnership with "Jewish profiteers"
rendered him a profoundly "un-German" figure.

"Here we are," Goss confided to his officer-controller in Berlin, "a
very small circle of people who have made it their deliberate aim to foster Germanism."[204] Within this circle of veteran agents and informants
from World War I, Canaris's name was not invariably uttered in a
"tone of commendation." Goss: "Herr Canaris maintains his informants
in quarters whose Germanism has not always stood the acid test . . .
That is to say, Herr Canaris is very close to the banking community of
Messrs. Ullmann and partners and derives his information from there.
These items of knowledge and information are, one and all, founded on
the said persons' endeavour to make money, nothing more."[205]

Goss itched to uncover Canaris's entire network in Spain but had to restrain himself while still employed by the Marineleitung. His chance came when German naval intelligence was merged with the Army's counterespionage service in April 1928. In June, by which time he was responsible to the Intelligence Section of the Reichswehr, he obtained his new superiors' permission to do some research on "Herr C." It took him only a few days to uncover the latter's Spanish espionage network.

While thus engaged, Goss stumbled on examples of such amateurism that his belief in the tale of Kika the master spy was banished for good. His inference: Canaris's operations in Spain were "a waste of time."[206] On September 27 he reported to Berlin: "If . . . I, a novice at this job, have managed to discover the broad framework of associated factors in four days, a trained man—and one who is not fully employed like myself—could unearth the whole edifice in twenty-four hours." Goss boldly concluded that Canaris was unfitted for secret missions, at least in Spain, "because the confidentiality essential to this work has in no way been preserved. Herr C. is an open book at sundry parties. He circulates with the soup like a mysterious figure to be winked at. 'Have you heard? Naval gentleman willing exchange contacts and information —person of importance."[207]

It may readily be imagined what effect these strictures had on admirers of Canaris. Lieutenant Commander Suadicani, his successor as adviser to the Marineleitung's Chief of Staff, put the following "observation" on record on October 21: "Our agent in Madrid is instructed to cease reporting on these naval matters."[208] Erich Raeder, the new Navy chief who had stepped into Zenker's shoes on October 2,[209] took a different view. He banned Canaris from further excursions into the political arena.

Raeder and Canaris had never got on. A petty and career-minded man whose foible was self-discipline, the admiral found Canaris too politically ambitious to be congenial and too many-faced to inspire trust. He had never forgotten Canaris's equivocal manoeuvrings prior to the Kapp Putsch or his own fierce arguments with Captain Loewenfeld of the *Berlin* and his executive officer—Canaris—in the days when he was inspector of naval training.[210] Furthermore, Raeder had a personal interest in keeping Canaris at arm's length. He himself had a rebel aura to dispel because he was reputed to have been the real brains behind the Navy's defection from the Republic during the Kapp adventure— reason enough to demonstrate his loyalty by steering clear of this pet target of the left-wing press.[211]

Reichswehr Minister Groener also discouraged any further political activity on Canaris's part. In company with Raeder, he turned down all requests to involve him in fresh negotiations with the Spanish Navy Ministry. In May 1929, when Echevarrieta asked the Marineleitung to send Canaris to Spain, Suadicani noted: "Dispatch of C. categorically rejected by the minister."[212] Canaris vainly rallied his friends in an attempt to lift the ban. Echevarrieta assured the Marineleitung that negotiations in Madrid would fail without Canaris and Messerschmidt darkly threatened that "the Spaniards who count" would be offended if "the person who has done all the spadework is now disowned." Even the German Embassy in Madrid intervened on Canaris's behalf, but Raeder and Groener remained adamant.[213]

Canaris reluctantly concentrated on his duties aboard the *Schlesien*, immersing himself in every detail of the work with almost frenzied single-mindedness. "Boundless devotion to duty" (to quote an entry in his confidential report) was Canaris's way of compensating for what Berlin had denied him.[214] He drove his officers and men unmercifully, insisted on the most sedulous performance of all duties and adopted a tough approach which made him feared despite his ability to show kindness.[215] As the *Schlesien*'s captain anxiously remarked, care would have to be taken to ensure that he did not "drive himself too hard." At the end of 1929 he went on vacation with his family and visited Corfu—a sad reflection on his state of mind, because he detested such joy rides and generally regarded spells of leave as an undesirable and thoroughly dispensable encroachment on his duties.[216]

Canaris displayed such drive aboard the *Schlesien* that his superiors were compelled to find something more substantial for his ambition to gnaw on. His new post was equally remote from the central offices of the Marineleitung. On September 29, 1930, Commander Canaris became Chief of Staff, North Sea Station,[217] but even this appointment fell short of his aspirations. He felt ill at ease with his colleagues and, in particular, with his Staff Officer, Grade 1, Commander Karl Dönitz. Hitler's last Navy chief recalls: "In those days we used to refer to him as the man with many souls in his breast. We did not get on with each other."[218]

Canaris still hoped against hope that he would be recalled to Berlin, where friends in the Marineleitung were trying to arrange a comeback. Then his name hit the headlines again and a public scandal blighted any prospect of a new career in Berlin.

Its author was Berthold Jacob of the *Weltbühne*, a journalist who had specialized in exposés of the armed forces and extreme right-wing organizations. In 1928 he was brought before the Reichsgericht [Supreme Court] on a charge of treason.[219] Counsel for the prosecution was Reichsanwalt [State Attorney] Jorns, the man who had prosecuted at the trial of Liebknecht's and Luxemburg's murderers in 1919. Recalling the lawyer's controversial role at that hearing, Jacob wrote an article in which he accused Jorns of aiding and abetting the assassins.[220] Canaris, who had been an associate judge, also came in for a squirt of poison. He had not, as Jacob put it, "hurt" the accused.[221]

Jacob's article had scarcely been published—anonymously—in the March 24, 1928, issue of *Das Tagebuch* when Reichsanwalt Jorns hit back. He brought charges of libel and defamation against the responsible *Tagebuch* editor, Josef Bornstein.[222] This was the moment which friends and admirers of the murdered Communist leaders had been awaiting for years. In April 1929 they submitted their evidence against the assassins and their accomplice, Jorns, to Central Berlin's Schöffengericht [Lay Assessors' Court]. The result: Bornstein was acquitted because the court considered it "proven" that the plaintiff's conduct in 1919 could have "redounded to the culprits' advantage."[223]

But the disappointed lawyer did not rest until he secured a new hearing from a criminal court under the auspices of Berlin's Landgericht III.[224] Jorns had better luck this time because the president of the court was in sympathy with him. Bornstein's counsel, Georg Löwenthal, spotted this at once and played his last card. On January 22, 1931, he called a former colleague into the witness box to confirm his allegation that Jorns had connived at the escape of Liebknecht's and Luxemburg's murderers. It was a man whom Canaris had every reason to avoid in public: ex-lawyer Bredereck of the National Association of German Officers, whose money had financed the murderers' escape.[225]

Bredereck presented a detailed account of how he had collected funds for the accused on behalf of the National Association, contacted the sister of the prisoners Horst and Heinz Pflugk-Hartung and finally handed the money to her and a male companion. Löwenthal seized on this.

"Who was this companion?"

Bredereck hesitated for a moment. Then he said, "Lieutenant Canaris."

Löwenthal: "Did Canaris know what purpose this money served?"

Bredereck: "He did."

The President intervened: "Was the money also intended for Vogel's escape?"

Bredereck: "I don't know if Vogel was still in prison at the time. The money was primarily intended for the officers detained in the Liebknecht case."

Löwenthal: "Was any reference made to whether Herr Jorns knew of this money?"

Bredereck: "No such reference was made. In fact I'm convinced that Herr Jorns knew nothing. The only people who did know were the contributors, Canaris and I—and, of course, the committees of the officers' organizations."[226]

Canaris's friends in the Marineleitung were dismayed to read reports of Bredereck's evidence in the morning papers on January 23.

Commander Flies, Lohmann's former aide, telephoned Canaris in Wilhelmshaven and asked for his comments. "He states," Flies noted in writing, "that he did not procure money for an escape by the Pflugk-Hartungs. Since their sister and parents were very badly off, C. urged the officers' organizations to obtain them some financial assistance. There had been absolutely no mention of an escape plan by the Pflugks at this stage."[227]

This did not, however, satisfy the heads of the Marineleitung, who asked Canaris for a written statement. On January 25 he submitted that Fräulein Pflugk had told him her family "was being subjected to constant threats from Communist sources." Canaris went on: "Under these circumstances, a sum of money was to be held in readiness so that, in the event of a Communist coup, the gentlemen [i.e. prisoners] and their endangered relatives would have a chance of eluding tyrants who had publicly adopted the most ruthless intimidation of all political opponents as an item on their agenda."[228]

It cannot have been lost on Canaris's readers at the Marineleitung that each of his statements told a different tale. According to one version, the fund-raising drive was intended to relieve the Pflugk-Hartung family of financial embarrassment; according to the other, its purpose was save the brothers and their relatives from political persecution. Neither story was accurate, because on January 30, 1931, the mother of the two men indignantly wrote to her lawyer instructing him to publish the following disclaimer in the press: "Neither they [the family] nor either one of the two accused and acquitted brothers V.P.H. has ever received or even asked for money in this connection. It is equally untrue that the family was persistently threatened by Communists and left Berlin on that account."[229] The lawyer had some difficulty in talking the Pflugk-Hartungs out of the idea of a press statement. It took them a while to realize "that we may possibly harm Canaris if we cause such a statement to be issued," as Ilse von Pflugk-Hartung put it.[230]

Pressure was likewise brought to bear on Bredereck—in fact the Marineleitung threatened to denounce him for perjury—but he refused to retract his story.[231] The Berlin district chairman of the National Association of German Officers was also approached by the Marineleitung but declined to be enlisted against Bredereck. A Marineleitung memo recorded that he "attached no importance to public controversy over this case."[232]

That left the Reichswehr Ministry with no choice but to issue an official statement incorporating the story about Communist intimidation. "Fräulein von Pflugk-Hartung addressed a request for assistance to Lieutenant Canaris, who was known to her, because she and her family were being persistently threatened by Communists . . . After the acquittal of the brothers Pflugk-Hartung . . . he [Canaris] learned that further funds from the National Association of German Officers were available for the Pflugk-Hartung family. He consequently decided . . . to arrange for the release of these funds to Fräulein von Pflugk-Hartung so that she and the members of her family could leave Berlin."[233]

Canaris's critics naturally remained unconvinced by this *démenti*. "Another Denial from the Reichswehr" and "Fresh Attempt to Bury the Truth" were only two of many headlines in the press.[234] "Such a statement," argued the Social Democratic *Volkswacht*, "does not in any case suffice to refute Bredereck's evidence under oath, especially as Reichswehr disclaimers are not to be trusted on principle because they have too often proved to be wholly false in the past."[235]

Worse still from Canaris's point of view was that the press embarked on a fresh investigation of every phase of his past career. "If Bredereck's evidence was true," wrote the *8-Uhr-Abendblatt*, "Captain Canaris committed a crime which is happily unprecedented in the history of German law, namely, that he did, as a judge, abet the escape of an accused person."[236] *Montag-Morgen* considered that the "exposure" of Captain Canaris had rendered him such a liability to the Reichswehr Ministry that it would necessarily be "compelled to intervene."[237]

The Marineleitung did just that: it barred Canaris's return to headquarters in Berlin. Raeder made sure that he did not leave his post at the North Sea Station under any circumstances. Canaris had come to a standstill at last, but his mercurial temperament rebelled against the torpid tranquillity of life on the staff. Not even his promotion to captain on October 1, 1931, could stifle the realization that he was approaching a terminal point in his career. He could foresee the inescapable road ahead. Having attained the rank of captain, he would end up in some naval backwater, a victim—as he saw it—of pacifist zealots and military careerists. The Republic had virtually no future to offer him.

But an alternative existed. It was taking shape in the streets of German towns and cities at that very moment—noisy, crude and violent but afire with faith in the future. Tramping through the streets and squares of Wilhelmshaven came the brown-uniformed contingents of National Socialism's private army, which followed a new Messiah: Adolf Hitler and his men were preparing to seize power.

Was this the long-awaited answer—the chance of escape from all the cares and concerns that weighed Canaris down? He didn't know, but he didn't want to let the opportunity slip. If this was the boat to the promised land, Wilhelm Canaris was determined not to miss it.

5

The Labyrinth

"He's coming!" The news spread like wildfire through the offices of HQ North Sea Station. Every interested party heard it and knew what it meant. The Chief of Staff, Wilhelm Canaris, heard it too. None of the naval officers stationed at Wilhelmshaven could resist its peculiar fascination. "He" was on his way.

He arrived on May 23, 1932, the most controversial party leader in Germany—the man who, at the head of a mass movement the like of which no German had ever seen before, was directing a venomous, spiteful and recriminatory campaign against the hard-pressed Republic yet was already regarded by millions of its citizens as their country's last hope. Adolf Hitler, leader of the National Socialist German Labour Party (NSDAP), was preparing to raise the banner of the Führer cult at Wilhelmshaven, a city steeped in naval tradition.

Even beside the route to Wilhelmshaven-Rüstringen, "people in every village awaited the Führer outside their cottages and trim little houses," as the *Völkischer Beobachter* reported in its own inimitably Byzantine style.[1] The closer he got to the meeting place where he was due to speak, the bigger the crowds that lined the streets. His car drew up outside the Schützenhof, a Rüstringen restaurant. "The large hall could accommodate only a fraction of those waiting outside. Thousands upon thousands stood in the open and listened to the Führer's speech relayed through loudspeakers."[2]

Many naval officers had donned civilian clothes in order to hear the party leader whose name had dominated political discussion in their messes for months past. They were rather disenchanted by the sight of the man with the dark forelock and the strange brown party uniform. Nothing in Hitler's appearance or demeanour gave a hint of the demagogue he was reputed to be. As soon as he mounted the speaker's rostrum and uttered his first few halting words, however, he became a man transformed. Every one of his staccato sentences disclosed that no one could give better expression to the malaises and anxiety neuroses of German society.

The time was ripe for such a man. Germany was in the throes of a seemingly hopeless political and social crisis and reeling under the impact of a worldwide economic recession. Germany's unemployed numbered 5.4 million, and the middle class, already impoverished by inflation, had seen the basis of its material existence melt away. Mass poverty was threatening to destroy such cohesion as the Republic had preserved in the face of every previous crisis.[3]

The Weimar Republic had never been popular. To the Socialist Left it remained "afflicted with the stigma of neglected socialization,"[4] whereas the bourgeoisie regarded their unfamiliar multiparty state as an anarchic jumble of sectional interests rather than an orderly political system. Nowhere could a majority be found to defend the Republic. Although it had been established in 1919 by a "Weimar coalition" made up of Social Democrats, Democrats and Centre Party members, its supporters had lost their parliamentary majority a year later. Since then the German democracy had subsisted "purely on the sufferance of its more moderate opponents."[5] The parties strove laboriously to form coalitions of which many embraced the most incompatible groups and few survived a twelvemonth.

One such coalition had been in power when Germany was hit by the great slump. Responsibility for surmounting this crisis devolved on a Social Democrat Chancellor, Hermann Müller, and a government drawn from the SPD, Centre Party and German People's Party, but these ill-matched partners failed to agree on a programme of reform. The government fell, but the Reichstag proved incapable of forming another because the strongest party—the SPD—was internally divided and refused to join a new coalition. This tempted the elderly President, Paul von Hindenburg, a lifelong devotee of monarchic and authoritarian rule, to govern without the parties and rely solely on the aid of his trusted associates.

But the presidentially appointed Chancellor, Heinrich Brüning, also failed to stem the tide. The last bastions of democracy were undermined by a mood of panic aggravated by unemployment and party-political strife. When Brüning finally called an election in September

1930, the hour of the National Socialist rabble-rousers struck. Hitler's
NSDAP became the second-strongest party in the Reichstag. The help-
lessness of those in power had provoked a trend towards disengagement, notably among the middle class, which robbed the Republic
of its sheet anchor. Fearful of social degradation and weary of the
placebos fed them by Republican politicians, members of the lower
middle class rallied in protest against the democratic multiparty state.
This occurred mainly in rural districts and the smaller towns, where
every shopkeeper's bankruptcy and every surrender of an independent
economic position was construed by eagle-eyed neighbours as a symptom of social decay.

The privations of the middle class and a section of the working class
triggered fears and desires which the purveyors of democratic enlightenment had long thought dead and buried. There were widespread calls
for a strong man, a redeemer whose coming seemed to have been
foreshadowed years earlier. Writing in 1922, the military historian Kurt
Hesse had enthused about the man eagerly awaited by "all of us . . .
who take Germany's tribulations so deeply to heart that he is pictured
by thousands upon hundreds of thousands of minds, invoked by millions of voices and sought by a single German soul."[6] The Germans
who identified Hitler with this Messiah steadily gained in number.
Within a few years, his party had absorbed over half the traditional
supporters of the middle-class parties of the Right and Centre. From
1930 onwards it broke up a succession of regional coalition governments, pledged to one idea and one objective alone: the seizure of
power at all costs.

Heard by ever-growing audiences up and down the country, Hitler
preached political upheaval and the transformation of the political and
social scene. Never had a tribune of the people more intuitively or
unerringly sensed a nation's hopes, resentments and dreams. Whether
solemnly intoning like a missionary or ranting like a demagogue,
Hitler struck a chord in his listeners and played on their credulity.

Wherever he spoke, he felt a communion with the masses who were
his medium, stimulus and object of aggression. He generally began his
speeches in a tentative manner, groping his way through the first few
noncommittal sentences, taking the pulse of his audience, sensing their
inclinations and aversions and swiftly attuning himself to their mood
until, with an ever faster, louder and more insistent flow of words, he
forged towards his climax. "The miracle of our age," he once declared,
"is that you should have found me—that you should have found me
among so many millions of people. And that I should have found you
—that is Germany's good fortune!"[7]

Even in the restrained North German atmosphere of the Schützenhof on the night of May 23, 1932, Hitler held his audience spellbound,

moved them to frenzied applause and drew enthusiastic cheers. "In their mind's eye," noted the correspondent of the *Völkischer Beobachter*, equally carried away, "there arose the future German National Socialist Reich of freedom, honour and social justice, as opposed to a system encumbered with the sins of fourteen long years."[8] When Hitler finally left the platform to an incessant barrage of acclamation, countless people crowded round him. His companions had difficulty in clearing a path to his car.

The naval officers among his audience dispersed in a thoughtful frame of mind. Their ears still rang with Hitler's words as they drove back to their quarters. Not only were they familiar with many of his theories; they themselves had entertained or voiced them in the past. One officer was particularly impressed by the Nazi leader's performance. Captain Schröder of the cruiser *Köln*, which was berthed at Wilhelmshaven, invited him to pay the ship a visit.[9]

On May 26 Hitler was welcomed aboard the *Köln* with full naval honours. Despite his private detestation of the sea, he surprised the ship's officers with his intimate knowledge of naval armaments. He was clearly versed in all the technical aspects of naval construction, little though he grasped the subtleties of strategic planning. Many of the *Köln*'s officers were delighted, and one of them made a note of Hitler's remarks: "1. I shall stamp out all treason. 2. I shall expand the Fleet within the framework of the Versailles Treaty. 3. If I say a ship is ten thousand tons it is ten thousand tons, no matter how big it really is."[10]

From then on, almost every officer in the *Köln* looked on the man who was piped back over the side as a confirmed friend and patron of the Reichsmarine. Before leaving, Hitler inscribed the cruiser's visitors' book as follows: "In the hope that I may play my part in reconstructing a navy worthy of the Reich. Adolf Hitler."[11] Reports that the Republic's fiercest opponent had been welcomed aboard a warship flying the Republic's colours spread like wildfire. Although many senior naval officers disapproved of Schröder's gesture, most of their juniors were in sympathy with the NSDAP. Naturally susceptible to authoritarian solutions by tradition and shipboard custom, and constantly threatened with professional extinction by the Republic's left-wing parties, many naval officers had already joined Hitler's ranks.

His fresh election victory in July 1932, which made the NSDAP the strongest and most influential party, assured him of wholehearted support from the bulk of the naval officer corps. By autumn, Chief of Staff Baltic Station was reporting to Admiral Raeder, head of the Marineleitung, that the overwhelming majority of his commanders doubted their units could be relied on in the event of a National Socialist coup.[12] Even Raeder himself, still an official advocate of unswerving loyalty to the Republic, was already putting out feelers in Hitler's direction and secretly pushing his own claims to the post of Reichswehr Minister in a cabinet with NSDAP participation.[13]

It was hardly surprising that Captain Wilhelm Canaris, Chief of Staff North Sea Station, should have seen just as little point in turning his back on the rising tide of National Socialism. His Republican links had dissolved and his loyalty to the Weimar democracy, never strong, had been undermined by banishment from Berlin and left-wing press campaigns. As one who had felt distrustful of public demonstrations and rallies of all kinds ever since the revolutionary days in Kiel, he regarded the mass cult of National Socialism with some misgiving. At the same time, he sensed that it possessed an elemental strength which could break down the barriers to a brighter future for the Navy and might release him, too, from the mental straitjacket he had worn since the collapse of 1918.

Canaris had never managed to overcome his attitude of cool detachment towards the Republic. He remained a monarchist whom the fall of the imperial regime had deprived of a political focus and plunged into spiritual exile—a condition which he painfully strove to offset with an abstract concept of service and duty. He later declared that the collapse of 1918 had "wrested the officer from a personal relationship to his supreme commander and placed him in an unrealistic, unsoldierly and abstract relationship to an equally unrealistic and unsoldierly 'constitution.'"[14] There was only one way out of this blind alley, and that was a concept of government and nationhood which branded the Weimar Republic as a temporary and transitional expedient.

Because Canaris never for a moment entertained the idea that the interests of the Navy and the nation might one day cease to coincide, he fashioned himself a dream image of "eternal Germany" which had nothing in common with the dismal postwar Republic and all its unsolved problems, political, economic and social. Having experienced the "concept" of Germany "in all its nobility and grandeur" during the war,[15] he could not come to terms with the depressing facts of everyday life, the more so because he had never ceased to believe that Germany was destined to attain world-power status by means of a super-fleet.

This made him receptive to the slogans of the National Socialist movement, which proposed to build just such a Germany and possessed the socially integrative aura which the Navy had lost during the war. It offered a prospect of fulfilling all that Canaris dreamed of: the establishment of an authoritarian state centred on a charismatic leader, relief from the constraints and inconveniences of modern democracy and removal of the limitations imposed on German military and foreign policy by the Versailles Treaty. Canaris deemed it a German officer's duty "to preserve the spiritual values of soldierliness . . . [until the advent of] an era in which the national community again became a community under arms."[16] Nobody subscribed more vigorously to this ideal than Hitler's party.

But there were other aspects of the Nazi programme which drew Canaris closer to the movement. Extreme anti-Communist slogans could not fail to appeal to an erstwhile Freikorps fighter who, even in 1931, still recalled the Red "tyrants who had publicly adopted the most ruthless intimidation of all political opponents as an item on their agenda."[17] Canaris shared the strange and almost panic fear of Communism which dominated wide sections of the German middle class, far out of proportion to the real dangers. He had belonged from the outset to that majority of naval officers who were alarmed by the German military authorities' flirtation with the Red Army and condemned all forms of co-operation with the Soviet Union.

Marineleitung policy had been governed by anti-Soviet ideas throughout Canaris's time in Berlin. The Marineleitung, which had long opposed visits by Soviet warships to German ports, only sanctioned one in 1929 provided there was no contact between Soviet ships' crews and home-grown Communists.[18] It even refused to approve the screening of Soviet naval films. In 1927, when *The Battleship Potemkin* was scheduled for presentation at a large Berlin cinema, it brought pressure to bear on the major film distributors and cinema chains until they undertook to show it at a small theatre only.[19]

Canaris and his then superior, Loewenfeld, did their utmost to ensure that the Navy forged no links with the East. In July 1926 Loewenfeld treated senior naval officers to a lecture entitled "Guiding Principles and Objectives of German Naval Policy." Its gist was that Bolshevism was "the greatest foe of Western civilization" and that Germany's natural allies were Fascist Italy and France. Loewenfeld even thought it possible that Poland would "for economic reasons" return the German territories annexed after 1918 and "heal itself at the expense of Russia, Lithuania, Courland, et cetera." However, Germany must "deliberately and discreetly" seek "a connection" with Britain because, "were Britain to disintegrate through Communism or . . . through the defection of her colonies, the threat of European Bolshevization would become direly imminent."[20]

It is quite obvious that Canaris's mentor was advancing propositions which Hitler had already incorporated in his *Mein Kampf* programme, and that no one who voiced them could steer clear of National Socialism for long. Many of Canaris's friends and comrades were already marching in the Brownshirt ranks. These included Friedrich Wilhelm Heinz, Hartmut Plaas and Manfred von Killinger. Even Ehrhardt, a long-time critic of Hitler, was toying with the idea of donning the uniform of an SS-Brigadeführer [major general].[21]

According to a brother officer, Conrad Patzig, it was not long before

Canaris likewise came to be regarded as an "enthusiastic National Socialist."[22] The next stage in his career brought him into even closer contact with the mood of the Navy and the country at large. On September 29, 1932, Canaris took command of the *Schlesien,* most of whose crew had written off the Republic long ago.[23] The battleship's frequent visits to ports on the North Sea and Baltic coasts were an insight into the climate of unrest prevailing in all sections of German society. It did not require clairvoyance to perceive that democracy's days were numbered.

Personal contact with leading National Socialists strengthened Canaris's belief that the impending "change-over," which was fatalistically awaited by friend and foe alike, would not degenerate into chaos and extremism. While visiting Hamburg he met the Nazi Gauleiter Karl Kaufmann, a founder member of the party who rated as one of the "reasonable" Nazis and was not an unqualified admirer of the Führer. Kaufmann's definition of the NSDAP programme appealed to Canaris, especially as he boasted one testimonial which never failed to impress: the Gauleiter was an ex-Freikorps man and had fought with the Ehrhardt Brigade.[24]

Thus, Canaris had long been acclimatized to the National Socialist era when January 30, 1933, "Assumption-of-Power Day," dawned over Germany. Although it found him at sea and preoccupied with naval routine (the *Schlesien* and another battleship, the *Hessen,* were carrying out torpedo and gunnery exercises in Kiel Bay), he too was fascinated by the mood of national reorientation.[25] Any misgivings he may still have had were swept away by the tide of enthusiasm which engulfed townsmen and countryfolk alike. On February 13, when he delivered the *Schlesien* to a Kiel dockyard for overhaul,[26] he saw a new Germany. Uniforms dominated the streets as they had in imperial days, nationalist slogans called for the salvation of the Fatherland, and the country seemed to be speaking with a single voice. Canaris was impressed by what he saw, like many—all too many—Germans of the time.

Not even the first signs of the Brownshirts' "co-ordinative" reign of terror could dissuade Canaris from giving the new regime a sympathetic welcome. He blithely dismissed occasional rumours of excesses on the part of Nazi overlords and their nationalist-conservative fellow travellers and trail blazers. Like millions of his compatriots, he cherished the hope that the new movement, however unbridled it might be, would liberate Germany from the sterile self-frustration of the democratic multiparty system and create a better form of government founded on authority and discipline. Even the coercion and intimidation practised by the "co-ordinators" seemed but a cleansing fire in which to consume the old and inadequate.

The apologists among Canaris's biographers have sought to purge their hero of political misjudgement by employing a variety of nebulous formulas to sidestep any admission that he was at this time a supporter of the Nazi regime. Abshagen claims that the regime's brutality and violence were "fundamentally distasteful" to him. "Canaris, of course, had no difficulty in seeing through the farce of the Reichstag fire. As things went on and on, and as no opposition—at least, no serious and effective opposition—made itself felt, he became more and more sceptical and more and more filled with misgiving."[27] Klaus Benzing likewise asserts that Canaris was "soon" filled with "a deep aversion to the Nazis' reign of terror" and that by the time of the Röhm affair in June 1934, at the latest, he had "finally [become] an opponent of Hitler and the National Socialist regime."[28]

So far from having seen through the Nazis' machinations at this stage, Canaris found it quite natural to co-operate wholeheartedly with the new regime. "Being a patriot in the best sense of the word, which he was," recalls his friend Otto Wagner, "all he felt at first, like most Germans, was the dynamic vitality which the NS movement transmitted to the nation as a whole, the better to extricate it from the internal and external entanglements of national existence. We nearly all followed suit at first."[29] This is confirmed by another witness, the former SS general Werner Best: "As an inveterate nationalist, he then believed that the new regime was infinitely better than anything that had gone before, and that, for the time being, there was absolutely no alternative."[30] Further evidence to the same effect stems from one of Canaris's less emotionally involved associates, ex-Lieutenant Colonel Erich Pruck, who headed a group in the Abwehr: "[His] development from a submissive servant of the state into a supporter of the opposition was only gradual."[31]

During the early years of the Hitler era, at any rate, criticism of the regime was alien to him. Canaris would firmly have rejected any opposition to the government and party. Even after the St. Bartholomew's Massacre of the so-called Röhm Putsch, the Third Reich's first essay in organized murder, Canaris preached wholehearted co-operation with the new regime. On November 1, 1934, the following addition to Canaris's personal file was made by his superior officer, Rear Admiral Bastian: "I must stress that, for the second year running, Captain Canaris has been tireless in his efforts to acquaint his crew, through the medium of personal lectures, with the ideas of the national movement and the principles underlying the development of the new Reich." Bastian's admiring summary: "Has performed exemplary work in this field."[32]

Although the text of these lectures has not survived, their drift may readily be inferred from the theories he advanced a few years later. Canaris: "Just as any officer was a natural monarchist before the World

War, and just as he naturally strove to preserve the legacy of combat experience thereafter, so it is quite as axiomatic today, when all our combat experience has found fulfilment in the National Socialist state, for him to be a National Socialist. And we, as servicemen, are fortunate in being able to profess its political ideology, which is soldierly in the extreme."[33]

But what, he asked, *was* National Socialism? "It is nothing more nor less than what the combat soldier experienced and endured in those days: performance of duty, obedience, comradeship and acceptance of one's obligation to the national community. Side by side with the subsequent political harbinger and shaper of this idea, Adolf Hitler, the German officer and ranker laid the foundation stone of a new Germany . . . Thus the combat soldiers of the World War were the first effective National Socialists."[34] Canaris also considered it proper that "we officers, in particular, should always recognize that without the Führer and his NSDAP the restoration of German military greatness and military strength would never have been possible. The Reichswehr could never have become a national army of itself."[35]

From this there emerged a "personal inference which every officer . . . must draw": "Although an unpolitical attitude was not pernicious or harmful in imperial times and during the early part of the war, and was positively beneficial in the Reichswehr of the Weimar state, it would, in the National Socialist state, be an act of sabotage and a crime . . . The officer's duty is to be a living example of National Socialism and make the German Wehrmacht reflect the fulfilment of National Socialist ideology. That must be our grand design."[36]

Any officer holding such sternly conformist Nazi views was bound to attract the attention of Germany's new masters sooner or later, but Canaris's relations with the leaders of the regime got off to an inauspicious start. He caught his first glimpse of them on May 23, 1933, when Hitler, Reichswehr Minister General Werner von Blomberg and Hermann Göring, Minister-President of Prussia, visited the assembled fleet at Kiel to watch some tactical exercises at sea. Göring was accommodated in the *Schlesien,* which had since January been the flagship of Commander in Chief Ships of the Line [an obsolete classification applied to old battleships customarily used for training purposes].[37]

Göring's visit ended on a sour note. The exercises took place in such stormy weather that Hitler's vain and ambitious henchman was sick (or "sacrificed to Neptune," as German sailors call it). Promptly, a couple of fun-loving lieutenants cracked a joke at their exalted guest's expense. When Göring ventured into the wardroom looking pale and queasy, one of them accosted him with a dead straight face: "Excuse me, Minister-President, but the following signal has just been received: 'Neptune to Minister-President Hermann Göring. With effect from today, you are appointed Reich Fish-Feeder in Chief and entitled to wear a string vest.' "38

Göring flounced out of the wardroom in a rage, whereupon Canaris sent for the humorist and reprimanded him. However, Göring addressed a complaint to the Marineleitung in Berlin alleging unseemly conduct and demanded that the lieutenant should be punished. This Canaris rejected because he had already dealt with the culprit and considered that Göring was trespassing on his official preserves.39

Trivial though this minor incident was, Canaris failed to secure the closer contact with government leaders for which he doubtless hoped. Not even the National Socialists' assumption of power retrieved his career from the backwater where it had been rusting since the Lohmann affair. His disappointment vented itself in crabbed and moody behaviour which vitiated his relations with Bastian. The bluff, conventional admiral and his sensitive subordinate got on so badly that they avoided one another whenever possible.

Bastian complained in writing of the absence of any "close personal ties between commander in chief and flagship commander." Canaris should urgently endeavour "to attune himself better to my personality and do justice to my views and opinions, and, in particular, curb his touchiness, which undoubtedly goes hand in hand with a somewhat excessive sensitivity."40 Canaris did his best to satisfy the commander in chief but Bastian came increasingly to realize that his quirks and frequent fluctuations of mood made him a far from ideal commanding officer.

"It will be advisable," Bastian wrote on September 19, 1933, "to employ him in spheres of command where keen observation and diplomatic skill are required, but also in posts which exploit his great intellectual abilities while preventing his bouts of scepticism, which do not arise from everyday experience, from communicating themselves to an unduly wide circle."41 A year later Bastian knew what post Canaris was specially fitted for. In a personal assessment, he noted: "Reichswehr Minister (initially as head of section—Abwehr Section)."42

The Fleet commander, Vice-Admiral Foerster, also confirmed that Canaris was "better suited by bent and disposition to politico-military rather than military employment,"43 but the Marineleitung wanted nothing more to do with Canaris the political officer. It finally shunted him into a siding—a dead-end job. On September 29, 1934, he was obliged to take up his duties as officer commanding Fort Swinemünde.44

Canaris had virtually reached the end of his tether because, to a volatile spirit like his, the fortress resembled a prison. Although the officer commanding Swinemünde came directly under Baltic Station HQ and rated as the coastal defence chief of his area, his authority and powers of inspection vis-à-vis the coastal artillery detachments were defined with extreme imprecision.[45] Resignedly, Canaris bowed to the inevitable. Early in October, he and his family went into provincial exile.

But he had barely settled into his new job when news broke which made him prick up his ears. As rumour yielded to certainty, it became clear that a dispute had arisen in the Reichswehr Ministry over who was to head the Abwehr, or military intelligence service, and that no one could resolve it but Canaris. The controversial head of the Abwehr, Captain Conrad Patzig, had been forced to resign. As Patzig himself recalled: "I nominated Canaris because I knew of no one in the Navy who would have been better suited without a long running-in period."[46] Bastian's recommendation had paid off after all.

Intelligence, espionage, counterespionage—Canaris, who had always been enthralled by the subject, hurriedly seized the chance of a lifetime. By October 15 he was standing in Patzig's Berlin office, being briefed on the Abwehr's uneasy position in the no man's land between the armed forces and the Gestapo.[47] But Canaris paid little heed to his predecessor's cautionary references to the fiendish machinations of the party and police. All he saw was what fate had put his way: he, Wilhelm Franz Canaris, was to take over one of the new regime's most potent and influential machines and follow in the footsteps of Goltz, Gruner, Stieber, Nicolai and all the other luminaries of German espionage.

With a light heart, Canaris abandoned an unpromising naval career in favour of this unique opportunity. He was familiar enough with the nature and history of the German secret service to know that, from now on, he would be one of the handful of initiates who helped to steer the ship of state. The secret service had always been an important trail blazer and travelling companion of Germany's authoritarian governments, just as those who headed it had always belonged to the ruling political and military caste. Discounting the Ludendorff-Hindenburg military double act, no German had wielded more influence during World War I than Lieutenant Colonel Nicolai, the unobtrusive spymaster who had directed Germany's espionage, military intelligence and propaganda operations.

The German secret service was as old as the expansionism of Prussia, whose most celebrated monarch had also, and not by accident, been its founder. Frederick the Great, often referred to by historians as the father of espionage,[48] found an ideal spy-master in Bernhard Wilhelm Baron von der Goltz, an agent, diplomat and soldier who established the first systematic intelligence service in German history at Frederick's behest.[49] His agents infiltrated foreign embassies in Berlin, assessed the preparedness of foreign armies, broke the seals on diplomatic dispatches and conspired in the antechambers of foreign chancelleries.

Frederick's intelligence service became one of his most dreaded and effective secret weapons. It brought him much information and many spectacular successes. In 1741 a female spy posing as a Catholic nun infiltrated a circle of Breslau ladies and foiled their secret plan to turn the city over to the Austrians.[50] In 1755 a Saxon government clerk was bribed to furnish the King with copies of secret correspondence between the governments of Russia, Austria and Saxony, which were forming an alliance against him.[51] At the end of 1745 Prussian spies warned of an impending Austro-Saxon invasion of Brandenburg, and Frederick forestalled it.[52]

Whenever Frederick's armies took the field and wherever he was planning a diplomatic coup, Prussian spies were in evidence. "Marshal Soubise," he once sarcastically remarked of an enemy general, "is always followed by a hundred cooks. I am always preceded by a hundred spies."[53] Although he declared that spies were people whom "one uses but does not esteem," he took an interest in every aspect of secret service operations.[54] The intelligence service was responsible to him personally, and Goltz received his orders from the King direct. They were usually couched in urgent and peremptory language. "Off you go! Here is a chance to prove yourself . . . [I] shall perceive from the success of your endeavours if you have wit enough to satisfy me regarding all the matters I wish to know."[55]

Under Frederick's unimaginative successors, however, "wit" was no longer expected of Prussian spy-masters. The politico-military intelligence service disintegrated and its components fell into the hands of that classic instrument of power in the age of absolutism, the political police. The secret service split into two parts, political and military, engendering the welter of intrigue and strife that has afflicted the history of German espionage for two whole centuries.

The Allgemeines Kriegsdepartement [General War Department] established a Geheime Policey [Secret Police] which gathered military intelligence about the enemy and recruited its personnel from the Army, whereas the Höhere Policey [Higher Police] was directed by an official responsible to the Prussian Minister of State [Premier].[56] Modelled on the *haute police* of Louis XIV, who had founded the first political police apparat of modern times, this organization was charged with neutralizing all threats to the monarchic regime.[57]

However, this royal network of police informers quickly became the mainstay of the Prussian espionage and counterespionage service when liberal reformers began to gird Prussia for the final struggle against Napoleon after the twin defeats of Jena and Auerstädt. In March 1809 the Westphalian administrative reformer Justus Gruner was appointed police commissioner of Berlin and given charge of the Höhere Polizei as well.[58] Gruner made it his first task to improve the latter's efficiency. He established a close-knit and nationwide intelligence network whose

GENEALOGY OF THE GERMAN SECRET SERVICE

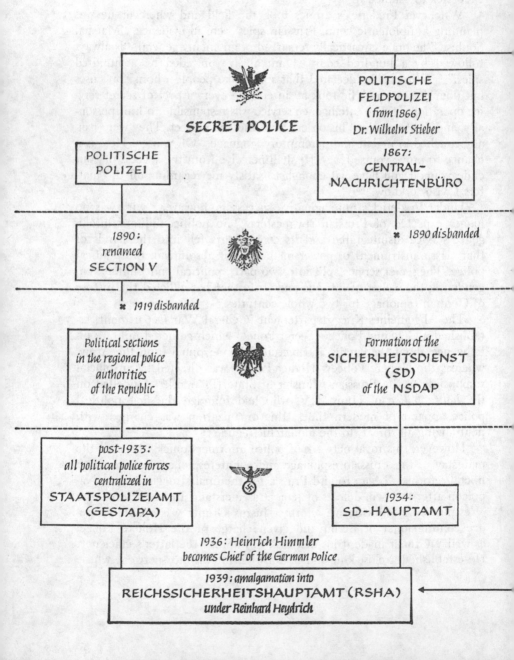

SECRET POLICE

POLITISCHE
FELDPOLIZEI
(from 1866)
Dr. Wilhelm Stieber

1867:
CENTRAL-
NACHRICHTENBÜRO

POLITISCHE
POLIZEI

1890:
renamed
SECTION V

✳ 1890 disbanded

✳ 1919 disbanded

Political sections
in the regional police
authorities
of the Republic

Formation of the
SICHERHEITSDIENST
(SD)
of the NSDAP

post-1933:
all political police forces
centralized in
STAATSPOLIZEIAMT
(GESTAPA)

1934:
SD-HAUPTAMT

1936: Heinrich Himmler
becomes Chief of the German Police

1939: amalgamation into
REICHSSICHERHEITSHAUPTAMT (RSHA)
under Reinhard Heydrich ◄

```
┌─────────────────────────────────────────────────────┐
│ post-1740: Frederick the Great founds the first      │
│ organized espionage service under Bernhard Wilhelm   │
│ von der Goltz                                         │
└─────────────────────────────────────────────────────┘
```

SECRET POLICE   **MILITARY INTELLIGENCE**

```
┌──────────────────┐    C.1800       ┌──────────────────┐
│ HÖHERE POLICEY   │    split into   │ GEHEIME POLICEY  │
└──────────────────┘                 └──────────────────┘
```

C.1810

```
┌─────────────────────────────────────────────┐
│ The HÖHERE POLICEY applies itself to military │
│ intelligence under Justus Gruner (from 1809); │
│ the Geheime Policey ceases to function.       │
└─────────────────────────────────────────────┘
```

The following established in the Allgemeines Kriegsdepartement (Prussian War Ministry):

MILITARY INTELLIGENCE   **MILITARY EVALUATION**

```
┌──────────────────────────┐    ┌──────────────────────────┐
│ NACHRICHTENBÜRO          │    │ SECTION 1 (RUSSIAN)       │
│ of the Grand General Staff│    │ SECTION 2 (FRENCH)        │
│ (from 1867)              │    │ of the Grand General Staff│
└──────────────────────────┘    └──────────────────────────┘
```

```
┌──────────────────┐  ┌──────────────────┐  ┌──────────────────────────┐
│ 1899: renamed    │  │ New agency:      │  │ 1914: renamed INTELLIGENCE│
│ III B (headed by │  │ SECRET INTELLIGENCE│ │ SECTION   1917:          │
│ Walter Nicolai   │  │ SERVICE of the   │  │ renamed FOREIGN ARMIES   │
│ 1913-19)         │  │ Imperial Navy    │  │                          │
└──────────────────┘  └──────────────────┘  └──────────────────────────┘
```

✱ 1919 disbanded   ✱ 1919 disbanded   ✱ 1919 disbanded

Establishments in the REICHSWEHR MINISTRY:

```
┌──────────────────────┐  ┌──────────────┐  ┌──────────────────────┐
│ INTELLIGENCE AND     │  │ NAVAL        │  │ ARMY STATISTICAL     │
│ RECONNAISSANCE       │  │ INTELLIGENCE │  │ SECTION (T3)         │
│ SERVICE,             │  │ SERVICE      │  │ 1931: renamed        │
│ later ABWEHR, headed │  │              │  │ FOREIGN ARMIES       │
│ in 1932 by Conrad    │  │ 1928: to     │  │                      │
│ Patzig               │◄─│ ABWEHR       │  │                      │
└──────────────────────┘  └──────────────┘  └──────────────────────┘
```

1935: REICHSWEHR MINISTRY becomes REICH WAR MINISTRY

1938: HIGH COMMAND OF THE ARMED FORCES (OKW)

1935 under Wilhelm Canaris

1939: AMT AUSLAND/ABWEHR

1944: ABWEHR absorbed by RSHA as AMT MIL

```
┌──────────────────┐  ┌──────────────────┐  ┌──────────┐
│ INTELLIGENCE     │  │ FOREIGN ARMIES   │  │ FOREIGN  │
│ EVALUATION       │  │ WEST             │  │ AIR      │
│ (3/SKl)          │  │ and              │  │ FORCES   │
│                  │  │ FOREIGN ARMIES   │  │          │
│                  │  │ EAST             │  │          │
└──────────────────┘  └──────────────────┘  └──────────┘
```

agents and informants were to paralyse French espionage and begin active reconnaissance of enemy dispositions. Gruner's spies gained such swift successes that the Allgemeines Kriegsdepartement's Geheime Polizei wound up its operations.[59] The police had spawned a secret service.

By censoring the mails, Gruner's secret police managed to unmask one French spy after another. There was hardly a janitor or secretary employed by the foreign embassies in Berlin who was not furnishing the head of the Prussian secret service with confidential information. Dispatches to the French Embassy were intercepted and read, French spies in the postal bureaux of Prussia and other German states "turned" and invisible hosts of informants unleashed on the territories controlled by the French Army. Political surveillance of Prussian citizens was not, of course, neglected either. As Gruner was pleased to note: "No merchant receives letters without having to show them to me, and I vigorously squelch every rumour at once."[60]

Although Gruner's twinges of liberalism sometimes caused him to utter self-pitying complaints about "the most depressing, loathsome and melancholy business which the world can lay on mortal shoulders," he was always devising new ways of improving the work and organization of his secret police still further.[61] In October 1810 he addressed a report to Chancellor Hardenberg proposing that the powers of the secret police should be extended.[62] Gruner's "Fundamental Remarks on the Administration of the Higher Police" provided for the development of a super-police beside which even Heinrich Himmler's Gestapo pales into insignificance.

Gruner demanded that the Höhere Polizei be granted sole jurisdiction over all aspects of national security, external and domestic. This covered surveillance of relations between foreign powers and private individuals, control over Prussia's own citizens and government departments and the initiation of precautionary measures against potential trouble makers. But these tasks could not be accomplished unless the secret police possessed adequate machinery. It therefore required "informants at foreign courts, access to all incoming diplomatic notes and public information on policy, the surveillance of all private and literary correspondence and of all foreigners inside the country, the discovery and recruitment of spies, the gathering of information from foreign newspapers, the dissemination of news beneficial to the state and the censorship and direction of domestic newspapers."[63]

This secret police force, Gruner went on, should be responsible to the Chancellor himself, on whose behalf it would be controlled and directed by a Staatsrat [councillor of state] acting as head of the Geheimes Polizeibüro [Secret Police Bureau]. The Bureau should be empowered to request reports from all agents and embassies, remunerate informants, maintain mail censorship offices in Berlin and all the larger towns in Prussia and request regular reports from the provincial police authorities.[64] The work of the secret police should be unhampered by any court or form of civil protection under the law. As Gruner had written previously: "If the police force observes legal formalities it forfeits its peculiar character and purpose. Its most sacred object is the state, not the individual. Should this not be so—should the well-being of the individual remain permanently inviolable and the welfare of all be founded thereon—no police force would be necessary, or not, at least, a secret one."[65]

Hardenberg approved this scheme, and in February 1811 the King appointed its author a Staatsrat and head of the Geheimes Polizeibüro. The new organization was detached from the regular police authority and housed at No. 13 Kronenstrasse, Berlin.[66] From now on, the Geheime Polizei was an unassailable power in the land. It could stop and detain any Prussian citizen and request information from any government authority. The cases it handled were not brought before normal courts but heard by commissioners specially sworn to secrecy. On the other hand, no government department in Prussia was permitted to meddle in the affairs of the Geheime Polizei. It was hardly surprising that Gruner's apparat became the secret ideal of every future German police chief.

The Geheime Polizei's omnipotent status proved an aid to espionage and the gathering of information about foreign powers, but only briefly. It lost interest in foreign intelligence soon after the wars of liberation and turned more and more completely into an instrument of oppression wielded by the royalist regime. It had long outlived its moderate liberal creator and theoretician. Suspected of reactionary leanings, Gruner had been banished to an ambassadorial post and died in 1820.[67] He did not live to see the inordinate expansion of Prussian police powers. Although it was abolished within a few years, the establishment of a Police Ministry helped to perfect a network of political informers which extended to the farthest corners of the Kingdom of Prussia.[68] The powers of the secret police remained uncurbed until after the abortive revolution of 1848.

But organized espionage had ceased to exist. This sorely tried the Prussian General Staff, which had not maintained an intelligence service of its own since 1810 and could see no prospect of obtaining information about potential enemies. There was an urgent need for just such information, for gone were the days when it sufficed a general to ascertain the enemy's order of battle from a windmill or manor house roof and send mounted scouts to explore his intentions. The technicization of warfare had made reconnaissance more complicated. To assess an enemy one needed accurate information in advance—information about arms and equipment, operational objectives, the state of fortifications, roads and terrain.

The procurement of this largely secret information would have devolved on an espionage service. In default of this, the General Staff's experts had to obtain it by other means. They initially confined themselves to reading the military publications of the country in question, perusing diplomatic reports and sending staff officers on *voyages d'études*. Not content with this, they then revived a plan originally conceived by Colonel von Massenbach of Prussia in 1795: "Let there be assigned to every embassy an officer of the General Staff who has served several years in that corps; let military-cum-diplomatic envoys be trained."[69] A new form of quasi-legal spy—the military attaché—came into being.

The Prussian General Staff appointed its first military attaché to Paris in 1830, and others followed in the middle of the century.[70] But not even military attachés could quench the General Staff's thirst for information. They were not officially authorized to engage in espionage, and the non-secret material they culled from books and newspapers was insufficient to reveal the strengths and weaknesses of an army. Despite orders to the contrary, the military attachés took to employing spies of their own. Early in the 1860s, Paris, Turin, Vienna, Pest and Linz all saw the appearance of secret agents whom Prussia's military attachés employed to cultivate contacts in war ministries, barrack rooms and military units.[71]

Nevertheless, the General Staff proved lamentably ill-informed about Prussia's opponents in the crucial year 1866. Its foreign experts were supplied with "almost wholly unreliable and low-grade material."[72] The General Staff had no idea of the extent of Austria's military preparedness and was ignorant of her Army's deployment against Prussia.[73]

At this point, another policeman showed the military how intelligence work should be performed. Polizeirat [roughly, Chief Superintendent] Dr. Wilhelm Stieber, an ex-lawyer and pioneer of democratic rights, had headed Berlin's Kriminalpolizei for ten years until prematurely retired on account of his harsh interrogation methods. He then became head of a private detective agency and was often consulted by men in high places because of his far-flung international connections. Stieber's introduction to espionage was a matter of chance.[74]

Thanks to an unsuccessful attempt on the life of the Prussian Minister-President, Otto von Bismarck, in May 1866, this German Sherlock Holmes was appointed to recruit a secret police force for the protection of the monarch and the head of government. His agency was to be entirely separate from the political police.[75] Stieber resurrected Gruner's scheme. He had visions of developing a powerful secret police apparatus controlled by the Minister-President, responsible for the internal and external security of the state, and combining politico-military intelligence work abroad with the protection of the monarchic system at home. His first and limited task was to form a sort of secret service bodyguard for the King during the war against Austria. A royal decree dated June 23, 1866, appointed him to command a Politische Feldpolizei [Political Field Police, later renamed "Geheime Feldpolizei" or Secret Field Police] "for the performance of higher police functions in and around the King's headquarters."[76]

This took Stieber to the heart of the military intelligence system, because Article 5 of his commission read: "To support the military authorities by procuring intelligence about the enemy Army."[77] Stieber mobilized several informants known to him abroad, and the General Staff began to receive its first information about the Austrian Army's deployment. His secret serviceman's prestige was much enhanced by a renegade Hungarian officer, ex-Lieutenant Baron August von Schluga. "Agent No. 17," as Schluga was henceforth known, supplied Stieber with character sketches of every senior officer in the Austrian Army and news of enemy troop movements—preliminary contributions from a master spy who was often to surprise his employers in years to come.[78]

Stieber expanded his secret service when the war ended. He took over a few rooms in the Foreign Office and his organization was renamed the Central-Nachrichtenbüro [Central Intelligence Bureau]. Stieber's agents hounded Bismarck's opponents among the pro-Guelph Hanoverians and spied on the authors of anti-Prussian newspaper articles at home and abroad, but they also gathered military and political intelligence. The Central-Nachrichtenbüro maintained agents in Paris, London and Vienna who garnered such items of information as Stieber deemed valuable.[79]

But the chief of the Prussian General Staff, Helmuth von Moltke, considered Stieber's successes and the failure of military intelligence to be an unworthy reflection on the Army. He duly set up a secret service of his own. February 11, 1867, witnessed the birth of the Prussian General Staff's Nachrichtenbüro [Intelligence Bureau], the germ cell of the Abwehr-to-be.[80] Provided with an annual budget of two thousand thalers, two full-time agents and a director "devoid of thorough military knowledge," it began to gather military intelligence about the potential foe.[81]

Major von Brandt's Nachrichtenbüro could not, however, compete with Polizeirat Stieber's army of agents. During the Franco-Prussian War of 1870–71 Stieber expanded his secret service still further. He now maintained a staff of 182 assistants to keep in touch with the numerous intelligence networks he had established throughout France and Switzerland.[82] Although he was still far from employing the 36,000 spies which legend ascribes to him, he did have agents and informants in every major French city—another respect in which he took his cue from Gruner, who in 1815 had set up a secret police organization in occupied France on behalf of the anti-Napoleonic alliance.[83]

Continued failure on the part of the military intelligence bureau made Moltke's foreign experts more and more dependent on Stieber and his apparatus. Whenever the General Staff wanted situation reports on the enemy, it was forced to consult Stieber's Geheime Feldpolizei, but the military became increasingly averse to doing so because Stieber's agents did not confine their attentions to the enemy; they also spied on Prussian generals for Bismarck's benefit. And here, for the first time, we see the rudiments of a conflict that was to assume lethal proportions during the Hitler era: the clash between an esoteric military caste of purely professional character and secret police sleuths employed by a charismatic leader. Although the Geheime Feldpolizei was technically subordinate to the General Staff, Stieber regarded Chancellor Bismarck as his sole legitimate employer. If Bismarck had political reasons for mistrusting the extramural activities of his generals, whose overforceful operations had disrupted his first tentative approaches to the defeated French, Stieber, the revolutionary-turned-conservative, experienced a revival of his old liberal antipathy towards the "arrogance and insensitivity" of the military demigods.[84] Bismarck and Stieber both agreed that the military needed putting in their place.

For their part, the military scented that Stieber was a telltale who kept Bismarck apprised of what went on inside the General Staff. Eagerly, they awaited an opportunity to cut the policeman down to size. Their chance came in September 1870, when Bismarck appointed Stieber police prefect of Rheims. The Chancellor's man governed the city without regard for General Staff directives. When he put up posters calling on the French inhabitants to surrender all their arms, Chief of the General Staff Podbielski reprimanded him on the grounds that such matters were the prerogative of the military authorities. Stieber complained to Bismarck, who backed him up. The General Staff angrily retorted that Stieber was under direct military command. Bismarck disputed this but gave in when confronted with documents to that effect.[85]

The generals had learnt their lesson. Never again must a Chancellor's police spy be permitted to invade the sacred domain of the General Staff. Furthermore, the secret service must become an exclusive preserve of the military. In practical terms, this entailed the systematic expansion of the Nachrichtenbüro. Being unqualified to build up an efficient military intelligence service, Brandt was replaced in 1872. Although a more dynamic type, his successor soon discovered that the Büro possessed not a single competent agent apart from Schluga, who had meanwhile transferred his allegiance to the Army.[86] Funds were short and no proper organization existed.

But Brandt's replacement wrought a gradual change. By the late 1880s the new head of the Nachrichtenbüro, Major von Lettow-Vorbeck, possessed a small but solid network of agents. In 1889 the indefatigable "No. 17" kept watch on the French Army's grand manoeuvres and sketched the disposition of its various corps, as he did every year, but the Büro also maintained agents in Brussels, Luxemburg, Belfort and Nancy and contacts in other French cities.[87] Successful work was also performed by its seventy-five agents and informants in Russia. From 1889 onwards they furnished details of the mobilization plans and deployment of the Tsar's armies "by the crate."[88]

But the expansion of the military intelligence service encountered growing resistance from the Foreign Office, which viewed the Army's ambitions with disfavour. Diplomatic circles were particularly resentful of the military attachés and their secret informants, especially as the Foreign Office pursued intelligence objectives of its own. It had long maintained clandestine contacts with voluntary informants who kept the Wilhelmstrasse apprised of interesting developments abroad. The diplomatic representatives of Prussia-Germany also employed the services of local agents, while Bismarck generally relied on personal envoys whom he entrusted with secret missions.

Foreign Office hostility was not based on any political considerations and merely concealed the departmentalism of a diplomatic caste intent on defending its interests against a rival. Stieber, on the other hand, did have a long-term plan. He wanted to use his Central-Nachrichtenbüro to make the Foreign Office the mainstay of a foreign intelligence service run on political-police lines, thus regaining for it the central role in Prussian espionage which it had briefly (1808–11) played under Staatsrat Nageler, head of Secton 2 of the Foreign Office.[89] However, Stieber never really sold this idea to Bismarck. Badly stricken with gout in the mid-1870s, he was compelled to leave the Foreign Office and died in 1882.[90]

Stieber's departure made it easier for the Grand General Staff to fulfil its intelligence service plans. It is not only ensured that the Nachrichtenbüro was increasingly financed out of secret Foreign Office funds but eventually prevailed on the Foreign Office to furnish it with military information from countries where it maintained no agents of its own.[91] This inspired Count von Waldersee, the new Chief of the General Staff, to ordain a further expansion of the Nachrichtenbüro. The secret service was also renamed IIIB because, as an independent subsection, it came directly under Oberquartiermeister [Chief of Staff] III.[92]

From now on, nothing could shake the Army's grip on the secret intelligence system. The clandestine gathering of information about foreign countries became a General Staff domain and the mentality of German secret servicemen was governed by military considerations alone. Founded on the eve of a new era of arms races and global wars, IIIB was ignorant of any world but that of politico-military power and rivalry measurable in divisions, deployment plans and recruitment potential. The growth of military strength was all that counted. Officers of IIIB had no eye for political imponderables or economic pressures, nor did the psychology of other nations and foreign governments figure in the ABC of German military intelligence. Every attempt at political reconnaissance proved abortive.

The Prussian War Ministry never tired of stressing IIIB's sole competence in the field of espionage. "Only a military institution will be dependable and efficient," the Prussian War Minister wrote to the Chancellor in 1891.[93] Members of IIIB showed due vigour in blocking the emergence of new espionage agencies. When the Imperial Navy set up its own secret intelligence service and disputed the Army's monopoly, the War Ministry neutralized this challenge by extracting a provisional undertaking that the naval intelligence service would confine its operations to Britain.[94]

However, intensified activity on the part of foreign agents in Germany soon showed the military that there was a yawning gap in their intelligence set-up: Germany had not possessed a counterespionage system since Gruner's day. Working conditions in the country were almost ideal for foreign spies, who operated without hindrance from any police or supervisory authority. If a local policeman did venture to shadow foreign agents, they quite often complained to police headquarters alleging harassment by junior officials.[95]

German counterespionage was then, at most, a hobby pursued by one or two policemen who watched foreign agents on their own initiative. When French espionage threatened to run riot in Alsace during 1887, a police superintendent named Zahn established a counterespionage agency at police headquarters in Strasbourg and christened it the Central-Polizeistelle [Central Police Department].[96] His experiment was not immediately copied. Police chiefs and their superiors in the Interior Ministries of the various German states were too jealous of their departmental prerogatives to favour co-operation with the military. They required much coaxing from IIIB before they consented to release the odd policeman for counterespionage duties, and even then they haggled endlessly over spheres of authority and expenses.

The General Staff grew impatient and launched a campaign for the establishment of a counterespionage apparatus. This was not without historical irony. Having resisted police interference for so long, the military suddenly demanded a super-police force to combat the threat of espionage. The Chief of the General Staff called for the creation of a "political Reich police" and thus for a measure of police reform which effectively amounted to a change in Article 4 of the Constitution, whereby control over the police was vested in the states.[97]

On December 5, 1890, when this proposal had been rejected by the Reich Ministry of the Interior, the Chief of the General Staff lodged a new demand: the secret service must be furnished with police agencies responsible for keeping watch on foreign military attachés and journalists, safeguarding military installations and sealing the frontiers against foreign spies. This plan was likewise rejected because lawyers proved without difficulty that it violated the Constitution, which forbade the subordination of a civilian body—the police—to the military authorities.[98]

Far from giving in, the General Staff stepped up its demands and eventually tabled a full-scale review of the Wilhelminian police structure. Writing to the Chancellor, the Prussian War Minister declared that only a "complete break with the existing [federally organized] system" would make it possible to create an effective counterespionage apparatus.[99] The country's political leaders turned a deaf ear without ordering the military back to their constitutional kennel. The government and Reichstag merely limited themselves to tightening up the law against treason.

The military were about to back down when Kriminalkommissar [roughly, Detective Superintendent] von Tausch, the celebrated chief of Prussia's political police, came to their aid. There had been renewed co-operation between the secret service and the political police since it became customary for police officers from Section V to keep foreign visitors under surveillance during manoeuvres and guard important military installations.[100] Secret servicemen and secret policemen were united mainly by their common dissatisfaction at the half measures of the Hohenzollerns' pseudo-liberal authoritarian regime. Both groups believed in a well-organized authoritarian state and both still owed something to the tradition of government by Wilhelminian Geheimräte [privy councillors]: the police an effective secret-police structure which measured the life of every citizen against the requirements of national security, and the secret service an elaborate counterespionage network without whose protection the work of IIIB would have been pointless.

It was in the field of counterespionage that the interests of secret servicemen and secret policemen coincided. This encouraged Kriminalkommissar von Tausch to back the Army. In 1895 he drafted a memorandum proposing the expansion of his department into the headquarters of a counterespionage police apparatus to which all Prussian police authorities should be subordinated by decree and those of

Saxony, Württemberg and Bavaria by voluntary consent.[101] Tausch had little more success than the General Staff: the War Ministries of Saxony, Württemberg and Bavaria refused to defer to Berlin.[102]

The Tausch plan only resulted in a loose form of organization. The police authorities in Berlin, Munich, Dresden, Stuttgart, Karlsruhe and Hamburg took their cue from Polizeirat Zahn of Strasbourg and set up Central-Polizeistellen for the combating of espionage. From 1907 onwards the Berlin police authority was permitted—on sufferance—to impose some measure of co-ordination on the work of its fellow authorities.[103] In Mecklenburg, Thuringia, Hessen and other states, no counterespionage agencies existed. The General Staff rightly protested that large areas of Germany were "still at the mercy of espionage."[104]

Embittered General Staff officers devised police projects of an increasingly drastic nature—indeed, their plans and memoranda sound, in retrospect, like recommendations for a Gestapo à la Himmler. On November 9, 1911, the Chief of the Grand General Staff declared that "all requirements would best be met by a Reich police force which autonomously spreads its net across the entire Reich and has its headquarters in Berlin."[105] Although such demands went unheeded, the campaign for the creation of a counterespionage police agency was not without effect. It influenced the political ideas of German secret servicemen for decades, and the joint endeavours of secret servicemen and secret policemen founded a partnership that would later play a role in the Third Reich.

In default of an effective counterespionage system, Section IIIB had to find another means of detecting and thwarting the enemy's intentions. The secret service apparatus was enlarged and improved. In Landwehr [territorial reserve] districts near the frontiers IIIB stationed retired officers—so-called Bezirksoffiziere [district officers]—who recruited informants on both sides of the border.[106] They also kept in close touch with the frontier police, who were requested to help gather information. From this there developed a new plan: the joint establishment of intelligence centres by IIIB and the frontier police.[107]

The first of these centres came into being in April 1893. They were manned by a district officer and a frontier police superintendent. A directive from the Oberpräsident [chief provincial administrator] of Posen stated that their main task was "to discover and indicate to the district officers in question persons qualified to become agents for the gathering of information beyond the frontiers."[108] The intelligence centres soon attracted a brisk flow of information, though its quality tended to be poor because many district officers were untrained men with no knowledge of foreign armies or languages.

Then the IIIB officers had an idea. Why not replace incompetent district officers with young serving staff officers who were familiar with foreign armies and intelligent enough to deploy agents at key points in times of national emergency? Assigned to the headquarters of the nearest corps in peacetime, they would take over intelligence duties at the relevant Army headquarters when war broke out—or so it was envisaged in the plan submitted by the Chief of the General Staff to Karl von Einem, the Prussian War Minister, on March 6, 1906.[109] A new secret service figure had been born: the "Ic" [General Staff intelligence officer].

The War Minister was horrified. He found it monstrous on social grounds "to expose junior officers . . . to constant intercourse with persons of dubious reputation for several years on end."[110] Only continued pressure from the Chief of the General Staff induced him to permit one of the latter's subordinates to test the efficacy of the new scheme. This officer, Lieutenant Walter Nicolai, was soon to secure for IIIB a measure of political influence never before wielded by any military intelligence service. Himself the son of an Army officer, Nicolai had been reared in a Protestant and traditional Prussian society which found it only natural that Army officers should rule the destinies of the nation. Royalist, ultraconservative and ever insistent on the virtues of the allegedly "non-political" soldier, Nicolai nonetheless exemplified the political role played by the imperial officer corps.

On June 1, 1906, Nicolai took charge of the Königsberg intelligence centre and developed it into the headquarters of an informants' network in Russia.[111] His successes were sufficiently impressive to convince the War Minister. Einem raised no further objections, and from summer 1907 onwards nearly all army corps were assigned intelligence officers [Nachrichtenoffiziere or NO] to whom the more able district officers were attached as deputies.[112] This step did, however, provide fresh scope for jurisdictional clashes. The War Ministry, IIIB and the army corps became embroiled in a three-sided dispute over who controlled the NOs—corps headquarters or the Grand General Staff—and it continued to rage under the Third Reich.

The introduction of NOs heralded a further expansion of the IIIB apparatus as the gathering storm clouds of World War I spurred the secret service into ever more feverish activity. Its tempo was greatly accelerated by Lieutenant Colonel Erich Ludendorff, who at that time headed Section 2 of the Grand General Staff.[113] Ludendorff, who took an exceptional interest in intelligence matters, regarded the secret service as indispensable, not only to the total war of the future but also to his visions of an authoritarian regime.

Ludendorff kept a benevolent eye on the secret service from late 1908 onwards. He advocated its enlargement, got the IIIB budget increased to 450,000 marks and used his influence to ensure that Nicolai, by now a major, reached the top of the secret service tree in spring 1913.[114] Theirs was a meeting of minds united by the lofty condescension peculiar to a military caste which felt superior to any civilian administrator and was soon to usurp the authority of a weak political leadership. Seldom did a secret service chief take over his official duties with greater self-assurance than forty-year-old Nicolai, who was extremely young and junior by Wilhelminian standards. He promptly instructed his NOs to reduce their dependence on corps headquarters and forbade them to engage in counterespionage on the grounds that this was a police matter. Naturally enough, a man like Nicolai did not content himself with a simple subsection and requested that IIIB should be upgraded to section status, which it was in 1915.[115]

Nicolai repeatedly impressed on his officers that IIIB's efforts were focused on war alone. "Before any procurement or transmission [of intelligence] by proxy, the NO should ask himself of what use it is to war."[116] His language suggested that war could not come soon enough. "For us, war will bring a day of reckoning. The Army will then expect us to produce the fruits of our long peacetime activities in the shape of strategic reports."[117]

When the time for action came in August 1914, however, IIIB's "fruits" turned sour indeed. The secret service proved incapable of assuaging the General Staff's hunger for information. Its main deficiency was a detailed picture of the enemy's operational objectives and strategic dispositions. Worse still, Nicolai lost his best foreign-based agents in the first few weeks, with the result that France and Russia remained blank areas on his situation maps. It was symptomatic of the impotence of the German secret service that he should have been obliged to reactivate the veteran spy Schluga, who was now seventy-three years old. Although his nerves were shot, "No. 17" performed such sterling work in Paris that, as one historian of the Abwehr remarked with a certain unconscious irony, "he formed the nucleus of our secret intelligence service against France."[118]

These failures inevitably came hard to the foreign army experts for whose benefit the secret service had originally been founded. The Intelligence Section [from 1917, the Abteilung Fremde Heere or Foreign Armies Section], which had been combined with the first and third sections of the Grand General Staff, was largely dependent on conjecture, especially as reports from IIIB had too often proved inaccurate.[119] Mistrust between the two sections was rife.

It now became clear that the German intelligence system was suffering from a cancer which continued to affect it until the fall of the Third Reich: a clearcut division between the procurement and evaluation of intelligence. One section was ignorant of the other's activities. The secret service had no influence over the evaluation of the reports it compiled. Conversely, the Intelligence Section could not judge where a report came from and whether a "source" should be taken seriously because the secret service released no details about its informants. Foreign Armies experts communicated with IIIB by means of questionnaires only, which led to a variety of misunderstandings and resulted in one fiasco after another.

Nicolai did his best to improve the work of his organization. He set up new intelligence centres, developed a system of prisoner interrogation and recruited agents who penetrated the enemy lines on IIIB's behalf. The more he expanded his organization the greater his influence became inside the German military hierarchy. His great day dawned in 1916–17, when Ludendorff, who had meanwhile become Chief of the General Staff and Germany's unofficial dictator, gave him a long-awaited opportunity to expand the military secret service politically.[120]

The head of IIIB had never been content with military objectives alone. He regarded his secret service as a General Staff propagandist, a relentless inculcator of the will to win and a supervisor and initiator of patriotic self-discipline. What was more, his organization already had the power to invade those areas which had long ago been wearily surrendered by the political authorities. IIIB had been assigned to control the counterespionage activities which it pursued in conjunction with the police and the Geheime Feldpolizei. Nicolai was in charge of the War Press Office and the Censorship Department. German newspapers were forbidden to print a word about military developments which had not been approved by the officials and officers of IIIB. IIIB also ran a home intelligence service with informers in firms, government departments and private circles.[121]

The IIIB authorities became convinced that it was the job of the secret service to bring the entire nation up to scratch. A Supreme Command directive dated May 8, 1917, empowered Nicolai to "co-ordinate such military intelligence activities at home, in occupied territory and among the forces in the field as are essential to the conduct of the war."[122] In other words, he was to bolster the German people's morale. Nicolai duly set up a propaganda centre designed, as another directive put it, to function as "an initiatory and co-ordinative [agency] between the various departments concerned with propaganda." He also instituted "patriotic instruction" for serving soldiers and employed his officers on War Loan fund-raising drives.[123]

Nicolai stepped in whenever he saw a threat to the country's martial spirit or scented a yearning for peace. He was behind the founding of the Vaterlandspartei, with its reactionary and chauvinistic plans for military conquests, helped to influence public opinion against moderate Social Democratic leaders and fanned the flames of nationalistic indignation when the Reichstag dared to advocate peace settlements that fell short of total victory. Not a press conference passed without his urging journalists to give the German war effort their all-out support.

However much his colleagues in the Foreign Armies Section might have preferred the secret service to improve its intelligence work proper, Lieutenant Colonel Nicolai had recognized his true vocation. Month by month, his repressive secret service apparatus cast an ever darker shadow over Germany's editorial offices and political parties. It was not only his left-wing opponents for whom Walter Nicolai became "the Father of the Lie." His name, as the *Weltbühne* later declared, was associated with all forms of "systematic stupefaction, political agitation and scintillating mendacity."[124]

Never before had a secret service so completely degenerated into an instrument of propaganda as Section IIIB of the German General Staff. It fell apart more rapidly in November 1918 than even its most pessimistic officers had feared. Nicolai was removed, most of the Supreme Command's secret papers were burned and IIIB was disbanded.[125] The secret service remained discredited for years, a symbolic and deterrent example of how the powers of an intelligence service can be politically abused.

The revolutionaries who assumed power in Germany were naturally determined to abolish everything reminiscent of the secret service and secret police. Having for decades been the objects and victims of covert investigation by a secret service, they lacked all sense of the practical need for one. Never again, they promised themselves, would anyone spy on the people for the benefit of the class enemy. "Away with the secret political police, that shameful sink of the foulest corruption," an SPD pamphlet had urged in 1911.[126] The new rulers acted accordingly.

The left-wing socialist Emil Eichhorn, People's Commissioner for Public Security, dissolved Section V of the Berlin Police Authority, where the political police had been based. Its officers were dismissed and its files seized.[127] The revolutionaries made an equally clean sweep in every other German city suspected of maintaining a secret police force, and the Foreign Office was discouraged from any attempt to set up a new intelligence section. The word "secret" was taboo. The left-wing revolutionaries dreamed of an open society unclouded by any form of secret investigation, but their dream was short-lived. The moderate Social Democrats who succeeded these extreme left-wingers at the various police headquarters soon created a political police of their own. The aftermath of revolution and the constant threat of left- and right-wing coups made it essential for the Republicans to detect any extremist conspiracy in advance. The Kapp Putsch had taught them how essential a trustworthy political police force was to the preservation of democracy itself. If the government had been able to call on one then, it would not have been so sadly hoodwinked.

The rulers of the Republic did not, of course, venture to call their secret protective organization a political police force because they considered the name too fraught with evil associations. Instead, they shielded it from the public's wary gaze behind a variety of innocent-looking labels. Prussia's new secret police agency (IA), for example, came into being as an appendage of the unrelated Section I at Berlin's police headquarters. The police authorities' political desks and departments were gradually developed into a new organization known as the Centrale Staatspolizei [Central State Police] or C.St.[128]

This impressive title disguised the fact that the C.St.'s performance and efficiency left much to be desired. Counterespionage could hardly be effective when the combating of espionage had deteriorated rather than improved since the days of the would-be reformers on the Grand General Staff. The Republic's counterespionage police system lacked all structural cohesion. No central office evaluated incoming material and employed it as an aid to concerted operations. There had merely been an agreement to regard Section IA of the Berlin Police Authority as a sort of bank and clearinghouse for information, but it possessed no definite powers.[129] Based on inadequate legislation and only half-heartedly backed by the government, German counterespionage was no real match for foreign secret services.

This was particularly apparent in respect of Soviet espionage, which became steadily more active in the late 1920s. "The German police were surprisingly ignorant concerning the activities of the various Soviet apparats," writes David Dallin, the American expert on Soviet espionage.[130] They did not know the whereabouts or membership of Communist underground organizations, failed to penetrate the network of informants engaged on Soviet industrial espionage and were unaware of the Soviet secret service's lines of communication in Germany.[131]

The impotence of the counterespionage police prompted the military to regain control of the secret service and counterespionage functions. Although mistrustful democrats were quite as averse to a revival of the military intelligence service as they had been to the restoration of the political police, the Reichswehr's semiautonomous status blocked the emergence of any real opposition, especially as the most urgent task of the new secret service—combating left-wing extremism in the armed forces—was not distasteful to leading Republicans.

This purpose was served by a Nachrichten- und Erkundungsdienst [Intelligence and Reconnaissance Service] which had been established as early as autumn 1919 in the units of the Provisional Reichswehr and the Freikorps. Run by ex-IIIB officers who were not too politically suspect,[132] this service had the job of guarding the armed forces against political upheavals and warding off revolutionary tendencies—hence the title of the new organization, which later took permanent root: the Abwehr [literally, "Defence"; see Glossary].

"In all Military District Headquarters and Reichswehr Brigades," HQ Reichswehr Group I decreed on November 24, 1919, "Abwehr sections are to be established. Their functions are as follows: 1. (a) Frontier intelligence, (b) the combating of enemy espionage; 2. Internal intelligence; 3. Surveillance of own troops."[133] HQ Group II was even more explicit. An equivalent directive stated that the intelligence service was to cover "the supervision of all political activity, particularly by extreme left-wing parties."[134] This was an open admission that the Abwehr's immediate and primary functions were political.

A small band of agents and informers was soon available to act on the instructions of secret service officers. But, small as the "Reconnaissance Service" was, revolution-torn Germany possessed no more knowledgeable intelligence network. Its informants were directed to take an interest in everything, from "the political situation in the USPD and KPD, local organizations and plans, readiness to obey orders from headquarters" to "meetings: place, time, participants, subjects, resolutions, mood, identity of speakers. Impending disturbances, strikes, coups."[135]

The men at the head of the new secret service did, however, shrink from repeating Nicolai's political experiment. They realized that the Abwehr's success and survival depended on their emphasizing its defensive character. Consequently, its role was limited to protecting the armed forces from spies and subversives. The rulers of the Republic could hardly withhold their approval of such modest aims, so the military secret service was eventually permitted to resume an official existence.

In summer 1920, under the command of Major Friedrich Gempp, Nicolai's former deputy, three serving officers, seven salaried ex-officers and a handful of clerical staff moved into the third floor of Nos. 72–76 Tirpitz-Ufer, Berlin, once the headquarters of the Reichsmarineamt and now occupied by the Reichswehr Ministry.[136] On May 17 the Abwehr issued the first directive in its history: its task consisted "generally in protecting the Army against unexpected coups, combating revolutionary agitation in the ranks and carrying out local reconnaissance during operations for the restoration of peace and good order."[137]

Political circumstances and lack of funds compelled Gempp to tread carefully at first. He divided his Abwehr group into an Eastern and a Western desk, not that they engaged in espionage in the traditional sense.[138] Defence against espionage and sabotage claimed the foreground and little foreign military intelligence was gathered, especially as Gempp's organization still possessed no technical aids such as radio sets, passports and invisible inks.

Being as ineffective as it was, the Abwehr had every reason to seek co-operation and assistance from more influential quarters. Foremost among these was the old Foreign Armies Section, now called the Heeresstatistische Abteilung [Army Statistical Section] (T3) of the Truppenamt, which itself stood proxy for the outlawed General Staff. The Abwehr joined forces with T3, forming a group of its own within it. For the first time, the gatherers and evaluators of intelligence were united in a single department.[139]

Major von Boetticher, head of T3, was at last entitled to hope that the frequent wartime failures of communication between secret service-men and Army intelligence officers would in future be obviated. Co-ordination now seemed complete. The Abwehrstellen or "Asts" [Abwehr outstations] forwarded their reports to Boetticher, who in turn distributed them between T3's Western and Eastern groups and their foreign-country desks.[140] T3 encouraged the Abwehr to step up its efforts because the Truppenamt's foreign armies analysts were more than ever dependent on secret service reports now that the Allies had insisted on the withdrawal of all German military attachés.[141]

Gempp and his officers improved their intelligence-gathering organization, but the harmony between T3 and the secret service suffered in the process. This trend began in the mid-1920s, when the Abwehr cut down on its political functions after the stabilization of the Republic and became active in espionage work proper. Gempp reorganized the Abwehr Group, establishing a basic structural pattern which it retained from then on. There came into being three subgroups entitled Abwehr I (Reconnaissance), Abwehr II (Cipher and Radio Monitoring Service) and Abwehr III (Counterespionage).[142] At the same time, the Abwehrstellen in the seven military districts established foreign contacts, initially on Germany's eastern border, where the Reichswehr Ministry surmised that the restless Poles and their sabre-rattling Army posed the most dangerous threat to national security.

The Abwehr's expansion coincided with the growth of Colonel Kurt von Schleicher's designs on the chancellorship. Schleicher, who was then beginning to build himself a power base in the Reichswehr Ministry, detached the politico-military group from the Army Section of the Truppenamt in 1926 and converted it into an independent Wehrmacht section of the Reichswehr Ministry. Once at the head of this, he steadily extended his influence.[143]

Still dissatisfied, Schleicher planned to gain personal control of the secret service. He found a willing helper in Lieutenant Colonel Günther Schwantes, Gempp's successor, whom he rewarded with an undertaking that the Abwehr would be expanded still further. Schleicher simultaneously fulfilled one of Schwantes's dearest ambitions by merging the Army's Abwehr with its rival, the naval intelligence service. The latter had also been reorganized immediately after the war and was perpetuating the old practice of keeping its Army colleagues as much in the dark as possible. Although the naval intelligence service possessed some good contacts abroad, its organization seemed poor because too many naval authorities were engaged on intelligence work.

Captain Lohmann was not the only naval officer to have played the secret serviceman on his own initiative. "Defence," a Marineleitung memorandum stated in 1928, "is handled as a secondary object of study by the Mobilization Desk, attack by the Foreign Navies Desk. Only the Foreign Intelligence Service, with its several hundred correspondents . . . has a desk of its own."[144] The Army's Abwehr felt doubly tempted to absorb this unco-ordinated structure. When the Lohmann affair developed into a setback for naval intelligence as well, Schwantes urged his chief to get the two intelligence services amalgamated under the direction of an Army officer.

Schleicher, who spotted a chance to concentrate the whole of military intelligence in a super-department controlled by himself, set to work. Without notifying the naval authorities in advance, he produced a "Draft Order for the Formation of the Abwehr Section" and ensured that copies of it landed on their desks in mid-March 1928.[145]

Reichswehr Minister Groener's draft directive looked suspiciously like an ultimatum. "1. With effect from April 1," it announced, "the Abwehr Group of the Heeresleitung [Army Directorate] will cease to be the province of the Truppenamt and departments concerned with counterespionage, foreign intelligence, secret intelligence and monitoring and cipher duties will cease to be that of the Marine-Kommando-Amt [Navy department responsible for general operational control]. 2. These departments will, as of the same date, be merged in the 'Abwehr-Abteilung' (Abw. Abt.) [Abwehr Section]. This will be . . . directly responsible to me. Lieutenant Colonel Schwantes will assume command of the Abwehr-Abteilung . . . 4. As the sole such authority in the Reichswehr Ministry, the Abwehr-Abteilung will handle the entire organization of the Secret Intelligence Service and the Monitoring and Cipher Service, as well as all military and naval counterespionage . . . Every other department in the Reichswehr Ministry is forbidden to deal with matters falling into this sphere of activity. The Abwehr-Abteilung must receive prior notification of any external contacts made by other departments in the Reichswehr Ministry."[146]

Naval intelligence reacted with predictable annoyance. "A military impossibility," fumed Section AIIa of the Marineleitung, and the head of the Flottenabteilung noted: "A broken-backed decision . . . quite unwarrantable."[147] He took an even stronger line when submitting a report to the head of the Marineleitung. "It is, after all, a well-known fact that the efficiency of an intelligence organization is

commensurate with its decentralization because security and concealment are better assured . . . Moreover, a large organization is politically dangerous in this field and considerably more vulnerable to enemy
counterespionage."[148]

Although the Navy tried to squelch the Schwantes scheme by negotiating with Schleicher, Groener remained adamant. On March 30,
1928, he ordained a merger of the two rival services under Schwantes's
command.[149] A year later the enlarged Abwehr moved another step up
the ladder. Together with the Armed Forces and Legal Section of the
Reichswehr Ministry, it was attached to the newly formed Ministerial
Department, which Schleicher took over.[150] Schwantes did not, however, enjoy his accretion of power for long. At the end of 1929 he was
relieved as head of the Abwehr by one of Schleicher's cronies, Colonel
Ferdinand von Bredow.[151]

Naval intelligence officers, who disliked having to work under Army
supervision, still found it impossible to reconcile themselves to the new
set-up. Commander Wollanke, who headed the section's naval group,
seized every opportunity to snub his Army colleagues and often withdrew from official discussions when he thought naval interests were in
jeopardy.[152] Bredow was so irritated by Wollanke's opposition that he
eventually asked Navy Chief Raeder to replace him with someone less
intractable. Raeder found a suitable candidate in Commander Conrad
Patzig, an engaging character whom he judged adroit enough to break
down the existing barrier of hostility.[153]

Patzig soon succeeded in making peace between the two camps.
Above all, he quickly established a good working relationship with
Bredow. "Bredow was a rather vain man," Patzig recalls, "and vain
people are particularly easy to handle."[154] The two men got on so well
that Bredow recommended Patzig to succeed him when he took over
the Ministerial Department in June 1932, after Schleicher had become
Reichswehr Minister. Army intelligence officers were taken aback by
this unprecedented appointment of a sailor to command a traditional
preserve of the Prusso-German military. They were already gathering
for a counterattack when the head of the Truppenamt, General
Adam, stepped in with a declaration that he had every confidence in
Patzig and wanted all Army officers to co-operate closely with the new
head of the Abwehr.[155]

Patzig, who had meanwhile been promoted captain, soon convinced
his departmental critics that he was a good organizer. He ushered in a
period of explosive development which set the German secret service
back on the road to power politics and unbridled military expansion.
Largely responsible for this were the Abwehr's naval officers, whose past
association with the Freikorps and abortive *coups d'état* lent them an

SECRET INTELLIGENCE SERVICES IN THE POWER STRUCTURE OF THE THIRD REICH

Adolf Hitler
Führer and Reich Chancellor
Supreme Commander of the Armed Forces

OKW
High Command
of the
Armed Forces
Field Marshal
Keitel

including:

Amt
Ausland/Abwehr
Admiral Canaris

OKH
High Command
of the
Army
Field Marshal
v. Brauchitsch

Chief of the
General Staff
General
Halder

Foreign
Armies
West

Foreign
Armies
East

OKL
High Command
of the
Air Force
Reich Marshal
Göring

Chief of the
General Staff
Major General
Jeschonnek

Foreign
Air
Forces

OKM
High Command
of the
Navy
Grand Admiral
Raeder

Chief of Staff,
Directorate of
Naval Warfare
Vice-Admiral
Schniewind

Intelligence
Evaluation
(3/Skl)

Reichsführer-SS
and
Chief of the
German Police
Himmler

Reichssicherheitshauptamt
Heydrich

including:

Amt III
SD
Inland

Amt IV
Gestapo

Amt VI
SD
Ausland

aura of adventurism and conspiracy which was alien to most of their stolid and respectable colleagues in the Army.

It was Captain Patzig who first developed the Abwehr into an all-round military intelligence service. Its agents, officer-controllers and informants began to probe the secret places of potential foreign adversaries. Incipient German rearmament cast the Abwehr in an increasingly important role. German military ambitions having revived long before Hitler came to power, Captain Patzig's Abwehr helped in its own way to provide the wherewithal for Germany's daring excursion into new and hazardous politico-military waters. By 1932–33 the Abwehr possessed a skeleton establishment substantial enough to undergo threefold expansion whenever the Reichswehr was itself enlarged.[156] Aided by a steady build-up of foreign contacts, it ventured into hitherto forbidden realms of activity.

Major Grimmeiss, head of the Geheimer Meldedienst (Abwehr I) [Secret Intelligence Service], took care to expand his small network of agents in the East. Abwehr outstations in Königsberg, Stettin and Berlin were instructed to concentrate all their efforts on increased surveillance of Poland.[157] Not only were agents mobilized for use in the Soviet Union, but the Abwehr acquired its first confederates abroad. The Lithuanian secret service offered to assist German reconnaissance in the East, and Grimmeiss responded with Polish information from his secret files.[158]

Counterespionage (Abwehr III) also improved its working methods. Abwehr III's task was to protect military installations from saboteurs and conceal the Reichswehr's expansion from the Franco-British spies whom the Inter-Allied Control Commission had left to keep watch on German disarmament after its withdrawal from the country.[159] The spy catchers evolved new methods of counterespionage and began to infiltrate opposing secret service networks with agents of their own.

Because the Centrale Staatspolizei was too ineffectual to meet the challenge of the French, Polish and Soviet secret services, Abwehr III took to employing its own secret agents and counterspies in counterespionage operations extraneous to the armed forces. Abwehr trace-and-search teams kept such an effective watch on the activities of enemy spies that the police were happy to accept military guidance. As they saw it, the Abwehr possessed what C.St. lacked, an integrated organization directed by a central and universally accepted authority. "Police intelligence experts," reports Werner Best, onetime legal adviser to the Gestapo, "became so accustomed to relying on the 'military Abwehr' and acting on its instructions that many of them could not break themselves of the habit, even after the establishment of an autonomous and nationally integrated counterespionage police."[160]

At the same time, the Abwehr's spy-hunters realized only too well that they needed a strong counterespionage police agency to provide an effective shield against foreign intelligence services. The military authorities were neither capable nor desirous of protecting civilian sectors of society from spies—that was still a police function. Furthermore, the Abwehr possessed no executive powers. If it detected a spy and wanted him arrested, the police had to be called in. Once again, as they had in imperial times, the military began to devise plans for political reform, and once again they revived the idea of a centralized nationwide police force with counterespionage functions.

Then Hitler's "national revolution" flooded the police authorities with men who were determined to remedy the shortcomings of the police system after their own fashion. They had visions of an organization which left no room for political opponents, far less spies. The National Socialists promised what the police and the military had always wanted: more money and prestige, better counterespionage facilities, centralized police functions and immunity from public criticism of any kind. Germany's new rulers demonstrated that they meant every word of this undertaking. Within a few months they constructed a police apparat unlike anything the twentieth century had ever seen.

As if deliberately resurrecting Gruner's claims to police omnipotence, the Nazis created an almost consummate police state. Its founder was Hermann Göring, Minister-President of Prussia. He detached the special political sections of the Criminal Police—the Political Police (combating of high treason) and Counterespionage Police (combating of treasonable activities beneficial to a foreign power [for precise distinction see Glossary])—from the Criminal Police and combined them into an independent police authority which he christened the Geheimes Staatspolizeiamt [Secret State Police Department].[161] A mail clerk faced with the problem of devising a cancellation stamp for the new department came up with the acronym "Gestapa,"[162] but common parlance transformed this postal abbreviation into the most baneful word Germans would ever hear in the years to come: Gestapo.

The Gestapo soon left the orbit of public administration and became a power in its own right, sinister and all-threatening. The Political Police proper, or nucleus of the Gestapo, converted itself into Section III of the Geheimes Staatspolizeiamt and the Counterespionage Police into Section IV (to which were added another two sections, Organization/Administration and Law).[163] The secret police also expressed its new-found power in geographical terms. Deserting Berlin's police headquarters, as it had under Gruner in Napoleon's day, it moved into a vacant arts-and-crafts school at No. 8 Prinz-Albrecht-Strasse.

The Gestapo severed its links with government at the intermediate level too. In the provinces, Staatspolizeistellen or "Stapostellen" [district Gestapo headquarters] were only technically responsible to the various Land [see Glossary] premiers because, from the end of 1933, the Gestapo claimed to be an autonomous organization responsible to the Prussian Minister-President alone.[164] Add to this the fact that President Hindenburg had, on February 28, 1933, issued an emergency ordinance "For the Protection of People and State" which suspended all basic civil rights and empowered the police to conduct house searches, make arrests, confiscate property, tap telephones and open mail, and a more powerful police force than Göring's Gestapo can scarcely be imagined.[165]

The Gestapo's surveillance machinery was steadily reinforced and improved. A categorized system of lists and card indexes kept track of every potential spy and opponent of the regime, while an elaborate tracing system ensured that no fugitive escaped the Gestapo's all-seeing eye.[166] Control over the concentration camps, those treadmills of the National Socialist "co-ordinative" machine, later armed it with an additional weapon. Undesirable aliens could be consigned to a concentration camp until deported.[167]

The Abwehr's spy-hunters, who had a military fondness for authoritarian solutions and were impressed by the regime's nationalistic slogans, bent a satisfied gaze on the cold-blooded efficiency with which the new counterespionage police went to work. There is a long-standing myth to the effect that the Abwehr resisted the Gestapo's arbitrary powers from first to last. In fact, nothing could have been more welcome to Abwehr officers than the drive and efficiency of the Secret State Police. This was how they had always conceived of fighting enemy espionage: hard, wholeheartedly and in secret. They ignored the political concomitants—loss of individual liberty and the Brownshirt reign of terror—because all that mattered to an expert was the efficiency of the new apparatus.

Indeed, the Gestapo could not be too powerful for the officers and associates of Abwehr III. Abwehr personnel were quite often enjoined by their superiors to devise better methods of police counterespionage and lend assistance to their colleagues in the "Stapo" (its official designation).[168] The Gestapo and Abwehr quickly became accustomed to working in harness. "For the proper handling of current Abwehr cases," declared an official Abwehr III directive, "a close personal relationship with the sole executive body engaged in combating espionage, the Secret State Police, is of special importance."[169]

Collaboration bred cohesion. Between them, official pressure and personal contact built up a sense of community which not even the interdepartmental feuds of later years could entirely destroy. The men of the Abwehr and Gestapo were children of their time—products of a nationalistic age in which most people still believed in the absolute value of the state and nation and were quite prepared to accept that the state and its leaders could require the citizen to make any sacrifice.[170]

Abwehr and Gestapo co-operated with due success. Only a few months after starting work together they jointly smashed an organization led by one of the century's most dangerous spies, a Polish cavalry officer named Sosnowski, whose agents and informants—most of them women—had probed deep into the secrets of the German armed forces.[171] Canaris's friend Protze, who had been transferred to counterespionage duties in Abwehr III after the amalgamation of the naval and military intelligence services, uncovered Sosnowski's network with the aid of some counterspies. He then alerted the Gestapo, who clinched the case with a series of arrests on February 27, 1934.[172]

So relations between the Abwehr and Gestapo would have remained near perfect had not a new force proclaimed monopoly rights in the sphere of national security. Heinrich Himmler's Schutzstaffel [Protection or Guard Detachment], which had swiftly risen to become the NSDAP's elite order, Hitler's personal bodyguard and the party's police, now claimed authority over the police as a whole. In April 1934 the SS achieved a decisive break-through. After some fierce internal bickering between the Nazi hierarchs, Göring was compelled to cede control over the Gestapo to the SS authorities.[173] It suddenly dawned on many Abwehr officers that the Gestapo was a reflection of something more than the new regime's understandable desire for security. Behind it lurked the demonic spirit of a totalitarian movement which recognized no norms or standards save the right of the stronger.

One of the first officers to grasp this was the Abwehr chief himself. Patzig's disenchantment dated from a spring day in 1934, when he encountered that personification of Nazi devilry and Lucifer of the police state, Reinhard Heydrich, the onetime cadet and musical house guest of Canaris who now headed the Secret State Police. It was no consolation to Patzig that SS-Oberführer [Brigadier] Heydrich had once worn naval officer's uniform—on the contrary. Heydrich's appearance before a naval court of honour in April 1931 had led to his dismissal from the service for "impropriety" on the grounds that he had broken off an engagement in a peculiarly tasteless manner.[174] Ever since then—and this was not lost on Patzig—his attitude towards most naval officers had been one of hatred and condescension.

On June 14, 1931, the cashiered and unemployed ex-officer, who already sensed that the SS would become the elite corps of a future Nazi regime, called on Himmler at his chicken farm in Waldtruderingen.[175] There, in a brief twenty minutes, he sketched the outlines of an SS counterespionage service designed to protect the party from its enemies. Schoolmasterish but not without a sense of theatre, Himmler was impressed. He christened Heydrich's brainchild the "Sicherheitsdienst des Reichsführers-SS" (SD) [Security Service of the Reichsführer-SS] and appointed its author to head the new organization.[176]

Heydrich later evolved a close-knit and SD-controlled surveillance system whose task was to keep watch on every sphere of national life and ensure the total supremacy of the NSDAP, backed by the SS and a police corps under its direction. This new SS-owned police agency differed from its predecessors in one important respect. The police forces of earlier regimes had confined themselves to catching public enemies red-handed, as it were, and did not step in unless there was a definite threat to the state. Heydrich's policemen were assigned to track down opponents even before they had entertained a subversive idea, let alone committed an act of resistance. The police force ceased to be a defensive counterespionage organ of the state and went over to the attack. More than that, it became an omnipotent and inquisitorial body which purged the nation of all undesirable thoughts. This removed the legal restraints on traditional police work. Only one law counted, and that was the ruthless defence of the Führer's dictatorship.

Heydrich fulfilled his programme by stages. In March 1933 he set up the Bavarian Political Police, a counterpart of the Prussian Gestapo. He then spread his net wider, because the remaining sixteen Land police forces had no common master.[177] One police authority after another fell under Himmler's sway until only Göring's Gestapo was left. At the end of April 1934, Himmler and Heydrich gained control of the Prussian police too, Himmler as inspector of the Gestapo and Heydrich as head of the Gestapa.[178]

At the same time, Heydrich made increasing inroads into the secret service domain. On June 9, 1934, Rudolf Hess, the Führer's deputy, declared the SD to be the NSDAP's sole intelligence service and forbade all other NS bodies to engage in secret service activities—the start of a surreptitious campaign by which Heydrich hoped gradually to extend his control over the national intelligence agencies.[179] He had already manoeuvred one ambitious SD officer, the Oberregierungsrat [senior civil servant] and former public prosecutor Günther Patschowsky, to the top of the Counterespionage Police. Patschowsky adopted a new approach to the Abwehr,[180] letting it be known that its supremacy would no longer be tolerated and that sole authority to combat espionage belonged to the Gestapo.

Heydrich's and Patschowsky's men encroached on the Abwehr's activities to such an extent that Patzig fought back. Fearing a Gestapo and SD take-over, he persuaded Blomberg, the weak and Nazi-dominated Reichswehr Minister, to extract a directive from Hitler stating that the Abwehr was the Reich's only politico-military intelligence service. This was a delusion, of course, because the Foreign Office would never have permitted the Abwehr to be the sole source of intelligence reports. Patzig did, however, achieve a partial success in that Hitler issued an order confirming that the Abwehr was exclusively responsible for military intelligence and counterespionage within the armed forces.[181]

But the Gestapo continued to meddle in military matters. In summer 1934 Heydrich requested the Abwehr to furnish him with a list of all clandestine munitions factories in Germany. Patzig recalls: "I replied that I did not possess such a list because any such document would be far too dangerous if it fell into outside hands." The Gestapo chief promptly complained to Blomberg, who instructed Patzig to reach an understanding with Heydrich, but Patzig dodged any further discussion of the subject.[182]

Heydrich continued to ply the Abwehr chief with requests. Patzig: "I was always having trouble with Heydrich."[183] Then the series of murders on June 30, 1934, provided Patzig with a welcome opportunity to try and neutralize Heydrich. In putting down the so-called Röhm Putsch, the Gestapo's murder squads had overstepped the powers granted them by Hitler and Göring and liquidated some wholly innocent military personnel. Many Abwehr officers were resentful that the victims had included two ex-members of their own organization, Bredow and Schleicher.

A group of officers led by Captain Friede of Abwehrstelle Dresden urged their chief to call for Heydrich's dismissal. Patzig actually induced the Reichswehr Minister to take such a step. Having won the support of a few other cabinet members, Blomberg confronted Himmler with a request that Heydrich be dismissed. Himmler repudiated the suggestion. He was well aware, he said, that it was all an anti-Gestapo plot hatched by Friede.[184]

Blomberg backed down. He not only blamed Patzig for his discomfiture but seems, even at this stage, to have decided that Heydrich's troublemaking critic must go. From then on, friction between Blomberg and Patzig was continuous. The minister wanted the Abwehr to contact and work closely with the Italian secret service, but Patzig jibbed. The Italian intelligence service was not only behind the times, he said, but untrustworthy.[185] The two men were equally at odds over the question of aerial reconnaissance against Poland and France, which Blomberg insisted that Hitler had forbidden.[186]

The break came in October 1934. While visiting Kiel, Blomberg learnt that Abwehr aircraft were taking high-altitude photographs of the Maginot Line. Furiously, he summoned Patzig and told him that he had "no use for an Abwehr chief who indulges in such escapades."[187] Although the head of the Heeresleitung, General Baron von Fritsch, took Patzig's part and assumed responsibility for the aerial reconnaissance operations, Blomberg demanded Patzig's resignation and the appointment of a successor.[188]

The Abwehr chief made a last attempt to warn his colleagues, and superiors against the machinations of the Gestapo and SS authorities, but his words fell on deaf ears. His farewell report, which erred on the crude and unsubtle side, called the SS a catchment area for rootless individuals who balked at nothing in their pursuit of power. Blomberg forbade such criticism with the words: "The SS is an organization of the Führer's!" At this, Patzig blurted out, "Then I only regret that the Führer doesn't know what a rotten bunch he has under him."[189]

But Patzig's strictures were equally unacceptable to the man he had nominated to succeed him. Being a National Socialist, Canaris actually reproached him for having failed to come to terms with Heydrich and the Gestapo.[190] "I knew," Patzig recalls, "that Canaris had taken a very dim view of my original appointment as head of the Abwehr because he considered me too good natured and decent. He did not think me tough enough for such a post."[191] When he told Canaris somewhat heatedly that friction between the Abwehr and the Gestapo had become intolerable, his successor remained unmoved. "Don't worry," Canaris rejoined, "I'll deal with those boys."[192]

Though filled with uneasiness, Patzig called on Raeder and submitted his recommendation. The Navy chief's response was indignant: "Impossible! I can't work with that man."[193] Raeder, who disliked the inscrutable Kapp rebel and had deliberately given him the dead-end job at Fort Swinemünde, planned to retire him completely the following year. Patzig fell back on the only argument calculated to win Raeder's approval. "Then there's nothing for it but to hand the Abwehr back to the Army, lock stock and barrel." Being a Navy lobbyist, Raeder gave in.[194]

Wilhelm Canaris had made it at last. His long years of barren routine, self-doubt and professional bottlenecks were over. Ahead of him lay a fresh start and a different future. He resolved to make the most of what the moment offered.

6

Head of the Abwehr

The new chief arrived at 8 A.M. Gallmüller, a veteran Berliner and long-time doorman of the mysterious premises known as 72–76 Tirpitz-Ufer, stiffened to semi-attention as the short, silver-haired figure in naval uniform passed him. Gallmüller glanced at the calendar. Not that he realized it, January 2, 1935, was a historic day: Captain Wilhelm Canaris, head of the Abwehr Section of the Reichswehr Ministry, was taking up his new appointment.[1]

Canaris strode on. He was only too familiar with the route to the decrepit old elevator that would take him up to the Abwehr Section. The cramped and shabby apartment house beside Berlin's Landwehr Canal, locally nicknamed the "Fuchsbau" [Fox's Earth] on account of its labyrinthine passages, innumerable doors and gloomy offices, had once been the premises of the Reichsmarineamt where Canaris had himself served as Noske's aide soon after the war. He was also acquainted with the next-door building, which housed the Reichswehr Minister's private suite, and with the adjacent offices of the Reichswehr Ministry itself, which extended as far as Bendlerstrasse.

Canaris's own past came flooding back at every step. The Landwehr Canal was the scene of the Liebknecht-Luxemburg murder scandal that had dogged him for so many years. In the building next door he had experienced the illusions and humiliations of the Kapp Putsch, and in the Marineleitung next door to that his promising naval career had led down the blind alley from which Captain Patzig's troubles had just delivered him.

The elevator stopped at the third floor. Canaris got out and negotiated the folding metal grille that shielded the Abwehr Section from unwanted visitors. Few of the offices were manned at this hour. Canaris glanced into them as he passed. They were dark and dismal places. A former member of the Abwehr described them as follows: "A desk, a table, a few chairs, a clothes locker, a washstand and a camp bed, all of barrack-room type, plus a safe—those were the normal appurtenances of an office. In the case of group heads, the height of luxury was represented by one or two tattered armchairs, often on three legs, and possibly a sofa and a radio."[2]

The head of section's quarters lay at the end of the passage. They consisted of a small outer office in which his senior secretary, Wera Schwarte, was already awaiting him with a female colleague, and an inner office with a balcony overlooking the Landwehr Canal. Canaris started at the sight of his future abode. It was completely bare. Patzig had made a clean sweep, but it was not long before some removals men delivered Canaris's personal effects—a leather couch, a desk and a conference table, a few document stands, the inevitable camp bed, numerous books, a model of the light cruiser *Dresden* and a trio of bronze monkeys from Japan symbolizing the cardinal virtues of the secret serviceman ("see all, hear all, say nothing").[3]

Canaris was soon installed in some degree of comfort. He was seated at his desk behind the *Dresden* and the three wise monkeys when his group and subgroup heads first saw their new master at close quarters. The atmosphere was rather strained because most of them were upset by his predecessor's departure and the Nazi machinations that had brought it about.[4] They bent an expectant gaze on Canaris, who slowly rose from behind his desk.

Accustomed to the brisk and cheerful Patzig, they were startled by what they saw. The man who came forward to greet them looked limp by comparison. He was round-shouldered and spoke in a quiet, diffident voice. Nobody had prepared the Abwehr officers for such a spectacle and none would have accepted the truth of the formula which Canaris's friend Hartmut Plaas was later to use on visitors meeting him for the first time: "The Admiral doesn't look much, but he's as sharp as they come."[5]

Canaris did, in fact, look colourless and impersonal. There was "nothing specially impressive about him," as one of his subordinates noted.[6] The group and subgroup heads took in every detail of their new chief: height approximately 5 feet 3 inches, white hair, sailor's ruddy complexion, bushy eyebrows, air of fatigue, slight and frail-looking physique, unmilitary bearing, shabby uniform tunic adorned with the Iron

Cross First Class, reserved manner, occasional lisp, tendency to answer
one question by putting another. Was this the forceful and uncompromising character they had hoped for after Patzig's humiliating dismissal? None of them thought so and nearly all were disappointed.
"Compared with the brisk and energetic Captain Patzig," recalls ex-Abwehr officer Gerhard Henke, "he seemed too old and spent for the
job."[7] Then forty-eight, Canaris adopted a "rather casual" manner towards his senior subordinates at their first meeting.[8] Henke: "He read
out his opening address, which clearly betrayed the new National
Socialist spirit. Then he invited us to brief him. I got the impression
that he was nearer yawning than listening to my report."[9] Captain
Grosse later described him as looking more like "the impresario of a
worldwide music-hall agency . . . than a senior German officer,"[10] the
head of Abwehr III pronounced him an "absolutely impossible" head
of section[11] and a newly recruited Abwehr I lieutenant congratulated
himself on not having to work with the "pale and inscrutable" Canaris.[12]

What surprised his listeners most of all were the new man's Nazi
slogans. Propagandist utterances of this kind did not normally obtrude
on the internal workings of the Abwehr. Patzig had never concealed his
keen distaste for the National Socialist regime; Canaris affected to be
its representative. His clear-cut programme was hardly compatible with
the old Patzig maxims: harmonious contact with all organs of the
Brownshirt government, "comradely co-operation" between the Abwehr
and Gestapo combined with a sober and dispassionate defence of the
Abwehr's prerogatives against all encroachments by non-military institutions.

Puzzled and depressed, Canaris's subordinates returned to their
offices. Nothing they learned about him in the ensuing days and weeks
dispelled the nagging suspicion that they had acquired an unsuitable
master, and their misgivings were reinforced by many office anecdotes
which painted him a figure of fun.

Superstitious, hypochondriacal and an inveterate pill-popper, Canaris nursed an almost morbid fear of illness, tall people and animal
haters. One of his officers records that he "often suffered from neuralgia
and insomnia"[13] and needed an inordinate amount of sleep. He liked to
rest on his leather couch in the afternoons, and there was no official
meeting or private party from which he did not retire to bed at about
10 P.M.[14] Even after a good sleep, however, he sometimes looked nervous and physically exhausted. He was also afflicted by imaginary ail-
ments and often felt sicker than he really was.

Back in 1924, his ship's doctor had reported: "Condition aggravated
by a tendency to interpret all kinds of minor symptoms as signs of severe illness."[15] Canaris had such an unbridled fear of infection that a

harmless cold could send him into a panic. "One day," recalls a former group head, "when I came to brief him with a cold and ventured to sneeze, he leapt out of his chair as if he had been stung and ordered me, being a germ carrier, to go home at once and not show my face at the office until the cold had completely gone."[16]

This was more than a fad, of course. Behind it lay the sensitivity of a fatalist who felt fundamentally vulnerable and always expected the worst. The same sensitivity was reflected by his aversion to "lanky fellows" or those who radiated energy and excessive zeal. Canaris could not stand subordinates who remained on duty after 10 P.M. and detested spit-and-polish types, especially when they flashed their war medals.[17]

There were times when a few minor physical peculiarities could suffice to make or break a person in his eyes. Provided they were not too tall and gifted with a ready tongue, good-looking men quickly endeared themselves to him; men with small ears never did. Heuke once accompanied Canaris on a visit to Froboess, the Danzig police chief. Afterwards, Canaris asked him if anything had struck him about the man. He was quite put out when Heuke said no. "You mean you didn't notice those little ears of his? You'd better watch your step with him!"[18]

Canaris reserved his deepest antipathy for those who did not get on with dogs and horses. He genuinely believed that "nobody who mal-treats animals can be a good sort."[19] He severed personal contact with people who turned out to dislike animals and shunned hotels where dogs were not admitted. He also waxed aggressive towards anyone, however influential, who scolded his dachshunds. Once, when a host smacked one of them and it started to growl, the Abwehr chief soothed his pet by likening its chastiser to some drunken member of a students' duelling club.[20]

But woe betide the Abwehr officer who withheld due homage from his canine friends! Canaris took to bringing them with him as soon as he had settled in, and they quickly became the bane of his immediate subordinates' existence. These two wire-haired dachshunds, Seppel and Sabine, turned up daily in the black government Mercedes which conveyed their master to the Tirpitz-Ufer. They remained with him all day long, fouling the carpet with considerable regularity but cheering him in his darker moments. When fatigue overcame him, he would closet himself in his office and play with them.[21]

Canaris was so devoted to these animals that he made notes and wrote short psychological essays about them. No living creatures preoccupied him as often as Sabine, Seppel and the latter's successor, Kasper. He frequently meditated on his four-legged friends in diaries of later date. One of the few Abwehr officers to have read these diaries before their disappearance in 1945 testified that they contained "very substantial notes and comments on his dogs." His love of dogs recurred again and again in a manner which seemed "almost whimsical and precious," and he often remarked that he preferred them to human beings.[22]

The dachshunds even accompanied Canaris on official trips. He always booked twin-bedded hotel rooms so that they could sleep beside him and became irate if they were neglected by the staff. On the few brief occasions when he had to leave them behind, no distance was too great for him to telephone daily for news of their bowel movements and emotional state.

There was a story current in the Abwehr that the Spanish secret police chief, who had monitored Canaris's telephone conversations during his visits to Spain, became sorely puzzled as to why the head of German military intelligence should be so deeply concerned about the digestion of a pair of important Abwehr agents named Seppel and Sabine.[23] Whenever Canaris returned from a dogless trip abroad, his first question to his aides—"How are things at home?"—referred to the canine, not the human, members of his household.

The officers and secretaries at the Tirpitz-Ufer headquarters smiled at their chief's idiosyncrasies without suspecting that his abstruse love of animals concealed a human and personal tragedy. Few of his subordinates noticed how seldom he mentioned his family. Canaris had failed to find the personal happiness he may well have yearned for. His marriage to Erika Waag had been lacking in harmony from the first. The unaesthetic naval officer and the industrialist's daughter, with her refined and cultivated tastes, were poles apart.[24]

Beneath the surface, the couple had long led wholly separate lives, though a regular woman visitor to their home recalls that they "always presented a united front" to the outside world.[25] Frau Canaris devoted herself to music, shone at social functions and had taken up anthroposophy, which enthralled her because of its phenomenological study of the spiritual element in man and his environment.[26] Canaris was excluded from his wife's world. Although a person of intellectual bent himself (his office desk was always littered with new books), he believed that human life was ruled more by the stars than by the fruits of anthroposophical meditation.[27]

Erika's interest in the dormant spiritual resources of mankind did not prevent her—according to another female eyewitness—from being "extremely moody and ungracious." Canaris, who was easily hurt and pretty much of a sitting target for her barbed remarks,[28] retired into his shell and took little part in family life. The cramped confines of the apartment he had taken at 11 Dölle-Strasse, Berlin-Südende, coupled with the lack of human warmth he found there and his younger daughter's persistent violin playing, could not in any case have made for a particularly congenial home life. Evening visitors provided Canaris with his sole consolation. In their company he could be charming and good-humoured—even witty.[29]

Yet he still remained a stranger under his own roof. He may also have been irked by the sight of his two problem children, however little contact he had with them. Eva, born at Kiel on December 16, 1923, and her younger sister Brigitte, born in Berlin on January 16, 1926, were widely regarded as solitary, precocious little girls who did not play with other children and never dressed their age.[30] Unmaternal and rather hard by nature, Erika was ill equipped to ride the blow that struck the family when Eva betrayed progressive mental defects which compelled her to leave primary school and prevented her from ever attending a normal educational establishment (she was later admitted to the Protestant mental home at Bethel).[31] Erika's favourite was Brigitte, an intelligent but aggressive girl who had inherited her mother's musical talent, although friends of the family regarded her, too, as "slightly dotty."[32]

Given this sort of home life, Canaris inevitably sought happiness and fulfilment in his official domain. The man who seldom went on family vacations, abhorred weekends off and shunned his own home even on public holidays plunged into a hectic round of activity. The Abwehr, which was used to operating in a leisurely manner, soon found itself presented with a new range of tasks.

The Abwehr chief's subordinates quickly discovered that he was a hard worker. It was not long before Henke, one of his critics, conceded that "our first impressions were mistaken."[33] A few weeks' experience of Captain Canaris were enough to convince every last member of his staff that there was no more skilful champion of the Abwehr's interests. The new plans he was evolving with his closest associates would, if communicated to a wider circle, have delighted the Abwehr Section at large. They provided for its expansion into an effective instrument of German espionage and underpinned its status as the "authorized supervisory headquarters of precautionary security in the Reich," as Canaris phrased it.[34]

But before any demands were made on Canaris's talent for organization, he was called upon to exercise his diplomatic skills in helping to extricate the Reichswehr from an awkward predicament. A clash between the armed forces and the party seemed more imminent now than at any time since the latter's assumption of power. The country buzzed with wild rumours of an impending military coup, and the foreign press, relying on information supplied by German *émigrés*, published daily predictions of a civil war in Adolf Hitler's Reich.[35]

At the same time, Reichswehr and party figured in the regime's propaganda vocabulary as the "twin columns" on which the new order reposed. Hitler's regime did, in fact, owe its very existence to the pact concluded by the military and the Nazi Party early in 1933. Reichswehr Minister General Werner von Blomberg, who was fascinated by Hitler, and his closest adviser, Major General Walter von Reichenau, who headed the Wehrmachtamt [Armed Forces Department] at the Reichswehr Ministry, had from the first adopted a flexible and accommodating policy designed to secure the Reichswehr an adequate share in political power. Their slogan was "Forward to the new state!"[36]

There was no ideological change of tack, no sudden innovation or act of violence on the part of the Nazi regime, which Blomberg and Reichenau did not tolerate. The Reichswehr, whose generals still regarded themselves as the custodians of traditional decency, looked on calmly while the Nazis stormed one constitutional bastion after another. The "co-ordinative" reign of terror thrust political parties and trade unions aside, the regime launched a guerrilla campaign against non-conformist elements in the Christian Churches, concentration camps were established and certainty of the law declined, but still the generals said nothing.

More than that, the Reichswehr authorities actually armed the SS murder squads who on June 30, 1934, struck down Ernst Röhm, the intransigent SA leader whose schemes for military reform deliberately threatened the Reichswehr's prerogatives. To Blomberg and Reichenau, the bloody suppression of its Brownshirt rivals was a triumphant vindication of their "flexible" policy. "All catched," Reichenau telegraphed Patzig in faulty English when the last of the SA leaders had been arrested and shot, and Blomberg extolled the "soldierly determination" and "exemplary courage" with which the Führer had crushed these "traitors and mutineers."[37]

Suddenly, however, the Reichswehr itself fell foul of the Nazi leaders' totalitarian claims to power. The real victor of June 30, Reichsführer-SS Heinrich Himmler, was carving himself an ever larger niche in the political edifice. He had thrown off the tutelage of Röhm and the SA, was steadily strengthening his grip on the police and had already gained control of the sinister concentration camp empire. Now, with a military formation of his own, the SS-Verfügungstruppe [SS Special Duties Force, later renamed the Waffen-SS or Militarized SS], he was invading the preserves of the regular armed forces.

The Reichswehr soon suspected that it was being spied on by Himmler's Gestapo and SD. The Gestapo monitored telephone calls between senior military departments, the SD encouraged party members in the Army to submit reports on alleged antigovernment intrigues in the officer corps and there were frequent brawls between Reichswehr personnel and members of the SS-Verfügungstruppe.[38] Egged on by the SS, fanatical party members spread it about that the Army planned to curb the NSDAP by building up a counterforce. Military district HQs reported a "systematic campaign against the Wehrmacht" and the SS authorities methodically broadcast a rumour that the Army was plotting a coup.[39]

Alarming reports from all sectors of the armed forces prompted the head of the Heeresleitung, General of Artillery Baron Werner von Fritsch, to advise the Reichswehr Ministry to adopt a policy of strict delimitation. Fritsch seriously believed that the Army could cocoon itself and insulate its men from National Socialist influence, solely linked with the regime by a "Führer and Reich Chancellor" who was supposed to be above the party.[40]

But Blomberg and Reichenau were unwilling to see their political schemes wrecked by such tactics. Blomberg tended to dismiss any signs of impending conflict as rumours and misunderstandings. Reichenau, who was a shrewder power-political tactician, also opposed Fritsch. He considered his proposals disastrous because they would inevitably isolate the Reichswehr from government and society and deprive the military of precisely the influence his conformist policy was designed to secure. Reichenau favoured *rapprochement* in the belief that friendly gestures would keep the Reichswehr's enemies sweet and simultaneously hold them at arm's length.

This was just where Canaris came in, being the head of an oganization—the Abwehr—which maintained contact with the Gestapo and, like a seismograph, registered any tremors in the relationship between the feuding brothers. To the Machiavellian Reichenau, Captain Canaris was the right person in the right place. Men of his calibre were bound, he thought, to dispose of a crisis which threatened Hitler and the Wehrmacht's rearmament plans in equal measure.

Canaris was attuned to his new duties by a spectacular manoeuvre on Hitler's part. Only hours after moving into Abwehr headquarters, he received orders to present himself at the Prussian State Opera House in Prachtstrasse, Unter den Linden, on the afternoon of January 3, 1935. Hitler had been so perturbed by New Year's Day reports of squabbles between the Reichswehr and party that he resolved to counter them with an elaborate *coup de théâtre*. He convened a meeting of "the entire leadership of the party, government and Wehrmacht."[41]

"Within twenty-four hours," rhapsodized the *Völkischer Beobachter*, "the entire leadership corps of the Reich had converged on Berlin from all parts of Germany and all steps essential to the mounting of such an important function had been taken."[42] The stalls and boxes were already packed by the time Canaris arrived. Every German officer, civil servant and Nazi official who counted for anything had turned up. Canaris took his place in the third row of the stalls, immediately behind Major Friedrich Hossbach, Hitler's adjutant.[43]

Frenzied cries of "Sieg Heil!" greeted the Führer's appearance. After the proceedings had been opened by Rudolf Hess, his official deputy, Göring said a few words in his capacity as host. Finally, Hitler stepped up to the speaker's stand and delivered a ninety-minute speech which must be numbered among the all-time masterpieces of mind-bending rhetoric. Although his audience found it hard to recall exactly what he had said, he spoke so persuasively that the military long remembered Hitler's speech of January 3, 1935, as a grand gesture of reconciliation on the part of an almost "national-conservative" politician.

Hitler denied all "rumours" of dissension between the party and the Reichswehr and proclaimed that the new Germany would continue to repose on those twin columns. It was his "unshakeable resolve" to lead Germany to new international standing and national security with the aid of a reinforced Wehrmacht. In a deliberate reference to critics inside the party, he claimed to be glad that the Reichswehr had not backed him prior to 1933. Obedience and conservatism were essential to any armed forces, so he might otherwise have feared present disloyalty from a Wehrmacht which had broken faith in the past.[44]

Again and again, Hitler stressed his "absolute and unshakeable faith . . . in the ability and, above all, in the loyalty of the entire Wehrmacht."[45] He also inveighed against those who spied on the armed forces: "Suppose someone from the party comes to me and says, 'That's all very well, my Führer, but General So-and-So is talking and working against you.' My reply is, 'I don't believe it!' And if someone else says, 'But I've brought you written proof, my Führer!', I tear the bumf up because my faith in the Wehrmacht is unshakeable."[46]

Hitler's military listeners were so impressed that some of them even thought they heard him take the opportunity to rehabilitate Generals von Schleicher and Bredow, who had been murdered on June 30, 1934. According to Hitler's reported statement, he had satisfied himself that their execution was mistaken and illegal, so the names of both generals would be reinstated in their regimental rolls of honour.[47] Whatever the Führer actually said, military men and party functionaries sat shoulder to shoulder, almost reconciled, when the spectacular culminated in a gala evening performance of Wagner's *Tannhäuser*.[48]

Canaris's first experience of Hitler the orator left him deeply impressed—not surprisingly, in view of the enthusiasm he saw on every side. Lieutenant General Curt Liebmann, GOC Military District V, opined that the Reichswehr had been "in a positively stirring manner . . . shown a confidence which no man of honour can reject," and even Fritsch stated that Hitler's speech had been "a firm declaration, an option in favour of the Wehrmacht."[49] From now on, influential military figures subscribed to a Hitler cult which exalted the leader of the Third Reich above the squalor of party politics, as it were, and promoted him to the status of a surrogate monarch.

Canaris was just as concerned to help cement the alliance between the Reichswehr and the Nazi regime, though without jeopardizing the military's independence. In this he took his cue from Reichenau, who deemed it opportune to follow up Hitler's act of reconciliation on January 3 with a few good-will gestures towards the party, SS and police.

Canaris was again present on the night of January 13, when Blomberg hosted a communal beer-drinking session which the *Völkischer Beobachter* described as uniting the senior officers of the Reichswehr and SS in "comradely communion."[50] There he saw Himmler, commander of the hostile battalions which had to be won over or at least neutralized. Himmler, whom Blomberg had invited to give a lecture on the functions of the SS, delivered a vague and woolly address, but his words made it only too plain that the manifold SS organizations represented a growing threat and a force to be reckoned with.[51]

The black-uniformed and puritanical order of the SS was increasingly moulding itself into a state within a state, an elite composed of unscrupulous power technicians who had long since infiltrated all those vacua in the government, party and administration which Hitler left his feuding henchmen free to fill with an interplay of countervailing forces. Bodyguards of the Führer, defenders of his dictatorship, uncompromising apostles of the National Socialist ideology and guardians of national sentiment, the SS men were ever more openly assuming the guise of a new and arrogant ruling class. As Himmler put it: "Our Führer knows what the SS means to him. We are his favourite and most highly valued organization because we have never let him down."[52]

But the empire of the death's-head was still incomplete. Many gaps still yawned in the surveillance system to which Himmler aspired. Above all, he had yet to pocket the entire police apparatus. Himmler had always wanted to create a centrally controlled Reich police system independent of the administration and judiciary, but the decisive breakthrough still eluded him. Although he was now in control of all the Land police authorities, powerful forces continued to bar his path. In Prussia he had to contend with Minister-President Göring (who retained nominal control of the Gestapo while Himmler could only call himself deputy chief and inspector), and at national level the Nazi bureaucrat Wilhelm Frick, who had just merged his Reich Ministry of the Interior with its Prussian counterpart, was striving to gain control of the Reich police as a whole and place it under the command of one of Himmler's rivals, SS-Gruppenführer [Lieutenant General] Kurt Daluege.[53]

These intrigues over the establishment of a nationwide police force did not escape the notice of the officers in the Reichswehr Ministry. The dispute with Frick and his civil service backers was hardly an inducement to Himmler to cross swords with the armed forces as well.

Canaris took advantage of this to open a dialogue with Himmler and his subordinates because only a truce with the SS would enable the Abwehr to expand in peace. His aim was to improve relations between the Abwehr and Gestapo, which had been disrupted during the Patzig era, and to define and delimit the two parties' spheres of activity, if possible in writing.

Himmler greeted the new head of the Abwehr in a cordial, almost jovial fashion. The SS chief was a man of medium height, and quite sturdily built. His features were puffy and undistinguished. The small receding chin gave an impression of weakness, but the steel-blue eyes, which regarded the world alertly from behind a pair of pince-nez, betrayed considerable determination. Heinrich Himmler has passed into history as a servile henchman of his Führer, but nothing in his appearance conveyed this. Canaris found himself face to face with a courteous and not unlikeable person who might have been an intelligent but somewhat fussy schoolmaster.

The two men quickly came to terms, and Himmler approved most of the proposals submitted by Canaris on behalf of the Reichswehr Ministry: delimitation of authority between the Abwehr, Gestapo and SD, better co-operation, exchanges of information and regular conferences between heads of department.

Himmler treated the Abwehr chief with benevolent curiosity because Canaris was reputed to be an exceptionally adroit and able representative of the secret service arm—and, more than that, a spy *par excellence*. To a power-hungry and elitist mystic like Himmler, the myth of the diabolically successful master spy tallied perfectly with his bizarre conception of the world and the forces that dominated it. Fundamentally unsophisticated, completely ignorant of the outside world and embroiled for too long in the sectarian feuds of a political revivalist movement, there were few more unquestioning devotees of espionage romanticism than Himmler.

His subordinates also worshipped at the shrine of John Buchan. More than any other ruling class in twentieth-century non-Communist Europe, they nursed a genuine belief that the fate of nations and their political systems hung largely on the covert activities of skilful agents and efficient secret services. Himmler, Heydrich and their aides were avid readers of detective and adventure stories rampant with grotesque overestimates of the British secret service—reason enough for the leading death's-head disciples to aim at establishing a similar organization themselves. A modest start had already been made. Heydrich signed his internal correspondence "C" because he had read somewhere that this was the title borne by the head of Britain's Secret Intelligence Service.[54]

Given their naive delight in secret service frolics, Captain Canaris and his glamorous past could hardly fail to kindle the imagination of the SS leaders. His opponents were impressed by this "fox among the bears of the Prussian military hierarchy."[55] Himmler never overcame his almost superstitious respect for such a "born spy." Even in 1943, when the Gestapo's suspicions had been aroused, he ordered them to discontinue all surveillance of the Abwehr chief.

Before Himmler approved a written agreement, however, he referred Canaris to his senior aide, the head of the Geheimes Staatspolizeiamt and SD. Canaris had been steeling himself for this reunion with his former cadet on the training ship *Berlin*, SS-Gruppenführer Reinhard Heydrich, ever since his return to Berlin. He fully realized that his talks with Heydrich, the regime's "suspecter in chief," would not be easy. Heydrich was wily, intelligent, consumingly ambitious and keenly competitive in politics as in sport—not an ideologist, but a ruthless wielder of power and fanatical devotee of expediency. It was he who wanted to curb the Reichswehr's influence, he who was watching the Abwehr's activities with suspicion and he who had conceived the plan for a total police state.

But Canaris quickly established contact with Heydrich thanks to a chance meeting early in 1935. While strolling down Dölle-Strasse with his wife, he saw an SS officer coming towards him with a blonde pushing a baby carriage. After a moment's uncertainty, Canaris exclaimed, "Good heavens, it's Heydrich!" As he drew nearer, recognition dawned on Heydrich too. He clicked his heels from ingrained habit, saluted and asked what the "Herr Kapitän" was doing in Berlin. The two men shook hands. Lina Heydrich, who had been married to Himmler's aide since 1931, learnt that her husband and Canaris had not met for twelve years.[56]

It was indicative of the gulf between the Abwehr and the Gestapo that Heydrich did not know who had succeeded Patzig until this chance meeting in Dölle-Strasse. "My husband knew nothing about it until then," Frau Heydrich recalls, "but he was pleased that Canaris had taken over the job. They had both been in the Navy, after all, and that formed a bond between them."[57] This is confirmed by the Gestapo's erstwhile legal adviser: "When . . . Canaris took charge of military intelligence, Heydrich expressed a wish to improve relations between it and the counterespionage police."[58]

As chance would have it, the Heydrichs also lived in Dölle-Strasse, where they rented a house belonging to a bank. They invited Canaris and his wife over, and this visit proved to be the first in a series of regular social contacts. When spring came, the Canarises often played croquet in the Heydrichs' garden. Canaris returned their hospitality by inviting them to meals at his apartment.[59] He was a good cook whose favourite dishes included saddle of wild boar in a *croûte*

made of crumbled black bread and red wine and a herring salad served
with brandy and caviar.[60]

Later, when the two families moved almost simultaneously to the
Schlachtensee district of Berlin and lived at such close quarters that the
Heydrichs' hen house abutted on the Canarises' garden, Heydrich and
Erika Canaris resumed the music-making that had formed a link be-
tween them in the old days at Kiel. A string quartet used to gather at
Heydrich's home in Augusta-Strasse. The host played first violin and
Frau Canaris second, Heydrich's younger brother Heinz the cello and
Ernst Hoffmann, who was a friend of the Heydrichs and later became a
chemist, the viola.[61] The amateur musicians met nearly every week. Canaris seldom attended these concerts, but Lina Heydrich, who was usually pregnant, listened ("Somebody had to shout 'Bravo!' ") while she
darned baby clothes.[62]

Canaris approved of these soirees at the Heydrich home because
they drew the two families together. He often told Lina Heydrich that
her husband was a good friend of his, sometimes adding that he
regarded him almost as a son.[63] Was it all an act dictated solely by the
advisability of keeping in touch with the Gestapa chief? Custodians of
the Canaris legend favour such an interpretation because the peculiar
rapport between the two adversaries does not accord with their picture
of Canaris the antifascist.[64]

The truth was more complex. The "blond beast," as Heydrich was
nicknamed inside the SS itself, fascinated the Abwehr chief. Heydrich
knew better than anyone how to appeal to Canaris's whimsical side, his
fondness for sudden changes of tack and love of juggling with alternatives. As for Canaris, he took pleasure in his opponent's manoeuvres
and subterfuges. It was significant that, of all sports, Heydrich had
made fencing his favourite pastime. Detecting and parrying hostile
moves, responding to unforeseen contingencies at lightning speed—all
these things had become second nature to him and evoked similar
qualities in Canaris.

They had many other traits in common, including lack of human
contact and a solitary streak which placed an insuperable barrier between them and those around them. They were also linked by memories
of time spent together in the Navy and by their common dislike of
Navy Chief Raeder, whom Heydrich blamed for his dismissal from the
service. Heydrich so often reminisced about the Navy that Canaris hit
on the idea of persuading Raeder to rehabilitate him. After much hesitation, Raeder restored Heydrich's right to wear naval uniform, but the
SS man rejected this intervention on his behalf. As Canaris ruefully
remarked to Bruno Streckenbach, one of Heydrich's officers, "I suppose
I've fallen between *all* the stools now!"[65]

But communal evenings with his "friend" did not prevent Heydrich from regarding Canaris as a dangerous competitor. He never tired of warning his immediate subordinates against the machinations of "that Levantine"[66] and repeatedly complained that Canaris was always "snooping and nosing around." Even today, Heydrich's widow echoes these sentiments: "Canaris was a spy. He did it for himself, not for any Reich or Führer. He spied for spying's sake."[67]

Even minor incidents of a personal nature were enough to inflame Heydrich's suspicions. When one of Canaris's daughters showed undue interest in the Gestapa chief's desk while visiting his study, he burst out, "Don't tell me the children are spying already!"[68]

He was even more perplexed by a permanent addition to the Canaris household. "By the way," he said to his wife one day with a mixture of annoyance and amusement, "Canaris has bought himself a man in Bordeaux—cost him twenty marks." The following night the Heydrichs curiously inspected this newcomer. He was an Algerian named Mohammed, and had been engaged as a butler.[69] The silent Mohammed, who served drinks even during official discussions between Canaris and Heydrich, soon got on the latter's nerves. Heydrich: "Look, I don't like that fellow always slinking round." Canaris: "No need to worry, Heydrich, he doesn't understand a word of German." Heydrich's direst suspicions were confirmed when Schmidt, a detective who guarded his house, reported having seen Mohammed dallying with "a lady" in the adjacent Canaris garden and heard him talking German. As far as Heydrich was concerned, that settled it. "Canaris even has his own guests spied on."[70]

Heydrich's superstitious dread of the supposedly omniscient spymaster gave way to mounting mistrust. The two men would have clashed, even at this stage, but for the peacemaking efforts of a new recruit to Heydrich's staff.

A third SS officer swam into Canaris's orbit: SS-Obersturmbannführer [Lieutenant Colonel] Dr. Werner Best, who early in January 1935 became head of Hauptabteilung I, the Gestapa section responsible for legal and administrative matters. Born in 1903, Best was the son of a Hessian postal official and had become a lawyer of philosophical and literary bent. He had for years espoused a rather conservative brand of German nationalism and believed that the ideal of the liberal and constitutional state should be replaced by a system based on pure political expediency. Best stripped the law of almost all its generally accepted meaning.[71] He also advocated a boundless expansion of police powers. "The tendency of the state is to perfect its authority; the more perfect the authority, the more perfect the state."[72] Heydrich did not notice until later that, for all his theoretical disparagement of "egocentric" human rights, Best still preserved a vestige of respect for legal concepts.

The Gestapa's short and dapper legal adviser inspired confidence in

Canaris, who was agreeably impressed by his reasonable and conciliatory manner. They, too, had much in common. Best shared Canaris's interest in Spain (he had translated the political testament of Primo de Rivera, the now defunct dictator-general, into German), was an ardent admirer of the Freikorps' "heroic realism" and cherished a profound "dislike of mass agitation" which had long deterred him from joining Hitler's movement.[73]

Such a man was ideally equipped to promote Canaris's plans for a *rapprochement* between the Abwehr and the Gestapo and SD. Best and Canaris got on well together. Even after the collapse of the Third Reich, Best wrote that he had "seldom met a fellow negotiator who negotiated more candidly and fulfilled his undertakings more faithfully than Canaris"; he had "come to know and respect him as a thoroughly honourable, well-meaning and morally percipient character."[74] Not surprisingly, Canaris was soon playing host to the Bests as well as the Heydrichs. Erika Canaris recalls: "Best was a great idealist, I suppose, but he always struck me as rather *'exalté.'* "[75]

Thanks to his close contacts with the leaders of the Gestapo and SD, Canaris quickly attained his goal. On January 17, 1935, the new partners signed a written agreement defining the powers of their respective organizations.[76]

Defined as "functions of the Wehrmacht" were: "1. Military espionage and counterespionage. 2. Intelligence work in the Reichswehr and in Reichswehr-owned concerns . . . 3. Supervision and implementation of all regulations enacted as safeguards against espionage . . . 4. Control and supervision of enrolment [of new officers] in the Wehrmacht. 5. Direction and determination of policy in all matters affecting national defence." A supplementary article stated: "It is incumbent on all departments in the Secret State Police and the Security Police of the Reichsführer-SS, including those of the Grenzpolizei [Frontier Police], to work closely with the relevant Abwehrstellen."

The Gestapo's powers embraced: "1. All functions of the Political Police (sole authorized executive agency); combating of all public enemies. 2. Frontier police and frontier intelligence service, aliens control and passport system. 3. General counterespionage police and counterespionage intelligence service inside the Reich borders. 4. Industrial counterespionage police, industrial security, industrial counterespionage intelligence service. 5. Telephonic and postal surveillance." Then came the powers of the SD. In addition to political functions of an internal nature, these covered "assistance (without executive power) in the field of industrial security, the industrial counterespionage intelligence service and the frontier intelligence service." The signatories resolved to oppose all other secret services, whether party-run or private. "Other, unofficial, intelligence services," they stated, "are not recognized and must be suppressed by all available means."[77]

Canaris was entitled to feel satisfied with this document. At least in theory, it drew a line between the rival intelligence services of the Wehrmacht and the SS police, shielded the Abwehr from interference by the other side and—more important still—established the Abwehr's predominant role in espionage and counterespionage. Credit for this did not belong solely to the new Abwehr chief. While negotiating, Canaris was able to cite a cabinet order of which a senior Gestapo official indignantly wrote that it represented "probably the most comprehensive blanket clause ever granted to an official department in the Third Reich."[78]

The Reich cabinet, with Hitler presiding, had in fact adopted a resolution on October 17, 1933, which stated: "The Reichswehr Minister shall take all steps essential to the preservation of national security and of interests relating to military policy in the field of counterespionage and propaganda. He will set out the requisite guidelines, which shall be observed by Reich departments and the Land authorities concerned."[79] In other words, the Abwehr Section of the Reichswehr Ministry was given responsibility for all matters relating to counterespionage. This prerogative had been lost during Patzig's turbulent reign. Canaris now regained it on the Abwehr's behalf.

He was able to uphold most of the Abwehr's interests because its rivals were still comparatively weak. The organizational problems of the police remained unsolved, just as it remained to be seen who would ultimately gain control over the police apparatus once it was "nationalized." The SD was just a limbless torso. Its head office personnel numbered only a few hundred, its functions were in dispute (Himmler: "The Sicherheitsdienst is only interested in major ideological questions") and its structure was so amorphous that—to quote one of its future commanders—"in 1936 there was absolutely no SD apparatus in the sense of an organization with intelligence coverage."[80] However little Canaris may have known about his rivals' internal problems, he must have sensed their uncertainty.

The Gestapo and SD duly hastened to confirm the Abwehr's leading role. On January 19, 1935, the Gestapa forwarded a directive from Reich Interior Minister Frick to the regional offices of the Geheime Staatspolizei enjoining them "to transmit, as speedily as possible, all incoming intelligence about military preparations and measures undertaken by France and other powers to the Abwehr offices of the military district headquarters responsible for their area."[81] This was followed on January 25 by a Gestapa admonition that the Geheime Staatspolizei had a duty to render the Wehrmacht "effective assistance . . . in its national defence tasks."[82]

Heydrich decreed: "Because personal contact is essential to smooth co-operation, any heads of Stapostellen who have not already done so shall forthwith introduce themselves to the head of the relevant Abwehrstelle and agree on detailed co-operation with him."[83] He summoned the regional Stapo chiefs to Berlin and lectured them on the proper way to treat their comrades in the Abwehr from now on.[84]

Heydrich also accompanied Canaris on visits to Abwehrstellen, addressed joint meetings of Abwehr personnel and SS officers and urged them to co-operate more closely. On February 7, Heydrich and Canaris visited the Abwehr's regional headquarters in Kiel, where the Gestapa chief delivered a programmatic address. An Abwehr report summarized it as follows: "Gruppenführer Heydrich explained the purpose of the meeting and the need for the closest co-operation between Abwehrstelle, Stapo and SD. Abwehrstelle in charge, prestige considerations to be excluded."[85] A few weeks later Canaris turned up in Bremen and Wilhelmshaven accompanied by Abwehr and SS officers. Once again, personnel were told that "the co-operation of all departments and organizations engaged in counterespionage must be ensured under the command of the milit[ary] Ast [Abwehrstelle]."[86]

Best, too, emphasized the Abwehr's dominant role. Referring to a report delivered by him to a Gestapa meeting, an Abwehr officer noted: "Dr. Best read out the cabinet decision of 24.10.1933.[87] He emphasized the mil[itary's] leadership, but also the Stapo's autonomy in its own province."[88] Abwehr officers took such assurances at their face value. They requested files from the Gestapo, summoned Gestapo personnel to attend Abwehr courses (sometimes on the strength of orders issued by military district headquarters) and occasionally took such a hand in Gestapo interrogations that even Canaris had to apply the brakes. Abwehr officers, he warned, had "no right to interfere with interrogations in any way."[89]

There were even times when the Abwehr took over, or at least sponsored, Gestapo assignments. A directive from Abwehr headquarters laid it down that an Abwehrstelle was to meet "any unavoidable expenses incurred by Stapo officers during surveillances wherever the Gestapa's budget and the SD's organization are insufficient to cover them."[90] To improve security in military training areas, Abwehrstellen were encouraged to request more Gestapo personnel. A directive from Abwehr III stated: "Requests for the establishment of Geheime Staatspolizei outstations should, after prior consultation with the appropriate Staatspolizeistelle, be addressed to Abw. complete with detailed reasons and particulars of the strength required."[91]

The SS-Verfügungstruppe, that bone of contention between the Army and Himmler, also came within the Abwehr's sphere of jurisdiction. Although the SS authorities were permitted to appoint a

"counterespionage representative," Himmler's man, SS-Standartenführer [Colonel] Tscharmann, was subordinate to the Abwehr Section
and had to follow its instructions. Unit commanders of the Verfügungstruppe were also obliged—pursuant to an order from Blomberg—"to
co-operate with the Abwehrstellen from which, when necessary, they receive instructions relating to the counterespionage service."[92] Even the
Reichsführerschulen of the SS, or Junker academies-to-be, were
"tended" by the Abwehr.[93]

Heydrich could no longer keep leaders of the earlier anti-Patzig
campaign in the upper echelons of the Gestapo. Abwehrpolizei Chief
Patschowsky was removed from his post in spring 1935, and middle-
ranking officers like Geschke, the head of the Kiel Gestapo, had to go
too.[94] Best, who had meanwhile been promoted SS-Standartenführer
and put in charge of the Abwehrpolizei, declared that "the headquarters are in full agreement, so the same must be required further
down the scale."[95]

The Tirpitz-Ufer staff looked on with some surprise and admiration
as their new chief extended the Abwehr's power and authority without
meeting any open resistance from its rival in Prinz-Albrecht-Strasse. Although many Abwehr officers were dismayed by Canaris's flexible
dealings with the opposition (Henke later insisted that Patzig had "recognized the SD's claim to totality more clearly than his successor, Canaris"[96]), most of his subordinates were glad that he had so evidently
struck the right note with the Gestapo and SD. All too many members
of the Abwehr were infected with the universal euphoria of the "national revolution" and its early successes, and few of them wanted to
drag their feet or earn a reputation for having failed to help rebuild the
new Germany.

The regime soon demanded their entire loyalty, because Hitler
chose this moment to embark on a succession of weekend foreign policy
coups which were to plunge Europe into a new era of crisis and bloodshed. At a stroke, he renounced the arms limitations of the Versailles
Treaty and granted his generals their dearest wish: rearmament.

Step by step, Germany's new master had broken up the French-led
postwar alliance against the main losers of World War I. In 1934 he
succeeded in loosening Franco-Polish ties by concluding a non-aggression pact with Poland. Shortly afterwards, British politicians showed
signs of coming to terms with the growing strength of Germany, and
even Italy—though temporarily deterred by violent Nazi agitation in
Austria—did not seem averse to a *rapprochement*. Then the French
gathered themselves for a diplomatic counterstroke by planning an
Eastern pact inclusive of the Soviet Union and directed against the
unpredictable Führer.[97]

The sweeping success of the plebiscite on January 13, 1935, which restored the Saar to the Reich after its postwar interlude as a territory under League of Nations mandate, nudged the French into precipitate action. On March 6 they announced the introduction of a two-year term of national service, and shortly afterwards they renewed the Franco-Belgian military pact. Just for a moment, it seemed to the more unsophisticated that the well-armed French intended a threat to their still poorly armed German neighbours. Hitler, who happened to be undergoing medical treatment in Munich, saw his chance and acted on it.[98]

Hitler's adjutant, Hossbach, was summoned to Munich on March 13 and told to attend his master at the Hotel Vierjahreszeiten next day. When he reported there on the morning of March 14, Hitler announced that he intended to reintroduce universal conscription and increase the strength of the Army. To what level? Hossbach only knew that, in their wildest dreams, the Heeresleitung authorities hankered after thirty-six divisions—as compared with the Reichswehr's seven in 1933. Hitler accepted Hossbach's figure on the spot.[99]

Without consulting Blomberg or Fritsch, Hitler proposed to introduce universal military service as soon as the French parliament had approved the extension of the call-up period. It took Hossbach a long time to persuade him that Blomberg should be notified in advance of the special Reich cabinet meeting planned for March 15.[100] Blomberg was horrified when he heard of Hitler's plan. Lieutenant General Ludwig Beck, the new head of the Truppenamt, also questioned Hitler's sanity because he had rejected a far smaller increase in the Army's strength some months before on the grounds that any such move would amount to "mobilization rather than the expansion of a peacetime army."[101] "What alarms me," Beck said anxiously, "is that we may become involved in a war before we are in a position to defend ourselves with any prospect of success. We must do our best to prevent it coming to that."[102]

Blomberg did, in fact, oppose Hitler's plans in cabinet whereas the civilian ministers promptly and enthusiastically endorsed them.[103] The Reichswehr Minister could not forget how ill prepared for war the German Reich was. Hitler's coup would have the effect of a "bomb" abroad,[104] so an armed conflict might break out at any moment. A few days later General von Fritsch supported him by remarking that "a fight . . . if it does come, cannot be more [for the German Army] than a desperate act of self-defence."[105]

But the weak-kneed Reichswehr chief did not withstand Hitler's pressure for long. The Chancellor summoned him and Fritsch next day, March 16, and explained why he thought war unlikely. Blomberg caved in, and the entire Reich cabinet approved of a "Proclamation of German Military Sovereignty" the same day.[106] "The cabinet members," reported the official Deutsches Nachrichtenbüro [German News

Agency], "rose spontaneously to their feet, and Reichswehr General von Blomberg gave three cheers for the Führer, coupled with a pledge of continuing steadfast loyalty and solidarity."[107]

Now the Abwehr went to work. The Reichswehr authorities still feared a violent reaction from Germany's neighbours, who had been taken completely by surprise. The French, Italian and British governments had already lodged diplomatic protests, so Canaris was instructed to keep watch on any military moves by a potential enemy. On March 29, 1935, he alerted his organization with a directive in the style of Nicolai: "Times of great international tension are a test of the intelligence service, its organization and mettle. I therefore expect all members of the Abwehr Section to do their utmost to meet the extreme demands of these days for the good of the Fatherland."[108]

The Abwehr was spurred to even greater activity by reports that the French, Italian and British heads of government planned to hold a summit meeting at Stresa on April 11 to decide on concerted moves against Germany. Canaris: "All Abwehrstellen must employ the time between now and the conference to brief their Spannungsleute [crisis teams], ensure that reports are submitted in a prompt and timely manner, and hold sufficient personnel in readiness for action at various times."[109] He repeatedly enjoined his agents "to ascertain what military developments, if any, are occurring in neighbouring countries."[110]

Canaris proceeded to check the effectiveness of his own organization by inspecting one Abwehrstelle after another. Early in April he began to enlist the help of friendly foreign colleagues. On April 4 he visited the Hungarian intelligence service headquarters in Budapest and came away convinced that the Hungarians "already take it for granted that we shall fight on the same side in any future war."[111] A memorandum on the trip recorded: "There is universal enthusiasm and admiration for our moves in defence policy and the rearmament question."[112]

He also established preliminary contacts with the Italian secret service, even though Italy rated as the prime mover of the hostile "Stresa front." Patzig had warned him against any involvement with the "untrustworthy" Italians, but Canaris, being favourably disposed towards the Latin life-style and mentality, believed he could make better use of the Italian intelligence service than his predecessor.[113] He had further been advised to seek contact with the Italians by the Hungarians, who exchanged information with them. Intermediaries set up a direct link between Canaris and Colonel Mario Roatta, his Italian opposite number, and their partnership was to prove of vital importance in the Spanish Civil War a year later.[114]

A few weeks' concentrated intelligence work were enough to convince Canaris that Hitler's daring coup would be meekly accepted by all the major foreign powers. The summit conference at Stresa came to nothing. Something unprecedented had happened—something whose effects were disastrous: Hitler had spectacularly succeeded in his first all-out gamble and poured scorn on the fears of the military.

Any lingering doubts the Reichswehr authorities may have felt were dispelled by these reports from the Abwehr. Docilely, Hitler's generals proceeded with his rearmament programme—and why not? The Führer had accomplished all they had fought and conspired for, everything for which they had jeopardized their careers, and sometimes their honour, during those dark and desperate postwar days in the "black" Reichswehr, when rearmament was still prohibited. Few of them paused to reflect where his policy might lead. All that mattered was the fulfilment of their long-standing dream and the final attainment of their objective, a nation in arms.

All Germany resounded to the tramp of boots and the rattle of tank tracks as one division after another joined the Army's swelling ranks. Its growth was well-nigh explosive. The Reichswehr had been 115,000 strong when Hitler came to power; by now, there were 350,000 men under arms.[115] Recruits flocked to the colours in such numbers that they swamped the country's barracks and training facilities. The generals tried to cure the resulting disorganization by slowing the pace of rearmament, but Hitler would have none of it: more and better soldiers were his sole requirement.

This onslaught swept away the last vestiges of military allegiance to the unloved Republic. The Reichswehr became the Wehrmacht and the Reichswehr Ministry was renamed the Reichskriegsministerium [Reich War Ministry]. The Truppenamt turned into the Generalstab des Heeres [Army General Staff] and the heads of the Heeresleitung and Marineleitung (from the beginning of March onwards there was also an air force under the command of Göring, now promoted general) were entitled to call themselves commanders in chief.[116]

Canaris, too, was cheered by the advent of rearmament, especially as his superiors had fulfilled one of his boyhood dreams. From May 1935 he wore the uniform of a rear admiral and was outwardly the personage that has since become an undying legend, "Admiral" Canaris.[117] This promotion accorded with the Abwehr's wider operational scope. Canaris's organization was now responsible for shielding incipient German rearmament from foreign agents. "With the introduction of universal military service," he had notified all Abwehrstellen on March 3, 1935, "we must allow for renewed and intensified action against the Wehrmacht and the German munitions industry by rival intelligence services. To be successful, our counterespionage campaign needs organizing on the wildest possible basis."[118] Canaris had visions of a close-knit surveillance network comprising "informants from all sectors of society" and covering every sphere of national existence from the munitions factory to the dance hall. Its object, in his own words, was "to screen our military organization from the eyes of the opposing intelligence service."[119]

In practice, this meant expanding Abwehr Group III, which was responsible for counterespionage. Abwehr III was the best-organized of the three classical components of the Abwehr Section (Group I: Secret Intelligence Service; Group II: Cipher Service; Group III: Counterespionage). Because of its largely defensive functions, Group III had been free to expand soon after World War I. It possessed a nucleus of experienced personnel who not only enjoyed a close working relationship but had successfully co-operated for years with the Political Police. As such, it provided Canaris with a springboard for his new schemes.

The accelerated expansion of Group III brought him into close contact with a counterespionage virtuoso. Major Rudolf Bamler, born in 1896, was the son of a Stettin doctor. An artilleryman and staff officer, he had headed Abwehr Group III since 1933 and was regarded by many insiders as the real brains of the Abwehr.[120] "Intelligent, socially self-assured, skilled in dealing with people and . . . of good appearance" (to quote a brother officer), Bamler had drafted most of the basic Abwehr directives and operational guidelines relevant to the combating of hostile espionage during this period.[121]

Bamler's own ambition and his wife's social aspirations moved him to bestow absolute allegiance on National Socialism at an early stage. He had kept in close personal touch with Heydrich long before Canaris pronounced this the duty of all his departmental chiefs, though the Bamler-Heydrich link had an official motivation as well. Unlike the section's other groups, Abwehr III was dependent on the help of the Gestapo, which alone possessed the authority to carry out arrests. The speed with which Bamler joined the Nazis, as he later did the Communists (he became chief inspector of the East German Volkspolizei after World War II), has made him an ideal target of postwar abuse for West Germans eager to unload the burdens of the past.[122] To them, as Resistance writer Hans Bernd Gisevius puts it, Bamler is a sort of "tanned" [i.e. superficially Brownshirt] snooper—an "infamous fellow."[123]

In fact, Bamler was a popular and sympathetic superior whom many of his colleagues regarded as a "good pal."[124] Canaris, too, valued the expert knowledge of his shrewdest departmental chief while remaining somewhat aloof from him as a person. Together, they proceeded to draw a fine web of surveillance and supervision over the armed forces, munitions factories, seaports—even the press.

Canaris and Bamler started off with a propaganda campaign in the Wehrmacht. Old units and new were inundated with leaflets and pamphlets in which the Abwehr Section inoculated the troops with ever

CANARIS

more urgent injunctions to be on their guard against foreign spies. Canaris's men balked at no catch phrase or slogan, however crude, in encouraging the armed forces to remain alert and give the state their absolute loyalty. One of Abwehr III's effusions, a leaflet entitled "Espionage, Counterespionage and Treason," stated: "Treason is a crime which presupposes a treacherous disposition . . . Anyone who dares to raise a hand against his country is doomed to die!"[125]

The directives and guidelines issued by Abwehr headquarters placed the armed forces on a standing alert. Security regulations were tightened up and permanent checks instituted. "The private life of those privy to official secrets," declared the head of Abwehr III on March 9, 1935, "requires constant surveillance. Sporadic checks are essential, both on duty and off."[126] Those in possession of military secrets were to have their briefcases examined before leaving the premises, and private telephone calls were forbidden. Bamler: "During office hours, mutual visits by staff, and particularly by outside personnel, must be restricted to a minimum, both in frequency and duration, because they can lend themselves to treasonable purposes."[127]

Canaris harnessed the press and cinema to his "Vorsicht, Feind hört mit" [English equivalent: "Careless talk costs lives"] campaign. In 1936 he got the director Karl Ritter to make the spy film Verräter [Traitors] using Abwehr men and equipment—a production which the U.S. cultural historian Frederick V. Grunfeld has pronounced typical of the films designed to prepare the public mind for all-out mobilization.[128] Every Volksgenosse ["compatriot," the Nazi equivalent of the Communist "comrade"] had to join the fight against foreign espionage. Canaris aimed to enlist the whole of the press as well. Articles—naturally written by Abwehr officers—were to be "appropriate to a given circle of readers, interesting . . . and instructive."[129] Bamler announced that, for pieces considered especially suitable, the "Herr Chef Abw" was offering prizes of up to RM100.[130]

Canaris insisted on supporting the campaign with some contributions of his own. He repeatedly warned against the enemy's machinations. To quote one of his personal directives: "Foreign intelligence services have recently shown signs of systematic action in various parts of the Reich aimed at the forcible acquisition of material . . . Abwehrstellen must ensure that all departments of the three armed services are alerted forthwith."[131] Canaris, who was fascinated by the phenomenon of treason, retained an indelible memory of the journalistic treason practised by the ultra-left-wing Weltbühne and other organs of extremist opinion under the Republic. He could not have guessed what a fateful role the topic was to play in his own life.

Always loud in his abhorrence of foreign espionage and native treason, Canaris often reviled culprits in print. In 1937, when a German

Army captain named Dempwolf was executed for spying on behalf of Czechoslovakia, he roundly condemned the man. His readers were informed that Dempwolf had been induced to spy for the enemy by lack of funds and hope of financial gain. Canaris: "And for that, he—an officer—betrayed his native land, sacrificed his life and honour and plunged his own and other families into unutterable misfortune."[132]

The Abwehr's X-ray machine irradiated would-be members and employees of the armed forces with special intensity. Abwehrstellen were under strict orders from Canaris to screen recruits carefully before engaging them. Apart from checking the central card index at Abwehr headquarters, they had to consult the files of the Gestapo, which meant that Canaris's officers often borrowed the latter's ideological categories. "In every case," Canaris stipulated, "the applicant must be required to sign a written declaration . . . stating whether he has been an official of the Marxist parties . . . [and] that he unreservedly supports the government."[133]

Rear Admiral Canaris took it for granted that Adolf Hitler's Wehrmacht had no room for left-wing ex-Republicans. "For counterespionage reasons," he declared, "the following are precluded from enlistment": aliens, Germans with criminal records, "ex-officials of the SPD and KPD and persons who have been particularly active in the Marxist cause."[134] In August 1937, when Abwehrstelle Dresden recommended Hans Winter, a leading member of the since disbanded Reichsbanner, a pro-Republican organization, for service in the Wehrmacht, Canaris expressed strong reservations: "Senior rank in the Reichsbanner should be regarded as exceptionally active employment in the Marxist cause." He did, however, make the Winter decision dependent on "whether the said person has, or has not, demonstrated his political reliability since the [National Socialist] assumption of power. This question is to be settled by A[bwehr-]ST[elle] in conjunction with the Gestapo."[135]

Adopting propaganda language of this type, Canaris and Bamler refined and perfected the work of their counterespionage organization. The Abwehrstellen in the nine military districts (which had grown to thirteen by the end of 1937) were directed to set up their own intelligence and surveillance teams. A mini-organization came into being. "Hauskapelle" [private orchestra] was the term applied by outstations to a team led by a "Kapellmeister" [conductor, i.e. senior agent] and usually comprising between three and half a dozen agents. This team worked outside its Abwehrstelle but had to remain in constant touch with the Führungsoffizier ["guidance officer" or controller] based there. Its task: to keep watch on suspects.[136]

These Hauskapellen signalled the emergence of a new branch of the intelligence service—an Abwehr within the Abwehr, as it were—to which Canaris lent special encouragement. Until he was appointed, counterespionage and antisabotage operations had been confined to German territory, and the efforts of foreign secret services had been combated with the police resources available to traditional counterespionage. Canaris now proposed to supplement and reinforce his counterespionage system by going over to the offensive. Skilled agents were to penetrate foreign intelligence agencies and investigate their operations against Germany from within or cause disruption by feeding them "Spielmaterial" [doctored information].[137] The Admiral had a predilection for this kind of double game and took a growing interest in it, so it was only natural that he entrusted the new counterespionage subgroup (IIIF) to one of his closest associates, Lieutenant Commander Richard Protze, known to his friends as "Uncle Richard."[138]

One of the main tasks of the Hauskapellen was to recruit agents capable of infiltrating foreign intelligence services. They were joined by a second group of informants, the "Hotelorganisation."[139] This comprised waiters, porters and chambermaids who worked for Canaris's representatives at nearly all the hotels in the vicinity of each Abwehrstelle. Their job was to keep watch on suspected agents, but also to prospect for foreigners who might lend themselves to employment abroad on behalf of German counterespionage.[140]

IIIF officers based at outstations near the frontiers were to cooperate with the Grenzpolizei in persuading foreign nationals to engage in counterespionage across the border. IIIF also concentrated on diplomatic establishments in Berlin, where foreign intentions were gauged by agents insinuated into legations and embassies.[141]

Government departments and munitions factories provided another target for Canaris's spy-hunters. Hitler's rearmament policy gave birth to a new munitions industry which presented the Abwehr with additional problems. Together with the Gestapo and SD, the Abwehr screened the staff of militarily important concerns for "politically unreliable" elements. Bamler made a note of the lines on which the "counterespionage service" should be organized in arms-producing firms: "(a) inner circle: SD with illegal surveillance of firm; (b) outer circle: Stapo with surveillance of labour force, tourism, etc.; (c) counterespionage from abroad."[142]

Given that the Abwehr was charged with maintaining security in the munitions industry and ensuring compliance with all counterespionage regulations by civil authorities as well, few government departments in the Third Reich remained uninfiltrated by the Admiral's informants. At the request of Bamler's officers, government authorities and industrial concerns had to appoint security representatives who were responsible to the Abwehrstellen and whose activities were concealed from the rest of the staff.[143]

Abwehrstelle representatives even claimed supervisory powers in the field of foreign policy secrets. Rittmeister [Captain of Cavalry] Kratzer, an officer from the Stuttgart Abwehrstelle, called on the firm of Zeiss to take "all steps necessary to safeguard the military and foreign policy secrets entrusted to it from espionage and treason."[144] Bamler's group also produced a "Leaflet on Defence Against Espionage and Treason" which stated: "Persons to whom a military or foreign policy secret is entrusted must faithfully comply with the directives issued for its safekeeping."[145]

Before long, the whole country was shrouded in an invisible veil of Abwehr informants and agents. The counterespionage net drew tighter as more and more informants penetrated the farthest reaches of German society. Bamler set a good example. In the Königin-Bar, a rendezvous popular with foreign attachés and tourists, he employed fifteen hostesses to pump patrons on the Abwehr's behalf and quite often supervised their work in person from behind a glass of champagne.[146]

Canaris was always offering criticism and suggestions designed to improve his surveillance system. While visiting Bremen he inspected the security precautions of the Weser concern. Bamler noted shortly afterwards: "Management still lacks an understanding of counterespionage duties. Improvement expected after appointment of new counterespionage representative. Another visit . . . required in near future."[147] A little later Canaris wrote: "W[ilhelms]haven dockyard suffers in respect of security from overextensive visits [by] 'Kraft durch Freude' [Strength Through Joy, the Nazi recreational and tourist organization]. Should at least be restricted."[148] And in Münster he complained: "Problems in III field owing to Münster's very remote position . . . Own system of informants, not Stapo."[149]

He was also irritated by the fact that munitions factories still employed "politically unreliable" persons or that workers dismissed at the Abwehr's instigation consulted the legal advice bureaux of the Deutsche Arbeitsfront [DAF, or German Labour Front] for help against the "purgers." Abwehr IIIWi-W [Industrial and Economic Security] noted with some relief on July 2, 1936, that the president of the Reich Bureau of Employment and Unemployment Insurance had directed that "those workers or salaried employees who are debarred from employment in munitions factories or have been dismissed from the same for reasons of political unreliability shall have an 'O' entered in ink in the 'Remarks' section of their employment card."[150]

Canaris soon devised a means of forestalling interference by the DAF. Whenever workers were fired on security grounds, Abwehrstellen had to notify the DAF promptly and in confidence that all such dismissals had been made "in the interests of national defence."[151] But the Admiral had yet another way of dealing with protests by workers.

Canaris on July 3, 1936: "Abw[ehr] has requested the Wehrmacht Legal Section to submit draft legislation to the Reich Ministry of Justice under which complaints of unfair dismissal will be rejected by labour tribunals whenever the plaintiff has been dismissed from a munitions firm at the instance of an official department."[152]

Even the "co-ordinated" press sometimes attracted the Admiral's critical attention. Abwehrstelle officers were further instructed to supervise compliance with "guidelines for military reporting," which prescribed: "1. The reproduction of spy stories . . . and similar factual reports in newspapers and periodicals are [sic] forbidden. 2. All items of information about military and naval premises are subject to the strictest limitations on reporting . . . 3. Reports of promotions, transfers and appointments may be published only when released by the DNB [German News Agency]."[153] No journalist dared to violate these guidelines because Canaris's officers swiftly retorted with charges of treason.

Despite this, the Abwehr chief was sometimes annoyed by the press and, more particularly, by the "Situations Vacant" columns in trade journals.[154] He repeatedly admonished editors because—as he complained on June 30, 1937—"where press acceptance of notices advertising situations is concerned . . . these [security] measures in the interests of national defence do not everywhere receive sufficient attention."[155]

Press, munitions factories, government departments, armed forces— the influence of Canaris's surveillance system extended far and wide. Unbeknown to them, many Germans became objects and sometimes victims of covert Abwehr investigation, and many workers, branded by the Admiral's men with the often lethal stigma of political unreliability, lost their jobs because they failed to fit into the regime's mass mobilization programme. The Hitlerian system drew strength from the Abwehr as well as the Gestapo.

This expansion of the Abwehr's field of activities compelled it to recruit additional personnel at an ever increasing rate. Newly enrolled or freshly seconded officers, civil servants and clerical staff, informants, "Tipper" [tipsters] and other personnel streamed into the offices of the intelligence service with the same feverish haste that characterized the expansion of the armed forces as a whole. Within a few months the Abwehr had developed, at least outwardly, into an impressive secret service. By June 1937, having entered the Hitler era only 150 strong, it numbered 956 officers, civilian officials and clerical staff, of whom 327 were based at Abwehr headquarters alone.[156]

And still the Admiral continued to recruit more men. He combed every sector of society, buttonholed friends and acquaintances and scoured the personnel departments of the Army and other services in a constant quest for potential Abwehr employees. His advice to many acquaintances was: "Make sure you become a reserve officer. Then you'll have your Wehrmacht uniform and won't need to dress any other way —we're all in uniform these days."[157]

Canaris opened up the Abwehr, that long-time staff officer's preserve, to former combat and regimental officers who either had been forced to leave the Army's depleted ranks after the war or had, at best, returned to serve in the capacity of civilian employees. These men could now be re-engaged as E-Offiziere [Ergänzungsoffiziere—supernumerary or re-engaged officers], a designation which implied inferior status but did not preclude the possibility that its bearer might one day be readmitted to full membership in the serving officer corps.

Most of the ex-officers who worked as civilian Abwehr employees were appointed E-Offiziere by Canaris shortly after he took over. Among them was Major Hans Oster, who had been dismissed from the Reichswehr for a personal misdemeanour and had re-entered the Army's service by devious means. Oster headed Referat [Desk] IIIC1 (counterespionage outside the Wehrmacht but exclusive of industry) and was destined to play a crucial role in the Admiral's life.[158]

Then came the first wave of new Abwehr personnel, mostly brother officers and contemporaries of Canaris who were attracted by his reputation or had their own—political—reasons for entering the Abwehr's service. These included Friedrich Wilhelm Heinz, ex-member of the Ehrhardt Brigade, author of books on the "national revolution" (*Sprengstoff, Nation greift an*) and an ex-SA officer who had become disenchanted with the Nazis; the lawyer Franz Liedig, who had long acted as a contact man between Canaris and Ehrhardt; and the Stahlhelm [v. Glossary] leader Werner Schrader, an anti-Nazi who criticized Hitler's conservative partners for their feeble acquiescence and was seeking refuge from harassment by the Gestapo.[159]

These were followed by a second wave of Abwehr candidates—men whom Germany's rearmament had tempted to quit their civilian jobs and climb back into uniform. Ex-Major Joachim Rohleder, a product of the Lichterfelde cadet school who had seen war service with the 8th Leib-Grenadier-Regiment [Grenadier Guards], gave up his commercial post in Argentina;[160] the ex-naval officer Wilhelm Leissner wound up his publishing business in Nicaragua;[161] the ex-cavalry officer Heinz Schmalschläger bade farewell to his mattress factory;[162] and the ex-Air Force officer Nikolaus Ritter was moved to return to Germany by a change of ownership in the U.S. textile company of which he was a director.[163] In each of these cases, the main motive was an overriding desire to help expand the Wehrmacht.

But not all came voluntarily. The Russian expert Erich Ferdinand Pruck, who had just been invalided out of the Wehrmacht after a riding accident and was now attending the Oriental Seminar at Berlin University, was recruited under protest. He did not agree to join until some Abwehr officers hinted that further resistance might be construed as opposition to the state and put his pension in jeopardy.[164] As for SS-Hauptsturmführer [Captain] Otto Wagner, he joined only because he had fallen out with the party and SA and bowed to the advice of his friend Best, who recommended him for service in the Abwehr.[165]

Recruits were accepted regardless of background. Whenever Canaris saw a chance of acquiring new subordinates, he grabbed it. The NSDAP's Auslandsorganisation [Nazi agency responsible for the care and supervision of Germans abroad] suggested putting reliable party members at the Abwehr's disposal; Canaris accepted.[166] The Sudeten German Paul Fidrmuc, an ex-officer in the Austro-Hungarian Army, applied for a post in the Abwehr.[167] So did the Catholic cavalry officer Count Rudolf von Marogna-Redwitz, an anti-Nazi who had once belonged to IIIB. So did the veteran Nazi and friend of Himmler, Paul Thümmel, who applied for a job with Abwehrstelle Dresden. In all these varied cases, Canaris ensured that the applicants were accepted.[168]

Yet another group of candidates flocked to join. These were officers and employees of the Political Police anxious to leave Heydrich's orbit before the Gestapo entirely degenerated into a barbarous instrument of oppression. Government ministries, too, were deserted by officials and employees interested in acquiring Abwehr jobs and the right to wear military uniform.

The more the Abwehr's ranks were swelled by new recruits, the more heterogeneous—indeed, disharmonious—its composition became. Until 1935 the Abwehr mentality had been characterized by a single human type: the outwardly unpolitical Reichswehr officer who, dominated by an abstract ideal of service and remote from society, lived in accordance with the arrogant dictum of the Reichswehr's great preceptor Hans von Seeckt: "The Army serves the state and only the state, for it *is* the state."[169]

This type was personified by the officer who had grown up under the monarchy, whose direct relationship to his supreme commander had been the mainspring of his own existence, and who, during the postwar turmoil, had yielded to a nebulous "political militarism" based on nothing more nor less than the belief that no soldier could exist unless inwardly at one with the nation and state. The other, or third, type of officer was represented by young men already under the spell of National Socialism and seething with an activist belief in progress—with what the historian Klaus-Jürgen Müller describes as "a blurred and fuzzy idealism, a 'futuristic emotionalism' in which vague national-revolutionary and national-social ideas were allied with antiliberal and antiparliamentary sentiments."[170]

And here we perceive the signs of conflicts and differences whose resolution was bound to be hard. All that made them partially tolerable was that, whatever category they belonged to, most Abwehr officers hailed from the same social background (middle or upper middle class) and possessed a common conception of the state. They all believed in the renascence of Germany as a great power, dismissed the possibility of any but an authoritarian system of government prescribed by Germany's history and geographical position, and were, in consequence, sworn foes of democracy. None shed a tear for the Republic and each expected Hitler's national upheaval to herald a supreme resurgence of national strength.

There was no room here for criticism of the National Socialist regime, let alone outright opposition. "I welcomed the NS movement," Wagner confesses, "as a great and socially oriented party which promised to change the lot of the unemployed millions and release Germany from the shackles of the Versailles Treaty."[171] Fidrmuc noted later: "The National Socialist revolution could not manage without draconian measures, particularly in the early period. A clash with Russia was inevitable sooner or later."[172] Bamler's sloganeers reduced these sentiments to a simple formula: "Your watchword: Loyalty to the Führer! Protection for the German people! Death to the traitor!"[173]

This is not the language of that spirit of resistance which the Abwehr's literary apologists claim to have discerned in it at an early stage. Like every other institution in the Third Reich, the Abwehr reflected the National Socialist spirit of the age. Many of its officers were hardly aware of their bland reliance on the most dreaded instruments of Nazi repression. Referring to "Frontier Violations by Foreign Military Personnel," for example, the head of Subgroup IIIC had no qualms about noting: "Removal to concentration camp. Foreign Legionnaires to camp. Dispatch Abw-Offz [Abwehr officer] to interrogate."[174] Even the persecution of the Jews cast a shadow over the Abwehr. Excerpt from the minutes of a meeting of industrial experts from Abwehr III: "Jewish businesses to be directly or indirectly identified as such."[175]

Not even Captain (E) Heinz, the frustrated ex-Brownshirt who now headed Referat IIIC3 and was thus responsible for "statistics, educational material, propaganda and counterpropaganda/press, pictorial matter, films, radio," could resist the impact of German rearmament. His propaganda material called for the mobilization of the armed forces and the masses, and he often encouraged Abwehr headquarters in its rabble-rousing efforts to stigmatize all negligence and carelessness as unpatriotic.[176]

But the Abwehr lacked internal cohesion because of the widely differing mentalities that had to compete and come to terms within it. Political differentiation went hand in hand with variations in quality.

Not everyone who joined the Abwehr was suited to intelligence work, and too many of its staff were simply out for a new uniform or a new job. Although some of the newcomers proved to be competent intelligence officers (Rohleder distinguished himself as a wily counterespionage chief from 1938 onwards, Schmalschläger became a master of the counterploy and Leissner made a good controller), the bulk of the Abwehr's employees betrayed definite signs of amateurism.

No able and career-minded officer could be expected to fulfil his ambitions by drafting assessments of agents' reports and living in the monastic anonymity of a secret service. Consequently, most of the work at Abwehr headquarters devolved on inexperienced and hurriedly promoted E-Offiziere who had been wrested from civilian occupations unrelated to espionage and entrusted with tasks for which they were unequipped by general staff training or a practical knowledge of military intelligence.

The result was a lack of expertise and efficiency which prevented the Abwehr from exceeding a mediocre level of performance, either then or later, because the new men received no adequate in-service training. Rearmament proceeded at such a pace that the Abwehr never had time to consolidate its structure or even to revise its standing orders, which were long outdated. "For all their . . . devotion to duty," Pruck complains, "many of the officers thus recruited, who were swiftly promoted to senior rank on the strength of paper seniority unsupported by years of actual service, failed in numerous respects to meet the requirements of their status."[177]

Any motley and disunited body needs a leader with the personal aura and creative ability to reduce conflicting temperaments and sectional interests to a common denominator, mould a diffuse collection of heterogeneous personalities into an organization powered by a common resolve, and imbue it with enough team spirit to withstand any crisis. Canaris did not possess these qualities. He lacked the charisma without which no large body of men can be successfully led. His forte lay in private discussion, personal contacts and committee work. Faced with a sizeable crowd of people, he lost his powers of persuasion.

In this respect he fell far short of the ideal intelligence chief which superficial observers believed him to be. His appointment to the Abwehr was based on the popular but erroneous notion that a secret service should be directed by someone in the nature of a super-spy. He did not realize (and probably never discovered) that secret service chiefs are primarily bureaucrats and that, paradoxical as it may sound, their talent for espionage is less in demand than their administrative competence. The greatness of a secret service chief depends solely on whether he can lead and motivate people—whether he commands the ability to control a vast departmental apparatus and cope with the wearisome minutiae of bureaucratic routine.

Intelligence work is, first and foremost, paper work. The installation and maintenance of card indexes, the compiling of intelligence digests and situation reports, the systematic perusal and evaluation of published sources (periodicals and newspapers, specialized literature and official data)—all these occupy the forefront of intelligence work and take priority over the operations of secret agents. But the secret service chief must never lose sight of his organization's many and various activities. He must be able to co-ordinate and delegate without relinquishing his supervisory function. This chains him to his desk and makes him an indefatigable reader of files, analyses and operational reports, for there is nothing more disastrous than an intelligence chief who does not know what goes on under his own roof.

But Canaris was bored and fatigued by bureaucratic work of this kind. True to the habits of a lifetime, he would escape from Abwehr headquarters and vacate his directorial chair for days on end. Canaris felt drawn to the men "at the front," as the current phrase went—to the Abwehr outstations and substations whose primary task was to direct secret intelligence operations abroad. He often turned up unannounced, asked for a situation report and then issued new instructions which were so much at variance with the basic ideas of his departmental chiefs that it became customary for someone from Abwehr headquarters to follow in his footsteps and discreetly amend the orders he had just given.[178]

Canaris was also fond of visiting southern Europe, sometimes travelling incognito because conspiratorial behaviour accorded with his notion of a state-employed super-spy. He occasionally undertook minor intelligence operations for which any local agent would have been better qualified. Once, while driving through the Black Forest on his way home from an undercover trip to Spain, he ran into a snowstorm. Abwehr headquarters spent days trying to locate him because he had taken refuge in a remote farmhouse where, soaked to the skin, he persuaded a peasant woman to nurse him until the risk of pneumonia had passed. On hearing this, Heydrich scoffed, "Is *that* how they run the Abwehr?"[179]

The peculiar restlessness which drove this "eternal voyager"[180] from one country and one Abwehr outstation to the next had a detrimental effect on life at headquarters. The Admiral's impatience and lack of psychology bred a disagreeable working atmosphere. He had little time for subordinates of medium or junior grade, and many of those who briefed him were discouraged by his brusque interjections of "*Kürzer, kürzer!*" [Make it snappy!].[181] Although he almost invariably proved amenable when accosted by secretaries who buttonholed their boss as he strolled absently down the passage and asked for a raise, his arbitrary approach to personnel decisions was a frequent source of disquiet.[182]

"Canaris was the most difficult superior I came up against in my thirty-year career," one of his departmental chiefs wrote later, and called him "contradictory in his instructions, unjust, moody and unpredictable."[183] He was no judge of character, readily succumbed to flattery and promoted many incompetent opportunists. His benevolent interest could be aroused by anyone who acquired a dog or sprinkled birdseed on his window sill while the boss was looking. His arbitrary personnel policy was an incitement to intrigue. One authority confirms that there was "no *esprit de corps*, only mistrust, jealousy and suspicion."[184]

Even Wagner, who admired Canaris, sometimes shrank from the "positively grotesque fits of temperament" which earned the Admiral so many enemies at headquarters,[185] nor did it benefit his reputation to squash experts when their views conflicted with his own preconceptions. As one who was later to voice justified complaints about Hitler's reluctance to accept unvarnished intelligence reports, he sometimes had difficulty in swallowing unpalatable facts himself. His experts in Spain, Italy and the East found it hard to secure a hearing for views that clashed with his own. Many advisers got their reports back blue-pencilled by Canaris and adorned with the apodictic comment "This is utter nonsense!"[186]

More seriously, Canaris made only halfhearted efforts to supervise his ever expanding organization. His absences from headquarters were so frequent that, as one insider remarks, "Canaris was totally uninformed about many developments."[187] He relied too heavily on his group and subgroup heads to keep the big machine in running order. "Without them," observes another Abwehr critic, "the whole thing would have been complete chaos."[188] Not unnaturally, many of the great man's subordinates itched to step into his shoes.

Among those beset by this temptation was the coolly ambitious Bamler, who resented it that Canaris left the real work to his group heads without improving their official status. Bamler often paid Sunday visits to the Heydrichs and complained over the bridge table that Canaris was letting the Abwehr "go hang." Frau Heydrich says: "Bamler was the sort who couldn't keep quiet. He was our best contact man inside the Abwehr." Heydrich repeatedly urged him to join the Gestapo, but a sense of loyalty kept him with the Abwehr.[189]

Bamler did, however, devote some thought to plans which would have neutralized Canaris or at least relegated him to the political and diplomatic sphere. By August 1937 he felt secure enough to draft a memorandum proposing that the Abwehr be reorganized in his favour. Bamler's programme: Canaris to be appointed head of department, all group heads to be promoted heads of section, and the Admiral's burdens to be eased by the appointment of a deputy.[190]

. Couched in Bamler's veiled language, this read as follows: "The duties of the head of the Abwehr [are] now so extensive and fraught with such varied responsibilities that it has proved impossible for this burden to devolve on *one* head of section." In addition, the head of Abwehr Group III, alias Bamler himself, "despite his effective responsibility for the implementation of Abwehr duties inside the Reich and their organization beyond the Reich borders, currently occupies a position which is not, from the purely superficial aspect, commensurate with those duties." For all his careful phrasing, Bamler disclosed in a subsequent sentence that his projected reform was fundamentally aimed at Canaris himself. "The head of department shall be assigned a senior general staff officer to ensure the maintenance of a uniformly consistent line and the uniform representation of all sections, having additional regard to the head of the Abwehr's frequent absences."[191] There is no doubt that Bamler's "senior general staff officer" was an allusion to himself.

But Bamler's initiative came to nothing and his chief's authority remained intact. The Admiral's failures of leadership largely escaped the notice of his superiors at the War Ministry, not least because he was now expanding a branch of intelligence in which he seemed specially qualified—the Geheimer Meldedienst or secret service proper. Knowledge of foreign countries, familiarity with the world of conspiracy and intrigue, intuition and a flair for the irrational—all these attributes predestined Canaris for a leading role in what romanticisers of espionage like to call "the war in the dark."

Ever since moving into his Tirpitz-Ufer office, Canaris had seen himself as a spy-master—supreme commander of an unseen army of agents and informants who penetrated the enemy's key positions, detecting, observing and recording his every move. Fascinated by the world of dead-letter boxes, secret couriers and furtive goings-on, Canaris insisted on personally interviewing every Abwehr agent who visited Berlin. His interest in the minutiae of the spy's profession was insatiable. Invisible inks preoccupied him as deeply as modern radio equipment or the marvels of microphotography.

The Admiral's curiosity was intense enough to survive his initial disappointment at learning that the Abwehr by no means possessed the huge host of informants at whose head he thought he had been placed. Lieutenant Colonel Grimmeiss's Abwehr Group I, which controlled the Geheimer Meldedienst, only maintained a handful of Friedensagenten [peacetime agents] in Poland, France and Czechoslovakia to report on peacetime troop movements and reconnoitre defence installations. Being almost invariably foreigners, they attracted attention in the event of increased political tension or actual hostilities between Germany and the country where they operated. In such cases, "Spannungsagenten" [S or "tension" agents] and "Kriegsagenten" [A or wartime agents] were required. The former were supposed to furnish the Abwehr with reports on hostile mobilization measures and the latter to carry out intelligence assignments behind the enemy lines, but Grimmeiss possessed very few agents of this type.

Canaris tried to change things fast. Abwehr outstations were instructed to set up A and S networks as well as recruit more peacetime agents. While visiting Abwehrstelle Münster, Canaris told its officers that "the current priority" was to "build up a peace-and wartime organization."[192] The Abwehrstellen were also assigned new fields of intelligence work. More outstations and substations were created and existing offices transferred to other cities. Münster, for example, was instructed to cover Holland, and Canaris pronounced Abwehrstelle Wilhelmshaven to be merely "an armed forces canteen" and so badly sited that he had it transferred to Bremen.[193]

It was not long before the A and S agents percolated into their future operational areas. The Abwehr outstations slowly improved their intelligence work abroad. Abwehrstelle Bremen initiated "a systematic intelligence survey of the French Navy, as far at least as the Channel and the Atlantic seaboard were concerned, via Holland and Belgium (the so-called northern France route),"[194] while Abwehrstelle Münster sent its agents swarming into Holland with the help of the Cologne substation, which maintained S agents, forwarding offices and scouts ("travel agents") in Belgium and northern France.[195] German firms also placed their foreign representatives at the Abwehr's disposal. Canaris personally commended I Wi, Abwehr I's industrial and economic subgroup, for services rendered: "I Wi has accurately discerned its objectives: to keep watch on the enemy munitions industry, discover its productive capacity and ascertain the local situation."[196]

Uncertainty still prevailed over how S agents would transmit reports to their controllers in case of real emergency. Each agent was under orders to repair to his allotted area at a prearranged code word and report any sign of hostile military preparations. His reports had to be obliquely worded (though not encoded) and were usually mailed to a "U-Stelle" [cover address] in the frontier area, whence they were forwarded to Germany by courier.[197] For frontier-based S agents the Abwehr constructed photophones which transmitted oral messages via invisible beams of light.[198]

Early in 1936, when the S network's communications system was still undeveloped, Canaris had to activate his new apparatus because Hitler was pursuing his "strategy of crisis" to the brink of war. Once again the Führer took advantage of a move in the French policy of security and encirclement, and once again he presented his wavering generals with a *fait accompli*.

His target this time was the last remnant of the Versailles peace settlement, the demilitarized German territory on the west bank of the Rhine. Its status reposed not only on the peace treaty of 1919 but on the Locarno Pact of 1925, in which Germany, France and Belgium had joined Great Britain and Italy in guaranteeing the western frontiers of the Reich as laid down at Versailles. The German government of the time had agreed to the continued demilitarization of the Rhineland in return for an assurance from the French that they would launch no unprovoked attack on Germany. The practical effect of this was that, should a conflict arise between the two countries, France could "occupy the demilitarized zone even before advance elements of the German Army crossed the Rhine bridges."[199]

Such was the Achilles' heel which Hitler and his generals found so intolerable, but War Minister von Blomberg flinched when he heard that Hitler was thinking of occupying the demilitarized Rhineland. He did not take the Führer's ideas seriously, being only too aware that any such incursion might lead to war and that the Wehrmacht's ten divisions could never fight on several fronts against the two hundred-odd divisions of the other Locarno powers.

But the gambler in Hitler discounted any risk of war and hoped that French diplomacy would, as it had already done in the case of rearmament, furnish him with suitable grounds for a surprise move. He was right. On May 2, 1935, the French Government concluded a mutual assistance pact with the Kremlin, and a fortnight later the Czechs—with French encouragement—signed a similar treaty. Hitler promptly pointed out that the Franco-Soviet agreement might compel the French to intervene against Germany whereas the Locarno Pact had pledged them to refrain from armed conflict. Thus, the new treaty was an implicit violation of the Locarno Pact.[200]

Hitler's sixth sense dissuaded him from making any immediate use of the Franco-Soviet treaty. He was still unsure of the League of Nations' reaction and did not know what steps, if any, the guaranteeing powers would take. For the moment, he confined himself to instructing Blomberg to produce a general staff study for the occupation of the Rhineland. "Schulung" ["Training," the code name for this operation] would be "executed by a surprise stroke delivered with lightning speed" but was officially described as a military exercise.[201] Hitler's personal order was that "only the very smallest number of officers should be informed." The operation was, in fact, mounted so surreptitiously that even Beck, the Chief of the General Staff, believed "Schulung" to be a training exercise.[202]

Not even Blomberg believed that Hitler would dare send the Wehrmacht marching into the Rhineland. He failed to notice how greatly the Führer's plans were furthered by Italy's wanton attack on Abyssinia in autumn 1935. The League's abortive sanctions policy against the aggressor not only reduced its prestige to zero but alienated Italy and Britain, the two Locarno guarantors. All at once, Hitler saw that his moment had come. The French Chamber of Deputies had only just ratified the Moscow pact on February 27, 1936, when the German dictator struck.

For two days he closeted himself in his study at the Chancellery. Then he sent for Blomberg.[203] No one could have been more dismayed by Hitler's instructions than the naive commander in chief of the Wehrmacht, but he obediently complied with the order to put "Winterübung" ["Winter Exercise"], as the operation had been renamed, into effect. On March 2 he dictated an order to the heads of the three services: "Elements of the Army and Air Force will . . . unexpectedly and simultaneously be transferred to permanent quarters in the demilitarized zone."[204] Only the date of the operation was left blank.

Blomberg hung on to this order for three days before circulating it with the crucial addition that "Winterübung" would be launched on March 7.[205] He may still have hoped that Beck and Fritsch would try to talk Hitler out of his plan. In fact, both generals were shocked at the dictator's "act of folly." Beck implored him to combine the move with an announcement that Germany did not intend to fortify the west bank of the Rhine.[206] Blomberg, too, ventured to suggest that Wehrmacht units might be withdrawn if the French undertook to pull back some of their own forces from the frontier.[207]

Having brusquely rejected all these proposals, the Führer himself turned hesitant. On March 5 he asked Hossbach whether the whole operation could still be halted. Hossbach confirmed this, but Hitler recovered his confidence within a few hours.[208] On March 7, 1936, nineteen Wehrmacht battalions and thirteen batteries—a force of thirty thousand men—crossed the Rhine bridges. Operation "Winterübung" was under way.[209]

Hitler and his generals waited, almost panic-stricken, for Canaris's S agents to report on the other side's reactions. Germany's military leaders were still prepared to cancel the operation at a moment's notice. Blomberg's instructions had contained the following rider: "If the other powers which have signed the Locarno Pact respond to the transfer of German troops into the demilitarized zone with military preparations, I reserve the right to decide on any military countermeasures."[210]

Code words issued by Abwehr headquarters sent the S agents hurrying to their operational areas. Preliminary messages from France and

Belgium reached the Tirpitz-Ufer, but the Abwehr's informants reported nothing that did not become public knowledge within a few hours. The garrison of the Maginot Line was brought up to wartime strength, the French General Staff transferred some North African divisions from the South of France to the German frontier and leave was cancelled for garrison troops in northern and eastern France.[211] The S agents could detect nothing beyond this. There was no sign of any warlike reaction in France or of mobilization measures in Britain. The Abwehr's alarm bells never rang.

But the quieter Canaris's network became, the uneasier Blomberg felt. Far from reassured by the sparsity of reports from his intelligence chief, he still thought it likely that France and Britain would hit back. Canaris now fell foul of the (inaccurate) reports submitted by his agents late in December 1935. According to these, the British and French General Staff had worked out joint contingency plans to counter a German occupation of the Rhineland.[212]

When Canaris still reported no new developments, Blomberg completely lost his nerve. He advised Hitler to withdraw his troops from Aachen, Trèves and Saarbrücken on the grounds that the French might hourly launch an attack which German forces could not withstand. Hitler again declined, but Blomberg persisted. He urged Hossbach on three separate occasions to talk the Führer round.[213]

Then, on March 13, Blomberg received a telegram from the three German service attachés in London. All his misgivings were confirmed. Captain Wassner, the naval attaché, had come away from a conversation at the Admiralty convinced that the British were in the process of alerting their fleet and sending an expeditionary force to France, while Major General Geyr von Schweppenburg, the military attaché, believed that the prospects of peace were steadily dwindling. He persuaded his colleagues to sign a "Most Urgent" telegram drafted by himself and addressed to Blomberg. It read: "Situation grave, 50-50 peace/war. Geyr, Wassner, Wenninger."[214] This communication not only alarmed Blomberg but encouraged him to pay another call on Hitler and plead for a withdrawal. To his astonishment, Hitler casually took the telegram and stuffed it in his pocket unread. Blomberg was not to know that Göring had handed the Führer a copy only minutes before.[215] Once again, his warnings were brushed aside.

Hitler's predatory instincts had not deceived him. Britain and France undertook no countermeasures, and once again a surprise move by Hitler resulted in nothing more than paper protests on the part of his duped opponents. His temporary fit of apprehension was dispelled by the pealing bells and jubilant crowds that paid homage to him on his long triumphal progress through the Rhineland. Hitler alone knew what he had been through in the preceding hours. "Am I glad!" he exclaimed. "Good Lord, am I glad it's gone so smoothly! Yes indeed, fortune favours the bold . . ."[216] Almost disdainfully, he promoted his two most cautious military advisers: Blomberg was upgraded to field marshal and Fritsch to colonel general.[217]

The Abwehr did not share in these days of triumph. Its S agents had yet to prove their mettle. They had failed to probe the other side's positions in depth, and their few reports had been greeted with scepticism by the Wehrmacht's senior commanders. In practice, Canaris's agents had yielded no more information than their rivals in the press. While visiting Königsberg, Hitler asked Henke, who had been appointed head of the East Prussian Abwehrstelle, how Poland had reacted to the Rhineland occupation. Henke recalls: "I was able to tell him because I had just been briefed by the head of the DNB."[218]

What worried Canaris most of all was the abortive intervention of Wehrmacht attachés based in London. Although Blomberg sent the trio an admonitory letter in which he hypocritically declared that service attachés must keep their nerve, even under trying political circumstances,[219] the matter did not end there. What if service attachés were to engage in espionage on their own account—what if the General Staff intelligence sections, whose elitist members tended to scorn the usually inferior qualifications of their colleagues in the Abwehr, took to building up their own networks of informants aboard? If they did, the Abwehr's very existence would soon be in jeopardy.

Given the traditionally bad relations between the intelligence gatherers of the secret service and the intelligence evaluators of the General Staff, this threat to the Abwehr was a real one. General Staff intelligence officers were always complaining about the lamentable quality of Abwehr reports. The Rhineland crisis won them eager support from the service attachés, with their ingrained dislike of the Abwehr's conspiratorial methods. As one military attaché complained to Pruck: "Anyone who spends his whole time dealing with criminals ends up a criminal himself."[220]

It seemed significant to Canaris that the London attachés' counterblast should have been instigated by Geyr von Schweppenburg. The two men had already crossed swords because Geyr not only declined to assist the Abwehr's activities in England but remained unmoved when Canaris menacingly alluded to an order from the Führer himself. Geyr said later: "I told him bluntly that I wouldn't do it, and that I would remain in London as a gentleman."[221] It was small comfort to Canaris when Blomberg recalled this despiser of the Abwehr to Germany because he knew only too well that his organization was being hampered in its work by the professional rivalry of many other military attachés. There was only one way of dealing with this concerted threat from service attachés and staff officers, and that was to speed up the development of the Abwehr's Geheimer Meldedienst.

New orders from Canaris concentrated and systematized the gathering of foreign intelligence. This had originally been an exclusive preserve of Abwehr I, but the Geheimer Meldedienst had since acquired Groups V (Navy) and VI (Air Force). Canaris now decreed a merger of these three groups because it had "proved necessary for all branches of the Geheimer Meldedienst to be more closely integrated and better co-ordinated."[222] The three groups were placed under a Führungsgruppe [Operations Group] headed by Grimmeiss.

An official directive from Canaris to Grimmeiss stated: "Over-all control of the Geheimer Meldedienst, as exercised by Group Director I, will ensure the closest co-operation between Groups I, V and VI in intelligence-gathering, Spannunsdienst [the duties performed by S agents mobilized in times of international tension] and wartime organization. Group Director I will be responsible, in consultation with Directors V and VI, for the internal and external direction of the Geheimer Meldedienst from salient points of view."[223] The most urgent task facing the head of the Führungsgruppe was "to create a unified Spannungsdienst and a common wartime organization by means of joint efforts and co-ordinative leadership of the subgroups and desks subordinate to him."[224]

But Lieutenant Colonel Grimmeiss, a colourless man who had grown old in the Abwehr's service, lacked the authority to unify these often refractory groups. Looking around for a new co-ordinator, Canaris found one in the person of a cheerful Rhinelander whose appointment turned out to be the Abwehr chief's most successful essay in personnel selection. Major Hans Piekenbrock, born in 1893, had served as a volunteer in the 1914–18 war and been a lieutenant with the 11th Hussars before transferring to General Staff duties in 1927. Known to his friends as "Pieki," he quickly won the Admiral's respect, especially as he and his blithely ironical manner helped to offset Bamler's influence.[225] Canaris got so used to having Piekenbrock around that he eventually gave him the post which Bamler had devised for himself, that of deputy chief of the Abwehr.

Firmly but amiably, Piekenbrock brought the three groups comprising the Geheimer Meldedienst up to scratch and extended his Führungsgruppe's radius of operations. Until now, Abwehr I's intelligence work had been confined to France, Poland and Czechoslovakia. Piekenbrock changed this. He divided the map at Abwehr headquarters into countries of "primary" and "secondary" interest and countries where all secret intelligence work was banned. Of primary interest to Abwehr I were France, Czechoslovakia, Poland, Britain, Russia and Spain. Secondary interest centered on Belgium, Switzerland, Yugoslavia, Romania and the U.S.A. Prohibited countries were Austria, Italy, Hungary, Finland, Estonia, Japan and Bulgaria.[226]

In accordance with the new thrust of Hitler's revisionist policy, which was clearly aimed at a union with Austria, Piekenbrock reorganized the Abwehr's focuses of activity abroad. Under its microscope came all the countries which might be expected to offer strong resistance to an Austro-German union. New Abwehr agents percolated France, Czechoslovakia, Yugoslavia and Romania. Abwehr observation posts were even established on the Austro-Italian border, a "prohibited zone," "because Mussolini's attitude was temporarily hostile to the Anschluss," as Piekenbrock later explained.[227]

Canaris and Piekenbrock also secured the backing of friendly foreign intelligence agencies. The Lithuanian secret service, with which Captain (ret.) Klein maintained contact on behalf of Abwehr headquarters, gathered information about Russia and sneaked German agents into the Soviet Union,[228] while the Hungarian intelligence service diligently helped to keep watch on Czechoslovakia, Yugoslavia and Romania.[229] Canaris and Piekenbrock acquired a new partner during a joint trip to Vienna. The Intelligence Section of the Austrian Defence Ministry promised help against the Czechoslovak Republic, and the two German visitors received assistance from Lieutenant Colonel Erwin Lahousen, who was to become their colleague at Abwehr headquarters a year or two later.[230]

Month by month, Piekenbrock expanded his small nucleus of agents and clandestine contacts. Major Urluziano, a Romanian, obtained deployment plans and details of military organization from the War Ministry in Bucharest, a former tsarist general named Dostovalov studied Soviet military publications in Berlin and his compatriot ex-Colonel Durunovo compiled information about the Yugoslav and Soviet armies in Belgrade.[231]

Piekenbrock's band of agents multiplied in the West as well. In France, Captains Credle and Froge supplied the Abwehr with blueprints of the Maginot Line, Commissaire Flobert of the Sûreté handed over documents from the files of the French security police and a French naval lieutenant passed on information gleaned in the outer office of Admiral Darlan, the French Navy chief.[232] In England Piekenbrock's representatives pursued their ends by dint of "social" espionage and in America through the Schiffsbefragungsdienst [Marine Interrogation Service], which obliged the captains and officers of German vessels to compile information about foreign countries and carry messages to agents overseas.[233]

Wherever Major Piekenbrock's agents took up their positions along the invisible front, they were followed by secret weapons from the Abwehr's technical laboratories. New inventions facilitated and improved the surveillance and communications system. "Ultraphotography" made it possible for the camera to penetrate foreign defence installations obscured by fog or swathed in camouflage nets.[234] Microphotographic equipment enabled documents and maps to be reduced to the size of a typescript dot, and the new "Afus" [Agentenfunkgeräte—agents' radio sets] were sufficiently miniaturized to fit into a small suitcase.[235]

Gradually, Piekenbrock built up the espionage system which earned Canaris his reputation as head of one of the most efficient secret services in Europe—or so, at least, the Reich War Ministry came to believe. The Abwehr chief's influence in the Third Reich's military hierarchy grew accordingly. There were few plans or decisions affecting foreign countries on which Canaris was not consulted.

But he never forgot that there were individuals and organizations in Germany to whom the rise of the Abwehr and its chief was an object of distavour and suspicion. His black-uniformed rivals had also extended their influence. Himmler and Heydrich were at last in possession of what they had coveted from the first: absolute mastery of the police machine.

The fierce disputes between Himmler and Reich Interior Minister Frick, who wanted the SS chief's control over the police to be purely nominal, had been settled by Hitler in summer 1936. On June 9 Heydrich requested on his Reichsführer's behalf that Himmler should be granted ministerial rank, placed on a par with the commanders in chief of the armed services, appointed sole commander of the police with the designation Reichsführer-SS und Chief der Deutschen Polizei [Reich Commander of the SS and Chief of the German Police], and made only "personally" (i.e. not effectively) responsible to the Minister of the Interior.[236] Frick was outraged and called on Hitler to protest, but Hitler gave him to understand that Himmler's appointment had been decided on long before.[237]

Although Himmler dispensed with ministerial rank and elected to be "personally and directly" responsible to Frick—a piece of distorted Nazi gobbledygook which signified little—he attained his main objective. On June 17, 1936, Heinrich Himmler was appointed chief of the German Police.[238] He also founded an official police empire of his own. Two principal departments came into being: the Hauptamt Sicherheitspolizei [Security Police HQ] under Heydrich, which embraced the Gestapo and the Criminal Police, and the Hauptamt Ordnungspolizei [Regular Police HQ], incorporating the Schutzpolizei [Urban Constabulary], Gendarmerie [Rural Constabulary] and Gemeindepolizei [Municipal Constabulary] and headed by Frick's disappointed protégé Kurt Daluege.[239]

Thanks to Himmler's advancement, Heydrich too was elevated to unforeseen heights in the political hierarchy. As Chef der Sicherheitspolizei und des SD [Chief of the Security Police and SD], SS-Gruppenführer Heydrich now commanded a vast organization which strove to bring more and more sectors of national life under its control and gradually acquired, outside the law, a sphere of operations inaccessible to any organ of government or judicial authority. In line with this accretion of power, Heydrich's demands on the Abwehr multiplied and his language became steadily more peremptory.

Renewed disputes broke out between the Gestapo and Abwehr, and relations between the two organizations cooled appreciably. It annoyed Heydrich that the Abwehr's Hauskapellen pursued investigations on their own account and exercised quasi-police functions, but jurisdictional overlaps in the field of counterespionage were an even sorer point. Just as the Gestapo often disrupted IIIF work in current cases of espionage by conducting premature inquiries, so the Abwehr failed to notify the police when a counterespionage operation was complete and the Gestapo could step in.

Sensing this changed climate, Canaris reacted swiftly. Although he firmly rejected Heydrich's demand for the abolition of the Hauskapellen, he was amenable to a settlement of all questions relating to counterespionage.[240] In autumn 1936 he got together with Best and drafted an agreement entitled "Principles Governing Co-operation Between the Geheime Staatspolizei and the Abwehr Offices of the Wehrmacht." Nicknamed the "Treaty of the Ten Commandments" on account of its ten constituent points, it was regarded as the Magna Carta of the German security system—quite wrongly so, because it was fundamentally restricted to the vexed question of counterespionage and counterintelligence.[241]

"Counterespionage, i.e. investigation of the military espionage services of foreign countries," wrote Canaris and Best, "is the function of the Abwehr offices of the Wehrmacht. The Geheime Staatspolizei shall promptly transmit all such information reaching it to the relevant Abwehr office of the Wehrmacht. Geheime Staatspolizei offices shall, within the limits of their official competence, render the Abwehr offices of the Wehrmacht all requisite assistance in counterespionage." Conversely: "Counterespionage police [work], i.e. the investigation of culpable actions under Para. 163 of the StPO [State Police Ordinance relating to treasonable activities] and the requisite follow-up operations, is the function of the Geheime Staatspolizei. The Abwehr offices of the Wehrmacht shall promptly transmit to the relevant offices of the Geheime Staatspolizei any findings that imply the perpetration of culpable acts. The Abwehr offices of the Wehrmacht shall impart to the offices of the Geheime Staatspolizci all information required for the purpose of following up and investigating culpable acts."[242]

Every item in the agreement was formulated with a similar regard for balance. Only in Point 6 did Canaris manage to secure precedence for the Abwehr: "In dealing with individual cases, the interests of the Geheimer Meldedienst and of counterespionage take precedence over executive action by the Abwehrpolizei. If . . . measures taken by the Geheime Staatspolizei would frustrate the attainment of results by the Geheimer Meldedienst and by counterespionage, the Geheime Staats- polizei office handling the case shall, if so requested by the relevant Abwehr office of the Wehrmacht, refrain from implementing its meas- ures until, in the judgement of the [said] Abwehr office of the Wehr- macht, the interests of the Geheimer Meldedienst and of coun- terespionage have ceased to conflict therewith."[243]

Canaris and Best signed this document on December 21, 1936. The Abwehr chief hastened to impress on all his subordinates that its provi- sions must be strictly observed. "I expect," he warned on December 23, "any existing uncertainties of prior date to be frankly discussed with the relevant authorities and completely resolved." He also warned against any undue recourse to Point 6. "Objections based on No. 6 should only be lodged by Abwehr offices in important cases. Exchanges of ideas are necessary in all cases."[244]

Best, too, urged his colleagues to observe this agreement to the let- ter. Addressing a conference of regional Gestapo chiefs, he impressed on them that "Active espionage (Geheimer Meldedienst) [he said] was an exclusively military function. Agreement should likewise be sought on counterespionage. For the sake of the cause, the Gestapo must sub- ordinate itself in this respect."[245]

However, not every Abwehr officer welcomed the Canaris-Best ac- cord with open arms. Some of them subscribed to the theory (which many historians still espouse) that Canaris had acquiesced in the Ab- wehr's political adulteration.[246] Henke even accused his chief of having surrendered the Abwehr's political functions—a gross misjudgement, because its political security functions in the Wehrmacht and muni- tions industry (it had never possessed any others) not only remained intact but never came within the scope of the Canaris-Best agreement. Canaris dismissed this criticism "so ungraciously" that Henke consid- ered resigning, but next day he told him "not to do anything stupid" and assured him that he still had "complete faith" in him.[247]

Canaris felt that he had no choice but to co-operate as closely as possible with his chief competitors. He soon drew even closer to Heydrich, whom he invited to discuss official business while riding with him in the mornings. Heydrich agreed, and his horse was duly stabled with the Admiral's Arab mare, Motte. Best joined the party too.[248]

Together the trio went for early morning canters through the Tiergarten. The white-haired Abwehr chief was usually flanked by his two SS companions, presenting a not unsymbolic picture: Wilhelm Canaris had been firmly dovetailed into the National Socialist state.

7

Under the Führer's Spell

Adolf Hitler was awaiting his secret service chief at the Chancellery. Rear Admiral Canaris had requested an interview at the unusual hour of 8 P.M., hinting that he had some information of the utmost urgency to impart. He turned up punctually and was admitted to the Führer's study at once.

Canaris came bearing a secret document which had been handed to his best senior agent in Paris. Its source, he explained, was a Quai d'Orsay official who felt dissatisfied with the present trend in French foreign policy, and it contained the text of the secret protocol on military cooperation annexed to the Franco-Soviet pact of mutual assistance. The most important provision was that, in the event of war with Germany, French and Russian forces would invade the Reich in close collaboration with the Czechs.[1]

Hitler was so impressed by this document that he summoned War Minister von Blomberg the same night, February 11, 1936, and instructed him to speed up preparations for the occupation of the Rhineland.[2] The Abwehr chief's report seemed to confirm his own prediction to the leading generals of the Reichswehr on February 3, 1933: "The expansion of the armed forces will be a time of extreme danger. We shall then see if France possesses any statesmen. If so, she will not give us time but attack us (probably with [the aid of] Eastern satellites)."[3]

Although the Paris document later turned out to be a forgery, the scene at the Chancellery illustrates how close the contact between Hitler and his intelligence chief had become. Hitler's all-or-nothing brinkmanship brought Canaris to the Chancellery more and more often, and the Abwehr's reports exercised a growing influence on the Chancellor's weekend coups. In times of crisis Canaris became an almost regular visitor. No less than seventeen Hitler-Canaris interviews at the Chancellery are recorded for the period December 1935–March 1936 alone.[4]

Within a full year, Wilhelm Canaris had achieved all that seemed desirable to him when he took up his post at the Tirpitz-Ufer: a place at the hub of German power and a share in the decisions of those who wielded it. Whenever Hitler was planning a new move, whenever he defied the outside world with an unexpected stroke of policy and forestalled his opponents' countermeasures, the diminutive figure of Admiral Canaris was close at hand. He undertook secret missions to foreign countries on his Führer's behalf. He opened up the countries of the south to Hitler's expansionist designs. He explored the enemy's potential, spun a web of clandestine contacts abroad and supplied the Chancellery with confidential files and secret reports.

Canaris and Hitler became so close that even superficial observers were struck by how well they got on. When colleagues warned of Hitler's capricious and unpredictable temperament, Canaris brushed their misgivings aside. "One can talk to him,"[5] was his complacent response. Few other visitors to the Chancellery had a better command of this rare art. Hitler enjoyed the Admiral's briefings. He liked his calm, quiet voice and his precise and businesslike way of putting things, especially as Canaris was adroit enough at handling individuals to skirt round delicate topics. "He's reasonable and sees your point of view as long as you put it to him properly . . ."[6] Canaris genuinely believed this.

There was something else which facilitated their mutual dealings. Both men had a rooted aversion to routine paper work and an insatiable urge to move around. Just as Canaris hurried from one Abwehrstelle to the next, so Hitler and his entourage sped from town to town and village to village by car, train and plane. Hitler and Canaris were also at one in their detachment from family and private life and their curiously dispassionate and almost sexless relations with women.

But their strongest common feature tended to be divisive. Both were masters of dissimulation and both possessed such an ability to take on the colour of their current surroundings that all who talked to them felt they had found a sympathetic audience. This explains why Canaris took so long to see through Hitler and why Hitler's usually unerring instinct for danger completely failed him in the case of Canaris. Until the

last, Hitler believed the Admiral to be his trusty and devoted henchman.

At this stage, however, Canaris's loyalty to Hitler was beyond question. He testified by word and deed that, for him, life held no more exalted purpose than the service of the Führer and his regime. Canaris,
addressing some Abwehr officers: "I require you to stand foursquare by
the National Socialist state and to act accordingly."[7] He was firmly convinced that "Adolf Hitler's ideas are imbued with the following soldierly spirit: honour and a sense of duty, courage, military preparedness,
a readiness for commitment and self-sacrifice, leadership, comradeship
and a sense of responsibility."[8]

No one who believed this could have had any qualms about performing his duties in Hitler's immediate orbit. Indeed, Canaris clung so
assiduously to the Führer's side that other military men were denied access to him. National Socialists, too, watched the Admiral's burgeoning
influence with unease. Even Best, the well-meaning chief of the counterespionage police, referred darkly to the "moment of weakness" in
which the Führer had suffered Canaris to play such a major role.[9] As
for an out-and-out Nazi like the ex-Gestapo officer Gerhard Fischer, his
memoirs go so far as to complain that Hitler's "gentlemanly relations
with Canaris" converted the Abwehr chief into an "extreme exponent
of Hitlerism."[10]

In reality, Canaris was at once a beneficiary and a victim of the
Hitler cult which had fastened on all sectors of German society. He too
fell prey to the megalomania of Nazism and became infected with the
giddy enthusiasm that robbed an entire nation of its discernment and
maturity. He was too fundamentally unpolitical to grasp the full
subtlety of the National Socialist system, whose plebiscitary elections,
gigantomaniac demonstrations of loyalty to the Führer, vast parades
and forests of fluttering banners were cementing an outwardly indestructible alliance between Hitler and the German people.

Canaris certainly had no illusions about the inferior quality of the
party that had ruled Germany since 1933. He was repelled by the "mass
bustle" of National Socialism and sensed that there were those in the
NSDAP who aspired to overthrow the bourgeois social order and impose a sort of "second revolution" (on that of January 30, 1933). He
often referred in private to "brown Bolshevism," and even his official
speeches warned of the dangers inherent in burdening the Abwehr with
"internal political power struggles of a Socialist complexion."[11]

These admonitions were not, as his more credulous biographers suggest, a symptom of incipient resistance to the Nazi system. They merely
stemmed from the natural prejudices of a conservative whom no misgivings could dissuade from serving the state. The Hitler cult absolved
senior functionaries, at least, from bestowing approval on every aspect

of the National Socialist system because Hitlerism transcended the party. It even cast its spell over Germans who would strongly have denied any allegiance to National Socialism as such. Three years after his assumption of power, Hitler had hypnotized the bulk of the nation. More than any German politician before or since, he enjoyed an authority which surpassed the divine right of kings.

"In heartfelt sincerity, we say: God preserve the Reich Chancellor for our nation," Cardinal Faulhaber of Munich wrote to Hitler, and Heinrich Rendtorff, the Protestant Bishop of Mecklenburg, acclaimed him as "our God-given leader."[12] As early as October 1933, eighty-eight writers had hastened "most solemnly to swear to you, Herr Reich Chancellor, an oath of the most faithful allegiance"—the first in a whole series of flatulent "exegeses" of Hitlerism in which a wide variety of intellectuals strove to outdo each other.[13] The poet and novelist Ina Seidel felt "our efforts and endeavours gratefully and humbly merging with the work of our generation's sole elect—with the work of Adolf Hitler," and the poet Otto Bangert broke into rhyme:

> From out primeval depths ascending,
> more like a mountain than a man,
> he, while to exile we were wending,
> his great and sacred task began.

> With hands outstretched he towers there
> amid a world's downfall and doom.
> Despair is throbbing everywhere,
> but, as with torchlight's ardent glare,
> his spirit lights the barren gloom.

> He points towards dawn's distant glow,
> makes every heart a flaming brand.
> With vibrant hearts and hands we vow:
> O Master, build your people now
> a new, exalted, Fatherland.[14]

A miracle had come to pass: one lone man of obscure origins, a charismatic figure endowed with a unique talent for demagogy, had swiftly succeeded in persuading the majority of the German people that they lived in a proud land led by a genius—that they were "the envy of the entire world," to quote a stock Nazi propaganda phrase. Disoriented by Republican turmoil, humiliated by economic ruin and inspired by an old and predemocratic belief in authority, the Germans had entrusted themselves to a putative redeemer. In the prevailing mood of panic, all that mattered to many people was relief from social distress—and this Hitler's regime had accomplished.

Germany's most dramatic problem, that of unemployment, was

eliminated by a crash programme. This job creation scheme took only a few years to mop up the 5.6 million unemployed who had confronted Hitler on his assumption of power.[15] The economy was boosted to such an extent that it soon regained the level attained in the boom year of 1928. "Victory on the economic front," as Nazi jargon had it, received statistical confirmation. Industrial investment in 1938 was 60 per cent higher than in 1928 and the production index had doubled. Personal expenditure rose by 35 per cent between 1933 and 1938, and the gross national product rose even more, from 59,000 million Reichsmark in 1933 to 105,000 million in 1938.[16]

Even more impressive than these statistics were the regime's social achievements in respect of labour. Better working conditions, more housing, the creation of sports facilities and organized mass tourism fostered an illusion that Germany's workers were heading for a golden age. Young workers, in particular, enjoyed better promotion prospects. The German Labour Front, which all employees and employers had to join, moulded them into a "national community." By this and other means, the class barriers which had hitherto separated the two categories were largely abolished.

Few people acknowledged the price that had to be paid for social progress. Workers were condemned to political impotence by the destruction of trade unions, a total loss of freedom, rigorous direction of labour, restrictions on movement and surveillance by Nazi informers at places of work. A few workers steeled themselves to resist this curtailment of their liberties, but the overwhelming majority submitted to Gleichschaltung [co-ordination], or incorporation in the totalitarian "social state."

What material incentives accomplished with the working class, Hitler's nationalistic slogans wrought upon the old bourgeois-reactionary establishment. His political programme, a blend of Prussian authoritarianism and expansionist ideology, initiated a process of suffocating self-adjustment. Cultural authorities, the machinery of government and the armed forces all aligned themselves with Hitler's charismatic leadership.

Canaris was no exception. All his speeches contained an avowal of loyalty to the Führer and none omitted Hitler quotations promoted to the status of biblical truths. Canaris: "Officers and other ranks are once more pledged to their Supreme Commander by a personal oath calling upon Almighty God to bear witness. Any doubt as to its loyalty or National Socialist dependability would be the gravest aspersion on the Wehrmacht and its officer corps."[17] He subscribed to "a watchword of pride and satisfaction: 'One nation, one Reich, one Führer and one Wehrmacht!'"[18]

Canaris would tolerate no dilution of this creed. Anyone who clung to an unpolitical attitude, he declared, was committing "an act of sabotage and a crime."[19] He warned his officers "to eschew the least semblance of reactionary sentiment, so called, which is either completely absent or which, in the few isolated places where it may still exist—usually as a result of plain stupidity—must be eradicated."[20] He repeatedly emphasized that "the really good serviceman will also be a good National Socialist."[21]

Canaris's was only one, and not even the most strident, of the voices that chorused their homage to the new Messiah. Hitler's appeals to nationalism, his Social Darwinist and anti-Semitic ideology, his tirades against the injustice of Versailles and his visions of a Greater German Reich were echoed a thousandfold. Although many compliant individuals were troubled by the spiritual sterility of the new Germany and the regimentation of all aspects of life, just as they were deterred by the growing power of the police apparat and the concentration camp system, public protest had already been stilled by the seductive poison of totalitarianism.

Not even the persecution of the Jews, who were now represented as evil incarnate, provoked open resistance. Society, which had for years been accustomed to an anti-Jewish climate of opinion, remained as unmoved by anti-Semitic purges in every sector of public life as it was by the so-called Nuremberg Laws, which deprived Jews of citizenship.

Canaris, who had grown up in the atmosphere of "moderate" anti-Semitism prevailing among the Ruhr middle class and in the Navy, believed in the existence of a "Jewish problem." Like many who parroted the stock phrases of Nazi propaganda, whether from conviction or opportunism, he favoured "an awareness of the eternal values of faith, race and nationhood."[22] So assiduously did he cultivate them that some ex-Nazis have since claimed that Canaris was the true originator of the Jewish star, that cruel mark of Cain which branded Jews as social lepers during World War II and heralded the physical destruction of millions of human beings.

Canaris did, in fact, suggest during 1935–36 that German Jews should be identified by a Star of David as special-category citizens whose rights were only on a par with those of foreign residents. Being a nationalist, he took it for granted that Britain and France would one day return the German colonies that had been "stolen" in 1919. Here in this new German empire he proposed to reserve a few areas where Jews could settle and found a polity of their own. Any Jews temporarily remaining in Germany were to legitimize themselves as citizens of this Jewish state by wearing a Star of David, not least as a safeguard against excesses by Nazi racial fanatics.[23]

It was this last consideration which prompted Canaris's friends to characterize his proposal as a gesture in defence of the Jews. His postwar apologists have claimed that he was "still trying to exert a restraining influence on the National Socialist leadership."[24] They ignore the fact that compulsory mass resettlement of the Jews—which was what his proposal amounted to—formed part of a programme widely supported by the party and the SS authorities in particular. Hermann Göring aired these ideas in 1938 and discussed them with British politicians through an intermediary named Karl Heinz Abshagen, the German journalist who later became Canaris's first biographer.[25] So far from committing an act of resistance, the Abwehr chief doubtless believed that he was acting in line with his Führer's intentions.

It was one of the absurdities of the Third Reich that many who objected to excesses and abuses of power, for all their loyalty to the regime, sought redress from Hitler himself. With its exaggerated notions of order, the old ruling class could not conceive of the German Chancellor as other than a politician whose steadfast resolve was to uphold the authority of the state.

Military men cherished a particular belief in the need to distinguish between Hitler and his party. Field Marshal Erich von Manstein refers in his memoirs to a "widely held view" in the Army that "Hitler knew nothing about his men's misdeeds and would certainly not have approved had he learned of them."[26] These delusions gave birth to the immortal formula which later acquired a bitterly ironical aftertaste but was fervently espoused by many Germans of the period: "If only the Führer knew!"

Hitler contrived to preserve some distance between himself and the party. Not for nothing had he emerged, after assuming the chancellorship, as a traditional bastion of government authority, and not for nothing had he appealed for loyalty to the state. He was hailed as the liquidator of experiments in socialism by National Socialist hotheads; he had discontinued the party's attempt—originally encouraged by himself—to convert the Protestant Church into a National Socialist Church; and he had stopped the Gestapo and SD from spying on the armed forces. In reality, Hitler had no interest in the authority of the state and was primarily concerned with personal power. That which the faithful interpreted as statesmanlike responsibility and the emancipation of a party leader from his political rank-and-file was merely the unbridled egoism of an individual who set himself above nation and society. Nothing could have mattered less to Hitler than the fate of a country divorced from his person.

Nor did the Führer have any intention of sharing power with his paladins in the NSDAP. He instinctively balked at creating that "totality of the state" whose establishment he had been promising for years. In 1933 he blocked the process every party member had taken for granted: a party take-over of government. The NSDAP became the

Third Reich's sole political party without ever gaining absolute power. Although party members were permitted to assume government posts, government itself remained beyond their reach. Hitler converted the NSDAP into the driving-belt of his personal authority and the politico-ideological mobilizer of the nation.

Party and state were never allowed to merge, even though Hitler repeatedly forecast their "fusion." A Law for the Preservation of the Unity of Party and State was enacted, but it only assigned the party a propaganda function by naming it "the vehicle of German political thought." Hitler took care to deny this "vehicle" undue access to his plans. He even blocked the transfer of the party's national directorate from Munich to Berlin, with the result that only a small "NSDAP liaison staff" at the Reich Chancellery had any direct contact with him.[27]

Hitler also ensured that the party spawned no faction opposed to him. Leading party members proposed to form a senate of elders; Hitler turned them down. NSDAP Reichsleiter and Gauleiter [national and regional party chiefs] wanted to hold regular meetings; Hitler prevented them from doing so. Party veterans planned an organization of their own; Hitler banned it.[28] Whenever the party tried to establish itself beside him as an independent force, he cut the ground from under its feet. Shortsighted military men not unnaturally misconstrued such behaviour as a quest for independence on the part of a statesman who valued his supra-party profile.

The real truth was that, instead of sharing executive power with the party, Hitler entrusted chosen members of his immediate circle with a series of ever changing functions and thereby bound them to his person. Unwilling to depend on a hierarchy, he delegated such tasks to as many mini-hierarchs as possible. An instinctive rather than deliberate process of multiplication prevented any of these subordinates from conspiring against Hitler with a rival. Himmler, Göring, Goebbels, Darré and the rest were each allotted wide-ranging functions, but their powers were never so precisely defined that they could feel altogether sure of themselves.

The result was a bizarre system of perpetual self-obstruction based on the popular Darwinist views which Hitler applied to political life. According to this unwritten law of the jungle, the better department and stronger administrator would automatically prevail in the fight for departmental power. This ethic drove many functionaries to despair, among them the SS ideologist Otto Ohlendorf, who lamented that government had been replaced by "the pluralistic tyranny of the senior hierarchs."[29]

But amid this chaos of jurisdictions and hierarchies there still existed one force—the Wehrmacht—which steadfastly believed in the supreme virtues of state authority. Its leaders welcomed the estrangement of Führer and party—indeed, they were beguiled by the thought of completely detaching Hitler from the NSDAP and getting him on their side. The men round Blomberg, Canaris included, pinned all their hopes on Hitler because only partnership with him could guarantee them influence and a slice of power.

This drew the armed forces into a game of National Socialist charades more systematic than that played by any other professional class in the Third Reich. The Wehrmacht authorities jettisoned almost every item of ideological ballast that might have encumbered the special relationship they sought. The lengths to which they went are perfectly illustrated by Canaris's public pronouncements.

Few were the articles of Wehrmacht faith which he neglected to align with Nazi ideology, calmly reformulating German military history to accord with National Socialist requirements. The Great Elector of Brandenburg became a precursor of Hitler whose establishment of an independent army had been "a National Socialist decision in the profoundest sense," while the front-line troops of World War I were transmogrified *en bloc* into "the first effective National Socialists." In view of this, who could dispute that Hitler's national defence laws were "the logical consummation, uncompromisingly and unadulteratedly fulfilled by National Socialism, of true soldierly spirit" or that National Socialism was nothing if not "an aid to the rearing of good Germans"? "The true soldierly attitude and National Socialism," Canaris declared, "are one."[30]

These verbal salutes were, of course, fired largely to convey to Hitler that his true place was on the Wehrmacht's side and that any disputes between party and military authorities should be settled in the latter's favour. The Führer had "granted his special protection to every member of the Wehrmacht," Canaris argued. "As the Führer is to his Wehrmacht, so is his Wehrmacht to him."[31]

If Abwehrstellen complained of clashes with the party or Nazi attacks on the officer corps, Canaris knew of no better response than a recourse to the Führer himself. "Rest assured," he told his subordinates, "that senior officials of the party and its agencies do, in the main, condemn blunders on the part of junior officials or other persons and fully understand when the Wehrmacht swiftly and resolutely resists infringements, insults, et cetera, in just defence of its status and reputation in the state."[32]

These and similar speeches created a special relationship between Hitler and his armed forces which conveyed, if only to the officers at the War Ministry, that a unique bond of trust united them with their Führer. Canaris's exegeses also made it plain that he himself had risen to become one of the Wehrmacht authorities' leading spokesmen.

Canaris was rated the most intelligent and tactically experienced departmental chief at the Ministry since Major General von Reichenau, Blomberg's closest adviser and the real political brains of the Wehrmacht leadership, had quit his post as head of the Wehrmachtamt in August 1935.[33] The War Minister often included Canaris in discussions of military policy, one factor beneficial to the Abwehr chief being that Reichenau had been succeeded as head of department by the pedantic and unimaginative Major General Wilhelm Keitel, an unpolitical desk warrior who was quite incapable of successfully upholding military interests in the field of tension bounded by Hitler, the party and the Wehrmacht.

Keitel had need of Canaris, who seemed to possess all the sophistication, powers of persuasion and rhetorical skill he lacked. He soon became increasingly dependent on the Abwehr chief's advice, reports and suggestions, although he subsequently wrote that Canaris had always remained "an enigma and a closed book" to him.[34] Keitel: "I was later to pay dearly for my faith in Canaris."[35]

Neither Keitel nor Blomberg objected when Canaris took advantage of his visits to the Chancellery to represent Wehrmacht interests outside the scope of his own domain. The Admiral was well liked in Hitler's entourage and got on well with the controllers of the police machine. Above all, he knew how to interest Hitler and his chief foreign policy adviser, special envoy Joachim von Ribbentrop, in the Mediterranean countries which Canaris saw as future allies of the Reich and aids to the recovery of its world-power status.

Canaris was always harping on the subject of two countries, Italy and Spain, which he regarded as natural allies of Germany. He had long believed that both could help to extricate the Reich from its international isolation. His political mentor, Loewenfeld, had declared in 1926 that Fascist Italy would make a potential partner for Germany if only Benito Mussolini "were not, being a dictator and an avowed destroyer of Italian Social Democracy and Jewish freemasonry, an enemy of the German democrats."[36] Canaris had taken a similar view.

In this he saw eye to eye with Hitler, who had allotted Italy a central place in any German revisionist policy ever since 1922. Hitler's plans provided for the encouragement of Italy's imperial ambitions in the Mediterranean and, thus, for an early clash between her and France, the premier Mediterranean power. Conflict with France would enforce Italian dependence on a stronger Germany, which would in turn boost the value of an alliance between the Reich and France's partner, Britain, and might induce the latter to change sides. The result: France would become isolated and Germany recover her complete freedom of manoeuvre in foreign policy.[37]

But these were just daydreams. The Italian leadership showed no signs of accepting Hitler's outstretched hand. Mussolini was afraid of

Germany's growing strength and Hitler's plans to annex Austria, the buffer between their two countries. The Duce had even acted as the spokesman of a diplomatic anti-Hitler front at Stresa, and a visit to him by the Führer had gone off badly. His cautious attitude did not soften until Italy went to war with Abyssinia. Mussolini now needed a powerful ally in his diplomatic campaign against the British and French, who were opposing Italian expansionism. Again Hitler made overtures, but still the Italians wavered.

At this stage, Canaris helped the Führer after his own fashion by pulling the wires that linked him with the Italian military authorities via German intermediaries on the spot. His motley band of helpers included Professor Karl Haushofer, the geopolitician, Major Giuseppe Renzetti of the Italian secret service, ex-Major Waldemar Pabst, his old friend from the Kapp Putsch days, who had since become director of the Society for the Study of Fascism, and the German Ambassador in Rome, Ulrich von Hassell, who had assisted Canaris during his visits to Spain in the 1920s while serving as consul general in Barcelona.[38]

As his most effective transmitter of German requirements Canaris selected Colonel Mario Roatta, head of SIM (Servizio Informazioni Militari), as the Italian Army's secret intelligence service was called. The two intelligence chiefs had first met in Munich during September 1935.[39] They were somewhat alike. Roatta was exactly the same age as Canaris, possessed a similar reputation for inscrutability and—being a descendant of Spanish Jews expelled from Spain during the fifteenth century—shared the Admiral's interest in the Iberian Peninsula.[40] Last but not least, the Italian was delighted to have found a German partner who understood the Latin way of life. SIM officers had never got over the arrogant behaviour of Canaris's predecessor, Patzig, and his companion, Colonel Carl-Heinrich von Stülpnagel, who had clearly conveyed during a visit to Rome in 1934 what a "backward and, above all, untrustworthy" impression they had formed of Roatta's secret service.[41]

Even when SIM offered to work closely with the Abwehr, Patzig had brusquely rejected the proposal. Not long afterwards, when the Italian naval attaché in Berlin, Count de Courten, hinted to Patzig that King Victor Emmanuel III wanted to signalize his trust by conferring a high decoration on him, the then Abwehr chief remained cool. "Co-operation entails trust on both sides, and no decoration can alter that."[42] Patzig further recalls that he "urgently advised" his minister against "any collaboration with the Italian secret service."[43]

Canaris was, of course, equally aware that the Servizio Informazioni Militari, founded in 1900, did not function very effectively. It lacked money, personnel and departmental authority, was only responsible for the Army and suffered from insufficient representation abroad.[44] These, however, were the very weaknesses which Canaris proceeded to exploit. He offered Roatta German intelligence material relating to countries where SIM maintained no agents. The Italian accepted and promised information from the Balkan and Mediterranean areas. This was quite an advantageous deal because Canaris knew from Hungarian intelligence officers that the Italians had cracked the military code used by several Balkan countries.[45]

Even more important to Canaris was that the Abwehr should maintain a dialogue with SIM and thereby influence the Italian leadership. Blomberg was impressed by Canaris's negotiating skill, especially as he still bore Patzig a grudge for having "sabotaged" his ministerial instructions to establish contact with the Italians. The fact that co-operation with Rome was also favoured by the Führer, to whom he constantly deferred, earned Canaris the War Minister's particular approval, and he entrusted the Abwehr chief with sundry new assignments.

Canaris was also on hand when Blomberg proceeded to adapt the Wehrmacht's command structure to the requirements of the authoritarian Nazi state. Although the Reich War Minister was commander in chief of the entire Wehrmacht, he still lacked the organization needed to command and control it. His aim was to unite the largely autonomous armed services under a single Wehrmacht ministry run by a Wehrmacht general staff which would direct all military operations in time of war and assist the supreme commander, Hitler.[46]

One germ cell of this future Wehrmacht general staff already existed in the shape of Keitel's Wehrmachtamt (WA). A start had been made under Reichenau at giving the WA a command structure capable of controlling the Wehrmacht. In 1934 it acquired an Abteilung L[andesverteidigung—National Defence Section] designed to cope with the operational and organizational problems of the Wehrmacht as a whole. This was joined soon afterwards by an Abteilung W[ehrwirtschafts- und Waffenwesen—Military Economics and Ordnance Section]. The WA soon acquired so many powers and responsibilities that, in cases where it represented Blomberg's interests as commander in chief of the Wehrmacht, it was referred to in internal correspondence from 1936 onwards as Oberkommando der Wehrmacht [OKW—Armed Forces High Command].[47]

Into these new Abteilungen and Referate streamed officers who were enthralled by the Hitler cult. They not only found the Army's traditional style of leadership outmoded but strove to create what one of them described as "something new, something better attuned to the new state and its requirements."[48] Like Colonel Alfred Jodl, head of Abteilung L, they were uncompromising functionalists so devoted to "ardent professional fanaticism" that nothing seemed more natural to them than an insistence that the Wehrmacht should conform to the

"Führer principle" and that its sole resolve must be to serve as a combat-ready instrument of the political executive.[49]

However, Blomberg's structural reforms met with growing resistance from the Chief of the Army General Staff, Beck, who disliked such indiscriminate co-operation between Hitler and the Wehrmacht authorities. He also took exception to the instrumental view of the Wehrmacht's role, as espoused by Blomberg and his associates, because he was hoping to become Hitler's personal adviser on military policy and had composed some long and intricate papers casting himself in the role of a super-chief of the Wehrmacht General Staff.[50]

A traditionalist hidebound by ideas which had long ago been overtaken by events, Beck could never get over the fact that the Army Chief of Staff had lost his central role in the German military hierarchy. During the wars of the nineteenth and early twentieth centuries, the Chief of the Grand General Staff had been the dominant military figure. Now, the Army Chief of Staff possessed only limited authority. He had relinquished important powers within his own service to the new commander in chief of the Army and was only one of several chiefs of staff in the over-all structure of the Wehrmacht.

But Beck worked tirelessly to reverse this development. On the principle that the Army would bear the brunt of the fighting in any future war, he claimed that its chief of staff should be appointed operational commander of the entire Wehrmacht. Although he could not prevent the War Ministry from setting up something akin to a Wehrmacht General Staff, he at once did his best to render it impotent. Under his proposals, the Wehrmacht General Staff would have purely administrative and organizational functions, whereas the Army General Staff would assume operational control of the entire Wehrmacht and its chief resume his central role in the German conduct of war as Erster Generalquartiermeister [First Chief of the General Staff].[51]

Beck submitted his demands and Blomberg promptly turned them down. The rival heads of the Army and armed forces clashed with a ferocity peculiar to interdepartmental disputes conducted under the auspices of an authoritarian regime. Pedantic as ever, Beck refused to compromise and felt personally affronted because the officers he had lent to the Wehrmachtamt turned out to be ardent supporters of the Blomberg plan.[52] Each camp sealed itself off from the other. The WA regarded the Army General Staff as "the other side," to quote one of Jodl's letters, and Beck forbade his staff officers to have any dealings with the War Ministry.[53]

Beck's isolationist policy could not fail to affect Canaris, whose Abwehr was dependent on close co-operation with the Army General Staff. Relations between the Abwehr and the Foreign Armies Section of the General Staff, which had never been entirely easy, could stand no additional strain, but the Army Chief of Staff was undeterred and even toyed with the idea of severing the Army's links with the Abwehr.

This may have contributed to the relative lack of harmony between Canaris and Beck. The Army Chief of Staff, an erudite but cautious and finicky man who never leapt without looking, disliked the boyish unconcern with which Canaris sometimes performed the tasks assigned him by Hitler and Blomberg. As for the Abwehr chief, who was still obsessed with dreams of Germany's ascent to world-power status, he could not share the pessimism of a man who abhorred Hitler's strident approach to foreign policy and rearmament and continued to believe in the validity of what he had written in 1934: "Our international position is bleak . . . All the powers that matter are against us."[54]

Besides, Canaris left Beck in no doubt that he approved of Blomberg's command structure. This was another point on which the chiefs of the Abwehr and Army General Staff could not agree. Beck regarded the military as politically autonomous and credited senior Army officers with the function of paramount advisers to the political leadership. Canaris, on the other hand, regarded the Wehrmacht primarily as an instrument tailored to the National Socialist "Führer principle," the "mailed fist of the German Reich," the "strongest manifestation of the National Socialist will to power and National Socialist strength vis-à-vis the outside world."[55]

The sceptic in Beck wanted to discontinue his own and his intelligence evaluators' dependence on such an ingenuous attitude. He stepped up the activities of his military attachés and encouraged them to report on foreign countries without bothering about the Abwehr. There now occurred what Canaris had been dreading ever since the London attachés' initiative at the height of the Rhineland crisis: Beck developed new sources of information extraneous to the Abwehr.

Beck ascribed great importance to better co-operation between military attachés. The Army had lost its Attaché Section during the postwar period. Immediately after taking up his appointment Beck prised it away from the Reichswehr Ministry and reincorporated it in the Army General Staff (then entitled the Truppenamt).[56] He even lent personal support to opponents of the Abwehr. The German military attaché in London, Major General Geyr von Schweppenburg, who regarded all Abwehr activities as irreconcilable with the principles of loyalty and good faith and had been rebuked by Blomberg for his conduct during the Rhineland crisis, was heartened by an assurance from Beck that no such "restriction on freedom of speech" would in future be tolerated.[57] The Army Chief of Staff further instructed the military attaché in Belgrade, Major General Moritz von Faber du Faur, another critic of the Abwehr, to check the accuracy of Canaris's analyses.[58]

Outside his own official sphere, too, Beck acquired new intelligence

1. Admiral Wilhelm Canaris, chief of the German Abwehr, at the height of his power. (*Ullstein Bilderdienst, Berlin*)

2. Canaris with fellow students after matriculating at Duisburg in 1905 (standing, second from right) . (*Ullstein Bilderdienst, Berlin*).

3. German torpedo squadron drill, 1904 (*Süddeutscher Verlag Bilderdienst, München*)

4. Period illustration of an imperial ball on board a battleship, 1894. (*Bildarchiv Preussischer Kulturbesitz, Berlin*)

5. Patriotic postcard of the battle of the Falkland Islands, 19_4 (after the painting "The Last Man" by Hans Bordt). (*Bildarchiv Preussischer Kulturbesitz, Berlin*)

6. The Valiant, a Royal Navy 1-class. (Ullstein Bilderdienst, Berlin)

7. Foreground: U-35 in the Mediterranean. This submarine smuggled Canaris the secret agent out of Spain in 1916. (*Ullstein Bilderdienst, Berlin*)

8. Canaris in the 1920s. (*Ullstein Bilderdienst, Berlin*)

sources designed to keep him briefed on the situation abroad. Foremost among the countries that interested him was Italy. One of Beck's acquaintances, Major (ret.) Dr. Adolf Günther, and a young legation counsellor named Waldheim kept him informed about developments in Italy and Abyssinia. Largely based on soundings taken by German residents,[59] their reports only confirmed what Beck himself had believed ever since attending some Italian manoeuvres in 1932, which was that the Italians could not be relied on.[60]

Finally, Beck sent Faber du Faur to investigate the military and political situation in Italy. Although he had to accept Canaris's close associate Piekenbrock as a travelling companion, this did not prevent Faber du Faur from picking holes in the Abwehr's optimistic situation reports.[61] "According to the Abwehr," he scoffed, "every Mediterranean country possessed a government—naturally supported by the Abwehr—which was only waiting for the whole picture to change because its people were so enamoured of the Germans."[62] Faber du Faur likewise advised against any more intimate partnership with the Italians.

But Canaris had no wish to be lectured by outsiders on a field of operations which he regarded as his personal province. Why should he, an expert on the Mediterranean world and its mentality, take lessons from people who were blind to everything save armaments statistics, divisional strengths and budgetary appropriations? The Abwehr chief had ways and means of neutralizing his critics, as the military attachés soon found out. There was no demand for their reports at the Chancellery because Hitler disliked their so-called defeatist tone. "He didn't want us," complains Faber du Faur, "he only wanted Ribbentrop and Canaris . . . , and they gagged military attachés on principle."[63]

Canaris found it all the easier to ward off his critics because he was now catapulted to one of the peaks in his career by a politico-military upheaval. In summer 1936 civil war broke out in Spain and the political map of Europe was transformed. Under the auspices of an anti-Communist crusade, Germany and Italy combined to form an "axis" and the leaders of the Third Reich embarked on their first foray beyond the German borders. Apart from Hitler himself, no one played a greater part in this than the little man in the shabby blue naval uniform.

The outbreak of the Spanish Civil War came as no surprise to Canaris. Abwehr outstations in France and the Mediterranean area had been picking up storm warnings for weeks in advance. A democratic parliamentary republic since 1931, Spain was steadily drifting into a chaos of riots, assassinations, arson and mass strikes over which little control was exercised by the strategists of fascist revolution or the largely doctrinaire leaders of the left-wing parties which had joined the Communists in forming a popular-front government.

The political scene in Madrid seethed with all the outstanding social and political problems that had plagued the country for decades. The unbridled supremacy of the Catholic Church, the poverty of the rural proletariat, the agricultural neglect of landed property, separatist aspirations in Catalonia and the Basque country—all these things cried out for solution now that the masses' hopes of deliverance had been kindled by the electoral success of the popular-front parties in February 1936.

Supporters of the victorious government parties truculently celebrated their triumph for weeks after the election, provoking equally intolerant counterdemonstrations on the part of their right-wing opponents and triggering an alarming increase in urban terrorism. As if bombings and assassinations were not enough, the verbal extremism of politicians on both sides fostered the impression that Spain was on the verge of a Red revolution—that the day was fast approaching when the bourgeois Republic would take on a Socialist hue and a Soviet Spain arise from the ashes of Catholic and conservative society.

The armed forces, for long the iron band that had held Spain's numerous centrifugal forces in check, felt strengthened in their unpolitical and superstitious belief that democracy and parliamentarianism were harbingers of anarchy and political dissolution. The Army spawned a clandestine officers' association entitled Unión Militar Española (UME) and dedicated to overthrowing the Republic by means of a military coup.[64]

One member of the UME was the former Spanish military attaché in Berlin, Colonel Juan Beigbeder Atienza, who was in touch with Canaris.[65] From him and other Spanish sources the Abwehr chief got hints of what was brewing in Spain. For the first time, too, he heard the question which his Spanish friends were to ask so repeatedly from then on: would Germany support the "Alzamiento Nacional," or national uprising?

Canaris's initial response was probably evasive, but his Spanish friends persevered. Late in February he met General José Sanjurjo y Sacanell, "the Lion of the Rif," once Spain's most popular colonial soldier but now an exile in Portugal after an abortive military revolt in August 1932.[66] Canaris was interested in meeting this celebrated visitor because the general was said to be the likely head of any new coup. Sanjurjo was taking advantage of a visit to the Winter Olympics in Garmisch to have talks with the German authorities.[67]

Canaris took his Spanish visitor on a conducted tour of German munitions factories and held out the prospect of arms supplies from the Reich if Sanjurjo's coup materialized.[68] Sanjurjo's account of anarchic conditions in Spain reminded him of his days with the Freikorps in Kiel and Berlin. He felt as if he were back in the unloved Weimar Republic, reliving the torments of the 1920s. Once again, or so it seemed to him, an officer corps which believed in the eternal virtues of patriotism and nationhood, which abhorred party politics and was solely dedicated to good order and the interests of the state, had set out to combat the universal evils of Socialism, Communism and anarchy.

The very names of the leading conspirators were reminiscent of phases in his own career. Kindelán, Jordana, Magáz, Martínez Anido— he not only knew them all but was linked with them by common experience or kindred values. As head of German military intelligence, he could not turn his back when every name was an irresistible appeal to repay what his beloved Spain had once bestowed on him in the way of colourful experiences and *joie de vivre*. Canaris's attitude made him only too ready to accept antidemocratic pronouncements from the lips of reactionary Spanish officers. In his ultraconservative view, as in theirs, Spain's domestic political crisis was simply a brazen attack by the universal Bolshevik foe on a jewel in the crown of Western civilization.

Sanjurjo departed in the comfortable expectation of assistance from his new pro-Spanish friend, but bad news awaited him on his return. Nearly all the leading conspirators had been relieved of their commands by the Madrid government and posted to remote garrisons. A premonition of impending danger had prompted the government to transfer Army Chief of Staff Franco to the Canary Islands, Air Force Chief Goded to the Balearics and General Mola to Pamplona.[69]

General Francisco Franco, who reached Tenerife, the largest of the Canary Islands, on March 12, was placed under special surveillance.[70] The civilian governor had orders to report any suspicious move he made. Franco did not, of course, know that he was also pursued by the watchful but benevolent gaze of a German named Niemann, who worked in Las Palmas on the neighbouring island of Gran Canaria and served as the Abwehr's local watchdog.[71] Niemann was only one of the agents and informants who tried to note any change in the uneasy relationship between the Army and the government.

All surveillance notwithstanding, the UME conspirators pressed on with their plans for a coup. Mola undertook its organization from Pamplona and established contact with every major garrison in the country. He also dispatched secret envoys to the leaders of the disunited right-wing parties, notably the fascist Falange, but it took time for them to agree on a concerted plan of action.[72]

Reports from military bases disclosed that not every unit in the 115,000-strong Army would support the coup. Full reliance could only be placed on the two corps in Spanish Morocco, which formed the nucleus of the Army: the Foreign Legion and the Moroccan native troops, totalling 34,000 men.[73] If the coup failed to go smoothly these units would have to intervene at once on the Spanish mainland, but how were they to cross the Strait of Gibraltar? Franco knew the answer. On May 11 Santa Cruz de Tenerife was visited by a Spanish naval squadron whose commander, Admiral Javier de Salas, was initiated into the conspiracy by Franco. The admiral pledged his support and promised that the squadron would be standing by to ferry the African Army to Spain.[74]

Mola was still negotiating with the right-wing parties when Spanish political terrorism claimed its most prominent victim. During the early hours of July 13, policemen incensed at the murder of one of their officers by Falangists forced their way into the home of the monarchist opposition leader José Calvo Sotelo, who was arrested and later shot during a car ride. To conservative Army officers, this outrage accorded perfectly with their picture of the enemy. The assassins were members of Socialist and Communist youth movements, the arrest had been made in consultation with the Prime Minister and the crime itself had probably been committed on direct instructions from Communist Party headquarters.[75]

Mola could wait no longer. He urged the politicians to hurry, and shortly afterwards his couriers delivered a brief message to every leading member of the conspiracy: "the 17th at 17." In clear, this meant that the conspirators in every Spanish province and colony were to strike at 5 P.M. on July 17, 1936.[76]

Mola's message was received by Franco, who promptly gave his watchdogs the slip. On the pretext that they had to attend the funeral of the military commander at Las Palmas, he and his senior aides travelled to the neighbouring island on the morning of July 17 and booked into the Hotel Madrid. Then he waited.[77] At 3 A.M. on July 18 there came a knock at his door. An officer handed him a signal just received by the Tenerife radio station. It read: "Melilla. General Solans to General Franco: The Army has taken up arms against the government and seized all command installations. Viva España!"[78] The garrison at Melilla in the northeast corner of Spanish Morocco had unleashed one of the longest and most sanguinary civil wars in European history.

Franco boarded an aircraft chartered in England and flew to Tetuán, the capital of Spanish Morocco, where he assumed command of the African forces.[79] Even while leafing through the first reports to reach his new headquarters, however, he realized that there were no grounds for rejoicing. The Alzamiento had almost failed and the Army's response had been patchy. Apart from Morocco, the "Nationalists" controlled smallish areas of Southwest Spain and almost the whole of the Northwest. Central Spain and the entire East were in government hands. Moreover, the Republican regime had promptly mobilized the civil population against the rebels and alerted its foreign friends in Eastern and Western Europe.

On July 20 Franco sustained yet another blow. Sanjurjo, the Nationalists' titular leader, had been killed in Portugal when his plane crashed on take-off.[80] Three days after the coup was launched the conspirators had lost their figurehead and the Alzamiento's only prominent leaders, Franco and Mola, were hundreds of miles apart. Worse still, a counterrevolt broke out among the petty officers and junior ratings manning the ships that were to ferry Franco's army to Spain. Within a few hours, 70 per cent of the Spanish naval officer corps lay murdered on deck.[81] Franco knew only too well what this meant. The African Army was stranded and would be forced to look on idly while the government sent its troops and volunteers into action against the rebels.

"I don't see what the rebels are after," jeered the Socialist leader Indalecio Prieto. "They're crazy. Who do they imagine is going to save them?"[82] Franco's response was to enlist the aid of the fascist powers Realizing that a handful of aircraft would suffice to transport his African army to Spain, he asked Mussolini for an immediate loan of twelve bombers and three fighters.[83] The Duce had already promised material assistance in the event of an anti-Republican coup.[84] Now, Franco took him at his word.

But Mussolini found the whole venture too risky. Even before Franco's emissary reached Rome on July 21, he blue-pencilled the single word "No!" on the telegram conveying the Spanish general's requirements.[85] Mola thereupon dispatched a confidential envoy to Rome to remind Mussolini of his former undertakings.[86] The courier was still airborne when Beigbeder, who was now heading the Moroccan Department of Native Affairs, stepped in.

Beigbeder may have informed Franco of what had been discussed between Sanjurjo and Canaris earlier in the year. Canaris's name was not unknown to the future Caudillo, who had met the German intelligence chief in Madrid while attending the arms deal negotiations between him and Gil Robles, the Spanish War Minister, in summer 1935. Being fully alive to the importance of these links with Canaris, Franco at once instructed Beigbeder to mobilize his German friends. On July 22, by way of the German Consulate in Tetuán, Beigbeder sent a telegram to Major General Kühlenthal, military attaché at the German Embassy in Paris, requesting him to forward it to the Reich War Ministry. The gist of Beigbeder's telegram, whose safe arrival on Canaris's desk he must have taken for granted, was a request that ten transport aircraft be dispatched to Morocco via private German airfreight companies.[87]

Not content with this, Franco sought his own pipeline to Berlin. He remembered having noticed a German at Tetuán airport when he landed there. Inquiries disclosed that he was a businessman named Johannes Bernhardt who worked for the export-import firm of Wilmer in Tetuán and sold cooking stoves to the Spanish Army. The rebel general decided to exploit the amibitions of this former East Prussian sugar merchant, who had fled from Germany in the 1920s to escape his creditors.[88]

What lent a little colour to Bernhardt's drab existence in the German colony at Tetuán were his part-time activities as press officer and economic expert of the local branch of the NSDAP's Auslandsorganisation [AO—Foreign Organization].[89] He called on Franco accompanied by his superior, Adolf Langenheim, the local party boss. The two Nazis leapt at Franco's suggestion that they should fly to Berlin with a Spanish officer, Captain Arranz, and there deliver two personal missives, one addressed to Hitler and the other to Göring. Franco went on to explain that these letters contained an urgent appeal for German military assistance.[90]

Transport was quickly provided. The rebel authorities at Las Palmas had commandeered a Lufthansa machine (D-A POK) and were using it to ferry their senior officials around. This aircraft was now detailed to convey Bernhardt, Langenheim and Arranz to Berlin. The three emissaries took off on July 24 and landed at Tempelhof Airport the same day.[91]

At first, however, the visitors found few willing listeners. The head of the Political Section of the Foreign Office, Hans Heinrich Dieckhoff, had previously told the War Ministry that Franco's envoys should "not be received by any official military departments," arguing that support for Franco could have "exceptionally detrimental effects" on German nationals in Spain, the German export trade and German shipping in the Mediterranean.[92] While concurring with Dieckhoff, War Ministry officials left matters largely in the air because Blomberg was absent on a visit to the Bayreuth Festival with his Führer.

Although AO Chief and Gauleiter Wilhelm Bohle had also been "urgently advised" by Dieckhoff "not to introduce the two officers [sic] to party officials or further their plans here in any way,"[93] the loyal Nazis from Tetuán were so insistent that he referred the matter to his immediate superior, party administrator Rudolf Hess. Hess decided that the Führer must see Franco's letter at once, and three departmental chiefs from the AO accompanied the delegation to Bayreuth. They got there late on Saturday, July 25.[94]

Hitler had just enjoyed "the ultimate acoustic experience which Wilhelm Furtwängler brings to full fruition in *Die Walküre*" (thus the music critic of the *Völkischer Beobachter*) and was about to retire to his suite at Haus Wahnfried when Franco's envoys were announced.[95] He read the general's letter and listened to an oral account of his requirements. Bernhardt recalls that "Hitler dominated the conference with a monologue and some pertinent questions, thus deciding on his own that Germany should help Franco. After this—midnight had passed—he sent for Göring and Blomberg."[96]

Did Canaris play a part in this fateful conference? A short extant memo by Hitler's Präsidialkanzlei [personal staff] records that "an admiral present at Bayreuth" was also summoned to the night session in Haus Wahnfried, and many historians have therefore concluded that he must have been Canaris.[97]

As the only surviving witness of the Bayreuth conference, however, Bernhardt insists that the admiral was not Canaris but another naval officer by the name of Karl Coupette, head of the Naval High Command's shipping department. Is it conceivable that a naval officer with only technical functions was admitted to one of the most momentous prewar conferences in Hitler's Germany? Other doubts remain, since Bernhardt's account conflicts with the Präsidialkanzlei memo on other points of detail. First, an admiral is mentioned, whereas Bernhardt's Coupette held the rank of captain only. Second, Bernhardt maintains that the Navy man was called in *after* Hitler made his decision, whereas the memo states that the Führer sent for the admiral "at once." And finally, Bernhardt reports that Hitler had decided to intervene *before* he sent for his three paladins, whereas Göring testified to the Nuremberg IMT [International Military Tribunal] that he found Hitler stil undecided: "The Führer thought it over. I vigorously urged that support should be given at all costs."[98]

By the time Hitler and his advisers parted in the early hours of July 26, the die was cast: the Third Reich would give the Spanish rebels its backing.[99] Only two days earlier, Hitler had been concerned lest intervention in the civil war (with warships dispatched for the protection of Germans resident in Spain) might involve the Reich in an "incident" of unforeseeable dimensions. Now his misgivings had vanished.[100] His one thought was that developments in Spain would inevitably kindle Mussolini's Mediterranean ambitions, propel the Italians into a confrontation with France, the Spanish Republic's patron, and finally drive them into the arms of Germany.

Canaris must have been involved in organizing aid for Franco not later than July 26. Representatives of the Abwehr took part when a "Sonderstab W" [Special Staff W] met at the Reich Ministry of Aviation the same afternoon, charged with setting up an airlift to Spanish Morocco. Although Canaris was not familiar with all the details of the situation in Spain (who could claim such knowledge in those chaotic days?), he was more and more often asked for advice and assistance by Mola and Franco. It was no mere coincidence that Mola had been in charge of the Seguridad, with which Canaris had co-operated during

the Weimar Republic, and Mola now took advantage of the old ties between the Admiral and the Spanish secret police.[101]

Unternehmen "Feuerzauber" [Operation "Fire-Magic"] was soon
under way.[102] On July 27 the first Ju 52s took off from Tempelhof Airport, to be followed by others of the twenty which represented Hitler's
preliminary contribution.[103] Piloted by Lufthansa personnel, they flew
to Tetuán by the shortest possible route and landed in Morocco on July
28. Then they began to airlift soldiers belonging to Franco's African
army. Week after week the German planes shuttled between Tetuán
and Seville, ferrying unit after unit to the Spanish mainland. By mid-
October thirteen thousand men and 270 tons of supplies had been
transported to Andalusia.[104] Franco and his forces could take a hand in
the fighting at last. The juggernaut of the Spanish Civil War proceeded
on its murderous way.

Meanwhile, a second consignment of German aid had left for
Spain. During the night of July 31–August 1, eighty-six Luftwaffe men
dressed in civilian clothes and camouflaged as members of the "Union
Tour Party" sailed from Hamburg aboard the steamship Usaramo. The
ship's cargo included half a dozen He 51 fighter planes and a score of
antiaircraft guns.[105] The units which followed this vanguard of Air
Force "volunteers" steadily grew in size until it was rumoured that Germany planned to intervene in Spain with ground forces as well as pilots
and instructors.

Foreign Office advisers watched gloomily as outsiders plunged the
Third Reich into an unpredictable interventionist policy which was
bound, like the Rhineland crisis, to result in a drastic confrontation
with the Western democracies. Heedless of the Foreign Office, Canaris
and Göring were harnessing Germany to the uncertain fate of one particular side in a foreign civil war. Once again, a weekend coup by the
Führer had ignored the misgivings—indeed, the very existence—of his
diplomats. Foreign Minister Konstantin von Neurath grumbled but did
not venture to protest.

Not so Beck. The Army Chief of Staff dug in his heels at the very
mention of committing troops in Spain. He flatly rejected the idea,
hinting that the active involvement of German Army units would only
retard and jeopardize the rearmament programme.[106] His commander
in chief, General von Fritsch, never exactly noted for his political or
tactical acumen, proposed that Russian émigrés be sent to the Spanish
front instead. When his advisers drew attention to the logistical problems, he sent for a map. Having screwed a monocle into his eye and
stared at it for a few moments, he drawled, "Peculiar country—doesn't
have any railways."[107] Stülpnagel, too, was alarmed at the "nervous
haste and precipitancy" of German foreign policy: "We can probably

keep the world on edge for quite a while yet, but sooner or later it will get fed up and call us to order."[108]

But Canaris, who was blind to such dangers, had found a theme which gave him no rest. "I saw for myself," recalls Bamler of Abwehr III, "how Canaris dropped all other matters and spared neither time nor effort in getting the leaders of Germany and Italy interested in his [Spanish] schemes."[109] He was in his element. Nobody was going to prevent him from creating a durable alliance between Germany and Franco's rejuvenated Spain.

Before the Franco delegation left, Canaris asked Langenheim, who had worked for the Abwehr in the past, to send him regular reports from Tetuán. The local party boss was to stay close to Franco and notify Canaris of any major developments on the staff of the man who was increasingly becoming the acknowledged leader of the insurrectionary movement.[110] The Admiral kept an equally close watch on Franco's partner Mola. An old friend, Colonel Juan Vigón, was acting as chief of staff to Mola's Army of the North, and reports were dispatched from Mola's headquarters by the V-Mann Seydel. In addition, Canaris's representative in Paris, Captain Lietzmann of the German Embassy, contacted emissaries from other revolutionary generals— "never at the same place twice and observing every precautionary measure possible to avoid compromising a member of the embassy staff," as the head of mission noted.[111]

Canaris mobilized every available Spanish expert in his organization. Many of his associates from the 1920s were back in harness again, among them Reserve Lieutenant Commander Rüggeberg, his onetime representative in Barcelona, and Lieutenant (ret.) Messerschmidt, "Kika's" erstwhile senior representative in Madrid, who undertook reconnaissance trips to Portugal and specialized in evaluating the arms and equipment of the Spanish rebel army.[112] Canaris also had men working among the "Reds," as right-wing jargon now called the Republicans, and the Abwehr sustained its first casualty when V-Mann Eberhard Funk was caught and shot after reconnoitring some Republican ammunition depots.[113]

The German intelligence chief was sometimes better informed than Mola and Franco, who were still separated by a strip of Republican-held territory and often had no knowledge of each other's activities. "Because reliable communication with Franco" did not seem "invariably guaranteed at present" (to quote one of Seydel's reports to Canaris), Mola transmitted some of his messages for Franco to the Abwehr chief, who forwarded them to the commander of the Southern Army via a Berlin V-Mann.[114]

Reading Mola's and Seydel's reports, Canaris was spurred to even greater activity. As early as August 2 he received a detailed inventory

from Paris which disclosed how feverishly France was supplying the
Spanish Republican forces with arms and ammunition. In all the European democracies and the Soviet Union, volunteers were enlisting for
active service against what they or left-wing propagandists regarded as
fascism.[115] The rebel forces, on the other hand, were short of arms and
ammunition. Seydel reported: "Northern group very urgently needs aircraft, especially fighters, also bombs, rifle and machine-gun ammunition, hand grenades and bayonets."[116]

Soon afterwards, Blomberg sent Canaris off with instructions to persuade the Italians to join in. On August 4 Canaris met Roatta, his
fellow intelligence chief and Hispanophile, at Bolzano. The two men
were quick to reach agreement, largely because Mussolini had by now
revised his negative attitude.[117] Weak though Franco seemed, the Duce
felt tempted to back him by the prospect of strengthening Italy's Mediterranean position at the expense of bloodshed in Spain.

Roatta had nonetheless been told to inform his German partner
that Italy's support for the Franco cause would only be "unofficial." Canaris also learned that twelve Italian aircraft and a shipload of ammunition had been sent to Morocco on July 30.[118] This information was
sufficient for Canaris, in his turn, to recommend the Führer's approval
of fresh deliveries to Spain. Franco had asked for twenty more warplanes and vast quantities of ammunition, and Canaris eagerly backed
his requests.[119]

Hitler accepted this advice. Although the Reich had officially
applauded the principle of non-intervention adopted by the European
powers, he lent covert support to the rebel Nationalist movement (just
as other countries did to "their" side in the civil war). On August 24
Hitler decreed that General Franco was to receive "the most extensive
material and military support," though active involvement in hostilities
was "excluded for the present."[120] Next day, three German freighters
laden with twenty-eight aircraft, ammunition and other war material
set off for Spain.[121]

Canaris was again dispatched to ensure the closest possible co-operation with Italy. At another meeting with Roatta on August 27 he negotiated a co-ordinative agreement in respect of German and Italian aid
to Spain.[122] This provided that both countries should as far as possible
equalize their consignments, which were to be for Franco's benefit
alone. Military equipment had to be maintained and serviced by German and Italian personnel, though the latter were precluded from open
involvement in hostilities. This ban could only be lifted if the order
were expressly countermanded with the agreement of both parties.

Without knowing it, Canaris and Roatta had taken the first step towards a German-Italian alliance which was to speed Hitler on the road
to new ventures in foreign policy. Just how political the Canaris-Roatta

agreement really was, despite its seeming confinement to military technicalities, emerges from what Canaris gathered in conversation with Count Galeazzo Ciano, Mussolini's Foreign Minister and son-in-law, on August 28. This was that Italy and Germany had a duty to assist Franco, with men as well as material, in his campaign against "the common Red enemy"—a task which entailed joint planning and mutual consultation.[123]

Ciano insisted that Germany and Italy should both permit their airmen to take an active part in the fighting. Canaris told him that only the Reich War Minister could make such a decision but undertook to inform Blomberg from Rome.[124] The same day, Blomberg decreed that German airmen in Spain could fly combat missions. A few days later he issued an analogous order to warships escorting German freighters to Spain.[125]

Shortly afterwards, Lieutenant Colonel Walter Warlimont of Abteilung L (travelling under the name Waltersdorf) and Roatta (recently promoted general and cover-named Mancini) boarded an Italian cruiser and sailed to Tetuán. From there they flew to Cáceres, where Franco had established his headquarters,[126] and briefed the general on how Germany and Italy saw the future conduct of the war. The German-Italian alliance was taking shape.

Diplomats continued what Canaris had begun. German and Italian intermediaries warmed the atmosphere between their two countries until Mussolini finally resolved to seek an alliance with Germany. Ciano appeared in Berlin on October 20 and next day concluded a secret agreement with Neurath under which both powers would co-ordinate their policies in Europe. Three days later Ciano travelled to Berchtesgaden for an audience with Hitler.[127]

The Führer gave him a friendly reception and acclaimed Mussolini as "the world's greatest statesman, to whom none may even remotely compare himself." No country in Europe, not even Britain, would be a match for a German-Italian bloc.[128] Mussolini requited Hitler for these flattering remarks. Addressing a mass rally in Milan on November 1, 1936, he announced that a "Rome-Berlin axis" had been founded and that every country in Europe was invited to join it.[129] This "invitation" did not disguise the fact that the fascist powers had declared war on the European *status quo*. Their secret agreement had already allotted one sphere of influence to each party: the Mediterranean to Italy and Eastern Europe to the Reich.

Canaris remained curiously indifferent to these developments because his gaze was focused on Spain alone. The more fanatically the two sides clashed, transforming their country into a wilderness ruled by terror and savagery, the more passionate became his commitment to the Spanish "crusade." He devoured every report his agents sent him from the Spanish theatre of war and radioed a stream of queries and instructions in return. In September he received a long-awaited message: a general officers' council had elected Franco Generalissimo and Head of State under the terms of a resolution proposed by none other than Canaris's old friend Kindelán.[130]

Many other reports were less favourable in tone. Franco's advance on Madrid was progressing slowly and the resistance of the government forces hardening week by week. Furthermore, the involvement of foreign volunteers was taking effect. As early as August 17, V-Mann 110, one of Canaris's most reliable agents in Republican territory, had reported that the "large-scale transfer of French volunteers to Spanish Red Militia began some days ago. 100 to 170 men daily. Total number approximately 30,000."[131] Soviet tanks and aircraft had also arrived in Spain. On October 29 Berlin received the following report from Barcelona: "Twenty Russian aircraft, single-seater fighters and bombers, have arrived Cartagena with Russian personnel including mechanics and fitters."[132]

Worried by reports that military aid from the Soviet Union was increasing and that Franco's conduct of the war was cautious and dominated by considerations of safety, Blomberg sent his chief of military intelligence to Spain. Canaris set off at the end of October dressed in civilian clothes and armed with false papers identifying him as an Argentine citizen named Guillermo.[133] His destination was Salamanca, Franco's new base, where he was to study the rebel army's military position and, if necessary, hold out prospects of increased German aid.

Canaris landed at Salamanca and drove to the bishop's palace, where Franco had installed his headquarters. The Caudillo came to meet his visitor and embraced him. Whatever he may have thought of the Germans, and however much he later dissociated himself from the doomed Third Reich, he never forgot what Admiral Canaris had done for him, Francisco Franco y Bahamonde, and for the immortal cause of conservative Spain. Canaris felt equally drawn to Franco, whom he considered one of the world's few great men—perhaps the greatest of his generation—and whose photograph was the only likeness of a contemporary politician to adorn his office in later years.

But there was little time for sentiment on this occasion. Canaris found the Generalissimo in low spirits because his forces had just (on October 29) taken a hard knock south of Madrid. Two hundred tanks, twelve- and eighteen-tonners fresh from production lines in the Soviet Union and commanded by the Russian general Pavlov, had burst through the narrow streets of the township of Esquivia and inflicted a crushing defeat on Franco's cavalry—crushing in the literal sense.[134]

As if one piece of bad news were not enough, Canaris had on October 30 been directed by Blomberg to extract some humiliating concessions from Franco before promising him more German aid. He was to inform him that the Reich was prepared to send a Luftwaffe corps to Spain, but only if he agreed in advance that it should be commanded by a German officer to whom all German military personnel in Spain would be subordinated.[135] Franco must further undertake "to prosecute the war more methodically and actively by means of ground and air operations and to co-ordinate both with a view to speedier occupation of the harbours essential to Russian supplies."[136] Canaris had also received the following instruction from Foreign Minister von Neurath: "Given the possibility of increased help for the Reds, the German Government does not consider that the combat tactics of White Spain, ground and air, give promise of success."[137]

But Canaris managed to disguise the arrogance of these demands and persuaded Franco to concentrate on the positive aspect of the German gesture. The Reich was coming to the Spanish Nationalists' aid with combat forces of its own. Four bomber squadrons, four fighter squadrons, one squadron each of naval and reconnaissance aircraft, one experimental squadron, antiaircraft and antitank units and thirty tanks, —all these represented a substantial increment to Franco's strength. The Caudillo acquiesced.[138]

By November 6 the new 6,500-man Condor Legion was ready for action in Seville under the command of Lieutenant General Hugo Sperrle.[139] Elements of the Legion soon took such a successful hand in the fighting that Franco put his Air Force units under Sperrle's command.[140] The position of the Nationalist assault troops improved so steadily, or so it seemed, that the Berlin and Rome authorities confidently assumed that the capture of Madrid by Franco's forces would only be a matter of days. They reacted too soon: on November 18, 1936, Germany and Italy recognized the Franco regime as Spain's sole legitimate government.[141]

Franco himself realized that he had yet to make the decisive breakthrough. Again he called for assistance from his German friends, and again Canaris was urged to help. The Caudillo hinted that he needed at least one German and one Italian division in order to defeat the common foe,[142] but this time his tireless champion in Berlin came up against a brick wall. Army Chief of Staff Beck declined to send a single infantryman to Spain and Blomberg pronounced the German rescue operation complete. The Foreign Minister was just as adamant. "The dispatching of an entire division," Neurath dictated, ". . . [would be] unwarrantable under any circumstances."[143]

Blomberg strictly impressed on Canaris that he was not to sponsor Franco's appeal for ground forces. The occasion of this warning was another visit by Canaris to Rome, because Mussolini was taking advantage of Franco's new demands to extend Italy's sphere of influence in the Western Mediterranean. The dictator was already rhapsodizing about the prospect of Italian bases in the Balearics and had come to regard Majorca as a sort of Italian Gibraltar, a fortress and symbol of the Roman *mare nostrum*.

December 6 was the date set by Mussolini for a joint chiefs of staff conference to which Roatta and Canaris were also invited.[144] Mussolini and Ciano made it quite clear that they thought the time had come to commit ground forces in Spain. Since the Canaris-Roatta agreement stipulated that both countries should maintain an equal military presence there, Mussolini asked Canaris if the Reich was also prepared to send a division. The Abwehr chief just sat there, stony-faced and silent, thoroughly resenting the role assigned him by Blomberg.[145]

The Duce was so annoyed by Canaris's reserved attitude that his invitation to the next conference on January 10, 1937, was coupled with an injunction to the German Ambassador in Rome to apprise Berlin as follows: "Since the object this time will be to effect a genuine outcome in Spain and, consequently, to reach important decisions, Mussolini would welcome it if Admiral Canaris or whoever is sent to replace or accompany him comes armed with full powers of discretion and not, like last time, as a semi-observer."[146]

Canaris must have taken another initiative in favour of increased German support for Franco, but Blomberg stood firm. A War Ministry memorandum dated January 7, 1937, records: "Franco's material demands are proving so detrimental to German rearmament that help from another quarter is only to be welcomed, possibly from the foreign policy aspect as well."[147] Canaris set off with strict instructions to approve any military commitment Italy chose to make. He was slightly envious when, at the January 10 conference, his friend Roatta was appointed commander in chief of an Italian expeditionary force whose strength rose within a month to four divisions numbering fifty thousand men.[148]

Envious or not, he followed the fortunes of this corps with benevolent interest. Roatta seemed to be in luck. On February 8 his men won their first victory by capturing the Republican stronghold of Málaga in conjunction with Spanish units.[149] A month later the Italians were sent into action on the Guadalajara front, east of Madrid, and had their first brush with the Republic's International Brigades. "The collapse of the international forces," Mussolini wrote to Roatta, "will be a success of far-reaching importance, politically as well as militarily."[150] He was disastrously wide of the mark. The International Brigades, including the Thälmann Battalion composed of German Socialists and Communists, put the well-armed Italians to flight.[151]

"The Germans in Salamanca," report two French historians of the Civil War, "seethed with scorn and derision. The 11th International

Brigade might consist of Jews and Communists, they said, but they had learnt to fight like Germans and make mincemeat of Italians."[152] Spanish Nationalist troops also sang satirical songs about Roatta's grenadiers, and Italy's prestige in Spain took a hammering.[153]

Being pro-Italian, Canaris was dismayed. He forbade his officers to criticize or condescend to their Italian colleagues and dismissed even the most objective references to the shortcomings of Roatta's troops. Major Pruck, an Eastern expert at Abwehr headquarters, heard an account of the Italians' conduct from a Japanese officer who had actually been present at the battle of Guadalajara. When Pruck drafted a report on his informant's experiences, Canaris reacted fiercely. He blue-pencilled the document and scrawled on it "This is utter nonsense!" It seems that he was particularly displeased by the passages relating to the prowess of the Thälmann Battalion.[154]

Altercations between Spaniards, Germans and Italians periodically reached such a pitch that the Admiral had to pay several visits to Spain to mediate between them. He became one of Franco's most indispensable helpmates. Wherever conflicts loomed or bottlenecks formed, Canaris stepped in to relieve Franco of wearisome problems or even more wearisome allies.

The headquarters staff of the Condor Legion and the Italian expeditionary force were barely on speaking terms . . . Canaris urged Roatta to fraternize with his German comrades-in-arms.[155] The Caudillo resented the megalomania of General (ret.) Wilhelm Faupel, the Nazi whom the German Foreign Office had selected as its first ambassador to Nationalist Spain . . . Canaris saw to it that Faupel was recalled and replaced by an old acquaintance from his wartime days in Madrid, the career diplomat Eberhard von Stohrer.[156] General Sperrle's brusque and imperious manner was getting on the Caudillo's nerves . . . A report from Canaris was enough to ensure that the Condor Legion acquired a new commander.[157]

No German carried more weight in contemporary Spain than Rear Admiral Canaris. Thanks to his senior status in the Wehrmacht hierarchy and his growing network of agents in Spain, he was intimately acquainted with every new development in the fighting. His informants held posts at the various belligerents' headquarters and his agents infiltrated the remotest subsidiary theatres of war. The conflict had long ago abandoned its purely national character. This war on the Iberian Peninsula had become an irreconcilable clash between the interests and ideologies of the day, and, more particularly, between the totalitarian powers and their intelligence agencies. It was no coincidence that the German and Soviet secret service chiefs were both personally involved, Wilhelm Canaris in the guise of Guillermo the globe-trotter and his opposite number, Ian Karlovich Berzin, as Military Attaché Goriev of the Soviet Embassy in Madrid.[158]

War had been raging between German and Soviet agents ever since the Abwehr made its official entry into Spain with the Condor Legion. It hid beneath the uncommunicative title "S/88/Ic," which merely denoted that its officers were responsible for intelligence operations on behalf of the Legion (code name S/88).[159] This group was headed by Lieutenant Commander Wilhelm Leissner, alias "Colonel Gustav Lenz," who had established an Abwehr outstation in Algeciras immediately after the Civil War flared up. Throughout its duration, the "Büro Lenz" at Algeciras remained the nerve centre of all Abwehr activities. Canaris often visited Leissner, a former U-boat commander with whom he was on close terms, and Algeciras soon became his favourite Spanish town. (The Büro Lenz, which formed the nucleus of what later became "KO [Kriegsorganisation—War Organization] Spain," moved in June 1939 to San Sebastián and in autumn of that year to Madrid.)[160]

Leissner brought some of the most able intelligence evaluators in the Geheimer Meldedienst (Abwehr I) to Spain, among them instructors whom he seconded to Franco's secret service, the Servicio Información Policía Militar (SIPM).[161] Even more important than the men of the Geheimer Meldedienst were those belonging to Abwehr III [counterespionage and counterintelligence] because no war had more thoroughly perfected the art of infiltration and camouflage than the Spanish Civil War. Counterespionage was directed by probably the shrewdest German specialist in this field, Major Joachim Rohleder.[162]

The Condor Legion's Abwehr group was also joined by a team of Gestapo officers, who assumed executive functions. Canaris and his Gestapo partner Best had previously agreed on the establishment of a police force in the Wehrmacht's service whose name was a reminder of early attempts at co-operation between the military and the police, the Geheime Feldpolizei [Secret Field Police].[163] This GFP was under military command, however, and many Gestapo men resented the fact. Best was obliged to pacify them with a confidential memo: "The Führer has made this concession to Canaris and signed the relevant order . . . You must definitely bear in mind that the Führer granted precedence to the other party in a weak moment and that we shall now have to prevail under difficult circumstances!"[164]

But working relations between the GFP and Abwehr III were almost devoid of friction, partly because one of the Gestapo officers, Gerhard Fischer, found that Rohleder was an old acquaintance from Buenos Aires.[165] Being a "typical straightforward soldier," the major earned an unequalled reputation among the men from Prinz-Albrecht-Strasse which was to stand Canaris in good stead at a critical stage.[166] The GFP men willingly bowed to Rohleder's professional expertise.

Together the Abwehr and GFP set out to unmask Republican agents operating in Nationalist territory, most of whom were Soviet-trained Communists. Assisted by German-trained SIPM personnel, they detected many of the agents who had already infiltrated Franco's forces. But the underground struggle was not confined to Spain. The Soviet secret service had set up intelligence and administrative networks in Western Europe, and these also had to be smashed.

In The Hague, Soviet resident director (General) Walter Krivitsky had established a firm of arms dealers—most of them Russian secret servicemen—who were purchasing arms for the Spanish Republic in all parts of Europe. After Abwehr agents had succeeded in penetrating this network, Canaris procured defective military equipment, refurbished it and sold it to the Krivitsky organization.[167] German intelligence was equally alive to the existence of the import-export firms which Soviet intelligence was setting up in Paris, London, Prague, Zurich, Warsaw, Copenhagen, Amsterdam and Brussels as front organizations for the procurement of arms and the recruitment of volunteers for the Republicans.[168]

Canaris's sleuths also picked up the trail of a new clandestine organization, the Copenhagen-based sabotage group run by ex-KPD official Ernst Wollweber. Dedicated to the "neutralization" of German, Italian and Japanese freighters bound for Spain, Wollweber's twenty-man team always employed the same method. Having laid a charge of dynamite in the ship's bilge between the outer hull and the hold, they set the firing mechanism so that the charge would explode at sea.[169] The Germans took some time to track this organization down.

But the toughest battle between the German and Soviet secret services took place in Paris and was waged for control of the local Russian *émigrés*, many of whom felt tempted to earn a return ticket to Russia by joining one of the International Brigades. Sometimes Canaris's recruiting officers got there first, and quite a few Russian expatriates let themselves be lured to Spain by Krivitsky's and Berzin's agents without disclosing that they had already been enlisted by the Abwehr.[170]

For all their industrious detective work, the Abwehr and Gestapo failed to spot that the enemy had long been ensconced at the heart of the organization handling German aid to Spain. Harro Schulze-Boysen, an antifascist who had suffered from the "co-ordinative" reign of terror in 1933 and was now employed in the press section of the Reich Ministry of Aviation, gathered all the information he could about Sonderstab W—details of German consignments to Spain, of the officers and other ranks involved and of Abwehr operations in Republican territory.[171] This information he embodied in letters which a relative, Gisela von Poellnitz, posted through the letterbox of the Soviet Trade Mission in Berlin.[172]

Schulze-Boysen's courier would have escaped detection had not the Gestapo placed the Soviet Trade Mission under closer surveillance. Gisela von Poellnitz was arrested in 1937. Schulze-Boysen and a few sympathizers were about to flee the country when she returned, having given nothing away. Schulze-Boysen himself got off with a caution from the Gestapo.[173] They only realized later that he had betrayed "secret Abwehr business."[174] A Gestapo superintendent: "During the Spanish Civil War we sent some of our own men to the International Brigade as spies. Schulze-Boysen knew their names and passed them on to the Reds. Our men were thereupon put up against a wall."[175]

This affair discloses something of the passionate crusading spirit with which the Abwehr and Gestapo hunted down their common foe. Canaris never ceased to regard Communism and its Soviet habitat as the root of all evil. To a West German like Canaris, Russia remained a sinister and enigmatic world, a dark hotbed of lethal threats to Europe's bourgeois way of life. But he was not content to keep the secret service outposts of Stalin's empire under observation and, where possible, control. He wanted to know more about the Russian interior and explore the possibilities of undermining its destructive potential. The Abwehr could not manage this on its own, of course, so the German secret service required foreign partners. This was not the first time Canaris had toyed with the idea of an alliance between the Abwehr and its counterparts in the countries bordering Russia, their common and exclusive purpose being to probe the Soviet Union. The Admiral even included far-off Japan in his secret service strategy, thereby imparting yet another fillip to Hitler's latent expansionism.

The countries consulted showed little immediate inclination to be drawn into the Abwehr's crusade. Even Hungary, with its traditionally pro-German attitude, had hesitated when Canaris paid a preliminary visit in April 1935. "In view of the political situation in Europe," he dictated to one of his escorting officers, "no firm decision for or against Germany can be expected from Hungary at the present time. A small country surrounded by fiercely hostile enemies has to pursue a cautious and temporizing policy . . . Uncertainty about the direction favoured by Gömbös [the Hungarian premier] is also causing uncertainty among senior officers."[176]

Canaris himself harboured no such doubts: "The friendship of the military [for Germany] is sincere."[177] He contacted Hungarian officers who had served with him during World War I at the Adriatic bases of the Austro-Hungarian Navy, among them some former comrades-in-arms who were now employed by the Hungarian secret service. In this he was assisted by a junior staff officer named Szentpetery, whose photograph later adorned his desk.[178] In summer 1935 Lieutenant Colonel Major, head of the Defensive Group of the Hungarian General

Staff, came to Berlin and opened negotiations which led to an agreement on joint German-Hungarian intelligence work inside the Soviet Union.[179]

That autumn another partner appeared on the scene. In Estonia, a group of pro-German officers under Colonel Massing had assumed control of the country's secret service.[180] Shortly afterwards Massing made Canaris an offer of the closest co-operation against Russia, and the Abwehr chief had an agreement drafted under which German military intelligence would be given free rein in Estonia and both secret services would co-ordinate their Russian activities in return for German financial aid and technical equipment.[181] In summer 1936 Massing visited Berlin to sign this document, and Canaris later travelled to Estonia for further discussions.[182]

The next secret service to join the anti-Soviet alliance was that of Japan. The espionage system maintained by this up-and-coming Asiatic power was rated "remarkably well informed" by the Abwehr.[183] The Japanese secret service, to quote a former Abwehr captain, "had at its disposal the best and shrewdest brains in its own country."[184] Japanese infiltration of the Soviet Union earned special esteem from the Abwehr, which had barely managed to introduce a single competent spy into the Soviet administrative and military machine. Piekenbrock, who headed the Geheimer Meldedienst, was only too conscious that "Russia is the hardest country for an enemy intelligence service to penetrate."[185]

To gain the co-operation of such an admirably well-informed secret service struck the Abwehr as a worthwhile objective. Canaris, who was fascinated by Japan, encouraged these endeavours. His trip to the Far East in summer 1924 had made a deep impression on him, as had the sight of what was going on in Japan's naval bases. His plans for closer co-operation between the navies of both countries were frustrated by the Marineleitung in Berlin, but his interest in Japan had endured.

It received fresh impetus when he met a dapper, amiable little man whose family background made him a living symbol, as it were, of German-Japanese co-operation. Major General Hiroshi Oshima, Japanese military attaché in Berlin and director of the Japanese secret service in Europe, was the son of a War Minister who had learnt his trade from General Meckel, the German reorganizer of the Japanese Army, and in an artillery regiment at Ludwigsburg.[186] The two Oshimas, father and son, were united in their admiration for German military technique and cultural achievements.

This prompted young Hiroshi to regard National Socialism as a rebirth of German great-power status on which the Oshimas and an influential group of Japanese Army officers based grandiose schemes of their own. Hostile to the parliamentary system of government and

Japan's pro-Western foreign policy, these officers planned to found an authoritarian regime and, by waging war on the Soviet Union, to carve a large enough slice of *Lebensraum* out of the Siberian land mass to assure their overpopulated country of supremacy in the Far East. It would, however, be easier to bring the Russians to their knees if Japan found an ally on the western marches of the Soviet Union. To the military imperialists, Hiroshi Oshima seemed the ideal person to commend their aggressive schemes to the one country that qualified as a potential ally, Hitler's Germany.[187]

In Canaris Oshima found a listener who was not averse, at least in his own professional sphere, to furthering Japanese designs on Russia. The two men, who liked each other personally and often dined together, agreed that their intelligence services should co-operate in all matters relating to the Soviet Union. The Abwehr and the Japanese secret service were to exchange information about Russia and permit each other to share in the interrogation of any Soviet officials who defected to either party.[188]

The oral agreement between Canaris and Oshima was committed to paper in October 1935 but did not assume the guise of a treaty[189] because Japan was still ruled by governments opposed to any form of alliance with the Third Reich. It was not until February 1936, after a military revolt had been quelled at the eleventh hour, that power passed to a cabinet more inclined to fall in with the Army's anti-Soviet ideas.

This triggered the automatic process which had once before converted a secret service pact initiated by Canaris into a political alliance. Friedrich Wilhelm Hack, a German arms dealer who operated in the Far East and was a close friend of Oshima's, persuaded Hitler's chief foreign policy adviser, Ribbentrop, to take an interest in the Japanese military attaché. Hack, whose activities as an arms dealer made him no stranger to the secret service scene, had obviously heard of the Canaris-Oshima agreement.[190] Ever eager to boost his personal prestige at Foreign Office expense, Ribbentrop seized on Hack's suggestion and met Oshima at his Berlin apartment in October 1935.[191]

Ribbentrop inquired if Tokyo would be interested in concluding a "defensive alliance" against Russia and asked Oshima to consult the Japanese General Staff—very discreetly, though, because he made it clear that he was acting in a "private" capacity and not on behalf of Hitler or the German Foreign Office.[192] This was all right with Oshima because he, too, foresaw great problems with his own government. He cabled the General Staff and was authorized to open negotiations,[193] but the talks dragged on fruitlessly because the Japanese Government still feared Moscow's reaction to an alliance with Germany.

Then someone had a bright idea. Hermann von Raumer, a Ribbentrop associate and expert on Eastern affairs, remembered reading somewhere that the Soviet Government had officially disclaimed responsibility for the propaganda activities of the Moscow-based Communist International (Comintern). If two countries concluded a treaty aimed at countering this Comintern propaganda, argued Raumer, the Soviet Government could hardly interpret it as an unfriendly act directed against the U.S.S.R.[194] Raumer was so delighted with his brainwave that he sat down there and then, on the night of November 22, 1935, and drafted the text of a treaty.[195] It was the birth of the Anti-Comintern Pact.

But what did the document contain? Almost nothing that had not already been embodied in the agreement negotiated by Canaris and the Spanish security chief, Bazan, in February 1928: joint opposition to the Comintern, exchanges of information about Comintern activities and an invitation to third countries to join the pact. It was followed in due course by a "secret supplementary agreement" in which each party undertook not to favour the Soviet Union in the event of war and not to conclude any agreement with that country in default of the other party's consent.[196]

Hitler gave his approval, and so—eventually—did the Japanese Government. The Anti-Comintern Pact was signed on November 25, 1936, a first step towards the founding of that power bloc which was soon to cast its menacing shadow over the international diplomatic scene, the Berlin-Rome-Tokyo Axis.[197]

But Canaris had no misgivings. He also ignored the fact that most senior Wehrmacht officers had little taste for an alliance with Japan because their sympathies traditionally lay with China, whose forces (trained by a substantial number of German military advisers) were conducting a desperate campaign against the Japanese Army's strategy of large-scale infiltration in Manchuria. Despite this, Canaris forged still closer links with Oshima, especially as the German and Japanese intelligence services were both smarting because Soviet spies had gained access to the secret correspondence connected with the German-Japanese treaty talks.

What alerted the Abwehr was that the Soviet government newspaper *Izvestia* had published a report on these negotiations at a time when not even the German and Japanese foreign ministries knew of them.[198] In August 1936 the Russians again showed themselves so well informed that it was rumoured in Berlin that the Kremlin had got its hands on the actual minutes of the proceedings.[199] Canaris promptly instituted a search for the leak from which this confidential information was escaping.

German and Japanese agents hunted diligently for their hidden foe but failed to unearth him. They did not know that the Forschungsamt [Research Department], the Third Reich's central monitoring agency, harboured a Krivitsky informant who enjoyed access to all the encoded telegrams intercepted by his department. By August 8 Krivitsky was already in possession of a film recording all the cables exchanged by the Japanese military attaché in Berlin and the General Staff in Tokyo. Krivitsky had the Oshima texts deciphered and translated in The Hague, then radioed to Moscow via Paris.[200]

The only effect of this shared defeat was to reinforce the bond between the German and Japanese intelligence services. Oshima wanted to convert the Anti-Comintern Pact into an alliance without delay. By December, when he made his farewells at the Reich War Ministry before paying a visit to Japan, he had drafted a "German-Japanese Military Convention."[201] But the Wehrmacht authorities recoiled and Keitel intimated to Oshima that the conclusion of such a pact was "a matter for the political leadership of the Reich."[202] Canaris, too, was informed that a military alliance with the inscrutable Japanese was not on the cards at present.[203]

But Oshima refused to give up. He had scarcely returned to Germany in March 1937 when he submitted, on behalf of the Japanese General Staff, a new document providing for the closest co-operation between the two countries' armies and air forces. Its opening passages referred to military intelligence: "Article 1. The two armies shall exchange information received, both about the Russian Army and about Russia. Article 2. In regard to the subversive activities against Russia planned by both armies, they shall consult one another, guarantee mutual assistance and, in addition, co-operate as far as possible."[204] Oshima's new offer caused considerable embarrassment at the War Ministry because Blomberg and Keitel were reluctant to approve any formalization of German-Japanese military contacts.

Japan's invasion of northern China in July made it easier for the Wehrmacht authorities to decline. Hitler himself had no wish to be drawn into a Far Eastern war and opposed an alliance with Japan.[205] Keitel had told General Oshima, even before the outbreak of hostilities in China, that "the continuance of trustful co-operation between us requires no further written confirmation."[206] In the end, the only person who profited from these abortive talks was Canaris.

Keitel gave Oshima to understand that he himself had "no objection" to the Japanese military attaché's negotiating with Canaris directly "on the subject of exchanges of information and subversive activities against Russia" or to his agreeing "a clear-cut delimitation of your respective spheres of activity."[207] For his part, Canaris was appointed to negotiate with Oshima. In mid-June Keitel had approved a suggestion that the headquarters of the various armed services should in future "take no independent action" in matters relating to German-

Japanese co-operation but leave everything to the Wehrmachtamt and the head of the Abwehr.[208] Canaris and Oshima drew even closer.

Agreement was quickly reached on the subversive activities to be undertaken by the two secret services, and the German and Japanese spymasters divided Russia between them. The groups and desks at Abwehr headquarters derived much valuable information from Japanese intelligence sources (mistrustful and xenophobic though the majority of Japanese agents remained). The Canaris-Oshima agreement bore fruit a year later, when General Samoilovich Lyushkov, Russia's security chief in the Far East, sought asylum with the Japanese and Tokyo invited the Abwehr to be present throughout his interrogations.[209]

Canaris made a point of celebrating this alliance between the German and Japanese intelligence services whenever possible. He contrived to meet every Japanese intelligence officer who visited Berlin, and once, when Japan's foremost Russian experts were attending a conference there, he welcomed them with a surprise gesture. Relying on a smattering of Russian acquired during his days as a cadet, he delivered a speech which he had got Pruck to translate into that language and learnt by heart. Pruck recalls that his audience greeted it with "enthusiastic and well-earned applause."[210]

The Admiral's zeal demonstrated how much value he attached to anti-Soviet co-operation in the field of military intelligence. Nothing formed a closer bond between him and the forces of fascist authoritarianism than his own anti-Communist sentiments. This need to strike at the heart of international Communism was an article of faith which consistently pervaded his political ideas and emotions from the time of the Red soviets in postwar Germany to the conclusion of the Anti-Comintern Pact. Any summons to join battle against Communism drew a ready response from Canaris the Christian conservative.

He was not dissatisfied when the German-Japanese Anti-Comintern Pact aroused interest abroad, particularly in his favourite foreign countries. Italy subscribed to the pact in November 1937, followed a bare eighteen months later by Spain, Hungary and the Japanese puppet state of Manchukuo.[211] Canaris found Spain's membership especially gratifying because the treaty was signed by two men well known to him, Ambassador von Stohrer for the Reich and Foreign Minister Count Jordana for Spain.[212]

Canaris was too indiscriminately anti-Communist to perceive the essential hollowness of the pact which Hitler and Ribbentrop had thrust into being. Unlike him, the Führer and his henchmen looked on anti-Communism simply as a tactical and diplomatic gambit—an explosive charge with which to demolish Europe's postwar alliances and rearrange them in Germany's favour. This did not preclude temporary collaboration—or at least a game of cat-and-mouse—with Joseph Stalin's abominated Russia, even though it was to culminate in what Hitler had dreamed of since the 1920s: the "Ritt nach Ostland" [ride to the East], or violent seizure of territory in the wide expanses of Russia.

Unscrupulousness of this kind was not only alien to Canaris but beyond his ken. For far too long, he looked on the leaders of the National Socialist regime as natural allies in the fight against atheistic Communism. It took an occurrence of historic dimensions to open his eyes.

On June 11, 1937, he was surprised by a report from the Soviet news agency Tass to the effect that Marshal Mikhail Tukhachevsky, a former Deputy Commissar of Defence, and seven Red Army generals had been sentenced to death by a special tribunal for having "maintained treasonable relationships with leading military circles of a foreign power which is pursuing a policy hostile to the Soviet Union. The accused were working for this power's espionage service."[213] Whatever that might mean in detail, Canaris was sure of one thing. The struggle for power in the Soviet Union, detectable for months from the show trials of Stalin's rivals, had now reached the Red Army.

The verdict on Tukhachevsky and his friends heralded an orgy of bloodshed, terror and arbitrary violence. The more brutally Stalin fought for personal supremacy and eliminated every real or putative opponent in the Army, party and government, the longer and more puzzling the list of executions became. Thirty-five thousand officers were "purged" within a year, including 90 per cent of the Red Army's generals and 80 per cent of its colonels.[214]

The "Yezhovchina" (so called after Nikolai Yezhov, the state security chief) did not confine itself to the military. It also mowed down the heads of the Soviet secret service because the misanthrope in the Kremlin suspected them, too, of hatching plots against him. His victims included many dangerous opponents of the Abwehr. Berzin was recalled from Spain and later liquidated, Krivitsky just escaped his executioners, the Soviet secret service chief in Switzerland was gunned down and even the Soviet military attaché in London, General Putna, fell victim to a secret police firing squad. [215]

Canaris was helpless in the face of this eruption of Asiatic despotism. The Abwehr's Russian desk was insufficiently well informed to brief him on the background to this internal crisis and, in particular, on the part played by Tukhachevsky and the other generals. Although Pruck had met some of them at German manoeuvres prior to 1933, when the Reichswehr and the Red Army were secretly co-operating, and although Blomberg had also made their acquaintance during a lengthy visit to the Soviet Union, neither man could unravel the mystery of the Tukhachevsky affair.[216]

Blomberg and Canaris sought enlightenment from the appropriate section of the Army General Staff. When Lieutenant Colonel Dr. Karl Spalcke, Russian expert of the Foreign Armies Section, came to present his report at the War Ministry, a friend accosted him and asked "if I knew that Gestapo chief Heydrich had engineered Tukhachevsky's downfall." He had "heard from some SS men that Heydrich was claiming credit for having deprived the Red Army of its leading figures." Spalcke's sole response: "Pure swank!"[217]

However, Spalcke considered the rumour important enough to relay it to Canaris. The Abwehr chief, who had not heard it before, was thunderstruck. Spalcke failed to shed any further light on the Tukhachevsky mystery, so he got a couple of friends to make inquiries at Gestapo headquarters.[218] When these yielded nothing, he questioned Heydrich himself at their very next meeting.

Canaris returned from his talk with Heydrich in a state of "profound mental shock" (to quote an eyewitness). He told a friend at his office, Captain Heinz, that Heydrich had actually admitted having "consigned the entire leadership of the Red Army to destruction." He now had it on Heydrich's personal authority as chief of the Security Police and SD that his organization had procured documents dating from the period when the Red Army and Reichswehr were co-operating and used the reports and signatures they contained to forge a correspondence implying treasonable relations between Soviet generals and German officers. Four ex-members of the Soviet State Security Service had helped to produce these forgeries. The material was then fed to the Czechoslovak General Staff, which had forwarded it to Moscow.[219]

Canaris could hardly contain himself. "Why in heaven's name did you play such a game?" he asked, to which Heydrich replied: "The idea came from the Führer himself. The Russian armed forces had to be decimated at the top and weakened in consequence. The whole thing is a gambit on the Führer's part—it fits into his over-all plan for the next few years."[220]

Canaris was so preoccupied with the affair that he instituted further inquiries into Heydrich's Tukhachevsky operation. His sleuths did not get far because the SD's system of watertight bulkheads resisted their efforts. The Abwehr chief never discovered that Heydrich had only been a small and unimportant accomplice of Moscow's own State Security Service, which had very probably inspired the SD operation itself. The first reports drawing Heydrich's attention to the supposed existence of a dissident group centred on Tukhachevsky had been submitted in December 1936 by an exiled Russian general living in Paris, Nikolai Vladimirovich Skoblin, who worked for the SD *and* the Soviet secret service.[221]

The sequence of events that culminated in Tukhachevsky's downfall was itself a pointer to the guiding hand of the Soviet State Security

Service. At the end of September 1936 Yezhov was appointed People's Commissar of Internal Affairs.[222] Tukhachevsky's associate Putna was arrested before the month was out.[223] On January 27, 1937, during the show trial of the right-wing deviationist Karl Radek, Tukhachevsky was publicly referred to for the first time as a friend of the "traitor" Putna.[224] On March 3 Stalin referred while addressing the Central Committee of the CPSU to the tremendous harm which "a handful of spies in the Red Army" could do to the country.[225] On May 11 Tukhachevsky was relieved of his post as Deputy Commissar of Defence.[226] His arrest followed three weeks later.[227]

But the SD had not begun its "systematic work of forgery" until April 1937, by which time Putna had already been publicly denounced and Stalin had made his "handul of spies" allusion.[228] Tukhachevsky lost his deputy commissar's job on May 11, yet the SD did not pass its forged documents to the Russians until the middle of that month.[229] In other words, Tukhachevsky and his associates were not laid low by Heydrich or the SD (nor did German documents turn up at any stage in the trial of the Tukhachevsky group).

Canaris, who was unaware of these facts, had no choice but to believe Heydrich's vainglorious revelations. To an anti-Communist like Canaris, it seemed not only monstrous but incompatible with a German officer's code of honour that any Reich authority should have assisted Soviet secret policemen to murder almost every senior officer in the Russian Army, among them men who had been guests and fellow students at German military academies. For the first time since his appointment as head of the Abwehr, Canaris was shocked by the moral abyss that yawned ahead of him.

But his sense of outrage was that of a departmental chief and interdepartmental strategist as well as a moralist. The Tukhachevsky affair signalled the advance of a rival who might one day present a serious threat to the Abwehr's monopoly in the field of foreign intelligence. This the SD had invaded with agents of its own, and its network of informants, though still small, was hampering the work of the secret service proper. The Abwehr and SD were already at loggerheads in Paris, a difficult area of operations, and the two agencies were also obstructing each other in Poland and other East European countries.

Many clashes occurred in counterespionage as well. "Instances are multiplying," Bamler wrote on May 28, 1937, "in which it can with certainty be assumed that the SD of the Reichsführer-SS [Himmler] . . . is striving to acquire supervisory powers over the Geheime Staatspolizei and other official organs of the Reich. There can be no doubt that the SD is trying, at the very least, to discredit the counterespionage organization of the RKM [Reich War Ministry] with the munitions industry and government departments."[230] Canaris was as alarmed by reports of this kind as he had been by the events surrounding Tukhachevsky's downfall.

He had not taken the SD too seriously until then, being preoccupied with his largely successful efforts to neutralize the Gestapo and solicit its co-operation. It had escaped him that the SD was developing into a rival body whose leaders actually spoke of combining the political and military intelligence agencies into a Greater German Intelligence Service controlled by themselves. Even now, the SD was a force to be reckoned with. By 1937 its Berlin headquarters in Wilhelmstrasse already boasted a central staff of three thousand plus fifty thousand informants, some willing and others conscripted.[231]

Heydrich"s little empire steadily expanded, the more so because he had grasped that the party's secret service was a flexible instrument of power which the Gestapo's bureaucratic apparatus could never, for all its ideological indoctrination, hope to become. The Gestapo was still faintly redolent of the Prusso-German civil service tradition, whereas the SD attracted a stream of intellectuals who had been shaped by unemployment, postwar chaos and bourgeois dissolution—adherents of an essentially unprincipled dynamic and technology of human domination whose sole objectives were the acquisition of power for its own sake and the service of a charismatic leader.

Only this ice-cold atmosphere of amoral functionalism could have bred the idea of abetting the Soviet secret police in a murderous assault on Russia's military leaders. But the SD's lack of scruple was matched by its dilettantism. External espionage was handled by the inexperienced SS-Oberführer Heinz Jost, who headed Zentralabteilung III2 [Co-ordinating Section III2, Combating of Enemy Intelligence Services] at the SD-Hauptamt [SD Central Office], and there were few professional secret servicemen even in the SD outstations near the frontiers.[232] Many SD men made up for their lack of experience by espousing lunatic Nazi ideas. There was, for example, a certain unintended humour in what the SD believed about Russia.

It was an SD article of faith that the internal power struggles in Russia were nothing more nor less than a diabolical Jewish plot. A special "Strictly Confidential" report drafted by the SD Information Bureau in 1937 ascribed Stalin's gory purges to a struggle between two power blocs. "One may be generally labelled 'Western and freemason' and the other 'Eastern and ghetto-Jewish.'" Tukhachevsky belonged to the "Western-Jewish-freemason camp and has, albeit cautiously, taken action along these lines like other Trotskyists."[233]

Canaris had every reason to fear the SD's expansionary pressure. He paid several calls on Best and complained that SD informants were amateurishly disrupting the Abwehr's work (a charge which the SS officer found only too justified).[234] Although Heydrich took the trouble to instruct his intelligence officers to co-operate with the Abwehr, relations between the two services remained uneasy. Canaris could not prevail on Heydrich to make any further concessions and the SD persisted in its foreign intelligence activities.

The Admiral resented this so much that he reacted fiercely whenever any derogation of the Abwehr's authority came to his notice. He then became capable of tough and uncompromising intervention. When he heard, for instance, that the Reich Propaganda Ministry was planning to deploy its own agents in border areas in the event of war, he firmly opposed this encroachment on his department's functions. On April 24, 1937, he dictated: "It is requested that the Propaganda Ministry's attention be drawn to the impermissible nature of this activity. The Abwehr will take the strongest possible steps to counter any such breach of definite instructions."[235]

He was in an equally aggressive mood when his predecessor, Patzig, met him in autumn of the same year. "At the very outset of our conversation," Patzig recalled, "he told me they were all criminals from top to bottom, and bent on ruining Germany." Patzig: "Then you can't go on running your department. Ask to be relieved." Canaris: "If I go Heydrich takes over, and that'll be the end of everything."[236]

Patzig left his successor in a meditative frame of mind. Was this the man who had so blithely taken over his job in 1934 and promised to "deal with those boys"? Patzig, who had never got over his enforced resignation, must have noted and memorized Canaris's emotional outburst with a certain amount of glee (and may even have exaggerated it after the event). He could not tell whether Canaris really meant what he said or was just being moody.

In fact, Canaris had no cause to fear any threat to his position. Not only was his place in the Wehrmacht hierarchy unassailed, but he still felt that he was working in the shadow of a national leader who, if not a genius, was certainly a man of stature. His remaining illusions were soon to be dispelled.

8

The Turning Point

The War Minister's wedding was the event of the winter season. Canaris learned of it on January 22, 1938, when he returned from a trip to Spain and was met at Tempelhof Airport by Lieutenant Colonel Piekenbrock, who had been holding the fort in his absence. As the two men drove through the snowy streets of Berlin, Piekenbrock turned to him and said, "By the way, Blomberg has married again."[1]

The news came as no surprise. Canaris had heard members of his headquarters staff gossiping about the elderly widower's tours of the capital's night spots. There were also whispers about a barmaid at Der Weisse Hirsch [The White Hart] with whom he was reputed to be having an affair,[2] though nobody knew her name. Whether this was the woman Blomberg had now married did not emerge from the brief and almost laconic announcement that had appeared in the *Völkischer Beobachter* on January 13: "The Reich War Minister, Field Marshal von Blomberg, married Fräulein Gruhn on Wednesday, January 12. The Führer and Colonel General Göring were witnesses."[3]

It was nonetheless noteworthy that the wedding ceremony at the Reich War Ministry had lasted only an hour and that the newlyweds left on their honeymoon at once. This had given rise to all kinds of rumours which "Pieki" retailed to his boss. But Canaris grew bored with the subject. He was tired after the flight and eager to get home to his dachshunds. Monday would be soon enough for a more detailed account of the nuptials.

Canaris was not to know that on Monday the German political scene would be convulsed for no reason other than Blomberg's marriage. The unwitting authors of the crisis were the Criminal Police, who chose that day to unearth a secret whose publication plunged the Wehrmacht into the gravest crisis in its history and Germany into the depths of total dicatorship.

It all began in the office of Kriminalrat [roughly, Detective Chief Superintendent] Hellmuth Müller, who headed the Records Department at the Reichskriminalpolizeiamt [RKPA—Criminal Police Headquarters]. Müller's secretary, Richard Burkert, brought him one of those confidential missives he occasionally received from Kriminalrat Nauck of the Dezernat für Sittlichkeitsverbrechen [Vice Squad]. It contained some pornographic photographs to be reproduced for records purposes.[4]

Müller was about to lay the photographs aside when Burkert urged him to look more closely at a woman who appeared in six of them. Studying her, Müller saw a well-proportioned blonde, height approximately 5 feet 8 inches, with bobbed hair and nothing in the way of clothes but a string of pearls. Inscribed on the back of the pictures was her name, "Gruhn, Luise Margarethe."

The name rang a bell. Müller had seen it somewhere quite recently —just where, he couldn't recall, but his curiosity was aroused. He took one of the photographs and went to see Kriminalkommissar Hennig, who was in charge of the fingerprint section at Müller's headquarters. Consulting the records, they came upon the name Gruhn splashed across a double card in Hennig's index. Müller still recalls: "The said lady figured in our collection two or three times. Records had processed her for soliciting in a public place and theft in conjunction with sexual intercourse."[5] He thereupon requested the head of the Residents' Registration Office, Regierungsrat Mesch, to check on the precise identity of Luise Margarethe Gruhn.

"When Mesch heard the name," Müller recounts, "he grinned at me and produced a sheet of paper from a filing cabinet. It was Field Marshal von Blomberg's registration card."[6] All at once, Müller knew why the name Gruhn had seemed so familiar. It dawned on him that he had accidentally stumbled upon a time bomb of unimaginable potency. The Third Reich's most senior soldier and Adolf Hitler's closest military adviser had married a convicted prostitute.

Müller hurried to his boss, Reichskriminaldirektor [National CID Chief] and SS-Sturmbannführer [Major] Arthur Nebe, and informed him of his discovery. Nebe jumped up, took a quick look at the photographs and then—according to Müller—slumped back into his chair "looking pale." "Good God, Müller," the CID chief whispered, "and the Führer kissed that woman's hand!"[7]

Nebe felt half inclined to "lose" the pictures and record cards on his desk because he recognized only too clearly what a threat such evidence could pose to the Wehrmacht authorities if it fell into the wrong hands. Then at the height of his career, Nebe had long ago been stripped of his illusions about the regime he had helped to found as head of a National Socialist police association. He was quite as repelled by the unbridled supremacy of the SS within the police apparatus as he was by the totalitarian system of tutelage practised under the Führer's dictatorship, but caution prevented him from destroying the Gruhn evidence because too many people were already in the know.

But to whom should he entrust the material? Regulations prescribed that it be passed to his immediate superior, but in Nebe's case this was the very man from whom it had to be kept at all costs. As head of the Security Police and SD, Heydrich would have no hesitation in using it for purposes of blackmail in the covert struggle between the SS and the armed forces.

Completely at a loss, Nebe consulted the man who, being police commissioner of Berlin, still acted as "landlord" of the Reichskriminalpolizeiamt. Count Wolf-Heinrich von Helldorf, a veteran National Socialist and SA-Obergruppenführer [general], opposed the SS and shared Nebe's dislike of what he regarded as the degeneration of National Socialism into "un-German" megalomania. He too felt that the scandal must at all costs be kept from Heydrich and Himmler and that the Wehrmacht chiefs should be warned at once.

But how to approach them? The fatal evidence could not just be sent to Blomberg out of the blue. Then Helldorf remembered reading in the weekend edition of the *Deutsche Allgemeine Zeitung* that Lieutenant Karl-Heinz Keitel, son of General Wilhelm Keitel, had announced his engagement to Dorothee von Blomberg, the field marshal's daughter.[8] Keitel, Blomberg's closest associate, seemed the ideal person to warn his endangered superior and alert the senior members of his staff.

Helldorf drove to the War Ministry and asked to see Keitel. He produced Fräulein Gruhn's file and photograph from his briefcase and asked the general to confirm that the face in the picture was identical with that of the new Frau von Blomberg. Keitel could not do so for the simple reason that he had never met the woman. With a sudden note of insistence in his voice, Helldorf requested Keitel to show Blomberg the photograph without delay. Still in the dark, Keitel rang the minister's office but was informed that he had not yet returned from a weekend visit to Eberswalde to clear up his late mother's financial affairs. Helldorf had no choice but to tell Keitel the whole truth.[9]

Keitel was horrified when he heard what was looming over the

Wehrmacht authorities. He gripped the edge of his desk, bereft of inspiration. All he could suggest at first was that the records should be destroyed, but he quickly abandoned this idea when Helldorf explained that it was too late to hush things up. No other solution occurred to him, and he never for a moment thought of demanding that the police records be turned over to the War Ministry.

Nervous, opportunistic and engrossed in his world of command structures and mobilization plans, Keitel could not bring himself to take any action even when the police chief had left. He neither warned Blomberg, whom he could have reached at Eberswalde, nor sought any confirmation of Helldorf's disclosures. A phone call to Canaris would have sufficed to send the latter's minions hunting for the truth. The Abwehr would have taken less than an hour to discover which Fräulein Gruhn the field marshal had married. The Berlin telephone directory listed only four female Gruhns, of whom one lived near the Tirpitz-Ufer:[10] Luise Margarethe Gruhn of 118 Eisenacher Strasse.

So far from consulting the Abwehr, Keitel had recommended a course of action which precipitated and aggravated the crisis surrounding the Wehrmacht. He suggested that Helldorf should call on Göring, who, having been a witness at her wedding, was bound to know what the field marshal's bride looked like. Keitel set such store by this piece of advice that he took it upon himself to call Göring at the Reich Aviation Ministry and fix an appointment for Helldorf.[11] No inner voice warned him against involving someone whose qualifications as a friend in need were little better than Himmler's or Heydrich's. Hermann Göring, commander in chief of the Luftwaffe and the regime's second most powerful man, had long coveted the War Minister's job.

Helldorf's visit unexpectedly dealt Göring a hand of cards strong enough to warrant a bid for the post he wanted. He saw at a glance that the scandal could not be suppressed and that Blomberg was done for. The Prusso-German military code would not tolerate a discredited figure at the head of the armed forces for a single day longer, but who would automatically succeed him at the War Ministry? None other than General Baron Werner von Fritsch, commander in chief of the Army and the Reich's most respected senior officer.

Göring wanted to prevent this at all costs, and he already knew how to block Fritsch's appointment. It had come to his knowledge that the Gestapa still retained copies of an old interrogation transcript in which a convicted blackmailer had alleged that Fritsch was a homosexual and had consorted with a young male prostitute in the neighbourhood of a Berlin railway station. Although this file had officially been destroyed on Hitler's orders when first submitted to him in 1936, Göring's status as the Gestapo's original founder was influential enough for him to persuade some Prinz-Albrecht-Strasse officials to reconstruct it with the aid of extant copies.[12]

Thus equipped, Göring was able to drive to the Chancellery on the evening of January 24, 1938, and unleash the great crisis. With some theatrical skill he contrived to arouse a sense of impending doom among the aides and ministers who were awaiting Hitler's return from a weekend trip to Bavaria. He strode up and down, breathing hard and loudly complaining that it was always his misfortune to be the bearer of evil tidings. When Hitler's adjutant, Captain (ret.) Fritz Wiedemann, asked Göring's aide, Bodenschatz, what was up with his boss, Bodenschatz replied, "Blomberg will have to go." Wiedemann thought he had misheard until Bodenschatz repeated, "I told you, Blomberg will have to go—he's married a prostitute!"[13]

Hitler turned up shortly afterwards and retired to his study with Göring, who put him in the picture with a few well-chosen words. His story was graphically illustrated by the photographs in the Gruhn file, which he had brought with him. He also made some preliminary allusions to the Fritsch "case" and presumably gave notice of the Gestapo dossier, which landed on Hitler's desk next morning.[14]

Hitler was shocked. The Blomberg-Fritsch affair left him feeling compromised—indeed, it must have shaken his naive and lifelong faith in the Prusso-German military elite. The blow was a hard one, but he soon recovered. His unerring instinct told him that here was a chance to strip the Wehrmacht commanders of their power and place himself at their head.

Blomberg and Fritsch had voiced too many doubts and misgivings about their master's provocation of international crises and been overpersistent in advising him against a policy of breakneck rearmament. Hitler preserved an unpleasant memory of the two men's attitude at a high-level Chancellery conference on the afternoon of November 5, 1937, when their sole response to his exposition of the aggressive schemes which he loftily entitled a "political testament" (armed expansion of German *Lebensraum*, annexation of Austria and Czechoslovakia by 1943) had been to advance military objections of a technical nature.[15]

No, officers of this type made unsuitable companions for someone poised on the knife-edge between peace and war. Their simultaneous fall from grace provided a perfect opportunity to decapitate the party's only autonomous rival, the armed forces. Hitler's mind was made up. Blomberg must resign, Fritsch must be subjected to a highly embarrassing investigation and compelled to do likewise. Göring could be appeased with a field marshal's baton, and he, Hitler, would gain undisputed sway over the armed forces by becoming their supreme commander.

By January 26 at latest, Keitel realized what his own inertia had accomplished. "Deeply affected and with tears in his eyes" (wrote his close friend Colonel Jodl), the general swore his departmental chiefs to secrecy and informed them that Blomberg had "fallen."[16] This was how Canaris learned of events at the top of the Wehrmacht, though only in the veiled and nebulous terms which Keitel favoured even with his immediate subordinates.

The Abwehr chief was as surprised by Hitler's cool and calculated stroke as any of his colleagues at the War Ministry. Previously ignorant of what was being hatched against Blomberg and Fritsch, he failed to detect the interplay between Göring, the Gestapo and Hitler. He was still completely in the dark when two informants reported to him on January 27. The more they told him of what they knew about the Blomberg affair, the more pained his usually impassive face became. In the end he could contain himself no longer and blurted out, "But the whole thing's quite appalling!"[17]

Canaris only gradually became aware of how ill the Wehrmacht had been treated. Although he remained ignorant of Göring's central role (and, more especially, Hitler's), he did grasp that the Wehrmacht authorities had been ambushed by dark forces lurking safely behind the scenes. He also knew, or had done ever since the Tukhachevsky affair, that Heydrich and his henchmen would stop at nothing to advance the Führer's interests.

By degrees, the Blomberg-Fritsch scandal became a moment of truth and watershed in the Admiral's career. Slowly and reluctantly, yet conscious that he had passed the point of no return, Canaris abandoned the illusions of Hitlerism. "It was then that Canaris began to turn from Hitler," his friend Protze told a British journalist in later years. "If you're looking for one specific event that shook Canaris's allegiance to Hitler, there you have it."[18]

This process of disengagement was a painful one. Canaris took a long time to grasp what was going on around him, aided by a subordinate who helped to sharpen his political perception. This man, who was to accompany him throughout the vicissitudes that culminated in their death on the gallows at Flossenbürg, was the most controversial counsellor and companion ever to impinge on the Admiral's career: Lieutenant Colonel (E) Hans Oster of Abwehr III.

Although Canaris and Oster were long regarded as close, almost inseparable friends, their relationship was not without strain and conflict. If only on the surface, they made a strangely incongruous pair. Born in 1887, several times decorated for gallantry during World War I, temperamental, volatile and outwardly preoccupied with an unremitting quest for attractive women and new specimens of horseflesh, the Saxon parson's son went ill together with the diffident, lisping, introverted little admiral.[19]

They had first met at Münster in 1931, when Oster was serving on the staff of the 6th Division under Colonel Franz Halder. As General Staff Officer, Grade 2 (Ib), Oster was responsible for divisional supplies. He was also the appropriate person for Canaris, then Chief of Staff North Sea Station, to consult when he came over from Wilhelmshaven to discuss matters of common interest with the staff of the neighbouring military district.[20] He took such a liking to Oster that he invited Halder to send his Ib to represent the district on a naval staff outing aboard a small warship.[21]

The two men became better acquainted during this voyage and discovered that they had much in common. They shared the bond that united a generation of serving officers whose attitudes remained firmly in the imperial mould. Both were staunch monarchists, both were reluctant wearers of the Republic's uniform and both yearned for an end to the "brittle multiparty state" (Oster) and the restoration of a national authoritarian regime founded on discipline and ruled by a strong supreme master.[22] Their discussions in 1931 showed Canaris that Oster's veneer of cynicism and arrogance concealed a serious-minded man who subscribed to a simple and straightforward code of soldierly and Christian conduct, an officer who aspired to remain "a decent fellow to the last breath, as we were taught in the nursery and in training."[23]

Not every observer would have concurred with this glowing piece of self-appraisal. Oster was not overpopular with his colleagues, of whom many thought him a casual and superficial careerist and others were repelled by his brash and peremptory manner. Colonel Friedrich Hossbach, Hitler's adjutant and head of the Personnel Section of the Army General Staff, clung to his belief that Oster's character defects unfitted him for general staff duties, and even well-disposed superiors like Halder or colleagues like Henke found it hard to endure his "irresponsible carelessness."[24]

It was this insouciance which finally put paid to Oster's staff career in 1932. Although married, he embarked on an affair with the wife of a reserve officer professor from Trèves and, in Halder's words, "behaved so badly that I only just got him out of the Army before some extremely disagreeable steps were taken against him."[25] He was tried by a court of honour and compelled to resign on December 31, 1932, though Halder made sure he departed on generous terms. He retained his full pension entitlement and was later granted the right to wear uniform.[26]

Oster's resignation did, for all that, betoken a break with the past from which he never inwardly recovered. He struggled along for some weeks, doing part-time work, until Göring's telephone-tapping "Research Department" offered him a post with effect from May 1, 1933.[27] Oster did not stay there long. In September, friends (possibly Canaris himself) secured him an interview with the then head of the Abwehr, Patzig. "He made a shabby and dejected impression," Patzig recalls. " 'Captain,' he said, 'you've got to help me.' "[28] Patzig's account of the interview is indicative of his feelings towards Oster, whom he disliked. "I did not rate him highly as a character, but I thought I ought to make use of his abilities and engaged him as a civilian employee."[29]

Patzig allotted Oster an office which he promptly adorned with a board bearing a Serbian proverb: "An eagle eats no flies."[30] This was tantamount to a proclamation that Hans Oster was not a man to be content with trivialities—that he was capable of, and destined for, great things. Patzig soon spotted that the newcomer made a habit of courting secretaries and discontented colleagues "so as to acquire a growing influence in the Abwehr Section." He "wanted to take over my outer office and so help to decide which visitors I should or should not see."[31]

Patzig shunted Oster into Group III, where he took charge of Desk C1. IIIC1 was responsible for counterespionage in all government departments not under Wehrmacht jurisdiction (the economic sector excepted) and maintained contact with the Berlin ministries.[32] As a result, Oster soon became an expert on the manifold interdepartmental intrigues and squabbles in which Germany's new power blocs and institutions were embroiled. He had taken up his appointment at what was probably the most hectic moment in the Third Reich's existence. It was the eve of the so-called Röhm Putsch, and government and society were still being tyrannized by the brown-shirted rowdies of the SA.

It was also about now that a lanky civil servant at the Reich Ministry of the Interior—described by the historian Edward Crankshaw as "a born go-between and . . . accomplished intriguer"[33]—offered to guide Oster through this jungle of contending cliques. Just thirty years old, Dr. Hans Bernd Gisevius was an ex-German Nationalist youth leader who had transferred his allegiance to the NSDAP and become an Assessor [higher civil service probationer] at the Geheimes Staatspolizeiamt. He was currently seeking allies against the (first) Gestapo chief Rudolf Diels and the predominance of the SA—a campaign in which personal ambition and political motives were strangely commingled.[34]

Gisevius had once entertained serious hopes of ousting Diels from his post and taking over the Gestapo himself. In concert with his friend Arthur Nebe, who then headed the executive branch of the Gestapa, he had put it about that Diels was a crypto-Communist. The Gestapo chief's response was to fire him,[35] but Gisevius kept up his campaign from a new base at the Ministry of the Interior. Nebe continued to back Gisevius because he, too, believed that his chief was making insufficient efforts to combat the SA. Together, the two friends furnished

Himmler and Heydrich with incriminating evidence which they hoped would stop the SA's reign of terror for good.[36]

Oster's reappearance on the scene encouraged Gisevius to enlist the Abwehr against Diels and the SA. Before long he turned up at Patzig's office and urged him to act. "He presented detailed accounts of scandalous behaviour on the part of SA officers . . . and tried to persuade me to intervene."[37] Patzig refused, commenting that it was none of the Abwehr's business.

But Gisevius did not abandon hope of winning the Abwehr over. He made himself indispensable to Oster, employing the method he had already used on Nebe: "I stuck so close to him that he simply couldn't get rid of me."[38] Gisevius bombarded Oster with items of information, rumours and half-truths culled from ministerial, police and party offices. They painted a villainous picture which was in shocking conflict with Oster's vision of the new Germany.

Gisevius's revelations were largely responsible for transforming Oster's attitude to the regime. Like most soldiers, he had welcomed Hitler's "national revolution." What he expected from the Nazis, first and foremost, was a "return to earlier traditions."[39] What confronted him in Gisevius's reports was the dismantling of those traditions and a contempt for decency and propriety—a "revolution from below" in which the gutter had triumphed.

Whatever Gisevius left undiscovered or reported, Oster could see for himself: enforced compliance in all sectors of society, the destruction of the constitutional state and—something which the parson's son found peculiarly outrageous—a campaign against the Christian Churches. The wave of murders on June 30, 1934, provided Oster with a new and even more drastic illustration of the new masters' barbarous approach to law and order. For the first time, he awoke to what he later called "the methods of a band of robbers."[40]

Although Oster had yet to become an out-and-out opponent of the Nazi regime, his opposition to certain very specific repositories of its power had been aroused. More keenly than his colleagues, he discerned that a lethal force was threatening the traditional structures of the state and the armed forces, and that its representatives wore the dread black uniform of the SS. He found it monstrous that the Wehrmacht authorities should have tolerated the liquidation of Generals von Schleicher and Bredow on June 30 without calling their SS murderers to account. Oster's fury at the tactical acquiescence of the Wehrmacht's commanders became transmuted into a hatred of the SS so fanatical that it even alarmed his friends.

From then onwards he persistently demanded that the influence of "the Blacks" be curbed, though he himself remained vague on how to achieve this. Patzig paid little heed to Oster because he found his language too woolly and hysterical. He did not take Oster's jeremiads seriously (even though he was thinking along the same lines) and warned Canaris against him before leaving the Abwehr: "Be careful of that man. There's something wrong with his personality."[41]

Although Canaris naturally took a different view of his friend, he was just as disturbed by Oster's political fanaticism and unconvinced by his warnings about the SS, whom he felt competent to handle, so there was little common ground between them at first. Aided by Halder, Canaris secured Oster's readmission to the officer corps (though he remained permanently debarred from General Staff duties). He also helped victims of Nazi persecution—mainly casualties of the anticlerical campaign—at Oster's request, but politically they went their separate ways. Oster could no longer share the Admiral's optimistic view of Germany's position and political direction.

But Canaris was broad-minded (and careless) enough to let Oster carry on in his own way. The head of IIIC1 continued to develop his contacts with ministries and party authorities, eagerly assisted by Gisevius, who had gone into industry after leaving the Ministry of the Interior under SS pressure and making a brief guest appearance at Nebe's RKPA.[42] Gisevius established a direct link between Oster and Nebe, whose inside knowledge of the Gestapo's affairs was exceptional, and thus brought many a disenchanted National Socialist into Oster's intelligence network.

Inside the Abwehr, too, Oster built up a circle of colleagues who were critically disposed towards the regime. These included Alexander von Pfuhlstein, head of Abwehrstelle Hanover, and Canaris's friend Friedrich Wilhelm Heinz, who worked in the same subgroup as Oster and was responsible for recruiting Lieutenant Franz Liedig of Abwehr IM.[43] "In fact," Liedig stated, "Oster's office was a port of call for all those members or associates of the Abwehr who were self-acknowledged opponents of National Socialism."[44] Oster's network of informants soon acquired such a legendary reputation that it was grossly overrated by would-be authorities on the subject. The diplomat Werner von Hentig went so far as to claim in 1938 that "what already exists is the surveillance of the entire party by the Wehrmacht's Abwehr Section (Canaris)."[45]

The truth is that Canaris viewed Oster's network with distaste because he feared protests from the SD, which bore sole responsibility for domestic intelligence work. He later protested officially that "the gathering of intelligence about the internal political situation lay outside the [Abwehr's] field of duties and was expressly forbidden by myself."[46] Canaris regarded such ventures on the fringes of legality as bothersome rather than profitable, especially as he failed to see what the Abwehr could gain from a knowledge of political "trivia" at home.

He also nursed private misgivings about many of Oster's associates. He could not endure Gisevius, the very sight of whom made him fidget. Nebe he considered too inscrutable and Heinz he did not take seriously in spite of their long-standing friendship and common memories of the early postwar period. There were altogether too many outsiders in the Oster set. Oster, with his precarious attachment to the officer corps, Gisevius, who had been thwarted by his own ambitions, Nebe the frustrated police chief, Heinz the stranded politician and man of letters—none of them seemed suitable advisers for a secret service chief.

At the same time, Canaris overlooked the fact that outsiders can often see more clearly than functionaries inhibited by considerations of personal advancement and the need to compromise. Critical outside observers like Oster and Gisevius did, in fact, have a firmer instinctive grasp than Canaris of the political and moral abyss that underlay Hitler's Germany. Even Canaris, who had climbed the professional ladder in a steady and conventional fashion, must have been reluctant to dispense entirely with Oster's undesirable set of informants because he tacitly allowed them to pursue their activities. Indeed, he ended by welcoming their existence when the Blomberg-Fritsch storm broke over the armed forces.

Canaris first learned the true facts behind Blomberg's exposure and disgrace on January 27, 1938. His information came from the much-maligned Gisevius and its source was Nebe.[47] From something Keitel had said, however, he suspected that Fritsch was also involved. Canaris: "'There's supposed to be something wrong with Fritsch as well!'"[48]

By noon next day, January 28, he knew more—from Keitel, whom Hitler had summoned that morning and finally enlightened on the full extent of his radical changes in the Wehrmacht command structure. He himself, Hitler intimated, would take over the Reich War Ministry and "I would remain his chief of staff—I couldn't and mustn't abandon him at this juncture," as Keitel rather smugly noted.[49] Then came the most drastic announcement of all: Fritsch would have to go too—his presence could no longer be tolerated.[50]

Still bemused, Keitel called his section heads together and told them the news. Jodl recorded it in the form in which it must also have been transmitted to Canaris: "He [Hitler] further intends to replace the ObdH [Commander in Chief of the Army]. Evidence about the latter is with the Reich Minister of Justice. (Suspected of offences under Para 175—for two years now.) He [Keitel] is being entrusted with this investigation by the Führer and states that he has known of these matters for two years."[51]

A few hours later Gisevius called on Oster with some additional details. He had heard from Nebe that Fritsch was a marked man and had twice been questioned by the Gestapo. According to the chief of the

Criminal Police, the Wehrmacht was about to sustain a major blow.[52] This information sent Oster into a paraoxysm of rage. A senior general questioned by the Gestapo? It had for years been dinned into every last Army recruit that Gestapo personnel had no right to arrest or even question a soldier, yet they had now interrogated the commander in chief himself.

Oster stormed into Canaris's office. Whatever their differences in recent years, neither was in any doubt that Fritsch must be rescued and this assault on the Wehrmacht's authority repulsed. Canaris was prepared to employ his organization's resources to rehabilitate the unfortunate general. Oster was no less determined. Fritsch had been his regimental commander in 1928. He was now making "Fritsch's cause my own," as he put it later.[53]

Canaris hastened to gather information and mobilize the Army against inroads by the Gestapo. He got in touch with other section heads and officers at the War Ministry, consulted Wehrmacht lawyers and looked up friends and acquaintances on the Army General Staff. These included Colonel Hossbach, whose loyalty to Fritsch was to cost him his job as Hitler's adjutant, and Franz Halder, who had now been promoted general and appointed Oberquartiermeister II, which made him a sort of Deputy Chief of Staff of the Army.

The crucial question was how the Army's senior officers would respond to the smear campaign against their commander in chief. With Fritsch in limbo, all the Army's influence was wielded by Beck, on whom Fritsch's defenders now focused their attention. Canaris forgot the interdepartmental squabbles that had once estranged them and took the Chief of the General Staff into his confidence. He plied Beck with a continuous stream of information, most of it transmitted by Oster, who often spent whole mornings at Beck's office.[54]

But Beck did not react. The background of the Fritsch affair largely escaped him. He regarded it as a personal matter irrelevant to the Army —in fact he found it hard to make up his mind whether the charges of homosexuality against Fritsch were well founded or not.[55] He undoubtedly wanted to help his commander in chief, but only "with the utmost possible discretion."[56] Officially, he pronounced the Fritsch affair taboo and forbade any discussion of it by members of the General Staff, thereby destroying all chance of fighting the case.

When Halder rebelled against these tactics and asked him to tell the General Staff what was afoot, Beck curtly ordered him to pipe down and await instructions. Halder insisted that it was Beck's duty to inform the members of the General Staff. At this, Beck rounded on him: "Mutiny and revolution are words that have no place in a German officer's vocabulary!"[57]

In reality, Beck's attention was concentrated on the scandal surrounding the War Minister. Blomberg's departure and the resultant weakening of the War Ministry had encouraged him to revive the old controversy about the Wehrmacht's command structure and make another attempt to assert the Army's predominance over the other armed services. He was already talking of an independent Army Ministry and drafting new recommendations, one of which badly nettled Canaris by demanding that the Abwehr should come under Army control.[58]

Ruefully, Halder and Canaris watched "that unmitigated fool" Beck thwarting Fritsch's rescue because of his "notorious lack of sophistication and ignorance of human nature" (Halder).[59] It was already becoming evident that all the Wehrmacht could muster in its gravest hour was a breed of soldier drilled in obedience and the leadership cult and fittingly characterized by Marshal MacMahon's dictum: "Of all people on earth, generals have the least stomach for action."[60]

But Canaris, Oster and Fritsch's small and scattered band of allies did not give up. If the Army authorities would not make a move, the general must receive help from another direction. The charges against him had to be disproved—exposed as products of malicious conjecture and evil intent—but what was their exact nature? Canaris did not know. Once again, Oster mobilized his informants to discover more about them.

A new contact, Oberregierungsrat Dr. Johannes (Hans) von Dohnanyi, put him partly in the picture. As personal adviser to Reich Minister of Justice Gürtner, Dohnanyi had read the twenty-two legal documents, seven folders and two interrogation transcripts which comprised the so-called Fritsch case.[61] The material had been referred to Gürtner and by him to Dohnanyi because Hitler wanted an expert opinion on the point at issue between himself and the Wehrmacht's legal authorities, in other words, whether the Fritsch case should be dealt with by a special court (Hitler's preference) or by a court-martial (as demanded by the military lawyers). Dohnanyi told Canaris and Oster of the "knowing smile" with which Gürtner, a conformist but still undergoing "conversion" by the Nazis, had quoted Hitler's instructions to him: "I don't have to tell you which end of the rope to tug . . ."[62]

Dohnanyi himself needed no telling, because he had long been debating how to put paid to Hitler's regime. Son of a celebrated pianist and brother-in-law of the Protestant theologian Dietrich Bonhoeffer, Dohnanyi was a brilliant thirty-six-year-old lawyer who had been appointed a public prosecutor at the age of twenty-nine and an Oberregierungsrat at thirty-one. As in the case of other dissidents, it was a personal experience which had first made him fully conscious of his opposition to the regime.[63] In 1936 envious rivals at the Ministry had discovered a non-Aryan maternal grandfather in Dohnanyi's family tree, and he had been hard put to it to obtain a ruling from Hitler to the effect that Gürtner's aide should suffer "no detriment" as a result of the "doubts" surrounding his grandfather's pedigree.[64]

Dohnanyi began to compile a "chronicle" in which he recorded such Nazi misdeeds as came to the knowledge of the Ministry of Justice. "From murder and attempted murder in concentration camps," reports his wife, Christine von Dohnanyi, "from the . . . abominations in those camps to common-or-garden foreign exchange rackets run by Gauleiters and distasteful goings-on in the higher reaches of the Hitler Youth and SA, there were few offences this 'chronicle' failed to list."[65] Dohnanyi's notes revealed a system ruled by corruption and an abuse of power which he ultimately traced to a single man, Hitler. To Dohnanyi, the logical inference was that his elimination would rid the country of a moral cancer.[66]

But how to remove him? Dohnanyi flirted with the idea of an assassination to be carried out by one of the men who were always at Hitler's side. In 1937 he tried to interest Wiedemann in this plan, but Wiedemann balked: "A revolver is the only way out, I grant you, but who's to do it? I can't help to murder someone who trusts me."[67] In desperation, Dohnanyi contacted another potential ally, the austere and extremist Order of the SS. "My husband had a peculiar relationship with Himmler," wrote Frau von Dohnanyi, who could still recall what hopes he had pinned on the puritanical and elitist Reichsführer-SS.[68]

Having read the Fritsch file, however, Dohnanyi realized that the SS and SS-controlled Gestapo were simply stirring up mud in order to break the morale of their own or Hitler's opponents, or those whom they considered such. That left only one force capable of cooking Hitler's goose: the Wehrmacht. Dohnanyi resolved to enlist it for the purpose. He duly slanted his written opinion on the Fritsch case in such a way that the Führer had virtually no choice but to give the Wehrmacht judiciary a chance.

Dohnanyi was assisted in drafting his recommendations by an old acquaintance who had worked with him on the Penal Offences Board of the Ministry of Justice, Reichskriegsgerichtsrat [Reich Court-Martial Counsel] Dr. Karl Sack.[69] Sack was a member of the Reichskriegsgericht and sat on the bench responsible for trying cases of treason. Sack and Dohnanyi quickly reached agreement. A Court of the Supreme Commander of the Wehrmacht, comprising the commanders in chief of the Army, Luftwaffe and Navy, together with the two presidents of the Reichskriegsgericht, would investigate the Fritsch case and pass judgement in the course of a main hearing. A military judge would conduct the inquiry without the Gestapo participation envisaged by Hitler.[70]

Hitler accepted these proposals, though only with substantial reservations. He directed the Gestapo to conduct a parallel investigation and assigned Göring the role of presiding judge.[71] Göring promptly ensured that the inquiry was headed, not by Sack (as the Wehrmacht legal authorities had suggested), but by a timid and cautious colleague of his named Biron.[72] However, it still proved possible to sneak Sack into the hearing by appointing him Biron's assistant and minute-taker.[73]

It was Sack, too, who introduced Dohnanyi to Oster and Canaris.[74] Dohnanyi's approach to the officers at Abwehr headquarters did not come easily because the military world remained forever alien to him. He used to say that there were ardent soldiers and ardent civilians, and that he was one of the latter. Out of tune with the military's notions of order, he often "criticized . . . their narrow outlook and 'cadettish' conceptions of honour and patriotism."[75] Only a sense of outrage at the machinations of Hitler and his henchmen impelled him to call at the Tirpitz-Ufer, where he was enthusiastically hailed as one of Oster's most valued confederates.

Canaris was equally impressed by Dohnanyi's precise, almost dispassionate tone. Privately, he earmarked this lawyer-intellectual for future employment in the Abwehr. Although he could not endorse Dohnanyi's views on Hitler, he was attracted by the cool powers of reasoning which he so sorely missed in Oster. Besides, Dohnanyi made a particularly welcome informant because he could supply details of the charges against Fritsch.

These were based on the evidence of one Otto Schmidt, a Berliner and habitual offender who had been rearrested in 1935. Yielding to a strange fit of megalomania, Schmidt not only bragged about numerous cases of extortion but claimed to have blackmailed many homosexuals —hundreds of them, including a number of prominent figures. He also named names, among them a "General Fritsch."[76]

This case came within the jurisdiction of the Reichszentrale für die Bekämpfung der Homosexualität [Reich Central Office for the Combating of Homosexuality], which was based at the Gestapa and waged a merciless campaign against the sexual inverts whom all the resources of government and society had combined to anathematize. The Reichszentrale was headed by Kriminalrat Josef Meisinger, a crude veteran Nazi who had risen to senior rank in the Gestapo by virtue of his party connections. While reading the transcript of the Schmidt interrogation, Meisinger was brought up short by the name Fritsch. Could it refer to the Army commander in chief, a man reputed to be the great white hope of the conservative opposition and a sworn enemy of the SS?

Early in July 1936 Meisinger showed the prisoner a collection of photographs from which Schmidt grandly selected the one with the most illustrious label. Ever an advocate of sledge-hammer police

methods, Meisinger had captioned each photo with the subject's name
and rank. As soon as Schmidt saw "Colonel General Baron von Fritsch,
Commander in Chief of the Army," he swooped. "That's him!" he
said, and proceeded to dictate a highly colourful statement.[77]

One night in November 1933, in the concourse of Berlin's Wannsee
Station, he had observed a man dressed as follows: dark overcoat with
brown fur collar, dark hat, white scarf, monocle. This individual had
left the station with a young male prostitute nicknamed "Bayern-
Seppl" [Bavarian Joe] and accompanied him down an ill-lit side road.
He, Schmidt, had then seen the pair engage in a homosexual act.

After a while the man returned and went to the neighbouring tramway station in Potsdamer Platz. There Schmidt stopped him, introduced himself as "Kriminalkommissar Kröger" and accused him of immoral behaviour. The man said he was General von Fritsch and
confirmed this by producing an identity card with the name "von
Fritsch" clearly visible in the top right corner. Schmidt demanded
hush money. The man replied that a few thousand marks were neither
here nor there but that he only had a hundred on him. Schmidt then
accompanied him to Berlin-Lichterfelde, where he disappeared into No.
21 Ferdinandstrasse.

Ten minutes later the man emerged, handed him five hundred
marks and promised him another thousand next day. Schmidt took delivery of this sum too and was promised the same again. This instal-
ment he collected in the second-class waiting room of the Lichterfelde-
Ost tramway station, accompanied by a labourer friend named Heiter,
alias "Bucker."[78]

So much for Schmidt's statement in July 1936. Meisinger proceeded
to make some additional inquiries. Schmidt supplied further details at
another interrogation and the story was confirmed on August 20 by his
accomplice Heiter.[79] That was good enough for Meisinger. He reported
his lucky find to his superiors, who hurried to the Chancellery to impart
the sensational news to Hitler. Being still at pains to secure Fritsch's co-
operation in 1936, the Führer merely ordered Himmler to burn "this
filth."[80] The Gestapo were not inspired to reopen the case until the
Blomberg scandal broke and Göring expressed interest in the Schmidt
file.

Now Hitler, too, developed a lively interest in the Gestapo's records.
It was rather ironical that he should have sent Göring, the co-producer
of the Blomberg-Fritsch spectacular, to verify Schmidt's statements at
Prinz-Albrecht-Strasse.[81] Hitler would much have preferred Fritsch simply to resign—indeed, he assumed that the general would do so in return for a promise of silence and immunity from investigation[82]—but
this was the one favour Fritsch declined to bestow on his Führer.

When Hossbach informed him of the charges in defiance of Hitler's express wishes, he flatly denied them: "It's a stinking lie!"[83]

But he said no more, and his reticence was to prove disastrous. Fritsch accepted his lot in a spirit of fatalistic resignation, unable to grasp what his supreme commander had done to him. He was so much under Hitler's spell that he bowed to any imposition from that quarter. He stalked into the Chancellery to confront his blackmailer but offered no protest when Hitler refused to accept his word of honour and attached no more validity to it than he did to the allegations of a convicted criminal. He twice submitted to questioning by the Gestapo, still hoping that his Führer would see the light.[84]

As soon as Canaris pieced together what had happened from the accounts given him by Dohnanyi and Gisevius, he realized that Fritsch was going to be of no help to his friends. Fortunately for the general, however, he had acquired an astute defence counsel in Count Rüdiger von der Goltz, a cousin of Frau von Dohnanyi's. Together with Canaris and the heads of the inquiry, Biron and Sack, Goltz worked out a plan of campaign for Fritsch's rehabilitation.[85]

Canaris sent two Abwehr technicians to the lawyer's office to examine its telephones for Gestapo monitoring devices.[86] He also placed other personnel at his disposal. In particular, he instructed Oster to maintain contact with Dohnanyi and Sack so that Abwehr headquarters could be kept constantly informed of the progress of the official inquiry. The investigators' reports were usually passed via Oster to Canaris, who forwarded them to Hossbach, who in turn passed them to Beck.[87]

But the investigation proceeded at a snail's pace. Goltz, Biron and Sack laboriously followed up a wide variety of leads. Then, on the night of January 31, Gisevius called at Oster's home with some news which shed an entirely new light on the affair. Nebe had informed him that "the so-called Fritsch 'case' was one of mistaken identity. Heydrich and Himmler knew this, he said, but had done their utmost to hush it up."[88] Although the RKPA chief could not discover the name of the person with whom Fritsch had been confused, he knew that this *gaffe* had caused a tremendous row at the Gestapa.[89]

Nebe did not possess sufficient inside information to ascertain the full details of the Gestapo slip-up. They were as follows. Kriminaloberinspektor [Detective Chief Inspector] Josef Huber, who had been brought into the Fritsch investigation while deputizing for Meisinger, currently absent on leave, had questioned the general on February 27 and formed the impression that there was something amiss with Schmidt's story. He decided to pursue some inquiries on his own account, so he paid a visit to Meisinger's deserted department after office hours and, more particularly, examined the desk occupied by Kriminalinspektor [Detective Inspector] Fehling, who was in direct charge of the Fritsch case.[90]

In the process, Huber came upon some extracts from a Dresdner Bank passbook numbered 10220 and registered in the name of Rittmeister a.D [Captain of Cavalry, retired] Achim von Frisch. It listed a series of cash withdrawals which coincided with the blackmail payments mentioned by Schmidt. Huber felt as if he had been "bitten by a tarantula."[91] It was patently obvious that Fehling had long known the true identity of Schmidt's victim and realized that General von Fritsch was completely innocent. Huber promptly reported his discovery to Himmler and Heydrich. The SS chief just brought himself to murmur, "Thanks, you've done a good job." Then an iron curtain of silence descended over Prinz-Albrecht-Strasse.[92]

Although Canaris was unaware of these facts, Gisevius's information was enough to go on. If it could be confirmed that the Fritsch case involved a mix-up, the Gestapo would be discredited. Hitler, too, would be compromised and infuriated by the Gestapo's amateurish methods. This moment must be exploited so as to bring Himmler and Heydrich to heel, and Canaris knew how: as soon as Fritsch's innocence had been established, the Wehrmacht must rally round and demand the dismissal of the entire Gestapo leadership.

On February 1 Canaris called on Keitel and Beck and let them into the secret of the Gestapo blunder.[93] He also asked Gisevius to draw up a report listing all the items of circumstantial evidence that pointed to a confusion of identities. This report he distributed to Sack and a number of military commanders.[94]

But the Abwehr chief had to tread carefully to avoid antagonizing certain senior officers. Keitel, in particular, disliked Canaris's intervention in the Fritsch affair because he feared it would provoke a clash between the armed forces and the Gestapo, and nothing dismayed him more than the prospect of tangling with Himmler's powerful organization. He warned Canaris to be careful but let him have his way. Keitel had grown accustomed to the little admiral. He needed his ingenuity and cunning—in fact he had even assigned him wider powers in his plans for a reorganized Wehrmacht command structure.

Meanwhile, all was in readiness for the public unveiling of a new Hitlerian coup. It had taken some days to find a replacement for Fritsch. His successor was General Walter von Brauchitsch, a weak and ambitious character who had gained Hitler's ear by promising to "introduce" the Army to the National Socialist state.[95] The moment came. On February 4, 1938, the nation learned that the critics of Hitler's all-or-nothing policy had been eliminated—Blomberg and Fritsch retired, Foreign Minister Baron von Neurath replaced by Joachim von Ribbentrop, several ambassadors recalled, sixteen generals compulsorily retired, forty-four others transferred and the War Ministry renamed the Ober-kommando der Wehrmacht (OKW) under Keitel's direction.[96]

This move, which accelerated Germany's progress towards total dic-tatorship and war, took Canaris another rung up the ladder of success. He became an Amtsgruppenchef [head of branch] in the OKW. On February 7 Keitel dictated a directive in which he laid it down that the Armed Forces High Command would in future have two Amtsgruppen, Amtsgruppe Führungsstab [Operations Staff Branch] and Amtsgruppe Allgemeine Wehrmachtangelegenheiten [AWA—General Armed Forces Affairs Branch]. Canaris took charge of the latter. Keitel decreed: "Admiral Canaris [is appointed] Amtsgruppenchef, while re-taining his post as head of the Abwehr Section. Subordinate to him are the Abwehr, Interior and Supply Sections."[97]

Keitel's directive made Canaris the Wehrmacht authorities' leading political spokesman. He was now responsible, under Keitel, for the OKW's relations with the party, police, press and public. "There can be no doubt," he told his Io and Abwehr officers, "that the internal inter-ests of the Wehrmacht, notably in the field of press policy, are closely linked with the problems of counterespionage . . . The scope of our joint activities has thus been expanded and widened to cover the field of internal politics as well."[98]

The National Socialist press soon felt his touch on the reins. When the departure of Blomberg and Fritsch was hailed by a leader in the *Völkischer Beobachter* as signifying that "the process of fusion between the Wehrmacht and the party" was assuming "ever clearer organi-zational forms" and that the natural consequence would be "to rein-vigorate the German Army with the spirit of the party," Canaris protested to Reich press chief Dietrich that the article conflicted with the "twin columns" structure of the Third Reich.[99] He told his press officers that "further steps have been taken to correct the attitude dis-cernible in the aforesaid leader and obviate similar misconceptions in future."[100]

The Admiral's new powers also made it easier for him to furnish the OKW and Army chiefs with anti-Gestapo ammunition, a task in which he was actively assisted by his fellow Amtsgruppenchef, Lieutenant General Max von Viehbahn. Canaris and Viehbahn were old friends who had served together on the staff of Reichswehr Minister Noske and shared the same cell when taken into custody after the Kapp Putsch.[101] Canaris needed Viehbahn's help in bringing influence to bear on other Army generals.

Only Beck continued to disrupt the Admiral's plans by stirring up new interdepartmental disputes. At the end of January he had stated in conversation with Keitel that the Army's importance to Germany was paramount. Jodl's Landesverteidigungsabteilung [National Defence Sec-

tion] should therefore be transferred to the Army General Staff.[102]
He now worked out a programme which amounted, according to Jodl,
to "the complete neutralization of the OKW."[103] As if nothing were
more important at this juncture than a discussion of structural reforms,
Beck diverted the energies of his fellow military leaders to the wrong
battlefield altogether.

But Canaris now needed every available ally because the duel be-
tween the Gestapo and the Wehrmacht's legal branch had intensified.
The Gestapa sent out its sleuths to round up new evidence against
General von Fritsch while Biron and Sack did their best to probe the
Prinz-Albrecht-Strasse's guilty secret.

It must have tickled the Admiral's sense of humour to go for his regular morning rides in the Tiergarten with Heydrich and Best, who were
directing operations for the other side and had long been on his black
list. He enjoyed these double games, although he had to assume that
his two adversaries knew perfectly well who was masterminding the opposition. Meanwhile, the three men gave no sign of knowing what they
knew. Chatting brightly, they rode together until it was time to depart
for their respective headquarters and resume the battle.

Canaris continued his search for new recruits to the Fritsch cause.
He even went so far as to woo Göring, though he had no knowledge of
the latter's baneful part in the affair. Göring, who was capable of good
as well as evil and always backed the bigger battalions, changed tack.
Blomberg's departure having left him the only serving field marshal
and, thus, the most senior officer in the armed forces, he thought it expedient to pose as a custodian of military tradition. He may also have
felt tempted to commit a small and surreptitious act of revenge on the
man who had thwarted his designs on the War Ministry.

At all events, he turned a receptive ear to the Wehrmacht's complaints when Canaris and Keitel visited him at Karinhall, his country
seat, on February 10.[104] Their discussion must have gone off well, because Canaris added Göring's name to the list of those whom he kept
supplied with regular batches of pro-Fritsch material.

Next day, February 11, Canaris received glad tidings from Sack. The
two chief investigators had finally succeeded in locating the vital witness whom the Gestapo had "failed" to trace but were really holding in
custody: Weingärtner, the youth alleged to have committed a homosexual act with Fritsch.[105] Weingärtner stoutly denied that Fritsch had
been his partner, and the president of the Reichskriegsgericht, General
Heitz, considered his statement so conclusive that he volunteered to advise Hitler to quash the proceedings.[106]

Heitz and the two chief investigators were just preparing to leave
for the Berghof, Hitler's mountain retreat, when an order from Keitel
temporarily suspended Canaris's activities on behalf of Fritsch. Keitel

himself received a summons to the Berghof and the Abwehr was placed on the alert. The Führer was girding himself for a new foreign policy coup, this time against Austria.

Some historians have suggested that Hitler deliberately provoked the Austrian crisis in order to distract attention from the Blomberg-Fritsch scandal. This simple theory is wide of the mark. The crisis was triggered by Franz von Papen, the German Ambassador in Vienna, who had helped Hitler to assume power and was now one of the victims of the February 4 reshuffle. As soon as Papen learned that he had lost his cosy appointment he decided to retrieve it at all costs. Hurrying to see Hitler at the Berghof, he lamented that he had just prevailed on Kurt von Schuschnigg, the Austrian Chancellor, to approve the closer Austro-German relationship which the Führer had always wanted. Schuschnigg, he declared, was now prepared for a heart to heart talk with Hitler.[107]

Ever ready to make capital out of any opportunity that presented itself, Hitler pricked up his ears. He sent Papen back to Vienna with instructions to arrange a visit by Schuschnigg.[108] There seemed to be a chance of squeezing some fresh concessions out of the Austrian Chancellor, but for that Hitler needed politico-military pressure. He accordingly summoned Keitel and two other generals to the Berghof.

Schuschnigg and his delegation turned up at the Führer's eyrie on February 12. He was scarcely inside the study when a torrent of recrimination engulfed him. He, the Austrian Chancellor, had sabotaged the 1936 agreement on co-operation between the two German states and was pursuing an "un-German" policy. Then Hitler presented his demands: the Austrian government must appoint some National Socialists to the cabinet, the police force was to be commanded by a party member and the economic and foreign policy of both countries must be co-ordinated.[109]

Schuschnigg angrily left the study. This was the cue for the OKW chief's entrance. While the Austrians were withdrawing to confer in private, Hitler's voice rang out: "General Keitel! Where's Keitel? Tell him to come here at once." Keitel came dashing in. The Austrians heard him say, "What are your orders, my Führer?"—nothing more. Inside the study, Hitler smirked. "There aren't any," he said, "—do sit down." When Keitel still looked puzzled, he added, "The Federal Chancellor wants to confer briefly with Foreign Minister Schmidt. I don't have anything else."[110]

Schuschnigg and his party had gloomily concluded that the German invasion of Austria was only hours away when Papen talked them into approving an "agreement" under which Schuschnigg promised to appoint the moderate Nazi Arthur Seyss-Inquart Minister of the Interior, with authority over the police, and to promote administrative co-ordination between the two countries. For his part, Hitler undertook to ban all illegal activities by the Austrian National Socialists.[111]

Hitler was so pleased with this "Berchtesgaden Protocol" that he briefly considered the subject of Austria closed. A few days later he recalled the five leading Nazi extremists in Austria and announced to his closest associates that the Austrian question could "never be solved by a revolution." To quote a contemporary record: "There were only two alternatives, force and evolution, and he wanted the latter chosen irrespective of whether or not the possibility of success was already in sight."[112]

However, Hitler still feared that the agreement might not be accepted by Federal President Miklas. He promptly thought up a new assignment for Keitel, who was to return to Berlin and stage some shows of strength along the Austro-German border. The time had come for Canaris to take a hand in the proceedings.

On the afternoon of February 13 Keitel summoned Canaris and Jodl to his private apartment in Berlin and informed them that Hitler had given orders "to maintain milit[ary] pressure by shamming milit[ary] action until the fifteenth."[113] Canaris quickly came up with a scheme which provided for the dissemination of "false but plausible reports . . . implying military preparations against Austria, (a) by agents inside Austria, (b) by our customs personnel at the border, (c) by travel [i.e. mobile] agents."[114]

Canaris was ingenious enough to devise a few misleading reports for the bafflement of the Austrian authorities. "(a) Leave must be stopped in the area of VII AK [VII Army Corps]. (b) Empty rolling stock to be concentrated in Munich, Augsburg and Regensburg. (c) The military attaché in Vienna, Lieutenant General Muff, to be recalled to Berlin for consultations. (d) The Frontier Police posts on the Austrian border have called up reinforcements. (e) Customs officers to report manoeuvres by the Mountain Brigade imminent near Freilassing, Reichenhall and Berchtesgaden."[115]

Keitel conveyed these proposals to Hitler by telephone and requested his approval. The go-ahead was given at 2:40 A.M. on February 14.[116] Canaris was ordered to supervise the diversionary manoeuvre in person. He sent for Major Pruck, who headed the Southeast Europe desk of Abwehr I, and caught a late-night express to Munich.[117]

Shortly afterwards, false reports began to filter along the channels leading to the Austrian military authorities. Austrian secret service departments were informed by self-styled anti-Nazis in the Reich that they had seen troop trains and motorized Wehrmacht units near the frontier.[118] "The effect has been swift and potent," Jodl noted gleefully. "The impression arising in Austria is of serious milit[ary] preparations in Germany."[119] In reality, Austrian intelligence officers whose knowledge of their German colleagues was based on years of co-operation could only smile at the Abwehr's efforts. Lieutenant Colonel Lahousen of the Austrian intelligence centre in Vienna stated that he and his men did not "fall for this bluff,"[120] and even Pruck admitted that it was "a flop."[121]

Still preening himself on his apparent success, Canaris was about to fly back to Berlin from Munich's Riem Airport when he caught sight of SS-Brigadeführer Best, who had been lecturing at Bad Tölz. He cheerfully accosted this prominent member of the enemy camp and drew him into a conversation which lasted throughout their flight to Berlin. Pruck was dismayed to hear his chief initiate the Gestapo man into every detail of the Abwehr operation which had just been launched.[122]

Pruck's bewilderment persists to the present day. He surmises that this was "one of Canaris's well-meant attempts to gain trust and recruit allies on the other side. That sort of *rapprochement* policy escaped my comprehension and still does. With me, you're either one thing or the other. In my personal experience . . . Canaris was not fully alive to the impossibility of bridging the gulf between a liberal outlook and totalitarian ideas."[123] For the first time, a senior member of the Abwehr had been struck by something which was later to perplex so many people: the equivocal way in which Canaris veered between Germany's two internal lines of battle.

Oster and his friends were also compelled to acknowledge that, despite their united front against "the Blacks," they could not place full reliance on the Admiral's co-operation. The Fritsch affair had long ago inspired them to contemplate the use of force against the regime, or at least against parts of it. Oster and Gisevius, supported by Carl Goerdeler, the ex-mayor of Leipzig, and Hjalmar Schacht, Hitler's ex-Minister of Economic Affairs, were considering "an armed self-help operation by the Army against the SS and Gestapo" and a radical reform of the regime. Gisevius, Oster and Goerdeler had, in fact, visited Hanover, Münster and Leipzig at the end of January in the hope of persuading the military district commanders to launch a coup against the SS, but their plan had been thwarted by the generals' lack of information.[124]

Canaris regarded such endeavours as utterly unrealistic, being aware that Oster's schemes were deficient in everything from military backing and leadership to a political programme and a revolutionary situation. He must have shared Count von der Goltz's amusement when the latter told him of Oster's plea that "the whole Prinz-Albrecht-Strasse set-up must be smoked out and occupied"—a remark which Goltz dismissed as just one more hilarious illustration of how temperamental Oster could be.[125]

The Abwehr chief possessed too keen an eye for individual and tactical weaknesses to be swayed by Oster's schemes. Oster and Gisevius submitted new proposals almost daily. At one moment they dreamed of inciting military commanders in the provinces to overthrow the regime by force, at another of prodding Fritsch into opposing Hitler, at another of persuading the Wehrmacht legal authorities to institute proceedings against the SS. This prompted Canaris to label them "perpetual rebels" and created "an impression of insufficient gravity, if not of irresponsible recklessness" in other quarters too.[126]

The two men's revolutionary ardour could not fail to arouse mistrust in someone with Canaris's personal experience of the darker side of revolution, especially as he was not in full agreement with their basic political analysis. They inhabited two different worlds of opposition sentiment.

At the same time, Canaris had by now learned enough about the background of the Blomberg-Fritsch crisis to grasp the full extent of Hitler's perfidy and thirst for power. He was co-author (with Hossbach) of the remark that "the Führer may well have an accurate knowledge of the psyche of the mass of the people but is not alert to the preservation of the Wehrmacht's good name and that of its commanders."[127] No officer could have levelled stronger criticism at his supreme commander. On the other hand, Canaris still hoped that Hitler was capable of improvement and clung to his belief that the regime could regenerate itself from within. In this he resembled Nebe, of whom a close acquaintance wrote that he had detested Himmler but regarded Hitler as "more dangerous but more unpredictably capable of good."[128]

In short, Hitler and the regime were not under discussion from the Admiral's point of view. He did not even question the Gestapo's right to exist. All he wanted was to extricate Fritsch from the mire, expose the conspiracy against him and break the supremacy of the "Cheka" (his sarcastic analogy between the Gestapo and the Soviet secret police)—not, à la Oster, by force of arms, but by a legitimate move on the part of senior German generals.

Canaris waited patiently for a chance to put the military authorities into a suitably resentful frame of mind with some fresh horror stories about the Gestapo. The opportunity soon came, because the Fritsch controversy dragged on. When Heitz, Biron and Sack recommended on February 13 that the proceedings be quashed, Hitler rejected their submission.[129] This encouraged the Gestapo to reopen the campaign by inviting Fritsch to undergo further questioning. Goltz, Canaris and Oster advised the general to refuse, but he insisted on doing his "duty."

Keitel eventually produced a compromise plan. The Gestapo and Fritsch would meet on "neutral territory" at a Wannsee villa which, though SS-owned, was not an official Gestapo stamping ground. Fritsch agreed.[130] Reichskriegsgerichtsrat Ernst Kanter, a new addition to the Biron-Sack investigating team, was to accompany the general. Furthermore, an Army unit would be ostentatiously posted in the neighbourhood to dissuade the Gestapo from doing anything "foolish" because Oster was afraid they might browbeat Fritsch into committing suicide.[131]

The interrogation took place on February 20. Meisinger conducted it in such an uncouth manner that Kanter had to step in and request him to concentrate on matters relevant to the proceedings.[132] By this time, even Fritsch had had enough. On February 23 he asked Sack to read an additional statement into the record of the Wannsee interview: "No nation has ever suffered the commander in chief of its Army to be subjected to such outrageous treatment. I expressly state this for the record so that future historians shall know how the commander in chief of the Army was treated in 1938. Such treatment is not only discreditable to me but degrading to the Army as a whole."[133]

This was just the sort of salvo Canaris needed. Promptly informed by Kanter of what had happened in Wannsee, he ensured that the story received wide circulation. Keitel was furious that Kanter had told the Abwehr chief first. He demanded an explanation and ordered the lawyer to keep his mouth shut, especially where Canaris was concerned. As he himself put it: "You simply aren't acquainted with the Gestapo's way of doing things."[134]

But there was no holding Canaris, who retailed the story of the Wannsee outburst wherever he went. On February 26 Jodl noted: "Canaris describes the shameful way in which Colonel General von Fritsch was questioned by the SS."[135] When Vichbahn heard of the latest development, he thundered, "If the men get to hear of this, there'll be revolution."[136] Canaris continued to stir away, determined that every senior functionary in the Reich should hear of Fritsch's maltreatment. He scored many successes. At the annual meeting of the Schlieffen Society on February 28, the Gestapo's methods were stigmatized by the police chiefs of Berlin and Potsdam.[137]

Encouraged by this wave of indignation, the three judicial investigators made a renewed effort to establish Fritsch's innocence. They had already shaken many of Schmidt's allegations, for example by proving that Fritsch had never possessed an identity card of the type described by Schmidt and never lived in the Ferdinandstrasse area. Weingärtner's statement left them in no doubt that the incident at Wannsee Station had actually taken place, but with someone else. Who could this "third man" be?

Sack was reminded of the report alleging mistaken identity. Kanter, too, recalled that Kriminalinspektor Fehling of the Gestapo had once mentioned that Schmidt was prone to exaggerate the importance of his

victims.[138] Weingärtner's partner might therefore have been someone
who resembled Fritsch in name or social status. There might also be
witnesses who had seen this double in Schmidt's company, possibly
while hush money was changing hands. Biron and Sack instituted fresh
inquiries at the spot where money had actually been paid over, in the
waiting room at Lichterfelde-Ost.

On the afternoon of March 1 they called at the waiting room and
questioned the woman attendant. She eventually recalled that the place
had often been frequented by a retired Army officer who was usually accompanied by a woman and lived somewhere nearby, possibly in Ferdinandstrasse.[139] The two investigators decided to comb the houses
round 21 Ferdinandstrasse and look through the postal directory for
a name resembling Fritsch. Biron was so taken with this idea that he
telephoned Gisevius the same evening and told him about it.[140]

The lawyer was too impatient to await the outcome of another visit
to Ferdinandstrasse. He got hold of a postal directory, opened it at the
page listing the residents of Ferdinandstrasse and ran his finger down
the column of names. Suddenly he came to "von Frisch, Achim, Captain of Cavalry (ret.)." And where did the gentleman live? At 20 Ferdinandstrasse, or one door away from the house into which, according
to Schmidt himself, "General von Fritsch" had disappeared. Gisevius at
once informed Biron and Sack, who hurried to Ferdinandstrasse next
morning.[141] A few minutes later they were face to face with the invalid
captain and his nurse—the woman referred to by the waiting-room attendant.

It all added up. Captain von Frisch admitted the incident at Wannsee Station. He owned a fur-trimmed overcoat like the one described by
Schmidt and even produced receipts for the hush money he had paid.
Then his nurse chimed in with a piece of information which took the
visitors' breath away: Kriminalinspektor Fehling had called on the captain in January 1938 and removed his bank statements.[142] The Gestapo
plot stood revealed in all its perfidy.

Sack took down the captain's deposition and went with Biron to tell
Goltz. Fritsch's counsel hurried to his client and unceremoniously informed him of the good news: "General, you can fire a victory salute—
the matter has been completely cleared up." Fritsch remained glum.
"It'll take more than that to satisfy the Führer. He won't believe anything of the kind."[143] The general very nearly proved right, thanks to
the gullibility of Canaris, who still failed to grasp what lengths the
Gestapo could go to.

It occurred to Hossbach that, far from twiddling their thumbs, the
Gestapo would try to pocket the witness who had virtually demolished
their case overnight. Determined to prevent this at all costs, Hossbach
called on Canaris and implored him to think of some valid reason why

the Abwehr should take Frisch into protective custody. Canaris dismissed the idea—"This time you're really being *too* suspicious"— and declared that the witness could safely remain in his apartment.[144]

Next day Achim von Frisch was gone—arrested by the Gestapo.[145] At the last moment, Canaris had hit on the idea of posting an Abwehr photographer in Ferdinandstrasse. Counterespionage Chief Protze recalls that the Admiral gave him only an hour "to produce a photographer who could, if necessary, snap Frisch being taken away by SS men."[146] This photograph, coupled with Sack's record of the original interview, became Frisch's life insurance policy.

The military lawyers now felt sure of their ground. At the end of February they formally charged Colonel General Baron von Fritsch with an offence under Paragraph 175 of the Penal Code and set a date for the main hearing. The scene of this judicial battle was the Preussen-Haus in Berlin, once the defunct monarchy's "First Chamber," or equivalent of the British House of Lords.

The main hearing opened on the morning of March 10, 1938. Göring and his fellow judges, together with the commanders in chief of the armed services and the two divisional presidents of the supreme military bench, entered the courtroom. Everyone rose except Fritsch, who ostentatiously remained seated—the ex-commander in chief's sole mark of protest.[147] Hitler's tubby field marshal soon took charge of the proceedings, but he did not get far.

Prosecuting counsel had just launched into a preliminary examination of Schmidt when an aide from the Chancellery appeared with a message for Göring. A whisper ran the length of the judges' bench. A minute later Fritsch, too, learned that Hitler had summoned all commanders in chief to the Chancellery. The hearing was adjourned.[148] A new drama was unfolding—Austria's incorporation in the Reich.

The humiliated co-signatory of the Berchtesgaden Protocol had hit back after all, but belatedly and with inadequate resources. Federal Chancellor von Schuschnigg did not grasp the full implications of his surrender on February 12 until he returned to Vienna. Although he complied with the terms of the agreement by declaring an amnesty for convicted Nazi supporters and took Seyss-Inquart into the cabinet, his authority waned so rapidly that he evolved a surprise move which would compel the "national opposition" to acknowledge the existence of a "free and German, independent and social, Christian and united Austria" (Schuschnigg's own formula). During the night of March 8–9 he confided to five of his closest advisers, including Federal Minister Zernatto, that he proposed to advertise Austria's desire for national independence by holding a referendum in four days' time.[149]

However, Schuschnigg was so unsure of himself that he decided to guarantee the result of this plebiscite by rigging the conditions under which it was held. The minimum voting age was set at twenty-four so as to exclude the young, most of whom were attracted to National Socialism and the Greater German ideal, in favour of those who supported the authoritarian ruling party.[150] Surprise was Schuschnigg's main consideration. By not announcing the plebiscite until he addressed a rally at Innsbruck on the evening of March 9, he hoped to give his opponents as little time as possible to organize counter-measures.[151]

But Zernatto's secretary betrayed the plan to Berlin, where its details became known by about noon on the crucial day. At first, Hitler was incredulous.[152] He refused to accept that the victim of his bullying was preparing to outmanoeuvre the Führer of the German Reich. As so often when confronted by an unexpected turn of events, Hitler momentarily wavered. He sent an envoy to Vienna to talk Schuschnigg out of his plan.[153]

By next morning, he realized that Schuschnigg's imprudence had presented him with a unique opportunity. The Berchtesgaden Protocol had laid down common policy guidelines from which it might "legitimately" be inferred that the Austrian Chancellor should have consulted his German counterpart in advance. Hitler arbitrarily concluded that Germany had the right to send troops into Austria. He formed an audacious plan to overthrow the Schuschnigg regime by military pressure—if necessary by means of a short-term invasion—and bring the National Socialists to power in his native land.[154]

Hitler received an unpleasant surprise when he asked Keitel to produce contingency plans for an invasion—there weren't any. In June 1937, Blomberg had issued an Order Relating to Co-ordinated Preparations for War by the Armed Forces in which he requested the Army General Staff to work out an operational plan for "Sonderfall [Special Contingency] Otto," or the occupation of Austria in the event of an attempt to restore the monarchy. But Beck, who was at odds with the War Minister over structural issues, did not consider this directive sufficiently important to warrant taxing the ingenuity of his logistics experts.[155]

Brauchitsch, the new Army commander in chief, was attending the Fritsch trial, so Hitler sent for his chief of staff. This was the great moment for which Beck had been waiting. He informed Hitler that an invasion would require the deployment of VII and VIII Army Corps and an armoured division, which would have to be mobilized at once. In the absence of any mobilization plans, this presented obvious difficulties. "Everything would have to be improvised," but it could be done.[156] Hitler announced that he intended "to march in next Saturday, on the eve of the projected referendum." After a little mental arithmetic, Beck told him that the mobilization order would have to be issued that day, March 10.[157]

Usually a critic of Hitler's expansionist programme, Beck was like a man transformed. The Führer had given him orders and sought his advice—that was precisely how he conceived of his role as Chief of the General Staff. Assiduously, he urged his logistics officers to fulfil the Führer's wishes. Beck's head of operations, Major General von Manstein, had the plans ready in five hours. "They went out twenty minutes late."[158] If Ludwig Beck had ever entertained any doubts about a policy of annexation, he was oblivious of them now.

Next day, when troops had already been alerted and were moving into their assembly areas, Hitler began to stoke up the international crisis. Göring, who took temporary charge of the political campaign, maintained permanent contact with the German Embassy in Vienna and bullied the Austrian authorities by telephone. His demands became tougher by the hour. He insisted that the plebiscite be cancelled, called for Schuschnigg's resignation and Seyss-Inquart's appointment as Federal Chancellor—even demanded a telegram from the new National Socialist government "requesting" Germany to march in.[159]

The time had come for Canaris to alert his own organization. On March 11, as tension continued to mount, he assembled all his departmental chiefs at Abwehr headquarters and informed them that the Führer had decided to settle the Austrian question, if necessary by military means. All Abwehr offices were to be manned round the clock.[160] S agents in every major European country were set in motion and dispatched to their posts.

Three countries and their reactions were a particular source of anxiety from the German point of view Italy, France and Great Britain—and it was these that merited special attention from the Abwehr's spies. Italy presented the thorniest problem, having long been Austria's protecting power, but Canaris's hands were tied by the fact that his organization could not operate in the territory of an Axis partner. Hitler cleared the air himself. He wrote Mussolini an explanatory letter and sent it to Rome by Prince Philipp of Hessen. At 10:25 P.M. the prince reported by telephone that the Duce had taken "the whole affair in a very, very friendly way." Hitler: "Then please tell Mussolini I shall never forget him for this. Never, never, never, come what may."[161]

As Army units moved off, so the Abwehr's time of trial began. Tensely, without stirring from their posts, Canaris and his colleagues scrutinized the stream of reports from abroad. By the night of March 12, no V-Mann had noted any critical reaction on the part of France and Britain. Canaris spent the night on the camp bed in his office while Pruck remained on duty in the anteroom. The major took down telephone messages from Abwehr outstations and relayed them to interested parties, notably the Army General Staff and the Foreign Armies Section of the OKW. He recalls: "The Admiral assured me next morning that he had slept excellently."[162]

Canaris skimmed through the night's crop of reports. None of them betrayed any disquieting reaction in foreign quarters and each revealed the hopeless isolation of Austria and her Chancellor. At midnight Pruck had passed the following report to the Foreign Section for transmission to the Foreign Office: "1. Maginot Line fully manned but solely for defensive purposes. 2. No military action to be expected from France save in the event of an attack on Czechoslovakia."[163] No military preparations were reported from Great Britain. The Abwehr's conclusion on March 13: "Reports from agents in France refer generally to prevailing calm and routine military activity."[164]

Instead of alarming reports from abroad, Canaris received a steady stream of dispatches from the units advancing into Austria. They disclosed that Hitler was approaching the greatest triumph in his political career. The German authorities had allowed for the possibility of active resistance, or at least popular protest and resentment. What actually greeted the German troops was a reception which grew more and more jubilant the farther they progressed.

Hitler, whose recent mood had been less self-assured than any of his inner circle could remember, accompanied the invasion in a kind of trance. He drove into his native Linz and spent the night there, frantically acclaimed by his compatriots. He gave a speech described by Göring as "the most interesting speech I have ever heard from the Führer. That man, whose command of language is second to none, could scarcely speak."[165] Telephoning his satrap, who had remained in Berlin, Hitler said, "Göring, you can't imagine—I'd forgotten just how beautiful my native land is."[166]

The Führer was so bewildered that he hardly knew what to do with his new acquisition. He did not at first consider the possibility of total annexation but envisaged a second National Socialist state linked to Germany by a personal union alone. Then the new Federal Chancellor, Seyss-Inquart, called at his temporary headquarters in Linz and reported that the cabinet had decided on full union. Hitler wept, and could only say, in a choking voice, "Yes, the right political action saves bloodshed."[167]

Dispatch after dispatch enabled Canaris to follow the triumphal progress of the Wehrmacht and its supreme commander. Next morning an Abwehr report summarized: "Advance proceeding as planned. Luftwaffe making propaganda flights over Austria. Armoured elements and the 27th Infantry Division will enter Vienna at noon today. It is assumed that the Führer will also take part."[168] Eager not to miss this historic spectacle, Canaris hurriedly boarded a plane for Vienna.

He did not arrive a moment too soon, because Heydrich's SD squads were busy confiscating the secret service archives of the defunct Schuschnigg regime.[169] However, the Admiral's friends in the Austrian Defence Ministry, notably Lieutenant Colonel Lahousen, had salvaged all the most important files on behalf of their German colleagues and opposite numbers. This material soon enabled Protze's men to uncover the espionage networks maintained by the foreign intelligence agencies which had been operating against Germany from Vienna.[170]

Canaris was impressionable enough to drink in the Anschluss euphoria that greeted him at every turn. Two days later, when hundreds of thousands of people packed the square in front of the Hofburg in Vienna for a demonstration in Hitler's honour, Canaris was present too. Charged with emotion, the Führer's voice rang out from the Hofburg balcony. "I can thus inform the German people that my life's greatest mission has been accomplished. As Führer and Chancellor of the German nation and the Reich, I now proclaim, in the presence of history, that my homeland has entered the German Reich."[171]

Had Hitler dropped dead at that moment, most Germans would have pronounced him the greatest statesman in their history. He had made an ancient German dream come true. He had succeeded, where even Bismarck had failed, in fulfilling every German patriot's ardent desire for a union of all the Germans. Even critical souls like Baron von Weizsäcker, a future State Secretary at the Foreign Office and trusted friend of the Admiral's, was enthralled by this achievement. "Yesterday in Vienna," he wrote home, "was the most noteworthy day since [the founding of the Reich on] January 18, 1871. Watching Austrian dragoons parade with our troops to the 'Prinz Eugen March' and witnessing the demonstration from the balcony of the Hofburg was an experience I wish you could all have shared."[172]

As a nationalist, Canaris felt much the same. Legend has it that he disapproved of the Anschluss and "brusquely" called to an Austrian officer, "It's all your fault. Why didn't you open fire?"[173] This conflicts with everything we know about his attitude, as witness the following excerpt from a 1938 speech on the Anschluss: "We are all still under the spell of that event which has uplifted every German heart, the unification of Greater Germany. It was yearned for, worked for and fought for . . . under the watchword: One Nation, one Reich, one Führer!"[174]

Lahousen, who was acquainted with the Admiral's prevailing mood, also confirms that he was an open advocate of union: "It was one of Hitler's few moves in foreign policy which Canaris (and, I fear, some leading British politicians of the time) did not take amiss."[175] Canaris even urged some Hungarian officers to bestow their wholehearted approval on the Anschluss. "Reflect on this all-German commitment prior to the World War and, more particularly, during it—I need only mention the glorious victories won by Austro-German forces at Aspern, Leipzig, Gorlice-Tarnów and Tolmein-Karfreit—and you will have no sense of bitterness at the development of a Greater German Wehrmacht. It is no lost battle that brings you to us, and your coming neither should nor shall be associated with any desire or compulsion to stand aloof."[176]

It must have been hard to leave these bright uplands of nationalist euphoria for the dismal depths of the totalitarian regime. The Fritsch case was still unresolved and unexpiated. Having reconvened on March 17, the court listened to two days of legal argument which increasingly turned into an indictment of the Gestapo.[177]

Göring, who soon sensed that the Gestapo were on a losing bet, smartly joined the Fritsch camp. He bellowed at the chief prosecution witness until Schmidt admitted that he had been lying—that he had never seen the general before. Defence counsel asked if he had been threatened with dire consequences if he retracted his original statement. Yes, said Schmidt, Meisinger had threatened to have him liquidated. The Gestapo officer promptly testified that he had merely warned the witness to tell the truth.[178]

But the Gestapo had already lost. Biron moved that the court declare the accused's innocence proven. As for Count von der Goltz, his closing speech proclaimed that "a uniquely monstrous proceeding . . . [undertaken] by criminal hands" had "dwindled to nothing," and that the case against Fritsch, which was "a most outrageous affront to the entire Army," had collapsed.[179] On March 18, 1938, the court announced its verdict: "The main hearing has established the innocence of Colonel General (ret.) Baron von Fritsch on all counts."[180]

It was now time for Canaris to settle the score with his black-uniformed rivals. Having spent weeks preparing Brauchitsch and Beck for this moment, he was authorized by the Army commander in chief to make representations to Hitler as soon as his predecessor's innocence had been judicially confirmed. The object of these representations could only be to curb the power and influence of the Gestapo—a long-standing ambition which the Abwehr chief had summarized as "releasing the Wehrmacht from a Cheka nightmare."[181]

Canaris and Hossbach drafted some proposals designed to prod Brauchitsch into action. "The Gestapo," they wrote, "must be charged (a) with having arbitrarily resumed their investigations after the Führer had ordered the files to be destroyed; (b) with having neglected, in dereliction of their duty, to investigate circumstances tending to exonerate the accused; and (c) with having untruthfully informed the Führer that Colonel General von Fr.'s guilt was established when all that had taken place was a wholly inadequate investigation." Furthermore, Meisinger had threatened Schmidt with death if he broke down in court. "Meisinger will thus have to answer to a charge of extorting testimony under duress as defined by Para. 373 of the Reich Penal Code." It was also recommended that disciplinary action be taken against the other Gestapo officers involved in the case.[182]

Going still further, Canaris and Hossbach called for "a radical change in the system and its senior personnel." Their central demand: "Fundamental changes in the occupancy of senior posts in the Geheime Staatspolizei. Foremost among those to be considered: Himmler, Heydrich, Jost (SD), Best, Meisinger, Fehling, *et al.*" Their reasoning: "As things stand, the continuance of fruitful co-operation by the Wehrmacht with responsible and senior members of the Geheime Staatspolizei involved in the defamation of Colonel General Baron von Fritsch, and thus in a malicious and insulting attack on the Army, cannot be countenanced."[183]

Canaris must have realized that he was asking Brauchitsch and Beck to call for nothing less than the dismissal of the SS and Gestapo leadership. He and Hossbach warned the two generals that it would be "essential, in gaining the Führer's acceptance of this move, not to attack the institution of a Geheime Staatspolizei as such. It should simply be stated that there are enough decent and honest National Socialists capable of performing this confidential function." There should also be an avoidance of anything that might help the other side to represent the *démarche* "as a mutiny, military coup or other move hostile to the party."[184]

But who was to undertake this *démarche?* Apart from Brauchitsch and Beck, the authors suggested Generals von Rundstedt, von Bock and List. To bolster the military leaders' courage, they further proposed that Göring and Keitel be associated with the move.[185] This transformed the Canaris-Hossbach programme into an utter pipe dream, because it required a massive dose of naivety to picture an anti-SS phalanx inclusive of Göring the opportunist and General "Lakeitel" [a play on Keitel's name—"Lakai"="toady"], as the compliant OKW chief had come to be known.

But the Army authorities had no intention of accepting these proposals in any case. No influential military commander summoned up the courage to recommend such a purge to a leader who now enjoyed absolute and quasi-divine authority. Brauchitsch conveniently forgot his good resolutions and shelved the unwelcome document. As for Beck, he was even less amenable to opposition ventures than before, however carefully Canaris dressed them in conformist and legal attire.[186]

The third general on Canaris's list, Rundstedt, also declined to take action against Himmler and the Gestapo. This was brought home to Fritsch when, in a belated fit of rage, he challenged the SS chief to a duel with pistols and nominated Rundstedt as his second. Rundstedt, who was supposed to deliver Fritsch's written challenge to the Reichsführer-SS, quailed at the prospect. He carried the letter around for days before deciding to talk Fritsch out of the idea on the grounds that nothing should be done to widen the rift between the Army and the regime.[187]

Canaris had learnt a lesson he never forgot. Imprisoned in the battered armour of their traditions and professional attitudes, the generals left the smear campaign against their former commander in chief unavenged and refrained from finishing off a groggy opponent because they were dazzled by the aura of the one man they were prepared to serve at any price.

The Abwehr chief gave up, especially as his enemies nimbly disposed of their worst liabilities. Meisinger was banished to the records department at SD headquarters and Fehling brought before a disciplinary tribunal, while Hitler formally rehabilitated Fritsch and fobbed him off with an empty and honorary appointment as Colonel of the 12th Artillery Regiment.[188] There was now a bitter element of truth in what Canaris had, for purely tactical and evasive reasons, told a full meeting of Ic officers on March 3: "We must for the moment accept this pronouncement [by Hitler on the Fritsch case]. It is at present impossible even to say another word about it."[189]

Canaris temporarily shut his ears to anti-SS sentiments. When Pruck, in the course of a report, insisted that "unless we put paid to those SS men now, Admiral, it'll be too late—they'll do for us," Canaris merely gazed up at him and said, "You think so?" Pruck: "There was something in his expression which conveyed that he couldn't make me out."[190] Canaris chose the opposite course. He resumed his morning rides with Heydrich and Best, which had lapsed, and urged his subordinates to consort with the other side as much as possible.

Promoted vice-admiral on April 1, Canaris swiftly reconverted himself into a guarantor of smooth co-operation between the armed forces and the regime.[191] True, he impressed on his officers that it was "incompatible with the Wehrmacht's dignity and standing in the state" to swallow abuse or denigration, and that they were to inform him at once so that he could intervene. "Concealment, silence and acquiescence—in other words, doing nothing—can reinforce the resolve and opposition of others while impairing the Wehrmacht's reputation and the rank and file's faith in their leaders."[192]

He nonetheless insisted that every officer should at all times demonstrate his unqualified allegiance to the Nazi regime. "In your conversations with senior members of the party," Canaris declared, "you must convey your unequivocal attitude towards the National Socialist state. You must make it clear that the Wehrmacht's perseverance and endeavours during the Weimar period created an essential basis for the development of the Third Reich, and that the Führer's conduct of foreign policy is governed by the Wehrmacht's existence."[193]

As if he had once more subordinated all his powers of discernment to the Führer's spirit and policies, Canaris relapsed more abjectly than ever into Hitler-oriented Byzantinism. They should be grateful, he told his officers, that the Führer had made it possible for all the moral values of the soldier to "develop on a broad basis comprising the entire nation."[194] It may readily be imagined what effect such clichés had on Oster, who was once heard to grumble, "A fool always finds a bigger fool to admire."[195]

Nor did Canaris shrink from making such avowals in public. Addressing the latest batch of cadets at the Wiener Neustadt military academy on April 22, 1938, he explained why the officer corps ought to bestow a "wholehearted affirmative" on the National Socialist state and its military system. "The officer corps must advance in the living fulfilment of National Socialism. Only thus will it preserve the status assigned it by the Führer and bequeathed by its earlier achievements."[196]

The Admiral showed equal alacrity a few weeks later when Richard Donnevert, a Reichsamtsleiter [national bureau director] on the staff of the Führer's deputy, was recruiting collaborators for a book designed to preach the allegedly indissoluble partnership between the party and the armed forces. Canaris, who undertook to write the key chapter ("Politics and the Wehrmacht"), showed yet again how well he had mastered the flowery vacuities of Nazi propaganda. He expatiated on "the obligation imposed by the Führer concept," saw "with wondrous clarity" that the Wehrmacht had become "the instrument of the National Socialist resolve to educate" and—last but not least—failed to detect any difference whatsoever between the Wehrmacht and the party: "The more we familiarize ourselves with the National Socialist store of ideas, the more clearly we see that they are, in fact, truly soldierly trains of thought."[197]

However, Canaris soon lost the need for this kind of verbal agility because he was deprived of his political functions. With effect from June 1, 1938, Keitel reorganized the OKW's command structure, converting the two Amtsgruppen into four. Canaris had to surrender the Amtsgruppe Allgemeine Wehrmachtangelegenheiten and, with it, the Abteilung Inland [Interior Section].[198]

Although compelled to fall back on his original Abwehr functions, Canaris remained an Amtsgruppenchef. Keitel fashioned him a new branch out of the Abwehr and Foreign Intelligence sections, which he withdrew from the Amtsgruppe Führungsstab. This lent final shape to the Admiral's organization. The new Amtsgruppe Auslandnachrichten und Abwehr [Foreign and Counterintelligence Branch], or Ausland/Abwehr for short, was transformed into an Amt in 1939. It remained permanently associated with Canaris's name until stripped of its powers in February 1944.[199]

Canaris converted the existing Abwehr groups into sections and put them on a par with Abteilung Ausland [the Foreign Intelligence Section], so that its head, Captain Leopold Bürkner, became only one of four heads of section. He did not have to fear any encroachments on his authority from Bürkner, an honest, well-meaning and conformist individual who had last commanded the cruiser *Emden* and owed his recent appointment as head of the Foreign Section to the sponsorship of Ribbentrop, at whose side he had performed "all the spadework for the 33 per cent naval agreement with Britain." Bürkner quite accepted that, although he was the second most senior officer in the Amtsgruppe, his right to deputize for the Admiral was confined to general departmental business and did not extend to Abwehr matters.[200]

Canaris's acquisition of Abteilung Ausland had important consequences in that it associated him more closely than ever with Hitler's foreign policy. Rather akin to an OKW foreign ministry, Bürkner's section maintained contact with the Foreign Office and was responsible for briefing it on military affairs, kept the top military departments informed of developments in foreign policy, supervised German service attachés abroad and looked after foreign military attachés in Berlin.[201]

But Abteilung Ausland was not the only section with foreign policy relevance. In company with Amtsgruppe Ausland/Abwehr, a new section—Abwehr II—had come into being. This differed appreciably from the Abwehr group of the same numerical designation. Canaris had in autumn 1937 been compelled to relinquish the old Abwehr II, responsible for radio and cipher duties, to the newly established Abteilung für Wehrmachtnachrichtenverbindungen [Armed Forces Communications Section], whose task was to exercise central control over the Wehrmacht's entire radio and monitoring system.[202] Meanwhile, a new Abwehr II grew out of Subgroup S of Abwehr I and was officially termed Abwehr II from June 1, 1938, onwards. Its functions embraced psychological warfare, agitation among foreign minorities abroad and the mounting of what the mass media later christened a "fifth column."[203]

Germany's neighbours, particularly those in Eastern and Southeast Europe, harboured hundreds of thousands of Volksdeutsche [ethnic Germans] who were citizens of foreign countries and dissatisfied with the status that had so arbitrarily been thrust on them by the Versailles peace settlement. The object was to mobilize these and other national minorities and use them as an explosive charge to destroy or cripple the countries that stood in the path of Hitler's projected march to the East. Abwehr II was assigned an important part in this process. Its agents were instructed to seek out the leaders of German and foreign minorities, furnish them with men and material for armed insurrections and organize operational teams which would, when "X day" dawned, secure the German invaders' line of advance through foreign territory.[204]

The Abwehr was, of course, a late arrival in the jungle of ethnic German infiltration. Other National Socialist bodies had already possessed themselves of a variety of powers. The Foreign Organization of the NSDAP supervised all party activities in the countries concerned, the Volksdeutsche Mittelstelle [Ethnic German Centre], a province of the SS, was charged with co-ordinating the activities of German associations and ethnic groups abroad and the SD cast its intelligence net across the countries of Eastern Europe.[205] But Abwehrabteilung II managed to uphold its interests. Relying on the prestige of the Wehrmacht, it drew expatriate German nationalist politicians, student groups and associations into its orbit.

Thanks to a quirk of contemporary history, however, Abwehr II was directed by an officer who regarded himself as a sworn opponent of the Nazi regime. Born in 1898, Major Helmuth Groscurth ("Muffel" to his friends) was a parson's son like Oster. After serving as a volunteer infantry officer in World War I and resigning in protest over the suppression of the Kapp Putsch, he became a courier for Ehrhardt's right-wing Organisation Consul. He farmed for a while, then rejoined the Reichswehr and in 1935, after graduating from military academy, was posted to the then Abwehr Section. According to Bürkner, "hatred of the NS system was written all over his face."[206] A devout Christian whose courage and candour verged on imprudence, he was described by Liedig, who shared his views, as "the Siegfried of the small Abwehr of those days."[207] Canaris also had a high regard for Groscurth, even though he disapproved of the major's outspoken attitude. "Muffel," he once said jokingly, "you're just the man for the Abwehr because you always tell the truth, and in our service no one believes it."[208]

For all his opposition to Hitler, Groscurth was so steeped in traditional concepts of nationhood that he failed to grasp the incongruous nature of his work. With a touch of pride, he noted in his diary: "My work relates to all ethnic German and foreign minorities, also to preparations for wartime sabotage as a whole. These things have a strongly political complexion."[209] Functions of this kind involved Canaris, too, in the next phase of Hitler's policy of conquest—the annexation of the Sudeten German territories.

Canaris and the Abwehr found it quite logical that Hitler's next foreign policy coup should be aimed at the multinational state whose capital was Prague. It had for years been a Tirpitz-Ufer axiom that the fate of the 3.5 million Sudeten Germans would appear on Germany's foreign policy agenda as soon as an independent Austria was no more. As early as February 3, 1934, the Breslau Abwehrstelle had prophesied: "A National Socialist revolution in Austria would transmit fresh nationalist momentum to the Sudeten Germans, quite apart from the fact that Czech policy would thereby lose an important focus of permanent influence."[210]

The Abwehr had done as much to prepare the Sudeten Germans for the day of "liberation" as any official body in the Reich. Military intelligence work and nationalistic sentiments combined in equal measure to render the Abwehr sympathetic to the trials and tribulations of Germans resident in the Czechoslovak Republic. "The Sudeten Germans," wrote an Abwehr V-Mann, "are fighting in the important capacity of an outpost of the Reich itself. The Reich cannot remain indifferent when the enemy line thrusts closer and closer to the Reich border by a process of continuous erosion."[211] As Germany regained strength under Hitler, so the Abwehr cast a longer shadow over the field of multinational conflict that divided the Czechoslovak state.

The Abwehr's subversive activities in Czechoslovakia were aided by a nationalistic sin of omission. At the end of World War I, when the Czechs acquired political independence, the German ethnic group was denied any kind of self-determination. The Czech authorities adopted a harshly coercive policy designed to cement Czech supremacy in the Czechoslovak Republic and discipline the German minority. German place names were Czechized, German children forced to learn the Czech language and German schools subjected to disabilities. One regulation forbade all financial dealings with the outside world, another decreed the dismissal of German civil servants, and a land reform expropriated all German-owned land acquired after 1620.[212]

An obscure gymnastics instructor, wartime officer and former bank clerk named Konrad Henlein, now thirty-five years old, made it his aim to unite the five Sudeten German parties and secure his compatriots full autonomy within the Czechoslovak Republic. In 1933 he founded a new party, the Sudetendeutsche Heimatfront, which the Prague authorities later compelled him to rename the Sudetendeutsche Partei (SdP).[213]

Neither Prague nor Berlin paid much attention to this "virgin in a political brothel," as one of Henlein's political rivals called him.[214] Only the Abwehr gambled on his success. "It is to be expected that the 'Heimatfront' will, in the future course of developments, become a catchment for all nationally minded Sudeten Germans," reported a V-Mann on January 16, 1934, and other Abwehr agents continued to chart Henlein's progress with care.[215] A report from the Braunau district of Czechoslovakia dated May 1, 1934, declared: "The Henlein front is . . . firmly in the ascendant here. It is claimed at meetings of the Henlein front that the latter already has 120,000 members in the entire Reich area."[216]

Abwehr headquarters began to concentrate on Henlein and in 1935 established contact with his friend Friedrich Bürger, who maintained a liaison office in Berlin—hence Canaris's frequent boast that the Abwehr was responsible for Henlein's "discovery."[217] Although Henlein had been discovered by others, the Admiral's exaggeration contained a germ of truth. In contrast to other Reich authorities, the Abwehr quickly grasped how useful to Germany Henlein and his party could become. In a rare display of solidarity, the Foreign Office, party and SS joined forces against Henlein because, from their point of view, he had a dire defect: he was no Nazi. A romantic nationalist devoted to the doctrine of an authoritarian national community in which all social conflicts would remain frozen, Henlein did not look for deliverance from the Third Reich. His preferred source of salvation lay farther south. He regarded the Austrian Chancellors Dollfuss and Schuschnigg as his political mentors and Othmar Spann, the ideologist of the corporate state, as the greatest man of the age.

Heydrich's SD-Hauptamt declared in May 1936 that Henlein was "a slave to Rome" and "peculiarly disastrous from the all-German aspect" because he was "estranging the Sudeten Germans from National Socialist Germany."[218] What infuriated SD researchers most of all was that Henlein belonged to the Kameradschaftsbund, a two-hundred-strong association of young Catholic right-wing intellectuals who wanted to impose a federal system on the Czechoslovak Republic but were wholly averse to Germany's annexation of the Sudeten German territories.[219]

This did not worry Canaris, who felt gratified that it was he, not Heydrich, who enjoyed the confidence of this up-and-coming man in the Sudeten German community. Besides, events confirmed the accuracy of his agents' predictions. Henlein's SdP became the largest Sudeten German party and the largest in Czechoslovakia as a whole. The SdP chief now felt strong enough to demand autonomy for the Sudeten Germans—"racial self-government and corporate representation"—at a mass rally in Aussig [Ústí nad Labem] on February 28, 1937.[220]

Prague entered into negotiations with Henlein, but they led nowhere because the Czechoslovak President, Eduard Beneš, a cautious champion of the *status quo*, refused to make any concessions. The latent tensions between Prague and the Sudeten Germans developed into a genuine crisis which steadily worsened and had repercussions on the Abwehr. In the course of 1937 Canaris adapted his Czech network to the prospect of open conflict. More and more Abwehr agents slipped across the frontier. For the first time, Groscurth's emissaries began to establish ammunition dumps and partisan assembly points on Czech territory, supervised by the Breslau and Dresden Abwehrstellen, where most of the controllers for the Czech area of operations were based.[221]

One of the Abwehr's chief informants, the ex-bookseller and leading SdP official Karl Hermann Frank, was instructed to organize a network devoted to subversion in the Czech Army and keep the Tirpitz-Ufer posted on political developments in the Sudetenland.[222] Erwin Stolze, later a colonel in Abwehr II, recalls that "Hager" (Frank's code name) was also directed "to set up an organization which could with the utmost possible speed transmit and implement any orders from the German authorities in Sudeten-German-occupied territory, as, for example, keeping roads free from refugees in the event of war."[223]

Frank's selection as a chief informant was to prove disastrous. An extreme and peculiarly crude exponent of German racial superiority, he had contacted the SS-controlled Volksdeutsche Mittelstelle in 1935 and was thereafter regarded by the SD-Hauptamt as a willing collaborator in any plots against Henlein.[224] Frank's duties in the SdP (he became Henlein's deputy in 1937) were so numerous that he delegated some of his Abwehr functions to subordinates without, however, relinquishing over-all supervision.[225]

The Abwehr and the SdP authorities drew even closer when Henlein joined Hitler's camp in spring 1938. Prague's negative attitude and the loss of his Austrian backers left him virtually no choice but to enlist the aid of Greater Germany. Hitler eagerly seized on the Sudeten issue, which was just another step on his road to the East. Union with Austria had left him ever more prone to hectic dreams of power and conquest. The hysteria of the Anschluss had dispelled his last vestiges of moderation and circumspection, and the feeble protests that had greeted his *coup de main* abroad only reinforced his lunatic sense of mission.

On March 28, 1938, he summoned Henlein to the Chancellery and informed him of his plans. His next blow, he declared, was to be aimed at Prague, and the Sudeten Germans would have to lead the assault themselves. "The SdP must continue its subversive activities—it must put unacceptable conditions to the Czech Government." Henlein recapitulated: "In other words, we must always pitch our demands so high that we can never be satisfied." Hitler nodded.[226] Soon afterwards Keitel received orders to gird the Wehrmacht for a war against Czechoslovakia.

Henlein busily set to work. Addressing an SdP conference at Karlsbad on April 24, he demanded unconditional autonomy for the Sudeten Germans, reparation for injustices done them since 1918 and "complete freedom" to profess the National Socialist ideology.[227] This unleashed what historians call the Sudeten crisis. Greater Germany used its propaganda and power-political resources to back Henlein's demands and conjured up the spectre of an armed clash between the Reich and Czechoslovakia. This at once raised the crucial question which preoccupied both hostile camps from now on: would the Western powers come to Prague's assistance if Germany invaded?

The French wanted to help Prague, but only if the British did too. The British, who regarded a Sudeten German crusade as wholly unjustified from the moral standpoint, declined. Premier Daladier hurried to London at the end of April, hoping to win them over, but Chamberlain stood firm. "If Germany did decide to destroy Czechoslovakia, I do not see how this could be prevented." Britain was unprepared for war, he went on, and could not even put two divisions in the field.[228]

Gloomily, Daladier listened to Chamberlain's proposed solution of the Sudeten crisis: they must jointly urge Prague to make generous concessions and Berlin to be patient. Daladier agreed,[229] and this very fact prompted Beneš, the "Metternich of democracy,"[230] to devise a spectacular course of action calculated to manoeuvre the Western powers on to his side. Some dubious intelligence reports furnished him with a welcome pretext.

Early in May the Czech secret service received reports from its agents alleging "exceptional concentrations of German units on the borders of Saxony and Silesia."[231] On May 12 Czech agent A-54 reported that the SD was planning a Sudeten German insurrection to be sparked off by a code word broadcast from Germany on the eve of the Czechoslovak municipal elections (May 22).[232] Whether or not these reports were exaggerated by the Czech secret service chief, Moravec, who advocated a firm stand against the Germans, Beneš resolved to exploit them for his own purposes. During the night of May 20–21 he ordered partial mobilization of the Army and called up 180,000 reservists.[233]

The Czech Premier's move took the Germans by surprise. Rather at a loss, Canaris requested information from his agents in Czechoslovakia but did not feel satisfied that war was not imminent until twenty-four hours later. On the morning of May 22 his overnight report to Keitel read: "No incidents of note. Czech mobilization measures proceeding as ordered. Those called up comprise all members of the 1913 and 1914 age groups but only specialists from the age groups 1894–1911, excluding age groups '04, '05, and '09."[234]

It soon transpired that reports of German troop movements had been incorrect. However, the world's press construed official German denials as evidence that Hitler had knuckled under to the tough Czech Premier and the Western democracies. This gleefully publicized misconception enraged Hitler and clinched his resolve to make war on the source of his discomfiture.

"I have irrevocably decided," he wrote on May 30, "to smash Czechoslovakia by military action in the foreseeable future. To await or engineer the politically and militarily opportune moment will be a matter for the political leadership."[235] There could be little doubt about the date of the attack: Operation "Green" had to be launched "by October 1, 1938," at latest.[236] Hitler had armed a time bomb which was to hurl Europe into the abyss of a major war for the first time since 1914.

The head of OKW instructed Amtsgruppe Ausland/Abwehr to prepare for the attack by means of propaganda, subversion and reconnaissance. A "draft for the new 'Green' directive" dated May 20 told Canaris what Hitler expected from the Abwehr: "The propaganda war must, on the one hand, intimidate Czechoslovakia and undermine her resistance with threats, and, on the other, convey instructions to the national minorities to support the armed struggle."[237] Another passage stated that when German assault units had penetrated the Czech fortifications, "co-operation with the Sudeten German frontier population, deserters from the Czechoslovak Army . . . and elements of the sabotage service" could prove valuable.[238]

Hitler's adjutant, Rudolf Schmundt, kept a record of his ideas on the Abwehr's role during the first two days of the invasion: "October 1. Sabotage inside 'nerve centres.' Occupation of fortifications, 'Trojan Horse' system. October 2. Immediate follow-up by disguised security troops to occupy important points between fortifications and frontier."[239] The Abwehr would also prepare "1. Leaflets on the conduct of Germans in Grünland ["Green"-land, i.e. Czechoslovakia]. 2. Leaflets containing threats for the intimidation of the Greens."[240]

The Abwehr was so firmly integrated in the planning of the invasion that many people considered it the logical stage manager for any political murder that might be required. Hitler was still debating how to fabricate a pretext for war when an idea came to him: "Of course, it's always possible the ambassador may be murdered." Keitel: "Which ambassador?" Hitler: "After all, the 1914 war started because of an assassination at Sarajevo. These things happen."[241] Before long, Hitler's advisers were devoting such serious consideration to the possibility of staging an attempt on the life of the German Ambassador in Prague that Jodl doubted if the OKW had enough time to co-ordinate its operational orders with this "outrage." He did not, however, think it wrong that "the Abw.Abt. should be made responsible for staging the incident."[242]

Canaris and his heads of section put their general directives from Hitler and Keitel into effect. Abwehr II's situation maps divided Czechoslovakia into zones designated K1 to K7.[243] These were the operational areas assigned to the K[ampf—combat] and S[abotage] teams which Groscurth's section sneaked across the German-Czech frontier in readiness for the acts of sabotage and terrorism to be committed when X day came.

It was vital to ensure that these units received support from the Sudeten German population. Not all the Germans in Czechoslovakia approved of Henlein's policy. Detailed lists kept by Abwehr headquarters drew distinctions between their political attitudes, as witness the following assessment by Abwehr I's East-South Desk: "Most dangerous to the Czechs are the Egerland and Bohemian Forest Germans extending roughly as far as Wickwitz . . . Central and North Bohemian residential area: politically far more neutral, militarily less valuable, more indifferent to political oppression . . . Northeast Bohemian residential area: the Schluck and Friedland districts may be regarded as exceptionally German nationalist and almost 100 per cent National Socialist, whereas all areas east of Trautenau are strongly clerical and unreliable."[244]

Guided by these and other assessments, the [combat and sabotage teams] K- and S-Verbände took up their positions on the other side of the frontier. They reconnoitred landing places in the Freudenthal area for the 7th Air Division, which was to link up there with units of VIII Army Corps. They also formed combat groups for the lightning seizure of border towns, prepared to occupy bridges and railway stations on the day of the attack and planned minor insurrections with dependable Sudeten Germans in the interior.[245]

The Abwehr authorities were inundated with requests and instructions. With a mixture of pride and exasperation, Groscurth noted: "Our help is much in demand. We even have to draw up propaganda guidelines for the armies' propaganda companies. That job really belongs to the National Defence Section!"[246] Requests soon piled up to such an extent that Canaris feared for the quality of Ausland/Abwehr's work. Groscurth made another note: "Our completed leaflets are with the Führer, who is correcting them . . . His instructions via Major Schmundt are that the Admiral mustn't worry, he'll deal with the matter himself."[247]

But the more the Abwehr's unseen army moved into its final positions for X day, the uneasier Canaris became about the perfection of his own machine. It only gradually dawned on him that the whole thing was deadly serious and not just a repetition of those propagandist military manoeuvres which had prefaced all Hitler's weekend surprises to date. War . . . The word appalled him, realizing as he did that Germany was unprepared for a major European conflict. War . . . To Canaris, it was synonymous with "finis Germaniae," with the end of the Reich and the destruction of all that German suffering and sacrifice had accomplished in generations of endeavour.

The Admiral's nerves were frayed still further by reports reaching him from the Chancellery. Everything indicated that Hitler and his closest advisers were preparing to embark on a disastrous course of action—"reckless in its premisses, unscrupulous in its methods, hazardous in its audacity and aims," to quote a historian's description.[248] Hitler was bent on war, and no power on earth was going to dissuade him from marching on Prague. Canaris had an agonizing presentiment that the man who had created the Greater German Reich was destined to destroy it as well.

But Canaris was determined to bar Hitler's path to war. He was suddenly smitten with the schizophrenia from which he never managed to recover—that sense of being at once an initiator and a would-be inhibitor of Hitler's wars of conquest. It was the schizophrenia cited after World War II by Robert Kempner, the U.S. deputy prosecutor at Nuremberg, who declared that if ever history had produced a split personality à la Jekyll and Hyde, it was Canaris, "the man who organized the National Socialist fifth column, who . . . introduced the murderous weapons of sabotage and surreptitious infiltration and sent German soldiers on suicide missions, and who, on the other hand, permitted individual officers to conspire against the regime."[249]

Canaris had originally assumed that Hitler was bluffing, and that his sabre-rattling was merely a way of forcing Prague to grant statutory autonomy to the Sudeten Germans. Even in late July, when the Führer ordered "a sort of experimental mobilization" which the British military attaché in Berlin, Colonel Mason-MacFarlane, found "most dangerous and provocative," Canaris soothed the colonel by assuring him that the move was a wholly routine military measure and amounted to nothing more than a "wheel-oiling process."[250]

However, Canaris soon realized that Hitler meant war. On July 30 Keitel went on leave and appointed Canaris to deputize for him. The orders, directives and reports that passed across the Admiral's desk left him in no doubt that the Wehrmacht would march, though there were still some generals who opposed such folly. Fascinated, Canaris watched the final phase of a one-man campaign mounted by the Army Chief of Staff.

This time, Beck had at once recognized the deadly peril threatening the Army and the nation, even though his initial opposition was based on departmental considerations and not—as some benevolent historians assume—on moral repugnance. The Führer was again planning a campaign without reference to the Army Chief of Staff. As soon as he learned of Hitler's warlike plans, Beck took issue with the Czech venture in a memorandum dated May 5.[251] Although he too accepted the need for "an early settlement of the Czech question by force," he considered the moment inopportune. Germany was unprepared for a long war and Britain and France were jointly committed to Czechoslovakia. They also enjoyed background support from Russia and America.[252]

Hitler rejected the memorandum and Beck temporarily refrained from any stronger action. Instead of tackling the Führer man to man, as it were, he churned out some more memoranda. When Hitler's military aide, Captain Engel, invited him to the vital planning conference at the Chancellery on May 28, Beck declined: "There's no point, not with the Führer . . . Give him my best regards and tell him I'll send General Halder." He eventually turned up after all—and said nothing.[253]

He made up for his silence on the morrow by busily committing to paper all the objections he had failed to voice the day before. His strongest argument was that war against Czechoslovakia would inevitably develop into a European—indeed, a world—war. Thanks to the military aid which Prague could expect to receive from Britain, France and America, Germany would ultimately lose a war against the Czechoslovak Republic.[254] Hitler was furious. "He said it was a mendacious piece of paper," Engel noted, "but nobody could pull the wool over his eyes."[255]

Brauchitsch was too chary of Hitler to back the explosive recommendations of his Chief of Staff, so Beck relapsed into his former state of inertia. Canaris and Oster promptly tried to nudge him into renewed activity.[256] Oster spent hours with the general, discussing possible moves, while Canaris tried to persuade the more pugnacious Halder to exert more pressure on him. Although the head of operations refused to be drawn into any cabals against his Chief of Staff,[257] he did approach him privately on his own initiative. Beck's despairing rejoinder: "But I *did* send him a memorandum!"[258]

He was driven to write a new one when the Sudeten crisis worsened. On July 15, abruptly resorting to political arguments instead of the technical and military considerations he had stressed hitherto, he declared that the German people and a section of the Army did not want war with Czechoslovakia. The war issue now affected "the confidence of the nation and Army in the Army's supreme leadership," so the latter must react.[259] Beck concluded that the Army commander in chief should call on Hitler and persuade him to discontinue preparations for war.[260]

No sooner had Beck written this than he waxed still more energetic. Unwilling any longer to leave Brauchitsch to tackle Hitler on his own, he decided to expand his campaign into a concerted move by the entire Wehrmacht leadership—a species of general officers' strike. In other words, they would resign *en bloc* unless Hitler acceded to their demands. In a note dated July 16 he invited Brauchitsch to join him and the rest of the generals in tackling Hitler jointly "so as to avert a war against Czechoslovakia."[261]

His next note, dated July 19, was even more tempestuous. He had rediscovered the old Canaris-Hossbach plan and adapted it to the requirements of the Sudeten crisis. Collective action by the military authorities, he declared, must also lead to a "definitive settlement with the SS." What mattered was "to deliver the German people and the Führer himself from a Cheka nightmare and from symptoms of corrupt officialdom which are destroying the substance and welfare of the Reich by way of public morale and causing a revival of Communism."[262] This was no plot against the regime, Beck warned, but a campaign on the Führer's behalf, so "party members of integrity and ability" should be "persuaded of the need for such a step and induced to support it." The order of the day was: "For the Führer! Against war!"[263]

One can hardly fail to detect the hand of Canaris in these remarks and the ideas underlying them. Like Canaris, Beck still mistook the nature of the totalitarian system sufficiently to cherish the illusion that Hitler had only to be delivered from the "radicals" for his regime to be purged of its "excrescences" and, so to speak, rendered worthy of existence. Beck's paper of July 19, 1938, was in full accord with the Abwehr chief's ideas: on the one hand, prevention of war, abolition of SS ascendancy and removal of corrupt officialdom; on the other, retention of an authoritarian regime plus immunity for Hitler. Canaris waited impatiently to see if Beck would win Brauchitsch over.

The ever cautious Army commander in chief shied away from these proposals. He did undertake to invite the army group commanders and commanding generals to a conference in Berlin on August 4 and acquaint them with Beck's demands,[264] but he ensured that they remained ignorant of their crux (collective resignation in the event of refusal and a political shake-up at home). Although most of the generals agreed with Beck's assessment of the situation, they drew no practical conclusions from it.[265]

Beck gave up. A fortnight later he tendered his resignation to Brauchitsch.[266] Canaris, who was among the first to hear this piece of bad news, realized that Germany's descent into war had become almost irresistible. He could only construe the press campaign unleashed by Joseph Goebbels, with its reports of anti-German excesses in Czechoslovakia, as an acceleration of his country's progress towards war.[267]

"I can't take it any more," he snarled to Eberhard, Keitel's aide. "We won't be used as atrocity-mongers."[268] Meeting his friend Captain Wagner in one of the dimly lit corridors at Abwehr headquarters, he assailed him with "Goebbels ought to be shot. What do you think?" Wagner was taken aback, but he whispered, "I agree, Herr Admiral."[269] Canaris can hardly have meant the remark seriously because the assassination of Nazi potentates was not his style. He saw another way of applying the brakes to Hitler's war chariot.

On August 6 Bürkner reported that the British Ambassador, Nevile Henderson, had told him at a party given by Mason-MacFarlane that Britain would agree to "any reasonable settlement" of the Sudeten question "as long as it was not attempted by force."[270] This inspired Canaris to try and influence Hitler along the lines favoured by Beck. According to Bürkner, Canaris "still set store by approaching Hitler in person" and clung to his belief that the dictator was open to persuasion.[271]

But how to exert the necessary influence? The only way, as Canaris saw it, was to detach Hitler from hard-liners like Ribbentrop and Himmler and feed him intelligence reports calculated to shake his belief that Britain and France would abandon Prague in the event of war. Henlein, too, must be brought into play because the SdP leader could have no interest in a conflict whose first victims would be the Sudeten Germans.

Canaris confided in State Secretary Baron von Weizsäcker of the Foreign Office, who shared his view of the situation and was, in his eyes, one of the regime's most congenial senior officials. The two men had met during the war and renewed their acquaintanceship in 1935, when Weizsäcker was at the German Embassy in Berne.[272] A former naval officer, Weizsäcker had served in distant-waters cruisers like Canaris and admired the lofty sentiments and extreme cunning which combined to make the Admiral a "wily Odysseus."[273] He also sensed, precisely because of their fellow feeling, the "profoundly tragic element" in Canaris[274]—the fact that he had recognized Hitler's destructive potentialities but was bound to the man by a thousand ties of loyalty and tradition.

Not unnaturally, Weizsäcker welcomed an alliance with the Admiral. Both men agreed that the key to the crisis lay in Britain because an authoritative word from the British was all that might deter Hitler from his warlike course.[275] Proceeding on the (false) assumption that Britain would never desert the Czechs, they thought it opportune to prod the British into issuing Hitler a stern warning. Germany's allies, notably Italy and Hungary, would also have to be encouraged to dissuade him,[276] and here Weizsäcker promised Canaris some diplomatic backing.

Already awaiting Canaris at his Tirpitz-Ufer headquarters, mobilized by Oster and eager to be of service, was a suitable emissary in the person of Ewald von Kleist-Schmenzin, a scion of the old Prussian landowning nobility and one of the regime's most resolute opponents. Kleist was instructed to visit various British politicians of his acquaintance and impress on them how essential it was to take a firm line. The Chamberlain government must demonstrate beyond all doubt that a German march on Prague would automatically mean war with Britain.[277] On August 18 Kleist flew to London.[278]

He was still engaged in discussions on August 22 when Canaris and Groscurth set off for Budapest to deter the Hungarians.[279] Canaris's arguments had some effect. Groscurth noted: "The Hungarians say they cannot take part in a war. For them, that would mean the end . . . The Regent [Admiral Horthy] is firmly resolved to raise objections to the war with the Führer."[280] Back in Berlin on August 23, Canaris quickly proceeded to mobilize his next ally against Hitler.[281]

On August 27 Groscurth noted: "The Admiral is asking Henlein to apprise the Führer of his objections to war. Frank is surprised at our pessimism but shares it."[282] Henlein, who was genuinely perturbed by the idea that the world might go to war over his Sudeten Germans, had already asked Hitler to refrain from solving the Sudeten crisis by force during an interview at Bayreuth on July 23.[283] Even Frank, for all his extremism, had called at the Chancellery to demonstrate to Hitler with the aid of maps that the Sudeten German population of Bohemia and Moravia was distributed in such a way that to recognize the right of self-determination would cripple the Czechoslovak Republic without any resort to war.[284]

Again an aircraft's engines roared into life, and again Canaris set off in search of allies. This time it was the Italians' turn. Since Mussolini was eager to know when the Germans meant to strike, Canaris had been officially instructed to brief the Italians without naming an actual date. September found him in Rome with Alberto Pariani, Chief of Staff of the Italian Army, who obligingly expressed qualms about Hitler's warlike intentions.[285] Canaris informed Groscurth that the Italians "strongly advise against war and will not take part."[286]

Weizsäcker fulfilled his promise of diplomatic support. He alerted German ambassadors in the major capitals and got them to confirm that "they did not believe the Western democracies would stand aside in the event of a German-Czech conflict," to quote a memorandum addressed to Ribbentrop.[287] He also did his utmost, using an assortment of veiled but unmistakable hints, to persuade the British and Italians to intervene with Hitler.

But Kleist's report on his return from London held out little hope that the British would play the part allotted them by Canaris and Weizsäcker. Kleist's arguments "got nowhere with Chamberlain,"[288] especially as the old Prussian war horse had interspersed them with all kinds of rosy but unrealistic notions cherished by those who were close to him in resistance circles. He claimed that the bulk of the German people were "sick of the regime," that only a minority supported Hitler, and that the Army was "unanimously opposed to war" and only needed firm encouragement from Britain to dash Hitler's incendiary torch from his hand.[289]

In anti-Prussian Britons, this bred a suspicion that Hitler's Third Reich was to be succeeded by a Junker- and Army-dominated Germany whose foreign policy objectives would differ little from those of the

Nazi regime. Kleist's contacts had no intention of encouraging such a development, so he drew a correspondingly meagre response. The only concrete result of his mission was a letter from Winston Churchill, then in opposition, stating that a German invasion of Czechoslovakia would bring about a renewal of the World War.[290]

It had long been apparent to realists that Britian would make no serious effort to defend the Czechoslovak Republic. Late in July the British Government had induced President Beneš to accept a so-called mediator whose sole task was to approve the Sudeten German demands as they stood. Lord Runciman, a former president of the Board of Trade who knew nothing about the problems of Central Europe, was unimaginative enough to carry out Chamberlain's programme to the letter.[291]

In a sudden display of genuine interest, however, Runciman found that the Prague government's concessions to the SdP leaders were quite reasonable. This was because Beneš, purely for the benefit of his guileless British visitor, had drastically changed tack and donned the guise of a devout pro-German. Beneš excelled himself in anticipating every request the Sudeten German negotiators planned to make. He approved new language legislation, civil service appointments and measures of self-government.[292] The SdP leaders were taken aback. If Beneš conceded every demand they had ever made, what pretext would there be for a German invasion?

Hitler had made final arrangements for a German attack at the Berghof on September 3. "The troops are to assemble two days' march from the frontier . . . ," he decreed. "I shall notify OKW of X day on September 27."[293] The German war machine was already rolling, and now the Czech President's diplomatic gambit threatened to halt it. Hitler gave orders to sabotage the negotiations in Prague by provoking an incident. But who was to stage it? None other than Frank, Canaris's confidant and the man who was supposed to help him stop the drift to war.

Frank convened an SdP rally in the Red stronghold of Mährisch-Ostrau [Moravská Ostrava] on September 7. Serious clashes with the police ensued and an SdP deputy was manhandled by Czechs.[294] Henlein and Frank promptly broke off negotiations with Beneš[295] and took such a truculent line that even the most credulous observers grasped that their sole intention was to provoke civil strife. This, of course, was the object of the exercise. Hitler needed a Czech "reign of terror" in order to strike his blow.

This was the moment when Canaris returned from his trip to Italy, still believing that disaster could be averted. He hurriedly dictated a report on his talks with Pariani. The gist of this document, undoubtedly couched in stronger terms than the content of their discussions warranted, was that Italy would not join in. Canaris distributed it to interested members of the military hierarchy in the hope of mobilizing them against Hitler's aggressive policy.[296] He also fed the OKW and Army General Staff with other information of an antiwar tendency.

His silent campaign bore fruit. Groscurth noted that Brauchitsch had evinced "great concern at the [Italian] report and other unfavourable news,"[297] and even Jodl, that single-minded apostle of the Führer cult, wrote on September 8: "I must confess that I, too, have some misgivings."[298] Next day, Brauchitsch screwed up the courage to call on Hitler and spend hours trying to talk him out of his invasion plan.[299]

Keitel soon became so irked by the Abwehr chief's reports that he forbade their unauthorized distribution. On September 8 Groscurth noted: "The Admiral's report on his trip to Italy must be withdrawn at once."[300] A few days later Keitel informed his branch and section heads in the course of "a very heated talk" that people had already begun to "include the OKW in their accusations of carping criticism [addressed to the Führer]." The cause of this unwelcome development: "Abwehr reports."[301] The OKW chief proceeded to whip himself into a fury. He would "tolerate no officer in the OKW who indulges in criticism, misgivings and faultfinding." However, when his pep talk degenerated into "savage abuse of the Army" (Groscurth), Canaris firmly repudiated it and sprang to the generals' defence.[302]

But by now his hands were officially tied. Worse still, Hitler's orders were fully involving him in the gamble he had hoped to prevent. He was obliged to summon his Ic officers to Berlin from their posts in the East and inform them that the Abwehr and its Sudetenland agents would also take part in the projected uprising.[303]

The moment came on September 11. SdP demonstrators turned out in force and provoked clashes with the Czech police. Next day, thirteen rural districts rebelled against the Prague authorities with sanguinary results. On September 13 the government imposed martial law. The insurrection claimed twenty-three lives and hundreds of casualties, but it soon became clear that Henlein's and Frank's call to arms was being obeyed by only a small section of the Sudeten German population. Peace was restored by September 14, despite the SdP leaders' impassioned appeals for continued resistance. Henlein and his confederates fled to Germany followed by thousands of their panic-stricken compatriots.[304]

But the revolt had already served its purpose. On September 12 Hitler mounted the rostrum at Nuremberg and addressed the party's annual rally. Heaping abuse on Beneš, he insisted that Prague must at long last grant the "oppressed" Sudeten Germans "the free right of self-determination."[305] Before the entire world, Hitler had identified the

Reich with the leaders and slogans of the Sudeten Germans. Unless Prague suddenly capitulated, this could only mean war.

Was there no way at all of averting it? Oster and his friends were prepared to adopt the drastic expedient of eliminating Hitler and his regime by force. The impetuous colonel had persisted in trying to interest Canaris in the idea of a military revolt. In February–March 1938 he had recommended a coup against the SS alone, but he now declared that the whole regime must go, and, in contrast to the earlier occasion, could cite individuals and groups who were willing and able to topple the system before Germany was dragged into a war of annihilation.

Oster's arguments sounded plausible to Canaris, especially as the Abwehr chief had come to appreciate his drive and mental agility. The two men had drawn closer since the Blomberg-Fritsch affair. Although Piekenbrock remained Canaris's most trusted subordinate in the administrative and technical sphere, Oster was politically and personally closer to him than any other officer in the Amtsgruppe. There was no policy decision, no problem relating to national interests or personnel policy, which the Admiral did not discuss with him.

Oster became so indispensable to Canaris that he resolved on an outward expression of their intimate relationship. He had already drafted the directive that was to inform all Abwehr personnel of Oster's promotion: "With effect from 26.9.1938 a Central Group [Zentralgruppe] is to be formed in Amtsgruppe Ausland/Abwehr. Director: Lieutenant Colonel (E) Oster. In the event of mobilization he will be Chief of Staff of Amt Ausl./Abw."[306] Gruppe Z, which subsequently became Abteilung Z, was assigned to deal with the Amtsgruppe's personnel records, finances and legal affairs. It was also entrusted with the main filing section and later with the ultrasecret central card index.[307]

Although this enlargement of Oster's powers did not arouse universal enthusiasm, he was respected as an intimate of the chief. He had for weeks belonged to the team that attended the regular morning conferences in the Admiral's office. His influence was also detectable in personnel and internal policy, but Canaris's directive expressly stated: "The head of the Central Group will whenever possible be present when Abteilungen present their reports to the Amtsgruppenchef. The Central Group is to be consulted on all changes in organization and personnel changes undertaken by Abteilungen and Abwehrstellen."[308] The message was plain: nobody who hoped to prosper in the Abwehr could afford to bypass Oster from now on.

Daily contact with Oster made Canaris receptive to his scheme for a military *coup d'état*. Its broad outlines—occupation of the government quarter in Berlin, seizure of all major communications centres, neutralization of Gestapo and SS authorities, arrest of Hitler, proclamation of a military dictatorship—did not strike him as unreasonable.[309]

Canaris agreed to back the venture. All that mattered to him was speed.[310] While showing a curious lack of interest in the precise arrangements for this coup, he did express concern over Hitler's intended fate. He agreed with Oster that the dictator should not be killed but arrested and brought to trial or—another possibility—declared insane by a medical board.[311] Canaris remained aloof from the rest of the conspiratorial details, his routine response to overlengthy explanations being "Just get on with it!"[312]

Forever mindful of the crucial date—September 27—on which Hitler proposed to issue his final invasion orders, Canaris urged the plotters to hurry. He insisted that "action" must be taken at last but did not say what form it should take.[313] He never coveted a leading part in the preparations for the coup. It was, he told Liedig, "unthinkable that anyone from the Navy should occupy a key role in the military resistance movement." In view of the German mentality, this should go to a general.[314]

But the general on whom the conspirators were pinning all their hopes—Franz Halder, the new Army Chief of Staff—did not find Canaris's self-effacement helpful. "Canaris was a difficult person to talk to," he recalls. "He was very sparing with words and enjoyed being allusive. One often found it genuinely hard to guess what he meant to convey."[315] The general had hoped that Canaris would back him and share his burdens since being subjected to pressure by Oster, "whose burning hatred of Hitler . . . frequently conjured up visions unacceptable to the sober and objective listener."[316]

Halder was scarcely installed behind Beck's desk on September 1 when Oster turned up and asked if he was prepared to lead a military coup against the regime. The general agreed, having for years regarded Hitler as evil incarnate—a "bloodsucker" and "criminal" who was endangering the moral basis and very existence of the German state.[317] Oster then listed the military commanders who were prepared to join in. They included General von Witzleben, commanding Military District II (Berlin), his subordinate Major General Count von Brockdorff-Ahlefeldt, commander of the Potsdam-based 23rd Division, and Colonel von Hase, commanding officer of the 50th Infantry Regiment stationed at Landsberg an der Warthe. Nebe and Helldorf were also privy to the plan, Oster said, so there was no risk of a counterblow by the police (the Gestapo excepted).[318]

Halder sent for Witzleben, and the military district commander, a straightforward soldier and anti-Nazi like Halder himself, confirmed that he was ready to move if ordered to do so by the Chief of Staff or Commander in Chief of the Army.[319] Oster was then instructed by Halder to work out detailed plans for the coup and ascertain the most favourable time to launch it.

But the Chief of Staff was accustomed to precise planning and dispassionate assessments of the situation. Even his preliminary talks with Oster made him wonder if Canaris's subordinate was the right man to plan a coup in a model police state like the Third Reich. Halder knew his former supply officer only too well. Oster had not changed since his carefree days at Münster. He was too indiscreet—too talkative. Halder recalls: "When he showed signs of monopolizing me in the same way as my predecessor I kept him at arm's length and only sent for him when I had some special reason for so doing."[320]

Temperamental incompatibility was compounded with a difference of opinion over the vital matter of when and under what circumstances the *coup d'état* should be launched. A meeting at Halder's private apartment in Berlin-Schlachtensee was soured by the presence of an unwelcome outsider. Halder never forgot the cause of the row: "Much to my annoyance, Oster . . . brought Herr Gisevius to the meeting that night without notifying me in advance."[321]

Gisevius's proposals struck the Chief of Staff as hazardous. Instead of awaiting a suitable moment, the lawyer said, they ought to strike without more ado. The regime should be tackled from the criminal angle. Raids on Gestapo, SD and SS offices would turn up quite enough evidence to justify the coup in the eyes of the world. Halder refused to expose his men to the dangers of such a course. His own theory was that the Army could not strike until Hitler was discredited—until he had shown himself to be a public menace and destroyed his personal hold on the officer corps. And that would not happen until the first shot had been fired at Hitler's command.[322]

Halder rejected the idea of any further meetings with Gisevius but agreed that the former Gestapo adviser should move into an office at Witzleben's headquarters, where he was assigned to co-ordinate the activities of the military and police authorities in the event of a coup.[323] A gulf had opened between the conspirators, and Canaris seemed the man to bridge it. Halder's dependence on him steadily increased because the Admiral alone could supply him with what he so urgently needed: reliable information about the current state of the Sudeten crisis.

Halder's plan to strike at the very last moment—after September 27 —presupposed that he was kept fully and accurately informed of the progress of diplomatic negotiations. Only this would enable the Chief of Staff to gauge the precise moment at which Hitler opted for war and take steps to neutralize him. Nobody was better acquainted with the course of the negotiations than Weizsäcker, but Halder's military status did not justify any official contact between him and the State Secretary at the Foreign Office. He therefore needed a reliable intermediary, and the obvious person was Canaris.

The Abwehr chief kept him regularly informed, but in so sibylline a manner that "much of what I was supposed to learn from Weizsäcker via Canaris" did not reach its destination in a "clear enough" form.[324] Halder: "In order to act on an assessment of the political circumstances I needed reliable data. These I could only obtain from Canaris to a very inadequate extent."[325] Why this reticence? It cannot be sufficiently explained by the Admiral's innate reserve and love of the mysterious. Canaris obviously still clung to the hope that Britain would stand firm after all, inflict a manifest defeat on Hitler and thus, at the eleventh hour, preserve Germany from the imponderable effects of a domestic upheaval.

This makes it clear that Halder's strategic approach to the coup suffered from a fatal flaw. He, Canaris and Witzleben were placing their reliance on factors beyond their control: Britain's reaction and Hitler's behaviour. Furthermore, Halder was technically incapable of launching a *coup d'état* because, as Chief of the General Staff, he had no direct authority over military units. He could not set a single company in motion. That was the prerogative of the Army Commander in Chief, whom he planned to take into his confidence and win over at the last moment.

It is not surprising that the Oster-Gisevius group should have felt a dawning suspicion that Halder and Canaris were not genuinely interested in the coup. To rely on an unknown quantity like Brauchitsch struck them as the height of self-delusion. Oster, Gisevius and Heinz, of whom the latter was particularly impatient, soon became so mistrustful of the Army authorities that they hatched a counterplot, "a conspiracy within a conspiracy" (Müller) designed to oust Halder from his involvement in preparations for the coup.[326]

Oster and Gisevius urged Witzleben to act on his own if necessary. Although the practical effect of this would have been to transform a *coup d'état* into a mutiny, Witzleben agreed. He had no particular love for Brauchitsch and Halder and no intention of letting them thwart his efforts to save the country from Hitler. "He would have been perfectly content to lock them up during those crucial hours," Gisevius records.[327] At a meeting in Oster's apartment the conspirators decided to launch a coup of their own without delay. The final details were discussed by Oster and Witzleben, who instructed Heinz to recruit the volunteer assault detachment which was to storm the Chancellery on the day of the coup and take Hitler into custody.[328]

Witzleben had only just left the building when the others banded together in yet another conspiracy within a conspiracy, this time without the general—indeed, against him. Heinz submitted that it was not enough to arrest Hitler and put him on trial. The assault detachment's task should be to provoke an incident and shoot him in the process.

Hitler alive was a dangerous force, Heinz argued, and stronger than all the conspirators and Witzleben's army corps put together. The rest supported him and agreed to conceal their decision from Witzleben because he was known to oppose any attempt on the Führer's life.[329]

Oster concurred, regardless of the fact that he was breaking his agreement with Canaris.[330] He was in no doubt that the Admiral would never consent to Hitler's assassination. Canaris, says Liedig, had always "taken the view, based on his attitude to religion, that he would personally oppose the murder."[331] Oster duly thought it advisable to keep his friend in ignorance of the conspirators' decision. Canaris was only told that a raiding party was being recruited and needed arms.

The Admiral directed Groscurth to issue Heinz with carbines and explosives.[332] This seems to have been Groscurth's first intimation of the projected coup. Not only did personnel from his section join Heinz's team, but Abwehr II "safe houses" were used as assembly points for the members of the Chancellery flying squad. On the evening of September 14 Groscurth met his brother and sister-in-law. "Can you keep a secret?" he asked them. They nodded. Then he blurted out, "Hitler's going to be arrested tonight."[333]

But plans for the coup were short-lived. By the time September 15 dawned, the hard-line anti-Nazis had been robbed of yet another hope: Prime Minister Chamberlain was flying to Berchtesgaden with an olive branch for Hitler.[334] Dismayed by the Sudetenland revolt, unnerved by a crudely bellicose German press campaign and torn between resistance and acquiescence, the British and French heads of government had found a way out: a summit meeting at which the German demands would be approved and given formal shape. It was the Munich formula —a recipe for surrender.

Hitler did not find it hard to persuade the elderly gentleman from London of his pacific intentions and reconcile him to a settlement which he had long ago made up his mind to accept, in other words, the cession of the Sudetenland to Germany. Chamberlain undertook to recommend this scheme to his own cabinet and government circles in Paris and Prague.

The British cabinet agreed. So did the French. Then they jointly applied the thumbscrew to Prague. On September 19 Beneš received a visit from the British and French ambassadors, who informed him that their governments recommended the cession of all Sudeten territories with a German population exceeding 50 per cent, preferably without a plebiscite and under international supervision. Eduard Beneš's world collapsed in ruins. "So Czechoslovakia is being abandoned after all," he exclaimed.[335] Two days later Prague accepted the Franco-British proposals.[336]

Beneš was not the only person to be taken aback by the capitulation of Britain and France. Canaris and the conspirators saw all their assumptions and hypotheses cut to ribbons, and many of them were "speechless with horror" (Müller).[337] Major General Count von Brockdorff-Ahlefeldt announced that he could no longer count on his men. As for Witzleben, he felt a burgeoning mistrust of those who, like Canaris and Weizsäcker, had been so woefully mistaken in their political assessments.[338]

But the conspirators were given a second chance by Hitler's decision to fan the flames once more. He was so set on war that he refused to be appeased by the cession of the Sudeten German territories. He now wanted to bring the whole of Czechoslovakia under German control. His thoughts were increasingly dominated by the prospect of war. The Wehrmacht had completed its deployment and German divisions were ready to move at any time.

Once again it was the Abwehr whose help was enlisted in bringing the crisis to a head. A new Sudeten German revolt was planned on the Czech side of the frontier, and who better to mount it than the organization led by Admiral Canaris? He had received the relevant orders on the afternoon of September 15. The same evening Groscurth was instructed to smuggle three thousand Austrian rifles into Czechoslovakia.[339] Canaris impatiently telephoned Keitel, who was staying at the Berghof, and asked if the operation could begin. Keitel: "No, not for the moment."

Henlein, the Abwehr's erstwhile protégé, had intervened with a proposal whose effect was to abolish the Abwehr's secret role in the Sudeten war of nerves. Henlein was still smarting at the speed with which his insurrection had collapsed on September 11 and yearned to redeem himself in the Führer's eyes. On September 16 he sent Frank to the Berghof with an offer to recruit a refugee legion which could make forays into Czechoslovakia and provoke incidents there.[340]

Hitler approved the idea. He ordained the formation of a Sudetendeutsches Freikorps (SFK) to be trained by SA and Army instructors and furnished with equipment and a commanding officer by the OKW.[341] Canaris and Groscurth were infuriated at the Abwehr's exclusion. Fresh from their efforts to get rid of Hitler and prevent war, they now protested because the Abwehr had been denied an opportunity to aggravate the crisis. "A risky policy," Groscurth complained to his diary. "Our units will be smashed in the process."[342] Canaris was so angry that he began by refusing to co-operate with the Freikorps. On September 18, when Groscurth gave Abwehr II contrary instructions, there was a fierce altercation between him and the Admiral.[343]

Next day Canaris changed his tactics. Reassured, Groscurth wrote: "Admiral decrees fullest possible support for the Freikorps!"[344] Canaris now thought it more expedient to maintain the closest possible contact with Henlein's formations so as to preserve the Abwehr's control over the politico-military underground. All at once, nobody could back the Freikorps promptly or vigorously enough to satisfy him. When Abwehrstelle Dresden was slow to alter course, Canaris berated it "in an unseemly manner."[345]

Groscurth was hurriedly instructed to establish close links with the military commanders of the Freikorps. On September 21 he and Canaris set off to visit the staffs of the SFK groups in Leipzig, Dresden and Bayreuth.[346] The Admiral soon became a frequent visitor to Schloss Fantaisie, Henlein's headquarters at Bayreuth-Donndorf. SS-Brigadeführer Berger, Himmler's representative with the SFK, noted that he appeared at Donndorf "nearly every other day and conferred with Henlein."[347] One of Canaris's informants, Richard Lammel, once an intelligence officer but now an SdP official and associate of Frank's, kept him informed of what went on inside the SFK.[348]

Canaris was depressed by what he saw and heard at Donndorf. Henlein had long ago joined the SS camp and Frank was already assured of his promotion to the rank of SS-Brigadeführer. "Talks with Henlein," wrote Groscurth. "Very disagreeable impression. Henlein edgy, dictatorial manner!"[349] It did not escape the Abwehr men that Henlein often drove to the Hotel Bellevue in Dresden to visit the head of the Ausland-SD, SS-Standartenführer Jost, whose dismissal Canaris had demanded in March of that year.[350]

But Canaris stuck to Henlein, whom he considered too goodhearted to submit to total domination by the SS. Besides, the Abwehr was under orders to assist the SFK. It supplied the arms, the intelligence network and, last but not least, funds to the tune of RM100,000 a day.[351] Thus encouraged, SFK raiding parties sallied into Czech territory. Henlein's volunteers began attacking Czech frontier posts on the morning of September 19. They engineered so many incidents that substantial elements of the Czech Army had to be transferred to the frontier, an unwelcome move from the Wehrmacht's point of view.[352]

These border skirmishes provided Hitler with the background noise he needed in order to submit new demands. When Chamberlain met him at the Hotel Dreesen in Godesberg on September 22 and reported that the Czech Government had accepted the German demands of September 15, the dictator snapped, "I'm terribly sorry, but it's too late for that." He abruptly insisted that the Sudetenland should be ceded unconditionally and at once, not—as agreed at Berchtesgaden only a week before—gradually and under international supervision. Chamberlain angrily protested that this was an entirely new demand.[353]

Next day Hitler submitted a memorandum in which he stated that the Sudeten German territories marked on an accompanying map must be evacuated by the Czech authorities from September 26 onwards and handed over to the Reich by September 28. Chamberlain objected that this memorandum amounted to an ultimatum and might provoke a European war. Hitler retreated an inch or two. He would, he said, be content with an October 1 time limit. Despite the gravest misgivings, Chamberlain volunteered to convey these terms to the Czechoslovak Government.[354]

The world took a sudden lurch towards the brink of war, for this time the Western powers seemed unwilling to yield. Beneš decreed the full mobilization of the Czech armed forces, Londoners dug trenches against the possibility of German air raids and the French ordered partial mobilization.[355] On September 26 Chamberlain informed Berlin that Prague had rejected the new German demands. Hitler still insisted that his forces would occupy the Sudeten German territories on October 1.[356] When Chamberlain sent a special envoy to warn the German dictator that "if France, in fulfillment of her treaty obligations, should become actively involved in hostilities against Germany, the United Kingdom would feel obliged to support France," Hitler retorted that a world war would break out in six days' time, and that it would spell the destruction of Czechoslovakia.[357]

Oster's comment on this statement was: "Thank God, at last we have clear proof that Hitler means to drift into war at all costs. Now there can't be any turning back."[358] He alerted his friends, Heinz mustered his assault group and Halder thought it time to put Brauchitsch in the picture. Witzleben was confident that the commander in chief would join them. "Doctor," he said to Gisevius, "it's almost time!"[359]

Canaris saw equally little chance of preventing war. Hour by hour, reports reaching Abwehr headquarters strengthened his belief that the Western powers would not back down. The British Fleet was already reported as having sailed for an unknown destination. Other Abwehr sources claimed that the Czech Government had been replaced by a military cabinet and the German Embassy in Prague stormed by a mob.[360]

Although many of these reports proved false, Canaris expected war to break out hourly. Nothing could shake his conviction that the Western powers would stand firm—not even his daily perusal of the "brown birds," those buff-coloured eagle-adorned sheets of paper on which the Forschungsamt submitted its typewritten intercepts. Telephone conversations between foreign embassies and cabinet offices in London, Prague and Paris disclosed how little the British and French were prepared to commit themselves on the Czechs' behalf, but Canaris found it inconceivable, as a naval officer, that Britain's world-power status would permit her to tolerate Hitler's brazen tinkering with the map of Europe for very much longer.

Reporting to Keitel on the morning of September 28, he stressed the gravity of the situation and gave it as his firm belief that armed intervention by the French and British was a foregone conclusion. He also knew from Gestapo reports that "the mood of the German people could not be worse." Captain Eberhard, Keitel's aide, made a note of the Admiral's arguments: "We are not in a position to wage war on two fronts. Commander in Chief of the Army shared this view. France would take the offensive. Britain herself would lose little blood in the operation, but they would be able to deprive Germany of all her raw materials and supplies."[361]

Canaris was mistaken. A few hours later Hitler had disarmed his bomb and robbed the conspirators of their chance. Once again the *deus ex machina* was Chamberlain, who had that morning volunteered to travel to Berlin to discuss the cession of the Sudetenland with Hitler, together with representatives from France, Italy and Czechoslovakia. Shortly afterwards Mussolini requested his German partner to accept Chamberlain's proposal and postpone mobilization.[362] Just before 2 P.M. the British Ambassador heard the vital news: Hitler was inviting Chamberlain, Daladier and Mussolini to discuss a settlement of the Sudeten question in Munich next day. Mobilization measures in Western Europe, coupled with a manifest aversion to war in his own capital, had deterred Hitler once more. "You know, Göring," he remarked, "I thought the British Fleet might open fire after all."[363] Only a few days later, the Munich Conference gave him what he wanted without a shot being fired.

Hitler had done it again. His powers of ruthless self-assertion had banished all the Germans' doubts and fears, all their hopes of deliverance from the nightmare of dictatorship. Many of his critics and opponents quickly swallowed their misgivings and joined in the paean of exultation with which the Greater German masses hailed their leader's latest triumph.

Canaris, whose capacity for wishful thinking seemed inexhaustible, also joined the ranks of the jubilant and relieved. Besides, he had some grounds for wanting to re-establish contact with Hitler. Too many of the Abwehr's studies and reports on the Sudeten crisis had proved inaccurate, and he was very much afraid that his reputation as an intelligence chief had suffered in recent weeks. Oster and his cronies must have been dismayed to note how quickly Canaris made his peace with the Führer.

He readily joined the motorized columns that roared through the "liberated Sudeten German territories" (Groscurth) at the beginning of October.[364] In company with Oster, Groscurth and Jenke, his aide, he followed in the wake of Hitler's convoy but failed to catch it up. At Hörsin, a village near Eger [Cheb], the four Abwehr men finally learned that Hitler would be passing through. Canaris and his companions quickly drove to the outskirts of the village, piled out of their car and cleared a route through the waiting crowds. Then the Führer hove in sight. "Why, there's Canaris," he called, and told his driver to stop. The Admiral saluted. Hitler exchanged a few words and drove on. Groscurth was piqued. "As usual, the Admiral thought it unnecessary to introduce us."[365]

Canaris was so firmly rededicated to the regime that even Oster shrank from submitting Groscurth's reports without deleting their more anti-Nazi comments. He blue-pencilled them unmercifully. Out went a reference to the Führer's habit of "irresponsibly mentioning the most secret matters in public." So did the allegation that Hitler had dismissed a general's objection "with a wild air," that Minister of the Interior Frick was "impersonal and disagreeable" and that Education Minister Rust had delivered "a frightful speech."[366]

The intelligence chief of the Greater German Reich had no use for such strictures at a time when contentment and gratitude were the order of the day. He could be extremely brusque with any colleagues and subordinates who betrayed a lack of respect for the Supreme Commander. While visiting Abwehrstelle Hamburg he was greeted by officers in civilian clothes with their arms limply raised in a semblance of the Hitler salute. "Gentlemen," he snapped, "I insist on your saluting me with the arm properly extended. It's an indirect tribute to the Führer, don't forget."[367]

These moods never lasted long, however. Canaris had gazed too deeply into the chasm on whose brink his joyful and exultant fellow countrymen still stood poised. He had a dawning presentiment of something which another prominent victim of Hitler's callousness had already translated into the language of grim resignation. Hitler, wrote Werner von Fritsch, "is Germany's destiny for better or worse, and that destiny will run its course. If it ends in the abyss he will drag us all down with him—there's nothing to be done."[368]

9

The Road to War

The Foreign Office man had bad news for his naval visitor. On December 14, 1938, Baron von Weizsäcker confided to Canaris that difficulties were arising from the "conversion of a nationalist policy into an imperialist policy." Then he came out with it; Hitler was forcing the pace in the East so hard that war between Germany and Poland could not be ruled out.[1]

Weizsäcker painted a gloomy picture of impending developments. The Wehrmacht was superior to the Polish Army and Britain and France would probably remain neutral. On the other hand, Italy might take advantage of hostilities in Poland to attack France, and that would mean a world war. All that could prevent this was "internal action," or the removal of Hitler, but the conspiracy lacked firm leadership. With a verbal shrug of resignation, Weizsäcker opined that the German people had grown "used to living in a Napoleonic age."[2]

This was Canaris's first intimation of what was brewing between Germany and Poland. All he knew was that, two months earlier, Foreign Minister von Ribbentrop had suggested to Josef Lipski, the Polish Ambassador, that their countries should seek "a general settlement of all existing sources of friction." Ribbentrop's proposal sounded relatively moderate. Poland should consent to Danzig's reunification with the Reich and the construction of an extraterritorial road and rail link through Pommerellen, the so-called Polish Corridor. In return, Germany would grant Poland economic concessions in Danzig and guarantee the Polish frontiers—inclusive of the German territories surrendered to Poland after World War I.[3]

While not slamming the door on negotiations, the Polish Government had made a negative response. However, Lipski's "purely personal" view was that talks about a motor road were possible, and Colonel Józef Beck, Foreign Minister and strong man of the ruling military junta, showed some interest in keeping the dialogue alive.[4] As late as November 29, Canaris's Polish counterpart, Colonel Pelczynski of Section II (military intelligence) of the General Staff, considered that German-Polish relations were in line with the non-aggression pact of 1934 and that no serious political differences existed between the two countries.[5]

Canaris could not share Weizsäcker's misgivings, especially as his own ideas on the subject of a German-Polish war were altogether different. He was firmly convinced that the Western powers would never stand idly by while Hitler launched an attack on Poland. As for Mussolini risking a military venture against France, the poor condition of the Italian war machine made this seem highly improbable. No, Weizsäcker was taking an overpessimistic view of things.

One awkward feature was that Hitler kept urging the Poles to approve the proposed settlement, but Canaris doubtless ascribed this to the nationalistic euphoria prevailing among the leaders of the Third Reich since their spectacular resolution of the Sudeten crisis—that sense of power, midway between pride and megalomania, which had not only infected habitual wielders of authority in the armed forces and civil service but sometimes overcame a sceptic like Canaris himself.

Most Germans had all too quickly grown accustomed to Hitler's amoral *Realpolitik*. Millions of Third Reich citizens had "learned to accept sudden treaty violations with the sly satisfaction of accomplices and the unpolitical philosophy of the armchair politician. 'That's politics: now we're better at it than the others . . .'"[6] In the new Germany, nothing counted for more than national power politics and racial narcissism. Germany seemed to bestride the European scene as never before, exercising a right of arbitrament which she had not possessed since Bismarck's day.

Nazi Germany's accretion of power was sensational indeed. The Munich Conference had exposed Southeast Europe to German hegemony and hastened the collapse of the last British and French diplomatic strongholds in the Balkans. Nothing could have advertised this change more clearly than the Vienna Award of November 2, under which the Axis Foreign Ministers assigned the Czechs, Slovaks, Ruthenians and Hungarians their new role in Adolf Hitler's Europe.

But Canaris thought it possible to control these bouts of Teutonic muscle-flexing because he knew of Hitler's directives to the Wehrmacht implying that the time of conquest was past. General von Brauchitsch, the Army commander in chief, had just received orders to discontinue all preparations for deployment or military action—the Army could quietly proceed with its expansion plans and complete them by the target date of 1945.[7] The Führer even managed to find an unaggressive formula for the impending liquidation of the Czechoslovak rump state, which he had resolved to destroy immediately after the Munich Conference. The OKW already had a supplementary directive ready for signature in which Hitler was to explain that the invasion of Czechoslovakia's remains was merely a "pacifying operation" to be carried out only if "no appreciable resistance" could be expected.[8]

Like many military men, Canaris had yielded to the mistaken belief that Hitler's Reich was saturated, so Weizsäcker's forebodings struck him as unrealistic. Not unduly perturbed, he drove back to his Tirpitz-Ufer headquarters and described the conversation to "Muffel" Groscurth.[9] The head of Abwehr II was just taking leave of his colleagues and superiors before embarking on a routine spell of regimental duty as commander of a company stationed in Breslau.[10]

Fatigued after a round of farewell parties in the Berlin fleshpots, Groscurth pricked up his ears at the mention of Poland, a key word which reminded him of a sore point in his work to date. He had never approved of Hitler's flexible Polish policy. To his straightforward Prusso-German mind, the Führer was making undue concessions to Polish chauvinism. To the annoyance of the Foreign Office and with little support from Canaris, he had therefore ventured some slight adjustments to Germany's official Polish policy in his own sphere of operations.

Helmuth Groscurth prided himself on possessing a political secret weapon designed to uphold and safeguard German interests in Eastern Europe. He had drawn a cast-iron inference from the postwar crisis of German nationalism and the collapse of the German-speaking Kaiserreich, which had abandoned millions of Germans in Eastern Europe to succession states of a largely chauvinist character. This inference was that the German "bastion of civilization" in the East would crumble unless supported by a strong German nation-state. And this, in turn, meant the establishment of German supremacy in the East. For this the Reich would require a dependable ally, and Groscurth had found one in the smouldering embers of Ukrainian nationalism.

The Ukraine, that weakest link in the Soviet chain and promised land of German and Polish imperialists, straggled over large tracts of Eastern Europe. Apart from the Soviet Ukraine, pockets of Ukrainian territory existed in four other countries including Poland (Galicia) and Czechoslovakia (Ruthenia). If the Ukrainian heartland were wrested from the Soviet Union and combined with the Ukrainian areas of

Poland and Czechoslovakia to form an independent republic, Greater Germany would acquire a trustworthy confederate—especially as only the Germans could help the Ukrainians to fulfil their ancient dream of unity. Such was Groscurth's grand design, which he called "the creation of a free Greater Ukraine."[11]

The idea was not a new one. During World War I the armies of Germany and Austria-Hungary had stormed the Ukrainian corn belt to attain what Chancellor von Bethmann-Hollweg had declared to be their common war aim: "Russia must as far as possible be thrust back from the German frontier" by the creation of an independent Ukraine.[12] The first free Ukrainian state came into being amid the shellfire of advancing armies and the turmoil of the 1917–18 revolution.

But the Austro-German authorities, who were more interested in raw materials and grain than in other people's independence, soon found the Ukrainian separatist movement too left-leaning for their taste. A monarchist, Hetmann Pavlo Skoropadsky, came to power with their assistance but did not last long.[13] The Ukraine remained in the throes of internal conflict and external oppression until victorious Red Army units reconquered it for Russia. Thousands of Ukrainian nationalists fled the country, determined that they would some day return with the Germans (the only allies they could conceive of) and found a "true" Ukrainian state.

The Ukrainian idea was revived early in the 1920s by a National Socialist visionary named Alfred Rosenberg, the NSDAP's ideologist in chief. Rosenberg forged links with prominent Ukrainian exiles such as Colonel Eugene Konovalets, who had served in the Austro-Hungarian Army and commanded the Sichovi Striltsi, a crack unit of regimental strength, during the Ukrainian revolution.[14] In 1929 he joined with other exiled officers of his old regiment in founding a political movement which styled itself the Organization of Ukrainian Nationalists (OUN) and staged acts of terrorism in the Soviet Union.[15] The OUN programme was perfectly tailored to the militancy of Konovalets's fascist friends. Antiparliamentary and hostile to the Western democracies, the movement planned to use brute force to break open what it referred to as "Greater Russian imperialism's prison-of-nations."

But Rosenberg's ideological tirades soon proved insufficient for Konovalets. Eager to acquire a more substantial ally, the OUN chief learned that there were officers in Canaris's Abwehr who might be induced to take a special interest in the Ukraine. He was given a few names: Voss, Groscurth, Pruck. Discussions with these men convinced Konovalets that the Abwehr possessed a concrete and constructive programme for the Ukraine.

In 1937 he and his entire movement entered the Abwehr's service under the care and supervision of Voss and Groscurth.[16] At a meeting the same year Konovalets and Canaris resolved on the closest co-operation, notably in regard to subversion and propaganda.[17] The Abwehr chief was so impressed by the Austro-Hungarian ex-officer's personality and social manner that he sought his company on numerous occasions. Konovalets died in 1938, but Canaris preserved an enduring memory of the man and ensured that his grave was tended until his own career came to an end.[18]

His attitude to Groscurth's Ukrainian schemes was less unequivocal. Although he appreciated the Ukrainians' assistance to the Abwehr, he did not share Muffel's passionate devotion to the Ukrainian cause. "Canaris had a definite Western bias," says Pruck, another pro-Ukrainian. "At all events, his Eastern interests leapfrogged Poland and Russia and concentrated exclusively on the Japanese."[19] Canaris may also have sensed that Groscurth's policy could not be reconciled with the official line because it questioned one of the keystones in Hitler's Eastern policy: the enticement of Poland into a joint war of conquest against the Soviet Union.

As long ago as 1927, Rosenberg had written that the "prime requirement" of a German policy towards the Ukraine was "the removal of the Polish state."[20] Groscurth's scheme likewise presupposed the dismemberment of Poland, whose Galician territories were essential to the creation of a Greater Ukraine. Hitler's tactics were diametrically opposed. To encourage the Poles to make war on Germany's side he held out the prospect of supplementing the Ukrainian territories already under their control by acquiring the Soviet Ukraine as well.

In January 1935 Hitler sent Göring on a mission to Warsaw. Poland's elderly head of state, Marshal Pilsudski, was invited to conclude an anti-Russian alliance and assume over-all command of a German-Polish invading force.[21] Polish generals responded to Göring's proposal by outlining a partition of Russia under which "the Ukraine would become a Polish sphere of influence while Northwest Russia would come under German influence," as one observer noted.[22] The two dictatorships' joint future amid the ruins of Russia was acclaimed with chants of "Heil Hitler, Heil Pilsudski!" in Berlin and Warsaw.

But Pilsudski refused to be incited against Moscow, realizing that the collapse of the Soviet Union would expose Poland to the full force of German revisionism. Although Pilsudski's heir, Józef Beck, adhered to this maxim after his death, Hitler continued to hope that Poland could be talked into a concerted invasion of Russia.

The Abwehr officers were compelled to recognize, with some chagrin, that Hitler's Polish policy ran counter to their projected German-Ukrainian alliance. But Groscurth dug his heels in. He got his Ukrainian aides to draft plans for a Greater Ukrainian government and

army while OUN commandos trained for operations against Poland
and Russia in Abwehr II camps. OUN activities were primarily directed
at Poland. This was only natural because Galicia lay next door to Germany, the OUN's two leading figures—Konovalcts's successor, ex-
Colonel Andrei Mel'nyk, and another ex-member of the Austro-Hungarian officer corps, Ryko Yary—were Galicians, and many Ukrainians
in Galicia yearned for deliverance from the Polish yoke.[23]

Abwehrstelle Vienna received instructions from headquarters to
give the OUN an opportunity to disseminate propaganda. The Ukrainians were soon in possession of a radio transmitter which enabled
them to broadcast the fiction that the Soviet Ukraine would soon
be detached from Russia and united with the Ukrainian areas of
Poland. The work of the Vienna transmitter bore fruit. In mid-October
1938 disturbances broke out in Lvov, the capital of Galicia, a clear indication of the extent to which Polish Ukrainians were susceptible to
OUN propaganda.[24]

Polish intelligence agents soon discovered who was behind the
broadcasts from Vienna. The Polish Foreign Office promptly sent for
Ambassador von Moltke and lodged a protest[25]—in fact the Poles
waxed so vehement on the subject that Moltke began to fear that the
Abwehr and the Propaganda Ministry (which was formally responsible
for the Vienna transmitter) would succeed in vitiating German-Polish
relations.

When the Ukrainian campaign was joined by two more transmitters
based at Graz and Leipzig, Moltke alerted the Foreign Office. The ambassador's reports on the effect of OUN propaganda became more and
more dramatic. On October 19 he announced that Warsaw cherished
"the deepest possible mistrust of a German Ukrainian policy detrimental to Poland's interests,"[26] and a few days later he could "not understand" why the Reich was "using radio propaganda to touch the
vital nerve of the Polish state at its most sensitive spot."[27]

The Wilhelmstrasse put a stop to Groscurth's Ukrainian campaign.
On October 22 the Foreign Office requested Amtsgruppe Ausland/Ab-
wehr "to avoid any action which might foster an impression of co-
operation between official quarters in Germany and the Yary group or
the Ukrainian National Union."[28] The same day, Ambassador von
Moltke was empowered to inform the Polish Government that "steps
have been taken . . . to halt the Ukraine propaganda complained of."[29]
Canaris, who had no wish to oppose Hitler's Polish policy, compelled
his impetuous subordinate to spend less time on his Ukrainians.

However, the Admiral's account of his conversation with Weizsäcker
on December 14 prompted Groscurth to hope that the Ukrainian
scheme might yet have a chance of success. If German-Polish relations
were really as bad as the State Secretary feared, the Abwehr could re-

sume or even intensify its anti-Polish activities without risk of Foreign Office interference. This conjecture turned out to be partly correct, though Groscurth himself could not take advantage of the changed situation.

Groscurth's successor, Lieutenant Colonel Erwin Lahousen, also supported a pro-Ukrainian policy and carried on his work. The forty-one-year-old Viennese was personally and professionally associated with the tradition of Austro-German activity in the East. He came of noble Franco-Polish stock (styling himself Lahousen Edler von Vivremont until titles were abolished in Republican Austria), had fought against the Russians as an Austro-Hungarian infantry officer in World War I and had been responsible for Poland, Czechoslovakia and Hungary in the Austrian Defence Ministry's secret intelligence service.[30]

The lean lieutenant colonel, with his air of cool and urbane reserve, was more to Canaris's taste than the headstrong Groscurth, whom he had always found a trifle unrefined. A polyglot whose languages included Polish, Czech, Hungarian and French as well as German, Lahousen fitted the Admiral's picture of an "imperial and royal" Army officer to a tee.[31] "Give me Austrians, not Ostmarkers," he used to say.[32] [Ostmark being the official designation for Austria after the Anschluss, this implied a preference for Austrians of the old school.] Lahousen was just such a one: Austrian by upbringing and pan-German by sentiment but no lover of the Nazis.

Canaris began to view his officers' Ukrainian plans with greater favour, and not simply as a result of Lahousen's more rational lines of argument. What weighed even more heavily with Canaris was a tactical change of direction in Hitler's Polish policy. Some weeks earlier, the dictator had abruptly decided to play his Ukrainian card after all.

This was not the major alteration of course for which the pro-Ukrainians had been hoping. Hitler merely wanted to mobilize Ukrainian nationalism so as to put pressure on the Polish Government and force Beck to accept his October proposals. Whatever prompted this change of tack, the Ukrainian propaganda experiments or Moltke's reports, Hitler had discerned that the Ukrainian question was Poland's Achilles' heel. Six and a half million Ukrainians lived there, robbed of the right of self-determination and yearning for deliverance. This was reason enough for him to employ them as a lever against Warsaw.

In the immediate neighbourhood of the Polish Ukraine, right on its southern border, lay a tract of mountainous territory which lent itself perfectly to the Führer's blackmail attempt.[33] This area went by the name of Ruthenia or Carpatho-Russia—many called it the Carpatho-Ukraine—and was inhabited by half a million peasants whom ethnologists dubiously classified as members of the Ukrainian nation. Although the Ruthenians' dialect was more closely related to Ukrainian than to any other Slavic language group, they constituted an ethnic unit of their own. Moreover, their contact with the Ukrainian state was nil. Ruthenia had belonged to Hungary from early medieval times until 1918, when it passed to Czechoslovakia. It had then, after Ilitler's amputation of the Czechoslovak Republic, entered into the enjoyment of a long-denied autonomy.

Thereafter it had been the plaything of foreign powers and their intelligence services. Disheartened by the Munich surrender, the Czechs exercised few supervisory functions there. German agents (mainly representatives of the Volksdeutsche Mittelstelle) controlled the administration and economy, and the regional government was led by a Hungarian-backed Premier who hoped to reincorporate Ruthenia in the Magyar state.[34] The Hungarians had already acquired part of it under the Vienna Award, which assigned them a strip of frontier territory in the south.

Such was the bleak little country which Canaris had to alchemize into a jewel in the Ukrainian crown—a "Ukrainian Piedmont," as current propaganda called it. The implication was that, just as the North Italian principality of Piedmont had been the germ cell of Italian unification, so the Carpatho-Ukraine would become a loadstone to which every other splinter and fragment of the erstwhile Ukrainian state would be attracted. Obediently, Canaris and Lahousen sent forth their agents to accomplish this Ukrainian miracle.

The Abwehr was able to call upon Ukrainian émigrés from Galicia who had fled to the Carpatho-Ukraine years before and now wielded a decisive influence on the political and intellectual life of their host country. They willingly joined the Germans in ousting pro-Hungarian elements and Ukrainianizing the rest. Their position was reinforced by an opportune crisis. A few weeks earlier the Prague central government had arrested the pro-Hungarian Premier of the Carpatho-Ukraine for high treason and replaced him with a Greek Orthodox priest, Monsignor Augustin Vološin.[35] He was reputed to be one of the few Ruthenian politicians who felt truly Ukrainian, although he had always opted for the Czechs. Vološin was shrewd enough to seek help from German agents and joined forces with the Ukrainian émigrés, who were soon in control of the country.

"Vološin," declared a report from Abwehrstelle Vienna in January 1939, "is now entirely under the influence of the Ukrainian nationalists (i.e. numerous émigrés) who really carry on the government."[36] The new masters—"little more than puppets in the hands of back-stage German agents," as the U.S. diplomat George F. Kennan put it—took a leaf out of the fascist book. A one-party system came into being, pro-Hungarian groups were suppressed and concentration camps took shape.[37]

Abwehr II's Ukrainian allies consummated their authoritarian regime by forming an SA-like party militia called the Sich [Owl], whose grey uniforms and Hitler Youth dirks were reminiscent of its Greater German model.[38] One Abwehr officer boasted that "the best elements of the people" were now represented in the Sich, "notably members of the intellectual class who, sustained by the most exalted national fervour, are supporting the liberation of their people and the establishment of a Greater Ukraine."[39] Vološin soon felt secure enough to call a parliamentary election. On February 12, 1939, this produced the expected result: 98 per cent of all votes cast in favour of the government.

Ruthenia was inundated with Ukrainian propaganda demanding unity and freedom. Various organizations called for the unification of the Carpatho-Ukraine with other Ukrainian areas abroad and Galician émigrés fomented popular hostility towards the Poles. Abwehr observers were pleased to detect "hatred of Poland and Hungary," and one of them noted drily: "The Ukrainians expect simply everything of Germany."[40]

What happened next was perfectly in line with the whole manoeuvre's underlying purpose: a wave of pan-Ukrainian fervour slopped over into Polish territory. Fresh disturbances broke out in Galicia and Polish peasants sold their farms because they had ceased to feel safe among Ukrainians. Polish infantry and artillery units were transferred to the Carpatho-Ukrainian border and military personnel took over the frontier posts,[41] but they found it hard to prevent Galician émigré leaders from sending emissaries to their former homeland with orders to incite open resistance among the Ukrainians of Poland.

Reports from the Ukrainian territories were eagerly studied by Canaris and Lahousen. Captain Robert Nowak of Abwehr II, code name "Martin," informed his superiors on February 25 that Carpatho-Ukrainian circles were counting on "the outbreak of an armed Ukrainian insurrection in Galicia, perhaps even this spring. The general view in Galicia is said to be that the voivodeships of Stanislau and Tarnopol will pass to the [Carpatho-] Ukraine."[42]

The Polish Foreign Minister was quick to recognize this lethal threat to his country's national integrity. As Beck saw it, his only course was to cripple the activities of Galician conspirators in the Carpatho-Ukraine and prevent the area from being used as an aid to German extortion.

Formal protests achieved nothing. Face to face with Hitler at Berchtesgaden on January 5, 1939, Beck warned darkly that "Poland recognizes old foes in the agitators in what is now Carpatho-Ukrainian territory and fears that the Carpatho-Ukraine may sometime develop into a source of such disquiet to Poland that the Polish Government would feel bound to intervene, a step from which further complications might arise." Hitler played the innocent. "The Führer stated . . . that Poland had nothing whatever to fear from Germany in this respect."[43]

Beck then tried to undermine the German position from abroad by bringing in the Hungarians, who were resentful that the Vienna Award had given them such a small slice of Carpatho-Ukrainian territory. The Polish Foreign Minister prompted the Hungarian authorities to state their claims on the Carpatho-Ukraine more loudly than before. His argument was that its disappearance from the political map would create a common Polish-Hungarian frontier, which would perfectly suit the interests of both countries vis-à-vis their powerful German neighbour.

From now on, no one more zealously advocated a Hungarian takeover than the Polish Foreign Minister. Beck supported the Hungarian demands in every foreign capital he visited. He became so closely identified with them that he even dropped a few confidential hints on how to speed up Hungary's acquisition of the hateful little country. A few disturbances on the "open" frontier between Hungary and the Carpatho-Ukraine, he intimated in Budapest, might provide sufficient grounds for a Hungarian invasion.[44]

Early in March Beck actually sent the Hungarians a sabotage expert seconded from his military intelligence service. Major Charaszkiewicz, head of Branch 2, Section II, was to assist the Hungarian secret service in "diversionary activities," as a Polish historian puts it, or, more accurately, in staging incidents on the Carpatho-Ukrainian border.[45] Even prior to this, the German Foreign Office had opined that "Poland is seeking to achieve her purpose by all available means (money, agents, radio broadcasts, custom-built resolutions, etc.)" and considered it "not out of the question that Poland will combine with Hungary to produce a *fait accompli* in the near future."[46]

But Beck's efforts to whip up an appetite for the Carpatho-Ukraine were also directed at the leaders of Slovakia, which had likewise been granted autonomy within the CSR (or Czechoslovak Republic) after the Munich Conference. His intermediaries got in touch with the Slovak Premier, Josef Tiso, and painted glowing pictures of the important role that might be played in Europe by a Slovakia completely detached from the CSR and augmented by the Carpatho-Ukraine.[47]

The more vigorously Beck stirred the Ukrainian cauldron, however, the more strongly Hitler reacted. Beck's manoeuvres among Poland's southern neighbours implanted an *idée fixe* in the Führer's mind. What if he brought the remains of Czechoslovakia under his control, hemming Poland in from the south and simultaneously enfolding her in a steely embrace from the north and west? At odds with the Soviet Union in the east and estranged from the democracies in the far west, Poland would then—if she responded "sensibly"—become dependent on a *modus vivendi* with Germany.

Friction between the central government in Prague and the recalcitrant provinces of Slovakia and the Carpatho-Ukraine could furnish Germany with a pretext for invading the CSR at any time. It would not be hard to talk Slovak politicians into a freedom-from-Prague campaign and gain their consent to the dismemberment of the Czech multinational state, but what would become of the Carpatho-Ukraine? If he had to, Hitler was ready to abandon it to the Hungarians, whose support in his future crusade against Russia he valued more highly than the vague aspirations of the Ukrainian nationalists.

Canaris was not privy to this line of reasoning, which would have shocked him profoundly. Hitler's plan not only militated against the Abwehr's Ukrainian campaign but conflicted with all the foreign policy instincts of a man who believed that his country's territorial demands had already been fulfilled. Canaris strongly opposed putting renewed pressure on Czechoslovakia so soon after the commotion caused by the Sudeten crisis. Everything argued against such a course. Not only had Hitler joined in guaranteeing the territorial integrity of the rump CSR at Munich, but a Czechoslovakia which combined formal independence with strong German ties would benefit the Third Reich's interests more than a German annexed CSR with an alien and discontented population. Ever a nationalist, Canaris favoured indirect German sovereignty over the government in Prague.

This was what had prompted Abwehr II to stem the influx of Germans from elsewhere in Czechoslovakia when the Sudetenland was occupied in October 1938. The status and strength of the German element in the rump state had to be preserved as a lever for use against Prague. "On their own initiative," Groscurth proudly noted at the time, Abwehr detachments had at once issued a general call to "stand your ground in the CSR."[48] Far from being a solo effort by Abwehr II, this move had fully accorded with the views of Admiral Canaris.

Writing to the Foreign Office on October 6, Canaris explained why everything should be done to preserve an independent Czechoslovak Republic. He stressed that "the 'Czech and Slovak' rump state must and shall be substantially dependent on Germany in future. The preconditions for this are particularly in evidence at the present time because the mood in Czechoslovakia is strongly hostile to Britain and France, which are felt to have betrayed her." To break up the Czechoslovak Republic, for instance by encouraging Slovak separatism, might result in the formation on Germany's eastern frontiers of "a united bloc of succession states linked to southeast Europe," and that would be intolerable. "It is therefore in the military interest for Slovakia not to break away from the Czechoslovak union but to remain, with Czechia, under strong German influence."[49]

But this—the destruction of the Czechoslovak Republic—was just what Hitler was now planning. At the end of January 1939 he summoned a few of his most trusted senior SS officers to the Chancellery. They included SS-Gruppenführer Wilhelm Keppler, State Secretary assigned to special duties at the Foreign Office, and Heydrich. The SD was instructed to establish contact with separatist politicians in Slovakia and persuade them to call for their country's secession from the Czechoslovak Republic. This operation had to be ready to roll by mid-March at latest.[50] When the conference broke up, Hitler impressed on his visitors that "for the time being, no other department of the Foreign Office, Army or party was to know of it."[51]

This meeting at the Chancellery boded ill for Canaris's status in the Third Reich's power structure. Instead of consulting his intelligence chief, Hitler had for the first time entrusted the latter's keenest competitors with secret preparations for a foreign policy coup. "The Reich's expert arsonist," as Admiral Alberto Lais, head of the Italian Navy's secret intelligence service, christened his German colleague, no longer enjoyed the Führer's unbounded confidence. His misgivings during the Sudeten crisis had not been forgotten.[52]

The SD set to work all the more zealously to carry out Hitler's orders. Keppler and an SD team drove to Bratislava, where they contacted Slovak politicians favourable to the idea of detaching their country from the Prague confederation and placing it under German "protection."[53] Keppler persuaded Premier Tiso to boycott a conference called by the central government, which was eager to resolve the outstanding differences between Czechs and Slovaks, and to prepare for Slovak independence.[54]

Canaris was still unaware that his rivals were demolishing in Slovakia what the Abwehr was erecting in the Carpatho-Ukraine when the SD resorted to overt action. Early in March, SD saboteurs commanded by SS-Sturmbannführer Alfred Naujocks staged some bombing attacks in Slovakia which looked like the work of Slovak nationalists.[55] The roar of explosives in Slovakia—almost certainly coupled with reports of the secret talks at Bratislava—prompted President Emil Hácha to take a precipitate and ill-considered step. During the night of March 9–10 he dismissed the Slovak provincial government.[56] Hitler now had the Czech crisis he wanted.

Suddenly, however, the Slovaks turned unco-operative. Karel Sidor, the new Prague-appointed Premier, rejected the German plans and even Tiso, whom he had replaced, started to waver.[57] On March 11 Keppler paid another visit to Tiso and urged him to proclaim independence and solicit German help. Tiso did not cave in until Keppler threatened that the eastern part of Slovakia, if not more, might otherwise be occupied by the Hungarians.[58] As soon as the Slovak said yes, which he did during the night of March 12–13, he was packed into an SD plane and whisked off to see Hitler.[59]

Hitler, too, threatened Tiso with a Hungarian invasion at their meeting on the night of March 13, but Tiso was no longer in need of any such pressure. A few hours later he was winging his way back to Bratislava with a declaration of independence ghosted by Ribbentrop and a stern injunction to see that his wavering colleagues changed their minds. This they did next morning.[60] Meanwhile the German war machine prepared to enter Bohemia and Moravia by dawn on March 15 at latest. It was only now that Canaris learned what had been happening behind his back.

The Admiral found it bitterly ironical that ethnic Germans whom the Abwehr had prevented from leaving the CSR should now supply the customary pretext for Hitler's *coup de main*. "German blood flows again in Brno!" screamed the headlines dictated by the Propaganda Ministry on March 12, and beneath them appeared sanguinary reports alleging persecution of the German minority by the Czech authorities.[61] At the Foreign Office, the State Secretary was already drafting a telegraphic circular justifying intervention on the grounds that the Reich Government had "in cognizance of its duty to preserve peace in Central Europe" and for the purpose of eliminating "intolerable and chaotic conditions on its eastern frontier" been "compelled to initiate the necessary steps."[62]

On March 13 the Czechs made another attempt to forestall the impending German invasion by appealing to Hitler. Hácha sent for the German chargé d'affaires in Prague, but the latter had instructions to remain incommunicado.[63] This left the sick old President with no choice. On March 14 he offered to visit Berlin in person. He arrived late that evening and was coerced by Hitler, with unprecedented brutality, into signing a document which declared that he had "confidently placed the destiny of the Czech people and his country in the hands of the Führer of the German Reich."[64]

Canaris had meanwhile been sitting in his office following the gradual progress of Hitler's operation. Abwehr reports received during the night of March 13–14 indicated that all was going smoothly: no Czech troop movements on the German border, a call-up of reservists by the three army corps in northern Hungary, "no significant military measures" in France or Britain.[65]

Only the fate of the Carpatho-Ukraine remained in doubt. A report from Chust, the capital, reached Canaris early in the morning. Vološin, scenting the end of Czechoslovakia, had jumped the gun and proclaimed his country's independence even before the Slovaks. He was in such a hurry that he woke the German consul, Hofmann, at 1:30 A.M. and requested him to wire his declaration of independence to Berlin at once.[66] Vološin's telegram was at the Foreign Office by 6:15 A.M. Shortly afterwards Canaris read: "To the Minister of Foreign Affairs, Berlin, Germany. On behalf of the government of Carpatho-Ukraine I request that note be taken of our declaration of independence under the protection of the German Reich. Prime Minister Dr. Vološin in Chust."[67]

Fresh reports reached Abwehr headquarters a few minutes later. The Polish Army was deploying along the Carpatho-Ukrainian border. "In regard to Polish troop movements," noted Legationsrat von Heyden-Rynsch, the Foreign Office liaison officer with Amtsgruppe Ausland/Abwehr, "a movement towards the southeast, i.e. towards the deployment area facing Carpatho-Ukraine, is becoming steadily more apparent. Few forces have been dispatched to the Olza district, whereas troop transports from the north and west are building up on the Carpatho-Ukrainian border."[68]

But the Abwehr had hardly incorporated these reports in its picture of the situation when it was approached by someone with genuine designs on the Carpatho-Ukraine. During the morning of March 14 Canaris was telephoned by Colonel Rudolf Andorka, chief of the Hungarian military intelligence service, and brusquely reproached for keeping an old ally in the dark. The Honvéd [Hungarian Armed Forces] General Staff did not know what the Germans intended and would appreciate precise information. Canaris sent for Major Pruck, briefed him and instructed an aircraft from the Sonderstaffel [Special Squadron] Rowehl, a Luftwaffe unit at the Abwehr's disposal, to stand by to fly him to Budapest.[69]

The major took off at 10 A.M. Three hours later he landed in Budapest, where Hungarian intelligence officers were urgently awaiting him at the Hotel Carlton. "I informed Colonel Andorka of the [impending] occupation and the official reasons for it," Pruck relates, "though these were not taken seriously." He noted that the Hungarians were genuinely in the dark because Andorka had been instructed by his government to submit a formal statement of Hungary's claim to the Carpatho-Ukraine *and* Slovakia.[70]

It was also clear from everything the Hungarian colonel said that he was yet another victim of the Canaris myth that flourished in so many foreign intelligence centres. "However," Pruck goes on, "the real reason for the Hungarians' eagerness to discuss matters was a desire to lodge their political claim in good time because they assumed that Admiral Canaris wielded great political influence with Hitler."[71] When he reported back to Canaris at 5 P.M. Pruck realized that his boss was also groping in the dark. Canaris did not discover the nature of Hitler's intentions towards Hungary and the Ukrainians until he had consulted the Foreign Office and the Chancellery.[72]

His inquiries disclosed the full extent of the Führer's duplicity and lack of scruple. With a shrug of the shoulders, Hitler abandoned the Carpatho-Ukraine and gave carte blanche to the Hungarian Army.[73] Newly independent Slovakia he denied to Budapest, but the Carpatho-Ukraine he abandoned to the vengeance of Magyar nationalism. Although Vološin desperately flung his pitiful little force of Sich troops against the Hungarian invaders, the Honvéd put paid to the Abwehr's miniature Ukraine within a few hours.[74]

"All this has been an experience which the Ukrainian nationalists will not be quick to forget," Kennan wrote to Washington. "The result must undoubtedly be extensive disillusionment in the sincerity of German support and a certain degree of demoralization throughout the Ukrainian movement."[75] Canaris was depressed too. He received more and more reports disclosing the brutal and inhuman treatment to which the Carpatho-Ukraine was being subjected by Germany's Hungarian allies. Pruck recalls that the Hungarians "strung up all the freedom fighters—three thousand of them, reportedly."[76]

But Canaris had no time to dwell on the criminal aspect of this *Realpolitik*. On March 15 Wehrmacht units crossed the Czech frontier en route for new and even more distant horizons. The Führer triumphantly followed in their wake and proclaimed the end of the Czech state at Hradschin Castle in Prague. From now on the Czechs were to be enfolded in the iron embrace of a Reich Protectorate of Bohemia and Moravia. Hitler sent for Dietrich, his press chief. "Have you any reports of troop movements in France and the Soviet Union or a mobilization of the British Fleet?" When Dietrich said no, Hitler exclaimed, "I knew it! Everyone will have stopped talking about this in a fortnight's time."[77]

Nothing seemed capable of stopping him now. He was like a man possessed, blind to moderation and deaf to the dictates of reason. After Hácha's abject surrender he rushed out and exuberantly invited his secretaries to kiss him. "Girls," he exclaimed, "this is the greatest day of my life. I shall go down in history as the greatest German ever."[78] The Führer became almost unapproachable for a time. He seemed to be spurred on by a strange fever, a hectic sense of unrest, a "neurasthenic urge for activity," as his biographer Joachim Fest puts it.

A week later he boarded the pocket battleship *Deutschland* at Swinemünde, bound for a new crisis. This time he was demanding the return of Memel, a German port in the north of East Prussia which the Lithuanians had occupied and annexed after World War I.[79] Without awaiting the result of Ribbentrop's negotiations with Lithuanian representatives in Berlin, Hitler ordered the *Deutschland* to head for Memel and prepared to enter the city—even at the risk of being welcomed with rifle fire instead of flowers. The Lithuanian negotiators averted disaster by swiftly caving in, and Germany's strong man was able to make another of his wildly acclaimed entries into a "liberated" city.[80]

Then came the moment for which all the foreign policy intrigues and subterfuges of the past few weeks—indeed, all the diplomatic spadework of the preceding years—had been but a prelude. At long last, the Poles were to be made to show their colours. Ambassador Coulondre of France had reported weeks before that "the hour of Lebensraum" was now striking, and he was right.[81] At Hitler's wish, the struggle for territorial expansion in the Soviet East was about to enter a crucial phase. Only one prerequisite was missing: Poland's partnership, military strength and geographical scope for deployment.

On March 21 Hitler instructed Foreign Minister Ribbentrop to renew his offer to Lipski, the Polish Ambassador. He even raised it to include a German guarantee of all Polish territory, a twenty-five-year extension of the German-Polish non-aggression pact, the admission of Poland to the anti-Comintern club, German-Polish control of the Soviet Ukraine (when conquered) and an equal share of influence in pseudo-autonomous Slovakia. In return, Ribbentrop again insisted that Poland must agree to the construction of an extraterritorial road and rail link through Pommerellen—a corridor within a corridor, so to speak —and further concede that the free city of Danzig, officially under League of Nations supervision but already governed by the NSDAP, should return to the Reich.[82] Lipski was so intrigued by the German proposals that he immediately set off for Warsaw to convey and recommend them to his Foreign Minister.

Unfortunately for Hitler, Colonel Beck was a kindred spirit, a political gambler driven by ambition, haunted by dreams of national greatness and no less cunning than the German dictator himself. Adroit, shrewd and preoccupied with a utopian vision of Polish dominance on the eastern marches of Europe, Beck pursued a shuttle policy between the two hostile giants, Germany and Russia, in the blind belief that nothing and no one could ever bring them together. His theory was that both powers must be kept in a state of suspension so as to spare Poland the lethal necessity of siding with one or the other.

The inference was that Poland should join no coalition of powers in which the Germans or the Russians wielded a decisive influence. Despite the shock occasioned by Hitler's march on Prague, this had just prompted Beck to reject a proposal from the British Foreign Minister, Lord Halifax, that Poland should join with Britain, France and the Soviet Union in concluding a pact against the German troublemakers.[83] Józef Beck refused to reach an accommodation with his country's mortal enemy in the East, but neither would he side with Germany against Russia. In practice, this meant that Beck had to turn Hitler down. The problems of Danzig and the Corridor had to remain unresolved, an ugly obstacle solid and immovable enough to prevent any *rapprochement* between Germany and Poland.[84]

Studying Ribbentrop's proposals on March 22, Beck sensed that the Germans would not hold off much longer. The threat of German military superiority grew with every passing day. His conclusion was that a non-Soviet great power must be persuaded to guarantee Poland's safety. The only possible candidate was Britain, but the British had a traditional aversion to presenting foreigners with blank cheques. What was more, the bizarre status of the free city of Danzig had never been popular with them.

Beck still confidently hoped to secure a Polish guarantee from London. In Britain, the rape of Prague had left a bruise which did not fade after Hitler's predicted fortnight. On the contrary, March 15, 1939, had become a turning point in the tide of British public opinion and a deathblow to appeasement which simultaneously provoked an unexpected wave of opposition to German expansionism. Even Chamberlain had to take account of these sentiments. Britain was in a mood to believe the worst of a dictator who broke his word and violated his treaty obligations. This being so, it was not impossible that the British Government would take diplomatic action if Hitler laid hands on yet another country—Poland, for example.

Beck's only problem was that Hitler showed absolutely no signs of unleashing his troops against Poland. He had offered the Poles an alliance, not demanded their capitulation, and was prepared to await a definite response until late in the summer. Beck's dilemma arose from an absence of the German pressure which alone could induce the British to act. Since Hitler refrained from provoking a crisis, Beck staged one himself.

On March 23, as though anticipating the threat of a German invasion, Warsaw decreed the partial mobilization of the Polish armed forces. Trained reservists of the 1911–14 age groups were called up and all reserve officers of specialist status were ordered to join their units. Some of the new formations were dispatched by the Polish General Staff to the East Prussian and East Pomeranian borders, and Polish Army commanders were assigned their various roles in the operational plan known as "West."[85]

Puzzled observers at Abwehr listening posts monitored this Polish sabre-rattling while Canaris vainly strove to read a pattern into the reports from his Polish S agents. Was Poland planning a pre-emptive campaign against Germany? Although the idea seemed absurd, Canaris had to bear in mind that in Poland partial mobilization was the penultimate step towards a declaration of war. By recalling an additional 334,000 men to the colours, the Polish Army had doubled its peacetime strength overnight.[86] Mobilization was attended by so many economic hazards in a backward country like Poland that the Abwehr reasonably assumed that general mobilization of the Polish Army implied a decision to go to war.

But could Poland seriously want war with Germany? Canaris found it hard to believe, much as Abwehr reports might speak of government-sponsored agitation, mass demonstrations and anti-German slogans ("Down with Hitler!", "We want Danzig!").[87] On the other hand, he could not ignore the fact that the Polish secret service had been placed on a war footing. The wartime espionage and diversionary planning staff of Section II had started work at the beginning of the year, and the Polish wartime espionage network in Germany was activated shortly afterwards.[88]

Carefully though he followed up each lead, Canaris failed to draw the correct inference—that it was all a diplomatic gambit on Beck's part. It also escaped the Abwehr that Beck was having foreign capitals sown with the seeds of a (false) rumour that German military formations were moving up to the Polish frontier.[89] In this he was inadvertently assisted by a correspondent of the British *News Chronicle*, who had heard that certain anti-Nazi Wehrmacht generals knew of the German deployment and were anxious to warn Britain.[90]

This journalist, who had been ordered out of Germany, alerted the British Foreign Office on March 29. Panic ensued. Poland seemed to be in the gravest danger and swift action was called for.[91] On March 30 Chamberlain hand-drafted a formal British guarantee. In the event of any action which "clearly threatened Polish independence, and which the Polish Government accordingly considered it vital to resist with their national forces," His Majesty's Government would feel "bound at once to lend the Polish Government all support in their power."[92] That afternoon Chamberlain secured Beck's approval and next day he read out the text to cheers from all sides of the Lower House. The French associated themselves with his declaration.[93]

Colonel Beck had gained his objective and more besides. The Franco-British guarantee released him from the need to negotiate with Hitler. Nowhere did the text enjoin the Polish Foreign Minister to contribute to a settlement of the Danzig issue by making concessions, and nowhere did it stipulate that Poland's attitude should promote the establishment of a coalition between the Western powers and the Soviet Union, the sole bloc capable of halting Hitler's martial progress.

The British belatedly grasped that they had been lured down a dangerous byway. Unable to exert a moderating influence on the Poles and Germans, British politicians found themselves increasingly coerced into what a study produced by Canaris's Abteilung Ausland construed as "an attempt by Great Britain to organize world opposition to Germany under her leadership."[94] This was bound to evoke a furious response from Hitler, who had now thrown reason to the winds, and it duly did so.

Canaris happened to be presenting one of his infrequent reports to Hitler when the first news of the British guarantee reached the Chancellery. The Führer froze, then vented his wrath in a wild outburst of abuse directed at foreign politicians. Puce in the face and almost oblivious of the Admiral's presence, he stormed up and down his study and pounded a marble table with his fists, exclaiming that he would mix them "a devil's brew."[95]

Canaris had never seen Hitler lose control in this way. Gone was the man who could coolly weigh the odds in the throes of any crisis—whose very strength had reposed in the ability to turn an opponent's sudden and unexpected moves to his own advantage. Returning to the Tirpitz-Ufer, Canaris was greeted by Oster. The Admiral drew him into his office and whispered, "I've just seen a madman—I still can't take it in. He's mad, mad, do you understand? Mad!"[96]

Next day he saw Hitler again when, still fuming at the British and the Poles, he delivered a speech to mark the launching of the new battleship *Tirpitz* at Wilhelmshaven, Canaris's old naval station. Furiously, Hitler classified Poland as one of those "satellite states" whose sole function was to be "set . . . against Germany" and warned the Polish Government that "He who declares himself ready to pull the chestnuts out of the fire for these powers should realize that he will burn his own fingers!"[97]

The document that turned up on Canaris's desk a few days later fully disclosed the nature of the devil's brew which Hitler was concocting for his enemies. Dated April 3, it was a copy of a directive from the Führer to the Wehrmacht and contained an alarming announcement: "The present attitude of Poland requires the initiation of military preparations to remove, if need be, any threat from this quarter forever." Beck's show of mobilization and military deployment had borne bitter fruit, because Hitler decreed that, in default of an agreement with Warsaw, it would be the aim of "Contingency White" (the operation's code name) "to smash Polish military strength and create a situation in the East which fulfills the requirements of national defence." An ominous date made its first appearance: preparatory staff work for the operation was to be "carried out in such a way that it may be put into effect at any time from 1.9.1939 onwards."[98]

Reports reaching Abwehr headquarters left no doubt that the international horizon was darkening day by day. On April 6 Great Britain and Poland signed a provisional pact of mutual assistance to be succeeded in due course by a permanent treaty, on April 7 Mussolini unleashed his troops against Albania, on April 13 Britain and France guaranteed the independence of Greece and Romania and on April 17 the Western powers and the Soviet Union opened negotiations on a joint pact.[99] The fronts of World War II were beginning to take shape.

But the last bridges between the blocs had yet to be burned when Hitler exacerbated the situation once more. On April 28 he mounted the speaker's rostrum in the Reichstag and dealt with the British "policy of encirclement" in a speech that was subtly compounded of scorn, polemics and prophecy—"probably the most brilliant oration he ever gave," according to one American listener.[100] He repudiated the Anglo-German naval treaty of 1935 and the German-Polish non-aggression pact of 1934. His pretext: Warsaw had concluded an agreement with Great Britain which would "under certain circumstances compel Poland . . . to take military action against Germany." This would entail a violation of the German-Polish pact, which he consequently regarded as "no longer in existence."[101]

Canaris realized only too well that Hitler had set the Reich on a collision course which might lead to war. But war, he remained firmly convinced, was the last thing Germany could afford. His stock phrase was that the firing of the first shot would spell "the end of Germany." It had been his profound belief ever since the alarming scene in the Chancellery that his personal mission was to prevent a war whose probable effect would be to destroy all that went by the name of Germany.

There was still a chance of halting this voyage to perdition, even now. Hitler had yet to decide on war and would only strike if the Western powers did not come to Poland's aid—or such was the implication of Hitler's April 3 directive. Canaris had been assured by Weizsäcker that the Führer "believed the Western powers would not abandon Poland, so we could not take action."[102] He therefore concluded that it was essential to stress Britain's striking power and determination—even, perhaps, to make the land of the rolled umbrella seem more pugnacious on paper than it was in reality.

Canaris's biographers have tended to believe that their hero was an admirer of Britain. The truth is different. His picture of Britain was still definitely tinged with the "Gott strafe England" sentiments of Grand Admiral von Tirpitz. The British had too often crossed his path in a hostile role. He had never forgotten the "disgrace" of the *Dresden* scuttling and preserved a vivid memory of Britain's part in the destruction of the Imperial Navy and British opposition to secret German naval rearmament during the 1920s. Even in the field of military intelligence, he saw little reason to admire the British.

Canaris did not share the worldwide respect enjoyed by Britain's Secret Intelligence Service (SIS). His verdict was that the SIS was politically in good shape but militarily useless, and the military capabilities of a secret service were all that weighed with a military man like Canaris. He told his friend Piekenbrock that Britain's military intelligence service was "appreciably worse than that of France, Russia, Japan, Italy or Poland" and that its personnel were "amateurs."[103]

The Admiral's judgement was coloured by experience of an operation in which the Abwehr's counterspionage group had contrived during autumn 1937 to infiltrate Organisation Z, as the SIS's anti-German network was called. His friend Protze, who had officially left the Abwehr and IIIF, continued to worm his way into the Dutch-based headquarters of Z, assisted by double agents and a degree of internal corruption not commonly found even in the world of espionage.[104] From then on, Canaris advised against any involvement with British intelligence. "It has been my experience that the Secret Service will reward you poorly," he told the anti-Nazi conspirator Fabian von Schlabrendorff. "They do not pay particularly well, believe me, and if they have the least suspicion they will not hesitate to betray you to me or my colleagues in the Reich Security Service."[105]

Canaris nonetheless cherished a respect for the British bulldog spirit, and he never wanted it displayed to better advantage than in spring 1939, when his object was to deter Hitler from going to war. A Nazi propaganda myth was already circulating to the effect that the British had been sapped of too much strength by consorting with Jews and plutocrats for them to dare stand up to the new Germany. On April 16 Weizsäcker noted that his boss Ribbentrop had "pronounced the current so-called British encircling movement to be empty propaganda . . . Not one British soldier [he said] would be called to arms if we militarily destroyed Poland today . . ."[106]

But Canaris resisted this view. "Survey of European Developments in Foreign Affairs," a document prepared for the military authorities by his Amtsgruppe, painted Germany's position in realistic colours and sternly warned against underestimating British resistance to the Third Reich. Circumstances had been transformed by a "radical shift in British foreign policy," and London was making serious efforts to isolate the Reich "by means of an appropriate political configuration of all anti-German forces."[107]

"Public sentiment [throughout the Balkans] is becoming increasingly hostile to Germany and/or National Socialism," stated the "Survey" on April 27. It should "not be ignored that concern over the possible loss of political independence and freedom has resulted, especially among parties of a left-wing tendency, in demonstrations of open hostility towards the two Axis powers." Reading between the lines of the "Survey," one could detect some oblique criticism of the Führer's headlong course, for instance: "The restoration of the Memelland to Germany is unlikely to help calm the political atmosphere . . ."[108]

Canaris repeatedly stressed to Keitel that "Britain would oppose us by all available means if we took drastic action against Poland and bloodshed resulted."[109] He also warned of Britain's (allegedly) strong position in the Balkans, though his assessments were often mistaken. For example, he urgently advised Keitel not to count on traditionally pro-German Bulgaria. Bulgaria was useless to Germany, he said, "because she would immediately be attacked by Romania and Turkey"—a prediction which betrayed his lack of contact with the Romanian and Turkish intelligence services.[110]

The Admiral told a visitor from England that he was striving to make it clear to Keitel and the Wehrmacht commanders that Britain had the capacity to plug the gaps in her war machine and catch up with Germany in a short space of time.[111] A few weeks later he informed Admiral Lais that Britain was already militarily equipped and prepared for war.[112]

But where was the use of submitting objective situation reports designed to convey the realities of the outside world to military commanders blinded by their faith in the Führer, or even to the Führer himself? Critical intelligence surveys had not been popular since the Sudeten crisis and were incapable of influencing Hitler's actions or beliefs, still less of modifying or guiding them. Even the Admiral's immediate superiors had difficulty in mustering the patience to listen to anything that conflicted with the official line. Canaris had never forgotten the barbarous Kristallnacht [Night of Broken Glass] on November 9, 1938, when concerted attacks were made on Jewish persons and property. He had drafted a detailed report for Keitel describing the vandalism of the Nazi mob and warning of its disastrous effect on international opinion, only to be angrily rebuffed by the OKW chief.[113] He had also, for some considerable time now, been submitting regular reports on the misdeeds of the Gestapo, but Keitel only read them with reluctance.[114]

Any other man would long ago have given up and resigned his post as Patzig had suggested in 1937. What stopped him? Undoubtedly an awareness of his important role, of wielding one of the gear-levers of power, of belonging to the wafer-thin crust of functionaries who helped to determine the course of the Fatherland and Reich. Nothing could have been more off-putting than the bleak prospect of life in retirement at the side of an uncaring wife and two children in whom he was fundamentally uninterested. He was fascinated by power and remained under its spell to his dying day.

But that cannot be the whole answer. Canaris was so much a prisoner of the illusions and temptations of nationalism and so attached to the conservative and authoritarian system of government that he could not stop serving a regime which he still regarded as the best in German history bar the monarchy. Closely linked with this world of sentiment was another factor. Whatever may now have separated him from Hitler and however dangerous he considered the Führer's policy after Prague, the nationalist in Canaris had no basic objection to a crusade against Poland.

It was one of the peculiarities of the German position in 1939 that almost all Germans—supporters and opponents of the regime alike—breathed a sigh of relief when Hitler concentrated the full force of his aggressive designs on Poland. The Germans had never secretly approved of his co-operation with the Polish military junta, nor had the regime succeeded in its laborious efforts to suppress anti-Polish revisionism at home. Thus, many unpolitical Germans were all the readier to approve the new anti-Polish campaign because "in contrast to the question of annexing the remainder of Czechoslovakia, a revision of the German-Polish frontiers [was] popular with the army, the public and most members of the opposition."[115]

No one demonstrated this more clearly than Groscurth, the passionate anti-Nazi, who noted after Hitler's abrogation of the Polish pact: "The Führer's great Reichstag speech has given the go-ahead to [our] work in Poland. A good thing and high time."[116] Back in February, Weizsäcker had called it "domestically the most popular act of German foreign policy to cut Poland down to the size that suits us, as a buffer against Russia."[117] Few people contemplated war, however, because they were all dominated by the miraculous hope that Hitler would again prevail without a shot being fired. Canaris, who was also swept along by this tide of instinctive nationalism, joined the anti-Polish campaign almost as a matter of course. We are presented with the depressing spectacle of agents being mobilized to prepare for war by a man who desired to avert it.

Early in May Canaris summoned the heads of Abwehr I and Abwehr II, Piekenbrock and Lahousen, and issued them with preliminary orders for the preparation of "Contingency White." Priority was given to the agents of Abwehr I, who were instructed by Colonel Piekenbrock to explore the strength, dispositions and operational objectives of the Polish armed forces. The Polish S network was alerted. At the same time, Colonel Günther Rowehl transferred his special squadron of high-altitude aircraft, German precursors of America's U-2 spy planes, to the Budapest area. From there they embarked on an immediate reconnaissance of the little-known Polish-Slovakian-Moravian frontier zone.[118] Piekenbrock's agents also compiled information about Polish troops.

Piekenbrock and Rowehl submitted regular reports on the progress of their work, and Lahousen was sometimes present when Canaris studied the aerial photographs through a large magnifying glass, but the results of Abwehr I's reconnaissance activities remained meagre. A 3rd Army Group staff officer noted on June 14 that "reliable information about Polish deployment and operational objectives is lacking," and

Lieutenant Colonel Kinzel of the General Staff's Foreign Armies East Section complained bitterly of the blank columns in his enemy-strength tables.[119]

This rankled with Canaris. General Staff intelligence officers were hypercritical enough in their attitude to Abwehr matters, and it embarrassed him to confront them empty-handed. Doggedly, he urged Lahousen to fill in the gaps left by Abwehr I.

A special task awaited Abwehr II. Its commando teams were instructed to take advantage of a blunder committed by the Polish General Staff when planning its dispositions. Instead of deploying the bulk of its forces far to the rear, beyond the rivers Vistula and San, where they could fight a delaying action, it had concentrated two thirds of them near the frontier. Motivated by a wish to defend Poland's main industrial areas,[120] this strategy tempted the German military leaders to try and smash the Polish armies at the first assault. And this, in turn, meant that Abwehr II was assigned the crucial task of forestalling any attempt by the enemy to destroy industrial installations and communications links of use to the advancing Germans.

Canaris and Lahousen considered it essential that Abwehr II should strike before the first shot had been fired. Abwehr personnel in civilian clothes were to sneak into Poland and be ready for action on the last day of peace. Their most difficult task would be to locate the demolition charges with which the Poles intended to destroy major installations. The Germans would have to be quicker than their Polish adversaries, and that called for daring and ingenuity. Lahousen and his officers possessed both.

In the forefront of their plans were two strategically vital communications links, the bridge over the Vistula at Dirschau [Tczew], near Danzig, and the Jablunkov Pass in the Beskid Mountains. The Dirschau bridge carried the entire rail traffic from Danzig and East Prussia to the Polish interior, while the tunnels of the Jablunkov Pass, with their twin tracks, canalized the rail traffic between East Germany, Southern Poland and the Balkans. The object was to occupy these key points in the Polish communications system by surprising and overpowering their defenders while peace still reigned. The schemes devised by Lahousen's officers took appropriately fantastic forms.

Abwehrstelle Königsberg produced a plan "to embark a detachment of between thirty and forty men in a barge and have it towed by the quietest available tug to a point three to five kilometres north of Dirschau." The men would then split up into groups and work their way towards the bridge, startle the Poles with a sudden burst of fire, "snatch prominent figures such as the battalion commander, the engineer officer and station supervisor from their private quarters and ruthlessly compel them to disclose where the detonator is situated."[121]

The task of the raiding party in the Beskids sounded relatively simple by comparison: "Mosty Station to be taken by the Jablunkov and Sillein [Žilina] combat groups. Blowing of the tunnel beneath the Jablunkov Pass to be prevented by destroying the detonating apparatus located there. Thereafter, occupy tunnel and remove explosive charge."[122]

Canaris approved these operational plans and the teams began to assemble at their jumping-off points. Lieutenant Hans-Albrecht Herzner of Abwehrstelle Breslau was ordered to recruit a detachment of twenty-four men from SA and Grenzpolizei personnel and await the prearranged signal in Northern Slovakia.[123] Abwehr headquarters later issued similar instructions to the Dirschau team.[124]

Once the first operation was under way, Lahousen's organization received a second assignment: sabotage far behind the enemy lines. Abwehrstelle Breslau allotted different tasks to each S detachment. The Hailos Group was instructed to "blow the bridge over the Wisloka at Dembica," the Hessler Group to "inflict extensive damage on Tarnow Station," the Neumann Group to "blow up track on the Krakow-Bochnia section." Yet another group was given a special mission: "Pätzold and Krüger, disguised in Polish uniform, will render the bridge over the Morzyslawski Canal, northeast of Konin, unserviceable by blowing three structural intersections."[125]

Lahousen eagerly took advantage of any opportunity to reinforce his sabotage groups. Visiting Hochdorf on June 11, he accepted Prince Henckel-Donnersmarck's offer of help from the entire forestry staff of his Polish estates, including "thirty ethnic German gamekeepers for special assignments," and shortly afterwards he was scouring the East German Abwehrstellen in quest of new S teams.[126] Before long he had thirteen hundred combat-ready helpers in Poland. The arms and explosives they needed were smuggled into Poland from Romania by means of Unternehmen [Operation] "Georgey."[127]

A third wave of Abwehr II agents infiltrated the German-Polish frontier with orders to foment an insurrection. Not unsurprisingly, Colonel Mel'nyk of the OUN and his Ukrainians were once more in evidence and ready to take a gamble on the Germans. The Carpatho-Ukrainian tragedy seemed forgotten, and anyone overanxious to revive its memory—like ex-Premier Vološin—was simply put on ice. An Abwehr II memorandum dated June 13, 1939, stated: "You are requested to remove Vološin and Revay, who . . . are engaging in futile political activity, from Berlin and pack them off to a health resort with instructions to desist from all political activity."[128]

The plans of the Abwehr's OUN allies received correspondingly greater encouragement. A Ukrainian Military Staff was to recruit a legion (projected strength thirteen hundred officers and twelve thousand men) for service alongside the Wehrmacht and, at the same time, to stage a revolt in Galicia. The code name of the Ukrainian operation was "Berg-Bauern-Hilfe" [Hill Farmers' Relief"].[129] "Arrangements for the organization of a Ukrainian revolt," wrote Lahousen, "will be made pursuant to instructions from Abwehr II by the II representative at Abwehrstelle VIII (Breslau). This will necessitate close co-operation with the Ukrainian Military Staff."[130] An Arbeitsstab [Planning Staff] Zips, based in Slovakia, was to pass on the Ukrainian agents required to lead this insurrection.[131]

The army of agents and saboteurs expanded week by week, and Lahousen's reports to Canaris became increasingly confident. "The initiation of the projected sabotage, protective and combat operations," he wrote on July 3, "will automatically ensue on the first military action against Poland, of which news should quickly spread there. In view of the large number of agents to be informed and the attendant risk of provocation and betrayal, it is not recommended that they be initiated by disguised instructions broadcast over the German radio."[132]

Canaris was impressed. Lahousen's tidings of success whetted his imagination and satisfied his craving for the unusual. Secret agents with blackened faces and foreign uniforms, demolition teams creeping up on bridges guarded by unsuspecting sentries, couriers in the night, insurrections behind the enemy lines—that was the world he loved and understood. He became so thoroughly engrossed in the plans and operations of his Amtsgruppe that he scarcely noticed his transformation into a pacemaker for war.

The truth was not brought home to him until late in July, when he received a visit from SS-Standartenführer Heinz Jost, head of the SD's foreign intelligence service, who announced that the Führer had given orders for the Abwehr to assist in carrying out an "operation" for the Reichsführer-SS. Jost detailed his requirements, which included 150 Polish uniforms, the weapons and paybooks to go with them, and 364 men who would be temporarily attached to the SD.[133] The SD man did not explain their function, merely saying that it was highly classified and could not be divulged.

The Admiral was strangely disconcerted by Jost's visit. There was nothing so sinister about his request for a few Polish uniforms—after all, Canaris himself was violating international law by disguising agents as Polish soldiers and sending them into foreign territory on illegal missions—and yet . . . Being opposed to war, he must instinctively have sensed that the SD was planning something calculated to make war inevitable. Although he had no firm knowledge of its nature at this stage, he became certain within a few days that Heydrich's secret service was planning to provoke a conflict.

Lahousen later claimed that the Abwehr authorities "made every possible conjecture about this mysterious procurement of Polish uniforms" but did not come to the right conclusion.[134] Put like that, his statement is definitely inaccurate. On July 22 Canaris confided to his Italian colleague Lais that "in the Danzig gamble" there was a risk of provocation by Hitler, who had "entrusted the party police with the whole of the clandestine activity connected with it." Only a week before the outbreak of war Hitler was credited by Oster's friends or Oster himself with the following apocryphal remark: "I'll get a few companies in Polish uniform to attack in Upper Silesia or the Protectorate. I couldn't care a damn if the world is taken in or not."[135] Canaris guessed the SD's intentions, though he did not have detailed knowledge of them.

He was also unaware that Lieutenant General von Manstein, Chief of Staff of Army Group South, which was earmarked for the Polish campaign, had unwittingly set the SD scheme in motion. It had occurred to Manstein that the Germans would find it easier to gain possession of the Upper Silesian industrial belt if they launched a surprise attack with three battalions of shock troops dressed in Polish uniforms.[136] Hitler turned him down, but Heydrich heard of the proposal and modified it, converting a suspect military operation into a war crime— the first in the Third Reich's history.

Heydrich's plan was as follows. On the eve of the German invasion, SD men disguised as Polish troops and irregulars would stage frontier incidents and attacks on fellow SD men posing as frontier guards along the German-Polish border. The fake Poles were to occupy the German radio station at Gleiwitz for long enough to broadcast some anti-German propaganda slogans, attack the forestry station at Pitschen, near the frontier, and destroy the Hochlinden customs post between Gleiwitz and Ratibor.[137] Concentration camp mortuaries would furnish corpses to be left behind at the scene of the skirmish so that everything looked absolutely authentic. "Actual proof of Polish attacks is essential," Heydrich insisted, "both for the foreign press and for German propaganda."[138]

Jost's secretive attitude not only alerted Canaris but excited his professional jealousy. Fearing that the SD was planning to take over the Abwehr's Polish operations as well, for example the Dirschau bridge attack, he delayed issuing the SD with Polish uniforms and approached Keitel in an attempt to thwart Heydrich's plans.

But the OKW chief was only half in the picture as usual. He told Canaris that, although he set no store by "such ventures," the Führer's order could not be countermanded. He did, however, give the Admiral some advice on "how to dodge it." Keitel: "Say you don't have any Polish uniforms at all. You can simply say you don't have any, and that'll settle the matter."[139] Keitel's suggestion could hardly have been more naive because the SD was well aware that Abwehr agents sometimes turned out in Polish uniforms. All Canaris could do was persuade his superior not to allow any SD encroachments on the Abwehr's domain. "Regarding Dirschau," he noted, "he [Keitel] has decided that the operation shall only be carried out by the Army."[140]

Jost's manner demonstrated to Canaris how close the Reich already was to the brink of war. Torn between a realistic assessment of the situation and vestiges of his old faith in Hitler, the Admiral had for too long assumed that Hitler would keep the peace provided the Western powers seemed certain to intervene militarily on Poland's side. Weizsäcker's reports from Hitler's immediate entourage had strengthened his belief that, temperamental outbursts notwithstanding, the Führer was still open to persuasion.

For weeks, therefore, Canaris believed that a genuine risk of war stemmed from two sources only: from Poland and from what he termed "extremist sections of the party." The Amtsgruppe's "Survey" of June 26 stated: "Polish chauvinism, which dominates the entire nation, not excluding top military circles, has not diminished in strength. The result is that absolutely no basis exists for a convergence of the Polish and German viewpoints in respect of the free city of Danzig."[141] Canaris duly considered it less and less likely that the Danzig question could be resolved by peaceful means.

Even more dangerous than Polish obduracy, it seemed to him, were the machinations of Nazi extremists such as Ribbentrop, Himmler, Propaganda Minister Goebbels and Gauleiter Forster of Danzig. On July 22 he opined that the NSDAP wanted war and that (according to an Italian Foreign Office summary of his views) there was "a strong possibility that the Führer may be talked into an act of violence by extremist elements."[142] Hitler, he said, was particularly vulnerable to such influence because, being ill informed by Göring and Keitel, he overestimated the Wehrmacht's effectiveness and harboured illusions about the brevity of a war against Poland.[143]

Canaris concluded that nothing must be done to drive Hitler into the arms of the "extremists." Noisy British opposition no longer suited his scheme of things. He even feared that precipitate action by Britain might induce the Führer to provoke a conflict. In company with his friend Weizsäcker, Canaris pursued a complicated game designed, on the one hand, to encourage the British to demonstrate their readiness to fight and, on the other, to dissuade them from any show of aggression which might evoke a warlike response from Hitler.

It can scarcely have overjoyed him that German anti-Nazis were now visiting England on their own initiative and trying to prod the British Government into a vigorous show of strength. In July Lieutenant Colonel Count Gerhard Schwerin, anti-Nazi head of the England/America group of the Foreign Armies West Section, met leading members of the British secret service by arrangement with Major Kenneth Strong, Britain's deputy military attaché in Berlin, and the Hamburg insurance salesman Otto Hübener, an Oster associate who was to play a fateful role in the Abwehr's future history.[144] At a meeting on July 14 in the London home of Admiral John Godfrey, head of British naval intelligence, Count Schwerin detailed the steps Britain might take to deter Hitler from attacking Poland. These included dispatching a battle squadron to the Baltic, transferring two fully equipped divisions and a group of heavy bombers to France and inviting Winston Churchill to join the Chamberlain government.[145]

The German Abwehr chief was little consoled by the fact that Schwerin brought him friendly greetings from one of his British hosts, Colonel Stewart Menzies, who had crossed swords with Canaris in Spain during World War I and was shortly to become his rival as head of the SIS from November 1939 onwards.[146] Canaris could not have failed to repudiate Schwerin's proposals. Weizsäcker was currently trying to dissuade the Führer and his Foreign Minister from sending a German naval squadron to visit Danzig at the end of the month.[147] One clash between German and British naval forces in the Baltic, and the die would have been cast.

No wonder the head of the Italian naval intelligence service noted on July 22 that Canaris had "given it as his firm belief that Britain may aggravate the dispute by provoking incidents in Danzig."[148] This was not the sort of British reaction calculated to exert a moderating influence on Hitler. Canaris agreed with Weizsäcker that only stern but *covert* warnings from the British would deter the Führer from going to war.

But what if the "extremists" in Hitler's entourage gained the upper hand? In Canaris's view, there was still one power and one threat that might stay the dictator's hand. The name of that power was Russia, and the threat was a war on two fronts. Even if Hitler let himself be talked into risking a conflict with the Western powers, he would surely be alarmed by the prospect of an embroilment with the Soviet Union as well—by the very same disastrous predicament that had once sealed the fate of imperial Germany. And Hitler firmly counted on Soviet opposition, as did his generals. "Contingency White" presupposed that the Polish military authorities would "broadly speaking fight to gain time in the hope of prompt military assistance from Russia."[149]

Hitler had every reason to include Soviet intervention in his calculations. For weeks now, British and French diplomats had been negotiating a mutual assistance pact with the Kremlin, and on July 24 the three governments agreed to enter upon the staff talks phase. This began on August 1.[150] Canaris had no doubt that the ill-assorted partners would come to terms. He was already plying friends and colleagues with esti-

mates of the other side's steadily mounting strength. Franco-British air
power would shortly be augmented by three thousand Soviet warplanes,
quite apart from the fact that the U.S.A. had "guaranteed an American
contribution of five thousand fully equipped aircraft."[151]

Canaris was all the harder hit by the unexpected coup which enabled Hitler to seize the diplomatic initiative—a pact between the
Brownshirts and the Reds. On August 6 Weizsäcker noted in his diary:
"We are stepping up the pressure in Moscow."[152] Four days later the
Kremlin intimated to Berlin that the Soviet Government was prepared
for wide-ranging talks on the political situation, and from then on the
pace of events quickened. On August 12 Hitler informed Moscow that
he had resolved on an immediate settlement of all matters outstanding
between the Reich and the U.S.S.R. On August 16 the German Ambassador in Moscow reported that Foreign Minister Molotov had proposed
the conclusion of a non-aggression pact between their two countries. He
was instructed by return to tell Molotov that the Führer accepted his
proposal and recommended that talks be held in Moscow.[153]

The international situation had radically altered within a few days.
Hitler was in a radiant mood. He believed that he at last had a
stranglehold on his enemies—indeed, he seriously imagined that the
London and Paris cabinets would not survive the signing of a German-
Soviet pact. Weizsäcker's reports to Canaris made it clear that the
"hawks" had almost won the day. On August 13 he wrote: "Ribbentrop
guarantees British and French neutrality if we inflict crushing blows on
the Poles in the first three days, as he firmly believes we shall."[154]

This information prompted Canaris to make yet another effort to
halt the slide into war. He feverishly sought new allies in his campaign
against the warmongers, took friends and enemies, Germans and foreigners, into his confidence and finally found an ally in Fascist Italy.

Bound to the Third Reich since May 23, 1939, by the outwardly
indissoluble "Pact of Steel," Italy had been relying on Hitler not to
drag her into a precipitate military venture. The Axis partners had mutually pledged that three years of peace must elapse before they embarked on an era of military conquest. Belatedly but not too late,
Mussolini and Foreign Minister Ciano realized that the Führer was
bent on war. Canaris knew from his contacts in the Italian secret service that Rome had turned wary and was toying with the idea of a quick
descent from Hitler's war chariot. To gain an exact idea of Germany's
intentions Ciano invited himself to Schloss Fuschl, Ribbentrop's summer residence near Salzburg, on August 11.[155]

Canaris had decided to provoke a breach between the Italians and
Hitler by feeding them some unwelcome pieces of information. His
basic idea, as he frankly told them, was: "Hitler may yet be dissuaded
from war if the Italian Government formally conveys that it will not

make common cause with him."[156] A visit to Ribbentrop at Fuschl on August 10 had satisfied Canaris that the Foreign Minister's war plans were entirely based on the assumption that Italy would join in, so his object was to destroy this article of faith.[157]

Ribbentrop declared over the family dinner table that Italian sea power could prove an exceptional threat to the British. The former U-boat captain and Mediterranean voyager listened calmly as Hitler's neurotic paladin and armchair strategist described how the Italians would close the Strait of Gibraltar with a hundred submarines and deny the Royal Navy access. Canaris made no comment until he was driving back to the airport. Then he grinned at one of his companions and said, "Listen, if the great Mediterranean naval battle does come off, we'll sit there on a raft and watch the 'Beefs' cut the 'Italianos' to pieces."[158]

Having laid his first mine, Canaris heard that the two Foreign Ministers had clashed at Fuschl and that Ciano had requested a clarificatory interview with Hitler. On August 12 he called on his friend Roatta, who was now the Italian military attaché in Berlin, and warned him of Germany's warlike intentions.'[159] It was an ironical moment for both men. Having assisted at the birth of the Axis, they now agreed to kill it in the interests of peace.

Canaris described the talks between Ciano and Ribbentrop, strongly hinting that the choice between war and peace depended on Italy. Roatta asked him to elaborate. Canaris: "Ribbentrop will ask if Italy is ready to enter the war. Ciano will say no." Roatta: "Who told you that?" Canaris: "It's my own idea. We aren't ready for a general war either."[160]

Only two days after Ciano left Germany, unreassured by his talks with Hitler, Canaris paid another call on Roatta. The Abwehr chief had some bad news: "The Führer not only intends to annex Danzig, he plans to destroy Poland as well. Military operations will start in about two weeks time."[161] Roatta was so impressed that he promptly reported this piece of hearsay to the Italian chargé d'affaires, Count Massimo Magistrati, who lost no time in writing a report and handing it to the Rome courier. Canaris had expressly advised against sending a telegram for fear that it might be intercepted and deciphered. Magistrati, who knew the risk Canaris was running, added a marginal note: "On no account mention the name of Admiral . . ."[162]

Canaris took advantage of the Italians' aversion to war, which he himself had helped to foster, by spreading anti-Italian pessimism in the German camp. Wherever the Admiral went he dropped hints that Italy was not to be trusted and that the "Italianos" were in the process of abandoning the Germans as they had in 1914. He was always on hand with fresh tidings of doom, for instance, that Abwehrstelle Vienna had just reported "that the King of Italy had told [ex-] King Alfonso [of Spain] a few days ago that he would under no circumstances sign a mobilization order if Mussolini submitted one."[163]

This not only annoyed Ribbentrop and the advocates of a collision course but touched Keitel on the raw. He was vain enough to feel misled by his Führer, who had only just assured him that Italy would definitely come in. Canaris demonstrated to him at an interview on August 17 how ill informed he was. "I [Canaris] replied that I considered this out of the question in view of the Ciano-Ribbentrop discussion, which I again described in detail. He [Keitel] said that the Führer had told him the contrary. It therefore followed from my remarks that the Führer did not tell him—Keitel—everything."[164]

Keitel was so annoyed that Canaris had renewed hopes of enlisting him against the warmongers. He knew that the general sometimes doubted the wisdom of Hitler's policy. He had, after all, gone to Hitler a few weeks earlier and reported that his senior military commanders were extremely concerned at the Wehrmacht's unpreparedness for war, primarily because of the possibility of a war on two fronts. Although Hitler had brushed this aside, Canaris could not believe that the OKW chief had swallowed all his doubts and misgivings.[165]

He made repeated attempts to convince Keitel how disastrous Germany's position would be in the event of a war with the Western powers. Keitel, who disliked such talk, desperately resisted the Admiral's arguments. There would be no war with the Western powers, he protested—the British would never come to Poland's aid. "I tried to rebut this view," wrote Canaris, "telling him that the British would undoubtedly impose an immediate blockade and destroy our merchant shipping. Keitel said that this did not matter unduly as we would get oil from Romania. I replied that this was not the decisive factor and that we should not be able to withstand a blockade indefinitely."[166]

The argument raged to and fro. Canaris asserted that the British would open fire if the Germans took military action against Poland. Keitel disputed this. Canaris declared that the consequences of economic warfare would be insupportable from Germany's point of view. Keitel disputed this too. Canaris claimed that the Germans could only resist a British blockade "with meagre resources" and quoted a recent report that "we can only dispatch ten U-boats to the Atlantic."[167]

Disheartening as these talks with Keitel were, Canaris persevered in his belief that the OKW chief was open to persuasion. He enlisted other people to put pressure on him. These included Major General Thomas, head of the OKW's Military Economics Staff, who adduced overwhelming statistical evidence of the inferiority of Germany's long-term war potential, and other OKW officers who urged their chief to hold a war game which would convince Hitler how unequal the Reich

9. and 10. The leaders of the Spartacus group, Rosa Luxemburg and Karl Liebknecht, murdered by "Volunteer Corps" officers in January 1919. Canaris's role in the escape of the murderers is still in dispute. (*Bildarchiv Preussischer Kulturbesitz, Berlin*)

1. Soldiers of the Ehrhardt Naval Brigade during the Kapp Putsch. (*Bildarchiv Preussischer Kulturbesitz, Berlin*)

2. Canaris's Republican boss, Reichswehr Minister Gustav Noske. (*Bildarchiv Preussischer Kulturbesitz, Berlin*)

3. Republican soldiers during the Kapp Putsch in Berlin, 1920. The sign reads: "Halt. Anyone proceeding farther will be shot." (*Bildarchiv Preussischer Kultur-besitz, Berlin*)

14. Canaris as executive officer on board the battleship *Schlesien*, with his commander Captain Max Bastian. *(Foto-Drüppel, Wilhelmshaven)*

15. Canaris (second from left) as commander of the *Schlesien* in 1934. *(Ullstein Bilderdienst, Berlin)*

16. Canaris's headquarters on the Tirpitz-Ufer in Berlin. *(Bildarchiv Preussischer Kulturbesitz, Berlin)*

17. Canaris with SS Lieutenant General Reinhard Heydrich, Chief of the Security Police and the Security Service, at a meeting of Armed Forces and SS officers in Berlin during 1936. (*Süddeutscher Verlag Bilderdienst, München*)

18. Hitler chats with his commanders in chief—Göring, Blomberg, Raeder and Fritsch—during a Berlin parade held to mark his forty-eighth birthday in 1937. *(Süddeutscher Verlag Bilderdienst, München)*

19. Canaris with Spain's General Moscardo *(Süddeutscher Verlag Bilderdienst, München)*

20. Franco with Canaris's friend General Kindelán bidding farewell to the German Condor Legion in 1939. *(Süddeutscher Verlag Bilderdienst, München)*

was to a simultaneous war with Poland and the Western powers.[168] But Keitel refused to associate himself with any more criticism and sought refuge in the abstruse theory with which he evaded all his tempters: Poland would climb down "when she sees we're in earnest."[169]

News of the German-Soviet negotiations made Keitel wholly unapproachable. Pedantically, he now insisted on unquestioning compliance with his orders, and all of them were directed towards a single end: war. The military came to heel, Canaris included. On August 12, after the regular morning conference with his heads of section, he placed the Amtsgruppe on a full alert. Ausland/Abwehr was now making final preparations for war.[170]

On August 15 Canaris received orders to set his K and S units in motion and send them across the German-Polish frontier.[171] All the Abwehr's combat teams moved out with the exception of the Ukrainians —Germany's second betrayal of her Ukrainian allies, this time committed for the Russians' sake, though Lahousen had no inkling of this when he entered the latest directive in Abwehr II's official diary on August 18: "Arms for the Ukrainian insurrectionary movement are excluded from conveyance across the frontier."[172]

The previous day Lahousen had been summoned to OKW Abteilung L, where Colonel Warlimont insisted that the SD should be issued with its promised items of Polish equipment.[173] On August 19 two trucks from Abwehrstelle Breslau set off under the command of Sergeant Kutschke, whose orders were to deliver a batch of Polish uniforms and accoutrements to SS-Obersturmbannführer Rату of the SD.[174] Lieutenant Colonel von Frankenberg, Oster's departmental adviser on mobilization measures and the reinforcement of frontier posts, was simultaneously ticking off a list of the 364 Abwehr men who were to participate in Heydrich's lethal charade.[175]

The Wehrmacht evacuated the area round Hochlinden, where the SD operation was to take place. At the SD Leadership Training School in Bernau, SS-Oberführer Mehlhorn rehearsed night attacks and Polish words of command with personnel on loan from the Abwehr and members of the Upper Silesian SS regiments. Then he issued his men with arms, ammunition and clothing—one Polish uniform, one carbine and thirty rounds each. On August 20 Mehlhorn assembled them all in the school's lecture hall and briefed them on what he termed a "frontier mission."[176]

Then the men set off in closed trucks for their assembly areas, where they were awaited by Mehlhorn's subordinates: SS-Oberführer Rasch, who was to lead the attack on Pitschen forestry station; SS-Obersturmbannführer Hellwig, whose assault detachment would storm Hochlinden from the Polish side; and SS-Standartenführer Trummler, who was to command the "defenders" there. Mehlhorn, whose task was to co-ordinate the mock battle between the attackers and defenders, reported to Heydrich on August 22 that his teams were ready for action.[177]

It was a day Canaris would never forget. The day before, August 21, OKW had been instructed that all Amtsgruppenchefs were to assemble at noon next day for a conference with Hitler at the Berghof. On reaching the Führer's mountain retreat, Canaris saw that the others present comprised almost every senior general and admiral in the Wehrmacht, including army group and air fleet commanders and their chiefs of staff. Göring and Ribbentrop had also turned up. At Hitler's special insistence, every one was wearing civilian clothes.[178]

Then the dictator appeared. He welcomed his guests and invited them to join him for refreshments on the spacious terrace. When a storm gathered, they all withdrew to his study. Then the Führer spoke. "I have called you together," he began, "to give you a picture of the political situation so that you may have an insight into the various factors on which I have based my decision to act."[179] The longer he spoke the more vehement his tone became. Harsh and intolerant, aggressive and fanatical, the words poured forth until no one in the room could fail to grasp the truth. Here was a man who was burning his last boats behind him, obsessed with a single desire and intention: to make war on Poland.

Canaris slowly fished out a pad and pencil, bemused by Hitler's revelations. Then he began to make notes. He only caught scraps of what was said. "Political situation favourable to us: in the Mediterranean, rivalry between Italy, France and Britain; in the Far East, tension between Japan and Britain; in the East, tension . . . Britain in extreme danger . . . France's position has also deteriorated . . . Not all of these favourable circumstances will obtain in two to three years' time. Nobody can tell how long I shall live. Therefore, better a showdown now . . . Our relationship with Poland has become intolerable . . . We must shoulder this risk with ruthless determination."[180]

And always he returned to castigate his critics and opponents. "It is nonsense to say that Britain wants to wage a long war . . . The enemy continued to hope that Russia would emerge as our enemy after the conquest of Poland. The enemy reckoned without my strength of purpose. Our enemies are little worms . . . I brought about the change towards Russia by degrees . . . Proposal for a non-aggression pact . . . Von Ribbentrop will conclude this treaty the day after tomorrow. Now I have Poland where I wanted her . . . My only fear is that some dirty dog will submit an arbitration plan at the last moment."[181]

Hitler broke off and invited his military commanders to a brief lunch, after which he continued in an even more intolerant vein. Canaris's pencil began to speed across the paper again. "The most iron determination on our part . . . A life-or-death struggle . . . A long period of peace would do us no good. We have the better men . . . The destruction of Poland comes first. Our object is to eliminate vital forces, not to reach a definite line . . . I shall supply a propagandist reason for starting the war, plausible or not . . . Close your hearts to pity. Act brutally. Eighty million people must obtain their due. The stronger side is always in the right."[182]

Exhausted, the orator paused. He fixed his audience with an unwavering stare, then spoke his final words: "I have done my duty. Now do yours."[183] None of the generals moved. They stood there as though paralysed. Nobody uttered a word of remonstrance against the Führer's warlike speech—not one general cast doubt on his mixture of self-delusion, megalomania and the will to destroy. All that could be heard was the voice of Commander in Chief von Brauchitsch addressing his army group commanders and their chiefs of staff: "Gentlemen, return to your posts as soon as possible!"[184]

Canaris left the Berghof appalled. Hitler's speech had shattered any lingering illusions he may still have had about the man. He now realized that war was inevitable, but it would have been unlike him to abandon all hope that a miracle was still lurking in some hidden corner. He worked his notes into a digest of the Führer's remarks and presented it to a meeting of his departmental chiefs next day.

During the Amtsgruppe conference of August 23 he acquainted his subordinates with the content and purpose of Hitler's address. "In the Führer's view," Lahousen noted, "Germany's chances of resolving the eastern questions are extremely good. The Führer believes that the Western powers will not intervene . . . The time to strike has come."[185] Canaris further intimated that the German units deployed against Poland would be ordered to attack on August 26 or 27. The Amtsgruppe must switch to "a wartime footing" forthwith.[186]

As soon as his group heads and some of his heads of section had dispersed, Canaris read out the crucial passages in Hitler's speech to his closest colleagues. Only then did they notice the extent of his despair. "He was still utterly horrified," writes Gisevius, who describes the scene. "His voice trembled as he read. Canaris was acutely aware that he had witnessed something monstrous."[187] Unlike Gisevius, Oster was fascinated by the bellicose and malevolent tone of Hitler's remarks. They sounded like just the evidence he needed to spur the regime's opponents into a peace-preserving *coup d'état*.

Oster had been labouring for weeks under the absence of any basis for a move against Hitler. He had visited one dissident general after another, forged links with new opponents of the Führer and worked out plans for a military take-over, but no general was prepared to act. Now, Canaris's record of Hitler's speech provided him with a slender chance.

If the text could be fed to the British, perhaps in an even starker and cruder version, they ought to react so sharply and unmask the dictator so completely that even his generals would summon up the courage to move against their fallen demigod.

Oster got Canaris to give him a copy of his transcript of Hitler's speech—for his "collection," as he put it.[188] What happened to this copy is uncertain, but we do know that Oster and his confederates produced a version of it which bore only a remote resemblance to the original. Canaris's text was rewritten and, in effect, falsified by being translated into a sort of gangster's argot complete with freshly minted quotations.[189]

This new version teemed with "cretins and semi-imbeciles," as Hitler was reputed to have called the West European leaders, with "tired and greedy nations" (another reference to the West Europeans), with "a feeble-minded king and a treacherous rogue of a crown prince" (the Italian monarchy), with a "corrupt slave to his sexual urges" (the King of Romania) and a "weak, corrupt and indecisive emperor" (to wit, Hirohito). Other quotations were equally fictitious: "After Stalin's death—he is gravely ill—we shall smash the Soviet Union. Then will come the dawn of German world supremacy . . . Be merciless, act more swiftly and brutally than the others. The citizens of Europe must quake with horror."[190]

This revamping of Hitler's speech was a desperate step which only served to show how isolated his opponents were. Hermann Maas, an anti-Nazi and former Social Democratic youth leader, volunteered to pass it to the U.S. journalist Louis P. Lochner, who on August 25 transmitted it to a British Embassy official in Berlin. Lochner reported that the transcript came from a German staff officer "who had it from a general present at the [Berghof] meeting." The general had been shocked and hoped that "the madman" would be restrained by Britain,[191] but the transcript, which was on plain paper and unsigned, failed to impress its recipients.

Canaris, who would hardly have sanctioned the Oster group's initiative, awaited the hour of decision in a mood of apathy. He knew that Hitler would give the order to attack any day now. Although the dictator was still uncertain whether Britain and France would come to Poland's aid, his mind was made up. The hours went by, and still Canaris waited tensely for a call from the Chancellery. The German forces had completed their deployment along the Polish frontier. All that remained was to unleash them.

At 4:05 P.M. on August 25 Canaris received the fateful order from Keitel. Lahousen's diary entry read: "Group heads informed of the Führer's command, Ia and the entire group: Y day is 26.8.39."[192] This meant, in clear, that the Wehrmacht would commence operations against Poland on the morning of August 26. From now on, the telephones at the Tirpitz-Ufer headquarters were in permanent use. Prearranged code words were transmitted and the Abwehr's sabotage and combat teams left their bases. Heydrich's *provocateurs* moved off too.

Then, quite suddenly, there occurred the miracle which Canaris had somehow been expecting: Hitler's decision was opposed by the Italians. Canaris's efforts had borne fruit after all. Shortly after 6 P.M. Ambassador Attolico called at the Chancellery and handed Hitler a message from Mussolini informing him that Italy could render Germany no military assistance in a war against Poland. This was the Führer's second bombshell of the afternoon. A few minutes earlier news had reached him that Britain and Poland had concluded a long-term military pact.[193] The dictator was on the verge of a nervous breakdown.

He sent for Keitel and conferred with him. "Stop everything at once," he decreed, "Get Brauchitsch immediately I need time to negotiate."[194] The OKW chief could not believe his ears. Deployment was complete and units were already moving into position for a dawn assault—how could such a vast war machine be brought to a standstill? Spurred on by Hitler, Keitel dashed to a telephone—it was now 6:30 P.M.—and informed the Army commander in chief as follows: "Operation 'White,' already in progress, will be halted at 2030 because of changed political circumstances."[195]

At that very moment, still unaware of what had happened, three members of the resistance were on their way to enlist Canaris in a final attempt to avert war. General Thomas, former Reichsbank president Schacht and Gisevius had devised an audacious plan to compel the military authorities to rise against Hitler. They planned to call on Brauchitsch and his Chief of Staff, Halder, to launch a *coup d'état*, threatening that records of all their conspiratorial discussions would be turned over to the Gestapo if they refused. Canaris's role was to arrange an interview between the trio and Halder.[196]

The three men had just reached Abwehr headquarters when news came that the order to invade had been cancelled. Thomas, Gisevius and Schacht were greeted by a sea of exultant faces. Peace seemed to be assured and Hitler's reputation ruined. "A supreme commander who rescinded so definite an order, who changed his mind on the question of war and peace from one moment to the next" appeared to them to be "done for."[197] "He'll never recover from this blow," Canaris exclaimed. "Peace has been preserved for the next twenty years . . ."[198]

Even the wary Oster ("The Führer's finished!") was so optimistic that it never occurred to him to exploit Hitler's greatest fit of political weakness since 1933 by attacking the Nazi regime.[199] Almost all the men in Canaris's office felt relieved and none of them cared to draw any practical conclusions from the latest development. Canaris, too, basked in the mistaken belief that peace and the Reich were safe at last.

Lahousen jolted him out of these rosy daydreams by reporting that not all the Abwehr's combat teams had returned from Polish territory. In particular, radio contact had been lost with Lieutenant Herzner's group, whose task was to occupy the Jablunkov Pass tunnel. Lahousen feared that Herzner was roaming through Polish territory in ignorance that the attack on Poland had been cancelled. Canaris had a sinister presentiment. What if Abwehr personnel and Polish soldiers fired on each other and provoked the war that Hitler had just called off?

A similar situation had arisen with Heydrich's men. A gun-battle had developed between Hellwig's fake Poles and Trummler's mock defenders at Hochlinden.[200] There, Germans had fired on Germans, but in the Abwehr's case Germans might fire on Poles and spark off a grave international crisis. Canaris told the head of Abwehr II to institute an urgent search for Herzner's group. He had to be found before an accident occurred. Lahousen warned Abwehrstelle Breslau, which alerted its outstations in northern Slovakia and the Striegau communications centre, whose radio operators vainly tried to contact the missing detachment.[201]

On the morning of August 26 Canaris's worst fears seemed to have been realized. Lahousen noted: "Captain Ernst zu Eikern reports that Permanent Way Team No. 20 in Cadca reported heavy rifle fire from the Jablunkov Pass direction at 4:45 A.M. Ast VIII assumes its source to be a combat team commanded by Reserve Lieutenant Herzner, which is out of contact."[202] Soon afterwards the Striegau communications centre finally got through to Herzner. At 11:45 A.M. it reported: "Lieutenant Herzner still in Poland. Tunnel intact. Two wounded."[203]

In fact, Herzner had hours earlier sent a written message to VIII Army Corps HQ which proved to be the first dispatch of World War II. Herzner wrote: "26.8.39. 3:55 A.M., captured Mosty Station with Corporal Jung and twelve men of the Jablunkov combat team. Attack on station by tunnel garrison repelled."[204] An attempt to enter the tunnel with a locomotive failed. Soon afterwards Herzner received orders from 7th Division, which was deployed near the frontier, to fight his way westwards to the Slovakian border. When Herzner and his men tried to withdraw, however, they ran into some members of the Polish rural constabulary, who were now on the alert. The Poles fanned out to bar their route to the frontier, and it was not until 1:30 P.M. that the Germans reached the Slovakian border at Rakowa, still under Polish fire.[205]

Back in Berlin, Canaris anxiously followed the withdrawal of Herzner and his men by telephone. He was just breathing a sigh of relief when he heard that the Jablunkov combat team was "provisionally" to remain in Poland on orders from Keitel.[206] The Admiral pricked up his ears. Was war on the cards after all? Uneasily, Lahousen made the following note in Abwehr II's diary: "Mobilization continues because it is still within the bounds of possibility that negotiations will break down and that Germany's demands will be met by other means."[207]

These "negotiations" were, of course, simply an attempt by Hitler to detach the British from their Polish allies and reduce the dangers of a German attack on Poland. His chances of success were fair because the Chamberlain cabinet had never altogether renounced the concept of appeasement. The conclusion of the German-Soviet non-aggression pact on August 23, coupled with Poland's refusal to exchange a single word with Germany on the subject of Danzig's future, had alarmed the British. Not many of them felt like "dying for Danzig," as the popular saying went.

Lord Halifax himself told the Polish Ambassador that "the Polish Government would make a great mistake if they sought to adopt a position in which discussion of peaceful modifications in the status of Danzig was ruled out."[208] No one had a keener ear for discord among allies than Hitler, who promptly tried to drive a wedge between the ill-assorted partners by making outwardly moderate overtures whose rejection by Poland was bound to exacerbate the crisis in the allied camp. He announced fresh proposals for a Danzig settlement and urged the British to recommend them to their reluctant friends in Warsaw. Then he waited.

But Hitler had forgotten how to wait. His shrewd and subtle gambits were more and more often spoilt by a wanton urge for destruction, a fierce desire to have "his" war at last. Describing the atmosphere at the Chancellery, Weizsäcker wrote: "During the day there is a fluctuation between extreme friendship for Britain and war *à tout prix*. Late at night the mood is wholly in favour of war again: Poland will be finished in two months, then we shall have a grand peace conference with the Western powers."[209] Meanwhile, Hitler's mistaken belief that Britain would back out became a near certainty.

Even Abwehr agents succumbed to this wishful thinking, and many of their reports predicted that the British and French would desert. On August 26 a "reliable Abwehr III V-Mann" reported the French general Alphonse Georges as stating that "he was extremely doubtful if Britain would come in over Poland,"[210] and on August 29 it was learned "from a reliable source that Warsaw is being urged to adopt a more compliant attitude by the British and French governments"—a report quoted in the Amtsgruppe's "foreign and politico-military intelligence" survey.[211] Yet another Abwehr III report stated: "A markedly confident tone prevails in foreign stock exchanges with regard to the preservation of peace."[212]

Only a few Abwehr I agents correctly reported that Britain was preparing for war. Report timed 10 P.M. on August 30: "An informant who today visited approximately thirty industrial firms twenty miles from London is said to have been greatly surprised by the extensive preparations made there. The political situation is regarded as easier, but not appreciably so because great importance is attached to the opposition of Halifax and Eden. Halifax and Eden are calling for firm decisions or war."[213] Next day came another report: "Well-connected informant reports American circles in England as believing that British moves in the past few days are solely a way of gaining time for the proper implementation of mob[ilization] measures."[214]

Canaris needed all his unerring powers of persuasion to pick his way through this maze of conflicting reports and analyses. Whatever the Amtsgruppe's agents in Britain reported, nothing could wean him from his belief that the British would strike as soon as the Germans invaded Poland. He implored Weizsäcker not to abandon the fight for peace and to do his utmost to prevent Hitler from issuing the order to attack.

But Canaris and Weizsäcker had already lost the battle. Looking back, Weizsäcker wrote: "Quite obviously, a firm decision to wage war at all costs had been made by the night of August 30. I believe that Ribbentrop's advice clinched matters, because he severed all the links that still existed."[215] The attempt to drive a diplomatic wedge had failed. Britain refused to be detached from Poland, and Hitler issued the most momentous order of his career.

The blow struck Canaris at 5:30 P.M. on August 31.[216] It left him stunned. Slowly, in an almost trancelike state, he walked down the corridor with a handful of subordinates. A civilian bustled up to him. It was Gisevius, in a hurry as usual. Canaris drew him aside. "Well," he asked, "what do you say now?" Gisevius was at a loss for an answer. Then the Admiral spoke again—just one sentence, but it was full of grim foreboding and prophetic insight: "This means the end of Germany." Peering more closely at him in the gloom, Gisevius saw that he was weeping.[217]

10

The Last Chance

Resignedly, Canaris left it to Heydrich and his helpmates in the SD, SS and Abwehr to kindle the flames of war. Heydrich had already alerted them with the prearranged signal "Grossmutter gestorben" [Grandma's dead] on the afternoon of August 31.[1] The troops set off to do their dirty work. Naujocks, who had "proved himself" during the last Czech crisis, attacked Gleiwitz radio station while Hellwig's men launched their mock attacks on the German frontier and Trummler's fired back at the SD "invaders."

"Polish rebels cross the German frontier," the *Völkischer Beobachter* screamed next day, and Adolf Hitler's voice resounded from every loudspeaker in Greater Germany as he proclaimed to the Reichstag that fourteen border incidents had occurred the previous night and that German troops would now "return fire."[2]

Canaris's group and section heads had gathered in his office and were listening to the radio broadcast of Hitler's speech. At the mention of "border incidents" Piekenbrock broke the silence by exclaiming, "So now we know why we had to get hold of those Polish uniforms!"[3] Canaris, who was not in the mood for disclosures, said nothing. As so often in the past, he had quickly shaken off the depressing effects of the previous day and was concentrating on what he deemed to be his duty.

He was every inch the commanding officer when he summoned his principal subordinates at 9:15 A.M. on that historic day, September 1,

1939, and gave them a brief but trenchant pep talk. Every officer and man in Amtsgruppe Ausland/Abwehr was pledged to the strictest secrecy and most unconditional loyalty to Führer and Reich. The Admiral even managed an unwonted "Heil Hitler!"[4] This was no hypocrisy. It sprang from deep conviction and was the natural and unquestioned product of thirty-four years in the service of Germany. Even at the end of 1940, Canaris sternly insisted to an Abwehr II officer during court-martial proceedings that members of the armed forces had no duty save obedience. Although he himself was often puzzled by orders "from higher up," "One is a serviceman and has to obey."[5]

He now seemed to recognize only one task incumbent on himself and the Abwehr: to serve the Wehrmacht and smooth its path to final victory in Poland. Abwehr units in the East moved off, many of them miles ahead of the advancing German armies. They had punctually reached their operational areas when, at 4:45 A.M., five German armies —divided between Army Group North under General von Bock and Army Group South under General von Rundstedt—invaded Poland and swiftly pierced the enemy's outlying defences.[6]

Fascinated by the momentum of the German attack, Canaris called for detailed reports on the hourly changing situation, not only at the front but behind the lines. All disclosed the effective work performed by his Abwehr units. Although the two most strategically important missions, those directed against Dirschau and the Jablunkov Pass, failed because Polish demolition squads forestalled the German raiding parties, most of the other operations were successful. Abwehr detachments occupied the rail junction at Kalthof, saved the industrial installations at Rybnik, seized nearly all the coal mines in Upper Silesia and took Katowice before German troops got there.[7]

The majority of Abwehr personnel operated with such precision that the Tirpitz-Ufer was bombarded with urgent assignments. The Army General Staff requested that paratroops be dispatched immediately "to destroy the three railway lines from Romania to Poland," Abwehr II was asked to supply "interpreters, guides and propagandists" for use in a secret operation masterminded by Luftwaffe General Student and Army units called for Ukrainian agents to explore enemy dispositions in Galicia.[8] Lieutenant Colonel Lahousen busily recorded these and other details, for example: "A combat group of twelve hundred men posted to protect the occupied industrial zone . . . General Busch, commanding VIII Army Corps, has personally commended a four hundred-man combat group from Abwehrstelle Breslau."[9]

Reports of success from Poland put the officers at Abwehr headquarters in a euphoric mood which stifled all their fears and misgivings. As military men, they could hardly fail to greet Germany's triumphs in the East with satisfaction—indeed, with pride—and claim a major share of the credit for themselves. They had spent years helping to build up the Wehrmacht and using their secret professional resources to make it the best-led and most effective fighting force in German history. Now the long-awaited time of trial had come, and no Abwehr officer wanted to miss it.

Not even Groscurth, who had rejoined the Abwehr and was doing a difficult job as the Amtsgruppe's liaison officer with the anti-OKW Army General Staff, could dissociate himself from the general enthusiasm. The entries in his diary betray the strange schizophrenia that afflicted opponents of the regime who condemned its power-crazy brutality on the one hand and, on the other, served it because their own lives had been shaped by the national ideals to which it seemed harnessed. This explains why Groscurth could see "nothing but lies and deception, nothing genuine" in the Nazi system and, in the same breath, condemn the policy pursued by Hitler's foreign adversaries ("ferocious warmongering abroad, like July 1914")—why he could call Hitler's war "madness" yet rejoice at every German military success: "Good progress in the East . . . More good advances . . . The Poles encircled at four points. Let's hope the cordons hold!"[10]

Canaris was another who yielded to these moods. He showed no outward concern even when the British and French declared war, nor did he say anything to temper his subordinates' enthusiasm. This was clearly brought home to SS-Brigadeführer Best of the Abwehrpolizei, who invited the Admiral and his heads of section to drinks a few days after the outbreak of war.

Best was still labouring under the depressing news that both the Western powers had entered the war when his guests began to speculate on its duration. His wife, who had expressed some uneasiness, drew a soothing remonstrance from the head of Abwehr III: "But my dear lady, the war will be over in five or six weeks." Frau Best staunchly contradicted him: "Five or six years, you mean!" Best, who claims to have backed her up, recalls that Canaris himself "said nothing, though he could easily have endorsed our worried attitude in the circumstances." Canaris could, in fact, have afforded to do so because he must have known that Best, although a National Socialist, had been observing his Führer's foreign policy with growing alarm for a considerable time.[11]

But Canaris chose not to share these doubts. At a time when the war was claiming all his drive and ingenuity, qualms and caution seemed alien to him. He plunged into the fray with characteristic vigour. Scarcely a week went by without his visiting the Polish front, scarcely a day without his requesting plans for new Abwehr operations. His two secretaries seldom saw him. Restless and preoccupied, he hurried from one Abwehrstelle to the next.

On September 3 he set off on his first visit to the front with

Piekenbrock and Oster, who was now the Amtsgruppe's official chief of staff.[12] His trip took him to Army Group South, the Abwehr's main centre of activity in the East. At Rundstedt's headquarters he was greeted by auspicious news. The German Fourteenth Army had just occupied Krakow and was driving the enemy forces back to the Nida-Dunajec line, while the Tenth Army was blasting its way through to Kielce and Tomaszow. Impressed by what he had seen, Canaris returned to Berlin on September 5. Groscurth noted: "The Admiral returned two hours ago . . . back from the front, favourable impression."[13]

Next morning he faced his staff conference brimming with new ideas and projects. It was not enough for him that the Abwehr should be operating in the East and reconnoitring the West in almost hourly expectation of an Allied attack for the relief of Poland. His organization must "go worldwide" and hit Germany's Western adversaries, notably Britain, where it would really hurt: in the colonial empires whose downtrodden inhabitants seemed eager to rise against their hated oppressors with the aid of German arms and money.

During World War I, the German leaders and their intelligence agencies had tried to develop a revolutionizing strategy and sow rebellion against the Entente powers among discontented Irish, Indians, Ukrainians and Caucasians. This policy would now, said Canaris, be continued by the Abwehr. A certain amount of spadework had already been done. Contact with IRA bombers had existed since February 1939, and Welsh nationalists and Scottish separatists also appeared on the payroll of the German secret service. Abwehr II's conspiratorial feelers extended as far as Persia and India.[14]

All these activities were to be expanded and systematized. Radio contact with IRA headquarters had been broken and must be restored. Arms consignments had to be arranged with the IRA's representative, explosives expert Jim O'Donovan, whom the Tirpitz-Ufer listed as a German V-Mann under the code name "Held." Indeed, there was later a plan to transport IRA Chief of Staff Sean Russell to Germany from the United States, where he had gone to ground, set up a concerted attack on the province of Ulster and land him in Ireland by U-boat. Plans for a rebellion in India and British-controlled Iraq were just as detailed.[15]

Canaris was particularly attracted by the bright ideas of Oberregierungsrat Wöhrl, who functioned as Abwehr II's V-Mann in Kabul. Wöhrl had devised an ambitious plan. He wanted to reinstate Afghanistan's pro-German ex-King Amanullah by means of a coup and stage an anti-British revolt by mountain tribes on the Afghan-Indian border.[16] Canaris was fond of such schemes, with their echoes of Wilhelminian grandeur. Many were put forward, including an Abwehr expedition to incite the Tibetans against the British and a similar project in Thailand.[17]

Canaris encouraged the drafting of these studies because they helped him demonstrate how essential the Abwehr was to the German war effort. No sooner were they on paper than he had them submitted to Hitler. On September 6 Lahousen wrote: "Amtsgruppenchef issues instructions for the preparation of a memorandum for the Führer on: (a) Proposed operations in the West; (b) Success and casualty reports; (c) Wöhrl project; (d) Position of the Ukrainians; (e) Tibetan project."[18]

The same day Canaris found a new outlet for his energies. This time his task was to head off another war. Colonel Homlok, chief of Section V of the Hungarian General Staff, had requested a meeting in Dresden on September 9, and his coming boded no good. The Hungarians, as Canaris already knew, were itching to take advantage of the German-Polish war to attack Romania and recover the territories they had ceded to their neighbours in 1919.[19] Canaris's brief read: "The Hungarians must be persuaded to hold off. No action to be taken against Romania."[20]

The Admiral travelled to Dresden with Piekenbrock and Lahousen. On September 9 the three Abwehr men sat down with their Hungarian visitors in the Hotel Bellevue. Canaris knew how to handle Hungarians. After a few hours' friendly discussion Colonel Homlok headed for home, convinced that Hungary could not afford to risk the Führer's displeasure.[21] Once on the move, Canaris proceeded to the front, lured there by fresh reports of success from Army Group South. The Fourteenth Army had thrust as far as the fortress of Przemysl and one corps of the Tenth Army was already on the outskirts of Warsaw.

But the closer General von Kleist's tanks drew to the West Ukrainian metropolis of Lvov the more Canaris suffered from a political dilemma which was bound to hamper the Abwehr's activities in the East: the Ukrainian question had reared its head once more. On September 10 the OUN leader, Yary, turned up at the Tirpitz-Ufer and asked the question which the Abwehr had so studiously been avoiding: what was the German attitude to the Ukraine?[22] The Ukrainian Military Staff had completed its preparations for a revolt in eastern Galicia. Soured by years of impotence and oppression, the West Ukrainians needed only one word from the German authorities to vent their accumulated hatred on the Poles, but the word never came. How, after the conclusion of the Hitler-Stalin pact, could Germany still be interested in sparking off a revolt that might spread to the Soviet Ukraine?

Although Canaris deluded himself into believing that the Abwehr would not abandon its Ukrainian allies for a second time, he did intimate to his subordinates at the morning conference on September 11 that it must naturally be "borne in mind that a Ukrainian insurrection, once unleashed, will turn against Poland *and* Russia."[23] Shortly afterwards a call from the Foreign Office informed him that no Galician revolt would ever take place. Pursuant to a decision by the Führer, noted Lahousen, the Ukrainian insurrectionary movement was "not to be activated at all."[24]

For the umpteenth time, Canaris hoped to be able to change Hitler's mind. On September 12 he set off with Lahousen for Illnau in Upper Silesia, where Hitler's mobile headquarters—twelve coaches and two locomotives—had been installed on a branch of the Opole-Kluczbork line.[25] Although he was unable to discuss the Ukrainian issue with Hitler himself, Ribbentrop and Keitel expressed such contrasting views that he imagined the final decision had yet to be taken.

Keitel told his Abwehr chief that the Führer was considering three possible solutions of the Polish conflict. Lahousen noted them in a memorandum for insertion in Canaris's diary: "Contingency 1: A fourth [Russo-German] partition of Poland, with Germany renouncing all interest in the area east of the Narew-Vistula-San line in favour of the Soviet Union. Contingency 2: Establishment of an independent rump Poland (the solution that most appeals to the Führer because he can then negotiate peace in the East with a Polish government. Contingency 3: No rump Poland. (a) Lithuania is offered the Vilna area. (b) The Galician and Polish Ukraine becomes independent. (This presupposes a mutually agreeable foreign policy settlement with the Soviet Union.)"[26] Canaris inferred from this that the Ukrainian revolt still meshed with Hitler's plans.

In respect of Contingency 3(b), Keitel ordered Canaris to "make preparations with the Ukrainians to the extent that, should this contingency be activated by the Mel'nyk organization (OUN), a revolt will break out in the Galician Ukraine, its object being the annihilation of the Poles and Jews."[27] However: "Any political extension of this movement to the Soviet Union (Greater Ukrainian idea) must be prevented at all costs."[28] Canaris journeyed on to Krakow feeling reassured and confident that Hitler would approve the Abwehr's plans for a Ukrainian revolt.

Hitler did, in fact, give his qualified assent, and on September 15 Canaris instructed Abwehr II to set the Ukrainians in motion. The Ukrainian Military Staff and its units were to join the Fourteenth Army and Mel'nyk was to hold himself "permanently available" for consultations with the Admiral.[29] Ukrainians were already hurrying to Galicia when this dream edifice, too, collapsed like a house of cards: Hitler was presenting the (Polish) West Ukraine to the Russians.

Early on the morning of September 17 Bürkner brought his chief a Foreign Office report that Red Army units had crossed the Polish frontier between Polotsk and Kamenets-Podolski at 4 A.M. Central European Time, clearly intending to occupy the territory east of the Lvov-Brest-Litovsk-Bialystok line.[30] Canaris could not have been surprised by this development. Ribbentrop had been urging the Kremlin to make a military contribution to the Polish campaign ever since it began. The Soviet military attaché in Berlin was kept regularly informed of progress at the front, and Canaris had been in no doubt that Stalin would strike as soon as the Polish Army was defeated.

The Russian invasion depressed him nonetheless. Stalin's intervention was bound to destroy the Abwehr's work in this field. To its Ukrainian agents it came as a "hammer blow" because—to quote Captain Nowak of the Abwehr—they regarded it as "a national disaster of the first magnitude . . . the collapse of all the hopes that have been so amply nourished in recent times."[31] But Canaris could not allow such sentiments to smoulder for long. With the ambidexterity proper to a secret service chief, he stopped the OUN operation in Galicia, banned all preparations for a revolt and, on the other hand, pledged humanitarian assistance to West Ukrainians fleeing from the Russians.

Canaris summoned the most belligerent and troublesome OUN leader to Berlin (Lahousen memo: "Yary needs watching, preferably surveillance") and browbeat him into accepting the new scheme of things.[32] "Yary stated," wrote Lahousen, "that all political interests must now be relegated so as to salvage what is still retrievable after the Russian march into Ukrainian territory."[33] On September 19 Canaris, Piekenbrock and Lahousen took Yary with them on a trip to Lvov, where the four men planned to see what could be done for the Ukrainian refugees.[34]

It was a laborious journey through Galicia, with its burning villages, panic-stricken civilian refugees and columns of German soldiers. Poland was on the verge of collapse. The Polish cabinet and High Command had withdrawn to Romania on the morrow of the Russian invasion. Such units and garrisons of the Polish Army as were still intact continued to offer aimless and hopeless resistance, notably the troops defending Warsaw, where the brunt of the German attack was now concentrated.

Abwehr officers in Lvov briefed Canaris on the displacement of the Ukrainian population. Few Polish Ukrainians had chosen to await the Red Army's arrival and many were fleeing to the Germans. Canaris left Lahousen and Yary to set up an organization in Krakow, complete with reception centres and a small administrative staff.[35] He himself pressed on to visit the forward areas, where German troops were already in contact with Soviet units.

Here, despite the rules which Groscurth had devised for dealing with the Russians, he received alarming reports of friction between the two armies. There had been such a fierce exchange of fire between German and Soviet troops in the Lvov area on September 20 that the OKW next day withdrew its forces to a demarcation line agreed by Ribbentrop and Molotov at the end of August, before signing the non-aggression pact. This followed the course of the Pissa, Narew, Vistula and San.[36]

"The withdrawal," fumed Groscurth, "is more than short-term—[it is] a sort of headlong retreat. German blood has contributed to an effortless advance by the Russians and Bolshevism."[37] Canaris himself saw all this as just the start of an accelerating retreat from the Russians. Back in Berlin on September 23 he was handed a directive from Hitler stating that Ukrainians were, if necessary, to be forcibly prevented from leaving the Soviet-occupied zone and seeking refuge in German-held territory.[38] The Abwehr's Ukrainian activities were soon banned altogether. Lahousen: "The Russians have forbidden all discussion of the Ukrainian problem . . . One can only advise the Ukrainian leaders . . . to go to a neutral foreign country."[39]

Two days later, on September 25, Stalin proposed to his German partner that their countries' Polish boundaries should be redrawn, and that the requisite territorial adjustments to their spheres of influence should be regulated by treaty. Ribbentrop hurried back to Moscow and a new pact came into being, the German-Soviet Boundary and Friendship Treaty, which was signed on September 29, 1939. In return for Soviet-occupied areas of Poland, Ribbentrop conceded that Lithuania was a Russian sphere of influence and granted the right of Russian troops to be stationed there "at some future date." For his part, Stalin affirmed that all Germans resident in the U.S.S.R. could be resettled in the Reich—the start of an exodus which was to assume catastrophic dimensions a few years later.[40]

"A day of shame," commented Halder, the Army Chief of Staff, when he learned the provisions of the new treaty.[41] Canaris, already steeped in dark forebodings and prophecies of doom, went even further. To him it was the ruin of the German nation-state, a sacrilegious violation of the world order, an act of political barbarism fraught with unpredictable consequences. That which God, nature and history had erected for the defence of Germany and the heartlands of Europe against oriental despotism—or so it seemed to Canaris—was now being dismantled by the power-hungry amateurs who ruled the Reich.

The German-Soviet Boundary and Friendship Treaty disclosed the full extent of the gulf that separated Canaris from Hitler and his adherents. Every line of the text was a challenge to the cause which he, Wilhelm Canaris, had espoused throughout his lifetime as an officer, patriot, Freikorps fighter and anti-Communist. The Reich was chaining itself to the cornerstone of Bolshevism and estranging itself forever from Britain and the rest of Europe, without whose support Germany might one day become the appendage of an alien, Asiatic Russia and Hitler himself a satrap of Stalin. The abandonment of Lithuania was a step towards renouncing the Baltic as a "German sea."

Canaris was even more dubious of the pact's repercussions on the domestic situation in Germany. It was bound to reinforce what he, an archconservative, regarded as socialist tendencies. Fear of socialist experiments in government, society and the armed forces had become almost an obsession with Canaris. He scented "Brown[shirt] Bolshevism" everywhere. This term, which he sometimes interchanged with "National Bolshevism," embraced everything that smacked of an attempt to dismantle or demolish the hierarchic bourgeois social system, and he felt that all these destructive forces had been stimulated by the Hitler-Stalin pact.

Vaguely sensed at first, these premonitions were committed to paper a few weeks later by Liedig, the Admiral's friend. "As an accomplice of the Russians' newly awakened hunger for territory and access to the sea," wrote Liedig, "Germany is effectively and finally becoming a mortal enemy of Britain. And all she will acquire in exchange for this mortal enmity is an appointment to serve as the European glacis of the Asiatic Soviet empire, as the Bolshevized outpost of Asia in Europe." Why? Because vis-à-vis the Soviet Union Germany "can in no way gain supremacy but, at best, retain client status or even degenerate into a race of Russian helots."[42]

Liedig's conclusion: "So Hitler's opportunist policy is remorselessly drifting, unprincipled and out of control, into the maelstrom of a German decline of unimaginable dimensions."[43] Canaris, who still believed that this maze had an exit, continued his feverish search for new solutions and expedients. He was magically attracted by the front and made repeated visits to Poland.

But wherever he went he saw chaos, dissolution and misery. He was particularly appalled by the sight of Warsaw in flames, which left him close to tears. Canaris returned from Poland "completely shattered," wrote Ulrich von Hassell, because he had "seen the results of our brutal conduct of the war, especially in devastated Warsaw."[44] He spent days driving through the streets with Major Horaczek of the Abwehr. "How frightful!" he was heard to exclaim. "Our children's children will have to bear the blame for this."[45]

The scenes of devastation in Poland left an indelible mark on Canaris. Land warfare was something new to him. His knowledge of war was based on memories of cruisers duelling at long range and coloured by the rites traditional among gentlemen of the sea. This was another kind of war, an orgy of mass slaughter and total destruction, a battle between fanatical beliefs and ideologies waged amid burning cities and the ruins of a national culture. What he saw evoked a sense of personal and national guilt which soon became condensed into the realization that was to plague him more and more as time went by: "God will pass judgement on us!"[46]

His sensitivity to the monstrous things he witnessed was rendered still keener by personal experience. He heard on September 17 that his sister Anna's son, Lieutenant Rolf Buck, had been killed at Radom.[47] Weizsäcker had previously lost his son Heinrich on September 2.[48] Then, like a portent of doom, came the most distressing piece of news any German officer could have received. Colonel General Baron Werner von Fritsch had been mysteriously struck down in the Warsaw suburb of Praha on September 22, while riding aimlessly along with his old regiment. Like Groscurth, Canaris may well have thought: "What a shocking fate!"[49]

The Admiral's only source of relief from the Polish nightmare was to help any refugees or victims of circumstance who could not be regarded as active opponents of Germany. Abwehr outstations in Poland were instructed to convey prominent Poles to safety. Often, a personal appeal to Canaris was enough to launch a rescue operation.

The U.S. consul general in Berlin asked Staatsrat Wohlthat, an acquaintance of his, to locate a rabbi who had gone to ground in Warsaw and get him out of the country. Canaris ensured that this Jewish dignitary reached New York.[50] Fearing that the Ukrainian Archbishop of Krakow would be in danger from the Russians, he spirited him out of the country too.[51] The Bishop of Przemysl, Dr. Josafat, also owed Canaris a debt of gratitude. A nephew of his left "a cashbox containing 46,000 U.S. dollars and 40 gold ducats in [Canaris's] safekeeping" (Lahousen).[52]

While visiting Poznan Canaris was accosted and asked for help by a pale, bewildered-looking Polish woman. The Admiral stared at her in dismay as recognition slowly dawned. It was Madame Czimanska, wife of the Polish military attaché and a popular hostess in prewar Berlin.[53] Lieutenant Colonel Hartwig of Abwehrstelle Lublin had discovered her and her two children in a refugee camp.[54] She had no idea of her husband's whereabouts. Canaris preserved agreeable memories of Lieutenant Colonel Antoni Czimanski, who was a living symbol of the German-Polish tragedy. Born in Poznan, Czimanski had been educated in German schools and undergone training in the German Army before becoming a German expert on the Polish General Staff. He had opposed Colonel Beck's disastrous policy in his official reports and clung until the last moment to his belief that the German-Polish dispute over Danzig and the Corridor could be satisfactorily resolved.[55]

Sobbing, Madame Czimanska told Canaris the story of her escape and expressed shame at the Polish forces' apparent lack of determination. Canaris consoled her. "Don't distress yourself . . . The Polish armies have fought well and bravely." When she asked permission to join her mother in Warsaw, however, he shook his head. "I wouldn't go to Wąrsaw," he said. He walked over to a big wall map and ran his finger across it. "Switzerland," he told her, "that's the best place."[56]

Canaris procured papers which enabled Madame Czimanska and her children to settle in the neighbourhood of Berne, where she found an apartment which he sometimes visited on his subsequent trips to Switzerland.[57] He also acted as a staging-post for correspondence between her and her mother in Warsaw.[58] Having discovered that the latter was living in Ulonska Street, he enlisted Horaczek to drive him there. "We'll go to the old lady and pass on the news that all's well with her daughter and the children."[59]

But private rescue operations of this kind could not exempt Canaris from involvement in Hitler's war and the subjugation of Poland. Einsatzgruppen [operational task forces] of the Sicherheitspolizei and SD were already moving in, determined to carry out their orders with a barbarous precision that matched the biologico-racial fanaticism and purgatory zeal of the Nazi leaders who had issued them. Heydrich's men deployed with the object of reducing the Poles to helot status, skimming off the cream of Polish society and destroying Poland's national identity. Their method was murder, pure and simple.

"Whatever we have now discovered in the way of a Polish ruling class must be liquidated; whatever grows again we must take into our safekeeping and eliminate in due course."[60] Such was Hitler's judgement on Poland, and Heydrich's myrmidons proceeded to execute it with dreadful deliberation. Consulting prepared lists, they arrested Polish teachers, doctors, civil servants, priests, landowners and businessmen. These detainees were herded together in reception centres, most of which soon turned out to be death camps.[61]

Officially, of course, the Einsatzgruppen functioned as security forces of the armies to which they were attached. As an Eighth Army order implied, their ostensible purpose was to "combat all anti-Reich and anti-German elements in the rear of the fighting forces, particularly [by means of] counterespionage; to detain politically untrustworthy persons, confiscate weapons, obtain custody of documents valuable to the counterespionage police, et cetera."[62] But Canaris was not misled. Regular contact with Heydrich soon enabled him to fathom the true role of the Einsatzgruppen.

A conversation with Heydrich on September 8 put him fully in the picture. As Heydrich himself phrased it: "We'll spare the common folk, but the aristocrats, priests and Jews must be killed. After moving into Warsaw I shall arrange with the Army how to squeeze them all out."[63] The same day Canaris reported to Army Chief of Staff I that SS officers had been heard to congratulate themselves on shooting two hundred Poles a day, and that most of these executions took place without trial.[64] The Army General Staff's head of operations, Lieutenant General Carl-Heinrich von Stülpnagel, was already aware of this. Groscurth noted: "He says that the Führer and Göring mean to annihilate and exterminate the Polish people."[65]

Canaris, who was profoundly shocked, told Bürkner: "A war waged with no regard for moral principles can never be won. There's such a thing as divine justice on earth."[66] He instructed Abwehrstellen in the field to keep watch on the activities of the Einsatzgruppen and submit detailed reports. He further insisted that all his officers in Poland keep him informed about Heydrich's men. While visiting Abwehrstelle Krakow he asked the Abwehr III representative, Major Schirnick, how many Jews had been shot in the Krakow area. Receiving no answer, he snapped, "But you ought to know that—it's part of your job!"[67]

Canaris used this incriminating evidence to rouse the corps commanders in Poland against the Einsatzgruppen. The Army put a stop to the activities of Heydrich's worst unit, the Einsatzgruppe commanded by SS-Obergruppenführer von Woyrsch, following a Canaris memorandum and a report from the Fourteenth Army's Abwehr officer, who stated that great disquiet had been occasioned by the Einsatzgruppe's "sometimes illegal measures." It angered the rank and file "that young men should test their mettle on defenceless people instead of fighting at the front."[68]

However, Canaris usually took a back seat and left others to make an open stand against these SS crimes. A senior Gestapo officer, SS-Obersturmbannführer Georg Kiessel, later commented scornfully that "he was extremely cautious and didn't like sticking his neck out."[69] We do, in fact, know of only one occasion when Canaris lodged an official protest against the Polish murders, and that was during his visit to the Führer's train on September 12.

He told Lahousen to make the following note: "I pointed out to General Keitel that I knew that extensive shootings were being planned in Poland and, in particular, that the nobility and clergy were to be exterminated. The world would ultimately extend responsibility to the armed forces because these things had happened under their noses. General Keitel replied that the matter had already been settled by the Führer, who had made it clear to the ObdH [Army commander in chief] that, if the armed forces wanted no part of it, they could not object if the SS and the Gestapo put in an appearance alongside them."[70]

Canaris's remarks read more strongly on paper than they sounded in reality. He must have expressed himself rather vaguely, because after he had gone Keitel turned to Lieutenant Colonel Nikolaus von Vormann, the OKH liaison officer at Hitler's headquarters, and asked, "What was the fellow driving at?" Vormann was equally at a loss and "didn't understand either."[71]

The Admiral's inhibitions were not merely characteristic. He may also have felt depressed at the role to which the Abwehr had been condemned, cheek by jowl with the Gestapo and SD, by the political spinelessness of the Wehrmacht authorities. The latter were only too glad to be relieved of the dirty work in Poland by Himmler's organization and grateful to the Führer for permitting them to wink at the Einsatzgruppen's murderous activities behind the lines. This being so, Canaris had little scope for an all-out campaign against the killings perpetrated by Heydrich's men.

Besides, the planning of the OUN operations had already shown how easy it was for Canaris himself to become entangled in Hitler's arrangements for the East. Without a word of protest, he had unhesitatingly accepted Keitel's order to use a Ukrainian revolt for the "annihilation of the Poles and Jews."[72] Worse still, Canaris had since the outbreak of war maintained a species of personal Einsatzgruppe which, though clad in Wehrmacht uniform, was no less dedicated to the political objectives of the Nazi regime.

What were these men of the Geheime Feldpolizei (GFP) if not uniformed Gestapo officers and employees subordinate to the Abwehr? Not only had they all been trained by Heydrich's organization, but their commander, Colonel Wilhelm Krichbaum, was a friend of Heydrich's and had last served as an SS-Standartenführer and Regierungsrat at the SD-Hauptamt.[73] It was hardly surprising, therefore, that the standing orders of Amtsgruppe Ausland/Abwehr entrusted GFP units with duties closely resembling those performed by the Einsatzgruppen, namely: "to investigate and combat all activities harmful to the nation and state, in particular, espionage, treason, sabotage, hostile propaganda and subversion in the theatre of operations."[74]

The GFP took correspondingly drastic action against real and putative enemies behind the German lines. GFP personnel arrested as many Poles for sabotage and espionage as they thought fit and turned them over for execution to their colleagues in the Einsatzgruppen. When this practice got out of hand, Heydrich stepped in. On September 20 the Abwehr officer of Army Group South radioed the following message to its constituent army corps: "Head of Sipo [Security Police] requests that the GFP be directed to carry out their own executions."[75]

This incident discloses that the organizations headed by Canaris and Heydrich were more closely related than the Abwehr's literary apologists have been willing to grant. The two authorities had drawn still closer since the outbreak of war, though with slightly altered names and increased powers. On September 27 Himmler had amalgamated the Gestapo, Kriminalpolizei and SD into a Reichssicherheitshauptamt [RSHA—Central State Security Bureau] under Heydrich, which was intended to become a police super-authority, and on October 18 Canaris's Amtsgruppe re-emerged as OKW-Amt Ausland/Abwehr, which wielded increased supervision over personnel in all sectors of the armed forces and the munitions industry.[76]

The first few days of the war had produced a whole web of mutual relationships and interdependences which formed a seemingly indissoluble bond between the RSHA and Abwehr. Abwehr personnel and equipment contributed to the SD's provocation of border incidents just as members of the SD-controlled Grenzpolizei and SS personnel supported the Abwehr's commando operations during the Polish campaign. Herzner's most expert aide at the Jablunkov Pass was an officer from the Stapoleitstelle [regional Gestapo headquarters] in Brno, and SS-Standartenführer Neumann and SS-Obersturmbannführer Kriewald had assisted in the Abwehr's Dirschau operation.[77]

Most of the Abwehr agents operating in Poland (and earlier in Czechoslovakia) were staunch National Socialists and many came from local SS units, so Abwehr officers at the Tirpitz-Ufer regarded it as a natural duty to recommend their helpers for promotion and decorations by applying to SS headquarters. Major Klug of Abwehr II even managed to obtain—for those of his men who belonged to the SS—a status symbol much coveted by National Socialists: the Ehrenwinkel [chevron of honour] worn on the right sleeve of an SS uniform and normally restricted to Alte Kämpfer [veteran Nazis] who had marched under Hitler's banner long before 1933.[78]

But the two organizations had many other areas of common ground. Abwehr officers trained the SS-Verfügungstruppe in security and counterespionage duties just as RSHA lecturers schooled their colleagues in the Abwehr. Given these many points of contact, even Canaris could sometimes drop his guard. Groscurth angrily took issue with the Admiral because he had recommended him to engage a secretary whose brother was an SS aide on Hitler's staff. "That's all we need at this stage," Groscurth protested. "Frau C[anaris] was also shocked that her husband should have . . . assigned me this person."[79]

The two authorities maintained such close outward co-operation that the Abwehr came to be regarded as an extension of the Gestapo by anti-Nazis who did not know better. One of these was Wolfgang Gans Edler Herr von und zu Putlitz, a diplomat serving at the German Embassy in The Hague. Having fallen into the clutches of the British secret service because of his homosexual proclivities, Putlitz suspected that Abwehr agents were on his track and hurriedly absconded to England in mid-September with 250,000 gulden from the embassy.[80] In his own words: "Canaris would have hanged me had he caught me."[81]

Putlitz's suspicions were well founded. Holland was the scene of a joint Abwehr-SD operation designed to infiltrate the British espionage network in Western Europe. The story had begun in 1937, when Major Johannes Travaglio, I/Luft-Referent [head of Abwehr I's Air Force desk] at Abwehrstelle Stuttgart, succeeded in making contact with Fischer, a German who had emigrated to Amsterdam and was in close touch with British intelligence personnel in London.[82]

Fischer was one of those expatriates of the Hitler era who were eager to escape the tribulations of life in exile and purchase a return ticket to Germany by working for the Third Reich's intelligence agencies. He had special reasons for making a pact with the Abwehr because he was wanted by the German police and hoped that the charges against him would be dropped if he played ball with Canaris's organization. Travaglio must have guaranteed this, because Fischer offered him something calculated to appeal to any German secret serviceman: a chance to spy on the Secret Intelligence Service.[83]

In January 1938 Majors Travaglio and Diebitsch of the Abwehr met Fischer at the Carlton Hotel in Amsterdam. Here they made use of the myth which German agents had found most marketable when dealing with foreign intelligence services: they pretended to be peace loving individuals who were perturbed by Hitler's belligerence and needed help from abroad to clip his wings.[84] Fischer, who caught their drift, recommended this pair of self-styled anti-Nazis to his friends at SIS headquarters in London. Ever wary, the SIS conducted an eighteen month investigation before finally suggesting that Fischer might care to call at the Pharmisan Company in The Hague and ask for a Mr. Payton Best.[85]

Ex-Captain Best, a gentlemanly figure complete with monocle, bowler and umbrella, proved to be the head of an SIS centre in Holland which was extremely interested in contacting German dissidents. A meeting was arranged for mid-September at the Hotel Wilhelminia in the Dutch frontier town of Venlo. Best turned up accompanied by his partner, Major Richard Stevens, the head of another British intelligence outstation. Travaglio, who adopted the pseudonym "Dr. Solms," told the British all kinds of weird and wonderful tales about the revolutionary schemes being hatched by influential anti-Nazis in the German armed forces.[86]

Stevens and Best were so impressed that they asked to speak to the leaders of these resistance groups without delay. New rendezvous were arranged and more and more "resistance fighters" introduced. Then the SD stepped in. A twenty-nine-year-old Regierungsrat and SS-Sturmbannführer named Walter Schellenberg began to interest himself in the Abwehr's Dutch operation.

Previously employed at the SD-Hauptamt, Schellenberg had been transferred by Heydrich to the regional Gestapo headquarters at Dortmund early in October, there to familiarize himself with practical counterespionage police work as a future Amtsgruppenchef at the RSHA.[87] Because the newcomer was sitting around idly and disrupting normal office routine by asking questions, the executive head of the Stapostelle, Kriminalkommissar Heimbach, decided to keep him occupied with some old files. Among other things, they dealt with the Dutch activities of Stapostelle Dortmund, which was the Gestapo's chief source of information about German *émigrés* in Western Europe.[88]

With mounting interest, Schellenberg read that the Gestapo was in touch with anti-Nazi *émigrés* in Holland and had made repeated attempts to abduct prominent anti-fascists like ex-Chancellor Brüning.[89] It was then, Heimbach later surmised, that Schellenberg "must suddenly have become obsessed" with the idea of penetrating the British intelligence network and kidnapping its leaders.[90] He was so fired with enthusiasm that he promptly borrowed an unlimited-travel rail warrant from Heimbach and set off for Berlin to report to Heydrich.[91]

Schellenberg's arrival was well timed because another SD officer at the RSHA, SS-Sturmbannführer Helmut Knochen, had recently learned of Travaglio's Dutch activities from the informant Fischer, who worked for the SD as well as the Abwehr.[92] Heydrich approved Schellenberg's proposal, and from then on the SD collaborated with the Abwehr in Holland. Knochen ran the operation from Berlin while Schellenberg attended all subsequent meetings with Best and Stevens under the pseudonym "Captain Schemmel."[93]

The SD planned few moves without informing or consulting Travaglio in advance. Another meeting with the two British agents was arranged for the afternoon of November 9, once again in Venlo.[94] Schellenberg was in Dortmund early that morning, preparing for his next rendezvous, when the telephone rang. It was Himmler, sounding agitated. "Tonight, just after the Führer's speech at the Beer Cellar, an attempt was made to assassinate him. Luckily, he'd left the Cellar a few minutes before . . . There's no doubt that the British secret service is behind it all."[95]

As a member of the SS, Schellenberg was outraged to hear of this attempt on Hitler's life. He was equally startled, or so he claimed, when Himmler went on to say that the Führer's orders were to detain Stevens and Best and convey them across the German frontier. Meanwhile, an SD flying squad under Knochen and the omnipresent Naujocks was already on its way to Dortmund.[96]

At 4 P.M., when Best drove up to the rendezvous, a Venlo cafe near the border, accompanied by Stevens, Lieutenant Klop of Dutch military intelligence and a garage owner named Lemmens, Schellenberg came out to meet him. At that moment an SS convertible roared up, crashed the frontier barrier and screamed to a halt in front of Best's Buick. A submachine gun started chattering and the Englishmen drew their revolvers. Naujocks and his men piled out and overpowered them. Klop collapsed, fatally wounded, but was carted off too. So was Lemmens. The raiders' car was now overloaded, and it was not until they reached the German customs post that a Wehrmacht corporal named Fühlen solved their problem by lending them a car of his own.[97]

The two vehicles headed for the nearest Gestapo offices in Düsseldorf, where the prisoners' papers were examined. Next day, November 10, they were taken on to Berlin.[98] Klop was past saving. He died in Düsseldorf without regaining consciousness, not that this prevented Schellenberg from crediting him with a written statement alleging secret talks between the British and Dutch General Staffs—a "confession" designed to gloss over the Germans' breach of international law at Venlo.[99]

Canaris was not informed of the operation until November 10. Puzzled by the manifold conjectures circulating about who had masterminded Georg Elser's unsuccessful bomb attack in the Bürgerbräukeller —according to Groscurth "the so-called 'pigeon-post circle' (disgruntled party veterans) or even the Gestapo itself"—Canaris asked Heydrich for a copy of the Stevens-Best interrogation transcript.[100] Heydrich promised him one but delayed handing it over. The Admiral thereupon summoned his leading Dutch experts to a conference at the Park Hotel in Düsseldorf on November 11.[101]

Catching sight of Lieutenant Commander (ret.) Protze, the legendary *éminence grise* behind all the Abwehr's Dutch activities, he simulated an air of casual interest. "Well, Richard," he asked, "what are your friends Stevens and Best up to these days?" Protze clicked his heels. "They're under constant observation, Herr Admiral!" Canaris looked derisive. "At this very moment," he said, "they're both in Berlin, closeted with the Gestapo at Prinz-Albrecht-Strasse." Somebody present recalls that Protze "gaped at him." Then the Abwehr chief let fly: "This mess is Heydrich's doing!"[102]

On the basis of this scene, subsequent defenders of the Abwehr have claimed that Canaris and his department had no prior knowledge of the Venlo operation. However true this may be, Abwehr headquarters urged Schellenberg to concede at least a modicum of the credit to the Wehrmacht. When he, Knochen and Naujocks were awarded the Iron Cross First Class for their part in the venture, Lieutenant Commander Meissner, senior Abwehr liaison officer at the RSHA, asked the Sturmbannführer to help get an Iron Cross for Corporal Fühlen, who had put his car at the raiding party's disposal. Schellenberg declined.[103]

Canaris realized that Schellenberg, whom he had scarcely met, was one of the RSHA's rising stars and a man who would repay careful watching. He may already have learned from SS-Brigadeführer Best that Schellenberg was one of the chief beneficiaries of the restructuring of the police apparatus. Best had lost command of the Abwehrpolizei, which now came under RSHA-Amtsgruppe IVE and was thus controlled by Schellenberg, one of Heydrich's blue-eyed boys.

Canaris must have regretted this because he got on well with Best despite their official rivalry. The Brigadeführer had often mediated in the jurisdictional disputes between Canaris and Heydrich. Although Best temporarily remained a head of department at the RSHA, responsible for Amt I (Administration and Law), he had lost his central role in Heydrich's entourage.[104] But who was Schellenberg? He had for years functioned as Heydrich's ghost writer and ideas man in the SD-Hauptamt, since dissolved, and the RSHA's creation was partly attributable to his memorandums and proposals. His few sorties from the shadows of the SD bureaucracy included one appearance with Himmler in March 1938, when German troops entered Vienna, and another as his orderly officer during the Polish campaign. All in all, little was known about him.[105]

The son of a bankrupt piano manufacturer from Saarbrücken, Schellenberg had studied law and joined the SD after serving as a Referendar [civil service graduate undergoing in-service training] at district courts in West Germany. Unhappily married to a former dressmaker who had financed his studies but did not measure up to the exalted social demands of a Herr Regierungsrat, he was reputed to be an adroit and ambitious young opportunist.[106] But he was also extremely intelligent and realistic—a typical product of the middle-class German society which, unsettled by postwar turmoil and inflation, saw many of its sons take refuge in an empty world where functionalism reigned supreme and personal ties meant nothing. He was rumoured to be on intimate terms with Lina Heydrich (Frau Heydrich: "Idle gossip!"), but this was only a corollary of his reputation for unbridled careerism.[107]

Canaris thought it time to make personal contact with the new head of the Abwehrpolizei. On February 9, 1940, he invited Schellenberg and Best to his office, after which the three of them repaired to Ewers for a morning snack and a discussion of all the problems outstanding between the RSHA and the Abwehr. "It was readily apparent that Admiral Canaris meant to give Sturmbannführer Schellenberg the once-over," the new Abwehrpolizei chief noted in a memorandum.[108] He must have passed the test, at least superficially, because Canaris soon suggested that he might like to join him on his daily rides in the Tiergarten with Best and Heydrich.

Canaris and Schellenberg quickly discovered a basis for trouble-free personal relations. The older man appreciated the Sturmbannführer's lively imagination and intelligence; the younger made no secret of his admiration for the Abwehr chief. Schellenberg subscribed to the theory —still so prevalent in the upper reaches of the SS—that Canaris had been an agent of superlative brilliance, and he insisted to the end of his days that the Admiral was "Germany's finest spy."[109]

Once, when Legationssekretär Krammarz of the Foreign Office asked him overconfidentially if he thought Canaris "a sly old fox or a harmless individual," Schellenberg returned an answer worthy of any officer in the Abwehr's ranks. "I stressed," Schellenberg noted, "that I considered Admiral Canaris an extremely shrewd man who could, from the practical aspect, be trusted in any direction."[110] Yet fate had cast the Sturmbannführer and the Admiral in the role of archenemies. It was Schellenberg who ousted Canaris from his post in 1944, arrested him soon afterwards and consigned him to the treadmills of the Gestapo.

Schellenberg's ambition left no room for a Wehrmacht secret service or an autonomous intelligence chief. Like Heydrich, he was enthralled by the idea of an integrated and centrally directed super-secret service which would, in turn, be only one component of the great Staatsschutzkorps [State Protection Corps] in which the SS was preparing to find its own fulfilment. With Schellenberg's assistance, SS-Obergruppenführer [General] Heydrich had been gradually laying the foundations of an all-embracing security system in which there would some day be no separate military Abwehr, merely a Greater German Intelligence Service presided over—or so he dreamed—by none other than Walter Schellenberg himself.

Schellenberg's activities were particularly indicative that the ostentatious display of camaraderie between the RSHA and Abwehr masked insoluble conflicts which divided the two authorities to a far greater extent than the interdepartmental squabbles customary among rival intelligence agencies. Not a staff conference went by and not a major decision was taken at the RSHA without Heydrich and his assiduous lieutenant encouraging their subordinates to mistrust and dissociate themselves from the RSHA's rival at the Tirpitz-Ufer.

Contrary to the belief of naive postwar analysts, this mistrust was not prompted by any suspicion of treasonable activity on the Abwehr's part. The men in Prinz-Albrecht-Strasse seldom worried about their competitors' loyalty to the regime at this stage. What spurred them on was the expansile pressure of an apparatus geared to the acquisition of total power—the arrogance of police and secret service functionalists who considered themselves progressive in relation to an intelligence service which they dismissed as antiquated and ineffective, hidebound and corrupt.

Heydrich and Schellenberg never tired of impressing on their men that, in future, government policy decisions must be based solely on RSHA material. In conference with his immediate subordinates on September 19, 1939, Heydrich enthusiastically read out the minutes of a Reich cabinet meeting from which it emerged that Göring had made exclusive use of SD reports.[111] But this was not enough for Heydrich. He was determined that the Wehrmacht authorities, too, should some day be dependent on information and reports furnished by the Reichssicherheitshauptamt.

On January 22, 1940, Schellenberg drafted a memorandum in which he submitted that the RSHA should become the Wehrmacht's sole source of political intelligence so as to gain full control of the armed forces' political and ideological indoctrination. "In readiness for the final break-through," he went on, attention should be devoted to that OKW department "which already lays claim to this political intelligence in the home sector as well."[112] The same memorandum stated: "Consideration should already be given to launching the requisite discussions with the Wehrmacht shortly before peace is concluded. This is to ensure, for tactical reasons, that 'political intelligence' . . . is very early acquired as a province controlled by the Geheime Staatspolizei."[113]

Heydrich and Schellenberg repeatedly stressed at RSHA meetings that the SD and Gestapo must oppose all Abwehr claims to supremacy. Schellenberg on February 1, 1940: "Care should in future be taken not to speak of the Abwehrpolizei or counterespionage in case the Wehrmacht asserts its claim to all counterespionage functions and designates the Staatspolizei [i.e. Gestapo] its executive arm."[114]

However, the force of these injunctions was usually blunted by daily routine and the quasi-complicity that formed a bond between the junior members of both organizations. There were plenty of informants who warned the opposition of forthcoming moves by their own superiors. One example emerges from Groscurth's diary: "Dr. B[est] has confided to the Chief that H[eydrich] is gathering evidence against the Chief and plans to bring him down."[115] Canaris also received many secret tips from SS-Standartenführer Kanstein, head of Stapostelle Berlin, as well as from Arthur Nebe, the anti-Nazi who now headed Amt V of the RSHA and apprised the Abwehr of anything he gleaned from his meetings with Heydrich.[116]

Conversely, Abwehr officers prevented Canaris from taking unduly drastic action against his competitors. In February 1940, when Stapoleitstelle Düsseldorf used a Jewish agent to feed the Western powers with disinformation about the Wehrmacht which had not (contrary to standing orders) been cleared with the Abwehr, Meissner warned the Gestapo of Canaris's reaction because—according to Schellenberg—"he was afraid the Admiral would take advantage of this to hit [the Gestapo] hard."[117]

Meissner could afford to take this independent line because he had the Abwehr officer's lofty self-assurance and lack of inferiority complexes vis-à-vis the other side. The Polish campaign had boosted the Wehrmacht's public image to an unforeseen extent. Canaris's officers profited from this growth of prestige, especially the senior members of his organization, most of whom were staff officers. The war had brought them an accretion of authority and official powers which they were only too happy to wield against the Gestapo and SD.

Indeed, the officers on the Tirpitz-Ufer felt powerful enough to criticize the RSHA for gaps in its own security system. Abwehr III was always thinking up new proposals aimed at reinforcing police surveillance—ostensibly for the benefit of the armed forces and their security. Many extensions of police powers were originally suggested by the Abwehr, among them the establishment of a central visa office controlled by the Reichsführer-SS and Chief of the German Police [RfSSuChdDt-Pol], the creation of prohibited frontier zones, tougher standards of security clearance for personnel and the expulsion of gipsies from frontier areas and munitions factories.[118]

But the officers of Abwehr III were not content with excursions into police work. An Abwehr III report drafted early in 1940 complained that its demand for a "universal closure of frontiers" had been rejected by the RSHA. Nor was this an isolated instance. "Many of the proposals for intensified security measures repeatedly submitted by Abw III" had "not been implemented" by the Reichssicherheitshauptamt.[119]

Most of these complaints stemmed from a former imperial guards officer who had been the last of Canaris's section heads to join his team. (Staff) Lieutenant Colonel Franz-Eccard von Bentivegni, director of Abwehrabteilung III since March 1, 1939, was a relentless champion of Prusso-German authoritarianism who found it wholly natural that the nation—and, thus, the police—should steadfastly serve the interests of the military and state. A short, slim man, Bentivegni had a swarthy complexion which betrayed his descent from a line of Italian noblemen, but his dapper appearance and the monocle screwed into his right eye were unadulteratedly Prussian.[120]

"Benti," as he was known to Abwehr insiders, came from Potsdam and belonged to an old military family. His father, a lieutenant colonel, had been killed in the 1914–18 war. His own career had followed a predictably military course. Born in 1896, he had entered the Army immediately after leaving school and joined the 2nd Guards Field Artillery Regiment—an elite unit, naturally. Having served as a lieutenant in World War I and won the Iron Cross Second Class, he was absorbed into the Reichswehr and secured a staff appointment in 1931. As an intelligence section major (Ic) in Military District XII and two years later as General Staff Officer, Grade One, of the 26th Infantry Division he had attracted the attention of Canaris, who sent for him when Bamler, thwarted in his ambitions as head of Abwehr III, tendered his resignation and shortly afterwards accepted a regimental posting.[121]

Canaris appreciated Bentivegni's social graces and talent for organization, but the two men remained personally remote despite their common Italian descent. The Admiral confided less in Bentivegni than in any other head of section. This was due not only to Benti's cool manner and his close (officially prescribed) relations with the RSHA, but also to the trace of uneasiness with which Canaris watched his subordinate's zealous attempts to perfect the Abwehr's surveillance system.

Abwehr III already possessed far-reaching instruments of control which enabled it to screen the activities of servicemen and civilians. The Geheime Feldpolizei could detain any serviceman while engaged in combating crime and espionage within the armed forces. Members of the Verstärkter Grenzaufsichtsdienst [Augmented Frontier Surveillance Service] patrolled the prohibited zones, Abwehr III officers were attached to the Munitions Inspectorates and no member of Bentivegni's section could, if serving as an accredited security representative, be dismissed without Abwehr III's permission from the firm where he was employed.[122]

Group IIIN ensured that nothing which it considered a military secret was divulged by the press, cinema or postal service. IIIN representatives read the items that passed through the foreign mail and telegram monitoring centres, and even carrier pigeons came under increasing Abwehr III scrutiny.[123] Deterrent "Feind hört mit!" ["Careless talk costs lives"] posters, usually distributed by the police, originated in the offices of Abwehr III, and the police were further responsible for ensuring that all party authorities observed the section's ban on public references to espionage and sabotage.[124]

But Bentivegni called for an even "greater expansion of German counterespionage." On February 6, 1940, he dictated a detailed account of what he meant by this: "I. That the frontiers of the Reich be fully safeguarded against all undesirable border crossings, legal or illegal. II. That the frontier zone enclosing all Reich territory be developed into a cordon which (a) is free from untrustworthy elements and (b) cannot be entered or traversed by unauthorized persons. III. That the operational area and adjacent areas of denser military occupation be safeguarded by the establishment of a zone subject to more stringent counterespionage regulations. IV. That all foreigners and all unreliable nationals throughout Reich territory be carefully registered and watched."[125]

Bentivegni also got his assistants to draw up a varied list of proposals ranging from the erection near the frontier of "an electrified wire fence which will naturally have to be guarded as well" to the establishment of new supervisory authorities in Germany's diplomatic missions abroad.[126] The police-controlled visa office was, for instance, to extend its supervision to Germans travelling abroad so that "all persons crossing the Reich borders" could be "subjected to regular and repeated checks by Central Office in Berlin."[127]

Most of these proposals were put into effect, creating even closer links between Abwehr III and the Gestapo. Shortage of staff prevented the RSHA from fulfilling all Bentivegni's requests, however, so he decided to make greater use of his section's Geheime Feldpolizei. Although the GFP was only designed to protect the Army in operational areas, Bentivegni had already, in his "Dienstvorschrift für die Geheime Feldpolizei" [Secret Field Police Regulations] of June 1939, gained acceptance of a form of words that made it possible for the Abwehr to employ the GFP as its executive arm inside the Reich as well.[128]

"When following up cases of espionage, etc., which extend beyond the area of operations," it was stipulated, "the GFP is, in an emergency, empowered to act throughout the Reich inclusive of occupied enemy territories. The local Staatspolizeistelle or corresponding authority in occupied territory will where possible be promptly notified in advance."[129] In other words, the Abwehr was claiming for the GFP powers which had hitherto been reserved for the Gestapo alone. This was made even clearer by another passage: "GFP authorities and personnel enjoy the powers which legally pertain to the authorities and personnel of the police and Security Service."[130]

Canaris gave Bentivegni free rein because he could hardly object to the Abwehr's asserting its independence of the Gestapo through the GFP. Although Heydrich soon spotted what was going on, his hands were temporarily tied. He had to accept the fact that former members of his own organization were being played off against the RSHA because no power in Germany could prevent the Wehrmacht from conscripting policemen for military service. Bentivegni assiduously employed the Geheime Feldpolizei for his own purposes, and its men (maximum wartime strength five to six thousand) gained a formidable reputation as screeners of military personnel.[131]

The activities of Bentivegni's section disclose something of the self-assurance that permeated every officer, functionary and employee of the Abwehr. Its sections and groups were animated by a spirit of enterprise and humming with new ideas and projects. Few cared to stand aside

when all Germans had been summoned to strain every sinew on behalf
of their country and its armed forces. OKW-Amt Ausland/Abwehr
took the same attitude as every other national institution. The defeat of
Poland seemed to have made all things possible, and hardly anyone
stopped to wonder where such an inordinate expenditure of energy
would lead.

On September 29, 1939, Bürkner painted a rosy "general picture"
and claimed that "Germany's current political and strategic position"
was "substantially more favourable . . . than in the course of the
[First] World War."[132] He went on: "In this respect, the German
military successes in the East . . . are creating a boom in German prestige and international respect for German strength."[133] There was a corresponding air of optimism about the plans for expansion that were
being diligently and confidently drafted in every Abwehr section.

Canaris, who was still shocked by what he had seen in Poland, did
not altogether welcome this surge of energy in his ranks. Abwehr III's
perfectionism irritated him, especially as he had no taste for systematic
organization and planning. As one who drew inspiration from sudden
whims and flashes of ingenuity, he seldom felt inclined to concentrate
on long-term plans for the future. The result was that many of the Abwehr's innovations had to be carried out against initial opposition
from its chief.

When Captain Dr. Theodor von Hippel of Abwehr II suggested
during an official trip to Dresden that a combat unit should be
recruited from ethnic German agents in the Sudetenland and Poland
and employed on psychological warfare behind the enemy lines, Canaris sensed that the recommendation embodied "National Bolshevist"
ideas and turned it down, remarking that, in an authoritarian state, psychological and ideological warfare was the prerogative of the ruling
party.[134] His indignant response stemmed from a suspicion that Hippel
was a crypto-socialist and pro-Bolshevik. Formerly an officer with General von Lettow-Vorbeck's colonial troops in German East Africa, Hippel did take an interest in the Soviet politico-social experiment. He
dreamed of a socialist system under national auspices—a "synthesis between East and West, an 'individual socialism,'" as he later defined
it.[135]

His latest proposal was not, however, inspired by socialism but by
straightforward concern for ethnic German agents who had worked for
the Abwehr without any official or legal status and now, after the Polish campaign, had no idea where they belonged. Hippel wanted to reac-
commodate them in a military unit which would carry out clandestine
combat missions in enemy territory as part of the Wehrmacht. Canaris
would have none of this.

Undeterred, Hippel decided to consult Groscurth, his former head of section, who had originally summoned the ethnic German combat teams into being.[136] The two men conferred on September 27, and Groscurth backed the idea.[137] A few days later the Organization Section of the Army General Staff issued a directive authorizing Captain von Hippel to form (as Groscurth put it) "a company of saboteurs for the West" composed of ethnic German Abwehr agents.[138] Hippel and his men moved into the Brandenburg barracks of an artillery regiment serving at the front. The new unit, which came under Abwehr II, initially styled itself the Deutsche Kompagnie, from October 25 the Baulehrkompagnie 800 [800th Constructional Training Company], and from January 10, 1940, the Bau-Lehr-Bataillon z.b.V. 800 [800th Special Duties Constructional Training Battalion]. However, its real name— the one later inscribed in the annals of World War II—derived from its first permanent quarters: "die Brandenburger"—the Brandenburgers.[139]

The circumstances under which this Abwehr unit came into being did not prevent Canaris's apologists from transforming him into its spiritual father. Some of them actually speculated that his motive in "creating" the Brandenburgers was to provide the German resistance movement with an armed spearhead for use against Hitler.[140] The true founder of the force could only shake his head at such notions. Hippel: "I consider this line of reasoning mistaken. The Brandenburgers certainly accepted a large number of ardent Nazis after 1940, and their fighting spirit unfitted them for a popular insurrection."[141]

The Abwehr's further expansion in autumn 1939 took place with little active help from its chief. It was only when Keitel redoubled his insistence on safeguarding supplies of oil from Romania against British acts of sabotage that Canaris dispatched Pruck to Romania in mid-October and concluded an agreement with General Moruzov, head of the Romanian secret service, under which the Abwehr was permitted to establish a secret oil security network along the Danube.[142] Similarly, it was Warlimont's proposal to initiate a military survey of Azerbaijan that prompted Canaris to send Captain Dr. Paul Leverkuehn to Tabriz in the guise of a consul—the Abwehr's very first reconnaissance mission in the Near East.[143]

The Abwehr's next essay in expansion, the establishment of KO [War Organization] Bulgaria, was also attributable to chance. One day in January 1940 Canaris buttonholed his friend Major Otto Wagner of Abwehr III in the corridor. Canaris: "I gather you don't feel happy here at headquarters. Is that right?" Wagner nodded. Canaris again: "Where do you think your services would be better employed?" The major remarked that Bulgaria might repay closer attention. The country's proximity to Russia and the Dardanelles made it desirable to establish a KO there. Canaris: "Very well. Be sure to take up your duties in Sofia as soon as possible." On that note he departed without giving Wagner any precise instructions, either then or later.[144]

The Admiral's singular lack of interest was not, however, solely a product of his failings and shortcomings as a departmental chief. He was fully preoccupied at this period with a new Hitlerian edict which seemed bound to aggravate the Reich's predicament and hasten its progress along the road to ruin. The dictator had decided to launch an early offensive in the West, and it can scarcely have rejoiced the Admiral's heart that Hitler's scenario for this offensive gave an important role to the Abwehr unit he had never wanted in the first place.

On September 27, 1939, the very day after Warsaw surrendered, Hitler had summoned his commanders in chief and announced that the Wehrmacht must seize the initiative in the West. Even if this meant violating Dutch and Belgian neutrality, he argued, the Reich could not afford to wait for the Western powers to attack because their military strength was growing day by day.[145]

Looking at the shocked faces of his generals, who had been expecting him to announce the end of the war, not its prolongation, Hitler assumed a moderate tone. He would order an attack only if the Western powers refused to accept the peace proposals which he would be submitting to them in the next few days. Addressing the Reichstag on October 6, he called for a conference of leading European nations. Its objective would be a peace settlement, but based on the latest German conquests.[146]

"Why should war take place in the West?" he sanctimoniously demanded, and answered that it would be senseless "to annihilate millions of human lives and property worth hundreds of thousands of millions" in order to reconstruct the Polish state or give Germany a new regime. "No," he trumpeted, "this war in the West will solve no problems whatsoever." At the same time, he loaded his nebulous peace proposals with fresh demands, e.g. for German colonies and a "solution and settlement of the Jewish problem."[147]

Hitler's "peace" speech was merely a propaganda smoke screen calculated to shroud his long-formed intention of waging war in the West. On October 10, far from waiting for a reply from the British Government, he recalled his commanders in chief and issued them with firm orders: the Western offensive would be mounted later that same autumn.[148]

The previous day he had signed Directive No. 6 on the Conduct of the War, which stated that the aim of this operation was "to destroy the power and capacity of the Western powers ever again to oppose the continued development of the German nation in Europe."[149] Reluctantly, the officers of the Army General Staff set about preparing a plan of campaign.

Hitler drove them hard. He received his military advisers at the Chancellery almost every day, bombarding them with new ideas and brainwaves and insisting on their immediate inclusion in the Wehrmacht's operational plans. Nourished by Karl May's tales of the Wild West, his fevered imagination produced a never-ending succession of stratagems designed to catch his Western adversaries unawares. "They haven't got a *ruse de guerre* among the lot of them," he said derisively of his generals. "They should have read more Karl May!"[150]

But which national institution was better equipped to satisfy the Führer's cowboys-and-Indians romanticism than the Abwehr? A cascade of Hitlerian suggestions, marginalia and directives descended on the Tirpitz-Ufer, and Canaris and Lahousen were often summoned to the Chancellery to listen to the Führer's flights of fancy. These envisaged, for example, that Abwehr commandos wearing foreign uniforms should seize the enemy's bridges and paralyse his defences a few hours before the main assault—indeed, there was even a plan to drop paratroops on The Hague and abduct the entire Dutch cabinet.[151]

In Belgium, a surprise attack was to neutralize Fort Eben Emael and the Albert Canal, which had been developed into a defence line, while in Southern Holland the bridges over the Maas (Meuse), the Maas-Waal and Juliana canals and the Ijssel would be occupied by means of similar tactics. Hitler had devised a different plan for each operation. Abwehr men disguised as policemen and railwaymen would jump the bridge pickets, glider troops would land in the fortified zone of Eben Emael "before first light" and barges packed with infantry would head for the enemy side of the canal.[152]

The Abwehr authorities hastened to comply with Hitler's wishes. Pickenbrock instructed Abwehrstelle Münster and Captain Walter Schulze-Bernett, head of KO Holland, to procure Dutch uniforms and ascertain the whereabouts of the Dutch cabinet and High Command.[153] Schulze-Bernett's agents could not have found this difficult, judging by the captain's frequent boast that his men knew "every pebble in the country."[154]

Schulze-Bernett mobilized every available V-Mann in co-operation with agents belonging to NS-Landesgruppenleiter Otto Butting, the local party boss in Holland. Butting led the three-thousand strong Reichsdeutsche Gemeinschaft [German Nationals' Association] and reported to the headquarters of the party's Auslandsorganisation, where Piekenbrock maintained a liaison officer named Heinz Cohrs.[155] Abwehr men did an equally thorough job in Belgium, while at home in Germany "particulars of the Albert Canal (profiles, embankments, depth, bridge dimensions, demolition chambers)" were obtained from "German firms which had built the canal as a reparations payment after 1918."[156]

Meanwhile, Abwehr II organized the assault detachments that were to pave the way for the German advance. Captain Fleck of Abwehrstelle Oppeln formed 550 Abwehr men into the 100th Special Duties Infantry Battalion, whose orders were to seize and hold the bridges of Northern Belgium and Southern Holland for General von Reichenau's Sixth Army. Captain von Hippel had to surrender fifty men from his Constructional Training Company to the Fourth Army for its thrust into Southern Belgium, and Lahousen had to find eighteen agent-parachutists and about twenty interpreters and guides for the operation against Eben Emael, which had been assigned to the 7th Air Division.[157]

Not having enough men with a knowledge of the language and terrain, Lahousen contacted the head of a Dutch National Socialist organization based in Germany, Julius Herdtmann, and requested his help. Two hundred members of Herdtmann's group were dispatched to Abwehr II camps for military training.[158] Their task was to filter across the border dressed as Dutch military policemen and occupy enemy key points before the assault.

Lahousen soon had a thousand men ready and waiting for Hitler's order to strike.[159] Canaris found himself deeply involved in yet another of the dictator's acts of violence. Although Abshagen claims that the Abwehr chief "pretty sharply opposed" the procurement of Dutch and Belgian uniforms,[160] this cannot be proved and is highly unlikely. On the contrary, Canaris had every reason to impress Hitler with his zeal and ingenuity.

This was because the Wehrmacht's switch from East to West had shown up an embarrassing deficiency which could scarcely be concealed from the Führer. As in World War I, so in World War II, the German secret service had lost the bulk of its V-Mann network in France and Britain almost before the first shot was fired. No reliable source of intelligence existed on the soil of Germany's Western adversaries. Abwehr headquarters strove desperately to discover the identity and location of enemy units and the strength of the forces deployed along Germany's western frontier. No reports about the enemy were received for weeks on end.[161]

Being as ill informed as they were, Canaris and Piekenbrock resorted to guesswork. They usually guessed wrong because they could not shake off the idea—a hangover from World War I—that the French soldier was a tough and aggressive foe. Only incorrigible optimists like Bürkner believed that the French Army had lost its stomach for battle. Most Abwehr I officers took a contrary view.[162] They thought the French might strike at any moment and could not understand why, after a few skirmishes, the *poilus* settled back into an almost cosy "Sitzkrieg" [phony war].

Piekenbrock surmised that the French would "fire leisurely at the West Wall throughout the winter, wear us down and get us to squander our ammunition."[163] The fact that Hitler assessed French morale quite differently was bound to engender friction between him and the Abwehr. There had already been one minor clash during the Polish campaign, and Canaris had made a poor showing.

When Hitler asked for news of developments in the West during a conference in mid-September, the Admiral replied that "all available reports" suggested that the French were "systematically and methodically preparing for a major attack" by concentrating troops and artillery, principally in the Saarbrücken area. The Führer found this improbable. "I cannot conceive," he told Canaris sternly, "that the French would choose to attack in the Saarbrücken area, where our position is strongest. We have our fortifications there. Besides, they would come up against a second and a third line which are, if anything, even better consolidated."[164]

The Abwehr's blind ignorance was finally exposed when the Army Central Staff began to plan its Western offensive. The officers of the Foreign Armies West Section received so little information from the Abwehr that they had to base their first situation maps on reports dating from summer 1938, when the French mobilized during the Sudeten crisis.[165] As for the British Expeditionary Force, absolutely nothing was known about its movements, its command structure and deployment areas.[166]

The head of Foreign Armies West, Lieutenant Colonel Ulrich Liss, was so exasperated by "the total collapse of our military intelligence at the beginning of the war" that he drafted a long and truculent report condemning the Abwehr for having neglected its duties.[167] "Big rumpus at Abw. over Lieutenant Colonel Liss's crazy report," noted Groscurth.[168] Although Canaris had no real answer to these accusations by the General Staff's senior Foreign Armies expert, every Abwehr officer regarded "that troublemaker Liss" (Groscurth again) as a pet abomination from then on.[169]

By slow degrees, Foreign Armies West managed to gain a more accurate idea of the other side's strength. Improved radio monitoring and front-line reconnaissance, coupled with the interrogation of the few French prisoners taken and reports from the German military attaché in Brussels, enabled Liss to present the General Staff with a general picture of the enemy dispositions.[170]

The Abwehr's contribution was extremely modest. It even failed to provide its assault teams with uniforms obtained in neutral Holland and Belgium. Early in November Dutch police arrested an agent from Abwehrstelle Münster who had purchased several outfits from a second-hand dealer in Amsterdam and was trying to smuggle them across the

border into Germany.[171] This incident caused such a stir in the press
that Abwehr headquarters discontinued its efforts to acquire more uniforms (obviously the source of the story that Canaris had opposed their
procurement in the first place).

In fact, Lahousen went looking for people who could produce accurate drawings of Dutch uniforms for the Abwehr's tailors to copy. On
November 8 he noted: "Major von Schweinichen introduced Sergeant
Major Wewer, who is stationed on the Dutch border and seems very
well informed about the uniforms and equipment of the Dutch police
and frontier units."[172] The advice given to Lahousen's tailors does not
appear to have been flawless. In May 1940 many an Abwehr man's
fancy-dress uniform and papier-mâché helmet excited the suspicions of
the Dutch frontier guards.[173]

Hitler angrily demanded information about the uniform fiasco when
Canaris reported on "existing arrangements connected with the Western operation" at the next Chancellery conference.[174] Canaris, who had
still not lost the art of pacifying his Führer, quickly poured oil on troubled waters. Not a muscle in his impassive face revealed the extent of
his desperation. Each new move by Hitler and each new General Staff
decision only reinforced his fatalistic belief that he was on board a sinking ship. Nothing and nobody—no tactical success or strategic victory—
could wean him from that conviction. "Ehrhardt," he told his old
Freikorps friend after the Polish campaign was over,"—Ehrhardt, the
war is lost, no matter how many more victories we win. It's lost."[175]

His hopes had at first revived when Hitler informed the Wehrmacht commanders that the war in the West would go on. The
Führer's announcement dismayed his generals more than any he had
made before. Never had any of his decisions been so fiercely debated.
Almost to a man, Germany's senior military commanders regarded his
projected campaign against the West as suicidal.

The Wehrmacht's weaknesses and bottlenecks were all too apparent. The newly formed third- and fourth-wave divisions were not even
fully equipped for a defensive role, armoured units needed refitting
after the wear and tear of the Polish campaign and ammunition on
hand in October 1939 was only sufficient to supply one third of the
German divisions for a month. Then there were other problems such as
the limited operational capacity of tanks and aircraft in autumn or
winter weather conditions, the seeming impregnability of the French
defences and the numerical strength and firepower of their garrisons.[176]

Hitler's leading generals criticized his plans in a correspondingly
forthright vein. General Ritter von Leeb, whose Army Group C was
stationed in the West, was outraged "that they genuinely mean to
launch this insane attack by violating the neutrality of Holland, Belgium and Luxemburg," and his opposite number at Army Group B,

General von Bock, agreed that a Western offensive had absolutely no prospect of winning the war.[177] The commanders of the Fourth and Sixth Armies, the two main spearheads of the German assault, were equally opposed to the campaign.[178]

The extent to which Hitler's projected offensive had incensed the military was illustrated by General von Reichenau, whom his enemies decried as a "Nazi general." Reichenau betrayed the plan of campaign to an anti-Nazi, ex-Mayor Fritz Elsas, and urged him to warn the Dutch and British authorities through his contacts abroad. The general further suggested that the Dutch should immediately place their canals and waterways in a state of readiness. If this were done openly and ostentatiously enough to rob the German offensive of its surprise effect, Hitler might yet be deterred from unleashing it.[179]

Canaris was too alert and well informed not to sense that the mood of his military colleagues had turned against Hitler. Was this a last-minute opportunity, a providential sign that one more attempt should be made to stem the inexorable advance of the historical process and halt Germany's plunge into the abyss? For one brief moment, the mystical and fatalistic little admiral felt that destiny had summoned him to assist in ending Hitler's baneful regime. His own imagination, nourished by the many confidants who privately sought to influence him, suggested that the discontented generals might now be prepared to launch a coup, possibly even with the help of the Western powers.

The time had come, he felt, for a last personal effort to preserve Germany from finally and irrevocably severing her European ties, in other words, from total commitment to Russia. A beguiling picture took shape in the Admiral's mind: by eliminating Hitler the Germans would extend the hand of friendship to Britain and obtain a peace settlement that conserved what they had filched and extorted under the Führer's leadership. This naturally meant that the Nazi regime must be abolished—sacrificed, as it were, on the altar of reconciliation between Germany and Europe.

Once more ready and waiting were Colonel Oster and his friends, the men who had previously—during the Sudeten crisis of 1938— pinned their hopes on the Admiral's willingness to pave the way for a *coup d'état.* The head of the Central Section and Abwehr chief of staff had for weeks been waiting to enlist his manifold contacts in this great and worthy cause. He had taken full advantage of the superficially futile and inactive period since the outbreak of war to expand his network of like-minded officers and civilians. His friends in the Abwehr—men like Liedig, Heinz, Pfuhlstein and Groscurth—had now been joined by others.

Since August 25 the office next door to Oster's had been occupied by Reichsgerichtsrat Hans von Dohnanyi, his comrade-in-arms during the Fritsch affair. Oster had given Dohnanyi a desk of his own (ZB) whose task was to keep Canaris (and Oster himself) regularly informed of developments in foreign and military policy.[180] An antimilitarist who had been crammed into the unaccustomed uniform of a Sonderführer K [wartime supernumerary with officer status] and given the rank of captain, Dohnanyi looked a trifle bizarre in the well-ordered world of the Abwehr and lent Oster's entourage an element of unreality—a strong whiff of unmilitary "civilianism" which was bound to attract attention in an environment geared to efficiency and discipline.

The Oster circle came to be regarded as a foreign body, not least because Dohnanyi gradually introduced other civilians whose very appearance advertised the fact that they had never "seen service." Most of them were intimate friends and all were staunch opponents of the regime. Dohnanyi's recruits included his childhood friend Justus Delbrück, a civil lawyer and son of the historian Hans von Delbrück, in whose home Dohnanyi himself had grown up, and Baron Karl Ludwig von und zu Guttenberg, editor of the Christian and monarchist *Weisse Blätter,* a publication which was later banned.[181] Referat ZB also kept in touch with Christian resistance circles through the Protestant pastor and theologian Dietrich Bonhoeffer, Dohnanyi's brother-in-law.[182]

Oster and Dohnanyi maintained special links with several Abwehr outstations manned by friends and acquaintances who supported their political endeavours. Abwehrstelle Munich, in particular, was a secure haven for confidants of this type. They included Wilhelm Schmidhuber, a brewery owner and honorary Portuguese consul who came of old military stock but was a businessman by nature and had only joined Abwehrstelle Munich as a reserve officer working in a quasi-part-time capacity.[183]

Oster had even managed to improve his precarious relationship with Halder now that Groscurth had been promoted lieutenant colonel and attached to the Army General Staff in its new quarters at Zossen on the outskirts of Berlin. The Abwehr's one-man liaison staff had since become a Special Duties Section in which largely anti-Nazi Abwehr officers dealt with political and secret service matters under Groscurth's supervision.[184] As head of this section Groscurth was responsible to the Army's Chief of Staff IV [Foreign Armies]. Although he still regarded Canaris as "the Chief," he wanted to repair the damage which the Sudeten crisis had done to relations between Oster and Halder. This did not, however, mean that he took an uncritical view of his friend. "I don't intend," he wrote, "to rely exclusively on Oster's reports."[185]

All in all, the Oster-Dohnanyi circle had many influential connections to offer when Canaris summoned his Chief of Staff to help him mount a major attack on the regime. The Admiral was like a man transformed. Having at last seen a chance to strike, he could not wait for the blow to fall. "There's no time to lose—Hitler must go!" Preserved for us by Halder, this remark became the Abwehr chief's stock refrain.[186] Canaris and Oster switched roles. The latter had always thirsted for action. Now the former outdid him.

Feverishly, Canaris urged Oster and his friends to mobilize their undercover resources. He himself called on all the generals within reach and tried to recruit them for a coup against Hitler. "Vis-à-vis the inner circle of 'resisters,'" Halder wrote later, "Canaris unilaterally and unequivocally played the part of an instigator."[187] Sending for evidence of German crimes in Poland and analyses of Germany's military position, the Admiral hurriedly stuffed them into his briefcase before setting off to visit one Army commander after another.

At the end of September Canaris and Lahousen toured the headquarters of the army groups and armies in the West. The general commanding Army Group C, Ritter von Leeb, made no secret of his willingness to back a coup against the regime if so instructed by higher authority. Support was also expressed by General von Witzleben, commander of the First Army and a leading sponsor of the coup preparations in 1938.[188] Most of the other generals approached by Canaris were chary of committing themselves. Even Reichenau, who still opposed an offensive in the West, recoiled at the idea although Lahousen's subsequent report discreetly stated that his reaction to "Canaris's warnings" had been "far more cautious but, in sum, extremely thoughtful and shrewd."[189] Reichenau's Chief of Staff, the General von Paulus who later won dubious renown at Stalingrad, was more outspoken. He described the wholesale German crimes in Poland as "a necessity of war" and "in other respects fell back on his purely military sphere of duties."[190]

Canaris needed no further evidence that, so far from dissolving since 1938, the problems of organizing a military revolt against the regime had tended to crystallize. The knowledge that their juniors were inspired or at least influenced by National Socialism had robbed the older generation of Army officers of the will to act. Even discounting this pressure from below, however, they shrank from the idea of launching a *coup d'état* against their supreme commander while he was scoring one German victory after another. Still more unthinkable to them was the idea of rebelling in the middle of a war and inviting the enemy to overpower their country in its moment of weakness.

Canaris went his way, immeasurably disappointed and incensed by the generals' lack of instinct. He felt so bitter when he returned to Berlin on October 3 that he refused to see any Army general—not even Major General von Tippelskirch, Chief of Staff IV, who was eager to discuss his criticism of plans for an offensive.[191] Groscurth tried to persuade him to make a trip to Zossen, but in vain. Groscurth: "He wants nothing more to do with those weak-kneed generals."[192]

The Admiral's ill humour must have been short-lived, because only a few days later he heard rumours that genuine opposition to Hitler's plans was taking shape at Zossen itself. Halder had rediscovered his anti-Nazi convictions and was urging the Army commander in chief, General von Brauchitsch, to take steps to prevent the all-out war against the Western powers which he himself wanted to avert at all costs. He had been hoping that the British Government would approve Hitler's peace proposals, but on October 13 Weizsäcker informed him that Chamberlain had turned them down.[193]

Next day Halder and Brauchitsch sat down and discussed the alternatives open to the General Staff. Halder saw "three possibilities: attack, a waiting game, and fundamental changes. No firm prospect of any of these, least of all the last, because it is essentially negative and productive of weakness. Discounting this, a duty to set forth the military outlook soberly and canvass any chance of peace."[194] For the first time ever, an official Wehrmacht diary had recorded the possibility of a *coup d'état* against the supreme commander, for "fundamental changes" could mean nothing else.

But the diffident commander in chief flinched from such a distasteful solution and sold Halder on the idea of using military arguments to change the Führer's mind. On October 16, when Hitler was still insistent on an offensive, Halder and Brauchitsch committed an act of tacit sabotage.[195] They demonstrated their complete "lack of interest" in Hitler's intentions by drawing up a sketchy and superficial plan of campaign and submitting it to the dictator through OKW chief Keitel.[196] These tactics were only a short-term expedient. On October 22 Hitler sent Keitel back with his amendments and announced that the Western offensive must open on November 12.[197] The two generals flew into a panic. Even before this, Groscurth had noted: "Complete loss of nerve [on Halder's part]. Brauchitsch also flummoxed."[198]

Halder's friend and deputy, General Carl-Heinrich von Stülpnagel, Chief of Staff I, implored him to dissociate himself from the commander in chief's futile manoeuvres and take the initiative. Stülpnagel: "You're becoming unnecessarily dependent on that man Brauchitsch."[199] After much discussion the two friends agreed that, however risky it might be, only the "fundamental changes" option could effect a decisive improvement in the situation. Without confiding in his immediate circle, Halder sought allies and openings for a coup against Hitler.

Groscurth, who must have got wind of Halder's plans, urged his friends at Abwehr headquarters to focus all their efforts on the Chief of Staff and his deputy. Canaris and Oster were quick to visit Zossen, where they doggedly put pressure on the generals. On October 25 they tried a combined assault and were rebuffed. Groscurth noted: "Colonel O[ster] with OQuI [Chief of Staff I]—turned down. Afternoon, Canaris with OQuI. Equally unsuccessful. Oster and self accused of pushing too hard."[200]

Halder felt a renewed antipathy for Oster, especially as the latter was tactless enough to invoke the name of Halder's predecessor, Beck, whom he greatly admired. On his own authority, Oster anointed Beck head of the military resistance, heedless of the fact that most OKH officers were just as annoyed by the frustrated old general's frequent misjudgements as they were resentful of his caustic comments on Halder and Brauchitsch ("sixth-form schoolboys in their capacity for assessing the immediate military situation").[201] Major General von Tippelskirch, who was anything but a National Socialist, adorned an unsigned Beck memorandum with the following marginal note: "Was this paper written by an Englishman or a German? If the latter, he's overdue for a concentration camp."[202]

Halder's annoyance at being badgered by Oster and Canaris caused him to reject all the opposition's advances. He gave no verbal hint that he had long been grappling with the practicalities of a problem they still regarded as abstract. By October 31, when Dohnanyi began, with Gisevius's help, to summarize all the arguments against a Western offensive in a memorandum intended for submission to the generals, Halder had already sent Stülpnagel to the West to discover how many army and army group commanders would be prepared to back a coup.[203]

Only then, on October 31, did Halder think it opportune to take the Tirpitz-Ufer conspirators into his confidence. Sending for Groscurth, he plied the astonished liaison officer with such a barrage of threats against Hitler that Groscurth anxiously commended the virtues of "orderly procedure." Groscurth's diary reads: "In tears, H[alder] said he had been calling on Emil [Hitler] for weeks with a pistol in his pocket, intending to shoot him out of hand if the occasion arose." Halder inquired the names of candidates for political leadership if a coup took place. Groscurth mentioned Beck and Goerdeler. The Chief of Staff studiously ignored Beck's name but asked that Goerdeler should be "taken care of."[204] Still bewildered by Halder's disclosures, Groscurth dashed to his car and drove back to Berlin.

Canaris, Oster and Dohnanyi reacted at once. It took them only a few hours to resume contact with dissident politicians like Goerdeler, Schacht and Hassell, as well as with Count Helldorf, the Berlin police chief. Meanwhile, the two military activists became steadily more definite in their suggestions and instructions. On November 2 Stülpnagel summoned Groscurth and told him to "get preparations under way."[205] Back in Berlin, Groscurth and his immediate subordinate Captain Fiedler discussed details of the coup with Oster and Dohnanyi.

Stülpnagel continued to feed Groscurth with advice and information. On one occasion he listed the dispositions of the units that would lend themselves to use in a revolt, on another he confided the names of officers who could be trusted.[206] Even the much maligned Oster received a hearing at Zossen, not from Halder but from Stülpnagel, who saw him on November 4 and asked him to update and amplify his coup plans of summer 1938.[207]

Oster, who needed no such encouragement, had long since dug out his recommendations on how to strike at the regime's power base in Berlin. Committed to three sheets of paper innocuously headed "Study," these outlined the way in which rebel troops would cordon off the government quarter, occupy the central administration blocks and arrest prominent members of the regime. Other measures included a Wehrmacht take-over of the executive powers of government, the proclamation of a state of emergency and the formation of a Reich Directorate by military leaders and trustworthy civilians.[208]

Oster's recurrent question was "Whom to bag and how?"—in other words, which leaders of the regime to put out of action at once. His own answer was "Hi, Gö, Rib, Hi, Hey," meaning Hitler, Göring, Ribbentrop, Himmler and Heydrich. He made it quite clear that these five were to be summarily shot,[209] though his papers also included a plan by Groscurth, who envisaged a different solution. According to this, Hitler would be taken alive and examined by a medical board of inquiry. The results—a foregone conclusion—would then be published.[210]

Oster adapted his original scheme to the distribution of forces prevailing in November 1939. Groscurth supplied him with the necessary details and Canaris contributed many items of information gleaned from his trips to the Western front. The more Oster rewrote his plan, however, the more he realized that its technical execution would be harder than in 1938. There were not enough reliable units in the Berlin area. The other side—Gestapo, SD and militarized SS—had gained strength.

The main difficulty was that Germany was at war. Any leader of a coup had to recognize that the Western powers might take advantage of internal disorder, or even civil war, to mount a full-scale attack on the Reich. To some a source of genuine concern and to others a welcome pretext for doing nothing, this factor pervaded every discussion the conspirators held with senior military commanders. Oster concluded that they must approach the Western powers and extract some form of standstill agreement coupled, if possible, with a guarantee of the new Germany's territorial integrity.[211]

But how were the conspirators to contact the enemy without incurring the stigma of treason? Oster had a brainwave. The ideas and intentions of the German resistance movement must be conveyed to the Western powers by a respected and neutral head of state, preferably Pope Pius XII. This appealed to Canaris, who had known Pius during his nunciature in Berlin and had often met him while riding in the Tiergarten.[212]

That left the problem of how to approach the Pope and initiate him into the conspirators' plans. Canaris and Oster were still debating the choice of a secret emissary when help arrived in the person of Captain Schmidhuber of Abwehrstelle Munich, who was a frequent visitor to Berlin and a devoted admirer of Christine von Dohnanyi, the Sonderführer's wife. A man of many connections, Schmidhuber knew an astute Munich lawyer who was "well in" with the Vatican and had succeeded for years, with a mixture of cunning and candour, in preserving Catholics and Church property from the clutches of the Gestapo.[213]

This Josef Müller, who bore the peculiar nickname "Ochsensepp" [Joe the Ox], readily accepted Oster's invitation to a confidential interview in Berlin, where the two men soon discovered that—as Oster put it—they "spoke the same language."[214]

Forty-one years old, Müller was a farmer's son from Upper Franconia whose legal career had been preceded by a rugged boyhood spent driving hay wagons and herding cattle (hence his sobriquet). After serving as a lieutenant in a mortar battalion during World War I, he had become a close associate of Heinrich Held, the Bavarian Premier ousted by the Nazis in 1933. He was an out-and-out opponent of the National Socialist regime,[215] so Oster's veiled attempts to extort his allegiance—"We know far more more about you than you do about us!"[216]—were wholly superfluous.

Müller listened calmly to Oster's flights of fancy. "The central directorate of German military intelligence, where you now are," Oster told him, "is also the central directorate of the German military opposition."[217] This resistance group was headed by General Beck, who requested him, Müller, "in the name of a decent Germany . . . to re-establish contact with the present Pope."[218] The Western powers must be informed via the Pope that the military opposition was planning Hitler's overthrow in order to prevent an attack in the West. At the same time, they must be persuaded to guarantee a standstill in the event of a coup and a "just and honourable peace."

Müller agreed to visit Rome on the opposition's behalf. Although he wondered why he had not been taken to see Canaris, the official author of his invitation to Berlin, he was content to regard Oster as the real wire-puller. Canaris did, in fact, leave his Chief of Staff to get in touch with Rome and, thus, with the Western powers. Whether doubtful of the venture's chances or averse to contacts with his country's opponents in war, he remained in the background. His only personal contribution was a plausible front for the lawyer's secret mission.

The Admiral approved Müller's enrolment in the Abwehr as a lieutenant of the reserve and his posting to Abwehrstelle Munich, with the proviso that he must be permanently available to Abwehr headquarters for special assignments in Italy.[219] Playing on Keitel's inveterate mistrust of Germany's Italian allies, Canaris informed him that Lieutenant Müller would be keeping an eye on developments in that quarter. The version current at Amt Ausland/Abwehr was that Müller had been detailed to explore the Allies' attitude towards peace talks with Germany.[220]

Canaris, whose characteristic duplicity prompted him to confide in his chief opponent and neutralize him at the same time, told Heydrich a similar tale soon afterwards. His department, he said, was in contact via the Vatican with the British, who seemed strangely less interested in military intelligence than in news of the Reich's internal situation. Since the Abwehr did not have access to such material, he wondered if the RSHA would render some interdepartmental assistance. Heydrich dodged this request, commenting that the decision rested with Himmler and that he objected on principle to raising the matter.[221]

Armed with this insurance policy, Müller could now leave for Rome. Influential helpers smoothed his path. Schmidhuber provided him with some useful names at the Vatican, but his major asset was a letter of recommendation from Abbot Corbinian Hofmeister, who was indebted to him for help in restoring Niederaltaich Abbey in 1934.[222] Müller also had some important Vatican contacts of his own. These included Monsignor Schönhöffer, who had been a witness at his wedding, and Monsignor Ludwig Kaas, once chairman of the German Centre Party and now in the nature of a German adviser to the Pope.[223] Müller got in touch with these two clerics as soon as he was safely installed in the Flora, an unpretentious Roman hotel.[224]

It was Kaas who established the initial contact. He went to the papal summer residence at Castel Gandolfo, where Pius XII was staying until the end of October, and passed on what Müller had told him. The Pope agreed to forward messages from the German military opposition to the British Government but told Kaas to begin by sounding out the British Embassy at the Vatican.[225] He also declined to meet Müller in person. All communications were to be transmitted by way of Kaas and the papal private secretary, Robert Leiber, a Jesuit priest from Baden. Pius XII: "Father Leiber shall be our common mouthpiece."[226]

Müller and Leiber met often from then on, usually at the priest's private quarters in the Papal University. Topics of conversation were few at first because, as the former emissary recalls, "soundings dragged on for weeks without yielding any tangible result."[227] Kaas, who was far from convinced of the lawyer's serious intentions, had difficulty in finding the right moment for a talk with the British Ambassador, Sir Francis d'Arcy Osborne, and more than a month went by before he showed his hand.[228]

However, Müller's reports from Rome were sufficiently optimistic to intensify the conspirators' efforts. Some of his preliminary information found its way into the memorandum with which Dohnanyi and his associates hoped to persuade the generals to strike a blow for freedom. Final preparations for a coup were made at Abwehr headquarters and Zossen. Halder had already warned the leading conspirators to hold themselves in readiness for a military coup from November 5 onwards.[229]

On that crucial date Brauchitsch planned to make a last attempt to talk Hitler out of his Western offensive. Although it was a vain endeavour, Halder encouraged Brauchitsch to make it because his own plans would otherwise be doomed to failure. This was yet another immutable factor governing any German military coup. No revolt was feasible without the Army Commander in Chief because no unit would march against its supreme commander without an order from him. As Chief of the General Staff, Halder had no executive powers. He needed his commander in chief. Only if Brauchitsch were sent packing by Hitler—or so Halder may have reasoned—would he finally sign the order to rise in revolt.

Brauchitsch spent days rehearsing for his interview with the dictator. Halder had done everything possible to steel him against Hitler. At the beginning of the month he took Brauchitsch on a conducted tour of the army groups in the West and showed off their general mood of dissatisfaction with the political leadership.[230] General von Brauchitsch seemed determined to stake everything on a single throw of the dice. Accompanied by Halder, he drove to the Chancellery on November 5. At twelve noon precisely he was standing in the big Kongresssaal, face to face with Hitler.[231]

The commander in chief presented his objections to the Western offensive but did not get far. Hitler's proximity flustered him. He stumbled over his words and contradicted himself, giving the dictator a welcome opportunity to hit back. Hitler pelted him with accusations and demolished his arguments, one by one, with steadily mounting volume and venom. Keitel was angrily summoned to become a mute observer of the Führer's verbal onslaughts. Hitler scathingly called on the commander in chief to substantiate his allegations of military indiscipline during the Polish campaign. When Brauchitsch failed to produce any evidence on the spot, he brusquely turned and stalked out of the room. Brauchitsch and Keitel stared at each other in silence.[232]

A few moments later Brauchitsch rejoined the waiting Halder "as

white as a sheet—you might even say, looking convulsed" (this according to Engel, Hitler's adjutant) and hurried him from the scene.[233] At
the end of his tether, Brauchitsch tremulously described the clash in
the Kongresssaal. Halder became infected with the commander in
chief's panic. What mainly alarmed him were the threats Hitler had uttered at the end of the interview. He knew all about "the spirit of Zossen," he said. His patience was exhausted—he would mercilessly stamp
it out.[234]

Halder was smitten with the fear that Hitler had already learned of
his plans for a *coup d'état* and might hit back at any moment. There
was no chance of launching one with Brauchitsch, who had burst like a
balloon. Their tour at the beginning of the month had demonstrated
that no army commander would lend himself to a coup, even in the
West. How had General von Rundstedt, commanding Army Group A
and—according to Lahousen—a typical "general in the old Prusso-German military tradition, ready for anything," responded to Halder's inquiry about his attitude to a revolt? Rundstedt: "You can order one for
all I care, but my instrument of authority would fall to pieces in my
hand if I tried to use it for that purpose."[235]

Halder's sole inference was as bewildering as his sudden flirtation
with a *coup d'état:* he decided to abandon the conspiratorial ship while
there was still time. Hurrying back to his office, he sent for Stülpnagel
and ordered him to destroy all their plans.[236] There must be no evidence of his own treasonable ideas, no document that might expose the
coup to a surprise visit by the Gestapo. Stülpnagel informed Groscurth,
who confided to his diary: "We have orders to burn everything."[237]

Then Halder sent for Groscurth to explain his *volte-face.* Every military argument had been exhausted, he said. In default of anyone to
lead "the cause," the Western offensive would take place. Halder: "So
the forces that were counting on us are no longer committed. You
know what I mean."[238] Groscurth's secretary recalls that he returned to
his office "pale as death."[239]

His hopes revived for a brief spell. After a long talk with Colonel
Wagner, the anti-Nazi who headed Section 6 of the Army General
Staff [Supply and Administration], Groscurth went back to Halder and
suggested calling in Beck, Goerdeler and Schacht, who were in a position to lead a *coup d'état.* Halder rejected the idea. When Groscurth
insisted that action could not be deferred any longer and that Admiral
Canaris likewise advocated Hitler's immediate removal, Halder angrily
retorted that, if so, Canaris ought to "get rid of him himself."[240]

Groscurth hurried back to Berlin to inform the Tirpitz-Ufer conspirators of Halder's defection. It was during this car drive on the evening of
November 5, 1939, that there must have occurred what some historians
have called a "momentous misunderstanding" but might more accu-

rately have termed an act of desperation on Groscurth's part: he converted an angry retort into a firm injunction to act. Going to Canaris and Oster, he transmitted "an urgent request" from Halder that the Admiral should "arrange to have Hitler assassinated. If that condition were fulfilled, he, Halder, would be willing to 'take action.' "[241] Our account of the scene derives from Gisevius, a bitter enemy of Halder's, but Groscurth's diary also contains the words: "I was to brief Canaris and tell him to act."[242]

Canaris, who was absolutely infuriated, took umbrage at this alleged request and grumbled that "Herr Halder" was not going to turn him into an assassin. If the Chief of the General Staff wanted to discuss matters of supreme political import, let him do so in person.[243] Almost beside himself with rage, the Admiral reverted to Halder's supposed presumption again and again. He demanded that Halder should "shoulder the responsibility in a clear-cut fashion" and not seek to foist it on others.[244]

Canaris was so upset that he refused to spare another Abwehr officer for Halder's dubious schemes. Although he may soon have sensed that Groscurth had misled him, knowing as he did that Halder shared his own deep-rooted aversion to an attempt on Hitler's life, the Admiral's faith in the Army dwindled fast. It sank to zero when he was summoned to the Chancellery the following afternoon to present yet another report on Abwehr II's preparations for the Western campaign.[245]

Even though he learned that the offensive had been postponed for a few days, he returned from the Chancellery steeped in gloom. Being accustomed to their master's abrupt changes of mood, his subordinates were not unduly worried. "Canaris . . . asked us if he ought to resign," Gisevius reports, "but this question was largely a matter of form; he often asked it in order to have us confirm his indispensability."[246] However, it soon became clear that the Admiral's low spirits concealed something of greater significance. Canaris was steadily losing his taste for the conspirators' guessing games.

This became clear to Groscurth, who was already devising new ways of persuading the Army to act. He had heard tell of Halder's remark that, although he wanted a coup as such, he was powerless without Witzleben and the First Army. Groscurth promptly decided that Oster and Gisevius must call on Witzleben and try to enlist his Army Group C in a *coup d'état*.[247] Canaris declined to release Oster, so Groscurth resorted to a ruse. The trip became feasible on November 7, but only after he had telephoned Witzleben and asked him to request the colonel's presence—apparently on his own initiative.[248]

As it turned out, Oster behaved so tactlessly during his visit to Leeb's and Witzleben's headquarters next day that Halder's worst prejudices were confirmed and even Canaris lost faith in Oster's talent for conspiracy. Colonel Vincenz Müller, Ia at Army Group C's Frankfurt headquarters, took fright when Oster reeled off a whole string of plotters' names and read him excerpts from two draft proclamations of a *coup d'état* by Beck which he blithely carried around with him as if the Gestapo did not exist.[249]

Colonel Müller had some difficulty in persuading him to burn the two documents in an ashtray, but Oster had copies of both proclamations with him—plus a list of the leading conspirators—when he called on Witzleben at his headquarters in Bad Kreuznach that afternoon.[250] The old war horse, who was depressed and in poor health, rounded on him angrily: "What, you had this in the car with you? Then I never want to see you again!"[251] He eventually calmed down, but not before cautioning Oster against further indiscretions.

Witzleben was so alarmed that he instructed Colonel Müller, who was travelling to Berlin, to tell the Chief of Staff to hide all incriminating evidence and be on his guard against Oster's carelessness.[252] Neither he nor Müller knew that Oster was already guilty of another escapade. Dropping in at an officers' mess in Frankfurt on the return journey, he had delivered a furious tirade against the Nazis and left behind a list of prospective members of the revolutionary government. As luck would have it, an officer sympathetic to the cause pocketed this before it could fall into the wrong hands.[253]

Back in Berlin, Halder was enraged by Oster's irresponsibility and convinced that it would send them all to the gallows. The Chief of Staff washed his hands of Colonel Oster. He barred him from access to the Army General Staff and told Groscurth to apprise him of his extreme displeasure. He further recommended Groscurth to submit an official report which would compel Canaris to discipline his Chief of Staff.[254]

Groscurth was too attached to Oster to submit such a report, but Canaris was tired of his friend's political forays. Oster and Gisevius had only just returned to Berlin on November 9 when the Admiral sent for Oster and ordered him to desist from his conspiratorial activities against the regime.[255] He also warned Oster, Dohnanyi and Groscurth against having too much to do with "that eternal rebel" Gisevius, which amounted to a ban on the latter's admission to Abwehr headquarters.[256]

The Admiral's friends were surprised to observe his progressive dissociation from plans for the coup whose most fervent advocate he had so recently been. The dramatic events of the past few days were preying on his mind and making it quite intolerable for him to play a double role in which he prepared for war and, at the same time, plotted to destroy the regime. Halder's *volte-face*, Oster's recklessness, the Munich attempt to assassinate Hitler on November 8 and the SD kidnapping operation at Venlo a day later—none of these things could fail to make a sensitive and neurasthenic man wonder how much longer he could sustain a Jekyll-and-Hyde existence under Hitler's very nose.

His position had become far too equivocal. How, for example, were his British adversaries to discern a fundamental difference between the Canaris who camouflaged his Abwehr officers as members of the resistance in Holland and the Canaris who had sent a genuine anti-Nazi to negotiate in Rome? The busy and uncommunicative little Abwehr chief remained something of a mystery even to German opponents of the regime, who gradually became suspicious of him. They would have been still more suspicious had they known that on November 9, after despondently listening to Oster's report on Army Group C's lack of enthusiasm for the cause, he forwarded material to the Gestapo advising them that "a [fresh] attempt on the Führer's life" was being discussed by "officers, party officials and foreigners" at a boardinghouse in the Kurfürstendamm.[257]

These were internal contradictions too glaring for any one man to reconcile. Canaris might have summoned up more patience and courage if he had at least been able to credit the possibility of a coup against Hitler, but he had abandoned all hope of overthrowing him. Halder, with whom he had patched things up, brought him firm evidence that no military commander was ready for an insurrection. Canaris must have felt like General von Stülpnagel, whose initial dismay at Halder's withdrawal had been tempered by another tour of the army groups. "You're right," he said, "it's no good. The commanders and their men would never obey your call."[258]

Oster and his confederates dismissed this as cowardice, but Canaris could sympathize with the feelings of senior military commanders who wanted to safeguard their men from the political dynamite of civil war —officers to whom the preservation of units which were the soldier's true homeland meant more than the fate of their country. This attitude seemed incomprehensible to Groscurth and Oster, who had never commanded any sizeable body of men, let alone to civilian outsiders like Dohnanyi and Gisevius. Canaris, the former submarine commander and Freikorps officer, knew what it meant to preserve the solidarity of a unit in time of political collapse.

He drew little encouragement from the reports submitted by his emissary in Rome, who visited Berlin on November 13.[259] Although he did not actually see "Herr X," as Müller was called for security reasons, the latter's written report could not—for all its optimistic tone—disguise his continuing failure to establish contact with the British authorities. Müller had been assured by the Belgian abbot general of the Premonstratensians, Hubert Noots, that "influential circles in Britain,

France and Belgium" were "genuinely desirous of a fair peace" with Germany after Hitler's removal.[260]

Canaris must have realized that such expressions of opinion were merely glosses on the part of Vatican clerics and diplomats who had their own reasons for converting Müller into a mouthpiece. Nothing had more deeply disquieted the Vatican than the Hitler-Stalin pact, and nothing could have been more unnerving than the nightmare vision of a convergence between Communism and National Socialism. The worldwide interests of the Catholic Church prescribed their estrangement, so its representatives did not shrink from suggesting that a non-Nazi Germany should break with Moscow—nor even from dangling the carrot of new territorial acquisitions in the Soviet East.

Müller was naive enough to relay the Vatican's siren song to the German military authorities. Noots informed him that influential figures in the West regarded "war against Germany, if Hitler's pro-Russian government is removed, as pointless because our natural expansion is directed eastwards, and there our interests coincide."[261] According to Müller, Leiber's ideas all boiled down to "the creation of a European united front against Russia,"[262] and another Vatican diplomat openly proclaimed "a crusade against Russia in which the Germans, too, must participate" unless they wished to be "numbered on the same side."[263]

There could have been no more grotesque reversal of Müller's mission. Instead of peace with the Western powers, the Vatican was offering a military alliance against the Soviet Union. Although Canaris shared many of the Vatican's fears, post-Hitler Germany could have no interest in a war against Russia. Thus the talks in Rome offered no escape from the German impasse. On November 30 Hassell wrote: "He [Canaris] has abandoned all hope of resistance by the generals and thinks it pointless to try anything more in that line.[264]

But Oster was not the sort of man to renounce his crusade on orders from above. If the military establishment were unprepared to neutralize the dictator, he and his friends would find other ways of abolishing the pernicious Nazi regime—not only without Canaris but, if need be, despite him.

The simplest and most drastic means of extricating the generals from their bonds of allegiance was to murder Hitler. One of Ribbentrop's subordinates, the diplomat Erich Kordt, volunteered to do the deed. He had obtained plans of the Chancellery and knew every door and passageway leading to the Führer's quarters.[265] All Kordt lacked was the explosive needed to blow him up. This the Abwehr possessed, but Oster knew perfectly well that Canaris would be too opposed to the plan to release any. He decided to act without him.

In November he took Lahousen into his confidence because the head of Abwehr II was the only section chief authorized to issue explosive. When Lahousen heard what it was to be used for he asked Oster if the Admiral knew of the scheme. Oster: "No, the Old Man's nerves are shot as it is."[266] The more Oster expatiated on his plan, the clearer it became to Lahousen that "Canaris had no knowledge of these matters or did not appear to have been consulted by Oster."[267]

Lahousen swallowed his misgivings and procured the only available explosive not subject to the tighter checks on explosive substances that had been introduced since the November 8 attempt on Hitler's life, a "suitcase containing explosive and clockwork detonators" (Lahousen) which had been deposited at the Stockholm embassy for use in acts of sabotage in Sweden.[268] Lahousen asked Oster if he had already found an assassin. Oster: "Yes, but he knows nothing about detonators or explosives. He ought to undergo a short course of training at Abwehr II's laboratory in Tegel, possibly disguised as an agent."[269] It never came to that because Oster eventually came to the conclusion that Kordt was not the man for the job.

Canaris remained quite as ignorant of the assassination plan as he was of Oster's instructions to Müller on the subject of his future negotiations in Rome. Müller's original brief had been to discover the terms on which the Western powers might be prepared to conclude a peace settlement with Germany once Hitler was removed. His position now changed. Instead of waiting to hear the Allies' terms, he himself devised a programme that anticipated the other side's demands.[270]

On small slips of paper which he sneaked to his Vatican contacts as a basis for discussion, Müller tried to coax the British out of their shell by stripping Germany of one asset after another. He offered the return of Poland and Czechoslovakia (less the Sudetenland), promised that the Reich's centralism would be offset by the establishment of a loose federation and undertook to partition Germany into a West German state and, possibly, a South German state inclusive of Austria.[271]

Müller became so eager to make concessions that even the sceptical Monsignor Kaas felt impelled to contact the British. On December 1 he presented His Britannic Majesty's Ambassador with such a circumstantial account of prior developments that Osborne assumed he was warning the British against negotiating with Müller's principals. Kaas recalled the Venlo affair, described the proposal for secret peace talks as "premature" and suggested that the men on whose behalf the German intermediary was acting ought first to supply proof that they were in a position to overthrow the Hitler regime.[272]

Müller was unaware that "Onkel Ludwig" (Kaas's code name in his reports) had taken such an equivocal line. Heartened by the fact that Kaas had spoken to the British at all, he busily churned out more slips of paper bearing revolutionary scenarios, each more fanciful than the last. The coup, he informed Osborne, would be launched somewhere other than Berlin. There would be two German governments for a while, and the outcome would be a "comparatively serious civil war in Germany."[273]

Canaris would hardly have sanctioned such tactics had he known of them, but he did not. Müller said later that the Admiral had never discussed his talks in Rome. "He knew of my trips . . . but never asked for details. He always avoided being privy to them."[274] Oster took care not to give his head of department any precise information. Müller, too, knew why Canaris was "not initiated" and why "the central direction functioned independently though Oster."[275] Müller: "Canaris was an eminently shrewd man, but his very shrewdness prevented him from clearing hurdles because he had failed to overcome all his inhibitions."[276]

The Abwehr chief was only called in when the conspirators ran into trouble and needed his agile assistance. This they soon did. In December a V-Mann employed by Abwehrstelle Stuttgart, the Benedictine monk Hermann Keller, picked up Müller's trail and was soon within an ace of unearthing all his secret Vatican connections.

Keller, a Nazi conformist who was involved in a variety of clerical intrigues and had clashed with Müller in the past, heard of his mission by chance.[277] While travelling through Switzerland he bumped into a Berlin lawyer named Etscheit, whom he had met in the course of an ecclesiastical hearing and whom Canaris and Halder had sent abroad to open a dialogue with some leading German expatriates. Etscheit confided to the monk—over several drinks—that Halder, Hammerstein-Equord and Beck were planning a coup against Hitler. He himself was negotiating on their behalf in Switzerland while his colleague Müller was trying to initiate peace talks with the Western powers in Rome.[278]

Hearing the hated name Müller, Keller itched to foil the lawyer's game. He travelled to Rome and would soon have uncovered Müller's secret had he not boasted of the preliminary results of his inquiries to Father Augustin Mayer, a Vatican-based Benedictine who tipped Müller off.[279] Müller could not, however, prevent Keller from submitting an account of his investigations to Abwehrstelle Stuttgart. This report was forwarded through official channels to Abwehr headquarters, where it came to the notice of Oster and Dohnanyi.[280]

Keller's report greatly alarmed the two conspirators because they knew that the monk sometimes spied for the SD as well. Their worst fears were confirmed when they heard that Heydrich had summoned Keller to Berlin and asked him to repeat his story in person.[281]

What happened next cannot be established beyond doubt. Müller alleges that Dohnanyi summoned Keller to his office and questioned him in an attempt to discover how much he had told Heydrich, pleading that the details of the Rome report had to be verified for Canaris's benefit. It transpired that Müller's arrest was "only a matter of days." Still according to Müller, Canaris stepped in and encouraged him to write a report implying that Generals von Fritsch, Halder, Hammerstein-Equord and Reichenau had planned a coup before the war. At the mention of Reichenau, Müller objected that he was a Nazi. Canaris retorted: "You've still got a couple of things to learn, my dear Müller. Put down Reichenau and some day I'll tell you why." Canaris had then taken this report to Hitler, who dismissed it as "trash" because of its obvious absurdity and "flung it to the ground."[282]

This colourful story sounds dubious. If it is unlikely that Dohnanyi, whose membership of the Central Section precluded him from controlling Abwehr agents, requested an agent to submit a report, it is totally improbable that Canaris should have sent for a man he scarcely knew and dictated a report designed to hoodwink his omnipotent Führer—quite apart from the fact that a report signed by Müller would have been valueless because the original document came from Keller and a copy of it already reposed on Heydrich's desk.

Keller later insisted that he never spoke to Dohnanyi and that the course of his interview with Heydrich differed from the account given by Müller.[283] More important than this denial, however, is the fact that the other main victim of Etscheit's loquacity, Halder, preserves a far simpler recollection of the affair.

According to him, it was provoked by an article in a Swiss newspaper, not by Etscheit's indiscretion. Halder writes: "Canaris got hold of the article. He had a copy made, adding other names—e.g. Reichenau and Keitel—which Hitler would consider innocuous. This copy he deposited on Hitler's desk during a briefing. He [Hitler] glanced through it, said 'Nonsense!', and the danger was past."[284] Halder's version of this "minor episode" sounds more realistic than Müller's wild story, which would not, of course, have been complete without an intimation that Heydrich had hoped to use the Keller-Etscheit affair "to 'roll up' the whole of the Abwehr."[285]

Whichever reading is correct, one cannot help feeling that Canaris intervened for Halder's sake rather than Oster's. Even when the affair had blown over, Oster continued to deny the Admiral an insight into Müller's negotiations. Oster and Canaris drew no closer politically as a result of their common peril. On the contrary, they became separated by an almost unbridgeable gulf.

Oster had meanwhile been prompted by conscience and conviction to take yet another step towards the barrier beyond which, in Canaris's view, the mine field of treason began. If generals were deterred from launching a coup by implicit faith in Hitler, and if an attempt on the dictator's life proved impracticable, Oster reasoned, there was still one drastic means of releasing German soldiers from the Führer's evil spell.

During their next military adventure, Hitler and the Wehrmacht must sustain a reverse grave enough to shatter the myth of the Führer's invincibility and encourage the regime's military opponents to abolish the Nazi system. This theory enjoyed widespread support among the military themselves. Halder himself held a similar view because his pessimistic assessment of Germany's offensive strength made a setback in the West seem all too certain.[286]

However, what set Oster apart from other opponents of the regime was his fanatical and uncompromising determination that Germany's Western offensive should fail. Not content to wait for this setback, he planned to hasten it and make an active contribution to the Wehrmacht's defeat. This meant that the countries of Western Europe, which had become enemies of Germany against their will, must be warned of the forthcoming attack and acquainted with the plans and objectives of the German High Command. The sooner this new act of war occurred, the greater the chance that the Wehrmacht's ill-prepared offensive would grind to a halt.

Canaris would never have followed Oster down this road had he known of his friend's intentions. Their positions were becoming more and more distinct. Canaris wanted to avert the new campaign whereas Oster planned to bring it about because only a Western offensive could defeat the Wehrmacht and destroy the Hitler myth. To put it baldly, Oster feared nothing so much as a peace settlement that would conserve the Nazi dictatorship. Canaris, on the other hand, had always been anxious to preserve peace because he believed that any war would spell the end of Germany—and Germany, which possessed an intrinsic and quasi-religious value in the Admiral's world of emotions and ideas, meant more to him than any political system his country chose to adopt. This devotion to Germany set narrow limits on his opposition to the regime. As his conduct during the Sudeten crisis and prior to the Polish campaign had shown, he always resisted Hitler's warlike policy until the first shot was fired. Once that happened, his actions were governed solely by the criteria and traditions of military discipline.

There can be no clearer indication that Canaris was hobbled by his conception of the nation-state. Oster had long been aware that the war unleashed by Nazi totalitarianism transcended the traditional boundaries of national social systems and that, over and above the state and nation, there were values that had to be preserved from nihilism disguised as patriotism—if necessary by means which the conventional mind regarded as outright treason.

"There's no turning back, not for me," Oster murmured to his friend Liedig as they were driving through the streets of Berlin in October 1939. Liedig did not follow him at first. Then Oster confided: "It's far simpler to take a pistol and gun someone down—far simpler to charge into a burst of machine-gun fire for the sake of a cause—than to do what I have in mind. If it ever comes to that, please stay friends with me even when I'm dead. Be the friend who knows how things were with me and what moved me to do things which other people may never understand or would certainly never have done themselves."[287]

Oster had already found someone to help him leak details of Germany's military preparations to the Allies. Major Gijsbertus Jacobus Sas was the Dutch military attaché in Berlin and had known Oster since 1932. The two men had struck up a friendship because they agreed on basic political issues. As ex-head of the Operations Section of the Dutch General Staff, Sas seemed just the man to furnish a correct interpretation of Oster's hints and disclosures, especially as he himself had predicted at the beginning of October that war in the West was only a few weeks off—"and this time we [the Dutch] will not escape."[288]

Two weeks later Oster told him: "My dear friend, you were right. This time Holland's for it too."[289] From then on he fed Sas with rumours and items of information from the Abwehr and other OKW sources, hoping that their betrayal would enable the Dutch to strengthen their defences and withstand the German attack. Oster's disclosures were not intended for the Dutch General Staff alone, and he urged Sas to warn all the countries under threat from Hitler's Wehrmacht.

The self-appointed counterspy in Germany's espionage headquarters did not, however, find it easy to sound out his own organization. Ausland/Abwehr's competing sections and groups maintained a compartmentalized system which prevented Oster from gaining a precise idea of the German invasion plans. Agents' reports were not routed through his Central Section, nor did he have access to operational plans drafted by the Army General Staff at Zossen, miles from Abwehr headquarters. Thus, Oster was largely dependent on what he could glean at the morning conferences in Canaris's office or from conversations with his colleagues.

This made his material very sketchy, notably in regard to the crucial question on which the fate of Holland depended: when would the Germans attack? Hitler repeatedly postponed the offensive because of bad weather or military deficiencies, so Oster found it hard to ascertain the latest position. Last-minute postponements often escaped him,[290] and his cries of wolf became an increasing source of irritation to Sas's superiors. Little by little, they lost faith in the dramatic warnings of their military attaché and his mysterious informant.[291]

But Oster did not confine his disclosures to Sas. Müller was also enlisted to warn the Western powers of plans for a German offensive through his contacts at the Vatican. "A major German offensive," Ambassador Osborne cabled the Foreign Office on January 12, 1940, "has been prepared in every detail for mid-February, or possibly even earlier. It will be hard, fierce and relentless."[292]

Oster seized every opportunity to explore the intentions of the Wehrmacht authorities and communicate them to the West. It was grimly ironical that a German colonel should be betraying his brother officers' work for the salvation—as he saw it—of the Fatherland. His moral dilemma soon became even more acute because the Abwehr was to figure prominently in an impending military operation, the campaign against Denmark and Norway. The war was taking a new turn, and nobody had given it a stronger impetus than Canaris.

Reports reaching the Tirpitz-Ufer late in September 1939 indicated that the British military authorities were planning to occupy Norway.[293] For once, these Abwehr reports were on target. A few days earlier, on September 19, Churchill had suggested to the War Cabinet that Norwegian territorial waters should be mined to prevent freighters laden with Swedish iron ore from sailing to Germany via Narvik. He even canvassed the idea that Narvik itself should be occupied by British troops.[294] Although Canaris knew few details of the British plans for Norway, he submitted an immediate report to the commander in chief of the Navy, Grand Admiral Raeder.

"I attached all the more weight to this report from the head of the Abwehr," Raeder recalled, "because he delivered it in person—something he only did in exceptional cases."[295] Raeder was so impressed by the Admiral's information that he advised Hitler to forestall the British by occupying Norway first. The Führer, whose thoughts and energies were wholly concentrated on the Western offensive at this stage, the beginning of October, rejected the plan.[296]

But Raeder clung to his scheme and compiled new arguments in favour of a pre-emptive descent on Scandinavia. In mid-December Abwehr II sent him an occasional informant who had come to Berlin with fresh tidings of British invasion plans, the Norwegian fascist leader Vidkun Quisling.[297] Quisling's reports of an imminent British landing sounded so ominous that Hitler deigned to grant him an interview.[298] While impressing on his visitor that the Reich was only interested in a neutral Norway, he did, for the first time, entertain the possibility of occupying the country with German troops. The Wehrmacht High Command was instructed to prepare a study on the operation.[299]

Hitler was still debating the need to invade Scandinavia when reports of Franco-British plans for a Norwegian landing began to crystallize. The war that had since broken out between Russia and Finland provided the Western powers with an ideal excuse for stepping in. On the pretext of assisting the hard-pressed Finns, they could—coincidentally, as it were—occupy northern Norway and cut off Germany's ore supplies. General Gamelin, the French commander in chief, had something of the sort in mind. He proposed to land an auxiliary force in northern Finland which would, at the same time, occupy the harbours and airfields on the west coast of Norway and push inland towards the Swedish iron mines.[300]

Hitler could wait no longer. On January 27, 1940, he instructed the OKW to work out a plan for the occupation of Norway and Denmark.[301] The same day OKW-Abteiling L set up a working party to prepare for the invasion (code-named "Weserübung" [Weser Exercise]). Canaris was called upon to pave the way for yet another military adventure—indeed, to make it possible at all. This was because the military planning staff knew no more about Norway's armed forces than appeared in "Orientierungsheft Norwegen," a 1907 manual which some intelligence officer had unearthed in a dusty records office.[302]

Canaris offered Abteilung L's planning staff the services of Erich Pruck, now a lieutenant colonel. Pruck was instructed to move into the German Embassy in Oslo with a small team of Abwehr officers whose task it would be to observe "the activities of enemy nationals in Norway" and evaluate the military situation as follows: "(a) Strength, disposition and operational objectives of the Norwegian armed forces; (b) Condition of harbour installations in Oslo, Kristiansand, Stavanger, Bergen, Trondheim and Narvik with a view to landing troops."[303]

On January 30, armed with a passport identifying him as Oberregierungsrat Ernst Pohl, Pruck flew to Oslo. He and his team took only a few weeks to perform a brilliant feat of reconnaissance. Abwehr Outstation Norway succeeded in pinpointing units, military installations and coastal defences with such accuracy that the planning staff of Group XXI, headquarters of the German invasion force, completed their operational plans in double-quick time.[304]

Speed was essential because Pruck's agents noted that more and more British and French "volunteers" for the Finnish campaign were turning up in Norway. What the Germans did not know was that these "volunteers" had orders to seize Trondheim, Stavanger, Bergen and Narvik on March 20 with the help of other units landed by sea.[305] This plan was thwarted by the unexpected surrender of Finland on March 13. The British and French were compelled to leave Norway, but London and Paris agreed on a new plan to invade Norway in mid-April.[306]

Pruck repeatedly warned Berlin that an enemy invasion was imminent. He did not know that he was being kept under hostile surveillance from afar by a senior colleague who was determined to foil his efforts. Colonel Oster was only waiting for the ideal moment to wreck the German invasion.

Before finally crossing his Rubicon, however, Oster was given another chance to put pressure on those generals who opposed the regime.

Müller seemed to have achieved a break-through in Rome. Pope Pius XII had intervened with a request to the British Government to define its attitude to a potential military coup in Germany.

He had summoned Sir Francis d'Arcy Osborne on January 12 and disclosed the existence of German military leaders who wanted to replace the present regime with a "government capable of negotiating" provided they could be "assured of a peace with Great Britain which would be neither a new Compiègne nor a peace à la Wilson." The new government would restore the independence of Poland and Czechoslovakia but insisted that Austria remain with the Reich. The British Ambassador's response was wary. The proposal was probably too "nebulous and indefinite" to be taken seriously by His Majesty's Government, but he would nonetheless convey it to London.[307]

When Osborne made no further move, the Pope sent for him again. On February 7 he suggested to the ambassador that his government should respond to the German approach. What its authors wanted was "a guarantee that the territorial integrity of the Reich plus Austria . . . would be respected by the Allies' peace terms."[308] Pius XII took such a firm line that the British Government was forced to respond. Its reply reached Rome ten days later.

"It must be made clear from the outset," Lord Halifax wrote to the ambassador on February 17, "that His Majesty's Government can only act in this matter in concert with France. If His Majesty's Government were persuaded that the mediators who have approached His Holiness represent forces in Germany which have the determination and the power to fulfil their undertakings, His Majesty's Government would be prepared, in conjunction with the French Government, to answer any inquiry which those forces might have. His Majesty's Government cannot, however, discuss this matter with the French Government on the basis of ideas whose provenance is as uncertain and whose nature as vague as those that have been submitted to you. If progress is to be made, a definite programme must be submitted and authoritatively advocated." Osborne was also instructed to state that the Allied governments desired no territorial gains. On the other hand, they thought it proper that the Austrians themselves be permitted to decide whether or not they wished to belong to the projected German federation.[309]

Osborne hastened to convey the British reply to the Pope. Müller was informed of it soon afterwards. The upshot was that the other side remained cool and did no more than express polite interest in Müller's proposals. Osborne demonstrated what really lay behind all these diplomatic flourishes when he met the Pope again on February 19. "I simply said," he reported, "that if they meant to overthrow the government they should do so. I added that, even if a change of government occurred, I still failed to see how peace could be made as long as the German military machine remained intact."[310]

Nevertheless, Müller transmuted the sheet of paper on which Father Leiber had noted the disheartening contents of the British reply into a definite prearrangement with the British Government, "a sort of gentleman's agreement" whose existence was assumed even by discriminating historians before the official British records, with their very different wording, saw the light of day.[311] Müller was so eager to succeed that he stifled his lawyer's objectivity and grotesquely overrated the British response. He sped happily back to Berlin at the end of February and infected Oster's friends, who had already resigned themselves to failure, with his sturdy optimism. "Now we'll make it!" was Dohnanyi's enthusiastic reaction.[312] Müller read out his notes at the latter's home. The same night, Dohnanyi incorporated key phrases from his own notes on Müller's report in a memorandum some twelve pages long which he dictated to his wife and christened the X Report after Müller's code name.[313]

This document, which Müller saw next day, was an astonishing tribute to its author's capacity for misinterpretation and wishful thinking. His many and various inferences from the British reply included a belief that Britain approved the retention of Austria and the Sudetenland and would give Germany a free hand in the East.[314] Halder even recalled that the X Report (which has not survived) sanctioned the restoration of Germany's pre-1914 frontiers and the return of Alsace-Lorraine.[315]

Back-pedalling after the war, Müller claimed that the report must have been embellished with numerous overstatements which did not appear in his original notes.[316] Although the document was repeatedly modified later on, Müller ignored the fact that his (extant) reports from November 1939 were pervaded with an optimistic assumption that the Allies would, as it were, reward Germany for getting rid of Hitler. Kaas had assured him that the Polish problem would receive "benevolent attention" from the German point of view, Noots wanted to "return Eupen-Malmédy" to the Reich and Müller had even been told by the South African Ambassador that Germany could "again have colonies."[317]

Whoever doctored the X Report, its text appeared to provide military critics of the regime with the international guarantees required for a coup. The document turned up at an opportune moment because rumour had it that Halder had recovered from the shock of November 5, 1939, and was seeking fresh openings for a coup d'état. Even Brauchitsch, so it was said, would this time be amenable to suggestions from his Chief of Staff. Once again the conspirators pinned their hopes on the two Army chiefs.

But how to approach them? Contact with Halder had been severed since early February, when Brauchitsch dismissed Groscurth and relegated him to a battalion commander's job because of a dispute over one of Himmler's marriage decrees, which Groscurth considered an affront to traditional Christian and military standards.[318] Oster could no longer show his face at Zossen and few other intermediaries presented themselves, so weeks elapsed before Lieutenant General Thomas volunteered to deliver the X Report to Halder early in April 1940.[319]

The Chief of Staff was too shrewd not to detect the pitfalls in this "not entirely reliable terrain," as he put it. Puzzled though he later claimed to have been by Britain's alleged territorial concessions,[320] he passed the report to Brauchitsch. The commander in chief read it and turned pale with anger. "You should never have shown me this," he said. "What's going on here is downright treason." Brauchitsch was so furious that he ordered Halder to arrest the bearer of the document. Halder apparently retorted, "If anyone's to be arrested, you'd better arrest me!"[321]

It was finally borne in on Oster that nothing could prevent the invasion of Scandinavia—no generals' coup or act of disobedience—but his own self-sacrificial resort to treason. In retrospect, Liedig felt that Oster must have regarded the attack on Denmark and Norway as "the final turning point, the ultimate threshold" after which there would be "no turning back" and "Nemesis would take its course."[322] Oster may briefly have debated whether to confide in Canaris, because he seems to have made a tentative move in that direction.

After Liedig had presented Canaris and Oster with a report on the current state of preparations for "Weserübung" on April 1 or 2, the colonel began to speculate aloud on ways of preventing the invasion. "People just don't understand how the British can be so blind. They ought to recognize the possibility of provoking a British show of strength. I'm sure the whole operation would be called off if it were seen that the Grand Fleet was poised to hit back and thwart this attack on a neutral country."[323] Oster's unspoken conclusion was that the British should be warned.

But Canaris, whose concept of obedience precluded any such act, ignored the implication. To him, who had been wearing the gold rings and epaulettes of a full admiral since April 1, the time for hesitation was past. Hitler had timed the German attack for 5:15 A.M. on April 9.[324] Canaris now insisted that all his officers perform their duties to the letter and barked like a sergeant major at anyone rash enough to deviate from military routine.

This became painfully clear to Pruck, who was still ignorant of the date of the attack, when he travelled to Berlin a few days later. The object of his unheralded visit was to complain that the Admiral had consented to his being placed under the naval attaché in Oslo, an officer of the reserve, for the duration of the campaign. Canaris roasted Pruck unmercifully when he reported to Abwehr headquarters, telling him that he had left his post without authority and was liable to a court-martial. This was Pruck's first intimation that the Scandinavian fuse had already been lit. Canaris was afraid the Norwegians might learn the truth and refuse to let Pruck back into the country. Piekenbrock and Lahousen being absent from Berlin, Pruck asked Oster to intercede on his behalf, but the Admiral was already pacified. "Very well," he told Pruck, "we'll drop the [question of your] subordination [to the naval attaché]. All that concerns me is getting you back to Oslo in time."[325]

Oster construed this minor incident as final proof that an attack was imminent. On April 3 he told Müller to alert his contacts at the Vatican, and shortly afterwards he urged Sas to notify the Scandinavian, British and Dutch authorities. All his agents were given the same story: he was sure that the invasion would be launched in the early part of the coming week, or between April 8 and 10.[326]

On the morning of April 4 Sas cabled Oster's information to his superiors in The Hague accompanied by a request that the British secret service be notified without delay. At about the same time Müller telephoned Monsignor Schönhöffer in Rome and read him a message in a prearranged code.[327] Meanwhile, Sas was on the move again. He called at the Adlon Hotel and warned the Norwegian diplomat Ulrich Stang, who remained sceptical because he knew that a fleet of troopships destined for Norway was already assembling in British ports. Sas was dumbfounded. "What!" he exclaimed. "You mean the British intend to land in your country? Don't they know the Germans will be landing in Norway next Tuesday?" Stang retorted, "Impossible—nonsense!"[328] Sas hurried off to see the last person on his list, the Danish naval attaché Kjølsen, who at once dispatched a courier to Copenhagen.[329]

Oster waited tensely for some reaction from the countries he had warned. Those who stood to suffer from Hitler's extension of the hostilities now had a genuine chance of fighting back. Forewarned, they could await the German onslaught with confidence. Never had one of Hitler's military ventures seemed so inevitably doomed to disaster. The defenders were on the qui vive and the German Army's swoop on Norway would be one of the most precarious undertakings in military history, especially as a second and even more formidable adversary—the Royal Navy—was closing in from the west.

Oster felt absolutely positive that "Emil's" days were numbered, a belief in which he was strengthened by Beck's gloomy assessments of the situation. Even though the retired general's seclusion tended to put him more and more out of touch with reality, Oster was counting on a

German setback in Norway. Once, when visiting Abwehr headquarters, Müller found him bending over a map. Oster pointed to a spot in the North Sea south of the Norwegian coast. "That's where the British Fleet will attack the German troopships," he explained, "and then it'll be all over." Hitler, he added, would never survive such a reverse.[330]

But Oster was wrong. Nothing came of his personal initiative. The Dutch General Staff did not forward Sas's information to the British secret service and Stang left his government in ignorance even though the Norwegian Minister in Berlin dispatched a timely warning.[331] The Norwegian armed forces were not mobilized until a few hours before the German invasion, and the British Home Fleet, followed at one day's interval by the troop transports, sailed on April 7 without knowing the date of the German attack.[332] Hans Oster had gambled with his life and honour to no avail.

On April 9, 1940, the German invaders moved off with clockwork precision. They encountered no serious resistance in Denmark or Norway. Paratroops occupied airfields and barracks in a series of surprise operations and the invaders mounted lightning attacks as far north as the environs of Narvik. They had already seized Norway's key positions by the time the British Expeditionary Force reached the west coast on and around April 12. The British fought without success. Although they proved a match for the Germans in central and northern Norway and even drove them briefly out of Narvik, they gained no decisive victory. Fighting continued for another few weeks in the north, but they re-embarked at the beginning of May.[333] Despite heavy casualties sustained at isolated points, Hitler and his Wehrmacht had once more triumphed all along the line.

Frozen-faced, Oster distributed medals to the Abwehr men who had enabled Hitler to succeed in yet another act of aggression. Ten members of the Brandenburg company, now expanded to battalion strength, had prefaced the invasion by securing railway bridges in the German-Danish frontier zone and handed over suspects to the Gestapo (Operation "Sanssouci"), four agents under Major Klug had destroyed the communications links between Gedser and Nykøbing (Operation "G.V.")[334] and nobody would soon forget the bravery of Pruck's assistant Kempf, who had used a suitcase transmitter to direct German forces in the Oslo area from aboard the steamship *Widar*.[335]

The repercussions of Hitler's latest tour de force were disastrous. Not even the most critical of his military leaders contemplated active resistance or a coup now that their lingering doubts had been dispelled by the victory in Norway. The chances of a successful Western offensive seemed to improve week by week, and even Halder was optimistic enough to hope that a German military success in the West would modify and moderate the regime.[336] He blithely berated "all those who toyed with the idea of a coup but could not agree . . . most of whom were mere reactionaries and wanted to reverse the course of history."[337]

Hitler had no trouble with such men when he insisted that total victory must be achieved by hurling the bulk of Germany's divisions against the West. His generals obediently toed the line, especially when he abandoned the "old Schlieffen twaddle" (his own description) on advice from Lieutenant General von Manstein and presented them with a new strategic recipe for victory. This envisaged that the focus of effort would be transferred from the right wing to the left and the main blow delivered via the Ardennes, hitherto regarded as impenetrable.[338] Thirsting for success, Army Groups A, B and C deployed for an offensive in the West.

No one could have watched this macabre display of compliance and opportunism with deeper contempt than Oster, whose own circle of resistance sympathizers had so recently included many of these overnight converts to the Hitlerian creed. Oster himself remained incorruptibly dedicated to the course prescribed by his conscience and a presentiment of disaster to come. Once more he prepared to warn his country's enemies in the vain and irrational hope that a short-term defeat might yet bring the German generals to their senses.

Had he no qualms at all about sabotaging the work of his own colleagues? Did he feel no compunction when risking the lives of thousands of German soldiers? Anyone who poses such questions has failed to grasp what drives a man whose actions are dictated by moral and righteous indignation. To Oster, this was not the deciding factor. On the contrary, he calmly allowed for the loss of forty thousand German lives in the event of a defeat in the West because he believed that a German victory would be succeeded by a welter of blood and tears, a tide that would rise, year after year, until Hitler's Reich finally drowned in its own iniquities.[339] The death of German soldiers, whom he by then regarded as the passive instruments of a brutal dictatorship, was no deterrent to Oster.

He had burned his boats so thoroughly that he never stopped to wonder if his action could fulfil its underlying purpose. The most amazing aspect of Oster's treachery was that the Chief of Staff of one of the biggest espionage services in the world could seriously believe that a report of obscure provenance, let alone one that emanated from the cogs of the Greater German war machine, would persuade countries like Belgium and Holland to mobilize against Germany. No government would have dared to proclaim a state of emergency on the strength of a single agent's report, which might so easily have been German-inspired. After all, what better excuse for launching an attack than precipitate mobilization by an intended victim?

But Oster's actions were not governed by expedience and utility. His hatred of the Nazi system stifled any more rational considerations. Far from shunning the stigma of treason, he felt himself a better patriot than the bulk of his colleagues and fellow countrymen. Oster: "I could be called a traitor, but I'm not one really. I consider myself a better German than all the people who trot along behind Hitler. It's my aim and my duty to rid Germany and the world of this plague."[340]

Once again he initiated the process that had been tried to such little effect at the beginning of April. Sas and Müller were instructed to warn their friends on the other side of an impending German offensive in the West. Oster had not yet learned the exact date—he only knew that the attack would take place during the first two weeks in May. Sas wanted to wait a few days because his superiors at The Hague mistrusted him, but Müller went to work at once. He turned up in Rome on May 1 and informed Father Leiber, giving him a sheet of paper for the Pope on which was written: "Hitler is going to attack, and the attack is imminent."[341]

This was a form of words which Beck had approved, though in ignorance of Oster's intentions. He believed that "decent Germans" were still negotiating with the British at the Vatican (Müller had, in fact, withdrawn his feelers at the end of February) and must demonstrate their good faith by making at least a vague allusion to the impending Western offensive. However, Müller's Vatican friends were not content with these nebulous hints and wanted detailed information. Müller duly supplied it.

In the course of two conversations on May 1 and 3 he disclosed to Abbot General Noots that Hitler planned to invade France, Belgium, Holland and Luxemburg within the next few days. The Wehrmacht would attack the Western neutrals without any formal declaration of war and use all available weapons, among them "gas and bacteria." Müller also gave details of various operations including those of the Abwehr, whose task it would be to drop agents behind the lines by parachute, disrupt communications and seize strategic points.[342]

Müller's information set the Vatican's diplomatic wheels turning. On May 3 Papal Secretary of State Maglione cabled the nuncios in Brussels and The Hague instructing them to transmit the dire news to the Belgian and Dutch governments. On May 6 Pius XII informed Crown Prince Umberto of Italy and his Belgian wife. Next day Under-Secretary of State Montini, later Pope Paul VI, summoned the diplomatic representatives of Britain and France.[343] Osborne informed the Foreign Office of the Vatican's belief that a German offensive would be launched the same week.[344]

Meanwhile, Noots alerted the Belgian Ambassador, Adrien Nieuwenhuys, who had already received a call from another compatriot, Father Monnens, who in turn had been notified by Leiber. The two clerics implored the ambassador to inform the Belgian Government without delay. Nieuwenhuys was sceptical (like his British colleague, who had not been unduly impressed by the Vatican report).[345] On learning the source of the information, he looked incredulous and exclaimed, "No German would do a thing like that!"[346]

On May 2, after prolonged pressure from Noots, he sent an encoded dispatch to Brussels. "I have received . . . [information]," he reported, "according to which attack on Belgium and Holland set for next week. Author of information, always considered worthy of trust by nuncio, has asked [our] compatriot to apprise his government . . . [It should be] understood that I transmit this information without being able to verify it. Any form of surprise possible."[347] Nieuwenhuys remained sceptical. His doubts about the authenticity of Müller's report persisted next day, as he indicated in another telegram to the Belgian Foreign Ministry.

What worried him most of all was the nature of his German informant. Although he was a person "who derives his information from the General Staff, whose emissary he purports to be," he was extremely suspect. "This man is either betraying his country to our advantage or acting on Germany's behalf. He obviously presents himself in the former light as a loyal friend, that is to say, as a traitor, and it is quite possible that he is in this way deceiving our compatriot as to the true purpose of his mission." Shrewdly, or so he thought, Nieuwenhuys drew two inferences from this: Hitler either meant to intimidate Belgium "by stressing the horrors of an invasion" or was "attracting attention to our area prior to attacking in the southeast."[348]

The Belgian Ambassador was quite unaware of what he had done by indulging in these telegraphic meditations. Not having been forewarned by Müller or his contacts that Göring's Forschungsamt read nearly every diplomatic telegram sent in Western Europe, Nieuwenhuys left a trail which the sleuths of the German counterespionage service were bound to pick up sooner or later. Although Müller knew nothing of these telegrams he began to feel uneasy, and on May 4 he returned to Germany.[349]

He reported to Oster just after the latter had received his first definite indication of the date of the attack. Hitler had timed the Western offensive to begin on May 5, but he then postponed it for another twenty-four hours.[350] This process was repeated several times in the next few days. Müller, who was supposed to pass each new date on, could hardly spend the whole time shuttling back and forth between Berlin, Munich and Rome. By a fortunate coincidence, his friend and sponsor Wilhelm Schmidhuber was on the point of leaving for the Italian capital. Müller took Schmidhuber into his confidence and gave him a slip of paper for Father Leiber bearing the latest starting date (May

8)—a fatal decision which ultimately spelt disaster for the whole of Oster's circle.[351]

Müller also made an arrangement with Schmidhuber. If the offensive was postponed again he would telephone him at the Hotel Flora in Rome. Schmidhuber would then write down the revised date on another slip of paper and hand it to Leiber.[352] For cover purposes they agreed to discuss a forthcoming board meeting of the Eidenschitz Bank in Munich, where both of them had accounts. If Müller said this meeting would be held on a certain date, Schmidhuber would know that he really meant the new date of the German attack in the West. Schmidhuber set off on May 6.[353]

Müller phoned him twice at the Flora to inform him that the board meeting had been postponed until the following day.[354] Oster continued to await firm orders. At last, on May 9, the moment came. Every head of section at Abwehr headquarters knew that the decision would be taken that day. At 12:30 P.M. Lahousen noted: "The head of L announces that A[ngriff—Attack] day is expected to be May 10. X hour: 5:33 A.M. Final decision to be made at 8:45 P.M."[355]

Oster spent the early part of that evening at his apartment, pacing restlessly up and down. Sas joined him at about 7 P.M. and the two men went out for a meal to calm their nerves. Oster to Sas: "There's still a chance the thing will be postponed. We've already been through this three times. Let's wait a bit longer."[356] The final decision had still not been taken an hour and a half later. At eight forty-five Lahousen was informed that "the decision on A day" had been "postponed for an hour."[357] Three quarters of an hour later Oster's patience ran out. He took a taxi to the Tirpitz-Ufer. Sas waited outside in the cab while Oster hurried to his office.[358]

Twenty minutes later he emerged, having got there at the crucial moment. Abteilung L of the Armed Forces High Command had just— at 9:45 P.M.—signalled a definite decision to attack by issuing the code word "Danzig."[359] Oster ran to the waiting cab. "This is really it," he said breathlessly. "No orders have been countermanded. The swine has left for the Western Front—this is really and finally it." Oster had one last request: "Sas, do me a favour and blow the Meuse bridges!"[360]

"After that," Sas recalled, "I headed at the double for my embassy, where I had asked the Belgian military attaché to meet me."[361] As soon as the Belgian heard the bare essentials he hurried off. Sas, who was already reaching for the phone, asked to be connected with the Dutch War Ministry. It took him twenty minutes to get through to The Hague. The man at the other end was Lieutenant Post Uitweer, whom Sas "fortunately knew well."[362]

"Post," Sas said excitedly, "you know my voice, don't you? It's Sas, calling from Berlin. I've only one thing to tell you. Tomorrow morning at daybreak, watch out!—understand? Please confirm." The lieutenant rapped out the message, then added, "I see. Letter 210 received." This satisfied the major that his message had been understood because according to a prearranged code "Letter 200" meant simply "invasion" and the numerical additions denoted the date of the attack. Reassured, Sas signed off with the words: "Yes, Letter 210 received."[363]

But Dutch military intelligence again mistrusted the judgement of its representative in Berlin. Colonel van der Plaasche, the secret service chief, telephoned Sas an hour and a half later. "I've received such bad news from you about your wife's operation," he said, sounding highly sceptical. "So sorry to hear about it. Have you consulted all the doctors?" Sas, who knew that such conversations were usually intercepted by the Forschungsamt, suppressed his mounting fury. "Yes," he snapped, "and I can't see why you're bothering me in the circumstances. I've spoken to all the doctors. It's set for daybreak tomorrow." Then he slammed the receiver down.[364]

Müller, who had likewise been notified by Oster, was also glued to the phone. Schmidhuber recorded the final and definitive information about the start of the German offensive on yet another slip of paper and took it to Father Leiber—though the two men later differed over the time of its actual delivery.[365] There was a renewed flurry of diplomatic activity at the Vatican.

Once again, however, events were to demonstrate the utter futility of Oster's initiative. Sas's report arrived too late to improve his country's defensive posture. Even now the Dutch Government and High Command shrank from provoking the Germans by alerting their army.[366] Instead, they placed their whole reliance on a state of emergency proclaimed during April and on the subsequent reinforcement of their frontier garrisons. Brussels also neglected to decree the general mobilization of its armed forces. It took a sharp increase in German air activity over the Dutch and Belgian borders during the early hours of May 10 to set the victims' alarm bells ringing.[367]

But by then it was too late. The full fury of the German onslaught burst upon the defenders of Belgium and the Netherlands, mostly in places where they had not been expecting an attack. What principally threw them off balance was the multiple strategy of the German assault troops. While Major General Rommel's 7th Panzer Division stormed the Dutch frontier positions, the Luftwaffe simultaneously unleashed its Stukas at seventy-two airfields in the interior and carried the war into the heart of enemy territory by landing glider-borne troops at The Hague and Rotterdam.[368] The Belgian defenders, too, felt the impact of the German dictator's fearsome Karl May fantasies. Seventy-eight glider-borne engineers landed on top of Fort Eben Emael, overwhelmed the garrison and blew up armoured gun turrets and ammunition stores.

Other German shock troops employed similar daredevil tactics to surprise the Belgian guards on the bridges over the Albert Canal and take them prisoner.[369]

And wherever the German attackers went they were preceded by Abwehr commando detachments. The campaign had actually been launched during the early hours of May 10 by Lieutenant Walther and his platoon of Brandenburgers. Disguised as a party of Dutch policemen escorting some prisoners, they gained access to the Meuse bridge at Gennep, overpowered the sentries and secured the 7th Panzer Division's route into Holland.[370]

But the Abwehr men did not succeed in gaining control of every major bridge. One notable failure was their assault on the two most important Meuse bridges at Nijmegen. Captain Fleck's 100th Special Duties Infantry Battalion suffered heavy losses while charging the bridge details, who detonated their charges before falling back. An attack on the bridge at Arnhem also failed.[371] In Belgium, on the other hand, the Abwehr was almost invariably successful. The Brandenburgers' No. 3 Company occupied a number of bridges and viaducts there. Chronicling Abwehr II's part in the preliminary phase of the Western campaign, Lahousen was gratified to note that "in all, forty-two out of sixty-one objectives were secured and handed over to the units following behind."[372]

So the German attack developed unhampered. Irresistibly, Wehrmacht units pressed on into Holland and Belgium. The Dutch Army surrendered after five days and the Belgians gave up soon afterwards. Meanwhile, Abwehr III's disinformation experts were already setting the scene for the next act in the military drama. Agents and informants spread misleading reports which concentrated the attention of the Allied general staffs so exclusively on the annihilation of Holland and Belgium that it never occurred to them that the main German thrust was still to come.[373]

Abwehr units were again in evidence when the tanks of General von Kleist's III Army Corps—a concentration of armour unprecedented in the annals of warfare—burst through the Ardennes, crossed the Meuse and, in an operation conducted at lightning speed, headed for the Channel coast before the Franco-British armies could gather themselves for an effective riposte. But hardly had the bulk of the enemy forces in the north been defeated at the beginning of June when the Germans switched their main attack to the south. German divisions sent the enemy reeling back under a succession of swingeing blows. Paris drew steadily nearer, and with it the final defeat of France.

It was now clear that nothing could halt the German armies. Canaris followed their progress with surprise and admiration. Impressed by the achievements of his Abwehr units, he seemed oblivious of all the doubts he had voiced for months about Hitler's offensive plan. As a serving officer he was blind to everything save the exploits of his men and found it only natural that "his" Brandenburgers should march in the van of the German invading armies, loaded with more decorations and citations than almost any other Wehrmacht unit.

He proudly and contentedly took note of every official commendation that associated him, Admiral Canaris, with the Abwehr's combat troops. Lahousen promptly telephoned his chief after a visit to the Führer's headquarters on May 14 to inform him that "Abwehr II's activities relative to the commencement of operations" had been highly commended. Canaris may also have taken it as a mark of commendation when, on May 15, orders were received to expand Bau-Lehr-Bataillon z.b.V. 800 into Lehr-Regiment Brandenburg z.b.V. 800.[374] On May 27 Keitel assured Canaris in writing that the Brandenburgers had fought outstandingly well.[375]

Still out in the cold, Groscurth was touched to receive a letter from Hippel telling him how well his Brandenburgers had performed. "His operation seems to have been a huge success," Groscurth wrote on May 25. "Commended by the Führer, the Iron Cross for 75 per cent of his men (out of six hundred!), and expansion into a regiment, which he would like me to command."[376] Being a professional wire-puller, Canaris could not but welcome the Führer's interest in his own and the Abwehr's achievements.

Champagne glasses were already clinking in triumph at Abwehr headquarters when gloom abruptly descended on its senior personnel. In mid-June Canaris received word that the date of the Western offensive had been betrayed, in all probability by a German officer. This was disclosed by the "brown birds," the Forschungsamt's buff-coloured typewritten monitoring reports. Inevitably, the Forschungsamt had intercepted and deciphered Ambassador Nieuwenhuys's telegrams of May 2 and 3. It had also picked up Sas's telephone conversation on the eve of the German attack.[377]

Hitler, who had also seen the Forschungsamt report, immediately sent for Canaris and Heydrich and ordered them to find the traitor at once. The two rivals agreed to co-operate closely—in fact a senior Gestapo officer recalls that it was "agreed to exchange findings so that no time would be lost."[378] Amt IVE handled inquiries for the RSHA. At Amt Ausland/Abwehr the group head responsible for counterespionage, Lieutenant Colonel Joachim Rohleder, was ordered to unmask the culprit regardless of his rank or identity.[379]

The news that the Western offensive had been betrayed spread through Abwehr headquarters like a forest fire. Treason . . . No German soldier could conceive of a more heinous crime. Canaris's officers had still to learn that a government and its leaders can commit treason on the nation in their care. They clung to the traditional military concept of loyalty without realizing that its values had long ago been debased by a dictatorship whose totalitarianism was destructive of all moral standards.

Even the most resolute opponents of the regime despised treason. They drew a sharp distinction between *Hochverrat* and *Landesverrat* [for precise distinction v. Glossary]. Opposition to Hitler they considered justifiable, even in wartime, but collaboration with the enemy at the expense of their comrades was beyond the pale. "Every member of the Abwehr circle would firmly have eschewed Landesverrat," wrote Georg Duesterberg, the Abwehr's administrative chief, who was critical of the regime.[380] How much more dramatic must the betrayal of the Western offensive have seemed to the majority of unpolitical or even pro-Nazi Abwehr officers! "Landesverrat," stated an Abwehr III directive, "is a crime which presupposes a criminal cast of mind . . . Anyone who dares raise a hand against his native land is doomed to die!"[381]

No one could have felt this more keenly than Canaris himself, who was almost physically allergic to this form of treachery. He had never forgotten the treason committed by left-wing journalists under the Weimar Republic and had always condemned treasonable tendencies in society and the armed forces in the strongest possible terms. "To the enemy and his campaign," he dictated on January 6, 1940, "it makes no difference whether he gets his knowledge and information from wilful traitors or irresponsible gossips. The former kill with deliberate intent, the latter with careless talk."[382]

The Admiral had repeatedly enjoined every officer, ranker and civilian employee to report any circumstance, however trivial, that pointed toward treason. It was, he wrote, the duty of all who had custody of official secrets to "take ruthless action if they come upon the disclosure of genuine or supposed secrets pertaining to national defence."[383] His attitude to traitors was implacable. As for "the grave threats to the security of the Wehrmacht arising from negligence and carelessness," another Canaris directive stated that these must be "mercilessly checked."[384]

Be that as it may, Canaris had a feeling that the detection of the traitor mentioned in the Forschungsamt's intercept would be a bitter pill to swallow. He was too much of an old hand to be puzzled for long by the identity of the informant alluded to by the Belgian Ambassador's report from Rome—that "person who derives his information from the General Staff, whose emissary he purports to be." Who else could it be but Josef Müller, the man whose mission Oster had always cloaked in such mystery? Canaris told Oster to send for him at once.

Dohnanyi called the lawyer in Munich and summoned him to Berlin, but not without giving him some advice: he should watch out for Rohleder, travel inconspicuously—by car, if possible—and cover his tracks.[385] Müller knew only too well what this portended. "Giovanni, I think I'm done for,"[386] he told a friend, but he set off for Berlin accompanied by another friend, Captain Ickrath, who also worked for Abwehrstelle Munich and was on close terms with Schmidhuber.[387] Before reporting to the Admiral he called at Oster's home. "Cheer up," Oster told him brightly," the Almighty will help *us*, not the other rotten swine."[388]

Then Müller presented himself at Abwehr headquarters. Canaris showed him the intercept from the Forschungsamt and said, "Is this you?" Müller parried the question. "I can't be sure," he replied. "Maybe so, maybe not." "Surely you must know," Canaris said impatiently, but Müller stuck to his guns. "I don't know, believe me. I'm not sure of anything these days."[389]

The outcome of this conversation, according to Müller, was that Canaris suggested an ingenious way out. He proposed to appoint Müller his special representative and send him to Rome, where he could make all the necessary arrangements and persuade the Abwehr's local representative to hand over the entire investigation to Müller himself (a version accepted by Harold C. Deutsch).[390] Müller: "I naturally accepted this assignment. The Admiral made me my own chief investigator."[391] This, however, is an unlikely course of events. Not even Canaris could have overridden his department's separation of powers. IIIF had already been entrusted with the case and no Josef Müller was going to prevent Rohleder from setting his agents on the informer's trail.

One can only surmise that Oster or even Canaris himself (out of friendship for Oster) gave the lawyer a chance to revisit Rome and obliterate the traces of what he had done. Müller took advantage of this to concoct an apparently watertight story which he stuck to even when the Third Reich had collapsed. According to this, the German traitor was a member of Foreign Minister von Ribbentrop's staff and an agent working for his Italian opposite number, Count Ciano, who had communicated the date of the German offensive to the Vatican by way of the Italian Ambassador to the Holy See.[392]

This tale was hardly calculated to impress a counterespionage pro like Rohleder, who suspected that the most likely place to find the traitor was among the peculiar informants maintained on a semiofficial basis by Oster. Like Canaris, Rohleder immediately thought of Müller. Nieuwenhuys's telegram of May 3 contained a definite lead: "The man concerned, who left Berlin on April 29, arrived in Rome on May 1 and talked to our compatriot for several hours on Friday night (May 3)."[393] The essential thing, Rohleder told himself, was to ascertain whether Müller had been in Rome at the stated time and whether he had left Berlin for Italy on the date in question.

Rohleder's investigators soon struck oil. They discovered that Müller had indeed left for Italy on April 29 and returned to Germany on May 4.[394] All that remained in doubt was whether he had been in Rome on May 1 or 3. Group IIIF duly requested Abwehrstelle Munich to state whether Müller had undertaken an official trip to Rome and, if so, whether he had been there at the beginning of May. Munich replied in the negative.[395]

IIIF was not to know that its inquiry had been answered by a friend of Müller's, Karl Süss, an ex-member of the Munich customs investigation bureau who had got to know the lawyer during a currency-smuggling trial in 1936–37 and was now the IIIF Referent at Abwehrstelle Munich. "By arrangement with Dr. Müller," Süss recalled, "my desk reported, deliberately at variance with the facts, that he had been in Venice, not Rome, on the day in question."[396] Müller had, in fact, taken the precaution of obtaining a rubber stamp from an Italian customs officer during his return flight on May 4, and this he used to obliterate the entry and exit dates in his passport.[397]

However, Rohleder thought he knew an informant capable of piercing the veil of secrecy maintained by those in the Vatican who were well aware of the part played by Müller while in Rome. His name was Gabriel Ascher and he was a German Jewish émigré resident in Stockholm, where he scraped a living as the Swedish correspondent of a Swiss newspaper. Ascher had adopted the Catholic faith and was in touch with the Catholic Bishop of Sweden, a Bavarian who happened to be a namesake of Rohleder's quarry.[398] Armed with letters of recommendation from Bishop Müller, Ascher gained access to almost the same circles as those frequented by the other Müller.

Few of the Vatican excellencies and eminences were disposed to mistrust an anti-Nazi émigré from Sweden, so they talked to him freely. Rohleder's agent took only a few weeks to unearth a substantial proportion of Müller's circle of acquaintances in Rome. As Rohleder proudly testified after the war: "Ascher managed to elucidate all the surrounding circumstances in a logically complete and entirely conclusive manner. He named the then lawyer Dr. Josef Müller as the traitor."[399]

Rohleder collated one piece of evidence after another in a folder which he adorned with the code name "Palmenzweig" ["Palm Frond"].[400] His inquiries into the identity of Sas's informant also made gradual progress. It was common knowledge at Abwehr headquarters that the Dutch military attaché used to be friendly with a senior Abwehr officer. Sas and Oster had too often been seen together, even in the days immediately preceding Germany's Western offensive. Rohleder could not banish the suspicion that Müller and Sas had merely been assisting a third party based at Abwehr headquarters. This was because the same name—Oster—frequently recurred in both investigations.[401]

The more Rohleder's dossier grew, the uneasier its implications made him. Reared in the elite military environment of Leibgrenadier-Regiment Nr. 8 [8th Grenadier Guards], Lieutenant Colonel Rohleder was the type of officer who believed implicitly in the hierarchic virtues of the Prusso-German military and social system. As such, he could hardly take it in.[402] Were there really German officers who, in their distaste for the National Socialist regime, would go to the lengths of betraying their own comrades and trying to destroy the Army that was their common home and heritage? If Rohleder failed to grasp this as a patriot and moralist, he found it quite incomprehensible as an expert secret serviceman. Nothing could have been more amateurish than an ill-disguised betrayal of military secrets under the watchful gaze of the Gestapo and the Forschungsamt.

Rohleder did his duty. He took the "Palmenzweig" dossier and requested an interview with Oster. Dohnanyi was at Oster's side when Rohleder entered the colonel's office. With a chill demeanour which many of his critics ascribed to coldheartedness, Rohleder presented the results of IIIF's inquiries. His conclusion: the traitors were Lieutenant Müller and Colonel Oster himself.[403] Oster was momentarily struck dumb. Then he broke into a furious denial of Rohleder's insinuations, seconded by Dohnanyi, who declared that they were a pack of lies.[404]

Unmoved, Rohleder announced that he was going to present his case to the head of department and invited Oster to accompany him. The two officers stalked off to see Canaris. The Admiral gazed stiffly into space while Rohleder submitted an account of his men's findings. According to Rohleder, he was "visibly impressed."[405] Oster again defended himself, his main argument being that the bulk of IIIF's evidence derived from informants in Rome who had long begrudged Müller his position of trust in Vatican circles.[406] The Abwehr chief listened but made no immediate comment.

We shall never know for certain what Canaris felt at this moment —we can only surmise that Rohleder's report must have sent a whole world crashing in ruins and rent the bonds of trust and affection forever. Hans Oster, his friend and confidant, his partner in countless political discussions, his Chief of Staff and the man whose military privileges he had helped to restore after his indiscretion in 1932, was a traitor. Canaris must have realized that Oster had acted from the best of motives, true, but here lay the dividing line and insurmountable barrier that was to separate the two anti-Nazis until death claimed them both.

Even now, the Admiral's feelings of friendship proved stronger than his detestation of what Oster had done. He announced that Group

IIIF's evidence was insufficient to warrant pursuing the matter further. Rohleder disputed this. At the very least, he insisted, Müller's connections with the Vatican should be severed immediately. After approving this step, Canaris signified that Rohleder could go.[407] A few days later he summoned him back, not only because Rohleder had made no secret of his anoyance but because—to quote Lahousen—Abwehr III personnel were engaging in "a great deal of talk and conjecture" about the circumstances underlying the affair.[408]

Canaris asked for a copy of "Palmenzweig" and informed Rohleder that all contact between Oster and Müller would be severed. Still dissatisfied, Rohleder yielded to a sudden fit of anger. "On this occasion," he stated, "I was so annoyed that I curtly pointed out to Admiral Canaris that Oster's private intelligence service was very amateurishly run and dangerous in the extreme. The inquiries I had instituted in this matter could have been conducted with equal success by the Gestapa. In that event, I said, the repercussions on our department and the Admiral himself would hardly have been in doubt."[409]

Although Rohleder had to accept Canaris's decision, a new threat was looming over Oster and his friends. On June 11 Pruck was summoned back to Berlin from Norway because of a report in which he had sharply attacked the crude methods practised by the German occupation authorities, in particular the Gestapo and SD.[410] Canaris, who had no wish to tangle with the RSHA officially, was upset by indiscreet criticism of this kind.

While awaiting the Admiral's verdict, Pruck heard what was being whispered at Abwehr headquarters about the "Palmenzweig" case. Although thoroughly critical of the regime, he regarded any conspiratorial activities against the state in wartime as unwarranted and subversive. He passed on what he had heard to his wife, who was outraged that Abwehr officers should be plotting against the Führer and had already learned from another source that the SS-Führungshauptamt [SS Operations Department] had its own quota of persons who were dissatisfied with Hitler and conspiring to bring him down.[411]

Without telling her husband, Kaete Pruck went to work. She wrote Canaris a letter accusing irresponsible elements at Abwehr headquarters and the SS-Führungshauptamt of forging plans to destroy the regime. She also named names. Those conspiring against the Führer included SS-Sturmbannführer Hofmann of the SS-Führungshauptamt and Oster, Dohnanyi and Müller of the Abwehr.[412] Canaris could not fail to be highly alarmed by this indication that an outsider was on the track of Oster and his associates. His prompt reaction showed how ruthlessly he could drop a colleague, however well established, if his own position was in jepoardy.

He dictated a letter to Himmler reporting Frau Pruck's "insane" allegations against the SS-Führungshauptamt (though suppressing her references to the Abwehr) and suggesting that the Reichsführer-SS should have her detained and committed to a mental institution.[413] At the same time, he urged Lieutenant Colonel Pruck to divorce his wife and resign. Pruck was, in fact, dismissed the service in June 1940 on the classic grounds that his reports from Norway had disclosed views unbecoming to a German officer.[414]

Himmler followed up the Admiral's denunciation. Kriminalinspektor Hugo Hoffmann, a "special cases" expert in Amtsgruppe IVE of the RSHA, was ordered to detain Kaete Pruck for questioning. He soon began to doubt that the woman was mentally deranged. "Because Frau Pruck showed no signs of insanity when interrogated on the first day," Hoffmann reports, "I admitted her to the women's section of the police prison at Alexanderplatz in Berlin."[415] Hoffmann's next session with her convinced him that the Gestapo was being hoodwinked by the head of the Abwehr.

Frau Pruck stated during this interrogation that Canaris's report to Himmler contained an incomplete version of her own letter to him. She had referred not only to treason [Hochverrat *and* Landesverrat] in the SS-Führungshauptamt but also and more especially, to similar activities in Amt Ausland/Abwehr. Hoffmann was still in two minds about her when she suggested that someone should go to her home and pick up a copy of the letter. The carbon copy, which was duly found, corroborated her statement in full.[416]

All at once, Canaris's gambit threatened to boomerang. Investigations into the Western offensive leak had ground to a halt, but Kriminalinspektor Hoffmann was now in possession of an important lead that might enable the Gestapo to get them moving again. Once more, however, the conspirators were in luck. The Gestapo officer was no Nazi. Reluctant to alert his superiors and help launch a witch hunt against the Abwehr, he handled the case in a dilatory manner, noted vaguely that Frau Pruck had also made allegations against Canaris's department—"all isn't well there either"—and wound up his investigation.[417]

Hoffmann's restraint ensured that the case was shelved. Kaete Pruck was pronounced schizophrenic and temporarily confined in an East Prussian sanatorium on the strength of a medical report which enabled her husband to divorce her. The SS-Führungshauptamt remained exempt from investigation and no Gestapo officer laid a finger on the Abwehr.[418] Hoffmann's report came back adorned with a marginal note from Gestapo chief Müller to the effect that Admiral Canaris's disciplinary problems were his own affair.[419] Hoffmann: "I only realized after July 20, 1944, that Frau Pruck's statements concerning Canaris's department were entirely correct."[420]

This was the last favour Canaris performed for Oster's benefit. There was little political rapport between them thereafter. The Admiral urged Oster to sever his independent links with Müller and destroy anything that might connect the department with the *coup d'état* plans of 1938–40. Oster's and Dohnanyi's office safes still contained studies, proclamations and draft programmes revealing the full extent to which senior Abwehr personnel had been implicated in these conspiracies.

Oster passed the word to Dohnanyi, who protested. The two men wrangled for hours until an "official order" from Oster clinched the argument[421]—or so he thought. Actually, Dohnanyi had no intention of obeying his chief's instructions. The lawyer subsequently explained his act of disobedience in hoarding the papers as follows: "I refrained from destroying the documents so as to be able to prove that we civilians had done something too. If the thing had come off, you can be sure the generals would have done everything and we civilians nothing. I wanted to avoid that."[422]

Major Heinz suggested an apparently safe hiding place for these dangerous papers. Heinz had a stepbrother named Hermann Schilling, who was chairman of the Prussian State Bank and had helped him out of periodic financial difficulties in the past. He proved equally accommodating on this occasion. The Oster-Dohnanyi papers were locked up in one of the bank's safes, having been conveyed there in a car belonging to Major Schrader of Abteilung z.b.V. [Special Duties Section]. This ill-considered step was to prove disastrous.[423]

As for Canaris, he declined to be enlisted in the conspirators' plans. He believed that Germany was ineluctably doomed and that no one could stem the onset of ultimate disaster. Liedig: "The line which Canaris drew, as it were, on his desk before the eyes of those who conversed with him" dated from immediately "after the conclusion of the French campaign." To use the Admiral's own words, resolute opponents of the National Socialist regime had dwindled to such an extent that they could be counted on the fingers of one hand.[424]

This marked the end of his connection with the resistance. His friends and allies among the conspirators left him one by one. Liedig accepted a foreign posting, Heinz took command of a battalion of the Brandenburgers, Gisevius was shunted off to Zurich as an Abwehr informant and Groscurth never re-entered the Admiral's orbit.[425] Otto Wagner and sundry other Abwehr officers close to Canaris had already gone abroad. Even the Admiral's partner-cum-rival Werner Best had quit his post at the RSHA, happy to have escaped the diabolical pull of Heydrich's magnetic field.[426]

Canaris battened down his hatches more and more. Fatalistic as ever, he steered the Abwehr towards new and even more tempestuous outbursts of perverted Hitlerian ingenuity.

11

Tears for Heydrich

Travelling through Spain at the end of July 1940 was a little white-haired man whose efforts to escape attention were conspicuous in themselves. Señor Juan Guillermo, identified by his passport as a citizen of the Argentine Republic, wore a plain grey flannel suit and shielded his face beneath a broad-brimmed hat of outsize dimensions. His companion, a lanky man who chauffeured him in a car with Spanish licence plates, was similarly attired.[1]

The two tourists drove leisurely through town and countryside, apparently engrossed in the exotic charms of a foreign land but really noting every detail that might enlighten them on Spain's military position.[2] Señor Guillermo and his driver were on a reconnaissance mission. Their purpose was to discover whether Spain, after a year's freedom from the scourge of civil strife and a year's subjection to a semifascist, semimilitary dictatorship, had regained enough strength to wage war.

One strange feature of this secret mission was that the Spanish military authorities obviously welcomed the visitors' questions. Wherever they called a halt or spent the night, Spanish intelligence officers plied them with military information. In some of the hotels they stayed at, Spanish uniforms were provided to facilitate contact with the local military authorities and protect them from surveillance by foreign agents. Colonel Martínez Campos, head of the Spanish Army's secret intelligence service, had given orders that Guillermo and his companion were to receive every possible assistance.[3]

The two men had just reached Madrid on July 23 when a telephone rang on the top floor of the German Embassy in Calle Castellana. Oberstabschef Max Franzbach, financial head of the Abwehr's wartime intelligence network in Spain [KO Spain], picked up the receiver and heard a girl's voice say, "*El tío está aquí* [Uncle's here]." He recognized the caller as someone who worked at the home of the Abwehr III representative, Helm, with whom the white-haired man always stayed when visiting Madrid. Franzbach passed the message to his superior, KO chief Commander Wilhelm Leissner, known to embassy staff as "Honorary Attaché Gustav Lenz."[4] Leissner hurriedly prepared to receive a visit from "Uncle" and his companion, alias Admiral Canaris and Lieutenant Colonel Piekenbrock of the Geheimer Meldedienst (Abwehr I), because he knew that they had come to Spain on a mission of the utmost urgency.[5]

But the more Canaris told Leissner about the ulterior purpose of his mission the clearer it became that the Admiral's visit might have fateful repercussions on the neutrality of Spain and peace in the Western Mediterranean. Assisted by a team of engineer, airborne and artillery officers, Canaris was to explore the possibility of capturing the Rock of Gibraltar, barring the Royal Navy's access to the Mediterranean and cutting Britain's oil supply routes.[6]

Canaris was so enthusiastic about the scheme that he could not wait to submit it to his friend Juan Vigón, now a major general and Chief of the Spanish General Staff. He went with Piekenbrock and Leissner to see Vigón, who called in Colonel Martínez Campos as soon as he heard what had brought Canaris to Spain.[7] Canaris explained that he was in Madrid to prepare for a concerted German-Spanish attack on Gibraltar. He proposed to reconnoitre the British defences with the aid of a planning staff and was counting on additional help from Spanish military intelligence.[8]

Vigón seemed impressed. Although he thought it unlikely that Gibraltar would fall to a surprise attack of the sort envisaged by Canaris, he considered the Admiral's disclosures important enough to request a special audience with the Spanish head of state. Vigón and Canaris called on Franco the very same day, July 23.[9] The Gibraltar scheme clearly appealed to him, though he did express misgivings—which Canaris temporarily ignored—about the strength of the Royal Navy.[10]

It was enough for Canaris that the Spaniards so obviously wanted to participate in an attack on Gibraltar. Soon afterwards he received a visit from Lieutenant Colonel Ramón Pardo of Spanish military intelligence, whose orders were to install the German scouts in the Gibraltar area. Meanwhile, the other members of Canaris's team had also reached Madrid. They comprised Lieutenant Colonel Hans Mikosch, commanding officer of the 51st Engineer Battalion, which had distinguished itself by helping to storm Fort Eben Emael during the Western campaign, Major Wolfgang Langkau from the School of Artillery at Jüterbog, and Captains Witzig and Osterecht of the paratroops.[11]

Canaris was itching to get started. By July 24 the Germans were in sight of Gibraltar's brooding silhouette. They began their reconnaissance of the British stronghold almost at once, aided by Pardo, who gave them access to official premises. The town commandant's office at La Línea, next door to Gibraltar, provided a good view of the northern defence installations, while the lighthouse of Punta Camero did the same in the west.[12]

Each member of the Admiral's team was allotted a separate task. Mikosch squeezed his corpulent frame into a Spanish officer's uniform and unobtrusively surveyed Gibraltar from a passenger aircraft on the Seville-Ceuta run, which passed quite close; Langkau drove along the edge of the neutral zone in an attempt to discover how the frontier had been mined and where the main gun emplacements were; and Witzig and Osterecht had to decide whether the rocky terrain would lend itself to airborne operations.[13]

Canaris preferred to roam the neighbourhood alone, a pastime which fired his imagination and accorded with his long-held notion of how a secret service chief should operate—skulking on the enemy's doorstep in disguise, as befitted a master spy. No area seemed better suited to show off his talents than southern Spain, which he knew well. He had toured it as a young lieutenant in search of supply depots for German submarines operating in the Mediterranean. More recently, during the Spanish Civil War, he had selected Algeciras as the earliest base for what was later to become KO Spain. Gibraltar itself was a vivid reminder of his experiences in World War I, when he had often spent days lying in wait for British convoys east of the Rock.

He busily proceeded to fulfil the Führer's requirements in his own inimitable way. "Señor Guillermo" climbed into his car and flitted from place to place, never staying long. He inspected the three buildings on the western shores of the Bay of Algeciras from which Abwehr agents kept watch on enemy harbour traffic, visited the Hotel Reina María Cristina in Algeciras and listened to British naval officers from Gibraltar conversing at nearby tables, and got in touch with Spanish Army posts whose commanders were only too willing to share their meagre knowledge of what went on inside the fortress.[14]

The experienced soldiers on his team were a little surprised to observe how eagerly he explored the chances of an attack on paper. Even before they had evaluated their findings, the Admiral was picturing a major assault in which crack German units under Spanish command would storm the Rock, that rugged bastion and symbol of British imperialism, deprive Britain of access to the Mediterranean and compel her to make peace with Germany.

If ordinary soldiers marvelled at the Admiral's martial spirit, those of his friends who were sworn opponents of Hitler's war and the Nazi regime must have been utterly dismayed by his chameleon-like powers of adaptation. Though determined to resist any extension of the war and involved in preparations for an anti-Nazi coup only weeks before the Western campaign, Canaris was now trying to pave the Wehrmacht's way across neutral Spain and carry the din of battle into a still untroubled corner of the Mediterranean.

The Admiral's activities in Spain are inconsistent with the pacifist image of him that dominated German literature and historical writing after the fall of the Third Reich. Abshagen's biography declared that he regarded "every new ally chained to Hitler's war chariot as an extension of the senseless conflict," and even historians like Hermann Graml seriously believed that Canaris succeeded in "thwarting the dictator's policy" during this very same trip to Spain in 1940.[15] Unrepentant supporters of Hitler have also reflected such legends in their own perverted fashion. Even today they reproach Canaris for sabotaging the Gibraltar operation, thereby denying the Reich a unique opportunity to impose a peace settlement on Britain by sealing off the Mediterranean.[16]

The truth is that Canaris positively hankered after the conquest of Gibraltar. As early as mid-July 1939 he asked Franco whether, if war broke out in Europe, the Spaniards would join forces with the Axis powers and neutralize Gibraltar in its capacity as an enemy base, if necessary by taking it themselves.[17] The Caudillo's response was negative.

Admiral Lais, head of Italian naval intelligence, made the following note after discussing the matter with his German colleague: "General Franco told Admiral Canaris (a) that he feared a conflict in which Italy and Germany might be involved because France would at once march into Spanish Morocco and Spain was not in a position to wage war, neither today nor in the immediate future; and (b) that Spain did not propose to undertake any operations against Gibraltar in the event of a conflict."[18]

Canaris had since taken it for granted that an alliance with Spain in the event of war would be far "more of a hindrance than a help to Italy and Germany."[19] His travels in Spain and her Moroccan possessions reinforced this sceptical attitude. Economically devastated, smitten with famine, subjected to the vengeance of a victorious but internally divided civil war party and held together only by the Caudillo's skill as a tightrope walker, Spain was limping through a turbulent phase in her modern history. Canaris confided to Lais that he had seen "much poverty, disorder and discontent."[20] His conclusion: "No peace reigns in the country, and he would not be surprised if another civil war broke out."[21]

While abandoning Spain as an active ally, however, Canaris was determined to secure her as an adjunct to Germany's armed might. By arrangement with Franco he installed Abwehr observation and listening posts at Tarifa, a Spanish port situated at the neck of the Strait of Gibraltar, where they could monitor traffic to and from the British fortress.[22] Enemy shipping in the Atlantic and Mediterranean was kept under additional surveillance by the establishment of Abwehr bases in Vigo, Santander, Cádiz, Barcelona and Morocco.[23]

More and more German agents filtered into Spain under the supervision of Leissner, who transferred his headquarters from San Sebastián to Madrid in autumn 1939. He and his immediate subordinates moved into four attic rooms in the German Embassy, but the KO expanded so fast that it outgrew its original premises. Before long, "Lenz's" men occupied the whole of the embassy's top floor and basement. Further acquisitions included two more houses in Madrid and a growing number of apartments in the capital and provinces. KO Spain soon became the Abwehr's most heavily manned foreign dependency, with a maximum establishment in 1943–44 of 250 Abwehr personnel and 2,000 informants. Its total monthly expenditure at this peak period amounted to 100 million pesetas or RM20 million.[24]

But Canaris and Franco devoted no further discussion to the fate of Gibraltar until the political fabric of Western Europe seemed to be in ruins. Franco's calculations, too, were affected by the German armies' unexpectedly swift successes in summer 1940. When the Wehrmacht took a mere six weeks to defeat the French armed forces and expel the British Expeditionary Force from the Continent, even the wary Caudillo felt that Germany's triumph was complete and the end of the war only days away.

Franco was anxious not to miss the German victory celebrations and a share in the spoils of war. On June 3 he hurriedly dictated a "Dear Führer" letter to Hitler in which he conveyed the "delight and admiration" inspired in him by Germany's successes and declared "how greatly I desire not to be remote from your concerns and how pleased I am to render you at all times the services you deem most valuable."[25] He then instructed Major General Vigón to deliver this missive to Hitler's headquarters with all possible speed. Everything Vigón said must suggest that Spain was ready to enter the war at last.[26]

Vigón was still roaming through occupied Belgium in search of the châteaux where the German leaders were quartered when Franco gave practical effect to his written assurances. In a speech delivered on June 10 he announced that Spain was now "non-belligerent," not neutral, and two days later he ordered Spanish troops into the international zone of Tangier.[27] At once, the streets of Spain came alive with crowds chanting a slogan which was bound to galvanize Canaris: *"Gibraltar para España!"*—Gibraltar for Spain.[28]

Vigón had also been instructed to raise the question of the Rock with Hitler. When he finally caught up with him on June 15, he announced that Spain would entrust her interests to the German Reich when the war was over and hinted at his country's desire for the return of Gibraltar. Hitler asked how Spain proposed to gain possession of this fortress, but Vigón evasively replied that the Caudillo had still to crystallize his ideas on the subject.[29]

Three days later the Spanish Ambassador turned up with some rather more concrete proposals. The Marqués de Magáz, another of Canaris's acquaintances, informed Baron von Weizsäcker of the Foreign Office that Spain laid claim to Gibraltar, the whole of Morocco, the Oran area and other parts of the Sahara. In return, she would enter the war as an ally of the German Reich if Britain decided to fight on.[30] "In that event," stated a memorandum which Magáz had brought with him, "she [Spain] would require some support from Germany in the way of military equipment, heavy artillery and aircraft for the attack on Gibraltar."[31]

This Spanish emphasis on Gibraltar proved alluring to Canaris, who scented a chance to distinguish himself and the Abwehr in Hitler's eyes. Nothing had done more to boost the Admiral's prestige at OKW and the Führer's headquarters during the Western campaign than the undercover operations of his private army, the Brandenburgers, which had seized the enemy's bridges, fortifications and key points in a series of surprise attacks. Captain Hans-Jochen Rudloff's No. 3 Company, since expanded into the 3rd Battalion, had attracted particular attention, winning a total of ninety-two Iron Crosses (eight First and eighty-four Second Class).[32]

Late in June, the successes gained by Rudloff and his men encouraged Canaris to toy with an audacious plan. Given that Britain was still dazed by her recent reverse, what if he sneaked his Brandenburgers into Spain and got them to capture the proud British stronghold at one fell swoop? Without divulging this scheme to his OKW superiors, he decided to see if Unternehmen "Felsennest" [Operation "Eyrie"] was feasible.[33]

Summoning Rudloff at the beginning of July, Canaris dramatically announced that it was time for the Abwehr to give a renewed demonstration of its prowess.[34] Though willing enough to lead a surprise attack on the fortress,[35] Rudloff found the Admiral's project fanciful in the extreme. The 3rd Battalion of the Brandenburg Regiment was to sneak up on Gibraltar by land while ships transported an engineer bat-

talion to Tarifa and a battery of heavy artillery to Ceuta. Under cover
of a sudden bombardment, the Brandenburgers must storm the Rock so
unexpectedly that its garrison would be unable to offer any effective
resistance.[36]

The Admiral's conspiratorial ingenuity was particularly exercised by
the 3rd Battalion's method of approach. He already had visions of a
three-day military operation resembling a game of cowboys and Indians
on the grand scale. The battalion would be sneaked through Spain in
closed trucks without looking like a military unit. The men would wear
civilian clothes and shun all contact with the Spanish population.[37] A
former Abwehr officer recalls: "The intention was, of course, to use
unfrequented roads and avoid towns wherever possible. Arrangements
were also to be made to cook food and feed the men at a number of isolated points in the countryside."[38]

Rudloff refrained from disclosing his personal opinion of the Abwehr chief's ludicrous scheme and obediently caught a Lufthansa plane
for the South of Spain. Canaris now thought it time to inform someone, if only the Army Chief of Staff, of his latest project. On July 6
Halder made the following brief note in his diary: "11 A.M. Canaris re
ported on Spain. Matters relating to Abwehr operation."[39]

But Rudloff returned with bad news. He had discovered that Ceuta
harbour possessed no cranes capable of disembarking heavy pieces of
artillery.[40] More worrying still, there was no prospect of conveying the
Brandenburgers across Spain undetected, even for a single day. The
British secret service kept such a close watch on northern Spain that a
convoy of German trucks would immediately be spotted by its agents.[41]

Canaris shelved his scheme. He was just about to cross Gibraltar off
his shopping list when it unexpectedly acquired burning topicality.
Hitler and his military advisers had warmed to the idea of a full-scale
assault on the British fortress.

Almost at the same time as Canaris was outlining his Gibraltar
plan, Major General Alfred Jodl, head of the Wehrmachtführungsamt
[Armed Forces Operations Department] and Hitler's chief military
planning expert, had produced a paper in which he broached the same
subject.[42] This study was entitled "The Continuation of the War
Against England"—and its name spoke volumes. As early as June 30,
1940, Jodl was coldly and logically preparing his Führer for the disappointment and disenchantment that would inevitably succeed the first
flush of victory.[43] Few now believed that the British would make peace
with Hitler despite the surrender of France, Belgium and Holland and
the fact that Britain was an island standing alone. Hitler clung to this
delusion, still persuading himself that political disaster would overtake
the new Prime Minister, Churchill, who was pledged to prosecute the

war at all costs, and that his successor would offer to treat with the victorious Third Reich.[44]

But Hitler waited in vain for an olive branch from London. Instead, Churchill's call to battle rang out, loud and clear, across the Channel: "Hitler knows that he will have to break us in this island or lose the war."[45] It began to dawn on Hitler that, for all its military successes, the Third Reich was in a hopeless dilemma: confronted in the west by an undefeated Britain; shackled in the south to an ambitious and untrustworthy Italy which had entered the war during June in the hope of easy pickings; and threatened in the east by the Russians, who were pocketing a succession of countries, from the Baltic States to Bessarabia, as they pushed ever closer to the eastern marches of the Greater German domain.

Hitler could not but fear that British perseverance might one day join forces with the new-found expansionism of Soviet Russia. The only immediate preventive was to force the British into submission at once. This was the realization for which Jodl had been trying to prepare his lord and master. He presented Hitler with two alternatives: either a German-Spanish-Italian offensive against the British Empire, which would entail sealing the Mediterranean by the capture of Gibraltar and Suez, or a German frontal attack on England followed by military occupation.[46]

To all appearances, Hitler plumped for the second alternative. In mid-July he issued Directive No. 16, which stated: "Since England still shows no signs of any readiness to negotiate, I have decided to prepare for a landing operation against England and, if necessary, carry it out."[47] The Wehrmacht girded itself for yet another campaign, this time christened Unternehmen "Seelöwe" [Operation "Sea Lion"].[48]

But Hitler's heart was not in it. The once Anglophile dictator recoiled at the prospect of occupying and destroying Britain because not even he could, within a few short weeks, shake off his lifelong dream of a grand Anglo-German alliance. Although he let preparations for "Sea Lion" run on, his interest in Jodl's first alternative, the closure of the Mediterranean, steadily increased. His entourage devoted more and more discussion to one particular project: Gibraltar.

On July 12 Jodl produced a preliminary study on the capture of the Rock.[49] The Directorate of Naval Warfare, which also began to examine this possibility, discovered how little was known about local conditions and called for an on-the-spot reconnaissance.[50] Jodl agreed.

On July 22, with a precipitancy characteristic of the OKW, Jodl and Keitel resolved to dispatch a high-powered reconnaissance team at once.[51] No one seemed better qualified to lead it than the OKW head of department who looked on German-Spanish relations as his private preserve. Once again, Canaris became the man of the moment. Jodl's plan promised to take him further up the professional ladder than anyone would have thought possible only a short while before. For the first time, he was to be privileged to help shape the strategic plans of those who controlled the German war machine.

Canaris was all the readier to exploit this new means of enhancing his prestige because the Spanish mission might distract attention from a weakness that had just shown up in the Abwehr. The "Sea Lion" preparations had saddled him with the unwelcome task of using every available agent to gauge the enemy's war potential—unwelcome because the Abwehr maintained no effective network of informants in the British Isles.[52] A few hurriedly recruited agents had been dropped there by parachute and—not that Canaris knew this—promptly captured by British counterespionage.[53]

He could only be thankful, therefore, that Hitler's gaze had suddenly veered southwards. The Abwehr chief felt unbeatable in Spain, where a whole army of experienced agents awaited his orders. Besides, any gaps in the Abwehr's knowledge could be plugged by the Spanish secret service, which was grateful to "Guillermo" for his many tips on opposition groups and activities hostile to the Franco regime.

By the time Canaris and his companions returned to Madrid on July 27 after their reconnaissance mission in the Gibraltar area, his enthusiasm had waned a little.[54] The team agreed that a surprise attack on the Rock had no prospect of success, especially in default of adequate cartographic data.[55]

Notwithstanding this, Canaris, Piekenbrock and Mikosch drew up a plan of attack. One hundred and sixty-seven pieces of artillery, mainly 210mm. mortars and heavy antiaircraft guns, would open fire on British naval units and antiaircraft positions. This bombardment would be followed thirty minutes later by a Stuka attack designed to pulverize the northern sector of the fortress and block the gallery entrances. The guns would then resume their bombardment while assault engineers and mountain troops broke through from La Línea, penetrated the enemy's defences and turned his northwest flank by striking southeast in a wide arc. Canaris, Piekenbrock and Mikosch estimated that the Rock would be in German hands within three days.[56]

Canaris submitted this plan of attack to Keitel and Major General Warlimont, Jodl's deputy, on August 2.[57] Five days later Warlimont authorized the preparation of a study which was then submitted to Hitler.[58] Warlimont's planning staff defined the aim of the operation as follows: "Capture of the Rock by means of an attack from the landward, and if possible seaward, side. Full acceptance of Spanish over-all command essential, but it must be ensured through the person of the German commander that effective control of the operation should rest in German hands."[59] The plan was code named Operation "Felix."

From now on, Canaris was inseparable from the operational planning of "Felix." Not a phase or major detail of the scheme escaped his rapt attention. He often acted on his own initiative and hurried off on reconnaissance trips without any firm instructions from Keitel or Warlimont.

On August 12 Piekenbrock informed Warlimont on the Admiral's behalf that Canaris proposed to continue the reconnaissance of Gibraltar in person and requested precise orders.[60] Warlimont, who was rather disconcerted by this, could only impress on Piekenbrock that his chief should "under no circumstances draw the attention of the British to our own preparations for an attack before [the establishment of] adequate safeguards against British attempts to extend Gibraltar's defences northwards and westwards, [a move] which could then be definitely expected."[61]

On August 16 Canaris left for France accompanied by the head of Abwehr II, Lahousen, without any very clear conception of his aims and objectives.[62] The Admiral was suffering from another attack of itchy feet. After visiting the Abwehr's Paris headquarters he toured the subordinate outstations in German-occupied France.[63] On August 19 he abruptly set off for Madrid, leaving Lahousen behind. As usual, his first port of call in the Spanish capital was Vigón's office.[64]

He spent two hours passing on what he had gleaned from his conversations with the OKW authorities. The Führer wanted the Spaniards to improve the roads leading to Gibraltar, put the airfields at Antequera, Granada, Jerez, Morón, Seville and Tablada into an operational state and step up their intelligence work against the Rock. Vigón undertook to fulfil these requirements without delay. He also declared that Spain intended to enter the war at the earliest possible moment and would soon be submitting a list of the supplies she needed from Germany.[65]

Reassured, Canaris moved on to Algeciras. He conferred with the local Abwehr officer, Major Fritz Kautschke, and made another tour of the Rock's environs.[66] But he did not linger there either. Before long he was on his way to Portugal, again without a definite assignment, though he later put it about that he had gone there to ascertain whether fears of an impending British invasion of Portugal were justified.[67] A day later he was back at his desk.

Meanwhile, an important decision had been taken in Berlin. On August 24 Hitler had approved the Operation "Felix" plan—reason enough for Canaris to involve himself even more actively in its preparation.[68] He promptly called on Halder and staked his claim to a say in the matter. The Army General Staff was also involved by this time because ground forces—the Sixth Army under Field Marshal von Reichenau—were to deliver the blow against the British fortress.[69]

Halder noted: "Conversation with Adm. Canaris. He is offering the services of all reconnaissance officers operating in Gibraltar [area]."[70] Behind this lay Canaris's claim to be involved in and consulted on all military moves connected with "Felix." He took such a fervent interest in the minutiae of the OKH's plans that Halder's staff officers jibbed, unable to see why a secret service chief should meddle in their operational planning.[71] Canaris complained of their attitude to Halder.

"He is obviously offended," wrote the Army Chief of Staff, "because he has been accused of poaching on OKH preserves."[72] Realizing that no reconnaissance of southern Spain could bypass Canaris, Halder requested his department's help. Canaris duly sent for his man in Algeciras. With the aid of maps, tabular data and aerial photographs, Major Kautschke presented Halder and his staff officers with as detailed a picture of the military situation in and around Gibraltar as any member of the Army General Staff could have produced.[73]

Canaris soon became even more important to the planning of the campaign. Since the Gibraltar operation was entirely dependent on Franco's approval, the OKW and OKH again requested Canaris to discover how serious the Caudillo was in his intimations that Spain would soon be entering the war.

Despite Vigón's formal assurances, Canaris could not help feeling that Franco had long ago regretted his precipitate announcement of June 1940, nor could any number of belligerent speeches by the new Spanish Foreign Minister, Ramón Serrano Suñer, the Caudillo's brother-in-law, blind Canaris to the fact that, in Franco's eyes, the situation had radically altered. Britain was fighting on, and nothing suggested that the Germans were on the brink of final victory.

It had not escaped the Spaniards that Hitler's prospects of victory were steadily receding. Operation "Sea Lion" was a dead letter. On September 17, partly influenced by the unfavourable weather conditions affecting large-scale German air raids on Britain, Hitler had postponed the landing "until further notice."[74] All that remained of his ambitious invasion project was the air battle over England, in which the Germans fared less and less well as the weeks went by. Ever a brilliant opportunist, Franco drew his own conclusions. There were growing signs of Spanish reluctance and evasion—Canaris perceived them only too clearly. As early as August 27 Halder made the following notes on what Canaris had told him: "Spain's internal situation very difficult. Food supplies poor. Shortage of coal. Franco has the generals and the clergy against him. His only prop is Suñer, but he is more pro-Italian that pro-German."[75]

The leaders of the Third Reich believed, nonetheless, that they could coerce the Spaniards into joining them. In mid-September they invited the Spanish Foreign Minister to Berlin but treated him so arrogantly that Suñer was able, with obvious annoyance, to dodge the central issue.[76] Franco quite welcomed this ill feeling because it gave him a chance to sidestep the Germans' main demand. Cautiously manoeuvring in the no man's land between a still dominant Germany and the growing strength of Britain, he played for time.

Hitler decided to force the Caudillo's hand and extort his consent to "Felix" at a face-to-face encounter. Shortly after Suñer's visit the Führer suggested to his fellow dictator that they should meet on the northern frontier of Spain. Franco delayed the meeting for a month. Finally, on October 23, 1940, the two leaders met at the Franco-Spanish border town of Hendaye.[77]

Hitler immediately presented his demands. These were that Spain and Germany should conclude an alliance and that Spain should enter the war in January 1941, combining this move with an attack on Gibraltar. Having approved an alliance "in principle," Franco proceeded to heap Hitler's plate with innumerable problems. Spain needed huge consignments of foodstuffs. She also lacked modern armaments, notably the heavy artillery required for an operation against Gibraltar. Franco would not countenance an independent German assault on the British stronghold. Gibraltar could "only be taken by the Spaniards themselves"—his compatriots' honour was at stake.[78] Wearily, Hitler let the Caudillo's eloquence wash over him. He later complained to Mussolini that he would rather have three or four teeth extracted than go through another conference with Franco.[79]

At the same time, the Spaniard was wary enough to avoid a complete break. He undertook to subscribe to the three-power pact concluded in September by Germany, Italy and Japan. "In fulfilment of her obligations as an ally," he affirmed in a secret protocol, "Spain will intervene in the present war between the Axis powers and Britain when the military assistance necessary to her preparation has been granted."[80]

As soon as Canaris heard what had happened at Hendaye he instinctively sensed that Spain would never come in. Five days later the war took a new turn which rendered Spain's active partnership with the Third Reich completely illusory. On October 28 Italian troops invaded Greece from Albania and presented the British with an unexpected chance to regain a foothold on the continent of Europe.[81]

Few other events in 1940 brought Hitler and Canaris closer than Italy's military adventure in Greece. The dictator and his secret service chief were both caught napping by the Greco-Italian war and both tried to smother it before Germany's chances of ultimate victory were completely wrecked.

It had become clear since the end of the Western campaign that Mussolini would not rest until he engineered a "little" war of his own in which the Italian Army could gain a few cheap successes and put it-

self on a par with the Wehrmacht. The Duce's most obvious course
was to take on the British Mediterranean Fleet, but his Navy usually
avoided such encounters. The Italian General Staff resorted to surro-
gates. In August its East African forces occupied British Somaliland,
which was almost undefended, and in September there followed a large-
scale attack from Libya on the weak British forces guarding the Egyp-
tian frontier.[82]

But Mussolini's pride demanded more than this. He wanted the
Italian Army to win some resounding victories in the Balkans, never
mind at whose expense. Yugoslavia and Greece were the most likely victims, but Hitler proved obstructive. Anxious for peace and quiet on the
southern borders of his domain, he forbade any German-Italian staff
talks about a campaign against Yugoslavia and advised Mussolini and
his Foreign Minister, Ciano, against attacking Greece.[83]

Canaris, who found it perturbing enough that Italy should have en
tered the war at all, did his best to discourage an Italian foray into the
Balkans. As late as February 1940 he had impressed on General
Giacomo Carboni, Mussolini's chief of military intelligence, that Italy
must stay out of the war so as to act as Germany's "diplomatic stand-
by."[84] He then hoped that Germany might succeed in wriggling out of
the war with Italian help. Now that this illusion had evaporated, his
only remaining task was to prevent Italy from damaging German interests.

Reports from Italian sources provided an early indication that
Mussolini was planning a war against Greece. According to rumours
systematically spread by Rome, British warships were using Greek ports
as naval bases.[85] Canaris, who had been associated with Greece since
childhood and friendly with Greek naval officers since the 1920s, was
able to reject the Italian allegations out of hand.

Secret French General Staff documents seized by the Abwehr had
revealed that Ioannis Metaxas, the Greek military dictator, was surreptitiously negotiating with Britain.[86] In mid-July Canaris sent Major
Christian Clemm von Hohenberg, a former Abwehr officer now serving
as military attaché in Athens, to see General Tetsis, the head of the
Greek King's military cabinet. The Admiral urgently warned the
Greeks against pursuing a foreign policy at variance with their neutral
status and advised them to clarify their attitude towards the victorious
Third Reich. Berlin had long been aware, he said, that Greek ministers
had given undertakings to the British which were inconsistent with a
policy of neutrality.[87]

Though acting on his own initiative, Canaris was also reflecting
Hitler's views. A month later the Führer informed the Greek Ambassador in Berlin that he would never tolerate an Italian attack on Greece
but advised Athens to refrain from provoking the Italians in any way.[88]

The Greek Government's protestations finally convinced Canaris that the Italian charges were unfounded. The more Rome stepped up its propaganda campaign against Greece, the stronger his pro-Greek line became. On August 17 he told the head of his Abteilung Ausland, Rear Admiral Bürkner, to inform the Greek naval attaché, Konstantinides, that the Abwehr "naturally" knew that Rome's charges against Athens were false[89]—once again in accord with the Führer. On the same day, Hitler infuriated Ciano by appealing to the Italians to maintain "a complete standstill all along the line."[90]

Before long, however, Hitler's endeavours and those of his Abwehr chief began to diverge. Already preoccupied with thoughts of a Russian campaign, the Führer decided that to continue a hard line would only alienate an ally whose help he needed in the East. He therefore took a milder tone with the Italians, whereas Canaris warned them ever more strongly—via the German military attaché in Rome, Lieutenant General von Rintelen—against going to war with Greece.[91]

Sensing this change of climate at the Berlin Chancellery, the Italians struck without notifying the Germans in advance. Hitler, who was just on his way to confer with Mussolini in Florence, swore loudly at the incompetence of "liaison staffs and attachés who knew their way round the best restaurants but were the world's worst spies" when news of the Italian invasion reached him early on the morning of October 28.[92] He found it hard to contain his rage and disappointment when the Duce greeted him in Florence. "Führer," Mussolini announced with a radiant smile, "we're on the march!"[93]

It was little use informing the Wehrmacht that Italy's move was "not in line with the Führer's policy and general conduct of the war"— the damage was already done.[94] The Italian offensive collapsed after a few days. In mid-November the Greek Army launched a counteroffensive and drove the invaders far back into Albania.[95] Worse still, Royal Air Force units installed themselves in Crete and the prospect of a major Balkan war threatened to sever the Germans from their Romanian oil supplies. The military situation in the Balkans became so precarious that Hitler decided to bail his Axis partner out. Ciano was still assuring his father-in-law that he would sooner shoot himself than ask Ribbentrop for help when Warlimont's staff officers began to pore over a new plan of campaign (code-named "Marita") which provided for the invasion of Greece by German forces.[96]

The Italian débâcle inevitably made a deep impression on Franco and must have reinforced his determination to stay out of the war at all costs. Detwiler considers that October 1940 marked the end of Franco's lukewarm involvement in Hitler's military plans.[97] The Führer refused to acknowledge this fact, unlike Canaris, who had grasped it very quickly.

On November 12 the Admiral revisited Spain to take another look at Gibraltar and form an assessment of Spain's military preparations.[98] He again travelled in the capacity of the Abwehr's senior spy, his purpose being to determine how Abwehr units and combat teams could best contribute to the capture of the Rock. Canaris and Lahousen had decided that the main assault should be supported by an Abwehr operation of their own devising. From November 7 onwards this bore the code name "Basta."[99]

Picking up the threads of his original plan, Canaris proposed that Brandenburger commando detachments should preface the attack by blowing up the heavy steel fence in the neutral zone between Gibraltar and Spanish territory, occupy the Rock's northwest thoroughfare and hold it until German assault troops caught up. Sabotage operations were also planned. Petrol dumps, the airfield, the generating station and the water distillation plant would all be destroyed so as to break the defenders' morale.[100] Captain Rudloff, temporarily attached to KO Spain under the code name "Rodrigo," was instructed to plan the operation in detail.[101]

Lahousen noted on November 5: "The Lehrregiment [Brandenburgers] has been instructed to hold about 150 men in readiness. Of this special contingent, which will shortly be transported to the South of France, 50 men are for immediate and the remaining 100 for subsequent employment."[102] Sabotage-Organisation Spanien [SO Spain], which temporarily consisted of one man, Rudloff, was to confide in the Spanish secret service. Operation "Basta" personnel would be disguised as members of the Spanish Foreign Legion and carry Spanish weapons.[103] As for Canaris himself, he insisted on reconnoitring "Basta's" operational area in the guise of Señor Guillermo.

Increased contact with the Spaniards satisfied Canaris that Franco would make no contribution to a German attack on Gibraltar. He reported to Halder on his return that Spanish military preparations showed no perceptible signs of progress,[104] but Hitler and most of his military advisers still genuinely believed that Franco would swallow his misgivings and join in. The Balkan fiasco even inspired a plan to drive the British from the Western as well as the Eastern Mediterranean by delivering several blows at once. On November 19, Keitel instructed Jodl to frame the orders of the Wehrmachtführungsstab [Armed Forces Operations Staff] in such a way that "Felix" and "Marita" could be launched simultaneously—by spring 1941 at the latest.[105]

The Luftwaffe representative on Jodl's staff objected that it would be difficult to carry out both operations at once because the eight Stuka dive-bomber groups assigned to Gibraltar would also be needed for "Marita."[106] Germany's military planners suddenly found themselves pressed for time. If the blow against Greece was to be delivered by the beginning of March 1941 at the latest, Operation "Felix" would have to be tackled right away. This meant obtaining Franco's consent to the attack on Gibraltar and deploying German troops in Spain early enough for the operation to begin on February 4 or 5, 1941. OKW logistics experts put the deployment time at twenty-five days, so German forces would need permission to cross the Spanish frontier by January 10 at the latest.[107]

But who was to obtain the Caudillo's firm consent? In conference with Keitel on December 4 Hitler suggested that Franco be apprised of the reasons for this sudden military decision by a personal representative of the Wehrmacht authorities, preferably Jodl. Keitel had a better envoy in mind. He proposed that Admiral Canaris, who knew the Caudillo personally, should go to Madrid at once and secure his approval. Hitler agreed and said that Jodl could follow a few days later to discuss the military details with Franco.[108]

Canaris flinched when he heard of his mission. Bürkner preserved a vivid recollection of his chief's annoyance at being dispatched to Madrid.[109] Canaris knew that Hitler's assignment was impracticable and that the mission would inevitably fail because nothing on earth would induce Franco to go to war against his will.

He had said as much on November 2 to Halder, who made the following note: "General impression of Spain: fear of a conflict with Britain, hence deep concern about a British landing in Spain or Portugal and about the possibility of a British occupation of the Canary Islands . . . Franco, who has lost his backing and so cannot afford to take any risks, in an awkward position."[110] A man like that would never go to war—Canaris was convinced of it, but what if he returned to Hitler empty-handed? Neither the Admiral's nerves nor the Abwehr's shaky reputation could withstand the Führer's outbursts of fury.

Thoroughly uneasy, Canaris reported to Hitler on December 4 for a last-minute briefing on his interview with Franco. The two men conferred for an hour. Canaris's spirits must have risen, because the dictator gave him an unexpected job in addition to his Madrid assignment. Unbeknown to Germany's Italian allies and the German Foreign Office, Canaris was to pave the way for an armistice between Italy and Greece.[111]

The signs are that Canaris was the first to broach the subject of an armistice in the Balkans. He had been trying for days to gain Hitler's approval of moves towards a settlement of the Greco-Italian conflict. Acting on his own initiative, he had also tried to foster a climate of conciliation in Athens and Rome. In November he got Major Clemm to sound out the Greek authorities on the conditions under which they would be prepared to accept a cease-fire. On December 1 he told General von Rintelen that a definite attempt must be made to persuade the Italians to compromise.[112]

Canaris seemed to have caught Hitler at an opportune moment. The dictator, who had reached a crucial stage in his own career and his country's history, listened calmly to the Admiral's arguments. After the almost total failure of his attempts to subdue the British, he was wavering beween the various courses open to him.

These included stepping up operations against the British in the Mediterranean, organizing an anti-British continental bloc in concert with the Soviet Union, whose energies would have to be diverted from Germany's eastern borders and focused on India and the Far East, or an attack on the Soviet Union itself, that traditional target of Hitlerian expansionism and inspiriting element in the British determination to stand firm. Being quite as averse to a naval war with Britain as he was to a direct assault on the British Isles, Hitler felt increasingly attracted by the idea of a war with Russia.

But the Greco-Italian war did not fit into this scheme of things, nor did the rescue operation known as "Marita." The Wehrmacht's offensive momentum was gradually turning eastwards, and a campaign against Greece would be bound to misdirect it. Canaris's armistice project offered an escape from this dilemma, though the Admiral himself could not at first have perceived its tragic implications. By trying to end hostilities in the Balkans, he was only paving the way for a still more sanguinary conflict in the East.

So the Führer had no hesitation in sanctioning his intelligence chief's armistice proposal. Canaris's ideas must have impressed Hitler, because on December 5—only a day after their meeting—the military advisers who were reporting to him on "Felix" and "Marita" were surprised to be told that the latter operation might never take place. Puzzled, Jodl noted down a statement by Hitler to the effect that Germany would have to intervene in Greece unless the Greeks themselves stopped the war with Italy and compelled the British to leave Greek soil. Intervention would then become unnecessary because the struggle for European supremacy would not be decided in Greece.[113]

Canaris yielded to the proud and beguiling sensation that he was playing a key role at a fateful moment in his country's history. He once more succumbed to the old and erroneous belief that Hitler was open to persuasion by those who knew how to handle him. Nothing could have been better calculated to nourish his fertile imagination than the thought that Hitler had entrusted him with a mission of rare ambivalence: to make war possible at one end of the Mediterranean while ending it at the other.

He took off on December 5, accompanied by Piekenbrock, and flew to Bordeaux, where he had been asked by Halder to brief a military reconnaissance team before it left for Gibraltar. Next morning the Admiral summoned the team members from their Bordeaux hotels and lectured them on their duties. Every inch the Supreme Commander's mouthpiece, Canaris prefaced his remarks with "a saying of the Führer's": "If I want to catch a burglar in a room with two doors, I shut one door first and nab him at the other." The practical inference, Canaris explained, was that Gibraltar must be taken before the British could be defeated at Suez.[114] He went on to detail his instructions and supervise the distribution of false papers, Spanish currency and maps. The ubiquitous Lieutenant Colonel Pardo turned up to fit the German cars with Spanish licence plates and sneak them across the border.[115]

Canaris went on ahead of the reconnaissance team. It was time to prepare for his crucial interview with Franco. He reached Madrid on the morning of December 7 and got in touch with Vigón soon afterwards.[116] Everything his Spanish friend said and did was a foretaste of the response awaiting him at the Prado Palace, Franco's official residence. Canaris could not afford to make a single blunder that might discredit him with Hitler, so he asked Vigón to make a full transcript of his conversation with the Caudillo and place it at his disposal for submission to the Führer.[117]

The audience at the Prado Palace was set for 7:30 P.M. Canaris turned up punctually, escorted by Piekenbrock and Leissner. He conveyed Hitler's greetings to Franco and stated that Germany wished "to undertake the attack on Gibraltar in the near future, it being necessary that German troops should enter Spain on January 10." The Führer deemed this the most opportune moment because the troops available for use against the Rock would soon be required for other operations. Once they were on Spanish soil, Germany's economic aid programme would become effective.[118]

Then came the answer Canaris had been expecting. To quote Vigón's record of the proceedings: "The Generalissimo informed the Admiral that it would be impossible for Spain to enter the war on the date in question for previously stated reasons."[119] The risk of intervention by the Royal Navy, coupled with Spain's military unpreparedness and shortage of supplies, precluded an early declaration of war. Franco: "For these reasons, Spain cannot enter the war in the near future, nor could she wage a long war without imposing intolerable sacrifices on the Spanish people."[120]

Franco's reply tallied almost word for word with Halder's summary of what Canaris had told him in advance. Despite this, Canaris asked whether Franco could suggest another date on which the entry of German troops might be possible. "The Generalissimo replied," noted Vigón, "that, since the removal of difficulties did not depend solely on the will of Spain, he was unable to give any firm date, which might be affected by circumstances."[121] The audience was at an end, and Canaris rose. Franco saw his visitor out, but not before giving him "a renewed expression of his esteem and his pleasure at seeing him back in Spain."[122]

Canaris and his two companions drove back to the German Embassy. The same night he sent off a telegram to Bürkner, his acting deputy. On December 8, 1940, the OKW diary-keeper made the following entry: "Chef Ausl./Abw., Admiral Canaris, reports that on the evening of 7.12, pursuant to instructions received on 4.12, he urgently discussed the need for Spain's early entry into the war with Generalissimo Franco. Franco replied that Spain could not enter the war on the date requested by the Führer because she was unprepared . . . General Franco stressed in conclusion that his refusal was based on a regard for our common interests. It was to be feared that Spain would become a heavy charge on the Axis powers after the conquest of Gibraltar."[123]

Bürkner passed Canaris's telegram to Jodl, who left Keitel to convey the bad news to Hitler.[124] The dictator still found it impossible to believe that his Spanish colleague was deserting him. At 6 P.M. Keitel dispatched a telegram requesting Canaris "to ask General Franco the earliest possible date for an attack on Gibraltar."[125] Leissner had some difficulty in forwarding this communication because Canaris was going the rounds of the Spanish authorities with the military misson, whose members had now reached Madrid.

Canaris did not answer Keitel's query until December 10. He wired him that he had already, on December 7, "repeatedly and urgently asked [Franco] whether he would be prepared to enter the war at another date or could specify a later time." Franco had replied in the negative and stated that any such date would depend "on the future economic development of Spain . . . as well as on the future development of the war against Britain."[126] This was enough to convince even Hitler, who promptly cancelled the operation against Gibraltar. His dreams of sealing off the Western Mediterranean had been dispelled for good.[127]

Canaris was momentarily afraid that Hitler would be exasperated by his failure in Madrid, but the dictator remained calm. Not even this abortive mission to Franco could destroy his conviction that Canaris had a superlative talent for handling the Spaniards. SS-Oberstgruppenführer [Colonel General] Karl Wolff, Himmler's erstwhile adjutant in chief, recalled after the war that Hitler had been "full of praise for Canaris" because the Admiral "had in Hitler's view shown exceptional skill in preparing for the negotiations with Franco in Spain."[128]

In view of this benevolent attitude, Canaris did not find it hard to tackle the second of Hitler's assignments. Any attempt to mediate in the Greco-Italian war would have to be swift, however, because circumstances had changed. On December 9, 1940, the British had launched a North African counteroffensive and put the Italians to flight. The bulk of four Italian divisions had been smashed within twenty-four hours, and the British attack was still in progress.[129]

Canaris had to act before Italy's enemies gained such an advantage that his attempt at mediation became futile. Chance enabled him to make a start in Madrid, where the Hungarian Ambassador happened to be Colonel Rudolf Andorka, the ex-intelligence chief with whom he had worked for so long. Canaris outlined his scheme for ending the Balkan war and asked Andorka if he would help to implement it. The colonel agreed.[130]

Andorka was on good terms with Admiral Perikles Argyropoulos, the Greek Ambassador in Madrid. On December 17 he informed Argyropoulos that he had a German cease-fire proposal which should be communicated to his government without delay. Canaris's terms were that Germany should help to negotiate an armistice on the Albanian front and preserve the cease-fire by dispatching a force to separate the opposing armies. The Greeks would retain the Albanian territory occupied by their troops. The only proviso was that they should revert to a strictly neutral status and ensure that the British left Greek soil.[131]

Argyropoulos was so taken aback by these terms that he asked Andorka more than once if they constituted an official German proposal and could reasonably be transmitted to Athens.[132] His fears were not allayed until he heard who was behind the project. The historical parallel cannot have escaped him. A Greek admiral named Kanaris had once secured his country's independence; was a German admiral named Canaris destined to bring it peace? The ambassador immediately communicated the German offer to General Metaxas, and the Greek dictator, who had already been contemplating a cease-fire by arrangement with Germany, took it up.

Not even Metaxas, a friend of Britain and bitter opponent of the Axis powers, could fail to recognize that his country was in mortal danger. The Italians he could handle, but behind them loomed the might of Germany. If the huge German war machine bore down, Greece was lost. Britain would come to her aid, granted, but the price would be national devastation.

Alarmed by reports which left him in no doubt that German military intervention was imminent, Metaxas decided to avert it at all costs. On the very day when Canaris was confiding in his ex-colleague Andorka, he sent an intermediary to Canaris's confidant, Clemm, to convey his hope that Germany would try to arrange a cease-fire.[133] Still ignorant of developments in Madrid, the Greek head of government urgently requested that any attempt to mediate should be undertaken by Admiral Canaris, a proven friend of Greece, rather than by Ribbentrop's diplomats.[134]

So Metaxas was only too ready to back Canaris's mediation proposal when it was cabled to him by Ambassador Argyropoulos. He must have seen at once that the Admiral's suggested terms were far more favourable to Greece than his own. The Greek dictator's scheme was based on the prewar frontiers, whereas Canaris was conceding the Albanian territories conquered by Greece. Common to both sets of proposals was a Greek undertaking to ensure that British troops withdrew.[135]

Metaxas submitted the terms in cabinet, but his ministers failed to agree. Most of them, impressed by continuing Greek and British successes in the field, interpreted the Canaris feeler as a symptom of Italian weakness or a German attempt to undermine Greek morale. In face of such sentiments, Metaxas did not disclose that he himself had already been in touch with the German military attaché.[136] If the debate taught him one thing, it was that mediation by the Germans would provoke a grave political crisis at home.

The Greek dictator drew back but remained in touch with the Germans. Clemm was informed that he wanted Canaris to reiterate his proposal through diplomatic channels so that the Greek Government could officially inform the British. Clemm forwarded this hint to Canaris, who may have passed it on to Hitler.[137] However, the Führer hesitated out of consideration for the Italians, who would have been furious and might even have terminated their alliance with Germany had they learnt that Berlin was offering Athens parts of a country to which they themselves laid claim.

British military authorities, diplomats and secret servicemen redoubled their efforts to persuade the Greek Government to take a definite stand against Germany. London bombarded Metaxas with requests that British troops should at last be permitted to operate on the Greek mainland and mount a joint offensive against the common foe. Metaxas postponed this decision because he knew that what underlay Britain's insistence was Churchill's plan to extend the Greco-Italian war to the whole of the Balkans including Yugoslavia, Bulgaria and Turkey, thereby establishing a sort of second front against Germany.[138]

The Turkish Government had rejected Churchill's plan of campaign. The Bulgarians, who were traditionally pro-German, and the Yugoslavs, who were gingerly sitting on the fence, did not wish to be drawn into a war against Germany either. That left Greece, whose government was in a position to admit a British expeditionary force to the Balkan mainland in pursuit of its military endeavours against Italy. So far, however, Metaxas had withheld his consent. Although Royal Air Force units were stationed in Crete, the Greek head of government declined to grant the British any further concessions unless he had to.[139]

At this juncture, Canaris's attempts to mediate were threatened with total disaster by a pro-British visitor to Athens. Colonel William J. Donovan, President Roosevelt's special representative and the future head of the U.S. secret service, was a fervent advocate of American military intervention and thoroughly in favour of British plans for a Balkan campaign. He was visiting Greece partly at the suggestion of the British secret service, which had helped to arrange "Wild Bill's" Balkan tour.[140]

Wherever he appeared in the Balkans, Donovan called for a crusade against German Nazism and promised consignments of American arms to any government willing to join it. He visited Greek troops on the Albanian front, negotiated with Metaxas and his generals, called on King Boris of Bulgaria. Whatever offers, pledges and undertakings he made, his abiding concern was "to maintain Britain's crucial strategic position" and deliver a message from Roosevelt to the effect that "any nation which tamely submits on the grounds of being quickly overrun would receive less sympathy from the world than a nation which resists, even if this resistance can be continued for only a few weeks."[141]

Canaris kept a wary eye on the American's movements and instructed German agents to dog his every step. They searched his discarded overcoat and stole his passport while he was visiting King Boris in Sofia, with the result that the Orient Express to Belgrade had to be delayed for twenty minutes before the colonel could continue his journey with a duplicate.[142] German misgivings about Donovan's trip to Yugoslavia were not groundless because Belgrade was the most elusive of Greater Germany's foreign policy targets.

The multinational Yugoslav state had long spurned German embraces and British overtures alike. Considerations of neutrality and internal stress forbade Premier Cvetković to join either of the warring camps for fear that the Serbs would reject an alliance with the Axis and the Croats a war against Germany.[143] Hitler, who had become more and more fanatically engrossed in his plans for the Russian campaign, was now pressing hard for a decision. He needed Yugoslavia as a partner and deployment area for his war in the East, so he demanded her accession to the Tripartite Pact. Cvetković, who could see no alternative, was preparing to join the Axis powers.[144]

This was precisely what Donovan had set out to prevent. German agents carefully registered all his attempts to dissuade the Yugoslav authorities from taking this fateful step, but they missed one crucially important detail. Donovan managed to contact General Dušan Simović of the Yugoslav Air Force and a group of Serbian nationalist officers who were prepared to overthrow the government rather than accept an alliance with Germany. During a secret visit to Simović's headquarters at Semlin the colonel promised that the United States would render them full moral and material support.[145]

Donovan proved so openhanded that he later boasted of having "bought" General Simović's *coup d'état*.[146] Like the Yugoslav general, Metaxas was impressed by his guarantees. Donovan's pledges of assistance were largely responsible for the Greek dictator's decision to yield to British demands in mid-January 1941. He agreed that the British military authorities in the Middle East should secretly prepare to land troops at Salonika but only disembark them when German forces moved into Bulgaria and so made a war with Greece unavoidable.[147]

Metaxas died two weeks later, leaving behind a divided nation. This was enough to revive the hopes of Canaris and Clemm. Although the reins of government passed to some pro-British generals and politicians, hostility towards the idea of an alliance with Britain was stirring in the middle and lower reaches of the Greek establishment. Even before the dictator's death Clemm had reported "proposals from pro-German opposition groups aimed at removing the Metaxas government and bringing about a peace settlement." The military attaché also recalled in later years that "these circles proposed to grant Germany submarine and air bases in the Peloponnese for the duration of the war."[148]

Clemm now found himself increasingly in demand with Greek officers and politicians who wanted to end the war against Italy with Germany's help and had already secured the approval of Crown Prince (later King) Paul, the ex-Kaiser's son-in-law.[149] When Hitler summoned the major to Berlin at the end of January to brief him urgently on the situation in Greece, Clemm and Canaris saw a chance to resurrect their mediation project.

Face to face with the Führer on February 1, Clemm asked if he might speak "quite frankly." Hitler nodded, whereupon Clemm presented a report whose gist was that a German campaign against Greece was avoidable because influential figures there wanted peace and no British forces worth mentioning were stationed on Greek soil.[150] Hitler made no secret of his indecision. Before dismissing Clemm he pointed to Albania on a map of the Balkans. "And all because of that muck there!" he fumed. "If I attack, everyone will say I've stabbed a gallant little nation in the back—one that's defending its freedom like the Finns. If I don't, the Italians will defect."[151]

Hitler was still so undecided about the merits of a campaign against Greece that he called for a resubmission of the Canaris plan. On February 17 "official personages" in Berlin, one of whom must certainly have been Canaris himself, were authorized to present Rangabé, the Greek Ambassador, with a German proposal which was almost indistinguishable from Canaris's original offer of mediation. The only difference was that the Reich itself would be responsible for expelling British forces from Greek territory.[152] Rangabé, a frequent partner in discussions with Canaris, cabled the offer to Athens.

This suited Hitler, who was receiving the Yugoslav ministers Cvetković and Marković at Berchtesgaden the same day. The Yugoslavs had come to submit a scheme that would absolve their country from joining the Tripartite Pact. They proposed that Yugoslavia, Bulgaria, Greece and Turkey join in forming a Balkan league which would undertake to maintain the strictest neutrality and prevent the stationing of British troops in the Balkans. The Belgrade ministers further offered to help negotiate an armistice between Greece and Italy. Hitler agreed and recommended discussions with the Italians.[153]

But both attempts to mediate were thwarted, one by Italian opposition and the other by Greek intransigence. Canaris was in despair. On February 19 the new Greek Premier, Korysis, rejected the German offer on the grounds that it was unacceptable to a country "at war."[154] Nothing could now stem the tide of disaster. German armies deployed for an attack on Greece. On March 2 German units moved into Bulgaria via Romania, whereupon a British fleet left Alexandria to land an expeditionary force at Piraeus under the command of General Wilson.[155]

However, Canaris's peace plan was unexpectedly given a last-minute chance of success by some Greek generals who were appalled at the spectacle of British troops landing on their native soil. With political backing from Crown Prince Paul, the commanders of the Epirus Army badgered Premier Korysis into seeking an accommodation with Germany after all.[156] Lieutenant General Tsolakoglyu, Commander in Chief Northern Greece, did not bother to wait for the government to act. On March 12 he hurriedly presented the German Consulate in Salonika with a request for mediation resembling the old Canaris proposal.[157]

On March 16 Korysis endorsed the general's recommendation and officially requested Germany's good offices. His undersecretary notified the German Ambassador in Athens. At the same time, Ambassador Rangabé hurried to the Foreign Office in Berlin with a diplomatic note assuring Hitler of the Greek Government's submission. Its key sentence ran: "In all circumstances, the decision [on Greece] rests with the Reich."[158] But Hitler declined to accept the document. State Secretary von Weizsäcker, who had known this beforehand, commented, "It's all too late. There's nothing more to be done."[159]

On March 20 Rangabé made a despairing dash to the Tirpitz-Ufer and begged Canaris to see that Hitler himself received the note. Though dubious, the Admiral agreed to help. He told Bürkner to call at the Chancellery and hand the Greek Government's note to the Führer in person, but Bürkner did not get far. Chancellery officials took receipt of the document but forwarded it to the Foreign Office, where it was filed. Hitler never set eyes on it.[160]

The German dictator was far along the road to another war, and no argument or appeal to reason could hold him back. His destructive urges had been stimulated by another development. Yugoslavia had hardly subscribed to the Tripartite Pact when Donovan's Serbian friends struck. During the night of March 26–27 General Simović seized power and mobilized against the Third Reich.[161] Hitler did not wait a moment longer. On March 27 he recorded his determination "to destroy Yugoslavia militarily and as a political structure." The operation against Greece was developing into a full-scale Balkan campaign.[162]

On April 6, 1941, the German armies formed up for the attack. Foreign territory was again overrun by the Wehrmacht and another component of the old European order disintegrated. Canaris watched in dismay as the armies and divisions of the Reich stormed into ever more remote areas and dispersed in all directions. German soldiers patrolling the mountains of Serbia and stationed on the Acropolis, German soldiers in Bulgaria and Romania, German soldiers sent to rescue their routed Italian allies in the desert sands of Africa—when, if ever, would this insane conflict cease?

War without end—that was what Canaris saw, and saw with growing clarity. All at once, the failure of his Balkan peacemaking efforts and the campaign in Southeast Europe seemed but further steps along the road to suicidal embroilment in Hitler's policy and strategy, a process which unfolded with apparent automatism, remorseless and irreversible. The Admiral's spirits sank to a new ebb. A few months ago he had still been optimistic. Now, all he could foresee was an endless succession of bloody Pyrrhic victories, each more cruel and futile than the last.

Canaris may, in these hours of despair, have recalled a conversation with the writer Franz Josef Furtwängler in which he had predicted what was to come. Furtwängler had asked him in autumn 1939 who were likely to be regarded as the outstanding military leaders of the new war. The Admiral's fatalistic rejoinder was that lunacy would command in person, that the other military leaders were just interchangeable extras and "exalted supernumeraries," and—anyway—"technical warfare proceeds with the automatism of a machine and the predictability of an ant heap."[163] The Balkan campaign supplied fresh confirmation of this gloomy forecast.

Canaris felt an urge to visit the front and see what "lunacy in person" had accomplished this time. On April 15 he and his heads of section boarded a special plane at Tempelhof Airport and flew to occupied Belgrade. Canaris caught his first glimpse of the Yugoslav capital at about 4 P.M. German bombers had left it devastated and in flames, mortally stricken and littered with dead. "The city," Lahousen noted with characteristic understatement, "is without water, light, power and gas. The dead are put at more than seven thousand. The cloying smell of dead bodies throughout the municipal area seems to confirm this assumption."[164]

The environs of the airport were so badly damaged that Canaris and his party had to be flown into the city in a light Fieseler Storch aircraft. They arrived just in time to watch a defeated Yugoslav division march through the streets of Belgrade under guard. Canaris drove aimlessly round the capital, shocked by the sight of its smoking ruins and stunned inhabitants. He spent the night at nearby Semlin and almost went down with a capsizing ferry while returning to Belgrade across the Sava.[165] But the sight of the capital proved too much for him. "I can't take any more of this," he groaned. "We're flying out of here."[166]

However, the following month saw him off on another tour of the latest battlefields, which held a strange fascination for him. This time he was on his way to Athens, which his Brandenburgers had been the first to occupy. Men of the 2nd Battalion under Captain Jacobi had entered the Greek capital on April 27 and hoisted the swastika flag over the city hall.[167] One feature of Canaris's visit to Athens on May 17 was a meeting with Major Clemm von Hohenberg during which the two men discussed the reasons why they had failed in their attempt to mediate.[168]

Those who saw the Admiral at this period found him pale and out of sorts. Few people realized that he had been through weeks of mental torment, despair and resignation. His mood not only reflected the failure of all his efforts to prevent a war in the Balkans. Canaris was plagued by a far more disturbing prospect and preoccupied with a future development whose consequences were incalculable—one that filled him with a sense of impending doom: Hitler's invasion of the Soviet Union.

Ever since Canaris learned that Hitler was toying with the idea of attacking and eliminating the Soviet Union as a potential adversary before forcing Britain into submission, he had instinctively felt that the dictator was burning the last of his boats. Canaris regarded the wilful and needless self-imposition of a war on two fronts as political folly and military suicide. If the Wehrmacht failed to crush the Red Army at the first onset Germany would be exposed to a war of attrition on too many fronts, and that would spell the fulfilment of his long-standing "Finis Germaniae" prophecy.

For a while he had hoped that Hitler would, after all, be deterred from a war with Russia. The Führer's signs of hesitation were perceptible enough. Although he had informed the Army commander in chief, Field Marshal von Brauchitsch, on July 21, 1940, that "the Russian problem must be tackled," matters had not progressed beyond the stage of "theoretical preparations" (Hitler). The Army General Staff produced some preliminary operational plans, but they were only abstract constructions.[169] They remained mere paper for as long as Hitler still flirted with the idea of neutralizing the Russians politically by incorporating them in a united anti-British front and assuaging their appetite for territory in India and the Near East.

Not until this attempt had failed (during Foreign Minister Molotov's visit to Berlin in November 1940) did Hitler decide on war with Russia.[170] A new code name—"Barbarossa"—made its appearance, as ominous-sounding as was the whole operation that heralded the end of Nazi Germany. In his Directive No. 21, dated December, 18, 1940, Hitler issued OKW with the following general order: "The German armed forces must be prepared to crush Soviet Russia in a brief campaign before the end of the war with Britain."[171] Preparations were to be complete by early summer and deployment would take place eight weeks before the invasion was launched.[172]

By the beginning of 1941 Canaris could no longer be in any doubt that the directive meant what it said. He confided in his heads of section. Piekenbrock later recalled: "I received more detailed information about the timing of the German attack on the Soviet Union from Canaris himself. He told me that the attack . . . was scheduled for May 15."[173] This news could have come as no surprise because the Admiral had been keeping Piekenbrock, Bentivegni and Lahousen regularly informed of the progress of the ultrasecret "Barbarossa" debate since mid-summer 1940.

As early as August of that year Canaris summoned the head of Abwehr III to his office and, as Colonel von Bentivegni subsequently testified, "informed me that Hitler had now decided to take steps towards putting the Eastern campaign into effect."[174] A month later Foreign Armies East was bombarding the Abwehr with requests for more information about Soviet units in Eastern Europe, and in November Bentivegni received "instructions from Canaris to step up Abwehr activity at points where German troops were concentrated along the Russo-German border."[175] The Admiral's immediate subordinates realized that this could only mean war with Russia.

Despite this, Canaris continued to search for ways of averting the fateful campaign. He was more than ever convinced of what he had said in his quiet, lisping voice at one of the first "Barbarossa" conferences at Abwehr headquarters: "The German armies will bleed to death on the icy plains of Russia, and two years later there won't be anything left of them."[176] He opposed Hitler's plan with all his might and found some influential allies in the process. Few German dignitaries outside the Führer's immediate circle were anything but appalled by the prospect of a campaign against Russia. Even Ribbentrop, his vain and fatuous Foreign Minister, was shocked when he heard where the country was heading.[177]

The Admiral mobilized everyone who seemed likely to further his purposes, whether Nazi or anti-Nazi, soldier or civilian. He persuaded General Thomas, the military economics chief, to define the limits of Germany's war potential in a wide-ranging memorandum. He prompted his friend Weizsäcker to declare that a German attack on Russia "would only give a fresh boost to British moral. It would be construed . . . as [a sign of] German uncertainty about the success of our war against Britain."[178] Finally, he implored Keitel to guard the Führer against overoptimistic assessments of the enemy—and earned himself an icy rebuff. Keitel: "My dear Canaris, you may know something about military intelligence. Being a sailor, you surely don't propose to give us any lessons in strategic planning."[179]

Canaris also brought Theodor Oberländer into play. A young political economist and National Socialist, Oberländer was head of the Bund Deutscher Osten [German Eastern Association] and an expert on Eastern Europe whose conspicuously moderate views had brought him into conflict with Erich Koch, the rabidly racist Gauleiter of East Prussia. Canaris sent for Oberländer and inquired his opinion of a war against the Soviet Union. Oberländer made no bones about it: "Lunacy." Canaris agreed and asked him to elaborate his views in a memorandum for submission to Hitler. The non-conformist Nazi professor fell in with the idea, and a few weeks later an Oberländer broadside landed on the Führer's desk.[180]

Canaris even tried to enlist his rivals against "Barbarossa." Making the most of his daily rides in the Tiergarten with counterespionage police chief Schellenberg, he repeatedly pointed out how unsafe it was to assume that the Soviet system would suffer military and political collapse as soon as the Germans attacked. This line of argument was, of course, designed to impress an even more influential party. Schellenberg transmitted the Admiral's whispered forebodings to his boss, but Heydrich wanted nothing to do with "those two bellyachers" in the Tiergarten. When Schellenberg pressed the point, he angrily retorted, "I've had enough of your petty-minded, defeatist misgivings!"[181]

Despite his lingering hopes that Hitler would somehow be dissuaded from taking the ultimate step, Canaris obediently mobilized his organization to help in accomplishing what he secretly wished to prevent. Reluctantly, he issued his senior subordinates with preparatory orders for "Barbarossa." Quite apart from his fundamental opposition to the whole scheme, there were internal and departmental grounds for his uneasiness. The German secret service was simply not equipped to supply the information now being requested by the general staffs.

In fact, the "Barbarossa" preparations exposed an ironical state of affairs: Canaris the rabid anti-Communist had completely emasculated the Abwehr's Russian side. Poorly informed about Russia at the best of times, the German secret service had never been so methodically isolated from its Russian sources. As soon as the German-Soviet non-aggression pact was concluded in August 1939, Hitler forbade the Abwehr to engage in activities hostile to the Soviet Union. Since then, the Abwehr had ceased to operate there.[182]

Had Canaris measured up to his legendary reputation for being a sly, crafty, farsighted secret service chief, he would undoubtedly have found ways of getting round this prohibition. As it was, he followed his Führer's guidelines to the letter. The following Canaris directive, dated March 26, 1940, was recorded by Lahousen: "Nothing must be done to offend the Russians."[183]

The Abwehr appointed Beauftragte für Grenzfragen [border representatives] on the German-Soviet demarcation line were instructed to prevent agents from spying on Russian troops without orders. "Representatives cannot be expected to succeed in their work," Canaris wrote on June 22, 1940, "unless they are careful to maintain co-operation with Soviet representatives. This co-operation should be as close as possible. It calls for a special degree of tact and negotiating skill." Even when there was a threat of incidents on the Soviet side, Abwehr representatives were only to intervene in the last resort. "Relations with Soviet representatives must not be impaired by protests and warnings for which there are no wholly irrefutable grounds."[184]

Canaris not only meant what he said but actively discouraged Abwehr officers from trying to exploit fresh sources of information about Russia. When Lieutenant Colonel Pruck visited Bucharest in October 1939, General Moruzov of the Romanian secret service offered to make his department's excellent Russian material available to the Abwehr. Pruck was compelled to decline because "Admiral Canaris expressly instructed me before I left not to enter into any agreement concerning the Soviet Union."[185]

This was no isolated instance. In November 1940 General Okamoto, the Japanese military attaché in Berlin, mooted the possibility of bringing a party of Estonian agents by submarine to Danzig from the Soviet-occupied Baltic States, but Canaris declined "on the grounds that it might jeopardize the political situation."[186] He also saw to it that a former Latvian minister and informant of the Japanese military attaché in Stockholm was refused entry to German-occupied Holland, where he planned to establish a colony of Latvian émigrés.[187]

The Abwehr's Ukrainian agents suffered particularly badly from the Admiral's faithful compliance with Hitler's wishes. Until now, Lahousen of Abwehr II had tried to preserve an inconspicuous niche for

Ukrainians associated with the OUN leaders Mel'nyk and Yary. Canaris squelched even this possibility as soon as the Gestapo threatened to make trouble. In November 1940, when Gestapo chief Müller discovered that Abwehr II was still employing the services of leading OUN members in defiance of the Führer's express instructions, he proposed to have them arrested. This step required the consent of Abwehr headquarters. Canaris was promptly alerted by Lahousen but took a feeble line. While blocking the arrests, he ruled that the Abwehr was no longer justified "for reasons of foreign policy" in employing Ukrainian leaders like Yary.[188] On December 14, 1940, Lahousen was obliged to send for Yary and inform him that further co-operation with him and his organization was "out of the question"—and this at a time when anyone privy to Hitler's firm intention of invading Russia could have foreseen that Germany would again stand in need of Ukrainian assistance.[189]

The result of this self-inflicted paralysis was that the Abwehr had almost no idea of what was going on inside Russia. The intelligence evaluators of Foreign Armies East discovered this as soon as they came to assess the Soviet Union's military strength when planning Operation "Barbarossa." "Our knowledge of Soviet arms and equipment is extraordinarily sketchy," complained FHO [Foreign Armies East] Referent Goth, and Lieutenant Colonel Helmdach, former head of FHO's Soviet group, recalls that it was "almost impossible to obtain secret information."[190]

Unable to furnish a reliable picture of the Red Army's strength, the Abwehr failed completely when it came to Russia's armaments potential. "It was virtually impossible to gain an insight into the munitions industry," says Helmdach, "so the state of Soviet armaments remained a mystery."[191] Lieutenant General Paulus, co-author of the "Barbarossa" plan of campaign and no admirer of Canaris since the *coup d'état* discussions of winter 1939–40, later declared that it had been a "cardinal error" that "military intelligence afforded us no clear idea of what a powerful industrial base Russia possesses in the East."[192] (He was, of course, forgetting that private German firms like I. G. Farben were admirably well informed on the subject.)

So as not to lose face completely, Abwehr officers were obliged to rummage through documents captured during the Polish campaign in search of information about Russia—the "extremely rich material" which Captain Hermann Baun, Abwehr I's Russian expert, had promised his FHO colleagues back in July 1940.[193] But the Poles' outdated prewar information did little to augment FHO's store of knowledge—in fact it only confirmed the intelligence evaluators' lofty disdain for the Red Army when they read Polish analyses like the following: "Growth of anti-Stalin sentiment among senior [Red Army] officers resulting from purge. Middle-ranking officers: careerists devoid of independence and initiative . . . NCOs and men: confidence in superiors undermined."[194]

But the more FHO requested information about the Red Army the more keenly Abwehr officers felt their Russian deficit. From autumn 1940 onwards Canaris sanctioned a gradual relaxation of Hitler's ban on the gathering of intelligence. The Abwehr was now permitted to conclude a reciprocal agreement with the Romanian secret service. Before long, reports on the Soviet Union were flowing to the Abwehr from the intelligence sources maintained by all Germany's future allies in the Russian campaign. The Japanese, too, were welcomed back to the Tirpitz-Ufer.[195] For the time being, however, the Abwehr's own sources of Russian intelligence remained meagre. By another quirk of contemporary history they were virtually restricted to a pair of "non-Aryans" who supplied the world's most crudely anti-Semitic country with better Russian material than any other agents in the same field. One was the Jewish businessman Klatt of Sofia, an Abwehrstelle Vienna agent who also worked for Japanese intelligence and whose reports (known as "Max reports" after his code name) were to become famous during the Eastern campaign.[196] The other was Ivar Lissner of Harbin, a German Baltic writer and victim of the Nazi racial laws, who had hired himself out to the Abwehr to protect his parents. From Lissner the Abwehr received detailed reports by radio on developments in the Russian aircraft industry.[197] "Agent Ivar," stated Canaris, "is Amt Ausland/Abwehr's sole source of comprehensive reports on Asiatic Russia and the Manchukuo-Russian frontier zone. Reports received . . . provide the only intelligence documentation covering reserves, new formations, etc., in particular those of the Soviet Air Force in the Siberian area."[198]

But Canaris did not for long remain content with Max and Ivar. He urged Pickenbrock to expand and improve his Eastern network as quickly as possible. Abwehr I looked around for new recruits because Canaris realized that "Barbarossa" would present his organization with a new range of tasks. The typewriters in Keitel's anteroom were already tapping out secret orders summoning the Abwehr to take its place in the forefront of the invading armies.

On February 15, 1941, Canaris received a Geheime Kommandosache [secret military document] signed by Keitel. This appointed him co-ordinator of all intelligence and military operations whose purpose was to mask the deployment of German forces against Russia.[199] OKW-Abteilung L had devised what Keitel called "the greatest diversionary manoeuvre in military history." It was really a double bluff designed to persuade the Russians that German troop concentrations in the East were solely concerned with the impending invasion of England

and aimed at misleading the British into a belief that Hitler planned to attack the Soviet Union instead. What mattered, Keitel's order stressed, was "to maintain the prevailing uncertainty about our intentions during the first phase, i.e. until approximately mid-April. In the ensuing second phase, when preparations for 'Barbarossa' itself can no longer be concealed, they must be represented as a deception and distraction from the invasion of England."[200]

To someone who meant to oppose the Russian campaign with all his might, nothing could have seemed more agonizing than Keitel's directive. He, Wilhelm Canaris, had been ordered to disguise the true intentions of Hitler and his military commanders from the world at large —not only from the enemy but from Germany's allies and even from his own colleagues. Keitel's wording made this quite clear. "Sparing allusions to our over-all aim [will be made] only through channels to be determined by the head of Amt Ausland/Abwehr. The latter will also control the provision of our attachés in neutral countries and neutral attachés in Berlin with suitably misleading reports."[201]

No opponent of Hitler could have been given a more perfect opportunity to enlighten the world on the Third Reich's latest military plans. A man like Oster would have had no qualms about lacing false reports with genuine data and thereby warning the Russians as he had warned the Dutch, Danes and Norwegians in 1940. As a conventional serving officer, Canaris shunned such a course. All that mattered to him were his orders, and he carried them out—reluctantly, it is true, and confident that Hitler would change tack at the last minute, but faithfully and to the letter.

Besides, his inhibitions must soon have been suppressed by professional curiosity and love of experimentation. The latest directive was perfectly calculated to appeal to his conspiratorial nature. Nothing gave him greater pleasure than covering his tracks, disguising his intentions and leading opponents astray. Although half of him still rebelled at the inordinacy of Hitler's strategic aims, his oversupple mind was already rehearsing the deceptive twists and turns of which he felt himself to be a supreme exponent. Keitel's order gave him no rest. A few days later he set off by plane to tour the Abwehr outstations in the East and organize his grand diversionary manoeuvre.

On February 19 he sent Lahousen to Camp Zeppelin at Zossen, headquarters of the Army General Staff, to co-ordinate operations between the Army and the Abwehr. At the end of the month he himself visited Abwehrstelle Krakow for consultations on how to take the Russians by surprise.[202] By the beginning of March he was back in Berlin with Bentivegni, who recorded his instructions as follows: "(a) Preparing all branches of Abwehr III for active counterespionage work against the Soviet Union, as, for example . . . paralysing the activities of Soviet intelligence agencies. (b) Misleading foreign intelligence services through their own agents so as to suggest an ostensible improvement in relations with the Soviet Union and the mounting of an attack on Great Britain. (c) Security measures to preserve the secrecy of preparations for war against the Soviet Union and safeguard troop transfers to the East."[203]

Bentivegni alerted Group IIID, which collaborated with OKW-Abteilung L and the general staffs of the armed services in preparing false reports which were then fed to the enemy by counterintelligence agents and informants belonging to Colonel Rohleder's Group IIIF.[204] The neutral capitals of Europe were soon buzzing with rumors of the subtle German methods employed to disguise an impending invasion of the British Isles. Reports of unknown provenance suggested that the Germans were preparing to attack the British in the Mediterranean as well. There was talk of mysterious German "tourists" keeping watch on airfields and naval bases in French Morocco. Six thousand German soldiers had been seen in Morocco and sixty thousand Wehrmacht personnel were marching through Spain.[205]

On March 11 Canaris received fresh orders from Abteilung L. The Soviet military attaché in Berlin, Major General V. I. Tupikov, was to be disinformed.[206] This meant co-operating with the Foreign Office, whose intelligence agents had succeeded in "turning" Orestes Berlings, a member of the Soviet State Security Service stationed at the embassy in Berlin.[207] By exploiting this contact with the Soviet Embassy Canaris ensured that IIID's fake reports turned up on General Tupikov's desk.

A new diversionary campaign—Unternehmen "Haifisch" [Operation "Shark"]—opened in the following month. With the help of Army Commander in Chief von Brauchitsch, Canaris simulated troop transfers from Scandinavia to Brittany which would lend greater plausibility to reports of an imminent landing in England.[208] At the same time, secret telegrams were dispatched to the (unwitting) German military attachés in nine neutral countries. Intended for Soviet eyes, these contained the gratifying news that eight German divisions would shortly be withdrawn from the Russian frontier.[209] The Abwehr's spectacular even contained a bit part for the Reich Propaganda Minister. Goebbels was persuaded to hint darkly at a cross-Channel invasion in the June 13 issue of the *Völkischer Beobachter*, whereupon the Gestapo ostentatiously withdrew all copies so as to suggest to inquisitive foreign correspondents in Berlin that the Minister had made an appalling *gaffe*.[210]

Canaris followed the tortuous activities of his disinformants with satisfaction. Although more and more German divisions were deploying for the Russian campaign and moving into their assembly areas, the other side appeared to suspect nothing. The Abwehr chief would have been doubly delighted had he known how effectively his false reports were leading the opposition astray.

Although British and Soviet intelligence received early indications that German forces were deploying against Russia, they did not believe that the Wehrmacht would attack. Stalin dismissed all reports of German troop concentrations in the East as a dirty trick on the part of the British, its sole aim being to provoke a clash between Moscow and Berlin. "Rumours and documents implying that war with the Soviet Union is inevitable this spring," wrote General F. I. Golikov, head of the Red Army's intelligence service, on March 20, 1941, "must be regarded as false reports emanating from the British, and possibly even the German, intelligence service."[211] Golikov's British opposite number, Major General Francis Davidson, was equally in the dark. Summarizing the situation on March 13, the Director of Military Intelligence stated that there were "no grounds for believing [that] an attack on Russia is imminent."[212]

Canaris deserved to feel satisfied. No intelligence chief could have done a more successful job and no secret service have performed its allotted task with greater precision, yet he was gnawed by the uneasy awareness that he was promoting a war which he himself regarded as a national calamity. No feats of deception could compensate him for the fact that he was abetting a crime which might claim millions of lives. A more consistent man would have retired or taken active steps to overthrow his country's criminally irresponsible regime.

The Abwehr chief did neither—he remained at his post. Where does the root of the mystery lie? Personal weakness, ambition, devotion to duty—all these may have played a part, but his decision to stay must be ascribed to another and crucial factor: a suspicion that Hitler might ultimately be correct in believing that only an attack on Russia could forestall the certain prospect of a Russian attack on the Reich and deprive the British of their last potential ally in Europe. Whatever Canaris's objections to Hitler's plan of campaign, he could not dismiss the possibility that the massing of Soviet armies in Western Russia *before* the German deployment boded no good.

It is, of course, easy to demonstrate at this distance in time that Stalin was not planning an attack in summer 1941, if only because deficiencies in his own military strength (obsolete tanks and aircraft, no munitions industry beyond the Urals) ruled such a venture out.[213] But Canaris in 1941 did not possess the data available to historians of later years. He had to make do with the sketchy and unreliable information garnered by his intelligence service and reflected by the Abwehr's situation maps, and what he saw there could not fail to make him uneasy, if not panic-stricken. One by one, Soviet divisions were being transferred to the West and welded into armies and army groups of steadily increasing size. Sometimes they turned up here, sometimes there, but always in the neighbourhood of countries soon to be presented with new territorial demands by the Kremlin.

Canaris was bound to conclude that this type of deployment had an ulterior motive. After all, he himself had warned OKW about Soviet troop concentrations on the Reich's eastern borders in May 1940.[214] He derived this information not from Abwehr agents but from the Army's radio-monitoring service, which had identified individual units on the other side. Canaris counted one hundred Soviet divisions in Western Russia, of which sixty were split between Romania and the Baltic States, those perennial targets of Russian imperialism.[215]

This alarmed Canaris because the one hundred Soviet divisions were faced by only six German, the bulk of the Wehrmacht being engaged in the Western campaign.[216] There was a grave danger that the Russians might use their temporary military superiority to extort political concessions. As it to confirm the Admiral's fears, new troop movements began to show up on his situation maps. As May gave way to June, some of the Soviet forces on the Romanian border were transferred to the vicinity of the Baltic States.[217] Kremlin ultimatums followed, and in mid-June Estonia, Latvia and Lithuania yielded to overwhelming Soviet strength. Two hundred and fifty thousand Red Army soldiers marched into the Baltic States.[218]

Once again the flags on the Abwehr's situation maps regrouped. Thirty-six Soviet divisions left the Baltic States and turned up in new positions on the Romanian frontier. Late in June 1940 the Kremlin's military diplomats struck there too. Under Soviet pressure, the Romanian Government ceded Bessarabia and North Bucovina to the U.S.S.R.[219]

Canaris realized by now that it meant something when Soviet troops deployed on a country's borders. His gaze continued to dwell on the situation maps, which were continually registering new developments. From August 1940 onwards the Russians reinforced their troops facing Finland. The Red Army was brought up to wartime strength with ever-increasing speed. In February 1941 Russian units started closing up on the German-Soviet demarcation line, and on March 17 Moscow decreed mobilization measures in all western military districts.[220] No wonder Canaris felt concerned, especially as the German deployment for "Barbarossa" had scarcely begun.

He was so perturbed that he plied the enemy-strength evaluators of Foreign Armies East with more and more alarming estimates of Soviet strength. However, FHO mistrusted the Abwehr's data and did not believe that the Russians meant to attack. It repudiated such fears in an "Assessment of the Enemy." This stated: "The fact that earlier and far more favourable opportunities for a preventive war (weak [German] forces in the East, Balkan War) were not exploited by the U.S.S.R., coupled with the politically accommodating attitude and efforts to avoid potential sources of friction which have been particularly evident in recent times, make an intention to attack seem unlikely."[221]

But Canaris stuck to his guns. He urged FHO to revise its estimates of Soviet strength in the West, which had risen by January 1941 to 150 divisions, on the grounds that the Red Army had since been reinforced still further. For weeks FHO refused to accept the Abwehr's new computations and reports. It was not until April 4 that Halder noted: "Ostabteilung [Eastern Section] now concedes that the estimated strength of the Russian Army in European Russia should be higher than previously supposed. (The Finns and Japanese had always asserted this.) The total is now put at 171 divisions, 36 cavalry divisions and 40 motorized brigades."[222]

The Army Chief of Staff was so impressed by these figures that, in the words of one historian, "he had by the beginning of April largely renounced his scepticism in regard to the possibility of a [Soviet] preventive operation."[223] Did this mean that Canaris, too, had come round to Hitler's proposition that the German attack would be merely a pre-emptive strike designed to forestall a sudden swoop by the Russians? Surely not, but he must have shared the sentiments which Halder confided to his diary: "Discounting the slogan that Russia wants peace and will not launch an unprovoked attack, one has to admit that the Russian [military] set-up could readily facilitate a transition to the offensive." Genuine fear of the Russian menace made it easier for Canaris to remain at Hitler's side and read something fateful and ineluctable into a decision which he himself acknowledged to be catastrophic.

He therefore had no qualms about summoning the remainder of the Abwehr's sections and units to prepare for war against Russia. Lahousen and Piekenbrock had already mobilized their organizations and adapted them to the needs of "Barbarossa." Piekenbrock detached Abwehr I's Eastern groups from his section and combined them into an advanced operational command staff code-named "Walli" (later "Walli I") whose task was to direct the Abwehr elements in the various army groups, armoured groups and armies. "Walli" was entrusted to Baun, the Russian expert, who installed his new organization at Sulejowek, near Warsaw.[224]

Lahousen also moved his commandos, saboteurs and subversion specialists into position. Brandenburger units were distributed among the three army groups for whose benefit they were to seize key points in enemy territory, "some of them a few hours before operations commence and others later on, as our advance develops."[225] At the same time, Lahousen's agents set off to stage revolts in the Soviet interior and furnish resistance groups with arms and ammunition. Anti-Communist groups were particularly active in the Baltic States, the Caucasus and the Ukraine.

"The Amtschef has given orders that contact with the Ukrainian leader Mel'nyk is to be restored by Abwehr II."[226] This entry in Lahousen's diary brought the Ukrainian expatriates flocking back. Lieutenant Colonel Erwin Stolze, Lahousen's deputy, at once enlisted Mel'nyk (code name "Konsul I") and his supporters in the Abwehr's subversive army and issued them with instructions "to organize provocative coups in the Ukraine immediately after Germany's attack on Russia for the purpose of weakening Soviet forces in the immediate interior."[227] In readiness to assist the Ukrainian insurrection was a force of shock troops, the Gruppe Nachtigall [Nightingale Group], a battalion-strength Wehrmacht unit comprising three companies of Ukrainians and one company from the Lehrregiment Brandenburg. It was commanded by Lieutenant Herzner, who had led the abortive Jablunkov Pass operation during the Polish campaign.[228]

This alliance with *émigrés* from the East imbued the Abwehr with an anti-Communist crusading spirit which cried out for fulfilment in the beckoning expanses of Russia. Romantic visions of a German-Ukrainian partnership enjoyed a revival at the Tirpitz-Ufer, and many an Abwehr officer befogged by delusions of political grandeur suddenly felt that—as one of them put it—"war with Russia *had* to come."[229] Herzner wrote to his wife: "Poland and France, Holland and Norway, Yugoslavia and Greece were only preliminary battles. The outcome will not be decided until the possibility of a condominium in Europe has been wrested from the hand of Bolshevism.[230]

Such sentiments were alien to Canaris, who had never taken any particular interest in questions of Eastern policy. Still profoundly uncertain who would strike first, Hitler or Stalin, he only saw that disaster was looming ever closer. All that remained for him in such a desperate predicament was to warn his country's political and military leaders against the German propensity for arrogance which could move even a cautious man like Halder to believe: "One punch and the whole thing will fall to bits."[231]

On June 21, on the eve of the fateful day appointed for the launching of "Barbarossa," Canaris joined Heydrich and Schellenberg for a meal at Horcher's, the famous Berlin restaurant. Even at that late stage he expressed anxiety lest the Führer and his advisers were taking too rosy a view of Germany's prospects.[232] Heydrich reassured him. He told the Abwehr chief of a discussion between Hitler and his crony Martin Bormann which suggested that the Führer harboured no illusions. According to Schellenberg's account of Heydrich's statement, Hitler was "far less optimistic than his immediate military entourage."[233]

By the time Canaris returned from this encounter, Abwehr headquarters had already received an order which set the wheels of destiny in motion.[234]

The prearranged code word was "Dortmund." At 3:15 A.M. next day, June 22, 1941, the Wehrmacht unleashed a creeping barrage on Russian territory. Canaris's Brandenburgers dashed into the fray followed by the largest striking force ever assembled in the annals of warfare: 152 divisions, 3,580 tanks, 2,740 warplanes—3 million men in all.[235]

As before, Abwehr groups accompanying the attack inundated the Tirpitz-Ufer with tidings of success which confirmed how efficiently the Wehrmacht was overrunning the Russians' defences and smashing their hurriedly assembled formations. Abwehr units and combat teams saw plenty of action. They seized strategic points behind the Russian lines, opened up lines of advance for the German formations following in their rear and signalled enemy counterattacks and diversions. The Brandenburgers distinguished themselves yet again. Elements of the Lehrregiment occupied Przemysl, established a bridgehead on the enemy side of the San and took only a few days to reach Lvov, while other contingents seized bridges over the Dvina in the north and held them against Soviet counterattacks.[236]

Obstacles to the German advance were also removed by Abwehr II's resistance groups on Soviet soil. At Vilna, anti-Communist conspirators in a Lithuanian division shot their political commissars and handed the unit over to the Germans. In the Kovno area, Lithuanian "activists" seized twenty-four important bridges, a tunnel and a radio transmitter, and Ukrainian nationalists in Lvov stormed the city's NKVD jail.[237]

The invading armies' route was cleared by a whole series of Abwehr operations, each more audacious than the last. Sonderführer Schwarze of the Brandenburgers, a journalist in civilian life, set off with sixteen agents and two seaplanes to carry out Operation "Erich," whose purpose was to blow up the Arctic Canal. Eighty Estonian agents embarked on Operation "Erna," an attempt to wage guerrilla warfare against Soviet troops in Estonia.[238] Meanwhile, Caucasian parachutist-agents were preparing for Operation "Tamara," defined by Lahousen as a project aimed at "organizing and fomenting an insurrection in the Georgian ethnic region."[239]

Canaris was briefly reminded of the Polish campaign, which had opened with similar tidings of success. Then he began to receive reports from behind the German lines which rendered such comparisons illusory. Einsatzgruppen of the Security Police and SD had appeared in the wake of the combat troops and were herding Jews, Russians and even Ukrainians together like cattle. Their manifest aim was to establish a reign of terror in the occupied territories.

Canaris suddenly realized that this was a different sort of conflict from the Polish campaign—one that failed to fit the "normal" pattern of Hitler's military adventures. The dictator had at last got the war he had craved ever since becoming a politician and party leader, the war he intended to wage on his own terms, uncompromisingly and without external interference: the struggle for German Lebensraum in the East —half a colonialist's land-grabbing foray and half a racist's attempt to exterminate peoples of "inferior" stock.

Hitler had not disguised from his senior military advisers that his plans for the East included its total domination by the German master race and the biological suppression of its alien inhabitants. He began by cloaking this objective in anti-Bolshevik jargon. "The Jewish-Bolshevist intelligentsia, having hitherto oppressed the people, must be eliminated" was his political guideline to Jodl on March 3, 1941, and a fortnight later he told two hundred senior officers that the Eastern campaign would be the most barbarous war of all time.[240] Halder recorded the bare bones of this pronouncement as follows: "Wehrmacht to smash, state to be dissolved . . . struggle between two ideologies . . . Bolshevism equals antisocial criminality."[241] In private, however, the Führer dropped this anti-Communist façade and confined himself to the colonialist vocabulary. What mattered, according to him, was "to cut the gigantic cake into convenient slices so that we can (a) control it, (b) administer it and (c) exploit it." This did not, however, preclude the Germans from undertaking "all necessary measures— shooting, deportation, and so on."[242]

Hitler had—with the approval of the military authorities—entrusted those "necessary measures" to the Reichsführer-SS, whom he deputed to police the occupied Eastern territories. Himmler passed the assignment to RSHA chief Heydrich, who quickly set up four Einsatzgruppen totalling three thousand men and held them in readiness to fulfil the Führer's every command.[243] Following hot on the heels of the combat troops, they hunted down those whom the SS authorities anathematized as "subhumans"—in other words, Bolsheviks, Jews and Russian intellectuals. The principal targets of their extermination programme were Russia's 5 million Jews.

Scarcely had the Einsatzgruppen entered a city when its Jewish inhabitants found themselves locked in a lethal stranglehold which claimed countless thousands of victims, day by day and hour by hour. Heydrich's men shrank from no atrocity, trickery or barbarity in fulfilling the extermination quota stipulated by those in charge. Report after report, couched in the language of icebox manufacturers or pest-control officers, testified to the fanatical zeal of the Einsatzgruppen. Incident Report No. 153, submitted by Einsatzgruppe D: "Subunit's field of operations cleared of Jews, particularly in smaller localities. Those shot during period under review comprise 3,176 Jews, 85 partisans, 12 looters and 122 Communist officials. Running total: 79,276." Report from Einsatzkommando 6: "Of the remaining 30,000, approximately 10,000 were shot." Report from Einsatzgruppe C: ". . . as of 6.9.1941, Special Detachment 4a had disposed of a total of 11,328 Jews."[244]

Although Canaris did not see this testimony to unprecedented barbarism, reports reaching him from the Abwehr groups in Russia were enough to convey the monstrous nature of what was happening there. On October 23 Stolze referred to an officer who could not shake off "the most appalling nightmares" after being detailed for mass executions. An order issued by Rundstedt on August 10 and copied by the Abwehr officer attached to Army Group South stated that soldiers were participating in executions in such an "undesirable manner" that "drastic measures" must be taken. Abwehr officers serving with armies and army groups were even instructed to confiscate and collect photographs taken during "Jewish operations."[245] It was clear to someone of Canaris's Christian and conservative sensibilities that the Germans were committing the crime of the century and shouldering a burden of guilt of which no earthly power could acquit them. If any one factor imbued him with a fatalistic belief that Germany was doomed, it was this crime against the Jews.

Although the realization oppressed him and banished the last vestiges of his peace of mind, Canaris was not the man to make a stand against the mass crimes of the regime. He seemed strangely reluctant to take action against Heydrich's men, as Lieutenant Herzner of the Gruppe Nachtigall was among the first to discover.

On June 30, 1941, the battalion marched into Lvov and was enthusiastically welcomed by its Ukrainian inhabitants, who experienced a sudden resurgence of hope that the Ukraine would soon be independent. This nationalistic fervour was exploited by supporters of the left-wing revolutionary leader Stefan Bandera. Without consulting the Abwehr or Nachtigall, they proclaimed a "Ukrainian State" and formed a government under Bandera's deputy, Yaroslav Stetsko.[246] Herzner and other Abwehr officers were still trying to persuade Bandera to reverse this "premature" step when the Einsatzgruppe operating in the Lvov area intervened. The first of Bandera's supporters were detained on July 2, to be followed on July 12 by Stetsko and Bandera themselves.[247] The Einsatzgruppe's reason: the Führer did not want an independent Ukraine.

Only Canaris could help now, but he declined. On July 30 he reluctantly visited the Gruppe Nachtigall, which had since been transferred. He not only arrived two hours late but cut his visit as short as possible.[248] Herzner wrote angrily to his friend Oberländer: "I'd sooner tell you in person sometime *how* the Admiral inspected us . . ."[249] But the real shock was still to come. Two days later Herzner learned that the Admiral had ordered Nachtigall back to Germany. He noted in his war diary: "The Ukrainians were positively shattered that their fight for freedom seemed to be over before it had even begun."[250]

But Canaris had further occasion to impress on Abwehr officers who were enraged by the brutality and stupidity of the German occupation policy that it was their duty to steer clear of political matters. As early as June 23 he instructed Lahousen to point out, "expressly and unmistakably," that Abwehr II's functions were "purely military."[251] An entry in Abwehr II's official diary states that Abwehrstellen in the East were "particularly directed, in reiteration of previous orders, that the utmost restraint should be exercised in all political matters and that absolutely no political assurances, or even prospects, should be extended to agents in the field."[252] The RSHA had only to ask Abwehr headquarters whether OKW was "co-operating with Lithuanian rebels along political lines" for the Tirpitz-Ufer to reply that nothing could be further from the Abwehr's intentions.[253]

Canaris refused to commit himself openly even when the Wehrmacht and the Security Police began to treat prisoners of war in a manner that should have outraged any decent officer. On July 16, 1941, Heydrich had concluded an agreement with Lieutenant General Reinecke, head of the OKW's Allgemeines Wehrmachtamt [General Armed Forces Department], under which Gestapo and SD personnel were permitted to comb Wehrmacht POW camps for Soviet citizens whom they adjudged "carriers of Bolshevism" and summarily execute them.[254] They included Jews and "antisocial elements" as well as political commissars and officials of the Communist Party.

Even Canaris was roused to anger by the rough and ready way in which Heydrich's squads selected their victims from the POW camps. Lahousen reports that he soon "took the most stringent line against it . . . in our own ranks."[255] When it came to preventing the worst and most murderous excesses in the camps, however, Canaris shied away from an argument with Reinecke and "Gestapo" Müller and sent Lahousen into the firing line in his place. The head of Abwehr II produced a remarkable explanation for this. As a junior head of section he could use "plainer language" than Canaris, "who, being a head of department, did not wish to adopt an unduly 'negative attitude' towards the ideological drift of these orders [regarding the treatment of Soviet prisoners of war] vis-à-vis the RSHA representative."[256]

Lahousen pointed out at his meeting with Reinecke and Müller that these orders "ran counter to the conventions of international law, but were also having deleterious effects on the morale of the troops in whose presence executions of selected prisoners frequently took place."[257] Although Müller rejected Lahousen's protest, Canaris did not leap to his envoy's assistance. He reacted only when the OKW issued new and even harsher regulations governing the treatment of prisoners of war, but even then he left colleagues to make the first move.[258]

Abteilung Ausland's international law desk, to which belonged that active member of the resistance Count Helmuth James von Moltke, spokesman and host of the antifascist Kreisau Circle, was instructed by head of section Bürkner to draft a memorandum addressed to Keitel. The new directive, wrote Moltke, would "negate the validity of standards prescribed by the rules of war in the fight against Bolshevism, apart from setting aside much that has, in the light of previous experience, been regarded not only as militarily expedient but also as absolutely essential to the maintenance of discipline and efficiency among our own men." Moltke concluded that there were, "in the view of Amt Ausland/Abwehr, strong objections" to the OKW directive, "not only from the standpoint of principle but because of the adverse consequences that would certainly ensue from the political and military aspect."[259]

This memorandum, dated September 15, 1941, and identified by its heading as a communication from "Chef (Ausl[and])," was eventually signed by Canaris. As anyone could have predicted, it got nowhere with Hitler's devoted OKW chief. Keitel wrote on the document: "These objections accord with soldierly conceptions of a chivalrous war! What matters here is the destruction of an ideology. I therefore approve and endorse these measures."[260] It was significant that Keitel addressed his comment to Auslandschef Bürkner, not Amtschef Canaris.

This incident discloses how feebly Canaris responded to the basic politico-moral questions confronting every German of his day. Was he merely inhibited by natural diffidence or already paralysed by a sense of his own tragic involvement in the crimes of the National Socialist regime? He could not with a clear conscience have ignored the fact that he and his organization formed part of the system that was now showing its most fearsome side.

As late as the beginning of June, he himself had convened a meeting of the Wehrmacht's senior intelligence officers and prominent members of the Gestapo and SD, Heydrich and Schellenberg included, to discuss co-operation between the Abwehr, Geheime Feldpolizei and Einsatzgruppen.[261] A basic pattern was quickly agreed and the allocation of duties embodied in a memorandum: "Wehrmacht: to subdue the enemy. Reichsführer-SS: to combat the enemy by political-police action."[262] Another paper, entitled "Delimitation of Functions between GFP-SD and SP[Sicherheitspolizei]," stated: "Departments shall render each other the fullest assistance."[263]

This was the basis on which co-operation between the Wehrmacht and agencies of the RSHA proceeded in occupied Russia. From time to

21. Canaris and his favorite horse, the Arab mare Motte, in Berlin's Grüne-
wald. (*Otto Wagner, Säckingen*)

22. Hitler addressing a mass demonstration in Vienna's Heldenplatz in 1938, after the union with Austria. (*Ullstein Bilderdienst, Berlin*)

23. Hitler trundles into the Sudetenland at the head of his troops. (*Süd-deutscher Verlag Bilderdienst, München*)

24. German soldiers remove a Polish
border turnpike, signalling the start of
the Second World War. (*Bildarchiv
Preussischer Kulturbesitz, Berlin*)

25. Major General Hans Oster, Chief
of Staff of the Abwehr, who, with
Canaris, wanted to overthrow Hitler's
dictatorship. (*Ullstein Bilderdienst,
Berlin*)

26. Canaris with Nazi VIPs (Himmler facing him, Goebbels on his right and police chief Daluege on his left). *(Süddeutscher Verlag Bilderdienst, München)*

7. The cell block at Flossenbürg, where Canaris was put to
death. *(Bildarchiv Preussischer
Kulturbesitz, Berlin)*

8. Wilhelm Canaris as a
"prisoner of honor" at Burg
Lauenstein. *(Otto Wagner,
Säckingen)*

29. Wilhelm Canaris in 1944, in the garden of his Berlin home.
(Otto Wagner, Säckingen)

time, as at Minsk in July 1941, the Abwehr-controlled Geheime Feldpolizei helped the Einsatzgruppen to make their "selections" from POW and internment camps. Abwehr III officers attached to these camps often prepared the lists and particulars which made it easier for Heydrich's men to perform their grisly task, nor was it rare for GFP units (e.g. GFP-Gruppe 647 at Kodyma in August 1941) to be invited by their Einsatzgruppe colleagues to join in concerted Jew-hunts.[264] By December 1941, when Major Stephanus of the Eleventh Army's general staff instructed Abwehr and GFP personnel to hand over recaptured Jewish fugitives to the Einsatzgruppen, nobody could have termed his action exceptional.[265]

Many Abwehr officers had grown so used to co-operating with RSHA agencies that they failed to notice how thoroughly they had adopted their range of ideas and scale of values. Even before the advent of the "Final Solution," or wholesale extermination of the Jews, Colonel von Bentivegni could regard it almost as a normal counterespionage measure to request Goebbels, in his capacity as Gauleiter of Berlin, to ensure that the capital's Jewish inhabitants wore a distinguishing badge and were concentrated in the eastern part of the city. For this step, which was taken on the grounds that all Jews were potential spies, Bentivegni actually secured Canaris's reluctant but compliant approval![266]

Even in branches of the Abwehr more remote from the Gestapo, e.g. the Geheimer Meldedienst, there prevailed a conformist anti-Semitism which coloured many an official report. This is discernible in the language of Hermann Baun, head of "Walli I": "The awareness of having been under Jewish domination for twenty years is slowly gaining ground [in Russia]. Red Army men are beginning to grumble more and more about the Jews because the latter are virtually exempt from combat duty. Jewish doctors certify all Jews, without exception, as unfit for active service. The strong Jewification of the rear echelon and supply services is increasingly showing up the generic affinity of Jewry and the Bolshevist system. Remarks like 'The Germans know how to deal with the Jews' are falling on extremely fertile ground."[267] "Jewification," "the generic affinity of Jewry and the Bolshevist system"—could any Abwehr officer have more grievously succumbed to the anti-Semitic poison which the Nazis had been administering for years?

Canaris may have sensed that it was impossible to enlist Abwehr officers of this type in an unremitting fight against the mass crimes in the East. He did not feel strong enough to do so himself, but he did permit Abwehr officers of a different calibre to help Jews in trouble—as long as such assistance could be technically reconciled with the department's interests. He even allowed Jews to be employed as agents in the Abwehr's foreign service and thereby put them beyond the reach of the German authorities.

Consequently, he was ready to help when Abwehr officers in occupied Holland devised a way of sneaking five hundred Jewish residents out of the country. This plan originated in the office of Major Schulze-Bernett, who headed the Abwehrstelle in the Dutch capital. Early in March 1941, Captain Pannwitz suggested using his good offices with the diplomatic representatives of various Latin American countries to mount a Jewish rescue operation. Canaris approved this "infiltration of agents into South America," as it was officially described, and the HSSPF [Senior SS and police commander] in the Netherlands raised no objection. The "agents" set off in May, travelling via Spain.[268]

But artifices of this kind had not escaped the notice of Himmler and Heydrich, who were only waiting for a chance to trip their rival up. It came in February 1942, when German intelligence agencies were buzzing with the exploits of an Abwehr V-Mann stationed in Tangier who was, in Nazi parlance, a full-blooded Jew. Himmler got to hear of this, probably through Schellenberg, who made a habit of nosing around after Canaris's agents in Spain and North Africa. While in conference with Hitler the Reichsführer-SS caustically alluded to the Admiral's reputation for favouring Jews and added that it was no wonder he maintained so many Jewish contacts and go-betweens abroad.[269]

Stung by Himmler's remarks, Hitler sent for Keitel and became so heated during the ensuing discussion that he finally ordered Canaris suspended from duty until further notice. Keitel obeyed without uttering a word in his subordinate's defence. Overnight, Canaris saw his whole existence threatened. He had to relinquish his post to Bürkner. Worse still, the OKW chief rebuffed his attempts to secure an interview with Hitler and persuade the dictator to rescind his suspension.[270]

Canaris eventually flew to Hitler's field headquarters and asked his military adjutant, Colonel Engel, to arrange a meeting. "Going behind the backs of Keitel and Schmundt [Hitler's Wehrmacht adjutant], I did so the same morning," Engel recalls. Hitler consented to see Canaris. Engel goes on: "Canaris was admitted after lunch and reinstated at the end of the interview. He flew back to Berlin without seeing Keitel or Schmundt." But he was only just back in his old office when Keitel rang to congratulate him on his reinstatement. He had, he said, "gone to great lengths" to persuade the Führer of Canaris's innocence and obtain him an interview, but all was well again. A telephone call to Engel satisfied Canaris that he, not Keitel, had secured the audience. When Engel expressed surprise at the field marshal's attitude, Canaris cut him short: "No comment."[271]

This affair was an object lesson. It showed Canaris the hollow and precarious nature of his position in the regime's hierarchy. A few barbed remarks from Himmler had very nearly ruined him. Gone were the days when he had been the dictator's foremost intelligence adviser.

Hitler seldom sent for him now, and his comments on the Abwehr—as relayed to Canaris by those present—were usually irritable and sarcastic. The longer the war went on and the farther German armies advanced into the unconquerable expanses of Russia, the scantier the Abwehr's reports became and the less often Admiral Canaris was summoned to Hitler's court.

One school of thought stubbornly insists that Abwehr reports were unpopular at the Führer's headquarters because they painted an all too accurate picture of the worsening military situation. Although Canaris himself saw matters in this light, the above interpretation is only partially correct and based on a false premiss. Abwehr reports were seldom submitted to Hitler direct. The majority were fed into the intelligence channels of the general staffs, whose evaluators worked them into their own situation reports—and these staff officers took an unflattering view of the quality of the Abwehr's material.

"All we got from Canaris was rubbish," states ex-Major Horst Hiemenz, wartime head of Group II [General Situation Soviet Russia] in the Foreign Armies East Section.[272] The Abwehr was too weak and undermanned to meet the general staff's requests for more information, better reconnaissance and closer insights into the enemy's intentions. The general staff evaluators, notably the hypercritical FHO under its new head of section Reinhard Gehlen, often expected the Abwehr to work miracles which were naturally beyond it. FHO officers tended to be dissatisfied even with reports from good agents. "Max reports" came in for criticism and one of Lissner's earned the rebuke: "Ivar is serving up old stuff under a new date."[273]

The Abwehr's material and organization proved so inadequate that the general staff evaluators began to take over its long-standing sources of information. This went for "Walli I" under Baun, now a major, who established such close personal ties with Foreign Armies East that he soon came to regard Gehlen, not Canaris, as his real boss. It was not long before Baun and his organization were actually included in the FHO's personnel lists.[274]

The fate of the Baun organization heralded a process of decay which Canaris failed to combat with sufficient vigour. It was paralleled by that of the Brandenburg Regiment, which was made up to divisional strength in autumn 1942. The Abwehr chief tolerated the fact that his household troops, though trained to undertake the most complex intelligence operations, were increasingly used by the Army in a normal infantry role and uselessly slaughtered in the crucial defensive battles of winter 1942–43.[275] Yet Canaris had once reserved the right to decide
· which Brandenburger units should be attached to which army groups and armies. He had even ordained that the Brandenburgers be with-

drawn from Abwehr II's direct control and placed under his personal command.[276] Now they were steadily slipping from his grasp.[277]

The Admiral's subordinates were alarmed to note these signs of disintegration, which reflected his mental state. Canaris was going downhill. He looked ill and exhausted, and his response to the most trivial blunder or irregularity could verge on the hysterical. Even his personal appearance was suggestive of mental disorder. He often turned up at the office looking pale and unkempt, his uniform tunic wrongly buttoned and adorned with traces of cigar ash or specks of food.

More worrying still, he was losing his grip on current business and failing to keep up with major developments. Office routine and administrative planning had never particularly interested him, but his ignorance now extended to the conspiratorial ventures which had formerly exercised his keen intelligence. When Sonderführer Schwarze came to present a report on Operation "Erich," which he had led, Canaris had first to be laboriously reminded of the plan's original purpose.[278] Taking advantage of this apathy, the sections began to lead a life of their own. The outstations, too, stood in less and less fear of surprise visits from their lord and master.

The Admiral's subordinates were also struck by a pronounced tendency towards mysticism which had formerly escaped them. Canaris felt drawn to the mysterious gloom of Catholic churches, where he spent hours deep in meditation and devotion. Spanish churches held a particular appeal for him.[279] In hours like these he sought solace from the tensions and frustrations of his work and his own devious soul. Colleagues were surprised to see this, not realizing that his behaviour was a legacy from his forebears, the ultra-Catholic Ronges of Neisse.[280]

Many Abwehr men were equally bewildered by his outbursts of wry humour. Even the sympathetic Piekenbrock, who often called his boss "Your Excellency" for fun, found it hard to keep up with him. Once, while the two men were driving through Spain, they caught sight of a shepherd. Canaris stopped the car, rose from his seat, and gave a military salute. "What is it, Your Excellency?" inquired Pieki. Canaris: "You can never tell if there's a senior officer underneath."[281] His muttered comment on the departing figure of a much bemedalled Luftwaffe officer who had just presented him with an overoptimistic situation report was, "Imbecile with oak leaves and swords!" [an allusion to the various grades of the Knight's Cross of the Iron Cross].[282] More and more often now, Canaris caught himself thinking how pleasant it would be to "chuck the whole business" and become a private citizen. He redoubled his visits to Spain, usually to Abwehrstelle Algeciras, where he liked to cook and listen to the murmur of voices from the nearby Hotel Reina Cristina.[283] While visiting Sofia he asked his friend Wagner, the local Abwehr chief, "What do you plan to do after the war? Will you be staying in the Army?" Wagner replied that he wanted to remain in the Balkans, whereupon Canaris mapped out a common future for them. "We ought to open a little coffee shop in Piraeus harbour. I'll make the coffee and you can wait table. Wouldn't it be great to lead a simple life like that?"[284]

The Admiral's signs of professional ennui were not lost on his rivals in the RSHA, where the top jobs had just changed hands. In autumn 1941 Heydrich was appointed acting Reich Protector of Bohemia and Moravia, though without losing control of the RSHA apparatus, while Schellenberg took over the Ausland-SD (Amt VI of the RSHA, or Foreign Intelligence Department) from Jost, who had been posted to the East.[285] The third—and from Canaris's angle the most fateful—appointment was that of Regierungsrat and SS-Sturmbannführer Walter Huppenkothen, the new head of the Abwehrpolizei (Amtsgruppe IVE), a typical ice-cold functionalist who unquestioningly performed any task assigned him by the Führer's dictatorial regime.[286]

Canaris and Huppenkothen, the future victim and his chief investigator, first became acquainted over the now traditional inaugural meal at Horcher's in August 1941. "Canaris disappointed me at our first meeting," Huppenkothen recalls. "He made an old, tired and war-weary impression."[287] The Abwehr chief was just as unimpressed by the new man, whom he found stiff, colourless and impersonal.

Huppenkothen's career stamped him as an all-purpose cog in the SS police machine: born in 1907, Rhinelander son of an industrial craftsman, doctor of law; head of department with the Gestapo, then with the SD; commander of the Security Police and SD in Krakow and, later, Lublin; transferred to the RSHA in July 1941.[288]

This was the man who proposed to join Heydrich and Schellenberg in exploiting the Abwehr's obvious weaknesses. There were ample pretexts for such a campaign. The old jurisdictional problems of the counterespionage system remained unsolved, the SD's aspirations to sole dominion over the intelligence service unsatisfied and the Abwehr and Geheime Feldpolizei unequal to the growing activity of Communist espionage and sabotage organizations in the German-occupied territories of Western Europe.

Late in December 1941 Heydrich wrote Jodl a letter in which he stated that the powers of the Abwehr and RSHA were insufficiently well defined and that fresh solutions must be found.[289] Jodl passed the letter to Canaris, who agreed to confer with Heydrich. The two sides met at the beginning of 1942. Canaris brought Bentivegni with him; Heydrich turned up with Huppenkothen, "Gestapo" Müller and Streckenbach, head of the RSHA's Amt I [Personnel].[290]

Heydrich delivered a long and patronizing speech which culminated in the announcement that, although the RSHA really laid claim to all the functions hitherto fulfilled by the Abwehr, it was prepared, in view of the military situation, to make do with a partial settlement. "Surprisingly enough," says Huppenkothen, "Canaris accepted this statement without demur."[291] The parties then resolved on a programme: counterespionage powers to be extended to RSHA agencies, the Abwehr to confine itself to military intelligence reports, and the Geheime Feldpolizei to be incorporated in the Sicherheitspolizei. Huppenkothen was appointed to draft the relevant provisions, plus the directives required for their implementation, and agree them with Bentivegni.[292]

Heydrich, Huppenkothen and Schellenberg could fairly claim to have won the day because Canaris had consented to a substantial diminution of the Abwehr's powers. Deprived of sole responsibility for counterespionage, as of the right to submit political or at least politico-military reports, the Abwehr was no longer what it had been. Canaris's subordinates realized this at once. Although we cannot reconstruct what happened at Abwehr headquarters, the fact is that Bentivegni had to hammer out a counterdraft which retracted almost all the Admiral's concessions.[293]

Heydrich was infuriated by Canaris's "bad faith" and severed all contact with him. There were dark hints from the RSHA that Himmler would be taking further action. Accompanied by Bentivegni, Canaris nervously hurried to Prinz-Albrecht-Strasse and asked to see the RSHA chief, but he was "otherwise engaged." Canaris stayed put in Heydrich's outer office and repeatedly demanded an interview. After waiting in vain for a response, he finally left—but not before he had forbidden Bentivegni to budge from the spot until Heydrich saw him. Bentivegni was only persuaded to leave the building when asked to do so—on Heydrich's instructions—by "Gestapo" Müller.[294]

Next, Canaris asked Keitel to talk Heydrich round. This time the OKW chief actually lent a helping hand. One telephone call sufficed to sell Heydrich on a compromise. The two rivals arranged to lunch at a house beside the Wannsee, where on March 1, 1942, they came to terms. Having drawn up a document headed "Implementation directives relating to official dealings between military Abwehr agencies and agencies of the Security Police and SD," they signed it. More importantly, they approved another document entitled "Principles governing co-operation between the Security Police and SD and the Abwehr agencies of the Wehrmacht," though the exact text was not formulated until April. Canaris further agreed that the GFP should come under Sipo control, at least in Western territories.[295]

With one or two exceptions, Heydrich could feel satisfied with what he had achieved. Points 3, 4 and 5 of "Principles" granted the RSHA increased powers. Point 3: "The secret political intelligence service abroad, together with its internal points of contact, is solely a function of the Security Police and SD." Point 4: "The submission of political reports (inclusive of morale within the Reich) is solely a function of the Security Police and SD." Point 5 was not only crucial but couched in language intricate enough to leave the Abwehr room for manoeuvre. It read: "The function of counterespionage is to investigate and neutralize foreign intelligence services operating against the interests of the Reich. The function of the military Abwehr service in this respect is to combat the [enemy] secret intelligence service and the activity of foreign intelligence services directly related thereto. Given that foreign intelligence services also engage in political acts of subversion, sabotage and terrorism, counterespionage shall in future be an additional function of the Security Police and SD."[296]

Although Canaris did his best to conceal this grave loss of Abwehr authority behind a mask of official optimism, his immediate subordinates were undeceived. He not only instructed every section in Amt Ausland/Abwehr to co-operate closely with the RSHA but helped the process along. On May 17, by mutual arrangement, he and the RSHA chief held a conference of all the departmental heads of the Abwehr, Gestapo, SD and Kriminalpolizei in Prague, Heydrich's new base of operations. Object of the meeting: to discuss and sign the latest agreements between the two rival bodies.[297] Canaris travelled to Prague with his wife and stayed at Jungfern-Breschan, Heydrich's official residence on the outskirts of the city. "Ah yes," sighs Lina Heydrich, recalling the Canarises' visit, "they were happy days . . ."[298] The conference ended on an amicable note.

A few days later Canaris received word that Heydrich had been ambushed by Czech assassins and was fighting for his life. He flew back to Prague but never spoke to him again. Reinhard Heydrich succumbed to his wounds on June 4, 1942.[299] Canaris stood silently in the forefront of those who attended his elaborate state funeral, weeping. When he caught sight of Huppenkothen he shook hands, still with tears in his eyes, and declared that Heydrich was a great man whom he had held in the highest regard and esteem.[300] His letter to Heydrich's widow assured her that he had lost "a true friend."[301]

Was he being sincere or just play-acting? Lina Heydrich still denies that the Admiral's words of condolence were "all hot air."[302] Whatever the truth, the death of his partner-cum-rival was far from beneficial to himself or the Abwehr. The Reichssicherheitshauptamt was now ruled by men who could not be swayed by common memories of bygone days in the Navy or cosy musical soirees, nor could anyone predict who would inherit Heydrich's mantle as head of department. Canaris must have welcomed Himmler's temporary retention of control because he knew that the Reichsführer-SS still cherished a timid and quasi-superstitious respect for his reputation as a master spy.

He could not, however, fail to recognize the growing difficulties of his internal position. His feeble performance had not gone unnoticed by the Abwehr's heads of section, who were becoming more and more critical of his leadership. One symptom of weakness was the withdrawal of the concessions he had made to Heydrich in respect of departmental powers. It is clear that the cancellation of his original pact with the RSHA was occasioned by internal pressure from subordinates who were indignant at his undue appeasement of the Gestapo.

Piekenbrock, Lahousen and Bentivegni could hardly approve of the way Canaris was running Amt Ausland/Abwehr. They wanted a tougher and more energetic boss, and they must have let him feel it. But there was also criticism from the Oster-Dohnanyi associates, who were still toying with the idea of re-enlisting the Admiral in their resistance schemes. Depressed by his resigned attitude, they urged him to find new ways of terminating the war.

Canaris found it hard to evade this pressure from his immediate subordinates. He sometimes concealed his tracks from them as well as his enemies and engaged in manoeuvres designed to refurbish his departmental image. This emerges from an incident which occurred shortly after Heydrich's death and concerned the forcible recapture of General Giraud, a respected French army commander who had escaped from a prisoner-of-war camp. Lahousen has put it on record that his murder by the Abwehr was ordered by Keitel but foiled by Canaris.[303] This contention is inaccurate.

The story began at dawn on April 17, 1942, when the sixty-three-year-old general climbed down the rock face enclosing Königstein POW camp in Saxony and slipped past the German sentries. His escape remained undiscovered for several days, and it was not until April 20 that Kripo [Criminal Police] Chief Nebe dictated the following special priority teleprinter message to all police, SS and SD units: "Recapture extremely important. A reward of RM100,000 is offered."[304] But the police were too late—Giraud had already gone to ground in unoccupied France.

Hitler furiously demanded Giraud's return, seconded by Keitel: "We must get the general back, dead or alive."[305] Because Giraud had taken refuge in Vichy France, the diplomats were mobilized. In Paris, Ambassador Otto Abetz was instructed to appeal to Giraud to return. If he did, he would be appointed to supervise the welfare of all French prisoners of war in Germany; if not, it was menacingly added, his former fellow prisoners would regret it. Abetz got in touch with Giraud, and on May 2 he met the general at the Hôtel de Paris in Moulins-sur-Allier, a town on the border between occupied and unoccupied France.

Giraud rejected the German proposal.[306] He was about to leave when the commander of the German 337th Infantry Division, who happened to be staying at the same hotel, learned that Giraud was on the premises. He wanted to arrest him on the spot but took the precaution of telephoning Keitel, who put his foot down. "I immediately and categorically refused," Keitel recalled, "because I considered it a breach of good faith, given that the general had turned up in the expectation of befitting treatment."[307] Giraud was allowed to return to his hide-out in the South of France.

On hearing of the incident, Canaris suggested to Keitel that the Abwehr might attempt to recapture Giraud by other means. He knew that Giraud's family lived in German-occupied France, so it was conceivable that he might visit them in the near future.[308] "He proposed," Keitel testified, "that arrangements be made to recapture the general if he paid such a visit to occupied territory. He volunteered to make and initiate these arrangements personally."[309] Keitel not only agreed but christened the operation "Gustav."

This is the germ of truth in the story—which gained wide circulation in later years—that Keitel had ordered Canaris to "kill" Giraud. Keitel disputed this to his dying day: "I never even mentioned doing away with the general—never!"[310] Ambassador Abetz was equally insistent that he "never heard anything, even by way of rumour" about a plan to murder Giraud.[311] Lahousen's version is unsupported by any documentary evidence or independent testimony.

Yet there is no reason to doubt Lahousen's respect for the truth. He must have heard the phrase "kill Giraud" from somebody, and that somebody can only have been the usual channel of communication between Keitel and the Abwehr's heads of section. What would have inspired the Abwehr chief to make his own proposal for a kidnapping operation look like an assassination plan? Departmental weakness is one likely answer. Once again, as in the case of his original pact with Heydrich at the beginning of the year, it turned out that Canaris was incapable of keeping his promises to outsiders. His heads of section were disinclined to involve the Abwehr in a kidnapping affair, so he bowed to the prevailing mood and left Operation "Gustav" in abeyance. Keitel: "Nothing happened in the ensuing period."[312]

After a few weeks the OKW chief wondered why no more had been heard of the scheme and pressed Canaris to do something. This put the Admiral on the spot. He could not admit to Keitel that he had abandoned "Gustav" under pressure from his subordinates, nor could he prevail on his subordinates to act. If he could only foster a suitable mood of protest, he would be officially compelled to ask Keitel to withdraw the "Gustav" assignment.

In his dilemma, Canaris may have hit on the idea of using veiled language to intimate that what Keitel really expected from the Abwehr was Giraud's murder. "Getting rid of Giraud" and "settling the Giraud question" were the Admiral's phrases, and he used them one Friday evening in August when he rang Lahousen at his home and told him that Keitel was again insisting that something be done.[313] At a meeting next day, Canaris and his subordinates debated what action to take. Lahousen recalls: "Everyone present flatly rejected this request to initiate and carry out a murder operation . . . Canaris thereupon went downstairs to see Keitel and persuade him to keep military intelligence out of such matters altogether and leave this business . . . entirely to the SD"[314] The heads of section continued to fulminate while Canaris was out of the office, and Piekenbrock snapped: "It's time Herr Keitel was told point-blank to inform his friend Herr Hitler that we, meaning military intelligence, aren't a murderous organization like the SD or the SS."[315]

Canaris returned with his mission accomplished. Keitel had agreed that the Abwehr should relinquish "Gustav" to the RSHA and stand down.[316] In conveying this news to his immediate associates, the Admiral withheld one importrant detail, namely, Keitel's assertion that the Führer had "already told him more than once that he was going to hand it [Operation "Gustav"] over to Himmler."[317] Instead, Lahousen recalled quite clearly that Canaris had assured him of his intention to foil the murder plot "at all costs," and that "I was to help him."[318]

Lahousen genuinely believed in Canaris's ability to prevent the SD from taking over the assignment. He was not to know that Hitler had long ago discussed "Gustav" with Himmler and that the latter had instructed Schellenberg to lay plans for an operation against Giraud. Supervision of Unternehmen "Leiermann" [Operation "Organ-Grinder" —the SD's code name for "Gustav"] was entrusted to the head of the Sipo and SD in France, SS-Standartenführer Knochen, whose experience of kidnapping dated from the Venlo affair. Knochen set up an "active squad" for Giraud's recapture while some of his spies, led by Agent AG379, co-operated with the French police in keeping watch on the general's homes at Cap d'Antibes and Aix-les-Bains.[319] However, not even the SD planned to murder Giraud. "The local active squad," Schellenberg reported to Himmler, "has been ordered to trace Leiermann by all available means. The French members of this squad are still in the unoccupied zone, ready . . . to track Leiermann down and take immediate action."[320]

That would have been the end of the matter, both for Canaris and his department, had not Himmler complained to Keitel that Canaris was still working on the Giraud case despite its relinquishment to the SD. In September Keitel decided that Canaris must come to some arrangement with the RSHA.[321] The Admiral was in Paris, so Keitel telephoned the order to Lahousen instead. Keitel: "What about 'Gustav'? You know what 'Gustav' means, don't you?" Lahousen said he did. Keitel again: "Then you know the others are supposed to be handling it?" When Lahousen replied in the affirmative, Keitel finally told him what he wanted: "Then go to [Gestapo chief] Müller right away and find out how far the whole operation has progressed. I urgently need to know."[322]

Lahousen was panic-stricken. Imagining that Canaris had deliberately withheld "Gustav" from the SD so as to foil the operation, he now feared that a query addressed to "Gestapo" Müller would expose the whole manoeuvre. He hurried to Oster, who advised him to fly to Paris and warn Canaris.[323] Next day Lahousen's lanky figure barged into the Hotel Lutetia, where Canaris was sitting at table with some senior Abwehr officers. On being told what had happened he looked "very dismayed and could not at first see any way out" (Lahousen)— though not for the reasons assumed by the head of Abwehr II. This now turn in the affair threatened to disclose the fact that he had not told his subordinates the whole truth.[324]

Abshagen gives a credulous but colourful account of the scene. Canaris continued to sit there, brooding darkly. Then a sly grin stole over his face. He asked Lahousen to give him the precise dates of three occurrences: Giraud's escape, the Abwehr-RSHA conference in Prague and Heydrich's death. Lahousen had them at his finger tips: Giraud had broken out on April 17, the Prague meeting took place on May 17, and Heydrich died on June 4. Canaris chuckled and raised his glass, looking reassured. "Well, *Langer* ["Lofty"], is that right? Yes, that's right. Cheers!"[325] Lahousen slowly grasped what the Admiral had in mind. He later explained: "Canaris had based his plan on these three dates. It consisted in giving the impression that he had transmitted the order to . . . Heydrich at this [Prague] conference, in other words, taking advantage of Heydrich's death and thereby wrecking the whole scheme."[326] According to Lahousen, the Admiral succeeded.

By this time, even his most wholehearted apologists should have spotted a flaw in the story. The three dates quoted by Lahousen do not marry up with the fourth and crucial date on which Canaris and Keitel agreed that "Gustav" should be relinquished to the SD. This happened in August, when Heydrich had been dead three months. Lahousen's chronology is as faulty as his theory that Canaris thwarted a murder which was never actully planned. Knochen's agents were still lying in wait for Giraud in November 1942, when a Royal Navy submarine picked him up and took him to join the Anglo-American invasion force that was about to land in North Africa.[327]

This affair was only one example, if an extreme one, of the deviousness with which Canaris threaded his way through all the problems, crises and bouts of depression that afflicted him in autumn 1942. The military situation was disheartening enough in itself. The year

1942 had seen the failure of the Wehrmacht's second attempt to smash the Red Army for good, and the material superiority of the United States, which had also entered the war, was becoming more and more detectable in the Mediterranean area. Rommel had already been forced to cut short his victorious campaign in the East and General Eisenhower and his Anglo-American army were advancing in the West.

Canaris, whose awareness of impending disaster grew keener month by month, suffered from fits of apathy and despair. Even friends and sympathetic observers shrank from the gloomy, apocalyptic visions that haunted him with increasing frequency. Werner Best, who had left the Gestapo in 1940 to become chief civil administrator in Paris and sometimes played host to him there, found the Admiral's melancholy manner almost too much to bear. "The pessimism which was an integral part of his nature," writes Best, "became so much the dominant expression of Canaris's personality that his company had a positively oppressive effect on one."[328]

Abwehr officers critical of the regime were more dismayed than most by their chief's low morale, especially when, in his philosophical moments, he declared that man should avoid any undue interference with the historical process. Canaris could not be induced to strike a grand blow for freedom against the regime and the war. If he did act, it was generally because other people had forced him to. He himself was not a man of action, nor were his actions governed by the moral aversion to Hitlerism and fascism that moved others to resist them. As one Abwehr officer puts it: "Canaris had a pronounced sense of adventure, including the adventure of evil itself."[329] "As for the Nazis," says Wolf Werner Schrader, a member of the German resistance, "Canaris considered them to be thugs and crooks, but he had no objection to observing them. It was like getting absorbed in some well-written crime story."[330]

However, there were still some openings which encouraged even a fatalist like Canaris to act because he scented a possibility of ending the war before the Reich was completely destroyed by what the Christian and mystic in him regarded as the wrath of God. Here, too, the spadework had been performed by others—agents, go-betweens and a few genuine resistance fighters who enabled him to contact Allied representatives in neutral countries and explore the chances of a separate peace with the enemy.

Historians of the German resistance movement like to interpret these secret contacts between Canaris and members of the Allied camp as acts of opposition to the Nazi regime. This is largely a misconception. His primary concern was to end the war and save the German authoritarian state. Being fundamentally uninterested in domestic politics, he attached only secondary importance to the nature of the regime under which Germany would enter the postwar period. He realized, of course, that the Allies would never come to terms with Hitler, but he may have thought it quite possible to obtain Allied approval of a "liberalized" National Socialist government led by Hermann Göring. He did not even find it grotesque to contemplate deposing Hitler with the aid of Himmler and his power base, an idea which commended itself even to resolute anti-Nazis like Dohnanyi.

Another striking fact is that secret contacts with the Allied camp were established, not by resistance figures of historical note, but by the Abwehr go-betweens and information-peddlers of whom Halder once wrote, rather overcondescendingly, that they were "people you did not want to meet in public."[331] Among them was a Russian *émigré* of Baltic stock in whom Canaris probably reposed more confidence, politically speaking, than in any of his few friends. This was Baron Vladimir Kaulbars, a former staff captain in the Russian Imperial Army, who initiated many mysterious moves in the twilight zone between business and espionage.[332]

Canaris had known Kaulbars since 1920–21. His official status was that of a family friend who gave the Admiral Russian lessons for fun and occasionally worked as an Abwehr interpreter. Canaris had recruited him into Abwehr I as a species of Russian adviser shortly before the Eastern campaign opened.[333] Kaulbars maintained British and East European contacts through Colonel Juhlinn-Dannfeld, the Swedish military attaché in Berlin. The Gestapo later sought to prove, on the strength of a lost briefcase which found its way into their possession, that Kaulbars had worked as an agent for its owner, the said Juhlinn-Dannfeld, and furnished him with details of German military operations in the East.[334]

Kaulbars urged Canaris to get in touch with Britain or Russia at an early stage, though he advised him to negotiate with only one of the two. He also warned him repeatedly against overestimating Germany's resources. It seems clear that he knew of the Abwehr's unrealistic reports during the first year of the Russian campaign, for example its study on peace modalities dated June 18, 1941. This culminated in an assertion that "the end of Russia" would be succeeded by the formation of a new, conservative and conciliatory British cabinet whose members would be amenable to a negotiated peace.[335]

This was the first of the semiofficial peace plans to originate in Canaris's circle. In spring and autumn 1941 the German resistance movement's "outside right," Ulrich von Hassell, had with the Admiral's knowledge outlined another, more realistic, peace plan to an American who styled himself "Mr. Stallforth" but was really James D. Mooney, president of the General Motors Overseas Corporation.[336] Hassell proposed that hostilities should cease on condition that Hitler and his government were removed, Germany vacated all occupied territories except the Saar, Austria and Danzig, Poland got German East Prussia and Germany the Polish Corridor, and the Allies waived reparations.[337]

Neither Washington nor London would consider any such proposals, so Canaris had to fall back on the second of Kaulbars's suggested routes to a separate peace. In September 1941 Abwehr headquarters received its first intimation that certain members of the Soviet diplomatic corps and party leadership might not be averse to reaching an accommodation with Germany.[338]

An Abwehr agent named Edgar Klaus, who had been stationed in Stockholm since spring 1941 and was the third of the great Jewish Russian experts employed by the German secret service, possessed firsthand knowledge of these symptoms of Soviet irresolution. He regularly played bridge with the Soviet envoy and "old Bolshevik" Alexandra Mikhailovna Kollontay, whose prestige as a heroine of the pre-1917 Communist underground assured her of good relations with the party leaders in Moscow.[339]

The versatile Klaus, who was a Balt like Kaulbars and an ex-Communist who had worked for French and Soviet intelligence before switching his allegiance to the Germans, was perceptive enough to sense his Russian contacts' mood of panic.[340] Madame Kollontay, in particular, doubted whether the Soviet system could survive for much longer. She soon confided to Klaus that she was ready to throw in her lot with the Germans if Hitler granted her honourable terms.[341] Klaus travelled to Berlin and informed Canaris.

The Abwehr chief could hardly believe his ears. His Stockholm agent had to present two separate reports before the news sank in.[342] Then he conveyed the glad tidings to Hitler. On July 20, 1941, Ambassador Ritter of the Foreign Office noted that Canaris had informed Hitler "that, according to reports transmitted by Abwehr personnel, the Russian Minister in Stockholm, Madame Kollontay, intended to break with the Soviet Government and come to Germany if offered the necessary guarantees."[343] Madame Kollontay owned "assets worth 3 million dollars" and planned to "buy a house" in Germany. The Führer took a magnanimous line. His instructions to Jodl were that the lady from the Kremlin should be "generously accommodated in every way."[344]

From now on Canaris took an even closer interest in Klaus's reports on enemy morale. However, he construed his agent's observations merely as symptoms of Soviet collapse, not as an opening for serious talks with the Russians. Like so many other erstwhile critics of Operation "Barbarossa," he was intoxicated by the way in which the Wehrmacht had dealt the Red Army a succession of blows and was, to all appearances, speeding down the road to final victory.

Canaris did not become receptive to veiled Soviet proposals until the second year of the war against Russia. After the failure of the German summer offensive in 1942 the Kremlin again showed signs of a readiness to compromise. Although Madame Kollontay had since withdrawn her personal offer, Klaus was still picking up tidbits of information from his bridge partner.

Stalingrad was already signalling a major turning point in the war and the beginnings of defeat for Germany when Klaus informed Canaris that the Russians were genuinely prepared "to seek a compromise with Germany so as to end this destructive war."[345] We can only guess at the factors that prompted the Russians to put out feelers at this stage, late in 1942. Whether they were motivated by a sudden awareness of their own strength or by anger at the Western powers' continued postponement of their promised Second Front in Western Europe, the fact remains that the Russians were ready to negotiate. Klaus stated this quite categorically: "I guarantee you that if Germany agrees to the 1939 frontiers you can have peace in a week."[346]

Now would have been the time for Canaris to put these veiled proposals to the test, but he did not react. Imprisoned in the strait jacket of his anti-Communist beliefs, he could not countenance the idea of negotiating with Soviet representatives. He was more than ever convinced of the threat posed by Communism. The Communist resistance and espionage organization known as the Rote Kapelle [Red Orchestra] was currently being unmasked and dealt with, and Canaris had been appalled by what came to light during the hearings of the Reichskriegsgericht. German citizens, officers included, had spied for Moscow and betrayed his treasured ideals of loyalty to the state and devotion to duty.[347]

The Admiral's condemnation of these traitors became even fiercer when it transpired that Lieutenant Herbert Gollnow, Abwehr II's desk officer for Airborne and Parachute Troops, had also worked for the Rote Kapelle.[348] Called as an expert witness, Canaris firmly assured the Reichskriegsgericht that the Rote Kapelle's treachery had cost the Wehrmacht a hundred thousand lives—a gross exaggeration which only illustrates the extent of his emotional involvement.[349] In reality, Moscow's agents were responsible for the deaths of thirty-six men belonging to ten sabotage teams whose operations behind the Soviet lines Gollnow had (unwittingly) betrayed. Canaris was later corrected by counterespionage chief Rohleder, who declared: "The espionage activities [of the Rote Kapelle] were conducted in a pathetically amateurish way, and little military harm seems to have been done."[350]

Canaris did not follow up the Soviet proposals. He left it to someone of an altogether different stamp, the Nazi diplomat Peter Kleist, who worked for the "Ribbentrop Office," to contact the Russians in Stockholm with Klaus's invaluable assistance.[351] Meanwhile, the Russians were becoming increasingly explicit. In April 1943 the Soviet diplomats Mikhail Nikitin, Alexei Taradin and Boris Yartsev met German representatives at a country house near Stockholm, and talks were resumed in June at the Swedish Baltic resort of Saltsjöbaden. Some days later an Abwehr agent (presumably Klaus) informed the German Embassy that an official of the Soviet Foreign Commissariat named Alexandrov wished to meet "a gentleman of his acquaintance in the German Foreign Office."[352]

Kleist made the most of the opportunity. On June 17, 1943, he booked into Stockholm's Strandhotel, where Klaus soon turned up to inform him that Alexandrov proposed a meeting on July 7.[353] Although the Kleist-Alexandrov talks came to nothing because of Hitler's violent objections, Klaus remained on the lookout for ways of entering into a dialogue with Moscow.[354] Other Abwehr agents, too, saw openings for German-Soviet negotiations.

A Portuguese diplomat and Abwehr agent code-numbered RR 3174 reported to his controller at Abwehrstelle Hamburg that the Russians were interested in negotiating with Germany. On August 29, 1943, Hamburg sent Berlin the following urgent cable: "Portuguese Minister in Stockholm reports by telegram to Foreign Ministry in Lisbon that rumours are current of an impending Russo-German peace settlement. Portuguese Minister at the Quirinal has cabled to the same effect."[355] But Canaris was finished with the subject. If Hitler had forbidden further talks, that was that.

Kaulbars was furious. "Russia is now on the other side," he wrote to Canaris, "and becoming stronger and more united every day thanks to German policy. It is only a matter of time before the Ukraine becomes Russian again and the Baltic States are incorporated in the Russian empire—but thoroughly this time, because small and large nations alike have failed to grasp what Russia was and still is."[356] Even now, however, the baron did not abandon hope of steering Canaris in the direction of secret talks aimed at ending the war. If the Russians were out of bounds, a route must be found to the Western powers.

Kaulbars did his best to persuade Canaris to establish secret contacts with the British and Americans. "Here, as in America," he wrote on May 25, 1943, in a letter shrewdly calculated to tickle the Admiral's vanity, "the attitude towards you is friendly rather than hostile. The view taken here is that you have carried out your great and arduous tasks with extreme competence and devotion to duty, formed a very accurate picture of the general situation and earned no gratitude from the German authorities by so doing. It is said that you have, ever since the beginning of the war, had profound differences of opinion with the Führer, whom you have truthfully briefed on the actual situation. Being unable to replace you with anyone else, he was compelled to retain you in this responsible post."[357]

But what did professional responsibility and patriotic duty prescribe? The Baltic baron had only one answer to that: Canaris must talk to the enemy and negotiate for his country's sake. He confidently predicted the British reaction: "It would also be realized in England that you are one of the few men with whom it is possible to negotiate. Your influence and your connections would be rated so highly that you could achieve something under the most adverse circumstances. Here, too, you are considered too decent and, thus, too weak to make a timely withdrawal."[358]

Far from being hollow flattery, these remarks faithfully reflected the Admiral's reputation in at least some quarters of the British and American intelligence services. The majority of Allied spies regarded him, to quote the American chronicler of the OSS, R. Harris Smith, as "an evil genius of the Third Reich, the organizer of Nazi Fifth Columns throughout Europe, and the scourge of Allied agents and their resistance friends."[359] The directors of the Western intelligence agencies took a more discriminating view of their German opponent. Major General Stewart Menzies, the head of the British Secret Intelligence Service, formed a peculiarly accurate picture of Canaris.

Known in accordance with British secret service tradition as "C," Menzies compiled every available item of information about Canaris and reconstructed his daily life. In this he was aided by what one British historian has called "almost clairvoyant qualities in assessing men he had never even met."[360] "C understood Admiral Canaris better than he did me," sighed a Menzies subordinate,[361] and the SIS chief often succeeded in predicting German moves with total accuracy. Menzies conceived a great respect for Canaris from what he saw in his secret service kaleidoscope because it transmitted the image of a kindred spirit who, all obstacles and all national and political differences notwithstanding, cherished as ardent a desire to end the war as he did himself.[362] Once convinced of this, Menzies became titillated by the laudable but utopian idea of meeting Canaris in person and working out a peace formula with him.

Canaris may also have sensed that a kindred spirit was at work on the other side, moulded like himself by officer-and-gentleman traditions and steeped in the mental attitudes of a conservative and aristocratic pre-1914 society. Late in 1942 he sent Menzies a message via intermediaries in the Iberian Peninsula inviting the SIS chief to meet him on neutral ground.[363] This was the news for which Menzies had been so eagerly waiting. A fantastic plan took shape in his mind: together, he and Canaris would overthrow the war criminal who ruled Germany, cut the conflict short and bring about a reconciliation between their two related peoples.

Menzies was more than ready to meet Canaris. The Anglo-

American invasion of North Africa presented a favourable opportunity to confer with the German intelligence chief somewhere in Spain or Portugal. The general submitted his proposal to the Foreign Office, where it was promptly scotched—"for fear of offending Russia," as Menzies commented after the war.[364] "It would certainly not have pleased Stalin," writes Frederick Winterbotham, the SIS Chief of Air Intelligence, in whom Menzies confided at the time, "but why we should fall over backwards to appease those who were, and are, pledged to destroy our way of life I shall never understand."[365] Men like Menzies and Winterbotham were dissatisfied with the Foreign Office ukase and continued to hope for a fresh approach from the other side.

The Foreign Office, to which the SIS was officially responsible, distrusted its own intelligence chief and erected a barrier against all future overtures by Canaris. British diplomatic missions abroad were instructed that peace feelers from military or civilian members of the German resistance must be automatically rejected.[366] When the lawyer and diplomat Allen W. Dulles arrived in Berne to set up the European headquarters of the Office of Strategic Services (OSS), America's new intelligence agency, SIS representatives in the Swiss capital warned him to be careful of German secret service *provocateurs* posing as resistance fighters![367]

Anything Foreign Office directives had failed to achieve was consummated by a historic decision on the part of the Allied leaders. In January 1943 Franklin D. Roosevelt and Winston Churchill resolved never to negotiate with members of the German resistance but simply and solely to bring about "the unconditional surrender of Germany."[368] Menzies at once grasped the significance of this. It meant a fight to the last German bullet and a death blow to any internal movement whose determination to remove Hitler and his regime was based on hopes of preserving a nation-state that had taken centuries to evolve. Canaris would never send him another message—of that Menzies felt certain.

But then a minor miracle occurred. Strangely enough, the Casablanca Conference and the demand for Germany's unconditional surrender spurred Canaris into renewed activity. Now that total disaster threatened the very existence of a country for which generations had fought and striven—for which millions had sacrificed their lives on the battlefields of Europe—Wilhelm Canaris felt a compulsion to act. For one brief moment, all his anxieties and uncertainties evaporated. Devious no longer, he set out to conduct a dialogue with the Western Allies by direct means.

The British having barred his path, he looked around for a contact with the Americans and found one in Captain Paul Leverkuehn, head of KO-Nebenstelle [War Organization Suboffice] Istanbul, who had been one of Germany's few internationally known lawyers before being drafted into the Wehrmacht.[369] Leverkuehn had served on the Mixed Claims Commission, a body appointed to settle private war-damage claims after World War I. While working in Washington he had met fellow lawyer William J. Donovan, now head of the U.S. secret service.[370] Being aware of Leverkuehn's U.S. connections, the Americans in Istanbul had engineered an acquaintanceship between him and one of their men, an employee of the United States War Information Service.[371]

Leverkuehn knew from his conversations with this American, as well as from other sources, that the U.S. naval attaché in Istanbul, Commander George H. Earle, was an archconservative who yearned to end the ill-starred conflict between the non-Communist powers. One of America's few Balkan experts and an extremely influential politician to boot, Earle was a friend of Roosevelt's and a former governor of Pennsylvania. He had been stationed in Turkey since early 1943 as the President's Balkan observer.[372] When Leverkuehn heard that Canaris was seeking contact with the Americans he put forward Earle's name. The combination of two naval officers who were both rabid anti-Communists struck him as a promising one.

In establishing contact, however, Leverkuehn remained in the background and left the preliminaries to another German who had the advantage of holding no official post. Baron Kurt von Lersner, an ex-diplomat who had led the German peace delegation at Versailles in 1919 and was a friend of Franz von Papen, the German Ambassador in Ankara, had once served as a counsellor at the German Embassy in Washington. There he had become friendly with Roosevelt, then assistant Secretary of the Navy.[373] Both being friends of Roosevelt's, Lersner and Earle had plenty of conversational topics.

The two men got on so well that Earle readily agreed to meet a good friend of Roosevelt's good friend Lersner—Wilhelm Canaris. By the end of January 1943 Canaris was face to face with Earle and asking if he saw any prospect of an accommodation between Hitler's German opponents and the Western Allies, its purpose being to shorten the war and concentrate all available forces on the threat from Russia.[374] He argued that the only terrible alternative was the unconditional surrender formula, which would enable Hitler to call forth the most fanatical war effort in German history and prolong the conflict for an indefinite period. Because this would be quite as detrimental to the Western Allies as to Germany, he, Canaris, was offering a solution on behalf of all the forces he represented: an armistice in the West and a continuation of the struggle in the East.[375]

Earle expressed his good will and undertook to convey this proposal to the President. Meanwhile, Canaris left Baron von Lersner to whet Earle's interest in his plan with further veiled allusions. "Our friend Franklin Roosevelt informed me," the baron wrote later, "that he would promptly discuss any of my proposals with his allies in the most sympathetic manner because he trusted my word. I proposed to fly to see him with a great American [Earle] from Stamboul. The Pope, Papal Secretary of State Maglione, Nuncio Roncalli and Bishop Montini had all promised their fullest support."[376]

Then came Roosevelt's response to Canaris's proposal: he had turned it down.[377] Canaris braced himself for another attempt and requested a second interview with Earle, but the American dodged him—his orders from Washington precluded any further negotiations with Canaris.[378] Disappointed but not disheartened, the Admiral urged Lernsner to keep in touch with Earle at all costs.

In May 1943 the baron presented Earle with a new scheme which sounded, if anything, more hazardous than Canaris's. He confided to the U.S. naval attaché that German Army officers had devised a plan to storm the Führer's headquarters, arrest him and hand him over to the Western Allies with the help of a raiding force currently being formed in Army Group Centre's Russian area of operations.[379] Lernsner was referring to the Reiterabteilung [Cavalry Detachment] Boeselager, a three-thousand-strong cavalry regiment commanded by Captain Georg von Boeselager, which the anti-Nazi conspirators regarded as a sort of task force for use in the event of a *coup d'état*.[380]

In June Canaris sent Count von Moltke to Istanbul, where he presented two OSS-connected professors of his acquaintance with a proposal that read like a sequel to the Canaris plan. Moltke suggested that a German General Staff officer should travel to England—an officer with sufficient knowledge, as one historian puts it, "to arrange with the Western Allies to open up the German Western Front." The Eastern Front, on the other hand, would remain in being. Moltke echoed Canaris's January plea for a retraction of the Casablanca formula.

Although the professors considered this a vain hope,[381] Moltke's American contacts were sufficiently interested for OSS chief Donovan to take a personal hand in the matter. He got his old friend Leverkuehn to sign a statement, typed on official paper from the German Embassy in Ankara, in which Canaris's representative promised on behalf of the German opposition that German military commanders would offer no resistance if the Western Allies invaded France.[382] Donovan was so impressed by this document that he decided to tackle Roosevelt again.

Even before Donovan stepped in, Canaris had begun to extend the range of his peace feelers. Approaching the Americans from the Istanbul end was no longer enough for him. His emissaries turned up in the neutral capitals of Europe with instructions to find British and American representatives who were ready to talk. But Canaris proceeded very gingerly. One false move, one overeager offer to negotiate, and he immediately broke contact. When the head of KO Stockholm, Lieutenant Colonel Wagner, reported to him on April 20, 1943, that the British naval attaché, Captain Denham, had expressed himself "very interested"—via some Swedish officers—in "talking to a German gentleman," Canaris scribbled on the report: "Lt. Col. Wagner to decline. C."[383]

The Admiral could only use inconspicuous middlemen whose work was unconnected with their national agencies abroad. He found them. In addition to Sonderführer Gisevius, Vice-Consul Eduard Waetjen and Captain Theodor Strünck of the Abwehr maintained contact with OSS Resident Director Dulles, the Berlin lawyer Carl Langbehn cultivated Dulles's friend Gero von Gaevernitz, and an ex-diplomat and double agent named Hans-Eduard Riessner sought to restore the severed links with Henry B. Livingston, the British Consul in Geneva. Canaris also commanded the services of Prince Max Egon zu Hohenlohe-Langenburg, a German prince, Spanish landowner and Liechtenstein citizen who excelled at back-room discussions.[384]

Canaris's contacts with the Allies in Spain showed exceptional promise, so he returned to the country which had generated so many developments in his career. "Canaris told me," said Colonel Georg Hansen, Piekenbrock's successor, "that he was on such good terms with Franco that the latter would be prepared to mediate with the British at any time."[385] Because contact with the British was still inadequate, Canaris asked the Spaniards to help. Writing after the war, José María Doussinague, director general of the Spanish Foreign Office, declared: "To us, the war's solution had always meant an acceptance of our view that the National Socialist regime should be overthrown without, however, destroying Germany. And now Prince Hohenlohe had brought us proof that this was not only feasible but comparatively simple."[386]

The Spanish secret service lent a hand, especially as it was in the Admiral's debt. German intelligence had often put Franco's security forces on the track of groups hostile to the regime.[387] It was little wonder that Spanish diplomats and secret servicemen had no qualms about transmitting messages to the enemy camp. By summer 1943 the Abwehr chief had gained his first objective. Generals Menzies and Donovan intimated to their German counterpart that they were prepared to meet him in Spain, and the three secret service chiefs convened at Santander soon afterwards.[388]

It must have been a remarkable occasion, this clandestine encounter between three men who controlled the most powerful espionage networks in the contemporary world. Canaris presented Menzies and Donovan with his peace plan, which still embodied the same elements: a cease-fire in the West, Hitler to be eliminated or handed over, and continuation of the war in the East. The British general raised few objections and even the less polished American bowed to the German admiral's logic. In this topsy-turvy situation it must have seemed lightyears since Canaris and Donovan had conducted their undercover duel in the Balkans. F. Justus von Einem, an Abwehr officer who was present at Santander, recalls: "Donovan, his British colleague and C[anaris] reached agreement on the basis of C's proposal. It was my most exciting experience as a member of C's staff.[389]

But the espionage chiefs' pact was short-lived. Roosevelt called his presumptuous OSS chief to heel and the head of the SIS took pains to minimize the significance of his forbidden trip to Spain vis-à-vis the British Foreign Office.[390] Donovan and Menzies must have felt rather like the American Secretary of the Navy, James Forrestal, who one day bumped into Earle at the White House. Forrestal to Earle, who had come to submit a new Canaris proposal: "My God, George, you and I and Bill Bullitt are the only ones around the President who know the Russian leaders for what they are."[391]

As for Canaris, all his hopes of a last-minute escape from the war had been dashed. He even had cause to fear that his rivals at the RSHA would use this surreptitious flirtation with Allied representatives to deal him a mortal blow. The Admiral's secret contacts were certainly no secret to SD chief Schellenberg, who was also striving, in his opportunistic and cold-blooded fashion, to desert the Führer's sinking ship. Schellenberg's agents likewise haunted Dulles's outer office and many of his intermediaries were identical with those of Canaris.[392] Prince von Hohenlohe appeared in his list of informants and Langbehn made overtures to U.S. secret servicemen on his behalf as well as the Admiral's.[393] It would have been only too easy for Schellenberg to destroy the ageing Abwehr chief.

But Canaris scented danger from the wrong quarter. The direst threat of all emanated from his own ranks, not the RSHA. The curtain was rising on the final act in his dramatic career.

12

Downfall

Early in 1943 two men presented themselves in Canaris's outer office and asked to see him urgently. One of them bore a name which was enough to gain both visitors immediate access to the chief's office. SS-Sturmbannführer and Oberregierungsrat Hartmut Plaas, head of the Internal Affairs Section of the Forschungsamt, was one of the Admiral's oldest friends. The Abwehr chief and the SS man had known each other since their Freikorps days, when Plaas maintained close contact with Canaris in his capacity as adjutant to the commander of the Naval Brigade, Ehrhardt.[1]

They had all been members of the same political camp: Lieutenant Canaris, organizer and paymaster of extreme right-wing vigilantes, Lieutenant (ret.) Plaas, sentenced to two years' imprisonment for abetting the murder of Walther Rathenau, Lieutenant (ret.) Franz Liedig, who forcibly released his commanding officer, Ehrhardt, from a prison cell, and the Freikorps propagandist Friedrich Wilhelm Heinz.[2] Politically, they had gone their separate ways after the Nazis came to power. Heinz and Liedig were early recruits to the resistance whereas Canaris and Plaas had toed the line until the degeneration of the regime drove them into the anti-Nazi camp.

Contacts between Canaris and Plaas had multiplied in recent months because of threats to opponents of the regime. The SS man often knew whom the Gestapo was spying on. If a suspect's phone needed tapping the RSHA had to request telephonic surveillance from the Forschungsamt because the Gestapo possessed no monitoring facilities of their own. This had enabled Plaas and Canaris to discover that their friend, Hermann Ehrhardt, who now lived on his Austrian estate at Brunn am Walde and made a habit of vituperating against the Nazi regime, was under Gestapo surveillance.[3]

Canaris and Plaas made several representations about this to Himmler. A Gestapo observation report of December 1941 recorded Plaas's assurance that Ehrhardt was "exceptionally well disposed towards the SS and had a high regard for the Reichsführer-SS," nor did it fail to note that Ehrhardt "is still in close touch with Admiral Canaris."[4] This finally preserved Ehrhardt from further harassment by the Gestapo. Himmler's memorandum to the relevant department at Prinz-Albrecht-Strasse read: "No action against Ehrhardt required."[5]

This time, however, Plaas was not concerned with the safety of his old commanding officer or a few tips culled from the RSHA's phone-tapping requisitions. His errand on this particular day in January 1943 was, quite simply, a matter of life or death—a last-minute plea to Canaris to prevent the Gestapo's myrmidons from driving someone down the road that led with mechanical inevitability to the gas chambers and death factories of German racial fanaticism.

Plaas's companion, the writer Franz Josef Furtwängler, who worked for the Indian Desk at the Foreign Office, explained the nature of their mission. They had, he told Canaris, a Jewish friend who had left Germany quite legally in 1938 and settled in Holland, where he carved out a new life for himself and was at first left in peace by the German occupation authorities. Now the worst had happened. Like thousands of other Jews in Holland he was to be branded with the notorious "yellow star" and deported to Poland. Then came Furtwängler's crucial question. Would the Admiral do what he had done in previous cases and save their Jewish friend from certain death by enlisting him in the Abwehr's service?[6]

The words were hardly out of his mouth when, as he later recalled, "we suffered a shattering blow."[7] Canaris declared himself unable to help. "The head of the Abwehr," Furtwängler went on, "admitted quite frankly that he was pretty well 'hemmed in.' Himmler was on the verge of outright victory, and he, the Admiral, no longer had the power to protect a person or 'requisition' him on behalf of his agencies."[8]

Dismayed as well as disappointed, Canaris's visitors noted his air of complete physical exhaustion and the utter despair in his faltering voice. The Abwehr chief was almost unrecognizable. His face looked tired and sunken, his gaze was abstracted and the cigar in his right hand trembled—clearly, he was drinking more than he used to. Was this the wily tactician who had picked his way so nimbly through Ger-

many's bureaucratic jungle, who had once been regarded by Furtwängler himself as a "fox among the bears of the Prussian military hierarchy" or described by his friend Otto Wagner as "the father of the
outlaws?"[9]

Canaris had often helped those in need. He seldom dismissed an appeal for aid and comfort unless it seemed likely to provoke a head-on
clash with the regime. Jews, in particular, had been snatched from
mass destruction by many devious manoeuvres on his part. Thanks to
him, numerous Jews or "half-Jews" wore Wehrmacht uniform or at
least carried Abwehr papers guaranteeing them immunity from the
Gestapo. The rescue of five hundred Dutch Jews by Abwehrstelle den
Haag in May 1941, which would have been impossible without the Admiral's consent, was still fresh in his visitors' minds. Even in late summer 1942 Canaris had mounted an audacious rescue operation by securing exit permits for twelve elderly Berlin Jews who had been
represented to the Gestapo as Abwehr agents earmarked for use against
the United States.[10]

But that was past history. Now Canaris was either reluctant or unable to help. He accounted for his attitude by citing a factor which ostensibly explained everything: the growing power of Himmler and his
police machine. The Admiral's remarks made such a lasting impression
on Furtwängler that he yielded to a writer's natural penchant for
overdramatization and sought to tinge the scene in his office with tragic
finality. There was no doubt in his mind that Canaris was "in process
of losing his last battle on behalf of Prussian military resistance to the
'National Socialist Revolution.'"[11]

It escaped Furtwängler, in company with many later historians, that
the Admiral's uneasiness and irresolution could not be solely ascribed to
the power of the SS-police empire. There was, of course, no mistaking
the steady self-aggrandizement of Himmler's complex organization.
The Reichsführer-SS was welding his policemen, secret servicemen, bureaucrats and soldiers into a separate state, a species of counterforce
with a growing tendency towards independence of the party and government. Himmler controlled the police and security services, he was
supreme arbiter of the regime's cultural and racial policy, his representatives were ensconced in industry and diplomacy, occupation authorities and administrative departments, his Waffen-SS was developing into a serious rival of the Wehrmacht, and the time was not far
hence when he would also acquire that outward token of internal authority, the post of Reich Interior Minister.

The Abwehr, too, felt the unmistakable impact of its competitor's
growing power. Not only had Canaris been obliged to relinquish control over the Geheime Feldpolizei to the RSHA, at least in the occupied Western territories, but the Abwehr had also lost its monopoly po-

sition in counterespionage, that traditional preserve of the military intelligence service. The upper reaches of the SD were now dominated by politically fanatical reformers who made it increasingly plain to the Abwehr that the days of an autonomous military intelligence service were numbered.

For all that, Canaris feared Abwehr weakness more than SS superiority. The Wehrmacht command structure was still more or less intact. Had the Abwehr been a strong and successful organization, backing from the armed forces would still have sufficed to repel the other side's claims to dominance. But internal cohesion, a successful record and the promise of a settled existence were just what the Abwehr lacked. Canaris was too shrewd not to admit to himself that he presided over a shaky and crumbling edifice.

The Abwehr's decline seemed irresistible. Other rivals were disputing any Abwehr functions still unclaimed by the Gestapo and SD. Jodl's Wehrmachtführungsstab aspired to control the Abwehr's household troops, the Brandenburgers, who had been reorganized early in 1943 after suffering heavy casualties on the Eastern Front, and OKH intelligence officers were toying with the idea of taking over the Abwehr's front-line personnel, whose operational links with the Tirpitz-Ufer had become extremely tenuous, and converting them into a self-contained intelligence service responsible to the Army alone.[12] The Luftwaffe and Navy were also building up their intelligence agencies so as to lessen their dependence on the Abwehr and its shortcomings.

Many setbacks demonstrated that, despite isolated achievements of outstanding merit, the Abwehr was inefficient. It had failed to detect the Russian build-up in the Stalingrad area with sufficient speed and was taken completely unawares by the Anglo-American landing in North Africa in November 1942.[13] Analysts at the Seekriegsleitung [Directorate of Naval Warfare] adjudged that, although the Abwehr was in possession of reports about the North African venture, the enemy had bombarded it with so many rumours of projected landings in other areas that "none of these intelligence complexes was evaluated as resolutely as the organization of long-term resistance to the enemy operation would have required." The outcome: "In this intelligence battle, we lost the day."[14]

Still more disastrous were the failures which went unrecognized by Canaris and his spy-masters. They did not know, for example, that the whole of the Abwehr's British network had long ago been detected and "turned" by British counterintelligence. Almost all data reaching the Tirpitz-Ufer from Britain really emanated from the disinformation experts of the Secret Intelligence Service, whose false reports were to play a fateful role on the eve of the Allied invasion of France in summer 1944.[15]

Failure even attended the sabotage operations which had long been the most spectacular feathers in the Abwehr's cap. An attempt to land eight Abwehr saboteurs in the United States during June 1942 (Operation "Pastorius") was nipped in the bud because their leaders betrayed the scheme to U.S. counterespionage.[16] The code names of other operations also became synonymous with Abwehr inefficiency. Operation "Weisdorn" (incitement of a popular uprising in South Africa), Operation "Tiger" (incitement of Afghanistan and Western India against the British), Operation "Shamyl" (incitement of an anti-Soviet revolt in the Caucasus)—all these came to nothing.[17]

"Yet again, Canaris's imprudence and inconsistency has landed us in the soup," fumed Jodl after the North African débâcle.[18] Criticism of Canaris became so fierce that he seldom visited the Führer's headquarters. He generally left it to Bürkner, whose Abteilung Ausland had since been upgraded into an Amtsgruppe, to represent Amt Ausland/Abwehr, not that this prevented the Admiral from ridiculing his delegate's naive faith in Hitler.[19] Canaris's friends like to recount how once, when Bürkner was watching the situation map at the Führer's command headquarters being adorned with red flags (for Russian units) and blue (for German), he had a sudden dread that Hitler might take offence at such a massive concentration of Soviet forces. His solution to the problem: "Hey, don't put so much red on that map!"[20]

The Germans were paying dearly for the fact that Hitler's breakneck policy of conquest and Canaris's singular conduct of affairs had inhibited the growth of an effective secret service. The "bloated military intelligence system, with an officer corps whose members competed, intrigued, denounced each other and were riven with political dissension" (to quote a former Abwehr officer), could not muster the energy to reform itself.[21] Fatalist that he was, bereft of faith in the future and accustomed to the mechanical fulfilment of his allotted tasks, Canaris let his organization drift into a backwater.

But the scantier its output of information became, the faster the Abwehr developed into a mammoth machine which did no more than idle for much of the time. It now employed more office-bound Referenten than agents, and one expert has described the standard of performance and training of many Abwehr officers as "startlingly low."[22] Largely reservists who had been drafted from civilian jobs unconnected with espionage, they tended to lack the military know-how which alone could have enabled them to recognize the significance and value of the information they received. The same applied in even greater measure to the Kasemattenbären ["casemate bears" or old soldiers] as German Army slang termed the elderly gentlemen past retirement age who dozed and vegetated in the more remote reaches of the Abwehr.

Like Abwehr headquarters, the far-flung outstations, "war organizations," suboffices and communications centres pursued a daily routine notable for its bureaucratic red tape, low standards of efficiency and ossified secret service rituals. Because headquarters—meaning Canaris first and foremost—scarcely bothered to supervise the work of the Abwehrstellen and KOs, many of them turned into hotbeds of personal ambition. The Tirpitz-Ufer's generous expense allowances and salaries enabled many on its payroll to indulge in high living, and more than one Abwehr employee succumbed to the lure of attractive women, lucrative business connections and straightforward bribes from foreign intelligence agencies.

KO Portugal, the jumping-off point for German agents assigned to Britain, was renowned for what Oberstabsintendant Max Franzbach remembers as "its monumental binges, which often went on far into the night. There really was everything you can possibly imagine. Those parties never stopped. We hardly had time to sleep."[23] When the mistress of a KO chief accompanied her boy friend back to Germany, the forty pairs of shoes and other belongings she had acquired in a bare three years were too bulky for one truck to accommodate.[24] Some officers serving with Abwehrstellen or KOs abroad had surreptitiously sent for their wives, which was strictly forbidden, and many Spanish, Portuguese, French or Turkish mistresses retailed the Abwehr's official secrets to their friends.

It was not unheard of for Abwehrstellen to be ruled by women. Two such were the legendary "Mausi," secretary, mistress and later wife of Ludwig Kremer von Auenrode, head of KO Lisbon, a lady who had to be wooed by anyone eager for advancement at this important Abwehr outstation, and her no less celebrated counterpart in Algeciras, Fräulein Fehleisen, who married Fritz Kautschke of the local suboffice and often caused turmoil in the German secret service by losing valuable documents or mislaying the second key to the office safe.[25]

Not unnaturally, KO personnel regarded it as good form to keep dogs because C's example had permeated the farthest corners of his empire. Smart operators enlivened the Admiral's tours of inspection by producing a dog at the opportune moment, conscious that the sight of it would sweeten his temper at once. Sometimes, of course, dogs were also used for security purposes. British secret servicemen monitoring Abwehr radio traffic racked their brains over the identity of a mysterious V-Mann named "Axel" whose assignment to the Algeciras-based agent Karbe (code name "Cäsar") was heralded by a flurry of radio messages. The British did not catch on until they picked up the following admonition: "Watch out for Axel. He bites." It came too late. Algeciras radioed back: "Cäsar is in hospital. Axel bit him."[26]

No picture of the Abwehrstellen would be complete without an allusion to the growing band of agents and spy-masters referred to in German secret service parlance as "Schaumschläger" [literally "egg whisks," figuratively "hot-air merchants"], meaning informants who had no "sources" and invented their material instead. Probably the most controversial of these was Paul Fidrmuc of Lisbon, an Abwehr officer who had built up an intelligence network named "Ostro" which enabled him to furnish the Wehrmacht authorities with numerous items of military information gleaned from Britain, the United States and Canada. Ostro threw such a scare into the Allies that the Secret Intelligence Service dispatched some of its best agents to Lisbon to reconnoitre. They soon discovered that this seemingly formidable espionage organization consisted of one busy individual who sat at a desk and cracked the top-secret safes of the Allied general staffs in his fertile imagination.[27]

Almost every Abwehrstelle and KO had its "hot-air merchants," but it was rare for an outstation to consist of them alone. One example was the Athens communications centre established by a professor of Oriental studies and his friend, who rose to become Federal German Ambassador in Greece after the war. These two gentlemen fed Abwehr headquarters with reports about the Near East which were quite as fictitious as the agents and informants on which their office prided itself.[28]

Thanks to these Byzantine activities, substantial sections of the Abwehr became a self-service counter—a maze of multifarious cliques and cabals in which corruption and nepotism ran riot. Canaris was not the type to take stern action against corrupt elements inside his own organization. He hushed up many a scandal himself and all too frequently turned a blind eye when officers in outstations or at headquarters made lavish use of travel allowances, letters of credit, trips abroad and expenses in general.

The Abwehr chief, who happily imported fresh Spanish strawberries from Aranjuez by special plane, plied his favourites with handsome gifts from Abwehr funds (Fidrmuc once received a diamond-encrusted tobacco jar that had belonged to Napoleon) and was loath to back up his paymasters when they protested at unsupported claims for travelling expenses lodged by senior Abwehr officers.[29] He did, on the other hand, complain to a military judge that many goings-on in his department had escaped his notice. He further declared that this ignorance of the facts "had already caused him a lot of trouble, and mentioned a sizeable currency switch from Venice to Croatia."[30]

There was no lack of corruption in the Abwehr. Officers at Abwehrstelle Munich did a brisk trade in smuggling foreign currency, carpets and paintings across the Reich borders, and there were desk chiefs at Abwehr headquarters who took their wives on trips abroad or procured lucrative credits by getting wealthy businessmen exempted from military service.[31] Paymasters and non-commissioned officers of KO Bulgaria were "racketeers of the first order," according to one of their colleagues, and the Slovak Ministry of Finance was knee-deep in reports compiled by an official board of inquiry which had checked on smuggling operations conducted by Abwehr outstations.[32]

The Abwehr was dotted with friends and relations eager to help other friends and relations. Captain Schulz found an Abwehr niche for his school friend Ivar Lissner; Martin Toeppen protected the Yugoslav brothers Dusco and Ivo Popov in ignorance that they were working for the other side; Schmidhuber wangled his secretary, Ickrath, and his friend Josef Müller into Abwehrstelle Munich; and Dohnanyi managed to obtain Abwehr assignments for his brother-in-law, Dietrich Bonhoeffer, and a desk job for his boyhood friend Delbrück.[33] Even Canaris found room for some relations. Heinz Canaris was attached to KO Spain, though he was "only tolerated as a nephew of Admiral Canaris, being no great shakes" (to quote his former administrative chief). One of the Admiral's nieces, Fräulein Spindler, worked at the Madrid office and another was a secretary with KO Portugal.[34]

The Abwehr's Western adversaries considered it so corrupt that the Secret Intelligence Service stationed its infiltrators in places where Abwehrstellen were unusually exposed to the temptations of la dolce vita —in Lisbon, Madrid, Istanbul and other cities in the Eastern Mediterranean. Most of KO Lisbon had already been infiltrated by the British secret service, and Abwehr personnel in Istanbul were also preparing to change sides.[35] KO Madrid presented no more secrets to the British either, as the British-Soviet double agent Kim Philby proudly declares. "We knew the names, pseudonyms, addresses, cover functions and real functions of most of the staff at Madrid headquarters and at the many outstations such as Barcelona, Bilbao, Vigo, Algeciras, etc."[36]

The "inefficiency of the Abwehr" was an integral component of all SIS plans, and many British secret servicemen blenched at the thought that "new brooms would have swept away much which we were concerned to preserve," as John Masterman, one of the leading lights in British counterintelligence, frankly admitted after the war.[37] The SIS was second only to Canaris and his officers in fearing a "collapse of the Abwehr, with which as well as against which we had learned to work."[38]

But woe if this deplorable state of affairs came to the notice of the Gestapo and SD! That would seal the Abwehr's fate because nobody and nothing would be able to save the military intelligence service from liquidation by the ruthless apparatchiks of the RSHA. Canaris realized that a well-mounted Gestapo operation might prove fatal to the Abwehr, and this was just the threat that now confronted him. For some weeks, the Gestapo's interrogators had been focusing their spotlights on an officer who probably knew more about corruption and nepotism in the Abwehr than any other member of the military intelligence service, Major Wilhelm Schmidhuber of Abwehrstelle Munich.

Hans Oster had even more cause for concern than Canaris because Schmidhuber had been privy to the Oster circle's *coup d'état* plans in 1939–40. More worrying still, it was he who had received the dates of the Western offensive from Oster's confidant Josef Müller in May 1940 and transmitted them to the Vatican and, thus, to the Western powers. If a man with his kind of inside information talked, the game was up.

For Oster, now a major general, Schmidhuber's arrest could not have come at a worse moment. For the first time since 1940 he could see a chance of averting national disaster and felt confident of finding enough determined men to sweep away Hitler and his regime. Although Canaris declined to participate in these new schemes, which he considered fanciful, Oster had recruited some vigorous allies.

These men were on the staff of Army Group Centre, now fighting in Russia. Oster had first heard of them in 1941 through one of their number, Fabian von Schlabrendorff, a friend and long-time member of the resistance. Schlabrendorff confided to Oster that several of Army Group Centre's officers had banded together and intended to move against the regime at the earliest possible moment.[39] Their leader was the ranking staff officer, Colonel Henning von Tresckow, a man who would stop at nothing.[40]

Tresckow had drawn his own conclusions from the fact that no senior officer had yet been prepared to rebel against Hitler. As he saw it, no prominent general would lift a finger against the regime while Hitler was alive because the military were paralysed by their oath of allegiance, with its pseudo-religious trappings. There was only one way of resolving the dilemma, and that was to assassinate Hitler.

Colonel von Tresckow instructed his staff to draw up a plan. There were three possibilities: Hitler could be shot by a lone assassin, bombed by a team or killed during a raid on his command headquarters. Tresckow decided on a bomb to be detonated when he was either on the move or at headquarters.[41] The army group's Ic officer, Lieutenant Colonel Baron von Gersdorff, procured some suitable explosive while other officers explored the most favourable opportunities for an attack.[42]

But what was to happen if the attempt on Hitler's life succeeded? The conspirators could not expect the front-line troops to side with them automatically once he was dead. They needed some units of their own to resist a probable counterblow by forces loyal to the regime. Tresckow considered setting up a special force at Army Group Centre (the origin of the Reiterabteilung Boeselager), but that was not enough. The grand design would have no prospect of success unless substantial forces joined the revolt at home in Germany. And that was when Tresckow got in touch with Oster.

Emboldened by Tresckow's efforts, Oster resumed work on his own plans for a *coup d'état*. He had by this time acquired a new ally in Berlin as well, namely General Friedrich Olbricht, whose status as head of the Allgemeines Heeresamt [AHA—General Army Department] was of crucial importance. Together with Olbricht, Oster produced a merger between his earlier ideas on a military revolt and those of Tresckow.[43] Thus originated the strategic pattern which the coup of July 20, 1944, was intended to follow. Hitler's death would, it was hoped, trigger a process resulting in the seizure of key points throughout Germany and the occupied territories.

Late in March 1942 the Berlin home of Colonel General (ret.) Beck became a sort of operational headquarters and Oster its Chief of Staff. Schlabrendorff was appointed liaison officer between Berlin and Army Group Centre, though Dohnanyi also undertook to carry messages from Oster, his immediate superior, to Tresckow in Russia.[44] Preparations for a coup crystallized week by week, and signs of impending disaster at Stalingrad made its leaders even more impatient to act.

Meanwhile, General Olbricht was assembling troops for the great day. Trustworthy units would have to be on stand-by, particularly in Berlin, Cologne, Munich and Vienna, when "X hour" struck. The most crucial area was Berlin, where the eastern half of the city was to be occupied by troops held in readiness at Frankfurt an der Oder, but it was doubtful who would seal off the SS Artillery School at Jüterbog and secure the western quarters.[45] Oster came up with a solution, at least on paper. He proposed to bring in the Brandenburg Division, which was then being formed in the Berlin area, and saw to it that the new divisional commander was an opponent of the regime, Colonel Alexander von Pfuhlstein.[46]

Pfuhlstein's appointment proved to be a grave miscalculation because his mind worked along far too orthodox military lines for him to involve his unit in a *coup d'état*. Although he had taken an active part in Oster's conspiratorial discussions as head of Abwehrstelle Hanover during the late 1930s, his posting to a combat unit had driven something of a wedge between him and the resistance. Awarded the Knight's Cross as commander of the 154th Infantry Regiment during heavy fighting in the Demyansk pocket in 1942, he now had little more than verbal sympathy for Oster's plans.[47]

Pfuhlstein took a purely military view of how the Brandenburg Division should be formed and led, and he abhorred any introduction of politics into his unit. This he made abundantly clear to Oster's friend Heinz, who had been given command of the Brandenburg's 4th Regiment shortly before his own appointment. The new divisional commander conceived a peculiar antipathy for Lieutenant Colonel Heinz,[48] whom he dismissed as a "political figure" with no knowledge of military matters. "He was," says Pfuhlstein, "virtually incapable of commanding a company, let alone a regiment. Heinz knew next to nothing . . . about modern warfare in general. Similarly, he had no experience or knowledge of how to train and instruct a reconstituted unit."[49] Pfuhlstein's personal inclination was to relieve Heinz of his command at once. In deference to his reputed friendship with Canaris, however, he left him where he was and did not have him replaced until later.[50]

More crucial than these personal animosities was the fact that Pfuhlstein quickly grasped how the balance of power had shifted inside the Wehrmacht High Command. General Jodl, head of the Wehrmachtführungsstab, was unwilling to give Canaris exclusive control over the new division. He claimed it for the OKW and proposed to grant the Admiral limited powers only, as he made clear to Pfuhlstein on his appointment: "The Wehrmachtführungsstab has no unit of its own for OKW theatres of war. Every division has to be laboriously wheedled out of OKH, often with considerable difficulty . . . An undignified and intolerable state of affairs! As the Wehrmachtführungsstab's sole household formation, the 'Brandenburg' Division will thus be directly subordinated thereto and put to use by me."[51]

Canaris acquiesced and contented himself with a joint say in personnel and security matters. Only the 5th Regiment, from now on entitled the "Kurfürst," remained exclusively available to him for commando operations by Abwehr II.[52] This lopsided distribution of power made it quite impracticable to enlist the new division in a *coup d'état,* and no one knew that better than its commander. Soon promoted major general, Pfuhlstein cautiously vacillated between his former loyalty to Oster and his duty of obedience to Jodl. As a source of help to the conspirators he was a dead letter.[53]

Oster, who had no inkling of his old friend's mixed emotions, still believed that the Brandenburgers could be incorporated in his plans for a coup. Favourable reports were coming in from other military districts, almost all of which seemed to boast a few staunch unit commanders who were ready to take part. Only a few weeks elapsed before General Olbricht was able to give Schlabrendorff, whom Tresckow had again sent to Berlin as his courier, the vital message: "We are ready."[54]

And all this—the eleventh-hour rescue of the Fatherland by a *coup d'état*—was now endangered by the racketeer and speculator in German officer's uniform who languished in the RSHA's private jail and might easily prove the conspirators' undoing. It would be impossible to overestimate the gloom that must have descended on Oster at this stage. He had repeatedly cautioned his friends against Schmidhuber's business dealings and advised the Dohnanyis not to become too closely involved with him.[55]

But Dohnanyi and his wife had paid no heed. Their relations with the Bavarian brewery owner and honorary Portuguese consul had grown steadily closer over the years. Christine von Dohnanyi was fascinated by the dark-haired Bavarian, for whom—as she once confessed to Müller—she had a "soft spot."[56] Besides, Schmidhuber contrived to retain the Dohnanyis' friendship by doing them a variety of favours. His suitcase was always stuffed with presents when he stayed at their home on his visits to Berlin.[57] Consul Schmidhuber's gifts were legendary. There was hardly an officer at Abwehrstelle Munich who had not sampled his particular brand of generosity, and many members of the Tirpitz-Ufer staff valued his multifarious connections.

Oster had never quite known what prompted him to keep this glamorous anti-Nazi at arm's length. Whether it was a prejudiced Prussian disinclination to accept a Bavarian separatist and Salazar supporter as a full member of the resistance, or whether his soldierly sense of integrity was offended by a part-time officer's shady commercial transactions, Oster had never overcome his mistrust of the man.

He had not, therefore, been surprised to learn that Schmidhuber was implicated in a currency racket. All that took him aback was the extent of the scandal, for he had never imagined that even a racketeer like Schmidhuber could be quite as lax in his dealings. And it was the sheer scale of Schmidhuber's operations that threatened Oster and Canaris with ruin unless they found a way out of the morass.

The affair had begun, innocuously enough, with a report submitted to the head of the Customs Investigation Bureau in Prague, Regierungsrat Johannes Wapenhensch, at Whitsun 1942. One of his officers had heard that a substantial sum of U.S. dollars was to be offered for sale at one of Prague's two main-line stations in the next few days.[58] Although Wapenhensch doubted the accuracy of this report he sent his men to the station in question. They returned within a few hours accompanied by a black-marketeer named David who identified himself as the chief clerk of a large firm in Prague.[59]

David had been arrested while trying to sell $10,000 to a Czech at an exorbitant rate of exchange. His briefcase was found to contain, in addition to U.S. dollars, several envelopes full of precious stones. These envelopes bore two names: Schmidhuber and Ickrath.[60] David explained that Major Schmidhuber and Captain Ickrath were officers attached to Abwehrstelle Munich and that he had been trying to sell the gems and currency on their behalf. He added that he had previously undertaken trips abroad for both officers, to Switzerland among other places.[61]

Wapenhensch found David's story so farfetched that he half suspected the Czech of being an enemy agent. He notified Abwehrstelle Prague but was advised by an officer there to get in touch with the Gestapo.[62] Having questioned the black-marketeer, Stapoleitstelle Prague decided after a brief investigation that Wapenhensch's suspicions of espionage were unfounded.[63] That left the Regierungsrat no choice but to telephone Abwehrstelle Munich and satisfy himself that two of its officers were named Schmidhuber and Ickrath.

The head of the Abwehrstelle, Lieutenant Colonel Nikolaus Ficht, confirmed that Schmidhuber and Ickrath were Air Force officers attached to his department. Both worked for I/Luft, the Luftwaffe subsection of Abwehrabteilung I.[64] However, Ficht was so sparing with his information that Wapenhensch still gained no real idea of the peculiar links between two Air Force officers, Abwehrstelle Munich and a Czech currency racketeer.

In civilian life Heinz Ickrath was secretary at the Portuguese Consulate in Munich and, thus, an employee of Consul Schmidhuber. Their relationship at the Abwehrstelle was reversed. Ickrath was the boss there, being head of Referat I/Luft. Schmidhuber was only an assistant and, consequently, Ickrath's subordinate,[65] though he did not have to take his secretary's official status too seriously because his own links with the Abwehrstelle were extremely loose. After serving there as a captain from 1939 to 1941, Schmidhuber had been released from active military service and simultaneously designated "uk" [*unabkömmlich*—indispensable] so that, as Ficht put it, he could "pursue his civilian occupation on the one hand and, on the other, work for the Abwehrstelle without any external connection."[66] However, the prospect of becoming a major had inspired Schmidhuber to re-enlist at the beginning of 1942 and perform occasional duties at the Abwehrstelle.[67] Ficht paid little attention to his subordinate, especially as he was reputed to take all his orders from Berlin.

Though scanty, Ficht's information provided Wapenhensch with sufficient grounds for summoning Ickrath and Schmidhuber to Prague.[68] There Schmidhuber spun him a colourful yarn. The cash and jewels found on David were part of an ultrasecret deal through which a Czech woman resident in Switzerland, who enjoyed good relations with the British secret service, was to be recruited by the Abwehr. She had agreed to supply the Germans with information provided the Abwehr helped her to realize her remaining assets in the Reich Protectorate of Bohemia and Moravia. David's money had come from the Abwehr and was earmarked for the woman in question.[69] Schmidhuber used this story to back up the demand which he now submitted on the Abwehr's behalf, to wit, that David and the cash be released forthwith because there were vital Abwehr interests at stake.[70]

Wapenhensch now yielded to another mistaken impulse because he read more into Schmidhuber's allegations than they implied. Unable to account for David's black market activities in any other way, the customs investigator suspected that he had been using Abwehr funds to carry on a lucrative sideline of his own. Whatever the truth, he was not prepared to release David or the money. To him the case constituted a clear infringement of currency regulations, and he proposed to act accordingly.[71]

Wapenhensch's stubborn refusal evoked a sudden change in Schmidhuber's story. Having just represented David as a vital cog in the Abwehr machine, the major now insinuated that he might be working for the other side. Wapenhensch leapt at this abrupt confirmation of his original theory and opined that it should be possible to establish the truth because David often travelled to Switzerland and withdrew money from a certain bank account there.[72]

Schmidhuber promptly volunteered to make inquiries at the Swiss end. A few days later he returned to Prague with tidings of success. The Swiss bank account, he said, belonged to the British secret service and there was no doubt that David had drawn on it quite recently.[73] Wapenhensch felt inclined to believe this story, "being still unconvinced that Schmidhuber was the brains behind this currency business."[74] He at once confronted David, who was still on remand, with Schmidhuber's report.

Now that he had been branded a British agent, David quickly dropped his guard. "My neck's at stake now," he declared, "—now I'll have to come clean. What Herr Schmidhuber has told you isn't true."[75] He went on to relate that he had been helping Schmidhuber and Ickrath with their currency transactions for a long time. They had also built up a substantial trade in smuggled goods, mainly paintings and precious stones. Schmidhuber did not confine his activities to German territory but operated abroad as well. He had bought up large quantities of merchandise in Slovakia, for example, and smuggled them across the border. The Slovak authorities could supply further details because Schmidhuber had been in trouble with them.[76]

Wapenhensch travelled to Bratislava and visited the investigation department of the Slovak Finance Ministry, where he turned up some files relating principally to an agent employed by Abwehrstelle Vienna, a Hungarian ex-major whom the Slovak police had arrested for illegal currency deals. The ex-major had admitted transporting substantial amounts of foreign currency from Schmidhuber to a man named David in Prague. He further stated that David handled most of these transactions on Schmidhuber's behalf.[77] Back in Prague, Wapenhensch showed the Slovak findings to David, "who not only confirmed but amplified them."[78]

The Regierungsrat now felt convinced that he was on to "one of the biggest smuggling and currency cases in my career."[79] In view of Schmidhuber's position in the military intelligence service, however, the affair struck him as so delicate that he confided in his immediate superior, the president of the Higher Fiscal Board in Prague, who referred him to the Reich Ministry of Finance. Wapenhensch submitted his report, but the only advice the Finance Ministry authorities could give him was to approach Amt Ausland/Abwehr direct—preferably its legal section.[80] Wapenhensch duly went to the Tirpitz-Ufer.

At Abwehr headquarters he came up against the ZR group [Zentralabteilung, Rechtswesen—Central Section, Legal Matters], where Oster's and Dohnanyi's keenest opponents worked. Abwehr personnel rated the ZR a staunch Nazi stronghold, and it can have been no coincidence that its head, Ministerialrat Dr. Herzlieb, was also a member of the notorious Volksgerichtshof [People's Court].[81] Besides, many ZR experts had a personal score to settle with Oster's crony, ex-Reichsgerichtsrat von Dohnanyi, who had all too often been instructed by Canaris to check the validity of their legal opinions—sometimes with adverse results.[82]

It was also known in the ZR that Schmidhuber was a personal friend of the Dohnanyis' and a frequent visitor to Oster's office, so Wapenhensch received ready encouragement in his efforts to bring the racketeer to book. Needless to say, he was also advised on which official channel to explore. The ZR men told him to consult the Reichskriegsanwaltschaft [Judge Advocates' Bench], which would take the matter further.[83] Wapenhensch did so and received a definite answer. Since Schmidhuber and Ickrath were Luftwaffe officers attached to Abwehrstelle Munich, their case must first be heard by the Feldgericht [Field Court-Martial] of Luftgau [Air Force District] VII (Munich).[84]

Canaris and Oster still had no suspicion of what was brewing against Schmidhuber. They would have been taken completely by surprise if Wapenhensch had not made a blunder. Instead of going straight to Munich—it was now September 1942—and informing the local Luftwaffe court, he returned to Prague to complete his documentation. Back in Prague it occurred to him that he was wasting time, so he decided to effect the two men's arrest from the Prague end.[85]

But Wapenhensch had little experience of military authorities and no idea who was ultimately responsible for the detention of armed forces personnel. Then he remembered that a former colleague and customs officer named Karl Süss was stationed at Abwehrstelle Munich. Wapenhensch telephoned Süss and asked him to have the currency smugglers arrested.[86] He could not have picked a more unsuitable ally. Captain Süss, who headed Referat IIIF, was in sympathy with the political endeavours of Schmidhuber and his friends.

Süss informed Wapenhensch that he could not arrest Schmidhuber because he had not been empowered to do so by a military authority. Moreover, he was only a captain whereas Schmidhuber was a major.[87]

As soon as Wapenhensch had rung off Süss alerted Schmidhuber and Ickrath and their friend "Joe the Ox," Lieutenant Josef Müller. The word was quickly passed to Dohnanyi, who informed Oster and Canaris.[88] Schmidhuber's friends at Abwehr headquarters realized that an avalanche was bearing down on them. Speed was essential. Wapenhensch would be in Munich in a few days' time, and that portended the start of an investigation conducted with all the relentless punctilio of which German military justice was capable.

But Schmidhuber would never withstand such pressure. Christine von Dohnanyi had once described him as "a good-natured and entertaining man, but weak,"[89] and it was just these characteristics which led Oster and his circle to fear that Schmidhuber presented a grave threat. A weak accomplice could all too easily become a dangerous one. Once he fell into the hands of interrogators loyal to the regime, the Abwehr's anti-Nazis would be at risk from their generous but garrulous confederate.

Canaris had just as much reason to fear the major's loquacity. Although he had not been party to Oster's treason in May 1940, Schmidhuber was well aware of his role in the coup d'état discussions of 1939–40. What was to be done? Schmidhuber himself had a simple solution: the Abwehr authorities must certify that he had been acting on official instructions.

Canaris would not hear of this, [90] and his refusal confronted Oster's friends with the gravest moral dilemma that could possibly have afflicted any opponents of Nazi immorality. Could one man be permitted to endanger the chances of German salvation and imperil the lives of those who were trying to release their country from the bonds of barbarism? One lone individual, and not an especially virtuous one, was threatening a cause for which German patriots were risking disgrace, imprisonment, torture and execution. The most obvious and tempting solution was to silence him for good.

A proposal that Schmidhuber should be eliminated before he could betray them was, in fact, discussed by Canaris, Oster and Dohnanyi.[91] Schmidhuber claimed after the war that three attempts had been made on his life,[92] but Dohnanyi opposed the idea of murder and the melodramatic scheme was dropped.[93] The trio eventually decided on a rather less crude solution. Schmidhuber would be persuaded to go to Italy and remain there until the storm blew over. Ickrath was also to leave Munich and retire to the Wörthersee.[94] Meanwhile, Canaris would try to head the inquiry off.

Schmidhuber agreed, but without enthusiasm. He asked Ficht for special leave of absence, pleading important business in Italy, and was granted it on condition that he stayed away no longer than two to three weeks. The major and his wife set off for Merano, where they went to ground in a small hotel.[95] Ickrath made himself scarce too. This was the moment for which Süss and Müller had been waiting. As soon as Schmidhuber was out of the way they opened his safe in search of tell-tale clues.[96]

"To begin with," Süss recalled, "I myself proceeded to remove all incriminating evidence from the files. However, I soon realized that my knowledge of the circumstances was insufficient for me to expurgate them on my own. I therefore made them available to Dr. Müller, who dealt with them in my office by destroying or removing any incriminating material."[97] Müller not only eliminated every document refer-ring to the Oster group's activities abroad but destroyed bills, receipts and memorandums. He also hid a briefcase which Schmidhuber himself had handed over. Müller testified: "This briefcase contained lists of the presents he had given to various officers, and he had kept these notes with scrupulous attention to detail."[98]

But Schmidhuber's disappearance could not remain a secret for long. Wapenhensch turned up in Munich, furious that his quarry had escaped, and again demanded the major's arrest. Since Schmidhuber was also wanted for questioning by the Feldgericht of Luftgau VII, Ficht recalled him from Merano.[99] Schmidhuber failed to appear, so Ficht told Lieutenant Müller to go to Merano and induce him to re-turn.[100]

Müller reversed the object of his mission because the Oster group had no desire to see Schmidhuber back on German soil. He met the major in Merano and implored him to stay away at all costs because "his life was in danger."[101] Schmidhuber angrily retorted that he would never return to Germany except as the high commissioner of a British occupying force.[102] Müller then said it would be best for all concerned if Schmidhuber went to Portugal. He would not be safe for long, even in Italy, but Müller promised before leaving to warn him if his Italian refuge was threatened. Meanwhile, he was not to worry.[103]

Wapenhensch gave Müller no chance to keep his promise. He urged Ficht to take out warrants for the arrest of his two missing officers. On application from Ficht, the Feldgericht ordered Major Schmidhuber to be detained in Merano as a suspected deserter and brought to Mu-nich.[104] Ickrath, who surrendered voluntarily, returned to the Abwehr-stelle and was arrested there on October 13.[105] Schmidhuber's de-tention proved more difficult because Italy was, after all, a foreign country. Wapenhensch needed someone with enough military authority to persuade the Italians to extradite him.

He found the person he needed in Captain Brede, head of Abwehr I's Luftwaffe subsection and Schmidhuber's official superior at Abwehr headquarters. Once again, Schmidhuber's friends at the Tirpitz-Ufer failed to detect a vital move by the other side. Without informing Canaris and Oster, Brede and Wapenhensch travelled to the South Tyrol and prevailed on the Italians to extradite Schmidhuber.[106] On October 31, 1942, the Italian police arrested him in Merano, and two days later he was handed over to Brede and Wapenhensch at Bolzano.[107] Wapenhensch handcuffed him and delivered him to the Wehrmacht prison in Munich.

Oster and his friends realized too late that their efforts to keep Schmidhuber out of the hands of the military authorities had failed. Canaris made a last attempt to save the situation. He ordered Ficht to ensure that nobody questioned Schmidhuber until a representative from Abwehr headquarters arrived in Munich. He then dispatched Oberkriegsgerichtsrat [Senior Court-Martial Counsel] Walter Schoen, ZR's expert on security ordinances, to Munich with a vaguely worded brief "to uphold OKW interests" and ensure that Schmidhuber's interrogation was confined to "purely military matters."[108]

The Abwehr chief further decreed that Ficht should be represented at his interrogation by Süss, and it was made abundantly clear to both Ficht and Wapenhensch how little Admiral Canaris liked the whole inquiry.[109] Ficht's telephone never stopped ringing. He received repeated calls from senior Abwehr officers in Berlin instructing him "to convey [to Wapenhensch] that a continuance of the inquiries would be highly undesirable."[110] It was more than once suggested, point-blank, that Wapenhensch should simply drop the proceedings. Wapenhensch: "I refused to discontinue my investigations."[111]

His interrogation of Schmidhuber and Ickrath provoked an immediate clash with Canaris's watchdogs. Süss exasperated his former colleague by trying to block any questions about currency offences committed by other Abwehr officers. As he himself recalled: "Wapenhensch expressly asked me to modify my approach to these proceedings or risk my own neck."[112] "Differences" also arose between Wapenhensch and Schoen, but the former claims that these "were later resolved."[113]

Intervention by the Admiral's representatives proved unavailing. Schmidhuber, who thought Müller had betrayed him, began to represent his currency deals as matters of official policy. Testifying before the presiding judge of the Air Force court, Oberfeldrichter Karl Sauermann, he claimed that he had only traded in currency on the Abwehr's behalf and acted in accordance with top-level policy decisions known to Sonderführer von Dohnanyi and Lieutenant Müller.[114] This sounded like a final warning to the Oster group that he would betray Oster's and Dohnanyi's anti-Nazi activities unless they backed him up.

At this moment of extreme danger Oster's friends hit upon an idea which promised salvation but was fraught with disastrous consequences. On the principle that Schmidhuber's credibility must be destroyed before he could blurt out any resistance secrets, they hinted that he was a British agent.

Ficht was instructed to persuade the Feldgericht that Schmidhuber was under suspicion of treason [Hochverrat and Landesverrat—v. Glossary].[115] Judge Sauermann later recalled "the Abwehrstelle's charge that Schmidhuber was suspected of defecting to the enemy. There was talk of foreign passports which he had secretly procured without the Abwehrstelle's knowledge, and also of espionage links with the enemy against Germany."[116] The most important piece of circumstantial evidence was Müller's statement that Major Schmidhuber had told him in Merano that he would only return to Germany as the high commissioner of a British occupying force.[117]

The effect of this desperate diversionary manoeuvre was to transform a currency racket into a far more explosive case of treason. Feeling unequal to this, the Feldgericht relinquished it to the very body which Canaris and the Abwehr authorities had been at pains to avoid—the Geheime Staatspolizei. At the end of November 1942 Schmidhuber and Ickrath were transferred to the cells of the RSHA.[118]

Anxious to discover how events could have taken this catastrophic turn, Canaris hurried to Munich and sent for Müller.[119] The Admiral's first act when Müller entered his room at the Hotel Regina was to sound the walls for hidden microphones and drape his overcoat over the telephone. "I could see that he was pretty near the end of his tether," recalled Müller.[120] Almost inquisitorially, Canaris demanded to know what Müller had told Judge Sauermann. His old mistrust of Oster's men came to the surface again. "But Müller," he protested, "what Oster and Dohnanyi are doing is treasonable—surely you can see that?" Müller stared at him "rather bemusedly" before replying.[121] "Admiral," he said, "please don't start talking about treason or quoting the penal code. You must be aware that our glorious Führer has succeeded in putting Hochverrat and Landesverrat on a par. It doesn't really matter *why* we're in this mess."[122]

Müller's belligerent retort was hardly calculated to pacify an opponent of military betrayal in all its forms. Canaris sensed that he and the Abwehr were in for a rough ride. Confined in the cellars at Prinz-Albrecht-Strasse was someone capable of testifying to Oster's treason in 1940, and the Gestapo could be relied on to make a meal of the case. Sure enough, they tackled it with customary vigour because it afforded their first real opportunity to probe the secrets of the Abwehr. The fact that Schmidhuber knew something about the activities of Abwehr officers in Rome was particularly gratifying to them because relations between the Abwehr and the Vatican had long ago excited the suspicions of Referat 6 of the Abwehrpolizei (RSHA-Gruppe IVE).

The order to keep a close watch on all Abwehr activities within the Vatican's orbit had originally come from Heydrich. In 1940 the RSHA had formed a suspicion that Müller had betrayed the timing of the Western offensive by way of his Vatican contacts. Although the "Schwarze Kapelle" [Black Orchestra] case (the Gestapo's code name for the betrayal of this date) had never been solved, Müller still figured in the list of suspects.[123] In 1941–42 the Gestapo's attention was drawn to another Abwehr officer from whom secret military information had been stolen during a visit to Rome, manifestly for transmission to the British secret service. Inquiries revealed that these documents had not (as the officer claimed) been released for disinformation purposes by the Wehrmacht authorities.[124] Oberregierungsrat Count Peter Yorck von Wartenburg, who belonged to a department close to the Abwehr, was also placed under Gestapo surveillance shortly afterwards because he had likewise endeavoured to forge links with the Vatican.[125]

For years the Gestapo had wondered what the Abwehr was up to in Rome. Now they were holding a man who had been involved in Abwehr negotiations there and was ready to divulge at least part of what he knew. Denounced by his own confederates as a spy and traitor, Schmidhuber could see only one chance of saving his skin. He decided to be communicative.

He was first questioned on January 10, 1943, by Kriminalkommissar Walter Möller of Referat 6. "In the course of his interrogation," Möller recalled, "Schmidhuber made allegations about the existence of intelligence links between the OKW's Abwehrabteilung and the Vatican. I recorded these things at the time and, since the matter struck me as exceedingly delicate, handled their dictation myself . . . At all events, we were confirmed in our supposition that links with the enemy ND [intelligence service] existed in Abwehr quarters."[126]

The Gestapo authorities attached so much importance to Schmidhuber's revelations that they assigned a particularly expert investigator to question their talkative prisoner. Into the arena stepped one of the RSHA's shrewdest and most intelligent officers—one who could be so humane despite his tough and occasionally brutal manner that many of his victims preserved agreeable memories of him. Christine von Dohnanyi described him as "at heart, a man of strong left-wing leanings who only pursued so-called 'reactionaries' with genuine detestation,"[127] and even Müller did not object to helping such a "decent person" after the war.[128] Franz Xaver Sonderegger was and remained a complex and inscrutable figure. His personal particulars were as follows: born in 1898, son of a Palatinate basket maker, compositor, World War I soldier, assistant customs officer; joined the police, served with the Sittenpolizei before transferring to the Politische Polizei in 1930, joined the Nazi Party and left it again; employed from September 1939 onwards as a Kriminalsekretär and SS-Untersturmführer [second lieutenant] in Referat 6 of Amtsgruppe IVE at the RSHA.[129]

Even his preliminary exchanges with Schmidhuber convinced Sonderegger that he was on the brink of a political sensation. The prisoner "hinted at the existence of a treasonable association backed by General Beck, Goerdeler, Dohnanyi and other persons."[130] He also claimed to have heard that a "generals' clique" was pledged to overthrow the National Socialist regime and end the war. Peace talks had been conducted with the British through contacts in the Vatican. Another channel of communication with the Allies ran via the Protestant Churches in Switzerland and Sweden. This contact was maintained by Pastor Dietrich Bonhoeffer, who had been exempted from normal military service by Abwehr opponents of the regime so that he could work exclusively for them.[131]

Schmidhuber claimed that he had financially supported these foreign activities in ignorance of their precise nature. To the extent that this had involved illegal currency transactions he had only acted on orders from the Abwehr, which had always assumed full responsibility for them.

He cited an instance of this. Dohnanyi, he said, had secured immunity from National Socialist racial laws for a number of Jewish acquaintances, some of whom were friends of Canaris's, by enrolling them in the Abwehr and sending them to Switzerland, ostensibly for subsequent infiltration into the United States. The operation had at first involved seven persons, hence its code name, "V7," but the figure later rose to twelve. Dohnanyi had procured the necessary exit permits by negotiating with the RSHA. He, Schmidhuber, had been instructed by Dohnanyi to smuggle $100,000 into Switzerland and deliver this sum to the members of "V7." Dohnanyi had also asked him to deliver jewels worth RM20,000 to a personal friend in the party.[132]

The more Schmidhuber said, the more clearly Sonderegger could discern the complex outlines of a plot against the National Socialist regime. When the policeman asked for names, however, Schmidhuber became evasive. He was only prepared to name persons who could furnish information about others.[133] He was even vague about Müller, whose failure to warn him had bred a grudge which was to fill him with rancour for the rest of his days. He testified that he had no idea whether Müller had tried to get in touch with the British through the Vatican in 1940—nor, being unwilling to incriminate himself, had he attempted to find out.[134]

Sonderegger reported Schmidhuber as stating that Müller was "undoubtedly a patriotic man, but one who took a pessimistic view of the military situation." All he would say about Dohnanyi was that he supposed him to be "an old-fashioned conservative who nursed a particular regret for the destruction of almost every civilized value on the European continent and regarded the future course of hostilities in a very gloomy light." On the other hand, Dohnanyi had also said that "it must, after all, be realized that the collapse of the fighting fronts would entail the collapse of the political regime, so consideration should be given to a stand-by government that can bring the fronts to a standstill."[135]

Schmidhuber had already mentioned so many names that Sonderegger decided to act. "These names," he said, "had occurred so often that I sent for every available file."[136] Taken in conjunction with Schmidhuber's statements, the contents of these dossiers seemed significant enough for Sonderegger to go to Gestapo chief Müller and recommend a surprise raid on Abwehr headquarters. Early in February 1943 he drafted a report which expressed the view that the real brains behind the whole conspiracy was none other than Canaris.[137]

But that was when Sonderegger got the shock of his life. His report, which "Gestapo" Müller had forwarded to the Reichsführer-SS, came back adorned with the following note in Himmler's copybook handwriting: "Kindly leave Canaris alone!"[138] Sonderegger learned that he had instructed the Geheimes Staatspolizeiamt to drop the Schmidhuber case and return the relevant files to the Wehrmacht's legal branch.[139] The head of Sonderegger's Referat, Kriminalrat Schmitz, impressed on him that the Gestapo was entitled to act only as an adjunct of the Wehrmachtjustiz [Armed Forces Judicature], not as an authority in its own right; otherwise there was "a danger that Canaris would, under such circumstances, resign his post, and that must be prevented."[140]

The puzzled policeman consulted colleagues in other departments on how to interpret Himmler's directive. Himmler was always covering up for the Admiral, they told him—it was always the same old story.

Sonderegger asked for some examples and got them. 1. In 1942 an Abwehr officer named Nikolaus von Halem had been arrested for plotting an attempt on Hitler's life. He admitted that Dohnanyi had given him RM12,000 to help recruit an assassin. Halem's Gestapo interrogators even claimed to have formed the impression that his real employer was Canaris. Instead of authorizing proceedings against the Admiral, the Reichsführer-SS not only imposed a ban on further inquiries but decreed that all references to him and the Abwehr should be struck from the record.[141] 2. Ex-Legation Secretary Mumm von Schwarzenstein had likewise planned an attempt on Hitler's life and been betrayed by a subordinate. Schwarzenstein was an Abwehr agent, so Himmler forbade any investigations to be pursued at Amt Ausland/Abwehr.[142] 3. A Landgerichtsrat [district court counsel] named Strassmann had organized a resistance group at Dohnanyi's behest and been detained by the Gestapo. In his case, too, a ban was imposed on inquiries directed against the Abwehr. Sonderegger's conclusion: "My investigations disclosed that the relevant orders had in each case come from Himmler."[143]

By this time, readers accustomed to the clear-cut picture presented by so many postwar historians must have stopped in their tracks. Himmler protecting Canaris? According to Gisevius and Abshagen, Hoffmann and Shirer, Bracher and Brissaud, the grand assault on the Tirpitz-Ufer was the product of a "diabolical Gestapo plot," a manoeuvre on the part of SD chief Schellenberg, who wanted to absorb the Abwehr, and a cold-blooded *coup de main* by Himmler.[144] The truth is very different: Himmler was indeed protecting Canaris.

How are we to account for this strange attachment, which conflicts with all that historians have to say on the subject? Quite simply, Himmler had never shaken off the fascination which Canaris always held for him. He considered him a past master of espionage whom the Reich could ill afford to lose while the war lasted. Himmler was wedded to Canaris by an almost grotesque overestimate of his professional ability, even though—as with the Jewish agents in January 1942—he seized any opportunity to get in a dig at the Admiral because, in company with many others, he resented and overrated his influence on Hitler.

Like his subordinates, Himmler naturally wanted to smash the Abwehr machine and replace it with a new and all-embracing Nazi secret service. For all his ideological delusions, however, he preserved a realistic view of the adventurers, fanatics and dilettantes who played the secret service game in snappy SS uniforms. Himmler was prepared to tolerate the Abwehr for as long as the SD lacked qualified personnel because nothing frightened him more than Hitler's waspish and derisive strictures on his own intelligence service.

Besides, the rapidly deteriorating military situation had opened up an area of common ground between the Abwehr chief, who was shocked at the regime's wholesale crimes, and the leading perpetrator of those very same iniquities. Ever since the failure of the German offensive in Russia in autumn 1942, Himmler had flirted with the idea that he might be destined to make peace with the Allies in Hitler's stead.[145] Although Canaris and Himmler were poles apart, both humanly and in terms of tradition, their analyses of the situation largely coincided. Germany had lost the war and Hitler was the gravest impediment to an accommodation with the enemy. Only his removal could save the country—no other basis for negotiation was conceivable. Schellenberg, the slippery opportunist, kept dinning this into Himmler, but the SS chief wavered, torn between a realistic acceptance of the facts and many years of subservience to Hitler.

It now seems almost incomprehensible that genuine members of the resistance could have seen anything more in Himmler than a sinister personification of the greatest crime in German history. Abroad—in the Spanish Foreign Office, for example, or the British secret service—he was long regarded as the only German capable of overthrowing Hitler and halting the war. There were those in the German resistance movement who also thought they could briefly support the SS chief against Hitler—at least until the latter's downfall. One of them was Dohnanyi, who kept a line open to Himmler and, more especially, to the chief of his personal staff, Karl Wolff.[146]

Canaris, too, believed that the resistance movement's long history of failure left it with no alternative but to enlist Himmler's help in removing the Führer. Emissaries dispatched to the Allies by Canaris and Schellenberg were already engaged, separately but in concert, on preparations for Hitler's overthrow, and it was already thought that the leaders of the internal opposition should at some stage present Himmler with their plans for the "post-Hitler period." The SD even employed certain Abwehr agents like Carl Langbehn or Prince Hohenlohe in its own attempts to start a dialogue with the Allies.[147]

However deep the gulf between Canaris and Himmler remained, the Reichsführer-SS could have had no interest in destroying the Abwehr in February 1943, still less in a full-scale investigation that would expose secret contacts between the Abwehr and the Allies from which he himself stood to profit. But Himmler's notions of power were too crude for him to leave the Abwehr totally unscathed. Still uncertain whether to take Schellenberg's advice, he decided to keep all his options open. He may have reasoned that it would be advisable to preserve the Admiral's unofficial partnership but retain a means of absorbing the Abwehr into his SS empire when circumstances changed. In practical terms, this meant passing the Schmidhuber case to the Wehrmachtjustiz without altogether losing track of it. The prisoners were transferred to the armed forces remand centre in Berlin and the Schmidhuber-Ickrath file returned to the Feldgericht of Luftgau VII—doubtless with a heavy hint to the effect that RSHA officials would be ready to assist the military authorities in dealing with the case.[148] The file did not remain in Munich for long. That same month, February 1943, it was forwarded to Oberstkriegsgerichtsrat Dr. Manfred Roeder, presiding judge of the Feldluftwaffengericht z.b.V. [Special Duties Air Force Court-Martial] in Berlin, which only handled cases of particular importance.[149]

Having skimmed through the sixty-page file to see if officers belonging to other armed services were involved (which they were), Roeder passed it to his superior, Ministerialdirektor Baron Christian von Hammerstein, head of the Legal Division of the Luftwaffe High Command.[150] Hammerstein, who was alarmed by what he read, ordered

Roeder to get in touch at once with the head of the OKW Legal Division, Generaloberstabsrichter [Judge Advocate General] Rudolf Lehmann, and discuss what action to take.[151]

On March 5 Roeder met Lehmann in Paris. Lehmann took fright when he heard what was afoot. Although he regarded "all the accusations as nonsense," he recognized their explosive nature and the spectacular threat they posed to the Wehrmacht. He was also quick to realize that Canaris and the Abwehr's efficiency, if not its very existence, would be jeopardized unless the Wehrmacht legal authorities managed to conduct an independent investigation of Schmidhuber and the men behind him. He could not dismiss the possibility that Schmidhuber's testimony had been manipulated by the Gestapo for subsequent use in evidence against the armed forces.[152]

"The whole affair," he wrote after the war, "could have been the jumping-off point for a police assault on the military intelligence system. If the Abwehr had collapsed under such an accusation its functions would automatically have been taken over by the Geheime Staatspolizei. We should then have had the SD and the Geheime Staatspolizei plumb in the middle of the armed forces."[153] The Gestapo was still forbidden to poach on military preserves. The essential thing, therefore, was to take over the Schmidhuber-Ickrath case without delay and claim sole jurisdiction on behalf of the Reichskriegsgericht (RKG), or supreme military tribunal.

Lehmann returned to Berlin to work on Keitel. The OKW chief was "genuinely scared to death" when Lehmann briefed him on March 8.[154] Lehmann goes on: "But he too regarded the idea that Canaris might be maintaining prohibited contacts with the enemy as altogether absurd. Although he did not trust General Oster overmuch, he utterly rejected the idea that a general in the Abwehr might be pursuing such plans." He nonetheless insisted that the charges should be swiftly and thoroughly investigated, and concurred with Lehmann's view that "every effort must be made to deal with the case inside the Wehrmacht judicial framework."[155]

At this stage the Wehrmacht authorities still had it in their power to prevent the RSHA from interfering in a case which might so easily become an investigation of Canaris and the Abwehr. Just as Keitel's lack of perception had contributed to the Blomberg-Fritsch crisis in 1938, however, so his spinelessness on this occasion frustrated Lehmann's efforts and opened a chink in the Wehrmacht's armour which left the Gestapo free to meddle in Abwehr affairs whenever its masters chose.

When Lehmann asked Keitel to inform Hitler about the case and secure his consent to its being heard by the Reichskriegsgericht, the field marshal jibbed. Nothing would induce him to raise the matter with Hitler, who would, he said, be promptly informed about it by the other side.[156] The reason for Keitel's panic was that the RKG had often incurred the wrath of the Führer, who bore the senior judge advocates a grudge for clinging to vestiges of constitutional principle which the aiders and abettors of Nazi legal tyranny had long since eradicated from other sectors of the judicial system.

Mainly responsible for this were the professional lawyers who shared the bench with officer-judges and lent the RKG an independence which seemed well nigh sensational when viewed against the backcloth of Nazi totalitarianism. They had, for instance, opposed Hitler's wish to prefer charges against generals who had flouted his orders by withdrawing their troops from positions outside Moscow during the winter campaign of 1941–42.[157] The RKG's defiance of the party, Gestapo and Nazi judiciary became particularly noticeable when the professional lawyer's urge for independence coincided with the professional soldier's defence of Prusso-German military values. In such cases the court stuck to its constitutional guns. It was no wonder that the RKG judges' keenest foes included "Gestapo" Müller as well as Hitler.[158]

And this was the court whose claim to jurisdiction in the Schmidhuber case Keitel was expected to recommend to the Führer? Never one to grasp a nettle, the OKW chief advised Lehmann to adopt a course that would involve the RKG judges unobtrusively, as it were, and forestall any drastic reaction on the part of Hitler or the RSHA.[159] Lehmann thereupon consulted Dr. Alexander Kraell, president of the Second Chamber of the Reichskriegsgericht, who was due to take over the Reichskriegsanwaltschaft on April 1.[160]

Kraell was the most astute of those nationalistic and authoritarian military judges whose lingering constitutionalism and unbiased verdicts had so often aroused Hitler's ire. A former senior public prosecutor from Darmstadt, Kraell had been concerned with the military administration of justice since 1938. He was generally regarded as an erudite, courageous and tactically skilful lawyer—indeed, expert observers considered him one of the country's most distinguished judges.[161] Few people realized that his artful twists and turns were steadily sucking him into the conformist undertow and swamping the principles that really mattered to him.

Kraell's nimble mind went to work as soon as Lehmann confided in him. He quickly devised a seemingly perfect solution: "1. The matter must be investigated. 2. The Wehrmacht need not shrink from this investigation because a predictably favourable outcome will only reinforce its position. 3. The SD and Gestapo must be notified so as to rebut any charges of secretiveness."[162] The third point was vital. What did "notifying" the other side mean? Kraell proposed to bring in the RSHA in such a way that it did not feel left out but had no influence on the course of the inquiry. Lehmann supports this view: "There had to be a firm safeguard against the [RSHA] charge that we were investigating in our own interests and would try to cover everything up."[163]

This was a disastrous manoeuvre which occasioned precisely what Kraell and Lehmann had hoped to prevent—the intervention of the Gestapo. Even allowing for the two men's ignorance of Himmler's hands-off ukase, their plan was fundamentally misconceived. The RSHA had never laid any official claim to jurisdiction in the Schmidhuber-Ickrath case. The prisoners and their files had been returned to the Wehrmacht authorities. What else was this gambit but an act of conformist overanxiety and diffidence?

Even more disastrous was the next move devised by these two master strategists in their campaign to forestall an adverse reaction from the RSHA. Lehmann had the idea of entrusting the inquiry to someone who was in good odour with the RSHA but could be relied on to uphold the Wehrmacht's interests. The champion selected by Lehmann and Kraell was the man who had first reported the scandal, Oberstkriegsgerichtsrat [judge advocate of colonel's rank] Roeder. Born in 1900, Roeder was the son of a district court judge from Kiel. He had successively been a lieutenant in the 83rd Field Artillery Regiment during World War I, a student, a legal adviser, a farm manager and a student again. After a brief spell on the Berlin district court bench in 1934 he joined the military judiciary, since when he had rated as a protégé of Hermann Göring's and one of the toughest judge advocates in the Third Reich.[164] Ultraconservative but by no means a typical Nazi judge, Roeder considered his supreme purpose in life to be the relentless preservation of government authority, whether its emblem were the swastika or the red, white, and black banner of imperial Germany.

Roeder's harsh procedural methods, which were a frequent cause of complaint, had left a swathe of personal altercations, official protests and disciplinary proceedings in his wake. His grim reputation stemmed from the Rote Kapelle espionage hearings, in which he had appeared before the Reichskriegsgericht as chief investigator and prosecutor.[165] The accused and their associates had repeatedly and vehemently complained of his unfeeling and sarcastic attitude, so much so that even Kraell later pronounced Roeder "too cold and one-sided" and his manner "occasionally policemanlike."[166]

And yet, brusque as he was, Roeder endeared himself to subordinates by showing an almost touching interest in their welfare. He always put them first, and there could be no more steadfast upholder of the truth when it came to unearthing corruption and nepotism in high places. This he had demonstrated in 1941–42, when he and Kraell were members of an RKG commission appointed to investigate the mysterious suicide of "the Devil's General," Ernst Udet, head of Luftwaffe

Equipment.[167] He showed himself a resourceful investigator and an astute, perceptive and tenacious lawyer. Once he had picked up a trail, nothing could deter him from following it until he finally brought his quarry to bay.

Kraell was again in need of these detective qualities, hence his appointment of Roeder to head the inquiry into the "Fall Depositenkasse" [Sub-branch Case], as the proceedings had now been officially named after the Swiss bank account opened by Schmidhuber on behalf of Dohnanyi's "V7" Jews. On April 3 Roeder was seconded to the Reichskriegsgericht. The same day he called at the Reichskriegsanwaltschaft and repossessed himself of the Schmidhuber file, which had since found its way there.[168] Then he set to work.

Roeder was forced to conclude, after examining all the evidence, that he was on the track of a gigantic and treasonable conspiracy centred on no less a person than Admiral Canaris. The record of Schmidhuber's interrogation by Sonderegger contained an oblique reference to the Abwehr chief which intensified Roeder's existing suspicions. It concerned Sonderführer and Vice-Consul Hans Bernd Gisevius, who was ensconced in KO Switzerland and had also been in close touch with Schmidhuber.

According to Roeder's postwar version of the prisoner's statement, "Vice-Consul Gisevius had, at their most recent meeting in Switzerland only a few days earlier, poured out his heart to him, Schmidhuber, about the irresolute conduct of Admiral Canaris, who was now making trouble for him, Gisevius, although he should be looking out for himself. He had betrayed the [German] Voronezh offensive to the Russians. Oster, too, had informed the Dutch military attaché about the attack in the West, inclusive of Holland, prior to the said attack. Gisevius had been extremely angry with Canaris at the time."[169] Kraell likewise recalled Schmidhuber's testimony after the war and said that it "very gravely compromised" Canaris. "He was alleged to have betrayed German offensive plans to the enemy in three instances, to the best of my recollection, the last of them being the offensive in the Voronezh area."[170]

Roeder was in little doubt that the Abwehr authorities had engaged in treason [Landesverrat] and must be stopped before they could divulge anything more. The first step was to arrest those persons to whom Schmidhuber had alluded with particular frequency as partners in his activities. Roeder wasted no time. Still on April 3, he was empowered by the president of the Reichskriegsgericht to detain the suspects and search their offices.[171]

Roeder needed assistance for the raid he had in mind. Although it would have been usual to enlist the Geheime Feldpolizei in a case affecting the Wehrmacht, Roeder mistrusted the GFP because it was still partially controlled by Canaris. Having been accustomed to working with the Gestapo since the Rote Kapelle case, he called in the RSHA. The Reichssicherheitshauptamt was only too happy to oblige, even under the terms of Kraell's three-point programme. Sonderegger, Möller and Schmitz were placed at his disposal with instructions to act solely at the judge advocate's behest and not on their own initiative.[172]

Oster and his confederates were not unaware that the other side might launch a surprise attack at any moment. Kripo chief Nebe had warned them back in autumn 1942 that moves were afoot against Dohnanyi.[173] Guttenberg, Gehre, Moltke, Langbehn—all of them knew that Dohnanyi's correspondence and phone calls were being monitored and that he himself was being tailed in the street.[174] Nebe's warnings rose to such a pitch early in February 1943 that Dohnanyi recalled his brother-in-law, Bonhoeffer, when he had already departed for Munich on his way to Rome.[175]

Canaris was equally worried because he knew how careless Oster and his friends could be. In recent days he had redoubled his insistence on the removal of all telltale documents from Abwehr headquarters. Even on April 4 he asked Oster for an assurance that he had left no incriminating papers lying around in his office. The Abwehr chief had just received an admonitory phone call from Lehmann, who was perturbed by Roeder's feverish activity but doubted if he would make any move for the next few days.[176]

Although he reassured Canaris, Oster did not take an altogether serious view of these repeated warnings. In any case, the conspirators' attention was centred on other things. March had been a bitterly disappointing month for them. March 13 saw the failure of an attempt to kill Hitler on his return flight from Army Group Centre to the Führer's headquarters by smuggling a time bomb aboard his plane, and a second attempt during his visit to the Berlin Armoury on March 21 had also miscarried because he left the premises too soon.[177] The conspiracy still lacked a "trigger device," so new ways of assassinating Hitler had to be sought and found.

Oster was so engrossed in his preparations for a *coup d'état* that he barely discerned the dangers that threatened his work. Besides, he did not fear a surprise move by the Gestapo and could not conceive of one from any other quarter. The result was that, when the other side finally struck, he and his friends displayed an almost suicidal inability to cope.

Abwehr headquarters was invaded just before 10 A.M. on April 5, 1943. There was none of the commotion that might have been expected—no Gestapo flying squad, no thunder of feet or jingle of handcuffs. The enemy force, which made an unobtrusive entrance and proceeded through official channels, consisted of a short stocky man in Luftwaffe uniform and a civilian who studiously hugged the background. A few moments later Oberstkriegsgerichtsrat Roeder and Kriminalsekretär Sonderegger were shown into Canaris's office. Tersely, Roeder informed the Admiral that he had been empowered by the president of the Reichskriegsgericht to arrest Sonderführer von Dohnanyi and search his office. Dohnanyi, he explained, was strongly suspected of corruption, abuse of authority and numerous currency offences. It was also possible that he had engaged in treasonable activities. Roeder ended by requesting that an Abwehr officer should be present at the arrest.[178]

An outsider had proposed, with Gestapo help, to search the hallowed premises of the military intelligence service. It was a shocking and unparalleled moment in the Abwehr's history. Yet, far from protesting at such sacrilege or complaining to Keitel about this breach of precedent and security regulations, the Abwehr chief received Roeder's remarks in silence. All those present got a foretaste of the impotence and confusion into which Roeder's tactics were to plunge him.

Canaris rose heavily to his feet and told Roeder that he would witness the arrest and search himself. He accompanied Roeder and Sonderegger down one of the old building's narrow corridors and into Oster's office.[179] As soon as Oster heard that his principal subordinate was to be arrested, he barked, "Then kindly arrest me too, because Herr von Dohnanyi has done nothing I don't know about."[180] Canaris quickly shut him up and the four men trooped through the communicating door between Oster's office and Dohnanyi's.

Roeder formally arrested Dohnanyi and told him that he proposed to search the room for incriminating documents. He bore down on a green safe adorned with embossed scrolls and demanded the key, which Dohnanyi grudgingly produced after at first denying that he had it on him.[181] It now became obvious how ill prepared for this raid the conspirators were. Roeder removed file after file from the safe and deposited them on Dohnanyi's desk. They contained details of travelling expenses claimed by Oster's political informants, foreign currency forms, suggested code words for disguising secret missions abroad and reports on how Jewish fugitives had been smuggled out of the country.[182]

Dohnanyi stared with growing consternation at a folder inscribed "Z grau" [Z grey] which Roeder had just removed from the safe. He reached behind him and was in the process of extracting three sheets of paper from it when Roeder swung round and told him to replace them. Dohnanyi did so.[183] While Roeder was walking back to the safe, Dohnanyi glanced meaningfully at Oster and whispered, "Those papers, those papers!"[184] Roeder's indictment contained the following account of what happened next: "By arrangement between the accused [Oster and Dohnanyi], Major General Oster stood facing the chief investigator with his left hand behind his back, removed the said papers and concealed them beneath the jacket of his civilian suit. Having been observed by Kriminalsekretär Sonderegger, who was also present, and the chief investigator, he was promptly challenged and compelled to surrender the papers."[185]

Roeder asked Canaris to remove Major General Oster from the room at once. Canaris bowed to this demand and Oster withdrew.[186] Roeder then took a closer look at the three sheets of paper, which were covered with typescript. One of them was a memorandum alleging that military groups in Germany and certain elements in the Christian Churches were determined to help overthrow the National Socialist regime. The second document outlined the territorial structure of post-Hitler Germany, which was to be divided into a northern and a southern state.[187] Roeder found the third document particularly interesting. He read:

Copy!

For a considerable time now, a small circle of prominent clerics in the German Protestant Church have been debating how the Protestant Church can help in this war to bring about a just and lasting peace and construct a social system based on Christian foundations. It is intended to draw up a series of programmatic points and, on the basis of these programmatic principles, to produce some universally intelligible explanatory leaflets which can be made available to the public when the occasion arises. Work is already far advanced. It is possible that the Pope enunciated his basic peace aims in his last two Christmas messages and that the British and American (as well as the Dutch, Norwegian and French) Protestant Churches are already devoting very keen consideration to these same questions. Since it would carry great weight if all Christian Churches adopted a concerted approach to the problems of arranging a peace when the time came, and since —so far as one can tell at this stage—a consensus on all essential points should be possible to obtain, it appears extremely important and desirable that a German Protestant cleric should be enabled, not only to hold discussions on the subject with representatives of the Catholic Church in Rome, but also to familiarize himself with the relevant activities of the worldwide Protestant Churches in Geneva or Stockholm.[188]

Roeder did not have to be exceptionally acute to realize what had fallen into his hands. He had found what the Gestapo had been seeking in vain for years—evidence of the Oster group's subversive activities—and must have felt profoundly satisfied that the Gestapo's myrmidons were even at that moment rounding up Oster's principal friends and associates outside Abwehr headquarters as well. They picked up Dohnanyi's wife at Sakrow, on the outskirts of Berlin, and arrested Pastor Bonhoeffer soon afterwards. Müller and his wife were detained in Munich, to be joined a few days later by Müller's secretary and Lieutenant Breidbach, once a junior in his law firm.[189]

An even worse feature of the situation was that Oster, the resistance movement's business manager, could no longer take part in the conspiracy because he had compromised himself by his behaviour at the time of Dohnanyi's arrest. Roeder lodged a complaint of negligence against the Admiral's chief of staff with Keitel, who washed his hands of the suspect general. Canaris seems to have made equally little attempt to save his friend of so many years' standing. On April 15, 1943, he dismissed Oster from the Abwehr (Colonel Jacobsen, a group head in Abwehr III, took over the Central Section) and "formally instructed us to avoid all contact with Oster," as Pfuhlstein noted at a staff conference in the Admiral's office.[190] Oster was transferred to the so-called Officers' Reserve of the Wehrmacht. He was still permitted to wear uniform but lived in virtual captivity at his Berlin and Dresden homes because he had now been officially entered in Roeder's list of suspects.[191]

The custodians of the regime had managed to cripple the Oster group and destroy the operational headquarters of the projected anti-Nazi coup at one fell swoop. The immediate effect of what Gisevius later called "the direst stroke of fate that could possibly have befallen the resistance movement"[192] was to banish all hope of throwing off the Nazi yoke, perpetuate a lunatic war and leave the Nazis free to commit still more crimes. Months were to pass before another man, Colonel Count Claus Schenk von Stauffenberg, could pick up the threads of Oster's ruined enterprise.

Canaris's reputation for being a wily resistance sympathizer who shielded conspirators without actively participating in their work had also taken a hard knock. "The Canaris outfit," noted Ulrich von Hassell, "has completely compromised itself and utterly failed to live up to expectations. Unless the 'good guys' are as wise as serpents and harmless as doves, nothing will be achieved."[193]

During the days immediately following Dohnanyi's arrest Pfuhlstein often found Canaris "extremely agitated" and "downright desperate" because the Abwehr chief could not help fearing that he himself would now be exposed to Roeder's inquisitorial talents.[194] Roeder made every effort to get to the bottom of the treasonable conspiracy which had, he suspected, been masterminded by the Abwehr authorities. He sent his Gestapo assistants to follow up new leads, hammered away at those of the Oster set who were in custody and sifted confiscated documents for any evidence that would confirm his still nebulous suspicions.

He inveighed against the Abwehr's shortcomings with a strange blend of prejudice and self-righteousness. "Personally," he said later, "I never thought much of the Abwehr and took the view that all Abwehr officers should have been transferred after a year at most because of the many dangers besetting them, especially those of weak character."[195] What he now discovered about the Abwehr's internal condition only served to sharpen his disapproval. "There's no one left to cover for you!" he snapped at Lieutenant Breidbach. "General Oster's finished, thanks to me. I'm going to clean the whole place out."[196]

He started with the papers found in Dohnanyi's safe. The last of the three documents, which was signed "O," proved a special challenge to his powers of deduction. The text clearly conveyed that Abwehr personnel were trying, through the Vatican, to reach agreement with parties abroad on the political shape of Germany after the National Socialist regime had been overthrown. To Roeder this was treason in itself, but who had actually written it? When questioned, Dohnanyi freely conceded that it was a joint effort by himself and his brother-in-law, Dietrich Bonhoeffer.[197] In order to defuse this "dangerous document," as his wife later called it, Dohnanyi had concocted a simple story. He claimed that the text meant the contrary of what it seemed to imply. It was an agreed vocabulary for dealing with the enemy such as the Abwehr customarily employed—in other words, covert instructions to Pastor Bonhoeffer from "O," or Oster, to approach the Vatican authorities and tap them for information.[198]

Unfortunately for Dohnanyi, Oster declined to confirm this story. He denied almost everything. He had no knowledge of any agreed vocabulary or of the document in question. "O" was not his conventional signature, and there could be no question of dispatching Bonhoeffer to Rome as a V-Mann because the Central Section was not authorized to maintain agents of its own.[199] Bonhoeffer disputed this. He had, he said, been an agent of Amt Ausland/Abwehr since September 1, 1939, and was a collator of information on internal and ecclesiastical affairs.[200]

Canaris could not fail to be embarrassed by this because the Abwehr was forbidden to maintain a domestic political intelligence service. Roeder quickly exploded the Bonhoeffer-Dohnanyi story. He discovered that although Bonhoeffer had, at his brother-in-law's instigation, been declared "uk," or indispensable to the Abwehr and exempt from conscription by any other branch of the armed forces, he did not possess any form of V-Mann status in the Abwehr.[201] Bonhoeffer was not listed in the agents' card index which only Sections I and III were entitled to keep, nor had he sworn the customary oath of secrecy, nor did any reports from the self-styled agent appear in the Abwehr's files.[202] The discovery that Bonhoeffer was a rabid anti-Nazi who had been under Gestapo surveillance for years, not to mention subject to travel restrictions and a ban on public speaking, brought Roeder an additional thrill of confirmation.[203]

Roeder's next move was to get in touch with Canaris, who invited him to an "informal" afternoon get-together over coffee and cigars at his home in Schlachtensee.[204] Also present was an assistant of Roeder's, Oberkriegsgerichtsrat Noack, who witnessed a pathetic little rearguard action on the Admiral's part. Canaris smilingly conceded that Bonhoeffer's "uk" status was irregular and that he had no knowledge of the pastor's employment on internal intelligence work, an activity he would never have sanctioned because it ran counter to the Abwehr-Gestapo agreements.[205] A few days later he testified: "Dohnanyi did not inform me that police measures had been taken against Bonhoeffer while he was employed by the Abwehr. I was ignorant both of the public speaking ban and of the travel restrictions."[206]

Remarks like these encouraged Roeder to shine an even stronger light on the dark and diffuse recesses of the Abwehr organization. Instinct told him that Dohnanyi was his most important prisoner. It was he who had initiated the "V7" operation, he who had given Schmidhuber his orders, he who was reputed to be the brains and theoretician of the Oster circle, and his name which recurred whenever Roeder discovered new grounds for suspicion or unearthed old and long-buried clues.

Roeder's inquiries became increasingly focused on Dohnanyi, who put up a stout defence. The two men were soon conducting a fierce duel in which Roeder tended to use petty, vindictive and unfair tactics because he could not shake off the inferiority complex aroused in him by such a scintillating opponent. The mediocre judge advocate, who had earned a "Quite Satisfactory" mark for his in-service examination papers, was no real match for a perceptive Supreme Court counsel who had, even as a young man, been accounted one of Germany's most brilliant public prosecutors.[207]

Instead of a political plot, Roeder merely unearthed a private financial arrangement which later stung Josef Müller into proclaiming that Dohnanyi had "put the entire circle in jeopardy by combining political dissidence with personal advantage."[208] Even Lehmann, who used milder language, referred to "singular findings in matters of finance, extremely dubious methods of computing travel expenses, and foreign exchange transactions of a more than peculiar nature."[209]

In the course of his inquiries Roeder stumbled on a strange and multifarious network of contacts linking Dohnanyi, who was chronically impecunious, with a number of businessmen and wealthy private individuals. All were members of his circle. They included Stier and Oswald Hübener, partners in the Hamburg insurance company Jauch & Hübener, who had been exempted from military service on Dohnanyi's recommendation; Otto Hübener, another J & H partner whose brokerage firm had got into hot water with the Prague authorities and employed Dohnanyi as a legal adviser; Count Ostrowsky of Styria, whose friend Paul Struzzl owed Dohnanyi a job with Jauch & Hübener followed by a posting to the Abwehr's Kurfürst Regiment; and, last but not least, Schmidhuber, who had assisted Dohnanyi with letters of credit.[210]

If Dohnanyi paid an official visit to Italy and took his wife along, Otto Hübener happily obliged the influential tourist by making up his travelling expenses, without receipt, through another of his brokerage firms with offices in Milan and Rome. In Munich, Schmidhuber procured foreign exchange and augmented the official travel allowance already paid to Dohnanyi in Berlin.[211] The lawyer consoled himself with the thought that he would repay his friends' subsidies after the war—including gifts to the value of RM5,000 received from Schmidhuber.[212] Roeder: "Schmidhuber was an agent, and the acceptance of gifts or emoluments from agents was officially prohibited."[213]

Roeder applied himself with special acumen to elucidating the relationship between Dohnanyi and Otto Hübener, which centred on the purchase of a house. In June 1941 Dohnanyi had been offered a villa in Sakrow for RM83,000 plus RM4,150 property transfer tax. Part of this sum was raised through a bank, leaving him short of RM40,000.[214] He mentioned this to Hübener and hinted that he might shortly be joining the board of the Rheinisch-Westfälische Bodenkreditbank.[215] Hübener immediately volunteered to advance him the RM40,000. Dohnanyi expressed misgivings: "But I'm sure you could invest your capital in something better." Hübener retorted, "Don't tell me how to invest capital. I was investing capital when you were wet behind the ears."[216]

Hübener advanced the money on extremely generous terms, but Christine von Dohnanyi, always more of a go-getter than her husband, was still dissatisfied because she considered the duration of the agreement too short. Hübener had claimed the return of his money after ten years, but Frau von Dohnanyi insisted on twenty.[217] Hübener hurriedly took the agreement back, apologizing for the "oversight" on his secretary's part. The final version read:

1. Herr Otto Hübener hereby advances a loan in the sum of RM40,000 to Herr v. Dohnanyi. Herr v. Dohnanyi may draw this sum in the form of a cheque at any time, even in Herr Otto Hübener's absence, from his secretary's office.

2. The loan is advanced for an indefinite period. Herr v. Dohnanyi is at liberty to undertake repayment as soon as he deems it opportune.

3. For his part, Herr Hübener will refrain from calling in the loan for the next twenty years.

4. The loan shall bear interest at 2%. It is Herr v. Dohnanyi's wish to undertake higher interest payments (no such increase being demanded on Herr Otto Hübener's part) as soon as his income shall at some later date permit him to pay a higher rate of interest. Berlin, July 3, 1941.[218]

Roeder could not help noticing that the agreement provided for a sensationally low rate of interest. Nobody knew this better than Dohnanyi, who was paying the then normal rate of 6 per cent on his RM56,000 loan from the banking house of Seiler while shelling out only 2 per cent to Hübener.[219] He had not even switched to a higher rate after September 1941, when his appointment to the Rheinische Bodenkreditbank more than doubled his income. This fact he disguised from Hübener by claiming that the bank did not propose to pay him any director's fees until after the war.[220]

The judge advocate tried to represent this as acceptance of a bribe, but Dohnanyi's counsel fought back. Attorney Kurt Peschke protested that Dohnanyi had wanted to remit more than the agreed rate when the first payment fell due in February 1943. "The accused himself," Peschke wrote, "was disposed to remit 5 per cent without more ado, but his wife thought Hübener might be offended."[221] Christine von Dohnanyi's principle was that a new rate of interest could only be fixed by the lender, not the borrower.[222] Roeder was unimpressed. "The fact that the accused gave false information to Hübener about the moneys available to him for disbursement . . . forces one to conclude, in view of the terms of the loan, that Hübener was concerned to retain the accused's general good will."[223]

But Roeder was not content to unearth disciplinary offences and irregularities. He went hunting for a grand political sensation—a treasonable conspiracy—and found himself groping in the dark. He had originally thought that the investigation of Dohnanyi's "V7" venture would turn up some new leads in that direction, but he was mistaken. Even the hope that Dohnanyi might have used the Swiss account to line his own pockets came to nothing.[224]

Roeder dashed off down another trail—the one that led to the Vatican. Here too success eluded him, thanks not least to the steadfastness of Josef Müller, who proved under repeated questioning that his nickname was well earned. "Joe the Ox" often riled his inquisitors with a mixture of obduracy and peasant cunning. "Well," Roeder asked him at their very first encounter, "are we both agreed that Germany would be inconceivable without the party?" Müller simulated blind military obedience. He clicked his heels and barked, "Certainly, Colonel!"[225]

After the war, Müller recalled that he and Roeder soon became embroiled in "fierce altercations" during which the judge advocate "shouted, uttered threats and insulted friends of mine."[226] If Roeder and his Gestapo helpmates took too harsh a line "Joe the Ox" would moderate their tone by mysteriously hinting at his relations with the SS authorities.

The chief investigator came to realize that no break-through would be possible in this case of suspected treason, at least for the present, unless a miracle occurred. Every new trail proved to be a blind alley, nor did Roeder turn up any definite clues to the whereabouts of Schmidhuber's "generals' clique." However, he had so far kept his hands off someone who was becoming steadily more suspect because his reaction to the "Depositenkasse" case seemed edgier and more jumpy than that of anyone else connected with it. That someone was Canaris.

Kraell urgently advised Roeder to treat the Abwehr chief with due respect. To Kraell, Admiral Canaris was still an incontestably loyal and patriotic figure whom it would be an offence against nature to suspect. Any questions Roeder proposed to ask him had first to be submitted in writing to Kraell, who sometimes attended the ensuing interviews in person.[227]

Kraell could not, however, fail to notice how spent and dejected the old man looked. As he himself said: "I recall one interrogation of Admiral Canaris by Roeder at which Canaris made a positively helpless impression and . . . sounded thoroughly unconvincing. I had expected him to present a strongly worded defence . . . Instead, his pronouncements struck me as feeble and almost apologetic."[228] Other people who saw Canaris at this period took a similar view. The elimination of the Oster group and the Abwehr's invasion by outside investigators had hit Canaris hard. Lethargic, bemused and bereft of initiative, he tacked to and fro between Roeder and the Abwehr officers who were urging him to fight back.

The instinct for survival which had served Canaris during other crises in his career prompted him to sever all contact with the suspects. He never readmitted Oster to his office and coolly dissociated himself from those in custody. Denials became his staple form of defence. No, he had never lent approval to a domestic intelligence service. No, Herr von Dohnanyi must have known that he, as head of department, strongly disapproved of wives being taken on official trips and had always insisted that out-of-pocket expenses be accounted for in the most scrupulous fashion. No, Bonhoeffer had not been an Abwehr agent and the Abwehr had never maintained any kind of intelligence agency devoted to ecclesiastical affairs.[229]

Even in conversation with sympathetic members of the Reichskriegsanwaltschaft like Karl Lotter, a former close associate of the anti-

Nazi Army judge Karl Sack, Canaris dissociated himself from his old friend Oster. "In talking to Canaris and Oster," Lotter noted, "I came to the conclusion that no agreement had been reached on reconciling the statements to be made to the chief investigator, but rather the opposite. During these periodic consultations, one of them gave an account of the history of the alleged currency offences which differed substantially from that presented by the other."[230]

To the prisoners in their cells, alternately exposed to solitude and Roeder's concentrated verbal onslaughts, the Admiral's behaviour seemed incomprehensible. The notes and whispered messages with which they tried to enlist Canaris in their cause sounded like cries for help. "The guilt of the accused," wrote Dohnanyi, "cannot be established if Admiral Canaris confirms the following—wholly incontestable—facts: 1. Bonhoeffer's oecumenical connections were of great interest from the intelligence standpoint . . . 2. In the Struzzl case, it was Abwehrstelle Hamburg which proposed that Struzzl . . . be given intelligence service assignments . . . 3. Admiral Canaris will confirm that it was not officially incumbent on Dr. v. Dohnanyi to make 'discretionary decisions,' even in the form of advice to the Chief of Staff. He had nothing to do with the procurement of intelligence as such. If only because he lacked the authority, therefore, he could not have taken it into his head to maintain an official connection with Hübener . . . If interrogation of Admiral Canaris produces the expected result described above, the penal authorities will have no grounds for contesting a stay of proceedings."[231]

The Admiral's continuing silence prompted Dohnanyi and his lawyers to step up their pressure on him. Peschke's partner Justizrat Count von der Goltz, whom Canaris had known ever since their joint campaign to rehabilitate Fritsch, put it to him that Roeder's efforts were fundamentally and solely directed against him and the Abwehr as a whole. "This emerged," Goltz argued, "*inter alia* from the bringing of unsubstantiated charges against the head of department himself (e.g. 'having sneaked Jews across the frontier and tossed $100,000 after them'), from allegations against the Abwehr and the fate he [Roeder] had in mind for it . . . Interrogations of the accused [Dohnanyi] were predominantly intended to extract depositions against the Abwehr as such and Admiral Canaris personally, as well as to induce him by means of mental coercion and threats of physical coercion to 'come clean'—as the chief investigator put it—about his department and Admiral Canaris."[232]

But even these deliberate appeals bore little fruit. Canaris conveyed secret messages of encouragement to the prisoners but preserved an official silence. Frau von Dohnanyi, who had meanwhile been released from custody, later recalled: "Canaris sent my husband repeated assurances that he had done everything possible, [but said] that his political position was no longer strong enough for him to lay down the law. My husband thought otherwise to the very last."[233]

This weary, apprehensive and ultra-cautious figure is in sharp contrast to the radiantly heroic picture painted by the Admiral's biographers. Abshagen claims that his hero was "spurred into activity" and gave another display of his "old agility," and Brissaud faithfully takes his cue from the Admiral's first biographer by stating that Canaris became "extremely active" and "thwarted" Roeder's investigations.[234] Canaris did none of these things. The prisoners and he himself would have been done for, even at this stage, had not a few courageous Abwehr officers undertaken the defence of their own organization.

The group's spokesmen were Colonel von Bentivegni, who was sickened by the spectacle of his chief's decline, and a vigorous anti-Nazi who had only recently attracted the Admiral's attention. This was Stabs Intendant Dr. Georg Duesterberg, deputy head of Group ZF [Central Section, Finance] and son of the former Stahlhelm leader Theodor Duesterberg.[235] Canaris had appointed him his "mailman" for confidential messages to Roeder "because he did not trust the head of the Legal Division of Amt Ausland/Abwehr and the junior officers in the department."[236]

Duesterberg's meetings with Roeder soon convinced him that the chief investigator was after the Admiral's blood. He told how Roeder "was always drawing me into 'comradely' discussions in the course of which he plied me with leading questions about the current proceedings against Dohnanyi, [and] asked me for character assessments of the Abwehr high-ups."[237] He was so dismayed by Roeder's "cynicism" that he informed Canaris that the judge advocate was twisting his words and had evil designs on the Abwehr. When Canaris asked if he was prepared to submit a report in writing, Duesterberg agreed.[238]

Bentivegni, who spotted a chance of halting Roeder in his tracks, sent for Duesterberg. Rather than submit a written report to Canaris, he said, why not lodge an official complaint against Roeder with the head of OKW?[239] Duesterberg jumped at the idea. He was just drafting his complaint when Roeder became involved in a row which suited Bentivegni's scheme to a tee.

In mid-May Roeder had arranged an interview with Gisevius, from whom Schmidhuber claimed to have heard that Canaris had betrayed German offensive plans to the Russians. The resistance veteran declined to confirm this story of betrayal but admitted that he had criticized Canaris to Schmidhuber because of a recent clash over certain jurisdictional matters.[240] Roeder was wily enough to have Gisevius read his partial confirmation of Schmidhuber's statement into the record. Gisevius was due to sign the transcript next day.[241]

Again Bentivegni stepped in. When he heard what Gisevius had let slip, he persuaded him to think again. At a conference held in Canaris's office that evening, consideration was given to ways of retracting Gisevius's injudicious statement.[242] The witness reappeared before Roeder next day, but in a truculent and arrogant frame of mind.

"He demanded changes in the previous day's record, which he himself had dictated," Roeder testified. "I refused to amend the old record and told him he could read any additions or changes into a new one."[243] Gisevius declined to make any further statement at all, whereupon Roeder lost his temper and bellowed that, if he persisted in his refusal, he would be taken into custody.[244] Gisevius shouted back, and one angry remark led to another. It was some time before he deigned to answer any more questions, and even then he disclaimed all recollection of the previously recorded differences of opinion between himself and Canaris. He finally signed the new transcript and left, after which Roeder dictated a memorandum on the incident to his secretary.[245]

Gisevius, once described by a malicious critic as "the Karl May of the German resistance movement," presents quite another version of the scene in Roeder's office.[246] According to him, he broke off the altercation by asking Roeder for a one-hour recess during which he hurried to see Judge Sack. Roeder had already warned him that he would be arrested, but Sack postponed this step for twenty-four hours. He, Gisevius, had used this respite to draft "a comprehensive complaint" about Roeder's interrogation methods. Only a few days later, Keitel took Roeder off the case.[247]

The one authentic feature of this story is that Gisevius was indeed moved to lodge an official complaint, but only by Sack and Bentivegni, especially the latter, who was delighted to have found yet another witness against Roeder.[248] The fire-eating colonel then drummed up a third member of the Abwehr who was also prepared to lodge a written complaint against Roeder.[249] After that, Kraell recalls, "there came a spate of incidents." The RKG received one complaint after another, and there was "an interminable series of clashes and recriminations."[250]

But Roeder had taken out plenty of insurance and was immune to official protests lodged by those unversed in the law. Lehmann states that these complaints were "quite obviously part of the fierce campaign which the Abwehr was conducting against the proceedings themselves and the person of Roeder . . . We in the OKW felt that interested parties in the Abwehr were using extremely irrelevant complaints in an effort to torpedo the proceedings."[251] All these objections were considered by the RKG and ruled on by its president, and none of them was upheld.[252]

Oberreichskriegsanwalt Kraell considered these charges so shaky that he advised Sack, who was an old schoolmate of his, to dissuade his friends in the Abwehr from launching any more attacks on Roeder.[253] Kraell's own plan was to let the inquiry die a slow death and oust the Gestapo by degrees, quietly and without fuss. An all-out campaign against Roeder would bring the RSHA into the picture with a vengeance, he warned. Sack, who dismissed this as a tactical ploy, insisted that Roeder be tackled head on.[254]

The more Abwehr headquarters bombarded Roeder, however, the more doggedly he fastened on any piece of evidence likely to incriminate Canaris. He could not but interpret the campaign against himself as a desperate rearguard action on the Admiral's part. Roeder was not alone in surmising that Canaris had been privy to his subordinates' political and financial ventures—indeed, he came to be regarded as the real prime suspect in the "Depositenkasse" case. Keitel conveyed this after his own fashion by instructing the Reichskriegsgericht and Reichskriegsanwaltschaft not to give Canaris anything but a superficial outline of the investigation.[255]

Kraell informs us that "Canaris was not officially listed as an accused person because the grounds for suspicion fell just short of that, but he was considered highly suspect even so."[256] Lehmann, too, says that "relations with Canaris" remained "very uneasy," and adds: "By any normal standards he should have been kept regularly informed about the proceedings, but that was impossible. For one thing, he was under pretty close scrutiny himself. Apart from that, we had to allow for the possibility that—given the close personal ties between him and his two subordinates—he would not keep his mouth shut."[257] Not unsurprisingly, the Admiral responded to these signs of mistrust by retiring still further into his shell.

Vice-Admiral Bürkner found himself transformed into the *de facto* head of the Abwehr, which had almost ceased to function. Little effective work went on at headquarters, where the various departmental chiefs were becoming more and more mesmerized by the all-pervading question of when Roeder would tighten his stranglehold on their organization and have its chief led away in handcuffs. Bürkner, who bore day-to-day responsibility for these steadily increasing signs of chaos at Abwehr headquarters, was obliged to pay regular visits to the Führer's command headquarters and submit to Hitler's caustic questions about what "Herr Canaris's" department was up to.

Almost at the end of his tether, Bürkner confided in Lehmann and asked for help. Lehmann noted: "Bürkner told me . . . quite bluntly that work at Abwehr headquarters had virtually ceased as a result of this investigation."[258] He added that Canaris was "almost incapacitated as a working member of the staff and a commanding officer."[259] Lehmann took Bürkner's appeal to heart. Then he had a sudden flash of inspiration—a harebrained and audacious idea which offered such a simple way out that its cautious and diffident author often smiled at it in years to come.

Lehmann consulted Kraell, who marvelled at his colleague's ingenuity. "It was a quite unprecedented proposal," he wrote, "—one which I never again encountered in my professional career and which, strictly speaking, ran counter to the law."[260] Together they went to see the president of the Reichskriegsgericht, Admiral Max Bastian, who had once helped Canaris on the road to a career in military intelligence and was only too happy to deliver his former flagship commander from the nightmare that now loomed over him. He agreed with the other two that anything was worth trying in an emergency.[261]

At the end of June Lehmann summoned his senior subordinates to a meeting with Huppenkothen of the RSHA. As he himself puts it, he then "broached an idea which dumbfounded all present. Quite out of the blue, I said I was toying with the idea of advising Field Marshal Keitel that the proceedings should be dropped because there seemed no prospect of getting to the bottom of the matter. Investigations should, I said, be restricted to secondary factors devoid of political interest."[262] Lehmann awaited a favourable moment before testing his scheme on Keitel.

A new turning point in the war presented him with the opportunity he sought. On July 10 British and U.S. forces landed in Sicily and began their assault on the "soft underbelly" of Hitler's Europe.[263] The very first battles disclosed that Italian resistance was waning fast and that the collapse of Fascist Italy could not be far off. Lehmann seized his chance. He reported to Keitel and submitted his plan, which held certain terrors for the spineless OKW chief because he would have to clear it with Himmler.[264]

To Lehmann's surprise, everything went off smoothly. Kraell asked Roeder for an interim report on his investigations worded in such a way as to cause no trouble.[265] "His report," Kraell says, "approved criminal proceedings of a non-political nature but was cautious in its assessment of political charges."[266] Bastian contributed a supplementary report—drafted by Kraell—which "[dismissed] the possibility of convicting the accused of treason [Hochverrat and/or Landesverrat] on the strength of available evidence."[267] This gave Keitel, in his supreme judicial capacity, sufficient grounds for ordering the political proceedings to be dropped.[268]

The relief attack mounted by Canaris's legal sympathizers was accelerated when Mussolini fell from power on July 25, 1943. Next day, Roeder recalls, "there came a signed directive from Keitel thanking the president of the RKG for services rendered. He further stated that military developments in the Italian theatre of war called for the full utilization of all Amt Ausland/Abwehr's resources and that the additional burden laid upon it by my investigation must be removed."[269] Roeder obediently produced what Keitel expected of him, namely, a charge sheet almost innocent of political undertones. Schmidhuber and Ickrath were jointly accused of currency offences and malfeasance, Dohnanyi of malfeasance, currency offences and "undermining the war effort," Oster of complicity and Bonhoeffer of evading military service.[270] The prosecution was taken over by a court-martial officer and Roeder withdrew from the case, angrily and reluctantly but without demur. The taste of defeat was sweetened some weeks later by his appointment as chief justice of Luftflotte IV in Lvov.[271]

As for Himmler, he wanted no more accusations levelled at Canaris and told Keitel that "the old man should be left in peace."[272] Huppenkothen never forgot Keitel's marginal note on the top sheet of Roeder's interim report. According to this, Himmler had declined to read the report, had declared himself uninterested in taking proceedings against Canaris, had personally given Canaris his oral consent to Operation "V7" and considered himself bound by his promise. For the rest, Canaris should at long last get rid of the unreliable members of his entourage and be more businesslike in future.[273]

Such were the comments of the newly appointed Reich Minister of the Interior, who had already arranged a meeting for August 26 at which ex-Finance Minister Popitz, accompanied by Canaris's informant Langbehn, was to brief him on the political plans of the German resistance movement.[274] Schellenberg disliked the Admiral's rehabilitation because it again postponed his dream of bossing an all-powerful intelligence service.

The inconceivable had come to pass. Contrary to all expectations, Canaris had been rescued yet again and the substance of his department preserved. Keitel did, however, insist on radical reforms and a better standard of performance. All the heads of section were replaced. Bürkner was allowed to keep his job and Oster's successor Jacobsen remained unscathed, but Piekenbrock, Lahousen and Bentivegni all had to quit their posts.[275] This decision came hard to Canaris because the last three had been virtually running the Abwehr.

The old hands were replaced by new men whom Canaris took time to accept. Colonel Theodor Heinrich, an infantryman posted to Abwehr headquarters by the OKW late in June, inherited Abwehr III on September 15. He remained an amorphous figure to Canaris, especially as he sustained serious injuries in a road accident only five days after formally taking up his duties and so enabled the Admiral to recall Bentivegni.[276] Piekenbrock's successor, Colonel Georg Hansen, was seventeen years younger than Canaris. An ex-tank officer and anti-Nazi who had recently headed Foreign Armies West, he was slow to get on with his new head of department because he arrived with many of the trained General Staff officer's prejudices against the Abwehr.[277] Better suited to Canaris was the new head of Abwehr II, who took over on August 1. This was Colonel Baron Wessel von Freytag-Loringhoven, born in 1899, a Balt who had grown up in imperial Russia, trained with the Latvian Army and then transferred to the Reichswehr. An ardent horseman, he had most recently served as Ic of Army Group South, under whose auspices he had organized pro-German Cossack cavalry formations and, coincidentally, become acquainted with the criminal megalomania of the Nazi master-race policy as applied to the East.[278]

The arrival of these new men wrought a gradual change in the outward appearance of Amt Ausland/Abwehr. Intensified Allied air raids on Berlin and other German cities compelled Abwehr headquarters to move to Camp Zeppelin at Zossen on the southern outskirts of Berlin. This move had already begun during the second half of April. Part of the Abwehr went to ground in Zeppelin's Maybach II security zone, an area of small terraced houses which had been camouflaged and provided with intercommunicating air raid shelters on two levels. Other Abwehr offices were distributed round Berlin, some in Matthäikirchplatz, Bendlerstrasse and Grossadmiral-Prinz-Heinrich-Strasse, and some at the old Eiche Police College in Potsdam.[279] Canaris himself moved into Maybach II premises formerly occupied by Halder when Chief of the General Staff (replaced by Hitler in 1942).[280]

Canaris was unaware that a menacing shadow from the past had pursued him into his subterranean lair. Remembering the secret records of the Oster-Dohnanyi group which had been stored in a Prussian State Bank safe since 1942, Oster's friend Lieutenant Colonel Heinz had thought it time to retrieve them from their hiding place. Two carloads of these papers were transferred to Maybach II and locked up in another safe which Heinz considered Gestapo-proof.[281]

Meanwhile, Canaris's new heads of section worked hard to improve the Abwehr's performance. Colonel Heinrich felt that the department's immobility and bureaucratic routine were stifling the ingenuity and initiative of the secret service proper, so he decided to split the stationary counterespionage and counterintelligence units into mobile Frontaufklärungskommandos [FAK—forward reconnaissance detachments]. The heads of the Abwehrstellen in occupied territory took a jaundiced view of this projected reform, which Bentivegni adopted on his return, and did their best to sabotage it. With Canaris's backing, however, Bentivegni won the day.[282] Supervised in France, Belgium and Holland by a "Leitstelle III West für Frontaufklärung," the FAK did succeed in improving the Abwehr's intelligence work. Other FAKs were established in the East—the beginning of an "Abwehr on wheels."

Canaris did not sit out the reorganization of his intelligence service in Maybach II but took to the road again. He was enthralled by the collapse of Italian Fascism. To a German patriot like him, the toppling of Mussolini's regime seemed worthy of emulation as a preliminary step towards extricating his own country from the war. Eager for a personal look at the Italian scene and all the invaluable openings it presented, he soon got the opportunity he needed. Keitel instructed him to confer with the head of Italian military intelligence, General Cesare Amé, in Venice. The object of the meeting was to discover what attitude Mussolini's successor, Pietro Badoglio, took to the German-Italian alliance and the continuation of the war.[283]

On July 29 Canaris flew with Lahousen and Freytag-Loringhoven to Venice, where they were met at Amé and an Italian military delegation.[284] Amé had received some ominous reports. The Germans were transferring three divisions to Italy, not for use in the Sicilian theatre but so that Northern Italy, the Italian naval bases and Rome could be promptly seized if Italy ran out on her ally[285]—and Amé was in no doubt that defection from the Axis was precisely what Badoglio had in mind.

The two delegations met at the Hotel Danieli and exchanged pledges of steadfast comradeship-in-arms. Canaris dictated a final communiqué whose wording was primarily intended for the Führer's mistrustful eye and proclaimed a common determination to fight on.[286] He was too shrewd not to grasp that the Italians planned to do otherwise and happily accepted the fact. During a recess in the July 30 conference he took Amé aside and suggested a breath of fresh air. They left the hotel, followed at some distance by the other delegates, and strolled down the street. Suddenly Canaris said, "Heartiest congratulations." The Italian feigned incomprehension, but Canaris went on, "Congratulations on your July 25. We could use one too. Germany's one dream is to get rid of Hitler."[287]

All at once, Amé had a strange feeling that he could trust this smiling and unfathomable German. "Admiral," he blurted out, "I'm counting on your absolute discretion. All we're doing today is trying to gain time. An armistice [with the Allies] will be offered very shortly, but it's essential that Italy isn't paralysed by a harsh and immediate Nazi occution." Canaris: "There's only one way of achieving that. Prevent the Wehrmacht from reinforcing its troops in Italy by every possible means. To put it in a nutshell, try and let as few German soldiers into Italy as you can."[288]

The Italian digested this advice with raised eyebrows, but Canaris gave him no time to suspect an ulterior motive. "As far as I'm concerned, my dear General Amé, you can rest assured—I shall say nothing of this in Berlin. On the contrary, I shall strongly emphasize that Italy intends to fight on at our side." He paused for a moment. "It's impossible for you to hold out longer than a month," he continued more urgently. "You must withdraw from the fray—you don't have any choice. But remember, allow as few German soldiers across the Brenner as you possibly can."[289]

On July 31 Canaris flew home, convinced that Italy would be out of the war in a few weeks at most.[290] He evidently hoped that Italy's surrender would give the German authorities such a jolt that, as in Italy before the Duce's downfall, influential military leaders and moderate party officials would be prepared to neutralize Hitler and offer the Allies a cease-fire. Mussolini's inscrutable police chief Carmine Senise, a species of Italian Himmler, had played a leading part in the coup, so why shouldn't his example be followed in Germany?

This was wishful thinking, of course, but political pipe dreams were all that now kept Canaris at his post. He was determined, at any rate, that his report should inhibit the transfer of strong German forces to Italy in time to counter the Italians' defection from the Axis by occupying their country at lightning speed.

He duly informed every official contact he met on his return from Venice that Italy was certain to remain at Germany's side. Huppenkothen, too, was told over dinner in the Admiral's underground headquarters at Zossen that he, Canaris, "thought it out of the question, both personally and judging by the impression he had gained from Amé, that Italy would make any unilateral move to end the war."[291]

But Canaris had reckoned without Walter Schellenberg. Annoyed at his rival's recent escape, he mistrusted the Admiral's story and unleashed his agents on Amé in Rome. The Italian intelligence chief had talked, and a homosexual relationship with his chauffeur, who was privy to the secret, boded ill for Canaris's safety. Schellenberg's agents discovered the true gist of the Canaris-Amé discussions in Venice,[292] and their reports made such sensational reading that the SD chief felt he at last had enough ammunition to gun his competitor down. He drafted a report accusing Canaris of having persistently, and with treasonable intent, misled the German authorities about Italy's future intentions.[293]

Schellenberg was feeling his oats, especially as Heydrich's eventual successor at the RSHA, SS-Obergruppenführer Ernst Kaltenbrunner, shared his secret service ambitions. Even before taking over, Kaltenbrunner had more or less made it a condition of his appointment when conferring with Himmler in December 1942 that a unified German secret service should be created under SS control.[294] "I told him then," said Kaltenbrunner, "that no intelligence service could be based on an SD alone. Any intelligence service which had been as tightly and progressively condensed into an executive body as it had under Heydrich was fundamentally unsuited to the gathering of intelligence. Secondly, an intelligence service had to be smaller. Above all, however,

I thought it madness for a line to be drawn between the political and military intelligence services. No country in the entire world, apart from Germany and France, had adopted this practice of dividing an intelligence service in two."[295]

Himmler had promised to submit these merger plans to Hitler when the time was ripe. Kaltenbrunner: "I requested him to begin by obtaining a Führer's directive under which the Wehrmacht's intelligence system . . . would be amalgamated with the SD."[296] Himmler agreed but ordered Kaltenbrunner to take over the RSHA while waiting. Kaltenbrunner had been waiting ever since. Schellenberg's anti-Canaris operation may have struck him as promising because he himself had been at Maybach II with Huppenkothen when the Abwehr chief was rhapsodizing about Italy's "loyalty" to the alliance.[297]

Schellenberg presented Himmler with his report on the true content of the Canaris-Amé discussions, which had the desired effect. Himmler tapped his teeth with his thumbnail—a sure sign of annoyance. "Leave the file here with me," he ordained. "I'll bring it to Hitler's notice when the occasion arises."[298] Fortunately, Canaris learned of Schellenberg's gambit in time. At his next dinner with the RSHA leaders, including Huppenkothen and Schellenberg himself, he neutralized his opponent at a stroke.

Huppenkothen records that Canaris handed Schellenberg "a lengthy paper in which (Italy's armistice with the Western powers having since come into effect) he reproduced a summary of all the reports submitted to Keitel by military intelligence over the years. They made explicit reference to the fact that Italy's military leaders were systematically planning a separate peace and the simultaneous elimination of Mussolini. Keitel had declined to submit these and similar reports to the Führer, Canaris emphasized, because they . . . would have caused the Führer needless agitation."[299] Canaris even contrived to add a small and dramatic footnote which, though inaccurate, threw the RSHA men into confusion. Amé, that loyal friend of Germany, had been relieved of his post shortly after the Venice meeting and appointed a divisional commander. He had vanished en route for his new command, and Canaris suspected that he was a victim of foul play.[300]

The Reichsführer-SS was suitably impressed by this display of agility. Schellenberg buttonholed him three more times on the subject of his anti-Canaris report but complains in his memoirs that Himmler "could not steel himself to draw the obvious conclusions."[301] He goes on: "Having always previously held Canaris up to me as a shrewd intelligence chief from whom I still had much to learn, he now declared that the Admiral's blunders and his attitude to the regime were another matter, and one with which I should not concern myself."[302]

This was the Admiral's last major triumph over his adversaries in the RSHA. From now on his position steadily deteriorated. Germany's military reverses only aggravated the internal crises besetting the Abwehr and its chief. It soon turned out that Canaris's hopes of a turning point in Italy were unfounded. Though eager to surrender, the entire country became engulfed in war when the Badoglio government capitulated on September 3 and British troops invaded the Italian mainland on the same day. The rest of Italy was occupied by German forces and the opposing armies settled down to a long and dogged war of attrition in the south.[303]

The Abwehr proved unequal to the new military intelligence problems posed by war in Italy. Having long been forbidden to spy on an allied country, it now lacked personnel with local knowledge. But the department's work was also flagging in its traditional spheres of activity. Abwehrstellen and KOs in the Eastern Mediterranean ceased to operate, and most of the monitoring and observation posts in North Africa had been overrun by Allied forces. The clearest symptom of decline was that KO Spain, Canaris's largest and most successful espionage network and the fruit of his lifelong preoccupation with the Iberian Peninsula, had run into trouble.

This crisis had been provoked by the Spanish authorities, who were showing less and less inclination to tolerate the work of German spies. Ever since the Allies' victorious advances in the Mediterranean area and, more especially, since the collapse of Fascist Italy, the import-dependent Spaniards had come under growing economic pressure. British and American diplomats were redoubling their insistence that the Madrid government should stop Spanish wolfram exports to Germany, close the German Consulate General in Tangier and expel all German agents from Spain and Spanish Morocco.[304] If Franco complied with these demands, KO Spain would be finished.

Early in October Canaris hurried off to pacify the Spaniards,[305] but Spain was a changed country. Franco declined to grant him an interview, Vigón expressed misgivings about the activities of German military intelligence and even secret service chief Martínez Campos proved less co-operative than usual. Undeterred by these rebuffs, Canaris negotiated with Vigón and the new Spanish Foreign Minister, Count Jordana. They eventually withdrew their objections, perhaps in part because of a small dossier which Canaris had instructed Abwehr III to prepare in July.[306]

This detailed the frequent occasions on which German military intelligence and the Spanish police had combined to neutralize anti-Franco resistance groups backed by Allied intelligence agencies. Among these were "a monarchist resistance movement in the northern Spanish provinces directed by the British Embassy in Madrid," which Abwehr agents had uncovered in April 1943, and an Abwehr-detected network of U.S. secret service informants in the Barcelona area "for the recon-naissance of coastal fortifications in Spain and the Balearics."[307] Cana-ris must also have been glad of a chance to sling some mud at the prominent Franco appointee who had already begun to demand the ex-pulsion of all German agents from Spanish Morocco. "German military intelligence," the Admiral pointedly remarked, "had ascertained by mid-June 1943 that the monarchist and pro-British High Commissioner for Spanish Morocco, General Orgaz, is planning a *coup d'état* with other leading monarchists in important posts. Spanish Morocco is in close touch with Málaga, where special preparations for this *coup d'état* are in train."[308]

Vigón and Jordana let it go at that, and the Abwehr was provi-sionally allowed to continue its operations. Canaris must, however, have realized that this chapter in his life was also drawing to a close. KO Spain's signs of internal decay were all too apparent. That very summer a KO flying squad had gunned down an Abwehr employee working for the British, and each new Allied protest to Madrid was accompanied by precise details of the real names and functions of local German agents —just another indication of how threadbare the Abwehr's Spanish net-work had become.[309]

This crisis in the outstations spread to Maybach II, whose intelli-gence evaluators were saddled with sparse and uncommunicative re-ports from the Abwehrstellen. Abwehr headquarters had still to recover from the shock of Roeder's inquisition, and many believed that the dust had far from settled. More rumours went the rounds, one of them being that Roeder, who had definitely withdrawn from the "Deposit-enkasse" inquiry in August, was again under orders to investigate the political grounds for suspicion against Canaris and his immediate subor-dinates. Some said he had reappeared in Berlin, where he was, in fact, sighted at the end of November.[310]

The Admiral's response to these rumours was jumpy and overex-cited, partly because he now knew that another Abwehr officer had aroused the Gestapo's suspicions. Captain Gehre learned from Ober-regierungsrat Plaas that the Gestapo had since autumn 1943 been watching a dissident group centred on Hanna Solf, an ambassador's widow. One member of this circle, in which subversive plans were discussed, was Major Otto Kiep of Amtsgruppe Ausland.[311] Plaas confided that a Gestapo informer named Paul Reckzeh had wormed his way into the confidence of the Solf circle and briefed the RSHA on what was said at its meetings, notably at a tea party given by Elisabeth von Thadden.[312]

In an atmosphere already so fraught with tension and suspicion, this new rumour was enough to send Canaris haywire. Early in January 1944 he heard that Roeder had resumed work on the Oster-Dohnanyi interrogation transcripts.[313] Instantly, his hackles rose. Determined to prevent another inquisition à la Roeder but without bothering to check the accuracy of the latest reports, he staged a little drama whose only result was to inject a note of farce into the Abwehr's tragic decline and fall.

Inquiries would quickly have disclosed that the Roeder rumour was false. He was still off the "Depositenkasse" case, but Lehmann had recalled him to Berlin at the end of November 1943 because his offices had been damaged in an air raid and the "Depositenkasse" files destroyed by fire.[314] The judge appointed to reconstruct the interrogation transcripts had invited Roeder to Torgau, the temporary quarters of the Reichskriegsgericht, at the beginning of January. Roeder had assisted him there for three days before rejoining his Luftflotte—and that was as far as it went.[315]

Canaris, who only knew that Roeder had been recalled, decided to squelch his comeback so effectively that the judge advocate would become the laughingstock of the entire armed forces and so be precluded from further involvement in the "Depositenkasse" case. But how to achieve this? A written submission which the Admiral had just received from Dohnanyi's defence counsel, Count von der Goltz, pointed the way.[316] Having settled on a reliable if unwitting accomplice, Canaris rang up the curtain.

On January 10, 1944, he sent a radio message to Major General von Pfuhlstein, commander of the Brandenburg Division, who was flying from Friedrichshafen to Vienna in a military aircraft. The brief message read: "No landing Vienna. Return Berlin immediately. Canaris."[317] The plane turned back, and a few hours later the general's car entered the security zone surrounding Abwehr headquarters at Zossen. Hansen and Freytag-Loringhoven, who were waiting in the anteroom, shepherded Pfuhlstein into the Admiral's office at once. Canaris quietly closed the door behind them, picked up a document lying on his desk and told the general, "Read it, read it!" He paced restlessly up and down while Pfuhlstein began to read, then interrupted him. "Haven't you got there yet? Carry on reading!"[318]

Overcome with impatience, Canaris retrieved the document from Pfuhlstein and showed him the part that mattered. It was a remark by Count von der Goltz to the effect that Roeder had called the Brandenburg Division "a shirkers' club."[319] Pfuhlstein recalls: "When I had read this, Canaris said I must surely realize that it was an abject slur and slander on my men."[320] Canaris then asked what action the general intended to take. Pfuhlstein hesitated before replying that he supposed charges could be brought against Roeder, though Canaris would have to associate himself with them. Canaris ("That won't do!") was "obviously disappointed." Then Pfuhlstein had a more acceptable idea. "I replied that my only alternative was to go and see Dr. Roeder and 'sock him on the jaw.' "[321]

This satisfied the Admiral, who blandly advised him to consult Dohnanyi and Goltz about the remark before proceeding further. Pfuhlstein's doubts revived as soon as they told him that Roeder had been alluding to the case of Paul Struzzl. Dohnanyi had found Struzzl a place in the Abwehr's Kurfürst Regiment, but the Kurfürst no longer formed part of the Brandenburg Division and came directly under Amt Ausland/Abwehr.[322] Pfuhlstein found it equally off-putting when he asked Army judge Sack what a "sock on the jaw" would be likely to cost him and was told: "Instant dismissal as divisional commander and six to nine months' detention."[323]

Back in Canaris's office on the evening of January 11, Pfuhlstein refused to play. Roeder had been referring to the Kurfürst Regiment, he argued, so "any further action should be taken through the Abwehr, to which that unit was subordinated."[324] Canaris rounded on him at once. He must have been mistaken in the Herr General, he said—he obviously lacked "the necessary personal courage." At this Pfuhlstein jumped up, beside himself with rage, and shouted, "If aspersions are being cast on my personal courage, that settles it. There's only one thing to do." So saying, he marched out of the room.[325]

As soon as he returned to his quarters he was handed a note asking him to telephone Canaris. Freytag-Loringhoven, who took the call, warned Pfuhlstein on the Admiral's behalf that he would have to "shoulder all the consequences of his own decision."[326] This really infuriated Pfuhlstein. He angrily refused to be lectured further and wrote Canaris a letter stating, among other things, that "I didn't lack the courage to deal with the matter, but I also had the courage to shoulder the responsibility which he was unwilling to bear."[327]

Pfuhlstein sent for his ADC, Lieutenant Arnold von Gustedt, and flew to the headquarters of Luftflotte IV in Lvov. On January 18 the two officers presented themselves in Roeder's outer office, removed their greatcoats, belts and pistols and barged into the judge's inner sanctum.[328] Pfuhlstein said, "I have a question for you, Herr Oberstkriegsgerichtsrat. Was it you who worked on the Dohnanyi case?" When Roeder agreed, Pfuhlstein continued, "In the course of those proceedings you made the remark: 'The Special Formation Brandenburg is a shirkers' club.'" Roeder broke in, "May I inquire where the Herr General heard this?" But Pfuhlstein would brook no interjections. "I can tell you that later. I'm the commander of the Brandenburg Division. You have gravely insulted my men. I am here in their name. This is my answer!"[329]

"Whereupon," Gustedt later testified for the record, "General von Pfuhlstein struck Oberstkriegsgerichtsrat Dr. Roeder on the left side of the face with his right hand and immediately left the room. He withdrew to the outer office to put his coat on. I followed him. The Oberstkriegsgerichtsrat followed us out and made another attempt to address the general. On reaching the outer office he said, in my presence and that of a non-commissioned officer in his department, 'I shall submit an immediate report to Field Marshal Keitel. May I inquire your name and the name of the lieutenant?' General von Pfuhlstein replied curtly, 'I am General von Pfuhlstein and this is Lieutenant von Gustedt!' Without another word, he then left the building."[330]

On January 23 Keitel sentenced Pfuhlstein to seven days' confinement to quarters. The general never forgave Canaris for compelling him to act "in violation of his official standing."[331] The report he "respectfully" submitted to the Abwehr chief on January 18 did, however, contain the following noble sentiment: "I am grateful to my superiors for not having acted sooner because I consider it my special function and my special prerogative, as its commander, to take the lead in standing up for my gallant division."[332] This is the basis of the touching but apocryphal story that Canaris assumed responsibility for Pfuhlstein's action and told Keitel that he would not leave his own quarters until the general was set at liberty.

The truth is that outside developments left Canaris no time to indulge in such rituals or even to savour his hollow victory over an inquisitor who had long ago been rendered harmless. At this very juncture, Amt Ausland/Abwehr was swamped by a tidal wave of blunders, failures and scandals which plunged the German military intelligence service into the gravest crisis in its history.

The Gestapo had struck again, even before the Lvov incident, and punched another hole in the defences manned by Canaris and his associates. On January 12 they arrested all the members of the Solf circle including Major Kiep of the Abwehr.[333] His arrest had some unexpected repercussions. On January 19 Gestapo officers picked up Moltke, who had tried to warn Kiep in advance, and the finger of suspicion pointed so unmistakably at Captain Gehre that he was arrested too.[334] What hit Canaris hardest of all, however, was that Plaas, his source of tips from the Forschungsamt, also fell into Gestapo hands.[335]

Unable to await the preliminary results of this Gestapo operation, Canaris boarded his plane and flew to Rome. On January 21 he was on the northern outskirts of the capital visiting the headquarters of Commander in Chief Southwest, whose staff officers were trying, after an eighteen-hundred-mile retreat across North Africa and up through Italy, to establish a more permanent line of defence at the narrowest part of the peninsula south of Rome.[336] The burning question there was what information the Abwehr had about enemy plans for a landing behind the German lines. The intelligence evaluators at HQ Southwest were suspicious because they had noticed that almost all the Allies' battle-ships, cruisers and landing craft had vanished from the western and southern coasts of Italy. According to some reports, shipping of the order of 350,000 tons was concentrated in Naples harbour, a possible jumping-off point for amphibious operations by the enemy.[337]

The Abwehr chief's remarks, which were greeted with interest, sounded most reassuring. "Don't worry," Canaris announced, "we're keeping an eye on those ships."[338] Major General Siegfried Westphal, Chief of Staff to Commander in Chief Southwest, recalls that the Admiral "was unable to particularize but said there was absolutely no danger of another landing in the near future."[339]

Canaris had just left Kesselring's headquarters when, at 2 A.M. on January 22, 1944, three hundred Allied landing craft appeared off Anzio, fifty miles behind the German lines, laden with men of the U. S. VI Corps commanded by General Lucas.[340] Shortly afterwards the attackers stormed ashore and established a beachhead which would have proved disastrous to the Germans if only Lucas had exploited the effect of surprise by delivering a lightning thrust at the undefended Ital-ian capital.[341] Canaris and his department had disgraced themselves. General Westphal swore never to trust another of the Admiral's analyses. "That," he insisted, "is why I say he was a bad intelligence officer."[342]

Many people thought the same. Canaris's reputation as a master spy was damaged beyond repair. He had for many years been regarded as the espionage chief par excellence, shrouded in mystery and habitually well informed. Now he attracted little but mild sarcasm or even com-miseration. Reichskriegsanwalt Lotter was shocked when he met Cana-ris during a visit to the Führer's headquarters in January. "Canaris was extremely agitated. Physically, he made a thoroughly run-down and groggy impression."[343] The Abwehr chief had every reason to be worried because Hitler had ordered Jodl to determine precisely why military intelligence had been caught napping by the Anzio landing.[344]

Jodl's report exacerbated Hitler's furious and sarcastic strictures on the Abwehr's incompetence. Only a few months earlier he had been taking a more amiable line towards Canaris—in fact he even missed him at times. On the night of August 23–24, 1943, the Führer asked his crony Bormann what Canaris was up to, adding, "I haven't heard from him for ages." The Admiral brightened when told of this. "You see," he triumphantly remarked to his adjutant, Jenke, "he still needs me after all!" Then he turned pensive. "But what's the use now?"[345] These sudden recollections of the erstwhile partnership between Hitler and his intelligence chief had become few and far between. Canaris could feel a chill wind blowing from the Führer's direction.

The weakness of the Abwehr and its chief had given encouragement to an old adversary who persisted in regarding the secret service as a troublesome competitor. Joachim von Ribbentrop's Foreign Office had always resented being forced to co-operate with the Abwehr. Too many Abwehr officers and agents were ensconced in the Reich's diplomatic missions abroad, where they availed themselves of Foreign Office radio equipment and operated under the aegis of diplomatic immunity. Ribbentrop had gone to a lot of trouble to ensure that all KO reports to Abwehr headquarters were first submitted to heads of mission and that Abwehr personnel did not obstruct the work of German diplomats by committing provocative acts.[346] Despite these concessions, however, the two authorities had become involved in a number of jurisdictional disputes.

The more the Abwehr expanded its establishments in neutral countries and the more German diplomats lost their scope for political manoeuvre, the fiercer these clashes became. Heads of mission and their immediate subordinates soon got the feeling that they were being spied on by Abwehr officers, many of whom lived under the same roof, and that these secret servicemen were rivals whose increasing tendency was to supervise a mission's local reports or embellish them with information of their own. For their part, heads of mission were generally debarred from all knowledge of the Abwehr's clandestine activities, which often hampered the work of their own staff.

Nor had the Foreign Office ceased to pursue its own intelligence projects, which dated back to the Bismarck era. The Wilhelmstrasse's Intelligence Section maintained a small secret intelligence service whose agents were based in German diplomatic missions or operated independently of them. Not even the SD's development into a foreign intelligence service had persuaded the Foreign Office to abandon its own conspiratorial ambitions, although its agents had little or no secret service training.

When war broke out, Himmler and Heydrich had tried to neutralize this other SD rival by getting the head of the Intelligence Section, Marschall von Bieberstein, replaced by SS-Brigadeführer Walter Stahlecker,[347] but Ribbentrop soon saw through this manoeuvre and squeezed the SS man out of the Foreign Office.[348] Stahlecker's successor was Unterstaatssekretär Sandor Hencke, who continued (with a certain amount of help from Marschall von Bieberstein) to expand the Wilhelmstrasse's private agency.[349] The "Hencke Service" became the bane of the RSHA, which was already contemplating its total absorption into the SS empire.

But the Hencke Service did not remain the sole instrument of Foreign Office ambitions in the intelligence field. The head of the Ribbentrop Office, Rudolf Likus, a veteran Nazi and school friend of the minister, established a separate ring of informants who penetrated foreign embassies (as in 1941, when they successfully tapped Kobulov, the NKVD's resident director in Berlin) or built up intelligence networks abroad.[350] Also attached to this conspiratorial branch of the Ribbentrop Office were the Foreign Minister's so-called special representatives, whose assignments were kept secret even from the relevant head of mission. One of these men, Legationsrat [Legation or Embassy Counsellor] Erich Gardemann, was instructed to organize an anti-Franco conspiracy with the aid of informants inside the Spanish party and government machine, its purpose being to prod the reluctant Caudillo into war or eliminate him in favour of a more compliant successor.[351]

No minister with such multifarious interests in the field of diplomacy and intelligence could take kindly to competition from the political and military intelligence services. The fussy and irascible Ribbentrop, one of the most agile departmental duellists at the top of the Nazi tree, opened a fierce guerrilla campaign against the Abwehr, which he had quickly identified as the weaker of the Foreign Office's two main rivals. His mode of procedure was not without subtlety.

The SS authorities already knew how inadvisable it was to underrate Ribbentrop's talent for intrigue. In October 1939 the RSHA had extracted his consent to an arrangement whereby the SD was permitted to make use of German embassies and missions, the SD chief in each country being built into the embassy staff as a police attaché. German missions abroad soon found themselves subject to SD surveillance and unable to fight back because Ribbentrop had granted the RSHA the right to employ and procure information from agents without referring to the Foreign Office.[352] Ribbentrop decided to rescind this agreement, but without tackling his powerful competitor head on.

He patiently waited until the SD made a *gaffe*. In January 1941, when SD agents fomented a revolt by the fascist Iron Guard against Antonescu, Romania's ultraconservative dictator and Hitler's Wilhelmstrasse-backed ally, Ribbentrop went to his Führer and accused the SD of sabotaging German policy in Romania.[353] Hitler, whose ire was easily aroused, thundered that he would "wipe out" the "Black Plague" unless they toed the line.[354] Taking advantage of Hitler's anger, Ribbentrop cancelled his agreement with the RSHA and in August 1941 coaxed Himmler into concluding a new pact which stipulated that all communications between police attachés and the RSHA were to be seen by heads of mission and that the SD must not meddle in diplomatic matters.[355]

Ribbentrop's campaign against the weakened Abwehr followed a similar pattern. The Foreign Minister had a definite plan in mind. He wanted to oust Abwehr personnel from diplomatic missions, reduce their activities in neutral countries to a minimum and subject them to control by his own local representatives. Once again, the skilled departmental strategist waited for a favourable moment. He selected as his battlefield the country where Canaris felt most at home—Spain.

The arena was well chosen because no other neutral country could provide stronger confirmation of Ribbentrop's thesis that the Abwehr's indisciplined activities were harming the interests of the Third Reich. What was more, the ambassadorial post in Madrid had been held since April 1943 by a brother-in-law of Ribbentrop's with practical and personal reasons for clipping the Abwehr's wings. Hans Dietrich Dieckhoff, a Spanish expert two years older than Canaris and typical of the professional diplomats whom the Nazis had refashioned into willing instruments of their policy, was the same Foreign Office official who had tried to prevent the party and Wehrmacht from making contact with representatives of the rebel general Franco in summer 1936.[356] Dieckhoff could not forget how political outsiders like Canaris had coerced the Foreign Office into a course of action pronounced disastrous by its own advisers.

The time had come to settle that old score, especially as Abwehr personnel were once more, as in 1936, opposing the Foreign Office and hampering German diplomacy. The tasks that had brought Dieckhoff to Spain were hard enough in themselves. Spanish deliveries of wolfram were militarily important to Germany, and it was his job to keep them going despite the severe economic pressure exerted on Spain by the Western Allies.[357] This thought was uppermost in Dieckhoff's mind. Hitler had decreed that "every effort must be made to secure us the greatest possible abundance of raw materials from Spain, especially wolfram."[358] Dieckhoff was also bound by the Führer's dictum that "wolfram purchases take priority, and all quantities purchased must be conveyed to Germany with the utmost speed."[359]

But the Spaniards would not deliver the goods—and this applied to more than wolfram—unless the Germans behaved with tact. Any loud noises on the German side were bound to alert the Allied ambassadors, who had repeatedly asked the Spanish Government to discontinue wolfram exports to Germany and expel German agents. What Hitler's ambassador in Madrid needed most of all was peace and quiet, self-effacement and discretion.

For some time now, however, Canaris's Spanish organization had been stepping up its bombings and acts of terrorism against the enemy on Spanish soil. Captain Hummel, KO Spain's Abwehr II officer, had organized a network of saboteurs and explosives experts for the purpose of attacking installations in Gibraltar and British ships in Spanish harbours,[360] though he was circumspect enough to leave no evidence of German involvement. The explosives used were always British-made and most of the saboteurs were members of Communist resistance groups who had no idea they were working for Hitler's secret service.

Their sole object was to incense His Majesty's Government against the Franco regime by obstructing trade between Spain and Britain.[361]

The saboteurs' favourite targets were British freighters carrying oranges. Their cargoes became more and more lethal. Orange crates surreptitiously filled with explosive substances blew up at sea or in British ports. "Sabotaged crates," noted Freytag-Loringhoven of Abwehr II, "were switched beyond the harbour limits and remained unnoticed. According to reports from KO Spain, German responsibility cannot be proved."[362] Orange ships from Spain became the bugbear of British port authorities. Dockers sometimes refused to unload them and police had to search every crate for hidden bombs.[363]

The collapse of Fascist Italy presented Hummel's saboteurs with a new range of targets. These were Italian vessels berthed in Spanish ports and claimed by the Badoglio government but held by the Spanish authorities although their immediate release was another item on the Allied ambassadors' list of demands.[364] Hummel's men swam out to these Italian ships under cover of darkness and placed small charges which rendered them unnavigable, if nothing more. The result of several weeks' exertions, proudly noted by the Abwehr: "Approximately 40,000 tons of Italian cargo space [have been] immobilized and temporarily denied to the enemy."[365]

Dieckhoff looked on in impotent fury while these acts of sabotage in Spanish ports wrecked what he was trying to achieve by tactful and diplomatic means. The Allies and the Spanish authorities soon guessed who was behind the explosions, but as long as nothing occurred to refute the Abwehr's claim that German responsibility could never be proved the ambassador had to grin and bear it.

Then, as Dieckhoff had always known it would, something went wrong. One night early in January 1944 an Abwehr diver named Carl Kampen climbed down the side of the German ship *Lipari* in Cartagena harbour and boarded a dinghy manned by two of its officers, Walter Schröder and Hans Richter. Schröder and Richter rowed while Kampen kept an eye on the mine they were towing at the end of a long rope. They slowly neared their target, the Italian tanker *Lavoro*. Kampen was to attach the submerged charge to her hull. Once in position, however, he made a fatal blunder. The calibrations on the 8 cm. acid fuse did not—as he thought—indicate hours, only minutes. Kampen was still alongside the *Lavoro* when a gigantic explosion blew him to pieces.[366] A Foreign Office report stated: "Kampen did not surface again. The dinghy . . . was overturned. The First Officer sustained non-fatal injuries and the Third Officer was unhurt."[367]

Consul Carlos Fricke, one of Canaris's oldest associates, stepped in and pacified the Spanish port authorities, but the Spaniards' suspicions had been aroused.[368] Dieckhoff seized his chance and urged Ribbentrop to call for a ban on all sabotage operations in Spain. The Foreign Minister, who was only too happy to back his brother-in-law's request, advised the Abwehr to draw its own conclusions from the Kampen affair. Canaris gave in. Freytag-Loringhoven noted: "Abwehr II has . . . completely halted S[abotage] attacks on enemy shipping in Spanish ports and Gibraltar . . . with effect from 18.1.44."[369]

But the attacks persisted because sabotage chief Hummel was, in an almost literal sense, hoist with his own petard. What he had thought of as a subtle ploy now redounded to the Abwehr's disadvantage. No word of command from Germany could prevent anti-Franco Spaniards from smuggling their lightweight charges aboard British ships and persevering in their supposed crusade against the fascist regime. More orange freighters were rent by explosions, and again the trail led to Cartagena harbour.[370]

This time the Spaniards reacted sharply. On January 21 some launches manned by armed marines headed for the German vessels *Lipari* and *Karl Vinnen*. They were boarded a few minutes later and searched for hidden explosives.[371] Soon afterwards Admiral Bastarreche, commanding the naval station at Cartagena, instructed Consul Fricke in writing that the *Lipari's* German crew must vacate her the same day and hand her over to a Spanish military guard.[372] Generalissimo Franco also ensured that his extreme displeasure at German sabotage activities was conveyed to the embassy. "The *Lipari* move," Naval Attaché Menzell cabled to Canaris, "is a consequence of British *démarches* occasioned by numerous acts of sabotage in Spanish ports. The head of state himself has sharply condemned them and given orders that further attacks, whether against foreign or Spanish vessels, are to be prevented by all available means."[373]

Dieckhoff was determined to launch his long-prepared assault on the Abwehr. Being a cautious diplomat and tactician, however, he awaited the ideal moment. It came a few days later in connection with an affair which, though entirely unrelated to events in Spain, provided the Foreign Office with a final pretext for moving against its rival. On January 27, 1944, the Argentine Government broke off diplomatic relations with Germany on the grounds that a German espionage organization had lured Argentine officers into betraying their own country and had thereby damaged Argentina's vital interests.[374]

The fact was that Hans Harnisch, a senior clerk employed by the firm of Boker & Company in Buenos Aires, had been working for the Abwehr (and the SD). Originally assigned to report on industrial developments in the United States, Harnisch was on such good terms with persons close to General Pedro Ramírez, who had assumed the presidency after a military coup in June 1943, that he increasingly concentrated on political intelligence in defiance of the German Embassy and its service attachés.[375] Harnisch genuinely believed that he could help to forge a military alliance between Berlin and Buenos Aires, and for this purpose he recruited an Argentine officer named Helmuth whom he proposed to send to Germany to purchase arms under the aegis of the SD. When Allied secret servicemen arrested the Argentinian during the crossing and uncovered the Harnisch-Helmuth-Ramírez connection, the Argentine President decided to forestall Allied reprisals by taking the opposite tack.[376]

To professional diplomats, the Harnisch affair was a classic example of the Abwehr's clumsy interference in foreign policy. Dieckhoff acted at last. On January 28 he sent a long telegram to the Foreign Office citing the Harnisch case and demanding the virtual cessation of Abwehr activities in Spain. "I consider it absolutely essential," he cabled, "that the Abwehr presence in Spain be drastically reduced."

While arguing that, fundamentally, "the service attaché machinery should suffice to handle the intelligence tasks required in this field," Dieckhoff did not dispute that "some sort of Abwehr apparatus" had a *raison d'être* in Spain. That apparatus should, however, be "radically reduced." "All Abwehr equipment must be removed from official embassy premises and German consulates as soon as possible. I consider a heavily manned organization superfluous and harmful . . . Everything must be done to ensure that, in future, remaining Abwehr personnel are solely entrusted with assignments that can genuinely be justified to outsiders . . . Above all, so-called active assignments such as acts of sabotage . . . must now be rendered definitely impossible."[377]

Ribbentrop fielded his brother-in-law's bombshell and flung it even harder at the Abwehr authorities. On January 30 the Foreign Minister dictated a letter to Keitel complaining about the Abwehr's activities in Spain and Argentina and claiming nothing less than a right of veto over all "active" Abwehr operations in neutral countries. "For this reason," he wrote, "I should be much obliged if you would as soon as possible inform me of all Abwehr operations already initiated or now in progress so that I can ascertain whether their implementation can or cannot be countenanced from the foreign policy aspect. I would further ask you to ensure that new assignments of this nature are henceforth cleared in advance with the Foreign Office."[378]

Keitel was not the man to reject such outside interference in military matters. He promptly instructed Canaris to reach an understanding with the Foreign Office. On February 3 the Admiral was constrained to write to Ribbentrop as follows: "Head of OKW has forbidden further sabotage against British ships in Spanish ports. He does, however, think it desirable to continue sabotage attacks on Badoglio shipping in Spanish ports. Your views are requested on whether, in view of prevailing circumstances, the continuation of sabotage attacks . . . is still warranted."[379] No intelligence chief could more abjectly have renounced his powers in the middle of a war than Canaris did by inviting the Foreign Minister to rule on his department's activities.

Keitel's response to Ribbentrop on February 4 was just as feeble. While snubbing him to the extent of commenting that the Harnisch and orange-ship incidents had probably not been "the occasion of the enemy's political pressures, but merely a pretext of the moment," he conceded that sabotage in Spain would be discontinued and that Abwehr operations in neutral countries would be "agreed" with the Foreign Office.[380] Furthermore: "I have instructed Admiral Canaris to establish personal contact with Ambassador Dieckhoff as soon as possible with a view to adjusting our military intelligence service in Spain to the prevailing international situation while still fulfilling essential military requirements."[381]

But Ribbentrop, who was determined to manoeuvre the Abwehr into an even more subordinate position, persevered with his campaign. After receiving a Reuters report that a *German* time bomb had been discovered in a crate of onions aboard a British ship fresh from Spain, he complained to the Führer himself.[382] There is no detailed record of what was said, but the gist of his argument must have been that the Abwehr was unreliable and that Canaris's men were sabotaging German policy in Spain. The outcome of the Hitler-Ribbentrop interview was conveyed to Canaris in a memorandum from Legationsrat Baron Otto von Grote, the Foreign Office liaison officer at Abwehr headquarters, which arrived on February 8: "The Führer stated in conclusion that (1) all such acts of sabotage must cease and (2) no sabotage attacks were to be made on Italian ships either."[383]

Ribbentrop had set his trap with care. If another act of sabotage did occur in Spain it would do so in direct defiance of Hitler's orders and have disastrous repercussions on the Abwehr authorities. But this time the Foreign Minister was overtaken by outside events. RSHA chief Kaltenbrunner had already sent Hitler a report on yet another Abwehr fiasco.

Kaltenbrunner's memorandum, a seven-page document dated February 7, contained this passage: "The SD representative in Istanbul reports a nest of German traitors in Turkey to which the following are so far known to belong: Dr. Kurt [sic] Vermehren, Jr., a lawyer, and his wife, née Countess Plettenberg; Dr. Hamburger; Herr and Frau Kletschkowski; Herock, the Semperit-Werke representative in Istanbul; the legal director of the Deutsche Bank, Dr. Barth; and the director of Gummi-Werke Semperit of Vienna, Josef Ridiger. Strong suspicion also attaches to the clerical assistant of the air attaché, Major Schenker-Angerer, and his wife and daughter; also to Frau Henschel, formerly

Countess Wurmbrand. All the above-named belong to Abwehrstelle Istanbul or are closely associated with it."[384]

Just to complete his sense of betrayal, Hitler was additionally informed by the SD representative, SS-Obersturmbannführer Wolff, through Kaltenbrunner, that the Vermehrens had already defected to the British and that the other suspects would be following them shortly. Kaltenbrunner emphasized the value of their work to the enemy: "Vermehren has for the past three months been engaging in treasonable activities on behalf of Major Elliot and Major Gripp of British military intelligence. Vermehren further intends to carry on active anti-German propaganda over the London radio. The British plan to make a sensation of this case, especially as Countess Plettenberg is related to [Ambassador] von Papen."[385]

Hitler stopped short. A name had suddenly caught his eye. He read the passage again. "Dr. Vermehren has since December 1942 been assistant and confidential adviser to the head of Abwehrstelle I in Istanbul, Dr. Leverkuehn."[386] The name was all too familiar. Captain Paul Leverkuehn, head of KO-Nebenstelle [substation] Istanbul and a friend of Canaris's and Papen's had in spring 1943 been the subject of a rumour that he was secretly in touch with the Americans and wanted to arrange a separate peace with the Western powers.[387] Since then, the very mention of his name had been enough to send the Führer into a tantrum. And now this friend of a friend of Canaris's had gone over to the enemy after turning his office into a hotbed of treason. Kaltenbrunner said as much himself: "This has gravely prejudiced the activities not only of Abwehrstelle Istanbul but of our other military agencies in Turkey. The entire work of the Abwehrstelle has been exposed and its continuation seems impracticable."[388]

Hitler was so incensed at this new Abwehr fiasco that he began to consider dropping Canaris. He first alluded to this in conference with Himmler on February 9.[389] The SS chief must have sensed the imminence of the moment for which he, and Kaltenbrunner and Schellenberg in particular, had so long been waiting, but he was too discreet to take the initiative. He left the Führer's wrath to mature by itself.

Hitler did not know that the SD's report on the extent of the Istanbul leak was as inaccurate as the personal particulars it gave of Leverkuchn's "confidant." Erich Maria (not "Kurt") Vermehren, born on December 23, 1919, was a Lübeck lawyer who had only been drafted into the Landesschützen [local defence forces], not the Army, because of a gunshot wound sustained in childhood. Thanks to his knowledge of foreign languages, he was later employed by the OKW to minister to the "spiritual welfare" of British and American prisoners of war before ending up as a clerk in Leverkuehn's office. He certainly had no talent for practical espionage. "My position in KO-Nebenstelle Istanbul was far too unimportant for my defection to have had momentous consequences in itself," states Eric M. de Saventhem, as Vermehren now calls himself, and a former KO colleague confirms that there could have been "no more innocuous person holding a junior post in an intelligence centre which had anyway ceased to function."[390]

It was legal rather than intelligence considerations that had prompted Leverkuehn to remember the son of Vermehren Sr., a former Hamburg colleague, and engineer his transfer to KO Istanbul. Being a specialist in international maritime law, Erich Vermehren was assigned to press Germany's claims to the Danube fleet, whose vessels had been embargoed by the Turks. These lengthy legal proceedings did not occupy the whole of Vermehren's time, so Leverkuehn entrusted him with a variety of unexciting clerical tasks as well.[391]

Vermehren would hardly have contemplated anything as dramatic as defecting to the Allies had it not been for the woman he married in 1941. Countess Elisabeth Plettenberg was a forceful person eight years his senior and a devout Roman Catholic who had decided that it would be immoral to continue serving the Nazi system. A member of the Hencke Service with long-standing anti-Nazi connections in the Catholic branch of the resistance movement, she saw no prospect of destroying the Hitler regime from within. Vermehren, whose "originally instinctive and almost congenital opposition to the regime had—on his own submission—acquired "ideological depth" through his conversion to Catholicism, likewise concluded that the Nazi system could only be overcome by extraneous means.

It is hard to determine which of the Vermehrens first resolved to go over to the Allies. Erich Vermehren claims to have had the idea in summer 1943, though his colleagues and the Gestapo surmised that the initiative came from his stronger-minded spouse.[392] What is certain is that Vermehren and his wife agreed during his first spell of home leave in November 1943 that anti-Nazis like themselves had no choice but to defect to the British. "I was ingenuous enough to believe," Vermehren says, "that even my own modest knowledge might help to ensure that the political plans of the future occupying powers would be better tailored . . . to the realities of the situation inside Germany."[393]

Elisabeth Vermehren laid her personal plans with care. She distributed her assets among the banking accounts of her younger brothers and sisters and persuaded Marschall von Bieberstein to entrust her with a Turkish mission of which State Secretary Baron Gustav Adolf Steengracht von Moyland, Weizsäcker's successor at the Foreign Office, gave the following apologetic description: "Ever since Cardinal Spellman's visit to Turkey, President Roosevelt had been obtaining information from a certain set of people known there. Information acquired from this circle—relating to Roosevelt's electoral prospects, etc.—was to be communicated to the Foreign Office through Frau Vermehren. Herr Vermehren had stated that material would become available to him, and later to his wife, which held no interest for the Abwehr but might prove valuable to Foreign Office Intelligence."[394]

Armed with this diplomatic assignment, Frau Vermehren hoped to evade the "frontier and visa restriction" which had been imposed on her by the Gestapo in October 1943 and amounted to an exit ban.[395] The Vermehrens set off for Turkey in mid-December. As soon as Leverkuehn learned of their project, however, he instructed the Abwehr outstations in Bulgaria to detain Frau Vermehren and send her back to Germany.[396] A patrol of the Geheime Feldpolizei duly stopped her at Svilengrad on the Bulgarian-Turkish border. Captain Hans Hussl, head of the local KO-Nebenstelle, confiscated Frau Vermehren's passport and sent her back to KO Sofia, leaving her husband to continue the journey alone.[397]

But Frau Vermehren found a friend in need at the German Embassy in Sofia. The cultural attaché, Gesandtschaftsrat [Legation Counsellor] Garben, was prevailed on to telephone Marschall von Bieberstein at the Foreign Office. Bieberstein advised Frau Vermehren to dodge the frontier checks by flying to Istanbul in an Air Ministry plane in which seats were reserved for diplomatic personnel.[398] She took his advice and reached Istanbul on December 24.[399] Leverkuehn, who was appalled and feared trouble with the Gestapo, persuaded Vermehren to submit a written report formally dissociating himself from his wife's action.

"I beg to report," Vermehren wrote to HQ KO Near East on December 27, "that my wife arrived in Istanbul by courier plane on 24.12.43 without my prior knowledge [but] on express instructions from the Foreign Office, which employs her. My wife informs me that she is here to carry out some assignments given her by the Foreign Office. It has been envisaged that she would proceed to Ankara forthwith. However, her state of health has compelled her to undergo medical treatment here, and she may have to spend some weeks in hospital."[400]

A few days later Vermehren contacted the Istanbul centre of the Secret Intelligence Service and offered to defect to the Allies on three conditions. These were, first, that he and his wife should not be involved in any Allied military operations; secondly, that their flight should be made to look like an abduction; and thirdly, that they should be employed on "planning work for the postwar period." The British agreed. Their "well-devised kidnapping scheme," says Vermehren, "made us feel confident that the voluntary nature of our defection would remain undisclosed until after the war." No Abwehr man could more guilelessly have surrendered to an enemy intelligence service. The Vermehrens' defection was worthless to the Allies unless they could make capital out of it. For this they needed voluntary defectors who were guided by conscience and willing to testify publicly to the desperate and deteriorating position of the Hitler regime.

It was little wonder that the kidnapping story soon collapsed. On January 27, 1944, Erich and Elisabeth Vermehren allowed themselves to be "abducted" by British agents in Istanbul and taken to Izmir, where they joined some Greek refugees aboard a freighter bound for Syria. From there they were flown to Cairo. The "bitter truth," as Vermehren calls it, was brought home to them within three weeks. Their defection was first reported by the Basle *Nationalzeitung* on February 16 and semiofficially confirmed by a BBC spokesman a fortnight later. On March 3 Radio Cairo broadcast an anti-Nazi declaration from the renegade couple.

The affair caused such a stir that subsequent historians and Canaris's biographers have unanimously described it as the occasion of the Admiral's downfall—the last nail in his coffin, so to speak. It is even said that Goebbels ascribed "crucial military importance" to the incident, and that it was "splashed" by the German press and radio. None of this is true. Nothing was publicly known until Canaris fell from grace. The Foreign Office, OKW and Propaganda Ministry all decided, even after the Allies' propaganda broadsides, that "for the present, nothing should be undertaken in the way of propaganda for fear of needlessly investing the affair with even greater resonance."[401]

Not even the RSHA report of February 7 provided Hitler with an excuse for dismissing Canaris on the spot. Only one person took immediate advantage of the fiasco, and that was Ribbentrop.

Presumably unaware that the Hencke Service was involved in Frau Vermehren's escape, the Foreign Minister saw it as another means of setting Hitler against Canaris and the Abwehr. Once again, Abwehr agents seemed to be disrupting the work of German diplomats. Vermehren's predictable disclosures about KO-Nebenstelle Istanbul would inevitably make things awkward for German diplomatic representatives in Turkey because the Abwehr's local headquarters were installed in the German Consulate in Istanbul. Ribbentrop must have been only too tempted to exploit Hitler's anger at the Vermehren affair.

He felt so sure of his ground that he even considered putting the SD on his black list as well. At his behest, Steengracht cabled the heads of mission in Ankara, Stockholm, Berne and Lisbon on February 8 requesting their "firm and precise views" on the following questions: "1. What installations and personnel belonging to the Abwehr and SD are still acceptable locally? 2. What reductions may be warranted in this respect?" Steengracht encouragingly added: "Kindly conduct this examination without regard for sectional interests and government departments at home."[402]

On February 9 the Foreign Office requested each of its diplomatic missions in Spain, Portugal, Sweden, Switzerland and Turkey to select one official who was versed in intelligence work and qualified to suggest ways of restricting the Abwehr's activities.[403] Karl Ritter, who was responsible for liaison with the military authorities as head of Sonderreferat [Special Desk] Pol IM, made his meaning clear in a secret telegram: "Since the High Command of the Armed Forces has yet to be apprised of our intention to summon these officials to Germany, you are asked to refrain pro tempore from informing service attachés and Abwehr representatives of the proposed trip."[404]

Despite this precaution, Canaris already sensed that Foreign Office bureaucrats were tightening their noose round his department. He was just preparing to visit Spain for a heart-to-heart with Dieckhoff, as instructed, when the ambassador lodged a veto. On February 5 Dieckhoff cabled Berlin that he had just learned of the Admiral's intention and urgently advised him to cancel his trip because it would only furnish the British and Americans with another pretext for increasing their pressure on Spain.[405]

Next day Dieckhoff erected some more barriers against the Admiral's projected visit. A further telegram referred darkly to anti-Abwehr "operations by the Spanish authorities" and painted the situation in dismal colours. "A member of Hummel's staff has recently had his home searched, and there are recurrent rumours of more house searches to come. Apart from this, it has been intimated to me that the Spaniards are planning a wider-ranging campaign against the German espionage network." As for Canaris's good relations with the Spaniards and his decades-old friendship with senior Spanish officials: "The durability of such personal relationships should on no account be overestimated."[406]

Although he must have found it insufferable that his visit to Spain should be opposed by a German ambassador who had backed the wrong horse in the Spanish Civil War and seen himself refuted by history, Canaris backed down. Too weary to take up the cudgels, even with a man like Dieckhoff, he agreed to call off the Spanish trip and confer with Dieckhoff's deputy, Minister Baron Sigismund von Bibra, at Biarritz on February 10.[407] Grote accompanied him to the French resort and the KO chiefs of Spain and Portugal, Leissner and Kremer von Auenrode, were also summoned to attend.[408]

Canaris lodged in the villa of the local Abwehr representative. Bibra duly appeared, but no agreement was reached. The diplomat came to feel that Canaris bestowed more interest on his dachshunds Kasper and Sabine, which had both come with him, than on military intelligence problems in the fourth year of a world war. Auenrode's wife also expressed surprise at his listless manner.[409]

Canaris was, in fact, extremely perturbed by what Leissner told him about breaches of discipline inside his own organization, KO Madrid. These reports left him convinced that he ought to visit Spain and the Spanish capital in order to salvage and repair his disintegrating espionage network. He telephoned Bürkner in Zossen and dictated something very like a *cri de coeur* to the Foreign Minister. Bürkner took it down: "The director of KO Madrid had intimated that difficulties had arisen in the organization of the military intelligence service in Spain which made it desirable for Admiral Canaris to visit Madrid. Admiral Canaris would only confer with General Vigón and the head of Spanish military intelligence, but would ensure that there was absolutely no question of a meeting with Franco, Jordana or Muñoz Grande. In view of the general situation, the trip had become urgently necessary. It would be undertaken incognito, with no visa or contact with frontier posts."[410]

Bürkner passed the message to Ritter, who graciously informed him that, although he felt sure the Reich Foreign Minister would have no objection to the trip, he would have to consult him first.[411] Canaris waited, hour after hour, and still no answer came. He never saw Spain again. Whether or not Dieckhoff threw another wrench in the works, the Spaniards declined to receive Canaris. They even cold-shouldered his suggestion that General Martínez Campos should meet him in the South of France.[412]

At last the villa's teleprinter started to chatter a brief message from Abwehr headquarters. Canaris turned pale when he read it. "How could they do such a thing!" he exclaimed angrily. "This is quite impossible—now of all times!"[413] The message stated that a bomb had exploded on yet another British orange ship at Cartagena. Frau von Auenrode, who was standing beside him, is still convinced that it was "the things he heard in Biarritz which ultimately tripped him up."[414]

Canaris guessed at once that he would not survive this new disaster in his present post. Suddenly feeling as if he had all the time in the world to spare, he lost his usual sense of urgency and could hardly be induced to leave. When Major von Auenrode proposed to move on, he talked him out of it. "No, don't go—let's stay here for another day or two." Canaris and the Auenrodes took the dogs to a small lake with an adjoining golf course and spent hours roaming the countryside. "It was all rather sad," Frau von Auenrode recalls. "We all felt sure it would end badly, but we didn't know just how badly."[415]

On February 11 they went their separate ways. Canaris flew back to Berlin and the Auenrodes returned to Lisbon. None of them suspected that Canaris would be axed the same day. Meanwhile, with the Vermehren case still fresh in his mind, the Führer had been told of the latest bomb explosion at Cartagena.[416] Another wave of Hitlerian fury broke over the Abwehr and its chief.

Having heard, like everyone on the dictator's staff, that Hitler was sick of "Herr Canaris" and his entire organization, Himmler's senior representative at the Führer's headquarters swung into action. Almost casually, SS-Brigadeführer Fegelein suggested that Hitler should simply hand "the whole works" over to the Reichsführer-SS.[417] Hitler nodded and sent for Himmler. By the time Himmler left he had taken another gigantic stride along the road to absolute power in the Third Reich: Hitler had commissioned him to create a unified intelligence service out of the SD and the Abwehr—the super-service of which the Black Order had always dreamed.[418] Canaris was relieved of his post and Colonel Hansen put in charge of Amt Ausland/Abwehr pending its reorganization.

Next day Himmler summoned several close advisers—Kaltenbrunner, Schellenberg, Müller and Huppenkothen, together with desk chiefs Schmitz and Sandberger to a meeting at Posen.[419] There on board "Heinrich," the special train that served as his mobile headquarters, he invited brief suggestions on how the Abwehr and SD should be integrated and what form the relevant "Hitler directive" should take.[420] Huppenkothen recalls that Schellenberg wanted as far as possible "to take over everything hitherto controlled by Canaris on behalf of the Reichsführer-SS," whereas Himmler confined himself to the sections (Abwehr I and II) which the RSHA could "digest."[421] Kaltenbrunner, who had long ago seen through Ribbentrop's machinations, wanted to incorporate the Foreign Office intelligence service as well. A few days later he was complaining, "The Foreign Office is trying to use the Vermehren and Co. affair to neutralize the German intelligence services, whose competition it finds irksome."[422]

The SS leaders drafted a Hitler directive which Kaltenbrunner took to the Führer's headquarters on February 13 and showed to Keitel and Jodl, who approved its submission to the Führer. After signing the draft order Hitler asked the RSHA chief with a hint of sarcasm whether he now "had everything." Kaltenbrunner replied that the Foreign Office intelligence service was the only missing item.[423] The Führer's response was so vague that he decided to press ahead with plans to bring the diplomatic intelligence service under the RSHA's yoke. Whoever emerged victorious from these interdepartmental skirmishes and intrigues, Kaltenbrunner was determined that it should not be Joachim von Ribbentrop.

Before long, typewriters were clattering in the outer offices of the Führer's headquarters. The product of this activity was a ten-line directive which special OKW and RSHA couriers delivered to every command headquarters in the Third Reich. The recipients of this directive, which was classified as a Geheime Reichssache [secret document] and had to be signed for, read: "Führer's headquarters, February 12, 1944. I direct: 1. A unified German secret intelligence service is to be created. 2. I appoint the Reichsführer-SS to command this German intelligence service. Insofar as this affects the military intelligence and counterespionage service, the Reichsführer-SS and the head of the OKW shall take all requisite steps by mutual arrangement. Signed: Adolf Hitler."[424]

The independent Abwehr was dead and its chief overthrown. As the Third Reich neared extinction, German hubris entered a last and lurid phase marked by almost unbridled SS supremacy.

13

Murder at Flossenbürg

In mid-February 1944 a German jeep carrying two senior Wehrmacht officers approached the gate of security zone Maybach II in the military camp at Zossen. One brief glance from the guard commander assured the vehicle of uninterrupted passage because its occupants were known to every German soldier. Field Marshal Keitel, head of the Armed Forces High Command, and Colonel General Jodl, head of the Armed Forces Operations Staff, saluted mechanically as they drove on. Minutes later they pulled up outside a well-camouflaged grey-green bunker nestling among some tall pine trees.

Keitel and Jodl cannot have felt particularly happy as they climbed out. Hitler had assigned them an unpleasant chore. They were to call on the disgraced Abwehr chief, explain the reasons for his dismissal and announce what fate the Führer had in store for him.[1] Rather stiffly, Hitler's two henchmen strode towards the bunker. Another few minutes and they were face to face with Canaris.

There is no record of what was said. Only the gist of their message can be reconstructed. This was that, in view of the critical military situation and the Abwehr's manifold failures in the past, the Führer had decided to streamline the secret intelligence services by merging the Abwehr and SD under the command of the Reichsführer-SS. Canaris was to hold himself in readiness at Burg Lauenstein until the process of reorganization was complete.[2] The Führer consolingly added that he would decide on the Admiral's future employment in due course.

Stripped of its embellishments, this meant that Wilhelm Canaris had been relieved of his command overnight and placed under house arrest until further notice. To someone who had so often incurred the dictator's wrath in recent days, temporary banishment to a castle did not seem too much to bear. Besides, instead of handing him a Chinese emperor's silken cord, Keitel and Jodl actually conveyed a few words of gratitude from the Führer's lips. Thus originated the legend that Hitler's errand boys presented Canaris with the German Cross in Gold, one of the regime's highest decorations for gallantry—a confusion which doubtless arose from the fact that Hitler had only a few weeks earlier invested him with the German Cross in Silver for "exceptional contributions to the military conduct of the war."[3]

But Keitel and Jodl gave him little time to dwell on the dictator's gratitude or ingratitude. Canaris had to vacate his bunker within hours, and his departure entailed no elaborate preparations. He did not even have to bid his family farewell. He had already found his wife a refuge from Allied air raids at the Bavarian home of an old friend from Spain and his daughters were also clear of Berlin (Brigitte at boarding school and Eva in a special institution).[4] All he had to do before setting off into the unknown was pack a suitcase and get his dachshunds ready.

With driver Lüdecke at the wheel, Canaris's official Mercedes headed south towards Thuringia and Upper Franconia. Canaris and his companion entered the Frankenwald, a mountainous region between the Thuringian Forest and the Fichtelgebirge whose harsh and inhospitable climate the sun-loving Admiral found repellent. Southwest of Probstzella, on a mountaintop overlooking the Loquitz Valley, towered a romantic castle which Canaris, with his sense of history, came to regard as a sort of Elba. Burg Lauenstein, his future place of exile, was an old fortress whose dates he was soon to know by heart: built in the thirteenth century, destroyed in 1290, faithfully restored during the fourteenth century and enlarged during the sixteenth, then left to decay until its most recent restoration in 1896.

The castle was secluded enough to accommodate those Abwehr departments which had reason to draw a special veil of secrecy over their work. Lauenstein was, in fact, mainly reserved for the experts who furnished intelligence agents with the indispensable tools of their trade —forged passports, invisible inks, microphotographic and duplicating equipment.[5] Presiding over Burg Lauenstein's secret world of laboratories and research departments was Lieutenant Colonel Albrecht Focke, a staunch National Socialist who had formerly been Wirtschaftsreferent [head of the Economics Desk, or I/Wi] at Abwehrnebenstelle Cologne and now held the post of castle commandant.[6]

Berlin had already briefed Focke on how to treat the Admiral. His instructions were: complete freedom of movement within the castle precincts, as little contact as possible with the outside world. He showed Canaris and Lüdecke to their quarters, treating his former chief with a courtesy and respect which were only slightly tempered by his inability to grasp how such an important personage could fail to believe in the Führer's genius.[7] But not even Focke's stiff and formal civility could dispel Canaris's agonizing awareness that he had been shut away.

The Admiral learned little of what was happening outside in the weeks that followed. No word reached him of how the Abwehr was faring or whether his successor, Hansen, had managed to rescue the bulk of the old intelligence service from the RSHA's clutches. Any picture he tried to form of the state of the Abwehr was dependent on rumour and guesswork. His only concrete information came from the official letters and communications which conveyed with brutal directness that his number was finally up. On March 10 his old rival Dönitz, now commander in chief of the Navy, informed him that his removal from the active list would take effect on June 30, 1944.[8] The Navy Personnel Office stated in a letter dated March 21: "Admiral Canaris will be placed at the Navy's disposal. No re-employment is contemplated."[9]

Although he had already been written off on paper, Canaris still hoped for an act of clemency on the Führer's part. But no heartening messages reached him from the outside world and none of his former subordinates or old friends came to see him. Not even Erika Canaris, who visited him once at the castle, could coax him out of his shell.[10] More than ever, Canaris devoted himself to his dachshunds. The three of them spent hours roaming and communing in the castle grounds: a strange spectacle in the midst of so much military routine and secret service activity.

At long last, a familiar figure turned up at Lauenstein. Lieutenant Colonel Schrader, one of the few members of the Oster circle still at large,[11] had come to give his former chief a report on the state of the Abwehr. Canaris was infuriated by Schrader's account of the merger talks between the Abwehr, SD and Gestapo. Grossly misjudging the facts, he felt that Colonel Hansen was making far too many concessions and surrendering one Abwehr stronghold after another to his triumphant rivals.[12]

The truth was that Kaltenbrunner, Schellenberg and "Gestapo" Müller were dismantling the old Abwehr machine bit by bit, and that Keitel and a few other officers were having great difficulty in preventing its total dissolution and dismemberment. The negotiations were not in fact being conducted by Hansen, the new Abwehr chief, but by Colonel von Bentivegni, the head of section who maintained close official links with the RSHA and was well acquainted with its ideas.[13] Keitel had appointed him deputy Abwehr chief for the duration of the remodelling process and instructed him to assist the senior OKW negotiator, Lieutenant General Paul Winter, in hammering out an agreement with the RSHA.[14]

Bentivegni, the Abwehr III chief whom his critics suspected of covert collaboration with the RSHA, was really pursuing a simple objective. He hoped to incorporate the Abwehr in the new super-organization as a self-contained unit and simultaneously preserve his old section from any form of RSHA control. This meant leaving the counterespionage organization (Abwehr III) and Bürkner's Amtsgruppe Ausland with the OKW while amalgamating Sections I (Secret Intelligence Service) and II (Sabotage) into a "Military Department" and consigning it to the RSHA as a separate unit, no stipulation being made about the future status of Jacobsen's Central Section.

Such was the shape of the proposal which Winter and Bentivegni submitted to their opponents in March. But the RSHA authorities had other ideas on how the intelligence services should be merged under their command. They demanded that *all* parts of the Abwehr be absorbed by the RSHA—insofar as they were not directly related to counterespionage in the armed forces—and wanted to distribute the various desks, groups and subsections among their RSHA equivalents. What the OKW representatives were offering, on the other hand, was an autonomous Abwehr inside the SD but still under military—in other words, OKW—jurisdiction. Kaltenbrunner and Schellenberg had entertained a wholly different vision of their new super-service.

At the end of March or the beginning of April (the exact date cannot be ascertained) Keitel braved the other side's predictable objections and sent Kaltenbrunner a draft outline of the OKW's proposals for reshaping the intelligence agencies and their powers. These envisaged that Abwehr I and II would be transferred to the RSHA under Colonel Hansen in the form of a Military Department while the bulk of Abwehr III (minus Counterespionage IIIF) and the forward reconnaissance teams would come under a Truppenabwehr [Forces Security] section of the Armed Forces Operations Staff or be controlled by a newly constituted Frontaufklärung und Truppenabwehr [Forward Reconnaissance and Forces Security] chief in the Army High Command.[15]

Early in April Kaltenbrunner responded with a set of counterproposals. These called for complete RSHA supervision of all intelligence agencies, divided the Abwehr among existing SD and Gestapo departments, stipulated that all Abwehr personnel transferred to the RSHA be subject to SS discipline and jurisdiction, and claimed sole RSHA competence in matters relating to personnel and appointments.[16] This proved too much even for Keitel, who promptly fired off a teleprinter message addressed to Kaltenbrunner: "Reference the joint order affecting the secret intelligence and counterespionage service, I cannot approve the counterproposal conveyed to me today by Lieutenant B. because it exceeds the terms of the Führer's directive."[17]

On April 11 Keitel drafted a letter of protest to Himmler but carefully secured the backing of the separate general staffs before sending it. Colonel Gehlen and his OKH intelligence officers were particularly anxious that their superiors should resist Kaltenbrunner at all costs. A letter from Gehlen to Keitel dated April 16 contained the following passage:

"In my estimation, the proposed arrangement entails a very far-reaching dismemberment of the functions of the military intelligence service and their transfer to the domain of the Reichsführer-SS, my concern being that the work of the military intelligence service may be substantially impaired thereby."[18]

Thus armed, Keitel could at last approach Himmler direct. "After consulting the head of the Armed Forces Operations Staff," he wrote, "and in agreement with the Commanders in Chief of the Air Force and the Navy, as well as with the Chief of the Army General Staff, I consider it mistaken at this present stage in the war to disband the 'Military Department' of the Secret Intelligence Service on take-over." The OKW chief became more and more refractory as his letter progressed. The RSHA proposals "would lead to disintegration and thus, certainly for an appreciable period, to a decline in performance . . . Complete fusion would cause . . . at least temporary paralysis in the procurement and, above all, in the sifting and evaluation of military intelligence . . . Transfers [of personnel] to militarily senior commands, staffs, etc., on direct orders from the Chief of the Security Police cannot be countenanced."[19]

Himmler was impressed by this unexpected stand. Never one to court a head on clash with the armed forces, he signalled his subordinates to drop some of their demands. The RSHA authorities had to tolerate the existence of the Military Department (future designation: Amt M or Amt Mil) and permit its chief to deputize for Schellenberg as Amtschef VI in the event of his absence—though the converse also applied. Kaltenbrunner further conceded that military and civilian Abwehr personnel transferred to the RSHA should be "militarily and economically" under Wehrmacht control and exempt from SS jurisdiction,[20] though he covered his retreat with a makeshift verbal smoke screen: the new arrangement was to be only "provisional."[21]

The RSHA negotiators haggled all the harder over the fate of the Abwehr's individual components. Canaris's empire disintegrated bit by bit. The Central Section was completely dismantled and shared round the Reichssicherheitshauptamt. The Admiral's most brilliant creation, Group IIIF [penetration of foreign intelligence services], became a bone of contention between Schellenberg and "Gestapo" Müller; the desks responsible for security precautions were allotted to the RSHA or OKW according to their civilian or military range of duties; and the sabotage functions of what had once been Abwehr II were redivided into general sabotage (RSHA) and sabotage against enemy forces (OKW).[22]

This wondrous feat of administrative fusion was complete by the beginning of May. It was held together by a web of complicated status directives which determined with bureaucratic exactitude where in the new intelligence set-up the military powers of the Wehrmacht ceased and the effective authority of the Reichsführer-SS began. On May 14, 1944, Keitel and Himmler signed an agreement embodying the compromise negotiated by the RSHA and OKW.[23] A few days later they summoned the luminaries of the Abwehr, Gestapo and SD to Salzburg, where the birth of the new organization was fittingly celebrated by a conference lasting several days.[24] Everyone turned up. Hansen, Bentivegni, Schellenberg, Kaltenbrunner, Rohleder, Huppenkothen—never had so many members of the Greater German secret service élite been gathered under a single roof.

Only one face was missing, but Himmler was at pains during his hour-long address on the future functions of the foreign intelligence service to mention Canaris and recall "the meritorious work performed by military intelligence."[25] Hansen likewise referred to the work that had been done under his predecessor. The heads of the German intelligence agencies feigned such harmony that their new supreme master, Kaltenbrunner, was able to issue the following directive on May 23: "The existing Amt Abwehr will be disbanded with effect from 1.6.44 . . . Systematic preparations are to be made for the gradual fusion of Ämter VI and M [Schellenberg's Amt VI and the Military Department]. This task I delegate to Amtschef VI."[26]

Soon afterwards Schellenberg went to Burg Lauenstein to enlighten Canaris on the reorganized Secret Intelligence Service.[27] History does not relate what passed between them, but Canaris can scarcely have approved of the new set-up. To smash the old Abwehr, disrupt the most sensitive counterespionage agencies and deprive the Wehrmacht of all foreign reconnaissance-in-depth seemed to him an act of self-destruction perpetrated by madmen and amateurs. He never came to terms with the ruin of his life's work and never ceased to blame this sacrilege on Hansen's feebleness and his overfriendly relations with the RSHA.

At the same time, Schellenberg's visit struck him as a good omen—a sign that his sterile and soul-destroying days at Burg Lauenstein would soon be over. Focke's manner towards his distinguished semiprisoner did, in fact, become perceptibly easier after Schellenberg's departure.

He had evidently received fresh instructions from Berlin. Although Hitler had decreed the Admiral's removal from the active list on June 10, the order was rescinded a few days later. Canaris was reinstated, this time as an admiral "z.V." [zur Verfügung—available for duty].[28]

By the end of June he had reason to hope that his career might not be over after all. Focke brought him word that the Führer had appointed him head of the OKW's Sonderstab für Handelskrieg und wirtschaftliche Kampfmassnahmen" [HWK—Special Staff for Mercantile Warfare and Economic Combat Measures].[29] What is the answer to this apparent riddle? The obvious one is that Hitler had no wish to dispense entirely with one of the few Germans in good standing with the outside world. Baron Kaulbars, Canaris's friend and confidant, later told the Gestapo of a feeling in Swedish circles that "the Admiral's removal would destroy every possibility of some kind of accommodation [between Germany and the Western Allies]."[30] What may also have accounted for his comeback was Hitler's lingering affection for the ex-spy-master and, last but not least, some discreet support from Keitel (who assisted his family financially after he had been detained by the Gestapo).

Whatever the reason, Canaris was free again. He told Lüdecke to pack their bags, and they returned to Berlin—plus dogs—at the end of June.[31] Canaris moved back into his old home at 14 Betazeile, where Mohammed the Algerian manservant and a Polish cook were waiting to welcome him.[32] On July 1 Admiral (z.V.) Canaris reported to Eiche near Potsdam, as instructed, and took over his new department. Despite its resounding name,[33] the Special Staff for Mercantile Warfare and Economic Combat Measures was hardly a power in the land. An adjutant, a handful of officers unfit for combat duty and a few drafted civilians and secretaries—such was the full extent of the organization over which Canaris now presided.

The history of the HWK had mirrored the ebb and flow of Germany's aspirations to great- and world-power status. Originally a department centred on the triangle formed by the Navy, Foreign Office and Ministry of Economic Affairs, it had been geared to directing mercantile warfare throughout the world and, in particular, co-ordinating resistance to the Allied economic blockade. But the HWK's field of activities had shrunk year by year as one country after another reduced its commercial dealings with Germany. Turkey had stopped all chrome shipments in April, no wolfram had arrived from Spain and Portugal since May and June respectively, and there were even signs that Sweden and Switzerland might impose a total ban on exports to the Reich.[34]

This left the new head of department with little more to do than peruse files and hold conferences which were virtually sand-table exercises. Canaris, who had never enjoyed paperwork, was bored by the whole business. He performed his duties in a semimechanical fashion, dismayed and distracted by the dramatic developments now taking shape on the Eastern and Western fronts. The war had entered a new phase. This time it was the Allies' turn to smite the Wehrmacht with lethal intensity, delivering a relentless hail of blows which steadily sapped the Germans' powers of resistance. The Third Reich was tottering towards its inevitable doom.

On June 6 the British and American armies launched their long-awaited invasion of France. By nightfall they had carved out three beachheads on the Normandy coast, where the Germans had not been expecting them. Continuously reinforced, they pushed inland.[35] Three weeks later the Allied Supreme Commander, Eisenhower, was directing the largest invasion force ever assembled on French soil: 1 million men, 171,532 vehicles and 566,648 tons of equipment.[36] The Cotentin Peninsula was soon in Allied hands, and on July 18 British and American units thrust southwards to gain full operational mobility.[37]

The Western Allies' invasion was just under way when the Russians struck in the East. On June 22 Marshals Zhukov and Vasilievsky hurled four army groups at the positions held by Army Group Centre and overran them.[38] The bulk of the Third Panzer Army was cut off at Vitebsk two days later, the Ninth Army was encircled at Bobruisk on June 26, and by July 3 the Fourth Army had been confined to a pocket in the neighbourhood of Minsk. Army Group Centre lost 350,000 men and the remainder streamed westwards.[39] According to the historian Lothar Gruchmann, the German Army in Russia had sustained "a far graver catastrophe . . . than at Stalingrad."[40]

And still the enemy offensives continued, almost without respite. The German armies were caught in a vice whose jaws were inexorably closing. General Bagramyan was already deploying Red Army forces for a push towards Riga with the aim of driving a wedge between Army Group North and its neighbours, British troops had captured Caen and the Americans were in St Lô.[41] Hopelessly exposed to Allied air superiority and unable to make good their losses of men and material, the German forces could only hope to delay, not halt, their enemies' advance in the West.

The position became so critical that two senior German commanders in France, Field Marshals von Rundstedt and Rommel, jibbed at Hitler's routine order to "stand firm" and urged him to revise his strategic decisions.[42] Even among officers loyal to Hitler, the invasion battle had dispelled any lingering illusions about the Reich's true predicament. Rommel estimated early in July that the German line in Normandy would hold for another three weeks, after which an American break-through would probably result in the loss of France.[43] He concluded that the Führer had three weeks in which to devise a strategic or political solution capable of preserving the German forces from total collapse.

But Hitler avoided any serious practical discussion with the two field marshals—in fact, he replaced Rundstedt with someone more outwardly compliant.[44] Meanwhile, in Normandy, one regiment after another was bleeding to death—sacrificed by a dictator whom no military reverse, no degree of enemy superiority and no German soldier's exhaustion could awaken from his eerie delusions of grandeur. Rommel, who had always been one of Hitler's most uncritical admirers, finally decided to do something about this senseless slaughter. On July 15 he sent off a teleprinter message, destined for the Führer, which read like an ultimatum: "Our men are fighting heroically everywhere, but the unequal struggle is nearing its end. I must request you to draw the inferences from this situation without delay."[45]

Rommel's cry for help was echoed a hundredfold in the hearts and minds of all who hoped that a short sharp *coup de main* would save their country from annihilation and thousands or even millions of people from extinction. If Rommel, the Führer's erstwhile paladin, could consider a radical move to end the war, the eagerness of the dissidents who had been predicting disaster for years may well be imagined. They could wait no longer, especially as they had now been joined by an inspiring and commanding figure who was prepared to stop at nothing: Colonel Count Claus Schenk von Stauffenberg.

Canaris heard the name with mixed feelings when Lieutenant Colonels Schrader and von Freytag Loringhoven vaguely outlined Stauffenberg's plans to him at the beginning of July.[46] He had lost touch with the military resistance leaders since Oster's fall and his own removal from office. The new activists rated Canaris too conservative, cautious and unimportant to merit a hearing, so he was grateful to Freytag, Schrader and Sack for bringing him up to date.[47]

Although Stauffenberg was keeping his plans secret, even from prominent fellow conspirators, Freytag and Schrader had a tangible clue to his intentions. This was a packet of captured British plastic explosive which a Geheime Feldpolizei patrol had unearthed in the Mauerwald OKH camp during November 1943 and, after an abortive investigation, turned over to Schrader in his capacity as a group head responsible for such matters in the Heerwesenabteilung [Army Section —Groscurth's old Special Duties Section].[48] Late in June 1944 Stauffenberg expressed an interest in the package and was given it by Freytag, who had been in charge of the Heerwesenabteilung since the Abwehr's disbandment.[49] Schrader and Freytag could only conclude that Stauffenberg intended to launch the coup himself by assassinating Hitler.

Quite apart from his enduring opposition to such a step, Canaris doubted whether Stauffenberg was the right person to plan a coup and execute it with precision.[50] Their paths had occasionally crossed since Stauffenberg's appointment as Chief of Staff of the Replacement Army at the OKH's Berlin headquarters in Bendlerstrasse during October 1943. Although Stauffenberg had inherited the luckless Oster's mantle, his passionate idealism and woolly socialist principles did not appeal to the Admiral, who was put off by his dashing military manner, sense of élitism and socio-revolutionary fervour.

Canaris could not appreciate the consuming passion which drove Stauffenberg to act when he had barely recovered from the severe wounds that had deprived him of his right hand and left eye during the North African campaign. He feared that Stauffenberg's revolutionary ardour would wreck the planning of a *coup d'état* which had, in his view, to allow for every conceivable risk and contingency. Other observers shared the Admiral's misgivings. Hansen found Stauffenberg so nervous and moody that he pronounced him close to a mental breakdown, and the world-famous surgeon Ferdinand Sauerbruch declared that his state of health precluded him from leading a coup at this juncture.[51]

Canaris and Stauffenberg got on so badly that Sack had to mediate between them more than once.[52] It was more than a clash of personalities and generations: they had too little in common politically. To Canaris the name Stauffenberg symbolized a leftward shift in the anti-Hitler bloc. Not only had confirmed socialists like Julius Leber and Adolf Reichwein come to the fore, but Stauffenberg was actually planning a supra-party movement in which Communists would also participate. Canaris refused to contemplate an alliance with the latter. No man who had spent years "purging" German munitions factories of suspected Marxists and hunting Red spies would ever have accepted Communists as allies in the campaign against Hitler.

The Admiral's doubts were reinforced when the anti-Hitler bloc sustained a severe blow shortly after his return from Lauenstein. Stauffenberg had approved Leber's plan to contact representatives of the illegal KPD and enlist their co-operation. Undeterred by warnings that the Communist underground was infested with Gestapo spies, Leber and Reichwein went ahead. On June 22 they conferred in Berlin with three Communist members of a resistance group directed by Bernhard Bästlein, a Hamburg KPD functionary. What Leber and Reichwein did not know was that one of the Communist trio worked for the Gestapo.[53] They paid dearly for their ignorance. Gestapo officers arrested Reichwein at his next rendezvous with the Communists on July 4 and picked up Leber next day.[54]

Canaris could not fail to regard Stauffenberg's and Leber's behaviour as the height of conspiratorial amateurism. The Bästlein group was a lingering reminder of the Rote Kapelle, which the Abwehr and Gestapo had jointly liquidated in 1942. Its leaders had been taken into custody but subsequently released. Since then the Gestapo had kept the group under surveillance, preferring for tactical reasons to infiltrate Bästlein's organization and discover its links with other resistance circles.[55] To have sought contact with such obvious Gestapo targets verged on self-destruction. For his part, Canaris felt disinclined to stake his already precarious existence on the work of amateur plotters. Oster's fate had been an object lesson.

Thus the final arrangements for the *coup d'état* proceeded in isolation from the onetime patron of the internal German resistance movement. Canaris withdrew into his own private world, outwardly unconcerned by the shape of things to come. He led the life of an ordinary public servant who does his office work by day and spends his leisure hours at home or in the garden. He usually left Eiche early in the afternoon. The rest of the time he devoted to reading, gossiping over the garden fence and, when the fancy took him, cooking an occasional meal for fun.

He even came, during this spell of enforced solitude, to take pleasure in the house that had only known him as a fleeting visitor. He resumed his Russian lessons with Kaulbars and listened patiently to the playing of his pianist neighbour and long-time admirer Helmut Maurer, who often dropped in to pass the time of day. "Uncle Mau," as Canaris called him, was the only friend who still formed a link with the Abwehr. The Admiral had found him civilian employment with an Abwehr III desk since transferred to the RSHA, so Uncle Mau was able to report on the work of his former subordinates.[56]

But his real preoccupation was animals, not people. Canaris never tired of playing with Kasper and Sabine, and one whinny would be enough to make him lay aside a book and visit his horses in their nearby stable. Motte, his Arab mare, often ventured through the french windows and into the dining room for a sugar lump from the master of the house. "His splendid little white mare was so well groomed," Maurer recalls, "that her coat competed with his own snow-white hair."[57] Canaris felt safe among his pets. "Rely on the goodness of animals," he once said. "Look at my dachshunds—they're discreet. They'll never give me away."[58]

No forewarning of the fateful events of July 20, 1944, penetrated this atmosphere of privacy and semiretirement. In an attempt to save his country from total disaster at the eleventh hour, Stauffenberg had resolved to stake everything on a single throw. Armed with Schrader's packet of explosive he set out at dawn for Wolfsschanze [Wolf's Lair], the Führer's headquarters near Rastenburg in East Prussia.[59] Hitler's daily conference was scheduled for 12:30 P.M. and Stauffenberg had been summoned to attend. After crushing the acid capsule of his time bomb in a lavatory, Stauffenberg entered the conference hut on time, shoved the briefcase containing it as close as possible to Hitler beneath the massive table and withdrew with a murmured apology. If all went well, the dictator would be dead within ten minutes.[60]

Stauffenberg hurried out in search of a car to take him and his companion, Lieutenant Werner von Haeften, to the airfield. He was still looking for one at 12:50 p.m. when the conference hut was shaken by a violent explosion. An eight-cylinder Horch drove up at the same moment. Stauffenberg and Haeften jumped into the car and set off at once.[61] A suspicious guard commander who had also heard the explosion halted the two conspirators at the outer perimeter, but his attention was distracted by a telephone call. The coup was under way.[62]

Now came the decisive moment. "Valkyrie" was the code word that should have alerted every Army unit in the Reich and signalled the immediate seizure of all political key points and police headquarters on the pretext that civil war was imminent, but Stauffenberg's Bendlerstrasse confederates were slow to act. Lieutenant General Thiele, the OKH communications chief, lost his nerve and dived for cover, and it was 4 p.m. before General Olbricht of the Allgemeines Heeresamt steeled himself to act.[63] He transmitted the orders by teleprinter and notified his senior subordinates. Hitler, they were told, had been assassinated, the Wehrmacht had made itself responsible for internal security by assuming executive powers under the command of Field Marshal von Witzleben, and the country's over-all leadership was now in the hands of General Beck.[64]

Olbricht already knew that the attempt on Hitler's life had failed. Though deserted by his superior, Fromm, the opportunist commander of the Replacement Army, and out of touch with Stauffenberg, who was still winging his way back to Berlin, Olbricht unleashed the blow that was meant to smash the regime. His aides alerted Berlin Military District Headquarters and the units under its command, notably the Grossdeutschland Guards Battalion, while orders were teletyped to every other military district commander in Germany.[65] Teleprinters chattered and telephones rang incessantly, all transmitting the same message: "An unscrupulous clique of combat-shy party leaders has attempted, by exploiting this situation [Hitler's death], to take our hard-pressed combat troops in the rear and seize power for their own ends."[66] Then came the most pregnant passage: "The following are to be removed from office forthwith and solitarily confined under exceptionally secure conditions: all Gauleiters, Reich governors, ministers, Oberpräsidenten [senior administrative officials], police commissioners, senior SS and police commanders, Gestapo chiefs and heads of SS departments."[67]

The "decent Germans," as Josef Müller characterized them, were rising in revolt against those who had ruined their country, but Canaris knew nothing. No one had warned him what to expect. July 20, 1944, was just another date in his desk diary—a common or garden Thursday. Baron Kaulbars and Maurer turned up for afternoon coffee and an informal chat at 14 Betazeile. According to Maurer, it was not until about 3 P.M. that Canaris received a call from Stauffenberg. The colonel announced that Hitler was dead—killed by a bomb. With "incredible presence of mind" (Maurer), Canaris insured himself against the threat of Gestapo eavesdroppers by replying, "Dead? Good God, who did it—the Russians?"[68]

We are entitled to doubt the accuracy of this recollection on the part of so faithful a custodian of the Canaris legend as Helmut Maurer. Stauffenberg can hardly have phoned Canaris at 3 P.M. because he was still airborne and did not reach Bendlerstrasse until four-thirty. Apart from that, the turmoil prevailing at the Allgemeines Heeresamt would have left him no time for personal calls to idle onlookers like the former Abwehr chief.[69] It was not until after 5 P.M. that Canaris heard the news, and then through Sack, who had come straight from Bendlerstrasse.

Being a close associate of Olbricht's and Stauffenberg's in his capacity as a divisional chief at the Allgemeines Heeresamt, the judge advocate had been attending a birthday coffee party when one of Olbricht's aides telephoned and summoned him to Bendlerstrasse.[70] This was at about 4 P.M., while Olbricht was issuing the "Valkyrie" orders and briefing his officers. Sack got into uniform and drove to Bendlerstrasse. Olbricht must have confided to him that the coup had little prospect of success, because he left the OKH building fifteen minutes later. He drove home, climbed back into civilian clothes and hurried off to tell Canaris.[71]

A few words from the Army judge were enough to convince Canaris that the coup was bound to fail. Hitler was still alive, the "Valkyrie" procedures had been initiated too late and precious time had been lost. Germany's fate was sealed, but Sack refused to abandon hope. He stubbornly and angrily resisted the dawning realization that everything he and his friends had suffered, striven and yearned for through the years —all their plans to save the Reich from tyranny and perdition—had been in vain. As for Canaris, he was already sure that nothing could avert the downfall of Germany.

When Sack had gone the Admiral paced nervously up and down his drawing room, watched in silence by Maurer. Suddenly he paused and asked, "Well, where shall I go, Eiche or Bendlerstrasse?"[72] It was a purely rhetorical question. Canaris drove to Eiche and turned up in his office shortly after 6 P.M.[73] His adjutant was already drafting a telegram to the Führer's headquarters. This loyally affirmed that Admiral Wilhelm Canaris congratulated Adolf Hitler on his miraculous escape in the name of the Special Staff for Mercantile Warfare and Economic Combat Measures.[74]

One cannot fail to be astonished at the timing of this telegram. Canaris declared for Hitler soon after 6 P.M. Few if any opponents of the regime resigned so early in the game. At the time of the Admiral's submission, Wehrmacht units alerted by Olbricht and the military district commanders were only just moving out of their barracks to secure government and party offices against ostensible seizure by "combat-shy party leaders." Towards 6:30 P.M. the Grossdeutschland Guards Battalion surrounded the Berlin government quarter, at 8 P.M. Military District HQ in Vienna arrested the local heads of the SS, Gestapo and SD, and three hours later the military authorities in occupied Paris arrested the two most senior officers of the Security Police and confined twelve hundred policemen in Wehrmacht prisons.[75]

Many supporters of the *coup d'état* still hoped that it would be crowned with success. Members of the SS and police organizations in Vienna and Paris meekly submitted to arrest by Wehrmacht officers, and in Berlin the Leibstandarte-SS "Adolf Hitler" [Hitler's personal bodyguard regiment] companies remained in barracks while RSHA personnel stood helplessly at their office windows, watching the mysterious comings and goings of Army units in the streets below.[76]

But no news from Bendlerstrasse and no grievance against those in power could wean Canaris from his fatalistic certainty that the coup was doomed. He methodically sifted his papers at Eiche for incriminating evidence and re-examined the diary he had kept since 1943 (its predecessors were already in a safe place) for suspect passages because he knew, only too well, that the tottering regime would not take long to deliver a brutal riposte. He was right. Pro-Hitler officers had only just taken over Bendlerstrasse and shot Stauffenberg and his closest associates when RSHA-Amt VI set its juggernaut in motion.

Himmler used his SS machine to crush suspected traitors and their families without mercy, instituting a judicial reign of terror unparalleled in German military history. He was once more the fanatical executive agent of the leader he had so recently planned to depose with the aid of German dissidents. When Felix Kersten, his German-Finnish masseur and confidant, discreetly reminded him of his former attitude, he retorted: "By saving the Führer, Providence has given us a sign. The Führer lives. He is invulnerable. It is the will of Providence that he shall survive for our sake and that we shall bring the war to a victorious conclusion under his leadership."[77] Himmler fulfilled every one of the dictator's vengeful commands with the same quasi-religious fervour. "Shoot anyone who resists, no matter who," Hitler shouted. Himmler snapped back, "My Führer, you can depend on me."[78]

The SS chief went to Berlin to inaugurate the regime's campaign of vengeance in person. He appointed "Gestapo" Müller to set up a "Sonderkommission 20 Juli" to which were assigned four hundred investigators including Huppenkothen and Sonderegger, both of whom knew Canaris of old.[79] Under orders to root out every resistance fighter and all who had sympathized with the coup, Gestapo squads combed every corner of the Reich. The faintest breath of suspicion was enough to consign any German to the RSHA's interrogation cells. Even innocent relatives disappeared behind an iron curtain of ruthless and arbitrary police action. Hardly a single prominent resistance leader escaped the guardians of the regime. Hundreds trod the martyr's road that led from Gestapo prisons, via the People's Court, to the concentration camp and —in all too many cases—the gallows.

Canaris fleetingly hoped that this reign of terror might pass him by. He had taken no part in the coup and lost no time in proclaiming his allegiance on July 20. The Gestapo's first wave of arrests did, in fact, leave him unscathed. No shadow of suspicion appeared to fall on the man who even now commanded the RSHA chiefs' superstitious respect and had long been regarded as a master spy by Himmler himself.

But the special investigators were soon on his track. With characteristic attention to detail they began to unravel the plotters' communications network by following up every personal and documentary lead emanating from the Allgemeines Heeresamt. One AHA officer after another fell into their clutches, among them Major Egbert Hayessen, whose task on July 20 had been to assist the military commander of Berlin in surrounding the government quarter.[80] Under interrogation, Hayessen implicated someone who had hitherto been persona grata at the RSHA: Colonel Hansen, head of Amt Mil.[81]

Müller took some time to recover from this shock. It seemed almost inconceivable that Schellenberg's deputy and the second most important man in the Secret Intelligence Service should be an enemy of the regime, but Hayessen's testimony was quite clear on this point. The Gestapo précis read as follows: "Hayessen was informed by Lieutenant Haeften on July 15 that Colonel Hansen would co-operate in occupying the official premises of the Geheime Staatspolizei. Colonel Hansen's name also appeared after the Geheimes Staatspolizeiamt [Gestapa] on the piece of paper which was passed to Hayessen as a documentary basis for his operation. Hansen had been pointed out [to him] as someone with special knowledge of conditions inside the Geheimes Staatspolizeiamt."[82]

Hansen was summoned to Prinz-Albrecht-Strasse on July 22, never to leave the RSHA headquarters as a free man. Müller, who took personal charge of his colleague's interrogation, pressed the colonel for a detailed account of his links with the conspirators and taxed him repeatedly with Hayessen's statement. After hours of verbal wrestling, Hansen broke down and admitted his involvement in the plot. This was the first confession by an influential member of the anti-Hitler camp. It was also the first of many. Hansen wrote down a whole list of names on the sheet of paper Müller put before him.[83]

Only those who have been subjected to the mental and physical terrors of a Gestapo interrogation can afford to pass judgement on Hansen's conduct. Who, at this distance in time, can tell what drove the colonel to make these admissions—stark fear or the desire to settle old scores, a desperate attempt to save prominent fellow conspirators by naming others of lesser importance or the temptation to incite potential dissidents in the higher echelons of the SS and police against a corrupt and tyrannical regime by fully disclosing the motives and extent of the conspiracy? The dry and dispassionate Gestapo records are silent on this subject. The fact remains that Georg Hansen had talked.

As he was glancing through Hansen's deposition, Müller came to a sudden stop, electrified by one of the many names it listed. Hansen had written: "I regard Canaris as the spiritual instigator of the revolutionary movement that led to July 20 . . . Canaris made an important personal contribution to this by maintaining the requisite contacts abroad. Canaris was at pains to get people who did not agree with the National Socialist regime out of the country. These included numerous Jews, persons with religious affiliations, etc."[84] Although nothing could surprise Müller now that Hansen himself was unmasked, he still found it hard to believe that Admiral Canaris, for so many years the high priest of close Abwehr-Gestapo collaboration, had been a leading sponsor of the anti-Nazi movement.

Next day, July 23, Müller alerted his colleague Schellenberg and requested him to take Canaris into custody.[85] The SD chief must have felt personally embarrassed—if nothing more—at the prospect of arresting his former rival, host and riding companion. He claims to have jibbed at the assignment, but Müller, who had been granted extraordinary powers in order to crack the conspiracy, insisted on strict compliance. That afternoon, accompanied by SS-Hauptsturmführer Baron von Völkersam, a former Abwehr officer who had transferred to the SD, Schellenberg drove to Betazeile, where Canaris was having coffee with two guests, his nephew Erwin Delbrück and Baron Kaulbars.[86]

When Schellenberg was announced Canaris asked his visitors to leave the room for a moment. He guessed why the SS-Brigadeführer had come. "Somehow," he said, "I felt it would be you." With a certain prescience he added, "Tell me, have you found anything in writing by that fool Colonel Hansen?" Schellenberg nodded and confined himself to intimating that Hansen had some connection with the affair.[87]

Schellenberg later alleged that he gave Canaris a last-minute opportunity to escape. Schellenberg to Canaris: "I shall wait in this room for an hour, and during that time you can do whatever you choose. I shall say in my report that you went to your bedroom to change." Canaris is said to have replied, "No, Schellenberg, there's no question of my escaping. I shan't kill myself either. I know what I'm doing." He went upstairs to his bedroom and changed, then rejoined Schellenberg carrying a suitcase. He looked round for a moment, moist-eyed, and put his arm round the younger man's shoulders. Then he said quietly, "All right, let's go."[88]

Baron von Völkersam was waiting outside. They got into the car and drove off, but not, as Canaris doubtless expected, in the direction of Prinz-Albrecht-Strasse and its dismal labyrinth of cellars. Instead, they left Berlin and headed north to the Mecklenburg town of Fürstenberg an der Havel. Here the car drew up in the courtyard of the Frontier Police College, whose officers' mess already accommodated a score of senior officers being held under house arrest because the Gestapo suspected them of complicity in the events of July 20.[89]

The college commandant, SS-Brigadeführer Dr. Hans Trummler, described by Schellenberg as "a most disagreeable-looking man," strove to do the military honours by inquiring if the new arrivals had already eaten. Canaris and Schellenberg were shown to a table where they shared a bottle of red wine and chatted about old times. The Admiral asked Schellenberg to secure him an interview with Himmler (which Schellenberg claims to have done). As the SD chief was leaving, Canaris warned him to steer clear of the kind of trouble he himself was in. Then the two men said goodbye. They never saw each other again.[90]

Canaris's detention at Fürstenberg obscured his true predicament and tempted him to believe that he need not fear the worst. In fact, Müller and his investigating officers were uncertain whether Canaris had really been one of the ringleaders or instigators of July 20. His behaviour on that day seemed to contradict Hansen's allegations, which were in any case extremely vague on the subject of Canaris's role in the actual organization of the coup. Furthermore, the two men who had loosely connected him with it were past talking. Freytag-Loringhoven shot himself on the day of the Admiral's arrest and Schrader followed his example five days later.[91]

Once their suspicions were aroused, however, the Gestapo made every effort to prove that Canaris had at least been privy to the plot if not actually implicated in it. Nobody at the RSHA was better qualified to solve the Canaris mystery than a legal functionalist who not only pursued the regime's enemies with cold-blooded and mechanical precision but had already observed the former Abwehr chief at close quarters. Just on the verge of promotion to senior rank, SS-Standartenführer Huppenkothen had never got over the fact that Canaris and his immediate subordinates had eluded the Gestapo in the "Depositenkasse" case. The Gestapo man was determined to make amends for his defeat at the hands of the Wehrmacht's slippery legal experts.

Huppenkothen resumed his inquiries at the point where they had petered out in summer 1943—in the maze of personal friendships and political sympathies that linked Canaris with the Oster set.[92]

He also requested the services of Sonderegger, now a Kriminalkommissar and the Gestapo's leading expert on the "Depositenkasse" file. Sonderegger, too, had personal reasons for wanting to "unmask" the Admiral. It still rankled with him that Himmler's veto had blocked his 1943 proposal to clean out "the nest of traitors round Canaris" by launching a frontal attack on Abwehr headquarters.

One by one, all the surviving members of the Oster circle were subjected to intensive questioning by Huppenkothen and Sonderegger. The Wehrmacht legal authorities had already handed over three of them to the Gestapo after July 20. These were Hans von Dohnanyi, Dietrich Bonhoeffer and Josef Müller, who had been acquitted by the Reichskriegsgericht in March 1944 but remanded in custody at the RSHA's request (unlike Schmidhuber and Ickrath, who had been sentenced in February to four years' penal servitude and two years' imprisonment respectively for currency offences and tax evasion).[93] The Gestapo now arrested two of Dohnanyi's former clerical assistants: Erwin Delbrück, who had been transferred to No. 2 Interpreters' Company in Military District III during 1943, and Baron Karl Ludwig von und zu Guttenberg, who was now serving as a Ic officer on the staff of the general officer commanding German forces in Croatia.[94]

Before long, the RSHA landed its biggest fish of all. Officers from Stapostelle Halle had already detained Hans Oster at his Schnaditz manor house in Kreis Delitzsch on July 21, although the preliminary evidence against him was only circumstantial. Files at the Allgemeines Heeresamt had been found to contain complete lists of those whom the conspirators proposed to employ as liaison officers to the various military districts. One of these was named as Major General (z.V.) Oster, but the Gestapo quickly concluded that Oster must have played a more active part than they had at first supposed. Sonderegger discovered that the general had left his country house on July 20 and visited Berlin.[95] Proof of his sojourn in the capital—according to Sonderegger—was that he had "on that date signed a receipt for food ration cards at the ration card office responsible for his apartment, No. 8 Bayerischer Platz."[96]

When Oster's name cropped up in interviews with other detainees, Huppenkothen had the general transferred to Cell No. 20 in the RSHA's private dungeon at Prinz-Albrecht-Strasse. Sonderegger handled the personal and Huppenkothen the formal aspect of Oster's interrogation, exerting pressure on him by means of the stick-and-carrot technique which Gestapo officers regarded as the acme of inquisitorial psychology. Alternating between flashes of human sympathy and threats of physical torture, they strove to wring a confession out of their prisoner by questioning him day after day and hour after hour in an attempt to discover what part he and Canaris had played in organizing the coup.

Huppenkothen later claimed that Oster made a "partial confession" after three days of intensive questioning.[97] Accurate as most of Huppenkothen's statements have proved, extant Gestapo records suggest that his memory must be at fault here. Kaltenbrunner presented Bormann with reports on the progress of the interrogations throughout August, and none of these contained any definite indication of Oster's connivance or complicity. His interrogators knew little more about him than Kaltenbrunner wrote in a report dated August 17: "The conspirators had earmarked him as OKH liaison officer to Military District IV. Oster is still subject to proceedings before the Reichskriegsgericht for undermining the war effort and exempting agents from military service in contravention of orders."[98]

Oster skilfully managed to conceal his central role in earlier plans for a coup. Almost imperceptibly, he steered the interrogations into political and ideological waters, giving his Gestapo inquisitors to understand that they were dealing with a reactionary but harmless professional soldier whose only real vice was an inability to grasp the "historical significance" of the National Socialist revolution.[99] There was an almost laudatory ring about Kaltenbrunner's report to Bormann on August 25: "More clearly than any of those involved have so far put it, Hans Oster has spoken of the mental and political attitude of the older career officer."[100]

But not even these tactics could absolve Oster from enhancing his own credibility by divulging a few names and contacts. It was only natural, in view of his former official position, that frequent references should be made to Canaris. Discreet though Oster tried to be, his avid listeners gradually built up a picture of a defeatist and war-weary Abwehr chief whose faith in final victory had been far from unqualified.

The Gestapo authorities now considered the Admiral sufficiently suspect to ordain his transfer from Fürstenberg to their own remand centre at Prinz-Albrecht-Strasse. Escorted there by a Gestapo superintendent, he remained at the mercy of the secret police from then on. His new quarters in the RSHA's inferno of subterranean corridors, steel doors and prison cells were an invitation to despair. Locked up in a cell measuring barely 8 feet by 5 feet and shackled day and night, he endured his interrogations without knowing how much the other side had already been told about him.

Canaris only gradually came to terms with his new surroundings.

Contact with other prisoners was forbidden and there were no communal walks round the prison yard. Nothing depressed him more than solitude—and hunger, the effects of which became more noticeable day by day. The prisoners were kept on a near-starvation diet. One of them recalled: "For breakfast and supper there was a mug of coffee substitute and two slices of bread and jam; at midday some soup."[101] Many detainees received food parcels from their friends and relations and some were permitted visitors, but no friend or relation came to see Canaris—not even his wife Erika.

He only saw others of his kind during their morning ablutions together. At the end of the row of cells was a washroom where the prisoners regularly met in defiance of all restrictions on personal contact. The shower was noisy enough to enable Canaris to exchange an occasional word with prisoners he knew, Oster included. Their news depressed him still further. Almost all the leading conspirators had been unmasked. Most were in custody and some already under sentence. Few of Oster's former subordinates had escaped arrest.

Although Canaris must have realized what this augured for him personally, he put up a skilful defence when Müller summoned him for his first interrogation. He gave another display of his old rhetorical mastery and practised the arts of allusion, insinuation and evasion. It took the Gestapo chief only a few hours to realize that he was no match for his prisoner. He had taxed the Admiral with responsibility for the "Depositenkasse" affair and read him excerpts from his diary for 1943, found at Eiche, which implied that he had obstructed the Wehrmacht legal authorities in their investigation of the case. Last but not least, he had quoted statements made by Oster.[102] Canaris, who refused to be browbeaten, had a plausible answer to every charge. He declared that an intelligence chief had to be realistic and allow for every possible contingency, and that he could not have permitted his department's work to be endangered by outside institutions.

Canaris had triumphed over an intellectual inferior, but there were no grounds for optimism. The Gestapo now pulled in two men who had likewise been named as political sympathizers by Oster and posed a threat to Canaris. One of them was Lieutenant Colonel Friedrich Wilhelm Heinz, who had been appointed to command the Wehrmacht patrol service in Military District III after his disastrous spell with the Brandenburg Division, and the other his keenest critic and former divisional commander, Major General Alexander von Pfuhlstein. United by the shock of their arrest, Oster's warring associates joined forces to attack their former chief.

Fortunately for Canaris, the Gestapo soon released the more dangerous of these two witnesses, Heinz, because they were ignorant of his role in preparations for a coup between 1938 and 1940. However, even his brief interrogation sufficed to render Canaris still more suspect in Gestapo eyes. "The . . . interrogation of Lieutenant Colonel Friedrich Wilhelm Heinz," Müller reported to Bormann, "reinforces our suspicion that the Brandenburg Division was to be given special employment within the context of plans for a revolutionary upheaval."[103] And who had been responsible for the division at the OKW? None other than Canaris.

Heinz stated that an unmilitary atmosphere had reigned at Abwehr headquarters and that all his efforts while serving in Canaris's department had been directed towards returning as quickly as possible to "a wholesome military environment."[104] Canaris had repeatedly tried to prevent the Brandenburg from being assigned to combat duties. A Gestapo officer made the following note: "A typical example quoted by Heinz was that a sergeant in the regiment [the Brandenburg] had constructed an excellent silencer for submachine guns and carbines. Canaris's and/or Oster's reaction to this was to question the point of continuing to produce new instruments of murder—enough terrible things were happening in the world as it was. He—Heinz—then took Sergeant Wolf to Reichsminister Speer, who arranged for a demonstration and evaluation."[105]

Questioned by the Gestapo, Pfuhlstein vented his long-suppressed dislike of the "unmilitary" Abwehr chief with even greater vehemence. Canaris sensed that Pfuhlstein represented a serious threat as soon as the general made his first appearance in the RSHA washroom on September 2. Pfuhlstein preserved a vivid recollection of their encounter. "Canaris and Oster were standing side by side at the washbasin, naked. Oster, with his toothbrush in his mouth, went quite rigid and stared at me in utter horror. Canaris, who looked physically broken, gave me an equally horrified stare and clung to the washbasin to prevent his knees from buckling."[106]

Pfuhlstein's testimony was a merciless indictment of his former departmental chief. Canaris, he declared, had never devoted much attention to the Brandenburg and his pessimism had exerted a paralysing effect on every genuine soldier.[107] "I received absolutely no help towards refurbishing the unit, neither from the department nor from Admiral Canaris. I gradually came to the conclusion that Admiral Canaris was quite uninterested in speedily returning my unit to the front."[108] Pfuhlstein went on to surmise that the Admiral's sole concern had been to "retain control over a dependable unit against the possibility of a critical situation, as protection for Amt Ausland/Abwehr and as a bodyguard for himself."[109]

Sonderegger craned forward eagerly. What sort of critical situation? Pfuhlstein couldn't say for sure, but he did recall that Canaris, Oster and another senior officer had discussed "reorganizing the leadership of the armed forces" and mentioned that "the Führer would only temporarily retain supreme command of the Army."[110] How had he, Pfuhlstein, dared to associate himself with treasonable remarks of this kind? The answer was recorded in a Gestapo transcript: "Pfuhlstein excuses his tacit involvement in such conversations by stating that he was entitled to assume that no illegal activities would be pursued by army commanders and field marshals. He debated what prospect of success he would have had in the event of his submitting a report. He was not, after all, in possession of any proof [of treasonable intent]."[111] He had nonetheless decided "to preserve his division from improper use, discreetly and by covert sabotage."[112]

Pfuhlstein must have hoped that such disclosures would insure him against a death sentence. He was, in fact, relieved of his command at the end of 1944 and reduced to the ranks.[113] The ex-general claimed after the war that his statements from September 9, 1944, onwards had "only told the Gestapo what they already knew," adding that he had included "a few not unduly incriminating items for safety's sake."[114] This is as incorrect as the date ascribed to his first statement. Gestapo files prove beyond doubt that his far-reaching admissions were on record by September 8 and that they weighed heavily against all concerned.[115]

Pfuhlstein's testimony hurt Canaris more than anyone because it tended to confirm at least some of the Gestapo's suspicions about him. More particularly, it forced Oster to enlarge on his own statements and concede that the reorganization of the Wehrmacht command structure had actually been discussed.

Gestapo records put it as follows: "By the beginning of 1942 these discussions had reached a stage at which [it was envisaged that] a Commander in Chief East and, if possible, a Commander in Chief Army would have to be appointed, if necessary against the Führer's wishes. The idea at that time was still to seal off the Führer's headquarters . . . Then, in autumn 1942, these plans assumed more concrete shape. In exchanging ideas on the treasonable preparations in progress, Oster and Sonderführer von Dohnanyi were solely concerned as to how 'the party, the police, the administration, the working class and, finally, the Army' could be drawn into 'the framework of the measures [to be taken] . . .' On Oster's submission, the subject was discussed in spring 1943 by him and also, through Olbricht, with Major General Alexander von Pfuhlstein."[116]

This was nothing short of an ill-disguised admission that there had been a plan to depose Germany's Führer and supreme commander by force. Oster's statement also implicated Canaris in these subversive schemes. "According to Oster," the Gestapo record went on, "such matters were also discussed with Admiral Canaris, Count Schwerin von

Schwanenfeld, Lieutenant Colonel Schrader and others. Canaris listened to these things without expressing an opinion, favourable or adverse."[117] To all intents and purposes Oster had accused Canaris of connivance. It was hardly surprising that Kaltenbrunner's next report to Bormann drew the following inference: "Interrogation of Major General Oster, Lieutenant General [sic] Pfuhlstein and Colonel Hansen, in particular, has given rise to a strong suspicion that Admiral Canaris was at least aware of these subversive schemes."[118]

Canaris sensed that the statements made by Oster, Heinz and Pfuhlstein were drawing the Gestapo's noose steadily tighter round his neck and that he would be lost unless he acted at once. He could see only one way—one bitter, painful and deceitful way—of saving himself. He would have to deny his fellow prisoners' most incriminating allegations, destroy Pfuhlstein's credibility and dismiss his erstwhile friend, Oster, as a dreamer whom no one had ever taken seriously.

On September 13 Canaris again submitted to questioning, this time in order to dissociate himself from Oster. Yes, he said, he could recall having talks with Oster in which "consideration was given to the difficulties of conducting the war and possible ways of remedying the same," by which Oster had meant "(a) appointing a Commander-in-Chief East, (b) augmenting the influence of the said commander in chief and the General Staff over operations in the East, (c) ensuring that proposals for conducting the war in the East were decided upon by the relevant commander in chief without delay, (d) modifying [German] policy in the occupied territories and (e) granting more independence to responsible army commanders."[119] Oster had also made occasional references to the possibility of treating with Germany's enemies in the East and West, but he, Canaris, had been unimpressed. "I attached absolutely no importance to any of these remarks, nor—above all—did I ever suppose them to be the product of serious deliberation. It went without saying, from my own point of view, that the whole matter was impracticable and unworthy of discussion."[120]

Sentence by sentence, Canaris severed the tenuous links that still attached him to Oster. "I was never in doubt," he said, "that any change of government during the war would not only be construed as a stab in the back but would disrupt the home front. I was also convinced that neither our Western enemies nor the Russians would accept an offer of peace, which they would automatically regard as a sign of weakness. Were they actually to accept one in the first instance they would do so only for show, in order to submit a ruthless demand for unconditional surrender thereafter. It would be 1918 all over again, but in a far worse form."[121]

As for Pfuhlstein's allegations, they were wholly inaccurate. He, Canaris, had never predicted Germany's certain collapse by Christmas

1943, as Pfuhlstein claimed, nor was it true that he had been a disseminator of pessimism. His conversations with the commander of the Brandenburg Division had been coloured by a sense of "grave responsibility" but could never be said to have involved "pessimistic or defeatist" comments on the progress of the war.[122] Apart from this, Pfuhlstein had misunderstood him. His objections to employing the Brandenburg in a front-line role and in partisan warfare had applied only to its use as an infantry unit, which had "deflected the division from its real task," namely, operations behind the enemy lines.[123]

Having thus been branded unreliable witnesses, Oster and Pfuhlstein requested a personal confrontation with the Admiral. The three ex-colleagues clashed fiercely in Huppenkothen's interrogation room.[124] Vehemently though Oster and Pfuhlstein argued with their former chief and implored him to tell the truth, Canaris stuck to the line he had already taken: they had misunderstood him—he had never been involved in any conspiracy against the National Socialist regime. Unreconciled, the trio were escorted back to their cells.

On September 21 Canaris made a further statement in his own hand. "I have often expressed the view," he wrote, "which I still hold today, that the final phase of the war will make further heavy demands on us and can be surmounted only if we genuinely fight to the last. I . . . drew attention to the difficulties that might be expected to arise if the enemy neared our frontiers. It was obvious that one had to allow for such a development in the war without being able to predict it for certain.

"On the other hand," he continued, "I also stated that we would eventually emerge successful from the war despite our steadily mounting difficulties. We had, however, to realize that such a war, in which the entire nation had given its all and the people at home had been called on for achievements very different from those of the first war, would not immediately be succeeded by a golden age, but that all our resources would at first be required to rebuild Germany and create fresh openings for her continued development. It would have to be borne in mind that, even after the war, we should initially continue to encounter great internal foreign resistance which would inevitably make it hard for us to rebuild at speed and regain our footing abroad. This, too, would undoubtedly be overcome, but we should have to attune ourselves to the idea that everyone must continue to make sacrifices and place himself entirely at the service of the Fatherland . . . Everyone would have to accept the need to lead a simple life in order to lay the fundaments of better living conditions for the rising generation."

And the reason for these reminiscences? "I have briefly restated these ideas because I believe that many officers regarded such appraisals of the situation and of the future course of developments as pessimistic

. . . But my principal realization—and I said as much to the officers who discussed these matters with me—was that a war of such vast dimensions had been ordained by fate and could never have been prevented. Nor was I in any doubt—and I often stressed this, too, in conversation—that the great sacrifices which our nation had made at the front and at home under firm and united leadership could never have been in vain and would have a beneficial effect even if the war did not end as the optimists thought."[125]

A strange and uneasy document, this last literary relic dated seven months before the Admiral's death. Like a distorting mirror produced for his own inquisitors, it reflected the major elements in his world of ideas and emotions: fatalism, patriotism, submission to the powers-that-be, and an indestructible faith which resisted all his pessimistic impulses and led him to hope, till the very last moment, that he would somehow escape the vengeance of a doomed regime.

But Canaris's skilful phrasing did not mislead his interrogators for long. The ink on his statement of September 21, 1944, was hardly dry when Sonderegger received a visit from someone who demolished the Admiral's defences at a stroke. Kurt Kerstenhan, personal driver to the late Werner Schrader, sought him out and volunteered an important lead.

A veteran Nazi of socialist leanings who opposed the Third Reich and had once belonged to Otto Strasser's anti-Hitler Black Front, Kerstenhan has been described as an "extreme and unfathomable man—a species of professional revolutionary."[126] He was released from political detention by Schrader in 1939 and served him faithfully, but the shot with which Schrader ended his own life at Camp Zeppelin deprived Kerstenhan of a protector and drove him to co-operate with the Gestapo. Sonderegger had questioned him at Prinz-Albrecht-Strasse late in July but released him because he clearly had nothing to contribute on the subject of Schrader's suicide.[127]

The Gestapo man was doubly surprised to receive an unsolicited visit from Kerstenhan on September 21. Something had occurred to him since their last meeting. He recalled having helped Schrader and Heinz to transport two carloads of papers from Amt Ausland/Abwehr to a Berlin building with the inscription "Seehandlung" [Maritime Trade] over the entrance. That was in 1942. A year later he had been told to collect the same papers and deliver them to a certain bunker at Camp Zeppelin.[128] Sonderegger did not take long to find the premises in question. They were the headquarters of the Preussische Staatsbank, which was managed by Heinz's stepbrother, Hermann Schilling.

It dawned on Sonderegger that a vital witness had slipped through his fingers. He immediately gave orders for Heinz to be rearrested, but his flying squad returned empty-handed. Heinz had been tipped off and was never found.[129] Sonderegger had to be content with the arrest of Schilling, but all that could be extracted from the bank manager was an admission that he had done his stepbrother a favour by keeping some unidentified documents for him in one of the bank's safes.[130]

Far more important to Sonderegger were the papers' present whereabouts. He asked Kerstenhan if he would recognize the bunker to which he had delivered them in 1943. The driver described its location. Sonderegger telephoned the Maybach II security zone at Camp Zeppelin and was informed that the said bunker contained a safe which differed from the security zone's 130 other safes in one important respect: the main key and the spare key (normally kept under seal at the guard post) had both disappeared.[131] Unwilling to risk forcing the mysterious strongbox, Sonderegger requested the manufacturers, Pohlschröder of Dortmund, to send a locksmith to open it.[132]

On September 22 Sonderegger and Kerstenhan drove to the underground shelter in Maybach II, which the driver recognized at once. The locksmith, who appeared on time, did not take long to open the safe.[133] Eagerly, Sonderegger peered inside. One glance at the neat stacks of files, folders and cardboard boxes was enough to convince him that he had gained his objective—the plotters' secret archives.

The more he dipped into this cache, scanning one file after another with mounting excitement, the more unreal the whole thing seemed. The Nazi regime possessed one of the most formidable police machines in history. Could its opponents really have recorded every phase of their conspiracy with such truly Teutonic attention to detail—could they really have filed and listed everything so neatly? Franz Xaver Sonderegger, whose own misgivings about the National Socialist regime had been aroused by the aftermath of July 20, could hardly believe his eyes. Every memorandum, every draft analysis and excerpt from the records, every agent's report, every letter and sheet of paper might have been an admission of its author's guilt—nay more, a self-imposed death sentence.

The conspirators seemed to have left nothing unrecorded. There was Oster's three-page "study" on the implementation of a *coup d'état*, there were essays on the programme, policy and composition of a revolutionary government with handwritten amendments by Oster, Groscurth, Gisevius and Heinz, there were batches of files on the Blomberg-Fritsch affair, memorandums and reports on Josef Müller's negotiations at the Vatican, draft speeches by Beck and sheets torn from notebooks in which Dohnanyi had outlined methods of launching a coup with the least possible bloodshed. And, last but not least, there were a few carbon copies of pages from the diaries of Admiral Canaris, so long and eagerly sought for by the Gestapo.[134]

Sonderegger did not have to read far to realize that the papers in the safe demanded a radical revision of the RSHA's working hypothesis about the motives and origins of this subversive movement. The Gestapo's existing belief was that July 20 had originated in 1941–42 and was largely a product of the dissatisfaction felt by many officers at Hitler's conduct of the war. However, the Zossen documents dated almost exclusively from the years 1938, 1939 and 1940. This meant that the conspiracy had originated long before the war and could hardly have been a product of the worsening military situation.[135] Sonderegger's discovery at Zossen compelled the RSHA to follow up some entirely new lines of inquiry because the papers found there contained the names of anti-Nazis to whom the Gestapo had previously devoted little consideration. General Thomas, Kriminalpolizei chief Nebe, Gauleiter Wagner, General Halder, Field Marshal von Brauchitsch, Lieutenant Commander Liedig—the list of new suspects seemed endless.

Huppenkothen threaded his way uneasily through the mass of papers which Sonderegger delivered to his office. It took him several days to gain even a superficial knowledge of their contents, but his final conclusion was that the Gestapo had—thanks to Kerstenhan—made a vital discovery. Sonderegger recalls that Kerstenhan was rewarded with RM1,000,[136] though Schrader's son, the ex-Abwehr soldier Dr. Werner Wolf Schrader, refuses to believe that he volunteered the information and surmises that he was "brutally beaten."[137]

Schrader Jr. and Benzing, another Canaris biographer, have even advanced the surprising theory that the papers "ostensibly" discovered at Zossen were merely a device fabricated by Huppenkothen and Sonderegger to help them evade punishment by postwar German courts.[138] "The documentary finds are a pretext put forward by SS murderers," Schrader insists, and Benzing finds it "remarkable" that "all reports" of the find were based on "allegations by members of the SS." Benzing adds: "No neutral informant has ever seen the documents."[139]

Both commentators are mistaken. There is ample documentary evidence of the Zossen find dating from *before* the war's end, notably Kaltenbrunner's reports to Bormann. One of them, dated October 2, 1944, states: "It now emerges from confiscated material found in an Abwehr safe that plans were already afoot in earlier years to effect a change of government by military means."[140] What is more, the documents found at Zossen were not even seen by SS witnesses. Colonel Rohleder discovered that Huppenkothen was in possession of his earlier reports on the "Palmenzweig" affair, and Josef Müller was confronted by his interrogators with "full particulars of my talks in Rome."[141] According to Müller, they were "nearly all documents which Dohnanyi had collected over the years."[142]

The Gestapo authorities regarded their find as so potentially explosive that they kept it under wraps, even inside the RSHA. When Huppenkothen ventured a reference to Sonderegger's stroke of luck at the next regular meeting of the board of inquiry, Gestapo chief Müller cut him short and called for a special report after the meeting had adjourned. "During this private discussion," Huppenkothen relates, "Müller told me off for not having reported these matters to him alone because they were highly confidential. He then instructed me to make no further reference to them, even among friends, but to continue to treat the case as a 'Geheime Reichssache—Ministersache'—the highest security classification."[143]

Huppenkothen had to compile a so-called Führervorlage or brief for Hitler consisting of a report and analysis plus two separate appendices containing photocopies of the most important documents—160 pages in all.[144] This was ready by mid-October, and Hitler's decision followed soon afterwards: pursue inquiries in the strictest secrecy; inform the Führer as soon as all interrogations have been concluded; do not pass completed cases to the People's Court.[145] In other words, Huppenkothen was to continue his investigations and Canaris had gained a brief reprieve.

Hitler's order provides a formal explanation of the mystery that has so often puzzled the Admiral's biographers—the fact that Canaris and some of his immediate subordinates survived the next few months. They did so not only contrary to expectation but in contrast to the many other dissidents who, after being interrogated and tortured, ran the gauntlet of the People's Court under its vicious presiding judge, Roland Freisler, and were herded to the gallows.

One cannot help being struck by the very different treatment bestowed on Canaris. He was not, like colleagues in similar straits, dismissed the service while remanded for questioning and stripped of his rank so as to expose him to the civil jurisdiction of the People's Court. He continued to be addressed as "Admiral" Canaris even by Gestapo officers who now spoke of "ex-Colonel" Hansen or "ex-Gruppenführer" Nebe. There was something almost courteous about the farewell edict signed by Dönitz on September 19, 1944. Not for Canaris the undignified abuse of a brother officer with which members of the Wehrmacht's Council of Honour saw fit to sully themselves, just a note of chill dissociation: "Admiral z.V. Canaris (Wilhelm) will be discharged from active duty in the Navy with effect from 25.7.44. His z.V. status in the Navy will cease on the same date."[146] Even in his dark and comfortless prison cell, Admiral (ret.) Canaris remained a man in demand. Himmler is said to have paid him a visit (according to Schellenberg), and only a few weeks before his death a fellow prisoner saw him strolling beside Kaltenbrunner in the yard at Flossenbürg concentration camp, deep in animated conversation.[147]

But Canaris was enough of a realist to know that the find at Zossen had made his position almost hopeless. News of the discovery must have come as a profound shock and exacerbated his resentment of Oster's carelessness. How often had he told his friend to destroy the conspiratorial evidence preserved by Dohnanyi, and how vehemently he had warned him against further indiscretions! Now all their erstwhile schemes for saving the Fatherland lay exposed to the Gestapo like an open book. Worse still, Oster had clearly abandoned all hope of survival. As if the Zossen documents were not incriminating enough, he now gave vent to a quasi-suicidal spate of admissions which soon made him one of the Gestapo's most oft-interrogated prisoners and informants.[148]

Though well nigh defenceless against this threat, Canaris made another effort to neutralize his enemies and inquisitors. What exactly had they found in Maybach II? Some twenty pages from his diaries containing references to subversive discussions with German military commanders in the West, notes on conversations between him and Halder in 1939–40, revolutionary proclamations amended in his own handwriting and particulars of the betrayal of the Western offensive which implied that he had arbitrarily and unwarrantably terminated Rohleder's investigations. Many of the papers dealing with Müller's secret talks in Rome could also be used to incriminate him.[149]

In face of this evidence, Canaris naturally saw that his flat denial of involvement in any form of conspiracy was untenable in its present form. The only way to dispose of these lethal excerpts from his diary was to convert ignorance into innocence as quickly as possible. His new line of argument was that he had engaged in subversive discussions, but only with a view to foiling the conspiracy if the worst came to the worst —in fact it had been his duty to do so as head of the secret service.[150] This reference to undercover functions also helped to explain his equivocal attitude towards Rohleder's investigations and Müller's talks with the Vatican, especially as the relevant documents were couched in the obscure and ambiguous language of the intelligence service.

Of course, this argument had a chance of acceptance only if no more incriminating evidence came to light—for instance, the actual diaries from which the twenty pages found at Zossen had been taken. As for these big black ring binders in which he had recorded and commented on every major military and political development since 1938, Canaris believed them to be in a safe place.[151] The originals of the five diaries (plus another six containing accounts of his travels) reposed in a still undiscovered safe in Maybach II. The copies entrusted to Schrader had been destroyed after July 20, partly by Schrader himself and partly by his wife.[152]

But Huppenkothen and Sonderegger, spurred on by Hitler's personal directive, barred every means of escape. They pinned the Admiral down under a cross fire of questions and insinuations, subjected him to relentless pressure, urged him to confess and repent. All the inhumanity and brutality of the Gestapo system surged over him, and it was only by drawing on his last reserves of physical energy that he managed to defend himself against this latest onslaught.

His two interrogators pressed him all the harder because they felt they were on the track of something which promised total victory over their nimble quarry. While reading the Zossen material, Sonderegger and Huppenkothen became convinced that the former Abwehr chief had committed Landesverrat as well as Hochverrat [in other words, betrayed his country to the enemy in addition to plotting the government's downfall].[153] This the two Gestapo officers inferred from the documents originally filed by Dohnanyi, which detailed the betrayal of Germany's Western offensive and Müller's Vatican contacts with the Western powers. Huppenkothen thought it quite logical to assume that Canaris had been behind both these treasonable activities.

"It was also known," Huppenkothen reports, "that Denmark and Norway had received prior warning of the German invasion, but there were no clues to the method, as there now were in the case of Rome and Holland."[154] Yet another instance of treachery was on record. On the eve of the Balkan campaign in 1941 the Forschungsamt had intercepted a telephone call to Colonel Vauhnik, the Yugoslav military attaché in Berlin, warning him that his country was about to be attacked. When questioned by the Gestapo, the colonel stated that the call had come as a complete surprise and that he had not recognized the caller's voice.[155] The only explanation, as Huppenkothen saw it, was that Canaris had been behind this too.

Huppenkothen now recalled Schmidhuber's claim that Gisevius had referred to several instances in which Canaris had betrayed forthcoming German offensives in the East.[156] Huppenkothen thought this equally possible, especially as one man who appeared on his list of suspects— Baron Kaulbars—was a Canaris friend and confidant whom he considered quite capable of parleying with the Russians. The Gestapo had discovered that Kaulbars was in touch with Soviet sources through the Swedish military attaché, Juhlinn-Dannfeld, and had often been apprised of military developments by Canaris. A Gestapo informant at the Swedish Embassy in Berlin had even procured some carbon copies of Juhlinn-Dannfeld's reports from which Huppenkothen inferred that the military attaché was "very accurately informed about all military developments and intentions, particularly those on the Eastern Front."[157]

Huppenkothen further deduced that Canaris had supplied the Russians with treasonable information via Kaulbars and Juhlinn-Dannfeld.

He also believed that he could prove the Admiral to have been in touch with the West. Gisevius maintained contact with Swiss-based representatives of the Polish government-in-exile in London, nor were the Gestapo unaware of his links with Allen Dulles, the U.S. resident director.[158] Dulles's wastepaper basket had yielded a purloined copy of a paper on the treatment of Nazi supporters in postwar Germany under Allied occupation, and Gisevius was suspected of being its author.[159]

All these things prompted Huppenkothen to accuse his prisoner of treason [Landesverrat], but nothing could have been better calculated to revive the Admiral's waning strength than the imputation that he had betrayed his country. Canaris had not spent a lifetime fighting that form of treason to be branded a traitor by the Gestapo. He put up a stout defence against the charges which Huppenkothen and Sonderegger hurled at him more and more indiscriminately, demolishing their flimsy "evidence" bit by bit.

He had a plausible explanation for every charge and every suspicious feature. Contacts with Dulles and the Polish government-in-exile? An unauthorized initiative on Gisevius's part for which he, Canaris, bore no responsibility. The telephone call to the Yugoslav military attaché? A reprehensible act with which he had no connection whatever. His alleged betrayal of German offensive intentions in the East? A monstrous, foolish and irresponsible piece of gossip invented by Schmidhuber or Gisevius.[160] Canaris also clarified his relations with Baron Kaulbars. While conceding that he had told him about the projected invasion of Russia a fortnight before "Barbarossa" began, he stressed that he had complete faith in the baron who was, after all, an accredited OKW agent.[161] As for Müller's dealings with the Vatican, their sole purpose had been "the gathering of intelligence." Müller had furnished "extremely valuable information about the enemy powers, their scientific capacity, their war aims and plans."[162]

Other prisoners and witnesses failed to corroborate Huppenkothen's charges. Kaulbars, in particular, made mincemeat of the two inquisitors' theories. A Gestapo report states: "Kaulbars . . . firmly backed Canaris under interrogation."[163] The baron also contrived to place a harmless gloss on his relations with Juhlinn-Dannfeld. The Swede had put him in touch with the Soviet authorities, true, but these contacts had only served to facilitate the task he had been assigned by the OKW, which was to discover the condition and whereabouts of German POWs in the Soviet Union.[164]

The more slowly they progressed, the more often Huppenkothen and Sonderegger resorted to barbarous interrogation techniques and uncouth behaviour. Even Canaris, who still inspired a trace of respect in his persecutors, felt the effects of their anger. Although his prestige saved him from physical maltreatment, the Gestapo officers devised other ways of breaking his sensitive spirit. His ration was cut to one third of the normal prison quota, his sleep disturbed by incessant security checks and his morale sapped by the imposition of undignified daily chores performed to an accompaniment of derisive remarks from his guards.[165] "Well, sailor boy," one of them jeered, "I bet you never thought you'd have to scrub the decks again!"[166]

The Admiral's fellow prisoners were subjected to renewed intimidation and sadism in the hope of extracting fresh evidence to support a charge of treason. From his basement cell, Canaris could often hear the screams of prisoners undergoing what was known in Gestapo parlance as "intensified questioning" in a room on the third floor. Some were tortured so cruelly that they had to spend days being nursed and fed in the interrogation room before they could be returned to their cells.[167]

Prisoners were frequently roughed up during "normal" interrogations as well. On one occasion Sonderegger lunged at Baron Guttenberg and punched him in the face, then hit him so hard on the back and chest that Guttenberg, whose nerve had broken, confided to a fellow victim after his first session (others followed) that he planned to commit suicide.[168] Guttenberg was not the only one to be struck by his interrogators. Josef Müller fell foul of Kriminalrat Stawitzky, one of the RSHA's most vicious bully-boys, but Schilling was sufficiently intimidated by the sight of other prisoners showing obvious signs of maltreatment.[169]

Elisabeth Strünck, the wife of the arrested Abwehr captain, never forgot the scene that met her when she entered Sonderegger's office. Hans Koch, a Berlin lawyer who had also been detained, was seated on a chair with his feet bound and his hands manacled behind the chair back. "Take the bastard out," snapped Sonderegger, whereupon two Gestapo officers dislodged the prisoner by booting the chair with all their might. Koch nearly fell headlong but just managed to retain his balance. He hopped out of the room, bent double, and was propelled through the open door by more kicks in the rear—a living symbol of the subhuman level to which the Gestapo degraded their victims.[170]

Dohnanyi, who had been transferred to the RSHA's cells from the sick bay at Oranienburg concentration camp, was another victim of Gestapo inhumanity. In an attempt to avoid further bouts of painful interrogation he had swallowed some diphtheria bacilli which seriously affected his heart and induced partial paralysis. One side effect was an inability to control his bowels.[171] Instead of approving medical treatment, Huppenkothen left Dohnanyi to wallow helplessly in his own ordure. Huppenkothen: "Let him croak in his own shit!"[172]

But Canaris held out for as long as he could still see the faces of other prisoners and derive encouragement from their brief messages, false hopes and personal anecdotes. He sometimes got a chance to speak to them in spite of the official ban on communication and association. One day Müller was detailed to help him scrub the corridor. "Has Dohnanyi incriminated me?" he whispered to "Joe the Ox." Müller whispered back, "I couldn't say—have they confronted you with the documents?" Canaris: "Say 'du' [the familiar mode of address]. Old formalities go by the board in this hellhole. We'll both say 'du' from now on." They continued to work in silence until their guards were again out of earshot. Müller asked, "Have you been expelled from the Wehrmacht?" Canaris didn't know. "You can think yourself lucky, then," Müller pursued brightly. "You won't come up before the People's Court, so you'll gain time."[173]

Air-raid warnings, which were becoming more and more frequent, reunited the prisoners in the Himmler-Bunker, a shelter in the RSHA courtyard. Here Canaris picked up much of what was circulating in the Gestapo's remand centre. The outside world was a disastrous sight, by all accounts. Hitler's Thousand-Year Reich lay in ruins. In mid-January 1945 the Soviet army groups commanded by Marshals Zhukov and Koniev had launched a drive towards the Oder, the last remaining river barrier between them and Berlin. Early in February the armies of the Western Allies gathered themselves for a concerted assault on the Ruhr and South Germany. East Prussia and Upper Silesia had both been lost,[174] yet die-hard fanatics continued to celebrate gory triumphs in what remained of the Reich. Drumhead courts set up by the SS and local party leaders stamped out any inclination to surrender—to the greater glory of a dictator who, thrown back on the geographical origins of his rise to power, had been preparing since mid-January to direct the final self-destructive battle for "Fortress Germany" from the Chancellery in Berlin.[175]

One thought alone preoccupied the captives in the Himmler-Bunker. Would the Allies arrive in time to save them from extermination by the RSHA? They lived from one hope to the next, heartened by the fact that some Gestapo officers were gradually modifying their attitude towards those in custody. Many prisoners claimed to have observed a definite rift between Huppenkothen and Sonderegger. Huppenkothen remained the unfeeling functionary that he was, whereas Sonderegger was displaying certain deviations from the RSHA line. Müller could have confirmed these suppositions. Sonderegger had enabled him to remove an important document from the Zossen files. He had also sneaked another piece of evidence against Müller to Kriminalinspektor Hoffmann and asked him to destroy it.[176] He even helped Dohnanyi and got him a doctor, though on the ostensibly legitimate grounds that "a dead Dohnanyi is no use to us."[177]

The prisoners were still debating the reasons for this change of heart when Allied bombers opened up an apparently promising escape route from the cellars of Prinz-Albrecht-Strasse. On the morning of February 3 their guards herded them back into the Himmler-Bunker because U.S. bomber squadrons were heading for Berlin.[178] Soon afterwards, violent explosions shook the Gestapo's nerve centre. The main RSHA buildings were set ablaze and the underground installations, including part of the prison, were destroyed. The cells were left without water, light or heating.[179]

Gestapo chief Müller promptly decreed that the prisoners should be transferred to areas still safe from Allied air and ground attacks. On February 6 Josef Müller, Bonhoeffer, Liedig, Gehre and a few other "special prisoners" were taken to Buchenwald concentration camp.[180] Next day a coach drove into the RSHA courtyard. Canaris, Oster, General Thomas, Strünck, Schacht and ex-Chancellor von Schuschnigg, who still enjoyed "prisoner of honour" status, climbed aboard.[181] They were only told their destination—Flossenbürg concentration camp—while on the way there. Canaris's hopes revived. He had no inkling that he would never return.

The coach headed for northern Bavaria, drove through Hof and took the road to Weiden. It then proceeded eastwards to the small township of Flossenbürg near the former German-Czech frontier. There on the outskirts of Flossenbürg, during the evening hours of February 7, 1945, Canaris caught his first glimpse of what lay in store for him: festoons of barbed wire, watchtowers and interminable rows of huts.[182] Sonderegger reported to the camp commandant, SS-Obersturmbannführer Kögl, and presumably handed him a letter from "Gestapo" Müller. This must have contained precise instructions on how the "special prisoners" were to be kept: permanently shackled and deprived of correspondence but adequately nourished and fit enough to undergo further interrogation.[183]

Canaris and the others were conducted to the Kommandantur Arrest [headquarters detention centre] which stood in a special part of the camp. This was a long stone building, single-storeyed and running east-west, which contained forty cells and was locally known as "the Bunker." As its official name implied, it had formerly accommodated those sentenced to close confinement by the camp commandant. Since 1943 or thereabouts the cell block had been reserved for political prisoners of special status. The cells faced south and afforded no view of the yard on the north side of the building, where executions were carried out.[184]

The RSHA prisoners filed past the guardroom and were allotted a cell each. Canaris's SS guards turned left along the corridor and stopped at a door marked 22. They pushed him inside, handcuffed him and shackled his ankles to some chains embedded in the wall.[185] Then they slammed the door on the man whom Camp Adjutant Baumgartner entered in his list of special prisoners under the code name "Caesar."

The cell block soon received a visit from someone who rapidly convinced Canaris that the RSHA had not given up. The notorious Kriminalrat Stawitzky was under orders to pursue the Admiral's interrogation by "vigorous" means.[186] Huppenkothen may have been inhibited by memories of Canaris's hospitality, but Stawitzky had no such qualms. Furthermore, he was in possession of what the RSHA regarded as new incriminating evidence. According to an official at the German Embassy in Madrid, Canaris had divulged military secrets to Franco and advised him against entering the war on Germany's side in 1940.[187]

The Admiral's denial of these fresh charges only spurred Stawitzky into stepping up the pressure on him. Outwardly, Canaris remained calm and unmoved. He wore a pale-grey suit, was never seen without a clean white shirt and a carefully chosen tie, and always remembered to don his overcoat before exercising in the yard (one of Flossenbürg's few privileges),[188] but his well-groomed exterior belied his state of mind. In the solitude of his cell he yielded to despair.

One day he heard someone tapping indistinctly on the wall of the next cell, No. 21. Straining his ears, he gathered that his unknown neighbour was trying to communicate in Morse. Canaris could not reply—he had learnt the Morse code but forgotten it.[189] After a while the tapping stopped. Next day one of the guards, SS-Rottenführer [Corporal] Weissenborn, passed Canaris a slip of paper on which his next-door neighbour had written out the standard prison signalling system. This reduced the alphabet to twenty-five letters by omitting J and split it into groups of five. The first signal indicated the group and the second the letter within it. Canaris quickly grasped the code but did not immediately learn his neighbour's identity.[190]

It was not until some days later, while Canaris was waiting in the corridor to be taken away for further questioning, that the stranger in Cell 21 managed to introduce himself. He was Mathiesen Lunding, a cavalry captain and ex-member of the Danish military intelligence service.

Canaris was familiar with Lunding's story. He hailed from the former German territory of North Schleswig, had trained with the Berlin Horse Guards, was appointed to set up an espionage network in and against Germany from 1937 onwards and continued to serve in the small rump army which Hitler temporarily permitted Denmark to retain under the German occupation. In August 1943, stiffening Danish resistance prompted the German authorities to disband this force and arrest its officers. Lunding was consigned to a Wehrmacht prison but soon handed over to the RSHA despite protests from Canaris, who had originally placed Lunding under the protection of Abwehrstelle Copenhagen. The Dane had been imprisoned at Flossenbürg since July 6, 1944.[191] But Canaris and Lunding had no time to dwell on the strange way in which their paths had crossed—the Admiral's escort might return at any moment. The two ex-intelligence officers hurriedly arranged to continue their conversation with the aid of Lunding's code,[192] which they did the following night.[193]

As soon as Lunding heard the rattle of chains in the adjacent cell he put his ear to the wall so as to catch every signal. At first the Dane understood little of what his neighbour was trying to convey. Canaris often tapped too fast or muddled his signals and misread letters, but communication improved day by day.[194] Lunding gradually built up a picture of the Admiral's experiences, the story of his interrogations, his hopes and fears.

The signals from Cell 22 sounded reasonably optimistic because Canaris still hoped to survive the Götterdämmerung that was so patently in store for the Nazi regime.[195] Stawitzky's boorish interrogation methods had borne no fruit. The Gestapo lacked sufficient evidence to convict Canaris of betraying secrets to the enemy, or even of having conspired against the regime. What was more, the Gestapo's investigations abroad seemed to be dogged by misfortune. Police Attaché Paul Winzer, whom "Gestapo" Müller had summoned to Berlin from Madrid for a briefing on the Canaris inquiry, had been shot down by Allied fighters during his return flight to Spain.[196]

Not unnaturally, Canaris assumed that the regime would collapse before the case against him was complete, and he had some grounds for this expectation. The Third Reich was disintegrating fast. Columns of Allied infantry and armour were thrusting deep into Germany. The west bank of the Rhine was already in enemy hands. By the beginning of March the Allies had occupied Krefeld and reached Cologne. The Ruhr and twenty-one German divisions were cut off on April 1. American forces simultaneously launched an offensive against the Mainz-Mannheim area and Thuringia with the aim of reaching northern Bavaria.[197] Meanwhile, the main Soviet armies preserved a standstill on the Oder front, continuously reinforcing their assault troops with one sole objective and one sole prize in mind: Hitler's capital city.

Frantically, the dictator built up his defensive cordon round Berlin. Every man, woman and boy was summoned to "drown the Bolshevist onslaught in blood."[198] New operational staffs took up residence in the underground shelters at Camp Zeppelin in Zossen, determined to resist the Red Army to the last German soldier. One of these last-ditch enthusiasts was General of Infantry Walter Buhle, head of the Army Staff at OKW, who moved into the former Abwehr premises in Maybach II and looked round for further accommodation.[199]

That was when disaster struck. While in search of more office space,

Buhle (or his officers) came across a safe containing several black cloth-covered binders. These, in turn, contained between eighty and two hundred sheets of paper apiece, handwritten and dated.[200] Buhle had found the long-lost diaries of Admiral Canaris. He promptly informed the Gestapo. Whether or not he felt any qualms about denouncing a brother officer, General Buhle was still under the spell of a memorable experience. He had been standing not far from Hitler in the Wolfsschanze conference hut on July 20, 1944, and had sustained severe injuries when Stauffenberg's bomb exploded.[201]

Buhle notified SS-Brigadeführer Hans Rattenhuber, head of the security service responsible for Hitler's personal safety, and handed him the Canaris diaries.[202] Rattenhuber immediately passed them to the RSHA, probably to Kaltenbrunner or Müller.[203] This must have been on April 4 at the latest, because next day SS-Obergruppenführer Kaltenbrunner rose triumphantly to his feet at the midday conference in the Chancellery and reported the sensational find to his Führer.[204]

Hitler read a few of the passages marked by Kaltenbrunner and grasped the picture at once—or thought he did. Caught in the web of his own delusions, the dictator was finally convinced that he had for years been the victim of treachery and perfidy. A gargantuan plot took shape in his imagination, hatched by trusted associates whose sole aim had been to rob Germany of final victory and overthrow him, Adolf Hitler. Whatever the outburst of fury and torrent of Hitlerian invective that may or may not have descended on Canaris and his friends in that hour of disenchantment, it culminated in the terrible command which was all that Rattenhuber recalled of the scene: the plotters must be destroyed at once.[205]

The SS had been given a free hand. There was nothing to prevent its executioners from snuffing out the "traitors'" lives, but the "soft Austrian," as Kaltenbrunner was called at the RSHA, disliked straightforward and unvarnished killing. The lawyer in him insisted that everything should be neatly signed and sealed, even in a case of judicial murder. By the time he conferred with Müller early on the afternoon of April 5, he had found the answer. An SS court of summary jurisdiction, complete with judges and prosecuting counsel, would sentence the doomed men to death before their executioners went to work.[206] He also knew of an apparatchik who could be relied on to stage the final act with due regard for legal convention—Huppenkothen.

At 4 P.M. Kaltenbrunner sent for Müller and told him that the RSHA's orders were that "Dohnanyi should be sentenced by a summary court to be convened at Sachsenhausen on April 6. I [Huppenkothen] was appointed to indict and prosecute."[207] Huppenkothen claims to have raised some formal objections, but Müller overruled them. His orders were crystal-clear. The Oranienburg/Sachsenhausen concentration camp maintained a summary court presided over by an SS judge (probably named Hoffmann) and two associate judges, Camp Commandant Keindl and SS-Oberführer Somann. Sonderegger was to deliver Dohnanyi in good time.[208]

Standartenführer Huppenkothen carried out his assignment promptly. At the appointed hour on the morning of April 6 he presented himself in the annex of the Oranienburg/Sachsenhausen camp headquarters, where the "trial" was to take place.[209] The SS judge and his two associates were ready and waiting. Huppenkothen prepared to read the indictment he had drafted at short notice—a few brief sentences based on the "Führer report" he had submitted in October 1944, after the original discovery of documents at Zossen.[210]

Hans von Dohnanyi was carried in on a stretcher by SS guards, still paralysed, and the proceedings opened. Huppenkothen read out his indictment, which charged the prisoner with high treason and treason in the field. Unaided by counsel, unable to consult any court records and debilitated by the effects of his grave illness, Dohnanyi was a sitting target.[211] By evening the grim farce was over. Somann and Keindl withdrew to confer before sentencing Dohnanyi to death by hanging. Huppenkothen's secretary took down the grounds for the judgement at the court's dictation, a two-page document which the prosecutor delivered to Berlin without delay.[212] (It is still unknown when Dohnanyi died, but he was probably executed on April 9, almost at the same time as the prisoners in Flossenbürg.)

Huppenkothen had only just reported to Müller at 11 P.M. when the Gestapo chief presented him with another liquidation order. He was to proceed at once to Flossenbürg concentration camp and dispose of the "Canaris-Oster group" by means of another summary hearing.[213] This time Müller had prepared the ground with more than usual care. On April 5 itself, top-priority teleprinter messages had alerted RSHA headquarters, concentration camp commandants and the SS central court. An RSHA order halted the convoy which had already left Buchenwald for Schönberg and diverted Josef Müller, Gehre and Bonhoeffer to Flossenbürg. Otto Thorbeck, an SS judge based in Nuremberg, was likewise ordered to Flossenbürg to preside over a summary court there, and Oberverwalter [Senior Administrative Officer] Gogalla, head of the RSHA prison, received instructions to organize a convoy of vehicles to transport a few special prisoners, plus Huppenkothen, to the same destination.[214]

Each order was timed so that all the dramatis personae—prosecutor, judge and additional prisoners—would reach Flossenbürg by Sunday, April 8, 1945. Everything went as Müller had planned. At 3 A.M. on April 7 Huppenkothen met Gogalla's convoy on the Berlin Autobahn and boarded one of the cars. The first stop was Hof, where the prosecutor picked up some documentary evidence for the forthcoming trial.[215] Rereading Müller's instructions on the way to Flossenbürg, Huppenkothen found them all too clear. Oster, Canaris, Captain Gehre of the Abwehr, the theologian Dietrich Bonhoeffer and ex-Army judge Sack were all to be sentenced to death.

Huppenkothen's car drove into camp headquarters at Flossenbürg on the evening of April 7. Judge Thorbeck reported to him next morning,[216] and the judicial farce enacted at Oranienburg/Sachsenhausen was repeated. One of the headquarters buildings was converted into a makeshift courthouse. Huppenkothen laid out his documentary evidence in a side room and ran through it with Thorbeck and his two associate judges, Camp Commandant Kögl and another person who has never been identified.[217] Once again, this evidence came exclusively from Huppenkothen's old report to the Führer. No reference was made to the diaries which had initiated the whole proceedings and which Huppenkothen, acting on orders from Kaltenbrunner, was to burn three weeks later at Schloss Mittersill in Austria.[218]

Had they no qualms or misgivings about staging this summary trial? Huppenkothen and Thorbeck were qualified lawyers with enough experience to know that they were paving the way for murder or unlawful homicide. Even the laws and ordinances of the Third Reich prescribed that legal proceedings must be based on a determination to ascertain the truth and ensure that justice was done. The sole object on this occasion was to serve the unlawful purposes of a doomed dictatorship and confer a semblance of legality on the authorities' decision to exterminate their political opponents.

Huppenkothen and Thorbeck were also bent on flouting certain important legal formalities. Canaris and the other accused were members of the armed forces, so an SS summary court had no jurisdiction over them. They could only be tried by a military court,[219] but not even a summary court staffed by military judges would have been entitled to convict Canaris and his companions because the Kriegsstrafverfahrungsordnung [KStVO, or code governing criminal proceedings in wartime] laid it down that summary courts-martial could only be appointed to try serious cases whose immediate disposal was essential to the maintenance of discipline and security—whereas the offences ascribed to the accused had been committed years before.[220] The choice of venue was also an infringement of regulations. The court should have convened in Berlin, where Canaris and Oster—and Huppenkothen—were officially stationed. Flossenbürg was not only a seat of judgement but a predetermined place of execution.[221]

Every main feature of these summary proceedings demonstrated that their underlying purpose was murder and the perversion of justice. No military judges, an improper venue, no defence counsel, no intention of submitting the foregone verdict to confirmation or review by a supreme judicial authority—all these factors amply justified the 1955 decision of an Augsburg assize court to convict Huppenkothen and Thorbeck of abetting murder and sentence them to seven and four years' penal servitude respectively.[222] They showed not the slightest reluctance to furnish the Flossenbürg death-mill with the legal grounds it needed. Almost lightheartedly, both men lunched with the two associate judges in the officers' mess on April 8, 1945. That afternoon the summary court convened.[223]

At 4 p.m. SS guards escorted the first of the accused into the courtroom. It was Oster. Huppenkothen read out the indictment in a cold and biting voice. Like Dohnanyi, the general was charged with having committed high treason and treason in the field over a period of years. Huppenkothen quoted from the Zossen papers, producing one document after another as evidence that Oster had worked to overthrow the National Socialist regime from 1938 onwards and had collaborated with the Western powers by way of the Vatican.[224] Hans Oster, who had abandoned all hope of survival, vehemently admitted the charges. Sentence of death was passed that evening and ordered to be carried out at dawn next day.[225]

Canaris came next. Just before 8 p.m. Lunding heard the door of the adjacent cell being opened. There was a sound of footsteps in the corridor. The clink and rattle of the Admiral's fetters grew fainter, then died away.[226] Our only knowledge of what happened in court stems from the smoke screen of self-justification put up by Huppenkothen and Thorbeck, but there is no doubt that Canaris was faced with almost the same indictment as Oster: that he had since 1938 been privy to plans for a *coup d'état*, that he had done everything possible to conceal the activities of Oster's subversive group inside the Abwehr—indeed, that he himself had actively sought to incite German military commanders to rebel during the winter of 1939–40 and was aware of Josef Müller's secret negotiations at the Vatican. (The charge of betraying military secrets had been quietly dropped.)[227]

Even now, at this darkest moment in his life, Canaris refused to give up. He refuted Huppenkothen's charges against him whenever possible, doggedly denying the prosecutor's allegations or turning them to his own advantage. "He was extremely lively during the hearing," Huppenkothen recalled, "and disputed every count in an effort to save his skin. We had a lot of trouble with him."[228] When Canaris repeatedly insisted that he had only played along with the conspirators for appearances sake, intending to expose the coup at the last moment, Thorbeck interrupted the proceedings and recalled Oster for a personal confrontation.[229]

The two ex-friends clashed bitterly when Thorbeck told Oster what

Canaris had pleaded in his defence. Oster indignantly rejoined that the Admiral's contentions were untrue—of course Canaris had been involved in every activity undertaken by his resistance group. "I did it for show," Canaris cried desperately, "don't you understand?"[230]—"No," Oster snapped back at him, "that's not true. I can only say what I know —I'm not a rogue." Canaris had reached the end of his tether. When Thorbeck asked point-blank whether his former Chief of Staff was falsely incriminating him, he quietly replied, "No."[231] The outcome: a death sentence.

While the remaining three accused were being tried—with the same result—Canaris was taken back to his cell.[232] At 10 P.M. Lunding heard the door of the neighbouring cell clang shut and the all too familiar rattle of the Admiral's chains. He waited for a couple of hours until peace had descended on the cell block. Then he tapped on the wall. There was a momentary pause before his signal drew a response. Listening intently, Lunding deciphered Canaris's final message to posterity: "Nose broken at last interrogation. My time is up. Was not a traitor. Did my duty as a German. If you survive remember me to my wife."[233]

It is nonetheless doubtful whether Lunding preserved an accurate verbatim recollection of the Admiral's message in the excitement of those closing days of the war. Seven years later, when called as a witness at the Huppenkothen trial, he thought it improbable that Canaris had referred to an "interrogation." He, Lunding, had supplied the word himself because he gathered that Canaris had got "bogged down" during an interrogation and expected to be dispatched at once.[234] The phrase "nose broken" also presents problems. Did Canaris mean to convey (as his biographers have automatically assumed) that he was struck during the court hearing, or were his words a metaphorical indication that his goose was cooked? The second interpretation seems more likely, especially as Theodor Aichholzer, the sick-bay clerk who was later detailed to carry away his body, noticed no marks on the dead man's face.[235]

Lunding pondered the significance of Canaris's words until far into the night of April 8–9, but he was eventually overcome by fatigue and fell asleep at about 2 A.M. A few hours later he sat up with a start. Loud voices could be heard inside the cell block and the guard dogs were barking incessantly—an unmistakable pointer to brisk activity in the execution yard. Lunding put his eye to a crack in the cell door, through which he could see a stretch of corridor and—thanks to a large window at ground level—part of the yard as well. It was dazzlingly illuminated by arc lamps.[236]

Adjutant Baumgartner had completed arrangements for the execution shortly after 5 A.M. The camp guard was due to turn out for roll call at five-thirty. On his way to inspect it Baumgartner told Geisberger, the reporting officer, to station himself at the cell block entrance, twenty paces from the place of execution. Flossenbürg's garrison medical officer, SS-Sturmbannführer Dr. Hermann Fischer, had received his orders the previous night. He was to attend the proceedings, ensure that the condemned men were dead and fill in a certificate of execution which would refer to the victims by their code names only.[237] Baumgartner, Fischer and Geisberger were already in position when the SS executioners ran a final check on their instruments of death. A wooden roof projected from the wall at the west end of the yard, and affixed to its supporting beams were hooks and nooses. Beneath each of these stood a small stepladder.

Fischer entered the cell block just as the SS guards went to fetch the condemned men. It was close on 6 A.M. when Lunding heard a commotion in the cell next door. Someone opened the door and called, "Out you come!" Then he heard bare feet padding along the stone-flagged corridor. A fresh order rang out from the direction of the orderly room: "Get undressed!"[238] Although Lunding could not see them, Canaris and his four companions were made to undress in the bath cubicle near the guardroom. Bonhoeffer was conducted into a room on the left. Fischer saw his naked figure kneeling there in an attitude of prayer.[239]

In response to more shouted orders, the doomed men filed back along the corridor towards the yard. Lunding caught a final glimpse of his neighbour. He rushed to the crack in the door as the padding of bare feet returned and saw a pale body and grey head flit past. It was Canaris.[240] After him came the other four candidates for the gallows—Oster, Sack, Bonhoeffer and Gehre, though Lunding could not identify them. The procession halted at the end of the corridor, just inside the entrance to the yard. More orders rang out, barely intelligible against a background of hysterical barking. "The condemned men were herded across the yard to the gallows, one by one," Fischer reports. "They were made to mount a small pair of steps. Then the noose was placed round their neck and the steps pulled away from under them."[241]

Canaris was the first to enter the yard. He was escorted to the steps and calmly submitted to the noose. Fischer and Huppenkothen, of whom the latter was standing beside him, stared rigidly ahead as Wilhelm Franz Canaris, fifty-eight years old, retired admiral and former military intelligence chief of the Greater German Reich, fought his last battle. We can only view his final moments from the barbarous standpoint of his executioners. To quote an SS witness: "The little admiral took a very long time—he was jerked up and down once or twice."[242] The SS physician, Fischer, used more becoming language: "Admiral Canaris died a staunch and manly death."[243]

Although the deaths of "Caesar" and his companions in misfortune were meant to be a well-kept secret, almost every prisoner in the block discovered what had happened within a few hours. Evidence of the crime was only too abundant. Prince Philipp of Hessen, another inmate, saw the dead men's clothes lying in a heap in the guardroom together with Canaris's final choice of reading matter, Ernst Kantorowicz's biography of Emperor Frederick II, complete with the Admiral's marginal notes.[244] News of the executions was also spread by talkative SS guards. When Lunding learned of Canaris's death and asked Weissenborn if the Germans always treated their officers that way, the SS corporal angrily retorted, "He wasn't an officer—he was a traitor."[245]

At the same time, Lunding found the date peculiarly symbolic. Five years earlier, on April 9, 1940, German troops had—with substantial assistance from Canaris and the Abwehr—turned on Denmark and begun to transform what was still a local war into a conflict of earth-shaking dimensions. Josef Müller, who had miraculously escaped summary trial, was also struck by the fateful nature of this historic day when he heard what had happened early that morning. The food-hatch of his cell opened to reveal the face of a captured British officer who had just been consigned to Flossenbürg but was permitted to move about the block in comparative freedom.[246]

"Are you one of the senior officers they're supposed to be hanging?" the Englishman inquired. "Yes," Müller replied tersely. The stranger shook his head. "I don't think so. Your friends are already dead. They're just being cremated behind the cell block."[247] Not long before, Clerk Aichholzer and another prisoner has been ordered to collect a stretcher from the camp mortuary and carry five naked corpses from the place of execution, where they had been lying for some hours, to the crematorium. Aicholzer particularly noticed one of the dead men (he knew none of them) because he had a "big hooked nose" and a "very thin strangulation mark" round his neck. Next day Fischer told him that the body had belonged to Canaris, alias "Caesar."[248]

As soon as Müller detected "a definite smell of burning bodies" he rushed to his cell window and looked out. "Specks were eddying through the air—eddying through the bars and into my cell. I had the impression that they were fragments of human skin."[249] Müller stared into space for minutes before the full truth sank in. "So what the Englishman had told me was true. My friends had been murdered. Their bodies had been placed on a pyre and burnt—and now, shreds of their skin were whirling around in the air and drifting into my cell. I couldn't bear it. I was so grieved and shaken I wept."[250]

Wilhelm Canaris dead? Müller could hardly take it in. Although he had not known the Admiral well enough to form a detailed and discriminating assessment of him, he could never forget the fascination which the man and his name had once wielded over all opponents of

Hitler and the Nazi regime. How profoundly had he, the "father of the outlaws," patron of the conservative resistance movement and advocate of military chivalry, made them believe in a "decent" Germany and a better future in which patriotism and Europeanism, national pride and constitutional legality would no longer be at variance—in which all the bloodstains left on the German escutcheon by nationalistic excesses and political megalomania would at last be erased!

But there had been something in Canaris which prevented him, against his better judgement, from truly becoming one of their number. He had never been a wholehearted ally of those who, with a trace of despairing pride, had styled themselves traitors to the iniquitous Nazi regime. Whether hampered by the thought patterns of military convention and tradition, bound to Hitler by a spell which he never quite managed to break or inhibited by a fatalism which conveyed that all he did was futile, Canaris never once ventured to throw off his multitudinous allegiances to the wielders of political, social and military power. It was not in his nature to break new ground or bid farewell to prewar modes of thought and conduct which had already grown illusory by 1918. He clung with every fibre of his being to the ideal of an authoritarian nation-state—and realized too late that the supreme fulfilment of that system under Hitler contained the seeds of its own destruction.

Canaris accordingly remained, until the day of his senseless death, what he had always been: an imperial cadet and a champion of German claims to international dominance which became steadily less compatible with the realities of the twentieth century. Shutting his eyes to this, he bestowed his allegiance on an outwardly efficient regime whose motto was that politics is the art of the impossible. But was he alone? Far from it. There were millions of decent, well-meaning and courageous men who, like him, subscribed to a regime which gave promise of boundless national dynamism but were slow to recognize its murderous proclivities. All that distinguished Wilhelm Canaris from most Germans was the prescience with which he grasped, sooner than others, that all would end in doom and disaster . . .

A sudden sound jolted Müller out of his reverie. The cell door had opened and Kriminalrat Stawitzky was standing there, looking strangely affable. "Dr. Müller," he said, "would you care to hear the latest Wehrmacht communiqué?" For a moment the prisoner was baffled—the callous policeman's new-found civility seemed incomprehensible. Then Stawitzky blurted out, "Dr. Müller, are we completely done for?"[251] Müller caught on at last. Stawitzky had just heard the latest news— U.S. troops were little more than fifty miles from Flossenbürg itself.

The situation became so precarious in the next few days that the Gestapo authorities had Müller, Lunding and the rest of the special-category prisoners transferred to the apparent safety of Dachau concentration camp. On April 15 a truck pulled up outside the cell block.[252] Dusk was falling as Müller squeezed into its already crowded interior. In the west, General Patch's U. S. Seventh Army was advancing on Nuremberg, that symbolic focus of the Third Reich. What had Canaris prophesied? "Finis Germaniae!" Though not the end of Germany, it was the end of the Reich to which Wilhelm Canaris had devoted half a century of life and endeavour.

The truck moved off and soon left the precincts of Flossenbürg behind. The huts and watchtowers steadily receded, growing smaller and smaller, until they vanished over the skyline.

APPENDIX 1

NOTES

Abbreviations:

ADAP   Akton zur Deutschen Auswärtigen Politik (German Foreign Policy Documents).

BA   Bundesarchiv (German Federal Archives, civil agencies), Coblenz.

BDC   Berlin Document Center (of U. S. Mission, Berlin).

IfZ   Institut für Zeitgeschichte (Institute of Contemporary History), Munich.

IMT   Records of the International Military Tribunal (Trial of the Major German War Criminals at Nuremberg).

LStA   Akten der Lüneburger Staatsanwaltschaft (Records of the Lüneburg Public Prosecutor's Department).

MA   Militärarchiv (German Military Archives), Freiburg.

NA   National Archives, Alexandria, Virginia.

PA   Politisches Archiv des Auswärtigen Amtes (German Foreign Office Political Archives).

VfZ   *Vierteljahreshefte für Zeitgeschichte* (*Quarterly Journal of Contemporary History*).

1 The Kaiser's Cadet

1. Otto Schenk: *S.M.S. "Dresden" im Geschwader Spee*, pp. 131–32.

2. Erich Raeder: *Das Kreuzergeschwader*, p. 399.

3. Ibid.

4. Schenk: op. cit., p. 132. Raeder: op. cit., p. 399.

5. Raeder: op. cit., p. 400.

6. Ibid.

7. Schenk: op. cit., p. 133.

8. Ibid.

9. Chr. P. Christensen: *Letzte Kaperfahrt nach Quiriquina*, p. 132. Raeder: op. cit., pp. 401–2.

10. Raeder: op. cit., p. 402.

11. Ibid., pp. 402–3.

12. Confidential Report, period ending December 1, 1913, Canaris Personal File, photocopy in IfZ. Cf. also Helmut Krausnick: "Aus den Personalakten von Canaris" in *VfZ*, No. 3, July 1962. (Krausnick did not, however, publish the Personal File in its entirety, so present reference is always to the IfZ photocopy of the original.)

13. Schenk: op. cit., p. 134.

14. Raeder: op. cit., pp. 400, 402–3.

15. Karl Heinz Abshagen: *Canaris*, p. 20.

16. Ibid., p. 20.

17. Ibid., p. 19.

18. Ibid., p. 18.

19. Hugo Racine and Helmut Krausnick: "Canaris" in *Neue deutsche Biographie*, pp. 116–18. Bodo Herzog: "Der junge Canaris in Duisburg (1892–1905)" in *Die Nachhut*, May 10, 1972, pp. 16–17.

20. Krausnick: op. cit., p. 117.

21. Herzog: op. cit., p. 14.

22. Ibid., pp. 14–15.

23. Abshagen: op. cit., p 15.

24. Ibid.

25. André Brissaud: *Canaris*, p. 5.

26. Ulrich Klever: *Knaurs Hundebuch*, p. 179.

27. Paul Ronge: "Zur Ahnentafel des Admirals Canaris" in *Genealogie*, Vol. VI, No. 1/1962, p. 35.

28. Abshagen: op. cit., p. 21.

29. Herzog: op. cit., p. 15.

30. Ibid., p. 16. Abshagen: op cit., p. 21.

31. Herzog: op. cit., p. 16.

32. *Brockhaus' Conversations-Lexikon*, 1885, Vol. X, p. 60.

33. Abshagen: op. cit., p. 19.

34. Herzog: op. cit., p. 16.

35. Anon. (=Erich Ferdinand Pruck): "Wilhelm Canaris" in Annedore Leber-*Das Gewissen entscheidet*, p. 251.

36. Michael Freund: *Deutsche Geschichte*, p. 827.

37. Ekkhard Verchau: "Von Jachmann über Stosch und Caprivi zu den Anfängen der Ära Tirpitz" in Herbert Schottelins and Wilhelm Deist (eds.), *Marine und Marinepolitik 1871–1914*, p. 54.

38. Ibid., p. 59.

39. Ibid., p. 67.

40. *Brockhaus Enzyklopädie*, 1968, Vol. IV, p. 798.

41. Paul Simsa: *Marine intern*, p. 30.

42. Ibid., p. 61.

43. Ibid., p. 84.

44. Cf. Volker R. Berghahn: "Der Tirpitz-Plan und die Krisis des preussisch-deutschen Herrschaftssystems" in Schottelins/Deist: op. cit., p. 89 et seq.

45. Arthur J. Mader: *From the Dreadnought to Scapa Flow*, p. 106.

46. Simsa: op. cit., p. 105.

47. Friedrich Forstmeier: "Der Tirpitzsche Flottenbau im Urteil der Historiker" in Schottelins/Deist: op. cit., p. 35.

48. Herzog: op. cit., p. 17. Brissaud: op. cit., p. 6.

49. Simsa: op. cit., p. 135.

50. *Deckoffiziere der deutschen Marine*, p. 20.

51. Holger H. Herwig: "Soziale Herkunft and wissenschaftliche Vorbildung des Seeoffiziers der kaiserlichen Marine vor 1914" in *Militärgeschichtliche Mitteilungen*, No. 2/1971, p. 89.

52. L. Persius: *Menschen und Schiffe in der kaiserlichen Flotte*, p. 24.

53. *Weyers Flottenkalender*, pp. 102, 104.

54. Persius: op. cit., p. 26.

55. Herzog: op. cit., p. 18.

56. Persius: op. cit., p. 29.

57. Hermann Giskes: *Spione überspielen Spione*, p. 41.

58. Abshagen: op. cit., p. 23.

59. Written communication from Herr Otto Benninghoff, November 12, 1966.

60. Abshagen: op. cit., p. 23. (The witness, though anonymous, is identical with Abshagen's associate Benninghoff.)

61. Confidential Report, period ending December 1, 1909, Canaris Personal File.

62. Ibid.

63. Holger H. Herwig: "Zur Soziolo-

gie des kaiserlichen Seeoffizierkorps vor 1914" in Schottelins/Deist: op. cit., p. 78.

64. Ibid., p. 81.

65. Ibid., p. 80.

66. E. Alboldt: *Die Tragödie der alten deutschen Marine*, p. 16 et seq.

67. Ibid., p. 25.

68. Ibid., pp. 26–27.

69. Ibid., p. 21.

70. E. Alboldt: "Die Uraschen des Zusammenbruchs der Marine" in *Die Ursachen des deutschen Zusammenbruchs in Jahre 1918*, Vol. X, p. 81.

71. Alboldt: *Tragödie*, p. 20.

72. Herwig: "Zur Soziologie," p. 83.

73. Ibid., p. 83.

74. Ibid., p. 83.

75. Ibid., p. 87.

76. Service Record, entry dated November 20, 1907, in Canaris Personal File.

77. *Weyers*, p. 168.

78. Confidential Report, period ending December 1, 1909, Canaris Personal File.

79. Captain's Report on relinquishing command, November 12, 1908, Canaris Personal File.

80. Service Record, entry dated November 20, 1907.

81. Captain's Report on relinquishing command, November 12, 1908.

82. Confidential Report, period ending December 1, 1909.

83. Decorations conferred on Admiral Canaris, Canaris Personal File.

84. Confidential Report, period ending December 1, 1909.

85. Hopmann Diary, November 21, 1908, BA/MA N 326/5.

86. Report on decommissioning of Manoeuvre Flotilla, September 3, 1910, in Canaris Personal File.

87. Medical report dated January 15, 1924, Canaris Personal File.

88. Confidential Report, period ending December 1, 1911, Canaris Personal File.

89. Medical report dated January 15, 1924.

90. Confidential Report, period ending December 1, 1911.

91. Ibid.

92. Confidential Report, period ending December 1, 1913.

93. Else Lüdecke: *Kreuzerfahrten und Kriegserlebnisse: S.M.S. "Dresden," 1914/1915*, p. 8.

94. Ibid.

95. Abshagen: op. cit., p. 25.

96. Lüdecke: op. cit., p. 9.

97. Raeder: op. cit., p. 370.

98. Heinrich Schneider: *Die letzte Fahrt des Kleinen Kreuzers "Dresden,"* pp. 9, 15.

99. Ibid., p. 16.

100. Ibid., pp. 17–19.

101. Lüdecke: op. cit., p. 9.

102. Raeder: op. cit., p. 371.

103. Schneider: op. cit, pp. 26–28.

104. Ibid., pp. 28–29. Raeder: op. cit., p. 371.

105. Raeder: op. cit., p. 371.

106. Ibid.

107. Schneider: op. cit., p. 30.

108. Raeder: op. cit., p. 371.

109. Ibid.

110. Schneider: op. cit., p. 36.

111. Ibid., p. 37.

112. Raeder: op. cit., p. 371.

113. Eberhard von Mantey: "Das Kreuzergeschwader 1914" in Mantey: *Unsere Marine im Weltkrieg 1914 1918*, p. 81.

114. Ibid. Gerhard Bidlingmaier: "Zum 50. Jahrestag der Falklandschlacht" in *Marine-Rundschau*, No. 6/1964, pp. 319–20.

115. Bidlingmaier: op. cit., p. 321.

116. Obituary in *Die Nachhut*, No. 6, December 15, 1968, p. 24. Ian Colvin: *Chief of Intelligence*, pp. 11–12. Hopmann Diary, November 21 and 25 and December 24, 1908.

117. H. R. Trevor-Roper: "Admiral Canaris" in *The Cornhill Magazine*, Summer 1950, p. 390.

118. Raeder, op. cit., pp. 371, 373.

119. Ibid., p. 373.

120. Ibid., p. 373.

121. Ibid., p. 373.

122. Ibid., p. 374. Obituary, p. 24 (v. 116).

123. Obituary, p. 24 (v. 116).

124. Raeder: op. cit., p. 375.

125. Ibid., pp. 372–75.
126. Ibid., p. 379.
127. Ibid., p. 381.
128. Ibid., p. 382.
129. Ibid., p. 380.
130. Bidlingmaier: op. cit., p. 320 et seq. Mantey: op. cit., p. 82.
131. Raeder: op. cit., p. 142.
132. Ibid., p. 142.
133. Ibid., p. 147.
134. Bidlingmaier: op. cit., p. 325.
135. Ibid., p. 326. Mantey: op. cit., p. 89.
136. Bidlingmaier: op. cit., p. 326.
137. Decorations conferred on Admiral Canaris. Abshagen: op. cit., p. 27.
138. Bidlingmaier: op. cit., p. 327.
139. Ibid., p. 327.
140. Ibid., p. 327.
141. Ibid., p. 328.
142. Ibid.
143. Raeder: op. cit., p. 295. Schneider: op. cit., p. 95 et seq.
144. Raeder: op. cit., p. 295.
145. Ibid., p. 296.
146. Ibid., pp. 386–87.
147. Schenk: op. cit., p. 101.
148. Raeder: op. cit., p. 387.
149. Schneider: op. cit., p. 111. Raeder: op. cit., p. 387.
150. Raeder: op. cit., p. 387.
151. Ibid., p. 387.
152. Ibid., p. 320.
153. Ibid., p. 320.
154. Ibid., p. 387.
155. Ibid., p. 387.
156. Ibid., p. 389.
157. Ibid., p. 388.
158. Ibid., pp. 388–91.
159. Ibid., p. 390.
160. Ibid., p. 393.
161. Ibid., p. 391.
162. Schneider: op. cit., p. 126. Schenk: op. cit., p. 116. Raeder: op. cit., p. 395.

163. Raeder: op. cit., p. 395.
164. Ibid., p. 396.
165. Schenk: op. cit., p. 123.
166. Ibid., p. 123.
167. Ibid., p. 123.
168. Ibid., p. 130.
169. Raeder: op. cit., p. 398.
170. Fritz Lüdecke: "S.M.S. Dresden von der Falkland-Schlacht bis zum Untergang" in Reinhard Scheer and Willy Stöwer: *Die deutsche Flotte in grosser Zeit*, p. 167.
171. Raeder: op. cit., pp. 397–98.
172. Fritz Lüdecke: op. cit., p. 167. Raeder: op. cit., p. 398.
173. Raeder: op. cit., p. 398. Schenk: op. cit., p. 128.
174. Raeder: op. cit., p. 399.
175. Ibid., p. 403.
176. Ibid., pp. 402–3.
177. Ibid. Colvin: op. cit., p. 18. Schenk: op. cit., p. 136. Otto Mielke: *Das letzte Schiff des Kreuzergeschwaders*, p. 36.
178. Else Lüdecke: op. cit., p. 43. Raeder: op. cit., p. 403.
179. Raeder: op. cit., p. 403.
180. Christensen: op. cit., p. 139. Raeder: op. cit., pp. 403–4. Schenk: op. cit., p. 139.
181. Raeder: op. cit., p. 404.
182. Schenk: op. cit., p. 146.
183. Else Lüdecke: op. cit., p. 47.
184. Ibid.
185. Raeder: op. cit., pp. 405–6.
186. Christensen: op. cit., p. 155.
187. Ibid., p. 157.
188. Else Lüdecke: op. cit., p. 53. Schenk: op. cit., p. 155.
189. Admiralstab memorandum dated October 5, 1915, BA/MA RM 5/v.2228. Else Lüdecke: op. cit., p. 53.
190. Canaris Personal File. Christensen: op. cit., p. 213.
191. Christensen: op. cit., p. 217.

2 Mission in the Mediterranean

1. Chr. P. Christensen: *Letzte Kaperfahrt nach Quiriquina*, p. 218.
2. Otto Schenk: *S.M.S. "Dresden"* im Geschwader Spee, p. 155. Else Lüdecke: *S.M.S. "Dresden,"* p. 54.
3. Admiralstab memorandum dated

October 5, 1915, BA/MA RM 5/v.2228.

4. Karl Heinz Abshagen: *Canaris*, p. 28.

5. Admiralstab memorandum dated October 5, 1915.

6. Ibid.

7. Abshagen: op. cit., p. 28.

8. For a recent example see Charles Whiting: *Canaris*, p. 15 et seq.

9. Admiralstab memorandum dated October 5, 1915.

10. Canaris Personal File, IfZ.

11. Ibid.

12. Letter from Admiralstab N to HQ Baltic Naval Station dated October 20, 1916, Canaris Personal File.

13. Otto Schulze: "U-Boote im Mittelmeer" in Eberhard von Mantey: *Unsere Marine im Weltkrieg 1914–1918*, p. 315.

14. Ibid., p. 315.

15. Ibid., p. 316.

16. Ibid., p. 316.

17. Ibid., p. 319.

18. Ibid., pp. 317–18.

19. Ibid., p. 319.

20. Canaris Personal File.

21. Abshagen: op. cit., p. 30.

22. Ibid.

23. Friedrich Gempp: *Geheimer Nachrichtendienst und Spionageabwehr des Heeres*, Vol. IV, Part II, p. 243, NA ML 68.

24. Abshagen: op. cit., p. 30.

25. Medical report dated January 15, 1924, and signed by Naval Staff Physician Dr. Schulte-Ostrop, Canaris Personal File. Helmut Krausnick: "Aus den Personalakten von Canaris" in *VfZ*, No. 3, July 1962, p. 286.

26. Abshagen: op. cit., p. 31.

27. Marineleitung list of code names in Spain, 1928, BA/MA, OKM Box 20, 48903.

28. Gempp: op. cit., p. 243.

29. Ibid.

30. Report from a V-Mann (Ritter von Goss) to the Marineleitung dated September 27, 1928, BA/MA, OKM Box 20, 48903.

31. Diplomatist: "Ein König im Netz" in *Die Weltbühne*, January 10, 1928, p. 53.

32. Ibid., p. 54.

33. Ibid., p. 55.

34. Gempp: op. cit., p. 243.

35. Report by Canaris: "N-Arbeiten in Spanien während der Reise vom 28.I bis 17.II 1925," BA/MA, OKM Box 20, 48903.

36. André Brissaud: *Canaris*, p. 8.

37. Abshagen: op. cit., p. 31.

38. Report from a V-Mann (Ritter von Goss) to the Marineleitung dated June 29, 1928, BA/MA, OKM Box 20, 48903.

39. See Chapter 4.

40. On the Canaris-Ullmann Echevarrieta connection, see Canaris's report on his Spanish trip, May 9–June 10, 1926, BA/MA, OKM Box 20, 48903. Hugh Thomas: *The Spanish Civil War*, p. 27.

41. Canaris's report on visit to Spain, January–February 1925, BA/MA, OKM Box 20, 48903.

42. Ibid.

43. Heinz Kiel: *Canaris zwischen den Fronten*, p. 7.

44. Ibid., p. 8.

45. See Chapter 4.

46. Abshagen: op. cit., p. 33.

47. Ibid.

48. Telegram from Admiralstab N to HQ Baltic Naval Station dated February 28, 1916, Canaris Personal File.

49. Ibid.

50. Telegram from Chief of Naval Staff to HQ Baltic Station dated March 3, 1916, Canaris Personal File.

51. Abshagen: op. cit., p. 33. A further reference in Bodo Herzog: "Canaris wird am 2. Oktober 1916 aus Spanien abgeholt" in *Die Nachhut*, No. 21/22, January 8, 1973, p. 24.

52. Herzog: op. cit., p. 24.

53. Telegram from Chief of Naval Staff to HQ Baltic Station dated March 3, 1916.

54. Abshagen: op. cit., p. 34.

55. Ladislas Farago: *The Game of the Foxes*, p. 6. Abshagen: op. cit., p. 34.

56. Medical report dated January 15, 1924.

57. Telegram from Admiralstab N to HQ Baltic Station dated March 20, 1916, Canaris Personal File.
58. Ibid.
59. Schulze: op. cit., pp. 316–17.
60. Diplomatist: op. cit., p. 56.
61. Gempp: op. cit., p. 243.
62. Admiralstab N memorandum dated September 5, 1916, Canaris Personal File.
63. Memorandum from Captain Götting, March 24, 1931, BA/MA, II M 65/2.
64. Letter from Canaris to Götting dated March 23, 1931.
65. Krausnick: op. cit., p. 286.
66. Telegram from Admiralstab N to HQ Baltic Station, September 1916, Canaris Personal File.
67. Herzog: op. cit., p. 21.
68. Report by Lieutenant von Arnauld on picking up Lieutenant Canaris off Cartagena, October 21, 1916, BA/MA, RM 97/766.
69. Herzog: op. cit., p. 22.
70. Ibid., p. 23.
71. War Diary of *U35*, September 30, 1916, BA/MA, RM 97/776.
72. Herzog: op. cit., p. 23.
73. War Diary of *U35*, October 1, 1916. Arnauld: Report on picking up Canaris.
74. Herzog: op. cit., p. 24.
75. Ibid., p. 23.
76. Arnauld: Report on picking up Canaris.
77. Letter from Admiralstab N to HQ Baltic Station, October 20, 1916.
78. Ibid.

79. Krausnick: op. cit., p. 286.
80. Letter from Lieutenant Commander Eschenburg, September 11, 1917, Canaris Personal File.
81. Ibid.
82. Confidential Report, period ending December 1, 1917, Canaris Personal File.
83. Abshagen: op. cit., pp. 42, 52.
84. Ibid.
85. Confidential Report, period ending December 1, 1917.
86. Schulze: op. cit., pp. 319–20.
87. Confidential Report, period ending December 1, 1917.
88. Undated memorandum by Lieutenant Otto Schulze, Canaris Personal File.
89. Bodo Herzog: "Kapitänleutnant Wilhelm Canaris als U-Boot-Kommandant" in *Die Nachhut*, October 1, 1972, p. 11.
90. Ibid., p. 11.
91. Ibid., p. 11.
92. Ibid., p. 12.
93. Ibid., p. 14.
94. Ibid., p. 15.
95. Schulze memorandum.
96. Abshagen: op. cit., p. 19.
97. Herzog: "Canaris als U-Boot-Kommandant," p. 16.
98. Letter from Lieutenant Commander Schaper dated August 1, 1918, Canaris Personal File.
99. Ibid.
100. Schulze: op. cit., p. 323.
101. Ibid., p. 326.
102. Ibid.

3 Counterrevolution

1. War Diary of *UB128*, entry dated November 29, 1918, BA/MA.
2. J. Benoist-Méchin: *Histoire de l'armée allemande* (German edition), Vol. I, "Das Kaiserreich zerbricht," p. 104.
3. War Diary of *UB128*, entry dated November 29, 1918.
4. Ibid.

5. Gustav Noske: *Von Kiel bis Kapp*, p. 45.
6. War Diary of *UB128*, entry dated November 29, 1918.
7. Noske: op. cit., p. 45.
8. Ibid., p. 45.
9. Ibid., p. 46.
10. Ibid.
11. Benoist-Méchin: op. cit., p. 66.

12. Klaus Hildebrand: "Hitlers Ort in der Geschichte des preussisch-deutschen Nationalstaates" in *Historische Zeitschrift*, Vol. 217, No. 3, December 1973, p. 615.

13. Lothar Persius: "Erinnerungen eines Seeoffiziers" in *Die Weltbühne*, May 12, 1925, p. 693.

14. *Die Ursachen des deutschen Zusammenbruchs im Jahre 1918*, ed. by Dr. Albrecht Philipp, Vol. 9, Half-Vol. 1, p. 131.

15. Ibid., p. 126.

16. Paul Simsa: *Marine intern*, p. 243.

17. See Navy Secretary (ret.) Alboldt: "Die Ursachen des Zusammenbruchs der Marine" in *Die Ursachen* . . . , Vol. 10, Half-Vol. 1, p. 133 et seq.

18. Ibid.

19. Simsa: op. cit., p. 253.

20. For the latest findings on this subject see Wilhelm Deist: "Die Politik der Seekriegsleitung und die Rebellion der Flotte Ende Oktober 1918" in VfZ, No. 4, October 1966, p. 341 et seq.

21. Simsa: op. cit., p. 287 et seq.

22. Wolfgang Malanowski: *November-Revolution 1918*, p. 35.

23. Michael Freund: *Deutsche Geschichte*, p. 1027.

24. Simsa: op. cit., p. 298 et seq.

25. Canaris Personal File, photocopy in IfZ.

26. *Die 3. Marine-Brigade v. Loewenfeld*, publ. by the 3rd Naval Brigade Association, p. 5.

27. Wilfried von Loewenfeld: "Das Freikorps von Loewenfeld" in Hans Roden: *Deutsche Soldaten*, p. 150.

28. *Die 3. Marine-Brigade*, p. 5.

29. Ibid., p. 4.

30. Loewenfeld: op. cit., p. 150.

31. Ibid., p. 150.

32. Ibid., p. 149.

33. "Die Wirren in der Reichshauptstadt und im nördlichen Deutschland 1918–1920," publ. by the Kriegsgeschichtliche Forschungsanstalt des Heeres in *Darstellungen aus den Nachkriegskämpfen deutscher Truppen und Freikorps*, Vol. 6, Ser. 2, p. 47.

34. Ibid., p. 47.

35. Ibid., p. 47.

36. Ibid., p. 48.

37. Freund: op. cit., pp. 1043–46.

38. Ibid.

39. Harry Wilde: *Rosa Luxemburg*, p. 181.

40. Ibid., p. 185.

41. "Die Wirren . . . ," p. 48.

42. Malanowski: op. cit., p. 100 et seq. Wilde: op. cit., p. 184.

43. Noske: op. cit., pp. 68–69.

44. "Die Wirren . . . ," p. 48. Benoist-Méchin: op. cit., p. 127.

45. Benoist-Méchin: op. cit., p. 125.

46. Ernst Jünger (ed.): *Krieg und Krieger*, p. 170.

47. Ibid., p. 106.

48. "Die Wirren . . . ," p. 46.

49. Ibid.

50. Oral communication from Herr Otto Wagner, June 1973.

51. Benoist-Méchin: op. cit., p. 127. Simsa: op. cit., p. 302.

52. "Die Wirren . . . ," p. 48.

53. Pabst Personal File, *Spiegel* Archives.

54. Waldemar Pabst, *Der Spiegel*, No. 16/1962, p. 39.

55. Benoist-Méchin: op. cit., pp. 129–32.

56. Ibid., pp. 129–32.

57. Ibid., p. 133.

58. Elisabeth Hannover-Drück and Heinrich Hannover: *Der Mord an Rosa Luxemburg und Karl Liebknecht*, p. 29.

59. Malanowski: op. cit., p. 105.

60. See Wilde: op. cit., pp. 95–96, 204, 208–9, 213, 215, 235.

61. Notes of a conversation with Pabst made by Dr. Günther Nollau, December 1, 1959, *Der Spiegel*, Nos. 1/2, 1970, p. 49.

62. Peter Nettl: *Rosa Luxemburg*, p. 772. Max Hochdorf: *Rosa Luxemburg*, p. 234 et seq.

63. Paul Levi: *Der Jorns-Prozess*, p. 3. Hannover-Drück/Hannover: op. cit., p. 36.

64. Interview with Pabst, *Der Spiegel*, No. 16/1962, p. 42. "Pabst-Befehle,"

unpubl. report of a Süddeutscher Rundfunk television team, 1966, *Spiegel* Archives.

65. Nettl: op. cit., p. 775. Hochdorf: op. cit., pp. 238–39.

66. Wilde: op. cit., p. 192. Levi: op. cit., p. 4.

67. Wilde: op. cit., p. 193. Pabst interview, p. 43.

68. "Der dritte Mann" in *Der Spiegel*, No. 8/1967, p. 40.

69. Malanowski: op. cit., p. 107.

70. Ibid.

71. Gert Buchheit: *Der deutsche Geheimdienst*, p. 193. André Brissaud: *Canaris*, p. 10. Karl Heinz Abshagen: *Canaris*, p. 44.

72. "Die Wirren . . . ," p. 54.

73. Ibid.

74. Buchheit: op. cit., p. 192.

75. Canaris Personal File.

76. Richard Grunberger: *Red Rising in Bavaria*, p. 63 et seq.

77. Abshagen: op. cit., p. 42.

78. Ibid., p. 44.

79. "Die Wirren . . . ," p. 54.

80. Canaris Personal File.

81. Jost Dülffer: *Weimar, Hitler und die Marine*, p. 29. See also Deist: op. cit., p. 352 et seq.

82. *Die 3. Marine-Brigade*, p. 6.

83. Gabriele Krüger: *Die Brigade Ehrhardt*, p. 26.

84. *Die 3. Marine-Brigade*, p. 7. Krüger: op. cit., pp. 26–27.

85. Krüger: op. cit., pp. 26–27. "Die Wirren . . . ," p. 213.

86. See the Loewenfeld Brigade's list of appointments in *Die 3. Marine-Brigade*, p. 11.

87. Levi: op. cit., pp. 7, 14–15.

88. Ibid., p. 8.

89. Ibid., p. 16.

90. Ibid., p. 7.

91. Ibid., p. 7.

92. Ibid., p. 7.

93. Ibid., p. 9.

94. Ibid., p. 9.

95. Ibid., p. 15.

96. Ibid., p. 16.

97. Ibid., p. 10.

98. Ibid., p. 10.

99. Ibid., p. 11.

100. Ibid., p. 13.

101. Statement by Canaris to Lieutenant Commander Flies, January 31, 1931, Canaris Personal File, BA/MA, II M 65/2. Levi: op. cit., p. 20.

102. Levi: op. cit., p. 20.

103. Ibid.

104. Ibid.

105. Hannover-Drück/Hannover: op. cit., p. 59.

106. Levi: op. cit., p. 21.

107. *Berliner Börsen-Zeitung*, January 23, 1931.

108. Bredereck's testimony at the Jorns hearing, *Berliner Börsen-Zeitung*, January 23, 1931.

109. Bredereck's testimony, *Vorwärts*, January 23, 1931. Transcript Ib (Marineleitung), January 1931, Canaris Personal File.

110. *Berliner Börsen-Zeitung*, January 23, 1931.

111. Bredereck's testimony, *Vorwärts*, January 23, 1931.

112. Ibid.

113. Hannover-Drück/Hannover: op. cit., p. 125.

114. BS-Korrespondenz, January 31, 1931, Canaris Personal File.

115. Report of the USPD daily *Freiheit*, May 8, 1919, quoted by Hannover-Drück/Hannover: op. cit., p. 60.

116. Hannover-Drück/Hannover: op. cit., p. 42.

117. *Der Spiegel*, No. 8/1967, p. 42.

118. It is still uncertain who fired the fatal shot. A Süddeutscher Rundfunk television programme produced by Dieter Ertel and broadcast early in 1969 attributed the shooting to Souchon on the basis of Pabst's testimony. In February 1970 Stuttgart District Court directed the company to withdraw this allegation.

119. Hannover-Drück/Hannover: op. cit., p. 116 et seq.

120. Levi: op. cit., p. 21.

121. Ibid., pp. 11–12.

122. Ibid., p. 12.

123. Hannover-Drück/Hannover: op. cit., p. 134. "Pabst-Befehle," pp. 7–8. This account is supported by the historian Helmut Krausnick, who claims to

have been told by Vogel during the mid-1930s, after his return to Berlin, that it was Canaris who released him. Oral communication from Professor Krausnick, June 1970.

124. Telephone call from Judge Advocate Sohl to Lieutenant Commander Flies, noted January 31, 1931, also handwritten notes by Flies. Canaris Personal File.

125. Ibid. Abshagen: op. cit., p. 49.

126. "Pabst-Befehle," p. 7.

127. Canaris Personal File.

128. Hagen Schulze: *Freikorps und Republik 1918–1920*, p. 207.

129. Ibid., p. 213.

130. Ibid., p. 210.

131. Ibid., p. 212.

132. Ibid. Krüger: op. cit., p. 40.

133. Schulze: op. cit., p. 213.

134. Krüger: op. cit., p. 40. Schulze: op. cit., p. 213.

135. Schulze: op. cit., p. 213.

136. Ibid., p. 253. Krüger: op. cit., p. 41.

137. Schulze: op. cit., p. 253.

138. Ibid.

139. Johannes Erger: *Der Kapp-Lüttwitz-Putsch*, p. 110. Schulze: op. cit., p 248.

140. Erger: op. cit., p. 115.

141. Said by Reich Minister Koch-Weser. Schulze: op. cit., p. 249.

142. Erger: op. cit., p. 116.

143. Schulze: op. cit., p. 250. Erger: op. cit., p. 116.

144. Schulze: op. cit., p. 261. Erger: op. cit., p. 121.

145. Erger: op. cit., p. 119.

146. Schulze: op. cit., p. 262.

147. Erger: op. cit., p. 121. Statement by Canaris, March 7, 1923, and by Trotha, January 12, 1923. Luetgebrune Papers, NA, T-253/12.

148. Senior State Prosecutor's indictment against Lieutenant Commander (ret.) Hermann Ehrhardt, May 5, 1923, p. 12, NA, T-253/12.

149. Schulze: op. cit., p. 255. Krüger: op. cit., p. 50. Erger: op. cit., p. 112.

150. Statement by Trotha, February 12, 1923.

151. Statement by Canaris, March 7, 1923.

152. Ibid.

153. Erger: op. cit., pp. 121–22.

154. Ibid., p. 123.

155. Ibid., p. 124.

156. Ibid., p. 124.

157. Ibid., p. 124.

158. Ibid., p. 125.

159. Ehrhardt indictment, p. 19.

160. Erger: op. cit., p. 132.

161. Trotha statement.

162. Ibid.

163. Ibid.

164. Canaris and Trotha statements.

165. Statement by Ehrhardt, December 14, 1922, NA, T-253/12.

166. Trotha's evidence, December 10, 1921.

167. Trotha's report to the Kommandanturgericht, March 26, 1920, NA, T-253/12.

168. Submission by Trotha's counsel, Grünspach, to the Kommandanturgericht, March 26, 1920, NA, T-253/12.

169. Canaris's evidence.

170. Ibid.

171. Trotha's evidence, December 10, 1921.

172. Ibid.

173. Ibid.

174. Recorded by State Secretary Albert, June 10, 1920, BA, R43 I/2722 138 R.

175. Trotha's report to the Kommandanturgericht, March 27, 1920, NA, T-253/12.

176. Helmut Sprotte: *Die Reichsmarine in ihrer organisatorischen Entwicklung seit der Revolution*, p. 25.

177. Ibid., pp. 25–26.

178. Ibid.

179. For a detailed account see Schulze and Erger.

180. Abshagen: op. cit., p. 54.

181. Sprotte: op. cit., p. 26.

182. Canaris Personal File. Abshagen: op. cit., p. 54.

183. Otto Gessler: *Reichswehrpolitik in der Weimarer Zeit*, p. 146.

184. Ibid., p. 148.

185. Ibid., p. 134.

186. Canaris Personal File.
187. Kurt Stöckel: *Die Entwicklung der Reichsmarine nach dem ersten Weltkrieg*, p. 43.
188. Ibid., p. 27.
189. Service Report, period ending August 1, 1921, Canaris Personal File.
190. Captain Schüssler: "Der Kampf der Marine gegen Versailles 1919–1935" in IMT, Vol. XXXIV, p. 541 et seq.
191. Cf Krüger: op. cit., p. 70 et seq.
192. Stöckel: op. cit., p. 45.
193. Ibid., p. 45.
194. Ibid., p. 44.
195. Sprotte: op. cit., p. 25.
196. Ehrhardt indictment.
197. Schüssler: op. cit., p. 551.
198. Ibid., p. 541.
199. Ibid., p. 542. Oliver: "Das Geheimnis um Canaris" in *Die Weltbühne*, August 23, 1927, p. 287.
200. Schüssler: op. cit., p. 541.
201. Ibid., p. 541.
202. Ibid., p. 542.
203. Ibid., p. 543.
204. Krüger: op. cit., p. 72.
205. Ibid., p. 73.
206. Ibid., pp. 70–71.
207. Ibid., p. 78.
208. Ibid.
209. Oliver: op. cit., p. 286. Krüger: op. cit., p. 91.
210. Oliver: "Canaris an der Ostsee" in *Die Weltbühne*, September 6, 1927, p. 357.
211. Evidence given by Captain (ret.) Kurt Lieder during the Wiking-Olympia hearing in 1927, reproduced by Oliver in "Das Geheimnis um Canaris," p. 286.
212. Ibid., p. 286.
213. Ibid., p. 287.
214. Krüger: op. cit., p. 91.

215. Ibid., p. 89.
216. Oliver: "Das Geheimnis um Canaris," p. 286.
217. Ibid., p. 288.
218. Krüger: op. cit., p. 105 et seq.
219. Heinz Kiel: *Canaris zwischen die Fronten*, p. 11.
220. Krüger: op. cit., p. 106.
221. Oliver: "Das Geheimnis um Canaris," p. 286.
222. Reichstag speech delivered by the SPD deputy Philipp Scheidemann and reproduced in *Reichstag Proceedings*, 3rd Electoral Period 1924, Vol. 391, p. 8580.
223. Canaris Personal File.
224. *Die 3. Marine-Brigade*, p. 19.
225. Erich Raeder: *Mein Leben*, Vol. I, p. 187 (not in English edition).
226. Francis L. Carsten: *The Reichswehr and Politics*, p. 99.
227. Shlomo Aronson: *Heydrich und die Anfänge des SD und der Gestapo 1931–1935*, p. 26.
228. Ibid., p. 45.
229. Ibid., pp. 40–41.
230. Canaris Personal File.
231. Ibid.
232. Aronson: op. cit., p. 51.
233. Oral information from Frau Renée Wagner, a frequent visitor to the Canaris home, June 1973.
234. Resignation request submitted by Lieutenant Commander Canaris and dated January 15, 1924, Canaris Personal File.
235. Medical report dated January 15, 1924, and signed by Naval Staff Physician Dr. Schulte-Ostrop, Canaris Personal File.
236. Letter from Rear Admiral von Gagern to Canaris, February 6, 1924, Canaris Personal File.

4 *The Exploits of Herr Kika*

1. Karl Heinz Abshagen: *Canaris*, p. 57.
2. Captain Schüssler: "Der Kampf der Marine gegen Versailles 1919–1935" in IMT, Vol. XXXIV, p. 565.
3. Ibid., p. 566.
4. Ibid.
5. A. G. Ploetz: *Geschichte des Zweiten Weltkrieges*, p. 285. Cf. also Donald W. Mitchell: *History of the Modern American Navy*.
6. Ploetz: op. cit., p. 305.

7. Schüssler: op. cit., p. 566.
8. Ploetz: op. cit., p. 305.
9. Schüssler: op. cit., p. 566.
10. Ibid.
11. Abshagen: op. cit., p. 57.
12. Ploetz: op. cit., p. 285.
13. Ibid., p. 305.
14. Abshagen: op. cit., p. 57.
15. Schüssler: op. cit., p. 566.
16. Canaris Personal File, photocopy in IfZ.
17. Jost Dülffer: *Weimar, Hitler und die Marine*, p. 51.
18. Ibid., p. 61.
19. Ibid., p. 62.
20. Ibid., p. 90.
21. Ibid., p. 63.
22. Wolfgang Wacker: *Der Bau des Panzerkreuzers A und der Reichstag*, p. 10 et seq.
23. Dülffer: op. cit., p. 75.
24. Ibid., p. 75.
25. Ibid., p. 75.
26. Ibid., p. 89.
27. Personal Assessment dated November 1, 1925, Canaris Personal File.
28. Ibid.
29. Ibid.
30. Schüssler: op. cit., pp. 566–67.
31. Kurt Stöckel: *Die Entwicklung der Reichsmarine nach dem Ersten Weltkriege*, p. 57.
32. Francis L. Carsten: *The Reichswehr and Politics*, p. 284 et seq.
33. Schüssler: op. cit., p. 553.
34. Ibid.
35. Ibid.
36. Ibid.
37. Otto Gessler: *Reichswehrpolitik in der Weimarer Zeit*, pp. 444, 447.
38. Ibid., p. 447.
39. Report by State Secretary (ret.) Fritze on the Lohmann commercial enterprises, BA, R43 I/605, p. 46.
40. Gessler: op. cit., p. 443.
41. State Secretary (ret.) Fritze: "Material zur Frage des 'Ruhrfonds,'" p. 1, BA, R43 I/605.
42. Ibid., p. 1.
43. Ibid., p. 4.
44. Ibid., p. 20.
45. Ibid., p. 11.
46. Ibid., pp. 17, 21.

47. Structure of the Lohmann enterprises, BA/MA, OKM Box 7, 34428.
48. Ibid.
49. Ibid.
50. Ibid.
51. Schüssler: op. cit., p. 567.
52. Ibid.
53. Ibid.
54. Report by Lieutenant Commander Canaris on his visit to Spain, January 28–February 17, 1925, Marineleitung/Spanien-Akten, BA/MA, OKM Box 20, 48903.
55. Ibid.
56. Ibid.
57. Canaris: "N-Arbeiten in Spanien während der Reise vom 28.I. bis 17.II. 1925," BA/MA, OKM Box 20, 48903.
58. Ibid.
59. Ibid.
60. Ibid.
61. Ibid.
62. Report by Lieutenant Commander Canaris on his visit to Spain, January 28–February 17, 1925. Report by Lieutenant Commander Canaris on his visit to Spain, April 20–May 8, 1925, BA/MA, OKM Box 20, 48903.
63. Canaris report, January 28–February 17, 1925.
64. Ibid.
65. Ibid.
66. Ibid.
67. Ibid.
68. Ibid.
69. Ibid.
70. Ibid.
71. Excerpt from C 4310/28, BA/MA, OKM Box 20, 48903.
72. "Geheim-Stabssache, Stand der U-Boots- u. Torpedo-Angelegenheit," notes by Canaris, BA/MA, OKM Box 20, 48903.
73. Canaris report, January 28–February 17, 1925.
74. Ibid.
75. Undated notes by Canaris (about June 1926), BA/MA, OKM Box 20, 48903.
76. Progress of affairs in Spain after Lieutenant Commander Canaris's visit

in February 1925, BA/MA, OKM Box 20, 48903.

77. Ibid.

78. Ibid.

79. Ibid.

80. Canaris report, April 20–May 8, 1925.

81. Ibid.

82. "Stand der spanischen Angelegenheit," undated notes by Canaris (about summer 1925), BA/MA, OKM Box 20, 48903.

83. Ibid.

84. Ibid.

85. Ibid.

86. Schüssler: op. cit., p. 555.

87. "Betrifft Torpedofabrikation in Spanien," notes by Canaris dated February 22, 1926, BA/MA, OKM Box 20, 48903.

88. "Situationsbericht über das spanische Geschäft," notes by Canaris, BA/MA, OKM Box 20, 48903.

89. Ibid.

90. Captain Lohmann's report on his trip to northern Spain and the *Barbara*'s visits to Bilbao and Santander, August 18–19, 1926, BA/MA, OKM Box 20, 48903.

91. "Situationsbericht über das spanische Geschäft."

92. Statement by Lieutenant Commander Canaris relating to the Lohmann affair, 1927, BA/MA, OKM Box 20, 48903.

93. Note on Echevarrieta by Canaris, 1926, BA/MA, OKM Box 20, 48903.

94. Lieutenant Commander Canaris's report on his visit to Spain, June 9–10, 1926, BA/MA, OKM Box 20, 48903.

95. Ibid.

96. Ibid.

97. Ibid.

98. Ibid.

99. Captain Lohmann's report . . .

100. Schedule of engagements, August 17–20, 1926, BA/MA, OKM Box 20, 48903.

101. Captain Lohmann's report . . .

102. Ibid.

103. Ibid.

104. "Bericht, 16. Febr. 1927," note

by Lohmann, BA/MA, OKM Box 20, 48903.

105. "Nachtrag zu dem Bericht über die Spanien-Reise," note by Lohmann, BA/MA, OKM Box 20, 48903.

106. Captain Lohmann's report . . .

107. Personal Assessment dated November 1, 1926, Canaris Personal File.

108. "Bericht über Reise Spanien vom 28. April bis 18. May 1927," notes by Canaris, BA/MA, OKM Box 20, 48903.

109. Ibid., together with Canaris's list of code names.

110. "Bericht über Spanienreise, Februar 1928," notes by Canaris, BA/MA, OKM Box 20, 48903.

111. Ibid.

112. Mutual Relations Between the Police Authorities of Germany and Spain, February 17, 1928, BA/MA, OKM Box 20, 48903.

113. Letter dated May 13, 1930, from R. Mayrhofer to Suadicani, BA/MA, OKM Box 20, 48903.

114. Canaris report, April 20–May 8, 1925.

115. Ibid.

116. "Bericht über Reise Spanien vom 28. April bis 18. May 1927," notes by Canaris, BA/MA, OKM Box 20, 48903.

117. André Brissaud: *Canaris*, p. 193. Brian Crozier: *Franco*, p. 42.

118. Crozier: op. cit., p. 90 et seq.

119. Personal Assessment dated November 1, 1927, Canaris Personal File.

120. Ibid.

121. Ibid.

122. Canaris report, April 28–May 18, 1927, also undated note by Canaris (about summer 1927), BA/MA, OKM Box 20, 48903.

123. "Ölmonopol," note by Canaris (about summer 1927), BA/MA, OKM Box 20, 48903.

124. "Betrifft Angelegenheiten in Spanien," note by Canaris dated August 8, 1927, BA/MA, OKM Box 20, 48903.

125. Canaris report, April 28–May 18, 1927.

126. Ibid.

127. "Reise Spanien vom 8.11–19.11.1927," note by Canaris, BA/MA, OKM Box 20, 48903.

128. Ibd.

129. Personal Assessment dated November 1, 1927.

130. Canaris's statement on Lohmann affair.

131. Schüssler: op. cit., p. 569. For Messerschmidt's functions and financing, see Appendix to "Structure of the Lohmann Enterprises."

132. Fritze report, p. 54.

133. Ibid.

134. Ibid.

135. Canaris's statement on Lohmann affair.

136. Ibid.

137. Ibid.

138. Fritze report, p. 55.

139. Gessler: op. cit., p. 451 et seq.

140. *Berliner Tageblatt*, August 8, 1927.

141. Fritze report, p. 98.

142. Ibid., p. 62 et seq.

143. Ibid., p. 64 et seq.

144. Ibid., p. 109.

145. Ibid., pp. 67–71.

146. Ibid., pp. 71–73.

147. Ibid., pp. 74–77.

148. Ibid., p. 78.

149. Ibid., p. 98.

150. Ibid.

151. Gessler: op. cit., p. 450.

152. *Berliner Tageblatt*, August 9, 1927.

153. Ibid.

154. Ibid.

155. Fritze report, p. 27.

156. Gessler: op. cit., p. 453.

157. Ibid., p. 456.

158. Preliminary Report No. 1 by Minister of State (ret.) Saemisch, November 11, 1927. Letter of appointment for Fritze signed by Reich Chancellor Marx, May 22, 1928, BA, R43 I/604.

159. Fritze report, p. 271.

160. Carsten: op. cit., p. 286.

161. Canaris comments on Lohmann affair.

162. "Geheime Kommandosache, Besprechung mit Hausknecht am 5. und 6.X in Bremen, 8 Oktober 1928," note by Canaris, BA/MA, OKM Box 20, 48903.

163. Ibid.

164. Personal Assessment dated June 18, 1928, Canaris Personal File.

165. *Die Weltbühne*, May 22, 1928.

166. Thus Kurt Tucholsky's programmatic announcement in *Die Weltbühne* that "there is no secret relating to the German armed forces which I would not betray to a foreign power if it seemed necessary in the interests of peace," quoted from Alf Enseling: *Die Weltbühne*, p. 115.

167. *Die Weltbühne*, August 2, August 16, September 13, 1927, May 22, 1928.

168. Ibid., November 22, 1927.

169. Quoted from Enseling. op. cit., p. 118.

170. "Die Ursachen des deutschen Zusammenbruchs im Jahre 1918" in *Das Werk des Untersuchungsausschusses 1919–1928*, Vol. 9, Half-Vol. 1, p. 126.

171. Wilhelm Deist: "Die Unruhen in der Marine 1917/18" in *Marine-Rundschau*, 6/1971, p. 333 et seq.

172. "Die Ursachen . . . ," p. 126.

173. Ibid., p. 126.

174. Ibid., p. 131.

175. Ibid., pp. 132, 134.

176. Ibid., p. 139.

177. Ibid., pp. 140–43.

178. Ibid., p. 144.

179. Ibid., p. 165.

180. *Vorwärts*, January 23, 1931.

181. *Reichstag Proceedings*, 3rd Electoral Period 1924, Vol. 391, p. 8,579 et seq. Carl von Ossietzky: "Der Ponton-Prozess" in *Die Weltbühne*, March 20, 1928, p. 428.

182. Oliver: "Canaris an der Ostsee" in *Die Weltbühne*, September 6, 1927, p. 357.

183. *Welt am Abend*, January 23, 1931.

184. "Die Ursachen . . . ," p. 137.

185. Wacker: op. cit., p. 13 et seq.

186. Ibid., p. 114.

187. Ibid., pp. 21, 24.

188. Gabriele Krüger: *Die Brigade Ehrhardt*, p. 12 et seq.

189. Wacker: op. cit., p. 24.

190. Ibid., pp. 19–23.

191. Ibid., pp. 21, 23, 121.

192. *Die Weltbühne*, February 3, 1931.

193. Dülffer: op. cit., p. 96.

194. Personal Assessment dated June 18, 1928.

195. On June 1, 1929. Personal Assessment dated November 1, 1929, Canaris Personal File.

196. Schüssler: op. cit., p. 569.

197. Letter dated May 13, 1928, from Araoz to Donner, BA/MA, OKM Box 20, 48903.

198. Documented in Marineleitung/Spanien-Akten (autumn 1928).

199. Letter dated August 27, 1928, from Suadicani to Captain Gladisch, Chief of Staff, Fleet Command, BA/MA, OKM Box 20, 48903.

200. "Das Märchen von den Canarischen Inseln" in *Die Weltbühne*, November 22, 1927.

201. Excerpt from C4310/28, also letter from M1 (Suadicani) dated May 25, 1928, BA/MA, OKM Box 20, 48903.

202. Letter from Donner dated May 19, 1928, BA/MA, OKM Box 20, 48903.

203. Letter dated June 24, 1929, from Suadicani to Messerschmidt. Messerschmidt's comments on a report from Lieutenant Colonel Schwantes, head of the Abwehrabteilung, May 1929, BA/MA, OKM Box 20, 48903.

204. Letter from Goss dated June 29, 1928, BA/MA, OKM Box 20, 48903.

205. Ibid.

206. Letter from Goss dated September 27, 1928, BA/MA, OKM Box 20, 48903.

207. Ibid.

208. Ibid.

209. Dülffer: op. cit., p. 97.

210. Erich Raeder: *Mein Leben*, Vol. 1, p. 188 (not in English edition).

211. Carsten: op. cit., p. 288.

212. Handwritten note by Suadicani on a letter from Messerschmidt, May 18, 1929, BA/MA, OKM Box 20, 48903.

213. Memorandum by Messerschmidt dated June 1, 1929, BA/MA, OKM Box 20, 48903.

214. Confidential Report, period ending November 1, 1930, Canaris Personal File.

215. Ibid.

216. Confidential Report, period ending November 1, 1928. Abshagen: op. cit., p. 62.

217. Canaris Personal File.

218. Karl Dönitz: *Zehn Jahre und zwanzig Tage*, p. 299 (not in English edition).

219. Enseling: op. cit., p. 116 et seq. Elisabeth Hannover-Drück and Heinrich Hannover: *Der Mord an Rosa Luxemburg und Karl Liebknecht*, p. 133.

220. Reproduced in Hannover-Drück/Hannover: op. cit., p. 133.

221. Ibid., p. 133.

222. Ibid., p. 136.

223. Ibid., pp. 158–61.

224. Ibid., p. 169.

225. *Berliner Börsenzeitung*, January 23, 1931.

226. Ibid.

227 Note by Flies: "Fernspruch Kpt. Canaris vom 23.I.31 4.35 Nm. mit Kpt. Flies," January 23, 1931, BA, II M65/2.

228. Statement by Canaris, January 26, 1931, BA, II M65/2.

229. Letter dated January 30, 1931, from Ilse von Pflugk-Hartung to Rechtsanwalt Asch, BA II M65/2.

230 Letter dated February 2, 1931, from Ilse von Pflugk-Hartung to her brother Horst, BA II M65/2.

231. Note by Flies, January 23, 1931. Note by Canaris: "Niederschrift über Besprechung mit Rechtsanwalt Bredereck in Angelegenheit Kapitän-Canaris-Jorns-Prozess am 26.1.31," BA II M65/2.

232. Memorandum dated January 30, 1931, BA II M65/2.

233. Reichswehr Ministry statement published in the *Berliner Tageblatt*, January 29, 1931.

234. *Volkswacht*, January 29, 1931.

235. Ibid.

236. *8-Uhr-Blatt*, January 26, 1931.

237. *Montag-Morgen*, January 26, 1931.

5 The Labyrinth

1. *Völkischer Beobachter*, May 25, 1932.

2. Ibid.

3. Helmut Heiber: "Die Republik von Weimar" in *Deutsche Geschichte seit dem Ersten Weltkrieg*, Vol. I, p. 197.

4. Werner Conze: "Die Krise des Parteienstaates in Deutschland 1929/30" in *Von Weimar zu Hitler*, p. 34.

5. Heiber: op. cit., p. 50.

6. Quoted from Werner Maser and Heinz Höhne: Adolf Hitler: "Aufriss über meine Person," *Der Spiegel*, No. 19/1973, p. 145.

7. Ibid.

8. *Völkischer Beobachter*, May 25, 1932.

9. Jost Dülffer: *Weimar, Hitler und die Marine*, p. 222. Max Domarus: *Hitler*, p. 109.

10. Dülffer: op. cit., p. 222.

11. Werner Maser: *Hitler's Letters and Notes*, p. 129.

12. Walter Baum: "Marine, Nationalsozialismus und Widerstand" in *VfZ*, 11th Year, 1963, p. 44.

13. Dülffer: op. cit., pp. 128–29.

14. Wilhelm Canaris: "Politik und Wehrmacht" in Richard Donnevert: *Wehrmacht und Partei*, p. 47.

15. Ibid., p. 46.

16. Ibid., p. 47.

17. Note by Canaris: "Niederschrift über Besprechung mit Rechtsanwalt Bredereck in Angelegenheit Kapitän-Canaris-Jorns-Prozess am 26.1.31," Canaris Personal File, BA, II M65/2.

18. Dülffer: op. cit., p. 75.

19. Morus: "Der Fall Lohmann" in *Die Weltbühne*, August 16, 1927.

20. Dülffer: op. cit., p. 88.

21. Gabriele Krüger: *Die Brigade Ehrhardt*, p. 120 et seq.

22. Recollections of Admiral (ret.) Conrad Patzig recorded January 18–19, 1966, p. 5, BA/MA.

23. Confidential Report dated November 1, 1933, Canaris Personal File, photocopy in IfZ.

24. Karl Heinz Abshagen: *Canaris*, p.

66. Victor Reimann: *Dr. Joseph Goebbels*, p. 40.

25. Bodo Herzog: "Das letzte Bordkommando von Wilhelm Canaris" in *Die Nachhut*, Nos. 23/24, May 15, 1973, p. 10.

26. Ibid.

27. Abshagen: op. cit., p. 66.

28. Klaus Benzing: *Der Admiral*, p. 48.

29. Otto Wagner: "Wilhelm Canaris," p. 2.

30. Letter dated December 17, 1949, from Dr. Werner Best.

31. Erich Pruck: "Admiral Wilhelm Canaris," p. 2.

32. Confidential Report, period ending November 1, 1934, Canaris Personal File.

33. Canaris: op. cit., p. 48.

34. Ibid., p. 47.

35. Ibid., p. 48.

36. Ibid., p. 49.

37. Herzog: op. cit., p. 10.

38. Ibid., p. 10.

39. Ibid., p. 11.

40. Confidential Report, period ending November 1, 1933, Canaris Personal File.

41. Ibid.

42. Confidential Report, period ending November 1, 1934, Canaris Personal File.

43. Marginal note by Foerster on Confidential Report, period ending November 1, 1934, Canaris Personal File.

44. Canaris Personal File.

45. Kurt Stöckel: *Die Entwicklung der Reichsmarine nach dem Ersten Weltkriege*, p. 55.

46. Patzig recollections, p. 4.

47. Ibid.

48. Harry Howe Ransom: *The Intelligence Establishment*, p. 51. Felix Baumann: "Bilder zur Geschichte der Spionage" in *Die Weltkriegsspionage*, p. 527.

49. Nancy Mitford: *Frederick the Great*, p. 108. Pierre Gaxotte: *Friedrich der Grosse* (German edition), p. 450.

50. Franz Kugler: *Geschichte Friedrichs des Grossen*, p. 161.

51. Ibid., p. 20.
52. Ibid., p. 205.
53. E. H. Cookridge: *The Third Man*, p. 94.
54. Baumann: op. cit., p. 527.
55. Gaxotte: op. cit., p. 450.
56. Ursula Veit: *Justus Gruner als Schöpfer der Geheimen Preussischen Staatspolizei*, pp. 6–7.
57. Kriminalkommissar Wendzio: "Politische Polizei" in files of the Reichsführer-SS and Chief of the German Police, NA, T-175/432.
58. Veit: op. cit., p. 7.
59. Ibid., p. 7.
60. Ibid., p. 11.
61. Ibid., p. 7.
62. Ibid., p. 30.
63. Ibid., pp. 30–31.
64. Ibid., pp. 30–31.
65. Ibid., p. 18.
66. Ibid., pp. 31–33.
67. Ibid., p. 4.
68. Wendzio: op. cit.
69. Manfred Kehrig: *Die Wiedereinrichtung des deutschen militärischen Attachédienstes nach dem Ersten Weltkrieg*, p. 4.
70. Ibid.
71. Ibid.
72. *Denkwürdigkeiten des Generalfeldmarschalls Alfred Grafen von Waldersee*, p. 24.
73. Ibid.
74. *Denkwürdigkeiten des Geheimen Regierungsrathes Dr. Stieber*, p. 4 et seq.
75. Ibid., p. 220. Walter Horn: "Abwehrspionage in der Ära Bismarcks" in *Die Weltkriegsspionage*, p. 560.
76. Stieber memoirs, p. 222. Friedrich Gempp: "Geheimer Nachrichtendienst und Spionageabwehr des Heeres," Part I, p. 1, NA, ML68.
77. Stieber memoirs, p. 223.
78. Gempp: op. cit., p. 1.
79. Stieber memoirs, pp. 239–51.
80. Gempp: op. cit., pp. 2–3.
81. Ibid., p. 3. Waldersee memoirs, p. 10.
82. Stieber memoirs, p. 253.
83. The American People's Encyclopedia, Vol. VII, p. 301. *Brockhaus'*

Conversations-Lexikon, Vol. VIII, p. 573.
84. Stieber memoirs, p. 260.
85. Waldersee memoirs, p. 95.
86. Gempp: op. cit., p. 12.
87. Ibid., p. 17.
88. Ibid., pp. 18–19.
89. Veit: op. cit., p. 6.
90. Stieber memoirs, p. 308. Horn: op. cit., p. 564.
91. Gempp: op. cit., p. 20.
92. Ibid., pp. 21–22.
93. Ibid., p. 29.
94. Ibid., p. 32 et seq.
95. Walter Nicolai: *Geheime Mächte*, p. 19 (not in English edition).
96. Gempp: op. cit., p. 49.
97. Ibid., p. 23 et seq.
98. Ibid., p. 26.
99. Ibid., p. 51.
100. Ibid., p. 56.
101. Ibid., pp. 56–58.
102. Ibid., pp. 58–59.
103. Ibid., p. 81.
104. Ibid., p. 81.
105. Ibid., p. 87.
106. Ibid., p. 38 et seq.
107. Ibid., p. 41.
108. Ibid., p. 44.
109. Ibid., p. 75.
110. Ibid., p. 76.
111. Ibid., p. 77.
112. Ibid., p. 77.
113. Ibid., p. 79 et seq.
114. Ibid., p. 103.
115. Ibid., p. 105.
116. Ibid., p. 106.
117. Ibid., p. 107.
118. Gempp: op. cit., Part II, Vol. 10, Sec. 9, p. 81.
119. Ibid., Vol. 7, Sec. 7, p. 155 et seq. Ulrich Liss: "Der Nachrichtendienst in den Grenzschlachten im Westen im August 1914" in *Wehrwissenschaftliche Rundschau*, March 1962, p. 142 et seq.
120. Gempp: op. cit., Part II, Vol. 10, Sec. 9, p. 47 et seq.
121. Gert Buchheit: *Der deutsche Geheimdienst*, p. 31. Andreas Ziesenitz: "Spionage" in *Die Weltbühne*, December 9, 1920, pp. 673–75.

122. Gempp: op. cit., Part II, Vol. 10, Sec. 9, p. 47.
123. Ibid., p. 48.
124. Andreas Ziesenitz: "Der Vater der Lüge" in *Die Weltbühne*, July 29, 1920, p. 140.
125. Buchheit: op. cit., p. 31. Gempp: op. cit., Part II, Vol. 8, Sec. 8a, p. 166.
126. Hans Buchheim et al.: *The Anatomy of the SS State*, p. 144.
127. Ibid.
128. Ibid.
129. Ibid. For an account from the National Socialist standpoint see Werner Best: "Die deutsche Abwehrpolizei bis 1945," p. 25.
130. David Dallin: *Soviet Espionage*, p. 120.
131. Heinz Höhne: *Codeword: Direktor*, p. 22.
132. Albrecht Charisius and Julius Mader: *Nicht länger geheim*, p. 78.
133. Ibid.
134. Ibid.
135. Ibid.
136. Buchheit: op. cit., p. 33.
137. Charisius/Mader: op. cit., p. 80.
138. Buchheit: op. cit., p. 33.
139. Kehrig: op. cit., p. 39.
140. Buchheit: op. cit., p. 32. Kehrig: op. cit., p. 39.
141. Kehrig: op. cit., p. 39.
142. Buchheit: op. cit., p. 33.
143. Ibid., p. 40.
144. Vortrag AII beim Amtschef A, March 20, 1928, Akten der Marineleitung, BA/MA, OKM Box 6 34165/2.
145. Reichswehr Minister's draft directive for the formation of an Abwehr Section, March 1928, together with a communication from Schleicher to the Marineleitung, March 14, 1928, BA/MA, OKM Box 6 3416/2.
146. Ibid.
147. Letter from AIIa to AII, March 17, 1928, and a memorandum by Loewenfeld dated March 19, 1928, BA/MA, OKM Box 6 34165/2.
148. Vortrag AII beim Amtschef A.
149. Akten der Marineleitung.
150. Buchheit: op. cit., p. 40.
151. Ibid., p. 38.
152. Patzig recollections, p. 1.
153. Ibid., p. 1.
154. Ibid., p. 1.
155. Ibid., pp. 1–2. Letter dated November 10, 1953, from Patzig to Walter Baum, IfZ, ZS 540.
156. Buchheit: op. cit., p. 40.
157. Ibid., p. 35.
158. Ibid., p. 35.
159. Ibid., p. 102.
160. Best: "Die deutsche Abwehrpolizei," p. 25.
161. Hans Buchheim: *SS und Polizei im NS-Staat*, pp. 32–34.
162. Jacques Delarue: *The History of the Gestapo*.
163. Heinz Höhne: *The Order of the Death's Head*, p. 182.
164. Ibid., p. 102.
165. Ibid., p. 182.
166. Ibid., p. 183.
167. Ibid., p. 185.
168. Letter from Abwehrabteilung to all Abwehrstellen, March 27, 1936, NA, T-175/403.
169. Quoted in a letter from the Geheimes Staatspolizeiamt to all Staatspolizeistellan and Staatspolizeileitstellen, April 28, 1939, NA, T-175/403.
170. Directive from Heydrich to all Staatspolizeistellen, 1934, NA, T-175/403.
171. Buchheit: op. cit., p. 46 et seq. "Der ungeklärte Fall Major Sosnowskis" in *Polnische Wochenschau*, Issue 24–1971.
172. "Der ungekläite Fall . . ."
173. Höhne: *Death's Head*, pp. 175–76.
174. Shlomo Aronson: *Heydrich und die Anfänge des SD und der Gestapo*, p. 53 et seq.
175. Ibid., p. 58.
176. Ibid.
177. Höhne: *Death's Head*, p. 176.
178. Ibid.
179. Buchheim: *SS und Polizei*, p. 62.
180. Aronson: op. cit., p. 214.
181. Buchheit: op. cit., p. 42. Deposition by Walter Huppenkothen: "Canaris und Abwehr," p. 3, IfZ ZS 249.
182. Patzig recollections, p. 3.

183. Ibid.

184. Letter dated March 5, 1955, from Dr. Helmut Krausnick to Patzig, together with Patzig's reply dated March 21, 1955, IfZ, ZS 540.

185. Patzig recollections, p. 2.

186. Buchheit: op. cit., p. 50.

187. Ibid. Ian Colvin claims to have heard a different version from Protze in *Chief of Intelligence*, p. 14. According to this, Blomberg fired him because of reconnaissance against Poland.

188. Patzig recollections, p. 4.

189. Ibid., p. 4.

190. Ibid., p. 5.

191. Letter dated November 10, 1953, from Patzig to Baum.

192. Ibid.

193. Patzig recollections, p. 4.

194. Ibid.

6 Head of the Abwehr

1. Personal documentation, Canaris Personal File, copy in IfZ. Observator (Dr. Will Grosse): "Geheimdienst, Fahneneid und Hakenkreuz" in *Echo der Woche*, May 5, 1950.

2. Observator: op. cit.

3. Gert Buchheit: *Der deutsche Geheimdienst*, p. 83. Erich Ferdinand Pruck: "Admiral Wilhelm Canaris," additional sheet.

4. Gerhard Henke: "Bericht und Erinnerungen" in *Die Nachhut*, August 1, 1967, p. 11.

5. Franz Josef Furtwängler: *Männer, die ich sah und kannte*, p. 205.

6. Nikolaus Ritter: *Deckname Dr. Rantzau*, pp. 24–25.

7. Gerhard Henke: "Aus den Erinnerungen eines Ic/AO" in *Die Nachhut*, November 15, 1967, p. 13.

8. Buchheit: op. cit., p. 63.

9. Ibid.

10. Will Grosse: "Der Mann, der zuviel wusste" in *Hamburger Morgenpost*, October 24, 1950.

11. Oral information from Frau Lina Heydrich-Manninen, March 8, 1975.

12. Ritter: op. cit., p. 25.

13. Erich Ferdinand Pruck: "Warnzeichen Rot," XIII, p. 16.

14. Henke: "Aus den Erinnerungen eines Ic/AO," p. 13.

15. Medical Report dated January 15, 1924, Canaris Personal File.

16. Pruck: "Warnzeichen Rot," XIII, p. 16.

17. Oral information from Herr Otto Wagner, July 12, 1973.

18. Henke: "Bericht und Erinnerungen," p. 12.

19. Buchheit: op. cit., p. 85.

20. Ibid.

21. Klaus Benzing: *Der Admiral*, p. 108.

22. Heinrich Fraenkel and Roger Manvell: *The Canaris Conspiracy*, p. 192.

23. Oral information from Herr Otto Wagner, July 22, 1973.

24. Written communication from Frau Renée Wagner, March 1975.

25. Oral information from Frau Lina Heydrich-Manninen, March 8, 1975.

26. Written communication from Frau Renée Wagner, March 1975.

27. Ibid.

28. Ibid.

29. Ibid.

30. Oral information from Frau Lina Heydrich-Manninen, March 8, 1975.

31. Written communication from Frau Renée Wagner, March 1975.

32. Written communication from Herr Otto Wagner, March 21, 1975.

33. Henke: "Aus den Erinnerungen eines Ic/AO," p. 13.

34. Letter from Canaris dated June 30, 1937, BA/MA, RW 5/v.197.

35. Helmut Krausnick: "Vorgeschichte und Beginn des militärischen Widerstandes gegen Hitler" in *Die Vollmacht des Gewissens*, p. 247.

36. Klaus-Jürgen Müller: *Das Heer und Hitler*, p. 165.

37. *Frankfurter Allgemeine Zeitung*, May 10, 1957. Heinrich Bennecke: *Die*

Reichswehr und der Röhm-Putsch, p. 65.

38. Müller: op. cit, p. 173.

39. Ibid., p. 155.

40. Ibid., pp. 166–67.

41. Krausnick: op. cit., p. 251.

42. *Völkischer Beobachter*, January 5, 1935.

43. *Berliner Illustrierte Zeitung*, January 10, 1935.

44. Müller: op. cit., p. 159.

45. Ibid.

46. Krausnick: op. cit., p. 253.

47. Sir John W. Wheeler-Bennett: *The Nemesis of Power*, p. 337. Contrast Krausnick: op. cit., p. 251.

48. *Völkischer Beobachter*, January 5, 1935.

49. Müller. op. cit., p. 159.

50. *Völkischer Beobachter*, January 14, 1935.

51. Friedrich Hossbach: *Zwischen Wehrmacht und Hitler 1934–1938*, p. 71.

52. Heinz Höhne: *The Order of the Death's Head*, p. 68.

53. Ibid., p. 193.

54. Shlomo Aronson: *Heydrich und die Anfänge des SD und der Gestapo*, p. 275.

55. Furtwängler: op. cit., p. 207.

56. Oral information from Frau Lina Heydrich-Manninen, March 8, 1975.

57. Ibid.

58. Werner Best: "Wilhelm Canaris," p. 4.

59. Oral information from Frau Lina Heydrich-Manninen, March 8, 1975.

60. Ibid. Benzing, op. cit., p. 106.

61. Oral information from Frau Lina Heydrich-Manninen, March 8, 1975.

62. Ibid.

63. Ibid.

64. As in Karl Heinz Abshagen: *Canaris*: p. 102 et seq.

65. Oral information from Herr Bruno Streckenbach, January 21, 1966.

66. Deposition by Walter Huppenkothen: "Canaris und Abwehr," IfZ, ZS 249.

67. Oral information from Frau Lina Heydrich-Manninen, March 8, 1975.

68. Ibid.

69. Ibid.

70. Ibid.

71. Aronson: op. cit., p. 190 et seq.

72. Ernst Jünger: *Krieg und Krieger*, p. 158.

73. Aronson: op. cit., pp. 195–98.

74. Best: op. cit., p. 3.

75. Letter dated April 1, 1955, from Frau Erika Canaris to Erich Ferdinand Pruck.

76. Letter dated April 2, 1936, from the Political Police Commander of the Länder, including a copy of the agreement of January 17, 1935, NA, T-175/403.

77. Ibid.

78. Huppenkothen deposition.

79. Reich Government Resolution of October 24, 1933, BA/MA, RW 5/v.195.

80. "Wie kam es zu meinem Russlandeinsatz?" Statement prepared by Otto Ohlendorf for his trial by the U. S. Military Tribunal, undated. From Frau Kathe Ohlendorf's private papers.

81. Letter dated January 19, 1935, from the Geheimes Staatspolizeiamt, IIIH, NA, T-175/403.

82. Letter dated January 25, 1935, from the Geheimes Staatspolizeiamt to all Staatspolizeistellen, NA, T-175/403.

83. Directive from Heydrich to all Staatspolizeistellen, 1935, NA, T-175/403.

84. Ibid.

85. Report on head of Abwehr's visit to Ast Kiel on February 7, 1935, with the head of Group III, Captain Bartenbach, and SS-Gruppenführer Heydrich, dated February 9, 1935, BA/MA, RW 5/v.197.

86. Report on visits to Bremen and Wilhelmshaven, March 25, 1935, BA/MA, RW 5/v.197.

87. A reference to the resolution of October 17, 1933, whose engrossment was dated October 24, 1933.

88. Stapostellen-Leiter conference at the Gestapa on October 19, 1936, dated November 11, 1936, BA/MA, RW 5/v.194.

89. Letter from Canaris dated De-

cember 14, 1936, BA/MA, RW 5/v.194.

90. Report on Bremen and Wilhelmshaven visits, March 25, 1935.

91. Letter from Bamler dated March 27, 1936, NA, T-175/403.

92. Reich War Minister: "Abwehrdienst in der SS-V.T.," April 23, 1936, BA/MA, RM 5/v.194.

93. Letter from Canaris relating to counterespionage in the SS-Verfügungstruppe, August 4, 1936, BA/MA, RW 5/v.194.

94. Aronson: op. cit., p. 308. Oral information from Herr Dr. Werner Best, February 5, 1966.

95. Stapostellen-Leiter conference, November 11, 1936.

96. Henke: "Bericht und Erinnerungen," p. 11.

97. Martin Göhring: *Bismarcks Erben*, p. 245 et seq.

98. Ibid., p. 247.

99. Robert J. O'Neill: *The German Army and the Nazi Party*, p. 87.

100. Müller: op. cit., p. 208.

101. Ibid., pp. 208–9.

102. Ibid., p. 207.

103. Ibid., p. 208.

104. Ibid.

105. Ibid.

106. O'Neill: op. cit., p. 88. Müller: op. cit., p. 209.

107. *Völkischer Beobachter*, March 18, 1935.

108. Letter dated March 29, 1935, from Canaris to all Abwehrstellen, BA/MA, RW 5/v.197.

109. Ibid.

110. Ibid.

111. Report of visit by head of Abwehr and his Section I Luftwaffe expert to Budapest, April 4, 1935, dated April 7, 1935, BA/MA, RW 5/v.197.

112. Ibid.

113. Recollections of Admiral (ret.) Conrad Patzig, recorded January 18–19, 1966, Militärgeschichtliche Forschungsanstalt, p. 2.

114. Hugh Thomas: *The Spanish Civil War*, p. 263.

115. J. Benoist-Méchin: *Histoire de l'armée allemande* (German edition), pp. 240–41.

116. O'Neill: op. cit., p. 89.

117. Canaris Personal File.

118. Letter dated March 30, 1935, from Canaris to all Abwehrstellen, BA/MA, RW 5/v.195.

119. Ibid.

120. Bamler Personal File, private archives.

121. Written communication from Erich Ferdinand Pruck, March 13, 1975.

122. Bamler Personal File.

123. Hans Bernd Gisevius: *To the Bitter End*, p. 194.

124. Written communication from Erich Ferdinand Pruck, March 13, 1975. Oral information from Frau Lina Heydrich-Manninen, March 8, 1975.

125. Abwehr III, "Merkblatt über Spionage, Spionageabwehr und Landesverrat," June 1938, BA/MA, RW 5/v.196.

126. Abwehr IIIa, "Vorsorglicher Geheimschutz," March 8, 1935, BA/MA, RW 5/v.195.

127. Ibid.

128. Frederick V. Grunfeld: *The Hitler File*, p. 189.

129. Bamler, memorandum dated April 10, 1935, BA/MA, RW 5/v.197.

130. Ibid.

131. Letter from Canaris referring to violent methods employed by foreign intelligence services, December 14, 1936, BA/MA, RW 5/v.194.

132. Letter from Canaris dated January 7, 1938, BA/MA, RW 5/v.196.

133. Letter dated March 31, 1938, from Canaris to the High Commands of the Army, Navy and Air Force. BA/MA, RW 5/v.197.

134. Ibid.

135. Letter dated August 30, 1937, from Canaris to Abwehrstelle Dresden, BA/MA, RW 5/v.196.

136. Statement made by Lieutenant General Franz-Eccard von Bentivegni while a Soviet prisoner of war, quoted in Julius Mader: *Hitlers Spionagegenerale sagen aus*, p. 212.

137. Oscar Reile: *Geheime Westfront*, p. 19 et seq.

138. Bamler, Abwehr conference on June 21–22, 1935, NA, T-77/808.

139. Bentivegni statement, op. cit., p. 212.

140. Ibid.

141. Ibid.

142. Bamler, report on visit to Kiel, February 9, 1935.

143. Bentivegni statement, op. cit., p. 205.

144. Letter from Abwehrstelle in Military District V, June 8, 1934, quoted in Mader: op. cit., p. 67.

145. "Merkblatt für Abwehr von Spionage und Verrat," January 2, 1934, quoted in Mader: op. cit., p. 70.

146. Ian Colvin: *Chief of Intelligence*, p. 44.

147. Bamler, report on visits to Bremen and Wilhelmshaven, March 25, 1935.

148. Ibid.

149. Abwehr Ia, notes on visit by head of Abwehr to Abwehrstelle Münster on May 15–16, 1935, dated May 20, 1935, BA/MA, RW 5/v.197.

150. Letter to all Abwehrstellen dated July 2, 1936, and signed by Henke, BA/MA, RW 5/v.197.

151. Ibid.

152. Letter dated July 3, 1936, from Canaris to all Abwehrstellen, BA/MA, RW 5/v.197.

153. Reich War Ministry, "Richtlinien für militärische Berichterstattung," January 11, 1935, NA, T-77/808.

154. Letter from Canaris dated June 30, 1937, BA/MA, RW 5/v.197.

155. Ibid.

156. Bamler: "Organisation der Abwehrabteilung," August 1937, BA/MA, RW 5/v.207

157. Observator: op. cit.

158. Personal documentation of Hans Oster, IfZ.

159. Internationales Bibliographisches Archiv (Munzinger-Archiv), 28/54. Interrogation of Franz Liedig, IfZ, ZS 2125. Oral information from Herr Dr. Werner Wolf Schrader, March 12, 1975.

160. Rohleder File, private archives.

161. Leissner File, private archives.

162. Schmalschläger File, private archives.

163. Ritter: op. cit., pp. 22, 49.

164. Pruck: "Warnzeichen Rot," XIII, pp. 1–3.

165. Otto Wagner, "Bericht," pp. 1–3.

166. Bentivegni statement, op. cit., p. 215.

167. Paul Fidrmuc, Diary, Vol. 1, owned by Herr Günter Peis.

168. *Die Nachhut*, May 15, 1973, p. 41 et seq.

169. Müller: op. cit., p. 22.

170. Ibid., p. 39.

171. Wagner, report, p. 4.

172. Fidrmuc, Diary, Vol. 1, p. 95.

173. "Merkblatt über Spionage, Spionageabwehr und Landesverrat."

174. Abwehr IIIC, points for discussion, late 1936, BA/MA, RW 5/v.195.

175. Reich War Ministry, J Ic/d, report, December 20, 1937, NA, T-77/808.

176. Letter from Canaris reference Subgroup IIIC, April 22, 1937, BA/MA, RW 5/v.196.

177. Erich Ferdinand Pruck: "Gedanken über den geheimen militärischen Meldedienst," p. 4.

178. Observator: op. cit., March 17, 1950. Walter Hagen (=Wilhelm Höttl): *Die geheime Front*, p. 105.

179. Oral information from Frau Lina Heydrich-Manninen, March 8, 1975.

180. Erich Ferdinand Pruck: "Der Abwehrchef" in *Der Notweg*, No. 7/1954.

181. Observator: op. cit., May 5, 1950.

182. Ibid.

183. Lahousen, quoted by Pruck in "Admiral Wilhelm Canaris," p. 4.

184. Pruck: "Gedanken über den geheimen militärischen Meldedienst," p. 4.

185. Otto Wagner: "Canaris," p. 3.

186. Pruck: "Warnzeichen Rot," XIII, p. 24.

187. Observator: op. cit, March 17, 1950.

188. Ibid.
189. Oral information from Frau Lina Heydrich-Manninen, March 8, 1975.
190. Bamler, "Organisation der Abwehrabteilung," August 1937.
191. Ibid.
192. Abwehr Ia, notes on Münster visit.
193. Ibid. Paul Leverkuehn: *German Military Intelligence*, p. 91.
194. Leverkuehn: op. cit., p. 91.
195. Abwehr Ia, notes on Münster visit.
196. Ibid.
197. Leverkuehn: op. cit., p. 68 (not in English edition).
198. Statement by Lieutenant General Hans Piekenbrock quoted in Mader: op. cit., p. 74.
199. Benoist-Méchin: op. cit., p. 289.
200. Ibid., p. 279.
201. William L. Shirer: *The Rise and Fall of the Third Reich*, p. 290.
202. Ladislas Farago: *The Game of the Foxes*, p. 88.
203. Benoist-Méchin: op. cit., p. 290.
204. Wheeler-Bennett: op. cit., pp. 351–52.
205. O'Neill: op. cit., p. 129.
206. Wheeler-Bennett: op. cit., p. 352.
207. Ibid.
208. O'Neill: op. cit., p. 129.
209. Benoist-Méchin: op. cit., p. 292 et seq.
210. Wheeler-Bennett: op. cit., p. 352.
211. Benoist-Méchin: op. cit., p. 296.
212. Farago: op. cit., p. 88.
213. O'Neill: op. cit., p. 129.
214. Letter from General (ret.) Geyr von Schweppenburg, August 21, 1967, ED91/Vol. 8, IfZ.
215. O'Neill: op. cit., p. 129.
216. Joachim C. Fest: *Hitler*, p. 499.
217. Benoist-Méchin: op. cit., p. 304.
218. Henke: "Aus den Erinnerungen eines Ic/AO," p. 12.
219. Müller: op. cit., p. 215.
220. Pruck: "Gedanken über den geheimen militärischen Meldedienst," p. 4.

221. Letter from General (ret.) Geyr von Schweppenburg, February 6, 1968, ED91/Vol. 8, IfZ.
222. Letter from Canaris reference organization of the Secret Intelligence Service, September 9, 1936, BA/MA, RW 5/v.197.
223. Instructions to the Führungsgruppe signed by Canaris, September 1936, BA/MA, RW 5/v.197.
224. Ibid.
225. Piekenbrock File, private archives.
226. Piekenbrock statement, op. cit., p. 51.
227. Ibid., p. 52.
228. Statement made by Colonel Erwin Stolze while a Soviet prisoner of war, quoted in Mader: op. cit., p. 145.
229. Piekenbrock statement, op. cit., p. 52.
230. IMT proceedings, Vol. II, p. 488.
231. Stolze statement, op. cit., pp. 145–47.
232. Ladislas Farago: *Burn After Reading*, p. 19. Reile: op. cit., p. 36.
233. Report on Marine Interrogation Service, Hamburg area, January 30, 1945, in the possession of Heinrich Fraenkel, Esq.
234. Piekenbrock statement, op. cit., p. 73.
235. Ibid. Buchheit: op. cit., p. 121.
236. Hans-Joachim Neufeldt, Jürgen Huck and Georg Tessin: *Zur Geschichte der Ordnungspolizei 1936–1945*, p. 14.
237. Ibid., p. 14.
238. Ibid., p. 17.
239. Höhne: op. cit., p. 195.
240. Oral information from Herr Erich Ferdinand Pruck, July 12, 1973.
241. "Principles Governing Co-operation Between the Geheime Staatspolizei and the Abwehr Offices of the Wehrmacht," December 21, 1936, BA/MA, RW 5/v.194.
242. Ibid.
243. Ibid.
244. Letter from Canaris dated December 23, 1936, BA/MA, RW 5/v.194.

245. Stapostellen-Leiter conference at the Gestapa on October 19, 1936.
246. Buchheit (op. cit., p. 170) supposes the agreement to have stipulated that the Abwehr should cease to maintain a political intelligence service and surrender that right exclusively to the SD. The text of the agreement does not support such an assumption.
247. Henke: "Bericht und Erinnerungen," p. 12.
248. Written communication from Frau Lina Heydrich-Manninen, April 12, 1975.

7 Under the Führer's Spell

1. Ladislas Farago: *The Game of the Foxes*, p. 88.
2. Ibid.
3. Werner Maser and Heinz Höhne: "Adolf Hitler: 'Aufriss über meine Person'" in *Der Spiegel*, No. 22/1973, p. 113.
4. Farago: op. cit., p. 87.
5 Ian Colvin: *Chief of Intelligence*, p. 39.
6. Ibid.
7. Transcript of an address given by Rear Admiral Canaris during the Ic conference at OKW on March 3, 1938, p. 5, NA, T-77/808.
8. Ibid., p. 6.
9. Gerhard Fischer: *Die Irrlichter*, p. 160.
10. Ibid., p. 316.
11. Transcript of Canaris address, p. 1.
12. Maser/Höhne: op. cit., No. 21/1973, p. 114.
13. Ibid., p. 114.
14. Ibid., p. 114.
15. Ibid, p. 114.
16. Ibid., p. 155.
17. "Die nationalpolitische Stellung des Offiziers in der deutschen Wehrmacht," lecture delivered by Vice-Admiral Canaris in Vienna on April 22, 1938, p. 6, IfZ.
18. Ibid., p. 1.
19. Wilhelm Canaris: "Politik und Wehrmacht" in Richard Donnevert (ed.): *Wehrmacht und Partei*, p. 48.
20. Transcript of Canaris address, p. 8.
21. Canaris: "Politik und Wehrmacht," op. cit., p. 54.
22. Ibid., p. 53.
23. Will Grosse: "Der Judenstern—eine Idee von Canaris?", undated, p. 1.
24. Ibid.
25. ADAP, Series D, Vol. V, p. 763.
26. Klaus-Jürgen Müller: *Das Heer und Hitler*, p. 41.
27. Maser/Höhne: op. cit., No. 20/1973, p. 135.
28. Ibid.
29. Testimony given by Otto Ohlendorf at Nuremberg on October 8, 1947, Case X, court records p. 495, in the possession of Frau Käthe Ohlendorf.
30. Canaris: "Politik und Wehrmacht," op. cit., p. 45. Canaris: "Die nationalpolitische Stellung des Offiziers," pp. 2, 8.
31. Canaris: "Politik und Wehrmacht," op. cit., p. 50.
32. Transcript of Canaris address, p. 10.
33. Müller: op. cit., p. 175.
34. Walter Görlitz: *Generalfeldmarschall Keitel—Verbrecher oder Offizier?*, p. 182.
35. Ibid.
36. Jost Dülffer: *Weimar, Hitler und die Marine*, p. 88.
37. Klaus-Peter Hoepke: *Die deutsche Rechte und der italienische Faschismus*, p. 159 et seq.
38. Ibid., pp. 297, 307. Hans-Adolf Jacobsen: *Nationalsozialistische Aussenpolitik*, p. 197.
39. Farago: op. cit., p. 12.
40. Internationales Biographisches Archiv (Munzinger-Archiv), 17/53.
41. Recollections of Admiral (ret.) Conrad Patzig, recorded January 18–19, 1966, p. 2, BA/MA.
42. Ibid.

43. Ibid.
44. Ploetz: *Geschichte des Zweiten Weltkrieges*, p. 822.
45. Farago: op. cit., p. 12. Report on visit to Budapest by head of Abwehr and his Section I Luftwaffe expert, April 1935, BA/MA, RW 5/v.197.
46. Müller: op. cit., p. 219.
47. Ibid., pp. 217–18.
48. Ibid., p. 220.
49. Ibid., p. 219.
50. Ibid., p. 224 et seq.
51. Ibid., p. 226 et seq.
52. Ibid., p. 240.
53. Ibid., p. 242.
54. Wolfgang Foerster: *Generaloberst Ludwig Beck*, p. 54.
55. Canaris: "Politik und Wehrmacht," op. cit., p. 50.
56. Müller: op. cit., p. 227.
57. Ibid., p. 215.
58. Moritz von Faber du Faur: *Macht und Ohnmacht*, p. 234.
59. Müller: op. cit., p. 233.
60. Faber du Faur: op. cit., p. 168 et seq.
61. Ibid., p. 234.
62. Ibid., p. 234.
63. Ibid., p. 200.
64. Gabriel Jackson: *A Concise History of the Spanish Civil War*, p. 39.
65. Brian Crozier: *Franco*, p. 196. Hugh Thomas: *The Spanish Civil War*, p. 101.
66. Thomas: op. cit., pp. 62, 101.
67. Fischer: op. cit., p. 168. Thomas: op. cit., p. 101.
68. Thomas: op. cit., p. 101.
69. Jackson: op. cit., p. 39.
70. Crozier: op. cit., p. 171.
71. Statement by Colonel Hans Remer, May 16, 1946, in Julius Mader: *Hitlers Spionagegenerale sagen aus*, p. 226.
72. Jackson: op. cit., p. 40.
73. Thomas: op. cit., p. 60.
74. Crozier: op. cit., p. 176.
75. Thomas: op. cit., p. 117 et seq.
76. Crozier: op. cit., p. 182.
77. Ibid., p. 182.
78. Ibid. p. 183.
79. Ibid., p. 186.
80. Ibid., p. 189.

81. Ibid., p. 191.
82. Ibid., p. 192.
83. Ibid., p. 194.
84. Ibid., p. 193.
85. Ibid., p. 194.
86. Ibid., p. 194.
87. Ibid., p. 196.
88. Klaus-Jörg Ruhl: *Spanien im Zweiten Weltkrieg*, p. 106.
89. Manfred Merkes: *Die deutsche Politik gegenüber dem spanischen Bürgerkrieg*, p. 19.
90. Crozier: op. cit., p. 196.
91. ADAP, Series D, Vol. III, pp. 9, 11.
92. Ibid., p. 12.
93. Ibid.
94. Merkes: op. cit., p. 20. ADAP, Series D, Vol. III, p. 4.
95. *Völkischer Beobachter*, July 26, 1936.
96. Written communication from Juan Bernhardt, September 30, 1970.
97. ADAP, Series D, Vol. III, p. 4.
98. Ibid., Merkes: op. cit., p. 23.
99. Merkes: op. cit., p. 27.
100. Ibid.
101. Angel Viñas: "Los espías nazis entran en la guerra civil" in *Historia*, October 1975, p. 17.
102. Ibid., p. 29.
103. Ibid.
104. Ibid.
105. Ibid.
106. Müller: op. cit., p. 232.
107. Faber du Faur: op. cit., p. 160.
108. Müller: op. cit., p. 232.
109. Colvin: op. cit., p. 31.
110. Remer statement, op. cit., p. 227.
111. ADAP, Series D, Vol. III, p. 23.
112. Ibid., pp. 31, 78. Remer statement, op. cit., p. 228.
113. Mader: op. cit., p. 227.
114. ADAP, Series D, Vol. III, p. 31.
115. Ibid., p. 23.
116. Ibid., p. 36.
117. Merkes: op. cit., p. 30.
118. Crozier: op. cit., p. 194. Merkes: op. cit., p. 30.
119. Merkes: op. cit., p. 30.
120. Ibid., p. 30.
121. Ibid., p. 30.

122. Ibid., p. 30.
123. Ibid., p. 31.
124. Ibid., p. 31.
125. Ibid., p. 31.
126. Ibid., p. 32. Thomas: op. cit., p. 264–65.
127. William L. Shirer: *The Rise and Fall of the Third Reich*, p. 298. Hermann Graml: "Europa zwischen den Kriegen" in *Deutsche Geschichte seit dem Ersten Weltkrieg*, Vol I, p. 459.
128. Shirer: op. cit., p. 298.
129. Graml: op. cit., p. 459.
130. Crozier: op. cit., p. 210.
131. ADAP, Vol. III, p. 39.
132. Ibid., p. 105.
133. Thomas: op. cit., p. 316. Brissaud: op. cit., p. 39.
134. Thomas: op. cit., p. 316.
135. ADAP, Series D, Vol. III, p. 106.
136. Ibid., p. 107.
137. Thomas: op. cit., p. 316.
138. Ibid., Hellmuth Günther Dahms: *Der spanische Bürgerkrieg*, p. 142.
139. Dahms: op. cit., p. 142.
140. Merkes: op. cit., p. 97.
141. Ibid., p. 64.
142. ADAP, Series D, Vol. III, p. 148.
143. Merkes: op. cit., p. 76.
144. Pierre Broué and Émile Témime: *The Revolution and the Civil War in Spain*, p. 346. ADAP, Series D, Vol. III, p. 126.
145. Merkes: op. cit., p. 75. ADAP, Series D, Vol. III, p. 126.
146. ADAP, Series D, Vol. III, p. 162.
147. Merkes: op. cit., p. 76.
148. Broué/Témime: op. cit., p. 347.
149. Ibid., p. 351.
150. Ibid., p. 352.
151. Ibid., p. 352.
152. Ibid., p. 352.
153. Ibid., p. 353.
154. Erich Ferdinand Pruck: "Warnzeichen Rot," XIII, p. 24.
155. Merkes: op. cit., p. 97.
156. Fischer: op. cit., p. 166. Merkes: op. cit., p. 103.
157. Merkes: op. cit., p. 103.
158. Thomas: op. cit., p. 262.
159. Fischer: op. cit., p. 159.
160. Max Franzbach: "Geschichte der KO Spanien," undated, p. 1, in the possession of Herr Günter Peis.
161. Gert Buchheit: *Der deutsche Geheimdienst*, p. 137. Fischer: op. cit., p. 175.
162. Statement by Lieutenant General von Bentivegni in Mader: op. cit., p. 230.
163. Werner Best: "Die deutsche Abwehrpolizei bis 1945," p. 49. Almost all the officers came from Hauptabteilung III of the Geheimes Staatspolizeiamt and were subordinated to Group III of the Abwehrabteilung for the duration of the war.
164. Fischer: op. cit., p. 160.
165. Ibid., p. 159.
166. Ibid., p. 180.
167. Thomas: op. cit., p. 296.
168. Ibid.
169. David J. Dallin: *Soviet Espionage*, p. 128.
170. Anon.: "Zarenoffiziere für Spaniens Internationale Brigaden," about 1950, *Spiegel* archives.
171. Report from the Chef der Sicherheitspolizei und des SD, IVA 2-B, December 22, 1942, *Spiegel* archives.
172. Ibid.
173. Günther Weisenborn: "Rote Kapelle" (collected reports on the survivors), records of the Public Prosecutor's Office, Lüneburg District Court, criminal proceedings against Dr. Manfred Roeder, Vol. VIII, 64.
174. Report from the Chef der Sicherheitspolizei und des SD, p. 20.
175. Klaus Lehmann: *Widerstandsgruppe Schulze-Boysen/Harnack*, p. 29.
176. Report on head of Abwehr's visit to Budapest, April 1935.
177. Ibid.
178. Paul Leverkuehn: *German Military Intelligence*, p. 63.
179. Report on head of Abwehr's visit to Budapest, April 1935.
180. Edgar Siegfried Meos: "Hitlers Geheimdienst in Estland vor dem Überfall auf die Sowjetunion" in *Mitteilungsblatt der Arbeitsgemeinschaft ehemaliger Offiziere*, p. 9.

181. Ibid., p. 9.

182. Ibid., p. 10.

183. Observator (=Dr. Will Grosse): "Geheimdienst, Fahneneid und Hakenkreuz" in *Echo der Woche*, March 24, 1950.

184. Ibid.

185. Lev Bezymenski: *Sonderakte "Barbarossa,"* p. 245.

186. Erich Kordt: *Nicht aus den Akten*, p. 123.

187. Ibid.

188. Heinz Höhne: "Der Fall Lissner" in Ivar Lissner: *Mein gefährlicher Weg*, p. 233.

189. Memorandum by head of Abteilung Ausland, August 26, 1937, NA, T-77/884. Farago: op. cit., p. 13.

190. Theo Sommer: *Deutschland und Japan zwischen den Mächten*, p. 25.

191. Ibid., p. 25.

192. Ibid., p. 25.

193. Ibid., p. 26.

194. Ibid., p. 27.

195. Ibid., p. 28.

196. Ibid., p. 493 et seq.

197. Martin Göhring: *Bismarcks Erben*, p. 258.

198. Sommer: op. cit., p. 29.

199. Ibid., p. 39.

200. Ibid.

201. Draft of a German-Japanese Military Convention (by Oshima), NA, T-77/884.

202. Reich War Minister's decision (drafted by Keitel), December 15, 1936, NA, T-77/884.

203. Ibid.

204. Agreements between the German Army (including the Luftwaffe) and the Japanese Army, drafted by Oshima, undated, NA, T-77/884.

205. Neurath, notes on a conversation with Hitler, August 17, 1937, NA, T-77/884.

206. Notes on a discussion between Chef WA and the Japanese military attaché, General Oshima, on July 6, 1937 (made by Keitel), NA, T-77/884.

207. Ibid.

208. Letter from Chef Abteilung Ausland to Chef WA, June 8, 1937, NA, T-77/884.

209. Höhne: op. cit., p. 233.

210. Pruck: op. cit., XIII, p. 13.

211. Göhring: op. cit., p. 258. Merkes: op. cit., p. 251.

212. Merkes: op. cit., p. 251.

213. Heinz Höhne: *The Order of the Death's Head*, p. 231.

214. Sir Basil Liddell Hart (ed.): *The Red Army*, p. 75.

215. Robert Conquest: *The Great Terror*, pp. 230, 437, 203. Krivitsky did not survive long. On February 10, 1941, he was found shot in a Washington hotel room.

216. Pruck: op. cit, X, p. 13 et seq.

217. Karl Spalcke: "Der Fall Tuchatschewski" in *Die Gegenwart*, January 25, 1958, p. 47.

218. Jesco von Puttkamer: *Von Stalingrad zur Volkspolizei*, p. 105.

219. Friedrich Wilhelm Heinz first published his conversations with Canaris under the pseudonym Horst Falkenhagen in the *Neue Zeitung* on July 6, 1948. He later worked this article into the second edition of Puttkamer's book, which was published by the Michael-Verlag (owner: Heinz himself). Letter from Heinz to the *Spiegel* archivist Robert Spiering, March 14, 1949.

220. Puttkamer: op. cit., p. 106.

221. Walter Schellenberg: *The Schellenberg Memoirs*, p. 46. Conquest: op. cit., p. 219.

222. Conquest: op. cit., p. 155.

223. Ibid., p. 201.

224. Ibid., p. 212.

225. Ibid., p. 213.

226. Ibid., p. 214.

227. Ibid., p. 221.

228. Walter Hagen (=Wilhelm Höttl): *Die geheime Front*, p. 62.

229. Schellenberg: op. cit., p. 49.

230. "Vortragsnotiz für Herrn Generalfeldmarschall" (Bamler to Blomberg), May 28, 1937, BA/MA, RW 5/v.207.

231. Josef Wulf: "Die SS," p. 123.

232. Shlomo Aronson: *Heydrich und die Anfänge des SD und der Gestapo*, p. 155.

233. Heinz Höhne: *Codeword: Direktor*, p. 67.

234. Oral information from Dr. Werner Best, February 5, 1966.

235. Letter from Canaris to the Inland Section of the Reich War Ministry, April 24, 1937. NA, T-77/808

236. Letter dated November 10, 1953, from Admiral Conrad Patzig to Walter Baum, IfZ, ZS540 Buchheit: op. cit., p. 64

8 The Turning Point

1. André Brissaud: Canaris, p. 66.

2. Harold C. Deutsch: Hitler and His Generals: The Hidden Crisis, p. 84.

3. Völkischer Beobachter, January 13, 1938.

4. Written communication from Herr Hellmuth Müller, December 9, 1949.

5. Ibid.

6. Ibid.

7. Ibid.

8. Ernst Murmann: "Betrachtungen zum Fall Blomberg" in Frankfurter Allgemeine Zeitung, June 4, 1974.

9. Walter Görlitz: Generalfeldmarschall Keitel—Verbrecher oder Offizier?, p. 103.

10. Murmann: op. cit.

11. Görlitz: op. cit., p. 104.

12. Helmut Krausnick: "Wehrmacht und Nationalsozialismus" in Das Parlament, November 9, 1955, p. 679.

13. Deutsch: op. cit., p. 106.

14. Friedrich Hossbach: Zwischen Wehrmacht und Hitler, p. 123.

15. Hermann Foertsch: Schuld und Verhängnis, p. 76

16. Jodl Diary, January 26, 1938, in IMT, Vol. XXVIII, p. 356.

17. Deutsch: op. cit., p. 201.

18. Ian Colvin: Chief of Intelligence, p. 43.

19. Personal record of Hans Paul Oster, IfZ, F87.

20. Letter dated June 3, 1957, from General (ret.) Franz Halder to Professor Walter Baum, IfZ, ZS240/VII.

21. Ibid.

22. Spiegelbild einer Verschwörung: Die Kaltenbrunner-Berichte an Bormann und Hitler über das Attentat vom 20. Juli 1944 [reports from Kaltenbrunner to Bormann and Hitler on the July 20, 1944, bomb plot], p. 302.

23. Hermann Graml: "Der Fall Oster," VfZ, 1966, p. 29.

24. Report by Kriminalkommissar (ret.) Franz Sonderegger on his relations with the July 20, 1944, conspirators, Lüneburg Public Prosecutor's Office, record of criminal proceedings against Dr. Manfred Roeder (=LStA), Vol. IX, 81

25. Written communication from General (ret.) Franz Halder, April 26, 1955, IfZ, ZS 240/V.

26. Ibid.

27. Oster record.

28. Recollections of Admiral (ret.) Conrad Patzig, recorded January 18–19, 1966, p. 3, BA/MA.

29. Ibid.

30. Erich Ferdinand Pruck: "Warnzeichen Rot," XIII, p. 17.

31. Patzig recollections, p. 3.

32. Letter from Canaris re Subgroup IIIC, April 22, 1937, BA/MA, RW 5/v. 196.

33. Edward Crankshaw: The Gestapo, p. 52.

34. Enrolment declaration by Hans Bernd Gisevius, November 15, 1933, BDC. Völkischer Beobachter, June 10, 1933.

35. "Das Spiel ist aus—Arthur Nebe" in Der Spiegel, December 22, 1949, p. 24.

36. Ibid.

37. Patzig recollections, p. 3.

38. Hans Bernd Gisevius: To the Bitter End, p. 59.

39. Kaltenbrunner Reports, p. 302.

40. Ibid., p. 451.

41. Patzig recollections, p. 5.

42. Deutsch: op. cit., p. 51.

43. Ibid., p. 49. Interrogation of Rechtsanwalt Liedig by Dr. Krausnick

and Professor Deutsch, undated, IfZ, ZS 2125, p. 1.

44. Liedig interrogation, p. 2.

45. Ulrich von Hassell: *The von Hassell Diaries*, p. 27.

46. Indictment against Dohnanyi and Oster, September 16, 1943, p. 8, LStA, Vol. I.

47. Deutsch: op. cit., p. 200.

48. Ibid.

49. Görlitz: op. cit., p. 109.

50. Ibid.

51. Jodl Diary, January 28, 1938, op. cit., p. 359.

52. Deutsch: op. cit., p. 201.

53. Kaltenbrunner Reports, p. 430.

54. Halder communication, April 26, 1955.

55. Klaus-Jürgen Müller: *Das Heer und Hitler*, p. 262.

56. Wolfgang Foerster: *Generaloberst Ludwig Beck*, p. 90.

57. Peter Hoffmann: *Widerstand, Staatsstreich, Attentat*, p. 68. Müller: op. cit., p. 283.

58. Müller: op. cit., p. 283.

59. Letter dated September 6, 1952, from General (ret.) Halder to Major General (ret.) Hermann von Witzleben, IfZ, ZS 240/VII.

60. Quoted from Werner Picht: *Vom Wesen des Krieges und vom Kriegswesen der Deutschen*, p. 225.

61. Judgement of the Court of the Supreme Commander of the Wehrmacht in re General Baron von Fritsch, in the possession of Dr. Fabian von Schlabrendorff, p. 28.

62. Undated notes of Christine von Dohnanyi, née Bonhoeffer, p. 4, LStA, Vol. I.

63. Indictment against Dohnanyi and Oster, p. 1. Letter from Count von der Goltz and Kurt Peschke to the Oberreichskriegsanwalt, February 19, 1944, LStA, Vol. I.

64. Ibid.

65. Christine von Dohnanyi notes, p. 6.

66. Ibid., p. 3.

67. Ibid.

68. Ibid.

69. Hermann Bösch: *Heeresrichter Dr. Karl Sack im Widerstand*, p. 24.

70. Ibid., p. 24.

71. Ibid., p. 26.

72. Ibid., p. 25.

73. Ibid.

74. Deutsch: op. cit., p. 292.

75. Christine von Dohnanyi notes, p. 4.

76. Fritsch judgement, p. 3.

77. Oral information from Dr. Werner Best, February 5, 1966.

78. Fritsch judgement, pp. 4–9.

79. Ibid., p. 11.

80. *Der Spiegel*, No. 36/1965, p. 46.

81. Foertsch: op. cit., pp. 90–91.

82. Ibid., p. 118.

83. Hossbach: op. cit., pp. 126–27.

84. Ibid., p. 129. Foertsch: op. cit., p. 138.

85. Bösch: op. cit., p. 29.

86. Deutsch: op. cit., p. 295.

87. Ibid., p. 299.

88. Gisevius: op. cit., p. 243.

89. Ibid.

90. Deutsch: op. cit., p. 179.

91. Ibid., p. 181.

92. Ibid., p. 183.

93. Ibid., p. 295.

94. Ibid.

95. Müller: op. cit., p. 290.

96. Foertsch: op. cit., p. 106.

97. Keitel, order dated February 7, 1938, NA, T-77/908.

98. Address by Rear Admiral Canaris to the Ic conference at OKW on March 3, 1938, p. 1, NA, T-77/808.

99. *Völkischer Beobachter*, February 6, 1938.

100. Canaris address, March 3, 1938, pp. 11–12.

101. Karl Heinz Abshagen: *Canaris*, p. 54.

102. Müller: op. cit., p. 291.

103. Jodl Diary, March 1, 1938, op. cit., p. 367.

104. Jodl Diary, February 10, 1938, op. cit., p. 367.

105. Deutsch: op. cit., p. 304.

106. Ibid., p. 305.

107. Franz von Papen: *Memoirs*, pp. 406–8.

108. Ibid., p. 408.

109. Walter Goldinger: "Die geschichtliche Ablauf der Ereignisse in Österreich von 1918 bis 1945" in Heinrich Benedikt: *Geschichte der Republik Österreich*, p. 260. Papen: op. cit., pp. 415–17.

110. Keitel testimony, IMT, Vol. X, pp. 567–68. Papen: op. cit., p. 417.

111. Hermann Graml: "Europa zwischen den Kriegen" in *Deutsche Geschichte seit dem Ersten Weltkrieg*, Vol. I, p. 474. Papen: op. cit., pp. 417–18.

112. Memorandum dated February 28, 1938, by State Secretary Keppler, ADAP, Series D, Vol. I, p. 450.

113. Keitel testimony, IMT, Vol. X, p. 568. Jodl Diary, February 13, 1938, op. cit., p. 367.

114. Keitel/Canaris proposal, IMT, Vol. II, p. 450.

115. Ibid.

116. Jodl Diary, February 14, 1938, op. cit., p. 367.

117. Pruck: op. cit., XIII, p. 16.

118. Ibid.

119. Jodl Diary, February 14, 1938, op. cit., p. 367.

120. Keitel testimony, IMT, Vol. X, p. 568.

121. Pruck: op. cit., XIII, p. 16.

122. Ibid., p. 17.

123. Ibid.

124. Müller: op. cit., p. 278. Deutsch: op. cit., pp. 253–55.

125. Deutsch: op. cit., p. 315.

126. Müller: op. cit., p. 289.

127. Undated comments on the case of General Baron von Fritsch (by Canaris and Hossbach). Kindly made available to the author by Professor Harold C. Deutsch.

128. "Das Spiel ist aus," *Der Spiegel*, December 22, 1949, p. 24.

129. Bösch: op. cit., p. 30.

130. Ibid.

131. Deutsch: op. cit., p. 307.

132. Ibid., p. 309.

133. Bösch: op. cit., p. 31.

134. Deutsch: op. cit., p. 311.

135. Jodl Diary, February 26, 1938, op. cit., p. 368.

136. Ibid.

137. Deutsch: op. cit., p. 315.

138. Ibid., p. 316.

139. Bösch: op. cit., p. 32.

140. Deutsch: op. cit., p. 317.

141. Ibid., p. 317.

142. Ibid., p. 320.

143. Foertsch: op. cit., p. 121. Adolf Count von Kielmansegg: *Der Fritschprozess 1938*, p. 82.

144. Kielmansegg: op. cit., p. 82.

145. Ibid.

146. Colvin: op. cit., p. 43.

147. Deutsch: op. cit., p. 336.

148. Ibid. Foertsch: op. cit., p. 125.

149. Undated memorandum by Military Attaché Muff, ADAP, D/I, p. 460. Goldinger: op. cit., pp. 265–66.

150. Ibid., p. 266.

151. Ibid., p. 265.

152. Ibid.

153. Telegram dated March 9, 1938, from Weizsacker to the German Embassy in London, ADAP, D/I, p. 460.

154. Goldinger: op. cit., p. 267.

155. Müller: op. cit., p. 236.

156. Von Manstein testimony, IMT, Vol. XX, p. 658.

157. Ibid.

158. Ibid.

159. Goldinger: op. cit., pp. 268–70.

160. Gert Buchheit: *Der deutsche Geheimdienst*, p. 142.

161. Transcript of a telephone conversation between Hitler and Prince Philipp of Hessen on March 11, 1938, IMT, Vol. XXXI, p. 368 et seq.

162. Pruck: op. cit., XIII, p. 19.

163. Foreign Office note of March 13, 1938, ADAP, D/I, p. 482.

164. Note made by Legationsrat Altenburg of the Foreign Office, March 13, 1938, ADAP, D/I, p. 483.

165. Transcript of a telephone conversation between Göring and Ribbentrop on March 13, 1938, IMT, Vol. XXXI, p. 383.

166. Ibid.

167. Joachim C. Fest: *Hitler*, p. 548.

168. Altenburg note, March 13, 1938, ADAP, D/I, p. 483.

169. Walter Schellenberg: *The Schellenberg Memoirs*, p. 51.

170. Buchheit: op. cit., p. 143.

171. Fest: op. cit., p. 549.

172. Leonidas E. Hill (ed.): *Die Weizsäcker-Papiere*, p. 123.

173. Abshagen: op. cit., p. 127.

174. "Die nationalpolitische Stellung des Offiziers in der deutschen Wehrmacht," lecture delivered by Vice-Admiral Canaris in Vienna on April 22, 1938, p. 1, IfZ, F 6/1.

175. Letter dated October 23, 1954, from Major General (ret.) Erwin Lahousen to Otto Benninghoff, IfZ, ZS 658.

176. "Die nationalpolitische Stellung . . . ," p. 2.

177. Kielmansegg: op. cit., p. 90.

178. Deutsch: op. cit., pp. 352–53.

179. Ibid., p. 356.

180. Fritsch judgement, p. 1.

181. Comments on the Fritsch case, p. 3.

182. Ibid., p. 5.

183. Ibid., p. 3.

184. Ibid., p. 4.

185. Ibid., pp. 1–2.

186. Müller: op. cit., p. 284.

187. Deutsch: op. cit., p. 368.

188. Foertsch: op. cit., p. 129. Schellenberg: op. cit., p. 177.

189. Canaris address, March 3, 1938, p. 11.

190. Pruck: op. cit., XXIII, p. 6.

191. Personal record, Canaris Personal File.

192. Canaris address, March 3, 1938, p. 4.

193. Ibid., p. 8.

194. Ibid., p. 6.

195. Ladislas Farago: *The Game of the Foxes*, p. 13.

196. "Die nationalpolitische Stellung . . . ," p. 2.

197. Wilhelm Canaris: "Politik und Wehrmacht" in Richard Donnevert (ed.): *Wehrmacht und Partei*, pp. 43–54.

198. Robert J. O'Neill: *The German Army and the Nazi Party*, p. 233.

199. Ibid.

200. Vice-Admiral (ret.) Leopold Bürkner: "Die Abteilung, spätere Amtsgruppe Ausland in Amt Ausland/Abwehr," August 22, 1960, pp. 1, 4, BA/MA, RW 5/v. list.

201. Ibid.

202. O'Neill: op. cit., p. 224. Albert Praun: *Soldat in der Telegraphen- und Nachrichtentruppe*, p. 225.

203. Diary of Helmuth Groscurth in Helmut Krausnick, Harold C. Deutsch and Hildegard Kotze: *Tagebücher eines Abwehroffiziers*, p. 101.

204. Abwehrabteilung II instruction of August 1, 1942, NA, T-77/884.

205. Louis de Jong: *Die deutsche Fünfte Kolonne im Zweiten Weltkrieg*, pp. 260–66.

206. Krausnick/Deutsch/Kotze: op. cit., pp. 18–19. Transcript of a conversation between Vice-Admiral (ret.) Bürkner and Dr. Krausnick on March 15, 1954, IfZ, ZS 364/I.

207. Liedig interrogation, p. 22.

208. Krausnick/Deutsch/Kotze: op. cit., p. 32.

209. Groscurth Diary, later addition, ibid., p. 101.

210. Abwehrstelle Silesia to Abwehr I, February 3, 1934, NA, T-77/897.

211. Ibid.

212. "Letzte Ölung" in *Der Spiegel*, No. 37/1968, pp. 105–6.

213. Boris Celovsky: *Das Münchner Abkommen 1938*, pp. 108–9.

214. "Letzte Ölung," op. cit., p. 106.

215. Abwehrstelle Silesia, political report on the Czechoslovak Republic, January 16, 1934, NA, T-77/897.

216. Letter from Abwehrstelle Silesia, June 7, 1934, NA, T-77/897.

217. Personal report on visit to the Sudeten German territories, October 10, 1938, in Krausnick/Deutsch/Kotze: op. cit., p. 135.

218. Helmuth K. G. Rönnefarth: *Die Sudetenkrise in der internationalen Politik*, Vol. I, p. 128 et seq.

219. Ibid., p. 128 et seq.

220. Ibid., p. 164.

221. Statement by Colonel (ret.) Erwin Stolze in Julius Mader: *Hitlers Spionagegenerale sagen aus*, p. 150. Frantisek Moravec: *Master of Spies*, p. 116.

222. Stolze statement, op. cit., pp. 150–51.

223. Ibid.

224. Rönnefarth: op. cit., p. 132.
225. Stolze statement, op. cit., p. 151.
226. Rönnefarth: op. cit., pp. 218–19.
227. Ibid., p. 231 et seq.
228. A. J. P. Taylor: *The Origins of the Second World War*, p. 160.
229. Ibid., p. 160.
230. Ibid., p. 153.
231. Moravec: op. cit., p. 125.
232. Ibid., p. 126.
233. Ibid.
234. Undated teleprinter message from Canaris, IMT, Vol. XXV, p. 432.
235. Geheime Kommandosache dated May 30, 1938, IMT, Vol. XXV, p. 434.
236. Geheime Kommandosache dated June 18, 1938, IMT, Vol. XXV, p. 446.
237. Geheime Kommandosache, draft of the new "Green" directive dated May 20, 1938, IMT, Vol. XXV, p. 423.
238. IMT, Vol. XXV, p. 425.
239. Procedures for "Green," undated, IMT, Vol. XXV, p. 433.
240. Summary of discussion between Hitler and Keitel on April 21, 1938, dated April 22, 1938, IMT, Vol. XXV, p. 417.
241. Celovsky: op. cit., p. 159.
242. "Der Zeitpunkt des X-Befehls und die Frage der Vorausmassnahmen," memorandum dated August 26, 1938, IMT, Vol. XXV, p. 462.
243. Krausnick/Deutsch/Kotze: op. cit., p. 118.
244. Letter from Abwehr I East-South, November 3, 1934, NA, T-77/897.
245. Krausnick/Deutsch/Kotze: op. cit., p. 118.
246. Groscurth Diary, September 4, 1938, op. cit.
247. Groscurth Diary, September 2, 1938, op. cit.
248. Helmut Krausnick: "Vorgeschichte und Beginn des militärischen Widerstandes gegen Hitler" in *Die Vollmacht des Gewissens*, p. 323.
249. Concluding passage of comments on the alleged "resistance activity" of the accused, Ernst von Weizsäcker, Military Court IV, October 12, 1948, in the possession of Dr. Robert M. W. Kempner.
250. Rudi Strauch: *Sir Nevile Henderson*, p. 132.
251. Müller: op. cit., p. 301.
252. Ibid., p. 302.
253. Note made by Engel on May 22, 1938, in Hildegard von Kotze: *Heeresadjutant bei Hitler 1938–1943*, pp. 22–25.
254. Müller: op. cit., p. 309.
255. Note made by Engel on July 18, 1938, op. cit., p. 27.
256. Halder communication, April 26, 1955, p. 3.
257. Ibid., p. 4.
258. Müller: op. cit., p. 325.
259. Ibid., p. 318.
260. Ibid., p. 318.
261. Ibid., p. 321.
262. Ibid., p. 327.
263. Ibid., p. 328.
264. Ibid., p. 333.
265. Ibid., p. 335.
266. Foerster: op. cit., p. 142.
267. Fritz Sänger: *Politik der Täuschungen*, p. 225.
268. Extracts from the diary of Captain Eberhard, August 15, 1938, kindly made available to the author by Mr. David Irving.
269. Otto Wagner: "Wilhelm Canaris," p. 5.
270. Note made by Legationsrat von Heyden-Rynsch, August 6, 1938, ADAP, Series D, Vol. II, p. 429.
271. Transcript of Bürkner-Krausnick conversation, p. 1.
272. Ernst von Weizsäcker: *Erinnerungen*, p. 175.
273. Ibid.
274. Ibid.
275. Weizsäcker Diary, March 1938, Weizsäcker Papers, p. 122.
276. Weizsäcker Diary, May 22, 1938, Weizsäcker Papers, p. 128.
277. Hoffmann: op. cit., p. 83.
278. Ibid.
279. Groscurth Diary, August 20, 1938, op. cit.
280. Ibid.

281. Groscurth Diary, August 23, 1938, op. cit.

282. Groscurth Diary, August 27, 1938, op. cit.

283. Note by W. Schmidt (=Friedrich Bürger), June 3, 1958, IfZ, ZS 1905.

284. Ibid.

285. Groscurth Diary, September 4, 1938, op. cit.

286. Groscurth Diary, September 6, 1938, op. cit.

287. Note by Weizsäcker, September 1938, Weizsäcker Papers, pp. 142–43.

288. Hoffmann: op. cit., p. 84.

289. Rönnefarth: op. cit., pp. 402–3.

290. William L. Shirer: *The Rise and Fall of the Third Reich*, p. 380. Hoffmann: op. cit., p. 85.

291. Taylor: op. cit., pp. 168–70.

292. Rönnefarth: op. cit., p. 436 et seq. Taylor: op. cit., pp. 169–70.

293. Rönnefarth: op. cit., p. 502.

294. Ibid., p. 485.

295. Ibid., p. 486.

296. Krausnick/Deutsch/Kotze: op. cit., p. 113.

297. Groscurth Diary, September 8, 1938, op. cit., p. 114.

298. Jodl Diary, September 8, 1938, op. cit., p. 376.

299. Jodl Diary, September 13, 1938, op. cit., p. 378.

300. Groscurth Diary, September 8, 1938, op. cit., p. 114.

301. Jodl Diary, September 13, 1938, op. cit., p. 378.

302. Groscurth Diary, September 7, 1938, op. cit.

303. Ibid.

304. Celovsky: op. cit., p. 334 et seq.

305. Ibid., pp. 332–33.

306. Letter from Canaris dated September 21, 1938, BA/MA, RW 5/v. 60.

307. Ibid.

308. Ibid.

309. Hoffmann: op. cit., p. 118 et seq. Müller: op. cit., p. 359.

310. Written communication from General (ret.) Halder, July 14, 1955.

311. Hoffmann: op. cit., p. 122.

312. Abshagen: op. cit., p. 122.

313. Letter dated June 3, 1957, from General (ret.) Halder to Professor Walter Baum, IfZ, ZS 240/V.

314. Liedig interrogation, p. 16.

315. Halder communication, July 14, 1955.

316. Ibid.

317. Müller: op. cit., p. 348.

318. Hoffmann: op. cit., p. 116. Müller: op. cit., p. 354.

319. Bösch: op. cit., p. 54.

320. Halder communication, April 26, 1955.

321. Halder communication, July 14, 1955.

322. Müller: op. cit., p. 355.

323. Halder communication, July 14, 1955.

324. Ibid.

325. Ibid.

326. Müller: op. cit., p. 357.

327. Gisevius: op. cit., p. 317.

328. Hoffmann: op. cit., p. 124. Müller: op. cit., p. 361.

329. Müller: op. cit., p. 362.

330. Ibid.

331. Liedig interrogation, p. 17.

332. Hoffmann: op. cit., p. 125.

333. Krausnick/Deutsch/Kotze: op. cit., p. 35.

334. Celovsky: op. cit., p. 343.

335. "Letzte Ölung," op. cit., p. 112.

336. Taylor: op. cit., p. 179.

337. Müller: op. cit., p. 371.

338. Ibid.

339. Groscurth Diary, September 15, 1938, op. cit.

340. Martin Broszat: "Das Sudetendeutsche Freikorps" in VfZ, 1961, p. 36.

341. Ibid., p. 37. Jodl Diary, September 17, 1938, op. cit., p. 381.

342. Groscurth Diary, September 17, 1938, op. cit.

343. Groscurth Diary, September 18, 1938, op. cit.

344. Groscurth Diary, September 19, 1938, op. cit.

345. Ibid.

346. Groscurth Diary, September 21, 1938, op. cit.

347. Berger's testimony, IMT, Vol. IV, p. 177.

348. Stolze's testimony, IMT, Vol. IV, pp. 151, 155.
349. Groscurth Diary, September 23, 1938, op. cit.
350. Ibid.
351. Groscurth Diary, September 23, 1938, op. cit.
352. Jodl Diary, September 20, 1938, op. cit., p. 381.
353. Celovsky: op. cit., p. 394.
354. Strauch: op. cit., p. 162.
355. Shirer: op. cit, pp. 400–2.
356. Strauch: op. cit., p. 164.
357. Shirer: op. cit., p. 398. Strauch: op. cit., p. 165.
358. Müller: op. cit., p. 374.
359. Ibid., p. 376.
360. Jodl Diary, September 21 and 26, 1938, op. cit., p. 386.

361. Extracts from the Eberhardt Diary, September 28, 1938.
362. Jodl Diary, September 28, 1938, op. cit., pp. 388–89.
363. Strauch: op. cit., p. 169. Josef Henke: *England in Hitlers politischem Kalkül*, p. 182.
364. Personal account of travels, October 10, 1938, Krausnick/Deutsch/Kotze: op. cit., p. 129 et seq.
365. Ibid.
366. Personal account of travels from October 11, 1938, onwards, Krausnick/Deutsch/Kotze: op. cit., pp. 138, 143, 152.
367. Charles Whiting: *Canaris*, p. 232.
368. Foerster: op. cit., p. 96.

9 The Road to War

1. Groscurth Diary, December 1938, in Helmut Krausnick, Harold C. Deutsch and Hildegard von Kotze: *Tagebücher eines Abwehroffiziers*, p. 158.
2. Ibid.
3. Charles C. Tansill: *Back Door to War*, p. 509.
4. Ibid., p. 510.
5. Wladislaw Kozaczuk: "Die Schlacht um Geheimnisse" (German translator's MS), p. 299.
6. Karl Dietrich Bracher: *The German Dictatorship*, p. 333.
7. Klaus-Jürgen Müller: *Das Heer und Hitler*, p. 384.
8. Ibid.
9. Groscurth Diary, December 1938, op. cit.
10. Ibid.
11. Erich Ferdinand Pruck: "Warnzeichen Rot," XIII, p. 21.
12. Fritz Fischer: *Griff nach der Weltmacht*, p. 150.
13. Isidore Nahayewsky: *History of the Modern Ukrainian State 1917–1923*, p. 80 et seq.
14. Ibid., p. 170.
15. Gregor Prokoptschuk: *Der Metropolit*, p, 221. Alexander Dallin: *German Rule in Russia*, p. 114.

16. Oscar Reile: *Geheime Ostfront*, p. 234.
17. Ibid.
18. Prokoptschuk: op. cit., p. 221. Dallin: op. cit., p. 114. Gerald Reitlinger: *The House Built on Sand*, p. 163. Reile: op. cit., p. 235.
19. Written communication from Herr Erich Ferdinand Pruck, November 10, 1976.
20. Hans-Adolf Jacobsen: *Nationalsozialistische Aussenpolitik*, p. 11.
21. Richard Breyer: *Das deutsche Reich und Polen*, p. 182.
22. Ibid., p. 183.
23. Reile: op. cit., p. 235. Prokoptschuk: op. cit., p. 221.
24. Report dated October 19, 1938, from the German Ambassador in Warsaw to the Foreign Office, ADAP, Series D, Vol. V, p. 83.
25. Report dated October 15, 1938, from the German Ambassador in Warsaw to the Foreign Office, ADAP, Series D, Vol. V, p. 79.
26. As Note 24.
27. Letter dated October 25, 1938, from the German Ambassador in Warsaw to Legationsrat Schliep, ADAP, Series D, Vol. V, p. 90.

28. Ibid.

29. Ibid.

30. Charles Wighton and Günter Peis: *They Spied on England*, p. 21.

31. Ibid.

32. Oral information from Herr Otto Wagner, September 12, 1973.

33. Wenzel Jaksch: *Europas Weg nach Potsdam*, p. 338.

34. Ibid., p. 338.

35. Ibid., p. 336.

36. Robert Nowak: "Bericht über eine Informationsreise durch die rückgegliederten Gebiete Oberungarns," January 1939, IfZ, ED 63.

37. George F. Kennan: *From Prague After Munich*, p. 64.

38. Ibid.

39. Robert Nowak: "Bericht über eine Informationsreise in die Slowakei und die Karpatenukraine im Jänner-Februar 1939," February 25, 1939, IfZ, ED 63.

40. Ibid.

41. Ibid.

42. Ibid.

43. Note by Gesandter Schmidt (Büro RAM), January 5, 1939, ADAP, Series D, Vol. V, pp. 128–31.

44. Kennan: op. cit., p. 62. Report dated October 19, 1938, from the German Ambassador in Warsaw to the Foreign Office.

45. Kozaczuk: op. cit., p. 298.

46. Note by the head of the Political Section of the Foreign Office, November 12, 1938, ADAP, Series D, Vol. V, p. 106.

47. Telegram dated March 13, 1939, from the German Ambassador in Warsaw to the Foreign Office, ADAP, Series C, Vol. V, pp. 151–52.

48. Letters from Groscurth to Canaris (dated October 15, 1938) and Oster (October 24, 1938) in Krausnick/Deutsch/Kotze: op. cit., pp. 332, 334, 342.

49. Letter dated October 6, 1938, from Group Ausland Ic of Abwehr/Ausland to the Foreign Office, ADAP, Series D, Vol. IV, p. 39.

50. Walter Hagen: *Die geheime Front*, p. 174.

51. Walter Schellenberg: *The Schellenberg Memoirs*, p. 56.

52. Report dated July 22, 1939, from Admiral Lais to the Italian chief of Naval Staff, *I Documenti Diplomatici Italiani*, Vol. XIII, p. 486.

53. Hagen: op. cit., p. 174.

54. Ibid., p. 175.

55. Heinz Höhne: *The Order of the Death's Head*, p. 282.

56. Alan Bullock: *Hitler: A Study in Tyranny*, p. 480.

57. Ibid., p. 481.

58. Erich Kordt: *Wahn und Wirklichkeit*, p. 142.

59. Hagen: op. cit., pp. 176–77.

60. Bullock: op. cit., pp. 481–82.

61. Ibid., p. 483.

62. Jaksch: op. cit., p. 339.

63. Kordt: op. cit., p. 143. Jaksch: op. cit., p. 339.

64. Jaksch: op. cit., p. 339.

65. ADAP, Series D, Vol. IV, pp. 219–20.

66. Ibid.

67. Ibid.

68. Note dated March 14, 1939, by Legationstrat von Heyden-Rynsch, ADAP, Series D, Vol. IV, p. 220.

69. Letter dated January 20, 1966, from Erich Ferdinand Pruck to Dr. Helmut Krausnick, IfZ, ZS 2099/I.

70. Ibid.

71. Ibid.

72. Ibid.

73. Hermann Graml: "Europa zwischen den Kriegen" in *Deutsche Geschichte seit dem Ersten Weltkrieg*, Vol. I, p. 490.

74. Kennan: op. cit., p. 90.

75. Ibid.

76. Written communication from Herr Erich Ferdinand Pruck, November 28, 1975.

77. Kordt: op. cit., p. 144.

78. Joachim Fest: *Hitler*, p. 573.

79. Ibid., p. 574.

80. Ibid.

81. Krausnick/Deutsch/Kotze: op. cit., p. 40.

82. Tansill: op. cit., p. 511. A. J. P. Taylor: *The Origins of the Second World War*, p. 210.

83. Tansill: op. cit., p. 512.
84. For a detailed and novel account see Taylor: op. cit., p. 210 et seq.
85. Hans Roos: "Die militärpolitische Lage und Planung Polens gegenüber Deutschland vor 1939" in *Wehrwissenschaftliche Rundschau*, No. 4/1957, p. 194. *Documents on Events*, p. 212.
86. *Documents on Events*, p. 212.
87. New York *Times*, March 28, 1939.
88. Kozaczuk: op. cit., pp. 305–6.
89. Taylor: op. cit., p. 210.
90. Ibid.
91. Ibid.
92. Tansill: op. cit., p. 513.
93. Ibid.
94. Ausland I, "Übersicht über aussenpolitische Vorgänge in Europa," April 27, 1939, BA/MA, RW 5/v.350.
95. Hans Bernd Gisevius: *To the Bitter End*, p. 362.
96. André Brissaud: *Canaris*, p. 133.
97. William L. Shirer: *The Rise and Fall of the Third Reich*, p. 467.
98. IMT, Vol. XXXIV, p. 380 et seq.
99. Shirer: op. cit., pp. 469, 479.
100. Ibid., p. 471.
101. Ibid., p. 472.
102. Leonidas E. Hill: *Die Weizsäcker-Papiere*, p. 185.
103. Statement made by Piekenbrock while a Soviet prisoner of war, in Mader: *Hitlers Spionagegenerale sagen aus*, p. 83.
104. Ladislas Farago: *The Game of the Foxes*, p. 104 et seq.
105. Ian Colvin: *Chief of Intelligence*, p. 54.
106. *Weizsäcker-Papiere*, p. 153.
107. Ausland I, "Übersicht über aussenpolitische Vorgänge in Europa," April 27, 1939, BA/MA, RW 5/v.350
108. Ibid.
109. Note by Canaris of a conversation with General Keitel on August 17, 1939, BA/MA, RW 4/v.764.
110. Ibid.
111. Karl Heinz Abshagen: *Canaris*, p. 133.
112. Lais report, July 22, 1939, op. cit.
113. Müller: op. cit., p. 386.
114. Ibid., p. 408.
115. Ibid., p. 392.
116. Groscurth Diary, April 1939, op. cit.
117. *Weizsäcker-Papiere*, p. 150.
118. Lahousen's testimony, November, 30, 1945, IMT, Vol. II, p. 515.
119. Heeresgruppenkommando 3, Ia, June 14, 1939, IMT, Vol. XXX, p. 190. Army High Command, Abteilung 12 [Foreign Armies East] of the Army General Staff, re the military position in Poland on August 12, 1939, BA/MA, RW 5/v.150.
120. Sir Basil Liddell Hart: *History of the Second World War*, p. 28.
121. Letter dated July 3, 1939, from Abwehrstelle I, Referat II, to Abwehrabteilung II, BA/MA, RW, 5/v.123.
122. Hans-Albrecht Herzner: "Bericht über das Unternehmen gegen Bahnhof und Tunnel von Mosty in der Nacht vom 25./26. August 1939," Herzner papers in the possession of Herr Günter Peis.
123. Ibid.
124. Heinz Heumann: "Bericht über die 'Brandenburg,'" June 13, 1965, in the possession of Dr. Gert Buchheit.
125. Letter dated June 14, 1939, from Abwehrstelle VIII to Abwehrabteilung II, BA/MA, RW 5/v.123.
126. Abwehr II/1(ON) office minute summarizing discussion between Prince Henckel-Donnersmarck and Major Diebitsch at Hochdorf on June 11, 1939, with head of Abw. II in attendance, June 14, 1939, BA/MA, RW 5/v.123.
127. Lahousen Diary, August 15, 1939, IfZ.
128. Ibid.
129. Abwehr II/1(ON) office minute of conference with the Ukrainian Military Staff, June 13, 1939, BA/MA, RW 5/v.123.
130. Note by Lahousen re outcome of discussion with the II-Referenten of Asten VIII and XVII on June 27, 1939, dated July 3, 1939, BA/MA, RW 5/v.123.
131. Robert Nowak: "Bericht über

die Tätigkeit des Arbeitsstabs Zips," IfZ, ED 63.

132. Lahousen memorandum, July 3, 1939.

133. Lahousen: "Das Unternehmen 'Himmler,'" undated, IfZ, ZS 658. Lahousen Diary, August 17, 1939.

134. Lahousen: "Unternehmen 'Himmler.'"

135. Lais report, July 22, 1939, op. cit., p. 486. ADAP, Series D, Vol. VII, p. 172.

136. Lahousen Diary, August 17, 1939.

137. Jürgen Thorwald: "Der Mann, der den Krieg auslöste" in *Der Stern*, June 7, 1953.

138. Höhne: op. cit., p. 260.

139. Keitel's testimony, IMT, Vol. X, p. 579.

140. Note by Canaris on discussion with Keitel, August, 17, 1939.

141. Ausland I, "Übersicht über die aussenpolitischen Vorgänge in Europa," June 26, 1939, BA/MA, RW 5/v.350.

142. *I Documenti Diplomatici Italiani*, Vol. XIII, p. 395.

143. Lais report, July 22, 1939, op. cit., p. 486.

144. Rudi Strauch: *Sir Nevile Henderson*, p. 238.

145. Ibid. Müller (different dating): op. cit., p. 407. Anthony Cave Brown: *Bodyguard of Lies*, p. 174.

146. Brown: op. cit., p. 173.

147. *Weizsäcker-Papiere*, p. 156.

148. Lais report, July 22, 1939, op. cit., p. 486.

149. HQ Army Group III, Ia, June 14, 1939, re enemy strength, IMT, Vol. XXX, p. 191.

150. Kordt: op. cit., p. 159.

151. Lais report, July 22, 1939, op. cit., p. 486.

152. *Weizsäcker-Papiere*, p. 157.

153. Kordt: op. cit., pp. 160–61.

154. *Weizsäcker-Papiere*, p. 158.

155. Ferdinand Siebert: *Italiens Weg in den Zweiten Weltkrieg*, p. 205 et seq.

156. Report dated August 16, 1939, from Magistrati to Ciano, *I Documenti Diplomatici Italiani*, Vol. XIII, p. 46.

157. Abshagen: op. cit., p. 136.

158. Ibid., p. 137.

159. Siebert: op. cit., p. 252.

160. Ibid.

161. Magistrati report, August 16, 1939, op. cit.

162. Ibid.

163. Canaris note on discussion with Keitel, August 17, 1939.

164. Ibid.

165. Müller: op. cit., p. 408.

166. Canaris note on discussion with Keitel, August 17, 1939.

167. Ibid.

168. Müller: op. cit., p. 408.

169. Ibid., p. 415.

170. Lahousen Diary, August 12, 1939.

171. Lahousen Diary, August 15, 1939.

172. Lahousen Diary, August 18, 1939.

173. Lahousen Diary, August 17, 1939.

174. Lahousen Diary, August 19, 1939.

175. Ibid.

176. Raimund Schnabel: *Macht ohne Moral*, p. 386.

177. Höhne: op. cit., p. 262.

178. See also Winfried Baumgart: "Zur Ansprache Hitlers vor den Führern der Wehrmacht am August 22, 1939," VfZ, No. 16/1968, p. 120 et seq.

179. Führer's address to the commanders in chief on August 22, 1939, ADAP, Series D, Vol. VII, p. 167.

180. Ibid., pp. 168–70.

181. Ibid.

182. Führer's second address on August 22, 1939, ADAP, Series D, Vol. VII, pp. 171–72.

183. War diary of Admiral Albrecht, August 22, 1939, reproduced in Baumgart: op. cit., p. 149.

184. "Persönliche Erlebnisse des Generals der Infanterie a.D. Curt Liepmann in den Jahren 1938/1939," p. 30, IfZ, ED 1/3.

185. Lahousen Diary, August 23, 1939.

186. Ibid.

187. Gisevius: op. cit., p. 360.

188. Ibid.

189. Baumgart: op. cit., p. 136 et seq.

190. ADAP, Series D, Vol. VII, pp. 171–72.

191. Strauch: op. cit., pp. 277–78.

192. Lahousen Diary, August 25, 1939.

193. Strauch: op. cit., p. 278.
194. Shirer: op. cit., p. 557. Keitel's and Brauchitsch's testimony, IMT, Vol. X, p. 578, and Vol. XX, p. 625.
195. Helmuth Greiner: *Die Oberste Wehrmachtführung*, pp. 46–47.
196. Müller: op. cit., pp. 413–14, 420.
197. Gisevius: op. cit., p. 370.
198. Ibid., p. 371.
199. Heinrich Fraenkel and Roger Manvell: *Canaris*, p. 63.
200. Höhne: op. cit., p. 263.
201. Lahousen Diary, August 26, 1939.
202. Ibid.
203. Signal recorded by Striegau Communications Centre on August 26, 1939, Herzner papers, in the possession of Herr Cünter Peis.
204. Report to VIII Corps HQ, Ic/AOII, August 26, 1939, Herzner papers.
205. Herzner: "Bericht über das Unternehmen gegen Bahnhof und Tunnel von Mosty . . ."

206. Lahousen Diary, August 26, 1939.
207. Ibid.
208. Taylor: op. cit., p. 270.
209. *Weizsäcker-Papiere*, p. 162.
210. Ausland I, "Aussen- und militärpolitische Nachrichten," August 26, 1939, BA/MA, RW 5/v.352.
211. Ausland I, "Aussen- und militärpolitische Nachrichten," August 30, 1939, BA/MA, RW 5/v.352.
212. Ausland I, "Aussen- und militärpolitische Nachrichten," August 29, 1939, BA/MA, RW 5/v.352.
213. Ausland I, "Aussen- und militärpolitische Nachrichten," August 31, 1939, BA/MA, RW 5/v.352.
214. Ausland I, "Aussen- und militärpolitische Nachrichten," September 1, 1939, BA/MA, RW 5/v.352.
215. *Weizsäcker-Papiere*, p. 163.
216. Lahousen Diary, August 31, 1939.
217. Gisevius: op. cit., p. 373.

10 The Last Chance

1. *Der Spiegel*, November 13, 1963, p. 74.
2. *Völkischer Beobachter*, September 1, 1939. Jürgen Runzheimer: "Der Überfall auf den Sender Gleiwitz im Jahre 1939" in VfZ, No. 4/1962, p. 409.
3. Lahousen: "Das Unternehmen 'Himmler,'" undated, IfZ, ZS 658.
4. Lahousen Diary, September 1, 1939. Ladislas Farago: *The Game of the Foxes*, p. 168.
5. Letter dated December 17, 1968, from Theodor von Hippel to Hildegard von Kotze, IfZ, ZS 2055/I.
6. Sir Basil Liddell Hart: *History of the Second World War*, p. 29.
7. Lahousen Diary, September 2 and 5, 1939. Groscurth Diary, September 5, 1939, in Helmut Krausnick, Harold C. Deutsch and Hildegard von Kotze: *Tagebücher eines Abwehroffiziers*, p. 259.
8. Lahousen Diary, September 6, 1939.
9. Lahousen Diary, September 3 and 5, 1939.

10. Groscurth Diary, August 24, 1939, July 2, 1939, September 4, 1939, September 5, 1939, September 10, 1939, op. cit.
11. Werner Best: "Wilhelm Canaris," April 10, 1949, in the possession of Dr. Best. Oral information from Dr. Best, February 5, 1966.
12. Groscurth Diary, September 3, 1939, op. cit.
13. Groscurth Diary, September 5, 1939, op. cit.
14. Enno Stephan: *Geheimauftrag Irland*, p. 27.
15. Ibid., p. 32 et seq.
16. Lahousen Diary, September 13, 1939.
17. Lahousen Diary, September 5, 1939.
18. Lahousen Diary, September 6, 1939.
19. Lahousen Diary, September 8, 1939.
20. Ibid.
21. Ibid.

22. Lahousen Diary, September 10, 1939.

23. Lahousen Diary, September 11, 1939.

24. Ibid.

25. Lahousen Diary, September 12, 1939.

26. Lahousen, office minute of conference in Führer's train at Illnau on September 12, 1939, dated September 14, in Krausnick/Deutsch/Kotze: op. cit., p. 357.

27. Ibid.

28. Ibid.

29. Lahousen Diary, September 15, 1939.

30. Lahousen Diary, September 17, 1939.

31. Robert Nowak: "Zur ukrainischen Frage," December 4, 1939, IfZ, ED 63.

32. Lahousen Diary, September 17, 1939.

33. Lahousen Diary, September 18, 1939.

34. Lahousen Diary, September 19, 1939.

35. Ibid.

36. Lahousen Diary, September 22, 1939.

37. Ibid.

38. Lahousen Diary, September 23, 1939.

39. Ibid.

40. Philipp W. Fabry: *Der Hitler-Stalin-Pakt*, p. 156 et seq.

41. Franz Halder, War Diary, Vol. I, p. 80.

42. Franz Liedig: "Die Bedeutung des russisch-finnischen Zusammenstosses für die gegenwärtige Lage Deutschlands," December 7, 1939, p. 5, BA/MA, N 104/2.

43. Ibid.

44. Ulrich von Hassell: *The von Hassell Diaries*, p. 73.

45. Oscar Reile: *Geheime Ostfront*, p. 310.

46. Klaus Benzing: *Der Admiral*, p. 61.

47. Groscurth Diary, September 17, 1939, op. cit.

48. Groscurth Diary, September 7, 1939, op. cit.

49. Groscurth Diary, September 22, 1939, op. cit.

50. Karl Heinz Abshagen: *Canaris*, p. 150.

51. Reile: op. cit., p. 311.

52. Lahousen Diary, September 29, 1939.

53. Ian Colvin: *Chief of Intelligence*, p. 89.

54. Reile: op. cit., p. 310.

55. Wladislaw Kozaczuk: "Die Schlacht um die Geheimnisse" (German translator's MS), p. 271 et seq.

56. Colvin: op. cit., p. 90.

57. Ibid.

58. Ibid.

59. Reile: op. cit., p. 310.

60. Helmut Krausnick: "Hitler und die Morde in Polen" in VfZ, April 1963, p. 203.

61. Ibid., p. 203.

62. Ibid., p. 198.

63. Groscurth Diary, September 8, 1939, op. cit.

64. Ibid.

65. Groscurth Diary, September 9, 1939, op. cit.

66. Gert Buchheit: *Der deutsche Geheimdienst*, p. 219.

67. Reile: op. cit., p. 312.

68. Groscurth Diary, September 23, 1939, op. cit. Martin Broszat: *Nationalsozialistische Polenpolitik*, p. 28.

69. David Irving: *Hitler's War*, p. 741 (not in English edition).

70. Lahousen's note on conference in the Führer's train, quoted by Krausnick/Deutsch/Kotze: op. cit., p. 358.

71. Recollections of General Nikolaus von Vormann, p. 76, IfZ, F 34/2.

72. Lahousen's note on conference in the Führer's train on September 12, 1939.

73. Krausnick/Deutsch/Kotze: op. cit., p. 128.

74. Secret Field Police Regulations, p. 6, BA/MA, RW 5/v.198.

75. Krausnick/Deutsch/Kotze: op. cit., p. 272.

76. For the origins of the RSHA see Heinz Höhne: *The Order of the Death's Head*, p. 252. Buchheit: op. cit., p. 106.

77. Heinz Heumann: "Bericht über die 'Brandenburg,'" June 13, 1965, in the possession of Dr. Buchheit.

78. Letter dated July 4, 1939, from Major Klug to Bürgermeister Peter Denk, Hartmannitz, and further examples of the relations between Abwehr II and the SS-Hauptamt in BA/MA, RW 5/v.164.

79. Groscurth Diary, September 12, 1939, op. cit.

80. Wolfgang Gans Edler Herr von und zu Putlitz: *Unterwegs nach Deutschland*, p. 257 et seq.

81. Colvin: op. cit., p. 104.

82. Walter Schulze-Bernett: "Der Grenzzwischenfall bei Venlo" in *Die Nachhut*, Nos. 23/24, May 1973, p. 1.

83. Ibid., p. 1.

84. Ibid., p. 2.

85. Ibid.

86. Ibid.

87. Walter Schellenberg: *The Schellenberg Memoirs*, p. 78.

88. Lothar Heimbach: "Die Stevens-Best-Affäre," October 26, 1967, p. 9.

89. Ibid.

90. Ibid.

91. Ibid.

92. Schulze-Bernett: op. cit., p. 2.

93. Schellenberg: op. cit., p. 83. Groscurth Diary, November 15, 1939, op. cit.

94. Schulze-Bernett: op. cit., p. 5.

95. Schellenberg: op. cit., p. 94.

96. Ibid. Krausnick/Deutsch/Kotze: op. cit., p. 309.

97. Schulze-Bernett: op. cit., pp. 5–6. Schellenberg: op. cit., p. 97. Letter dated February 12, 1940, from Schellenberg to Meisner, NA, T-175/463.

98. Schulze-Bernett: op. cit., p. 6.

99. Ibid., pp. 7–8.

100. Groscurth Diary, November 9, 1939, op. cit.

101. Schulze-Bernett: op. cit., p. 9. Groscurth Diary, November 15, 1939.

102. Schulze-Bernett: op. cit., p. 9.

103. Letter dated February 12, 1940, from Schellenberg to Meisner.

104. Hans Buchheim et al.: *The Anatomy of the SS State*, p. 173.

105. Office Memorandum, United States Government, Subject; Friedrich Walter Schellenberg, December 29, 1947, IfZ, ZS 291/V. Oral information from Frau Lina Heydrich-Manninen, March 8, 1974.

106. Office Memorandum Schellenberg.

107. Oral information from Frau Lina Heydrich-Manninen.

108. Memorandum by Schellenberg, February, 10, 1940, NA, T-175/463. Schellenberg: op. cit.

109. Schellenberg interrogation, July 29, 1946, IfZ, ZS 291/I.

110. Memorandum by Schellenberg, January 30, 1941, NA, T-175/463.

111. Minutes of Amtschef conference on September 19, 1939, dated September 21, 1939, NA, T-175/463.

112. Memorandum by Schellenberg, January 22, 1940, NA, T-175/463.

113. Ibid.

114. Memorandum by Schellenberg, February 1, 1940, NA, T-175/463.

115. Groscurth Diary, June 18, 1939, op. cit.

116. Bernt Richter: "Interview mit Paul Kanstein," June 21, 1971, p. 2, in the possession of Dr. Richter. Examples in Clsevius: *To the Bitter End*, p. 388 et seq.

117. Memorandum by Schellenberg, February 23, 1940, NA T-175/463.

118. Abwehr III memorandum headed "Abwehrmassnahmen in Deutschland auf dem Gebiet der Personenüberwachung," February 6, 1940, NAT-175/463.

119. "Abwehrmassnahmen in Deutschland . . . ," pp. 1, 14.

120. Bentivegni File, *Spiegel* Archives.

121. Ibid.

122. Buchheit: op. cit., pp. 109–10.

123. Ibid., p. 109.

124. Abwehr III memorandum headed "Propagandamassnahmen," December 12, 1939, BA/MA, RW 5/v.198.

125. "Abwehrmassnahmen in Deutschland . . . ," p. 16.

126. Ibid., pp. 17, 23.

127. Ibid.

128. Secret Field Police Regulations, p. 7, BA/MA, RW 5/v.198.
129. Ibid.
130. Abwehr III "Merkblatt für Unterrichtung der Truppe usw. über Einsatz and Aufgaben der Geheimen Feldpolizei," p. 2, BA/MA, RW 5/v 198.
131. Schellenberg interrogation, November 21, 1946, IfZ, ZS 291/II.
132. Ausland I, "Aussenpolitische Mitteilung," September 29, 1939, BA/MA, RW 6/v. 198, Part 2.
133. Ibid.
134. Letter dated October 30, 1968, from Theodor von Hippel to Dr. Helmut Krausnick, IfZ, ZS 2055/I. Buchheit: op. cit., p. 308.
135. Ibid.
136. Ibid.
137. Groscurth Diary, September 27, 1939, op. cit.
138. Ibid.
139. Anon (=Friedrich Wilhelm Heinz): "Der historische Ablauf bei 'Brandenburg'" in Herbert Kriegsheim: *Getarnt, getäuscht und doch getreu*, p. 295. Georg Tessin: *Verbände der deutschen Wehrmacht und Waffen-SS im Zweiten Weltkrieg*, Vol. 12, p. 327.
140. See mainly Abshagen: op. cit., p. 161, and Heinz: op. cit., p. 289.
141. Letter dated December, 17, 1968, from Hippel to Hildegard von Kotze.
142. Lahousen Diary, October 13, 1939. Erich Ferdinand Pruck: "Warnzeichen Rot," XIV, p. 8 et seq.
143. Reile: op. cit., pp. 341–42.
144. Oral information from Herr Otto Wagner, September 12, 1973. Reile: op. cit., pp. 323, 342.
145. Klaus-Jürgen Müller: *Das Heer und Hitler*, p. 473.
146. Ibid., p. 475.
147. William L. Shirer: *The Rise and Fall of the Third Reich*, p. 641.
148. Müller: op. cit., p. 477.
149. Lothar Gruchmann: "Der Zweite Weltkrieg" in *Deutsche Geschichte seit dem Ersten Weltkrieg*, Vol. II, p. 33.
150. Irving: op. cit., p 46.
151. Louis de Jong: *Die deutsche fünfte Kolonne im Zweiten Weltkrieg*, p. 178.
152. Ibid., p. 179.
153. Ibid., p. 178.
154. Putlitz: op. cit., p. 225.
155. De Jong: op. cit., p. 73.
156. Statement by Piekenbrock while a Soviet prisoner of war in Julius Mader: *Hitlers Spionagegenerale sagen aus*, p. 65.
157. Lahousen Diary, November, 4, 1939.
158. De Jong: op. cit., p. 179.
159. Ibid.
160. Abshagen: op. cit., p. 162.
161. Sir Kenneth Strong: *Men of Intelligence*, p. 79.
162. Ausland I, "Aussenpolitische Mitteilung," September 29, 1939.
163. Groscurth Diary, September 11, 1939, op. cit.
164. Lahousen's note on conference in the Führer's train, September 12, 1939.
165. Strong: op. cit., p. 79.
166. Ibid.
167. Krausnick/Deutsch/Kotze: op. cit., p. 212.
168. Groscurth Diary, October 5, 1939, op. cit.
169. Groscurth Diary, October 10, 1939 and February 14, 1940, op. cit.
170. Strong: op. cit., pp. 81–83.
171. Lahousen Diary, November 5, 1939. De Jong: op. cit., p. 71.
172. Lahousen Diary, November 8, 1939.
173. De Jong: op. cit., p. 180.
174. Lahousen Diary, November 16, 1939.
175. Ehrhardt statement in "Kapitän Ehrhardt," a television programme by Wolfgang Venohr, Westdeutscher Rundfunk, 3rd Programme, October 9, 1971.
176. Gruchmann: op. cit., p. 31.
177. Müller: op. cit., pp. 476, 478.
178. Ibid., p. 478.
179. Harold C. Deutsch: *The Conspiracy Against Hitler in the Twilight War*, pp. 74–75.
180. Undated notes of Christine von Dohnanyi, née Bonhoeffer, p. 5, Lüneburg Public Prosecutor's Records, crimi-

nal proceedings against Dr. Manfred Roeder (=LStA), Vol. I.

181. Otto John: "Männer im Kampf gegen Hitler, Hans von Dohnanyi," undated, *Spiegel* Archives. Richard Korherr: "Karl Ludwig Freiherr von und zu Guttenberg," *Deutsche Tagespost*, April 28, 1965.

182. Christine von Dohnanyi notes, p. 2.

183. Schmidhuber's testimony, July 20, 1950, LStA, Vol. IX, p. 221. Testimony of ex-Abwehrstellenleiter Nikolaus Ficht, September 6, 1950, LStA, Vol. XIV, p. 15.

184. Deutsch: op. cit., p. 84.

185. Letter from Groscurth dated October 15, 1939, in Krausnick/Deutsch/Kotze: op. cit., p. 32.

186. Letter dated June 3, 1957 from Franz Halder to Professor Walter Baum, IfZ, ZS 240/V.

187. Ibid.

188. Lahousen statement, January 30, 1953, IfZ, ZS 658.

189. Ibid.

190. Ibid.

191. Groscurth Diary, October 5, 1939, op. cit.

192. Ibid.

193. Müller: op. cit., p. 479.

194. Halder War Diary, Vol. I, p. 105.

195. Müller: op. cit., p. 482.

196. Ibid., p. 483.

197. Ibid.

198. Groscurth Diary, October 16, 1939, op. cit.

199. Müller: op. cit., p. 494.

200. Groscurth Diary, October 25, 1939, op. cit.

201. Müller: op. cit., p. 489.

202. Ibid., p. 488.

203. Ibid., p. 496.

204. Groscurth Diary, November 1, 1939, op. cit.

205. Groscurth Diary, November 2, 1939, op. cit.

206. Müller: op. cit., p. 514.

207. Ibid., p. 516.

208. Ibid.

209. Walter Huppenkothen, undated copy, LStA.

210. Ibid.

211. Deutsch: op. cit., p. 106.

212. Ibid., p. 111.

213. Schmidhuber testimony, July 20, 1950.

214. Josef Müller: *Bis zur letzten Konsequenz*, p. 12.

215. Ibid., p. 19 et seq.

216. Ibid., p. 12.

217. Ibid., p. 14.

218. Ibid.

219. Ficht testimony, September 6, 1950.

220. Deutsch: op. cit., p. 117.

221. Deposition by ex-Kriminalkommissar Franz Xaver Sonderegger, August 31, 1950, LStA, Vol. IX, p. 211.

222. Corbinian Hofmeister testimony, November 25, 1948, LStA, Vol. V, p. 713.

223. J. Müller: op. cit., pp. 17, 64. Deutsch: op. cit., p. 114.

224. J. Müller: op. cit., p. 82. Deutsch: op. cit., p. 125.

225. Peter Ludlow: "Papst Pius XII., die britische Regierung und die deutsche Opposition im Winter 1939/40" in *VfZ*, No. 3/1974, p. 303.

226. J. Müller: op. cit., p. 85.

227. Ibid., p. 88.

228. Ludlow: op. cit., p. 305.

229. Müller: op. cit., p. 520.

230. Ibid., p. 513.

231. Deutsch: op. cit., p. 226.

232. Müller: op. cit., p. 521. Deutsch: op. cit., p. 226 et seq.

233. Deutsch: op. cit., p. 226.

234. Ibid., p. 229. Müller: op. cit., p. 521.

235. Lahousen statement, January 30, 1953. Müller: op cit., p. 510.

236. Müller: op. cit., p. 522.

237. Deutsch: op. cit., p. 232.

238. Groscurth Diary, November 5, 1939, op. cit.

239. Deutsch: op. cit., p. 232.

240. Letter dated June 3, 1957, from Halder to Baum.

241. Gisevius: op. cit., p. 387.

242. Groscurth Diary, November 5, 1939, op. cit.

243. Letter dated June 3, 1957, from Halder to Baum.

244. Gisevius: op. cit., p. 387.
245. Ibid.
246. Ibid.
247. Müller: op. cit., p. 530.
248. Ibid., p. 531.
249. Ibid., p. 534.
250. Deutsch: op. cit., p. 239.
251. Ibid., p. 240.
252. Ibid., p. 242.
253. Ibid., p. 241.
254. Groscurth Diary, November 11, 1939, op. cit.
255. Müller: op. cit., p. 536.
256. Ibid.
257. Groscurth Diary, November 9, 1939, op. cit.
258. Müller: op. cit., p. 544.
259. Ludlow: op. cit., p. 305.
260. "Besprechung in Rom beim Vatikan 6.–9.11.39," p. 15 (by Dr. Josef Müller), BA/MA, N 104/2.
261. Ibid., p. 16.
262. Ibid., p. 17.
263. Ibid., p. 19.
264. Hassell: op. cit., p. 90.
265. Peter Hoffmann: *Widerstand, Staatsstreich, Attentat*, p. 177. Deutsch: op. cit., p. 245.
266. Lahousen: "Zur Vorgeschichte des Anschlags vom 20. Juli 1944," IfZ, ZS 658.
267. Ibid.
268. Ibid.
269. Ibid.
270. Ludlow: op. cit., pp. 330, 334.
271. Ibid., pp. 330, 334.
272. Ibid., p. 328.
273. Ibid., p. 334.
274. Müller's testimony at the Huppenkothen trial, *Frankfurter Allgemeine Zeitung*, October 15, 1952.
275. "Fragen und Erläuterungen von Dr. Müller," July 1947, LStA, Vol. IX, p. 69.
276. Ibid.
277. Deutsch: op. cit., p. 129 et seq.
278. Ibid., p. 132.
279. J. Müller: op. cit., p. 96.
280. Ibid.
281. Deutsch: op. cit., p. 133.
282. J. Müller: op. cit., p. 98.
283. Deutsch: op. cit., p. 133.

284. Letter dated June 3, 1957, from Halder to Baum.
285. J. Müller: op. cit., p. 97.
286. Müller: op. cit., p. 572.
287. Interrogation of Liedig by Dr. Helmut Krausnick and Professor Harold C. Deutsch, undated, IfZ, ZS 2125.
288. Deutsch: op. cit., p. 94.
289. Sas testimony, March 16, 1948, Enquetecommissie Regeringsbeleid 1940–1945 (German translation), p. 7.
290. Deutsch: op. cit., p. 95.
291. Sas testimony, op. cit, p. 8.
292. Ludlow: op. cit., p. 330.
293. Farago: op. cit., p. 204.
294. Liddell Hart: op. cit., p. 52.
295. Erich Raeder: *Struggle for the Sea*, p. 158.
296. Liddell Hart: op. cit., p. 53.
297. Ibid., p. 54. Quisling's Abwehr contact was Captain von Hippel (code name "Hohenstein"); oral information from Frau Melitta Wiedemann, January 17, 1976.
298. Irving: op. cit., p. 65.
299. Ibid.
300. Liddell Hart: op. cit., pp. 54–55.
301. Ibid., p. 55.
302. Pruck: op cit., XV, p. 1.
303. Ibid., p. 1.
304. Ibid., p. 4.
305. Liddell Hart: op. cit., p. 57.
306. Ibid.
307. Report from Osborne to Lord Halifax in Ludlow: op. cit., p. 330 et seq.
308. Report from Osborne to Lord Halifax, February 7, 1940, in Ludlow: op. cit., p. 333 et seq.
309. Letter from Lord Halifax to Osborne, February 17, 1940, in Ludlow: op. cit., p. 336 et seq.
310. Report from Osborne to Lord Halifax, February 19, 1940, in Ludlow: op. cit., p. 337.
311. See also Klaus-Jürgen Müller, who actually speaks of an "agreement" (p. 560).
312. Müller: op. cit., p. 128.
313. Deutsch: op. cit., p. 289 et seq.
314. Ibid., p. 297.
315. Ibid., p. 299.
316. Ibid.

317. "Besprechung in Rom," pp. 6, 15.

318. Groscurth Diary, January 20–February 2, 1940, op. cit.

319. Deutsch: op. cit., p. 309.

320. Müller: op. cit., p. 565.

321. Ibid.

322. Liedig interrogation, p. 6.

323. Ibid.

324. Irving: op. cit., p. 94.

325. Pruck: op. cit., XV, pp. 12–13.

326. Deutsch: op. cit., p. 320.

327. Ibid., p. 319.

328. Ibid., p. 321.

329. Ibid.

330. J. Müller: op. cit., p. 137.

331. Deutsch: op. cit., p. 321. Liddell Hart: op. cit., p. 60.

332. Liddell Hart: op. cit., p. 57 et seq.

333. Ibid., p. 63.

334. Lahousen Diary, April 9, 1940.

335. Pruck: op. cit., XV, p. 14.

336. Müller: op. cit., p. 567.

337. Ibid.

338. Hildegard von Kotze: *Heeresadjutant bei Hitler*, p. 69. Ibid., p. 58 et seq.

339. Hoffmann: op. cit., p. 217.

340. Hermann Graml: "Der Fall Oster" in *VfZ*, No. 3/1966, p. 39.

341. Deutsch: op. cit., p. 336.

342. Ibid., p. 340.

343. Ibid.

344. Ludlow: op. cit., p. 341.

345. Deutsch: op. cit., p. 341.

346. Ibid., p. 340.

347. Ibid., pp. 340–41.

348. Ibid., p. 341.

349. Ibid., p. 337.

350. Ibid., p. 337.

351. Ibid., p. 337.

352. Ibid., p. 337.

353. Ibid., p. 337.

354. Ibid., pp. 337–38.

355. Lahousen Diary, May 9, 1940.

356. Sas testimony, op. cit., p. 16.

357. Lahousen Diary, May 9, 1940.

358. Sas testimony, op. cit., p. 16. Deutsch: op. cit., p. 328.

359. Lahousen Diary, May 9, 1940.

360. Sas testimony, op. cit., p. 16.

361. Ibid.

362. Deutsch: op. cit., p. 329.

363. Sas testimony, op. cit., p. 17.

364. Ibid.

365. Ibid.

366. Deutsch: op. cit., p. 329.

367. Ibid., p. 330. De Jong: op. cit., p. 73 et seq.

368. Irving: op. cit., p. 116.

369. Ibid., p. 115.

370. Ibid.

371. Buchheit: op. cit., p. 316.

372. Irving: op. cit., p. 117 (in German edition only). De Jong: op. cit., p. 180.

373. Lahousen Diary, May 26, 1940.

374. Irving: op. cit., p. 118 (in German edition only).

375. Lahousen Diary, May 14 and 16, 1940.

376. Letter dated May 25, 1940, from Groscurth to his brother, in Krausnick/Deutsch/Kotze: op. cit., p. 520.

377. Lahousen Diary, June 1, 1940.

378. Huppenkothen, copy, p. 12.

379. Ibid.

380. Opinion of Dr. Georg Düsterberg, February 2, 1951, LStA, Vol. XIII, p. 159.

381. Abwehr IIIC order re "Massnahmen gegen fahrlässige Preisgabe von Staatsgeheimnissen," January 6, 1940, BA/MA, RW 5/v.198.

382. Canaris order dated January 6, 1940, BA/MA, RW 5/v.198.

383. Ibid.

384. See Chapter 6, Note 123.

385. Final report by Staatsanwalt Dr. Finck on the judicial inquiry into Manfred Roeder, p. 655.

386. Deutsch: op cit., p. 343.

387. J. Müller: op. cit., p. 148.

388. Ibid.

389. Ibid.

390. Deutsch: op. cit., p 344. J. Müller: op. cit., p. 149.

391. Deutsch: op. cit., p. 344.

392. J. Müller: op. cit., p. 150.

393. Ibid., p. 152. Statement by Müller, October 21, 1948, LStA, Vol. V, p. 208.

394. Deutsch: op. cit., p. 347.

395. Ibid.

396. Sworn statement by Karl Süss,

December 19, 1946, LStA, Vol. XIV, pp. 10–11.
397. Ibid.
398. Deutsch: op. cit., p. 335.
399. Written communication from Herr Kurt English, September 22, 1969. Deutsch: op. cit., p. 348. Rohleder testimony, July 2, 1950, LStA, Vol. IX, p. 184.
400. Rohleder testimony, June 2, 1950.
401. Final report by Finck, p. 655.
402. Rohleder testimony, July 2, 1950.
403. "In memoriam Joachim Rohleder" in *Die Nachhut*, Nos. 29/30, July 15, 1974, p. 15.
404. Rohleder testimony, op. cit., p. 185.
405. Ibid.
406. Ibid.
407. Ibid. J. Müller: op. cit., p. 154.
408. Rohleder testimony, op. cit., p. 185.

409. Comments by Lahousen, October 15, 1952, IfZ, ZS 658.
410. Rohleder testimony, op. cit., p. 185.
411. Pruck: op. cit., XV, p. 24.
412. Deposition by ex-Kriminalinspektor Hugo Franz Hoffmann, June 15, 1950, LStA, Vol. IX, p. 233.
413. Ibid.
414. Ibid.
415. Pruck: op. cit., XV, p. 24.
416. Hoffmann deposition, op. cit., p. 233.
417. Ibid., p. 234.
418. Ibid., p. 234.
419. Ibid., p. 234.
420. Ibid., p. 234.
421. Ibid., p. 235.
422. Final report by Finck, p. 672.
423. Ibid.
424. Ibid.
425. Liedig interrogation, p. 16.
426. Ibid., p. 12.

11 Tears for Heydrich

1. Charles B. Burdick: *Germany's Military Strategy and Spain in World War II*, p. 24.
2. Ibid., p. 24.
3. Ibid., p. 25.
4. Interview with Max Franzbach, October 29, 1974, in the possession of Herr Günter Peis.
5. Burdick: op. cit., p. 24.
6. Ibid., p. 24.
7. Ibid., p. 25.
8. Ibid., p. 25.
9. Ibid., p. 25.
10. Ibid., p. 25.
11. Ibid., p. 24.
12. Ibid., p. 26.
13. Ibid., p. 26.
14. Ibid., p. 26.
15. Karl Heinz Abshagen: *Canaris*, p. 211 et seq. Hermann Graml: "Die deutsche Militäropposition vom Sommer 1940 bis zum Frühjahr 1943" in Helmut Krausnick: *Die Vollmacht des Gewissens*, Vol. II, p. 425.
16. Thus Karl Wolff in his undated

monograph "Hitler und Franco," p. 27 et seq.
17. Report dated July 22, 1939, from Admiral Lais to the Italian Chief of Naval Staff, *I Documenti Diplomatici Italiani*, Vol. XIII, p. 485.
18. Ibid.
19. Ibid.
20. Ibid.
21. Ibid.
22. Ibid.
23. Ibid.
24. Max Franzbach: "K.O. Spanien, die grösste Kriegsorganisation der Abwehr," undated (about 1946), in the possession of Herr Günter Peis. Klaus-Jörg Ruhl: *Spanien im Zweiten Weltkrieg*, p. 51.
25. Letter dated June 3, 1940, from Franco to Hitler, in Donald S. Detwiler: *Hitler, Franco und Gibraltar*, p. 106.
26. Ibid., p. 22.
27. Ibid., p. 18.
28. Ibid., p. 18.
29. Ibid., p. 24.

30. Ibid., p. 25.
31. Ibid.
32. Gert Buchheit: *Der deutsche Geheimdienst*, p. 317.
33. Burdick: op. cit., p. 20.
34. Interview with Hans-Jochen Rudloff, May 22, 1976, in the possession of Herr Günter Peis.
35. Burdick: op. cit., p. 29.
36. Ibid.
37. Ibid.
38. Oscar Reile: *Geheime Westfront*, p. 284.
39. Halder War Diary, Vol. II, July 6, 1940.
40. Reile: op. cit., p. 284.
41. Burdick: op. cit, p. 20.
42. Ronald Wheatley: *Operation Sea Lion*, p. 31.
43. Ibid.
44. Lothar Gruchmann: "Der Zweite Weltkrieg" in *Deutsche Geschichte seit dem Ersten Welkrieg*, Vol. II, p. 59.
45. Ibid.
46. Wheatley: op. cit., p. 31.
47. Gruchmann: op. cit., p. 60.
48. Ibid.
49. Burdick: op. cit., p. 21.
50. Ibid., p. 21.
51. Ibid., p. 24.
52. Günter Alexander (=Peis): *So ging Deutschland in die Falle*, p. 56 et seq.
53. Ibid., p. 170 et seq.
54. Burdick: op. cit., p. 26.
55. Ibid., p. 27.
56. Ibid., p. 27.
57. Ibid., p. 35.
58. Detwiler: op. cit., p. 32.
59. Ibid.
60. Burdick: op. cit., p. 37.
61. Detwiler: op. cit., p. 35.
62. Lahousen Diary, August 16, 1940.
63. Lahousen Diary, August 24, 1940.
64. Burdick: op. cit., p. 41.
65. Ibid.
66. Ibid.
67. Ibid.
68. Detwiler: op. cit., pp. 35–36.
69. Burdick: op. cit., p. 70.
70. Halder War Diary, October 27, 1940.
71. Halder War Diary, November 2, 1940.
72. Ibid.
73. Ibid. Burdick: op. cit., p. 67.
74. Gruchmann: op. cit., p. 61.
75. Halder War Diary, August 27, 1940.
76. Detwiler: op. cit., p. 41.
77. Ibid., p. 56.
78. Ibid., pp. 58–59.
79. Ibid., p. 59.
80. Ibid., p. 61.
81. Gruchmann: op. cit., p. 65.
82. Ibid., p. 82.
83. Ehrengard Schramm-von Thadden: *Griechenland und die Grossmächte im Zweiten Weltkrieg*, p. 73.
84. Ferdinand Siebert: *Italiens Weg in den Zweiten Weltkrieg*, p. 392.
85. Schramm-von Thadden: op. cit., p. 47.
86. Ibid., p. 51.
87. Ibid., p. 51.
88. Ibid., p. 77.
89. Ibid., p. 78.
90. Ibid., p. 74.
91. Ibid., p. 138.
92. David Irving: *Hitler's War*, p. 174.
93. Ibid.
94. Bernd Martin: *Friedensinitiativen und Machtpolitik im Zweiten Weltkrieg*, p. 395.
95. Gruchmann: op. cit., p. 84.
96. Ibid.
97. Detwiler: op. cit., p. 70.
98. Burdick: op. cit., p. 80.
99. Ibid., p. 94.
100. Ibid.
101. Ibid.
102. Lahousen Diary, November 5, 1940.
103. Burdick: op. cit., p. 94.
104. Ibid., p. 80.
105. Detwiler: op. cit., p. 80.
106. Ibid., p. 80.
107. Ibid., pp. 80–81.
108. Burdick: op. cit., pp. 102–3.
109. Ibid., p. 103.
110. Halder War Diary, November 2, 1940.
111. Schramm-von Thadden: op. cit., p. 139.

112. Ibid., p. 138.
113. Ibid., p. 139.
114. Burdick: op. cit, p. 106.
115. Ibid.
116. Detwiler: op. cit., p. 85. Burdick: op. cit., p. 103.
117. Reproduced in Detwiler: op. cit., pp. 123–25.
118. Record of Franco-Canaris discussion, December 7, 1940, in Detwiler: op. cit., pp. 123–24.
119. Ibid., p. 124.
120. Ibid., p. 124.
121. Ibid., p. 125.
122. Ibid.
123. OKW War Diary, Vol. I, December 8, 1940.
124. Ibid.
125. Ibid.
126. OKW War Diary, Vol. I, December 10, 1940.
127. Detwiler: op. cit., p. 87.
128. Postscript to Karl Wolff: "Hitler und Franco," January 27, 1972, p. 5.
129. Gruchmann: op. cit., p. 140.
130. Schramm-von Thadden: op. cit., p. 140.
131. Note by Admiral Perikles Argyropoulos, July 1952, in Schramm-von Thadden: op. cit., p. 217.
132. Ibid.
133. Note by Colonel (ret.) Clemm von Hohenberg, November 1952, in Schramm-von Thadden: op. cit., p. 218.
134. Ibid., p. 219.
135. Schramm-von Thadden: op. cit., p. 151.
136. Ibid.
137. Ibid.
138. Gruchmann: op. cit., p. 84.
139. Ibid.
140. Corey Ford: *Donovan of OSS*, p. 99.
141. Ibid., p. 100.
142. Ibid., p. 102.
143. Gruchmann: op. cit., p. 85.
144. Ibid.
145. Ford: op. cit., p. 103.
146. Johann Wuescht: *Jugoslawien und das Dritte Reich*, p. 151.
147. Martin: op. cit., p. 403.
148. Schramm-von Thadden: op. cit., p. 220.
149. Martin: op. cit., p. 406.
150. Schramm-von Thadden: op. cit., p. 219.
151. Ibid., p. 220.
152. Ibid., p. 169.
153. Ibid., p. 169.
154. Ibid., p. 170.
155. Gruchmann: op. cit., p. 85.
156. Martin: op. cit., p. 406.
157. Ibid.
158. Ibid.
159. Schramm-von Thadden: op. cit., p. 220.
160. Ibid., p. 172.
161. Wuescht: op. cit., p. 159 et seq.
162. Gruchmann: op. cit., p. 86.
163. Franz Josef Furtwängler: *Männer, die ich sah und kannte*, p. 208.
164. Lahousen Diary, April 15, 1941.
165. Lahousen Diary, April 16, 1941.
166. Abshagen: op. cit., p. 180.
167. Lahousen Diary, May 7, 1941.
168. Schramm-von Thadden: op. cit., p. 221.
169. Halder War Diary, July 22, 1940.
170. Philipp W. Fabry: *Der Hitler-Stalin-Pakt*, p. 367.
171. Erich Helmdach: *Überfall?*, p. 18.
172. Barton Whaley: *Codeword Barbarossa*, p. 18.
173. Deposition made by Piekenbrock while a Soviet prisoner of war, December 12, 1945, IMT, Vol. VII, p. 293.
174. Deposition made by Bentivegni while a Soviet prisoner of war, December 28, 1945, IMT, Vol. VII, p. 294.
175. Bentivegni deposition, op. cit., p. 300.
176. Hermann Giskes: *Spione überspielen Spione*, p. 16.
177. Fabry: op. cit., p. 393.
178. Ibid., pp. 389, 393.
179. Buchheit: op. cit., p. 256.
180. Written communication from Professor Theodor Oberländer, June 25, 1976. Buchheit: op. cit., p. 205. Kurt Ziesel: *Der rote Rufmord*, p. 63.
181. Walter Schellenberg: *The Schellenberg Memoirs*, p. 206.
182. Helmdach: op. cit., p. 88.

183. Lahousen Diary, March 26, 1940.

184. Order signed by Canaris re "Organisation zur Behandlung von Zwischenfällen an der deutsch-sowjetrussischen Grenze," June 18, 1940, NA, T-77/908.

185. Erich Ferdinand Pruck: "Warnzeichen Rot," XIV, p. 13.

186. Lahousen Diary, November 11, 1940.

187. Lahousen Diary, February 15, 1941.

188. Lahousen diary, November 30, 1940.

189. Lahousen Diary, December 14, 1940.

190. Letter from Goth dated May 4, 1940, NA, T-78/488. Helmdach: op. cit., p. 17.

191. Helmdach: op. cit., p. 17.

192. *Die Welt*, January 31, 1973.

193. Note by Baun, July 4, 1940, NA, T-78/488.

194. Hermann Zolling and Heinz Höhne: *Network*, cf. pp. 24–25.

195. Examples can be found in the records of Foreign Armies East, autumn 1940, NA, T-78/488.

196. Herbert Rittlinger: *Geheimdienst mit beschränkter Haftung*, p. 224 et seq.

197. Heinz Höhne: "Der Fall Lissner" in Ivar Lissner: *Mein gefährlicher Weg*, p. 243 et seq.

198. Ibid., p. 248.

199. Reproduced in F. A. Krummacher and Helmut Lange: *Krieg und Frieden*, p. 555.

200. Ibid.

201. Ibid.

202. Lahousen Diary, February 19 and 25, 1941.

203. Bentivegni deposition, op. cit., p. 301.

204. Whaley: op. cit., p. 171.

205. Ibid., p. 175.

206. Ibid., p. 256.

207. Ibid., p. 160.

208. Ibid., p. 173.

209. Ibid.

210. Ibid.

211. Georgi Zhukov: *Erinnerungen und Gedanken*, p. 227.

212. Whaley: op. cit., p. 232.

213. Detailed information in Gruchmann: op. cit., p. 91.

214. Fabry: op. cit., p. 410.

215. Ibid.

216. Ibid. Helmdach: op. cit., p. 10.

217. Fabry: op. cit., p. 410.

218. Ibid., p. 410.

219. Ibid., p. 411.

220. Ibid., pp. 415, 417.

221. Foreign Armies East, Assessment of the Enemy as at May 20, 1941, NA, T-78/479.

222. Halder War Diary, April 4, 1941.

223. Fabry: op. cit., p. 418.

224. Order establishing "Walli" signed by Piekenbrock and dated June 10, 1941, NA, 78/458.

225. Lahousen Diary, June 1941.

226. Lahousen Diary, February 25, 1941.

227. Deposition made by Stolze while a Soviet prisoner of war, December 25, 1945, IMT, Vol. VII, p. 302.

228. Note made by Herzner on June 28, 1941, Herzner papers in the possession of Herr Günter Peis.

229. Letter dated July 26, 1941, from Herzner to his wife, Herzner papers.

230. Ibid.

231. Lev Bezymenski: *Sonderakte "Barbarossa,"* p. 253.

232. Schellenberg: op. cit., pp. 222–23.

233. Ibid., p. 223.

234. Lahousen Diary, June 1, 1941.

235. Gruchmann: op. cit., p. 93.

236. Herbert Kriegsheim: *Getarnt, getäuscht und doch getreu*, pp. 308–9.

237. Lahousen Diary, June 29, July 29, 1941. Alexander Dallin: *German Rule in Russia*, p. 119.

238. Lahousen Diary, June 18 and 26, July 17, 18 and 22, June 21 and July 24, 1941.

239. Lahousen Diary, July 5, 1941.

240. Heinrich Uhlig: "Der verbrecherische Befehl" in *Das Parlament*, November 6, 1963, p. 431.

241. Ibid., p. 432.

242. Joachim Fest: *Hitler*, p. 650.

243. "Das Spiel ist aus—Arthur Nebe," *Der Spiegel*, January 2, 1950, p. 24.

244. Robert Kempner: *SS im Kreuzverhör*, pp. 25, 28.

245. Raul Hilberg: *The Destruction of the European Jews*, pp. 213–15.

246. Dallin: op. cit., p. 120.

247. Ibid.

248. Diary of the Nachtigall training course, July 30, 1941, Herzner papers.

249. Letter dated September 3, 1941, from Herzner to Oberländer, Herzner papers.

250. Nachtigall Diary, August 1, 1941.

251. Lahousen Diary, June 23, 1941.

252. Ibid.

253. Lahousen Diary, June 1941.

254. Hilberg: op. cit., p. 219 et seq.

255. Lahousen testimony, November 30, 1945, IMT, Vol. II, p. 501.

256. Lahousen deposition to Fred Kaufman, January 9, 1948, IfZ, 1948/56.

257. Ibid.

258. Lahousen testimony, op. cit., p. 501.

259. Memorandum on "Instructions for the Treatment of Soviet Prisoners of War," September 15, 1941, in Hans Buchheim, Martin Broszat, Hans-Adolf Jacobsen, Helmut Krausnick: *The Anatomy of the SS State*, p. 526.

260. Ibid.

261. Hilberg: op. cit., p. 189.

262. "Besprechung OKW/Abw. und OKH am 5./6. Juni 1941 in Berlin," recorded by Captain Keune, Ic, Arbeitsstab Ostpreussen, NA, T-78/482.

263. Office minute by Captain Keune, January 16, 1941, NA, T-78/482.

264. Hilberg: op. cit., pp. 198, 222, 244.

265. Ibid., p. 245.

266. Karl Bartz: *The Downfall of the German Secret Service*, pp. 75–76.

267. "Stab Walli" memorandum for Abwehr I, Berlin, signed by Baun and dated March 24, 1942, NA, T-77/1028.

268. Undated note by Dr. Gert Buch-

heit, kindly made available to the author.

269. Letter dated October 17, 1964, from Lieutenant General (ret.) Gerhard Engel to Dr. Krausnick, IfZ, ZS 222/Vol. I.

270. Ibid.

271. Ibid.

272. Oral information from Herr Horst Hiemenz, May 21, 1970.

273. On a Lissner report dated August 14, 1942, see Höhne: "Der Fall Lissner," op. cit., p. 249.

274. Oral information from Herr Gerhard Wessel, June 3, 1971. See also "Kriegsstellenbesetzung der Fremde Heere Ost, 1943," NA, T-78/499.

275. Kriegsheim: op. cit., p. 310 et seq.

276. Buchheit: op. cit., p. 323.

277. Ibid., p. 324.

278. Observator (=Will Grosse): "Geheimdienst, Hakenkreuz und Fahneneid" in *Echo der Woche*, March 17, 1950.

279. Abshagen: op. cit., p. 17.

280. Paul Ronge: "Zur Ahnentafel des Admirals Canaris" in *Genealogie*, Vol. VI, No. 1/1962, p. 35.

281. Buchheit: op. cit., p. 84.

282. Ibid.

283. Ian Colvin: *Chief of Intelligence*, p. 158.

284. Buchheit: op. cit., p. 85.

285. Heinz Höhne: *The Order of the Death's Head*, p. 369.

286. Huppenkothen papers, BDC.

287. Huppenkothen deposition on "Canaris und Abwehr," undated, IfZ, ZS, 249, p. 1.

288. Huppenkothen papers, BDC.

289. Huppenkothen deposition, p. 4.

290. Ibid., p. 4.

291. Ibid., p. 4.

292. Ibid., p. 5.

293. Ibid.

294. Ibid.

295. "Implementation directives relating to official dealings between military Abwehr agencies and agencies of the Security Police and SD," signed by Canaris and Heydrich and dated March 1,

1942; reproduced in *Die Nachhut*, No. 3/32, February 1, 1975, p. 28.

296. Ic/AO re functions of the SD, military Abwehr and GFP, October 2, 1942, reproduced as in Note 295.

297. Buchheit: op. cit., p. 189 (though with inaccurate particulars of the timing and signing of the Abwehr-RSHA agreements).

298. Oral information from Frau Lina Heydrich-Manninen, March 8, 1975.

299. Höhne, *Death's Head*, p. 495.

300. Huppenkothen deposition, p. 5.

301. Information from Frau Heydrich-Manninen.

302. Ibid.

303. Lahousen deposition in IMT, Vol. II, p. 512 et seq.

304. General Giraud: "Mes évasions" in *Point de vue images du monde*, May 12, 1949. Criminal Police Headquarters priority teleprinter message, April 20, 1942, NA, T-175/498.

305. Keitel testimony, April 5, 1946, IMT, Vol. X, p. 647.

306. Ibid. Bartz: op. cit., pp. 123–24 (German edition only).

307. Keitel testimony, op. cit., p. 647.

308. Ibid., p. 647.

309. Ibid., p. 648.

310. Ibid., p. 649.

311. Bartz: op. cit., p. 126 (German edition only).

312. Keitel testimony, op. cit., p. 648.

313. Lahousen testimony, op. cit., p. 512.

314. Ibid.

315. Ibid.

316. Ibid.

317. Keitel testimony, op. cit., p. 648.

318. Lahousen testimony, op. cit., p. 512.

319. Priority teleprinter message from Schellenberg to Himmler, November 9, 1942, NA T-175.

320. Ibid. Also, interrogation of Schellenberg by Dr. Robert Kempner, December 18, 1947, IfZ, ZS 291/V.

321. Keitel testimony, op. cit., p. 648.

322. Lahousen testimony, op. cit., p. 513.

323. Ibid.

324. Ibid.

325. Abshagen: op. cit., p. 196.

326. Lahousen testimony, op. cit., p. 514.

327. Priority teleprinter message from Schellenberg to Himmler, November 9, 1942.

328. Werner Best: "Canaris," April 10, 1949, Best Archives.

329. Heinrich Fraenkel and Roger Manvell: *Canaris*, p. 193.

330. Ibid.

331. Allen Welsh Dulles: *Germany's Underground*, p. 75.

332. Abshagen: op. cit., p. 241. Walter Huppenkothen, copy, p. 15, kindly made available by Herr Huppenkothen.

333. Abshagen: op. cit., p. 241. *Spiegelbild einer Verschwörung* (the Kaltenbrunner Reports), p. 425.

334. Huppenkothen, copy, p. 15.

335. Martin: op. cit., pp. 454–55.

336. Whaley: op. cit., p. 38.

337. Peter Hoffmann: *Widerstand, Staatsstreich, Attentat*, p. 263.

338. Martin: op. cit., p. 464.

339. Alexander Fischer: *Sowjetische Deutschlandpolitik im Zweiten Weltkrieg*, p. 181.

340. Ibid., p. 180.

341. Ibid., p. 181.

342. Ibid.

343. Martin: op. cit., p. 464.

344. Fischer: op. cit., p. 181.

345. Ibid., p. 41.

346. Ibid.

347. Heinz Höhne: *Codeword: Direktor*, p. 155 et seq.

348. Ibid., p. 141.

349. Oral information from Generalrichter (ret.) Dr. Manfred Roeder, March 5, 1968.

350. Testimony of Joachim Rohleder, July 2, 1950, Lüneburg Public Prosecutor's Records, Roeder proceedings, Vol. XII, p. 193.

351. Fischer: op. cit., p. 40 et seq.

352. Ibid., pp. 42–44.

353. Ibid., p. 44.

354. Ibid., p. 45.

355. Telegram dated August 29, 1943, from Ast Hamburg to Chef I

Ausl./Abw., in the possession of Dr. Gert Buchheit.

356. Letter dated May 25, 1943, from Baron Kaulbars to Canaris, BA/MA, RW 4/v.764.

357. Ibid.

358. Ibid.

359. R. Harris Smith: OSS, p. 210.

360. Richard Deacon: A History of the British Secret Service, p. 282.

361. Ibid.

362. Ibid.

363. Ibid.

364. Ibid.

365. F. W. Winterbotham: Secret and Personal, p. 162.

366. Smith: op. cit., pp. 210–11.

367. Ibid., p. 211.

368. Gruchmann: op. cit., p. 260.

369. Hoffmann: op. cit., p. 278.

370. Colvin: op. cit., p. 181.

371. Franz von Papen: Memoirs, p. 499.

372. Albert C. Wedemeyer. Wedemeyer Reports!, pp. 416–17.

373. Papen: op. cit., p. 15. Letter from Baron Kurt von Lernsner to his brother Horst, autumn 1945, in the possession of Herr Otto Wagner.

374. Mario Rodriguez Aragon: "Operación KN" in Pueblo (Madrid), August 21, 1958.

375. Heinrich Brackelmanns: "Ein Beitrag zur politischen Geschichte des II. Weltkrieges," p. 5, kindly made available to the author. Wedemeyer: op. cit., p. 417.

376. Lernsner letter, autumn 1945.

377. Wedemeyer: op. cit., p. 417.

378. Rodriguez: op. cit.

379. Ibid.

380. Hoffmann: op. cit., pp. 327–29.

381. Ibid., p. 277.

382. Ibid., p. 278.

383. Gert Buchheit: "Eine Dokumentation" in Die Nachhut, February 15, 1968, p. 11 et seq.

384. Deposition made by Gero von S.-Gaevernitz in the Wolff trial, September 1, 1964, Public Prosecutor's Records, District Court II, Munich. Hoffmann: op. cit., p. 287. Martin. op. cit., pp. 280–81.

385. Kaltenbrunner Reports, November 29, 1944, p. 505.

386. José María Doussinague: España tenía razón, p. 295.

387. Canaris memorandum for Chef OKW, July 1943, NA, T-77/856.

388. Letter dated December 29, 1967, from F. Justus von Einem to Dr. Josef Müller, in the possession of Heinrich Fraenkel.

389. Ibid.

390. Ibid.

391. Wedemeyer: op. cit., p. 417.

392. Höhne, Death's Head, p. 522 et seq.

393. Letter dated April 30, 1943, from SS-Hauptsturmführer Ahrens to RSHA, IVD, in the possession of Lev Bezymenski. Dulles: op. cit., p. 185 et seq.

12 Downfall

1. Gabriele Krüger: Die Brigade Ehrhardt, p. 71.

2. Ibid., p. 106.

3. Note by Chef der Sicherheitspolizei und des SD, IVA3a, re Lieutenant Commander (ret.) Ehrhardt, December 1941, NA, T-175/128.

4. Ibid.

5. Letter dated July 26, 1943, from the Personal Staff of the Reichsführer-SS to RSHA Referat IVA3a, NA, T-175/128.

6. Franz Josef Furtwängler: Männer, die ich sah und kannte, pp. 210–11.

7. Ibid., p. 211.

8. Ibid., p. 211.

9. Ibid., p. 207.

10. Gert Buchheit: "Aktion 'V7,'" undated, kindly made available by the author.

11. Furtwängler: op. cit., p. 211.

12. See Chapter 11.

13. Günter Alexander (=Peis): So

ging *Deutschland in die Falle*, p. 200 et seq.

14. Seekriegsleitung War Diary, November 8, 1942, quoted by Alexander, op. cit., p. 220.

15. Alexander: op. cit., p. 187 et seq.

16. Ibid., p. 217.

17. Ibid., p. 220 et seq.

18. Ibid., p. 202.

19. Ian Colvin: *Chief of Intelligence*, p. 187.

20. Ibid.

21. Letter dated March 12, 1975, from Herr Erich Ferdinand Pruck to the author.

22. Dr. Werner Best in conversation with the author, February 5, 1966

23. Tape recording of a conversation between Max Franzbach and Günter Peis, October 29, 1974, p. 3 of transcript, in the possession of Herr Peis.

24. Ibid.

25. Alexander: op. cit., p. 182. Charles B. Burdick: *Germany's Military Strategy and Spain in World War II*, p. 107.

26. Kim Philby: *My Silent War*, p. 38.

27. Ladislas Farago: *The Game of the Foxes*, p. 519.

28. Herbert Rittlinger: *Geheimdienst mit beschränkter Haftung*, p. 54 et seq.

29. Alexander: op. cit., p. 139.

30. Testimony of Manfred Roeder, May 23, 1947, Lüneburg Public Prosecutor's Records, Roeder proceedings (=LStA), Vol. II, p. 219.

31. Charges against Dohnanyi and Oster, September 16, 1943, LStA, Vol. I, p. 3 et seq.

32. Rittlinger: op. cit., p. 71. For account given by Johannes Wapenhensch, see details under Note 59.

33. Heinz Höhne: "Der Fall Lissner" in Ivar Lissner: *Mein gefährlicher Weg*, p. 242. Alexander: op. cit., p. 270. Franz Xaver Sonderegger's report on his relations with the July 20, 1944, conspirators, LStA, Vol. IX, p. 81 et seq.

34. Franzbach-Peis tape recording, p. 29.

35. Alexander: op. cit., p. 182.

36. Philby: op. cit., p. 38.

37. Sir John C. Masterman: *The*

Double-Cross System in the War of 1939 to 1945, pp. 151–52.

38. Ibid., p. 152.

39. Peter Hoffmann: *Widerstand, Staatsstreich, Attentat*, p. 309 et seq.

40. Ibid., p. 311.

41. Ibid., p. 321.

42. Ibid., p. 322.

43. Ibid., p. 327.

44. Ibid., p. 319.

45. Ibid., p. 325.

46. Ibid.

47. Gert Buchheit: *Der deutsche Geheimdienst*, p. 324.

48. Alexander von Pfuhlstein: "Bericht über meine Erlebnisse in Verbindung mit Herrn Heinz," June 10, 1953, kindly made available by the author.

49. Ibid., p. 2.

50. Ibid.

51. Buchheit: *Geheimdienst*, p. 324.

52. Ibid., p. 323.

53. "Zur Kritik an Pfuhlstein," letter dated February 2, 1951, from Georg Duesterberg to the Senior Public Prosecutor, Lüneburg, LStA, Vol. XIII, p. 161.

54. Hoffmann: op. cit., p. 332.

55. Questions and statements by Dr. (Josef) Müller, dictated in July 1947, LStA, Vol. IX, p. 73.

56. Ibid., p. 66.

57. Ibid.

58. Final report by Staatsanwalt Dr. Finck, Lüneburg, re judicial proceedings against ex-Generalrichter Dr. Manfred Roeder for obtaining evidence under duress, p. 681, Ministry of Justice Archives of Land Niedersachsen.

59. Deposition by Johannes Wapenhensch, September 16, 1950, LStA, Vol. XIV, p. 23.

60. Ibid.

61. Final report, p. 681.

62. Wapenhensch deposition, p. 23.

63. Ibid., p. 24.

64. Deposition by Nikolaus Ficht, September 6, 1950, LStA, Vol. XIV, p. 15.

65. Deposition by Heinz Ickrath, September 8, 1950, LStA, Vol. XIV, p. 1.

66. Ficht deposition, p. 15.

67. Ibid.
68. Final report, p. 683.
69. Wapenhensch deposition, p. 24.
70. Ibid., p. 24.
71. Ibid., p. 24.
72. Ibid., p. 25.
73. Final report, p. 684.
74. Wapenhensch deposition, p. 25.
75. Ibid.
76. Ibid.
77. Final report, p. 684.
78. Wapenhensch deposition, p. 25.
79. Ibid., p. 25.
80. Ibid., p. 26.
81. ZR's distribution of functions, January 21, 1942, BA/MA.
82. Undated note by Christine von Dohnanyi (about 1948–49), LStA, Vol. I, p. 126.
83. Wapenhensch deposition, p. 26.
84. Ibid.
85. Final report, p. 686.
86. Deposition by Karl Süss, September 6, 1950, LStA, Vol. XIV, p. 7.
87. Ibid.
88. Final report, p. 686.
89. Christine von Dohnanyi note, p. 127.
90. Final report, p. 688.
91. Ibid., p. 710.
92. Ibid., p. 707.
93. Ibid., p. 710.
94. Ibid, p. 688.
95. Ficht deposition, p. 16.
96. Final report, p. 687.
97. Affidavit by Karl Süss, December 19, 1946, LStA, Vol. XIV, p. 10.
98. Deposition by Josef Müller, September 22, 1950, LStA, Vol. XIV, p. 29.
99. Ficht deposition, p. 16.
100. Ibid.
101. Final report, p. 688.
102. Ibid., p. 688.
103. Ibid., p. 689.
104. Ficht deposition, p. 16. Final report, p. 689.
105. Ickrath deposition, p. 2.
106. Wapenhensch deposition, p. 27.
107. Deposition by Wilhelm Schmidhuber, July 20, 1950, LStA, Vol. IX, p. 222.
108. Final report, p. 691. Deposition

by Walter Schoen, September 11, 1950, LStA, Vol. XIV, p. 21.
109. Final report, p. 691.
110. Wapenhensch deposition, p. 26.
111. Ibid., p. 27.
112. Süss affidavit, p. 11.
113. Wapenhensch deposition, p. 27.
114. Final report, p. 692.
115. Ibid., pp. 704, 707.
116. Deposition by Karl Sauermann, September 7, 1950, LStA, Vol. XIV, p. 18.
117. Final report, p. 689.
118. Ibid., p. 704.
119. Josef Müller: *Bis zur letzten Konsequenz*, p. 165.
120. Ibid., p. 166.
121. Ibid., p. 167.
122. Ibid.
123. Walter Schellenberg: *The Schellenberg Memoirs*, p. 360.
124. Deposition by Franz Xaver Sonderegger, August 31, 1950, LStA, Vol. IX, p. 244.
125. Ibid.
126. Final report, p. 727.
127. Christine von Dohnanyi note, p. 140.
128. Questions and statements by Dr. Müller, p. 4 et seq.
129. Deposition by Franz Xaver Sonderegger, September 9, 1948, LStA, Vol. III, p. 435 et seq.
130. Ibid.
131. Ibid.
132. Christine von Dohnanyi note, p. 127.
133. Sonderegger deposition, Vol. IX, p. 248.
134. Ibid., p. 250.
135. Ibid., p. 246.
136. Ibid., p. 248.
137. Ibid., p. 250.
138. Ibid.
139. Sonderegger deposition, Vol. III, p. 437.
140. Ibid., p. 438.
141. Sonderegger deposition, Vol. IX, p. 299.
142. Ibid.
143. Ibid.
144. Hans Bernd Gisevius: *To the Bitter End*, p. 471.

145. Heinz Höhne: *The Order of the Death's Head*, p. 524 et seq.
146. Deposition by Josef Müller, October 21, 1948, LStA, Vol. V, p. 209.
147. Höhne: *Death's Head*, p. 518 et seq.
148. Final report, p. 764.
149. Ibid., pp. 774–75.
150. Ibid., p. 775.
151. Note by Rudolf Lehmann, June 30, 1947, LStA, Vol. XIV, p. 78.
152. Ibid., p. 79.
153. Ibid., p. 79.
154. Ibid., p. 80.
155. Ibid.
156. Ibid.
157. Final report, p. 67.
158. Ibid.
159. Lehmann note, p. 80.
160. Ibid.
161. United States Military Intelligence Service Center, Subject: Alexander Kraell, July 18, 1946, David Irving Archive.
162. Alexander Kraell, report on the "Depositenkasse" proceedings, August 25, 1948, LStA, Vol. III, p. 402.
163. Lehmann note, p. 80.
164. Final report, p. 1.
165. Heinz Höhne: *Codeword· Direktor*, p. 181.
166. Kraell report, p. 398.
167. Deposition by Christian von Hammerstein, July 22, 1948, LStA, Vol. VIII, p. 54.
168. Deposition by Manfred Roeder, December 9, 1947, LStA, Vol. II, p. 328.
169. Deposition by Manfred Roeder, May 9, 1947, LStA, Vol. II, p. 201.
170. Kraell report, p. 400.
171. Roeder deposition, Vol. II, p. 328.
172. Sonderegger deposition, Vol. III, p. 438.
173. Eberhard Bethge: *Dietrich Bonhoeffer*, p. 686.
174. Christine von Dohnanyi note, p. 126.
175. Bethge: op. cit., p. 689.
176. Christine von Dohnanyi note, p. 130.
177. Hoffmann: op. cit., pp. 332–41.

178. Final report, p. 802.
179. Roeder deposition, Vol. II, p. 329.
180. Indictment against Dohnanyi and Oster, p. 23.
181. Roeder deposition, Vol. II, p. 329.
182. Ibid.
183. Ibid.
184. Gisevius: op. cit., p. 472.
185. Indictment, p. 9.
186. Roeder deposition, Vol. II, p. 329.
187. Final report, p. 804. Kraell report, p. 404.
188. Indictment, pp. 9–10.
189. Final report, p. 805.
190. Indictment, p. 5. Deposition by Alexander von Pfuhlstein, March 10, 1950, LStA, Vol. IX, p. 140.
191. Pfuhlstein deposition, p. 140.
192. Gisevius: op. cit., p. 471.
193. Ulrich von Hassell: *The von Hassell Diaries*, p. 271.
194. Pfuhlstein deposition, p. 140.
195. Roeder deposition, Vol. II, p. 336.
196. Letter dated November 10, 1943, from Josef Müller to the Oberreichskriegsanwalt, LStA, Vol. V, p. 705.
197. Christine von Dohnanyi note, pp. 130–31.
198. Ibid. Indictment, p. 10.
199. Indictment, p. 10.
200. Ibid., p. 8.
201. Ibid., p. 5 et seq.
202. Ibid., pp. 8–9.
203. Ibid., p. 7.
204. Roeder deposition, Vol. II, p. 330.
205. Ibid., p. 208.
206. Indictment, p. 8.
207. Final report, p. 2.
208. Questions and statements by Dr. Müller, p. 66.
209. Lehmann note, p. 82.
210. Indictment, pp. 11–17.
211. Ibid., p. 18.
212. Ibid., p. 19.
213. Ibid., p. 19.
214. Ibid., p. 15.
215. Ibid., p. 16.

216. Written declaration by Rechts-anwalt Kurt Peschke, undated (early 1944), LStA, Vol. I, p. 70.

217. Ibid., pp. 71–72.

218. Indictment, pp. 15–16.

219. Ibid., p. 18.

220. Ibid., p. 16.

221. Peschke declaration, p. 74.

222. Ibid.

223. Indictment, p. 17.

224. Bethge: op. cit., pp. 708–9.

225. Müller: op. cit., p. 171.

226. Müller deposition, Vol. V, p. 698.

227. Roeder deposition, Vol. II, p. 330.

228. Deposition by Alexander Kraell, June 19, 1950, LStA, Vol. IX, p. 165.

229. Indictment, pp. 8, 21, 23.

230. Deposition by Karl Lotter, August 30, 1950, LStA, Vol. IX, p. 241.

231. Written defence by Hans von Dohnanyi, undated (autumn or late 1943), LStA, Vol. I, p. 17.

232. Written declaration by Count von der Goltz, February 19, 1944, LStA, Vol. I, p. 21.

233. Christine von Dohnanyi note, p. 135.

234. Karl Heinz Abshagen: *Canaris*, p. 234. André Brissaud: *Canaris*, p. 301.

235. Letter dated November 16, 1950, from Georg Duesterberg to the Lüneburg Public Prosecutor's Office, LStA, Vol. XIII, p. 139.

236. Ibid.

237. Ibid.

238. Ibid.

239. Ibid.

240. Roeder deposition, Vol. II, p. 336.

241. Ibid.

242. Final report, p. 838.

243. Roeder deposition, Vol. II, p. 336.

244. Ibid.

245. Ibid. Kraell report, p. 411.

246. Gisevius: op. cit., p. 473.

247. Ibid.

248. Final report, p. 839.

249. Kraell report, p. 416.

250. Ibid., p. 412.

251. Deposition by Rudolf Lehmann, September 28, 1948, LStA, Vol. IV, p. 535.

252. Lehmann note, p. 83.

253. Kraell report, p. 412.

254. Ibid., p. 412.

255. Ibid., p. 409.

256. Ibid.

257. Lehmann note, p. 82.

258. Ibid., p. 83.

259. Ibid.

260. Kraell report, p. 413.

261. Ibid.

262. Lehmann note, p. 83.

263. Lothar Gruchmann: "Der Zweite Weltkrieg" in *Deutsche Geschichte seit dem Ersten Weltkrieg*, Vol. II, p. 170.

264. Kraell report, p. 414.

265. Ibid., p. 413.

266. Ibid., p. 413.

267. Ibid., p. 414.

268. Final report, p. 866.

269. Roeder deposition, Vol. II, p. 217.

270. Ibid.

271. Final report, p. 2.

272. Kraell report, p. 166.

273. Deposition by Walter Huppenkothen, July 12, 1950, LStA, Vol. IX, p. 199.

274. Allen W. Dulles: *Germany's Underground*, p. 161 et seq.

275. Schellenberg: op. cit., p. 408.

276. Heinrich papers, in the possession of Herr Robert Spiering.

277. Hansen papers, in the possession of Herr Robert Spiering.

278. Freytag-Loringhoven papers, in the possession of Herr Robert Spiering.

279. Buchheit: *Geheimdienst*, p. 426. Address and telephone number list of OKW-Amt Ausland/Abwehr, 1943, BA/MA, RW 5.

280. Colvin: op. cit., p. 186.

281. Final report, p. 1157.

282. Buchheit: *Geheimdienst*, p. 424.

283. Ibid., p. 407.

284. Lahousen Diary, July 29, 1943.

285. Melton S. Davis: *Who Defends Rome?*, p. 219.

286. Schellenberg: op. cit., p. 407.

287. *Frankfurter Allgemeine Zeitung*, May 23, 1970.

288. Ibid.

289. Ibid.
290. Lahousen Diary, July 31, 1943.
291. Walter Huppenkothen: "Canaris und Abwehr," p. 5, IfZ, ZS 249.
292. Schellenberg: op. cit., p. 407.
293. Ibid.
294. Deposition by Ernst Kaltenbrunner, IMT, Vol. XI, p. 266.
295. Ibid., p. 267.
296. Ibid., p. 268.
297. Huppenkothen: op. cit., p. 5.
298. Schellenberg: op. cit., p. 408.
299. Huppenkothen: op. cit., p. 5.
300. Ibid.
301. Schellenberg: op. cit., p. 408.
302. Ibid.
303. Gruchmann: op. cit., p. 173 et seq.
304. Klaus Jörg Ruhl: *Spanien im Zweiten Weltkrieg*, p. 239.
305. Ibid., p. 238.
306. Ibid.
307. Memorandum for Chef OKW, signed by Canaris, July 1943, NA, T-77/856.
308. Ibid.
309. Alexander: op. cit., p. 249 et seq.
310. Final report, p. 889 et seq.
311. Hoffmann: op. cit., p. 678.
312. Walter Huppenkothen: "Der Fall Kiep und andere," undated, LStA, Vol. I, p. 123 et seq.
313. Final report, p. 889.
314. Ibid., p. 889.
315. Ibid., p. 893.
316. Christine von Dohnanyi note, p. 137.
317. Pfuhlstein deposition, p. 141. Alexander von Pfuhlstein: "Ein Faustschlag und seine Folgen," February 25, 1948, IfZ, ZS 592.
318. Pfuhlstein: "Faustschlag."
319. Pfuhlstein deposition, p. 141.
320. Ibid., p. 141.
321. Ibid., p. 141.
322. Ibid., p. 142.
323. Letter dated July 18, 1969, from Alexander von Pfuhlstein to Hans Rothfels, IfZ, ZS 592.
324. Pfuhlstein deposition, p. 142.
325. Ibid., p. 143.
326. Ibid.

327. Ibid.
328. Record of the interrogation of Lieutenant von Gustedt, January 18, 1944, in the possession of Herr Alexander von Pfuhlstein.
329. Ibid.
330. Ibid.
331. Letter dated January 20, 1951, from Staatsanwalt Finck to Regierungsdirektor Schierholt, LStA, Vol. XIII, p. 155. Letter dated July 11, 1969, from the Central Information Office of the BA to Alexander von Pfuhlstein, in the latter's possession.
332. Report dated January 18, 1944, from Alexander von Pfuhlstein to Canaris, in Herr von Pfuhlstein's possession.
333. Hoffmann: op. cit., p. 448. Huppenkothen: "Fall Kiep," p. 7.
334. Hoffmann: op. cit., p. 448. Huppenkothen: "Fall Kiep," p. 8.
335. Huppenkothen: "Fall Kiep," p. 8.
336. Siegfried Westphal: *The German Army in the West*, p. 155.
337. Ibid., p. 156.
338. Colvin: op. cit., p. 191.
339. Westphal: op. cit., p. 156.
340. David Irving: *Hitler's War*, p. 601.
341. Gruchmann: op. cit., p. 176.
342. Colvin: op. cit., p. 191.
343. Lotter deposition, p. 21.
344. Irving: op. cit., p. 605.
345. Colvin: op. cit., p. 186.
346. More particulars may be found in the teleprinter message from Legationstrat Kramarz to Ambassador Ritter, August 5, 1942, NA, T-120/366.
347. Schellenberg: op. cit., p. 281.
348. Ibid.
349. Ibid.
350. Barton Whaley: *Codeword Barbarossa*, p. 160.
351. Ruhl: op. cit., p. 54 et seq.
352. Letter dated June 20, 1941, from Heydrich to the Foreign Office, NA, T-175/199.
353. Walter Hagen (=Hoettl): *Die geheime Front*, p. 288.
354. Schellenberg: op. cit., p. 364.
355. Paul Seabury: *The Wilhelmstrasse*, p. 128.

356. Ruhl: op. cit., p. 54.
357. Ibid., p. 236.
358. Ibid., p. 239.
359. Ibid.
360. Memorandum dated January 29, 1944, for head of Wehrmacht operations, signed by Freytag-Loringhoven, PA, Records of the Political Section, IM, in the possession of Herr Günter Peis.
361. Letter dated January 27, 1944, from Grote to Steengracht, PA.
362. Memorandum for head of Wehrmacht operations, January 29, 1944.
363. Ibid.
364. Ruhl: op. cit., p. 239.
365. Letter dated January 27, 1944, from Grote to Steengracht, PA.
366. Memorandum by Grote re Kampen, January 26, 1944, PA.
367. Ibid.
368. Report addressed to Canaris by Naval Attaché Menzell, January 31, 1944, PA.
369. Memorandum for head of Wehrmacht operations, January 29, 1944.
370. Menzell to Canaris, January 31, 1944.
371. Ibid.
372. Ibid.
373. Ibid.
374. Farago: op. cit., p. 610.
375. Amt Ausland/Abwehr memorandum re arrest of Harnisch in Buenos Aires, January 30, 1944, NA, T-120/366.
376. Ibid.
377. Telegram dated January 28, 1944, from Dieckhoff to the Foreign Office, NA, T-120/366.
378. Letter dated January 30, 1944, from Ribbentrop to Keitel, NA, T-120/366.
379. Letter dated February 3, 1944, from Canaris to Ribbentrop, PA.
380. Letter dated February 4, 1944, from Keitel to Ribbentrop, NA, T-120/366.
381. Ibid.
382. Letter dated February 8, 1944, from Grote to Amt Ausland/Abwehr, PA.

383. Ibid.
384. Report from Chef der Sicherheitspolizei und des SD concerning German traitors in Turkey, February 7, 1944, NA T-120/784.
385. Ibid.
386. Ibid.
387. Abshagen: op. cit., p. 238.
388. Report from Chef der Sicherheitspolizei und des SD, February 7, 1944.
389. Irving: op. cit., p. 605.
390. Rittlinger: op. cit., p. 246. Written communication from Dr. Eric M. de Saventhem, May 17, 1976.
391. Saventhem communication.
392. *Genealogisches Handbuch des Adels*, Gräfliche Häuser, A, Vol. IV, p. 298. Sonderegger's report on his relations with the July 20, 1944, conspirators, LStA, Vol. IX, p. 86. Rittlinger: op. cit., p. 246.
393. Saventhem communication.
394. Steengracht's report to Ribbentrop, May 6, 1944, NA, T-120/784.
395. Comment of the Chef der Sicherheitspolizei und des SD on the Reich Foreign Minister's memorandum, April 20, 1944, NA, T120/874.
396. Ibid.
397. Hans Hussl: "Flucht des Vermehren mit seiner Frau," note of July 2, 1965, in the possession of Dr. Gert Buchheit.
398. Comment of the Chef der Sicherheitspolizei und des SD, April 20, 1944.
399. Ibid.
400. Ibid.
401. Saventhem communication. Memorandum by Legationsrat Frohwein, March 3, 1944, NA, T-120/366.
402. Steengracht's telegram to the heads of mission in Ankara, Stockholm, Berne and Lisbon, February 8, 1944, NA, T-120/366.
403. Ritter's telegram to the diplomatic missions in Ankara, Berne, Stockholm, Lisbon and Madrid, February 9, 1944, NA, T-120/366.
404. Ibid.
405. Farago: op. cit., p. 611.
406. Telegram from Dieckhoff to the Foreign Office, February 6, 1944, PA.

407. Ritter's telegram, February 9, 1944.

408. Diary entries of the German Embassy in Madrid, 1944, Vol. I, kindly made available to the author by Dr. Werner Maser.

409. Tape recording of a conversation between Frau Kremer von Auenrode and Günter Peis, p. 115 of transcript, in the possession of Herr Günter Peis.

410. Note by Bürkner, February 10, 1944, in the possession of Dr. Buchheit.

411. Ibid.

412. Farago: op. cit., p. 612.

413. Report from Chef der Sicherheitspolizei und des SD, February 26, 1944.

414. Auenrode transcript, p. 416.

415. Abshagen: op. cit., p. 368 (German edition only).

416. Irving: op. cit., p. 605.

417. Huppenkothen: "Canaris und Abwehr," p. 6.

418. Ibid.

419. Ibid.

420. Report from Chef der Sicherheitspolizei und des SD, February 26, 1944.

421. Huppenkothen: "Canaris und Abwehr," p. 6.

422. Report from Chef der Sicherheitspolizei und des SD, February 26, 1944.

423. Huppenkothen: "Canaris und Abwehr," p. 6.

424. Order headed "Der Führer, Chef OKW Nr. 1/44," February 12, 1944, NA, T-78/497.

13   Murder at Flossenbürg

1. Anthony Cave Brown: *Bodyguard of Lies*, p. 456.

2. Ibid.

3. Orders and decorations conferred on Admiral Canaris, Canaris Personal File, photocopy in IfZ.

4. Oral information from Herr Otto Wagner, May 15, 1976.

5. Ibid.

6. Ibid.

7. Ibid.

8. Letter dated March 21, 1944, from the Naval Personnel Department, OKM, to HQ Baltic Command, Canaris Personal File.

9. Ibid.

10. Oral information from Herr Otto Wagner, undated.

11. Klaus Benzing: *Der Admiral*, p. 150.

12. Karl Heinz Abshagen: *Canaris*, p. 224.

13. Walter Huppenkothen: "Canaris und Abwehr," p. 6, IfZ.

14. Ibid., p. 7. Gert Buchheit: *Der deutsche Geheimdienst*, p. 430.

15. Huppenkothen, op. cit., p. 7. Buchheit: op. cit., p. 430.

16. Letter dated April 11, 1944, from Keitel to Himmler, NA, T-78/497.

17. Undated teleprinter message from Keitel to Kaltenbrunner, NA, T-78/497.

18. Letter dated April 16, 1944, from Foreign Armies East (Staub), NA, T-78/497.

19. Letter from Keitel to Himmler, April 11, 1944.

20. Kaltenbrunner's order concerning reorganization of the Secret Intelligence Service, May 23, 1944, NA, T-78/497.

21. Ibid.

22. Huppenkothen, op. cit. p. 7 et seq.

23. Agreement between Keitel and Himmler on the functions of the Secret Intelligence Service, May 14, 1944, NA, T-78/497.

24. Huppenkothen, op. cit., p. 9. Buchheit: op. cit., p. 432.

25. Buchheit: op. cit., p. 432.

26. Kaltenbrunner order, May 23, 1944.

27. Buchheit: op. cit., p. 433.

28. Personal record of Canaris, Canaris Personal File.

29. Ibid.

30. Kaltenbrunner's report to Bormann, September 29, 1944, in *Spiegelbild einer Verschwörung* (Kaltenbrunner's reports to Bormann and Hitler on the July 20, 1944, bomb plot), p. 425.

31. Buchheit: op. cit., p. 433.

32. Benzing: op. cit., p. 108.

33. Abshagen: op. cit., p. 240.

34. W. N. Medlicott: *The Economic Blockade*, Vol. II, p. 611.

35. Lothar Gruchmann: "Der Zweite Weltkrieg" in *Deutsche Geschichte seit dem Ersten Weltkrieg*, p. 222.

36. Ibid., p. 222.

37. Ibid., p. 222.

38. Ibid., p. 192.

39. Ibid., p. 193.

40. Ibid., p. 193.

41. Ibid., p. 224.

42. Ibid.

43. Hans Speidel: *We Defended Normandy*, pp. 126–27.

44. Gruchmann: op. cit., p. 224.

45. Ibid., p. 225.

46. Buchheit: op. cit., pp. 437–38.

47. Ibid.

48. Peter Hoffmann: *Widerstand, Staatsstreich, Attentat*, p. 394.

49. Ibid., p. 395.

50. Abshagen: op. cit., p. 236.

51. Hoffmann: op. cit., pp. 377–78.

52. Walter Huppenkothen: copy (of his account of investigations into the Canaris-Oster group), p. 25, kindly made available by Herr Huppenkothen.

53. Hoffmann: op. cit., p. 429.

54. Ibid., p. 430.

55. Heinz Höhne: *Codeword: Direktor*, p. 195.

56. Abshagen: op. cit., p. 235.

57. Benzing: op. cit., p. 104.

58. Ibid., p. 107.

59. Hoffmann: op. cit., p. 466.

60. Ibid., pp. 469–70.

61. Ibid., pp. 470–71.

62. Eberhard Zeller: *Geist der Freiheit*, p. 381.

63. Hoffmann: op. cit., pp. 487, 491.

64. Ibid., p. 492.

65. Ibid.

66. HOKW [OKW Building] tele-printer message No. 02165, July 20, 1944; Kaltenbrunner Reports, p. 24.

67. Teleprinter message to HQ Military Districts I–XIII, XVII, XVIII, XX, XXI, also Government General of Bohemia-Moravia, July 20, 1944; Kaltenbrunner Reports, p. 25.

68. Abshagen: op. cit., p. 242. David Irving: *Hitler's War*, p. 849 (German edition only).

69. Hoffmann: op. cit., p. 491.

70. Hermann Bösch: *Heeresrichter Dr. Karl Sack im Widerstand*, p. 83. This tallies with Huppenkothen: copy, p. 24.

71. Bösch: op. cit., p. 83.

72. Abshagen: op. cit., p. 242.

73. Ibid.

74. Ibid.

75. Hoffmann: op. cit., pp. 575, 555, 562.

76. Dieter Ehlers: *Technik und Moral einer Verschwörung*, p. 220.

77. Felix Kersten: *Totenkopf und Treue*, p. 242 (not in English edition).

78. Zeller: op. cit., p. 251.

79. SS report on July 20 in *Nordwestdeutsche Hefte*, February 1947, p. 5.

80. Kaltenbrunner's report to Bormann, July 25, 1944; Kaltenbrunner Reports, p. 47.

81. Ibid., p. 48.

82. Ibid.

83. Karl Bartz: *The Downfall of the German Secret Service*, p. 148.

84. Kaltenbrunner's report to Bormann, November 29, 1944; Kaltenbrunner Reports, p. 503.

85. Walter Schellenberg: *The Schellenberg Memoirs*, p. 409.

86. Ibid., p. 410. Huppenkothen: copy, p. 2.

87. Schellenberg: op. cit., p. 410.

88. Ibid., p. 411.

89. Ibid.

90. Ibid.

91. Hoffmann: op. cit., p. 613.

92. Huppenkothen: copy, p. 1.

93. Personal report by ex-Kriminalkommissar Franz Xaver Sonderegger on his relations with the July 20, 1944, conspirators; LStA criminal proceedings against Manfred Roeder, Vol. IX, p. 81

et seq. Final Report by Staatsanwalt Dr. Finck on the Roeder judicial inquiry, p. 965; Archiv des niedersächsischen Justizministeriums.

94. Sonderegger report, p. 84.

95. Ibid., p. 81.

96. Ibid.

97. Huppenkothen: copy, p. 2.

98. Kaltenbrunner's report to Bormann, August 17, 1944; Kaltenbrunner Reports, p. 248.

99. "Die geistige Haltung des Offiziers," Kaltenbrunner Reports, p. 301.

100. Ibid.

101. Eberhard Bethge: *Dietrich Bonhoeffer*, p. 810.

102. Bartz: op. cit., p. 153.

103. Müller's report to Bormann, September 8, 1944; Kaltenbrunner Reports, p. 370.

104. Ibid., p. 371.

105. Ibid.

106. Alexander von Pfuhlstein: "Bericht über meine Erlebnisse in Verbindung mit Herrn Heinz," June 10, 1953, p. 10.

107. Müller's report to Bormann, September 8, 1944; Kaltenbrunner Reports, p. 370.

108. Ibid., p. 370.

109. Ibid., p. 371.

110. Kaltenbrunner's report to Bormann, September 21, 1944; Kaltenbrunner Reports, p. 407.

111. Ibid., p. 407.

112. Ibid., p. 408.

113. Notes by Alexander von Pfuhlstein: "Die Vernehmung, die Wartezeit im Kerker," February 25, 1948; IfZ, ZS 592.

114. Ibid., p. 19.

115. Müller's report to Borman, September 8, 1944; Kaltenbrunner Reports, p. 370.

116. Ibid., pp. 369–70.

117. Ibid., p. 369.

118. Kaltenbrunner's report to Bormann, September 21, 1944; Kaltenbrunner Reports, p. 405.

119. Ibid., p. 406.

120. Ibid., p. 407.

121. Ibid., p. 408.

122. Ibid., p. 406.

123. Ibid.

124. Ibid.

125. Handwritten statement by Canaris dated September 21, 1944; Kaltenbrunner Reports, pp. 409–10.

126. Written communication from Dr. Werner Wolf Schrader, March 16, 1968.

127. Final Report, p. 1,157.

128. Sonderegger report, p. 86.

129. Ibid.

130. Ibid.

131. Will Grosse: "Im Hintergrund Admiral Canaris," p. 5.

132. Bartz: op. cit., p. 156.

133. Assize court (Landgericht München I) judgement against Walter Huppenkothen, February 16, 1951 (=Munich Judgement), p. 8; photocopy in the records of Kammergericht Berlin, p. 1,157. Bartz: op. cit., p. 157.

134. Huppenkothen: copy, p. 2 et seq.

135. Ibid., p. 11.

136. Sonderegger deposition; Final Report, p. 1,157.

137. Oral information from Dr. Schrader, undated.

138. Heinrich Fraenkel and Roger Manvell: *Canaris*, pp. 190, 240.

139. Ibid. Benzing: op. cit., p. 140.

140. Kaltenbrunner's report to Bormann, October 2, 1944; Kaltenbrunner Reports, p. 430.

141. Roeder deposition, July 2, 1950; LStA, Vol. IX, p. 185. Josef Müller: *Bis zur letzten Konsequenz*, p. 215.

142. Müller, p. 214.

143. Huppenkothen: copy, p. 13.

144. Ibid.

145. Ibid.

146. MPA VI, 7479, September 19, 1944; Canaris Personal File.

147. Schellenberg: op. cit., p. 412. Abshagen: op. cit., p. 254.

148. See Kaltenbrunner's report to Bormann, October 2, 1944; Kaltenbrunner Reports, p. 430 et seq.

149. Huppenkothen: copy, p. 8 et seq.

150. A line of defence repeated be-

fore the SS summary tribunal at Flossenbürg; see Note 229.

151. Grosse: op. cit., p. 2.
152. Ibid., p. 6. Fraenkel/Manvell: op. cit., p. 191.
153. Huppenkothen: copy, p. 11 et seq.
154. Ibid., p. 14.
155. Ibid., p. 14.
156. Ibid., p. 16.
157. Ibid., p. 15.
158. Ibid., p. 16.
159. Ibid., p. 16.
160. Ibid., pp. 15–17.
161. Ibid., p. 15.
162. Ibid., p. 17.
163. Kaltenbrunner's report to Bormann, September 29, 1944; Kaltenbrunner Reports, p. 425.
164. Huppenkothen: copy, p. 15.
165. Abshagen: op. cit., p. 244.
166. Ibid.
167. Munich Judgement, p. 22.
168. Ibid., p. 20.
169. Ibid., p. 22.
170. Ibid., p. 15 et seq.
171. Ibid., p. 11.
172. Ibid.
173. Müller: op. cit., p. 229.
174. Gruchmann: op. cit, pp. 314–15.
175. Ibid., p. 314.
176. Final Report, p. 1,151.
177. Munich Judgement, p. 12.
178. Bethge: op. cit., p. 810.
179. Bartz: op. cit., p. 189.
180. Judgement of the Augsburg Assize Court in the proceedings against Walter Huppenkothen and Otto Thorbeck (=Augsburg Judgement), October 15, 1955, pp. 16–17; photocopy in the records of Kammergericht Berlin.
181. Ibid., p. 17.
182. Ibid.
183. Bartz: op. cit., p. 261 (not in English edition).
184. Augsburg Judgement, p. 17. Abshagen: op. cit., p. 249.
185. Hans M. Lunding: sketch of "special prisoners' block" in *Die Nachhut*, Nos. 13/14, September 15, 1971, p. 13.
186. Munich Judgement, p. 33.
187. Huppenkothen: copy, p. 17.

188. Abshagen: op. cit., p. 251.
189. Augsburg Judgement, p. 43.
190. Ibid. Gert Buchheit: *Im Würgegriff der Politik*, p. 183.
191. Hans M. Lunding: *Stemplet fortroligt*, pp. 18, 39 et seq.
192. Augsburg Judgement, p. 43.
193. Abshagen: op. cit., p. 252.
194. Augsburg Judgement, p. 43.
195. Abshagen: op. cit., p. 252.
196. Huppenkothen: copy, p. 17.
197. Gruchmann: op. cit, pp. 319–27.
198. Ibid., p. 329.
199. Buchheit: *Geheimdienst*, p. 444.
200. Ibid. Grosse: op. cit., p. 3.
201. Hoffmann: op. cit., p. 476.
202. Huppenkothen deposition, record of witnesses' testimony in the trial of Walter Huppenkothen, February 4–14, 1951, Day 1, p. 193; photocopy in IfZ.
203. Ibid. Grosse: op. cit., p. 3.
204. Huppenkothen deposition, transcript, p. 205.
205. Buchheit: *Geheimdienst*, p. 445.
206. Huppenkothen deposition, transcript, p. 205.
207. Ibid.
208. Augsburg Judgement, p. 18.
209. Ibid., p. 21.
210. Munich Judgement, p. 30.
211. Augsburg Judgement, p. 21.
212. Munich Judgement, pp. 31–32.
213. Ibid., p. 33.
214. Augsburg Judgement, p. 19.
215. Ibid., p. 25.
216. Ibid., p. 26.
217. Ibid., pp. 26, 31.
218. Huppenkothen deposition, transcript, p. 193.
219. Augsburg Judgement, p. 51.
220. Ibid., p. 51.
221. Ibid., p. 52.
222. Ibid., pp. 2, 51–58.
223. Ibid., p. 31.
224. Assize Court (Landgericht München I) judgement against Walter Huppenkothen and Otto Thorbeck, February 16, 1953 (=Munich Judgement II), p. 10; photocopy in the records of Kammergericht Berlin.
225. Munich Judgement II, p. 15.
226. Augsburg Judgement, p. 43.

227. Munich Judgement II, p. 11.
228. *Die Welt*, October 1, 1955.
229. Augsburg Judgement, p. 31.
230. Ibid. Munich Judgement II, p. 16. *Die Welt*, February 14, 1951.
231. Ibid.
232. Augsburg Judgement, p. 43.
233. Lunding: op. cit., p. 107. Augsburg Judgement, p. 44. Buchheit: *Würgegriff*, p. 183. *Die Welt*, February 10, 1951.
234. Munich Judgement II, p. 23.
235. Aichholzer deposition, *Frankfurter Rundschau*, November 4, 1952.
236. Lunding: op. cit., p. 107. Müller: op. cit., p. 251.
237. Munich Judgement II, pp. 26-27.
238. Munich Judgement, p. 37.
239. Augsburg Judgement, p. 48.

240. Lunding: op. cit., p. 107. Munich Judgement, p. 37.
241. Fischer deposition, *Die Welt*, October 1, 1955.
242. *Neue Zeitung*, February 10, 1951.
243. Fischer deposition, *Die Welt*, October 1, 1955.
244. Augsburg Judgement, p. 45.
245. Lunding deposition, *Die Welt*, February 10, 1951.
246. Müller: op. cit., p. 252.
247. Ibid.
248. Aichholzer deposition, *Frankfurter Rundschau*, November 4, 1952.
249. Müller: op. cit., p. 252.
250. Ibid., p. 252.
251. Ibid., p. 253.
252. Ibid., p. 255.

APPENDIX 2

GLOSSARY

N. B. Extensive glossaries of German military and political terms, titles, acronyms etc. may be found in Heinz Höhne: *The Order of the Death's Head*, Secker & Warburg, 1969, and Hans Buchheim et al.: *The Anatomy of the SS State*, Collins, 1968, to whose compilers the present translator stands indebted. German military organization and its structural changes after 1933 are very fully treated in Robert J. O'Neill: *The German Army and the Nazi Party*, Cassell, 1966.

A-Agent   See Kriegsagent.

Abt.   See Abteilung.

Abteilung   1. A branch, section or subdivision of a department, head office or government authority (Amt, Amtsgruppe, Hauptamt, etc.), here translated "section." 2. A military unit or detachment up to battalion strength or equivalent level of command.

Abteilung Ausland   Foreign Intelligence Section of Amtsgruppe Auslandnachrichten und Abwehr. Later upgraded into Amtsgruppe Ausland (q.v.).

Abteilung L   Abteilung Landesverteidigung—National Defence Section of the Wehrmachtamt, formed late 1933.

Abteilung W   Abteilung Wehrwirtschafts- und Waffenwesen—Military Economics and Ordnance Section of the Wehrmachtamt, formed November 1934.

Abwehr   Lit. "defence," loosely applied to military intelligence in general and Amt Ausland/Abwehr in particular.

Abwehrnebenstelle   Abwehr suboffice or substation.

Abwehrpolizei   The Counterespionage Police. A branch of the Gestapo.

Abwehrstelle   Abwehr district headquarters or outstation.

a.D.   See ausser Dienst.

Adjutant   A far more elastic term in German than English, this may be applied to a regimental adjutant, flag lieutenant, personal staff officer to a ship's captain, aide-de-camp (ADC) or military assistant (MA).

Admiralität Admiralty of the Weimar Republic, previously known as the Reichsmarineamt, renamed the Marineleitung in 1920.

Afu See Agentenfunkgerät.

A.G. See Aktiengesellschaft.

Agentenfunkgerät Abwehr agent's portable radio transceiver.

Aktiengesellschaft Joint stock company, corporation.

Allgemeines Heeresamt General Army Department.

Allgemeines Wehrmachtamt General Armed Forces Department. Wartime (August 1939) successor of the Amtsgruppe Allgemeine Wehrmachtangelegenheiten.

Amt Head office, branch or directorate of a ministry. Sometimes an independent ministry, e.g. Auswärtiges Amt (q.v.). Here translated "department."

Amt Ausland/Abwehr The armed forces espionage, counterespionage, sabotage and foreign intelligence department headed by Admiral Canaris. Formed in August 1939 out of Amtsgruppe Auslandnachrichten und Abwehr; disbanded in 1944 and absorbed by the RSHA.

Amtsgruppe Branch or division of a central office or directorate (Amt). Here translated "branch."

Amtsgruppe Allgemeine Wehrmachtangelegenheiten General Armed Forces Affairs Branch of the OKW.

Amtsgruppe Ausland Foreign Affairs Branch of Amt Ausland/Abwehr (originally Abteilung Ausland).

Amtsgruppe Auslandnachrichten und Abwehr Foreign and Counterintelligence Branch of the OKW, formed June 1, 1938. Precursor of Amt Ausland/Abwehr.

Amtsgruppe Führungsstab Armed Forces Operations Staff Branch of the OKW, formed June 1, 1938.

AO See Auslands-Organisation.

Ast See Abwehrstelle.

Ausland/Abwehr Abbreviated form of Amt Ausland/Abwehr (q.v.).

Auslandsorganisation NSDAP agency charged with the care and supervision of Germans abroad.

ausser Dienst Retired, removed from the active list.

Auswärtiges Amt Foreign Office, Ministry of Foreign Affairs.

AWA See Amtsgruppe Allgemeine Wehrmachtangelegenheiten, also Allgemeines Wehrmachtamt.

"Barbarossa" Code name for the German invasion of Russia, June 22, 1941.

Bau-Lehr-Bataillon z.b.V. 800 See Brandenburg.

Baulehrkompagnie 800 See Brandenburg.

Brandenburg Appellation of Abwehr II combat unit formed in 1939 by Captain von Hippel and successively expanded from company to battalion, regimental and, finally, divisional strength.

Bürgerwehr Militia or citizens' defence force (early post-1918 period).

Chef der Sicherheitspolizei und des SD Chief of the Security Police and

Security Service. Heydrich until 1942, then—after an interregnum—Kaltenbrunner.

DAF   See Deutsche Arbeitsfront.

Deutsche Arbeitsfront   German Labour Front. An umbrella organization comprising "all working Germans," employees and employers alike.

Deutsches Nachrichtenbüro   German News Agency.

DNB   See Deutsches Nachrichtenbüro.

Einsatzgruppe   Operational group or task force of the Sipo and SD employed on special missions (usually liquidations) in occupied territory. Consisted of up to six Einsatzkommandos.

Einsatzkommando   Sipo detachment forming part of an Einsatzgruppe.

Einwohnerwehr   Home Guard or citizens' defence force (early post-1918 period).

E-Offizier   See Ergänzungsoffizier.

Ergänzungsoffizier   Supernumerary or re-engaged officer.

Etappe   Staging post or base, specifically applied to depots and intelligence-gathering centres of the German Navy on foreign soil.

F-   In compound words relating to Abwehr functions, denotes "peacetime" or "on a peacetime footing," e.g. F-Agent.

F-Agent   See Friedensagent.

FAK   See Frontaufklärungskommando.

"Fall Weiss"   "Contingency White." Code name for German invasion of Poland.

Feldgericht   Field court-martial.

FHO   See Fremde Heere Ost.

FHW   See Fremde Heere West.

Forschungsamt   Research Department. The Third Reich agency controlled by Göring and responsible for telecommunications monitoring (e.g. phone tapping, telegraphic and teletype intercepts).

Freikorps   Volunteer Corps. Military or paramilitary formations recruited to oppose post-1918 revolutionaries in Germany, commonly identified by the names of their commanding officers.

Fremde Heere Ost   The Foreign Armies East Section (12. Abt) of the OKH.

Fremde Heere West   The Foreign Armies West Section (3. Abt) of the OKH.

Friedensagent   Abwehr agent employed in peacetime.

Frontaufklärungskommando   Forward Reconnaissance Detachment.

Führer   Leader, chief, commander. Except when used in compounds, e.g Gruppenführer, a title reserved for Hitler alone.

Führungsoffizier   Officer-controller responsible for supervising Abwehr agents at base, "control."

Garde-Kavallerie-Schützen-Division   Guards Cavalry Rifle Division. Freikorps formation employed to crush the Spartacists in January 1919.

Garde-Kavallerie-Schützenkorps   Expanded GKSD, three divisions strong.

Gau   Main territorial unit of the NSDAP. Germany was divided into forty-two Gaue, with the Auslands-Organisation (q.v.) constituting the forty-third.

Gauleiter Highest-ranking NSDAP official in a Gau, responsible for all political and economic activity, mobilization of labour and civil defence.

Geheime Feldpolizei Secret Field Police. Originally a force of security personnel formed to guard the King and Chancellor in Wilhelminian Germany. Under the Third Reich, the executive arm of the Abwehr charged with maintaining security inside the armed forces. Largely taken over by the Sipo and SD in 1942.

Geheime Kommandosache A secret military document (civilian equivalent: geheime Reichssache).

Geheime Reichssache Secret document (military equivalent: geheime Kommandosache).

Geheimer Meldedienst Secret Intelligence Service. Officially designated Abteilung I of Amt Ausland/Abwehr, this section performed intelligence tasks abroad and constituted the secret service proper.

Geheimes Staatspolizeiamt National headquarters of the Gestapo, absorbed into the RSHA in 1939.

Geheime Staatspolizei Secret State Police, or Amt IV of the RSHA.

Gemeindepolizei Municipal police.

Gendarmerie Rural police, including motorized traffic control units.

Generalstab des Heeres Army General Staff, formed on June 1, 1935, out of the old Truppenamt (q.v.).

Gesandtschaftsrat Legation or embassy counsellor in the Foreign Service.

Gestapa See Geheimes Staatspolizeiamt.

Gestapo See Geheime Staatspolizei.

GFP See Geheime Feldpolizei.

GKSD See Garde-Kavallerie-Schützen-Division.

GKSK See Garde-Kavallerie-Schützenkorps.

Gleichschaltung A term denoting co-ordination, alignment or streamlining, specifically applied to the Nazification of all sectors of German national life after 1933.

GmbH "Geschäft mit beschränkter Haftung"—limited liability company (="Ltd.").

Grenzpolizei Frontier Police, a force controlled by the Gestapo.

Gruppe Group, a multipurpose term applied to an *ad hoc* military formation or an administrative section.

Hauptamt Central office, directorate or administrative headquarters.

Hauptamt Sicherheitspolizei Headquarters of the Security Police (Gestapo and Kripo), integrated in the RSHA in 1939.

Hauskapelle Lit. "private orchestra." Intelligence-gathering team of three to half a dozen agents recruited and controlled by individual Abwehr outstations.

Heeresanwalt Army legal officer or counsel.

Heeresleitung Army Directorate, renamed Oberkommando des Heeres (OKH) May 21, 1935.

Hencke-Dienst Foreign Office intelligence service headed by Sandor Hencke.

Hochverrat High treason. An attempt to overthrow the government or change the constitution by force, as defined in Articles 80–87 of the Reich Penal Code (cf. Landesverrat).

Höherer SS- und Polizeiführer Senior SS and Police Commander. Himmler's personal representative in each Wehrkreis and liaison officer with the military district commander and other senior regional authorities. Also established in occupied territories. Nominally commanded all SS and police units in his area.

HSSPf See Höherer SS- und Polizeiführer.

Ic Intelligence (staff) officer in a military headquarters or formation.

Justizrat Title conferred on distinguished lawyers, judges, etc.

K- In compound words relating to Abwehr functions, denotes "wartime" or "on a wartime footing," e.g. K-network.

Kapellmeister Lit. "conductor" or "band leader," i.e. the senior agent in a Hauskapelle (q.v.).

KO See Kriegsorganisation.

KO-Nebenstelle Suboffice or substation of a KO (q.v.).

KPD Original Communist Party of Germany (as distinct from the DKP or reconstituted German Communist Party legalized in West Germany during 1968).

Kriegsagent Agent mobilized at, or just before, the outbreak of war.

Kriegsgericht Court-martial.

Kriegsgerichtsrat Court-martial counsel.

Kriegsorganisation An Abwehr wartime intelligence network based abroad.

Kriminalassistent (Roughly) detective sergeant.

Kriminalinspektor (Roughly) detective inspector.

Kriminalkommissar (Roughly) detective superintendent.

Kriminaloberinspektor (Roughly) detective chief inspector.

Kriminalpolizei The Criminal Police or Criminal Investigation Department, which combined with the Gestapo to form the Sicherheitspolizei and became RSHA-Amt V in 1939.

Kriminalrat (Roughly) detective chief superintendent.

Kripo See Kriminalpolizei.

K-Verbände Abwehr combat detachments or combat teams assigned to sabotage or capture enemy key points ahead of an invasion force.

Land (pl. Länder) One of the fifteen territorial divisions of Republican Germany, each with its own government.

Landesverrat Treasonable activity against the state in its relation to other countries, e.g. divulging official secrets to a foreign power (cf. Hochverrat).

Landgericht District court of the first instance.

Landgerichtsrat District court counsel.

Legationsrat Legation or embassy counsellor in the Foreign Service.

Lehrregiment Brandenburg See Brandenburg.

Leiter Head, chief or principal of an office, department or authority.

Leitstelle A regional headquarters of the Gestapo or Kripo established at a military district headquarters or in the administrative capital of a Land or territory annexed after 1939.

Marineamt See Reichsmarineamt.

Marineleitung Navy Directorate (the German Admiralty of the Republican and immediately post-Republican period).

Ministerialdirektor Head of department in a ministry. Senior civil servant approximating to an Assistant Secretary.

Ministerialrat Senior civil servant, usually head of a ministry section.

Nationalsozialistische Deutsche Arbeiterpartei National Socialist German Labour Party—the official title of the Nazi Party.

Nebenstelle Substation or suboffice of an organization or agency.

NS National Socialist, Nazi.

NSDAP See Nationalsozialistische Deutsche Arbeiterpartei.

ObdH See Oberbefehlshaber des Heeres.

Oberbefehlshaber des Heeres Commander in Chief of the Army.

Oberkommando der Luftwaffe High Command of the Air Force.

Oberkommando der Marine High Command of the Navy.

Oberkommando der Wehrmacht High Command of the Armed Forces.

Oberkommando des Heeres High Command of the Army.

Oberpräsident Senior administrative official in a Prussian province.

Oberquartiermeister I, II, III, IV and V (Deputy) Chiefs of the Army General Staff responsible for various functions thereof, e.g. Operations (1. Abt.), Organization (2. Abt.), Training (4. Abt.), Military Science (7. Abt.), etc. (as of September 1939).

Oberregierungsrat Senior government counsellor in the Higher Civil Service.

Oberstkriegsgerichtsrat Judge advocate of colonel's rank.

OKH See Oberkommando des Heeres.

OKL See Oberkommando der Luftwaffe.

OKM See Oberkommando der Marine.

OKW See Oberkommando der Wehrmacht.

Oqu I–V See Oberquartiermeister I, II, III, IV and V.

Ordnungspolizei Regular uniformed police.

Orpo See Ordnungspolizei.

OSS Office of Strategic Services. U.S. intelligence agency established during World War II for the purpose of acquiring and evaluating information about the enemy and enemy-occupied territory.

Politische Feldpolizei Original name of the (Wilhelminian) Geheime Feldpolizei (q.v.).

Politische Polizei Political Police of the Weimar period, absorbed by the Gestapo and expanded after 1933.

Referat Specialist subsection of a department or headquarters, here translated "desk."

Referendar Higher Civil Service probationer undergoing in-service training between passing the first state examination and attempting the second.

Referent Official in charge of a Referat.

Regierungsrat Government counsellor. The lowest grade in the Higher Civil Service.

Reichsbanner Nominally non-party defence founded in 1924 by SPD politicians to protect the Weimar Republic against extremist elements.

Reichsführer-SS und Chef der Deutschen Polizei Reich Commander of the SS and Chief of the German Police. Himmler's title from June 1936.

Reichsgericht Germany's Supreme Court between 1879 and 1945.

Reichskriegsanwaltschaft Judge Advocates' Bench.

Reichskriegsgericht (Supreme) Reich Court-Martial.

Reichskriegsgerichtsrat Reich court-martial counsel.

Reichskriegsministerium Reich War Ministry, constituted May 21, 1935 (formerly Reichswehrministerium).

Reichskriminalpolizeiamt Headquarters of the Kripo, or RSHA-Amt V.

Reichsleiter Highest-ranking Nazi Party official, usually holding a ministerial or senior administrative post.

Reichsmarine Republican Navy.

Reichsmarineamt German Admiralty founded under Wilhelm II. Also temporarily applied to its Republican successor.

Reichssicherheitshauptamt Central State Security Bureau (RSHA). Formed in 1939, this combined the Sicherheitspolizei (Gestapo and Kripo) and the SD.

Reichswehr Republican Armed Forces (a term retained by the Nazis until May 21, 1935, when it was changed to Wehrmacht).

Reichswehrgruppenkommando Republican military area command headquarters.

Reiseagent Lit. "travel agent," i.e. Abwehr scout or mobile informant.

RfSSuChdDtPol See Reichsführer-SS und Chef der Deutschen Polizei.

Rittmeister Captain (of cavalry).

RKG See Reichskriegsgericht.

RKM See Reichskriegsministerium.

RKPA See Reichskriminalpolizeiamt.

RSHA See Reichssicherheitshauptamt.

S- In compound words relating to Abwehr functions, stands either for "sabotage," as in S-Verbände (q.v.), or for "tension" (*Spannung*), as in S-Agent (q.v.).

SA See Sturmabteilung.

S-Agent See Spannungsagent.

Schiffsbefragungsdienst Marine Interrogation Service, an Abwehr I agency responsible for procuring intelligence from the crews of German ships entering foreign ports.

"Schulung" "Training." Original code name for Rhineland reoccupation.

Schupo See Schutzpolizei.

Schutzpolizei Lit. "Protection Police." Regular uniformed municipal and rural constabulary forming the bulk of the Ordnungspolizei.

Schutzstaffel Lit. "Protection Detachment." The SS, formed 1925.

SD See Sicherheitsdienst des RfSS.

SD-Hauptamt Headquarters of the SD, or Central Security Department.

Seekriegsleitung Directorate of Naval Warfare.

Servicio Información Policía Militar Spanish military intelligence and internal security service (under Franco).

Servizio Informazioni Militari Italian military intelligence service.

SFK See Sudetendeutsches Freikorps.

Sicherheitsdienst des RfSS Security Service of the Reichsführer-SS, formed under Heydrich in 1932 and designed to be the NSDAP's sole intelligence agency.

Sicherheitspolizei The Security Police, comprising the Gestapo and Kripo.

SIM See Servizio Informazioni Militari.

SIPM See Servicio Información Policía Militar.

Sipo See Sicherheitspolizei.

SIS (British) Secret Intelligence Service.

Sittenpolizei Division of Kriminalpolizei responsible for investigating sexual offences, pornography, etc.—loosely, Vice Squad.

Sonderführer K Civilian employed as a wartime supernumerary of officer status.

Sonderstab W Special working party set up to administer German aid to Franco.

Sozialdemokratische Partei Deutschlands German Social Democratic Party, thus entitled in 1890 after its precursor, the German Social Democratic Labour Party, had been legislated out of existence by Bismarck. The SPD lost its left wing (USPD) to the radical socialists in 1916–17 but emerged as the strongest single party in the early years after World War I. It lost its dominant role after the 1920s and was banned by the Nazis in 1933.

Spannungsagent Lit. "tension agent." Abwehr agent mobilized in times of international crisis.

SPD See Sozialdemokratische Partei Deutschlands.

Spielmaterial False or doctored data fed to an enemy—disinformation.

SS See Schutzstaffel.

SS-Brigadeführer SS major general.

SS-Führungshauptamt Operations Department of the entire SS, responsible for every aspect of its activities except the tactical employment of Waffen-SS units in the field.

SS-Gruppenführer SS lieutenant general.

SS-Hauptsturmführer SS captain.

SS-Oberführer SS brigadier (U.S.: brigadier general).

SS-Obergruppenführer SS general.

SS-Oberstgruppenführer SS colonel general (no British or U.S. equivalent).

SS-Obersturmbannführer SS lieutenant colonel.

SS-Rottenführer SS corporal.

SS-Standartenführer SS colonel.

SS-Sturmbannführer SS major.

SS-Untersturmführer SS lieutenant.

SS-Verfügungstruppe The militarized formations of the SS, renamed the Waffen-SS in winter 1939–40.

Staatspolizei Originally the Prussian Political Police. Later the Nazi Political Police, i.e. the Gestapo.

Staatspolizeileitstelle Regional Gestapo HQ.

Staatspolizeistelle District Gestapo HQ, co-ordinated by but not subordinate to a Stapoleitstelle.

Stahlhelm Nationalist ex-servicemen's association founded in 1918. Compulsorily absorbed into the SA in 1933.

Stapo See Staatspolizei.

Stapoleitstelle See Staatspolizeileitstelle.

Stapostelle See Staatspolizeistelle.

Stelle A very broad term meaning (a) place, post or position; (b) official establishment or department.

Sturmabteilung Lit. "assault detachment." The SA ("Brownshirts" or Stormtroopers) who formed the original shock troops of the NSDAP. Founded 1921, purged 1934 and thereafter eclipsed by the SS.

Sudetendeutsches Freikorps Sudeten German Volunteer Corps, formed September 1938.

S-Verbände Abwehr sabotage teams.

Totenkopf-Verbände Death's Head SS units employed as concentration camp guards. In 1939 they constituted the nucleus of the SST Division, an early field formation of the Waffen-SS.

Truppenamt Effectively the Reichswehr's Army General Staff (an institution prohibited by the Versailles Treaty). It became the Generalstab des Heeres under Wehrmacht auspices on June 1, 1935.

Unabhängige Sozialdemokratische Partei Deutschlands Independent German Social Democratic Party. Radical splinter group of the SPD, formed in 1917. The left wing joined the Communists in 1920, the remainder merged with the so-called "Majority Socialists" in 1922.

Unternehmen "Barbarossa" Code name for invasion of Russia.

Unternehmen "Felix" Code name for OKW plan to capture Gibraltar.

Unternehmen "Felsennest" Operation "Eyrie." Code name for Canaris's original plan to capture Gibraltar.

Unternehmen "Feuerzauber" Operation "Fire-Magic." Code name for German airlift of Franco troops and supplies from Morocco to the Spanish mainland.

Unternehmen "Grün" Operation "Green." Code name for German invasion of Czechoslovakia.

Unternehmen "Haifisch" Operation "Shark." Code name for diversionary manoeuvres in the West to mask preparations for "Barbarossa."

Unternehmen "Marita" Code name for German invasion of Greece.

Unternehmen "Seelöwe" Operation "Sea Lion." Code name for German invasion of England.

USPD See Unabhängige Sozialdemokratische Partei Deutschlands.

U-Stelle Cover address for use by Abwehr couriers and agents.

Verfügungstruppe The militarized formations of the SS, renamed Waffen-SS in the winter of 1939–40.

Vestärkter Grenzaufsichtsdienst Augmented Frontier Surveillance Service. A function of Abwehr III.

Vertrauensmann German equivalent of the French *homme de confiance*. "Trusted person," i.e. intelligence agent or informant.

V-Mann See Vertrauensmann.

Volksdeutsche Mittelstelle Ethnic German Centre. One of the organizations through which contact was maintained with Germans abroad. Largely SS-run.

Volksdeutscher Ethnic German. Member of a German minority in a foreign country.

WA See Wehrmachtamt.

Waffen-SS Fully militarized SS formations, initially composed of the Verfügungstruppe and Totenkopf-Verbände, later including non-German units.

Wehrkreis Military district, specified by Roman numeral.

Wehrmachtamt Armed Forces Department, established late 1933 as a successor to the Ministerialamt of the Reichswehr Ministry.

Wehrmachtführungsamt Armed Forces Operations Department. Wartime (August 1939) successor of Amtsgruppe Führungsstab.

Wehrmachtjustiz Armed Forces Judicature.

Weserübung "Weser Exercise." Code name for German invasion of Norway.

WFA See Amtsgruppe Führungsstab, also Wehrmacht-Führungsamt.

Winterübung "Winter Exercise." Final code name for Rhineland reoccupation.

z.b.V. zur besonderen Verwendung—for special employment. Used attributively, "special duties . . ."

ZR Zentralabteilung, Rechtswesen. The legal division of the Abwehr's Central or Co-ordinating Section.

z.V. zur Verfügung—available (for duty, reassignment, etc.). Of an officer not holding a specific appointment but still on the active list.

APPENDIX 3

BIBLIOGRAPHY

UNPUBLISHED SOURCES

Akten der Staatsanwaltschaft am Landgericht Lüneburg (LStA), Criminal Proceedings Against Dr. Manfred Roeder, 15 vols.

Akten des Politischen Archivs des Auswärtigen Amtes, Bonn (photocopies in the possession of Herr Günter Peis).

Anon.: "Zarenoffiziere für Spaniens Internationale Brigaden" (about 1950); private archive.

Augsburg Judgement (Urteil des Schwurgerichts beim Landgericht München I gegen Walter Huppenkothen und Otto Thorbeck), October 15, 1955; Archives of Kammergericht Berlin.

Best, Werner: "Die deutsche Abwehrpolizei bis 1945"; in the possession of Dr. Werner Best.

———: "Wilhelm Canaris," undated. Privately owned by Dr. Best.

Bidlingmaier: "Gedächtnisprotokoll über die Befragung des Admirals a.D. Conrad Patzig am 18./19. 1.1966"; Militärgeschichtliches Forschungsamt, Freiburg.

Buchheit, Gert: "Aktion 'V7,'" undated; in the possession of Dr. Buchheit.

Bundesarchiv (BA), Koblenz.

Bundesarchiv/Militärarchiv (BA/MA), Freiburg.

Document Center, West Berlin.

Final Report by Staatsanwalt Dr. Finck on the criminal proceedings against Dr. Manfred Roeder, Lüneburg 1951; Ministry of Justice Archives, Land Niedersachsen.

Franzbach/Peis. Tape recording of a conversation between Max Franzbach and Günter Peis, October 29, 1974; in the possession of Herr Peis.

Gempp, Friedrich: "Geheimer Nachrichtendienst und Spionageabwehr des Heeres"; National Archives (NA), Alexandria (U.S.A.), Microfilm Groups ML68 and T-77.

German Embassy, Madrid. Diary entries 1941–45; Dr. Maser Archive.

Grosse, Will: "Der Judenstern—eine Idee von Canaris?", undated; Grosse estate.

Bibliography 673

————: "Im Hintergrund der Admiral Canaris," undated; Grosse estate.

Heimbach, Lothar: "Die Stevens-Best Affäre," October 26, 1967; Heimbach estate.

Herzner papers; in the possession of Herr Günter Peis.

Heumann, Heinz: "Bericht über die 'Brandenburg,'" June 13, 1965; in the possession of Dr. Buchheit.

Hussl, Hans: "Flucht des Vermehren mit seiner Frau," notes dated July 2, 1965; in the possession of Dr. Buchheit.

Institut für Zeitgeschichte (IfZ), Munich. Documents and written depositions.

Kapp Putsch records; National Archives (NA), Alexandria (U.S.A.), Microfilm Group T-235.

Kozaczuk, Wladislaw: "Die Schlacht um Geheimnisse" (German translator's MS), undated; in the possession of Dr. Buchheit.

Kremer von Auenrode/Peis. Tape recording of a conversation between Frau von Auenrode and Günter Peis; in the possession of Herr Peis.

Luetgebrune estate; National Archives (NA), Alexandria (U.S.A.), Microfilm Group T-253.

Miscellaneous material privately owned by Dr. Gert Buchheit, Boris Celovsky, Professor Harold C. Deutsch, Heinrich Fraenkel, David Irving, Dr. Robert M. Kempner, Günter Peis, Alexander von Pfuhlstein, Erich Ferdinand Pruck, Dr. Bernt Richter, Franz Seubert, Robert Spiering and Otto Wagner.

Munich Judgement (Urteil des Schwurgerichts beim Landgericht München I gegen Walter Huppenkothen), February 16, 1951; Archives of Kammergericht Berlin.

Munich Judgement II (Urteil des Schwurgerichts beim Landgericht München I gegen Walter Huppenkothen und Otto Thorbeck), February 16, 1953; Archives of Kammergericht Berlin.

Ohlendorf, Otto: "Wie kam es zu meinem Russlandeinsatz?" Statement prepared by Otto Ohlendorf for his trial by the U. S. Military Tribunal, undated; in the possession of Frau Käthe Ohlendorf.

OKH records; National Archives (NA), Alexandria (U.S.A.), Microfilm Group T-78.

OKW records; National Archives (NA), Alexandria (U.S.A.), Microfilm Group T-77.

Personal Staff of the Reichsführer-SS and Chief of the German Police, records thereof; National Archives (NA), Alexandria (U.S.A.), Microfilm Group T-175.

Pfuhlstein, Alexander von: "Bericht über meine Erlebnisse in Verbindung mit Herrn Heinz," June 10, 1953; in the possession of Herr von Pfuhlstein.

Pruck, Erich Ferdinand: "Admiral Wilhelm Canaris," undated; in the possession of Herr Pruck.

————: "Gedanken über den geheimen militärischen Meldedienst," undated; in the possession of Herr Pruck.

————: "Warnzeichen Rot," undated; in the possession of Herr Pruck.

Richter, Bernt: "Interview mit Paul Kanstein," June 24, 1971; in the possession of Dr. Richter.
Sas, Gisbertus. Deposition by Lieutenant Colonel Gisbertus Sas, March 16, 1948, Enquetecommisserie Regeringsbeleid 1940–45 (German translation); in the possession of Rechtsanwalt Seidel, Munich.
Wagner, Otto: "Bericht"; in the possession of Herr Wagner.
————: "Wilhelm Canaris," undated; in the possession of Herr Wagner.
Wolff, Karl: "Hitler und Franco," undated; in the possession of Herr Wolff.
Wulf, Josef: "Die SS," 1965; Wulf Archive.

PUBLISHED SOURCES

Akten zur Deutschen Auswärtigen Politik (ADAP), Series D, 5 vols.; Baden-Baden, 1950–56.
American People's Encyclopedia, The; New York, 1969.
Brockhaus' Conversations-Lexikon; Leipzig, 1885.
Brockhaus Enzyklopädie; 1968.
Domarus, Max: *Hitler—Reden und Proklamationen 1932–1945;* Würzburg, 1962–63.
Freund, Michael: *Deutsche Geschichte;* Gütersloh, 1973.
Genealogisches Handbuch des Adels, "Gräfliche Häuser, A," Vol. VI; Limburg, Lahn, 1970.
IMT (proceedings of the International Military Tribunal, Nuremberg), 42 vols.; Nuremberg, 1949.
Internationales Bibliographisches Archiv (Munzinger Archiv).
Kriegstagebuch des Oberkommandos der Wehrmacht; Frankfurt am Main, 1965.
Neue Deutsche Biographie; Berlin, 1957.
Philip, Dr. Albrecht (ed.): *Die Ursachen des Deutschen Zusammenbruchs im Jahre 1918,* Vols. 9 and 10, Half-vols. 1 and 2; Berlin, 1928.
Ploetz, A. G.: *Geschichte des Zweiten Weltkriegs;* Würzburg, 1960.
Reichstag Proceedings, 3rd Electoral Period 1924, Vol. 391.
Tessin, Georg: *Verbände und Truppen der deutschen Wehrmacht und Waffen-SS im Zweiten Weltkrieg 1939–1945;* Osnabrück, 1975.
Weyers Flottenkalender.

BOOKS

Abshagen, Karl Heinz: *Canaris,* translated by A. H. Brodrick; Hutchinson, London, 1956.
Alboldt, E.: *Die Tragödie der alten deutschen Marine;* Berlin, 1928.
Alexander, Günter: *So ging Deutschland in die Falle;* Düsseldorf, 1976.
Aronson, Shlomo: *Heydrich und die Anfänge des SD und der Gestapo 1931–1935;* Berlin, 1966.

Bartz, Karl: *The Downfall of the German Secret Service*; Kimber, London, 1956.

Baumann, Felix: *Die Weltkriegsspionage*; Munich, 1931.

Benedikt, Heinrich: *Geschichte der Republik Österreich*; Vienna, 1954.

Bennecke, Heinrich: *Die Reichswehr und der Röhm-Putsch*; Munich and Vienna, 1964.

Benoist-Méchin, J.: *Histoire de l'armée allemande*; Paris, 1964–66.

Benzing, Klaus: *Der Admiral*; Nördlingen, 1973.

Bethge, Eberhard: *Dietrich Bonhoeffer*, translated by Erich Mosbacher and others; Collins, London, 1970.

Bezymenski, Lev: *Sonderakte "Barbarossa"*; Stuttgart, 1968.

Bösch, Hermann: *Heeresrichter Dr. Karl Sack im Widerstand*; Munich, 1967.

Boveri, Margret: *Treason in the Twentieth Century*; MacDonald, London, 1961.

Bracher, Karl Dietrich: *The German Dictatorship*; Weidenfeld & Nicolson, London, 1971.

Breyer, Richard: *Das Deutsche Reich und Polen 1932–1937*; Würzburg, 1955.

Brinkmann, Jürgen: *Orden und Ehrenzeichen des "Dritten Reiches"*; Minden, 1976.

Brissaud, André: *Canaris*, translated and edited by Ian Colvin; Weidenfeld & Nicolson, London, 1973.

Broszat, Martin: *Nationalsozialistische Polenpolitik*; Stuttgart, 1961.

Broué, Pierre, and Témime, Émile: *The Revolution and the Civil War in Spain*, translated by Tony White; Faber, London, 1972.

Brown, Anthony Cave: *Bodyguard of Lies*; W. H. Allen, London, 1976.

Buchheim, Broszat, Jacobsen and Krausnick: *The Anatomy of the SS State*, translated by R. H. Barry, Marian Jackson and Dorothy Long; Collins, London, 1968.

Buchheit, Gert: *Der deutsche Geheimdienst*; Munich, 1966.

———: *Im Würgegriff der Politik*; Landshut, 1974.

———: *Soldatentum und Rebellion*; Rastatt, 1961.

Bullock, Alan: *Hitler: a Study in Tyranny*; Odhams, London, 1952, rev. 1964.

Bund der Deckoffiziere: *Deckoffiziere der Deutschen Marine*; Berlin, 1933.

Burdick, Charles B.: *Germany's Military Strategy and Spain in World War II*; Syracuse, 1968.

Carsten, Francis L.: *The Reichswehr and Politics: 1918–1933*; Oxford University Press, 1966.

Celovsky, Boris: *Das Münchner Abkommen 1938*; Stuttgart, 1958.

Charisius, Albrecht, and Mader, Julius: *Nicht länger geheim*; East Berlin, 1969.

Christensen, Chr. P.: *Letzte Kaperfahrt nach Quiriquina*; Berlin, 1934.

Colvin, Ian: *Chief of Intelligence*; Gollancz, London, 1951 and Mann, Maidstone, 1973.

Conquest, Robert: *The Great Terror*; Macmillan & Co., London, 1968.

Cookridge, E. H.: *The Third Man*; Arthur Barker, London, 1968.

Crankshaw, Edward: *The Gestapo*; Putnam, London, 1956.

Crozier, Brian: *Franco*; Eyre & Spottiswoode, London, 1967.

Dahms, Hellmuth Günther: *Der spanische Bürgerkrieg*; Tübingen, 1962.

Dallin, Alexander: *German Rule in Russia 1941–1944*; Macmillan & Co., London, 1957.

Dallin, David J.: *Soviet Espionage*; Geoffrey Cumberledge, Oxford University Press, London, 1956.

Davis, Melton S.: *Who defends Rome?*; Allen & Unwin, London, 1973.

Deacon, Richard: *A History of the British Secret Service*; Frederick Muller, London, 1969.

Delarue, Jacques: *The History of the Gestapo*, translated by Mervyn Savill; Macdonald, London, 1964.

Detwiler, Donald S.: *Hitler, Franco und Gibraltar*; Wiesbaden, 1962.

Deutsch, Harold C.: *Hitler and His Generals: The Hidden Crisis, January–June 1938*; Oxford University Press, 1975.

————: *The Conspiracy Against Hitler in the Twilight War*; Oxford University Press, London, 1968.

Deutsche Geschichte seit dem Ersten Weltkrieg (3 vols.); Stuttgart, 1971–73.

Dönitz, Karl: *Zehn Jahre und zwanzig Tage*; Frankfurt and Bonn, 1964. *Ten Years and Twenty Days*, translated by R. H. Stevens; Weidenfeld & Nicolson, London, 1959.

Donnevert, Richard: *Wehrmacht und Partei*; Leipzig, 1938.

Doussinague, José María: *España tenía razón*; Madrid, 1950.

Dülffer, Jost: *Weimar, Hitler und die Marine*; Düsseldorf, 1973.

Dulles, Allen W.: *Germany's Underground*; Macmillan, New York, 1947.

Ehlers, Dieter: *Technik und Moral einer Verschwörung*; Bonn, 1964.

Enseling, Alf: *Die Weltbühne*; Münster, 1962.

Erger, Johannes: *Der Kapp-Lüttwitz-Putsch*; Düsseldorf, 1967.

Faber du Faur: *Macht und Ohnmacht*; Stuttgart, 1953.

Fabry, Philipp W.: *Der Hitler-Stalin-Pakt 1939–1941*; Darmstadt, 1962.

Farago, Ladislas: *The Game of the Foxes*; New York, 1971.

Fest, Joachim C.: *Hitler*, translated by Richard and Clara Winston; Weidenfeld & Nicolson, London, 1974.

Fischer, Alexander: *Sowjetische Deutschlandpolitik im Zweiten Weltkrieg*; Stuttgart, 1975.

Fischer, Fritz: *Griff nach der Weltmacht*; Düsseldorf, 1961.

Fischer, Gerhard: *Die Irrlichter*; Valparaiso, 1953.

Foerster, Wolfgang: *Generaloberst Ludwig Beck*; Munich, 1953.

Foertsch, Hermann: *Schuld und Verhängnis*; Stuttgart, 1951.

Ford, Corey: *Donovan of OSS*; Robert Hale, London, 1971.

Fraenkel, Heinrich, and Manvell, Roger: *The Canaris Conspiracy*; Wm. Heinemann, London, 1969.

Furtwängler, Franz Josef: *Männer, die ich sah und kannte*; Hamburg, 1951.

Gaxotte, Pierre: *Friedrich der Grosse* (German translation); Frankfurt, Berlin, Vienna, 1973.

Gehlen, Reinhard: *The Service*; New York, 1972.

Gessler, Otto: *Reichswehrpolitik in der Weimarerzeit*; Stuttgart, 1958.

Gisevius, Hans Bernd: *Bis zum bitteren Ende;* Hamburg and Berlin/Frankfurt, 1947 and 1964. *To the Bitter End,* translated by Richard and Clara Winston; Jonathan Cape, London, 1948.

Giskes, Hermann: *Spione überspielen Spione;* Hamburg, 1959.

Goebbels, Joseph: *The Goebbels Diaries,* edited and translated by Louis P. Lochner; Hamish Hamilton, London, 1948.

Göhring, Martin:*Bismarcks Erben 1890–1945,* Wiesbaden, 1958.

Görlitz, Walter: *Generalfeldmarschall Keitel—Verbrecher oder Offizier?;* Göttingen, Berlin, Frankfurt, 1961.

Greiner, Helmuth: *Die Oberste Wehrmachtführung;* Wiesbaden, 1951.

Gröner, Erich: *Die deutschen Kriegschiffe 1815–1945;* Munich, 1966.

Grunberger, Richard: *Red Rising in Bavaria;* Arthur Barker, London, 1973.

Grunfeld, Frederic V.: *The Hitler File;* Weidenfeld & Nicolson, London, 1974.

Hagen, Walter: *Die geheime Front;* Linz/Vienna, 1950.

Halder, Franz: *Kriegstagebuch Band I und II;* Stuttgart, 1963.

Hannover-Drück, Elisabeth, and Hannover, Heinrich: *Der Mord an Rosa Luxemburg und Karl Liebknecht;* Frankfurt, 1967.

Hassell, Ulrich von: *Vom anderen Deutschland;* Zurich, Freiburg, 1946. *The von Hassell Diaries;* Hamish Hamilton, London, 1948.

Helmdach, Erich: *Überfall?;* Neckargemünd, 1975.

Henke, Josef: *England in Hitlers politischem Kalkül 1935–1939;* Boppard, 1973.

Hilberg, Raul: *The Destruction of the European Jews;* W. H. Allen, London, 1961.

Hill, Leonidas E. (ed.): *Die Weizsäcker-Papiere 1933–1950;* Frankfurt, Berlin, Vienna, 1974.

Hochdorf, Max: *Rosa Luxemburg;* Berlin, 1924.

Hoepke, Klaus-Peter: *Die deutsche Rechte und der italienische Faschismus;* Düsseldorf, 1968.

Hoffman, Peter: *Widerstand, Staatsstreich, Attentat;* Munich, 1970.

Höhne, Heinz: *The Order of the Death's Head,* translated by Richard Barry; Secker & Warburg, London, 1969.

————: *Codeword: Direktor,* translated by Richard Barry; Secker & Warburg, London, 1971.

Hossbach, Friedrich: *Zwischen Wehrmacht und Hitler 1934–1938;* Wolfenbüttel and Hanover, 1949.

Irving, David: *Hitler's War;* Hodder & Stoughton, London, 1977.

Jackson, Gabriel: *A Concise History of the Spanish Civil War;* Thames and Hudson, London, 1974.

Jacobsen, Hans-Adolf: *Nationalsozialistische Aussenpolitik 1933–1938;* Frankfurt and Berlin, 1968.

Jaksch, Wenzel: *Europas Weg nach Potsdam;* Stuttgart, 1958.

Jasper, Gotthard (ed.): *Von Weimar zu Hitler 1930–1933;* Frankfurt, 1963.

Jong, Louis de: *Die deutsche Fünfte Kolonne im Zweiten Weltkrieg;* Stuttgart, 1959.

Jünger, Ernst (ed.): *Krieg und Krieger;* Berlin, 1930.

Kaltenbrunner, Ernst: *Spiegelbild einer Verschwörung* (the Kaltenbrunner Reports to Bormann and Hitler on the coup of July 20, 1944), edited by Archiv Peter für historische und zeitgeschichtliche Dokumentation; Seewald Verlag, Stuttgart, 1961.

Kameradschaft der 3. Marine-Brigade: *Die 3. Marine-Brigade v. Loewenfeld*; Kiel/Plön, 1963.

Kehrig, Manfred: *Die Wiedereinrichtung des deutschen militärischen Attachédienstes nach dem Ersten Weltkrieg*; Boppard, 1966.

Kempner, Robert M. W.: *SS im Kreuzverhör*; Munich, 1964.

Kennan, George F.: *From Prague After Munich*; Princeton, 1968.

Kersten, Felix: *Totenkopf und Treue*; Hamburg, 1952. *The Kersten Memoirs 1940–1945*, translated by Constantine Fitzgibbon and James Oliver; Hutchinson, London, 1956.

Kiel, Heinz: *Canaris zwischen den Fronten*; Bremerhaven, 1950.

Kielmansegg, Adolf von: *Der Fritschprozess 1938*; Hamburg, 1948.

Klever, Ulrich: *Knaurs Hundebuch*; Munich/Zurich, 1959.

Kordt, Erich: *Nicht aus den Akten*; Mannheim, 1949.

————: *Wahn und Wirklichkeit*; Stuttgart, 1947.

Kotze, Hildegard von: *Heeresadjutant bei Hitler 1938–1943*; Stuttgart, 1974.

Krausnick Helmut: *Die Vollmacht des Gewissens*; Frankfurt and Berlin, 1960.

Krausnick, Helmut; Deutsch, Harold C., and Kotze, Hildegard von: *Tagebücher eines Abwehroffiziers*; Stuttgart, 1970.

Kriegsgeschichtliche Forschungsanstalt des Heeres: *Die Wirren in der Reichshauptstadt und im nördlichen Deutschland 1918–1920*; Berlin, 1940.

Kriegsheim, Herbert: *Getarnt, getäuscht und doch getreu*; Berlin, 1959.

Krüger, Gabriele: *Die Brigade Ehrhardt*; Hamburg, 1971.

Krummacher, F. A., and Lange, Helmut: *Krieg und Frieden*; Munich and Esslingen, 1970.

Kugler, Franz: *Geschichte Friedrichs des Grossen*; Leipzig, 1936.

Leber, Annedore: *Das Gewissen entscheidet*; Berlin/Frankfurt, 1957.

Lehmann, Klaus: *Widerstandsgruppe Schulze-Boysen/Harnack*; East Berlin, 1948.

Leverkuehn, Paul: *German Military Intelligence*, translated by R. H. Stevens and Constantine Fitzgibbon; Weidenfeld & Nicolson, London 1954.

Levi, Paul: *Der Jorns-Prozess*; Berlin, 1929.

Liddell Hart, Sir Basil: *History of the Second World War*; Cassell & Co., London, 1970.

Liddell Hart, Sir Basil (ed.): *The Red Army*; Weidenfeld & Nicolson, London, 1956.

Lissner, Ivar: *Mein gefährlicher Weg*; Munich, 1975.

Lüdecke, Else: *S.M.S. "Dresden" 1914/1915*; Berlin, 1915.

Lunding, Hans M.: *Stemplet fortroligt*; Copenhagen, 1970.

Mader, Julius: *Hitlers Spionagegenerale sagen aus*; East Berlin, 1970.

Malanowski, Wolfgang: *November-Revolution 1918*; Berlin, 1969.

Mann, Rudolph: *Mit Ehrhardt durch Deutschland*; Berlin, 1921.

Mantey, Eberhard von: *Unsere Marine im Weltkrieg 1914–1918*; Berlin, 1927.

Martin, Bernd: *Friedensinitiativen und Machtpolitik im Zweiten Weltkrieg*; Düsseldorf, 1974.

Maser, Werner: *Hitler's Letters and Notes*; Heinemann, London, 1974.

Masterman, Sir John C.: *The Double-Cross System in the War of 1939 to 1945*; Yale University Press, 1972.

Medlicott, W. N.: *The Economic Blockade*, Vol. II; HMSO, London, 1959.

Merkes, Manfred: *Die deutsche Politik gegenüber dem spanischen Bürgerkrieg 1936–1939*; Bonn, 1961.

Mielke, Otto: *Das letzte Schiff des Kreuzergeschwaders*; Munich, 1954.

Mitchell, Donald W.: *History of the Modern American Navy*; New York, 1946.

Mitford, Nancy: *Frederick the Great*; Hamish Hamilton, London, 1970.

Moravec, Frantisek: *Master of Spies*; Bodley Head, London, 1975.

Müller, Josef: *Bis zur letzten Konsequenz*; Munich, 1975.

Müller, Klaus-Jürgen: *Das Heer und Hitler*; Stuttgart, 1969.

Nahayewsky, Isidore: *History of the Modern Ukrainian State 1917–1923*; Munich, 1966.

Nettl, John P.: *Rosa Luxemburg*; Oxford University Press, 1966.

Neufeldt, Hans-Joachim; Huck Jürgen; and Tessin, Georg: *Zur Geschichte der Ordnungspolizei 1936–1945*; Coblenz, 1957.

Nicolai, Walter: *Geheime Mächte*; Leipzig, 1925. *The German Secret Service*; Harrap, London, 1929.

Noske, Gustav: *Erlebtes aus Aufstieg und Niedergang einer Demokratie*, Offenbach, 1947.

————: *Von Kiel bis Kapp*; Berlin, 1920.

Oertzen, F. W. von: *Die deutschen Freikorps 1918–1923*; Munich, 1936.

O'Neill, Robert J.: *The German Army and the Nazi Party*; Cassell & Co., London, 1966.

Papen, Franz von: *Der Wahrheit eine Gasse*; Munich, 1952. *Memoirs*, translated by Brian Connell; André Deutsch, London, 1952.

Persius, Lothar: *Menschen und Schiffe in der Kaiserlichen Flotte*; Berlin, 1925.

Philby, Kim: *My Silent War*; MacGibbon & Kee, London, 1968.

Picht, Werner: *Vom Wesen des Krieges und vom Kriegswesen der Deutschen*; Stuttgart, 1952.

Praun, Albert: *Soldat in der Telegraphen- und Nachrichtentruppe*; Würzburg, 1965.

Prokoptschuk, Gregor: *Der Metropolit*; Munich, 1955.

Putlitz, Wolfgang, Gans Edler Herr zu: *Unterwegs nach Deutschland*; East Berlin, 1957.

Puttkamer, Jesco von: *Von Stalingrad zur Volkspolizei*; Wiesbaden, 1951.

Raeder, Erich: *Der Kreuzerkrieg in ausländischen Gewässern*; Berlin, 1922.

————: *Mein Leben* (Vol. I); Tübingen, 1956. *Struggle for the Sea*, translated by E. Fitzgerald; Wm. Kimber, London, 1959.

Ransom, Harry Howe: *The Intelligence Establishment*; Cambridge (U.S.A.), 1970.

Reile, Oscar: *Geheime Ostfront*; Munich, 1963.

————: *Geheime Westfront*; Munich, 1962.

Reiman, Victor: *Dr. Joseph Goebbels*; Vienna, Munich and Zurich, 1971.

Reiners, Ludwig: *Friedrich*; Munich, 1952.

Reitlinger, Gerald: *The House Built on Sand*; Weidenfeld & Nicolson, London, 1960.

Ritter, Nikolaus: *Deckname Dr. Rantzau*; Hamburg, 1972.

Rittlinger, Herbert: *Geheimdienst mit beschränkter Haftung*; Stuttgart, 1973.

Roden, Hans: *Deutsche Soldaten*; Leipzig, 1935.

Rönnefarth, Helmuth K. G.: *Die Sudetenkrise in der internationalen Politik*; Wiesbaden, 1961.

Ruhl, Klaus-Jörg: *Spanien im Zweiten Weltkrieg*; Hamburg, 1975.

Sänger, Fritz: *Politik der Täuschungen*; Vienna, 1975.

Scheer, Reinhard, and Stöwer, Willy: *Die deutsche Flotte in grosser Zeit*; Braunschweig, Berlin and Hamburg, 1926.

Schellenberg, Walter: *Memoiren*; Cologne, 1956. *The Schellenberg Memoirs*, translated by Louis Hagen; André Deutsch, London, 1961.

Schenk, Otto: *S.M.S. "Dresden" im Geschwader Spee*; Berlin (undated).

Schnabel, Raimund: *Macht ohne Moral*; Frankfurt, 1957.

Schneider, Heinrich: *Die letzte Fahrt des Kleinen Kreuzers "Dresden"*; Berlin and Leipzig, 1926.

Schottelius, Herbert, and Deist, Wilhelm: *Marine und Marinepolitik 1871–1914*; Düsseldorf, 1972.

Schramm-von Thadden, Ehrengard: *Griechenland und die Grossmächte im Zweiten Weltkrieg*, Wiesbaden, 1955.

Schulze, Hagen: *Freikorps und Republik 1918–1920*; Boppard am Rhein, 1969.

Seabury, Paul: *The Wilhelmstrasse*; Berkeley, Los Angeles, 1964.

Shirer, William L.: *The Rise and Fall of the Third Reich*; Secker & Warburg, London, 1961.

Siebert, Ferdinand: *Italiens Weg in den Zweiten Weltkrieg*; Frankfurt, 1962.

Simsa, Paul: *Marine intern*; Stuttgart, 1972.

Smith, R. Harris: *OSS*; University of California Press, 1972.

Sommer, Theo: *Deutschland und Japan zwischen den Mächten*; Tübingen, 1962.

Speidel, Hans: *Invasion 1944*; Tübingen and Stuttgart, 1961. *We Defended Normandy*, translated and edited by Ian Colvin; Herbert Jenkins, London, 1951.

Sprotte, Helmut: *Die Reichsmarine in ihrer organisatorischen Entwicklung seit der Revolution*; Berlin, 1922.

Stephan, Enno: *Geheimauftrag Irland*; Oldenburg, 1961.

Stieber, Wilhelm: *Denkwürdigkeiten des Geheimen Regierungsrathes Dr. Stieber;* Berlin, 1884.

Stöckel, Kurt: *Die Entwicklung der Reichsmarine nach dem Ersten Weltkrieg (1919–1935);* Göttingen, 1954.

Strauch, Rudi: *Sir Nevile Henderson;* Bonn, 1959.

Ströbinger, Rudolf: *A/54;* Munich, 1966.

Strong, Sir Kenneth: *Men of Intelligence;* Cassell & Co., London, 1970.

Tansill, Charles Callan: *Back Door to War;* New York, 1952.

Taylor, A. J. P.: *The Origins of the Second World War;* Hamish Hamilton, London, 1961.

Thomas, Hugh: *The Spanish Civil War;* Eyre & Spottiswoode, London, 1961.

Veit, Ursula: *Justus Gruner als Schöpfer der Geheimen Preussischen Staatspolizei;* Coburg, 1937.

Wacker, Wolfgang: *Der Bau des Panzerschiffes "A" und der Reichstag;* Tübingen, 1959.

Waldersee, Alfred von: *Denkwürdigkeiten des Generalfeldmarschalls Alfred Grafen von Waldersee;* Stuttgart, 1922.

Wedemeyer, Albert C.: *Wedemeyer Reports!;* New York, 1958.

Weizsäcker, Ernst von: *Erinnerungen;* Munich, 1950.

Westphal, Siegfried: *Heer in Fesseln;* Bonn, 1952. *The German Army in the West;* Cassell & Co., London, 1951.

Whaley, Barton: *Codeword Barbarossa;* Cambridge (U.S.A.) and M.I.T. Press, 1973.

Wheatley, Ronald: *Operation Sea Lion;* Oxford University Press, 1958.

Wheeler-Bennett, Sir John W.: *The Nemesis of Power;* Macmillan, London, St. Martin's Press, New York, 1953, 2nd ed., 1964.

Wighton, Charles, and Peis, Günter: *They Spied on England;* Odhams Press, London, 1958.

Whiting, Charles: *Canaris;* Ballantine, New York, 1973.

Wilde, Harry: *Rosa Luxemburg;* Vienna, Munich and Zurich, 1970.

Winterbotham, F. W.: *Secret and Personal;* Wm. Kimber, London, 1969.

Wuescht, Johann: *Jugoslawien und das Dritte Reich;* Stuttgart, 1969.

Zeller, Eberhard: *Geist der Freiheit;* Munich, 1963.

Zhukov, Georgi K.: *Memoirs;* Macdonald, London, 1969.

Ziesel, Kurt: *Der rote Rufmord;* Tübingen, 1961.

Zolling, Hermann, and Höhne, Heinz: *Network,* translated by Richard Barry; Secker & Warburg, London, 1972.

PERIODICAL AND NEWSPAPER ARTICLES

Baum, Walter: "Marine, Nationalsozialismus und Widerstand"; *Vierteljahreshefte für Zeitgeschichte,* No. 2/1963.

Baumgart, Winfried: "Zur Ansprache Hitlers vor den Führern der Wehrmacht am 22. August 1939"; *Vierteljahreshefte für Zeitgeschichte,* No. 16/1968.

Bidlingmaier, Gerhard: "Zum 50. Jahrestag der Falklandschlacht"; *Marine-Rundschau*, No. 6/1964.

Böhm, Anton: "Canaris"; *Rheinischer Merkur*, January 7, 1955.

Broszat, Martin: "Das Sudetendeutsche Freikorps"; *Vierteljahreshefte für Zeitgeschichte*, 1961.

Deist, Wilhelm: "Die Politik der Seekriegsleitung und die Rebellion der Flotte Ende Oktober 1918"; *Vierteljahreshefte für Zeitgeschichte*, No. 4/1966.

————: "Die Unruhen in der Marine 1917/1918"; *Marine-Rundschau*, No. 6/1971.

Diplomatist: "Ein König im Netz"; *Die Weltbühne*, January 10, 1928.

Drascher, Wahrhold: "Zur Soziologie des deutschen Seeoffizierkorps"; *Wehrwissenschaftliche Rundschau*, No. 10/1962.

Falkenhagen, Horst: "Gespräche mit Canaris"; *Neue Zeitung*, July 6, 1948.

Forstmeier, Friedrich: "Probleme der Erziehung und Ausbildung in der Kaiserlichen Marine in Abhängigkeit von geistiger Situation und sozialer Struktur"; *Marine-Rundschau*, No. 4/1966.

Graml, Hermann: "Der Fall Oster"; *Vierteljahreshefte für Zeitgeschichte*, 1966.

Grosse, Will: "Der Mann, der zuviel wusste"; *Hamburger Morgenpost*, October 24, 1950.

Hartmann, Sverre: "Zwischen Staat und System"; *Deutsche Rundschau*, April 1955.

Henke, Gerhard: "Bericht und Erinnerungen"; *Die Nachhut*, August 1, 1967.

————: "Aus den Erinnerungen eines Ic/AO"; *Die Nachhut*, November 15, 1967.

Herwig, Holger H.: "Soziale Herkunft und wissenschaftliche Vorbildung des Seeoffiziers der Kaiserlichen Marine vor 1914"; *Militärgeschichtliche Mitteilungen*, No. 2/1971.

Herzog, Bodo: "Kapitänleutnant Wilhelm Canaris als U-Boot-Kommandant"; *Die Nachhut*, October 1, 1972.

————: "Der junge Canaris in Duisburg (1892–1905)"; *Die Nachhut*, May 10, 1972.

————: "Das letzte Bordkommando von Wilhelm Canaris"; *Die Nachhut*, May 15, 1973.

Hildebrand, Klaus: "Hitlers Ort in der Geschichte des preussisch-deutschen Nationalstaates"; *Historische Zeitschrift*, Vol. 217, No. 3, December 1973.

Kisch, Egon Erwin: "Rettungsgürtel an einer kleinen Brücke"; *Die Weltbühne*, May 29, 1928.

Krausnick, Helmut: "Wehrmacht und Nationalsozialismus"; *Das Parlament*, November 9, 1955.

————: "Hitler und die Morde in Polen"; *Vierteljahreshefte für Zeitgeschichte*, April 1963.

Ludlow, Peter: "Papst Pius XII, die britische Regierung und die deutsche Opposition im Winter 1939/40"; *Vierteljahreshefte für Zeitgeschichte*, No. 3/1974.

Lunding, Hans M.: sketch of the "special prisoners' block"; *Die Nachhut*, September 1, 1971.

Maser, Werner, and Höhne, Heinz: "Aufriss Über meine Person"; *Der Spiegel*, Nos. 19/1973 and 22/1973.

Meos, Edgar Siegfried: "Hitlers Geheimdienst in Estland vor dem Überfall auf die Sowjetunion"; *Mitteilungsblatt der Arbeitsgemeinschaft ehemaliger Offiziere*, East Berlin, June 1969.

Merkel, Harald: "Ein Admiral kämpft für Frieden und Menschlichkeit"; *Marine-Rundschau*, No. 6/1965.

Morus: "Der Fall Lohmann"; *Die Weltbühne*, August 16, 1927.

———: "Alle Mann an Bord"; *Die Weltbühne*, March 13, 1928.

Murmann, Ernst: "Betrachtungen zum Fall Blomberg"; *Frankfurter Allgemeine Zeitung*, June 4, 1974.

Nollau, Günther: "Rosa Luxemburg als Faust II"; *Der Spiegel*, Nos. 1/2/1970.

Observator: "Geheimdienst, Fahneneid und Hakenkreuz"; *Echo der Woche*, February 17–May 5, 1950.

Oliver: "Gregory in Kiel"; *Die Weltbühne*, March 6, 1928.

———: "Canaris an der Ostsee"; *Die Weltbühne*, September 6, 1927.

———: "Das Geheimnis um Canaris"; *Die Weltbühne*, August 23, 1927.

Ossietzky, Carl von: "Der Ponton-Prozess"; *Die Weltbühne*, March 20, 1928.

———: "Das glückhafte Schiff von Kiel"; *Die Weltbühne*, January 24, 1928.

———: "Canarisfilm und Völkerbundstheater"; *Die Weltbühne*, September 13, 1927.

Pabst, Waldemar: "Ich liess Rosa Luxemburg richten"; *Der Spiegel*, No. 16/1962.

Persius, Lothar: "Der Seekrieg"; *Die Weltbühne*, April 17 and June 19, 1919.

———: "Der Schwindel über die Marine"; *Die Weltbühne*, May 13, 1920.

———: "Die Tragödie der alten Marine"; *Die Weltbühne*, November 6, 1928.

Pruck, Erich Ferdinand: "Der Abwehrchef"; *Der Notweg*, No. 7/1954.

Rodriguez Aragon, Mario: "Operación KN"; *Pueblo* (Madrid), August 21, 1958.

Ronge, Paul: "Zur Ahnentafel des Admirals Canaris"; *Genealogie*, Vol. VI, No. 1/1962.

Roos, Hans: "Die militärpolitische Lage und Planung Polens gegenüber Deutschland vor 1939"; *Wehrwissenschaftliche Rundschau*, No. 4/1957.

Scheurig, Bodo: "Helfer, Zauberer, Aussenseiter"; *Vorwärts*, April 8, 1960.

Schulze-Bernett, Walter: "Der Grenzzwischenfall bei Venlo"; *Die Nachhut*, May 15, 1973.

Selle, Erich von: "Mann im Schatten"; *Welt am Sonntag*, January 8, 1950.

Spalcke, Karl: "Der Fall Tuchatschewski"; *Die Gegenwart*, January 25, 1958.

Thorwald, Jürgen: "Der Mann, der den Krieg auslöste"; *Der Stern,* June 7, 1953.

Trevor-Roper, H. R.: "Admiral Canaris"; *The Cornhill Magazine,* Summer 1950.

Uhlig, Heinrich: "Der verbrecherische Befehl"; *Das Parlament,* November 6, 1963.

Viñas, Angel: "Los espías nazis entran en la guerra civil," *Historia,* October 1975.

Ziesenitz, Andreas: "Spionage"; *Die Weltbühne,* December 9, 1920.

————: "Der Vater der Lüge"; *Die Weltbühne,* July 29, 1920.

"Das Märchen von den Canarischen Inseln"; *Die Weltbühne,* November 22, 1927.

"Das Spiel ist aus—Arthur Nebe"; *Der Spiegel,* September 29–April 20, 1950.

"Der ungeklärte Fall Major Sosnowskis"; *Polnische Wochenschau,* No. 24/1971.

"Im Reichsmarineamt erscheint Herr Dillenz mit einem ausländischen Rechtsanwalt . . ."; *Die Weltbühne,* May 22, 1928.

"In memoriam Joachim Rohleder"; *Die Nachhut,* July 15, 1974.

"Korvettenkapitän Canaris"; *Die Weltbühne,* February 3, 1931.

"Letzte Ölung"; *Der Spiegel,* No. 37/1968.

"SS-Bericht über den 20. Juli"; *Nordwestdeutsche Hefte,* No. 2, February 1947.

"Stabsoffizier, Das alte Heer"; *Die Weltbühne,* June 10, 1920.

NEWSPAPERS AND PERIODICALS

Berliner Börsenzeitung, 1931.
Berliner Illustrierte Zeitung, 1935.
Berliner Tageblatt, 1927, 1931.
Der Spiegel, 1948–76.
Die Nachhut, 1969–75.
Die Weltbühne, 1920–33.
Frankfurter Allgemeine Zeitung, 1950–55, 1975.
Völkischer Beobachter, 1930–45.

INDEX

STRUCTURE OF AMT AUSLAND/ABWEHR

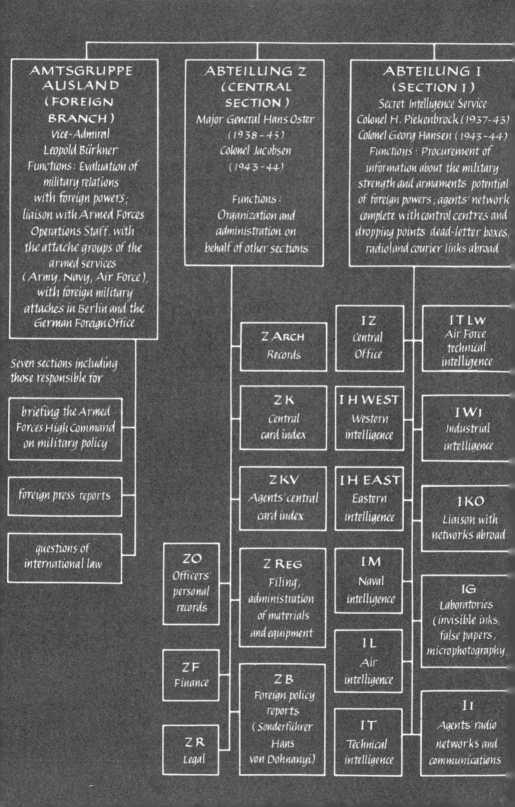

AMTSGRUPPE AUSLAND (FOREIGN BRANCH)
Vice-Admiral Leopold Bürkner
Functions: Evaluation of military relations with foreign powers; liaison with Armed Forces Operations Staff, with the attache groups of the armed services (Army, Navy, Air Force), with foreign military attaches in Berlin and the German Foreign Office

Seven sections including those responsible for

- briefing the Armed Forces High Command on military policy
- foreign press reports
- questions of international law

ABTEILUNG Z (CENTRAL SECTION)
Major General Hans Oster (1938–43)
Colonel Jacobsen (1943–44)

Functions: Organization and administration on behalf of other sections

- ZO — Officers' personal records
- ZF — Finance
- ZR — Legal
- Z ARCH — Records
- ZK — Central card index
- ZKV — Agents' central card index
- Z REG — Filing, administration of materials and equipment
- ZB — Foreign policy reports (Sonderführer Hans von Dohnanyi)

ABTEILUNG I (SECTION I)
Secret Intelligence Service
Colonel H. Piekenbrock (1937–43)
Colonel Georg Hansen (1943–44)
Functions: Procurement of information about the military strength and armaments potential of foreign powers; agents' network complete with control centres and dropping points dead-letter boxes, radio and courier links abroad

- IZ — Central Office
- IH WEST — Western intelligence
- IH EAST — Eastern intelligence
- IM — Naval intelligence
- IL — Air intelligence
- IT — Technical intelligence
- ITLw — Air Force technical intelligence
- IWI — Industrial intelligence
- IKO — Liaison with networks abroad
- IG — Laboratories (invisible inks, false papers, microphotography)
- II — Agents' radio networks and communications